# The Ultimate Plant & Garden Book

# The Ultimate Plant & Garden Book

Edited by
R. G. Turner Jr

CROWN PUBLISHERS, INC. NEW YORK

*Chief consultant* R. G. TURNER Jr
*Consultants* DUNCAN HIMMELMAN
STIRLING MACOBOY
ROGER MANN
IAN PERCY
TONY RODD

*Additional writers*

*Text*

*Your Garden* Roger Mann
*Annuals & Perennials* Dalys Newman
Robin Simon

*Shrubs* Peter Lavelle
Dalys Newman
*Trees* Henry Barrkman
Heather Jackson

*Bulbs, Corms & Tubers* Julie Silk

*Lawns, Ground Covers & Ornamental Grasses* Heather Jackson
Robin Smith

*Vegetables & Herbs* Gina Schien (vegetables)
Denise Grieg (herbs)
Heather Jackson

*Fruit Trees, Nut Trees & Other Fruits* Heather Jackson
Gina Schien

*Indoor Plants* Heather Jackson
Marnie Roper

*Climbers & Creepers* Denise Grieg
Heather Jackson

*Chapter Introductions* Roger Mann
Judy Moore

*Field Trips*
Andy Clements *(Dochu La);* John Forlonge *(Magallanes Region);* Maurie Kellett *(Fortin de las Flores);* John Manning *(Darling and Malmesbury);* Kristo Peinaar *(Cape Floral Kingdom);* Graeme Platt *(Coromandel Peninsula);* Julie Silk *(Blue Mountains, Mount Kinbalu, Norfolk Island);* Paul Sterry *(Grindelwald, Lundy);* Angus Stewart *(Guadalupe Mountains National Park)*



First Published in 1996

Published by Crown Publishers, Inc., 201 East 50th Street, New York, New York 10022.
Member of the Crown Publishing Group.

Random House, Inc. New York, Toronto, London, Sydney, Auckland

http://www.randomhouse.com/

Crown is a trade mark of Crown Publishers, Inc.

Library of Congress Cataloging-in-Publication Data available upon request.

ISBN 0-517-70189-8

10 9 8 7 6 5 4 3 2 1

First American Edition

Managing Editors: Margaret Olds, Lisa Foulis

Senior Editor: Marie-Louise Taylor

Copy Editors: Deb Brown, Susan Page, Stephanie Campion, Kate Etherington, Margaret McAllister, Marnie Roper, Dawn Cockle, Heather Jackson, James Young

Art Director: Stan Lamond

Designer: Joy Eckermann

Maps: Stan Lamond

Index: Lisa Foulis

Color Separations by Pica Colour Separation Overseas Pte Ltd

Printed in Hong Kong by South China Printing Co. Ltd

Photographers: Ardea (London), Tony Bomford, Geoff Bryant, Brinsley Burbidge, Claver Carroll, Andy Clements, Densey Clyne, Tony Curry, John Forlonge, Denise Grieg, Joanne Van Gruisen, Sarah Guest, Ivy Hansen, Joy Harland, James Hyett (ARPS), Maurice Kellet, Stirling Macoboy, Brett McKay, Leo Meier, Geoff Moon, Kristo Pienaar, Gordon Roberts, Tony Rodd, Lorna Rose, Paul Sterry, Oliver Strewe, Ben Wallace, Gerry Whitmont, Brent Wilson, Australian Picture Library, Random House Picture Library

*Page 1: Aquilegia* 'Crimson Star', a native North American species

*Page 2:* A very colorful collection of mixed flowers

*Page 5:* The romance and beauty of old roses (Gil Hanly)

*Pages 8–9:* A lush, cool-climate garden (Gil Hanly)

# Contents

CHAPTER 1

# Your Garden

*Everything You Need to Know to Plan, Develop and Maintain Your Garden*

*We walk in a world of our own creation; and the pleasures of the gardens we create are many and lasting. True, the flower fades, the perfect tomato is brought to the table and is no more: but tomorrow there will be new flowers, other fruit; still the sunshine will sparkle on the lawn; the newly dug earth gives its sweet smell, rich with promise; and as the years and seasons pass, the garden matures in beauty. In our hectic and alienated times, what price an activity that brings us back in touch with the slow rhythms of nature?*

*But first we must begin to create our garden. A beautiful garden grows out of the interaction between the site, the climate, the soil, and the needs and desires of its owner; and there are as many ways to bring these together as there are gardeners. There is no "right" way to make a garden—there is only the one that works best for you.*

## PLANNING THE GARDEN

### Design for living

Most of us make our garden on the land about our house, and it augments the house's living space. Thinking about how you (and your family) want to live in your garden is as good a starting point for planning as any. Do you need a place to wash the car, to entertain friends at a barbecue, for children to play; to hang out the washing, hide the garbage can, make a compost heap; to sunbathe, to sit in the cool of a summer evening with a cold drink? Would you like a swimming pool, a spa, a place to grow vegetables and fruit? To grow flowers for cutting? Do you need a shed, or can tools, the lawnmower, portable garden furniture and what have you be kept in the garage? How important is privacy to you?

Think, if you like, in terms of "garden rooms", remembering, however, that "rooms" in a garden need not have the clearly defined functions that those in a house normally do. A sunny lawn can serve just as well for the children to throw a ball as it can for adults to relax; and if you have a party, guests can wander out onto it and sit on the grass. On the other hand, the feet of chairs and tables tend to sink into grass if it is soggy from rain, and you may find yourself wishing for a paved area—a terrace, patio, call it what you will. Paving can get uncomfortably hot in summer, so this suggests the patio should be shaded: but you will probably want the winter sun, so you start thinking in terms of deciduous trees or of vines on pergolas. The patio probably should link up in some easy way with the living rooms, and in turn open out onto the lawn; perhaps it is the spot to display some extra-choice flowers or a

*Vine covered arbors, favorite sitting places since the days of the Romans, are still an effective way to link house with garden.*

fine piece of sculpture ... or should the flowers or the sculpture be placed at the other side of the lawn to draw people out to admire them? Before you know it, a design for a garden room is taking shape ...

## *Plan for the climate*

When gardeners think of climate, it is usually in terms of how it affects the choice of plants, but it influences the basic layout of a garden also. Barbecues and swimming pools flourish where summers are sunny and pleasant; in a hot climate shade is a necessity; and in any climate you will almost certainly face winds, hot or cold, that you want to break.

If you can arrange a balance of sun and shade, you have the option of sitting in either, and you gain a greater choice of plants you can grow. But shade doesn't stay in one place—the sun moves around all the time. It moves daily from east to west of course; but it also shifts with the seasons, being higher in the sky in summer than in winter. So the pool of shade cast by a tree, for instance, is larger in winter than in summer—and a corner behind the shed may get sun in summer but not during the winter months.

It is a general rule that (in the northern hemisphere) the south side of the house is the sunny one, and the north is in the shade of the house itself. Most of us like the morning sun, but on a hot summer day the last thing we want is the hot afternoon sun streaming in the windows. If you can arrange trees on your western side to shade the house on summer afternoons, it will make life more comfortable. The south side can do with summer shade too, but here you will probably welcome the winter sun. Deciduous trees, which drop their leaves as the summer cools into fall and clothe themselves again in spring, will fill the bill here, and so might grapes or wisteria trained on pergolas. Beneath them is the ideal place for a terrace for sitting out and entertaining; but what if your living rooms face some other aspect? It doesn't really matter. An easy link with the living rooms is more important. (You don't really want to be taking guests out through the bedrooms or laundry, do you?)

East is marginally better than west; most people entertain in the evenings and in summer a west aspect will still be hot. But it doesn't really matter; arrange suitable shade and you can make yourself comfortable on most aspects. (My own two patios face east and west, which gives me one for the morning and one for the afternoon.) The north side of the house can be tricky. For most of the year it is in shade, but in midsummer the sun will have moved around enough to reach it. A north side patio should have deciduous shade also!

When you are planning for sun and shade, think of your comfort inside the house as well as in the garden. Curtains or no, once the sun has gotten in through a window, its heat is in too,

*A spot for outdoor living amidst lush greenery, the brightly painted walls adding color.*

*Climbers can provide much-needed shade.*

*Creeping fig softens and shades this house well.*

*The massive trees and expansive lawn sit well with this grand house.*

*An inviting white summer house stands out against varied greens.*

and it is very difficult to evict; shading the outside of the glass is the only way to keep it out. Architects employ a variety of devices—cornices, eaves, verandahs—to achieve this. Gardeners use plants: trees, shrubs, climbers which can be allowed to climb the walls and hang trails of greenery over the windows (few sights are more romantic) or trained over pergolas to form green roofs. Plants give cooler shade than structures do, by virtue of their constant transpiration of water.

## Wind

Say "windbreak" and most people immediately think of the rows of poplars or conifers that march across fields in the country. If you have a country garden you'll probably be thinking of belts of large trees. In the suburbs there is unlikely to be room for them, and so you'll be thinking of shrubs, small trees, and maybe fences and trellises. Nonetheless, you will want to screen the garden from the cold winds in winter and the hot ones of summer. Not only for your own comfort, but because wind dries out the garden as effectively as it does the washing on the line. Trees and shrubs are more effective than structures for the purpose. If the wind hits a wall it just rebounds and comes down with renewed force, but foliage filters the wind and gives you shelter for a distance downwind about eight times the height of the planting. In a hot climate, you can use greenery as an air-conditioner simply by turning a sprinkler on it, converting a hot dry breeze into a gentle cool one.

Not all wind is undesirable. In most areas there are evening summer breezes that you won't want to block, and you'll be thinking of less dense plantings on that aspect. It isn't possible to give rules for all this, as wind patterns vary so much from place to place. On the east coast and in the Midwest, the hot summer winds come from the west; in Portland or San Francisco they blow from the east. Everywhere, it is the local geography that determines the prevailing winds. At the seaside, a strong wind off the sea is a major factor in garden-making, but seaside gardens are a special case and we will look at them later.

It can be a worry when the prevailing wind (or the hot summer sun) comes from the same direction as a wonderful view. Perhaps the best way to deal with it is to use fairly open-growing trees which will break the wind or sun a bit but not block the view too much, or to group the plants so that they frame segments of the view, the way a photographer arranges interesting things in the foreground of a picture. If the problem is essentially a summer one, you might use deciduous trees, which will at least give you back the view in winter. However you deal with the problem, the answer will be a compromise between view and shelter—but in gardening, as in life, compromises can often have the happiest results.

## Privacy

How much privacy you need in the garden is a matter of temperament; some people like more seclusion than others. A new garden is apt to be dominated by fences and the neighbors' houses, but before you rush to surround yourself with dense growth like Sleeping Beauty in the fairy tale, take a careful look. Ignore the fence for a moment—you can mask it with creepers and shrubs—and concentrate on the neighbors' houses. If you arrange some trees or tall shrubs to mask these from your view, leaving the skyline open elsewhere, will that be sufficient?

It can be difficult to visualize how this is going to look; try taking snapshots and sketching some foliage on them to give you an idea of how much cover you'll need. (This can be a good way of visualizing any changes you propose to the garden—and before-and-after pictures of the garden are worth taking and provide a valuable record.)

A low-maintenance garden that gives a very pictureque first impression.

## Front gardens

Almost always, the house is set on the land so that you have front and back yards. As it is usually more private, the back yard is frequently where most people enjoy their family activities. It can be difficult to contrive privacy in a front garden. Even where local ordinances allow a front fence, the front garden is still basically a threshold to your property, a link between the street and the front door. It may be possible to screen a section to make a front patio (using hedges where fences aren't permitted), but there is still the need to have access to the house, and that really can't be forbidden to the person who comes to read the meters, let alone your invited guests. You do need to have a clear path from the entrance to the front door, and to ensure it is well lit at night.

The front yard is the scene of the visitor's first and last impressions. Also it is neighborly to have a garden that looks pleasing from the street and you will want to show off the architecture of the house to advantage. If you are a keen gardener, you may seize the opportunity to show off your skills. But on the other hand you may not want to spend a high proportion of your gardening time on an area you don't use much yourself and you may opt for a low maintenance design. It's up to you, but a word to the wise: in these days of high crime, it isn't a good idea to shroud the front of your house too much in greenery or with high fences. Burglars appreciate privacy too!

## Inner-city gardens

In some ways, a city garden is the ideal for busy people—there simply isn't room to overindulge in gardening! But a confined space does call for some editing of the wish list—you just can't include all the activities or all the plants you might want. The answer is to develop the garden as a living room; think of it as a courtyard and pave most of it—a garden that is all patio, in fact (and it is interesting to recall that the Spanish word 'patio' originally meant a paved courtyard garden just like this).

The walls and fences can be clad with climbing plants or with shrubs trained as espaliers. If space allows, you might be able to contrive a pocket-handkerchief-sized lawn; but city conditions are against it. Surrounding buildings often block the sun, and few lawn grasses like shade. Chances are you'll wear the grass out underfoot anyway; and you need to consider where you are going to store the lawnmower.

The big problem is apt to be privacy.

A cherry tree trained espalier to soften a wall.

Even with the high fences (6 ft/about 1.8 m) that most planning regulations allow, the dominant feature of your view is likely to be the neighbors' walls and windows. Sure, they will be as much concerned about you as you might be about them: but it is still desirable to screen them. Trellises might do it; trees are effective too, though they will probably eventually confine your choice of plants to shade lovers. Also you need to choose carefully to be sure that the trees don't have structure-damaging roots. One splendid tree spreading its leafy (and why not flowery?) canopy over the whole garden can set the style far more effectively than several smaller ones can.

## Side gardens

If the areas beside the house are large enough to use as living spaces, you can usually extend a screen (built or planted) from the facade of the house to the side fence and thus incorporate the area into the back yard. Depending on aspect, this can be a nice place for a secluded patio, for the vegetable garden or for the compost heap; and trees planted there can be useful in framing the house. Often, however, it is simply a narrow strip, just wide enough to separate the house from the neighbors. Here there is little to do but treat it as a passageway, putting down a path and training plants on the fence and the house. Make the plants interesting enough to be worth visiting. Watering a long narrow area is difficult and tedious. Even if you elect to use hand-held hoses and movable sprinklers elsewhere in the garden, consider an in-ground system here.

*In a large garden, a variety of places to sit—and a whole succession of different pictures.*

*A formal vista like this needs a focal point—here, the comfortable white-painted seat.*

## Country gardens

A garden in the country gives you more scope than one in the suburbs; you don't have to worry about being overlooked by neighbors, and you can develop just as much ground as you please. Sweeping driveways, vistas through trees and across whole fields of flowers to the countryside beyond are all possible; but beware lest ambition outrun resources. If you are dependent on water from dams or rainwater tanks, the sweeping lawns can all too easily go brown and the flowers wilt in a dry summer. There is a tradition in England of country gardens divided by hedges into distinct flower-filled rooms; many people feel that this doesn't suit our more open landscape and wider horizons. They suggest a freer style, open to the surrounding country, is more appropriate.

You will almost certainly need to plant windbreak trees if they don't exist already; hot winds will dry the garden faster than you can keep the water up to it. In some areas of the west, lawns are something of a luxury and people often must save their bath water to water them—they make such a pleasant relief to the eye from the glare of summer dryness and dust. You could try laying the area in gravel, which needs no water; but shade it, or the glare and reflected heat will be ferocious. The idea of having the country sweep right up to the windows is a bold approach unless fire is a worry; in that case, be sure to plant a 30 ft (about 9 m) swath of fire-resistant or low fuel plants around the house.

## Making a plan

The easiest way of developing a layout for the garden is to make a plan on paper. An empty yard is apt to look larger than it is, and a plan can tell you whether you can in fact fit in all the things you want to accommodate. Start by making a plan showing the land as it exists. It doesn't have to be a work of art, but it is desirable that it be fairly accurately to scale, and that it shows the features that might influence your design. These include the boundaries and fences; any pavings, paths, driveways, immovable rocks and trees that might already be there; and, of course, the house itself, with its external doors and windows.

Don't forget to note desirable views that you will want to frame, undesirable ones that should be screened; the location of such nuisances as overhead wires or underground sewers and telephone lines; and the direction of north, which tells you where the sun comes from. You may have architect's plans for the house that show many of these things; your municipal building department may still have them; or you may need to spend a few hours with a long tape measure and paper to create the plan for yourself.

Then you can start to arrange your garden rooms—the patio near the living room, the vegetable patch in that sunny place near the kitchen door, the swimming pool, the path to the front door. Get them in the right places first, and then the decisions about what shapes they are to take, where the trees and shrubs are to go to frame them (and block out the view of that nosy neighbor), whether to give them floors of paving or grass, and what sort of plants to have, can follow.

Plan generously, allowing yourself room to move. If you make a lawn or terrace for sitting out, 32 sq ft (about 3 sq m) is about as small as you can get away with; paths less than around 4 ft (about 1.2 m) wide are too narrow for two people to stroll comfortably along; a row of shrubs tall enough to give privacy will grow at least 6 ft (about 1.8 m) wide.

Remember that a plan is flat, and most plots of land are, at most, flattish. It is a rare garden that will not have some changes of level to negotiate, even if only the provision of a couple of steps leading up into the house. Welcome them, and make them features in your design. You can even go to the extent of creating level changes in your garden just for the sake of the interest they add!

Two hints on plan making: Don't make your plans too big in scale or you'll spend a great deal of time drawing on unmanageably large sheets of paper. A scale of 1 in: 4 ft (used on most builders' drawings) is large enough. Do your basic "as is" plan on good stout paper (graph paper makes setting out easier), and develop your ideas on tracing paper laid over it—it saves redrawing the house and fences.

*Brick steps, simply designed but generously proportioned.*

*The formal garden at its most magnificent; the garden of the palace at Versailles.*

*A colorful and informal combination gains quick attention.*

## CHOOSING A STYLE

Don't worry that this care over the plan and layout will lead to a stereotyped garden. You can develop your ideas in any style you like, and clothe them with your favorites among the plants that your soil and climate allow. You might opt for a rigidly formal, symmetrical design, like the old gardens of Italy and France, making much use of clipped hedges and statuary, with flowers used only as accents at key points; or you might go to the opposite extreme, and make flowers the theme, disposing them with total informality in drifts and masses, maybe in English-style borders. If you concentrate on "old-fashioned" flowers, blending them (perhaps) with scented herbs and maybe the more decorative vegetables and fruit trees, you have a cottage garden. (Picket fences and arches covered with climbing roses are very much a part of the cottage style.) Taking your cue from the presence of a tree or several, you might decide on a woodland theme, treating your living spaces as woodland glades. Here you have several possibilities—you might use mostly deciduous trees with such plants as camellias, azaleas or bluebells beneath; or you might prefer to use native trees and shrubs to re-create a patch of local forest; or you might go tropical with palm trees and exotic foliage, if climate permits. There are endless possibilities.

The different styles of gardening are more about the kinds of plants you choose and how you display them than about how you cultivate them. But, in deciding which you would like, do be realistic about the time you will be prepared to devote to your garden. If sports or family activities already take most of your leisure hours, will you be able to cope with extensive plantings of flowers or vegetables? Might you not be wiser to develop a love for easy-care trees and ground covers?

## REMODELLING

What if you are remodelling an existing garden? The procedure is in fact the same as if you were planning a new one on a clean slate; start with considering how the existing garden fits your lifestyle. What changes would help it fit better? To some extent, the style will be already set, though garden styles aren't rigid categories. Your predecessors may, for instance, have been native plant buffs while you long for a cottage garden—who says you can't keep the best of the native trees and shrubs and blend them with your cottage flowers?

It is always wise to proceed slowly when you take over an established garden; live with it for at least a year before deciding on major changes. Mature trees and shrubs are assets that take time to replace, and you should give them time to reveal their beauties, especially if they are species you aren't familiar with. Who knows what hidden treasures may appear and flower with the change of season; that sunny place behind the shed (why didn't they put the vegetable garden there?) may turn out to be in heavy shade all winter and therefore totally inappropriate.

## *Engaging a professional*

Designing a garden can be one of life's most rewarding challenges, but there is no shame in deciding that you need some assistance. A professional has done it all before, many times, and will be placing the benefit of that experience at your disposal. He (or she) will be doing for a living what you do for a hobby, so don't begrudge him his fee—chances are, he will save you that much money and more. Anyone with a truck and a shovel can set himself up as a landscaper, so you need to be careful in your search; but there are trained professionals around. There are landscape architects, many of whom specialize in big projects like airports or parks, though equally many are only too delighted to take on the more intimate challenge of a private garden; many of the bigger nurseries and landscape contractors offer a design service, sometimes as a part of a design-and-build package, sometimes not; and there are smaller, independent designers also. Feel free to shop around, asking to see some of that firm's work to see whether you like their style, talking to previous clients if you wish; and don't be shy about discussing money. Be absolutely clear about your wishes and tastes, and your budget—mental telepathy isn't part of a designer's skills.

# BUILDING THE GARDEN

Having made your plans for the garden, you can elect to have your designs carried out professionally. Financial institutions are far more willing to finance landscaping than they used to be. Or you can save money—and gain a great deal of personal satisfaction—by doing some or all the work yourself. This will mean that you will have to make a considerable input in time and energy, so it will save much frustration and back-tracking if you develop a game plan for doing the work in stages; don't be afraid to take anything up to two to three years to achieve this.

If you are impatient, remember that staging the work allows you time to ponder and to add the touches that lift a garden out of the ordinary. These can be difficult to anticipate on paper. They might be unusual and effective combinations of plants, pieces of furniture or sculpture, cleverly arranged lighting, even something as simple as laying a paving pattern in one way and not another—the sorts of inspirations that strike only while you are getting your hands dirty.

If you are starting from scratch, the best plan is the one that most landscape contractors follow. First, do any major reshaping of the ground which will need heavy equipment, build any retaining walls needed to hold the reshaped earth in place, and lay any soil drains needed. (All this is disruptive, messy work if you do it later.) Then you might lay your basic pavings: the driveway comes first or you will be getting the car bogged on the way to the garage. (Chances are, the builder will have installed a basic, concrete drive as part of the house package.) If you can afford to lay paths and terraces at this stage, do it, but if not, you'll need to at least provide some cover for the bare ground. This needn't be the final lawn; there is sense in growing a cover crop of clover to improve the soil—and this won't cause heartache if it gets dug up or torn around later.

Then, as early as possible, you should plant your most important trees: the earlier you get them in, the earlier you'll be enjoying their shade. This might be enough for your energy and budget in the first year. If the garden looks a bit unfinished, fill in with inexpensive, fast return annuals to give you something to look at.

If you haven't laid your pavings already, they should be the big project for the second year, with the final grading and installation of the lawn to follow. However if your budget calls for it, you can sow the lawn now, leaving the future terraces simply in gravel or grass. Structures like pergolas might also form part of this second stage.

Stage three is the more detailed planting of things like shrubberies and ground covers. Stage four is the fine-tuning, the trying out of new plants, the adjusting of color schemes, and so on. This can go on for as long as the garden is yours.

This sort of plan, whether carried out over two years, three or more, works for most people and situations, but don't treat it as obligatory. Use it as a basis for tailoring a strategy that will suit you.

*A beautifully detailed trellis fence.*

## *Garden construction*

The actual construction of fences, walls, pergolas and their like is a matter both of taste and flair in design, and of handyperson skill. While much garden construction is well within the scope of the amateur carpenter, if you're at all doubtful about your skills, it is better to call in a professional. Nothing looks worse than clumsy workmanship—and surprisingly often, you don't save all that much money; not when you factor in the cost of your own time and of hiring the equipment which the professional builder already owns. But don't let this put you off. Doing your own building can be fun, and if your work isn't as finely finished as it might be, you can always call on foliage to camouflage this.

## *Fences and walls*

Fences are worth spending time on, as they can set the tone and feeling of the garden. You need them for privacy and to keep out intruders, but you want them to work for your design, not against you.

Most builders and developers provide

*Adding a panel of trellis at the top of the paling fence has gained greater privacy without making the whole thing too dominating.*

a basic fence with the house. Usually, this is tallest around the back garden, though surprisingly often it is only about 4 ft (about 1.2 m) high, tall enough to keep the children and the dog from straying but not really tall enough for privacy, for which it really ought to be 6 ft (about 1.8 m) or a shade taller.

The material used will vary from one part of the country to the other, but timber boards on a wooden post and rail frame are the most common. Though in theory the maintenance of boundary fences is the joint responsibility of the two adjoining property owners, in practice if you want to heighten the fence, or replace it with a more decorative material, it is likely you'll be bearing the cost yourself. Don't despair; a coat of paint (choose the sort of olive drab, khaki, dark brown or grey the army uses for camouflage rather than green which stands out in the landscape instead of receding) or the application of a wooden trellis can work wonders in dressing up the fence; or you can attach a wire-mesh trellis and cover the lot with vines. Alternatively, call on foliage to provide screening—6 ft (about 1.8 m) or taller shrubs or small trees will do the trick. They needn't be evergreen; many deciduous shrubs are sufficiently thick in growth to provide screening.

If you prefer a fancier fence there are many alternatives, better shown in pictures than described.

In many suburbs, front fences are frowned upon, and even where you are allowed them, it is not often that you will be able to build anything tall enough for privacy forward of the building line. Here, the fence is part of the foreground to the house, and its style will depend very much on that of the house itself. Wooden pickets, plain or fancy, suit colonial style cottages, whether colonial in date or not; cast-iron pickets are the standard accompaniment to a Georgian, Federalist or Victorian house; and modern houses can be flattered by brick walls and stone as well as wood. The choice is limited only by your imagination. Also, any fence can be decorated with flowering vines. Be careful, though, with thorny plants like roses and bougainvilleas: if they injure a passer-by, you may be liable.

Fences are usually thought of as fairly light constructions; when they are made of masonry (brick or stone) they

*Spaced laths, painted white.*

*A cream picket fence hung with bougainvillea.*

are walls. Walls can look mighty handsome, but cost usually limits their use to enclosing courtyards, where their style should closely match that of the house. There is no reason why you shouldn't put windows or gates in them to allow access or to frame a view. The circular moon gate is one of the happiest ideas to come from Chinese gardens. Unless you are skilled at building, leave masonry and its heavy foundations to the professional.

Gates go with fences, and they offer nearly as infinite a range of options. The only rule is that the gate shouldn't look stronger than the fence it interrupts.

While we usually think first of boundary fences, don't forget that fences and walls can be used within the garden too, to set off and enclose your garden rooms. Here, where security is not the issue, they can be open, light and decorative in construction, but not flimsy. You don't want them blowing down in the first storm.

## *Retaining walls and steps*

Retaining walls are heavy engineering rather than art, and you shouldn't attempt to design or build one more than around 3 ft (about 90 cm) high without the assistance of a professional. Lower walls are safer, provided you adhere to two rules.

First, the wall should be battered, that is leant back into the earth that it supports. The pressure of the earth is constantly trying to push the wall over, and once a vertical wall starts leaning outwards, it not only looks unstable, it is unstable. Second, water builds up behind the wall and, unless you give it somewhere to go, its pressure will endanger the stability of the wall. You can lead it away by a drain behind the foot of the wall, or provide holes so that it can flow out through the wall face; either is effective.

With these two rules in mind, you can make your wall from a variety of materials—brick, stone, concrete blocks, treated timbers. All can look effective, and all can be clothed with plants to soften their appearance. Often, there is no need to make the wall in one lift; you can make it as a series of steps, with plants growing at each level—a terraced bank if you like. If you have the room to simply make a bank at a slope of 1:1 (no steeper), you can dispense with the wall altogether, using a dense ground cover to hold the bank against erosion. There will be run-off at the foot of any bank; ensure that there is some way of carrying the water away—a drain or a slope.

Whether you have retaining walls or banks, changes of level call for steps to get from one level to the other. They can be focal points in the garden design, but need to be designed with care, because they should not only be attractive to look at, they must be safe and comfortable to use. If you are going to use them at night, ensure they are well lit; but it is even more important that they should fit the feet of those who walk up and down them.

The rule to ensure good, comfortable steps is that twice the height of the step (the riser) plus its length (the tread), in inches (centimetres), equals 26 or 27 (66). The maximum height for a garden step is around $6^1/_2$ in (about 16 cm), but the ideal proportion is a riser of 5 in (about 12 cm) with a tread of 17 in (about 42 cm). It is preferable to have an uneven number of steps, and to keep all in the same flight the same dimensions; if you must change the proportions to accommodate a changing slope, separate the two sets with a landing.

The width of steps is a matter of proportion, though it is an accepted rule that the fewer you have, the wider they should be. The steps must not be slippery when wet; usually you can make them in any material suitable for paving. If they are wide enough, you could make the risers in brick or timber and the treads in grass—but that will involve you in some careful trimming. Whatever you make them of, ensure they are firm; a wobbly step is as dangerous as a slippery one.

## *Paths and paving*

A path needn't be made of paving (in situations like a formal rose or vegetable garden you may well want to make your paths of grass) but they usually are, so we can consider them as narrow strips of paving, to be made of the same sorts of materials as you might use for a more extensive terrace or patio.

The choice of paving materials is enormous, but they break down into two main categories: those you lay as a continuous sheet and those you assemble from small units.

The continuous sheet pavings start with gravel, the oldest of all, and the cheapest. It has the disadvantages of being uncomfortable to bare feet, tending to track into the house and onto the lawn, and on any but the very slightest of slopes it washes away. But it does look soft and natural and flatters any plants associated with it. (It can look very attractive to plant a few plants in the gravel itself, to look as though they have escaped the adjacent planting beds, but don't overdo it.) If you have a choice, a fine, well-rounded river gravel is the best. Initially it should be laid to give you a layer around 3 in (about 7.5 cm) deep.

*A long flight of steps needs to be well lit for night-time safety and well upholstered with plants.*

Lay the gravel on a weed-free, well-rolled bed of soil. It will bed down into the soil over time, so you'll need to topdress it occasionally. To look its best it should be raked smooth every so often. Japanese gardens often feature a very fine white gravel which is raked daily into patterns. Nothing looks so authentic in a Japanese style garden—but unless you are a Zen monk you may find the constant raking a bore.

Wood chips and tanbark are softer equivalents of gravel and can look very pleasing in an informal woodland style garden—but are they pavings or mulches?

Then there is asphalt, a functional pavement, and, alas, looking it—it is very hard to make it look like anything except a car park. It needs professional laying, so it isn't really cheap. Few gardeners would want to use it.

Last of the continual sheet paving is concrete. Plain grey concrete is tiresome. You can color it, but it is a bit like a bore at a party who hopes that a martini or two is going to make him witty. The only really attractive surface is "exposed aggregate", achieved by using a good quality gravel and gently hosing off the surface excess before the concrete is quite set. This is a skilled job. If you would like to try it, you should practise behind the shed before tackling the patio where your visitors will see it. You can buy the sand, cement and gravel and mix the concrete yourself, but these days most gardens are within reach of a ready-mix place that will supply small orders. They will make a better, stronger mix than you can.

Have everything in readiness before the truck arrives. This involves leveling your bed and placing the timber formwork that will hold the concrete in place while it sets. You can't cast concrete paving in wide, seamless sheets—it will crack even if it is reinforced. Divide it with expansion joints every 6 to 10 ft (about 2–3 m). These can be the formwork, left in place; and you can have great fun arranging patterns. If this all sounds like a stretching of handyman skills to the limit, you hear correctly; if you are planning a cast concrete patio or driveway, you'll be thinking of calling in an expert to lay it for you.

Concrete can be colored to look like brick, but why not lay the paving in brick anyway? The real thing always looks better. Brick is probably the most popular of the pavings you can assemble yourself. And brick is just the thing for the do-it-yourselfer; it's easy to lay, and you can do just as much at a time as you have the time and energy for. The easiest way to lay it is on a carefully leveled bed of sand 4 in (about 10 cm) deep. The sand should be held in place with the same sort of 2 by 4 timbers you use for concrete formwork. Start at one end, and tap your bricks into place with a mallet, and when you are finished, spread more sand over the top and sweep and water it in to fill the joints. There are many patterns in which you can lay the bricks, but the easiest, and in many ways the most

*A simple gravel pathway, edged with an equally simple planting in white, yellow and blue.*

attractive, is basket weave. Stretcher bond, the kind you use in walls, is dependent on high accuracy, both in the making of the bricks and in the laying if the lines of the pattern aren't to go crooked. The same is true of "herringbone", which gives the strongest pavement, a factor that might be important if you are planning a brick driveway. The actual color is a matter of taste, and it will soften with weathering and dirt. One that matches or is a darker tone than the brick walls of the house is always a good choice.

Concrete pavers are a substitute for brick and are laid in the same way, though their proportions are such that the variety of possible patterns is less. They come in a range of colors, and which to choose is a matter of personal taste. They all fade a bit with age and sunlight, and that is usually an improvement.

You can also buy precast concrete slabs, usually around $2^1/_2$ in (about 6 cm) thick, in a variety of sizes and proportions. They are cast in steel molds. Plain-surfaced slabs can be so smooth they get slippery when wet; try laying them upside down (the bottom is rougher) or pay the extra for an exposed aggregate finish. They look very well laid an inch or so apart, with grass growing in between. A sand bed is best, and two pairs of hands will make the laying of the heavy slabs a lot easier.

Stone is the choicest of paving materials, but it isn't cheap. The type available will depend on what your local quarry can supply, and you can either set big, squared slabs with wide grassed joints the way you lay concrete slabs or butt them closer and point up the joints in cement. Or you can lay crazy paving, which calls for much care in arranging the irregular pieces of stone to fit the space. Some trimming is usually called for. A sand bed will normally suffice, but you might prefer the added strength of a 3 in (about 7.5 cm) concrete base.

Slate, whose grey surface can be very sympathetic to plants, must be laid on concrete as it is very brittle. The same is true of marble—but if you can afford marble, the expense of having a marble mason lay it for you won't be a problem! Be careful of stone and brick in shaded places, as they can develop a surface growth of algae in wet weather. This is not only dirty looking and unsightly, but it makes the paving as slippery as ice. If it starts to develop, you should wash the

*Low plantings on either side of this mellow brick path enhance the feeling of space.*

*A long flight of steps, but of such an easy grade that they aren't tiring. The material is bluestone.*

*A rockery is planted so lavishly that the rocks are almost hidden.*

paving down with either swimming pool chlorine or diluted bleach, sweeping it on with a stiff broom to remove as much of the algae as possible. The treatment is not permanent—in wet weather cleaning the pavement can be a regular chore. Concrete isn't so troubled by the problem.

Finally, no pavement except gravel should be perfectly level or there will be puddles everywhere when it rains. There should always be a fall, not less than around $^1/_8$ in per foot (about $^1/_2$ cm per 30 cm) to carry the water away—to a lawn, to planting beds, anywhere but towards the house.

## Swimming pools

Building a swimming pool is not a do-it-yourself project, and the local swimming pool company (choose carefully; the trade is notorious for attracting the disreputable) is the best source of advice on styles and whether you should go for fiberglass or concrete. Let us here only note a couple of factors that might affect the garden.

Plan for the pool from the very beginning, even if it is a to-be-done-later project. Unless you have a vast acreage where you can tuck it away, it will be the dominant feature of the garden. It should look as though it belongs, and not be an afterthought. It's difficult to make a pool look natural, and a simple shape is almost always the best. Try to arrange the pool itself to be in the sun, but some shade nearby will be a pleasure to retreat to. You don't want plants overhanging the water and dropping leaves into the pool. Allow room for the pool builder to get in later with his equipment—don't plan some feature like a patio or a major planting that will obstruct him or the price will skyrocket. Many local authorities these days require swimming pools to be securely fenced. So make sure you plan for enclosure. Finally, make sure that the surrounding pavements drain away from the pool, or every time it rains it will be flooded with dirty water and your filter system will be forced to work overtime.

## Getting the soil in shape

If the builder has just left you with a brand new house, the first thing to do is to get rid of the inevitable heaps of trash. Call in a trash removal contractor, or yell at the builder to come and clean up after himself. You will, hopefully, have remembered to put it in his contract to remove the topsoil from the areas he is building over so that you can spread it on the garden-to-be later. But before you can spread topsoil, you need to do some thorough cultivating. His trucks and heavy equipment will have been driving everywhere, and they will have compacted the soil. Digging with a spade is hard work, though good exercise for the young and fit. You may prefer to hire a rotary hoe, complete with operator, for a day. This is the time to do the shaping of the ground, so that your lawns won't be full of bumps and hollows. Then you can spread your reserved topsoil. If you are in the position of having to bring in soil, buy the best "garden" grade. Imported soil is often scraped from old farm fields and may have weed killer residues. "Garden" grade should have some humus added.

This is part of the joy of a brand new house, and buyers of old houses are spared it. But it is still worth checking your soil and cultivating if need be. Before you plant is the best time to improve soil in old garden beds, and the best way to do that is to dig by hand, to a spade's depth—as far, that is, as the blade of the spade will go. Turn the soil over and incorporate as much organic matter—manure, compost and the like—as you can lay your hands on. Leave it to settle a few days, and you're ready to plant. (More about soil and how to improve it in the section "Looking after the garden".)

## Installing the lawn

Most of us think of installing a lawn as part of the construction of the garden—after all, you need to have something to keep the dust down. You can do it at any time of year, but remember that grass takes longer to establish in winter, and at the height of summer you will be driving yourself crazy keeping the new lawn watered. Spring and autumn are the best times, with a preference for spring if you have the choice.

The bed for a lawn should be prepared as scrupulously as you would for any other plants, by cultivating and enriching the soil as much as you can; but you also need to ensure that it is properly even in grade, with no bumps and hollows. Dragging a long straight piece of timber over it helps, and for the final grading you need a fine-tined rake. Pick up any stones lying on the surface and get rid of them—you don't want the mower to find them later. Then, you water. Not only will this help show up any spots that still need leveling, it will encourage the weeds to germinate. When they have come up and are looking dreadful, zap them with glyphosate. Yes, we know: this takes a month or so, and you are impatient to be getting on with the lawn; but starting clean will be a great help in keeping things that way in the years to come.

With the weeds gone, it is time to think about grass. Different parts of the country have their own favorites, and this is one area where you should be guided by local custom. The only thought we offer is that you should go for the finest grass mixture available for your area, even if it is more expensive and slower to establish than cheaper, fast-growing blends designed for parks and playgrounds. Think of all the time you'll save by having to mow less frequently. (Don't, don't be tempted by either perennial rye or kikuyu unless you really love mowing.)

The cheapest way to establish the lawn is by sowing seed. Follow the directions on the packet as to quantity, and then divide your seed supply in two. You can hire a gadget like a carpet-sweeper that dribbles the seed out evenly, or you can broadcast by hand. Either way, you do it twice, first going up and down and then from side to side—you get a more even coverage that way. Follow up with a light raking which will cover the seed, and instruct the cat to chase the birds away from it. Water with the finest spray the hose will give, and keep the bed evenly moist until the grass is well up. Normally germination takes about ten days, but you need to keep watering (twice a day if needed in hot weather) until it is around 2 in (about 5 cm) high, when you can taper off. About then, you can give the grass its first mowing to encourage it to branch low, but set the mower blades as high as they will go. By the second or third mowing you should be down to your regular watering schedule of no more than once a week.

*Lawns usually look best uncluttered; here, a bright garden bed sets off the perfect sward.*

Sod is easier and faster—"instant lawn"—but very much more expensive, and you are likely to have a more limited selection of grasses than you would find on the seed shelf. Still, if you are laying only a fairly small lawn, or don't have the time to devote to nursing seedling grass, it will be worthwhile. The bed needs to be prepared as before, but laying the sod is easy. You just unroll it and put it on the ground face up like so much carpet, trimming it around the edges with scissors. Stand back and admire while you can, for the next job is to spread fine topsoil over it until the green almost disappears. Water it in and most of the green will return, and keep it all well watered at least until the grass is due for its first mowing.

For economy with some lawn types, you can cut each turf into plugs around $1^1/_2$ in (about 3 cm) square, which you then plant out like seedlings around 4 in (about 10 cm) apart, watering them in and keeping an eye out for weeds that might grow in while the grass is growing together. Or you could pull the turf apart into runners, which you sprinkle all over the bed and then rake over to cover with soil. You have to work fast though, for the runners dry out quickly, and you'll have to water nearly as assiduously as you water seed.

Remember, sod doesn't keep. If you are planning to lay it on the weekend, order delivery for Thursday at the earliest.

*In a sloping garden, steps and paths of neatly tailored concrete pavers are softened by lavish plantings.*

*The beautiful* Cornus florida.

## PLANT SELECTION

### *Choosing plants for the design*

Half the art of successful planting design is learning to see plants as a whole. Don't just focus on the flowers, however gorgeous. Does the plant have attractive foliage, and what is more, is it attractive for a long time, even all year? If it isn't, is its moment of glory sufficient to keep you looking fondly at it during its off-days? Does it have an attractive habit, graceful and open, or neat, rounded and compact, boldly upright, cascading or whatever: or is it just a scruffy support for the flowers? What sort of texture does it suggest to the eye: fine, medium, coarse or bold, matt or glossy? Does it offer features other than flowers or fancy leaves—interesting bark or fruit perhaps, or fragrance? Is it easy to grow in your soil and climate, or will it be an unhappy invalid, needing constant attention? And, if your temperament suggests, does it carry pleasant associations, childhood memories perhaps? There are some plants that will seem to have that indefinable quality of distinction, that makes you say, "Yes, you will do fine in my garden!" and those are the ones you should choose to plant.

The other half is learning to think of plants in terms of the role you want them to play in your garden design. This is particularly useful if you don't know everything there is to know about plants—and there are so many in the world that none of us can have even a nodding acquaintance with them all. It's much easier to talk to someone from a nursery or search through an illustrated book like this one if you have already

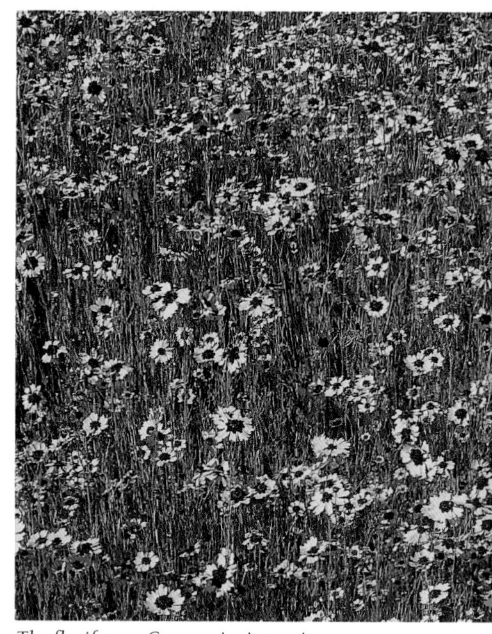

*The floriferous* Coreopsis tinctoria.

focused your desires by thinking in terms of, say, a deciduous shrub, around 9 ft (about 3 m) tall, with yellow flowers, or an evergreen, cascading ground cover to trail over the retaining wall, than if you just ask "What would look pretty?"

The art of all art is simplicity. Don't think you will be bored by having several plants of the one kind; it is much easier to arrange just a few species effectively than to try to weave an intricate tapestry with just one plant each of many.

A word of warning. The commonest mistake in planting is to crowd your plants. Sure, the baby plants look so lonely; but space them in accordance with their mature spread or you'll end up with a tangle. Where we have given the width of a plant take note; where it isn't given, assume that it will spread to a width about two-thirds to three-quarters of its height, unless it is noted as "spreading" or "upright", in which case you can assume a greater or lesser figure.

*Big trees can lend dignity to a house the way no combination of smaller plants can, provided there is room.*

## *Native or exotic?*

Gardeners have always used their native plants. The cypresses, umbrella pines and box of the great formal Italian gardens are all Italian natives and the camellias and chrysanthemums of Japanese gardens are native to Japan, though after centuries of cultivation they can scarcely be described as wildflowers. So the idea that American gardens should contain American plants and that their presence will help to create a distinctive American style of gardening, in perfect harmony with the American landscape as the gardens of Italy and Japan are with their landscapes, is scarcely a radical one.

On the other hand, gardeners have always taken delight in importing choice plants from foreign lands—there are carvings on ancient Egyptian and Assyrian temples praising the rulers who had the benevolence to introduce trees and flowers that had never grown in those countries before. So whether you belong to the "natives only" school, prefer the beautiful garden plants of other countries, or prefer to blend the two, you will have plenty of tradition behind you.

It is true that native plants can create a feeling that the garden belongs to this land which is sometimes hard to achieve with exotics (using the term in the strict scientific sense of "coming from a foreign place or environment"). However this is a big country with many diverse climates and ecosystems. Can you really call a tree from the deciduous forests of New England "native" in San Francisco or Phoenix; or pretend that a prairie wildflower is anything other than foreign to the very different soils and climates of the humid Southeast? True, it is American, and thus pleasing to the patriotic breast in a way that a plant from, say, Australia won't be; but it isn't native in the sense that a local wildflower is.

Local plants do have the practical advantage that they are born to your own environment, and the chances are that they will flourish with little attention. And wherever you might live there will be native plants of great beauty to choose from: trees, shrubs or flowers, even grasses, though the use and development of the various drought-tolerant American prairie grasses for lawns is still in its infancy.

Most gardeners ignore the debate and grow what they like, no matter where it comes from, mixing native and exotic plants as their fancy suggests. And why not?

## *Trees*

Trees are the most important plants in any garden—they grow bigger, and live longer than any others, and they are the main creators of the form and structure of your garden. More than any other plants, they are the ones that enhance not only your garden but the entire street. They can provide, according to the type and how you place them, shade, shelter or privacy. Some give flowers in their season, and there is no better way of having the sensation of swimming in flowers than from a flowering tree. However flowers are not the prime consideration: elegant habit, attractive foliage and suitability for the position and use are more important.

*Whether low or tall, hedges introduce long horizontal lines to a garden and call for trees to balance them.*

*Seaside daisies set off the intricate patterns of tiled pavings. A mix of flowers would look restless here.*

Think of deciduous trees for summer shade and winter sun; of evergreens for screening and backdrops. Think too of trees that branch high enough to walk under, so that you can look up and see the sun shining through the branches as well as those that sweep the ground to be looked at from the outside as it were. Don't forget to think of the mature height and spread of your chosen tree, and how quickly it will reach full size. Scale is important: will it be too big for the garden, or just right? If you garden on a grand scale, you can think of forest giants; in small gardens, small trees are more appropriate.

## Shrubs

Shrubs are the workhorses of the garden, filling in the structure at and below eye level. They can act as screens for privacy, soften the lines of the house, or be given starring roles by virtue of their flowers, fruit or handsome foliage. They provide detailed interest for less expense and work than any other plant. But don't forget to allow them room to do their job; most shrubs will grow nearly as tall as they are wide, and it would be a pity if you have to be constantly trimming to get past them.

Try to value shrubs as much for their habit and foliage as for their flowers. It can be very telling to set some small, rounded shrubs in front of a tall, arching one; to set dense foliage against shrubs which feature an open tracery of branches; to contrast an upright grower against one of spreading, prostrate habit. And don't forget those shrubs which can be clipped to form hedges, or which lend themselves to training flat against a wall, in the the technique known as espalier. These can create a note of formality, and there are times when that is just what is needed.

## Ground covers

Low plants that carpet the ground with foliage, suppressing weeds, ground covers will grow in the dense shade beneath low branching trees and shrubs where few other plants will grow. They are often modest in foliage and flower, and their great asset is the unity and simplicity they can bring to a garden. Always planted in masses of a single species (you can make patterns of several types, but you'll always be fighting to keep them in balance), they tie together collections of disparate plants that rise above them. If you have a fine tree or group of trees, their beauty will be enhanced by allowing them to rise unencumbered by a clutter of fancy plants at their feet. Simple panels of ground cover can relieve the arid appearance of large areas of paving.

## Climbing plants

Do you have an unsightly fence or shed that you wish would vanish from your sight? Climbing plants (or vines) to the rescue. Do you want to soften the lines of the house and make it blend well with the garden? Try decorating the walls with a climber. Do you want shade in a hurry, and can't wait for a tree to grow? Build a pergola and grow a vine over it. In two or three years you will have the shade, while a shade tree is still only a sapling.

You can train some vines to grow flat

on the ground as ground covers—ivy is the classic example—or place them at the top of retaining walls to cascade down in a foam of greenery and flowers. Or, if you have a worthy but dull tree, try training some flowery climber into it to wreathe it in color. Just beware that it doesn't grow so heavy that it brings the tree down on top of you.

## Annuals and perennials

They don't have permanent woody stems, but annuals and perennials bear some of the brightest and most beautiful of all flowers, and no flower lover would be without them. The distinction according to the botanist is that annuals don't live to see their first birthday, ensuring their future by setting abundant seed; perennials live and flower for many years.

But matters in the garden are not as clear cut as that. There are many subtropical plants, perennial in frost-free climates but always grown as annuals where winter cold cripples them—petunias, gazanias, scarlet salvias and the busy lizzie *(Impatiens wallerana)* for instance. Conversely, other perennials need winter cold and rarely flourish beyond their first summer in mild climates. A notable example is the delphinium; long-lived in Britain where it is one of the glories of the classic perennial border, but best discarded after flowering in mild winter regions of California and the Southeast. The Iceland poppy is another; and then there are such plants as gaillardias, carnations and rudbeckias, which come in both truly annual and perennial versions. So we have decided to list all our annual and perennial flowers together. And there is no reason other than horticultural convention why you shouldn't mix and match them in your plantings also.

Some gardeners are prejudiced against annuals, which only live for a few months and thus put their owners to the bother of replacing them when they die. But if annuals' lives are short, they are filled with gaiety; in fact, some of the world's best loved flowers are annuals—sweet peas, marigolds, poppies, larkspurs, everlasting daisies. Annual flowers are generous with their blooms, and they are a great boon to the owner of a new garden. They grow quickly and give you something to admire while your slower growing, permanent plants are developing. In an established garden, they provide continuity of flower while perennials and shrubs are coming into bloom and passing out again, and you can use them to draw attention to focal points in your design. Cluster them at the front door, around the patio, on either side of steps; they don't call for a permanent commitment, and you can change your color schemes from year to year, even season to season. If you love novelty and variety, they are for you. Just don't make the mistake of building the garden

*The unmatched brilliance of summer flowers—here zinnias, begonias and roses—calls for a simple green backdrop such as the leafy wisteria in this garden.*

*Formal bedding needs to be on the grand scale of this bed of tulips and white daisies to look really stunning, and is most successful in public spaces.*

around them—you do need those permanent plantings!

With the current fashion for cottage gardens, perennials are enjoying a great revival. No wonder, for they are the flowers of Grandma's garden, and if you have childhood memories of beautiful flowers there, chances are that many of them were perennials. Coming up unfailingly year after year, they can be displayed in borders in the English manner, or you can just tuck a few here and there among and in front of shrubs, or beside a path: or blend them with annuals and shrubs for a kaleidoscope of color. Many have handsome foliage too, and some are providers of the boldest, most architectural foliage the garden contains. Use these in the way you use pictures and accessories and ornaments in a room; they draw the eye and provide the finishing themes. Their ease of propagation allows you to expand your holdings year by year; and many a lifelong friendship has begun with the gift of a piece of some choice perennial flower.

## Bulbs

If you want to initiate a friend into the joys of gardening, a sure-fire gift would be a packet of bulbs. If nature ever developed a foolproof way of packaging a plant it is this; just plant, add water, and before too long there will be flowers. We always associate bulbs with spring and with cool climates, but there are summer flowering bulbs and bulbs for warm climates too. They all share a perfection of form and color which is their own—but most only give a few flowers per plant each year. So plant them as generously as your purse will allow, in clumps, in bold masses under trees, in containers, in with other flowers. Plant great drifts of bulbs as though they were wildflowers in long grass. You can "naturalize" bulbs in ground cover plantings too.

*Daffodils can brighten a winter garden.*

## *Vegetables and herbs*

There once was a time when it wasn't quite nice to admit you had a vegetable patch. The master and mistress of the house may have taken the keenest interest in the vegetable garden, but no visitor ever saw the vegetables growing. They only saw them after they had been harvested and the cook had had her way with them.

Nowadays, many of us take great pride in our vegetables, and for many people they are the most important part of the garden. If that includes you, why not display them with pride? Not in the front garden, perhaps (we don't want to place temptation in the way of light-fingered passers-by) but in a choice position in the back garden, where they get the sun they need and where you don't have to make a safari out to the back of the shed to admire their progress. Lay the plot out with care, casting an eye over the proportions of your beds and laying attractive paths between them (grass, brick and gravel all have their admirers) and giving them a flattering backdrop of shrubs or fruit trees, not just a bare fence or a shed.

The problem is that a vegetable bed is never full. Just as the plants are beginning to develop sufficient growth to be worth looking at, the cook descends on them, and great gaps appear in your plantings. What to do? You could edge the beds with low-growing flowers (and why not include some annuals among the cabbages, to provide cut flowers for the house?) but it is even nicer to edge the bed with herbs. Most herbs are fairly low-growing, and their scent is a pleasure as you plant and weed. Their varied greens and textures offer much scope for developing garden pictures. Think, for instance, of the gray-green of sage in front of the darker, matt green of cabbages or the brighter color of lettuces ...

There is an old tradition of growing herbs in small formal gardens by themselves, and a small herb patch can be a pleasant accompaniment to a patio, but you needn't isolate them. Plant them as edgings to flowers, or set them among the blooms in a cottage garden mix. Their soft textures and varied greens will help stop a riot of colors turning violent with clashes—and again, their fragrance is definitely to be sniffed at.

Don't forget, too, that fruit trees (unless they are pruned into grotesqueness) are as beautiful to the eye as any other trees. Let them take places of honor in your garden design.

*Herbs lend themselves wonderfully to formal treatment as in this traditionally styled herb garden.*

*Tropical water lilies. A pond yielding flowers such as these is a garden in itself.*

## *Water gardens and water plants*

Even in the driest of climates, water in the garden adds a special dimension of pleasure. It needn't take the form of the elaborate fountains that Italian and Islamic gardens specialize in; just a simple pond reflecting the sky and cradling a water lily or two can bring great joy too.

In designing a garden pond, the important thing to remember is that it is the water that is the purpose of the exercise. It is so easy to get excited by water lilies, lotuses, Japanese irises and all the other water garden plants that the

*Even in the tiniest of ponds, you need to allow sufficient clear water to catch the light.*

*A butterfly on a scarlet canna.*

water vanishes in the greenery and you might as well have planted a regular flower bed. As a general rule, whether your pond be informal and naturalistic or frankly formal and artificial (and this is a matter of which will best suit the style of your garden as a whole), the water plants should cover no more than a half of the surface.

A second rule is to make your pond a good deal bigger than you first thought of it as being. The pond itself is just a hole in the ground with a waterproof liner. You can buy ready-made fiberglass pool liners, though they tend to be sized for portability and to end up looking like puddles. The choice for liners is really between concrete and plastic sheeting. Both have their devotees. Plastic is certainly easier and cheaper, though you must hold down its edges and conceal them with rocks or a strip of paving. If you choose blue plastic the pool will always look unnatural. Simply lay plastic over a sand base, taking great care that there is no unevenness or any sharp objects that will tear it. A layer of pebbles over the bottom will mask it from sight. Pebbles will help the appearance of a concrete pool too.

The plants need rich soil to grow in, and this is usually provided by planting in containers, wooden boxes being traditional. (You can't use plastic pots, which tend to float; it is a bit disconcerting to see a water iris topple over in full growth because its roots are trying to rise to the surface.) Give the plants rich soil, and, at the point where the pond can overflow when it rains, plant some of the many desirable perennials that love wet feet. If the water garden bug really bites, you could make it the theme for the entire garden, taking your cue from some of the old gardens of China and Japan, where the "lake" occupies most of the garden and the viewers stroll around it. If you fancy artificial waterfalls and rock work, go ahead. But first, spend a day or two looking at natural streams and waterholes to see how nature arranges rocks, water and plants. You'll learn more from her than from a torrent of words; but don't come back with the car loaded up with rocks. Those rocks are part of the natural ecology of the area, and are home to many wild creatures. It is scandalous to dispossess them.

Don't forget when you plant the pond to include as well as the water lilies some floating and submerged plants to provide oxygen to the water. These are essential if you aren't to have the pond all choked up with algae, and they are needed for the fish. Of course, you will have fish to keep the pond from becoming infested with mosquitoes. Goldfish in their various forms and varieties are the easiest to keep as well as the most decorative. Buy them from a good aquarium supplier, and, as soon as you introduce any new fish to your pond, treat it against fish diseases with methylene green. The people who raise fish take every care, but it is better to be overcautious. The aquarium shop will advise you about all these things.

## Birds and butterflies

While there are some forms of wildlife that you won't want to encourage in the garden—poisonous snakes, skunks, and the assorted bugs that will try to eat your plants—you will want to encourage birds and butterflies. This is easy to do.

Most of the birds we want to see are natives, and the recipe for encouraging them to visit the garden and hopefully take up residence is simple. First, you put a bell (or preferably two) on the cat. It's surprising how cats can learn to silence one bell when the urge to go hunting seizes them. Then, you plant as

*A pleasing arrangement of color is a personal thing; some may not have placed the yellow tulips in this display.*

wide a variety of native plants as you can accommodate. Honeysuckle, trumpet vines and sages are much loved by hummingbirds, and so are such exotic plants as butterfly bush and the South African tecomarias. Seed-eaters will go for coreopsis, cosmos, and sunflowers; fruit-eaters will eat the berries of wild cherries, huckleberries, and viburnums, as well as cotoneasters and their like too. Insect-eaters will come, too, for the native plants and trees provide their food without asking. Regular spraying not only cleans out the insects, it can poison the birds too. If you don't spray, the birds may well act as pest-control agents for you.

Don't forget that many native birds nest in hollow trees and branches, and you should think twice about removing these unless they are really unsafe.

We always think of providing food for adult butterflies. Any flat-faced summer flowers will attract them, not just the buddleias that are so much frequented by them they are called the butterfly bush. But don't forget that they start out life as caterpillars, and if you want butterflies in the garden there has to be a source of caterpillar food somewhere nearby. Many of the preferred caterpillar plants are weeds, and a lazy gardener will often be rewarded with more butterflies than an industrious, conscientious one. It's not fair, is it?

## Color

It is fashionable for gardening books to give learned dissertations on the "rules" of arranging color schemes, so that you are burdened with terms like "analogous harmonies", "complementary contrasts" and "color wheels"; and to give lists of colors that do and don't, in the opinion of the writer, go together. This book won't do any such thing, because the careful color schemes which might be appropriate in arranging wallpaper and furnishing fabrics fail to take into account that colors in the garden (by which most people mean the colors of flowers) are displayed and arranged against a background of green. The green of foliage comes in infinite variety, from the brilliant green of grass to the dark, almost black-green of some tropical plants to yellow-greens, olive greens, gray-greens, and the steely tones that gardeners are pleased to describe as "blue," as in the blue spruce and some cedars. All these greens are constantly changing with the time of year and time of day.

In any case, pleasing arrangement of color is such a personal thing; some people adore bright pink flowers, others don't; some find bright yellow shrill, others think it cheerful and sunny. Let

*A quiet scheme in grays and pale colors.*

your own taste and sense of the appropriate be your guide—and keep your eyes open when you see other people's gardens. They might have ideas that you can borrow!

## Fragrance

It used to be common to make scented gardens for the delectation of blind people, but the fashion has lapsed, fortunately, for most blind people found such gardens patronizing. They like to smell the flowers in the same sort of gardens that everyone else does. Indeed, scent on the air is one of the great delights of gardening.

The problem with writing about scent is that you can't describe it in any meaningful way except by comparison—and most flowers smell more like themselves than anything else. Nor can you photograph it.

Francis Bacon suggested that scented flowers should be planted along paths where you can sniff them as you pass by, and that still holds true. But he also reminded us that there are many plants whose fragrance is in the leaves, not to be released unless they are brushed against or crushed, and that these should be planted right at the edge of paths, "where you may enjoy them as you walk and tread."

In this book, we have noted when a plant is fragrant. In choosing plants for the delight they offer to the eye, don't forget the nose. Develop the habit of sniffing every new plant you meet, and plant your favorites in your garden with a lavish hand.

## Climate

We have discussed the influence of climate on the design of the garden, but mainly from the point of view of your, the garden user's, comfort. But your climate also determines, more than anything else, the selection of plants you can grow. The earth has many types of climate, from tropical to arctic, and nature has evolved plants to grow in all of them. Take those plants from the wild and bring them into a garden, and they will be happiest and easiest to grow where the climate matches that of their homeland. If it is markedly different, the plant will either not grow at all or it will lose its character. And it is not only the familiar phenomenon of a tropical plant freezing to death when struck by frost; the reverse is true too. Cold-climate plants need their winters to flourish. For example, we always say that cherries need a cold climate to grow, but this is not strictly true. There was, some years ago, a cherry tree in the Botanic Gardens in Singapore. It grew, but it never flowered or even lost its leaves; in the tropical climate it had become a non-flowering evergreen.

Nevertheless, it is frost that provides the sharpest division. Though it is true that plants that can stand frost vary in the amount they can survive, plants from warm climates with no frosts have never evolved defensive mechanisms to allow themselves to cope with being frozen. Take them to a frosty climate, and they die from having their cell walls ruptured by the freezing and expansion of their sap. In the USDA, "hardiness zones" have been worked out for the entire country plus Canada, based on the minimum temperatures expected and how long they occur. Gardeners have developed the habit of saying that a plant is hardy to zone 7 (or 3 or whatever) or "suitable for zones 5 to 9," say; if you are unfamiliar with a plant's cold tolerance, use the hardiness zone rating as a guide. In the mild West the worry is just as likely to be trying to grow some cool-climate plant in a climate too warm for it as the reverse and the limiting factors are likely to be drought and heat.

So for this book, in the plant entries we have described the growing conditions each plant requires, and its hardiness zones for all outdoor plants. And we have also noted if a plant is drought-tolerant; summer humidity, not just rainfall, is important.

## Buying plants

These days, gardening is big business. Every suburb, even inner-city ones, has its garden center; florists do a flourishing trade in pot plants; even supermarkets sell plants. It has never been easier to buy what you need to furnish the garden. If you can't find just what you are looking for, you can often find it advertised in the gardening press by one of the many mail-order nurseries.

Supermarkets and chain stores tend to buy nationally from one or more of the big wholesale growers. The fact they are selling a particular plant doesn't guarantee its suitability for your climate—you need to use your own knowledge. Also, conditions in an artificially lit, air-conditioned store aren't always ideal for plants (except indoor plants, usually a good buy). It is good fortune to find a salesperson who knows anything about them. Try to buy as soon as possible after the plants arrive. Walk by any that look like they are suffering stress. Bulbs and perennials in picture packets can often be a good buy here, but check them carefully—sometimes stock gets left on the shelves long after the planting season has finished and they are dead.

At garden centers and nurseries, you can expect the staff to be able to give good advice about the plants they sell. Often they will also have encyclopedic knowledge of what does well in their area, knowledge that can save you making costly mistakes. You should still look carefully at the quality and condition of the plants. Are they healthy, vigorous-looking and free from disease. Not potbound from hanging around too long (telltale signs are a plant that's just too big for the pot, with roots poking out of the drainage holes or at the surface), or obviously having suffered drought at some stage? Naturally, there shouldn't be weeds in the pots. Be prepared to pay a fair price; bargains are often plants left over from last season, offered cheap to get rid of them. They may grow well, or they may not; why spend money to take the risk?

Bare-rooted stock, like roses, fruit trees and perennials in season, should be

*A display of annuals like these pansies and double daisies takes a lot from the soil, which you have to put back if you want to repeat it season after season.*

plump and healthy, with plenty of roots. Reject any that look shriveled and dried out, or which seem to be trying to grow prematurely. Bulbs should be firm; if you find any that feel squashy or mildewed, examine the others even more carefully. But a good nursery knows that it trades on its reputation for quality ...

The same is true of the mail-order houses. Here you can't examine before you buy, but you should take a critical look at the plants the minute they arrive. Notify the nursery at once if they arrive in less than perfect condition. (A nursery that regularly supplies inferior stock won't stay in business for long.) Don't forget, however, that the nursery may be a very long way from you, and it is up to you to be sure that your chosen plants will grow in your area. The mail-order nurseries are often the best places to find rare, choice plants your local nursery may not even have heard of. When you find yourself reading their catalogues with the same eagerness as movie fans do the latest gossip about the stars, you know that gardening has you hooked.

## LOOKING AFTER THE GARDEN

### Preparing and cultivating the soil

Just what sort of soil you have doesn't influence the basic planning of the garden much as there are trees, ground covers and grasses suitable for just about any soil. But it does matter when it comes to choosing your plants, and then when you look after them. Geologists have developed many different classifications for soils, but the gardener needn't learn them. Garden soils are classed as light (or sandy), medium (or loam) and heavy (or clay), the terms referring to how easy they are to dig. (Sand is in fact weightier than clay.) Then, we want to know how deep our topsoil is before we strike the less-fertile subsoil or even rock; how well drained it is; whether it be acid or alkaline; and, finally, how fertile it is.

Let us look at each in turn. To find out whether you have sand, loam or clay is easy. Make a ball of just-moist soil in your hand. Does it feel gritty and crumble as soon as you open your hand? Sand. Does it feel gritty, but holds its shape, more or less? Sandy loam. Does it feel just slightly sticky and holds its shape but crumbles if you poke it? Medium loam—and go and open a bottle of champagne, because this is the sort of soil that gardeners' dreams are made of. Does it feel greasy, holds its shape, and polishes if you rub it with your fingers? Clay loam, heavy to work but not to worry; it will grow most things. Can you not only polish it, but mold it into delicate shapes like modeling clay? Clay.

Be prepared for hard work, but don't despair—clay soils are usually fertile. Away from the beach, pure sand is rare, and so is pure clay; most soils will fall in the range from sandy to heavy loam.

Strictly speaking, you should measure the average size of the rock particles that make up your soil to arrive at a more scientific classification. But these are measurements you can't make outside a laboratory, and for practical purposes the ball in the hand will tell you what you need to know.

Below the topsoil, you'll find the subsoil, which is usually, but not always, of the same type, but distinguished from it by a different color, due to its lesser humus content. It is normally more tightly packed than the topsoil, so that plant roots don't penetrate it as easily. As it contains less humus, it is less fertile. You don't usually want to dig it up and mix it with the more fertile topsoil, but if a little of that happens, it is no great worry. Below the topsoil and subsoil you will eventually come across rock. Sometimes this is quite close to the surface, sometimes many yards down; but as long as you have around 12–20 in (about 30-50 cm) of topsoil before striking it (or a solid subsoil) you have sufficient depth to grow almost anything.

It is the subsoil that normally determines how well drained your soil is. This is perhaps the most important thing to know about your soil. While plant roots need water, they also need air; if the spaces between the soil particles remain clogged with water for too long, they suffocate. Test your drainage by digging a hole around 16 in (about 40 cm) deep, which is as deep as most of us can take a spade without strain, and fill it with water. Come back in 24 hours, and if it is quite empty, you have no worries about drainage. If there is still a puddle in the bottom, you will have to do something to improve it, unless you are content to specialize in wet ground plants. There are a lot of these; but, alas, many choice trees and shrubs, lawn grass, and most vegetables aren't included on the list.

*The arum lily* (Zantedeschia aethiopica), *an obliging plant that actually loves wet, poorly drained soil.*

There are two ways to improve drainage. If your garden design suits, you can make raised beds. These can be an advantage if you don't like bending. Hold the soil with a wall (brick, heavy timber or whatever) and you can sit down rather than crouch to garden. Or you can lay agricultural drain pipes, leading the excess water to a sump or to a convenient ditch or creek. Thanks to the introduction of flexible plastic pipes, this isn't the difficult job it used to be, but it's still heavy work to dig a network of trenches to lay the pipes in. The usual arrangement is to lay branch lines across the slope, feeding to a main which should direct the water away from the house.

Happily, poor drainage is rare in suburban gardens—wet ground is not prime land for building development. Generally, the sandier the soil, the better drained it will be—sometimes too well, so that you barely seem to have finished watering before you have to start again—and sloping sites are usually well drained too. Poorly drained soils are often clays.

Then there is the matter of acidity and alkalinity to consider. This is a great business for show-off gardeners who like to be "scientific" and say things like "Oh, my soil is ideal—slightly acid; pH 6.8, you know." The pH scale measures acidity and alkalinity, with 1 representing a strong acid, strong enough to eat the end off your spade, 14 an alkali just as strong. The mid-point, 7, is completely neutral, like pure water, and each step is ten times as large as the next; thus a soil of pH 5 is ten times as acid as one of pH 6. Most soils fall within the range of 5.6 to approximately 8.6. The significance is that the higher the pH, the more alkalinity there is in the soil.

Some plants, like rhododendrons, azaleas, camellias and blueberries, prefer their soil acid (i.e. with pH less than 7); others, notably bearded irises, the cabbage tribe, and lilacs are lime-lovers and like a soil with a pH of about 8. If your soil is too acid for these, it is simply a matter of adding a little lime; if it is too alkaline (limy) for the acid-lovers, you are in trouble, as it isn't easy to acidify a soil. (Adding sulphur is the standard way, but worms and most soil-living microorganisms dislike it; you can grow the acid-lovers in containers of special soil.)

*Raised beds are a classic way to overcome less than perfect drainage—but they also are a great showcase for flowers.*

So the ideal is to have the soil neutral or slightly acid. (In our plant descriptions, we draw your attention to any special likes or dislikes in soil that a plant may have.)

You can buy soil-testing kits that will tell you just what the pH of your soil is, or you can send a sample away to your state department of agriculture who will test it for you. Easier, perhaps, is checking out what sort of plants are growing in the neighborhood. If you see many camellias and azaleas flourishing, you can assume your soil to be acid; if they are looking miserable, with odd russet and yellowish tints to their foliage, you can bet it is alkaline. Hydrangeas are even better indicators: in acid soils their flowers are blue, in alkaline ones pink. As a very general rule, sandstone or shale-derived soils or those in regions of high rainfall tend to be acid; those in dry areas inland, or where the parent rocks are limestones, alkaline.

Finally, there is the big question: is the soil fertile? To an extent, this depends on its type. Sandy soils tend to be "hungry," because the large spaces between their particles don't hold the water and the plant nutrients contained in the water. Clay soils, with their smaller pores, hold the water and nutrients more readily and are often more fertile. Loam is the perfect balance. But fertility depends even more on the amount of humus the soil contains. This substance, the end-product of the rotting of the remains of plants and animals—organic matter for short—gives fertile soil its instantly recognizable dark color. It provides the nourishment for all the microscopic life (bacteria, fungi, algae, tiny insects) which hold and release nutrients to the plants we grow. It also improves the soil texture, simultaneously aiding its water-holding capacity and its drainage. So if you want to improve your soil and maintain its fertility, the recipe is simple: add as much organic matter in the form of compost, well-rotted manure, and what have you, as often as you can. (Yes, we know it might be possible to overdo it; but where is the lucky gardener who has that much compost available?)

It used to be said that soil wasn't properly prepared for planting unless it had been dug to two spades' depth by a laborious process called "double digging." These days we are content to dig it over to as deep as the spade will go, breaking up the clods, softening and opening up the structure and just folding in (as a cook would put it) our compost. After the bed is planted, it is impossible to dig that deep without disturbing the roots of our plants, so we cultivate more shallowly, just sufficient to break up the crust that develops on the surface with the pressure of rain and watering. And if we put a protective blanket of mulch on the surface, we don't have to do that very often.

Don't fret about the type of soil you have. Sure, a slightly acid, crumbly medium loam is the ideal, but few desirable plants insist on it. Attend, if needed, to the drainage; and then, with regular cultivation, and keeping up the humus supply, any soil will become more fertile as the years go by.

## Fertilizing

To listen to some of the advertising fertilizer manufacturers have put out since factory-made fertilizers were invented about a hundred and fifty years ago, plants are made up entirely of the things they market. Not so; most of a plant's substance is made up of hydrogen, carbon and oxygen—elements that don't appear on the analyses given on fertilizer packages. The plant extracts these from air and water by the wonderful process known as photosynthesis. As a by-product, green plants release oxygen into the air, thus making life possible for animals, including ourselves.

Both the oxygen and hydrogen are derived from water. That's why plants grow ahead so strongly after a drought breaks; a plant deprived of water isn't just thirsty, it is actually starving too.

But living things are more complex than that, and there are many other elements that a plant needs to live. These it gets from the soil, absorbing them in very dilute solutions through its roots. Chief among these are nitrogen, phosphorus, potassium and calcium. Others, like magnesium, manganese, boron, iron, copper and what have you, are only wanted in tiny amounts and so are called trace elements.

Calcium is pretty abundant in most soils, and it is only if we want to grow lime-loving plants in acid soils that we need to add it in the form of lime. Lime (calcium oxide) comes in various forms. There is quicklime, the pure oxide; slaked lime is prepared by putting quicklime in water. Both of these will burn the skin off your hand if you are silly enough to touch them. Leave them to builders for their mortar mixes. If you want to apply lime use it in the form of pulverized limestone (calcium carbonate). Better yet, use dolomite, which contains magnesium as well. Not that magnesium (a vital component of the green pigment chlorophyll which makes photosynthesis work) is usually in short supply, but it won't hurt to add a little. The other three elements, nitrogen, phosphorus and potassium, are used up by plants. In nature most of these elements are eventually returned to the soil when plants die and decay. But in the garden there is always some waste—we harvest our vegetables and eat them, flowers are cut and taken into the house, prunings burnt or carted away. A prudent gardener establishes a recycling depot, otherwise known as the compost heap.

Nitrogen forms most of the air, but in that form it is of no use to plants. They need to absorb it in combination with oxygen (as nitrates) or with hydrogen (as ammonia). These come into the soil by several routes: they are formed by lightning in thunderstorms; they are released by the decay of once-living organisms; and they can be formed ("fixed") out of atmospheric nitrogen by certain bacteria that live in nodules on the roots of legumes, plants of the pea family. Nitrogen is a vital part of proteins, without which life can't exist. It is essential to plants if they are to grow and make abundant foliage. This is why high-nitrogen fertilizers are prescribed for lawns and for leafy crops like lettuces and cabbages. Sulphate of ammonia is the standard source of nitrogen in artificial fertilizers; blood meal (which is mostly protein) is the richest organic source. Compost and manure contain nitrogen too, in varying amounts depending on their origin, how old they are, and so on.

Phosphorus and potassium are needed for almost all life processes, but they play especially important roles in flowering and fruiting, and in the creation of woody tissue. Consequently, plants that we grow for their flowers or which we want to make firm branches (trees and shrubs) need them in abundance. A fertilizer designed for them will be proportionately higher in these two elements than in nitrogen, too much of which can promote luxuriant leaves and

*Here a raised bed takes the place of a front fence. Scarlet cannas bring bright color, contrasted with the soft blue trailing* Convolvulus sabatius.

*Spring bulbs are ideal for busy gardeners; they will bloom reliably with minimal care.*

few flowers. Nitrogen deficiency shows up in stunted growth and pale, wan-looking leaves, which usually drop prematurely.

Phosphorus doesn't occur pure in the soil, but in various salts. Most of these are very insoluble, and it is something of a mystery how plants actually get hold of them. It is thought that the soil micro-organisms are involved—and as these need humus to thrive, this is another reason for the compost heap. Soluble or not, phosphorus eventually leaches from the soil. The main organic source of phosphorus is bone meal. Phosphorus deficiency manifests itself in stunted growth, with leaves showing odd russet tones.

Potassium salts are highly soluble, and the element washes from the soil very easily. Fortunately, micro-organisms can fix it; but if you let a potassium-containing fertilizer get wet, you'll have lost much of its nourishment. Various potassium salts are used in the making of fertilizers; the main homemade source is wood ash (not coal ash!), which should always be kept under cover if it isn't going to be spread on the garden as soon as the fire has died. Seaweed is very rich in potash; if you want to collect it at the seashore, make sure you wash the salt water out before putting it on the compost heap. Potassium deficiency shows first in yellowing of the tips and edges of older leaves, which eventually die.

These are the big three. An artificial fertilizer containing all of them can be described on the label as "complete". The amount the fertilizer contains is usually given as a percentage by weight, and you will see such indications as N:P:K 7:6:7 or N:P:K 5:8:12 on the bag. (K stands for potassium which was originally known to 18th-century chemists as kalium.) Most companies make a range of blends for different purposes. Thus a nitrogen-high blend like 9:4:6 might be recommended for lawns, the lower-nitrogen 5:8:12 for shrubs or roses. Whether it is economical to have different bags for different plants is up to you to decide; many people find it easier to just buy a standard, evenly balanced mix, say 8:8:8, and use it for everything. You might also look for one that contains trace elements too.

The various trace elements each have their own functions, and each deficiency has its own symptoms (like the mottled yellow pallor of young leaves caused by iron deficiency or the between-the-veins yellowing of older leaves associated with lack of manganese). So if you suspect a trace element deficiency—and they aren't common, these elements being needed only in tiny amounts—it is better to give the plants a complete trace element mix or a general fertilizer containing them. Treat just the one you suspect and the chances are you will overdo it and throw the soil out of balance, leading to a deficiency of something else: and your last state will be worse than the first.

### *ORGANIC OR ARTIFICIAL?*

So we are going to fertilize our soil. The question is whether to do it with organic materials (the various forms of manure, compost, blood meal or bone meal) or with factory-made artificial fertilizers. In the short term, it makes little difference to the plants, which can only take in their nourishment in the form of solutions of chemical salts, and don't discriminate as to how they got there. In the long term it matters very much indeed, because if the soil is to remain fertile, it must have its humus content continually replenished so that the soil micro-organisms continue to flourish. So the thinking gardener always prefers organic fertilizers. Never mind that their N:P:K ratios are much lower than those of the artificials. They are feeding all the life of your soil; the plants you planted are only a part of this. Take an analogy, but don't stretch it too far—vitamin pills are richer in vitamins than food, but would you try to live on a diet of pills? You can give your plants a quick boost with artificial fertilizers occasionally, but make their main diet organic. The analogy holds true in terms of quantity too—artificial fertilizers must always be used with a sparing hand or you will overdose. It's really better to halve the manufacturer's recommended dose and apply it in two lots a couple of weeks or so apart. Don't increase the dose—a little may be good but more won't be better! Never apply artificial fertilizer to dry ground, and water heavily as soon as you have spread it. Otherwise you risk burning any roots and stems it comes in contact with.

### *MANURE*

There's a story told of First Lady Bess Truman, in the audience while her husband was lecturing a group of farmers on the virtues and uses of manure. A prim friend whispered to her, "Can't you get him to say something politer than 'manure'?", to which Mrs Truman replied, "Honey, if you only knew how hard it was to get him to say 'manure'!"

Even now, primness becomes us; let us simply note that manure is the rotted dung of animals. Until it has been rotted (mellowed if you like), it is far too sharp and strong to put on the garden. It will burn any plant it touches, and the neighbors will turn up their noses as they go by. If you do acquire it fresh, put it in a heap in an out of the way place, or spread it on top of the compost pile, and leave it to settle for six weeks or so, throwing an old tarpaulin or a piece of plastic sheet over it to keep rain from washing out the soluble nitrogen and to discourage flies. When it stops smelling like ... when it starts to smell less offensive, it is ready to use.

Dig it into the beds you are preparing to plant, or spread it as a mulch. Or make liquid manure out of it; simply put some in a cloth bag and steep it in a garbage can full of water like a teabag. When the water is the color of tea, it will be as rich in nitrogen as any artificial fertilizer. You can pour it around plants that need a quick boost, and throw the bag and its contents on the compost heap. Artificial fertilizers designed to be mixed up in water are available to give much the same effect without making you hold your nose. They are usually applied dilute enough to be absorbed by the leaves as well as the roots, and shouldn't burn. Even so, the makers usually suggest you pour them on in the cool of the evening. They can be applied with a hose-end sprayer or with a watering can.

Manure varies in richness and "heat" according to the animal it comes from. Pig manure, not often seen for hygienic reasons, is the "coldest", poultry manure the "hottest". Horse and cow manure fall somewhere in between. If in doubt, heap it up and wait; well-rotted manure is almost always safe to use. Exception: human manure. Only use it if you have a compost toilet that works properly; there is too great a risk of horrible diseases like cholera and dysentery otherwise. The Chinese have used "night soil" for centuries, and fertile stuff it is, but they always compost it first—and even so the history of China is studded with epidemics. Treated sewage sludge is indeed safe to use on paddocks and fields, but that has been prepared under skilled attention.

How much manure? Old garden books that assumed you had a horse or two give recipes that boggle the mind, calling for layers of manure 6 or 8 in (about 15–20 cm) deep to be spread over beds and dug in, and this often twice a year. Nobody can afford to buy the stuff in such quantities these days, but take the point: you can feel free to be as lavish as you can afford.

Dehydrated, pelleted, fairly odor-free poultry manure is a recent development. It's great stuff, but concentrated, and it needs to be applied nearly as carefully as an artificial fertilizer. Follow the suggestions on the bag, and store it in a dry place—if it gets wet in the bag it will putrefy.

Blood meal is a by-product of the meat industry and is the strongest organic source of nitrogen, with some potassium and phosphorus. It should be used as sparingly as an artificial fertilizer, just coloring the ground with the powder (think of a cook sprinkling powdered sugar on a cake) and watering it in thoroughly. Keep the dog off for a few days, or the smell will have him digging like crazy. Bone meal is similar, but is made from animal bones. It is slow acting and the best purchasable organic source of phosphorus, the best being wood ash. (Wood in this case includes paper.)

## *Compost*

No garden should be without its compost heap. Compost is the most readily available source of organic matter, and it is free but for the labor in making it. That isn't all that great either; you can simply gather together all the fallen leaves, grass clippings, bean stalks and other once-

*A small compost heap held with bricks.*

*A plastic compost bin.*

*The traditional, triple compost heap.*

living debris of the garden, throw them on a heap in an out-of-the-way corner, and come back a little while later to find compost. That little while may be several months or even a year, but sooner or later you'll find, under a skin of leaves and twigs that haven't completely rotted, a pile of the black, moist crumbly stuff that works such magic on any soil.

Compost freaks will throw up their hands in horror. "Compost making is a scientific process!" they'll say. "A heap like that takes too long to rot, half the nitrogen will have evaporated as ammonia, and the compost won't be as rich as manure, as it would have been had it been made properly." True; but compost isn't all that rich in N:P:K—that is not the point. It is mainly intended to keep the soil supplied with humus, its direct value as fertilizer being only secondary. Let us, however, look at the standard recipe for compost making, with the understanding that apart from piling up the heap just about all the manipulations directed are optional.

*While bark chips are a favorite mulch, they rot very slowly and don't add much to the soil.*

First, you gather together roughly a cubic yard of compostable stuff. This can be almost anything of organic origin, though the bulk will be plant matter. (Don't put meat in the heap or you'll attract flies and rude remarks from the neighbors.) Ideally, you want a mix of coarse and fine material, so that the heap will neither be too open to rot properly nor so well-packed that air can't get into it. Coarse stuff includes cabbage and tomato stalks from the vegetable garden, straw, weeds complete with roots and a bit of dirt, twiggy prunings (no thorns, please) and the like; fine includes lawn clippings, shredded paper, small fallen leaves and their like. Cooked vegetables are apt to go soggy and putrefy, and left-overs from the salad bowl are dubious—the oil tends to set like lacquer and preserve them. Perfectionists will keep the coarse and fine stuff separate, so that they can put them on in layers, like a layer cake.

You need to keep the heap compact. The best way to do this is to put it in a compost bin. Better yet, have two, side by side. Bins can be made of wood, bricks, or chicken wire stretched between four stakes, as you please and as your handyperson skills allow. (You can buy compost bin kits made from treated pine if you want to save head-scratching and trouble.) No need for a concrete floor; sitting the bin on the ground allows worms to enter the heap and assist with the rotting.

Into the bin you throw around 8 in (about 20 cm) of stuff, and on that you sprinkle a nitrogen-rich "starter", to encourage the bacteria and fungi that will do the rotting to begin their work. Poultry manure or blood and bone will be just fine; urea is even better. You can buy compost starters that claim to contain cultures of the bacteria and fungi. No doubt they do, but it is a rare garden (a roof top in the city, perhaps) that doesn't already contain plenty of them blowing about in the air. To the mix, add left-over artificial fertilizer, manure (rotted or otherwise), ash and the like. They will all help enrich the compost.

Keep piling in layers of stuff and starter, and when the bin is full, water it. Then you should cover it with a tarpaulin to keep the rain off; you don't want it all to get too wet or it may putrefy and smell of rotten eggs and worse. (If it does, it's a sign of it being too compact and too wet. Take the tarpaulin off, and stab the heap several times with a sharp stake to let some air in. That is really the only thing that can go radically wrong.)

Almost at once, there will be frantic activity from the bacteria and friends, the heap will start to get very hot in the middle, and there will be a smell of ammonia. No doubt this represents nitrogen being lost, but most of it will stay in the heap. Don't get obsessive ... When the ammonia smell passes (in a couple of weeks to a month) the heap is ready to be turned inside out, so that the bits on the outside get the benefit of the heat and activity of the middle. This is what the second bin is for—simply pitchfork everything into it, and the compost should be well turned. (Then you can start on making a new heap in the first bin.) Once again, the smell of ammonia; but this time when it fades there is no need to turn. That would disturb the worms, which will now come in and polish the compost. When most of them leave, it is ready to be shoveled out onto the garden. It will be black, crumbly and sweet-smelling, and free from weeds and diseases, which will have been killed by the heat of fermentation.

Even so, it isn't wise to count on this last quality—diseased material and such horrors as oxalis bulbs are better burnt to make ash. They should not be added to compost heaps.

The compost will keep for a while, but don't just sit and gloat over how gorgeous it is. Compost is not an end in itself; it is meant to be put on the garden to improve the soil. The lazy gardener can make compost without even going to the trouble to make a heap. Just spread your compostable material straight on your beds as mulch, sprinkle it with a bit of blood meal to ensure it doesn't take nitrogen from the soil as it starts to rot, and let it rot down in place. This has the fancy name of "sheet composting." There are neater mulches, more suitable for putting in the front garden where the neighbors might see them, but it's fine for the vegetable garden.

The makers of horticultural gadgetry have jumped on the compost bandwagon. In small gardens, the plastic compost bins are very useful; they take up less room than a full-sized bin and don't look quite so untidy. Some even come on a mount which enables you to turn them over and over, which the makers claim will accelerate the rotting process and give you compost in a couple of weeks. They don't hold much and are really only useful in a small garden or for the impatient. Shredders, alias chippers, are useful gadgets—they chop up prunings and other garden waste into small pieces. This allows you to compost bigger, woodier stuff than otherwise, and the neat same-sized pieces are great for sheet composting. The mulch looks so much better than when it is thrown on as it came. Like dishwashers a few years ago, they are moving up from being just gadgets to don't-know-what-I-did-without-it status. Most of us will only need a smallish, electric model.

*Planting seedlings into well-prepared soil.*

*Well-spaced plantings of ageratums.*

## Mulching

Mulches have become so much a part of gardening that it is hard to realize our parents found them a novelty. Basically, a mulch is a blanket you lay across the surface of bare soil to protect it against the crusting effect of rain and watering, to conserve moisture by blocking its evaporation from the surface, and to smother weed seedlings, and it can be of any of a wide variety of materials.

Cut-rate landscapers are fond of black plastic, which certainly holds moisture in and stops weeds; but it also blocks moisture getting in, and eventually suffocates the soil. It is a fine way to kill off weeds without digging or using weedkillers, but don't leave it on for more than six months or so. It is usually hidden beneath a layer of pebbles, which would make an effective mulch by themselves. Gravel or crushed rock or brick would serve too. These conserve a surprising amount of moisture, and by reflecting heat they keep the soil cool. But they are apt to be glary, and they look artificial except in a desert-style landscape.

Rocks don't add any fertility to the soil; organic mulches eventually rot down and add humus. There is an enormous variety you can use: grass clippings (don't pile these on more than ½ in (about 1 cm) thick at a time, or they will ferment, get hot, and clog into a thatch that suffocates the soil), fallen leaves, pine needles; compost, well-rotted manure; shredded prunings; straw; bark chips; shredded tanbark; old mushroom compost (careful, it tends to make the soil alkaline) and others which you'll find at the garden center, the precise selection varying from place to place. Sawdust is common, but it takes a lot of nitrogen to start it rotting, and it is best heaped up with a bit of compost starter and left for a few months.

Which of these you choose depends on which is easy and cheap to get, and how you like the look of it. Some, like straw or bark chips, can look a bit raw when they are new, but will presently weather into inconspicuousness. Just be wary of nitrogen starvation unless, as with compost, the rotting process has already taken place. Sprinkle some blood and bone over the mulch when you lay it.

How thick to apply mulch depends on how much you can afford, but the ideal with most materials is to have the mulch 1½ in (about 3–4 cm) thick, thinning it out a bit immediately around the stems of the plants. Less isn't so effective at smothering the weed seeds. Notice weed seeds; if weeds are already established, they will benefit from the mulch. Remove them first, and water the soil. Never, never, mulch dry soil—there has to be water to conserve! And a dry mulch will rob moisture from the soil beneath; water it after you spread it. That's it; but don't forget that the rotting eventually shrinks the mulch. You'll need to topdress it from time to time, though there's no need to use the same material as before.

You can, as our grandparents used to do, hoe the soil after every rain to create a dust mulch. The hoeing encourages the top inch or so to dry out, and the dust acts as a mulch, stopping further evaporation. It does work, but it's scarcely labor saving and the dust blows about in the wind.

## Planting

The actual planting of a plant only takes a few minutes, but how you do it is as important as anything else you ever do to it. Plant with care, and you get it off to a good start; do it carelessly and badly and you can cripple it for life. Don't be alarmed; there are only four rules.

*Rule 1.* Never put a ten dollar plant in a one dollar hole. If you haven't been able to dig the whole bed, dig as much as you can. Make your hole generously wider than the plant's roots, so that it has plenty of nice, soft soil to spread its roots into. People often dig a small hole in the middle of a lawn, pop a tree into it, and then wonder why it doesn't grow. They should have made a bed at least 3 ft (about 90 cm) wide, preferably wider, and planted the tree in that. Plenty of

*Nemesias, ideal cool weather flowers.*

*Cinerarias, almost always sown in flats or pots (the seed is very small) and then planted out.*

time to let the grass grow up to the trunk when the tree has had a chance to become established.

*Rule 2.* Disturb the roots as little as possible. If the plant is growing in a container, it has to be removed, and there is a right and wrong way to do it. The wrong way is to grab the poor thing by the stalks and tug. You'll get it out of the pot all right, but like as not you'll leave half the roots behind. The right way is to tip the pot upside down, holding the plant in the fingers of one hand, and give the rim a sharp tap to release the pot from the root ball. It can then just be lifted off. If the pot is too big to do this, lie it on its side and tap; the plant should slide out sideways. Advanced trees and shrubs are often grown in large plastic bags. These are best cut away with scissors, and then you can lift the plant (cradling the roots, not grabbing the stem and expecting it to take the weight of the soil) off the bottom.

If the plant is at all potbound and the roots are showing signs of going around in circles, gently release them and tease them out, or they will continue to circle forever and not break out into the surrounding ground. (Fast-growing trees and shrubs are very prone to this.) This might sound like breaking the rule, but not so if you do it gently and quickly, so that the roots don't get a chance to dry out. (If you're reluctant to do this, cut the circling roots by slashing the root ball in two or three places with a sharp knife; new, outward-going roots will grow where you cut.)

Seedlings growing in flats are tipped out the same way as other plants are removed from pots. The easiest way to separate them is to cut their roots apart with a sharp knife. Try to pull them apart, and you'll invariably lose soil and maybe bits of root.

Growing bags are on the way to superseding the technique of growing trees in the field and then lifting them and bundling up their root balls in burlap and string, but if you do acquire a "balled and burlapped" tree, they are easy to handle. Simply carry them by the root ball and undo the string when the tree is safely in its hole. Leave the burlap in place; it will soon rot and the roots will grow through its remains. If the burlap has been plasticized, remove it completely; it will not rot.

Fruit trees and roses are often sold bare-root, that is, without soil. These need care to ensure they don't dry out. Plan on planting them as soon as you get them home. Once they are unwrapped, keep them in a bucket of water. If need be, disentangle the roots, and trim any broken ones with sharp pruners. (Planting is simple enough: make your hole, spread the roots out over a small mound in the bottom, fill up with crumbly soil and water heavily to settle the soil around the roots.)

Drying out is the worst disturbance you can inflict on any roots—once you have plants out of their containers, don't dawdle.

*Rule 3.* Set the plant at the same depth as it was originally. This is simple enough with container-grown plants, and balled-and-burlapped and bare-rooted trees usually show a mark on the stem where the soil was in the nursery. Add or take away soil to adjust the hole's depth. With most plants, a whisker or two too deep or shallow won't matter, but do try not to set the roots too deep or there is a real danger of smothering them.

Grafted plants are normally set with the graft union just at soil level, though there are two major exceptions, citrus and lilac. Citrus are prone to collar rot, which is almost certain to occur if the graft is buried. Lilac, on the other hand, must have the graft set well below the surface. This is because it is normally grafted on the closely related privet, which is really too vigorous for it. Burying the graft enables the lilac to make its own roots and eventually smother the privet, which otherwise would push the lilac off after a few years.

Annuals can go in a shade deeper than they were in the flat, and most perennials are set with 2–3 in (about 5–7.5 cm) of soil above the crown. Bulbs, as a general rule, are set so they have twice as much soil over their noses as they are tall, though most won't mind if they are a bit shallower or deeper. Many have the remarkable ability to pull themselves down to where they feel comfortable.

*Rule 4.* Water the plant in well. First of course you need to fill the hole in around the roots with well-crumbled soil, and many people like to enrich this with a bit of compost to help the plant make the transition from the enriched soil of its container to the garden soil. Time was when people told you to trample it well to stick it to the roots, but that is no longer the fashion. Just water in well with the hose or water poured from a bucket, and that will settle the soil well enough.

Some gardeners like to water with a plant hormone to encourage new roots; others think it makes no difference. Naturally, you will water and mulch the new plant for as long as it needs it.

*A few don'ts.* Don't plant any plant while it is making active growth if you can avoid it. Even minimal disturbance to the roots will affect their ability to support the activity above, though if the choice is between planting and any risk of the plant drying out in its pot, plant. Don't plant out of the correct season for the plant unless you really have to, but especially not when the weather is hot and dry.

Warm weather planting from containers is fine, and most plants will establish quicker than they would in winter; but you do need to take extra care—its new home is probably less sheltered than the nursery was. Give it some shade for a few days (a newspaper teepee is just the thing for seedlings, a few leafy twigs or some shade cloth for a shrub) and water regularly at least until fall.

## *Watering and conserving water*

It may seem superfluous to suggest that watering is a skill; after all, any child can turn on a tap and wave a hose around. Yet it is a skill. The water we put on our gardens accounts for a surprisingly high percentage of our total water usage, and an alarming percentage of that water is, in fact, wasted.

*Often thirsty and prone to wilt if the soil gets a bit dry, hydrangeas tell you the garden needs watering.*

The golden rule is to water only when the plants actually need it and then to water thoroughly, so that the water actually penetrates to where the roots are. Frequent light sprinklings only encourage roots to stay near the surface, where they suffer as soon as the soil dries out again; deep watering sends them deep where the soil dries out more slowly.

It isn't possible to give rules like "water twice a week for twenty minutes." It depends on the weather and even more on your soil. Sandy soils absorb moisture more quickly than clay soils do, but they don't absorb so much, so excess runs away more easily and what has been held is used up faster. Clay soils are the opposite; they only absorb water slowly (especially when they are quite dry) but they hold onto it for longer. Watering heavy soils takes patience—you can't apply the water as fast as you can on sand. Loam, as in so much else, is the best balance, absorbing the water fairly quickly and holding onto it well. On any soil, you shouldn't apply water faster than the soil can absorb it—if the water is running away it is being wasted.

Similarly, you shouldn't waste water by evaporation. This will happen if you water in the heat of the day, especially if a dry wind is blowing, and the loss will be worse if you deliver the water in a fine spray. Much of it will evaporate even before it hits the ground! Early morning or evening, when the air is cooler and stiller, is better; better yet is the middle of the night, when the air is coolest and water pressure highest.

Not that anyone would want to leave a plant that is actually wilting till the evening—water at once! Plants send signals that they are suffering water stress long before they actually wilt, and the observant gardener learns to recognize them and act promptly. Leaves and flowers go, not exactly limp, but unhappy-looking and lusterless; grass retains your footprints instead of springing back; in many plants the stems and leaves lose the appearance of firm plumpness they have when they are well-filled with water. Some plants react faster than others, and you may want to plant such things as hydrangeas or acanthus as an early warning system. When they start to droop, it is a signal to get out the hose.

In drought-prone areas it is wise to make the backbone of your plantings

*Night time is the best time to water to conserve moisture.*

species that will survive and flourish with little assistance beyond the local rainfall. It is frustrating not to be able to give lists of these, but so much depends on your climate.

The best way to find out what plants are drought-hardy in your area is to make a tour of the neighborhood next time a summer drought strikes, and note the plants that are obviously bearing up without help. There will be plenty, and they should form the basis of your planting designs, with the more tender plants placed at key positions where they will give the best value for water.

*WATERING SYSTEMS*

Watering by hand can be a relaxing way to spend time in the evening, but to do it thoroughly takes more time than you would think. It can save time and water to install a sprinkler system. Almost every big hardware store these days can give you a choice of do-it-yourself systems, and if you want something more sophisticated there are plenty of more complex ones which need professional design and installation. These can be of mind-boggling complexity, with sprinklers that pop up out of the ground, electronic gizmos that sense when the soil is dry, and timers that can be set to turn the system on late at night when conditions are optimum and the chances of giving a visitor a surprise shower are least.

Somewhere along the range is one that will suit your needs and pocket. Designs and gadgetry are always changing and you should take the advice of the people who market the systems or an independent irrigation consultant. Let us only note here that in most gardens do-it-yourself systems can be perfectly adequate, and that the drip systems are the most economical of water, though the most fiddly to install (you need far more drip emitters than you do sprinklers) and to maintain, the tiny pipes clogging up easily and the absence of water only being noticed when a choice plant dies. If you install any watering system, do give it a test run every few weeks to ensure all is working properly, and install an in-line filter unless you can swear on the Bible to the purity of your water supply. And do arrange your system so you aren't watering pavement and driveways. They don't need it, you know!

You may prefer the old-fashioned but still effective method of sprinklers on the ends of hoses. Shifting these about is troublesome, and it is best to have several strategically placed taps rather than just one. That way you can run two or three sprinklers simultaneously. Short hoses last longer and are less fuss to handle than long ones too. It's a good idea to place a timer on each tap. They are quite cheap, and save the annoyance of finding that you have left the sprinkler on all night.

Three final thoughts on saving water. Mulching protects the soil from drying out; a single dripping tap or leaking pipe wastes thousands of gallons a year; and the single most important thing you can do to save water is to keep your garden weeded. One of the things that allows a plant to become a weed is super-efficiency at taking water from the soil. Why allow plants you don't even want to rob water from the garden?

## *Looking after a lawn*

Ask anyone who announces a dislike of gardening what they dislike about it, and chances are "mowing the lawn" will be high on the list. This is understandable; it is a chore with little creativity about it. Yet it is the most important part of managing a lawn. Leave the grass unmown, and eventually it becomes a meadow—the grass gets long, and the weeds come in. How often and how short to mow depends on the type of grass and also, to an extent, on the

*A massed planting such as this will help keep the weeds down.*

season. Fine grasses like creeping fescue and bent can take closer cropping than the coarser types like buffalo or tall fescue, and in a dry summer it is wise to leave the grass a little longer than usual.

As with any plant, cutting back the foliage takes strength from it, and when it is growing slowly you shouldn't weaken it too much. As a general rule, the fine grasses can be cropped to 1 in (about 2.5 cm) or a shade more, the coarser ones to 2 in (about 5 cm). Don't make the mistake of cutting as short as the mower will go in the hope of mowing less often. Scalping the grass only weakens it and allows weeds to get in—and then you'll be mowing more often, as the weeds grow taller and faster than the grass and look dreadful.

The actual layout of the lawn can make mowing easier or more difficult. Don't clutter it with flower beds and specimen trees any more than you really have to; and avoid sharp corners and wriggly curves, which make it difficult to get the mower right to the edge without much backing off and returning. Ideally, no corner should be sharper than a right angle, no curve smaller than you can easily sweep the mower round. If you fancy grass paths, in the vegetable garden or in a formal rose garden for instance, don't make them narrower than the mower! It is easy to make them exactly the same width, and that way you only have to push the machine down them once: but in practice that requires such careful handling that you might as well have them wider and make two passes. The same applies to the space between two trees, should you plant a grove on the lawn. Here don't forget to allow for the eventual thickening of the trunks. A gentle slope is easy enough to mow, but anything steeper than about 1 in 4 is both uncomfortable and dangerous. Consider planting banks with no-mow ground covers rather than grass.

*THE LAWNMOWER*

The mower itself is probably the most expensive item of gardening equipment you'll buy, so choose with care and look after it. There is nothing that gives the perfect velvet sward better than the old-fashioned hand-mower with its cylinder of blades kept razor sharp; but it needs cleaning and oiling after every use, the blades are fiddly to sharpen, and it takes energy to push it. Most of us aren't such perfectionists (or can think of more enjoyable ways to get our exercise) and will opt for a power-driven mower. Gas or electric is up to you. Electric mowers are quieter and save the bother of storing fuel, but the charging of their batteries takes time and they aren't as useful for a big or rugged lawn as the commoner gas-powered type. These come in either reel or rotary models, the reel being essentially a mechanized hand-mower. The rotary is easier to maintain, and better at tackling thick or wet grass; but it doesn't give the striped effect for which you must have a cylinder. Most people aren't that fussy, and opt for a rotary, with a grass catcher to save raking up. (Leaving the clippings on the lawn, to filter down between the grass blades and rot, is a better idea since the cut leaves compost in place, returning nutrients directly to the root zone of the grass; this works best, however, when the lawn is cut frequently to avoid the build-up of a thick thatch preventing air and water from reaching the roots.)

Whichever mower you buy, look after it as the manufacturer directs, and develop an obsession with safety in its use. Make sure the blades of rotaries are screwed on properly lest they fly off and amputate your foot; remove sticks, stones, children and toys from the lawn before you start; do not go away and leave the mower running, even for a minute; wear solid, protective shoes; and never, never, put your hand down near the business end while the machine is running.

*One of the greatest joys of* Camellia japonica *is that it needs so little pruning.*

*EDGES*

Trimming edges is as time consuming a job as mowing. There is no real substitute for the old-fashioned edging shears for this, though the mechanical edgers that operate with a flailing nylon line are adequate for the non-perfectionist. You can save a lot of work if you make your edges such that you can ride the mower over them. If you don't like the effect of brick, timber or concrete edging strips, at least keep the edges of your beds level with the grass and avoid the gutter so admired by professional gardeners. And don't edge your plantings with fragile things like lobelias or wax begonias that can't take the odd bump from the mower wheels! Beware the junction of ground cover and grass. They will tend to invade each other and have you down on your hands and knees separating them. You can just mow over the edge, but it will get messy-looking. If you can't make a mowing strip without introducing an unwanted element of formality, use ground covers or massed shrubs tall enough to have an overhang under which the mower can be tucked and which will hide the planting/grass interface.

*KEEPING WEEDS OUT*

The second arduous job is weeding. It sounds like "I told you so," but most sessions of hands-and-knees labor on the lawn could have been avoided, simply by starting with clean soil and keeping the grass growing strongly enough so that weeds don't get a chance to get in. (Yes, we know it will then need mowing!) If you do need to weed, it is often easier to cut the weeds out with a heavy kitchen knife than to use a trowel or hand fork. Just make sure you get all the root. Or you can try painting the weed with a small brush dipped in glyphosate, relying on the vigor of your grass to cover the bare patch. (If you are unfortunate enough to inherit a lawn that is more than 35 per cent weeds, you might be better off plowing the whole thing under and starting again.)

How to encourage the grass to grow strongly enough to be weed repellent? First, you need to water it: and here, more than ever, the golden rule of watering—infrequently but heavily—applies. A few minutes' sprinkling will revive the grass and have it looking fresh after a hot day, but grass roots are lazy, and this will only encourage them to stay close to the surface where they are likely to suffer as soon as the surface soil dries out.

Thorough watering, sufficient to wet the soil down deep, and only repeating it when the surface soil has really dried, will force the roots deeper and you'll have a much more vigorous, drought-resistant lawn. Water properly and you shouldn't have to water more than once a week, even at the height of summer.

Fertilizing is easy. Choose a good

brand of lawn fertilizer, and apply it according to the manufacturer's directions. Better yet, halve the quantity, and put it on in two lots two weeks apart. Spring and fall are the best times; and don't forget to water the fertilizer in thoroughly and at once, or you'll burn the grass. Organic fertilizers like manure and compost aren't really much use on the lawn—too bulky—but you might try blood meal. Old-time gardeners used to set much store by an annual top-dressing with sandy soil, but this is more a ritual than any real benefit; fertilizer is better unless you want to even out any hollows.

Lawn pests are basically two. Various grubs live under the soil, eat the roots and leave dead, brown patches. You can usually dig them up and leave them for the birds, or simply water the scene of their activities with a strong insecticide, or with a culture of *Bacillus thuringiensis*. (See the section on caterpillars later in this chapter.) Dollar spot is a fungus that attacks bent and Bermuda grasses and is worst in wet weather. It tends to leave lawn both dead and mildewed-looking; water with a fungicide. If dead patches are more than 12 in (about 30 cm) or so wide, it's desirable to sow some fresh grass on them; if less, the lawn will usually grow over them, but watch for weeds trying to get in first!

Constant traffic can compact the soil so that it sets like cement and water and air can't get in to the roots. The grass, no matter what you do, just doesn't grow vigorously. The solution is to hire an aerator, a kind of spiked roller, roll it over the lawn a couple of times to break the crust, and resolve not to park the car on the grass in future. The problem is worst on heavy soils, where it is a good idea to aerate every spring.

## *Pruning*

It may seem paradoxical, but the reason we cut bits of plants is to encourage growth. Yet that is the purpose of pruning. Bear it in mind, asking yourself, "If I cut here, what sort of growth will come?," and you should be able to prune just about any tree or shrub with confidence.

Indiscriminately "cutting back" isn't pruning; it's butchery, and the usual result is a misshapen, unhappy plant. Still, some gardeners love cutting back their plants, and can never see a shrub or tree flourishing without saying, "That is really getting beyond itself. It needs cutting back!" There is no need to become one of their company.

The golden rule is always to prune to a place where growth will come. Most trees and shrubs grow by first extending their branches, and then making side shoots from growth buds in the axils (the "armpits") of the leaves. To encourage these buds (the lateral buds) to grow, you shorten the branch, cutting to just above a leaf; to encourage the main branch (or the trunk of a young tree) to grow taller, you shorten any side shoots to divert the plant's energy into the end shoot, the terminal bud. And if you want to remove the branch altogether, you cut it right back to a junction with another, diverting the energy to that branch. However you cut, don't leave stubs. If you are cutting to above a leaf, cut just above it; if back to another branch, cut close. Stubs and stumps won't grow, they'll only rot, and the rot may spread into the living wood. Cut at the right place, and the wound will heal over nicely.

That's really all there is to it—to encourage side shoots, shorten leading shoots; to encourage leading shoots, shorten side shoots. The art is in deciding which to do. Many shrubs, though not all, bear most of their flowers and fruit on side shoots, and shortening the leaders encourages not only a bushier plant, it leads to more flowers. On the other hand, you might want to encourage the leading shoots, as when you are trying to get a young tree to grow tall in a hurry. Then you would shorten the side branches.

When do you remove a branch altogether? It might be dead, when it is no use to the plant; it might be senile, and the plant is already replacing it with strong new growth, as when you remove a branch of a mock-orange, say, or a rambling rose that has already flowered; it might be weak and feeble, its energy better diverted to other branches; it might be spoiling the desired shape of the plant, when you might want to shorten it simply for symmetry; or it might be crowding out other, better placed or stronger branches.

This last is the key to pruning trees. Usually, trees can grow perfectly well without pruning, though the prudent gardener removes dead branches before they fall on someone; but often a tree is a bit too big or too densely shady for its position. All too often, it gets cut back (topped) to make it smaller. This is usually a disaster. Topping may indeed make the tree smaller, but at the cost of ruining its shape; and the poor thing usually responds by making great bunches of new shoots, so that it is shadier than before. Controlled, regular cutting back, called pollarding, has its place in a formal garden where a lollipop-shaped tree can look appropriate: in most gardens, you are almost always better to thin out the crown of the tree, removing superfluous branches to let in the light.

With shrubs, thinning is often the wisest course also, as it reveals the lines of the branches and allows the light into the plant to encourage strong new growth; but every species is different, and you need to study how the plant grows. If, like a mock-orange, a hydrangea, a poinsettia, a raspberry or a rose, it grows by renewing itself, annually making new shoots to take the place of those that have spent their energy in flowers, then the basic job is thinning out the old wood to make way for the new, and these are the plants that call for the most attention from the pruning shears. (You can usually recognize them by their thicketing, multi-stemmed habit, with unbranched young stems and twiggy older ones.) If it grows more like a miniature tree, as camellias, bottlebrushes, hibiscus or crepe myrtles do, then it will need less pruning; usually the judicious removal of weak or overcrowded branches is all that is needed.

Nature doesn't prune, and you shouldn't get the idea that it is something that you must do every year or your plants will languish. Even roses, normally pruned each winter, can be let go for a while, and you only have to see a neglected rosebush covered with roses in some old garden to wonder whether we don't prune too much. When a description says "prune in winter," take it as meaning that is the time to prune if you think the plant will benefit from it. Many trees and shrubs can flourish without ever feeling the pruners or the saw.

Fruit trees are a special case. Here the aim is to keep the tree small enough to make spraying and harvesting of the fruit easy, as well as to encourage the plant to put its energy into maximum numbers of fruit. You can leave fruit trees unpruned (this is the rule with citrus, avocados, and most subtropical fruit) if you don't mind getting out the ladder to tend them. They can look very romantic growing naturally.

The next question is when to prune.

First, never prune anything during the period when it is actively growing and the sap is running; you risk having it bleed to death. There are a few exceptions; for example, you can pinch back the tips of such things as lavender, rosemary and boxwood to encourage the growth to be bushy, and you can pinch the long shoots of wisteria to keep the plant from getting out of bounds; but if you find yourself cutting into strong wood at this time, you will regret it.

The golden rule here is that unless you are hoping for fruit or berries to follow, prune after flowering and before growth begins. This means that spring bloomers, almost all of which bloom on the growth they made last year, are pruned in late spring or summer; they include such things as forsythia, weigelas, flowering peaches and their ilk, and wild roses. Prune them in winter, and you are cutting away the wood that will shortly be flowering. (You can do your pruning while the plants are in bloom, taking the cut off branches inside for flower arrangements.) Summer bloomers usually flower on growth made in spring, and in their case "after flowering" means during winter.

Unless you expect spring flowers from them, most trees can be thinned in winter; but the after-flowering rule applies here also, so you can do the job in late summer or early fall after growth has slowed down. This can be the better time if the aim is to let in sunshine; you can see the effect more easily if you prune a deciduous tree while the leaves are still on it.

The next rule is to use the right tools; you'll do far more harm by tearing your plant about with the wrong tool than from ignorance. If the branch is too big for pruning shears, you will need long-handled loppers or a pruning saw; if you find yourself wishing for a chainsaw, call in a professional. Tree surgery is dangerous work, and chainsaws lethal in the hands of the inexperienced. You don't want to find yourself falling out of a tree and breaking a leg or worse. And keep your tools sharp so they cut cleanly. Ragged cuts heal poorly and infections can get in. If you aren't used to using a whetstone, send your tools to be sharpened professionally.

## Propagating

It has never been so easy to buy plants, but there is still satisfaction to be had in propagating your own—it's cheaper too.

*Impatiens are easy to propagate—just pick a few stems and stand them in a glass of water to root.*

The basic way is from seed, the way most plants propagate themselves in the wild. Almost any garden plant can be grown from seed (unless hybridity or doubling, which transforms the reproductive organs into petals, has made it sterile), and seed-grown plants have the advantage that they start out life healthy—very few plant diseases are transmitted through the seed. But gardeners can be an impatient lot, and don't always want to wait for seedlings to take their time about flowering, as most trees shrubs and perennials do. Also, many highly bred plants don't "come true" from seed. These we propagate by division, from cuttings, or by layering or grafting, according to the type of plant. Collectively, these are known as "vegetative" means of propagation, and they give you new plants exactly the same as their parents. A group of plants propagated vegetatively from a single original is called a "clone." The named varieties of roses or fruit trees are examples of the clonal method of propagation.

### *GROWING SEEDS*

Plants differ in the ease with which they can be raised from seed, but basically it isn't difficult. The first thing to note is that your seeds must be fresh. If you have bought them, they should be fine if sown by the "sow by" date, provided you haven't broken the seal on the packet. Don't try to save unsown seeds for next year; the germination rate falls off markedly. (Saving some for a second sowing in a few weeks, as one does with many vegetables, is fine.) If you save your own seeds from the garden, make sure they are quite dry before you store them, a sealed container in the vegetable drawer of the fridge being the best place. Sow at the right time of year, which will be given on the seed packet or can be looked up in books like this one.

Whether you sow your seeds in a nursery bed or in pots, the soil should be fine and crumbly. A bed can be improved by the addition of some sand or vermiculite. For sowing in pots you can buy special seed-raising soil mixes. Naturally, you'll make sure there are no weeds or weed seeds to confuse matters. Water your seed bed well to encourage weeds to germinate and zap them with glyphosate, then wait a few days before sowing. The basic rule is to sow seeds so that they are covered by their own thickness of soil, and this is easiest if you make furrows to sow them in. A pointed stick will do the job nicely. Very fine seeds need only a light dusting of soil to cover them, and it can be easier to distribute them along the furrow if you bulk them up with some dry sand. Large seeds like nasturtiums or pumpkins can be placed individually. Such plants are often sown where they are to spend their lives, in the regular garden beds, as are many vegetables. Smooth the soil over, pat it down very gently, and water with the finest spray your hose or watering will deliver. Until the seeds have germinated, you need to keep them constantly, evenly moist, which will mean daily attention in warm weather.

How long the seedlings will take to come up depends on the species. Most annuals, including vegetables, appear in ten days or so, but perennials and shrubs can take much longer, some preferring to be sown in the fall and given a spell of cold before germinating in spring. Be patient!

If germination is as good as it should be, the baby seedlings will be crowded. As soon as they are big enough to handle, prick them out into another container or another bed until they are big enough to transplant to their final homes. If they are already in their permanent bed, thin them out, leaving only the strongest at the required spacing.

The biggest potential problem with young seedlings is damping off, a fungus that rots them. Poor drainage in the seedling bed encourages it, and so does too humid an atmosphere which you might get if you are sowing in a greenhouse or have enclosed the pots in plastic bags to keep them from drying out. Take the precaution of watering with a dilute fungicide as soon as you see signs of germination.

### *DIVISION*

Division is the easiest method of vegetative propagation. At the appropriate planting time, you dig up a clump of perennials or bulbs, and shake the excess soil off its roots. The clump may simply fall into pieces, but often you'll have to pull it apart or cut it apart with a sharp knife or pruning shears. The result is several new plants, which you can plant in their new homes immediately. Don't try to make the divisions any smaller than what comes easily, and give preference to the strong new sections from the outside of the clump.

### *CUTTINGS*

Cuttings are the standard means of propagating most shrubby plants. All they are is a piece of stem around 4–6 in (about 10–15 cm) long, detached from the plant and put in soil in the expectation that it will make roots. Not all shrubs will strike from cuttings—eucalypts are impossible and rhododendrons and lilac recalcitrant—but most are easy enough. Cuttings are classed as follows: softwood or tip cuttings, taken from the ends of actively growing shoots in spring or summer (fuchsias, impatiens, lavender); semi-mature or half-ripe cuttings, taken after growth is complete but before it is quite ripe, usually about the middle of summer (camellias and most spring-flowering shrubs); and hardwood cuttings, taken in fall or winter from wood which has fully matured and might even be dormant. Roses are the classic example of these.

All cuttings are prepared in much the same way. Take the piece of stem you want, allowing about 4 to 6 joints where the leaves arise, and trim the bottom end of the stem just below a leaf, using a razor sharp knife or blade so as not to bruise it. Cut off any leaves that will be buried, and trim the remainder in half to stop moisture loss. Then you simply insert your cutting in a very sandy soil, either in a pot or a suitably sheltered bed, and keep it moist. Softwood and semi-mature cuttings are best given some protection from dry air, the standard way being to enclose pot and all in a clear plastic bag. Nurseries now use misting systems that keep the air of a greenhouse as humid as a Turkish bath, and these have allowed many plants to be propagated from cuttings that were regarded as too difficult before.

Dipping the end of the cutting in rooting hormone does help the "take," but make sure the stuff is fresh. It loses potency quickly and has a short shelf life.

The speed with which roots will form varies greatly. Be patient; as long as your cutting hasn't withered it will be trying to root. After a fortnight or so, you can tip the cuttings out of a pot to check on progress provided you don't disturb them. When you see roots growing, the plants can be potted on or transplanted, treating them as gently as seedlings.

*Ivy cuttings will often root in water, but ground-cover plantings usually layer themselves.*

### *LAYERING*

Layering is used for shrubs that don't root easily from cuttings, but it is useful also for any shrub when you only want a couple of new plants. It's simple to do; you bend a branch down to the ground and bury a section, holding it firmly in place with a short stake. Roots will form—eventually—where the stem was buried. Then the new plant can be severed from its parent and transplanted. Some shrubs like rhododendrons will take their time about it. You can nick the stem where you want the roots, but take care not to cut right through. A wipe with rooting hormone won't go astray. Many sprawling or creeping plants—raspberries, rambling roses, hypericum, ivy ground covers—will layer themselves naturally, and they are the easiest of all plants to propagate. Rummage around the base of an old plant, and chances are you'll find new ones waiting for you.

### *AIR-LAYERING*

The only problem with layering is that you have to be able to bend the stem down to the ground. If this isn't possible, you can try air-layering. This always looks like magic, but isn't difficult. Spring or early summer is usually the best time. Select a suitable branch, and trim off any leaves, then cut it part-way through, being careful not to cut it off. If you are worried about it breaking, brace it with a stick. Then pack around the cut with wet sphagnum moss, and wrap that in a sheet of plastic, tying it on firmly. You'll need to check that the moss doesn't dry out; when it is evidently full of roots, you can detach the new plant, unwrap, and plant it in a pot.

### *GRAFTING*

Grafting is one of the high points of the gardener's art, and also one of the most ancient. It has many different techniques, but they all involve the uniting of a piece of stem from one plant to the roots of another. It seems a lot of fiddling; why not just take a cutting? The answer is that by selection of the plant that provides the roots (the understock), you can influence the growth of the plant grafted on it (the scion). Thus you might want to give a cultivated plant the strength of wild roots, which is why roses are almost always grafted despite many of them doing quite well from cuttings. Conversely, you might want to reduce the vigor of the scion. This is the often the case with fruit trees. A cutting-grown apple tree, for instance, will normally grow unmanageably tall: but graft it onto a less vigorous, "dwarfing" stock, and you produce a smaller (and often more fruitful) tree. But the two plants keep their genetic identity—graft a white grape onto a red one, and you'll get white grapes, not pink ones.

Grafting needs to be done at the optimum time, when the stock is growing strongly and the sap will run straight up into the scion and keep it alive while the tissues are growing together. To make the union requires exquisite care in matching the cambium layers, the band of green tissue just beneath the bark where the sap runs and cells are dividing. Fail in this, and the graft won't take. This is delicate surgery, calling for sharp knives and a steady hand.

Budding, the method used for roses and fruit trees, is the simplest form of grafting, and the one you should start with before graduating to cleft grafting and the more exotic types like veneer and approach grafting.

### *MERICLONAL PROPAGATION*

There is yet another method of vegetative propagation which we should note, though you probably won't be able to use it yourself. This is mericlonal propagation, which involves cutting out, under a microscope, the very tip of a growing shoot—just the few cells that are actively dividing—and placing them on a sterile growing medium. The tip gives rise to a mass of undifferentiated cells called callus, which can be cut into pieces that then are placed in a different growing medium to grow into plants. The method has had huge success in making formerly intractable plants readily available, and has allowed outstanding orchids to be propagated in quantity much more quickly and cheaply than before. It can also be used to create virus-free clones of old cultivars whose vigor has declined through infection. Wine-growers are hoping it will be able to restore old, virus-ridden but still ultra-choice varieties to health and productivity. We will be hearing a lot more of mericlonally propagated plants in the future.

*Snails.*

*Slugs.*

*A "snail trap."*

*Cabbage butterfly caterpillars love nasturtiums.*

## *Controlling pests and diseases*

Nothing is more off-putting than a long list of the bugs, grubs and fungi that are just lying in wait to attack your plants and destroy your garden in the twinkling of an eye—unless it be an equally long list of the dangerous chemicals that you have to douse them with. Some of these kill one bug, some another. Identification of the precise nature of the trouble is evidently crucial; you wouldn't want to mistake a greenfly for a blackfly, or brown rot for black rot.

Happily, things aren't nearly as bad as that. For one thing, many pests are specific in the plants they attack, and unless you grow these you'll never see them. Then, most plants do have a certain amount of resistance—it's rare for major harm to be done before you can notice and take action. The multifarious pests and diseases really only fall under a few headings; and once you have decided what group the problem falls into, deciding the appropriate remedy is usually easy.

### *SNAILS AND SLUGS*

Perhaps the most bothersome of all pests are in a group of their own: snails and slugs. They eat leaves, any sort of leaves that are soft enough, with a particular fondness for newly planted seedlings. They'll climb into plants to get their dinner, and have no compunction about eating flowers. If you can catch them, you can simply squash them; but that calls for constant vigilance. Night-time and wet weather (the times when most of us prefer to stay indoors) are the best times to go snail hunting. The standard way to control slugs and snails is to scatter anti-snail pellets, which you can buy in many suburban supermarkets as well as at garden centers. Some people worry about them, as there is a risk of poisoning other wildlife feeding on dying snails. You can protect delicate plants by surrounding them with a circle of ash or diatomaceous earth, across which the snails can't slither; or you can use salt for the purpose if you don't mind its disastrous effects on the soil. Also time-honored is setting saucers or small dishes up to their rims in the soil, and filling them with beer, which snails adore. They drown in it, making a revolting mess ...

*CATERPILLARS*

Perhaps the next tribe of pests is the caterpillars, the juvenile stage of moths and butterflies. No one would like to be without butterflies in the garden, but happily the most desirable and decorative butterflies rarely come in such numbers that their caterpillars do much damage. It is usually the ones which are least attractive as adults that cause the most trouble as juveniles. Chief of the caterpillars is that of the cabbage white butterfly, which chews up the leaves of not only cabbages but their kith (broccoli, cauliflowers, Brussels sprouts and the various Chinese cabbages) and kin (wallflowers, stocks, honesty) and other plants as well. They are especially fond of nasturtiums. Then there are the tent caterpillars whose web-like nests cover branches of cherries and other trees; budworms, the tiny pests that curl up in the young leaves of roses and other plants and eat the developing growth; the tomato hornworm that feeds on tomatoes; the corn earworm, which eats the developing ears of corn; the loopers, which walk by doubling themselves up as they eat just about anything green; and finally the cutworms, white grubs that live below the soil and eat roots. These curl up if you dig them up and expose them to the air, a defense that might protect them against birds, but leaves them defenseless against the gardener who promptly squashes them.

Squashing them if you can catch the beasts—fortunately very few caterpillars

*Tomato caterpillars.*

*A cut worm.*

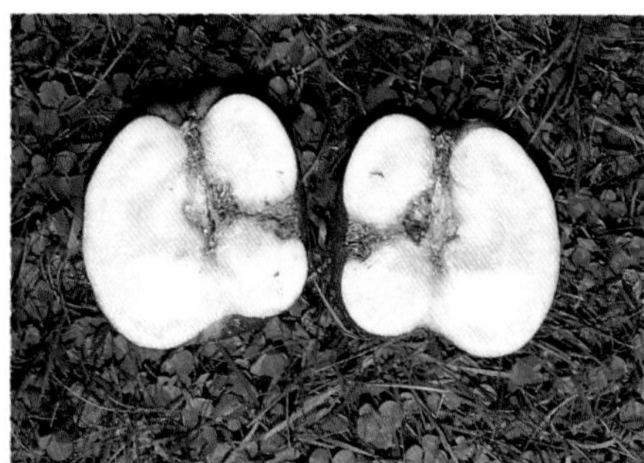

*Codling moth damage.*

move quickly—is the easiest way of dealing with caterpillars if there aren't many. If you see a shoot rolled up by a budworm, squash the shoot before you open it up or the caterpillar will escape. Processional caterpillars are best sprayed. You will want to spray any kind of caterpillar if they invade in greater numbers than can be controlled by squashing. The standard anti-caterpillar spray is carbaryl, which is certainly effective but poisonous both to people and birds that might eat a dying caterpillar. A better alternative is the cultures of the bacterium *Bacillus thuringiensis*, which gives caterpillars a disease (milky spore disease) fatal to them but not to birds or other animals. Look for the name in the small print on the packet; the best known preparation is marketed as Dipel. Mix it up according to the package directions, and spray it on; if you suspect cutworms, water it into the ground where you think they are. The only problem is that it doesn't persist;

*Borer damage.*

*Sawdust evidence of borers.*

*Borers in an angophora branch.*

once the caterpillars have all died, the bacterium dies also, and if new caterpillars arrive you have to spray them with a fresh culture.

Borers, which burrow into the stems of trees, are caterpillars too. Their activities are revealed by masses of stuck-together sawdust around the entries to their tunnels, and if you see this you should take action at once, as a severe borer attack can kill a tree. The standard treatment is to poke a wire down the tunnel in the hope of impaling the caterpillar; if you can't reach it,

Harlequin bug.

Red spider mite damage.

Mealy bug.

squirt some kerosene or methylated spirits into the hole. (It is very hard to get any sort of spray into the holes.) Borers are particularly fond of wattles and of some conifers. There are types that molest cherry and pear trees too.

Borers usually have trouble invading a vigorous and otherwise healthy tree, and borer attack is often a sign that the tree is unhappy. Water and fertilizer are called for.

Another caterpillar that gets inside the plant where milky spore disease has trouble reaching it is that of the codling moth, a major pest of apples, pears and quinces. The moth lays its eggs on the developing fruit, which by the time it ripens is ruined by being full of little grubs. When the caterpillars are fully grown, they leave the fruit to pupate in crevices in the bark and in litter at the base of the tree. The first step in controlling them is to clean off loose bark and rubbish from the base of the trees. If you like, you can tie a collar of corrugated cardboard around the trunk, where the pupas will make themselves at home; you can then burn cardboard, pupas and all, before they turn into moths. But if the moth is bothersome in your area, you will have to spray with carbaryl every two or three weeks from the time the flower petals fall until the fruit is approaching ripeness. Remember too that if you grow fruit trees, the law may well compel you to control pests such as codling moth and fruit fly or face a fine.

### BEETLES

Beetles are not usually a great nuisance, except for a few which become troublesome on certain fruit or vegetable crops. Watch for asparagus beetles, Colorado potato beetles, cucumber beetles, Mexican bean beetles and plum curculios—each feeding on a few plants other than those suggested by their names. The imported Japanese beetle has the broadest appetite, including many garden flowers. The simplest control—

Aphids on a rose bush.

and least toxic—is to systematically search suspect plants for the beetles and crush them when found.

Rotenone or pyrethrum sprays work on most offending beetles. Try killing the ground-dwelling white grubs of the Japanese beetle by soaking infested areas with a solution of milky spore disease *(Bacillus papilliae).*

### SUCKING INSECTS

Caterpillars and their ilk are chewing insects, which need to be poisoned directly—you have to get the poison onto them, which means thorough spraying. The big tribe of sap-sucking insects includes beetles, aphids, mealy bugs and scale insects. They don't do the immediately obvious damage that caterpillars do, but they can severely stunt the growth of a plant. Just as importantly, they can spread virus diseases. The suckers can be controlled by most insecticides, but their control has been made much simpler by the development of systemic insecticides, the most important of which is dimethoate. These are absorbed by the plant and render its sap poisonous to the pests. (To people too, so you need to be very careful about using these on plants which you plan to eat. The poison dissipates after a while, and you should be scrupulous about observing the "withholding period" noted on the label.) The great advantage of systemic insecticides is that not only do they not

White wax scale.

Red scale on a lemon.

get washed off by rain, they protect parts of the plants which the spray didn't reach. They are most effective against the sap-sucking tribe; the chewers have to do a fair amount of damage before they take in enough poison to affect them, and there is no substitute for dousing them with insecticide.

### SCALE INSECTS

The grand exception to all this is the scale insects, sap-suckers which live sedentary lives, secreting a carapace of wax to protect themselves. This it does very effectively, and they don't seem to pick up systemic insecticides much. The most familiar are the white wax scale and red scale which affect citrus and many other shrubs, and the white scale of roses.

The gardener's strategy here is to wreck the carapace, destroying the tiny breathing tubes the insect builds into it, so that the insect suffocates in its own wax, and this is done by spraying with horticultural oil, which dissolves the wax. This is tricky stuff to use, as it can burn the foliage in summer heat—check whether you are about to use "summer" or "winter" oil. If the plant or the infestation is small, you can avoid using horticultural oil by brushing methylated spirits onto the scales. An old toothbrush is ideal, and if it scrubs the insects off, so much the better—they can't crawl back on.

### *NEMATODES*

Nematodes or eelworms are microscopic worm-like creatures that live in the soil and attack the roots or bulbs of a range of plants. The destruction of the roots causes the plant to wilt and often die, and they cause bulbs to rot. They are especially fond of tomato roots and daffodil bulbs, but they are not very common. Fortunately, as they are very difficult to eradicate. The soil can be fumigated to kill them, but this calls for professional help; the chemicals are very dangerous and shouldn't be used by the home gardener. African and French marigolds secrete substances into the soil that drive the nematodes away, which is why they are often planted with tomatoes. Daffodil bulbs can be treated in hot water. But if you are unfortunate enough to suffer eelworms, crop rotation—planting different crops in the same ground in consecutive plantings—is the only real defence.

### *BACTERIA*

The bacterial diseases are the rarest, which is just as well as they are difficult to treat. The most common bacterial diseases are those that cause cankers and galls on the stems and sometimes the leaves of stone fruit, tomatoes and oleanders. Here you can do little except remove and burn the affected parts in the hope of destroying all the bacteria, a course of action to follow too if you get bacterial leaf spots on ivy or geraniums. Gladiolus bulbs are sometimes affected by bacterial scab, which manifests itself in black, rotted areas. Burn any affected bulbs, and don't replant new bulbs in the same place.

### *FUNGI*

The fungi are the main diseases. There are many of them and they tend to be specific in their choice of plants to attack. They fall into two categories: those that spread through the soil and those that attack the leaves, flowers or stems. Let us look at the latter first, as they are the most common.

The fungi that attack leaves, flowers and stems fall into two categories: those that stay mostly on the surface and those that burrow into the plant to do their damage from within. The surface-living types like the assorted mildews, molds and rusts, are simple enough to deal with. Spray at the first signs of infection, using the fungicide currently fashionable for the particular fungus, and keep spraying at weekly or ten-day intervals until the problem clears up. The important thing is to get in as early as possible and spray thoroughly, making sure that all the leaf surfaces, including the undersides, are coated with the spray. Fungicides are mostly based on copper, the old standby being copper oxychloride, though this is pretty potent stuff and can damage soft foliage. Many old-time gardeners swear by Bordeaux mixture, originally developed in the nineteenth century to protect the French vineyards against mildew; it incorporates both copper and sulphur, another traditional fungus killer, but it needs to be applied in large quantities and is anything but biodegradable. More recent fungicides are less damaging to the environment and need less chemical to do their job, which is of course a good thing. They aren't all copper based, some incorporating zinc (Zineb) or manganese (Mancozeb). Don't worry over much about what goes into a fungicide—read the label and it will tell you which fungus it is designed to kill.

The systemic fungicides, which work in much the same way as systemic insecticides, are no longer new, and they have proved the best defence against the fungi that get into the plant tissues the way black spot of roses and some vegetable rots do. They are effective against the surface dwellers also. Like systemic insecticides, they don't have to be applied quite so meticulously. Fungi

*Mildew on a grape leaf.*

*Sooty mold.*

*Hollyhock rust.*

mutate and develop resistance to chemicals even faster than insects do, so any list of remedies for specific fungi becomes outdated surprisingly quickly. The best way to deal with any disease (or insect) is to take the advice of the people at your local nursery, showing them a sample of the problem if you are uncertain about it, and then read the directions on the packet of any chemicals they give you with care.

Soil-borne fungi, like soil-dwelling insects, are a headache to deal with. Drenching the soil with fungicide is not very effective and can wreak havoc on the humus-producing micro-organisms. The most feared is root rot, *Phytophthora cinnamomi,* alias cinnamon fungus. This can kill and cripple the roots of a very wide range of trees and shrubs. By the time you see the plant suddenly wilting, it is too late to save it. The fungus flourishes best in damp ground, and the best preventive and remedy is to improve drainage, or to plant plants that like wet feet, which are often resistant to the fungus, and to be obsessive about not transferring infected soil to other parts of the garden.

Honey fungus, *Armillaria,* is nearly as bad, particularly in the West and in the South. It ringbarks the roots. While it usually starts out on the roots or stump of a dead tree, it can spread to a live one. To guard against it, always remove the stump and as much of the roots as you can if you have to cut down a tree. It eventually produces small, honey-scented mushrooms—delicious eating but poor compensation for the loss of a fine tree or shrub. It can be eradicated by fumigating the soil, a job for a specialist professional. Club root affects the cabbage tribe and their relatives. Sufficient to note that it cripples the plants and crop rotation is your best defence.

### VIRUSES

It is a general rule that viruses are untreatable. The only thing to do is to destroy the infected plant before the virus gets a chance to spread, which it can do by the activities of aphids and by careless gardeners exchanging plant fluids by way of unclean pruning shears. But don't act in haste. Some viruses, such as rose wilt and the viruses that affect lilies and tomatoes, are indeed fatal and to be viewed with fear and loathing; others are more-or-less harmless. But they do generally reduce the vigor of an infected plant.

*Black spot on a rose leaf.*

*Mosaic virus on an apple tree.*

Where you are offered the choice of certified virus-free stock of *anything*, pay the extra money for it. Some viruses are indeed viewed as desirable: many variegated-leaved plants get that way through virus infection, as do some striped and blotched camellias; and the classic desirable virus is the one that "breaks" the color of tulip blossoms into stripes. (In seventeenth-century Holland, these "broken" flowers were much prized, and were so expensive that speculators started trading in tulip bulb futures, to the enrichment of some and the ruin of many. Eventually the government had to step in to stop the "tulipomania.")

Happily, few virus diseases are transmitted through the seed, and you can often save your stock of a plant dying of a virus by saving some seeds and growing them.

### SAFETY FIRST

It is easy to speak glibly as we have been doing about spraying, but all these chemicals are poisonous and you need to handle them with care. Don't even try to spray if there is a breeze blowing, or you'll get spray everywhere you don't want it, including on yourself. Wear protective clothing. Long trousers, long sleeves, gloves and safety goggles, and even a handkerchief over your mouth and nose, are the minimum. When you have finished spraying, wash both your clothes and yourself. This even applies if you are using the relatively non-toxic insecticides like pyrethrum or its derivatives. And take great care when mixing different chemicals as they may not be compatible. At best they may not work; at worst the mixture may be poisonous to plants. If you want to mix, say, an insecticide and a fungicide, check the labels on the packets. If that doesn't give you clear answers, phone the manufacturers or the local office of your state department of agriculture to get advice before you start mixing chemicals.

Naturally, keep all garden chemicals securely stored out of the reach of children and pets. There is no need to arm yourself with a whole arsenal of spray guns. For small jobs you can often buy the sprays ready mixed in aerosol cans; medium-sized jobs can be adequately dealt with by a pump-up pressure gun which holds a quart or so of spray. For big tasks like a whole bed of roses or a fruit tree, there is nothing easier than one of the gadgets that attaches to the end of the hose. These are apt to only give a coarse spray, but that probably won't bother you too much. Wash your equipment thoroughly with warm water and detergent when you have finished; and if you are in the habit of spraying weedkiller, keep a separate gun, prominently marked, for it.

Don't forget that there are many, many beautiful plants that are not bothered by pests and diseases. If you concentrate on these, you won't have to be alarmed by what you have just been reading.

## Weeds

Console yourself. *Every* year is a dreadful one for weeds. If your soil won't support a decent crop of weeds, it won't grow anything else.

Weeding is still everyone's least favorite gardening chore, and it is one that you can't really design away. No matter what you do, weeds *will* appear, to rob your desired plants of light, nourishment and water and make your garden unattractive.

What is a weed? There is an old saying that it is simply a plant in the wrong place. The classic example is Bermuda grass, one of the most desirable of lawn grasses but apt to provoke the gardener to unprintable language should it escape from the lawn into nearby flower beds. And some plants that are great pests in one area may be desirable plants in another. Another definition is that it is a plant which a local government authority has declared to be a weed and which you are, therefore, obliged to remove from your land should it appear. Not all such "declared weeds" meet the usual gardener's definition of an uninvited, unlovely plant that would take over the garden (and the wild!) if you let it. Your local authority should be able to give you a list of the declared weeds for your area, and the fines, if any, for harboring them.

While the invention of the non-persistent herbicides like glyphosate (Zero or Roundup being well-known brands) that do not poison the soil has given the gardener the upper hand in the battle against weeds, the victory still goes to the swift. Pull weeds out as soon as they come up and they won't get a chance to go to seed. Eventually, the reservoir of weed seeds in your soil will diminish and the standing army will go away. Seeds will still blow in from next door or down the road, but you will be ahead. Just remember that most weed plants have long-lived seeds and there is truth in the old adage, "One year's seeding, seven years weeding." You can either pull by grasping the weed at its base, or dig it out with a trowel—a bit of practice will soon show which suits you better; just make sure you get the whole plant.

Mulching, provided the stuff you do it with isn't full of weed seeds, gives you an advantage in the war, as mulches smother most weed seeds and prevent

*Little hop-clover* (Trifolium dubium).

*Bermuda buttercup* (Oxalis pes-caprae).

*Creeping oxalis* (Oxalis corniculata).

*St Augustine grass killed by herbicides.*

*Onion weed* (Nothoscordum inodorum).

*Bermuda grass escaping from the lawn.*

*The edible dandelion* (Taraxacum officinale).

*Petty spurge* (Euphorbia peplus).

*Purslane* (Portulaca olearea).

*Crabgrass* (Digitaria sanguinoles).

them germinating. If any do come up, the soft texture of the mulch makes it easier to pull them out.

Weeds can be annuals, perennials, or even shrubs or trees. The annuals are perhaps the easiest to deal with. Pull them up before they go to seed and put them on the compost heap. Then you can mulch to smother the germination of any seeds that might still be lurking. (Don't leave any weed just lying there; they have an alarming ability to re-root themselves.) Paradoxically, the shrubs and trees like blackberries, privet or unwanted Norway maples are nearly as simple, as they grow slowly in their youth. All you have to do is make sure you get all the roots when you pull them up. (This does get harder as they get bigger!) The most difficult are the perennial weeds that proliferate from underground runners or bulbs—horrors like oxalis, onion weed and nut grass, *Cyperus rotundus*. With these, you must, must get every last root, tuber or bulb or there will shortly be an even bigger crowd of baby weeds waiting for you. You can't get rid of them by mulching; they just come up and grow all the stronger.

Dealing with these is when glyphosate really comes into its own. Spray it on, and it should kill the whole plant. But watch you don't overspray and kill plants you want. In close country, you might want to paint the weed with a small paint brush. This is worth doing in lawns too;

if you are careful you won't kill so much grass that it can't grow quickly over the bare spot where the weed was. There are selective weedkillers that will kill broad-leafed weeds and not the grass but their safety is suspect to say the least. Few of us would want to use them these days.

You can also eliminate weeds in lawns by successive tillings. Established weeds will be destroyed the first time round and will bring new weed seeds to the surface. Get these a couple of weeks later. Till two or three times to eliminate resident weeds.

Weedkillers, like all garden chemicals, are poisonous. Take the greatest care in using them. Don't breathe the fumes; don't get them on your skin; wash up thoroughly after using them; and don't store them where they might fall into the hands of children.

One last thought on weeds: before you pull out a tiny seedling, do make sure it is a weed. Sometimes garden plants seed themselves, and you might be pulling out something choice by mistake. Give the suspect a chance to identify itself first.

## ORGANIC GARDENING

With the growing awareness of the importance of conserving the environment, organic gardening has become fashionable. We may not, as individuals at least, be able to do much about saving the Amazon rainforests, but we can do something about the patch of land we have in our own stewardship, keeping it healthy and free from poisons, in harmony with nature.

After such a lofty beginning, it can be a disappointment to find that organic gardening has no hidden secrets. It is easier to define organic gardening in terms of what it is not. Basically, it is gardening without the (often dubious) benefits of modern chemicals. Organic gardeners don't use weedkillers; they pull weeds out by hand. They don't spray bugs and fungi with chemicals, or at least not with the newer ones developed by the petrochemical industry. They prefer to squash caterpillars or, when spraying can't be avoided, to use old-fashioned chemicals like Bordeaux mixture or home-made sprays like garlic water. (Infuse a few garlic cloves in 2 cupfuls or so of boiling water, as though you were making tea; when it reeks of garlic, it is ready to use. Tobacco water is made the same way, using the highest-tar cigarettes you can buy.) Organic gardeners don't use chemical fertilizers, relying on compost and on manure.

The basic philosophy of organic gardening—returning what we can to the soil and avoiding chemicals that might damage the environment—is simply common sense. A fertile soil is one which contains a flourishing population of micro-organisms, and they cannot long endure without the constant replenishment of humus that comes from compost or manure. Chemical fertilizers don't help them, and, what is more, fertilizers do leach from the soil to pollute waterways and other soils. Sprays, no matter how non-toxic their manufacturers hope them to be, should always be regarded as poisonous and dangerous to the environment until proved otherwise.

Any gardeners who really care about their soil and garden will make compost;

*The most widely accepted marriage of companion plants—French marigolds protecting tomatoes against soil-dwelling nematodes (eelworms).*

*Nasturtiums are said to enhance the growth of most vegetables. Here they are with broccoli.*

will give preference to organic fertilizers like manure and blood and bone rather than chemicals like superphosphate and sulphate of ammonia; and will use chemical sprays only when absolutely necessary, after less drastic controls of pests and diseases have failed. Most gardeners garden like this. The days when people used to spray their gardens from fence to fence every season just in case there was a bug lurking somewhere are long over.

Whether the result of strict organic gardening practices is indeed more flavorful, more nutritious vegetables and healthier flowers is hard to say. Some scientific research suggests no, that the nourishment contained in an orange is the same whether it was "organically" or "chemically" grown. But it will be as free as it might be of chemical residues: and the soil that grew it will, or should, be still healthy and fertile; and that is worth aspiring to.

## COMPANION PLANTING

The idea that some plants exert a beneficial effect on others growing nearby and others inhibit their growth is an ancient one that is enjoying renewed popularity. Many of the companion plantings suggested even now tend to be among the vegetables and herbs that interested the old herbalists and alchemists. Scientific evidence shows that there is some basis for the belief. It is known, for example, that African and French marigolds secrete substances from their roots that repel nematodes and that the reluctance of grass to grow under eucalypts is due to its being poisoned by the secretions of certain insects that live on the gum leaves. Planted among tomatoes, which are prone to nematode attack, the marigolds offer some protection. Some of the widely accepted companionships follow.

### HAPPY

Roses and garlic (the garlic protects the roses from aphids, and it is claimed, intensifies the roses' perfume)

Beans and sweet corn (train the beans up the cornstalks, and remember to water and fertilize for both); beans also grow well with potatoes

Tomatoes and marigolds; tomatoes like onions and garlic also

Potatoes and cabbages; and maybe the other members of the cabbage tribe also

Nasturtiums and most vegetables

### UNHAPPY

Walnuts and most other plants (fallen walnut leaves and walnut roots poison the soil and prevent other plants growing beneath the trees)

Sunflowers and almost everything else

Cabbages and beans

Peas and onions

## LOW-MAINTENANCE GARDENING

Non-gardeners are apt to wish for no-maintenance gardening. "I want a beautiful garden that never needs any work!" is one of the cries most familiar to a professional garden designer's ears. Gardeners know better; gardening, even the boring bits like weeding, is one of the happiest of hobbies. Even so, there are times when we would like to do something else with our spare time; just as houses should be labor saving, so gardens should be too.

There are many ways to achieve the low-maintenance garden; here are two of the easiest.

The celebrated English garden designer Russel Page used to say "trees, grass and water." That sums up one approach, that of concentrating on plants that need little attention to grow well and look handsome. (Grass might seem an odd inclusion; but unless you are a perfect-lawn freak, it isn't really all that demanding to maintain, not compared with beds of annuals or vegetables, anyway.) The best trees certainly fit the bill, but there are many shrubs, and indeed ground-cover plants too, that need little care other than admiration.

You need to take your climate and soil into account here. Any plant that needs extra watering, sheltering from the cold, or spraying because it is growing in

*These brick pavers are set slightly below the level of the grass, so the mower can just ride onto it and trim the edges automatically.*

*A raised stone edge like this keeps the lawn out of the flower bed.*

conditions that aren't exactly right for it can't be called "low maintenance," however it might behave in other climates and gardens. Neither can a plant that needs constant pruning, dividing, or dead-heading to look presentable be called low maintenance.

This may sound awfully boring, but in fact there is a good range of beautiful, easy-care plants: and if limiting your choice leads to simplicity of design, so much the better. There is no need to be purist and banish your own favorite flowers—just don't go overboard on them, and place them at key points where they give maximum effect for the work you put into them. Search among the flowers, and you'll find many that need only once- or twice-a-year attention, among them the evergreen daylilies, the shrub roses, the daffodils that come up, flower, and then obligingly disappear beneath ground covers or mulches. Remember though, that if a plant doesn't appeal to you, you will

*Where the plants are being massed like these regal pelargoniums, unattractive plastic pots will be largely hidden by foliage.*

resent *any* care that it asks for ...

Native plants are often touted as easy-care, as they were bred by nature to our soils and climates. Moreover, few have been subjected to the ministrations of the plant breeder which can so often lead to bigger flowers or fruit at the expense of health and vigor. True, but only up to a point. Some of the most desirable native (by this we mean American) plants are easy care but short lived, and after 10 or 15 years lazy gardeners may find themselves facing the major job of replanting much of the garden.

The other approach is to be meticulous in your layout, so that the chores of gardening are minimized. Thus you would arrange to surround a messy tree with a ground-cover planting into which its fallen leaves, twigs and so on will vanish to make a mulch, rather than a paving or lawn where they would have to be swept up. Lawns can be given mowing strips of brick or concrete to eliminate the chore of trimming the edges, and to keep the grass from invading nearby plantings. Paving should be set so that it meets the lawn at the same level, instead of a few inches higher, for the same purpose. Pavings and ground covers could take the place of some areas of grass; and you could try using neat, dense shrubs instead of having clipped hedges.

The prudent gardener combines both approaches, and remembers that no garden can truthfully be called "low maintenance" until it is well established. Immature trees and shrubs will need watering, fertilizing, protecting from such nasties as snails and caterpillars, and maybe pruning; ground covers won't be weedproof until they have grown to make a solid mat of foliage, and newly planted grass needs pampering. Any garden, low maintenance or not, needs some attention from time to time—wouldn't it be somewhat boring if it didn't?

## *GARDENING IN CONTAINERS*

At first thought, growing plants in containers seems a perverse thing to do. Why imprison a plant in a pot where it is utterly dependent on you to water and fertilize it, and where it will need more care than it would if it were growing in the ground? There are many reasons.

First, you can give a potted plant individual care, with a soil mix designed to suit it, watering or not just as it needs it, and a position in sun or shade as it needs. Some plants with specialized needs such as epiphytic orchids and some cacti are usually grown as pot plants for this reason. Baby plants, whether grown from seeds or cuttings, are usually grown on in pots while they are too delicate to take their chances in the competition of the open garden. They will suffer less shock when they are transplanted than they would if they were lifted from the open ground; and most modern nurseries grow most of their plants in pots for this very reason. You and I can buy them, take them home and plant them at almost any time with reasonable certainty of success.

Then, you might want to grow your plant on a paved terrace, on a verandah, even on a balcony or roof. Here, pots can make the difference between having plants or not having them. Or you might be renting your house on a short lease, and want to be able to take your plants with you when you go—plant them in the ground and you are making a present of them to your landlord.

Put a plant in a handsome container, and you give it importance. It's a bit like setting a statue on a plinth or a picture in a frame. And you might want to use a potted plant or a group of them to create a focal point—next to the front door, at the head of a set of steps, around a swimming pool for instance. You might then want to take advantage of container plants' portability to arrange a changing display, retiring one plant as its flowers fade and bringing in another that is just coming into bloom. This way you can have interest all year.

Just about any plant can be grown in a pot, at least for the time being. Full-sized trees can be grown in containers, and many a city tree is growing in a huge planter box while cars park in a basement beneath its roots; but few gardeners will want to deal with something so cumbersome. A half-barrel is about as big as most of us can cope with—and even that will need two people to shift it—but it is quite big enough to grow a shrub. Bearing in mind that a container plant like this draws the eye, choose one that looks good for much of the year. Think of long-flowering, handsome evergreens like dwarf pines, hibiscus, camellias, azaleas, cotoneasters, even citrus. There are also many others.

Smaller pots offer their own possibilities. Annuals, spring bulbs (which often flower a week or two earlier in the warmth of a pot than they do in the open ground), those frustrating fall bulbs like nerines and blood lilies that won't bloom without summer drought (shift them out of the rain when they die down); ferns; even vegetables and climbing plants. (Try training a moonflower or a honeysuckle up a tripod of tall stakes to make a column of bloom—an eye-catcher indeed.)

A cluster of small or medium-sized pots has more impact than just one, and you can mix and match your plants just as the mood takes you—one of the joys

*A complete garden growing in containers on a balcony. The pink and white flowers are petunias, which take very happily to container life.*

*This handsome glazed Chinese pot holds a complete spring garden of primulas, violas and lobelias (which haven't started to flower yet).*

of container gardening.

Window boxes are enjoying renewed interest. They dress up the front of a plain house like nothing else can, and to an ornate one they add an extra touch of gaiety. Geraniums and petunias are the traditional plants for them, but you can plant any sort of low or trailing things you fancy. Ferns and fuchsias would be nice in a shaded spot; and what about some herbs conveniently outside the kitchen window? The important things are to make the box itself generous in size—8 in (about 20 cm) is a minimum width and depth—and to fix it securely in place.

The containers themselves offer great choice. Plastic pots have been much improved in recent years, and there are more to choose from than just the old black ones, useful as they are as temporary homes for plants that are going to be planted out. The material doesn't age well, however, and though its lightness

*Bring potted spring bulbs out to show them off, then retire them after they have finished flowering.*

*Nothing dresses up a facade the way window boxes do, and the simplest plantings are always the most effective, like the impatiens and lobelias here.*

*A collection of different terracotta pots, given unity by a common theme of gray foliage: catnip* (Nepeta), *lamb's ears* (Stachys) *and sun roses* (Helianthemum).

*Some of the variety of sizes and shapes available in terracotta. The bright flowers in the center are* Colchicum autumnale.

is usually an asset, it won't be if you are planning a tall plant which might get blown over in a high wind.

Terracotta is the material with several thousand years' tradition behind it, and even in the plainest models its warm color is flattering to almost any plant displayed in it. It has an advantage over plastic in that it is porous; it is harder to overwater a plant in terracotta. Salts from fertilizer tend to make a white bloom on the surface, which isn't pretty. It does wash off easily, but also it can be minimized by painting the inside of the pot with olive oil before you plant—a trick practised by the ancient Romans. As long as you don't have an accident, terracotta will last for hundreds of years, mellowing in beauty all the time.

Glazed earthenware and porcelain pots have been fashionable for years. The best come from Italy (but are very expensive) and the Orient (rather cheaper), though there are potters making attractive ones here. They offer good accommodation for plants, with three caveats: they are sometimes rather fragile; the fancier ones are apt to distract from the plants they are supposed to be showing off; and some of the large Chinese ones have no drainage holes. That's because they aren't flower pots at all, but egg jars or goldfish bowls. You can drill holes in them, but it's a risky business.

Wood is traditional for containers too, whether in the form of cut-down barrels or in more elaborate designs like the *caisses de versailles* originally designed for the gardens of Louis XIV. Wood has the great ability to keep the roots of any plant growing in it cool, no matter how hot the summer. Choose wooden containers as much for their durability as their looks. Teak, cedar and redwood are the timbers of choice; treated pine is a reasonably economical alternative. All will last longer if they are oiled or painted.

Reinforced concrete is the material of the most daring modern architecture, but did you know it was first developed to make flower pots? That was back around 1800, and concrete pots have been with us ever since. Their walls have to be thick, so there is no point in trying to make them small; most concrete pots are tub sized and heavy. The weight is a disadvantage; few concrete tubs are truly portable. So is the ease with which the material can take molded decoration, usually with unhappy results. The most attractive concrete pots are simple in design, and these days are often colored and finished to resemble stone. You can paint them, though moisture from inside usually flakes the paint off in a couple of years and they then look tatty.

Splendidly carved urns and vases of stone and marble are sometimes available, though they are fabulously expensive. Should you be fortunate enough to have one, you have a work of art which could be the focal point of the entire garden.

*A container need not sit in spendid isolation. This decorative urn filled with pansies adds a graceful note to a bed of flowers in fetching blue and yellow tones.*

Whatever the material, make sure your container has adequate drainage holes; nothing will kill your plants faster than wet feet. For the same reason, it isn't wise to stand an outdoor pot in a saucer, which will stay full in wet weather. Only do this for real water lovers like arum lilies, willows or Louisiana irises. Over the holes it is customary to place a few pieces of broken pot to keep the soil from washing out. (Unless you are in the habit of breaking pots, these crocks are hard to come by; try pieces of brass or aluminum window screen, which will also keep out worms, which rapidly wear out their welcome in the confines of a pot.) Then add your potting soil and plant, ensuring an inch or so (about 2.5 cm) between the finished level of the soil and the rim for water.

A time-honored potting mix, suitable for most plants, can be made from equal parts of good garden soil, sharp sand, and peat moss or the coarser stuff from the compost heap, with a handful of complete fertilizer added to each barrowful. Unless you are planning on a lot of pot plants, you'll probably find it easier to buy one of the ready-made potting mixes which every garden center carries these days. Premium grade is worth the extra money, and you can buy special mixes for acid-loving plants like azaleas. Recently, water-retaining granules which you add to the potting mix have become available. They aren't cheap, but they do reduce the need for frequent watering a little. A point to watch: always use fresh potting mix; it can be tempting to re-use soil that has held annuals or bulbs, but don't. It will have lost structure and nutrients and the new plants will suffer accordingly.

Planting is just the same as when planting in the open ground—follow the four rules. Make sure your plant is accurately centered in the container, or it will annoy you every time you look at it. Looking after container plants is simple. Water them when they need it (in summer this can mean every day) and fertilize them regularly, as the constant watering leaches nutrients from the soil rather quickly. Here slow-release fertilizers are well worth their high cost.

Annuals are simply discarded at the end of their season, but other plants will eventually need repotting when they exhaust their soil. If they can go into a larger container, fine; if not, you may have to prune the roots. This is easy—simply tip the plant out of its container, shave $^{1}/_{2}$ inch (about 1 cm) or so off the sides of the root ball with a sharp knife, and replant.

# *Hardiness Zone Map*

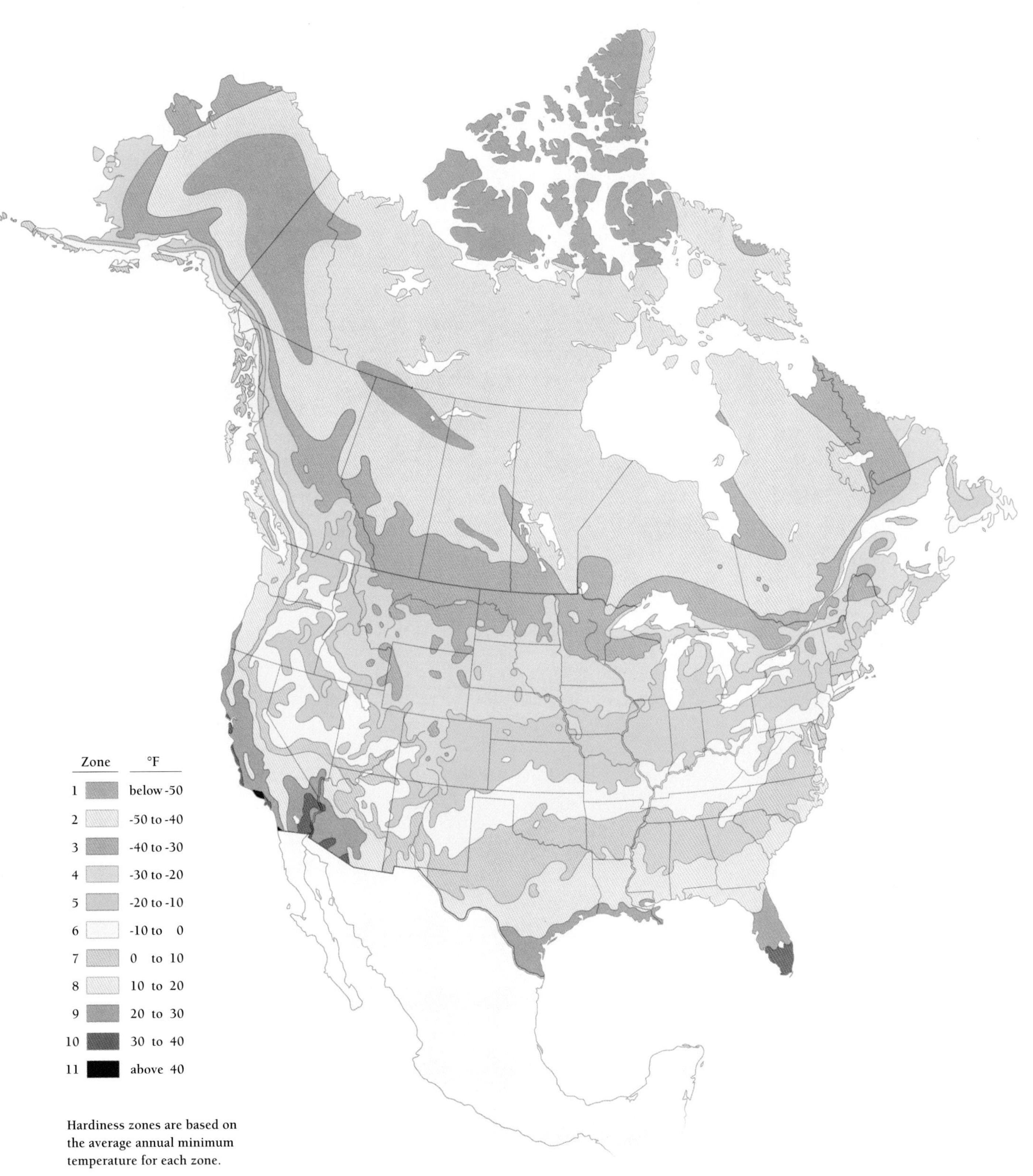


Hardiness zones are based on the average annual minimum temperature for each zone.

CHAPTER 2

# Annuals & Perennials

*Annuals and perennials, the mainstay of a garden, can provide year-round color and interest. Horticulturally, annuals are those plants which complete their life cycle, from seed to seed, in a season, while perennials generally live for three years or more.*

Within the vast group of perennials are evergreens, such as the hardy agapanthus and iris, which are ideally suited to temperate climates, and the herbaceous types, such as asters and gentians, which are able to cope with severe winters as they die back at the end of the summer and form new shoots after a dormant period.

Traditionally these plants were used for massed displays called carpet bedding, where plants were selected to form disciplined color displays. Today this type of formal, high maintenance display is usually restricted to very large private gardens or parks for special events, while the keen gardener experiments with plants to provide varied and interesting combinations.

Annuals are ideally suited to this experimentation as they are not permanent. One summer the garden could be a subtle combination of creams and soft blues of the newer viola hybrids, another season a completely different effect could be achieved by using bright blue salvias and bold yellow marigolds in the same position. In this way the novice gardener can decide which color combination is the most pleasing and go on to repeat these colors in the permanent planting of a garden.

## Planting Combinations

By combining perennials with annuals in a more informal manner the garden loses that "all or nothing" effect which is so evident when a bed of annuals has "finished" and is again planted out with tiny seedlings. By placing clumps of perennials besides drifts of annuals the eye is drawn from one accent to another, say from a group of low-growing annuals in front to the taller perennial flower spikes behind. Annuals are marvellous for providing a festive welcome to an entrance or a splash of color to a shrub border when the garden is to be used for a special event. For a continuous effect, group them with perennials, staggering the flowering times of the plants so that when a small pocket of annuals is nearly past its prime a perennial just behind is about to strut its stuff. This complementary display can take a few seasons to achieve as many perennials need two years to bloom, but don't give up as experimenting in this way is one of the most rewarding aspects of gardening.

Apart from color combinations within a garden, try to tie in the house color to that of a garden display so they complement one another—a red or red-orange toned house looks good surrounded by bright oranges/yellow/rusty reds and creams while a white or muted pastel painted house blends well with soft blue, mauve, pink and white flowers plus masses of silver foliage.

*Chrysanthemums can provide a spectacular display of color.*

Just as important as linking the houses to the garden is the overall siting of the garden beds. Most annuals demand a position in full sun to flower well so be sure to choose an aspect where the plants will receive as much light, particularly morning sun, as possible. Give them generously wide beds ensuring the colorful display will not be overwhelmed by shrub foliage or robbed of nutrients by the roots of nearby permanent plants.

## Instant Color Effects

One of the most welcome developments in recent years is the increase in the number of annuals and perennials available in "instant color" pots. Once red geraniums were the only available way to provide a splash of color in early spring, now, right through the seasons a pot or tray of mature, flowering annuals can be purchased to add instant color to a garden dead spot or patio. And don't overlook hanging baskets filled with annuals to highlight a garden color scheme. If potting up seedlings to make your own instant color, take care to choose plants that fall gracefully over the edge of the basket. Both upright and sprawling types can produce a very decorative display in large pots or tubs.

As discussed earlier annuals, by their very nature, aim to set as many seeds as possible within a very short life span. Gardeners can extend the flowering period by cutting the blooms for indoor use or by nipping off any faded flowers before they set seed and therefore decide it's all over for another year. Remember, if you follow this procedure it is good practice to provide regular nourishment to the plants in the form of a quick-acting fertilizer designed to promote flowers, rather than foliage growth.

## Soil Preparation and Planting

To ensure good strong growth and maximize flowering, prepare your garden beds soundly. If the area to be planted has not been dug over before, it is a good idea to double dig. This means that the topsoil, say a fork's depth, is weeded and put aside and the soil under this layer is dug over to the depth of a fork. Humus, such as well-rotted manure, or compost can be added to this layer to help break up heavy clay particles or to add moisture retentive qualities to sandy soils. This double digging is particularly beneficial to perennials which can be left in the same position for some years. Replace the top layer of soil and prepare this surface in accordance with your planting needs. If planting perennials, a dressing of well-rotted manure or compost or a complete fertilizer can be added while roughly digging the soil over, whereas if hardy annual seeds are to be sown directly into the soil in temperate areas this top layer needs to be well dug over to remove any clods, then raked evenly to ensure a smooth, even surface.

*With their large spikes of showy, pea flowers,* Lupinus *species will enhance any garden.*

In many areas the local climate determines when and if seeds can be planted directly into the ground. A much greater success rate is ensured, should there be a possibility of a late frost, if seeds are sown in a greenhouse or on a warm, weather-proof veranda or similar sheltered spot. This guarantees that the seedlings are ready to be transplanted as soon as weather permits.

Whereas annuals are grown from seed each season, perennials have various ways of being propagated. Most can be grown from seed, however this usually takes longer for blooms to form. If established crowns or rhizomes are divided, new plants, true to form, are generally established more quickly and often produce flowers the following season.

For gardeners in all climatic zones annuals provide welcome displays of color, especially in the early spring, while perennials put on a color parade once a year, often as a bonus to distinctive foliage. What's more, perennials pay handsome dividends, providing the gardener with a source of plant material with which to experiment with design and color combinations each season.

*Achillea filipendulina* 'Gold Plate'

*Achillea millefolium*

*Achillea* 'Taygetea'

*Acanthus spinosus*

*Aconitum napellus*

*Abelmoschus moschatus* 'Mischief'

*Acanthus mollis*

## *ABELMOSCHUS*

### *moschatus* 'Mischief'

MUSK MALLOW

This bushy, fast-growing annual becomes an 18 in (about 45 cm) mound with narrowly divided leaves, sometimes tinged with pink. It bears white-centered red flowers 3–4 in (about 7.5–10 cm) across from summer through fall, each flower lasting only one day. Other named selections with pink or scarlet flowers are available. The flowers resemble the hibiscus; when crushed, both flowers and foliage have a musty smell. It grows well as a pot plant, or in the summer border. It prefers heat and sun, but will flower in light shade. Provide plenty of water and a rich garden soil. Propagate from seed in spring. Rust disease can be a problem.

ZONES 9–11

## *ACANTHUS*

BEAR'S BREECH

These ancient perennials are grown mainly for their handsome leaves and curious spikes of flowers. They make spectacular feature plants and are useful for covering steep banks. Native to the Mediterranean region of southern Europe, they will grow in sun or shade in well-drained soil. They prefer a moist situation, but tolerate the annual summer drought of the West by going dormant after flowering in early summer. Remove spent flowers, stems and dead leaves and propagate by division in fall or from seed sown in spring. Watch for snails and slugs. They have persistent roots which may be difficult to eradicate; even tiny pieces will grow into new plants. This genus has been immortalized by the Greeks, who used the leaf as a motif in the decoration of Corinthian column capitals.

### *A. mollis*

This strong, upright-growing, semi-evergreen has large, deeply serrated and veined, bright green leaves. It produces 4–6 ft (about 1.2–1.8 m) tall spikes of densely clustered white flowers, each surrounded by light rosy-purple bracts, in early summer. The mound of foliage is 3 ft (about 1 m) tall with a spread of 4 ft (about 1.2 m). It prefers partial shade.

ZONES 8–11

### *A. spinosus*

This species has very large, deeply divided, arching dark green leaves with spiny points. In summer it bears bold spikes of white flowers tinted with purple. It grows to 3½ ft (about 1 m) high with a spread of 3 ft (about 90 cm).

ZONES 7–11

## *ACHILLEA*

YARROW, MILFOIL

There are about 85 species of *Achillea*, most native to Europe, Asia and North America. Foliage is fern like, and masses of large, flat heads of tiny daisy flowers are borne in summer in shades of white, yellow, pink and red. They are hardy perennials, easily grown and tolerant of poor soils but doing best in sunny, well-drained sites in temperate climates. They multiply rapidly and are easily propagated by division in early spring or from cuttings in early summer. Flowering stems may be cut when spent or left to die down naturally in winter, when the clumps should be pruned to stimulate strong spring growth. Fertilize in spring. Achilleas are suitable for massed border planting and rockeries, and flowerheads can be dried—retaining their color—for winter decoration. This genus is named after Achilles, who in Greek mythology used the plant to heal wounds. On St John's Eve the Irish traditionally hang yarrow in the house to ward off evil.

### *A. filipendulina* 'Gold Plate'

FERNLEAF YARROW

A strong-growing, erect cultivar reaching 3½ ft (about 1 m) or more with a spread of 24 in (about 60 cm). It has aromatic, bright green foliage and in summer bears flat, rounded heads of golden-yellow flowers, 4–6 in (about 10–15 cm) wide. It is a valuable border plant.

ZONES 3–10

### *A. millefolium*

COMMON YARROW

A widespread and invasive plant growing to 24 in (about 60 cm) tall with feathery, dull green foliage and white to pale pink flowers in summer. It will tolerate mowing and light foot traffic and makes a useful ground cover. The cultivars are to be preferred in the garden for their less invasive nature and for better colors; 'Cerise Queen' is bright rose pink, while 'Rosea' has softer pink flowers. Numerous hybrids from Germany are now available in a wider array of colors.

ZONES 2–11

### *A.* 'Taygetea'

Low mounds of finely divided, gray-green foliage provide a perfect backdrop for the flat heads of soft, lemon-yellow flowers carried on 18 in (about 45 cm) high stems. This hybrid species has an excellent color that works well with purple and blue flowers, and is less invasive than other species.

ZONES 3–10

### *A. tomentosa*

WOOLLY YARROW

This species is a low, spreading plant with feathery gray-green leaves and bright yellow flowerheads on 12 in (about 30 cm) stems. It is excellent in the rock garden or as an edging plant.

ZONES 3–0

## *ACONITUM*
### *napellus*

MONKSHOOD, HELMET FLOWER

Native to northern Europe, this fall-flowering perennial is good for cooler climates. Plant in bold groups or allow to naturalize in woodland conditions. It has tall slender spires of helmet-shaped, violet-blue flowers (some forms have pink or white flowers) and deeply divided mid-green leaves. It grows to $4^1/_2$ ft (about 1.3 m) in height with a spread of 24 in (about 60 cm). It will do best in a moderately rich, well-drained soil in sun or partial shade, and must not be allowed to dry out during the growing season. Plants are easily increased by root division in winter, but once established they are best left undisturbed for several years. Transplant when dormant in winter. The poison aconite is extracted from the roots of this plant.

ZONES 2–9

## *ACORUS*
### *calamus*

SWEET FLAG

This grass-like plant is a marginal water plant, accepting a depth of up to 10 in (about 25 cm) of water. It is a semi-evergreen perennial with aromatic, tangerine-scented, leathery, sword-like leaves. *A. calamus* grows to 4–6 ft (about 1.2–1.8 m) high with a spread of 24 in (about 60 cm). Plant in full sun. Propagation is by division of the rhizomes in winter or early spring. Plants should be divided every three or four years. The leaves of the cultivar *A. calamus* 'Variegatus' have a cream variegation, while the smaller *A. gramineus* also has variegated forms.

ZONES 5–11

## *ADONIS*
### *aestivalis*

This herbaceous perennial has ranunculus-like red blooms in early spring and feathery mid-green foliage. It grows in clumps with a height and spread of 10–12 in (about 25–30 cm). Best results are obtained when planted in a moist, fairly light soil that contains a considerable amount of composted material, peat or leafmold. It flowers in sun or light shade but wilts badly in extreme heat. Fertilize and water regularly and propagate from seed in late summer or by division after flowering.

ZONES 6–8

## *AETHIONEMA*
### *armenum* 'Warley Rose'

syn. *A.* x *warleyense* 'Warley Rose'

A member of the mustard family and native to the Mediterranean area, this low, evergreen, short-lived sub-shrub is grown for its profusion of small, bright rose-pink flowers in spring and summer. Foliage is handsome, with narrow, elongated bluish green leaves. It is a compact 6 in (about 15 cm) high and wide, making it an ideal plant to grow between paving stones or in a rock garden. It enjoys well-drained, coarse-textured soil and full sun, and is quite tolerant of mild winter climates. Trim lightly after flowering and propagate by softwood cuttings in spring or by seed in fall. It will self seed readily.

ZONES 5–9

## *AGAPANTHUS*

LILY-OF-THE-NILE, AFRICAN LILY

Native to southern Africa, these strong-growing perennials are popular for their fine foliage and showy flowers produced in abundance over summer. They have dark green, glossy, gracefully arching, strap-shaped leaves. Flowers are blue or white, in many flowered umbels, borne on a long erect stem often 3 ft (about 90 cm) or more tall. Agapanthus are ideal for background plants or for edging along a wall, fence or driveway. Cut flowers are useful for bold arrangements in large containers and the plants also make excellent tub and container specimens. The genus is extremely tough, thriving in conditions of neglect on hillsides and near the coast, but only in the milder climates. The plants enjoy full sun but will tolerate some shade, and will grow in any soil; though they prefer moisture, they are admirably drought tolerant. They naturalize readily, soon forming large clumps. Propagate by division in late winter, or from seed in spring or fall. Remove spent flower stems and dead leaves at the end of winter. All species make good pot plants; in cold winter areas they can be brought indoors for the winter.

### *A. africanus*

Blue flowers are produced on 18 in (about 45 cm) stems from midsummer to early fall; each flowerhead contains 20 to 50 individual blossoms. The leaves are shorter than on *A. praecox.*

ZONES 8–11

### *A. praecox* subsp. *orientalis*

This is probably the best known agapanthus, with its large dense umbels of rich blue flowers carried on strong 4–5 ft (about 1.2–1.5 m) tall stems over broad dark green leaves in late summer; the flowerheads have as many as 100 blossoms each. The foliage grows to 3 ft (about 90 cm) high with a spread of 24–36 in (about 60–90 cm). Various dwarf selections are available including 'Peter Pan' with small heads of blue flowers freely produced above 10 in (about 25 cm) mounds of foliage; these make excellent edging plants.

ZONES 8–11

## *AGASTACHE*
### *cana*

MOSQUITO PLANT

These sage relatives are extremely popular with hummingbirds, producing bright rose-pink tubular flowers on 24–36 in (about 60–90 cm) stems through late summer and fall. Though rare in its native New Mexico, it is well adapted throughout the Southwest and up to 6000 ft (about 1830 m) in the mountains. It prefers full sun to partial shade, a well-drained soil and only moderate amounts of water. The crushed foliage releases a distinct fragrance of bubblegum. It is a good plant for a mixed border in a dry climate region, or for naturalizing.

ZONES 5–9

*Agapanthus africanus*

*Acorus calamus*

*Adonis aestivalis*

*Aethionema armenum* 'Warley Rose'

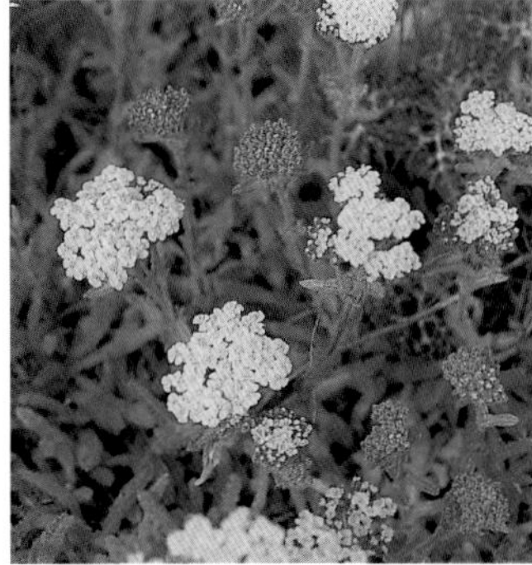

*Achillea tomentosa*

*Alcea rosea*

*Agrostemma githago*

*Ageratum houstonianum*

*Alchemilla mollis*

*Ajuga reptans* 'Atropurpurea'

*Alpinia zerumbet*

## AGERATUM
*houstonianum*

FLOSS FLOWER

Native to tropical Mexico, this member of the Aster family is a popular and easily grown annual with dull, hairy, heart-shaped leaves and showy blue, lavender, mauve-pink or white fluffy flowerheads. It should flower throughout summer and into fall if the ground is kept moist and dead flowerheads are removed regularly. The tall cultivars form clumps 24 in (about 60 cm) high and wide and are useful for bedding and cut flowers. The dwarf varieties form clumps 6–12 in (about 15–30 cm) high and wide and are excellent for edging and containers. Any well-drained soil is suitable, preferably compost enriched. They prefer a sunny position with protection from cold wind. Keep moist, especially during spring and summer. Young plants benefit from tip pruning and spent flowers should be removed. Propagate from seed sown in spring.

ZONES 2–10

## AGROSTEMMA
*githago*

CORN COCKLE

This fast-growing showy annual reaches a height of 3 ft (about 90 cm) with a spread of 12 in (about 30 cm), making it ideal for planting at the back of an annual border. It has a slender, many branched, willowy habit with lance-shaped leaves. Open, trumpet-shaped pink flowers, 3 in (about 8 cm) in diameter, appear throughout summer. It grows best in full sun in a well-drained soil. Propagate from seed sown in early spring or fall. Young plants should be thinned to around 10 in (about 25 cm) spacing and may need light staking if growing in exposed areas. The tiny, round, dark brown seeds are poisonous.

ALL ZONES

## AJUGA
*reptans*

CARPET BUGLEWEED

This excellent perennial ground cover forms a showy carpet in sun or part shade. Bright blue flower spikes appear in early spring above the metallic green crinkled leaves. There are various cultivars with different colored leaves: 'Burgundy Glow' has cream and maroon variegated leaves; 'Atropurpurea', dark purplish bronze; 'Multicolor', white and pink and purple; 'Variegata', light green and creamy white; and 'Jungle Beauty', dark green with a tinge of purple. They grow 4–12 in (about 10–30 cm) high and spread rapidly from runners. They grow in most conditions but prefer shade and cool moist soil. Those with bronze foliage do better in sun. Propagate by division in spring. Remove spent flowerheads and watch for fungus disease. *Ajuga* has been widely used as a healing agent for wounds.

ZONES 3–10

## ALCEA
*rosea*

HOLLYHOCK

A native of the eastern Mediterranean and central Asia, this stately biennial was one of the first flowers to be cultivated in the southern hemisphere. They are popular for their tall spikes of flowers which can reach 6 ft (about 1.8 m). Flowers appear in summer and early fall and come in a range of colors including red, pink, cream and yellow; some are double. Foliage is roundish and rough and the plant spreads to around 24 in (about 60 cm). They need shelter from wind, benefiting from staking in exposed positions. They prefer sun, a rich, heavy, well-drained soil and frequent watering in dry weather. Propagate from seed in late summer or spring. Rust disease can be a problem; spray with a fungicide.

ZONES 2–10

## ALCHEMILLA
*mollis*

LADY'S MANTLE

This old-fashioned, low-growing perennial is ideal for ground cover, for massed plantings on slopes, the front of borders or for rock gardens. It is clump forming, growing to a height and spread of 16 in (about 40 cm). It has decorative, wavy-edged leaves which hold dew or raindrops to give a sparkling effect. In summer it bears masses of small sprays of greenish yellow flowers, similar to *Gypsophila*. They prefer partial shade, moist, well-drained soil and a humid atmosphere. Propagate from seed or by division in spring or fall, and cut back to $1^1/_2$ in (about 3 cm) when they finish flowering.

ZONES 3–9

## ALPINIA
*zerumbet*

SHELL GINGER, SHELL FLOWER

A genus named in honor of the sixteenth-century Italian botanist Prospero Alpino, they are grown for their very showy flowers. Gingers are not easy to grow successfully in pots and will only flower in a warm, moist position. They prefer a mild to subtropical climate. They need full sun to part shade and will not survive temperatures below 61–64°F (about 16–18°C). Propagate by division of rhizomes in spring or early summer. Although edible, it is not the ginger used commercially. The flowers are used in the Pacific Islands to make garlands. *A. zerumbet* is a tall plant, growing to 9 ft (about 2.7 m). Originally from China, it bear racemes of waxy, ivory or white flowers with yellow lips and pink or red throats in summer. It needs partial shade, good soil and plenty of water to flower well.

ZONES 9–11

## *ALSTROEMERIA*

PERUVIAN LILY

Native to South America, these tuberous plants are among the finest of all perennials for cutting, but they do drop petals. Flowers are showy and multicolored, resembling miniature trumpet lilies held on thin wiry stems. They flower profusely from spring to summer. About 50 species exist, all growing well in sun or light shade in a well-enriched, well-drained acid soil. They soon form large clumps, bearing dozens of heads of flowers. Propagate from seed or by division in early spring. In cold winters protect the dormant tubers by covering with loose peat or a leafy mulch. Best left undisturbed when established, but one-year-old seedlings transplant well. Alstroemerias do well naturalized under trees or on sloping banks.

### *A. aurea*

**syn. *A. aurantiaca***

This is the most common and easily grown species, with heads of orange flowers tipped with green and streaked with maroon. Leaves are twisted, narrow and lance shaped. Several cultivars exist with deeper or more golden flowers. They reach a height of 3 ft (about 90 cm) with a spread of 24–36 in (about 60–90 cm).

ZONES 7–11

### *A.*, Ligtu hybrids

Leaves are narrow and twisted and flowers are widely flared in shades of pink, salmon, yellow or orange, sometimes streaked and spotted with other colors. They grow 2–4 ft (about 60-120 cm) tall with a spread of 2–3 ft (about 60-90 cm).

ZONES 7–11

*Anaphalis margaritacea*

*Alstroemeria,* Ligtu hybrids

*Alstroemeria aurea*

## AMARANTHUS

These bright, showy annuals, native to the tropics, are grown for their brilliant foliage, curious flowers and adaptability to hot, dry conditions. They are popular bedding plants, with large and attractively colored leaves and minute flowers borne in drooping, tassel-like spikes. A sunny, dry position with protection from strong winds is essential, and they enjoy a fertile, well-drained soil, mulched during hot weather. Pinch when young to thicken growth and propagate from seed sown in spring. Prepare soil for planting with plenty of manure, and water seedlings regularly. Protect from snails when young and watch for caterpillars and aphids.

### *A. caudatus*

This tall species, growing to 4–5 ft (about 1.2–1.5 m) high and 24–36 in (about 60–90 cm) wide, has oval, pale green leaves and dark red flowers in long, drooping cords, their ends often touching the ground. Flowers appear in summer through to fall. In many old gardens this plant was used to give height in the center of circular beds.

ZONES 2–11

*Amaranthus tricolor* 'Joseph's Coat'

*Amaranthus caudatus*

*Anagallis monellii*

### *A. tricolor* 'Joseph's Coat'

A bushy annual, growing to 3 ft (about 90 cm) high and 24 in (about 60 cm) wide, this plant is grown for its brilliant bronze, gold, orange and red, variegated, 8 in (about 20 cm) long leaves, which retain their coloring into late fall. Tiny red flowers appear in summer. Protect from snails when young.

ZONES 2–11

## AMSONIA *tabernaemontana*

BLUE STAR, BLUE DOGBANE

This is a delightful perennial from the northeastern and central United States. Stiff stems, 24–36 in (about 60–90 cm) tall, are topped by pyramidal clusters of small, star-shaped flowers of pale blue in early summer, flowering along with peonies and irises. The leaves are narrow-elliptical and 3–6 in (about 7.5–15 cm) long. This species needs minimal care if given a moist, fertile soil in full sun to light shade. They are good in the perennial border or in a damp wildflower meadow.

ZONES 3–9

## ANAGALLIS *monellii*

**syn. *A. linifolia***

This charming little plant is grown for its brilliant blue or scarlet flowers of $^1/_2$ in (about 1 cm) in diameter. They are good small rockery plants or can be used for edging large containers. They flower during summer and are low growing to under 18 in (about 45 cm), with a spread of 6 in (about 15 cm) or more. This species requires a sunny, well-drained spot in fertile, moist soil. They benefit from some shade in hot areas. Propagate from seed or by division in spring.

ZONES 7–10

## ANAPHALIS *margaritacea*

PEARLY EVERLASTING

Native to the northern hemisphere, this perennial member of the aster family is valued for its papery, small, white flowers which can be dried for indoor decoration. It has lance-shaped, silvery gray leaves and the flowers are borne on erect stems in late summer. Bushy in habit, it grows to 24–30 in (about 60–76 cm) high and 24 in (about 60 cm) wide. Easily grown, it prefers a sunny situation (but will grow in semi-shade) and well-drained soil. It will accept either damp or dry conditions. Propagate from seed in fall or by division in early spring. Prune back hard in winter.

ZONES 3–9

*Amsonia tabernaemontana*

*Antirrhinum majus*

*Anchusa capensis* 'Blue Angel'

*Anchusa azurea*

*Anthemis tinctoria*

## ANCHUSA

BUGLOSS, ALKANET

Natives of Europe, north and south Africa and western Asia, this genus consists of about 50 species of annuals, biennials and perennials. They are larger than the forget-me-not (*Myosotis*) and have clearer, true blue flowers that do not fade easily. All species are suitable for herbaceous borders and are easily grown in beds and containers. They grow best in a sunny position in deep, rich, well-drained soil. Feed sparingly and water generously. The taller species benefit from staking and the plants require plenty of room as they make large root systems. Cut flower stalks back after blooming to promote new growth. Propagate perennials by division in early spring (winter in the West), annuals and biennials from seed in fall or spring. Transplant perennials before growth begins in early spring. These plants are popular with bees.

### *A. azurea*

**syn. *A. italica***

This tough Mediterranean perennial grows to 3–3½ ft (about 90–120 cm) high and 24 in (about 60 cm) wide. It has coarse, hairy leaves and an erect habit with tiers of brilliant blue flowers borne in spring to summer.

ZONES 3–10

### *A. capensis* 'Blue Angel'

CAPE FORGET-ME-NOT, SUMMER FORGET-ME-NOT

A bushy biennial grown as an annual, this *Anchusa* reaches a height and spread of 8 in (about 20 cm). A native of southern Africa, it forms a compact pyramid of shallow, bowl-shaped, sky-blue flowers in early summer. 'Blue Bird' is a taller— 20 in (about 50 cm)—but equally striking cultivar.

ZONES 8–11

*Anemone* x *hybrida* 'Honorine Jobert'

## ANEMONE

### x *hybrida*

**syn. *A. japonica***

JAPANESE ANEMONE

One of the most elegant plants for growing under trees or large shrubs, this vigorous perennial grows to a height of 2–4 ft (about 60–120 cm) and a width of 24 in (about 60 cm). The leaves are deeply divided and dark green; tall, erect flower stems bear many large, saucer-shaped flowers in late summer and early fall. Flowers are white, pink or soft carmine red, and single, semi-double or double; cut back stems as they fade. Plant in humus-rich, well-drained soil in full sun to half-shade (in hot summer areas). They adapt to almost any position. Propagate by division of an established clump in early spring before growth begins, or from seed sown in late summer. Fertilize in late winter or early spring. The cultivar 'Honorine Jobert' has slightly cupped white flowers with yellow stamens.

ZONES 6–10

## ANIGOZANTHOS

### Bush Gems series

KANGAROO PAW

Native to southwestern Australia, these perennials are noted for their unique paw-shaped, hummingbird-attracting flowers. The best of the kangaroo paws for their resistance to the ink disease, the Bush Gems hybrids grow 2–4 ft (about 60–120 cm) tall and 12–24 in (about 30–60 cm) wide. The flower color ranges fom yellow, gold and green through to orange, red and burgundy. Plant in a warm, very well-drained sandy or gravelly soil in a sunny, open position. Most tolerate summer drought, although flowering will be prolonged with summer water. They will tolerate some frost, but do best in mild coastal regions of the West Coast and mild winter areas in the desert southwest.

ZONES 9–11

## ANTHEMIS

### *tinctoria*

GOLDEN MARGUERITE, DYER'S CHAMOMILE

An easily grown perennial that is covered in late spring and summer with a dazzling display of daisy-like yellow flowers above fern-like, crinkled green leaves. The foliage is very aromatic when crushed; the flowers are the source of a yellow dye. They prefer sun and will thrive even in poor sandy or clay soils as long as they are well drained. Short-lived but strong growers, they form clumps 3 ft (about 90 cm) high and should have spent flowers trimmed off to prolong flowering. Propagate in spring from basal cuttings.

ZONES 3–10

## ANTIRRHINUM

### *majus*

SNAPDRAGON

Native to the Mediterranean region, this annual is valued for its showy flowers borne over a long period from spring to fall. It is a good source of winter color in mild regions. There are many cultivars, ranging from tall (30 in/76 cm), to medium (20 in/ 50 cm), to dwarf (10 in/25 cm). They have a spread of 12–20 in (about 30–50 cm). Erect plants, they form dense bushes of many upright stems carrying spikes of frilly, two-lipped, sometimes double, flowers in a range of colors including orange, yellow, red, purple, pink and white. They prefer a fertile, well-drained soil in full sun with some protection from wind. Plants should be deadheaded to prolong flowering; early growth should be pinched to in-

crease branching. Propagate from seed in spring or early fall. Rust disease can be a problem.
ZONES 2–11

## AQUILEGIA

COLUMBINE

These graceful, clump-forming perennials native to Europe, North America and Asia are grown for their interesting form and varied color range. They are also useful cut flowers, and the dwarf and alpine species make good rock garden plants. Foliage is fern like and the flowers are mainly bell shaped and spurred. They flower during early summer and prefer a well-drained, light soil enriched with animal manure. Plant in an open, sunny site protected from strong winds and with some shade in hot areas. They look their best in broad drifts amongst low, evergreen foliage. Keep moist and give plenty of liquid fertilizer during growth. In cold climates columbines are perennial and need to be cut to the ground in late fall; treating them as annuals usually gives good results. Propagate from seed in fall and spring. The plants are short lived, but self seed readily. The common name, columbine, comes from the Latin for dove, as the flowers were thought to resemble a cluster of doves.

### *A. caerulea*

ROCKY MOUNTAIN COLUMBINE

This alpine species is a short-lived, upright perennial growing to 18 in (about 45 cm) in height with a spread of 6 in (about 15 cm). Big, powdery blue or white nodding flowers on branching stems appear in spring and early summer. It sometimes produces a few blooms in fall. It does best in rich soil, but does not like heat. *A. alpina* is similar but has short spurs and usually all blue flowers.
ZONES 3–10

### *A. canadensis*

WILD COLUMBINE

This native of eastern and central North America produces masses of red and yellow flowers on 18 in (about 45 cm) stems in late spring and early summer. It is tolerant of full sun, provided there is plenty of moisture. It will also tolerate heat if some shade is provided. Hummingbirds love the nectar-rich flowers.
ZONES 3–9

### *A. chrysantha*

GOLDEN COLUMBINE

These are among the showiest of the North American columbines, with large, long-spurred, fragrant yellow flowers on stems often exceeding 3 ft (about 90 cm) in height. Native to the Southwest, it is more tolerant of sun and heat than most species. White and double-flowered cultivars are available.
ZONES 3–10

### *A.*, McKana Giants

A clump-forming, leafy perennial growing to 30 in (about 76 cm) tall with a spread of 12 in (about 30 cm). This hybrid strain includes an extensive range of pastel shades and bicolors. Flowers are large and are noted for their delicate long spurs behind the petals. They flower in spring or early summer.
ZONES 5–10

### *A. vulgaris*

GARDEN COLUMBINE, EUROPEAN COLUMBINE

This is the true columbine, one of the parents of the modern short-spurred hybrids. It is a variable species, growing to 24–36 in (about 30–60 cm) high with a spread of 20 in (about 50 cm). It bears funnel-shaped, short-spurred flowers in colors of pink, crimson, white and purple on long stems from the center of a loose rosette of gray-green foliage that resembles maidenhair fern. It flowers from spring to early summer.
ZONES 3–10

## ARABIS

### *caucasica*

**syn. *A. albida***

WALL ROCKCRESS

This tough, evergreen perennial is suitable for ground cover in a rock garden, for crevices in walls or for bedding. It is sometimes used to overplant spring-flowering bulbs. Easily grown, it forms dense clusters of thick foliage up to 6 in (about 15 cm) high with a spread of 18 in (about 45 cm). In spring it has white flowers on loose racemes above gray-green leaf rosettes. Double-flowered forms, such as 'Plena', are available. It requires a light, well-drained soil rich in organic matter. Plant in full sun (semi-shade in warmer climates) and cut back hard after flowering. Propagate from softwood cuttings in summer, or from seed or by division in fall.
ZONES 4–10

## ARCTOTIS

### × *hybrida*

AFRICAN DAISY

Native to southern Africa, these colorful, profusely blooming flowers are excellent for ground cover or mass planting on sloping sites. They are compact perennials, often grown as annuals, and reach a height of 20 in (about 50 cm) or more and a spread of 16 in (about 40 cm). Daisy-like, 3 in (about 7.5 cm) flowers in shades of pink, white, yellow, red and orange, all with contrasting black and gold centers, are produced abundantly from winter until late summer. The blooms close in dull weather and in late afternoon. Leaves are chrysanthemum like. These plants require full sun, regular watering and a light, well-drained soil; they do not like heat combined with humidity. Dead-head consistently to ensure a long bloom period. Propagate from seed in spring or fall, or from year-round stem cuttings.
Sow seed where they are to be planted.
ZONES 9–11

*Aquilegia*, McKana hybrids

*Aquilegia caerulea*

*Aquilegia vulgaris*

*Aquilegia canadensis*

*Arabis caucasica* 'Plena'

*Arctotis* × *hybrida*

*Armeria maritima*

*Argyranthemum frutescens*

## ARGEMONE
*platyceras*

PRICKLY POPPY

This annual has prickly, white-marked grayish green leaves and white to yellow poppy-like flowers. The flowers are 3 in (about 8 cm) wide and appear in summer. It has a spreading habit, growing to 24 in (about 60 cm) high and 12 in (about 30 cm) wide. They grow best in full sun and very well-drained soil. Sow seed in early spring where they are to flower. This species self seeds readily and can become invasive. Native to Mexico, the genus is named from the Greek *argema*, a cataract, as the local Indians believed the plants had medicinal properties that would cure cataracts.

ALL ZONES

## ARGYRANTHEMUM
*frutescens*

syn. *Chrysanthemum frutescens*

MARGUERITE

Native to the Canary Islands, this bushy evergreen perennial is available in white, pink and yellow. They bear many daisy-like flowerheads, both single and double, in spring and summer. Most grow to a height and spread of 3 ft (about 90 cm). Pinch out growing tips regularly to maintain shape, and cut back severely in summer.

ZONES 9–11

## ARISAEMA
*triphyllum*

JACK-IN-THE-PULPIT

This is one of the distinctive native wildflowers of North America's

*Argemone platyceras*

*Artemisia* 'Powys Castle'

northeastern woodlands, flowering in spring before the trees leaf out. One or two sets of medium green leaves, divided into three leaflets, increase in height to over 12 in (about 30 cm) after flowers fade. Tiny purple or green flowers cover a slender spadix which is enclosed by a leafy spathe of pale green to purple-brown; the tip of the spathe flops over, like a canopy over a pulpit. Bright scarlet berries line the spadix in fall, by which time the leaves have died down. The tuberous roots should be planted in a rich, woodsy, moisture-retentive soil in dappled shade.

ZONES 4–9

## ARMERIA
*maritima*

THRIFT, SEA PINK

One of the best of the old cottage garden plants, thrift was in cultivation as early as 1578. It is a tufted evergreen perennial with a mound-like mass of narrow, dark green leaves and dense flowerheads of small pink to white flowers on slender 6–12 in (about 15–30 cm) stems. Flowers are produced in a flush in early spring and continue to bloom for most of the year. The plant grows to 4 in (about 10 cm) high and spreads to 8 in (about 20 cm), making it good for edging. Sandy soil and good drainage are essential and they thrive in hot, dry, sunny situations, particularly near the coast. The species is native to the mountains and rocky coasts of the Mediterranean, Asia Minor and the west coast of North America, and resents wet conditions or heavy soils. Propagate from seed

*Artemisia stellerana*

in fall, or from semi-ripe cuttings in summer.

ZONES 3–10

## ARTEMISIA

WORMWOOD

This is a large genus, mostly native to arid regions in the northern hemisphere. They are grown for their decorative silvery foliage which is often aromatic and sometimes repellent to insects. They have insignificant flowers but are an attractive addition to a flower border where their feathery foliage provides interest throughout the year. There are both shrubby and herbaceous, evergreen and deciduous species. They prefer an open, sunny situation with light, well-drained soil. Prune back lightly in spring to stimulate growth. Propagate from softwood or semi-ripe cuttings in summer or by division in spring. Transplant during winter or early spring, before growth begins.

### *A. arborescens*

Evergreen perennial with silvery white foliage, reaching a height of $3^1/_2$ ft (about 1 m) and a spread of 30 in (about 76 cm). Small, bright yellow flowers are borne in summer and early fall. Trim well in spring. It does not like heat with high humidity; it is a good plant for the back of a border.

ZONES 9–11

### *A. lactiflora*

WHITE MUGWORT

A tall-growing, attractive Chinese species which grows like a Michaelmas daisy with many-

*Artemisia arborescens*

branched heads of tiny, milky white flowers blooming in summer. Foliage is dark green, fern like and aromatic. This is a useful plant for the rear of a border; it prefers a moister, richer soil than other *Artemisia*. It needs staking, as it grows $3^1/_2$–$4^1/_2$ ft (about 1–1.3 m) tall with a spread of 20 in (about 50 cm).

ZONES 4–10

### *A.* 'Powys Castle'

This assumed hybrid between *A. absinthium* and *A. arborescens* is one of the most useful of the wormwoods, with its finely dissected silvery leaves and its gentle 24–36 in (about 60–90 cm) mounding habit. Because it seldom flowers it remains more compact and less leggy than other species; older plants, nevertheless, benefit from a hard cutting back in early spring as new shoots develop from the base. Use it to introduce a distinct foliage effect into a mixed border of perennials and shrubs; contrast it with deep reds and purples. It prefers full sun but does well in light shade provided the soil is well drained. Propagate from cuttings in summer; in cold climates, grow indoors over winter for planting out in spring.

ZONES 6–11

### *A. stellerana*

BEECH WORMWOOD, DUSTY MILLER

Excellent planted in light sandy soils, this evergreen perennial has serrated, white-haired silver leaves, and slender sprays of small yellow flowers are borne in summer. It has

*Artemisia lactiflora*

*Aruncus dioica*

a rounded habit and grows 12–24 in (about 30–60 cm) high and spreads up to 3 ft (about 90 cm).
ZONES 4–10

## ARUNCUS
*dioica*
syn. *A. sylvester, Spiraea aruncus*
GOATSBEARD

A graceful woodland perennial useful for shady spots and moist situations. This clump-forming plant produces a mass of rich green, fern-like foliage and arching plumes of tiny silky white flowers in summer. Grows to a height of 6 ft (about 1.8 m) and spread of $3^1/_2$ ft (about 1 m). It is a good specimen for planting beside a pool or creek. The plant naturalizes readily and thrives in any well-drained, moist soil, in full light or partial shade. Propagate from seed in spring or by division in spring or fall.
ZONES 3–9

## ASCLEPIAS
*tuberosa*
BUTTERFLY WEED

One of North America's brightest meadow wildflowers, this 24–36 in (about 60–90 cm) mounding perennial produces broad heads of small orange (sometimes yellow or red) flowers during summer. It is very popular with butterflies. The slender, bladder-like pods that follow are interesting and release tiny seeds that fly off on silky hairs. Adaptable to both moist and very dry soils, it demands full sun and good drainage.
ZONES 3–10

## ASTER
MICHAELMAS DAISY, ASTER

Native to the northern hemisphere, this large genus of perennials and deciduous or evergreen sub-shrubs contains over 250 species. Easily grown, they vary in height from miniatures suitable for rock gardens to 6 ft (about 1.8 m) tall giants suitable for the back of an herbaceous border. Leaves are sometimes dark colored, sometimes hairy. Showy, daisy-like flowerheads are usually produced in late summer or fall in a wide range of colors, including blue, violet, purple, pink, red or white, all with a central disc of yellow or black. Grow in sun or partial shade in hot areas in a well-drained soil. Keep moist at all times. Propagate by division in spring or late fall, or from softwood cuttings in spring. Replace plants about every three years.

### A. alpinus

A clump-forming plant, growing 6–12 in (about 15–30 cm) high and 12 in (about 30 cm) wide. Large, violet-blue daisies with yellow centers appear from late spring until early summer and the foliage is dark green. This species is popular as a rock garden plant. It prefers full sun and is easily grown.
ZONES 4–9

### A. x frikartii 'Mönch'

A bushy, free-branching plant producing large, single, soft lavender-blue, daisy-like flowers with yellowish centers over a long period from mid-summer until late fall. It grows to a height of 30 in (about 76 cm) and a spread of 18 in (about 45 cm).
ZONES 5–10

### A. linariifolius
STIFF ASTER, SAVORYLEAF ASTER

Low, somewhat stiff mounds 12-24 in (about 30-60 cm) high and 12 in (about 30 cm) wide are covered in late summer and early fall with 1 in (about 2.5 cm) daisies of soft lavender-pink. This species does not need staking, and makes a good low, flowering hedge. It likes full sun and a well-drained but fertile soil.
ZONES 3–10

### A. novi-angliae
NEW ENGLAND ASTER, MICHAELMAS DAISY

Vigorous clumps of mostly vertical, 3-6 ft (about 0.9-1.8 m) stems are likely to lean with the weight of large, loose clusters of daisies opening in late summer or fall. Staking is often necessary, except on the most compact of cultivars. The natural color is violet, although many cultivars such as 'Harrington's Pink' (clear pink and late blooming) and 'September Ruby' (cerise) have been selected for their different colors. Native to the eastern US, these asters prefer a moist, rich soil in full sun.
ZONES 4-9

### A. novi-belgii
NEW YORK ASTER, MICHAELMAS DAISY

Usually more compact than the New England asters, this species may vary in height from 12 in (about 30 cm) to over 4 ft (about 1.2 m). It is also more prone to mildew. The original violet color has now been replaced in cultivars by pure white ('Boningdale White'), deep crimson ('Alert'), bright red ('Mulberry') and powder blue ('Marie Ballard'). The Oregon-Pacific strain is very compact.
ZONES 4–9

## ASTILBE

Native to the Orient, these easily grown perennials are ideal used as a trouble-free ground cover in damp spots. They grow best on the edge of ponds and in damp hollows, but are also suitable for borders and rock gardens. Foliage is attractive and fern like, and in young plants often a coppery red. Flowers appear in summer in tall, fluffy, plume-like panicles in white, cream, many shades of pink, red and purple. Plant in rich, deep soil in partial shade and give plenty of water; do not allow to dry out. Propagate by division of established clumps from late winter to spring, or from seed or division in fall. Astilbes make good cut flowers.

### A. x arendsii

A leafy, clump-forming plant growing to 24–36 in (about 60–90 cm) tall and as wide. These are hybrids produced from several different species, the height of which vary from 18 in to 4 ft (about 45 cm to 1.2 m), with a spread of 18–30 in (about 45–76 cm). They are available as named cultivars in a range of colors from red through pink to white. 'Fanal' is scarlet, 'Bridal Veil' is white and 'Rheinland' is deep rose, to name just a few. Flowers are produced on spikes in late spring to early summer. It has broad leaves with oval leaflets.
ZONES 4–10

*Astilbe* x *arendsii*

*Aster alpinus*

*Aster* x *frikartii* 'Mönch'

*Aster novi-belgii* 'Mulberry'

*Aster novi-angliae* 'Harrington's Pink'

### *A. chinensis* 'Pumila'

An attractive clump-forming plant with toothed, hairy, dark green leaves and dense, fluffy spikes of small, star-shaped mauve-red flowers. It grows to a height of 12 in (about 30 cm) and spreads quickly. Ideal for moist, shady borders or rock gardens.

ZONES 4–9

## ASTRANTIA
### *major*

MASTERWORT

Deeply lobed palmate leaves form a loose mound of foliage 18 in (about 45 cm) tall from which rise nearly bare stems to 24 in (about 60 cm) or more, each topped by intricately formed, soft pink or white, daisy-like flowers. Each flower is actually many tiny flowers in a domed cluster, surrounded by petal-like bracts in the same colors. Flowers are produced almost throughout summer. They prefer rich, moist soil in full sun or dappled shade.

ZONES 4–10

## AUBRIETA
### *deltoidea*

FALSE ROCK CRESS

This miniature, trailing perennial is an ideal plant for rock gardens, sunny dry banks, or for border edges. It is a compact plant with greenish gray leaves and masses of starry flowers in mauve-pinks, mauve-blues and violets. It flowers for a long period in spring. It forms a dense mat to 2 in (about 5 cm) high with a spread of 8 in (about 20 cm), and spills prettily over the edges of beds or containers. It thrives in sun and any well-drained soil. Propagate from semi-ripe cuttings in late summer or fall or from seed sown in spring.

ZONES 4–9

## AURINIA
### *saxatilis*
**syn. *Alyssum saxatile***

BASKET-OF-GOLD

Native to southeastern Europe, this perennial blooms in early spring. It forms a neat mound of grayish green leaf rosettes and has showy flower sprays in shades of vivid yellow and gold that last for months. It is a woody-rooted, evergreen plant growing to 10 in (about 25 cm) high with a spread of 12 in (about 30 cm). It needs sun and a moderately fertile, coarse, gritty, well-drained soil. Propagate from seed in fall or softwood or greenwood cuttings in early summer.

ZONES 4–10

## BAILEYA
### *multiradiata*

DESERT MARIGOLD

Low mounds of silver gray foliage mark this desert dweller. Bright yellow daisies (even the centers are yellow) rise above the foliage on slender 18 in (about 45 cm) stems nearly all year round. Best where summer humidity is low, soils are well drained and sunlight is plentiful, the desert marigold is best started from seed sown in place in early fall. It will naturalize where it is happy.

ZONES 6–10

## BAPTISIA
### *australis*

Native to the eastern United States, this summer-flowering perennial is beautiful in both flower and foliage. The lobed leaves are blue-green and form a loose mound around 4 ft (about 1.2 m) high and 24 in (about 60 cm) across. The lupin-like flowers are borne on spikes from early to mid-summer; they are an unusual shade of deep blue. The seed pods can be dried for indoor decoration. This plant does best in full sun and in a good, moisture-retentive soil. It has a deep root system and does not like being transplanted or disturbed, so propagation is best done by seed collected and sown as soon as it is ripe in fall.

ZONES 3–10

## BEGONIA

BEGONIA

This large genus of perennial plants are grown for their colorful flowers and ornamental foliage. Most of the 1000-odd species can be grown outdoors only in areas with warm temperate to subtropical climates. Tuberous rooted or fibrous, they range in habit from dwarf to tall and scandent. All require a light, rich, well-drained soil that is slightly acidic. They need shelter from wind and strong sunlight.

### *B. grandis*

HARDY BEGONIA

This is the only begonia that can be expected to survive moderately cold winters. It is a low, bushy begonia with red stems to 3 ft (about 90 cm) tall, growing from tuberous roots. Leaves are roughly oval in outline, somewhat fleshy, and generally reddish or copper. Flowers are fragrant, pink, around 1 in (about 2.5 cm) across and are produced in nodding clusters all summer. It prefers shade and moist, woodsy soil.

ZONES 7–11

### *B.* Semperflorens-Cultorum hybrids

WAX BEGONIA, BEDDING BEGONIA

Bushy, evergreen perennials, cultivars within this group are often grown as bedding annuals. They are also useful for bordering, especially in shaded gardens. Freely branching plants with soft succulent stems, they have rounded, glossy green, bronze or variegated 2 in (about 5 cm) long leaves. Flowers are showy, single or double in colors of bright rose-pink, light pink, white or red. They grow best in partial sun or shade and a well-drained soil. Propagate in spring from seed or stem cuttings and pinch out growing tips to encourage bushy growth.

ALL ZONES

### *B. metallica*

METAL-LEAF BEGONIA

A tall-growing, shrub-like begonia from Mexico with bronze-green leaves often splashed with white. The leaves are borne from white-haired stems and are covered with fine silver hairs, red beneath. In summer to fall pink flowers with red bristles appear.

ZONES 4–10

*Astrantia major*

*Aubrieta deltoidea*

*Aurinia saxatilis*

*Begonia metallica*

*Begonia* 'Orange Rubra'

*Baptisia australis*

*Astilbe chinensis* 'Pumila'

*Bergenia cordifolia*

*Browallia americana*

*Bergenia stracheyi*

*Bergenia* hybrids

*Bellis perennis*

*Brachycome iberidifolia*

*Brunnera macrophylla*

### B. 'Orange Rubra'

This cane-stemmed begonia can reach 24 in (about 60 cm) in height. It has large, oval, light green leaves, sometimes with white spots that disappear with age. Clusters of orange flowers are produced throughout the year.

ZONES 4–10

## *BELLIS*
## *perennis*

ENGLISH DAISY

Often treated as a biennial, the semi-double to double flowerheads of the garden forms come in red, crimson, pink and white, all with a gold center. They grow to a height and spread of 6–8 in (about 15–20 cm) and make ideal front border, edging or rockery plants. They flower in spring and grow in sun or semi-shade and prefer well-drained, rich, moist soil. They are usually grown as annuals or biennials from seed sown in summer. Remove spent flowerheads regularly to prolong flowering.

ZONES 4–10

## *BERGENIA*

A group of perennials with large, handsome, leathery leaves. The species are native to Asia, and there are also many garden hybrids that have been developed over the last one hundred years or so. Clusters of flowers are borne on short, stout stems in spring. The evergreen foliage makes excellent ground cover, which is especially useful as bergenias thrive in sun or shade and are tolerant of exposed sites. The leaves often develop attractive red tints in winter; these colors develop best when the plants are grown in sun and on poor soil. Propagate by division in spring after flowering.

### *B. cordifolia*

HEART-LEAFED BERGENIA

Native to Siberia, this tough perennial has large, roundish, crinkle-edged, heart-shaped leaves and produces racemes of rosy red flowers on 12–16 in (about 30–40 cm) stems in spring. Growing to a height of 18 in (about 45 cm) and a spread of 24 in (about 60 cm), it makes an excellent border plant or trouble-free ground cover among deciduous trees and shrubs, and thrives in sun or shade. It requires a fairly good soil with plenty of humus. Propagate by division in fall or after flowering in spring. It does best with regular summer watering. Remove spent flowerheads to prolong flowering.

ZONES 3–10

### *B.* hybrids

ELEPHANT'S EARS

There are many handsome bergenia hybrids in a range of colors. They include 'Abendglut' (also known as 'Evening Glow') with deep magenta flowers and leaves that develop maroon tints in winter; 'Ballawley', which bears bright crimson flowers; and 'Silberlicht' (also known as 'Silver Light') with pure white flowers. They all flower in spring. Sizes range from 12–24 in (about 30–60 cm) in height and spread. Propagate by division in spring after flowering.

ZONES 6–10

### *B. stracheyi*

Native to the Himalayas, this evergreen perennial has relatively small, wedge-shaped, hairy-margined leaves that are carried more erectly than on most of the other bergenias. It produces sprays of cup-shaped, pale pink or white flowers in spring. Clump forming, it reaches a height of 9 in (about 23 cm) with a spread of 12 in (about 30 cm).

ZONES 6–10

## *BRACHYCOME*

Native to Australia, these low-growing annuals and evergreen perennials are suitable for use as ground cover. They are mound-forming plants with finely divided, soft, fern-like foliage and bear hundreds of daisy-like flowers in many shades of blue, mauve, pink and white, centered in black and gold. They are showy border or bedding plants, the smaller species being excellent for rock gardens. They require a sunny situation, in sandy loam or well-drained garden soil. Do not overwater as they prefer dry conditions. Pinch out early shoots to encourage branching and propagate from ripe seed or by divisions or stem cuttings in spring or fall. The Swan River daisy (*B. iberidifolia*) grows to a height and spread of 20 in (about 50 cm). It is fairly fast growing with lacy green foliage. Small, fragrant, daisy-like flowers of blue, pink, mauve, purple or white appear in summer and early fall.

ALL ZONES

## *BROWALLIA*
## *americana*

syn. *B. elata*

BUSH VIOLET

This moderately fast-growing perennial, related to the petunia, is usually grown as an annual. A bushy plant, it grows to a height of 24 in (about 60 cm) and a spread of 6 in (about 15 cm). In summer and early fall it bears clusters of showy, semi-star shaped, 2 in (about 5 cm) wide flowers in a rare shade of intense blue. It has oval, mid-green leaves. It can withstand temperatures down to 40°F (4°C), and grows best in partial shade in a rich soil with good drainage. Propagate from seed in spring, or in late summer for winter flowers. Pinch out young growing tips to encourage bushiness. The cultivar 'Sapphire' is a compact selection with dark blue flowers with white eyes.

ALL ZONES

## *BRUNNERA*
## *macrophylla*

SIBERIAN BUGLOSS

The small but intensely blue flowers show their relationship to the forget-me-nots; they are held on slender stems 18–24 in (about 45–60 cm) tall above the bold mounds of heart-shaped basal leaves. Flowers appear in late spring to early summer, after which the new leaves grow to their full 6–8 in (about 15–20 cm) width. Clumps spread slowly underground but self seed readily, making an excellent ground cover under trees and large shrubs. It prefers a rich, woodsy, moist soil, especially in sun; it is more tolerant of dry conditions in the shade.

ZONES 3-10

*Callistephus chinensis*

*Calceolaria* x *herbeohybrida*

## *CALCEOLARIA*

SLIPPER FLOWER, POCKETBOOK FLOWER

Mostly native to Central and South America, these charming annuals, biennials, evergreen perennials, sub-shrubs and scandent climbers make spectacular pot plants and garden plants, and are valued for their ability to flower profusely in partial shade. Flowers are pouch like, usually yellow, sometimes red and heavily spotted on the lower lip. Most prefer sun, but several species will flower well in a shady, cool site in moist, well-drained soil with added compost and sharp sand. Propagate from seed in fall or softwood cuttings in summer or late spring. Provide shelter from heavy winds as the flowerheads are easily damaged.

### *C.* x *herbeohybrida*

A compact, bushy annual popular as an indoor plant, especially for spring display. There are many named varieties, growing to a height of 8–16 in (about 20–40 cm) and a spread of 6–10 in (about 15–25 cm). It flowers during spring and summer, bearing heads of red and yellow pouched flowers around 2 in (about 5 cm) wide. The leaves are oval and slightly hairy.

ZONES 9–11

### *C. integrifolia*

An evergreen, sub-shrubby perennial growing to 3½ ft (about 1 m) high with a spread of 24 in (about 60 cm). It has soft green, heavily wrinkled, clammy leaves, rust-colored beneath, and in summer bears crowded clusters of wide, brilliant yellow to red-brown flowers. It is sometimes grown as an annual and during very cold winters may die down to near ground level. It prefers a well-drained, acid soil and only occasional watering; it flowers very well when rootbound in a pot.

ZONES 9–11

## *CALENDULA officinalis*

CALENDULA, POT MARIGOLD

This is a popular winter- and spring-flowering annual that remains in bloom for a long time. There are tall and dwarf forms, both bushy, the tall growing to a height and spread of 24 in (about 60 cm) and the dwarf to 12 in (about 30 cm). These fast-growing plants are among the easiest of all annuals to grow, and are useful for filling gaps in the winter and spring garden. They also provide good cut flowers for the cooler months. All forms have lance-shaped, strongly scented, pale-green leaves and daisy-like single or double flowerheads. Tall strains include 'Pacific Beauty', with pastel-shaded double flowers, and 'Radio', with cactus-like quilled petals. Dwarf strains include the Fiesta series, with double flowers in colors ranging from cream to orange; the Bon Bon strain, with very early flowers of orange, apricot and yellow; and the Dwarf Gem strain with double flowers from pale yellow to orange. All cultivars will thrive in almost any well-drained soil in a sunny situation. Propagate from seed sown in late summer for winter bloom in mild climates, or in early spring for late spring to early summer bloom elsewhere. They also self seed readily. Remove spent flowerheads to encourage prolonged flowering.

ZONES 4–11

## *CALLISTEPHUS chinensis*

CHINA ASTER

An erect, bushy annual that is reputedly difficult to grow, this species needs sun, protection from wind and extremes of heat and a light, sandy, fertile, well-drained soil with added lime. Water plants well and mulch in hot weather to keep the root system cool. It is a fairly fast-growing plant. There are various cultivars available, ranging from tall, up to 24 in (about 60 cm) with a spread of 18 in (about 45 cm) to very dwarf, up to 8 in (about 20 cm) with a spread of 12 in (about 30 cm). Leaves are oval, toothed and mid-green and the plants flower in summer and early fall in a wide range of colors including white, blue, pink and red. Stake tall cultivars and remove spent flowers regularly. Sow seed in spring after the danger of frost has passed, and watch for virus disease, aphids, and stem and root rot. Select wilt-resistant strains.

ALL ZONES

*Calceolaria integrifolia*

*Calendula officinalis*

Caltha palustris

Campanula isophylla

Campanula carpatica

## *CALTHA palustris*

MARSH MARIGOLD, KINGCUP

Native to the temperate and cold regions of the northern hemisphere, this marginal water plant is grown for its attractive flowers. It is a deciduous or semi-evergreen perennial with glistening, buttercup-like golden yellow flowers borne in spring and dark green, rounded leaves. It grows to a height and spread of 12 in (about 30 cm). It is suitable for the margins of streams or ponds or in any damp spots and prefers an open, sunny position and wet soil. Propagate by division in early spring, or from seed or by division in fall. Treat any rust with a fungicide.
ZONES 3–10

## *CAMPANULA*

BELLFLOWER

Native to the temperate parts of the northern hemisphere, this large genus includes about 250 species of annuals, biennials and perennials. They are among the most showy of plants and are useful specimens for rockeries, borders, wild gardens and hanging baskets. Many of the species are classed as rock and alpine plants. Leaves vary in shape and size, sometimes appearing on upright stems and sometimes only as a cluster at the base. Flowers are mostly bell shaped and blue, with some whites. All do best in a moderately enriched, moist, well-drained soil. They grow in sun or shade, but flower color remains brightest in shady situations. Protect from drying winds and stake the taller varieties, which make good cut flowers. Remove spent flower stems. Feed regularly, particularly during the growing season. Propagate from seed or by division in spring or fall, or by softwood or basal cuttings in spring or summer. Transplant in fall or early spring.

### *C. carpatica*

CARPATHIAN BELLFLOWER

The slowly spreading clumps of basal leaves of this species make it good as an edging or rock garden

*Campanula persicifolia* 'Alba'

plant. From late spring through much of summer 12–15 in (about 30–38 cm) stems rise above the foliage, carrying up-facing, 1–2 in (about 2.5–5 cm) wide bowl-shaped flowers in blue, lavender or white. The most common cultivars available are the compact-growing 'Blue Clips' and 'White Clips', and the bright violet blue 'Wedgwood Blue'. Full sun to light shade is preferred, along with a well-drained soil. Divide established clumps in early spring as growth begins, or sow from seed in fall.
ZONES 3–10

### *C. isophylla*

ITALIAN BELLFLOWER

A dwarf, evergreen trailing perennial, growing to 4 in (about 10 cm) high with a spread of 12 in (about 30 cm). Native to the mountain slopes of northern Italy, it has star-shaped blue or white flowers in summer. The leaves are small and heart shaped. 'Alba' has white flowers. This is an ideal hanging basket specimen.
ZONES 7–10

### *C. lactiflora*

A strong-growing perennial reaching a height of 3½ ft (about 1 m) and a spread of 24 in (about 60 cm). In summer it produces immense pyramidal spikes containing large, bell-shaped, lilac blue (occasionally pink or white) flowers. The leaves are narrowly oval. If cut back immediately after flowering they may bloom again in late fall. These plants can be naturalized among light grass and will thrive in either sun or semi-shade.
ZONES 6–10

Campanula lactiflora

### *C. medium*

CANTERBURY BELL

A biennial species, this is a slow-growing, erect, clump-forming plant. It produces spires of bell-shaped single or double, white, pink or blue flowers towering 3 ft (about 90 cm) over a rosette of lance-shaped fresh green leaves that spreads to 12 in (about 30 cm). Dwarf cultivars grow to 24 in (about 60 cm). It flowers in spring and early summer. Grow as border plants in semi-shade.
ZONES 6–10

### *C. persicifolia*

PEACH-LEAVED BELLFLOWER

Perhaps the best known *Campanula* with nodding, bell-shaped blue or white flowers borne above narrow, lance-shaped bright green leaves in summer. *C. p.* 'Alba' has white flowers. Pinch spent flowers off stems as they fade. It is a spreading, rosette-forming perennial reaching a height of 3 ft (about 90 cm) and a spread of 12 in (about 30 cm).
ZONES 3–10

Campanula medium

*Catharanthus roseus*

*Campanula poscharskyana*

*Campanula portenschlagiana*

*Canna* x *generalis*

*Celosia argentea* var. *cristata*

*Catananche caerulea* 'Major'

### *C. portenschlagiana*

Native to the mountains of southern Europe, this is a low-growing, evergreen plant well suited to rock gardens. It grows to a height of 6 in (about 15 cm) with an indefinite spread. It has dense, small, ivy-shaped leaves, and a profusion of deeply lobed, bell-shaped, violet flowers are borne in late spring and early summer. Plant in cool, partly shaded positions with good drainage.

ZONES 5–10

### *C. poscharskyana*

A rampant, low-growing, spreading perennial with sprays of star-shaped, mauve-blue flowers from late spring onwards. It mounds up from 4–6 in (about 10–15 cm) with an indefinite spread and is ideal for use as a ground cover, on walls and banks and in the front of mixed borders. Partial shade will prolong flowering.

ZONES 3–10

## CANNA
### x *generalis*

Native to tropical America, these robust, showy perennials grow from rhizomes and are valued for their striking flowers and foliage. Ideally suited to summer bedding displays and containers, they grow from 4½–6 ft (about 1.3–1.8 m) tall and spread to 24 in (about 60 cm). The sturdy stems have bold, lance-shaped, green or bronze leaves and the summer flowers are red, pink, orange or yellow. They require a sunny position and moist soil with plenty of well-decayed animal manure. Water well during summer to prolong flowering. Propagate in spring by division. In cold areas protect roots with mulch.

ZONES 8–11

## CATANANCHE
### *caerulea* 'Major'

CUPID'S DART

Native to the Mediterranean region, this fast-growing, herbaceous perennial reaches 24 in (about 60 cm) in height with a spread of 12 in (about 30 cm). Clump forming, the slender leaves are gray-green while thin, leafless stems topped with daisy-like, lavender-blue flowerheads are borne freely throughout summer. The flowers are suitable for drying. Requiring full sun, it is easily grown in most soil conditions and is fairly drought tolerant. Relatively short lived, it is best divided frequently; it will self seed readily. It looks good among grasses in a meadow garden as well as in a sunny border.

ZONES 4–10

## CATHARANTHUS
### *roseus*
syn. *Vinca rosea*

MADAGASCAR PERIWINKLE, ROSE PERIWINKLE

This small relative of the oleander is an evergreen spreading shrub in its native Africa, but is usually grown in the US as an annual or tender perennial. It is popular for its dark-centered, rose-pink to white phlox-like flowers, which bloom from spring to fall or into winter in warm areas. It grows to 24 in (about 60 cm) in height and spread. It loves heat and sun but will flower well in part shade; it prefers a rich, well-drained soil and demands little water once established. Older plants may become untidy and require pruning to promote a bushy habit. A useful summer bedding plant in cool climates, flowering quickly from seed sown in spring after the danger of frost has passed.

ZONES 10–11

## CELOSIA
### *argentea* var. *cristata*

COCKSCOMB

Native to the tropics, this is a fast-growing annual cultivated for summer bedding displays. The leaves are mid-green; the erect, bushy plants may range from 10–24 in (about 25–60 cm) in height with a spread of 8–12 in (about 20–30 cm). The flowers are of two types—coral-like rippled crests, or feathery plumes—both in hot colors of yellow, orange and red. They are long lasting and make excellent cut flowers. It requires a moderately rich, well-drained soil and loves a sunny site; it will tolerate dryness. Sow seed in spring after the danger of frost has passed.

ZONES 4–11

## CENTAUREA

KNAPWEED

Mostly native to Europe, Asia and Africa, this large genus of annuals and perennials are grown for their graceful flowerheads which have thistle-like centers surrounded by finely rayed petals in shades of bright red, deep purple, blue and golden yellow. Some species are inclined to sprawl and need trimming back. All are suitable for cutting. They need sun and well-drained soil and are particularly useful in dryish conditions on alkaline soils. Propagate by division or seed in fall, late winter or spring. Transplant during winter or spring. Centaureas have been grown since ancient times and were once used as a love divination.

### *C. cyanus*

CORNFLOWER, BACHELOR'S BUTTONS

One of the best known annuals, this fast-growing upright plant reaches a height of 3 ft (about 90 cm) with a spread of 12 in (about 30 cm). It has lance-shaped leaves and a spring or early summer display of double, daisy-like flowerheads in shades of pale and deep pink, cerise, crimson, white, purple and blue. Tall and dwarf cultivars are available. Best displayed in large drifts and will flower for months if deadheads are removed regularly. Once known as bluebottle, the wild form was used to make ink.

ZONES 3–10

### *C. dealbata*

PERSIAN CORNFLOWER

A very leafy plant with light grayish green, deeply cut foliage. Lilac-purple to lilac-pink flowerheads appear in a mass from late spring onwards. An erect perennial, it grows to around 30 in (about 76 cm) high with a spread of 24 in (about 60 cm). The cultivar 'Steenbergii' has larger, deep pink flowers.

ZONES 3–10

### *C. hypoleucha* 'John Coutts'

Deep rose-pink flowers are produced singly on stalks up to 24 in (about 60 cm) high in early summer, often with a second flush in fall. This spreading perennial has long, lobed leaves, green on top and gray underneath, and forms a clump 18 in (about 45 cm) across.

ZONES 3–9

### *C. moschata*

syn. *Amberboa moschata*

SWEET SULTAN

A sweet-scented cottage garden plant introduced to cultivation over 350 years ago, this is a fast-growing, upright annual with lance-shaped, grayish green leaves. Fragrant, fluffy, thistle-like flowers to 2 in (about 5 cm) across are produced in a wide range of colors in summer and early fall. Grows to 24–36 in (about 60–90 cm) tall and spreads to 12 in (about 30 cm). It loves heat; avoid overhead irrigation.

ZONES 8–10

## *CENTRANTHUS*

### *ruber*

RED VALERIAN

Native to Europe, this perennial is often seen as a naturalized plant on dry banks and is ideal for dry rock gardens. It is grown for its dense clusters of small, star-shaped, deep reddish pink flowers that are borne for a long period from late spring to fall. The cultivar 'Albus' has white flowers. It forms loose clumps of fleshy leaves and grows to a height of 24–36 in (about 60–90 cm) and a spread of 20–24 in (about 50–60 cm). One of the easiest plants to grow, it requires sun and good drainage and will tolerate exposed positions and poor, alkaline soil. It is very drought tolerant but will grow more lushly with regular water. Cut back straggly growth to invigorate the plant and force a second bloom. Propagate from seed in fall or spring; it self seeds readily and may naturalize.

ZONES 4–10

## *CEPHALARIA*

### *gigantea*

GIANT SCABIOUS

This handsome giant of a perennial is native to Siberia. It need plenty of space to spread as it grows to around 6 ft (about 1.8 m) high and 4 ft (about 1.2 m) across. It forms a huge clump of dark green, divided leaves from which rise many tough, thin stems around 3 ft (about 90 cm) high, topped with primrose-yellow flowerheads that are rather like those of a scabious. Propagation can be done by division in spring or by seed in fall. This plant is not particular as to soil, and does best in a site in full sun.

ZONES 3–10

## *CERASTIUM*

### *tomentosum*

SNOW-IN-SUMMER

A vigorous, fast-growing ground cover, this perennial is ideal for a well-drained, hot, dry bank or rockery. It has tiny, silvery gray leaves, and masses of star-shaped white flowers are borne in late spring and summer. It is particularly attractive when used as an underplanting beneath greener-leafed plants. The foliage is dense and is an effective weed suppressant. It grows to 3 in (about 7.5 cm) high and spreads indefinitely. Water regularly but allow to dry out between soakings. Propagate by division in spring. After flowering, remove spent flowers by clipping the top of the plant with shears.

ZONES 3–11

## *CERATOSTIGMA*

### *plumbaginoides*

DWARF PLUMBAGO, LEADWORT

Native to western China, this bushy perennial grows to 12 in (about 30 cm) high with a spread of 18 in (about 45 cm). Valued for its tough constitution and attractive foliage and flowers, it has oval, mid-green leaves that turn a rich orange and red in fall. Single, cornflower-blue flowers appear in clusters on reddish, branched stems in late summer and fall. Preferring a sunny situation, it also thrives in shade but with somewhat reduced flowering and less fall color in the leaves. Give it a light, well-drained soil and moisture until well established, after which it adapts to varying levels of soil moisture. Good planted among spring bulbs, as its bushy form will fill the gaps when bulb foliage dies down.

ZONES 5–10

*Centaurea cyanus*

*Ceratostigma plumbaginoides*

*Centaurea moschata*

*Centaurea dealbata*

*Centranthus ruber*

*Centaurea hypoleucha* 'John Coutts'

*Cerastium tomentosum*

*Clarkia amoena*

*Chrysanthemum carinatum*

*Cleome hassleriana*

## CHELONE
*obliqua*

TURTLEHEAD

Of the several species of turtleheads native to eastern North America, this is the showiest and most garden worthy. Pairs of rich green leaves line 3 ft (about 90 cm) tall vertical stems topped with short spikes of curious rosy-purple tubular flowers in late summer and fall. Best along streams or pond edges, they also adapt well to a moist border planting with rich soil in full sun or part shade. Propagate by dividing clumps in early spring.

ZONES 3–9

## CHRYSANTHEMUM

CHRYSANTHEMUM

Native to temperate zones, this large genus is valued for its ease of culture, rapid growth and showy flowers. It includes annuals, perennials and sub-shrubs, most of which are evergreen. All have daisy-like flowers, each flowerhead in fact made up of a large number of individual florets. Color range includes yellow, orange, brown, white, pink, red and purple. Leaves are usually deeply cut or divided, often feathery, and oval to lance shaped. Stems are upright and often woody. Chrysanthemums grow best in an open, sunny site in a rich, friable, well-drained soil. Feed and water regularly. Stake tall plants and pinch out growing tips of young plants to encourage lateral branching. Suckers should not be allowed to develop until the plants have flowered. Propagate annuals by seed sown in spring; perennials by dividing basal growth or by striking cuttings taken from plant material that is in active growth in spring; and sub-shrubs by softwood cuttings in spring or hardwood cuttings in winter. The genus *Chrysanthemum* is currently undergoing revision. Some species have been reclassified and will be found in this chapter under their new names. Diseases include chrysanthemum rust, powdery mildew, petal blight and botrytis.

### *C. carinatum*
**syn. *C. tricolor***

SUMMER CHRYSANTHEMUM

This spectacular annual species is from Morocco and grows to 24 in (about 60 cm), spreading to 12 in (about 30 cm) with banded, multicolored flowers in summer and early fall, or winter to early spring in mild regions. The Court Jesters strain comes in red with yellow centers or white with red centers. Excellent as bedding plants and cut flowers. Sow seed in spring for summer/fall bloom or in early fall for winter/spring bloom.

ALL ZONES

*C. frutescens* see *Argyranthemum frutescens*

*C. maximum* see *Leucanthemum* × *superbum*

*C. morifolium* see *Dendranthema* × *grandiflora*

## CIMICIFUGA
*racemosa*

BUGBANE, BLACK COHOSH, BLACK SNAKEROOT

These eastern American natives are bold additions to the summer garden, at the back of borders or in open woodland situations. Above large, divided, astilbe-like foliage rise 3–8 ft (about 90–240 cm) tall racemes of tiny, fragrant, white flowers. They prefer a deep, rich soil with regular watering but are generally carefree perennials. Plant in spring or fall, but do not disturb for years; they flower best when well established, and seldom need staking.

ZONES 3–9

## CLARKIA

FAREWELL-TO-SPRING, GODETIA, MOUNTAIN GARLAND

Free-flowering annuals native to the western United States, Mexico and South America, this genus is particularly common in California where they color the hills in late spring after the winter rains have ceased. They normally dry up by early summer, dispersing their seeds for the next year's bloom. In gardens, flowering can be extended through the summer with occasional irrigation. The best growth and flowering occurs in areas of cool, dry summers (like the West Coast and the mountain states), but it is worth experimenting with elsewhere. Soil should be fast draining and not too rich; choose a sunny spot for the most compact growth. Sow seed in fall in mild winter regions, or in very early spring where winters are cold; sow where they are to bloom since they do not transplant well. Dead-head regularly to extend bloom; let some seed ripen and fall for next year's flowers. They make excellent cut flowers. Watch for botrytis. *Clarkia* are named for Captain William Clark, one of the early explorers of the West.

### *C. amoena*

FAREWELL-TO-SPRING

Named for its flowering period at the beginning of summer, this is a fast-growing western American native to a height of 24 in (about 60 cm) and a spread of 12 in (about 30 cm). It has lance-shaped, mid-green leaves, thin upright stems, and in summer bears short spikes of 2 in (about 5 cm), open, cup-shaped flowers in shades of pink. Numerous named seed strains are now available with either single or double flowers in a range of colors that includes white and soft reds, and with heights varying from 8–24 in (about 20–60 cm).

ALL ZONES

### *C. unguiculata*
**syn. *C. elegans***

MOUNTAIN GARLAND

This species is usually taller than *C. amoena* but with smaller flowers, only 1 in (about 2.5 cm) across and often frilled and doubled. The flowers are produced along the tops of slender reddish stems, 3 ft (about 90 cm) or more in height. The color range is broader, including orange and purple.

ALL ZONES

## CLEOME
*hassleriana*

**syn. *C. spinosa***

Mainly native to tropical America, this fast-growing, bushy annual is valued for its unusual spidery flowers. An erect plant, it grows to 4–5 ft (about 1.2–1.5 m) tall with a spread of up to 3 ft (about 90 cm). It has hairy stems and palmate leaves topped in summer with heads of airy pink or white flowers with long protruding stamens. Flowering lasts until winter. A good background bedding plant and useful in new gardens for their rapid growth, they require sun and fertile, well-drained soil as over-watering will cause rank growth. Shelter from strong winds. Propagate by seed in spring or early summer. Watch for aphids.

ZONES 4–11

## *CODONOPSIS clematidea*

Native to Asia, this perennial thrives in cooler areas. The bell-shaped, pale blue blossoms are borne in late summer; they are prettily marked with orange and red on the inside. The grayish green foliage forms a rounded clump around 24 in (about 60 cm) high and wide, though the plant can reach double that height if it can twine up a support or through a shrub. For the best effect, plant it in a raised bed or on a bank where the inside of its nodding flowers can easily be seen. It does best in a light, well-drained soil in part or complete shade. Propagate by seed in fall or spring.
ZONES 5–9

## *COLEUS*

Native to the tropics of Asia and Africa, these annuals, perennials and evergreen sub-shrubs are grown for their brightly colored and variegated foliage. In milder climates they are popular pot plants and are useful for bedding in sheltered places. *Coleus* grow best in bright, indirect light or partial shade and a rich, well-drained or moist soil in a sheltered position. Feed and water liberally during the growing season to encourage strong leafy growth. In winter potted plants should be kept fairly dry. Potted plants develop brightest colors when pot bound. Pinch out young shoots to promote bushy growth. Propagate from seed sown indoors in late winter or spring, or from softwood cuttings in spring or summer. Botanists have begun assigning species of *Coleus* to either *Solenostemon* or *Plectranthus*; these new names are given here as synonyms.

### *C. blumei*
**syn. *Solenostemon scutellaroides***
COLEUS, PAINTED NETTLE

Native to Java this bushy, fast-growing perennial is grown as an annual in more temperate climates. The leaves are a bright mixture of pink, green, red or yellow and are a pointed oval shape with serrated edges. It grows to 20 in (about 50 cm) high with a spread of 12 in (about 30 cm), and prefers partial shade. Remove flower spikes. Most of the forms available are probably hybrids with other species.
ZONES 4–11

*Coleus blumei*

### *C. thyrsoides*
**syn. *Plectranthus thyrsoides***
FLOWERING BUSH COLEUS

A fast-growing bushy perennial also grown as an annual. This is a larger species, growing to 3 ft (about 90 cm) high with a spread of 24 in (about 60 cm). The leaves are oval, and mid-green with serrated edges; panicles of tubular bright blue flowers are borne in winter.
ZONES 4–11

*Coleus thyrsoides*

## *CONSOLIDA ambigua*

ROCKET LARKSPUR, ANNUAL DELPHINIUM

A showy annual with upright, 2–5 ft (about 60–150 cm) spikes of delphinium-like flowers in blue, violet, pink, carmine and white. The leaves are deeply lobed, like birds' feet. Plants bloom heavily in late spring and early summer, then gradually wither away. Sow seed in fall for bloom the following year; once planted, they self seed readily. Give them a sunny situation and a well-drained soil. Water regularly for best growth. There are numerous seed strains with variations in height and flower color and with single or double flowers.
ZONES 4–11

## *CONVOLVULUS*

This is a large genus of dwarf, bushy and climbing perennials, annuals, evergreen shrubs and sub-shrubs from warm to temperate climates. Some species are now naturalized and strongly invasive; others of only moderate vigor are useful for spilling over walls, for rock gardens, hanging baskets and as a ground cover. They flower most prolifically in a sunny situation in poor to fertile, well-drained soil. Little pruning is needed. Dead-head plants to prolong flowering. Propagate from seed sown in mid-spring, or from softwood cuttings in late spring and summer for perennials and sub-shrubs.

*Convolvulus cneorum*

### *C. cneorum*
BUSH MORNING GLORY, SILVERBUSH

A dense, shrubby, evergreen growing to 24 in (about 60 cm) or more with narrow, silky, silvery green leaves and large white flowers, sometimes tinged with pink or cream, with yellow centers. It flowers from mid-spring to late summer and is a useful plant for hot dry places and average soil. It flowers best if trimmed back every year.
ZONES 7–11

### *C. sabatius*
**syn. *C. mauritanicus***
GROUND MORNING GLORY

A trailing perennial with profuse, open, trumpet-shaped, mauve-blue flowers from spring to fall. Slender stems and small, oval leaves. An excellent specimen for draping over walls and hanging baskets, it grows to a height of 6–8 in (about 15–20 cm) and a spread of 24–36 in (about 60–90 cm).
ZONES 8–11

*Convolvulus sabatius*

*Consolida ambigua*

*Coreopsis verticillata*

*Coreopsis grandiflora*

*Corydalis lutea*

*Convolvulus tricolor*

*Coreopsis tinctoria*

*Cosmos atrosanguineus*

### *C. tricolor*
**syn. *C. minor***
DWARF MORNING GLORY

An interesting bedding annual with profuse trumpet-shaped blue or white flowers with banded yellow and white throats. Leaves are lance shaped and mid-green. It grows to a height of 12 in (about 30 cm) and a spread of 18 in (about 45 cm) or more. It blooms continuously through the warm weather.
ZONES 7–11

## *COREOPSIS*
TICKSEED

This genus of easily grown annuals and perennials, all native to North America, are valued for their daisy-like flowers in shades of gold or yellow, some bicolors. They are mainly summer flowering. The perennials make excellent herbaceous border plants, looking striking with shasta daisies and blue delphiniums. They prefer full sun and a fertile, well-drained soil but also grow well in coastal regions and on poor, stony soil. Propagate perennials by division of old clumps in winter or spring, or by spring cuttings. The annuals also prefer full sun and a fertile, well-drained soil; they will not tolerate a heavy clay soil. Taller varieties may need staking. Propagate annuals from seed in spring or fall, and dead-head regularly.

### *C. grandiflora*

Among the easiest of perennials, this bright golden-yellow daisy provides color for most of the summer. Somewhat hairy leaves and stems form a loose mound to 12 in (about 30 cm) tall and wider, the flower stems rising to nearly 24 in (about 60 cm), or usually flopping on their neighbors. Ideal for a wild meadow, but for the well-maintained border use the cultivars selected for a more compact habit such as 'Sunray' or 'Early Sunrise'.
ZONES 5–10

### *C. tinctoria*
ANNUAL COREOPSIS, CALLIOPSIS

A fast-growing showy annual that produces clusters of bright yellow, daisy-like flowerheads with red centers throughout summer and fall. It grows to a height of 24–36 in (about 60–90 cm) and a spread of 8 in (about 20 cm). Provide support with branched twigs or fine bamboo stakes. Makes good cut flowers. It is a popular plant in meadow and prairie gardens.
ZONES 4–10

### *C. verticillata*
THREAD-LEAF COREOPSIS

A strong, dependable perennial, growing to 30 in (about 76 cm) with a spread of 24 in (about 60 cm). Produces abundant, large, daisy-like, rich yellow flowers on elegant stems and is useful for cutting. Leaves are bright green and very finely divided. Flowers from late spring until winter and does best in light, poorish soil. 'Moonbeam' is a selection with pale yellow flowers.
ZONES 3–10

## *CORYDALIS*
### *lutea*

Related to the bleeding hearts (*Dicentra*), this long-blooming perennial covers itself with racemes of soft yellow flowers from spring to fall, beautifully presented against the lush, fern-like foliage. The mounded plants are only 12 in (about 30 cm) tall and wide, but self seed readily to form quite an acceptable ground cover. The best growth will be achieved in dappled shade, though more flowers are produced in full sun; they prefer a woodsy soil and steady moisture through the growing season. They are excellent for naturalizing in stone walls, between paving stones or in a woodland garden.
ZONES 5–10

## *COSMOS*

Native to Mexico and central America, this small genus of annuals and perennials has been grown in gardens for over a century. Some annual species are particularly tall, ideal for the back of borders and excellent for late summer and fall cutting. They require a sunny situation with protection from strong winds and will grow in any well-drained soil as long as it is not over-rich. Propagate annuals from seed in spring, perennials from basal cuttings in spring.

### *C. atrosanguineus*

BLACK COSMOS

A clump-forming perennial growing to 24 in (about 60 cm) in height and spread, black cosmos has very dark, blackish red flowers that have a chocolate scent, which is most noticeable on warm days. It flowers from late spring to fall. The pinnate foliage is broad compared to that of the annuals. Partially evergreen but it may die back completely in cold areas. Demands excellent winter drainage or the rootstock may rot. It is not as dependable a garden plant as the other species of cosmos. Good as a cut flower.

ZONES 7–10

### *C. bipinnatus*

COSMOS

An upright, bushy annual growing to nearly 6 ft (about 1.8 m) in height with a spread of 20 in (about 50 cm). Though too tall for bedding, it is a fine border plant with large rose-pink, white or maroon flowerheads held against delicate feathery foliage. It flowers in late summer and fall. It can be used as a filler or temporary screen in gardens that are just establishing themselves; allow it to naturalize among shrubs and perennials. Many seed strains are available offering variations in height and flower color, including some with bicolored, striped or frilled petals and one with rolled petals.

ZONES 7–10

### *C. sulphureus*

YELLOW COSMOS

This annual has coarser foliage and blooms in many shades of yellow and orange in summer and early fall. It is moderately fast growing, reaching a height of 24 in (about 60 cm) and a spread of 20 in (about 50 cm). It is very tolerant of heat and drought; it will also tolerate poor soil.

ZONES 7–10

*Crambe maritima*

## *CRAMBE maritima*

SEA KALE

This robust, small perennial forms a mound of wide, silvery green leaves and carries branching sprays of tiny white flowers in summer. Sea kale prefers an open sunny position, but will tolerate light shade, and a well-drained, neutral to alkaline soil. It grows to a height and spread of 24–36 in (about 60–90 cm). The young leaf shoots are edible. Propagate from seed in spring or fall or by division in early spring. *C. cordifolia* is similar but much larger and produces clouds of small, white, 4-petaled flowers in summer.

ZONES 6–9

## *CYPERUS papyrus*

PAPYRUS, EGYPTIAN PAPER REED

This large perennial evergreen sedge has an indefinite spread and grows $4^1/_2$–$7^1/_2$ ft (about 1.3–2.2 m) tall. Its sturdy, leafless stems carry enormous umbels of spikelets in summer. It prefers a sunny situation in wet soil and can be grown in water. This is the bulrush of the Bible. Ancient Egyptians made paper from the stems.

ZONES 9–11

## *DAHLIA*

DAHLIA

This genus of bushy, tuberous-rooted perennials, native to Mexico, are named after the Swedish botanist Andreas Dahl, a pupil of Linnaeus. Grown as bedding plants, they are valued for the wide range of colors, color combinations, sizes and shapes of their flowers, which are excellent as cut flowers. Named varieties come and go with amazing speed and every country has a different selection, so we have simply given representative examples of each type. Dwarf forms are also suitable for containers. Fast growing, they have a long flowering period from late spring to late fall. They grow best in a warm sunny position, preferably sheltered from strong winds, and in well-fertilized, well-drained soil. They must be fed monthly and watered well when in flower. Old and faded blooms should be removed to help prolong the flowering season. Flower size can be increased by disbudding—pinch out the two buds that grow with the center bud on each stem and cut off the immediate laterals and all superfluous shoots. In very hot weather they benefit from a mulch around the stems. The dwarf forms will flower in the first year from seed sown in spring. All can be propagated by division of tuberous roots before planting in spring, or from basal shoots in late spring.

### Cactus dahlias

Derived from crosses between *D. variabilis* and *D. juarezii* from northern Mexico, this most popular type is distinguished by the long, recurved ray florets which give the flower a graceful outline. The varieties are classed as miniature, medium and giant, the size range being about the same as the decoratives. All are tall and need staking.

ALL ZONES

Cactus dahlia

*Cosmos bipinnatus*

*Cosmos sulphureus*

*Cyperus papyrus*

# A Field Trip to Lundy

Viewed from the mainland on a clear day, the windswept island of Lundy looms out of the sea haze, providing a tantalizing and imposing view of its fortress-like profile. A safe haven for pirates and marauders in centuries past, Lundy is now a sanctuary for wildlife, both land-based and marine. It has been owned by the National Trust for the past 25 years. As a measure of its importance, the surrounding waters were recently declared Britain's first Marine Nature Reserve.

Lundy lies 11 miles (about 17 km) off the coast of Devon in southwestern England. Boat trips there operate regularly from the small, north Devon port of Bideford. After an invariably choppy sea-crossing lasting a couple of hours, the towering cliffs of Lundy are a welcome sight. After stepping ashore, regain your land legs and climb the steep slopes to admire stunning coastal scenery of granite headlands and cliffs stretching into the distance. The island comprises a flattish plateau, which in places rises almost 400 ft (about 120 m) from the sea, some cliffs being almost sheer. The eastern side is relatively sheltered from prevailing westerly winds while the western side is often battered by the full force of Atlantic gales. If your visit coincides with the peak flowering period, many of the views are framed by a foreground carpet of purple foxgloves *(Digitalis purpurea)*.

Lundy's flowers are fascinating and varied. In May and June, thrift, or sea pink *(Armeria maritima)*, and sea campion

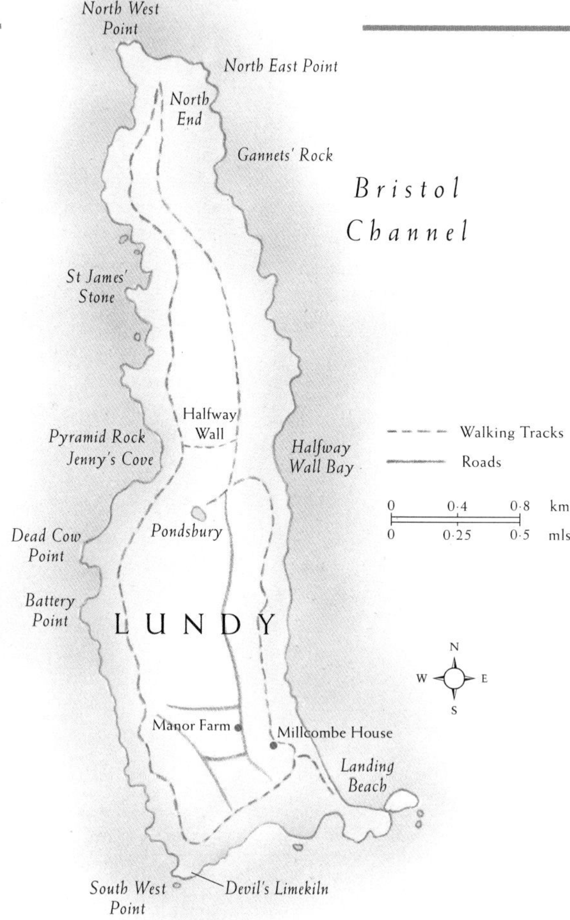


*Foxgloves grow profusely on the islands off southwestern England.*

*(Silene vulgaris* subsp. *maritima)* provide a floral display on the western side, while short-cropped turf on the top of the island harbors Britain's best population of the intriguingly named dwarf adder's tongue-fern *(Ophioglossum azoricum).* There is even an endemic plant here—the Lundy cabbage *(Coincya wrightii),* which is found nowhere else in the world. The impact of these is diminished, however, by the abundant spikes of purple foxgloves that thrive in the eastern and southern parts of the island.

Although the foxglove is sometimes perennial, especially in ornamental settings, it is mostly considered a biennial in the wild. In the first year it produces rosettes of broad, oval to lanceolate leaves up to 12 in (about 30 cm) long with a distinctly hairy upper surface. In the second year a tall flowering spike is produced, which is usually branched and stands up to 6 ft (about 2 m) in height. Flowers appear on the spike over a period of a few weeks between May and August, opening from the bottom of the spike upwards as the spike itself lengthens. The individual flowers, lasting approximately one to two weeks, are tubular with an elongated, bell-shaped appearance. In the wild they are usually deep pink or purple, although white flower spikes are occasionally seen. In cultivation, the paler varieties tend to be more popular. The inner surface of the flower is usually spotted and hairy; this latter assists bees to pollinate the flowers.

Foxgloves are common along the north Devon coast and grow wild in a wide range of habitats. They do, however, prefer comparatively well-drained, neutral to acid soil. Typical sites would include sunny woodland glades, forest clearings, hillsides with broken or rocky soils and coastal cliffs; they will grow quite happily on recently disturbed ground. On Lundy they thrive on slopes which, although covered with bracken *(Pteridium aquilinum),* are almost completely lacking in tree cover. Growing in these conditions, the plant has to be tolerant of salt-spray and constant, sometimes violent, wind.

Rainfall in the west of Britain is comparatively high—40–50 in (about 1000–1200 mm) per year is not unusual—so the plant will need regular watering in a garden setting; however it will not tolerate becoming waterlogged. Foxgloves will also grow both in the open and in a sheltered position although they will not survive for long where the shade is too dense. Since it occurs from sea-level to moderate elevations inland, the foxglove is clearly tolerant of climatic variation.

If you want to see foxgloves at their best on Lundy, visit in mid-June. One of their most attractive settings is among the quarries and spoil workings halfway along the eastern side. Here you can see signs of where blocks of granite were hewn from the cliffs, although much of the evidence is now masked by plant growth, including introduced clumps of rhododendrons. For an alternative view, make your way to the top of the island where you may see small numbers of the rare Soay sheep and Lundy ponies (a breed exclusive to the island). A track runs north–south down the island's spine.

Whether you visit Lundy to see garden plants such as the foxglove growing in their native setting, or simply to experience the rugged splendor of the untamed coastal scenery, you will find it a captivating island, one which few visitors can bear to see only once.

*Digitalis purpurea*

## Digitalis

*Digitalis,* the foxglove genus, consists of around 18 species of biennials and perennials and a few soft-wooded shrubs. Geographically they are centered on the Mediterranean (including North Africa), the majority growing wild in Britain and Europe. Apart from *D. purpurea,* several other *Digitalis* species are sometimes grown for ornament.

Despite being poisonous, the foxglove is one of Britain's most striking and distinctive plants, both in overall size and flower structure. The medicinal properties of *D. purpurea* are important—the leaves are a source of the drug digitalin, which is used to control and alleviate the symptoms of heart disease.

Foxgloves are represented in gardens chiefly by the ornamental strains of *D. purpurea,* for example, the well-known 'Excelsior' strain. The garden forms are more robust than the wild *D. purpurea* plants, and the flowers are packed more closely on the stem. Breeders have aimed for larger, more widely flared and richly spotted flowers displaying a more varied mix of colors. Garden foxgloves are also remarkably adaptable, thriving almost anywhere in temperate zones and in any normal, well-drained garden soil.

*Digitalis* is just one of almost 250 genera of the worldwide Scrophulariaceae family. Snapdragons (*Antirrhinum* ssp.), a genus of annuals popular among gardeners, also belong to this family.

*Digitalis purpurea*

### Collarette dahlias

These old-fashioned dahlias have single flowers with a ruffle of short petals surrounding the disc like a lace collar. Both tall—6 ft (about 1.8 m)—and dwarf—12 in (about 30 cm)—forms are available.

ALL ZONES

### Decorative dahlias

Growing to around 6 ft (about 1.8 m), these have informal, fully double flowers with broad ray petals. They come in giant, medium and miniature varieties, the miniatures having flowers around 4 in (about 10 cm) across and the giants around 10 in (about 25 cm) or more. All need staking.

ALL ZONES

### Dwarf or bedding dahlias

Often grown as annuals, dwarf dahlias grow 14–16 in (about 35–40 cm) tall. The flowers are 2–4 in (about 5–10 cm) across and either semi-double or fully double. They are much used for bedding and may be grown from seed sown in spring or by division of the tubers.

ALL ZONES

### Pompon dahlias

These are tall growing—6 ft (about 1.8 m)—but bear small flowers, 2 in (about 5 cm) across. They are usually fully double, so much so that the flowers open into perfect spheres. They are very useful for cutting, to contrast with the larger types. Show dahlias, not often seen now, are similar in form.

ALL ZONES

### Waterlily dahlias

These have fully double flowers with broad ray petals, smaller and more formal than the decoratives; most varieties are around 5–6 in (about 12–15 cm) wide. They grow 4½–6 ft (about 1.3–1.8 m) tall and need staking.

ALL ZONES

## *DELPHINIUM*

This is a large genus of annuals and herbaceous perennials, most native to the northern hemisphere. The splendid, mainly blue, pink, purple or white spikes of cup-shaped, spurred flowers are useful for massed displays or for cutting. They range from tall spikes up to 6 ft (about 1.8 m) to dwarfs suitable for bedding. Best suited to cooler climate gardens, they can be grown as annuals in warmer climates. Grow in a sunny position, preferably sheltered from wind—the taller cultivars will need to be staked. A well-drained, moist, slightly alkaline, rich loam is ideal. Feed with a complete fertilizer, water well and provide a surface mulch of compost during the growing season. Remove flower spikes after they fade to encourage a second flush in late summer. Spray with fungicide for powdery mildew and black spot, and protect from slugs and snails. The name delphinium derives from the Greek *delphin*, for the dolphins the buds were thought to resemble.

### *D.* x *belladonna*

These hybrid perennials have an upright branching form and 1 in (about 2.5 cm) wide flowers in shades of blue or white. The single, sometimes semi-double, flowers which appear in summer on 12 in (about 30 cm) long spikes are useful for cutting. It grows to a height of 3–4½ ft (about 90–130 cm) and spread of 24 in (about 60 cm). Propagate by division or from basal cuttings in spring.

ZONES 3–10

### *D.* x *cultorum* hybrids

These erect perennials flower in a range of colors from white to purple, usually with contrasting eyes. They grow to 4½–6½ ft (about 1.3-2 m) high with a spread of 2½–3 ft (about 70–90 cm). Tall, tapering spikes of evenly spaced semi-double flowers appear from summer to fall. Cultivars include: 'Blue Bird', medium blue flowers with a white eye; 'Galahad', pure white; 'King Arthur', royal-purple with a white eye; 'Summer Skies', light blue with a white eye; 'Black Knight', violet-blue with a black eye; and 'Astolat', blush pink to rose. Some seed strains (Blue Fountains strain) can be grown from seed sown in spring or fall.

ZONES 3–10

### *D. grandiflorum*

**syn. *D. chinense***

CHINESE DELPHINIUM

Perennial in its native Asian home, this plant is best treated as an annual in mild winter climates. It grows to a height of 18 in (about 45 cm) and a spread of 12 in (about 30 cm). It has bright blue flowers and is useful as a bedding plant as it flowers over a long period during the summer months. Remove spent flowerheads regularly. 'Blue Mirror' is gentian blue and 24 in (about 60 cm) tall.

ZONES 3–10

## *DENDRANTHEMA*

### x *grandiflora*

**syn. *Chrysanthemum morifolium***

GARDEN OR FLORISTS' CHRYSANTHEMUM

These hybrids make up the vast majority of perennial cultivated chrysanthemums and include a variety of flower forms, sizes and growth habits. Most flower in mid-

Waterlily or Nymphaea dahlia

Decorative dahlia

Dwarf or bedding dahlias

Pompon dahlia

Collarette dahlia

*Delphinium* x *belladonna*

*Delphinium* x *cultorum* hybrid

or late fall, but flowering is often artificially delayed to fit in with exhibition seasons. Of the hundreds available, the best cultivars for garden display are those identified as "cushion" mums; these branch naturally, needing very little pinching, to form attractive mounds with "pompon" flowers in a range of colors. The more serious lover of mums will select from intermediate decorative, reflexed decorative, anemone-flowered, single or spider categories of flower shape. Most of these will require pinching twice before 4 July to promote sturdy branching and generous flowering. Most potted mums obtained from a florist at any season can be set out in the garden after flowering, then cut back hard, watered and fertilized.

ZONES 4–10

## *DIANELLA tasmanica*

FLAX LILY

Native to southeast Australia, including Tasmania, this upright perennial is fibrous rooted, spreading from underground rhizomes and sending up evergreen, straplike leaves. Nodding, star-shaped, bright blue or purple-blue flowers are borne in branching sprays in spring and early summer, followed by shining deep blue berries. The plants grow from 20 in–4½ ft (about 50–130 cm) in height with a spread of 20 in (about 50 cm). They make interesting accent plants in sun or partial shade and require a well-drained, neutral to acid soil. Propagate by division, from rooted offsets, or from seed in spring and fall. It can be invasive.

ZONES 8–10

## *DIANTHUS*

PINK

A very large genus including the carnation, maiden pink, cottage pink, sweet William, Chinese or Indian pink and many other cultivated annuals, biennials and evergreen perennials. Most species are popular as massed border plants and for cutting. Perennial species include some small-flowered plants, excellent for rock gardens and chinks in stone walls and between paving stones. The taller perpetual and spray carnations are generally grown in glasshouses. *Dianthus* likes a sunny position and well-drained, slightly alkaline soil. Regular watering and twice-monthly feeding produces good flowers. The taller varieties will require staking. Prune stems back after flowering to encourage new growth. Propagate perennials by layering or from cuttings in summer; annuals and biennials from seed in fall or early spring.

*Dianthus caryophyllus* cultivars

### *D.* 'Allwoodii'

syn. *D.* × *allwoodii*

COTTAGE PINK, BORDER CARNATION, ALLWOOD PINK

Densely leafed, tuft-forming perennials of hybrid origin with gray-green foliage and an abundance of erect flowering stems, each carrying four to six fragrant, single to fully double flowers in shades of white, pink or crimson, often with dark centers and with plain or fringed petals. Flowers over a long season from late spring until early fall. Grows 12–18 in (about 30–45 cm) tall with a spread of 18 in (about 45 cm).

ZONES 4–10

### *D. barbatus*

SWEET WILLIAM

A short-lived perennial, usually treated as a biennial, it self sows readily and is useful for bedding and cut flowers. It is slow growing, to a height of 20 in (about 50 cm) and a spread of 6 in (about 15 cm). In late spring and early summer it bears many small, fragrant flowers in bright reds, pinks and bicolors in flat-topped clusters. It has bright green, grassy leaves.

ZONES 4–10

### *D. caryophyllus* cultivars

CARNATION

Fairly fast-growing evergreen perennials of short duration, carnations have a tufted, erect habit with lance-shaped, gray-green leaves and showy, perfumed, semi-double or double flowers. The range of colors includes pink, yellow, white and red. Striped flowers are called fancies; those edged in a contrasting color, picotees. The numerous cultivars are classified as either florists' carnations or border carnations. The former are best grown in greenhouses, as the plants are untidy, disease prone and the flowering undependable unless conditions are just right. The border carnations make somewhat better garden plants, but may still need staking to keep floppy stems from muddying the flowers; they perform best in areas of cool summers and mild winters.

ZONES 8–10

*Dendranthema grandiflora*

*Dianthus* 'Allwoodii'

*Delphinium grandiflorum*

*Dianthus barbatus*

*Dianella tasmanica*

### *D. chinensis*

CHINA PINK, RAINBOW PINK

This popular annual has a short, tufted growth habit and gray-green lance-shaped leaves. In late spring and summer it bears masses of tubular, single or double, sweetly scented flowers in shades of pink, red, lavender and white. Modern strains, such as 'Snowfire' (white with a red eye), are fast growing to a height and spread of 6–12 in (about 15–30 cm) and will flower in as little as 10 weeks from seed.

ZONES 3–10

### *D. deltoides*

MAIDEN PINK

Ideal for a rock garden or as a ground cover, this dwarf, mat-forming, evergreen perennial is easily grown from seed or cuttings. It has tiny, lance-shaped leaves and bears small, single, fringed flowers in pink, cerise or white, mostly with a red eye, in spring and early summer. It grows to 6 in (about 15 cm) high with a spread of 12 in (about 30 cm). Cut back after flowering.

ZONES 3–10

### *D. gratianopolitanus*

syn. *D. caesius*

CHEDDAR PINK

Tidy mounds of blue-gray linear foliage in time become broad mats 6 ft (about 1.8 m) tall and 12 in (about 30 cm) or more wide. In spring, delightfully fragrant, single, pink blossoms with toothed ("pinked") petals top 6–12 in (about 15–30 cm) wiry stems; flowers will often continue until frost. It requires a very well-drained, alkaline soil and full sun. The best know cultivar is 'Tiny Tim', with 1/2 in (about 1 cm), double, deep pink flowers on 4 in (about 10 cm) stems.

ZONES 5–10

### *D. plumarius*

COTTAGE PINK, GRASS PINK

A loosely tufted, evergreen perennial growing 6–12 in (about 15–30 cm) in height with a spread of 10 in (about 25 cm). There are many named cultivars, bearing sprays of single or fully double sweetly scented flowers in red, pinks, purple-reds, mauves and whites. Many have fringed petals and a contrasting eye. It flowers in late spring and is useful at the front of the border or in rockeries.

ZONES 4–10

## *DIASCIA*

TWINSPUR

The twinspurs are delicate but long-blooming perennials from South Africa that have recently become popular as garden plants on the West Coast; they are treated as annuals or pot plants elsewhere. Difficult to tell apart, they all have flat flowers, generally pink, with the characteristic double nectar spurs on the back of the flower. They mass nicely in the foreground of a border, at the top of a wall or in the rockery. Full sun is best, with afternoon shade in the hottest areas. A well-drained soil is critical, with regular watering through the summer. They do not like the combination of heat and humidity. Propagate from cuttings in late spring. Apart from those mentioned below, other twinspurs to look for are *D. fetcaniensis*, *D. vigilis* and 'Ruby Field', a quite dependable hybrid.

*Diascia rigescens*

*Dianthus chinensis*

### *D. barberae*

This low-growing, rather fragile perennial is usually treated as an annual and makes a useful addition to rock gardens and borders. It has small, heart-shaped, pale green leaves and bears clusters of twin-spurred, salmon pink flowers in spring through to early fall. It grows to a height of 6–12 in (about 15–30 cm) with a spread of 8 in (about 20 cm). Pinch out growing tips to increase bushiness and cut back old stems after flowering has finished. Propagate from seed in fall, softwood cuttings in late spring or from semi-ripe cuttings in summer.

ZONES 8–11

### *D. rigescens*

This vigorous twinspur has a sprawling form with dense 6–8 in (about 15–20 cm) spikes of pink flowers at the upturned ends of each stem; clumps may be 24 in (about 60 cm) across. It flowers nearly all season if faded flower spikes are removed.

ZONES 8–10

## *DICENTRA*

Herbaceous perennials native to the colder regions of northern Asia and North America, these plants are grown for their attractive sprays of pendent, heart-shaped pink, red or white flowers, which are carried on arching stems above lacy, blue-green leaves. They flower from spring through summer and grow from 12 in to 3 ft (about 30–90 cm) in height with a comparable spread. Plant in a rich, well-drained soil of coarse texture. Propagate by late winter divisions, from spring basal cuttings or seed in fall.

*Dicentra formosa* 'Alba'

*Dicentra spectabilis*

### *D. eximia*

FRINGED BLEEDING HEART

Orderley mounds of finely dissected foliage provide year-round interest. Narrow, heart-shaped, purplish-pink flowers hang on gentle 12–15 in (about 30–38 cm) stems above the foliage through spring and summer. 'Bountiful' is very showy with carmine red flowers but may be a hybrid.

ZONES 3–11

### *D. formosa*

WESTERN BLEEDING HEART

This spreading plant grows to 18 in (about 45 cm) high and has a spread of 12 in (about 30 cm). Dainty pink and red flowers appear throughout spring and summer. *D. f.* 'Alba' is a white-flowered form.

ZONES 3–10

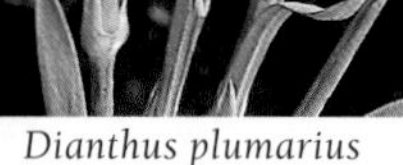

*Dianthus plumarius*

*Dicentra eximia*

*Diascia barberae*

*Dianthus deltoides*

### *D. spectabilis*

BLEEDING HEART

This species is a popular garden perennial. It grows to a height of 24–36 in (about 60–90 cm) with a spread of 18–24 in (about 45–60 cm). Pink and white flowers appear in late spring and summer. After flowering, the foliage usually dies down to the ground; late-growing hostas and ferns can help fill the gap in the garden.

ZONES 3–10

## *DICTAMNUS*
### *albus*

GAS PLANT

Native to southern Europe and Asia, this long-lived, herbaceous perennial is grown for its early summer spikes of fragrant, star-shaped, white or pink flowers with long stamens. The flowers are good for cutting. It has an upright habit, growing to 3 ft (about 90 cm) tall with a spread of 24 in (about 60 cm) with lemon-scented, glossy, leathery, light green leaves. It requires full sun, fertile, well-drained soil and regular water. It is a slow-growing plant, taking 3 or 4 years to reach flowering size. Propagate from seed sown in late summer. Resents being disturbed once established. The whole plant gives off an inflammable oil which may ignite if a flame is held near it.

ZONES 2–9

## *DIERAMA*
### *pulcherrimum*

FAIRY WAND

South African members of the iris family, these upright, summer-flowering plants have evergreen, strap-like foliage and arching stems which bear long, swinging tassels of tubular or bell-shaped deep pink flowers. The effect is particularly enchanting in a breeze or reflected in a pool. It grows to a height of $4\frac{1}{2}$ ft (about 1.3 m) and a spread of 24–36 in (about 60–90 cm). Requires sun and deep, rich, moist, well-drained soil; it will however adapt to summer drought in cooler areas of the West Coast. It dies down partially in winter. Propagate by separating the bulb-like corms in spring. They resent disturbance and may be left in the ground for years.

ZONES 8–11

## *DIETES*

FORTNIGHT LILY, AFRICAN IRIS

Native to southern Africa these evergreen, rhizomatous perennials are grown for their attractive iris-shaped flowers. The flowers usually last only for a day but new buds open over a long period in spring and early summer. They have strong, sword-like leaves which form large and attractive clumps. All species will thrive in semi-shade or sun and in humus-rich, well-drained soil that does not dry out too quickly. Do not remove flower stems as they continue to flower for several years. They are tough enough to use as low hedges. Propagate from seed in spring or fall or by division in spring.

### *D. grandiflora*

Wild iris grows to a height of 3–4 ft (about 0.9–1.2 m) and a spread of 24–36 in (about 60–90 cm) and bears 4 in (about 10 cm) wide, white, iris-like flowers marked with mauve and orange-yellow. Its blooms last several days in summer.

ZONES 9–10

### *D. vegeta*

**syn. *D. irioides***

A smaller version of *D. grandiflora,* this species has branching, wiry stems carrying $2\frac{1}{2}$–3 in (about 6.5–7.5 cm) wide, iris-like flowers, white with central yellow marks. It grows to a height of 24 in (about 60 cm) and a spread of 12–24 in (about 30–60 cm), forming dense clumps. Its native habitat is in semi-shade under tall open trees.

ZONES 9–10

## *DIGITALIS*

FOXGLOVE

Natives of Europe, northern Africa and western Asia, these biennials and perennials, some of which are evergreen, are grown for the strong accent value of their tall flower spikes in the summer border. They are very effective planted in groups in a shrub border under taller trees to provide shade and wind protection. They come in many colors including magenta, purple, white, cream, yellow, pink and lavender. They grow in most conditions, doing best in cool, humid climates in semi-shade and moist, well-drained soil. Cut flowering stems down to the ground after the spring flowering to encourage development of secondary spikes. Propagate from seed in fall; they self seed readily. The medicinal properties of digitalis have been known since ancient times.

### *D.* × *mertonensis*

Clump forming, this perennial grows to 24–36 in (about 60–90 cm) in height with a spread of 12 in (about 30 cm). Summer flowering, it bears spikes of tubular, coppery rose flowers over a rosette of soft, hairy, oval leaves. Divide after flowering.

ZONES 5–10

### *D. purpurea*

COMMON FOXGLOVE

This short-lived perennial is grown as a biennial. It is ideal for providing a vertical accent in a border or for naturalizing in open woodlands. It reaches a height of $3–4\frac{1}{2}$ ft (about 90–130 cm) and a spread of 24 in (about 60 cm). Tall spikes of tubular flowers in shades of purple, white, pink, rosy magenta and pale yellow appear between late spring and early fall, above a rosette of rough, oval, deep green leaves. All parts of the plant, especially the leaves, are poisonous. They self seed readily.

ZONES 4–10

*Digitalis purpurea*

*Dietes vegeta*

*Dietes grandiflora*

*Digitalis* × *mertonensis*

*Dictamnus albus*

*Dierama pulcherrimum*

Dorotheanthus bellidiformis

Dimorphotheca sinuata

Dodecatheon meadia

Dimorphotheca pluvialis

Echinacea purpurea

Duchesnea indica

## DIMORPHOTHECA

AFRICAN DAISY, CAPE MARIGOLD

Indigenous to South Africa, these annuals, perennials and evergreen sub-shrubs are valued for their glossy, daisy-like flowers which appear over a long season from early spring, or winter and spring in the mildest regions. They are useful for rock gardens, dry banks and the front row of borders—particularly as temporary fillers. They require an open, sunny situation and a light, well-drained soil. Ideal for beach gardens. They are not good as cut flowers as they close on cloudy days and remain closed indoors. Deadhead to prolong flowering. Propagate annuals from seed sown in spring and perennials from semiripe cuttings in summer. Watch for botrytis.

*D. pluvialis*

This annual is an excellent bedding plant producing small flowerheads, snowy white above, purple beneath, with brownish purple centers. It is low growing, reaching 8–12 in (about 20–30 cm) high with a spread of 6 in (about 15 cm).

ALL ZONES

*D. sinuata*
**syn. *D. aurantiaca, D. calendulacea***

This expansive annual species grows up to 12 in (about 30 cm) in height. Its roughly serrated, spoon-shaped leaves grow to 3 in (about 7.5 cm) long. Daisy-like flowers with yellow centers and orange outer petals which occasionally have yellow bases appear in winter and spring in milder areas or from spring through summer elsewhere.

ALL ZONES

## DODECATHEON
*meadia*

SHOOTING STAR

This perennial, a member of the primrose family and native to eastern North America, is good for hillside and mountain gardens and is a beautiful poolside or bog plant. In spring it bears distinctive, nodding, cyclamen-pink flowers with reflexed petals and extended stamens. It has primula-like, clumped rosettes of pale green leaves, and ranges in height from 6–20 in (about 15–50 cm) with a spread of around 12 in (about 30 cm). Best grown in semi-shade in a moist, well-drained acid soil. Propagate from seed in fall or by division in very early spring. Dormant after flowering and difficult to transplant as it resents disturbance.

ZONES 4–9

## DOROTHEANTHUS
*bellidiformis*

LIVINGSTONE DAISY

Native to South Africa, this small, succulent annual is ideal for spring and summer display in rockeries, banks, beds and planter boxes, particularly if sown thickly so the plants can intermingle. It has daisy-like flowerheads in dazzling shades of yellow, white, red or pink. It grows to a height of 6 in (about 15 cm) and a spread of 12 in (about 30 cm). Plant in an open sunny position—the flowers close in dull weather or if grown in shade. Grows well in poor but well-drained soil, and because of its salt resistance is good for seaside gardens. Do not overwater. Sow seed in fall in mild winter areas, otherwise spring after the danger of frost has passed.

ALL ZONES

## DUCHESNEA
*indica*
**syn. *Fragaria indica***

INDIAN MOCK STRAWBERRY

A semi-evergreen, trailing perennial that spreads rapidly by runners and is useful for ground cover, bed edging, hanging baskets and pots. It has dark green leaves and bright, 1 in (about 2.5 cm) wide yellow flowers from spring to early summer. Ornamental, strawberry-like, small red fruits appear in late summer. Grows to a height of 4 in (about 10 cm) with an indefinite spread. It is best grown in sun or semi-shade in well-drained, rich, cultivated soil. Propagate by division in spring, from seed in fall, or by rooting plantlets.

ZONES 4–11

## ECHINACEA
*purpurea*
**syn. *Rudbeckia purpurea***

PURPLE CONEFLOWER

Native to North America, this showy, summer-flowering perennial has large, daisy-like, rosy purple flowers with high, orange-brown central cones. The 4 in (about 10 cm) wide flowers, borne singly on strong stems, are useful for cutting. Leaves are lance shaped and dark green. Of upright habit, it grows to 4 ft (about 1.2 m) and spreads 20 in (about 50 cm). It prefers a sunny situation and a rich, moist but well-drained soil. Regular dead-heading prolongs flowering. Propagate by division or from root cuttings from winter to early spring.

ZONES 3–10

## ECHINOPS
*ritro*

GLOBE THISTLE

This perennial of a genus native to northern Africa, Europe and western Asia is a useful plant for the herbaceous border, and its globe-like, spiky flowers can be cut and dried for winter decoration. It has large, deeply cut, prickly leaves, downy beneath, with silvery white stems and round, thistle-like, purplish blue heads of flowers in summer. Of an upright habit, it grows to 4 ft (about 1.2 m) in height with a spread of 30 in (about 76 cm). It requires full sun and a well-drained soil and is generally drought resistant. Propagate from seed in spring, from root cuttings or by division in fall, or by division in late winter. Transplant during the winter or early spring months.

ZONES 3–10

*Eremurus* × *isabellinus* Shelford hybrids

## *ECHIUM*

Indigenous to the Mediterranean, Canary Islands and Madeira, this genus of annuals and evergreen shrubs, perennials and biennials are grown for their spectacular tall spires and bright blue or pink flowers in late spring and summer. They require a dry climate, full sun or semi-shade and a well-drained soil of only moderate fertility; they grow unwieldly in soil that is too rich or damp. Coastal planting is ideal; they are all best adapted to California gardens. Propagate from seed or cuttings in spring or summer. In mild climates they self sow readily.

### *E. vulgare* [dwarf]

This biennial has an erect, bushy habit. In its dwarf form it grows to a height of 12 in (about 30 cm) and a spread of 8 in (about 20 cm). It has lance-shaped, dark green leaves and white, blue, pink or purple tubular flowers. It is fast growing and may become invasive.

ZONES 9–11

### *E. wildpretii*

**syn. *E. bourgaeanum***

TOWER OF JEWELS

A striking biennial from the Canary Islands, this evergreen plant makes a lovely rosette of narrow, silvery leaves and, in its second season, bears a single, bold spike of small, funnel-shaped, rich coral-pink flowers. It dies after flowering and setting seed. It has an erect habit, growing to a height of $7^{1}/_{2}$ ft (about 2.2 m) or more with a spread of 24 in (about 60 cm).

ZONES 9–11

## *EPILOBIUM* *angustifolium*

FIREWEED, GREAT WILLOW HERB

A tall, vigorous perennial found throughout the northern and mountainous parts of North America, most widespread in areas that have been burned or logged recently. Drifts of rose-pink flowering spikes cover moist mountainsides in late summer, creating a memorable sight. In the garden, fireweed is useful in a border or naturalized in a moist meadow. Growing 3–5 ft (about 90–150 cm) tall, it will

*Epimedium grandiflorum*

spread indefinitely unless confined by reducing watering or by pruning or containing the root system. It is easily grown in most soils in full sun or light shade. Propagate in spring by division of the roots; it also self seeds readily.

ZONES 2–9

## *EPIMEDIUM*

BARRENWORT

Among the most important of low-growing perennials for shady situations, the barrenworts produce elegant foliage, sometimes evergreen, and are pinnately divided into heart-shaped or angel wing-shaped leaflets. Delightful sprays of delicate, spurred flowers appear in late spring or early summer just above the foliage. Slowly spreading to form a broad mound, they serve well as ground covers in open woodland or in the foreground of borders and rockeries. Many are drought tolerant, especially in the shade. All prefer a woodsy, well-drained soil. Divide in early spring or early fall. Old leaves are best cut back in early spring to better display the new foliage and flowers.

### *E. grandiflorum*

BISHOP'S HAT, LONGSPUR EPIMEDIUM

This species is deciduous, except in mild climates, and has toothed leaflets often margined in red. Spidery, red-violet flowers with white spurs are held above the foliage on 12 in (about 30 cm) slender stems. It is best displayed as a specimen clump rather than as a ground cover. The selections 'Rose Queen' (pink) and 'White Queen' are the most readily available.

ZONES 4–8

### *E. pinnatum* subsp. *colchicum*

PERSIAN EPIMEDIUM

This subspecies is the one most commonly grown for its larger, yellow flowers in clusters at the top of 18 in (about 45 cm) stems. The leaves are bronzy and generally not toothed or spined, and are nearly evergreen. This makes an excellent ground cover, and is one of the best for dry shade.

ZONES 5–10

*Echium wildpretii*

### *E.* × *rubrum*

This hybrid can be variable, but generally has spiny leaves that are strikingly veined in red. Low mounds are topped by 12 in (about 30 cm) stems with crimson and white, 1 in (about 2.5 cm) flowers in spring. It can be used as a ground cover.

ZONES 4–9

### *E.* × *warleyense*

Somewhat sparse as a ground cover, this species nevertheless works well in a woodland garden and produces beautiful flowers that combine coppery red with yellow centers. The leaves are spiny and semi-evergreen. It is one of the best hybrid epimediums.

ZONES 4–9

## *EREMURUS* × *isabellinus* Shelford hybrids

SHELFORD FOXTAIL LILY

This group of perennials is grown for its lofty spikes of close-packed flowers, magnificent for floral arrangements. They produce rosettes of strap-like leaves and in midsummer each crown yields spikes of bloom with strong stems and hundreds of shallow, cup-shaped flowers in a wide range of colors including white, pink, salmon, yellow, apricot and coppery tones. It grows 4–6 ft (about 1.2–1.8 m) tall with a foliage spread of 3 ft (about 90 cm). They prefer a sunny, warm position, protection from heavy winds and a well-drained, preferably sandy soil. May require staking. Protect roots with a layer of mulch in cold winters. Propagate from seed in fall or by division in late winter and early spring. Transplant when dormant.

ZONES 6–8

## *ERIGERON*

FLEABANE

This is a large genus of annuals, biennials and perennials, some evergreen, that are predominantly native to North America. They have mainly erect stems capped by masses of pink, white or blue, daisy-like flowers that are striking in the front row of a mixed herbaceous

*Echinops ritro*

*Epimedium* × *rubrum*

*Echium vulgare* [dwarf]

*Epilobium angustifolium*

border or rock garden. They flower between late spring and mid-summer. They prefer a sunny position sheltered from strong winds and moderately fertile, well-drained soil. Most are able to survive periods of drought with little problem, but all thrive on regular water. Propagate by division of an established clump in spring or fall and remove spent stems after flowering. It can become invasive.

### E. glaucus

SEASIDE DAISY

A perennial bearing lilac-pink flowers in spring and summer. Clump forming, it grows to 10 in (about 25 cm) in height with a spread of around 12 in (about 30 cm). The leaves are long and hairy. It does best in cooler coastal areas along the West Coast.

ZONES 6–10

### E. karvinskianus

MEXICAN DAISY, SANTA BARBARA DAISY

This spreading perennial is useful as an informal ground cover in mild climates where it will bloom profusely throughout the year. The small, 1 in (about 2.5 cm) wide, daisy-like flowers open white, fading to pink and wine-red. It grows 10–20 in (about 25–50 cm) high with an indefinite spread; it can be mowed or sheared to only 4 in (about 10 cm) and still flower steadily. It is excellent in wall crevices, between pavers or in hanging baskets and is quite drought tolerant. It has lax stems and narrow, lance-shaped, hairy leaves. Cut back hard from time to time. Native to Mexico.

ZONES 9–11

*Erigeron glaucus*

*Erinus alpinus*

*Erigeron karvinskianus*

### E. speciosus

OREGON DAISY

A native western American perennial with lilac flowers produced in abundance through the summer. Clump forming, it varies from 6–30 in (about 15–76 cm) in height, the taller ones often needing staking. Commonly available selections such as 'Azure Fairy' and 'Prosperity' may actually be hybrids of this species.

ZONES 3–10

## ERINUS
### alpinus

This small, semi-evergreen perennial is native to the European alps and is ideal for planting in wall crevices and rock gardens. It forms rosettes of soft, medium green leaves and bears a profusion of starry, rosy purple or white flowers in late spring and summer. It grows 2–3 in (about 5–7.5 cm) in height and spread. It is short lived but self seeds freely. *E. alpinus* grows well in either full sun or partial shade and requires a well-drained soil. Propagate from seed in fall.

ZONES 6–10

## ERODIUM

HERONSBILL

Long-blooming perennials in the geranium family, the long, slender fruits of this genus resemble the bill of a heron. Most are small, like *E. reichardii*, and are best suited to the rock garden or for cracks in a stone wall. A few make fine additions to the front of a border. The five-petaled flowers are tiny versions of the garden geraniums. The evergreen foliage is often finely divided and is quite attractive. All prefer full sun, generally doing well in warm, dry regions. Soils must be well drained and not too fertile.

*Eryngium* x *oliverianum*

*Eryngium variifolium*

### E. absinthoides

A sprawler, this species has fern-like, finely divided foliage of a soft gray-green. The simple flowers, 3/4 in (about 1.8 cm) across, are violet, pink or white, often with very attractive veining in a darker color; flowers are produced for most of the summer. Mounds are 8 in (about 20 cm) tall and 12–18 in (about 30–45 cm) wide.

ZONES 6–10

### E. reichardii
**syn. *E. chamaedryoides***

Native to the Balaeric Islands and Corsica, this choice little rock garden plant flowers through spring and summer, with tiny 1/2 in (about 1 cm) flowers of white or pale pink on dense mounds of evergreen foliage. Only 2 in (about 5 cm) tall and 6–8 in (about 15–20 cm) across, it works well between pavers in a lightly shaded situation or in full sun. Give it good drainage and average moisture.

ZONES 7–10

## ERYNGIUM

Native to Europe and the Americas, these biennials and perennials are members of the carrot family and are grown for their interesting foliage and spiny-collared blooms that usually have a bluish metallic sheen. They flower over a long period in summer and may be cut and dried for winter decoration. They require a sunny situation, good drainage and a sandy soil. Plants tend to collapse in wet, heavy ground during winter. Propagate species from fresh seed; selected forms from root cuttings in winter or by division in spring. Transplant when dormant in winter. The spiny appearance of the strongly colored, thistle-like bracts that surround the central flower give rise to the common name 'holly'.

### E. alpinum

Considered one of the most beautiful of the genus, this has green, heart-shaped, spiny basal leaves but with the upper stems and leaves suffused with a soft blue. The 1 1/2 in (about 3.5 cm) flowers continue the blue theme with the very intricately cut bracts being a steel blue. Plants are 30 in (about 76 cm) high with a spread of 18 in (about 45 cm) and are superb in the border, where they will tolerate very light shade.

ZONES 3–10

### E. x oliverianum

This upright perennial grows to a height of 24–36 in (about 60–90 cm) and a spread of 18–24 in (about 45–60 cm). In late summer it bears large, rounded, lavender blue thistle heads. Leaves are jagged, mid-green and heart shaped.

ZONES 5–10

### E. variifolium

Distinct for its variegated white and green foliage which forms an attractive evergreen mantle, this species has silvery-blue stems to 18 in (about 45 cm) which are topped by 1 in (about 2.5 cm), thistle-like flowers surrounded by similar silvery-blue bracts. It is good for the front of the border, where the foliage will provide interest all year round.

ZONES 7–10

## ERYSIMUM

WALLFLOWER

These perennial, flowering plants have been part of the cottage garden for centuries. Some species are suitable for rock gardens, other fit nicely into the border. Short-lived species are best grown as biennials. Some of the perennials form woody bases and become leggy after a few years, at which time they are best replaced with younger specimens. A number of species are fine winter-spring-flowering plants, while some flower all winter or all year in very mild regions. The older types are sweetly scented, while the newer cultivars have no fragrance but bloom well over a long season. They do best in well-drained, fertile soil in an open, sunny position. Propagate from seed in spring or softwood cuttings in summer. Cut back plants occasionally so only a few leaves remain on each stem. Botanists have now placed all plants in the genus *Cheiranthus* into this genus.

### E. x allionii
**syn. *Cheiranthus* x *allionii***

SIBERIAN WALLFLOWER

This hybrid of indeterminate parentage is a bushy evergreen perennial suitable for rock gardens, banks and borders. It is short lived and should be grown as a biennial. It has toothed, mid-green leaves and bears bright yellow or orange flowers in spring, putting on a dazzling display for a long period. Slow growing, it reaches a height and spread of 12 in (about 30 cm). It prefers light, well-drained, fertile soil and a sunny position. Propagate in summer from cuttings, which

root very easily, or from seed in spring—it self seeds freely. Cultivars include 'Orange Bedder', which has scented, brilliant orange flowers.
ZONES 3–10

### *E.* 'Bowles Mauve'

A shrubby, evergreen perennial that flowers almost continuously in mild climates like California's. The deep rosy-purple flowers on elongating stems are nicely set off against the glaucous foliage. Plants develop into uniform mounds 30 in (about 76 cm) tall and 3 ft (about 90 cm) wide. Prune back lightly when flowering slows to encourage another flush of blooms. Flowering ceases in extremely hot weather, but will continue through the winter in spite of occasional light frosts.
ZONES 6–11

### *E. cheiri*

syn. *Cheiranthus cheiri*
ENGLISH WALLFLOWER

A bushy perennial grown as an annual or biennial. Cultivars vary in height from 8–24 in (about 20–60 cm) and spread to 16 in (about 40 cm). Fragrant, 4-petaled flowers appear in spring, or during winter in mild winter regions. Colors range from pastel pink and yellow to deep browns, bronze, orange, bright yellow, dark red and scarlet. All have lance-shaped leaves. They do best where summers are cool. Provide them with a fertile, well-drained soil and do not let them dry out in summer. Cut back hard after flowering. Sow seeds in spring for bloom the next year.
ZONES 8–10

## *ESCHSCHOLZIA californica*

CALIFORNIA POPPY

This, the state flower of California, is one of the brightest garden annuals, suitable for rock gardens, the front of borders and gaps in paving. They are superb in wildflower meadows in the arid West, but are so vigorous that they may overwhelm other species. The cup-shaped flowers open above feathery, gray-green foliage in vivid shades of orange or yellow, although hybridizers have produced seed strains in cream, red, mauve and rose. They flower from late winter through early summer in their native range in the West, but in irrigated gardens or colder climates they will flower through summer. They close in dull weather so should be planted in a sunny situation. Of a slender, erect habit, they grow 12–24 in (about 30–60 cm) in height with a spread of 12–18 in (about 30–45 cm). They grow well in poor, very well-drained soil and should be dead-headed regularly to prolong flowering. Propagate from seed sown in spring in cold climates, or in fall in mild ones. They do not transplant easily, so sow where the plants are to remain. Watch for snails.
ZONES 8–11

## *EUPATORIUM purpureum*

JOE-PYE WEED

These are massive perennials, reaching 5–9 ft (about 1.5–2.7 m) in height with a spread of 4 ft (about

*Erysimum* 'Bowles Mauve'

1.2 m) or more. They provide a bold accent for the fall garden, with their 12 in (about 30 cm) long leaves and large heads of tiny, purplish flowers. Native to eastern and central North America, they are usually found where there is plenty of water. Useful in the large border, they perform best alongside water where they can get all the water they need for full growth. Give them full sun to part shade and a rich, humusy soil. Cut to the ground each winter. Propagate in spring or fall by division. There are forms that are more compact and that have darker purple flowers.
ZONES 3–11

## *EUPHORBIA*

SPURGE

This large and varied genus of shrubs, succulents, perennials and annuals have in common a milky sap which may irritate the skin and can be poisonous. The spectacular flowerheads consist of a series of highly colored, cup-shaped bracts or modified leaves. There are many succulent species which are suitable for pot plants and for sandy or desert gardens. They require either sun or partial shade and a moist but well-drained soil. Plants are increased from young basal cuttings in spring, or by division in early spring or early fall. They may also self seed if conditions at flowering time are suitable.

### *E. characias* subsp. *wulfenii*

Beautiful blue-green leaves densely line the erect stems, which in spring are topped by broad flowerheads of intense chartreuse. Color remains in the flowerheads until seeds ripen, when foliage yellows; cut to the ground to make room for new shoots that have already started. Plants are upright to 4–5 ft (about 1.2–1.5 m) with a spread of 3 ft (about 90 cm). They are fairly drought tolerant.
ZONES 8–10

*Erysimum cheiri*

*Erysimum* x *allionii*

### *E. marginata*

SNOW-ON-THE-MOUNTAIN

Native to central areas of North America, this bushy annual makes an excellent foil for brighter flowers. It has pointed, oval, bright green leaves, sharply margined with white, and broad, petal-like white bracts surrounding small flowers in summer. Fairly fast growing to 24 in (about 60 cm) tall with a 12 in (about 30 cm) spread. It will endure colder conditions.
ZONES 5–11

### *E. myrsinites*

This trailing species is only 6–8 in (about 15–20 cm) tall but spreads to over 12 in (about 30 cm) wide. Blue-green, oval leaves spiral around the stems, each stem ending in a small flowerhead of soft chartreuse in spring. They are excellent in a rock garden or at the top of a low wall. Cut out old stems as the leaves yellow to make room for new growth. It self seeds readily and will tolerate poor soils, heat and drought.
ZONES 5–11

*Euphorbia marginata*

*Euphorbia myrsinites*

*Euphorbia characias* subsp. *wulfenii*

*Eschscholzia californica*

*Felicia amelloides*

*Exacum affine*

*Filipendula rubra* 'Venusta'

*Eustoma grandiflorum*

## *EUSTOMA grandiflorum*

PRAIRIE GENTIAN

Native to America's Midwest right down to Texas and New Mexico, this short-lived perennial is grown for its flowers which are excellent for cutting, lasting up to 3 weeks in water. They are also useful as container plants. It has lance-shaped, deep green leaves and 2 in (about 5 cm) wide, flared, tulip-like flowers in colors of rich purple, pink, blue or white. Flowers appear in spring and again in fall. If dead-headed, flowers will continue from early summer through fall. The most commonly available as potted plants in nurseries are the selected forms, sometimes double flowered, developed in Japan. Of an upright habit, the plant is slow growing to a height of 24 in (about 60 cm) and spread of 12 in (about 30 cm). It requires a sunny situation and well-drained soil. In frost-free areas propagate from seed sown in early fall.
ZONES 4–10

## *EXACUM affine*

PERSIAN VIOLET

Native to the Yemeni island of Socotra, this showy miniature is useful both as an indoor pot plant and as a plant for outdoor sun or semi-shaded positions. It has shining, oval dark leaves and bears a profusion of tiny, fragrant, 5-petaled, saucer-shaped purple flowers with yellow stamens throughout summer. A biennial usually treated as an annual, it has a bushy habit and grows to a height and spread of 8–12 in (about 20–30 cm). It enjoys rich, moist but well-drained soil. Indoors, they like diffused sun and a night temperature not below 60°F (15°C). Propagate from seed sown in early spring or late summer.
ZONES 9–11

*Gaillardia pulchella* 'Lorenziana'

*Francoa appendiculata*

## *FELICIA amelloides*

BLUE MARGUERITE

Native to South Africa, these annuals and evergreen sub-shrubs include some of the finest species of blue daisy flowers. They require full sun and a dryish, well-drained, gravelly soil enriched with organic matter; they will not tolerate wet conditions. *F. amelloides* is a bushy, evergreen shrub with roundish, bright green leaves and sky-blue flowerheads with bright yellow centers borne on long stalks. It has a spreading habit, growing to 18 in (about 45 cm) in height and 24 in (about 60 cm) or more in width. It is fast growing in mild winter climates and is useful for small formal hedges, rock gardens, path edgings, indoor pot plants or as a seaside plant. The flowers, appearing nearly year round if properly dead-headed and thus making this a particularly useful container plant, cut well for small bouquets. Give them full sun and regular water for best growth after flowering. Prune hard as soon as it becomes straggly to encourage new growth. Propagate by cuttings taken in fall or spring. Numerous named selections are available which have a more compact habit or bluer flowers.
ZONES 9–11

## *FILIPENDULA rubra*

QUEEN-OF-THE-PRAIRIE

This herbaceous perennial is grown for its attractive, deeply cut, fern-like foliage and showy, crowded heads of tiny peach-blossom pink flowers; the cultivar 'Venusta' has deeper pink flowers. Flowers are long lasting and the foliage remains lovely long after flowering. These plants do well at the back of larger perennial borders, as long as the soil remains moist, and in waterside positions. They also do well in damp meadows. Upright in habit, it grows to a height of 4–6 ft (about 1.2–1.8 m) and a spread of 4 ft (about 1.2 m) and has fleshy, swollen roots. This species prefers a moist soil in full sun or in semi-shade. Propagate by division in winter or from seed in spring and fall, and cut back when dormant in colder areas. Watch for powdery mildew.
ZONES 3–9

## *FRANCOA appendiculata*

BRIDAL WREATH

From summer to early fall this evergreen perennial bears racemes of delightful pale pink flowers on graceful, erect stems. It bears crinkled, hairy, oval, dark green leaves and will thrive best in full sun or partial shade. Plant in fertile, well-drained soil. It grows to a height of 24 in (about 60 cm) with a spread of 18 in (about 45 cm). Propagate from seed or by division in spring.
ZONES 8–10

## *GAILLARDIA*

BLANKET FLOWER

These annuals and perennials from the central and western United States have vividly colored, daisy-like flowers. Some varieties make good cut flowers. The perennials are often short lived and are better grown as biennials in cooler climates. They are easy to grow, requiring sun and any ordinary well-drained garden soil. Suits coastal areas. Propagate from spring cuttings taken before the plants have bloomed or from seed in fall or spring.

### *G.* × *grandiflora*

These are hybrids of *G. aristata* and *G. pulchella*, and are the most commonly grown of the blanket flowers. Upright to spreading, their hairy leaves are narrow and slightly lobed; the plants form mounds up to 24 in (about 60 cm) high and wide. The flowerheads are 3–4 in (about 7.5–10 cm) in diameter, in a variety of hot colors (red, yellow, orange and burgundy). Often grown from seed and treated as short-lived perennials, they may also be propagated by division or from cuttings; this is particularly important if the named cultivars are desired, such as 'Burgundy' or 'Goblin' (dark red with a yellow border).
ZONES 3–10

### *G. pulchella*

An annual or short-lived perennial, this upright species has hairy, lance-shaped, gray-green leaves. The cultivar 'Lorenziana' is the most common in gardens; its flowerheads are globular with many tubular florets, making a pompon effect. It is summer flowering and comes in shades of crimson, red or pink and yellow. Useful for creating bright patches in the border. Fast growing to a height of 12–20 in (about 30–50 cm) and a spread of 12 in (about 30 cm).
ZONES 3–9

## *GALIUM*
### *odoratum*
syn. *Asperula odorata*

SWEET WOODRUFF

A beautiful pattern of whorled leaves is offered by this delicate perennial, which will spread into a ground cover only 6–8 in (about 15–20 cm) in a shady situation. The tiny white flowers are produced in few-flowered clusters in late spring. The fragrant foliage was traditionally added to white wine to produce May wine in Europe. In gardens, this is an excellent plant for moist, shaded situations, particularly on slightly acid soils as around rhododendrons. It can be invasive.

ZONES 3–10

## *GAURA*
### *lindheimeri*

Native to North America, this bushy, long-flowering perennial is useful for mixed flower borders and naturalized in meadows. It has loosely branched stems covered with tiny hairs, and from spring to fall produces beautiful, pink-suffused, small white flowers which give a misty pink effect. The leaves are lance shaped and mid-green. It grows to 4 ft (about 1.2 m) in height with a spread of 3 ft (about 90 cm) and is easily grown, thriving in hot dry climates and preferring full sun and a light sandy, well-drained soil. Propagate from seed in spring or fall or from cuttings in summer.

ZONES 6–10

## *GAZANIA*

These low-growing perennials, some grown as annuals, are valued for their ease of culture and large, brightly colored flowers. Most modern variants are hybrids from a number of South African species. They are useful for bedding, rock gardens and for binding soil on sloping land; in cold winter climates they are still useful for summer bedding, pots and tubs. Leaves are either entire or deeply lobed, long and narrow and are usually dark green on top, silver-gray and woolly beneath. The large daisy flowers come in a range of colors from cream to yellow, gold, pink, red, buff, brown and intermediate shades, usually marked with bands or spots of contrasting color at the base of the petals. They open in full sun and glow with a metallic sheen. Flowering is over a long period from early spring until summer. Grow in full sun in sandy, fairly dry soil. Give an annual mulch of compost and water during dry periods. They are salt resistant so are useful in coastal areas. Propagate by division or from cuttings in fall, or from seed in late winter to early spring.

*Gazania rigens* var. *leucolaena*

*Gentiana acaulis*

*Gazania*, Sunshine hybrids

*Galium odoratum*

*Gaura lindheimeri*

Remove spent flowers and dead leaves, and tidy up at the end of the growing season.

### *G.* hybrids

This covers a large range of gazanias of uncertain parentage. Some are clumpers, others are trailers. The cultivars must be propagated by cuttings to be assured of the correct one; seed strains are likely to be more varied. Popular in the West is the Mini-Star strain (either yellow or orange) and the Sunshine strain which includes a wide array of colors, mostly with stripes or zones of a second or third color. 'Aztec Queen' (multicolored) and 'Copper King' are readily available cultivars.

ZONES 9–11

### *G. rigens* var. *leucolaena*

TRAILING GAZANIA

This trailing species is distinct for its foliage, which is silvery on both top and bottom. Flower color is typically yellow, but newer selections offer orange, white and bronze as well. This is one of the best species for use as ground cover or in hanging baskets. The flowering period does not last as long as for the hybrids.

ZONES 9–11

## *GENTIANA*

GENTIAN

Natives of alpine meadows throughout the world, these annuals, biennials and perennials, some of which are evergreen, are valued for their brilliant blue flowers. They are useful plants for rock gardens, peat beds and sloping hillside gardens, doing best in cooler regions. They prefer a well-drained, acid, peaty-sandy soil with some humus. Some species grow naturally on limestone soils. Plant in either sun or semi-shade. Propagate by division in spring or from seed in fall. Divide fall-flowering species every 3 years in early spring, planting out in fresh soil. They are named after Gentius, an Illyrian king who discovered the medicinal value of their bitter roots.

### *G. acaulis*

An evergreen, clump-forming perennial best adapted to the rock garden. In spring, and sometimes fall, it forms a striking carpet of trumpet-shaped, vivid blue flowers with green-spotted throats. Its foliage is compact, with tufted clumps of glossy green, narrow leaves. Grows to 1 in (about 2.5 cm) in height with a spread of 2–3 in (about 5–7.5 cm). It needs a deep root run and an acid soil. Propagate by division in spring or from seed in fall.

ZONES 3–9

### *G. andrewsii*

BOTTLE GENTIAN, CLOSED GENTIAN

This is distinctly different from the other species in that it has dark blue tubular flowers which never open; the flowers appear in mid-summer. Native to moist meadows and woodlands of eastern North America, *G. andrewsii* adapts with relative ease to moist borders or streamside gardens. The dark green foliage is attractive on stems that reach 12–24 in (about 30–60 cm) in height; the plants have a spread of 12 in (30 cm).

ZONES 3–9

### *G. asclepiaea*

WILLOW GENTIAN

Arching stems are clad with slender, willow-like leaves. In early fall, many rich blue flowers are borne in the leaf axils on the upper part of the stems. This perennial forms a loose clump around 3 ft (about 90 cm) high and 24 in (about 60 cm) across. It does best in deep, moist, humus-rich soil.

ZONES 5–9

### *G. lutea*

GREAT YELLOW GENTIAN

This perennial produces tubular yellow flowers in clusters on tall stems in summer. Erect and unbranched, it grows to 3–6 ft (about 90–180 cm) high and spreads to 24 in (about 60 cm). Its oval leaves grow to 12 in (about 30 cm) in length. This species is the main commercial source of gentian root, which is used medicinally and as a flavoring in vermouth.

ZONES 6–9

### *G. sino-ornata*

An evergreen perennial flowering in fall and bearing trumpet-shaped, deep blue flowers that are paler at the base and banded purplish blue. It is an easily grown species of prostrate, spreading habit, reaching a height of 8 in (about 20 cm) and spread of 12 in (about 30 cm).

ZONES 6–9

## *GERANIUM*

CRANESBILL

There are over 400 species of perennial geraniums, some of which are evergreen, found all over the world in cool, temperate and alpine regions. Grown for their attractive flowers, they are useful for rock gardens, as informal ground covers and as plants for the front of the border. They make showy clumps with pink to blue or purple flowers around 1½ in (about 3.5 cm) across. All flower in spring to summer. Most species prefer a sunny situation and damp, well-drained soil. Propagate from semi-ripe cuttings in summer, from seed in spring or by division in fall. Tidy up regularly to encourage bushy growth. Transplant during winter or early spring.

### *G. dalmaticum*

A dwarf plant suitable for the rock garden or as a small ground cover, this species spreads slowly and has glossy, deeply divided leaves forming a dense 3–4 in (about 7.5–10 cm) tall mat. Soft pink flowers are held above the foliage in spring through mid-summer. 'Album' has white flowers.

ZONES 5–10

### *G. incanum*

This tender, South African, evergreen perennial grows up to only 8–10 in (about 20–25 cm) and spreads broadly to 3 ft (about 90 cm) or more. Its gray-green leaves are very finely divided and have a spicy aroma. The flowers are cup shaped and a deep magenta pink. Shear after each flush of bloom to encourage dense growth and more flowering.

ZONES 9–11

### *G.* 'Johnson's Blue'

This rhizomatous perennial has cup-shaped, lavender-blue flowers throughout summer. The leaves are deeply divided. It has a spreading habit, growing to a height of 12 in (about 30 cm) and spread of 24 in (about 60 cm).

ZONES 5–10

### *G. macrorrhizum*

An excellent ground cover for dry shade, as well as for sunny situations. The evergreen foliage is aromatic, deeply lobed and medium green with bronze tints, especially in winter. Flowers appear on 12 in (about 30 cm) stems above the foliage in spring and sporadically throughout the year; color varies from pink or purplish pink to pure white. 'Ingwersen's Variety' has pale pink flowers and smoother leaves.

ZONES 3–10

### *G. maculatum*

Native to eastern American woodlands, this species is best used in woodland gardens as it is less showy and more open than other species. Pale pink flowers are produced in spring above deeply lobed leaves on plants that reach 24 in (about 60 cm) in height with a spread of 18 in (about 45 cm).

ZONES 3–10

### *G. phaeum*

MOURNING WIDOW

Native to Europe and western Russia, this clump-forming perennial has soft green, densely lobed leaves and 1 in (about 2.5 cm) wide lilac to brownish purple flowers that may or may not have a paler eye or basal zone. The flowers are borne on 24 in (about 60 cm) stems in late spring or early summer. It reaches a height of 30 in (about 76 cm) with a spread of 18 in (about 45 cm). The strain 'Lily Lovell' has white flowers.

ZONES 5–10

### *G. sanguineum*

BLOODY CRANESBILL

This perennial, useful as ground cover, bears cup-shaped, bright purple-crimson, notched-petaled flowers throughout spring and summer. It has deeply divided, dark green leaves. It develops into a mound around 12 in (about 30 cm) high and 18 in (about 45 cm) wide. A pretty pink version called *G. s.* var. *striatum* is also available.

ZONES 4–10

## *GERBERA*

*jamesonii*

GERBERA DAISY, TRANSVAAL DAISY

Native to the Transvaal in South Africa but much developed and

*Gentiana lutea*

*Geranium sanguineum*

*Gentiana sino-ornata*

*Geranium* 'Johnson's Blue'

*Gentiana asclepiaea*

*G. macrorrhizum* 'Ingwersen's Variety'

*Geranium incanum*

*Geranium phaeum* 'Lily Lovell'

*Geranium maculatum*

*Gerbera jamesonii*

improved in Holland, this is one of the most decorative of all daisies and is an excellent cut flower. It has orange-red or flame-scarlet flowerheads up to 4 in (about 10 cm) wide, borne singly on long stems in spring and summer from basal rosettes of large, jagged leaves. An evergreen perennial of upright habit, it grows to 24 in (about 60 cm) in height with a spread of 18 in (about 45 cm). It requires an open, sunny position and a light, fibrous soil with free drainage. Keep somewhat dry during fall and winter. Fertilize monthly in spring and summer to produce large blooms. Propagate from cuttings of side shoots in summer, from seed in fall or early spring, or by division from late winter to early spring. Watch for crown rot, slugs and snails.
ZONES 9–11

## *GEUM*

AVENS

These evergreen and herbaceous perennials are valued for their long flowering period from late spring until early fall. Flowering can be prolonged by regular dead-heading, and in frost-free areas they will flower almost continuously all year. They form basal rosettes of hairy, lobed leaves and bear masses of red, orange and yellow, single or double flowers with prominent yellow stamens. Good plants for mixed herbaceous borders and rock gardens, although they require a lot of room to produce a good display. They prefer a sunny, open position and moist, well-drained soil. Propagate by division in winter or early spring, or from seed sown in fall.

### *G. chiloense* 'Mrs Bradshaw'

A taller cultivar with rounded, double, orange-scarlet flowers borne in small sprays. It grows to a height of 24 in (about 60 cm) and a spread of 18 in (about 45 cm) and is good for mixed herbaceous borders. Water well during hot weather.
ZONES 5–10

### *G. coccineum* 'Werner Arends'

**syn. *G.* × *borisii*, *G.* 'Borisii'**

A clump-forming perennial with a constant succession of single, bright

*Gomphrena globosa*

*Glechoma hederacea*

orange flowers borne on slender, branching stems above irregularly lobed leaves. Low growing, it reaches a height and spread of 12 in (about 30 cm). A good rock garden plant.
ZONES 5–10

## *GILIA*
## *capitata*

BLUE THIMBLE FLOWER

Native to the western mountains of the Americas, this erect, branching annual has mid-green, fern-like leaves and tiny, soft lavender-blue flowers that appear in a nearly spherical, pincushion-like form in summer and early fall. It is a good cut flower and useful border plant and grows to a height of 20 in (about 50 cm) and spread of 8 in (about 20 cm). It prefers a cool climate and requires full sun and a fertile, well-drained soil. Water lightly and regularly. The intensity of flower color can vary with soil type and situation. Propagate from seed sown outdoors in early spring.
ALL ZONES

## *GLECHOMA*
## *hederacea*

GROUND IVY

A European native, this evergreen perennial makes a good carpeting ground cover but is very invasive and should be kept away from heavily planted beds and from lawns. Useful as a container and hanging basket plant. It has heart-shaped leaves and bears small clusters of insignificant, mauve-blue, trumpet flowers in summer. A pretty variegated cultivar has white

*Gilia capitata*

*Globularia cordifolia*

marbling on the leaves. It grows to a height of 6 in (about 15 cm) and spreads rapidly. It can be grown in either sun or shade in a moist, well-drained soil. Propagate by division in spring or fall, or from softwood cuttings in spring.
ZONES 6–11

## *GLOBULARIA*
## *cordifolia*

GLOBE DAISY

An evergreen dwarf shrub found in Europe and the Mediterranean, this plant is ideal for sunny rockeries in cool temperate climates. It has creeping woody stems with unusual, tiny, spoon-shaped leaves and produces solitary, stemless, round heads of fluffy mauve stamens from late spring until early summer. It forms a dome-shaped hummock, growing to a height of 2–4 in (about 5–10 cm) and gradually spreading to 8 in (about 20 cm). It requires full sun and well-drained neutral to alkaline soil. Water sparingly. Propagate by division or from seed in fall, or from softwood cuttings in summer.
ZONES 6–10

## *GOMPHRENA*
## *globosa*

GLOBE AMARANTH

This bushy bedding annual from Southeast Asia is valued for its papery, pompon-like flowers which are attractive dried for winter decoration. Cut flowering stems just before blooms are fully open and hang upside down in a cool, well-ventilated place until dry. The plant has oval hairy leaves and produces

*Geum chiloense* 'Mrs Bradshaw'

*Geum coccineum* 'Werner Arends'

clover-like flowerheads in shades of pink, purple, yellow, orange or white in summer and early fall. Of an upright habit, it reaches a height of 24 in (about 60 cm) and spread of 12 in (about 30 cm) and is moderately fast growing. It prefers a sunny situation and light, well-drained soil. Propagate from seed in spring when the danger of frost has passed. The plants benefit from mulching in hot weather.
ZONES 4–11

## *GYPSOPHILA*

BABY'S BREATH

Native to Europe, Asia and North Africa, these annuals and perennials, some of which are semi-evergreen, are grown for their masses of small, dainty, white or pink flowers which make an excellent foil for bolder flowers. They are also a valuable cut flower for use with other flowers or foliage. Plant in full sun with shelter from strong winds. They will tolerate most soils but do best in deep, well-drained soil that contains some organic matter in the

*Helianthemum nummularium*

*Gypsophila elegans*

*Hedychium gardnerianum*

*Hedychium coronarium*

*Helenium* 'Moerheim Beauty'

form of compost or peat. They will grow well on limestone soils. Cut back after flowering to encourage a second flush of flowers. Propagate from cuttings of small lateral shoots in summer or from seed in spring or fall. Transplant when dormant during winter or early spring.

### *G. elegans*

Of dainty, erect habit, this bushy annual grows to a height of 18 in (about 45 cm) and a spread of 12 in (about 30 cm). It makes delicate, pretty clumps in the garden and bears masses of tiny white, or sometimes pink, flowers in branching heads from summer to early fall. The leaves are lance shaped and grayish green.

ZONES 3–10

### *G. paniculata* 'Bristol Fairy'

A relatively long-lived perennial grown for its sprays of tiny white flowers in spring; 'Bristol Fairy' is the best selection, distinctive for its double white flowers. An excellent garden plant, it should be sheared after flowering to prevent seed production and encourage a second flowering. It grows 18 in (about 45 cm) to 4 ft (about 1.2 m) in height and spread. Propagate from cuttings.

ZONES 3–10

## *HEDYCHIUM*

GINGER LILY

Natives of Southeast Asia, these semi-tropical perennials with fleshy rhizomes and sweetly scented flowers are ideal for sheltered borders. The large, deep-green, paddle-shaped leaves are attractive in summer and die down in winter in cold areas. The showy flowers are short lived but are borne profusely. In some species the flowers are followed by capsules with red or orange seeds. Grow in full sun or partial shade and rich, moist soil with good drainage. Water well in summer. Propagate by division of rhizomes from late winter to spring. Cut down to ground level as soon as the flowers have finished.

### *H. coronarium*

WHITE GINGER LILY

A satiny, white-flowered, sweet-scented species that in summer bears dense spikes of butterfly-like flowers with pastel yellow blotches. Leaves are lance shaped with downy undersides. It has an upright habit and grows to 5–6 ft (about 1.5–1.8 m) in height with a spread of up to 3 ft (about 90 cm).

ZONES 9–11

### *H. gardnerianum*

KAHILI GINGER

The best-known and easiest grown species, this plant produces spikes of short-lived, fragrant scarlet and yellow blossoms in late summer and early fall. Its leaves are deep green and broadly lance shaped. It grows to 5–6 ft (about 1.5–1.8 m) in height and 3 ft (about 90 cm) wide.

ZONES 9–11

## *HELENIUM* 'Moerheim Beauty'

SNEEZEWEED

This upright perennial, native to North America, is grown for its sprays of daisy-like, rich orange-red flowers with prominent, chocolate-brown central discs. Flowers are borne in summer and early fall above dark green foliage. Easily grown, they give a vivid splash of color to borders and are useful as cut flowers. They grow to a height of 3 ft (about 90 cm) and spread of 24 in (about 60 cm). They enjoy hot summers and are best grown in full sun with shelter from strong wind, otherwise staking may be necessary. A rich, moist, well-drained soil is ideal. Dead-head regularly to prolong the flowering period, and propagate by division of old clumps in winter or early spring or from seed in spring or fall.

ZONES 3–10

*Gypsophila paniculata* 'Bristol Fairy'

## *HELIANTHEMUM nummularium*

SUN ROSE

Native mostly to the Mediterranean countries and North America, these evergreen, sun-loving, sub-shrubby perennials are grown in rock gardens or as a ground cover for their brightly colored flowers and neat, prostrate habit. The flowers last a day, the petals falling off in the afternoon; double forms hold their flowers until the evening. They have attractive foliage, varying from deep to grayish green, and in spring are smothered with flowers in shades of red, pink, orange, yellow and white. They should be lightly cut back as soon as flowers fade to encourage a second flush of bloom in fall. They enjoy a warm, sunny position in a freely drained, coarse soil; they do not do well in strongly acid soils. They do best in the arid regions of the West Coast, or where winters are cold but dry. Propagate from semi-ripe cuttings in late summer and fall.

ZONES 5–10

## *HELIANTHUS*

SUNFLOWER

Native to the Americas, these tall, showy-flowered annuals and perennials are grown for their large, daisy-like, golden-yellow blooms, which are on prolonged display from summer to fall. The plants have coarsely hairy, sticky-feeling leaves and tall, rough stems which bear mostly yellow flowers with brown or yellow discs. They are effective planted against a dark green background. They prefer full sun and protection from wind, otherwise staking will be necessary to support the tall stems. Soil should be well drained. Fertilize in spring to promote large blooms and water deeply in dry conditions. They may become invasive and should be cut down to the base when they finish flowering. Propagate from seed or by division in fall or early spring. Watch for snails. These flowers were once worshipped by the Incas as living images of their Sun God.

### *H. annuus*

COMMON SUNFLOWER

An upright annual, fast growing to a height of 9 ft (about 2.7 m) or more. Large, daisy-like, 12 in (about 30 cm) wide yellow flowerheads with brown centers are borne in summer. They are coarse, leggy plants with heavily veined, mid-green leaves. The seeds are a good source of protein and starch for humans and birds alike, and are pressed to produce a valuable oil.
ZONES 4–10

### *H. salicifolius*

An upright perennial that is valuable for background planting. It grows to $6^1/_2$ ft (about 1.9 m) in height and bears brilliant yellow, 3 in (about 7.5 cm) wide, single, daisy-like flowers on branching stems in late summer or fall. The rich, dark green shining leaves are willow like. They look good planted with late-flowering blue asters or salvias.
ZONES 4–10

## *HELICHRYSUM*

STRAWFLOWER, EVERLASTING

This large genus of mainly annuals and short-lived perennials are notable for their papery, daisy flowers, commonly called strawflowers. The most spectacular species occur in Australia. They require a warm, sunny situation and a moderately fertile, sandy or gravelly soil with free drainage. They adapt to most soils except heavy clay. Water regularly and shelter from strong winds. To use as dried decoration, cut flowers when just open, tie in bundles loosely wrapped in a paper sheath and hang upside down in a well-ventilated place. Propagate perennials by division, or from seed or suckers in spring, and annuals from seed in spring.

### *H. bracteatum*

STRAWFLOWER

Native to Australia, this annual or short-lived perennial has an upright, branching habit and grows to a height and spread of 30 in (about 76 cm). It has tough, hollow stems, rough, narrow leaves and from summer to early fall bears clusters of daisy-like blooms. Flowers are multicolored and have a crackly, papery finish. 'Dargan Hill Monarch' is the name of the golden-flowered cultivar commonly grown that often lives for two or three years, while the many-colored garden hybrids (red, pink, yellow and white) are definitely annuals.
ZONES 9–10

### *H. petiolare*

LICORICE PLANT

This South African native is an excellent foliage plant; it has gray, heart-shaped leaves covered with a soft, felt-like wool, as are the stems. They are sprawling sub-shrubs, well adapted to sun or shade and to dry conditions. The flowers, only occasionally produced, are not showy. Most popular are the cultivars 'Limelight', with pale chartreuse foliage, and 'Variegatum', with a creamy variegation; both do better in shade and make superb summer container plants in cold climates.
ZONES 9–10

## *HELIOPSIS*

### *helianthoides* 'Light of Lodden'

Native to North America, this herbaceous perennial puts on a bright display in the summer border. It has rough, hairy leaves and strong stems which carry neatly shaped, bright yellow, double flowers in late summer. The flowers are dahlia like and are good as cut flowers, particularly in large arrangements. The plant grows to a height of $3^1/_2$ ft (about 1 m) and a spread of 24 in (about 60 cm). It requires sun and a moist but well-drained soil. Dead-head regularly to prolong the flower display and cut back to ground level after flowering finishes. Propagate from seed or by division in spring or fall.
ZONES 4–9

## *HELLEBORUS*

HELLEBORE

Native to southern Europe and western Asia these perennials, some of which are evergreen, are useful winter- and spring-flowering plants for cooler climates. They bear beautiful, open, cup-shaped flowers in shades of green and purple and are effective planted in drifts or massed in the shade of deciduous trees. They grow best in semi-shade and a

*Helichrysum bracteatum*

*Helianthus salicifolius*

*Helichrysum petiolare* 'Limelight'

*Helianthus annuus*

*Heliopsis helianthoides* 'Light of Lodden'

*Helleborus foetidus*

*Helleborus niger*

*Helleborus argutifolius*

*Hemerocallis* hybrid

moisture-retentive, well-drained soil that is heavily enriched with organic matter. Never let the plants completely dry out in summer. Cut off old leaves of deciduous species in early spring just as buds start to appear. A top-dressing of compost or manure after flowering is beneficial. Propagate from seed or by division in fall or early spring, and watch for aphids. The plants have poisonous properties.

### *H. argutifolius*

CORSICAN HELLEBORE

This is one of the earliest flowering hellebores, with blooms appearing in late winter and early spring. It is a robust evergreen that produces large clusters of cup-shaped, nodding, 2 in (about 5 cm) wide green flowers on an upright spike above divided, spiny, blue-green to gray-green foliage. It has a clump-forming habit, growing to a height of 24 in (about 60 cm) and a spread of 24–36 in (about 60–90 cm). This is the most sun and drought tolerant of the genus.

ZONES 6–11

### *H. foetidus*

STINKING HELLEBORE

A clump-forming, poisonous perennial with attractive, dark green, divided leaves that remain all year. In winter or early spring the clusters of pale green, bell-shaped flowers, delicately edged with red, are borne on short stems. It thrives in sun or shade in any reasonable soil. Propagation is best done by seed in spring, though established plants will often self seed readily.

ZONES 5–10

### *H. niger*

CHRISTMAS ROSE

Popular for its white, mid-winter flowers, often appearing in the snow, this is one of the more temperamental species. Dark green, deeply lobed leaves are evergreen; mounds are 12 in (about 30 cm) high with a spread of 12–18 in (about 24–45 cm). They prefer shade and a rich soil that is slightly alkaline; they also need steady moisture.

ZONES 3–9

*Hemerocallis fulva*

### *H. orientalis*

LENTEN ROSE

The most easily grown of the genus, this species is evergreen and clump forming, growing to a height and spread of 18 in (about 45 cm). The large, nodding flowers come in a great variety of colors from white, green, pink and rose to purple, sometimes with dark spots. It flowers in winter or early spring. The dense foliage fades and can be trimmed back before flowering. Good cut flowers.

ZONES 3–10

## *HEMEROCALLIS*

DAYLILY

Native to Europe and Asia these perennials, some of which are semi-evergreen or evergreen, are grown for their showy, often fragrant flowers which come in a vibrant range of colors. Individual blooms last for only a day, but they are borne in great numbers on strong stems above tall, grassy foliage and continue flowering from early summer to fall. Grow in the herbaceous border, among shrubs, or naturalize in grassy woodland areas. Position carefully when planting as the flowers turn their heads towards the sun and the equator. They prefer sun but will grow well and give brighter colors in part shade. Plant in a reasonably good soil that does not dry out. Propagate by division in fall or spring and divide clumps every 3 or 4 years. Cultivars raised from seed do not come true to type. Watch for slugs and snails in early spring. Plants may also suffer from aphid or spider mite attack. The botanical

*Hesperis matronalis*

name derives from the Greek and means beautiful for a day.

### *H. fulva*

TAWNY DAYLILY

Clump forming, growing to a height of 4 ft (about 1.2 m) or more and spread of 3 ft (about 90 cm). It bears rich orange-red, trumpet-shaped, 3–5 in (about7.5–12.5 cm) wide flowers from mid- to late summer. This plant has been in cultivation for centuries, and has naturalized in parts of North America. 'Kwanso Flore Plena' is double flowered.

ZONES 3–10

### *H.* hybrids

In the last 50 years plant breeders in the USA, and lately Australia and the UK, have developed a huge range of daylilies. These bloom in late spring and intermittently until fall, and have flowers 3–6 in (about 7.5–15 cm) wide on plants ranging in height from 20–36 in (50–91 cm) or more. Colors vary from cream to brilliant yellow, pale pink to red; many have contrasting shades in the throat. Evergreen types are best suited to mild climates; deciduous to cold regions. Catalogues carry an ever-changing selection.

ZONES 3–10

## *HESPERIS*

### *matronalis*

SWEET ROCKET, DAME'S ROCKET

This perennial, found mainly in the northern hemisphere, is grown for its flowers which become very fragrant on humid evenings. It has

*Helleborus orientalis*

smooth, narrowly oval leaves and branching flowerheads with white to lilac flowers borne in summer. Upright in habit, it grows to 30 in (about 76 cm) in height with a spread of 24 in (about 60 cm). It prefers a sunny situation and will tolerate poor soil as long as it is well drained and is not allowed to completely dry out. Plants have a tendency to become woody and are best renewed every few years. Propagate by division or from seed in spring or fall.

ZONES 3–9

## *HEUCHERA*

ALUM ROOT, CORAL BELLS

These evergreen perennials, indigenous to North America, are useful cultivated as ground cover or as rock garden or edging plants. They form neat clumps of scalloped leaves, often tinted bronze or purple, from which arise very slender stems bearing masses of dainty, nodding, white, crimson or pink bell flowers over a long flowering season. They grow well in either full sun or semi-shade, and like a well-drained, coarse, moisture-retentive soil. Propagate species from seed in fall or by division in spring or fall; cultivars by division in fall or early spring. Remove spent flower stems and divide established clumps every 3 or 4 years.

### *H.* x *brizoides*

HYBRID CORAL BELLS

This ever-enlarging group of hybrids represents the combined traits of several species. Most flower over a long period on stems reaching 24–30 in (about 60–76 cm) in height. 'Chatterbox' has large pink flowers; 'June Bride' is pure white; and 'Spitfire' is rose-red. New cultivars are introduced each year, many now displaying variegated foliage.

ZONES 3–10

### *H. micrantha* 'Palace Purple'

This species is grown for its striking, purple, heart-shaped foliage and sprays of small white flowers in summer. It is clump forming, growing to a height and spread of 20 in (about 50 cm). The leaves last well for indoor decoration.

ZONES 4–10

### *H. sanguinea*

CORAL BELLS

This is the most important species, with sprays of scarlet or coral-red flowers over round dark leaves. British and American gardeners have used this species in producing the hybrids listed under *H.* x *brizoides*.

ZONES 3–10

## HIBISCUS *moscheutos*

ROSE MALLOW, SWAMP ROSE MALLOW

Native to North America, this herbaceous perennial grows to a height of 6 ft (about 1.8 m) and a spread of 3–3½ ft (about 0.9–1 m). Single, hollyhock-like flowers, 4–8 in (10–20 cm) wide, are carried on robust, unbranched stems in late summer and fall. Colors vary from white to pink to deep rose, usually with a crimson throat. Leaves are large, toothed and softly hairy beneath. Suitable for the back of the herbaceous border and should be protected from strong winds. This hibiscus requires full sun and a well-drained, moderately rich soil. Remove spent canes in winter after the wood has died back to ground level. Transplant when dormant during winter. Fertilize in spring to encourage growth and water well during the flowering season. Prune to maintain shape and extend flowering. Propagate from seed or cuttings. Watch for root and collar rot and for attacks by aphids, Japanese beetles, white fly and caterpillars.

ZONES 4–9

## HOSTA

PLANTAIN LILY

Natives of Japan and China, these easily grown perennials are valued for their decorative foliage. They all produce wide, handsome leaves, some being marbled or marked with white, others a bluish green. All-yellow foliage is also available. They do well in large pots or planters, are excellent for ground cover and add an exotic touch planted on the margins of lily ponds or in bog gardens. Tall stems of nodding, white, pink or mauve bell flowers appear in warmer weather. Both leaves and flowers are popular for floral arrangements. They prefer shade and rich, moist, neutral, well-drained soil. Feed regularly during the growing season. Propagate by division in early spring, and keep an eye out for attacks by snails and slugs.

### *H. fortunei*

This is probably a very old hybrid form that has been in gardens for years. It originally had green to gray-green leaves, but is now seen mostly in its variegated forms. 'Aureomarginata' has mid-green leaves with creamy yellow edges and tolerates full sun; *H. f.* var. *marginata alba* has sage green leaves with white margins, gray beneath, and is good for waterside planting; *H. f.* var. *albopicta* is pale green with a yellowish center. All bear racemes of trumpet-shaped, violet flowers in summer. They grow to a height of 18 in (about 45 cm) and a spread of 24 in (60 cm).

ZONES 3–9

### *H. lancifolia*

NARROW-LEAVED PLANTAIN LILY

A clump-forming plant growing to 12 in (about 30 cm) with a spread of 18 in (about 45 cm). It has narrow, lance-shaped, glossy, mid-green leaves and is one of the smaller-leaved species. Racemes of trumpet-shaped, pale lilac flowers are borne in late summer and early fall.

ZONES 3–9

### *H. plantaginea*

FRAGRANT PLANTAIN LILY, AUGUST LILY

Popular for its pure white, fragrant flowers on 30 in (about 76 cm) stems, this species has medium green leaves forming a mound 3 ft (about 90 cm) across. It flowers in late summer. 'Royal Standard' has deeper green leaves and more but smaller flowers.

ZONES 3–9

### *H. sieboldiana*

A robust, clump-forming plant growing to a height of 3 ft (about 90 cm) and spread of 4½ ft (about 1.3 m). It has large, puckered, heart-shaped, bluish gray leaves and bears racemes of trumpet-shaped white flowers in early summer. There are many beautiful variegated cultivars.

ZONES 3–10

*Heuchera sanguinea*

*Hosta fortunei* cultivar

*Heuchera* x *brizoides*

*Hosta sieboldiana*

*Hibiscus moscheutos*

*Hosta plantaginea*

*Heuchera micrantha* 'Palace Purple'

*Hosta lancifolia*

*Iberis sempervirens*

*Hypericum calycinum*

*Iberis umbellata*

*Hypericum cerastoides*

*Hunnemannia fumariifolia*

## HOUTTUYNIA
### *cordata* 'Chamaeleon'

**syn. *H. cordata* 'Variegata'**

A native of the Himalayas, Indonesia and Japan, this water-loving, deciduous perennial makes a good ground cover but may become invasive. It is a vigorous plant, growing up to 24 in (about 60 cm) in height with an indefinite spread. It grows from underground runners which send up bright red branched stems bearing aromatic, leathery, heart-shaped leaves splashed with yellow and red. Small sprays of white flowers are borne in summer. It prefers a damp, semi-shaded position and will grow in shallow water at the edge of streams and ponds. Propagate from runners in spring.
ZONES 6–10

## HUNNEMANNIA
### *fumariifolia*

MEXICAN TULIP POPPY

One of the best yellow-flowered perennials, this relative of the Californian poppy is usually grown as an annual. It has an upright habit and is fast growing to a height of 24 in (about 60 cm) and spread of 12–18 in (about 30–45 cm). It has decorative, oblong, divided, bluish green leaves and bears rich, glowing, clear yellow, single, 3 in (about 7.5 cm) wide, tulip-shaped flowers in summer and early fall. It prefers a warm, sunny position and slightly alkaline, well-drained soil. Deadhead plants regularly to prolong flowering and provide support in exposed areas. Water liberally in hot weather to keep plants in bloom. Propagate from seed in spring—the plants do not transplant well so seed should be sown where the plants are to remain.
ZONES 9–10

*Iberis amara*

*Houttuynia cordata* 'Chamaeleon'

## HYPERICUM

This large genus of perennials and deciduous, semi-evergreen or evergreen sub-shrubs and shrubs are grown for their bright yellow flowers with prominent showy stamens. In a mild temperate climate they provide year-round color. There are prostrate species excellent for rock gardens and large flowered species striking in garden displays. Larger species need semi-shade and a fertile, not too dry, soil; the smaller types prefer full sun and well-drained soil. Most are frost resistant. Propagate perennials from seed or by division in spring or fall, and sub-shrubs and shrubs from softwood cuttings in summer. The leaves are occasionally attacked by rust and should be sprayed with a fungicide if this occurs. Most of the species benefit from winter mulching.

### *H. calycinum*

ST-JOHN'S-WORT

An evergreen or semi-evergreen dwarf shrub with dark green foliage that grows to a height of around 12 in (about 30 cm) with an indefinite spread. It is a good ground cover and bears large yellow flowers up to 4 in (about 10 cm) wide from midsummer to mid-fall. It grows in sun or shade, and is ideal for massed planting. Propagate by softwood cuttings in summer.
ZONES 6–10

### *H. cerastoides*

A perennial with dense, oval, gray-green leaves and terminal clusters of bright yellow, star-shaped flowers with showy stamens produced in late spring and early summer. It has an upright, slightly spreading habit and grows to 12 in (about 30 cm) tall with a 20 in (about 50 cm) spread. Useful in rock gardens. Plant in full sun, in well-drained soil.
ZONES 6–10

## IBERIS

CANDYTUFT

These annuals and perennials are mainly from southern Europe, western Asia and the Mediterranean area. They are highly regarded as decorative plants and are excellent for rock gardens, bedding and bordering. Showy flowers are borne in either flattish heads in colors of white, red and purple, or in erect racemes of pure white flowers. They are widely used in floral arrangements. Some species are only short lived, flowering themselves into oblivion. They require a warm, sunny position and a well-drained, light soil, preferably with added lime or dolomite. Water regularly. Propagate from seed in fall or semi-ripe cuttings in summer.

### *I. amara*

ROCKET CANDYTUFT, HYACINTH-FLOWERED CANDYTUFT

Native to the United Kingdom and Europe, this fast-growing annual has lance-shaped, mid-green leaves and produces showy racemes of fragrant, pure white flowers in early spring and summer. Of an erect, bushy habit, it reaches a height of 15 in (about 38 cm) and a spread of 6 in (about 15 cm). The Hyacinth-flowered Series has flattish heads of large, scented, 4-petaled flowers in a variety of colors.
ZONES 4–10

### *I. sempervirens*

PERENNIAL CANDYTUFT

A low, spreading, evergreen perennial, this species is ideal for rock gardens. It has narrow, dark green leaves and dense, rounded heads of white flowers in spring. It grows to a height of 6–12 in (about 15–30 cm) and a spread of 20-24 in (about 50-60 cm). The cultivar 'Snowflake', which also has white flowers in spring, is most attractive.
ZONES 3–10

### *I. umbellata*

GLOBE CANDYTUFT

Native to the Mediterranean region, this upright annual has lance-shaped, mid-green leaves and flattish heads of mauve, lilac, pink, purple, carmine or white flowers in late spring and summer. Of a bushy

*Impatiens sodenii*

*Incarvillea delavayi*

*Impatiens balsamina*

*Impatiens wallerana*

habit, it grows to a height of 16 in (about 40 cm) and a spread of 12 in (about 30 cm). A useful cut flower, it lasts well in fresh arrangements while the seed heads can be used for dry arrangements. Plant in part or full sun in average soil. Sow seed where they are to be planted.
ZONES 3–10

## *IMPATIENS*

BALSAM, TOUCH-ME-NOT, JEWELWEED

This large genus of succulent annuals and mainly evergreen perennials are from the subtropics and tropics of Asia and Africa. They are useful for colorful summer bedding displays and for indoor and patio plants. Flowers come in an ever-increasing range of colors. Many hybrid strains are perennial in mild climates but in colder climates are usually grown as annuals. They will grow in sun or semi-shade, many species doing well under overhanging trees. They prefer a moist but freely drained soil, and need protection from strong winds. Tip prune the fast-growing shoots to encourage shrubby growth and more abundant flowers. Propagate from seed or stem cuttings in spring or summer. Their botanical name refers to the impatience with which the seeds explode from their pods.

### *I. balsamina*

GARDEN BALSAM

An erect, bushy annual with lance-shaped, bright green leaves and small, camellia-like single or double spurred flowers produced in abundance throughout summer and early fall. Color range includes blood-red, purple-red, pink, yellow and white, some spotted. It is fairly fast growing to a height of 30 in (about 76 cm) and a spread of 18 in (about 45 cm). It is good for bedding displays in sunny situations.
ALL ZONES

### *I.*, New Guinea hybrids

BUSY LIZZIE

A group of fast-growing perennials that are also grown as annuals in cool climates. The result of extensive hybridizing from an extremely variable New Guinean species, they grow to a height and spread of 12–20 in (about 30–50 cm). Leaves are oval, pointed and bronze-green, or they may be variegated with cream, white or yellow. Flowers are flat, spurred, pink, orange, red or cerise, sometimes with white markings. 'Tango' has deep orange flowers, while 'Red Magic' has scarlet. They do well in brightly lit positions indoors.
ZONES 10–11

### *I. sodenii*

This vigorous and profusely flowering, softwooded perennial has whorls of 4 to 10 waxy, oval, pale green leaves with toothed margins. Many white or pale lilac single flowers appear nearly all year round in mild climates. It grows to a height of 4 ft (about 1.2 m) with a spread of 24 in (about 60 cm). Propagate from seed or stem cuttings in spring or summer.
ZONES 9–11

### *I. wallerana*

IMPATIENS, BUSY LIZZIE, PATIENCE PLANT

Native to tropical East Africa, this succulent, evergreen perennial is grown as an annual in cool climates. It has soft, fleshy stems with reddish stripes, oval, fresh green leaves and flattish, spurred flowers ranging through crimson, ruby red, pink, orange, lavender and white, some variegated. Some forms have double flowers that look like miniature roses. There are many cultivars. Fast growing and bushy to a height and spread of 8–24 in (about 20–60 cm). Flowers from late spring to late fall. A popular indoor plant and useful for bedding in partial shade. Water well.
ZONES 10–11

## *INCARVILLEA*

### *delavayi*

HARDY GLOXINIA

This fleshy-rooted, clump-forming perennial is useful for rock gardens and borders. It has handsome, fern-like foliage and erect stems bearing 3 in (about 7.5 cm) long, trumpet-shaped, rosy purple flowers in summer. Best suited to cool, temperate climates, the plants grow to a height of 24 in (about 60 cm) and a spread of 12 in (about 30 cm), but die down early in fall. Grow in a sunny situation in rich, well-drained soil but protect with a compost mulch during cold winter. Propagate from seed or by division of old clumps in spring or fall.
ZONES 6–11

## *IPOMOPSIS*

### *aggregata*

SCARLET GILIA, SKYROCKET

Native to the mountains of western North America, this showy biennial adapts easily to gardens where the summer humidity is low. Finely divided leaves delicately clothe slender stems to 30 in (about 76 cm) tall with a spread of only 8 in (about 20 cm). Terminal clusters of slender, 1 in (about 2.5 cm) long trumper flowers light up the landscape with their bright scarlet or soft silvery-pink (or occasionally yellow or white) colors. Sow seed in place in spring or early summer for next summer's flowers. Give them full sun and a well-drained soil. Plant in masses for the best effect; ideal for mountain wildflower meadows.
ZONES 4–11

## *IRIS*

IRIS

This genus of more than 200 species, almost all of which are worth cultivating, are native to the temperate regions of the northern hemisphere. The majority are clump-forming, rhizomatous perennials, although a significant number grow from bulbs (these can be found in that chapter). The rhizomotous irises are divided into four groups: the bearded irises, distinguished by the tuft of hairs (the "beard") on the three lower petals; the beardless irises, which have none; the crested or Evansia irises, which have a raised crest in lieu of a beard and are mostly rather tender in cold climates; and the very rare and beautiful Oncocyclus irises, allied to the bearded types. These last are native to the eastern Mediterranean and need cold winters and hot, dry summers to flourish; the pale gray *I. susiana* is the most likely to be seen in specialist catalogues. All the rhizomatous irises have sword-shaped leaves, sometimes evergreen. As a rule they are cold hardy and prefer sun; some of the beardless types like very moist soil. All are easily grown and are propagated by division in late summer after flowering. There are many hybrids in all divisions, and the selection is constantly being updated. The varieties illustrated are simply indicative of the range available.

# A Field Trip to the Guadalupe Mountains National Park

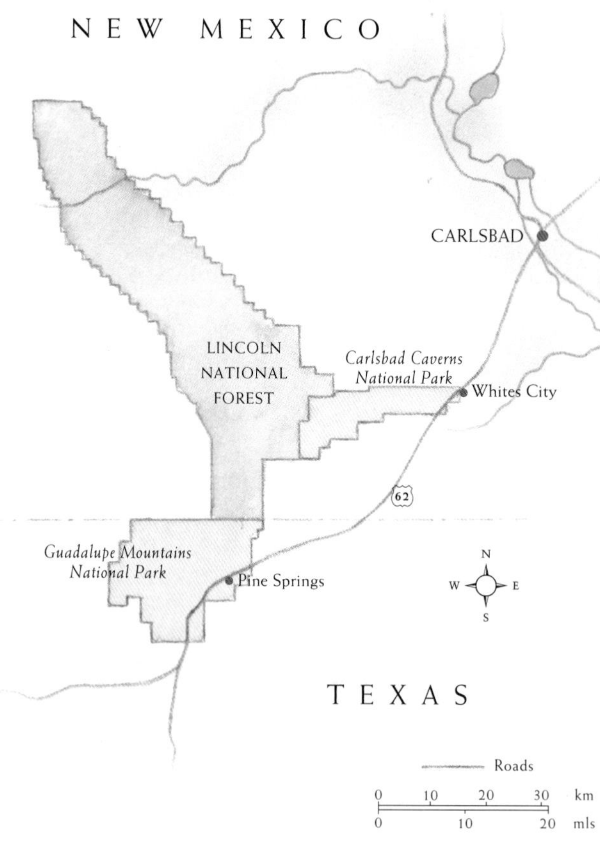


The prairie country of the USA is home to a host of wildflowers, a number of which have found their way into gardens all over the world. Although the prairies are large, relatively flat expanses of many different grasses, extensive stands of one or a few wildflower species can sometimes occur, creating a wildflower lover's delight.

Driving along any of the major highways in Texas from March through to May, particularly following a season of good rainfall, you are likely to be greeted with a kaleidoscope of wildflowers.

Although the prairie country consists mainly of vast flat regions, you are always close to mountains, and the adventurous wildflower lover can move between different elevations to extend the viewing range, as the delayed spring of higher altitudes causes the lowland species to flower later.

One of the most distinctive of these prairie wildflowers is the daisy, Indian blanket (*Gaillardia pulchella*), with its bright, almost gaudy, color scheme. Native to a wide area of the southern and central USA—from Arizona to Texas, north to Colorado and Nebraska and south into Mexico—it is found

*A huge drift of Indian blanket creates a colorful expanse.*

mainly on the sandy prairies and in the desert regions. Its scientific name, *Gaillardia pulchella*, which incorporates the name of Gailard de Charentoneau, a French patron of botany, and the Latin word for "pretty," hardly conveys the vividness of its floral display. Its common name, Indian blanket, more appropriately describes its habit, after a good rainfall season, of spreading over wide areas of the prairie in a series of flamboyant patterns.

One of the best places to view *G. pulchella* is in the Guadalupe Mountains National Park, on the border between New Mexico and Texas. Traveling east from El Paso, take Route 62 for approximately 100 miles (about 160 km) until you reach the town of Pine Springs, just inside the park. From here, drive in a northeasterly direction, skirting the southern side of the park through the foothills of the Guadalupe Mountains and up to the border with New Mexico, which forms the park's northern boundary. Among these foothills, you will see that the Indian blanket is well adapted to colonizing roadside verges, making it easy to find. At first you will see the odd flash of color on a roadside bank and then, if you are lucky, a large expanse of pure Indian blanket will appear over a meadow or a disturbed area of soil. It is worth stopping at these spots to explore the subtle variations in size and color of each population. These areas usually run into larger expanses of wildflowers further from the roadside—walking through these is a memorable experience.

The prairies often produce spectacular fields of wildflower mixtures and you may find the adaptable *G. pulchella* near other equally appealing flowers, such as the delicate white Queen Anne's lace *(Daucus carota)* and the strikingly blue Texas bluebonnet *(Lupinus texensis)*.

The Indian blanket can grow on high plains to 3300 ft (about 1000 m) above sea level, where there are dramatic fluctuations between day and night temperatures, and is adaptable enough to grow in conditions ranging from desert to humid coastal areas. Being a prairie species, the Indian blanket needs full sun and room to spread. It is best suited to porous, well-drained soils which mimic those found in its natural habitat.

A fascinating aspect of the Indian blanket is the natural variation it shows when it is grown from seed. A wonderful range of colors is obtained with interesting zigzag patterns on the florets. It is frequently grown as an annual, and seed should be sown in fall. Alternatively, it can be easily propagated from soft-tip cuttings which, if renewed every six months or so, can produce flowers all year round. The Indian blanket itself can form a sprawling specimen up to 32 in (about 80 cm) if not kept in check by tip pruning. The flowers are, of course, its most outstanding feature, the individual heads being 1.5–2.5 in (about 4–6 cm) wide, with bristly scales found among the florets. The leaves are a pleasing gray-green, approximately 3 in (about 7 cm) in length, often with toothed margins.

The Indian blanket is a star attraction of the prairie wildflower country. Whether you wish to appreciate its ephemeral charm in the wild or cultivate it in your own garden, *G. pulchella* will always reward you with both its adaptability and inspirational coloring.

*Gaillardia pulchella*

## *Gaillardia*

*Gaillardia* is a genus of about 28 species of annuals and perennials in the daisy (Asteraceae) family, within which it falls into the sunflower tribe (Heliantheae). *Gaillardia* is centered in the USA and Mexico, with three of its species also being found in South America. Only two species are generally known in gardens, the yellow-flowered perennial *G. aristata* and the bicoloured annual Indian blanket, *G. pulchella*. Both have been selected over a hundred years for their size and for the coloring of the flowers. A range of hybrids has arisen between them, the earliest of which were believed to have appeared spontaneously. The results of deliberate breeding for new strains are known collectively as *G.* × *grandiflora*.

The most distinctive feature of *Gaillardia* is the circle of "petals" (the ray-florets), which are wedge-shaped and toothed at the apex. These contrast in color with the prominent dark center of the flowerhead. Cultivated gaillardias are among the hardiest of garden flowers, tolerating extreme heat as well as cold and dryness, strong winds and poor soils.

Daisies form one of the largest flowering plant families with some 25000 species in 1100 genera, including *Coreopsis*, *Cosmos*, *Rudbeckia* and *Echinacea*.

*Gaillardia pulchella*

*Iris* Pacific Coast hybrids

*Iris japonica*

*Iris ensata*

*Iris* bearded hybrid

## *I.* bearded hybrids

FLAG, BEARDED IRIS

Often classed under *I. germanica,* which is only one of their ancestral species, the bearded irises are among the most beautiful and widely grown of late-spring flowers. Their sword-shaped, grayish foliage is handsome in its own right and the flower stems bear several flowers. They are available in an enormous range of colors—everything but true red—with many varieties featuring blended colors, contrasting upright petals ("standards") and lower petals ("falls"), or a broad band of color around basically white flowers (this pattern is called "plicata"). They can be divided into three groups: the dwarfs, which grow 6–15 in (about 15–38 cm) tall and flower earlier than the others; the intermediates, which are usually 15–28 in (about 38–71 cm) tall and flower two to three weeks later; and the tall bearded irises, last to bloom and growing 3 ft (about 90 cm) or more tall. These are the most popular, and new introductions are available every year from breeders in the United States, the United Kingdom, Australia and New Zealand. Some of the newer varieties, described as "remontant", flower a second time in late summer or fall, though rather erratically. All prefer a temperate climate, sun and an alkaline, well-drained soil.

ZONES 3–10

## *I. cristata*

CRESTED IRIS

A woodland iris native to the southeastern United States, this delightful 6–10 in (about 15–25 cm) creeper makes a satisfactory ground cover in shaded gardens. Pale blue to lavender or purple flowers are held just above the foliage in spring and offer a faint but sweet fragrance; the crest on the falls is yellow or cream. It prefers a woodsy, moist soil in the shade; it spreads slowy by rhizomes. 'Alba' is a vigorous cultivar with white flowers.

ZONES 6–9

*Iris pallida* 'Variegata'

*Iris cristata*

## *I. ensata*

syn. *I. kaempferi*

JAPANESE IRIS, JAPANESE WATER IRIS

Native to Japan and cultivated there for centuries, the beardless *I. ensata* grows to a height of 3 ft (about 90 cm) and bears purple flowers with yellow blotches in late spring. The many named garden varieties bear huge flowers, sometimes as much as 10 in (about 25 cm) wide, in shades of white, lavender, blue and purple, often blending two shades. The foliage dies down for the winter. The plants prefer rich, acid soil and plenty of moisture, even growing happily in shallow water provided they are not submerged in winter. The similar but slightly smaller flowered *I. laevigata* can grow in water all year. Both feature in Japanese paintings.

ZONES 5–11

## *I. japonica*

JAPANESE CRESTED IRIS

This 20 in (about 50 cm) tall species from Japan is the best known of the crested species. It forms large clumps of almost evergreen, midgreen leaves and bears sprays of many $2^1/_2$ in (about 6.5 cm) wide, exquisitely ruffled, pale blue or white flowers in late winter and spring. It likes acid soil and a lightly shaded spot, and prefers a more or less frost-free climate. There is a variety with white-striped leaves, although this is rather shy flowering.

ZONES 8–10

*Iris* Louisiana hybrid

## *I.* Louisiana hybrids

Mainly derived from *I. fulva* and its allied species from the southern United States, these beardless irises are evergreen and bear flat, often ruffled flowers. In late spring several flowers appear together on stems which are usually a little over 3 ft (about 90 cm). They come in a very wide range of colors—white, cream, yellow, blue, mauve, magenta and purple. They prefer sun and very moist soil and will grow permanently in shallow water at the edge of a pond. The flowers are excellent for cutting.

ZONES 4–10

## *I.* Pacific Coast hybrids

These almost evergreen, beardless irises are mainly derived from *I. innominata, I. douglasiana* and other species native to the West Coast of the United States. In late spring they bear 3 in (about 7.5 cm) wide flowers, usually beautifully marked and veined in a wide range of colors—cream, yellow, blue, mauve and bronze. They prefer acid soil and sun or light shade, and have the reputation of being difficult to transplant. Once a clump is established, leave it undisturbed. Water freely while the plants are growing from fall through spring, less in the summer, but do not let them completely dry out. Foliage is narrow and dark green.

ZONES 8–10

## *I. pallida* 'Variegata'

ORRIS

This splendid bearded iris from the Middle East features handsome leaves which are striped in graygreen and cream. Its pale blue, lightly scented flowers are borne on $3^1/_2$ ft (about 1 m) high stems in late spring. Cultivation is the same as for the bearded irises.

ZONES 3–10

### *I. pseudacorus*

YELLOW FLAG, WATER FLAG

A beardless iris from Europe, the water flag has handsome, mid-green leaves and profuse bright yellow flowers in late spring. There is also a form with variegated leaves. Both prefer to grow in shallow water and rich soil, and are delightful, easily grown plants for a garden pond.

ZONES 4–9

### *I. pseudacorus* 'Variegata'

This strain has yellow and green-striped foliage during the spring months, then often turning green in summer. It is less vigorous than *I. pseudacorus*.

ZONES 4–9

### *I. siberica*

SIBERIAN IRIS

Among the best of the irises for the border, the Siberians make strongly vertical clumps of slender bright green leaves to a height of 2–4 ft (about 60–120 cm). In late spring or early summer stems rise above the foliage and present one to several narrow-petaled, blue, purple or white flowers, often veined in a deeper color. They prefer full sun to a very light shade (particularly in hot areas), a moderately moist, rich soil that may be slightly acid and water during the hottest periods.

ZONES 4–10

### *I. spuria* hybrids

While *I. spuria, I. orientalis* and their allied species, mainly from eastern Europe and western Asia, are beautiful plants in their own right, they have been much hybridized. The more common hybrids bear many flowers on 3½ ft (about 1 m) high stems in early summer. The colors are mainly in the white, yellow and blue range. All prefer sun, rich soil, and lavish watering while they are growing and flowering, but need minimal watering during the summer.

ZONES 7–10

### *I. unguicularis*

WINTER IRIS

This evergreen, beardless species from north Africa is valued for its habit of bearing its scented flowers from fall to spring. Whenever the weather is mild they are lovely for cutting and will last 3 or 4 days if cut in bud. The typical form is pale blue but there are also white and darker blue varieties available. All flower best in a warm, sunny position where they don't get too much summer sun, and in slightly alkaline soil. The flowers on their 8 in (about 20 cm) stems will be more conspicuous if the luxuriant foliage is cut back in late fall.

ZONES 8–11

*Iris unguicularis*

## *KIRENGESHOMA palmata*

From Japan comes this unusual perennial which thrives in cool, moist conditions and needs a deep, lime-free soil in order to flourish. In late summer it bears pale yellow, shuttlecock-shaped flowers on arching stems 3 ft (about 90 cm) high, forming a clump about the same distance across. It does best in part or complete shade. Propagate by division in fall or spring.

ZONES 5–9

*Kirengeshoma palmata*

## *KNIPHOFIA*

RED-HOT POKER, TORCH LILY

Native to southern Africa these stately perennials, some of which are evergreen, can be relied upon to make a brilliant display in the garden for a long time. They are upright, tufted plants with long, grass-like foliage and tall, bare stems carrying showy, brightly colored tubular flowers in dense racemes. They require an open position in full sun and a well-drained soil; though they prefer plenty of water during the growing season, many have proven drought tolerant in the dry summers of the West. They tolerate wind well and are often seen growing close to the coast. From spring on, fertilize monthly to increase size and quality of blooms. Remove dead flower stems and leaves in late fall. They are excellent cut flowers, looking very good when combined with agapanthus. Propagate species from seed or by division in spring; cultivars by division in spring. They are attractive to hummingbirds.

### *K.* hybrids

A great many hybrids have been developed over the years, using *K. uvaria* and other species. Heights range from 12 in (about 30 cm) to 4 ft (about 1.2 m). Flower color varies from creamy whites through yellows and oranges to hot corals and scarlet; many have two or three colors per flower. 'Little Maid' has spikes of creamy flowers; 'Atlanta' has soft red flowers.

ZONES 7–11

### *K. uvaria*

POKER PLANT

A tall perennial with large, strap-shaped, strongly channeled leaves and dense racemes of tubular scarlet flowers that become orange-yellow with age. Flowers in late summer and fall and grows to a height of 3½ ft (about 1 m) with a spread of 20 in (about 50 cm).

ZONES 6–11

*Iris siberica*

*Iris pseudacorus*

*Kniphofia uvaria*

*Kniphofia* 'Atlanta'

*Iris pseudacorus* 'Variegata'

*Iris spuria* hybrid

*Lavatera trimestris*

*Lamium maculatum*

*Lamiastrum galeobdolon* 'Variegatum'

*Leonotis leonurus*

*Leucanthemum* × *superbum*

*Kochia scoparia* f. *trichophylla*

*Lavatera thuringiaca*

## *KOCHIA*

### *scoparia* f. *trichophylla*

**syn. *Bassia scoparia* f. *trichophylla***

FIRE BUSH, BURNING BUSH

A very bushy annual native to southern Europe and grown for its narrow, lance-shaped, 2–3 in (about 5–7.5 cm) long, soft, light green leaves that turn a brilliant purplish red in fall. The flowers are dull and inconspicuous. It is useful for bedding and for pot plants. Moderately fast growing, it reaches a height of 3 ft (about 90 cm) and a spread of 24 in (about 60 cm). It prefers a warm, open, sun-exposed position sheltered from harsh winds—provide support in very windy areas. Soil should be moderately fertile and well drained. Tip prune young plants to encourage denser growth. Propagate from seed in spring; it readily self seeds and can become invasive.

ALL ZONES

## *LAMIASTRUM*

### *galeobdolon* 'Variegatum'

**syn. *Galeobdolon argentatum*, *Lamium galeobdolon* 'Variegatum'**

YELLOW ARCHANGEL

This semi-evergreen carpeting perennial is much favored as ground cover in shaded places, particularly under deciduous trees. It spreads fast from runners, producing long trailing stems of oval, coarsely toothed, silver-marked, mid-green leaves. It is inclined to be rampant but can easily be controlled. Yellow flowers, similar in form to those of *Lamium*, are produced in summer. It grows to around 12 in (about 30 cm) in height with an indefinite spread. Culture as for *Lamium*. Cut back lightly after flowering.

ZONES 3–10

## *LAMIUM*

### *maculatum*

SPOTTED DEAD NETTLE

A semi-evergreen perennial, this is a popular flowering ground cover for the shade. It has mauve-tinged, deeply toothed leaves with central silvery stripes and carries clusters of pinkish flowers in spring and summer. Mat forming, it grows to a height of 10–12 in (about 25–30 cm) with a spread of 3 ft (about 90 cm). The plants prefer full to partial shade and a moist, well-drained soil. Propagate by separating rooted stems in spring. There are several cultivars with more silver in the leaves and more compact growth: 'Beacon Silver' with pink flowers; 'White Nancy' with white flowers; and 'Pink Pewter' with silvery-pink flowers.

ZONES 3–10

## *LAVATERA*

MALLOW

Closely related to the hollyhock and hibiscus, this group of annuals, biennials, perennials and soft-wooded shrubs are popular for their usually large, colorful mallow flowers, generally produced over a long season. Unfortunately, however, even the perennials are not long lived. Upright in habit with simply to palmately lobed leaves, often woolly to the touch. All prefer a sunny site with any well-drained soil. Pruning after a flush of blooms will encourage branching and more flowers. Propagate from seed sown in place as cuttings do not strike well.

### *L. thuringiaca*

TREE LAVATERA

A fairly recent introduction to American gardens, this shrubby perennial produces a glorious display of rosy-pink, hollyhock-like flowers all summer on sturdy bushes to 5 ft (about 1.5 m) in height. Softly hairy, grayish green leaves are an attractive foil for the flowers. Native to the Mediterranean, they prefer full sun, a well-drained soil and average water. Use at the back of a border or as a colorful hedge. Easy from seed, there are now several cultivars available with distinct flower colors: 'Barnsley' is nearly white with a deep pink center; 'Bredon Springs' is a rich pink.

ZONES 6–10

### *L. trimestris*

ANNUAL MALLOW

This shrubby annual, native to the Mediterranean, is grown mainly for its brilliant white or pink, silken flowers which closely resemble a hibiscus. Flowers are 3 in (about 7.5 cm) wide and appear from summer to early fall. They are short lived but are borne in profusion, benefiting from regular dead-heading. Leaves are oval, lobed and mid-green. It has an erect, branching habit and is moderately fast growing to a height of 2–4 ft (about 60–120 cm) and spread of 24 in (about 60 cm). 'Silver Cup' has lovely dark pink flowers; 'Mont Blanc' is pure white.

ZONES 4–10

## LEONOTIS
*leonurus*

LION'S TAIL

Native to Africa, this evergreen shrubby perennial is popular in warm, dry gardens. A striking plant, growing to 6 ft (about 1.8 m) or more, it bears vertical stems with whorls of tawny orange, furry, tubular flowers in late summer and fall. Leaves are lance shaped and aromatic. It requires a sunny position and well-drained soil. Do not over-water. These plants are dependably drought tolerant and do well in coastal situations. Propagate from seed in spring or softwood cuttings in early summer. To control height and encourage vigorous flowering stems, cut back hard in spring. There is a white variety.

ZONES 9–10

## LEUCANTHEMUM
× *superbum*

syn. *Chrysanthemum maximum*

SHASTA DAISY

This robust perennial grows to a height and spread of 3 ft (about 90 cm). It has large, daisy-like, white flowerheads with golden centers. The flowers are carried high over the dark, shiny, toothed leaves in summer. Cultivars are available with either single or double flowers, some with fringed petals. Give full sun, a well-drained soil and average water. Divide and replant every two years for best flowering.

ZONES 4–10

## LIATRIS
*spicata*

syn. *L. callilepis*

SPIKE GAYFEATHER, BLAZING STAR

This upright perennial from the prairies of central North America is a desirable cut flower and a good butterfly and bee-attracting plant. The flowers are lilac-purple and are produced in crowded, fluffy spikes—like a feather duster—in late summer. They open from the top downwards, the opposite of most flowering spikes. The species has thickened, corm-like rootstocks and basal tufts of grassy, mid-green foliage. Clump forming, it grows to a height of 2–4 ft (about 60–120 cm) with a spread of 24 in (about 60 cm). The plants require a sunny situation and well-drained, light soil of reasonable quality. They do not like high humidity. Propagate by division in early spring or from seed in spring or fall. Transplant when dormant during late winter or early spring.

ZONES 3–10

## LIGULARIA

Originally from the temperate regions of Europe and Asia, these perennials produce large clusters or racemes of daisy-like flowers in summer. Some species grow up to $7^1/_2$ ft (about 2.2 m) tall and 3 ft (about 90 cm) wide. They prefer a moist, well-drained soil and will grow in either sun or semi-shade. Propagate by division in spring or from seed in spring or fall. Prone to attack by slugs and snails.

### *L. dentata* 'Desdemona'

syn. *Senecio clivorum* 'Desdemona'

GOLDEN GROUNDSEL

A compact perennial grown for its striking foliage and showy heads of daisy flowers. It has kidney-shaped, long-stalked, leathery, brownish green leaves and bears clusters of large, 3 in (about 7.5 cm) wide orange-yellow flowerheads on long branching stems in summer. Clump forming, it grows to a height of 4 ft (about 1.2 m) and a spread of 24 in (about 60 cm). This species will grow happily at the edge of ponds.

ZONES 4–10

### *L. tussilaginea* 'Aureomaculata'

LEOPARD PLANT

This herbaceous perennial is grown for its foliage and flowers. It has variegated gold and green leaves with clusters of daisy-like flowers arising from branched stems in late summer. This species grows to a height and spread of 24 in (about 60 cm). A frost-tolerant plant ideal for a damp, shady area, although it will also grow in the sun. Plant in damp, fertile soil. Cut stems down to the base in fall. Propagate by division in spring or from seed in spring or fall. Keep a look out for slug and snail attacks.

ZONES 7–11

## LIMONIUM

STATICE, SEA LAVENDER

These sub-shrubs and perennials, sometimes grown as annuals, are popular for their papery, many colored flowers, which can be cut and dried for decoration. Flowers should be cut just as they open and hung upside down to dry in a cool, airy place. They are good mixed border plants and excellent rock garden plants and are easily grown in full sun and well-drained, sandy soil. Their need for minimal maintenance and tolerance to seaspray and low rainfall make them a good choice for seaside and second home gardens. Plants will benefit from light fertilizing in spring while flowerheads are developing. Propagate by division in spring, from seed in early spring or fall, or from root cuttings in late winter. Transplant during winter or early spring.

### *L. latifolium*

SEA LAVENDER

A tall-stemmed perennial bearing clusters of lavender-blue or bluish white flowers for a long period over summer. Clump forming, it grows to a height of 24–36 in (about 60–90 cm) and a spread of 18 in (about 45 cm), with large leaves. The dried flower stems have a delicate, misty appearance. They are attractive to bees.

ZONES 3–10

### *L. sinuatum*

ANNUAL STATICE

This statice is a bushy, upright perennial almost always grown as an annual. It produces dense rosettes of oblong, deeply waved, dark green leaves and bears masses of tiny blue, pink or white papery flowers on winged stems. Flowers in summer and early fall. It is fairly slow growing to a height of 20 in (about 50 cm) and a spread of 12 in (about 30 cm).

ZONES 3–10

*Ligularia dentata* 'Desdemona'

*Liatris spicata*

*Limonium latifolium*

*Limonium sinuatum*

*Ligularia tussilaginea* 'Aureomaculata'

## LINARIA

### *maroccana* 'Fairy Bouquet'

TOADFLAX, BABY SNAPDRAGON

Native to Morocco, this fast-growing, bushy annual is a useful bedding plant, giving a long and colorful display of flowers in spring. It bears sprays of small, snapdragon-like flowers in colors of gold, pink, mauve, apricot, cream, purple and yellow. It has lance-shaped, pale green leaves and grows to a height of 9 in (about 23 cm) and a spread of 4 in (about 10 cm). It prefers sun or light shade and a well-drained, neutral soil. Water well in the early stages of growth. Propagate from seed in spring or fall; it also self seeds freely.

ALL ZONES

## LINUM

FLAX

These annuals, biennials, perennials, sub-shrubs and shrubs, some of which are evergreen, are distributed widely in temperate regions. They are grown for their profuse blooms and are useful in a rock garden or border. Grow in a sunny spot with average, well-drained soil; some species need shelter in cool climates. Propagate the annuals, biennials and perennials from seed in fall and perennials by division in spring or fall. Most species self sow readily.

### *L. grandiflorum* 'Rubrum'

SCARLET FLAX

Native to Algeria, this annual has small, rounded, flattish, deep red flowers and lance-shaped, gray-green leaves. The flowering period is short but can be extended by sowing seed at monthly intervals. It has a slim, erect habit and is fairly fast growing to a height of 20 in (about 50 cm) and spread of 6 in (about 15 cm).

ZONES 5–10

### *L. narbonense*

FLAX

The most handsome of all the blue flaxes, with deep, sky-blue, funnel-shaped flowers that last for many weeks in summer, borne on slender stems and forming a clump 18 in (about 45 cm) high and wide. It needs a well-drained soil and a sheltered site in full sun.

ZONES 5–10

### *L. perenne*

BLUE FLAX

A vigorous, upright perennial forming an open, bushy plant 12–24 in (about 30–60 cm) high with a spread of 18 in (about 45 cm) or more. It has slender stems with grass-like leaves and clusters of open, funnel-shaped, light blue flowers that are borne throughout summer.

ZONES 5–10

## LIRIOPE

### *muscari*

BIG BLUE LILYTURF

This clumping evergreen perennial—one of 5 species of a genus native to China, Japan and Vietnam—is a useful casual ground cover or path edging. It has grass-like, shining, dark green leaves (*L. m.* 'Variegata' has variegated leaves), and bears erect spikes of rounded, bell-shaped, violet flowers in late summer. It grows to a height of 12–24 in (about 30–60 cm) with a spread of 12 in (about 30 cm), with flower spikes held just above the foliage. It will grow in sun but prefers shade and well-drained, moderately fertile soil. Propagate by division in early spring or from seed in fall.

ZONES 5–11

## LOBELIA

This large genus of annuals and perennials is widely distributed in temperate regions, particularly America and Africa. Growth habits vary from low bedding plants to tall, herbaceous perennials. They are all grown for their ornamental flowers and neat foliage and make excellent edging, flower box, hanging basket and rock garden specimens. Some are suitable in wild gardens or by the waterside. They are best grown in a well-drained, moist, light loam enriched with animal manure or compost. Most grow in sun or semi-shade. Prune after the first flush of flowers to encourage repeat flowering, and fertilize weekly with a liquid manure during the season. Propagate annuals from seed in spring, perennial species from seed or by division in spring or fall and perennial cultivars by division only. Transplant from late fall until early spring.

### *L. cardinalis*

CARDINAL FLOWER

A clump-forming perennial useful for growing in wet places and beside streams and ponds. From late summer to mid- fall it produces spikes of brilliant scarlet-red flowers on branching stems above green or deep bronzy purple foliage. Grows to a height of 3 ft (about 90 cm) and a spread of 12 in (about 30 cm). It requires moist soil and semi-shade and is very attractive to hummingbirds.

ZONES 2–10

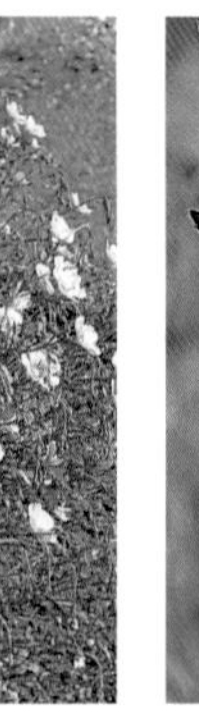

*Linum perenne*

*Linum narbonense*

*Linaria maroccana* 'Fairy Bouquet'

*Lobelia cardinalis*

*Liriope muscari* 'Variegata'

*Linum grandiflorum* 'Rubrum'

*Lobelia erinus*

*L. erinus*

EDGING LOBELIA

This slow-growing, compact annual is native to South Africa. It has a tufted, sometimes semi-trailing habit with dense oval to lance-shaped leaves. It bears small, two-lipped flowers from spring through early fall; the typical color is blue. It grows to a height of 4–8 in (about 10–20 cm) and a spread of 4–6 in (about 10–15 cm). Water sparingly and feed regularly. Excellent for edging, rockeries, pots and hanging baskets. 'Cambridge Blue' is a pale blue; 'Crystal Palace' is dark blue; 'Sapphire' is a good blue trailer. White and pink cultivars are also available.

ZONES 4–10

*L.* × *gerardii* 'Vedrariensis'

A hybrid of *L. cardinalis* and *L. syphilitica,* this clump-forming perennial is an excellent border plant, growing to a height of 3 ft (about 90 cm) and a spread of 12 in (about 30 cm). It produces racemes of two-lipped, violet-blue flowers in late summer. Leaves are dark green and lance shaped. It prefers full sun.

ZONES 4–8

## *LOBULARIA*
*maritima*

**syn. *Alyssum maritimum***

SWEET ALYSSUM

Native to southern Europe and western Asia, this fast-growing, spreading annual is a widely popular edging, rock garden or window box plant. It produces masses of tiny, honey-scented, 4-petaled white flowers over a long season from spring to early fall. Lilac, pink and violet shades are also available. It has a low, rounded, compact habit with lance-shaped, grayish green leaves and grows to a height of 3–6 in (about 7.5–15 cm) and a spread of 8–12 in (about 20–30 cm). It grows best in a dryish position in full sun and likes a fertile, well-drained soil. Good for coastal and beach situations. Shear back after flowering to encourage continuous flowering. Propagate from seed in spring.

ZONES 4–10

*Lobularia maritima*

## *LOTUS*
*berthelotii*

PARROT'S BEAK

Native to the Cape Verde and Canary Islands, this semi-evergreen, trailing perennial is suitable for hanging baskets, ground cover or spilling over rockeries, banks or the tops of walls. It has hairy, silvery branches of fine needle leaves and clusters of pea-like, scarlet flowers cover the plant in spring and early summer. Grows to 12 in (about 30 cm) tall with an indefinite spread. It requires a fairly sunny situation and well-drained, coarse soil, preferably with a little added peat or other organic matter. It is best suited to warm coastal gardens. Tip prune young shoots to encourage dense foliage. Propagate from cuttings taken in summer or from seed in spring or fall.

ZONES 9–11

## *LUNARIA*
*annua*

**syn. *L. biennis***

MONEY PLANT, HONESTY

A fast-growing biennial native to southern Europe and the Mediterranean coast, this plant is grown for its attractive flowers and curious fruits. It has pointed, oval, serrated, bright green leaves and bears heads of scented, 4-petaled rosy magenta, white or violet-purple flowers in spring and early summer. These are followed by circular seed pods with a silvery, translucent membrane, which are used in dried floral arrangements. Erect in habit, it grows to a height of 30 in (about 76 cm) and a spread of 12 in (about 30 cm). It will grow in either sun or shade, but prefers partial shade and a moderately fertile, well-drained soil. Propagate from seed in spring or fall. This plant self sows readily in most climates.

ZONES 4–10

*Lobelia* × *gerardii* 'Vedrariensis'

## *LUPINUS*

LUPINE

A large genus of annuals and perennials mainly native to North America and southern Europe, grown for their ease of culture, rapid growth and large spikes of showy pea flowers in a range of colors including blue, purple, pink, white, yellow, orange and red. They are useful grouped with bearded irises in bedding schemes and are good naturalized. Grow in an open, sunny position in a well-drained soil; water during the growing season and mulch in dry areas. They enjoy high humidity and should be mulched in dry areas. Spent flowers should be cut away to prolong plant life and to prevent self seeding. Propagate species from seed in fall and selected forms from cuttings in early spring. Watch out for slugs and snails.

*Lotus berthelotii*

*Lupinus hartwegii*

*Lunaria annua*

*L. hartwegii*

HAIRY-FOLIAGED LUPIN

Native to Mexico this annual has compact, erect growth to 28 in (about 71 cm) high with a spread of 16 in (about 40 cm). It has hairy, palmate, dark green leaves and slender spikes of pea flowers in shades of blue, white or pink are borne abundantly in late winter, spring and early summer.

ZONES 4–10

### *L.*, Russell hybrids

This fine strain of perennial lupines bears long spikes of large, brilliant, strongly colored flowers (in shades of cream, pink, orange, blue or violet), some of which are bicolored, in late spring and summer. They produce a magnificent clump of handsome, deeply divided, mid-green leaves, growing to a height of 3 ft (about 90 cm) with a spread of half that. There are also dwarf strains, such as the 24 in (60 cm) high 'Little Lulu'. Cut back flowering stems to ground level in late fall and divide and replant clumps between fall and early spring every two or three years. These hybrids require a richer, slightly acid soil than do most of the species and prefer cool summers with high humidity. Even under the best of conditions they are prone to a number of pests and diseases.

ZONES 4–9

### *L. texensis*

TEXAS BLUE BONNET

A fast-growing, bushy annual reaching a height of 12 in (about 30 cm) and spread of 8 in (about 20 cm), this species has bright green palmate leaves and bears dark blue and white flowers in late spring. Easily grown, it thrives in poor soils and is quick to flower from seed. This is the state flower of Texas.

ZONES 4–10

## *LYCHNIS*

CAMPION

Native to the temperate regions of the northern hemisphere, these annuals, biennials and perennials are grown for their attractive summer flowers, borne in cymes in white through to reds and magenta. They are easily grown in sunny sites in any well-drained soil on an westerly or northerly slope to minimize soil temperatures, and an annual feeding in late winter to early spring is beneficial. Remove spent stems after flowering and dead-head frequently to prolong the flowering period. Propagate by division or from seed in fall or early spring. They self seed readily. These plants have been cultivated for many centuries.

### *L. coronaria*

ROSE CAMPION, MULLEIN PINK

A clump-forming perennial, sometimes grown as a biennial, this plant grows to a height of 24 in (about 60 cm) and a spread of 18 in (about 45 cm). It is native to Africa, Asia and Europe. It forms a dense clump of silvery white, woolly leaves; branched, gray stems carry bright cerise flowers throughout summer. It thrives in most areas and self sows readily. Plant it in moist, rich soil in a sunny position. 'Alba' is a white-flowered cultivar. In ancient times the flowers were used for garlands and crowns.

ZONES 3–10

### *L.* × *haagena*

A short-lived, clump-forming perennial growing to a height of 18 in (about 45 cm) with a spread of 12 in (about 30 cm). In summer it bears clusters of large, 5-petaled, white, salmon, flame and scarlet flowers. Foliage is mid-green. Plant in a sunny position in well-drained soil. It is weak growing and should be regularly propagated from seed.

ZONES 4–9

## *LYSICHITON*

### *camtschatcensis*

SKUNK CABBAGE

Native to Siberia and northern Japan this deciduous perennial is a marsh plant useful for planting in damp, boggy soils and on pond edges. It has handsome, arum-like, pure white spathes surrounding spikes of small insignificant flowers. These are borne in spring and are followed by tufts of bold, bright green foliage arising from a creeping rhizome. It grows to a height of 30 in (about 76 cm) and a spread of 24 in (about 60 cm). It prefers full sun but will tolerate semi-shade. They require a cold and frosty winter climate and are happy growing in both running and still water. Propagate from seed in late summer.

ZONES 6–9

## *LYSIMACHIA*

### *punctata*

YELLOW LOOSESTRIFE

A clump-forming perennial with mid-green leaves and lightly branched stems that in summer carry a great massed display of brilliant yellow, starry flowers produced in whorls. They are suitable for bedding, rock gardens or beside pools and streams. It grows erect to a height and spread of around 28 in (about 71 cm). It prefers a sunny situation and moist but well-drained soil. Propagate by division in fall, winter or early spring, or from seed in fall. Its common name is derived from 'louse-strife', as the plant was grown to repel lice.

ZONES 4–10

## *MACLEAYA*

### *cordata*

syn. *Bocconia cordata*

PLUME POPPY

Native to China and Japan, this tall perennial grows to 8 ft (about 2.4

*Lysichiton camtschatcensis*

*Lychnis coronaria*

*Lychnis* × *haagena*

*Lysimachia punctata*

*Lupinus texensis*

*Macleaya cordata*

*Lupinus*, Russell hybrids

*Matthiola incana*

m) in height. It belongs to the poppy family. It has large, rounded, deeply veined, heart-shaped, gray-green leaves and bears large, feathery, terminal flower spikes of cream tinted with pink in summer. It is one of the most attractive foliage plants available for the herbaceous border. It requires a sunny, sheltered situation and well-drained soil, and prefers cool summers. Water well during the growing season and mulch during winter. Propagate by division in early spring or from root cuttings in winter. It spreads from underground stems and may become invasive.
ZONES 4–10

## MALCOLMIA
*maritima*

VIRGINIA STOCK

An attractive little annual from the Mediterranean, this plant is valued for its ability to flower in as little as 4 to 6 weeks after seed is sown. It is very useful for edging, for paths, crevices and window boxes, and for growing over spring-flowering bulbs. It has oval, gray-green leaves and bears 1 in (about 2.5 cm) wide fragrant flowers in shades of pink, red, mauve and white from spring to fall. It has an erect habit and is fast growing to a height of 8–15 in (about 20-38 cm) and a spread of 4–8 in (about 10–20 cm). It requires sun and fertile, well-drained soil. Propagate from seed sown at frequent intervals from spring to early fall for a long flowering season. It self seeds readily.
ALL ZONES

## MALVA
*moschata*

MUSK MALLOW

Useful for naturalizing in a wild garden or odd corner, this perennial has narrow, lobed, divided leaves with a sticky, hairy texture which emit a musky, cheesy odor when crushed. A native of Europe, it bears profuse spikes of saucer-shaped pink flowers in summer. 'Alba', the white cultivar, is also very popular. It has a bushy, branching habit and can grow to a height of 3 ft (about 90 cm). It requires a sunny situation and will thrive in a wide range of soil and climatic conditions. Propagate from seed in fall and cut plants back after the first flowers have faded. Watch for rust disease.
ZONES 3–11

## MATTHIOLA

STOCK

This genus of annuals, biennials and perennials is native to the Mediterranean region. They are grown for their soft, gray-green foliage and densely clustered, highly scented flowers in shades of white, lilac and purple, deep reds and pinks, and yellow. They are fragrant and long lasting as cut flowers. Grows best in a sheltered position in sun or light shade and in a fertile, well-drained soil. There are many improved seed strains available, developed for a wider color range (reds to pure white), double flowers or compact habit. Tall cultivars may need support. Over-fertilizing will encourage leaf growth at the expense of the flowers. In mild regions, sow seed in early fall for winter flowering, or in early spring for later spring bloom.

### *M. incana*

STOCK

This upright biennial or short-lived perennial from southern Europe is best grown as an annual. It has a bushy habit and grows up to 30 in (about 76 cm) in height with a spread of 12 in (about 30 cm). *M. incana* has an unforgettable, pervading and spicy fragrance. These stocks have lance-shaped, gray-green leaves and fragrant, 3–6 in (about 7.5–15 cm) long spikes of mauve flowers which are borne during cool weather—winter in the mildest regions, spring elsewhere.
ZONES 4–10

*Malva moschata*

### *M.* 'Mammoth Column'
**syn. *M.* 'Giant Column'**

This is a cultivar from *M. incana* which grows taller, reaching 3 ft (about 90 cm) in height. Each plant produces a single, 12–16 in (about 30–38 cm) tall spike of scented flowers in spring, in mixed or separate colors. When the main spike is finished, cutting the plant back will promote more flowers. It is sensitive to the temperature and needs a long, cool spring.
ZONES 4–10

## MAZUS
*reptans*

This prostrate, carpet-forming, Himalayan perennial has stems that root as they trail and are lined with 1 in (about 2.5 cm) long bright green leaves. Small flowers appear in spring on short, upright stems; flowers are lavender with white and yellow spots. Only 2 in (about 5 cm) tall but spreading to 12 in (about 30 cm) or more, this makes a good small-scale ground cover or addition to a rock garden. It likes an average soil and moderate watering. It will often invade nearby lawns, but looks attractive there and will tolerate light foot traffic. It also works well in cracks between paving stones. Give afternoon shade in hot areas, otherwise full sun.
ZONES 3–11

*Matthiola* 'Mammoth Column'

## MECONOPSIS

A genus of short-lived perennials that are mostly native to the Himalaya, and which includes the superb Himalayan blue poppy (*M. betonicifolia*). They bear large, exotic flowers with papery petals and a bold, central boss of stamens on tall stems in early summer. Most meconopsis species are exacting in their requirements, needing a moist but not over-wet, lime-free soil with plenty of humus and a cool site in part or full shade which is sheltered from strong winds. One exception is the Welsh poppy (*M. cambrica*), a

*Malcolmia maritima*

native of Europe with bright lemon-yellow or orange flowers borne on short stems. This species thrives in most soils and usually self seeds freely. Propagate meconopsis by fresh seed in late summer.

### *M. betonicifolia*

BLUE POPPY

Native to the Himalayas, this clump-forming but short-lived perennial bears pure sky-blue, saucer-shaped, 2–3 in (about 5–7.5 cm) wide, satiny flowers with yellow stamens in late spring and early summer. Oblong, hairy, mid-green leaves are produced in basal rosettes. It grows to a height of 3 ft (about 90 cm) and a spread of 18 in (about 45 cm). A woodland species, it must be grown in a sheltered position in humus-rich, moist, neutral to acid soil and in a cool climate. Plants usually bloom in their second year, and often die unless they are prevented from setting seed by dead-heading. Propagate from seed in late summer. Best in the Pacific Northwest; a distinct challenge elsewhere.

ZONES 7–9

### *M. cambrica*

WELSH POPPY

Native to western Europe and including Great Britain, these perennial poppies are more easily grown than the blue poppy and make a welcome addition to the garden when allowed to naturalize with shrubs and bulbs or when added to flower borders. The slightly hairy, mid-green leaves are deeply divided and form basal tufts. Lemon-yellow or rich orange blooms are freely borne in late spring. It has a spreading habit, reaching 12 in (about 30 cm), with a height of 12–18 in (about 30–45 cm). It is a short-lived species that nevertheless self seeds readily.

ZONES 7–9

## *MERTENSIA virginica*

VIRGINIA BLUEBELLS

Native to the cooler parts of eastern North America, this perennial is one of the loveliest of all blue spring flowers. It bears clusters of rich blue, tubular, 1 in (about 2.5 cm) long flowers, 20 or more on each stem, and has smooth, oblong, soft blue-green foliage; the foliage dies back in early summer after flowering. It is effective planted with daffodils and polyanthus primroses and is seen at its best naturalized in woodlands or alongside streams. It grows to a height and spread of around 18 in (about 45 cm). Plant in shade and a deep, well-drained soil. Propagate by division in spring or from seed or by division in fall. Watch for slugs. *V. ciliata* is very similar but is native to the Rocky Mountains.

ZONES 3–9

## *MIMULUS*

MONKEY FLOWER

These annuals and perennials are characterized by tubular flowers with flared mouths, often curiously spotted and mottled, which have been likened to grinning monkey faces. The flowers come in a large range of colors including brown, orange, yellow, red and crimson. Mainly native to the cool Pacific coastal areas of Chile and the USA, most species are suited to bog gardens or other moist situations, although some are excellent rock garden plants. The bright flowers are particularly effective in containers and in groups at the edge of flower beds. Grow in full sun or partial shade in a wet or moist soil. Propagate perennials by division in spring and annuals from seed in fall or early spring.

### *M. cardinalis*

SCARLET MONKEY FLOWER

Striking for its tubular, two-lipped flowers of bright scarlet, this clump-forming perennial from western North America makes an excellent addition to the damp border or a streamside garden. Medium green hairy leaves are nicely backlit by the sun. Clumps reach 4 ft (about 1.2 m) in height with a spread or around 24 in (about 60 cm). With plenty of moisture flowers are produced from late spring through fall, especially if dead-headed and cut back when flowering slows to encourage new flowering stems. A rich, moist soil is important in a sunny situation. Very popular with hummingbirds.

ZONES 7–10

### *M.* × *hybridus*

MONKEY FLOWER

A showy group of hybrids derived from *M. guttatus* and *M. luteus*, these are low-growing and short-lived perennials often grown as annuals. It forms a spreading mound and is good for containers or for bedding displays. 'Calypso' and 'Malibu' are the most readily available seed strains, each around 12 in (about 30 cm) tall and wide and offering a range of warm colors—yellow, orange, red and mahogany—and usually with spotted and speckled throats. All will do well in a rich, moist soil in full sun in cool areas, light shade elsewhere. They grow best in cool weather; start seeds in spring for summer bloom.

ZONES 6–11

### *M. moschatus*

MUSK PLANT, MUSK FLOWER

A small, creeping, water-loving perennial growing to a height and spread of 6–12 in (about 15–30 cm). It bears snapdragon-like, pale yellow flowers, lightly dotted with brown, in summer to fall. The leaves are pale green, hairy and oval. This plant was once grown for its musk scent but, mysteriously, it has been odorless for many years.

ZONES 7–10

*Meconopsis cambrica*

*Meconopsis betonicifolia*

*Mimulus cardinalis*

*Mertensia virginica*

*Mina lobata*

*Mimulus moschatus*

## *MINA*

*lobata*

**syn. *Ipomoea versicolor, Quamoclit lobata***

Native to Mexico and central America, this vigorous, short-lived, twining climber is a perennial usually grown as an annual. It is deciduous or semi-evergreen with three-lobed bright green leaves, and bears racemes of small, tubular, dark red flowers fading to orange then creamy yellow. Flowers appear from late summer until late fall. The plant climbs to a height of 15 ft (about 4.5 m) and quickly provides a dense leafy cover over a suitable supporting structure. It requires a warm, sun-exposed position and a rich, well-drained soil that does not dry out. In cold climates the plant rarely survives the winter and should be replaced by fresh sowings in spring.

ZONES 9–11

## *MIRABILIS*

*jalapa*

FOUR O'CLOCK

This bushy, tuberous perennial is grown for its fragrant, trumpet-shaped, crimson, pink, white or yellow flowers which open in late afternoon and remain open all night, closing again at dawn. Although it is not as showy as some annuals, it is a tough plant that is easy to cultivate. Good as pot plants, bedding plants or as a dwarf hedge. They are native to tropical America, are summer flowering, and grow to around 3 ft (about 90 cm) high with a similar spread. They require a sheltered position in full sun in a fertile, well-drained soil and will tolerate any heat that is reflected from buildings or pavements. In frosty areas tubers are best lifted and stored like dahlias over winter; in mild climates they can be left undisturbed and gradually make large clumps. Propagate from seed or by division of tubers in early spring.

ZONES 8–10

## *MOLUCCELLA*

*laevis*

BELLS OF IRELAND, SHELL FLOWER

This summer-flowering annual, native to Syria, is grown for its flower spikes which are very popular for fresh or dried floral work; each tiny white flower is surrounded by a shell-like, apple-green calyx. Rounded leaves are pale green and nettle like. The plant is fairly fast growing to a height of 24 in (about 60 cm) and spread of 12 in (about 30 cm), and has an erect, branching habit. It grows best in a sunny, open position in a rich, very well-drained soil. Propagate by sowing seed directly into its flowering position in early spring. Water moderately and feed monthly with a balanced fertilizer.

ALL ZONES

## *MYOSOTIS*

FORGET-ME-NOT

This genus of annuals and perennials includes 50 or so species, but those most commonly cultivated come from the temperate regions of Europe, Asia and the Americas. They are grown for their dainty blue (sometimes pink or white) flowers that complement plants of stronger color in the spring garden. Most species are useful in rock gardens, border displays or as ground cover under trees and shrubs. They prefer either a semi-shaded woodland setting or a sunny spot with the protection of other, larger plants. Soil should be fertile and well drained. They are rarely affected by pests or diseases and respond well to feeding in the pre-flowering period. Discard plants after flowering. Propagate from seed in fall. Once established they self seed freely. Myosotis is derived from the Greek for "mouse ear", referring to the pointed leaves. The flowers have long been associated with love and remembrance.

### M. 'Blue Ball'

This slow-growing perennial is usually grown as an annual. It has a bushy, compact habit, growing to a height of 8 in (about 20 cm) with a spread of 6 in (about 15 cm) and bears tiny, five-lobed, deep blue flowers in spring and early summer. Its leaves are lanced shaped. It is good for edging. Propagate from seed in fall.

ZONES 5–10

### M. *scorpioides*

FORGET-ME-NOT

A deciduous to semi-evergreen perennial similar to *M. sylvatica* but generally lower, this species has shiny leaves, is more likely to be perennial and spreads by rhizomes. The small blue flowers will have a yellow, white or pink eye on stems 12–18 in (about 30–45 cm) high over a longer period than *M. sylvatica.* They appear throughout summer. It is a marginal water plant and can be grown in mud or even in very shallow water.

ZONES 5–10

### M. *sylvatica*

GARDEN FORGET-ME-NOT

This biennial or short-lived perennial is usually grown as an annual for its cheery, bright blue, yellow-eyed flowers in spring and early summer. It forms mounds of fuzzy foliage 18 in (about 45 cm) tall and 12 in (about 30 cm) wide, with taller, slender, curled stems unfurling as their flower buds open. Easily grown in most soils with moisture in spring, the plants fade shortly after flowering and are best pulled up; seedlings will appear in following years for a repeat of the spring bloom. For great effect, plant it among daffodils, tulips and other spring bulbs. Numerous named selections are available with more compact habit (8–12 in/20–30 cm) or brighter blue flowers (occasionally pink or white).

ZONES 5–10

*Myosotis sylvatica*

*Myosotis scorpioides*

*Mirabilis jalapa*

*Moluccella laevis*

*Myosotis* 'Blue Ball'

*Nemesia strumosa*

*Nelumbo nucifera*

## NELUMBO
### *nucifera*
SACRED LOTUS

A deciduous, perennial, aquatic plant in the water lily family growing 3–4½ ft (about 90–130 cm) above the water surface and spreading to 3½ ft (about 1 m). Large, fragrant, pink or white, 10 in (about 25 cm) wide flowers are borne above large, shield-shaped, pale green leaves. It is a subtropical species and requires an open, sunny position and 8–12 in (about 20–30 cm) of water over the tubers. Flowers develop into unusual seed pods, resembling salt shakers. Remove faded foliage and divide overgrown plants in spring. Propagate from seed in spring. This vigorous plant grows well in large ponds. Buddha is often depicted sitting in the center of a lotus.

ZONES 8–11

## NEMESIA
### *strumosa*

Indigenous to southern Africa this colorful, fast-growing annual is popular as a bedding plant for winter bloom in the milder regions and summer bloom elsewhere. They are also useful for planting between summer-flowering bulbs, in rock gardens and window boxes. They are bushy plants with lance-shaped, pale green and prominently toothed leaves, growing to a height of 12–18 in (about 30–45 cm) and a spread of 10 in (about 25 cm). Large, two-lipped, snapdragon-like flowers in colors of yellow, white, red or orange are borne in spring on short terminal racemes. The plants prefer a well-drained, moderately fertile soil and a wind-sheltered, sunny position. They prefer cool weather and do not do well in hot, humid summers. Prune spent flowers to prolong flowering and pinch out growing shoots of young plants to encourage a bushy habit. Sow seed in early fall for winter blooms, or spring for early summer bloom. The most cultivated of its genus, *N. strumosa* has spawned a range of hybrids and cultivars of varying heights and colors.

ALL ZONES

*Nemophila menziesii*

*Nertera granadensis*

*Nepeta × faassenii*

## NEMOPHILA
### *menziesii*
BABY-BLUE-EYES

A charming little Californian wildflower, this fast-growing, spreading annual is a useful ground cover under shrubs such as roses, in rock gardens and edges, and is particularly effective overplanting a bed of spring bulbs. In spring or early summer it bears small, bowl-shaped, sapphire-blue flowers with a well-defined concentric ring of white in the center. It has dainty, serrated, mid-green foliage and grows to a height of 8 in (about 20 cm) and a spread of 6 in (about 15 cm). It is best planted in a cool, partly shaded site in fertile, well-drained soil; it will continue flowering as long as the soil is moist and the temperature remains cool. Sow seed where they are to grow in early fall in mild areas or in early spring. Watch for aphids.

ALL ZONES

## NEPETA
### × *faassenii*
CATMINT

A bushy perennial useful for separating strong colors in the shrub or flower border and very effective when used with stone, either in walls, paving or rock gardens, or as an edging plant. It forms spreading mounds of grayish green leaves that are aromatic when crushed, and the numerous flower stems carry hundreds of small, pale violet-blue flowers throughout summer. Grows to a height and spread of 18 in (about 45 cm). It prefers cool conditions and a sunny situation, but does not like high humidity. Any moderately fertile, well-drained soil will suit. Cut back old growth to within 3 in (about 7.5 cm) of soil level in winter; shear when flowers fade to encourage a new flush of blooms. Propagate by division in early spring or from softwood cuttings in spring and summer.

ZONES 3–10

## NERTERA
### *granadensis*
syn. *N. depressa*
BEAD PLANT

A carpeting perennial grown for the mass of spherical, orange or red, bead-like berries it bears in fall. It has a prostrate habit, growing to ½ in (about 1 cm) in height with a spread of 4 in (about 10 cm) and forming compact cushions of tiny bright green leaves with extremely small, greenish white flowers in early summer. It thrives in a cool, sheltered, semi-shaded site in gritty, moist but well-drained sandy soil.

Water well in summer but keep dryish in winter. It is an excellent alpine house plant. Propagate by division or from seed or tip cuttings in spring. There is a variety with purple-tinged foliage.
ALL ZONES

## *NICOTIANA*

TOBACCO

These annuals and perennials, some of which are grown as annuals, are mainly of South American origin and are an ornamental species of tobacco. The older species are grown for the fragrance of their warm-weather flowers which usually open at night; the newer strains have flowers that remain open all day but have limited perfume. They require full sun or light shade and a fertile, moist but well-drained soil. Propagate from seed in early spring. The flowers are good for cutting, although the plants are sticky to handle. Watch for snails and caterpillars.

### N. *alata*

**syn. *N. affinis***

FLOWERING TOBACCO

A short-lived perennial usually grown as an annual, this flowering tobacco bears few-flowered stems of trumpet-shaped flowers that are white inside and the palest green outside. The flowers open towards evening and fill the garden with scent on warm, still nights. Rosette forming, it has oval, mid-green leaves and grows to a height of 3 ft (about 90 cm) with a spread of 12 in (about 30 cm). It flowers through summer and fall. There are hybrid forms with different flower colors.
ZONES 4–10

### N. × *sanderae*

HYBRID FLOWERING TOBACCO

These hybrids, derived from *N. alata* and *N. forgetiana,* are somewhat bushy annuals with heights varying from 12 in (about 30 cm) to 3 ft (about 90 cm) and a spread of 12 in (about 30 cm) or more. From early summer through fall they bear long, trumpet-shaped flowers in shades of green, white, pink, red, cerise, crimson and purple. Flowers stay open during the day, although not all are fragrant. The Nikki series are heavy bloomers on compact plants, but with little fragrance. The Domino strain is more heat and sun tolerant. 'Fragrant Cloud' is tall, white and fragrant at night.
ZONES 4–10

## *NIEREMBERGIA*
## *hippomanica* var. *violacea* 'Purple Robe'

CUPFLOWER

Native to Argentina, this small, bushy perennial, best grown as an annual, is ideal for edgings and massed beddings, rock gardens and window boxes. In summer and early fall it bears a profusion of cup-shaped, open, dark bluish purple flowers with yellow throats. It has much-branched, thin, stiffly erect stems and narrow, lance-shaped, deep-green, slightly hairy leaves. Moderately fast growing to a height and spread of around 12 in (about 30 cm). It prefers a moist but well-drained soil and a sunny situation. Cut back well after flowering. Propagate by division in spring, from semi-ripe cuttings in summer or seed in fall. Fresh stock should be raised every two or three years.
ZONES 7–11

## NIGELLA
## *damascena*

LOVE-IN-A-MIST

This annual is grown for its attractive flowers and is native to the Mediterranean and western Asia. It has spurred, many-petaled blue, pink or white flowers in spring and early summer, almost hidden in the bright green feathery foliage and followed by rounded, green seed pods that mature to brown. Both flowers and seed pods are good for floral decoration. Upright and fast growing, it reaches 24 in (about 60 cm) in height with a spread of 8 in (about 20 cm). Plant in a sunny situation in a fertile, well-drained soil; water regularly. The plants have a short blooming season and can be dead-headed to prolong flowering; successive sowings can also be made. Propagate from seed in fall. It self sows readily.
ALL ZONES

## *NYMPHAEA*

WATER LILY

This genus of deciduous and evergreen, perennial, aquatic plants with fleshy roots is named for the Greek goddess Nymphe. They are grown for their floating leaves and attractive bright flowers that come in shades of white and cream, brilliant yellows and oranges, pinks and deep reds, blues and purple. There are hardy and tropical varieties. Hardy water lilies grow in all climates and flower freely throughout summer, both flowers and foliage floating on the water surface. Faded foliage should be removed. Divide the tuber-like rhizomes and replant in spring or summer every three or four years. Tropical water lilies are all frost tender, requiring a very warm, sunny situation. They flower from mid-summer into fall and have large, scented flowers held above the water surface. In cooler areas the tubers should be lifted and stored in moist sand over winter. All species need still water and annual fertilizing as they are gross feeders. Propagate from seed or by separating plantlets in spring or early fall. Watch for insects, particularly aphids; goldfish in the pool will eat most pests.

### N. *alba*

EUROPEAN WHITE WATER LILY

A deciduous, hardy species with floating dark green leaves and cup-shaped, semi-double, fragrant 4 in (about 10 cm) wide white flowers with golden centers. It spreads to 9 ft (about 2.7 m).
ZONES 5–11

### N. 'Aurora'

A smaller, hardy cultivar, also deciduous, with floating olive green leaves blotched with purple. Semi-double flowers are star-shaped, 2 in (about 5 cm) wide and turn from cream to yellow, to orange, to blood-red. Spreads to 30 in (about 76 cm).
ZONES 5–11

### N. *candida*

This dainty, dwarf species is ideal for a miniature pond. It bears small, pure white, cup-shaped flowers. Plant with around 6–9 in (about 15–23 cm) of water over the crown of the plant.
ZONES 7–11

### N. × *helvola*

A true miniature water lily which bears soft yellow, star-shaped, semi-double flowers. The leaves are handsome too, being dark olive green splashed with maroon. Plant with around 9 in (about 23 cm) of water over the crown of the plant.
ZONES 7–11

### N. Laydeckeri hybrids

These compact hybrids are excellent for small ponds, as they are very free flowering yet produce comparatively little foliage. Colors range from soft rose-pink to deep pink and rosy crimson. Plant with 9–12 in (about 23–30 cm) of water over the crown of the plant.
ZONES 5–11

*Nicotiana alata*

*Nicotiana* × *sanderae*

*Nierembergia hippomanica* var. *violacea* 'Purple Robe'

*Nigella damascena*

*Nymphaea alba*

*Nymphaea* 'Aurora'

### *N. marliacea* 'Carnea'

This elegant water lily has dark green leaves and star-shaped, semi-double, soft pink flowers with golden centers 6–10 in (about 15–25 cm) across. It flowers in summer. Propagate from seed or by separating plantlets in spring or early fall.

ZONES 7–11

### *N. odorata*

WHITE POND LILY

This perennial, native to America, has large, white, fragrant, many-petaled flowers appearing in summer. It prefers the still waters of ponds and marshes in an open, sunny position. It is frost resistant. Propagate by division.

ZONES 5–11

## *OENOTHERA*

EVENING PRIMROSE

Native to the Americas but naturalized elsewhere, this genus of annuals, biennials and perennials is grown for the masses of short-lived flowers borne during summer. Most species are pollinated by night-flying insects and only release their lovely fragrance at night. Some members of the genus do not even open their petals during the day. They grow best in a well-drained, sandy soil in an open, sunny situation. They will tolerate dry conditions. Propagate from seed or by division in spring or fall, or from softwood cuttings in late spring.

### *O. biennis*

COMMON EVENING PRIMROSE

A showy plant, this upright biennial has large, scented, yellow flowers that grow in long sprays and open in the evening. Foliage is light green. It is fast growing to a height of 5 ft (about 1.5 m) and a spread of 24 in (about 60 cm). Oil from the seeds has been used medicinally.

ZONES 4–10

### *O. missouriensis*

OZARK SUNDROPS

A spreading perennial that forms mats of dark green leaves and has short-stemmed, bell-shaped, 4 in (about 10 cm) wide, canary yellow flowers, sometimes spotted red. Flowers open at sundown and are borne over a long period throughout spring and summer. It grows to a height and spread of 12 in (about 30 cm).

ZONES 5–10

### *O. speciosa*

WHITE EVENING PRIMROSE

A short-lived, rhizomatous perennial bearing spikes of fragrant, saucer-shaped, pink-tinted white flowers in profusion. Fresh flowerheads open daily throughout the summer. The small leaves often turn red in hot or cold weather. It spreads aggressively by rhizomes to 3 ft (about 90 cm) or more with a height of 12–18 in (about 30–45 cm). It can become invasive.

ZONES 5–11

## *ORIGANUM*

### *laevigatum*

ORNAMENTAL OREGANO

A very ornamental oregano with spreading roots serving a low, dense mass of evergreen leaves, from which rise flowering stems to 18–24 in (about 45–60 cm). Tiny flowers create a cloud of lavender at the top of the stems all summer long, and provide nectar for bees and butterflies. An excellent filler for the perennial border as well as the herb garden. Provide full sun, a well-drained soil that is not too fertile, and occasional water during dry periods. Cut flower stems to the ground at the end of the season; they make delightful additions to dried flower arrangements. 'Hopleys' and 'Herrenhausen' are recent cultivars with richer flower color.

ZONES 7–11

## *OSTEOSPERMUM*

This genus of annuals and evergreen, semi-woody perennials is mostly indigenous to South Africa. The tough plants are useful for rock gardens, dry embankments or the front rows of shrub borders, particularly as temporary filler plants. They produce large, daisy-like flowers in the white and violet, purple and blue range and flower for many weeks in winter and spring. They prefer a warm, temperate climate and require moderately fertile, well-

*Oenothera speciosa*

*Nymphaea marliacea* 'Carnea'

*Origanum laevigatum*

*Oenothera biennis*

*Nymphaea* hybrid

*Osteospermum ecklonis*

*Oenothera missouriensis*

drained soil. An open, sun-exposed position is essential. Shearing after flowering helps maintain shape and extend the plant's life span. Propagate from cuttings of non-flowering shoots or from seed in summer.

### *O. ecklonis*

An evergreen with either upright or straggling habit, this sub-shrub grows to a height and spread of 3 ft (about 90 cm). It has lance-shaped, mid-green leaves and bears 3 in (about 7.5 cm) wide daisies, glistening white with deep reddish violet centers and streaked with bluish mauve underneath the petals. Flowers from early summer to fall.
ZONES 9–11

### *O. fruticosum*
**syn. *Dimorphotheca fruticosa***
FREEWAY DAISY

An evergreen perennial with prostrate or trailing stems which spread to cover vast areas when planted along freeways in coastal California. Flowering stems carry masses of palest lilac daisies around 12 in (about 30 cm) above the ground; the heaviest bloom is in winter, with some blossoms at any time. Named selections are available with pure white, burgundy or purple flowers.
ZONES 9–11

### *O. jucundum*
**syn. *Dimorphotheca jucundum***

This evergreen perennial grows to a height and spread of 18 in (about 45 cm). It is clump forming with mid- to dark green, lance-shaped to rectangular leaves and produces abundant purplish pink daisies with darker central discs from fall to early summer. The flowers close on cloudy days.
ZONES 9–11

## *OXYPETALUM*
### *caeruleum*
**syn. *Tweedia caerulea***
SOUTHERN STAR

Pale blue starry flowers, aging to purple, are borne in summer and early fall on this weakly twining herbaceous climber. They are followed by 6 in (about 15 cm) long, boat-shaped, green seed pods similar to those of other members of the milkweed family. The flowers are suitable for picking but the cut stems must be burnt to seal the sticky white sap. The plant has heart-shaped, gray-green leaves covered with a hairy down, and grows to a height of 3 ft (about 90 cm). It requires a sunny situation and rich, well-drained soil and should be grown as an annual in cooler climates. Propagate from seed in spring and pinch out tips of buds to encourage a branching habit. This species, from Uruguay and Brazil, is the only member of its genus to be cultivated widely.
ZONES 9–11

*Oxypetalum caeruleum*

## *PACHYSANDRA*
### *terminalis*

This creeping perennial, a native of Japan, has leathery, ovate leaves with saw-tooth tips clustered at the ends of short stems. Tiny white flowers, sometimes pink or purple tinted, appear in terminal clusters in early summer. This evergreen makes a good ground cover and likes moist, well-drained soil in a shady site. It grows to a height of 8 in (about 20 cm) with a similar spread. Propagate by division in early spring. There is a silver-edged form that is less vigorous.
ZONES 5–10

*Pachysandra terminalis*

## *PAEONIA*
PEONY

Some species of these deciduous shrubs and perennials display showy seed pods in addition to the lobed foliage and full, round flowerheads for which this genus is renowned. Many species are from western China and the Himalayas; some from Siberia and Mongolia. Others are of European origin, including *P. officinalis* which has been used medicinally. Propagate by carefully dividing the fleshy roots in early fall, or early spring in the South. Soil should be deep and rich, moist but well drained, especially in winter. Plant in full sun, except in the hottest of areas. Best in regions with a long, cold winter. They are not well adapted to mild winter zones (8–10); try early-blooming cultivars there. 'Sarah Bernhardt' has fragrant, double white flowers flecked with red. Staking is often necessary for the large-flowered kinds. Botrytis is the most serious disease of peonies; treat with a fungicide. Peonies do not like to be disturbed; they flower better with age.

*Osteospermum jucundum*

*Osteospermum fruticosum*

*Paeonia* 'Sarah Bernhardt'

# A Field Trip to Grindelwald

Visit the picture-postcard town of Grindelwald between December and March and you will find thousands of brightly clad skiers trudging through the slush and ice. Return again in July and Grindelwald will have undergone a transformation, with colorful windowboxes full of geraniums adorning attractive alpine houses.

The town nestles in the mountains of the Bernese Oberland, sitting against the backdrop of the Swiss Alps, These mountains, with their wooded lower slopes, alpine meadows and snow-capped peaks, include among their number the towering Eiger.

Although Grindelwald at times suffers from an inundation of visitors, it does have two important advantages for the plant enthusiasts who visit. Firstly, it is surrounded by some superb alpine meadows and pastures which are incredibly rich in colorful species; secondly, the same chairlifts that transport hopeful skiers to the *piste* during the winter months operate throughout the year and can save hours of foot-slogging toil. Within a few short minutes, you can be free of the hustle and bustle of urban Grindelwald below and admire the clear views and brilliant flowers which in summer include one of the Alps' most spectacular species, the great yellow gentian *(Gentiana lutea)*.

*The great yellow gentian, with a spectacular mountain backdrop.*

The Grindelwald chairlift has intermediate stations before you reach the highest point. One of the best ways to explore the region, assuming you are sufficiently fit and energetic, is to walk down the slopes from one of these stop-off points. The network of paths and tracks are signposted and route maps are available.

The highest ski-station is well above the tree-line and in the highest zone of vegetation before areas of permanent snow are reached. A succession of flowers appears from May onwards, as the snows retreat, and these include the spring gentian *(G. verna)* and the trumpet gentian *(G. acaulis)*. One of the region's most enchanting plants also occurs here, the aptly named alpine snowbell *(Soldanella alpina)*, and it is one which usually cannot wait for the snow to melt. Nodding flower spikes of these fringed flowers often force their way through the snow itself.

After you descend a few hundred feet (a hundred meters or so) you come to some truly vivid alpine meadows. Throughout the summer months these flower-rich pastures are home to small herds of cattle, noisily identified by their jangling cow-bells. Everywhere you look there are such plants as alpine pasque-flower *(Pulsatilla alpina)*, alpine bartsia *(Bartsia alpina)* and alpine butterwort *(Pinguicula alpina)*, as well as numerous cranesbills, bedstraws, cinquefoils and orchids. It is in this region, on slopes and banks, that you are most likely to come across some brightly colored stands of great yellow gentian.

Further down the mountainside, towards Grindelwald, the meadows become increasingly lush and full of grasses and rich flowers such as red campion *(Silene dioica)* and dandelion *(Taraxacum officinale)*.

Here and there, as you are descending the slopes above Grindelwald, you walk through stands of native conifer forest. These are mainly comprised of white fir *(Abies alba)*—in winter their sagging, snow-laden branches make a delightful spectacle. On the forest floor colorful plants such as the yellow wood violet *(Viola lutea)* and the twinflower *(Linnaea borealis)* are there to be seen. If you look carefully you may find the diminutive and easily overlooked lesser twayblade orchid *(Listera cordata)*.

*Gentiana lutea* is among the most striking and distinctive of all these plants, and its appearance is enhanced by the invariably stunning settings in which it grows.

The species produces a robust basal rosette, each leaf of which is broadly lanceolate or ovate in outline and pointed at the tip. The leaves are bluish green in color with strongly marked veins, and can be up to 12 in (about 30 cm) long. From June until August, stout and upright flower-bearing spikes appear, rising from the basal rosette. These reach a height of up to 6 ft (about 2 m) or more and are hollow and unbranched. Whorls of large, bright yellow flowers are arranged up the stem with pairs of clasping leaves below. These are similar in appearance to the basal leaves but smaller in size. The individual flower corollas are colored deep yellow, or occasionally reddish, and are about 1 in (about 2 cm) long; they have five to nine lobes which spread out in star-shaped fashion.

Great yellow gentian is a hardy, long-lasting perennial, like all the species that grow in the Alps and central European mountains, Here the combination of a short growing season and a prolonged winter has favored the adaptation of very hardy plants indeed. The first heavy snows in the Alps can come as early as October, although the lower slopes are not usually covered until Christmas. Freezing temperatures and a blanket of snow are then the norm until April, when the thaw begins.

Great yellow gentian can be found in many of the mountainous areas of Europe, but while some of these may rival the Bernese Oberland for scenic splendor, few can match it for the ease with which you can reach the plant's natural habitat. Whether you visit Grindelwald or one of the many other alpine resorts, you will surely have a botanical field trip to remember and cherish.

*Gentiana lutea*

## *Gentiana*

Gentians are members of the genus *Gentiana* and its more recent sister-genera *Gentianella* and *Gentianopsis*. The group consists of around 400 species of mostly perennial herbs found in most parts of the world, although in the tropics only in higher mountain regions. The areas richest in gentian species are the mountains of western China and the neighboring Himalayas. The Alps of Europe boast equally attractive species, including *G. lutea* which is widespread throughout the upland and mountain regions of central Europe. The roots of *G. lutea* are important in herbal medicine and its infusions and brews serve as useful tonics; a potent liqueur is also distilled from the fermented root.

Intense deep blues and sky blues are the flower colors most commonly associated with gentians, but whites and creams are also frequent, and *G. lutea* has a brilliant yellow flower.

The family Gentianaceae contains about 80 genera, including woody shrubs, annuals and perennials. Others that may be familiar to gardeners include the prairie gentian *(Eustoma)*, popular as a cut flower, and the Persian violet *(Exacum)*, which is grown as an indoor plant.

*Gentiana lutea*

### *P. lactiflora* hybrids

COMMON GARDEN PEONY

A mainstay of the early summer border, these long-lived perennials are among the most popular of garden flowers in America. Great mounds of excellent, deep green foliage provide interest from spring to fall. Flowers appear above the leaves on stems that may need staking, especially for the double-flowered forms. Colors range from pure white to pink, red, salmon and peach; flowers may be single, with a great burst of yellow stamens in the center, semi-double or double. These hybrids are derived mostly from *P. lactiflora*, but a number of other, lesser known species have been involved over the years. 'Festiva Maxima' has fragrant, double, pure white flowers flecked with red. 'Coral Charm' represents more recent breeding, its coral buds opening to semi-double, peach-colored blossoms.
ZONES 2–9

### *P. officinalis*

COMMON PEONY

A tuberous species, this perennial reaches 24 in (about 60 cm) in height and spread, bearing single, purple or red rose-like flowers in spring through mid-summer. It is a native of Europe and likes good soil and ample water. Of similar size, the hybrid 'Rubra Plena' bears flowers that are fulsome clusters of many small, mid-magenta petals.
ZONES 2–9

## *PAPAVER*

POPPY

With their characteristic cupped petals and nodding buds turning skywards upon opening, poppies are popular flowers for bedding and for borders. They prefer a well-drained soil, average water and full sun. Dead-head for longer flowering. Sow seed in spring or fall; the annual species self seed readily.

*Papaver somniferum*

### *P. alpinum*

ALPINE POPPY

This alpine poppy is a miniature Iceland poppy. A short-lived perennial, this tuft-forming semi-evergreen grows 8–12 in (about 20–30 cm) high and wide, and has finely cut grayish leaves. It bears white or yellow flowers through summer. Use on banks or in rock gardens.
ZONES 5–10

### *P. nudicaule*

ICELAND POPPY

This tuft-forming perennial is in fact almost always grown as an annual. It bears large, scented flowers, colored white, yellow, orange and pink and with a crinkled texture, in winter and spring. The plant has pale green leaves, long, hairy stems and grows to a height of 12–24 in (about 30–60 cm) with a 4 in (about 10 cm) spread. Give this native of subarctic regions full sun. Sow in late summer to early fall. The species is good for rock gardens, bedding and cutting.
ZONES 3–10

### *P. orientale*

ORIENTAL POPPY

This perennial bears spectacular single or double flowers in early summer. Originally from Asia, varieties offering different colors abound but a common feature is the dark basal blotch on each petal. Their hairy, lance-like, bluish green leaves become straggly and die down completely after flowering. Propagate when dormant in late summer by lifting and dividing or by taking root cuttings. These plants will grow to a height of 2–4 ft (about 60–120 cm) and a spread of nearly 3 ft (about 90 cm).
ZONES 3–9

### *P. rhoeas*

FLANDERS POPPY

The cupped flowers on this fast-growing annual from Asia Minor are small, delicate, scarlet and single, although cultivated varieties (Shirley poppies) offer hues including reds, pinks, whites and bicolors. Double-flowered strains are also available. It will grow 24–36 in (about 60–90 cm) high with a 12 in (about 30 cm) spread. Flowering time is early summer, and the leaves are light green and lobed. Give them all full sun.
ZONES 5–10

### *P. somniferum*

BREADSEED POPPY, PEONY POPPY

The green leaves on this fast-growing annual have a grayish cast and are lobed and elliptical with serrated edges. It blooms in early summer, displaying big flowers in white, pink, red or purple, often as doubles. From the Middle East, it likes sun. Opium poppies are cultivated for the milky sap extracted from their seed capsules, source of the narcotic drug opium and its derivatives. Though technically illegal to grow as the source of opium, the garden forms readily self seed (and in fact have naturalized) in the warmer areas of the United States, and are a source of the poppy seeds found on breads and bagels.
ZONES 5–10

*Papaver orientale*

*Papaver rhoeas*

*Papaver nudicaule*

*Paeonia officinalis*

*Papaver alpinum*

*Pelargonium × hortorum*

*Pelargonium odoratissimum*

*Parochetus communis*

*Pelargonium graveolens*

*Pelargonium crispum*

## PAROCHETUS *communis*

SHAMROCK PEA

It is the flowers that are pea like on this evergreen, ground-hugging, wide-spreading perennial. The flowers are bright blue and bloom for most of the year; the leaves resemble clover. In mild winter climates it is a successful ground cover, and is a good pot plant or basket plant elsewhere. Plant it in partial shade in moist, coarse soil. Use rooted runners to propagate by division at any time of year. Don't be alarmed if it vanishes without apparent cause; marginal bits will live from which you can make divisions to re-establish it.

ZONES 9–11

## PELARGONIUM

GERANIUM

These tender perennials are often grown as annuals for summer bedding in colder climates. In warmer climates with long hours of daylight they flower almost all the time, although they do not do well in extreme heat and humidity. Keep in a greenhouse in winter in colder climates. Plant in pots or beds. The site should be sunny with light, well-drained, neutral soil. If in pots, fertilize regularly and cull deadheads. Avoid over-watering. Use softwood cuttings for propagation in spring through fall. The species in this genus are mainly from South Africa. Including hybrids and cultivated varieties, the genus can be divided into four groups: zonal, ivy-leaved, regal or show, and scented-leaf geraniums.

### *P. crispum*

LEMON GERANIUM

The lemon-scented leaves on this upright plant are small and lobed with crinkled margins. Pink flowers up to 1 in (about 2.5 cm) across often have darker markings. It grows to 3 ft (about 90 cm) with a 12–20 in (about 30–50 cm) spread. *P. c.* 'Variegatum' has variegated leaves.

ZONES 10–11

### *P. × domesticum*

MARTHA WASHINGTON GERANIUM, REGAL GERANIUM, SHOW

Often just called "pelargonium," the regal types are shrubby perennials with stiff, pleated leaves and clusters of large flowers, wide open and often blotched or particolored. They flower in late spring and come in shades from white through pink to red and purple. They have the showiest flowers of any of the geraniums and are often likened to azaleas. They are much grown as pot plants and are tender—in cool areas a greenhouse is needed. Cut back hard after blooming to keep the bushes compact.

ZONES 10–11

### *P. graveolens*

ROSE GERANIUM

The deeply lobed, furry leaves give off an aroma of roses when crushed. This is a shrubby species, growing 12–24 in (about 30–60 cm) tall and as wide. The flowers are rose-pink with a purple spot on the upper petals. There are a number of hybrids that also carry a rose scent; all are derived from this species.

ZONES 9–11

*Pelargonium × domesticum*

### *P. × hortorum*

**syn. *P. × zonale***

COMMON GERANIUM, ZONAL GERANIUM

These popular hybrids of several South African species are bushy, aromatic perennials with round leaves, often marked with a darker zone, and clusters of bright flowers. Elsewhere they are grown as summer annuals, propagated from either seed or cuttings. Flowers can be single or double, in red, orange, salmon, pink, lavender or white, and there are several cultivars with variegated leaves.

ZONES 10–11

### *P. odoratissimum*

APPLE GERANIUM

A strong, pungent smell of apples comes off the small, roughly heart-shaped, lobed, gray-green leaves of this very bushy, many-branched geranium, which reaches a height and spread of 12 in (about 30 cm). The flowers it bears are small and white, sometimes with red veins in the upper petals. In warm temperatures flowers may be borne almost continuously, although it dislikes hot, humid conditions. Plant it in a well-drained, neutral to alkaline soil.

ZONES 10–11

*Pelargonium peltatum*

*Penstemon digitalis* 'Husker's Red'

*Peltiphyllum peltatum*

*Penstemon barbatus*

*Pelargonium* 'Orange Ricard'

*Penstemon* hybrid

*Pelargonium tomentosum*

### *P.* 'Orange Ricard'

Masses of large, semi-double coral flowers bloom on this variegated-leaved zonal geranium. It grows vigorously to 24 in (about 60 cm), spreading over half that.

ZONES 10–11

### *P. peltatum*

IVY-LEAVED GERANIUM

Originating in South Africa, this species has narrow trailing or climbing stems up to 3 ft (about 90 cm) long. Its bright green leaves have five sharp lobes and are up to 3 in (about 7.5 cm) across. The foliage is similar in appearance to ivy. Flowers can range from purplish red-pink to white and appear in spring and summer.

ZONES 10–11

### *P. tomentosum*

PEPPERMINT GERANIUM

A strong, refreshing smell of peppermint comes from the large-lobed, heart-shaped, grayish green velvety leaves on this sprawling geranium. It produces insignificant, purple-veined white flowers in clusters. Give it at least partial shade. The species climbs to 24 in (about 60 cm) and spreads widely or hangs. Limit its spread by pinching out the growing tips. Older plants present poorly.

ZONES 10–11

## *PELTIPHYLLUM*

### *peltatum*

UMBRELLA PLANT

A good plant for around ponds this perennial, indigenous to western North America, has lobed, peltate leaves (hence the species name, meaning shield shaped) that grow up to 24 in (about 60 cm) across. In spring it bears pale pink flowers, some forming into panicles, on hairy stems. Foliage growth follows flowering. It grows 4 ft (about 1.2 m) in height and half that in spread. Plant this species in moist soil in a sunny or shaded location. Propagate by division in spring. In full growth the umbrella plant is not easily contained.

ZONES 6–10

## *PENSTEMON*

BEARD-TONGUE

This large genus includes subshrubs, annuals and perennials, all of which do best in fertile, well-drained soil and full sun. Most of the species are native to North America, but hybrids are grown worldwide for their showy flower spikes in blues, reds, white and bicolors. Tall varieties suit sheltered borders; dwarf strains are bright in bedding schemes. Cut plants back hard after flowering. Propagate from seed in spring or fall, by division in spring, or from cuttings of non-flowering shoots in late summer. The genus comprises mainly evergreens and semi-evergreens. They are attractive to hummingbirds.

### *P. barbatus*

syn. *Chelone barbata*

BEARD-LIP PENSTEMON

The scarlet flowers on this perennial are tubular with two lips. They bloom on racemes from the middle of summer to early fall above narrow, lance-shaped, green leaves. The plant grows to 3 ft (about 90 cm) high, with a spread of 12 in (about 30 cm). Plant this semi-evergreen in well-drained soil in a sunny location. 'Prairie Fire' (scarlet) and 'Prairie Dusk' (purple) are two commonly available cultivars, each around 24 in (about 60 cm) tall. There are many other cultivars with varied flower colors, including pink, purple, white and orange.

ZONES 3–9

### *P. digitalis* 'Husker's Red'

This species is native to eastern North America and is usually seen with white or pale lavender flowers, neither particularly exciting. This cultivar, however, is notable for its deep reddish-purple foliage, which adds a strong color accent to the border. It is a robust plant, reaching a height of 30 in (76 cm) and spread of 24 in (about 60 cm). Give it good soil and regular water in a sunny situation. It is attractive to hummingbirds.

ZONES 3–9

### *P. heterophyllus* subsp. *purdyi*

FOOTHILL PENSTEMON

A good addition to rock gardens, this semi-evergreen shrub reaches 10 in (about 25 cm) in height and somewhat more in spread. In late spring through early summer blue, tube-shaped flowers bloom from short side shoots. Its lanceolate leaves are pale green. Used for ground cover, this North American native has been dubbed 'Blue Bedder' in some regions. Propagate from seed in spring or fall, or by division in spring.

ZONES 5–10

### P. hybrids

The many named hybrid penstemons are mostly derived from *P. hartwegii* and either *P. campanulatus* or *P. cobaea*. All tend to be more or less shrubby, evergreen, long flowering and make excellent plants for the middle or rear of the border. Among the hardier ones are 'Evelyn' (rose-pink) and 'Garnet' (wine-red); slightly more tender ones are 'Midnight' (deep purple) and 'Holly's White'. Removing flower stems after a flush of bloom will encourage more branching and more flowers.

ZONES 8–10

### P. pinifolius

This is a sprightly perennial best suited to a well-drained rock garden. A native of the Southwest of the United States, it loves heat and needs little in supplemental water beyond the normal rainfall. Flowers are typically two lipped and bright orange-red, and are produced for much of the summer. The leaves are needle like.

ZONES 7–10

## PEROVSKIA
## *atriplicifolia*

RUSSIAN SAGE

This tall, tough sub-shrub produces soft, gray-green foliage, beautifully complementing the haze of pale, lavender-blue flowers that appear on panicles in late summer and fall. Plants are upright to 5 ft (about 1.5 m), with a spread of 3 ft (about 90 cm) or more. Given full sun, a well-drained, not too rich soil and only moderate water, these plants will live for a long time. Cut to the ground in late fall. Divide in fall or early spring.

ZONES 5–10

## PETUNIA
## × *hybrida*

PETUNIA

*"Petun"* means "tobacco" in a South American Indian dialect and petunias are indeed relatives of the tobaccos *(Nicotiana)*, their leaves having a similar effect on humans. Always grown as annuals, these perennials like well-drained, fertile soil and a sunny location. They thrive where summers are hot, but need shelter from the wind. Available are hues of white, pale yellow, purple, red, blue and pink, as well as blends and mixtures of all these colors. Fairly fast growing, the branching plant has dark green elliptical leaves. Flowers of some of the larger Grandiflora hybrids are damaged by rain but others, mainly the Multiflora hybrids, are more resistant. Sow seed early in spring. Pinching back hard encourages branching. Give fertilizer every month only until the onset of hot weather. Cucumber mosaic and tomato spotted wilt can attack these species, which need regular deadheading. Petunias are some of the most popular flowers in the world, finding widespread use as bedding plants and in window boxes, hanging baskets or planters. Of the many types available the Grandifloras remain the most popular, due to their large flower size, although they are more susceptible to disfiguring botrytis; look for the Cascade (trailing) or Magic series. The Floribunda type is the most weather resistant and flowers very heavily; try the Madness series. The Multifloras have smaller flowers but make up for size with prolific flowering; the Plum series have delightfully veined flowers.

ZONES 4–11

## PHACELIA
## *campanularia*

CALIFORNIA BLUEBELL, DESERT BLUEBELL

True to its common name, the flowers on this fast-growing annual are blue and shaped like bells. Appearing in spring and early summer, the flowers are small, only 1 in (about 2.5 cm) across. The bushy, branching plant is delightful in a rock garden or border; it grows around 6–18 in (about 15–45 cm) tall with a 6 in (about 15 cm) spread. Its leaves are dark green and serrated. Plant in well-drained, fertile soil and full sun. Propagate from seed in spring or early fall.

ALL ZONES

*Petunia*, a double Multiflora

*Petunia*, a cascading Grandiflora

*Phacelia campanularia*

*Penstemon pinifolius*

*Penstemon heterophyllus* subsp. *purdyi*

*Perovskia atriplicifolia*

## PHLOMIS
### *russeliana*

A native of Syria, this easily grown plant thrives in any ordinary soil given a reasonable amount of sun. The large, heart-shaped, fresh green leaves make excellent ground cover, forming clumps around 12 in (about 30 cm) high and up to 24 in (about 60 cm) across. In summer it bears stout stems around 3 ft (about 90 cm) high topped with several whorls of hooded, butter-yellow flowers. Propagate by division in spring or from seed in fall.
ZONES 4–10

## PHLOX

These evergreen and semi-evergreen annuals and perennials, mostly native to North America, are grown for their profuse, fragrant flowers. The name phlox means "flame," an appropriate epithet for these brightly colored, showy flowers popular in bedding and border displays. Grow in fertile soil that drains well but remains moist. Choose a sunny or partially shaded location.

### *P. drummondii*
ANNUAL PHLOX

This annual grows fairly rapidly to a bushy 16 in (about 40 cm) in height, half that in spread. The species has a number of cultivars, including some dwarf strains which grow to 4 in (about 10 cm). *P. drummondii* bears closely clustered, small, flattish flowers with 5 petals in summer and fall in reds, pinks, purples and creams, and has lanceolate, light green leaves. It is resistant to frosts but not to droughts. Sow seed in spring.
ZONES 3–9

### *P. paniculata*
GARDEN PHLOX, SUMMER PHLOX

This tall perennial can grow to more than 3 ft (about 90 cm), although height varies a little among the many named varieties. In summer it bears long-lasting, terminal flowerheads comprising many small, 5-petaled flowers. Colors range through violet, red, salmon and white according to variety. Watch out for spider mites and powdery mildew. Propagate by division in fall or early spring. Give it mulch in winter.
ZONES 3–9

### *P. stolonifera*
CREEPING PHLOX

A native of the woodlands of southeastern North America, this delightful creeper makes an excellent ground cover in shaded situations. Low mats of deep green evergreen foliage increase by rhizomes. Spring flowers in pink, blue or white are held above the foliage on 12 in (about 30 cm) stems. It will tolerate sun in cool areas; otherwise it needs shade and a woodsy soil.
ZONES 3–9

### *P. subulata*
MOSS PHLOX

The flowers that bloom through spring in terminal masses on this prostrate perennial are mauve, pink, white and shaped like stars, the petals being notched and open. This evergreen species is suited to growing in rock gardens where it will get sun. Its fine-leaved foliage will grow carpet like to 4 in (about 10 cm) high with a spread twice that. Start in spring or summer using cuttings from non-flowering shoots.
ZONES 2–9

## PHORMIUM
NEW ZEALAND FLAX

Grown for the dramatic effect of their stiff, vertical leaves, often multicolored, these large, clumping plants are tough and adaptable. In summer they produce tall panicles of dull reddish or yellow flowers. *P. tenax* grows to 6 ft (about 1.8 m) tall, while *P. colensoi* about half that height. They make splendid container plants in colder climates, where they can be brought indoors for the winter, and are useful garden accents in milder regions of the country. They respond well to average soil and to generous watering, but adapt well to the summer droughts of the West Coast. Propagate from seed or by division in spring.

### *P. cookianum* 'Tricolor'
NEW ZEALAND FLAX

This handsome plant with bold spiky leaves is ideal for adding some foliage interest to the garden. It prefers full sun and a reasonably retentive yet well-drained soil. The erect, sword-like leaves, reaching around 4 ft (about 1.2 m) high in a clump 18 in (about 45 cm) across, are prettily striped with red, yellow and green. Propagate by division in spring. Frost damage can be a problem in colder areas, in which case the plant can be grown in a large container and overwintered in an unheated greenhouse.
ZONES 8–10

### *P.* hybrids

These hybrids of *P. tenax* and *P. colensoi* are the most varied in foliage color, and are often of more compact growth habit than their parents. Foliage color varies from bronze or purplish to chartreuse to pink and salmon; the leaves may be variegated with vertical stripes of two or more colors. New cultivars are introduced from New Zealand each year; some have the unfortunate habit of reverting to a plain green foliage with age. Among the best are 'Bronze Baby' (reddish-brown to 3 ft/90 cm), 'Maori Chief' (green and rose-red stripes to 5 ft/1.5 m), 'Surfer' (olive green with burgundy margins to 24 in/60 cm) and 'Tom Thumb' (green with bronze margins to 24 in/60 cm).
ZONES 8–11

*Phlox subulata*

*Phlomis russeliana*

*Phlox paniculata*

*Phlox drummondii*

*Phlox stolonifera*

*Phormium tenax*

*Polemonium caeruleum*

*Polygonatum* x *hybridum*

*Polygonum affine*

*Physostegia virginiana*

*P. tenax*

This is the largest of the New Zealand flaxes, with olive green leaves reaching 6–10 ft (about 1.8–3 m) in height and clumps 6 ft (about 1.8 m) across. They grow well by the sea, and can be used as a hedge or windbreak. 'Purpureum' has maroon foliage; 'Variegatum' is striped creamy yellow and white.
ZONES 8–11

## *PHYSOSTEGIA*
*virginiana*
OBEDIENT PLANT, FALSE DRAGONHEAD

If you move a flower on this herbaceous perennial it will not spring back into position but will obediently stay put, thanks to a stalk with a hinge-like structure. The showy flowers, which bloom in erect terminal spikes late in summer, are tubular, have two lips and are available in pale pink, magenta ('Vivid') or white. The leaves are lance shaped and serrated. Plant this species in sun in fertile soil that drains well but remains moist. Propagate by division in spring. This native of eastern and central North America will grow to 3 ft (about 90 cm) and make a striking display in a mixed border.
ZONES 3–10

## *PLATYCODON*
*grandiflorus*
BALLOON FLOWER

This perennial originates from Japan and China. In summer, balloon-like buds open out into 5-lobed flowers like bells, colored blue, purple, pink or white. The serrated, elliptical leaves with a silvery blue cast form in a neat clump up to 24 in (about 60 cm) high and half that in spread. Plant it in full sun in well-drained, sandy soil. Use rooted basal cuttings of non-flowering shoots to propagate in summer, sow seed in spring or fall, or divide clumps in spring.
ZONES 3–10

## *PLECTOSTACHYS*
*serphyllifolia*
**syn. *Helichrysum petiolare* 'Microphyllum'**

Resembling a miniature version of *Helichrysum petiolare*, this sprawling sub-shrub has felt-like stems and tiny leaves of silvery gray. Though the flowers are insignificant, the foliage and form provide an excellent addition to container and windowbox gardens in cold regions, or a year-round low mound of silver for mild gardens. They adapt to either full sun or part shade, but need a well-drained soil and only moderate amounts of water. Pinch growing tips to encourage branching. Propagate from cuttings in summer.
ZONES 9–11

## *PODOPHYLLUM*
*peltatum*
MAY APPLE

A popular eastern American wildflower, appearing before the leaves on deciduous forest trees. Deeply lobed, peltate leaves around 12 in (about 30 cm) tall shelter creamy white blossoms resembling single roses, almost hidden under the leaves. Edible yellow fruits follow. Deep, woodsy soil is preferred, with ample water in a lightly shaded position. It spreads rampantly to form a bold ground cover, so it is not for the small garden. Propagate by dividing the rhizomes in early spring.
ZONES 3–9

## *POLEMONIUM*
*caeruleum*
JACOB'S LADDER

Yellowy orange stamens provide a colorful contrast against the blue of this perennial's bell-shaped flowers when they open in summer. The flowers cluster above pinnately divided leaves resembling the rungs of a ladder, hence its common name. The plant grows in a clump to a height and spread of up to 24 in (about 60 cm) or more. The stem is hollow and upstanding. Grow this species in well-drained soil in sun or semi-shade. Propagate by division in early spring, from seed or by division in fall. A native of temperate Europe, it suits cooler climates.
ZONES 3–9

*Phormium tenax* 'Purpureum'

## *POLYGONATUM*
x *hybridum*
SOLOMON'S SEAL

The elegant Solomon's seal is native to temperate areas of the northern hemisphere. It does best in cool to cold areas where it will produce tubular, bell-shaped flowers in spring. A gently arching stem grows to around 3 ft (about 90 cm) with white, green-tipped flowers hanging from the underside at each leaf axil. The broadly oval leaves rise off the stem like sets of wings. Rhizomes should be planted in fall to winter in a moist, shady spot in well-drained soil.
ZONES 4–10

## *POLYGONUM*
*affine*
HIMALAYAN FLEECE-FLOWER

The green of this evergreen perennial's small, shiny, lance-like leaves becomes bronze in winter. It spreads 12 in (about 30 cm) or more, forming a mat to about the same height. The flowers it bears in dense spikes in late summer and fall are small, red and funnel shaped. Sunny or lightly shaded locations are fine for this plant; a moist but well-drained soil of average fertility is preferred. Use it in a rock garden or at the front of a border. Sow seed or propagate by division in spring or fall. The genus name means "many knees", referring to the plant's swollen nodes.
ZONES 3–9

*Plectostachys serphyllifolia*

*Podophyllum peltatum*

*Platycodon grandiflorus*

*Pontederia cordata*

*Potentilla nepalensis* 'Miss Willmott'

*Portulaca grandiflora*

*Pratia angulata*

## PONTEDERIA
*cordata*

PICKEREL WEED

This marginal water plant from North America grows to 30 in (about 76 cm) with an 18 in (about 45 cm) spread. Its tapered, heart-shaped leaves are dark green and shiny. Blooming in summer, the deciduous perennial produces intense blue flowers in dense, terminal spikes. Plant it in full sun in up to 10 in (about 25 cm) of water. Cull flowers as they fade. Sow seed or propagate by division in spring.
ZONES 3–11

## PORTULACA
*grandiflora*

MOSS ROSE

This annual, native to South America, grows quickly, attaining a height of up to 8 in (about 20 cm) and a spread of 12 in (about 30 cm). Its small, lance-shaped, fleshy leaves are bright green and its branching stems are prostrate. Its large, open flowers, which may be single or double, bloom in red, pink, yellow or white, in summer through early fall. This is a very good plant for hot, dry sites. Plant it as a summer ground cover in a rock garden or in containers in well-drained soil in full sun. The flowers close in dull conditions and overnight. Sow seed in spring. Watch out for aphids.
ZONES 4–10

## POTENTILLA

CINQUEFOIL

The flowers of this large genus of deciduous shrubs and perennials are small and rounded, growing in clusters. Although the species all thrive in full sun in temperate climates, cultivars producing pink, red and orange blooms will be better colored if protected from very strong sun. Tall species, and in particular the shrubs, are useful in borders, while dwarf potentillas have their place in rock gardens. Plant all in well-drained, enriched soil. The species is indigenous to the northern hemisphere, from temperate to arctic regions. Perennials are propagated by division in early spring or fall, or from seed in fall. Some species have been used medicinally.

### *P.* 'Gibson's Scarlet'

This red-flowered cinquefoil is one of a number of hybrids that are worthy additions to the summer garden. At 18 in (about 45 cm) tall and with somewhat floppy stems, it is best at the front of a border; it reaches a similar width. The foliage is a soft green, with each leaf divided into three leaflets.
ZONES 5–9

### *P. nepalensis*

NEPAL CINQUEFOIL

A profusion of flowers in shades of pink or apricot with cherry-red centers appears on the slim branching stems of this Himalayan perennial throughout summer. With bright green, strawberry-like leaves, this species reaches a height of 30 cm (about 12 in) or more and twice that in breadth. 'Miss Willmott' has a cherry-red, crimson-centered flower and is exceptionally floriferous.
ZONES 5–10

## PRATIA
*angulata*

This New Zealand creeper has $^1/_2$ in (about 1 cm) wide, nearly round, deep green leaves with roughly serrated edges. It forms a low carpet, flat to the ground, and makes a good small-scale ground cover if there is no foot traffic; it may also be used in the rock gartden. In spring white, starry flowers with purple veins appear in the leaf axils, followed in fall by globular, reddish purple fruits. This species will tolerate full sun and enjoys damp soil.
ZONES 7–11

## PRIMULA

PRIMROSE, PRIMULA

Fragrant, colorful flowers on stems above a rosette of basal leaves are characteristic of this genus, mostly from the temperate regions of the northern hemisphere. The flowers can be flat, trumpet shaped or bell shaped. Primulas like fertile, well-drained soil, partial shade and ample water. Propagate from seed in spring, early summer or fall, or by division or from root cuttings. Remove dead-heads and old foliage after blooming. There is a primula for virtually every position and purpose. Some alpine species are a challenge to grow and are best left to the specialists, while others are among the simplest of perennials for the garden. All are perennial, though some are treated as annuals.

## *P. denticulata*

DRUMSTICK PRIMULA

The species name of this Himalayan native refers to the toothed profile of the leaves, which are mid-green and broadly lanceolate. A neat and vigorous grower, it reaches a height and spread of 12 in (about 30 cm). It blooms in early to mid-spring, when open flowers of pink, purple or lilac with yellow centers crowd in rounded terminal clusters atop thick hairy stems.

ZONES 3–9

## *P. florindae*

TIBETAN PRIMROSE

Growing 24–36 in (about 60–90 cm) high, this perennial blooms in spring. The flowers—up to 60 of them to an umbel—are bright yellow and hang like little bells against a backdrop of broad, mid-green leaves with serrated edges. This species prefers very wet conditions, thriving at the edge of a pond or stream.

ZONES 6–10

## *P. japonica*

JAPANESE PRIMROSE

Forming a clump up to 24 in (about 60 cm) high and 20 in (about 50 cm) across, this native of Japan flowers in tiers on tall, sturdy stems like a candelabra in spring and early summer. Its flowers range in color through pinks, crimsons and purples to nearly pure white, usually with a distinct eye of another color. The leaves are elliptical, serrated and pale green. This species also does best in a moist situation.

ZONES 5–10

## *P. malacoides*

FAIRY PRIMROSE

Small, open flowers bloom in spiral masses on this perennial, which is usually grown as an annual for winter bloom in mild regions. It is a native of China. The single or double flowers range in color from white to pink to magenta. Its oval-shaped, light green leaves have a hairy texture, as does its erect stem. The species reaches a height and spread of 12 in (about 30 cm).

ZONES 8–11

*Primula vulgaris*

*Primula florindae*

## *P. obconica*

POISON PRIMULA

Dense flower clusters grow in an umbellate arrangement on hairy, erect stems on this perennial. A native of China, it grows to 12 in (about 30 cm) high and as much or more in spread. Flowering time is winter through spring. The yellow-eyed, flattish flowers, 1 in (about 2.5 cm) across, range in color from white through pink to purple. The light green, hairy leaves are elliptical; the hairs sometimes cause an irritation to the skin when touched. This is a popular container plant.

ZONES 8–11

## *P.* × *polyantha*

POLYANTHUS PRIMROSE

This perennial, sometimes grown as an annual, reaches 12 in (about 30 cm) in spread and height. Large, flat, scented flowers in every color but green bloom on dense umbels in winter through spring. Polyanthus are cultivars derived from *P. vulgaris* crossed with the cowslip (*P. veris*) and have been grown since the seventeenth century.

ZONES 3–10

*Primula malacoides*

## *P. viallii*

This 24 in (about 60 cm) tall perennial species from Yunnan Province in China is remarkable for carrying its lilac flowers in dense spikes, quite unlike any other primula. The buds are crimson, giving the inflorescence a two-tone effect. Foliage is lush and bright green. A cool, moist climate is needed.

ZONES 5–10

## *P. vulgaris*

ENGLISH PRIMROSE, COMMON PRIMROSE

This is one of the most familiar wildflowers in Europe. It is low growing to around 6 in (about 15 cm) and produces a carpet of bright flowers in spring. The flattish flowers are pale yellow with dark eyes and bloom singly on hairy stems above rosettes of crinkled, lance-shaped, serrated leaves. Both leaves and flowers are edible.

ZONES 5–9

*Primula obconica*

*Primula denticulata*

*Primula viallii*

*Primula japonica*

*Primula* × *polyantha*

*Pulsatilla vulgaris*

*Prunella grandiflora*

*Raoulia australis*

*Pulmonaria angustifolia*

*Ranunculus aconitifolius*

*Reseda odorata*

## *PRUNELLA grandiflora*

SELF-HEAL

Purple, two-lipped flowers grow in erect spikes above leafy mats in spring and summer on this semi-evergreen perennial. A native of Europe, it is good for ground cover or rock gardens, having a spread of 18–20 in (about 45–50 cm) and a height of 12 in (about 30 cm). Plant in moist, well-drained soil in a sunny location. Propagate by division in spring. Trim out old flower stems before they seed. The species is a member of the mint family, and was considered to be of medicinal value.

ZONES 4–10

## *PULMONARIA angustifolia*

BLUE LUNGWORT, COWSLIP LUNGWORT

Dark blue flowers, sometimes tinged pink, bloom through spring on this European perennial. The flowerheads have a 5-lobed tubular shape and are held above basal rosettes of mid-green foliage. The plant grows to a height and spread of 10–12 in (about 25–30 cm). Plant in moist, well-drained soil in shade. Propagate by division in spring or fall. Its close relative, the Bethlehem sage (*P. saccharata*), is very similar but its broad, lance-shaped leaves are usually speckled or streaked with silver and gray. It makes a handsome ground cover, bringing a little sparkle of light to a shady area.

ZONES 4–10

## *PULSATILLA vulgaris*

syn. ***Anemone pulsatilla***

PASQUE FLOWER

Nodding, 6-petaled flowers bloom in spring on this perennial from Europe. The yellow centers of the flowers are a stark color contrast to the petals, which can range through white, pink and red to purple. The finely divided leaves are pale green and are covered with silky hairs which glisten in the sunlight. Reaching 10 in (about 25 cm) in height and spread, the species is good in a sunny rock garden, in well-drained soil rich in humus. Avoid disturbing the roots. Sow seed when fresh or propagate using root cuttings in winter.

ZONES 4–9

## *RANUNCULUS*

BUTTERCUP

This is a genus of some 250 species, mostly annuals and perennials, grown for their colorful flowers. The name derives from the Latin for "frog", as some of the genus are aquatic plants (although these are not widely cultivated). Most species are tuberous and thrive in cool, moist conditions in sunny or shady locations. Sow seed when fresh or propagate by division in spring or fall. The genus includes some species that are common weeds.

### *R. aconitifolius*

FAIR MAIDS OF FRANCE

Cultivated to produce pure white, single or double flowers, this perennial flowers in terminal clusters on robust branched stems from spring to summer. Its dark green leaves have 3 or 5 lobes with saw edges. The plant grows to 24 in (about 60 cm) high over a slightly lesser spread and is native to southern and central Europe.

ZONES 5–9

### *R. gramineus*

With bluish green leaves like grass, this perennial has a compact spread and grows 20 in (about 50 cm) tall. It blooms in late spring and early summer, producing cupped yellow flowers. Plant it in rich soil.

ZONES 7–10

## *RAOULIA australis*

Suitable for rock gardens, this native of New Zealand lays down a solid carpet of silvery leaves $^1/_2$ in (about 1 cm) deep over a spread of 10 in (about 25 cm). In summer it produces miniscule flowerheads of fluffy yellow blooms. Plant this perennial in moist, well-drained, acidic soil that has been well composted. Give it an open, sunny location. Sow seed when fresh or propagate by division in spring.

ZONES 6–10

## *RESEDA odorata*

MIGNONETTE

A moderately fast-growing annual, renowned for the strong fragrance of its flowers. The conical heads of small greenish flowers with dark orange stamens are otherwise unspectacular. Flowering is in summer through early fall. Remove dead-heads to prolong flowering. Plant it in well-drained, fertile soil in sun or partial shade. Sow seed in spring or fall. It will grow to 24 in (about 60 cm) high and about half that in spread.

ALL ZONES

*Rheum palmatum* 'Atrosanguineum'

*Rodgersia aesculifolia*

## *RHEUM*

### *palmatum* 'Atrosanguineum'

A cousin of the rhubarb we eat, this perennial bears panicles of small, bright red flowers that open in early summer. It has deep green leaves with decoratively cut edges, and reaches up to 6 ft (about 1.8 m) or more in height and 4-6 ft (about 1.2-1.8 m) in spread. Grow in deep, rich soil that drains well but retains moisture. Give it a sunny or partially shaded location. Propagate from seed or by division in spring or fall.

ZONES 5–9

## *RHODOCHITON*

### *atrosanguineum*

**syn. *R. volubile***

PURPLE BELLS

A native of Mexico, this evergreen leaf-stalk climber is mostly grown as an annual. The flowers it bears in late spring through late fall comprise a long, finger-like, dark purple corolla protruding from a bell-shaped calyx in a redder hue of purple. Its leaves are ovate to heart shaped with sparsely spiky edges. The plant is good for ground cover or for planting on trellises or fences, where it will grow to 9 ft (about 2.7 m). It thrives in sun and well-drained soil. Propagate from seed early in spring.

ZONES 9–11

## *RICINUS*

### *communis*

CASTOR BEAN

The purgative of universal renown comes from the seeds of this species, native to Asia. The evergreen shrub, which is alone in its genus, is mostly grown as an annual. Rounded, prickly seed pods appear following the summer display of woolly clusters of red and greenish flowers. The plant's leaves are large, glossy and deeply divided into elliptical lobes; the leaves are often red or bronze in color. It grows rapidly, reaching 6 ft (about 1.8 m) in height and spread. This drought-resistant species takes to most soils and likes a sunny, open location. Propagate from seed sown in spring after the danger of frost has passed. The seeds are deadly poisonous if eaten; touching the leaves may cause dermatitis for some individuals.

ZONES 4–10

*Ricinus communis*

## *RODGERSIA*

Native to China and Japan, these handsome, moisture-loving perennials are attractive both in foliage and flowers. However, they tend to be grown more for their bold, architectural leaves than for their plumes of fluffy flowers which are borne in mid- to late summer. The stems unfurl in mid-spring and spread out to form a fan of leaves on top of stout stems. Their liking for moist soil makes them excellent plants for marshy ground at the edge of a pond or in a bog garden in sun or part shade. They are best grown in a site sheltered from strong winds, which can damage the foliage. Propagate by division in spring or from seed in fall.

### *R. aesculifolia*

Large, lobed, bronze-tinted leaves are borne on hairy stalks, forming a clump around 24 in (about 60 cm) high and wide. The large, cone-shaped clusters of small, starry flowers are cream or pale pink, and are borne in mid- to late summer on stout stalks up to 4 ft (about 1.2 m).

ZONES 5–9

### *R. pinnata*

The bold, dark green leaves are arranged in pairs, above which are borne clusters of creamy pink flowers. The height and spread reach approximately 3 ft (about 90 cm).

ZONES 5–9

*Rodgersia pinnata*

*Rhodochiton atrosanguineum*

*Roscoea cauteloides*

*Rudbeckia fulgida* var. *sullivantii* 'Goldsturm'

*Rudbeckia hirta*

*Salpiglossis sinuata*

### *R. podophylla*

Suited to pond surrounds, this rhizomatous perennial has unusual leaves comprising 5 to 9 large leaflets with a touch of copper to their green color. Multi-branched panicles of star-shaped flowers bloom in mid-summer in a froth of cream. Plant in moist soil and protect from strong wind. Tolerates full shade, but is better in partial shade. This species grows to a height of 3–4 ft (about 90–120 cm) and a spread of 30 in (about 76 cm).

ZONES 5–9

*Rodgersia podophylla*

## *ROMNEYA coulteri*

MATILIJA POPPY

This summer-flowering, shrubby Californian perennial produces large, sweetly scented, poppy-like white flowers boldly accented by the gold of fluffy stamens. The silvery green leaves are deeply divided, their edges sparsely fringed with hairs. Sensitive to disturbance but a vigorous grower once established, this species forms a bush up to 8 ft (about 2.4 m) high, with a spread of 3 ft (about 90 cm). Grow it in well-drained soil in full sun; fully drought tolerant in the West, it adapts to moderate summer water elsewhere. In colder climates, protect the roots with mulch. It can be a rampant spreader, especially with summer water.

ZONES 7–11

## *ROSCOEA cauteloides*

Bearing a yellow flower similar to an orchid in summer, this tuberous perennial grows to 18 in (about 45 cm) with a 6 in (about 15 cm) spread. Glossy leaves are lance shaped, erect and wrap into a hollow, stem-like structure at their base. Grow this species in cool soil that is rich in humus. Keep the soil moist in summer. Choose a sunny or semi-shaded location. When it dies back, top dress with mature compost or leafmold. Propagate by division in spring or from seed in winter or fall.

ZONES 8–9

*Romneya coulteri*

## *RUDBECKIA*

CONEFLOWER

These North American annuals, biennials and perennials are popular for their bright, daisy-like flowers with a prominent dark-colored central cone (hence their common name). Plants range from 2–6 ft (about 60–180 cm) tall, depending on species, and spread up to 3 ft (about 90 cm) wide. The summer and fall blooms provide good cut flowers. Grow in moist soil in a sunny position. Start from cuttings in spring. Propagate from seed or by division in spring or fall.

### *R. fulgida* var. *sullivantii* 'Goldsturm'

This upstanding perennial bears flowerheads like daisies, orange-yellow with central black cones. Growing 24 in (about 60 cm) high with a spread of 12 in (about 30 cm) or more, the plant has narrow, lanceolate, green leaves. Sunny locations are preferred. It is very well suited to mass planting in meadow gardens.

ZONES 3–10

### *R. hirta*

BLACK-EYED SUSAN, GLORIOSA DAISY

The flowerheads on this branching annual are big, daisy like and bright yellow, with central cones of green or purple. Its leaves are mid-green and lance shaped. It reaches 1–3 ft (about 30–90 cm) tall, with a spread of 12 in (about 30 cm). Hybrid forms, called gloriosa daisies, have yellow, gold, red, mahogany and bicolored flowers up to 6 in (about 15 cm) in diameter. *R. hirta* is very easily grown.

ZONES 4–8

## *SALPIGLOSSIS sinuata*

PAINTED-TONGUE

Offering a variety of flower colors including red, orange, yellow, blue and purple, this species from Chile blooms from summer until frost. The 2 in (about 5 cm) wide, heavily veined flowers are like small flaring trumpets. The lanceolate leaves are light green. A fast grower, this branching annual reaches a height of 16–20 in (about 40–50 cm) and a spread of at least 16 in (about

*Salvia uliginosa*

40 cm). It is both frost and drought tender. Grow it in a rich, well-drained soil in a sunny location; do not over-water, and support weak stems. Watch out for aphids. Sow seed from early spring indoors; plant out after the danger of frost has passed.
ALL ZONES

## *SALVIA*

SAGE

This large and widely distributed genus of annual and perennial herbs and shrubs includes species whose leaves are used as edible herbs as well as for a host of folk remedies. The genus is named from the Latin "salvere," to be healthy. The leaves of most species are aromatic, and many produce decorative garden displays with spikes of small, thimble-shaped flowers with two lips. Establish these species in fertile, well-drained soil in a sunny location. Propagate annuals from seed and perennials by division in spring or from softwood cuttings in spring and summer.

### *S. azurea*

BLUE SAGE

Long spikes of clear blue flowers appear in late summer and fall on this eastern American native perennial. The narrow green leaves have a gray cast. Blue sage grows to around 6 ft (about 1.8 m) and usually needs staking. It prefers a poor, relatively dry soil but adapts well to increased moisture. Best in full sun.
ZONES 4–10

### *S. farinacea*

MEALY-CUP SAGE

This species is grown as an annual in regions that have cold winters and sometimes also in warmer climates. Growing to 24-36 in (about 60-90 cm), it bears its violet-blue flowers in slender spikes on white stems. 'Blue Bedder' is an improved cultivar; there are also white and purple cultivars available.
ZONES 8–11

### *S. splendens*

SCARLET SAGE

This native of Brazil, which is grown as an annual, produces stiff, terminal spikes of harsh scarlet flowers continuously from early summer to frost. The leaves are toothed ellipses on plants that grow to 30 in (about 76 cm) in height and spread to 12 in (about 30 cm) or more. Provide full sun, except in the hottest climates.
ZONES 5–10

*Salvia azurea*

### *S.* × *superba*

syn. *S. nemorosa*

Many slender, erect spikes of pinkish purple flowers appear through summer on well-branched perennial plants. It grows to around 3 ft (about 90 cm) high, with an 18 in (about 45 cm) spread.
ZONES 5–10

### *S. uliginosa*

Long racemes of blue flowers appear on this branching species in summer and fall, amid serrated, elliptical to lance-shaped leaves. It grows to 6 ft (about 1.8 m) with a spread of 18 in (about 45 cm). Its soil should be moist.
ZONES 7–10

## *SANGUISORBA canadensis*

BLOODROOT

A native of eastern North America, this vigorous perennial loves full sun and a moist soil. The handsome, pinnate leaves are fresh green and form a clump around 18 in (about 45 cm) wide, above which are borne masses of white, bottlebrush flowers in late summer. It grows to around 8 in (about 20 cm) in height. Propagate by division in spring or from seed in fall.
ZONES 3–9

*Salvia splendens*

*Salvia farinacea* 'Blue Bedder'

*Salvia* × *superba*

*Sanguisorba canadensis*

## *SANVITALIA procumbens*

CREEPING ZINNIA

A native of Central America, this summer-flowering annual produces masses of bright yellow flowerheads like 1 in (about 2.5 cm) daisies with black centers. It is a prostrate species with mid-green, ovate leaves, growing to 6 in (about 15 cm) high and spreading easily twice that. Grow it as ground cover or in a hanging basket in fertile, well-drained soil in a sunny position.

ALL ZONES

## *SAPONARIA ocymoides*

ROCK SOAPWORT

Ideal for banks, rock gardens or trailing over walls, this tough alpine perennial, a native of Europe, forms a thick carpet from which profuse terminal clusters of small, flattish flowers, colored pink to deep red, bloom in late spring and early summer. Grow in sun in sandy, well-drained soil. Propagate from softwood cuttings in early summer or seed in spring or fall. Its names refer to the juice of the plant's crushed leaves which can be used as a soap substitute.

ZONES 2–10

## *SARRACENIA flava*

YELLOW PITCHER PLANT

This insectivorous plant, native to North America, has cylindrical, yellowish green pitchers (modified leaves) marked in red and with a hooded top. The pitchers secrete nectar which, together with the bright colors of the plant, attract insects which become trapped and are absorbed into the plant. Strongly scented, yellow or greenish yellow flowers are borne on long stems in late spring to summer. During the growth period it requires wet conditions and in winter, when dormant, cool, moist conditions are preferred. Grow in full sun or part shade.

ZONES 7–9

## *SAXIFRAGA*

SAXIFRAGE

This genus comprises some 370 species of evergreens and semi-evergreens. Their natural territory includes temperate, alpine and sub-arctic regions but many garden hybrids have been cultivated, and they serve well in rock gardens, in edges and as ground cover. Generally they dislike a warm, humid climate and demand a gritty, well-drained soil with moderate water during dry periods. The flowers are mostly white, sometimes spotted with pink, but other colors are also available. Use rooted offsets for propagation in winter or seed in fall. The genus name combines the Latin roots for rock or stone and for "to break", suggestive of the plant's apparent ability to grow in cracks in rocks and break them apart with their sturdy roots.

### *S. caespitosa*

MOSSY SAXIFRAGE

The mossy saxifrages are among the easiest to grow, preferring light shade and a moist but well-drained soil. The leaves are deeply cut, giving an almost fringed effect. In spring the 3–4 in (about 7.5–10 cm) mounds are covered with small pink or white flowers.

ZONES 4–9

### *S. paniculata*

This summer-flowering evergreen perennial from central Europe bears terminal clusters of 5-petaled white flowers, often with spots of reddish purple, on erect stalks. The bluish green leaves form a rosette below the flower stems. The species grows to a height and spread of 8–10 in (about 20–25 cm).

ZONES 2–9

### *S. stolonifera*

**syn. *S. sarmentosa***

STRAWBERRY GERANIUM, MOTHER-OF-THOUSANDS

Geranium-like leaves are a feature of this perennial, which is a native of eastern Asia. The rounded, glossy leaves are olive green with silver veins, purplish pink on the under-

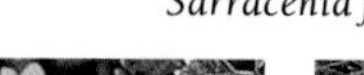

*Sarracenia flava*

*Sanvitalia procumbens*

*Saponaria ocymoides*

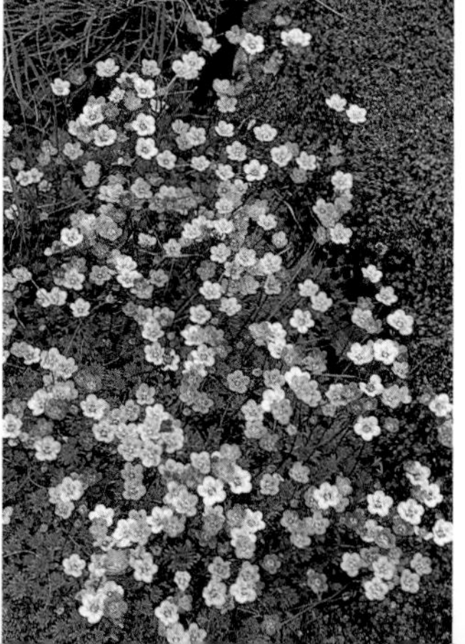

*Saxifraga caespitosa*

*Saxifraga paniculata*

*Scaevola aemula*

*Scaevola* 'Mauve Clusters'

*Scabiosa atropurpurea*

*Saxifraga stolonifera*

*Schizanthus pinnatus*

sides. In summer, curious white flowers are borne in delicate panicles on thin, erect stalks. Two petals on the tiny flowers seem to outgrow the 3 companion petals. This surprisingly hardy species makes a good ground cover or container plant both indoors and outdoors. It grows to a height of 6–8 in (about 15–20 cm) and spreads to 12 in (about 30 cm) by runners.
ZONES 6–11

## *SCABIOSA*

PINCUSHION FLOWER, SCABIOUS

This genus of annuals and perennials, found widely in temperate climates, produces long-stemmed flowers suitable for cutting or drying. Dome-shaped flowerheads contain numerous individual florets, each with protruding stamens, creating a pincushion effect. Flower colors range from white through pinks and reds to blue and purple. Most species will thrive in full sun in well-drained, alkaline soil. Propagate annuals from seed in spring; perennials from cuttings in summer, seed in fall, or by division in early spring.

### *S. atropurpurea*

PINCUSHION FLOWER, MOURNING BRIDE

This bushy annual produces flowers from summer through to early fall, provided blooms are cut or deadheaded. The dome-shaped flowerheads are some 2 in (about 5 cm) wide and are fragrant and mainly dark purple but also come in white, pink, crimson and blue. Sizes vary from 20 in (about 50 cm) for dwarf forms, up to 3 ft (about 90 cm) high for taller plants. This species has lobed, lance-like foliage.
ALL ZONES

### *S. caucasica*

PERENNIAL PINCUSHION FLOWER, SCABIOUS

Flat flowerheads in blue, pink or white with pincushion-like centers surrounded by longer-petaled florets make these summer-flowering perennials popular for borders and cut flowers. It has lobed, gray-green leaves for a 12–18 in (about 30–45 cm) wide basal rosette, with flower stems rising to 18–24 in (about 45–60 cm). Originally from the Caucasus, there are now a number of named selections available.
ZONES 3–10

## *SCAEVOLA*

FAN FLOWER

This genus of evergreen perennials and small shrubs is found in Australia and the islands of the Pacific. The flowers are 5 petaled, often split into a fan-shaped arrangement. Their colors range from white to blue and mauve. The plants are excellent as ground cover or in rockeries or hanging baskets. They like sun or partial shade and well-drained soil. Propagate from cuttings in spring and summer.

### *S. aemula*

FAIRY FAN FLOWER

The thick, coarsely toothed, dark green leaves on this perennial herb grow along spreading stems to form a mound 20 in (about 50 cm) high with a spread of 3 ft (about 90 cm). Open spikes of blue flowers with yellow throats appear in spring and summer. This species, native to the sandy coastal regions of Australia, resists drought and salt spray.
ZONES 9–11

### *S.* 'Mauve Clusters'

This spreading perennial flowers profusely in spring and summer. The small flowers present as mauve masses against a backdrop of bright green leaves. This cultivar spreads as much as 6 ft (about 1.8 m).
ZONES 9–11

## *SCHIZANTHUS*

### *pinnatus*

**syn. *S. wisetonensis***

POOR MAN'S ORCHID, BUTTERFLY FLOWER

These attractive plants, native to Chile, are grown for their exotic blooms and pale green, fern-like foliage. The orchid-like flowers come in a range of colors from white, pinks and mauves to scarlet and purple, all with speckled yellow throats. They need fertile, well-drained soil, partial shade, and protection against both frost and heat. They grow into a bush up to 18 in (about 45 cm) high and wide. They make excellent winter bedding plants in mild winter regions, or spring and early summer flowers elsewhere. Propagate from seed in late summer and fall. Encourage young plants into bushy growth by nipping off growing tips.
ALL ZONES

*Scabiosa caucasica*

# A Field Trip to Dochu La

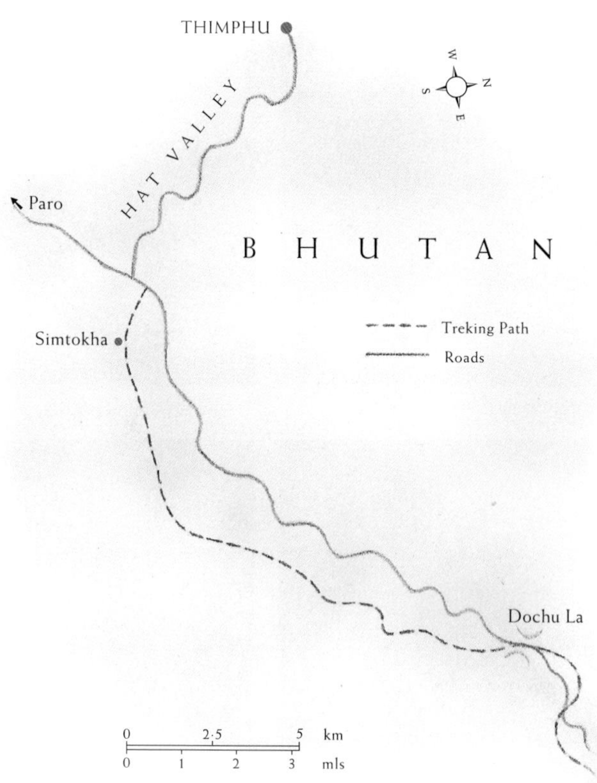


The flight to Bhutan from the cities of Calcutta and Delhi passes over a region of stark contrast. As your light aircraft crosses the flat expanse of the Bangladesh plains, which can be either dry and dusty or completely flooded, you will see far to the north the snow-covered peaks of the world's tallest mountains, hanging suspended above an ever-present haze. As your descent begins, you pass closely over a myriad of ridges and slopes still completely clothed in pristine forest. Soon you slip into the Paro valley and land at the airstrip which services Bhutan's capital, Thimphu, which has a population of 20000. Walk down the steps and treat yourself to the rarified Himalayan air, with spectacular scenery whichever way you look.

This was certainly not the way that plant collectors in the nineteenth and early twentieth century arrived in the kingdom, but Bhutan's diversity of plant species was a big enough incentive for them to endure the hardship of a long overland journey through India to reach these botanical crown jewels. Many of our most attractive garden plants originated in the forests of Bhutan, ranging from large-flowering *Magnolia* and *Rhododendron* species, shrubby *Pieris* and *Daphne* species, to *Impatiens* and *Primula*. Nowhere else in the world can you see as many species from the *Primula* genus. The best time to see *Primula denticulata* in Bhutan is April. Spring weather is often clear and cold at night but pleasantly warm during the day.

*A carpet of drumstick primulas at Dochu La.*

Bhutan is a small Bhuddist country to the east of the famous Indian districts of Darjeeling and Sikkim, with Tibet to the north. The interior is protected physically by ranges of forested hills and a scarcity of roads, while its culture is maintained intact by a monarchist government committed to conservation of the environment. Fortunately for both the visitor and the Bhutanese, its policy of sustainable tourism, designed to protect the country's fragile natural and cultural riches, allows only limited access.

Thimphu, the base for your field trip, lies 19 miles (about 30 km) to the east of the airstrip. The road from here climbs east out of the Thimphu valley and, after about 12–15 miles (about 20–25 km), reaches a pass called the Dochu La. Most visitors travel to the pass by taxi, coach or jeep, the hardy returning part of the way on foot. A trekking path winds downhill for about 9 miles (about 15 km), passing through open forest with clearings. The walk back to the road junction at Simtokha takes about four hours.

The view from Dochu La at 9100 ft (about 2800 m) allows a glimpse of distant snowy peaks, but the forests in the foreground are even more spectacular. The birches, oaks and firs always make an impressive combination, but in spring the gaze is really drawn to the multiple splashes of bright color. These include the intense red of the tree rhododendron (*Rhododendron arboreum*), the stark and beautiful candles of the

Campbell magnolia *(Magnolia campbellii)* on branches otherwise bare of leaves; and the bright pink *Rhododendron kisangi*, this last species only recognized as a separate species in the 1980s and named after the queen of Bhutan.

In clearings on the ground and along the sides of the path, the round pink heads of the drumstick primula or primrose *(Primula denticulata)* can be seen. Common throughout the mid-altitudinal range and the most easily seen member of its genus in the Himalayas, *P. denticulata* is particularly impressive, with tall, flowering stalks and large, round umbels of flowers—a growth form which gives the plant its colloquial name. The leaves form a compact rosette. At flowering time they are a fresh, pale green, often closely packed in the rosette and tending to curl downwards along the edges. After flowering the leaves become much larger, up to 12 in (about 30 cm) long. The flowers are usually pink or purple, the intensity of color varying considerably, although occasionally they can be white. Around Dochu La, drumstick primulas are mainly tall with purplish pink flowers. In other areas, where Bhutan's wild deer and yak or domestic flocks of sheep have been grazing, the stem may be very short and the flowers appear to sit down on the leaves.

In this area the drumstick primula can be found in shrubberies and on open slopes, but not in the shade of the forest interior. Like other primulas it grows close to water, often along the damp edges of paths. In the 1930s, the plant collector, Frank Kingdon Ward, said during one of his Himalayan expeditions: "Primulas have a strong social sense. They hate to be alone. On the other hand they loathe all but their own kind. Each primula species stands up for its own rights, but once security is attained, then it is primulas against the world; at least the alpine world."

The drumstick primula's natural range covers a wide diversity of habitat and climate. The species can withstand heavy frosts and in its highest Himalayan locations, up to 14 750 ft (about 4500 m), it will often spend some months under snow. In summer, its presence in open, rather than shaded, situations shows its ability to withstand long days of intense sunshine and heat.

In the Dochu La pass groups of tall pink drumstick primulas compete for your attention with the wildlife. Parties of small, brightly colored birds move through the trees and understory of bamboo and daphne—warbler-sized babblers and flycatchers, and the iridescent red and green sunbirds which perch among the rhododendrons to sip nectar. Overhead the occasional mountain hawk-eagle soars, and yellow-billed magpies flap across to their fir tree perches. It may be possible to glimpse muntjac deer or yellow-throated marten; these forests also hold small numbers of the elusive lesser, or red, panda.

Yet despite these distractions, a swathe of *P. denticulata* is spectacular enough to halt your progress. In this area particularly, the species grow in large concentrations, making the area flush with pink, with the whole scene framed by tall Himalayan firs and a glorious blue sky. It is a scene not easily forgotten, a reminder of the magnetic attraction which originally drew explorers to these mountains—and to their botanical treasures—a hundred years ago.

*Primula denticulata*

## Primula

Primulas, or primroses, are botanically members of the genus *Primula*, which consists of as many as 500 species. They are concentrated in temperate Asia, more particularly in China and the Himalayas; smaller numbers of species occur in other areas of the world. *Primula denticulata* occurs right throughout the Himalayas, from Afghanistan to southeastern Tibet and to Burma in the east. Its seed only reached England in the mid-nineteenth century. Some of the most popular English wildflowers are *Primula* species, namely the primrose, cowslip and oxlip (*P. vulgaris*, *P. veris* and *P. elatior* respectively).

Hardly any other genus offers such a treasury of perennials to the cool-climate gardener. With spikes of flowers in almost every color known in nature and often with two or more color zones in a flower, they attract the attention of enthusiasts and collectors. Their scale is generally small though there are a few that send up spikes 3 ft (about 1 m) in height. In warmer temperate climates a few species succeed, for instance fairy primula *(P. malacoides)*, which is usually treated as an annual, poison primula *(P. obconica)* and the more brilliantly colored polyanthuses, *(P. × polyantha)*, which are treated as spring annuals in warmer areas.

The Primulaceae family contains 20 or so genera, most of them confined to the northern hemisphere. Another well-known genus *(Cyclamen)* contains the tuberous cyclamens.

*Primula denticulata*

*Schizostylis coccinea* 'Grandiflora'

*Sempervivum arachnoideum*

*Sedum spurium*

*Sempervivum tectorum*

*Sedum spectabile*

*Sedum* 'Autumn Joy'

## *SCHIZOSTYLIS*

### *coccinea* 'Grandiflora'

KAFFIR LILY

Spikes of open, gladiolus-like flowers provide bright splashes of crimson against long, grassy foliage on this rhizomatous perennial, which blooms in fall. A South African native, it grows to a height of 16 in (about 40 cm) or more and a spread of about half that. It is a good source of cut flowers. Grow this species in moist, fertile soil and give it some shade only where exposed to hot weather. Water amply during summer. Propagate by division every three years in spring. There are white and pink cultivars, the best known being the pale pink 'Mrs Hegarty'.

ZONES 7–11

## *SEDUM*

STONECROP

There are about 600 species and eight groups in this genus, comprising annuals, biennials, perennials, shrubs and sub-shrubs, mostly succulents. They serve well along borders and in rock gardens. Common features are the small, overlapping leaves and the star-shaped flowers in flat heads. Their natural territory is wide: from the Far East and Europe to tropical mountain regions. Any soil is suitable, but they need sun. Propagate perennials from seed in spring or fall, or by division or from softwood cuttings in spring through mid-summer. Propagate annuals and biennials from seed sown under glass in early spring or outdoors in mid-spring.

### S. hybrids

An increasing number of very garden-worthy hybrid sedums are becoming available. Most include *S. spectabile* and *S. telephium*. All provide late summer or fall color for the border or rockery. 'Autumn Joy' (24–36 in/60–90 cm tall and wide) has bright salmon flowers that age to bronze, providing a long season of interest. 'Ruby Glow' is more compact (only 12 in/30 cm tall) with blue-gray leaves and ruby red flowers.

ZONES 4–10

### *S. spectabile*

SHOWY SEDUM

Spoon-shaped, fleshy, gray-green leaves grow in clusters on the branching, erect stems of this perennial. Butterflies flock to the flattish heads of little, pink, star-like flowers which bloom late in summer. This Asian native grows to a height and spread of 18 in (about 45 cm). 'Brilliant', 'Indian Chief' and 'Meteor' are selections with richer flower colors.

ZONES 4–10

### *S. spurium*

This summer-flowering, semi-evergreen perennial bears small blooms in big, rounded flower-heads; colors range from white to purple. Hairy stems carrying saw-edged, elliptical leaves spread widely into a carpet 4 in (about 10 cm) deep, suitable for covering banks and slopes. It is an easily cultivated, low-maintenance plant for a sunny position.'Dragon's Blood' is a rosy-red flowered, purple-leaved cultivar.

ZONES 4–10

## *SEMPERVIVUM*

HEN-AND-CHICKENS, HOUSELEEK

These evergreen perennials with distinctive small rosettes of fleshy, elliptical or strap-shaped leaves spread into a dense carpet, making good cover for walls, banks and rock gardens. Found in Europe, northern Africa and western Asia, their star-shaped flowers appear at the top of stems rising from the center of the oldest rosettes. Flowering does not begin for several years. A well-drained soil and sun are preferred. Propagate in summer from offsets left after the rosettes die following flowering.

### *S. arachnoideum*

COBWEB HOUSELEEK

The web of white hairs covering the green, triangular-leaved, 1 in (about 2.5 cm) wide rosettes of this species undoubtedly inspired its name. This evergreen produces pink to crimson flowers in loose terminal clusters on 12 in (about 30 cm) tall stems in summer.

ZONES 5–10

### *S. tectorum*

HEN-AND-CHICKENS, COMMON HOUSELEEK

The rosettes of this species are reddish tipped, sometimes red throughout. The flowers are a purple to rosy red and appear in one-sided terminal clusters on 12 in (about 30 cm) high stems in summer. The rosettes are 4–6 in (about 10-15 cm) wide. Applying bruised leaves to the skin has a cooling effect and is said to relieve burns, insect bites, skin problems and fever.

ZONES 5–10

## *SENECIO*
*cruentus*

CINERARIA

This species, which grows 12 in (about 30 cm) tall and as wide, is a multi-purpose bloomer for grouping or for formal bedding in semi-shaded spots, for windowboxes or for containers on balconies or in protected courtyards. The color of the daisy-like flowers ranges from pink, red, purple and crimson through to white, as well as the traditional blue. They are very heat and drought, salt air and poor soil tolerant, but they suffer from high humidity or excessive rain.

ZONES 8–11

## *SIDALCEA*
*malviflora* 'Rose Queen'

PRAIRIE MALLOW, MINIATURE HOLLYHOCK

The flower spikes borne in summer by this perennial resemble hollyhocks. The large, cupped flowers are dark pink, while the divided leaves form a basal clump with a spread of 24 in (about 60 cm). Overall height of this species is 4 ft (about 1.2 m) and tall plants may need staking. Establish in well-drained soil in sun. Propagate from seed or by division in spring or by division in fall.

ZONES 5–11

## *SILENE*

CAMPION, CATCHFLY

These annuals and perennials feature 5-petaled summer flowers, baggy calyces and a multitude of small, elliptical, often-silky leaves. Some of the species do well potted; others make good ground cover, with numerous stems forming a mound. Widely distributed throughout temperate and cold climates of the northern hemisphere, these evergreens like fertile, well-drained soil and full or partial sun. To propagate, use seed in spring or early fall or softwood cuttings in spring.

### *S. coeli-rosa*
syn. *Agrostemma coeli-rosa, Lychnis coeli-rosa*

This upstanding annual bears pinkish purple flowers with white centers in summer, or in winter-spring in mild regions. Its green leaves have a grayish cast. It grows rapidly to 20 in (about 50 cm), with a spread of 6 in (about 15 cm).

ALL ZONES

### *S. vulgaris* subsp. *maritima*
syn. *S. uniflora*

SEA CAMPION

This deep-rooted perennial bears a multitude of white flowers (sometimes double) on short-branched stems in spring or summer. Its calyces are greenish and balloon like; its lanceolate leaves have a grayish cast. Reaching around 8 in (about 20 cm) in height with a 15 in (about 38 cm) spread, it can be grown on top of walls or in beds or containers. Cut the stems occasionally to bring on new growth.

ZONES 4–10

## *SISYRINCHIUM*

These natives of North and South America are clump-forming perennials with long, slender leaves typical of the iris family. Establish them in moist soil that drains well. Although tolerant of semi-shade, they prefer sun. They readily self seed, or can be propagated by division in late summer. It is easy to mistake the narrow leaves of the seedlings for grass.

### *S. angustifolium*
syn. *S. graminoides*

BLUE-EYED GRASS

This semi-evergreen perennial blooms in spring, producing terminal clusters of small, pale blue to deep purple flowers like small, flat irises; they also have yellow throats, some yellow with darker veins. The stalks are flattened and winged. The plant grows to 12–18 in (about 30–45 cm). *S. bellum* is a western species with similar flowers.

ZONES 5–9

*Silene coeli-rosa*

*Silene vulgaris* subsp. *maritima*

*Sisyrinchium angustifolium*

*Sidalcea malviflora* 'Rose Queen'

*Senecio cruentus*

*Sisyrinchium striatum*

### *S. striatum*

Long, narrow and sword shaped, the leaves on this semi-evergreen perennial are gray-green. In summer it bears slender spikes of little cream flowers striped purple. The species, which originates in Chile, grows 18–24 in (about 45–60 cm) high, with a 12 in (about 30 cm) spread. There is also an attractive variegated form.

ZONES 7–11

## *SMILACINA*
### *racemosa*

FALSE SOLOMON'S SEAL, FALSE SPIKENARD

Red fleshy fruits appear on this perennial after it blooms in spring through mid-summer, producing lemon-scented white flowers in feathery sprays above fresh green, elliptical leaves. Growing to 3 ft (about 90 cm) high and a spread of about half that, this plant likes semi-shade and moist soil of acidic pH. It is a native of North America.

ZONES 3–9

*Soleirolia soleirolii*

*Solanum pseudocapsicum*

## *SOLANUM*
### *pseudocapsicum*

JERUSALEM CHERRY, WINTER CHERRY, CHRISTMAS CHERRY

The small, scarlet berries that appear on this species after flowering are poisonous to eat but are used as Christmas decorations in some northern hemisphere countries. The starry white flowers, precursors to the berries, bloom in summer. A native of the Mediterranean, this evergreen grows sedately into a bushy, velvety-leaved shrub around 4 ft (about 1.2 m) high and wide. It is perhaps best grown as an annual, even in wild areas, in which case it should grow to 26 in (about 66 cm) tall. Several varieties with differently colored fruit are available. The species is related to the potato, eggplant and tomato, as well as some less edible plants. The genus name refers to the narcotic qualities of some species. It is well suited to being an indoor plant.

ALL ZONES

## *SOLEIROLIA*
### *soleirolii*

syn. ***Helxine soleirolii***

BABY'S TEARS

Indigenous to the Mediterranean, this creeping, herbaceous perennial has small, round, bright green leaves and tiny, insignificant white flowers, which occur singly in the leaf axils. Grow in moist soil and shade. It makes an acceptable substitute for the traditional moss of a Japanese garden. Beware of using it between paving stones, as it is extremely slippery even when dry. It spreads widely and can be invasive unless contained; hanging baskets are ideal.

ZONES 9–11

## *SOLIDAGO*
### species and hybrids

GOLDENROD

The poor goldenrod has never achieved much garden status in North America, due in part to the assumption that it is a primary cause of hay fever. In fact it does not contribute to this allergy prob-

*Smilacina racemosa*

*Solidago* hybrid

lem at all, since its pollen is too heavy to float in the air. The current surge of interest in America's native plants will hopefully result in broader acceptance for these colorful perennials of the fields, prairies and mountains. Most are rhizomatous and can become invasive if allowed, but many new cultivars are more compact in their growth habit. Bright yellow is the standard color of goldenrod, with occasional diversions into cream. Growth is generally upright, with heights varying from 12 in (about 30 cm) to 4 ft (about 1.2 m) or more. Flowering occurs in late summer and fall, the tiny flowers clustered in large masses on racemes or panicles. They are easily grown in full sun, average soil and with moderate water. Divide in fall or spring. 'Golden Mosa' is a good, light yellow.

ZONES 4–10

## X *SOLIDASTER*

### *luteus*

**syn. x *S. hybridus, Aster luteus***

When this perennial's daisy-like flowers first open at their mid-summer blooming both their disc and rays are gold, although the rays quickly fade to creamy yellow. The flowers cluster in flattish heads, 4 in (about 10 cm) across, on downy stems branched near the top. The leaves are narrow and mid-green. It grows to 24 in (about 60 cm) high and spreads somewhat more than that. This species likes well-drained soil and full sun.

ZONES 4–10

## *STACHYS*

BETONY

This genus in the mint family has long been used in herb gardens, many of them having supposed medicinal value. Those listed here are fine perennials for the border, rockery or naturalistic landscape. Some betonies are more vaulable for their foliage, others for their flowers. All like a well-drained soil in full sun, with only moderate amounts of water. Divide in early spring.

x *Solidaster luteus*

### *S. byzantina*

**syn. *S. lanata, S. olympica***

LAMB'S-EARS

The leaves give this perennial its common name: shaped like a lamb's ear with the same white woolly feel—wonderful to touch. Unfortunately, the leaves turn to mush in very cold, humid or wet weather. Lamb's-ears makes a good ground cover or border plant, growing 12–20 in (about 30–50 cm) high, with a 24 in (about 60 cm) spread. Mauve-pink flowers appear in summer. 'Silver Carpet' seldom flowers, remaining more compact than the species. Establish in well-drained soil in full sun.

ZONES 5–10

### *S. coccinea*

SCARLET HEDGE NETTLE

A long-flowering perennial native to the Southwest United States and Mexico, bearing tubular, two-lipped, red flowers. The flowers are almost irresistible to hummingbirds. Flowering continues from spring through fall on plants that grows 12–36 in (about 30–90 cm) tall and as wide.

ZONES 5–11

## *STOKESIA*

### *laevis*

**syn. *S. cyanea***

STOKES' ASTER

This perennial from the southeast of North America has evergreen rosettes, its narrow leaves green, basal and divided. The summer-flowering, blue-mauve or white blooms have a shaggy appearance. The plants grow to a height of 12–24 in (about 30–60 cm) and a spread of 18 in (about 45 cm). Establish in well-drained soil in full sun. Propagate from seed or root cuttings.

ZONES 5–10

## *TAGETES*

MARIGOLD

These annuals are used in beds or for edgings. Plant seed in spring, after the danger of frost has passed. Give marigolds maximum sunlight, any well-drained soil and average moisture. To prolong flowering, dead-head regularly. Japanese beetles can be a problem; excess rain or humidity will rot the flowers. Dozens of seed strains are available for each species of marigold.

*Tagetes erecta*

### *T. erecta*

AFRICAN MARIGOLD

A strong aroma comes from the glossy, dark green leaves of this bushy annual from Mexico. It grows to around 2–4 ft (about 60–120 cm) tall with a spread of 18–24 in (about 45–60 cm). Very large double flowerheads in orange or yellow are produced from summer through the first heavy frost of fall. The flowers can be as much as 4 in (about 10 cm) across.

ALL ZONES

*Stokesia laevis*

*Stachys byzantina*

*Solidago* 'Golden Mosa'

### *T. patula*

FRENCH MARIGOLD

The double flowerheads produced in summer and early fall by this bushy annual resemble beefy carnations in hot reds, yellows, oranges and mahogany. Look for the Bonanza or Aurora series. The leaves are deep green and aromatic. This fast grower reaches 12 in (about 30 cm) in height and spread. This marigold was introduced to European gardens via the south of France—hence its common name.

ALL ZONES

### *T. tenuifolia*

SIGNET MARIGOLD

Much more delicate in its lacy foliage than other species, the signet marigold grows to a height and spread of only 8 in (about 20 cm), making it suitable for edgings and bedding. The flowers are smaller as well, to 1 in (about 2.5 cm) across, in either soft yellow or orange 'Tangerine Gem' has small, single, deep orange flowerheads.

ALL ZONES

## *TANACETUM*

TANSY

Immortality came to Ganymede as a result of drinking tansy, a species of this genus that is still considered of medicinal value. Confined mainly to the northern hemisphere, tansy are grown more for their finely cut foliage and daisy-like flowers. They are relatives of the chrysanthemum. The foliage of many of the perennials carries a strong fragrance. Grow them in sun in well-drained, dryish soil. Propagate by division in spring.

### *T. coccineum*

**syn. *Chrysanthemum coccineum, Pyrethrum roseum***

PAINTED DAISY, PYRETHRUM

The leaves are feathery and scented on this perennial. Its single, or sometimes double, flowerheads may be pink, red, purple or white, appearing from late spring to early summer. 'Brenda' is a striking magenta. The species grows 24 in (about 60 cm) high with a spread of 18 in (about 45 cm) or more.

ZONES 5–9

### *T. ptarmicifolium*

**syn. *Chrysanthemum coccineum, Cineraria candicans***

DUSTY MILLER, SILVER LACE

The dusty miller is a bushy perennial growing from a woody tap root to a height of 18 in (about 45 cm) or more and a spread of 15 in (about 38 cm). Its silvery, elliptical leaves are intricately cut, perfect for introducing a lacy texture in a perennial border. In summer it bears white flowerheads in terminal clusters; they are very useful in floral arrangements.

ZONES 9–10

## *THALIA*
## *dealbata*

WATER CANNA

This aquatic perennial from the southeast of North America tolerates cool water. Growing to 6 ft (about 1.8 m) in height and 24 in (about 60 cm) or more in spread, it carries blue-green leaves that are broadly elliptical to lanceolate with long stalks and a mealy whitish coating. Its stems are erect and unbranching. Its summer blooms are followed by decorative seed heads. The flowers, which occur in tall spikes, are violet and waxy, their six petals forming a tube. Establish this species in loamy soil in full sun under 6 in (about 15 cm) of water.

ZONES 9–10

## *THALICTRUM*

MEADOW RUE

Known for their fluffy, showy flowers, these perennials overall have a delicate presentation. The branches of their slender, upstanding stems hold leaves that are finely divided and columbine like. Blooming time is spring or summer, the flowers having four or five sepals and conspicuous tufts of stamens. They serve well in borders, particularly as contrast to perennials with bolder blooms and foliage, and in the margins of woodland gardens. Establish them in rich, damp soil with shade from the hot afternoon sun. Propagate from seed when fresh or by division in spring.

### *T. aquilegiifolium*

This spring-flowering perennial bears lilac or greenish white flowers in fluffy clusters on strong stems; the leaves are gray-green and delicate. Growing 3 ft (about 90 cm) high, the species has a spread of 18 in (about 45 cm).

ZONES 5–10

### *T. delavayi*

**syn. *T. dipterocarpum***

Rather than fluffy heads, this species bears a multitude of nodding, lilac flowers in loose panicles, their yellow stamens prominent. Flowering time is from the middle to the end of summer. Reaching 4–5 ft (about 1.2–1.5 m) high, this species has a spread of 24 in (about 60 cm).

ZONES 5–10

## *TIARELLA*
## *cordifolia*

FOAMFLOWER

This vigorous, spreading evergreen, a North American native, blooms

*Thalictrum aquilegiifolium*

*Thalia dealbata*

*Tanacetum coccineum*

*Tagetes tenuifolia* 'Tangerine Gem'

*Tagetes patula*

*Tanacetum ptarmicifolium*

*Thalictrum delavayi*

profusely in early to late spring, producing terminal spikes of tiny, pink-tinged white flowers with 5 petals. Its leaves are mostly pale green, lobed and toothed with dark red marbling and spots, although the basal leaves take on an orange-red hue. Its height and spread when in flower are 12 in (about 30 cm) or more. Establish in moist, well-composted soil in semi-shade. Propagate from seed or by division.
ZONES 3–9

## *TITHONIA*
### *rotundifolia* 'Torch'
MEXICAN SUNFLOWER

Flowerheads resembling bright orange or red daisies up to 3 in (about 7.5 cm) across appear on this slow-growing annual in summer and early fall. Growing to 4–6 ft (about 1.2–1.8 m) high with a spread of 24 in (about 60 cm), this species carries rounded, lobate leaves. Establish it in well-drained soil in full sun. Propagate from seed sown under glass in late winter or early spring.
ALL ZONES

## *TORENIA*
### *fournieri*
WISHBONE FLOWER

This branching annual from tropical Asia has light to dark green, ovate or elliptical leaves with toothed edges. Its flowers, borne in summer and early fall, are like small gloxinias, deep purplish-blue, turning abruptly paler nearer the center and with a touch of yellow. It grows fairly rapidly to a height of 12 in (about 30 cm) and a spread of 8 in (about 20 cm). Establish in rich, moist soil that drains well, in partial shade. Propagate from seed. Red, pink and white varieties are available.
ALL ZONES

## *TRADESCANTIA*
### *virginiana*
COMMON SPIDERWORT

A native of eastern North America, this perennial has dull green, strap-like leaves that grow to 12 in (about 30 cm) or more in length. It has an erect stem with spreading branches, and reaches a height of 18–24 in (about 45–60 cm) with a spread of 24 in (about 60 cm) or more. It bears small, 1–1 1/2 in (about 2.5–3.5 cm) wide, deep blue flowers with three petals in late spring to fall. This species is one parent of most of the named garden hybrids now available in white, pink, and purple as well as blue. Give it a protected location in average to poor soil; do not over-water or fertilize, which encourages rampant vegetative growth at the expense of the flowers. Propagate by division in early spring.
ZONES 5–10

## *TRILLIUM*
WAKE ROBIN

Among America's most beautiful wildflowers, trilliums are members of the lily family, having three simple petals held just above a whorl of three leaves. There are numerous species found in woodland habitats, flowering in spring before the deciduous leaves appear then remaining green until fall. They all prefer a moist, woodsy soil with ample water and shade from the hot afternoon sun. Slow to propagate from seed or by division, they are long lived once established.

### *T. chloropetalum*
GIANT TRILLIUM

A western species, the giant trillium is found from California to Washington in wooded or streamside situations. Growing up to 24 in (about 60 cm) tall, its flowers may be green, white, pink or maroon, with the three petals held upright. This species is more tolerant of dry shade than other species.
ZONES 6–9

### *T. grandiflorum*
SNOW TRILLIUM

This showy trillium is native to eastern American woodlands and is the easiest to grow, reaching 12–18 in (about 30–45 cm) in height. The pure white flowers fade to pink as they age. The double-flowered form is beautiful but rare. *T. ovatum* (the coast trillium) is very similar on the West Coast.
ZONES 3–9

## *TROLLIUS*
### *europaeus*
GLOBEFLOWER

The stem on this perennial from northern and central Europe is smooth, hollow and upstanding, branching at the apex. Its spring flowers are yellow and terminal, its 5 to 15 petal-like sepals forming a rounded shape 2 in (about 5 cm) across. Forming each mid-green leaf are 3 to 5 lobes arranged palmately, each lobe incised deeply. This species grows to a height of 24 in (about 60 cm) with an 18 in (about 45 cm) spread. Establish it in moist, rich soil in a protected location with some shade. Propagate from seed in spring or fall, or by division in spring or fall.
ZONES 3–10

*Tradescantia virginiana*

*Torenia fournieri*

*Trillium chloropetalum*

*Tiarella cordifolia*

*Trillium grandiflorum*

*Tithonia rotundifolia* 'Torch'

*Trollius europaeus*

*Tropaeolum majus* 'Alaska'

*Verbascum nigrum*

*Verbascum olympican*

## *TROPAEOLUM*

NASTURTIUM

Bright flowers are the attraction of this genus of annuals, perennials and twining climbers, whose natural territory extends from Chile to Mexico. Most species prefer moist, well-drained soil and a sunny or semi-shaded location. Propagate from seed, basal stem cuttings or tubers in spring. Watch out for aphids and the cabbage moth caterpillars.

### *T. majus*

GARDEN NASTURTIUM

The stem is trailing and climbing on this fast-growing, bushy annual. Its leaves are rounded with radial veins. It blooms in summer and fall, its large, 5-petaled flowers spurred, open and trumpet shaped in many shades of red or yellow. It will spread to 24 in (about 60 cm) or more, and will climb to 3–4 ft (about 90–120 cm). There are numerous seed strains with single or double flowers on either compact, bushy plants (12 in/30 cm tall and wide) or trailing and climbing plants. The Alaska strain has single flowers and prettily variegated leaves. Give nasturtiums average soil, full sun to part shade and moderate water; avoid fertilizing, which only encourages foliage at the expense of the flowers. The spicy-flavored leaves and flowers are used to accent salads.

ZONES 4–11

### *T. peregrinum*

**syn. *T. canariense***

CANARY CREEPER

This South American annual vine climbs to over 6 ft (about 1.8 m). Its gray-green leaves have 5 broad lobes and radial veins. In summer to early winter it bears small, trumpet-shaped, yellow flowers; the upper pair of its 5 petals are bigger and fringed. The stems are slender and trailing or climbing. It is adaptable to most acid soils in a protected, partially shaded position.

ZONES 4–11

*Veratrum nigrum*

*Tropaeolum peregrinum*

## X *VENIDIO-ARCTOTIS CULTIVARS*

MONARCH OF THE VELD

In summer, these branching perennials bear large flowers like daisies in numerous hues. Most commonly grown as annuals, the plants carry lobate green leaves that have a grayish cast on the upper side and are almost white beneath. They grow sedately to a height and spread of 20 in (about 50 cm). They are from a hybrid genus that enjoys well-drained, fertile soil and sun. The plants are best propagated in late summer using semi-ripe cuttings. In frosty climates they are grown as annuals.

ALL ZONES

## *VERATRUM*

### *nigrum*

BLACK FALSE HELLEBORE

This species is a rare perennial from southern Europe and Asia. It carries long, narrow, terminal spikes of small, purplish brown flowers with six petals that bloom in late summer. The big, pleated, elliptical leaves are arranged spirally into a sheath around the stout, erect stems. This species grows to a height of 6 ft (about 1.8 m) and a spread of about half that. Establish it in moist, rich soil in a protected location in sun or semi-shade.

x *Venidio-arctotis* cultivars

Propagate *V. nigrum* in early spring from seed or by division. *V. album,* with cream flowers, and *V. viride,* with pale green flowers, are very similar to this species. Protect all from snails. All species are poisonous.

ZONES 3–9

## *VERBASCUM*

MULLEIN

Large, basal rosettes develop on the biennial and perennial members of this European and Asian genus. Including both very large and some very coarse species, the genus offers much variety in the foliage, with leaves ranging from glossy to velvety. Summer flowering is mainly in the form of tall, narrow spikes. Establish all species in well-drained soil and an open, sunny location, though they do tolerate shade. Propagate from seed in spring or late summer or root cuttings in winter. Some species self seed readily.

### *V. nigrum*

DARK MULLEIN

Long spikes of yellow flowers with almost black centers appear on this native of Morocco in summer through fall. The species' mid-green leaves taper to a point and carry a dense layer of hairs. This semi-evergreen grows to a height of 3 ft (about 90 cm) and a spread of 18 in (about 45 cm).

ZONES 5–10

### *V. olympican*

Not a long-lasting species, this semi-evergreen perennial grows sedately up to $4^1/_2$ ft (about 1.3 m) with a spread of 24 in (about 60 cm). Its stems and leaves are hairy. The rosette-forming leaves are large, elliptical and silver-gray and spikes of 5-lobed yellow flowers appear in summer.

ZONES 6–10

## *VERBENA*

VERVAIN

Because of a susceptibility to powdery mildew, these biennials and perennials are considered best grown as annuals. Originating in the

Americas, they are characterized by small, dark, irregularly shaped and toothed leaves. The flowers are presented in short spikes over a long season from summer through fall; butterflies find some of them irresistible. Establish in medium, well-drained soil in sun or at most semi-shade. To propagate, use seed in fall or spring, stem cuttings in summer or fall, or division in late winter. You can also propagate in spring by division of young shoots. An agreeably spicy aroma is associated with most verbenas.

### *V. bonariensis*

This tall perennial is often grown as an annual, primarily for its deep purple flowers which top the sparsely foliaged 4–5 ft (about 1.2–1.5 m) stems. Deeply toothed leaves cluster in a mounded rosette, which easily fits in the front or middle of a border; the floral stems give a vertical line without much mass. It self seeds readily and survives with only minimal water, even in the dry west.

ZONES 7–10

### *V. canadensis*

ROSE VERBENA, CREEPING VERVAIN

This native of eastern North America is a trailing or sprawling, short-lived perennial quite easily grown as an annual. It grows to 18 in (about 45 cm) in height with a spread of 24 in (about 60 cm). Dark purplish pink flowers appear from summer through fall. 'Homestead Purple' is a sturdy cultivar with rich red-purple flowers.

ZONES 5–10

### *V.* × *hybrida*

GARDEN VERBENA

This tender, trailing perennial is usually grown as an annual. It bears slightly hairy leaves. It blooms in summer to fall, its fragrant flowers appearing in dense clusters 1 in (about 2.5 cm) across, many showing off white centers among the hues of red, mauve, violet, white and pink. Use this species in summer beds and containers. Avoid being heavy handed with fertilizers or the plants will yield more leaves than flowers. Where hardy, shear to the ground in late winter to encourage vigorous new growth.

ZONES 10–11

## *VERONICA*

SPEEDWELL

These perennials are widespread through temperate regions. Although their flowers are usually blue, they encompass a wide variety of foliage types and a range in height from a few inches to around 4 ft (about 1.2 m). Some are evergreens, some semi-evergreens. Establish them in rich, well-drained soil in full sun to light shade. To propagate, use seed in fall or spring, division in early spring or fall, or either softwood or semi-ripe cuttings in summer.

### *V. austriaca* subsp. *teucrium*

A spreading perennial forming a low mound of foliage around 18 in (about 45 cm) across from which rise the flower stems 12 in (about 30 cm) high, which comprise many tiny blooms in deep true blue. The flowers are borne in late summer. This plant prefers full sun and a well-drained soil.

ZONES 6–9

### *V. gentianoides*

This mat-forming plant has wide, dark green leaves from which rise stems of the palest blue, almost white flowers in late spring. They reach 18 in (about 45 cm) in height and spread.

ZONES 4–9

### *V. incana*

WOOLLY SPEEDWELL

Notable for its spreading clumps of silvery, woolly leaves, this speedwell grows 12–24 in (about 30–60 cm) tall and wide. The flowers are on typical spikes and are a deep violet blue. Though it does not flower as reliably as other species, the foliage is attractive enough. It will brighten the front of a terrace and is good also in borders and rock gardens. Several hybrid offspring are excellent garden plants, including 'Minuet' which is a soft pink.

ZONES 3–10

### *V. prostrata*

**syn. *V. rupestris***

This perennial from Europe has trailing stems and somewhat variable foliage. The flowers are small and blue, with widely flared petals, occurring in upright spikes in spring and early summer. This species spreads widely into a mat of indefinite coverage, however it only reaches 12 in (about 30 cm) in height.

ZONES 5–10

*Veronica gentianoides*

*Veronica prostrata*

*Veronica austriaca* subsp. *teucrium*

*Verbena canadensis*

*Veronica incana*

*Verbena bonariensis*

*Verbena* × *hybrida*

*Viola reichenbachiana*

*Veronica spicata*

*Vinca minor*

*Viola cornuta*

### *V. spicata*

SPIKE SPEEDWELL

A European species, this perennial reaches a height of 12–24 in (about 30–60 cm) and a spread of 12 in (about 30 cm). Its stems are erect, hairy and branching. Spikes of small, star-shaped, usually blue flowers appear in summer; named selections are available with pink or white flowers, although some of these may actually be hybrids. The leaves of this species are mid-green, linear to lanceolate in shape. Plant in full sun to light shade.

ZONES 3–10

## VINCA

PERIWINKLE

Shiny green leaves are common on these vining perennials and subshrubs from Russia and Europe. The flowers are widely flared with five lobes. Any soil is good provided it is not too dry. If ground cover is desired, provide these evergreens with shade to semi-shade. For flowers, let them have more sun. Propagate by division in fall through

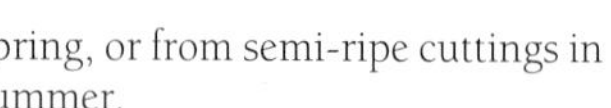

spring, or from semi-ripe cuttings in summer.

### *V. major*

LARGE PERIWINKLE

The leaves have a dark green gloss and are heart shaped to pointed ovate on this tenacious evergreen vine from the Mediterranean. Widely spreading and with an erect, woody stem, the species climbs to 12 in (about 30 cm) in height with a spread of 3 ft (about 90 cm). Brilliant blue flowers 2 in (about 5 cm) across are borne in early spring through early fall. It can be aggressive and invasive.

ZONES 7–10

### *V. minor*

COMMON PERIWINKLE

The slender woody stems on this European evergreen creeper will cover ground over a distance of 3 ft (about 90 cm) to lay down a mat of glossy, dark green leaves of pointed elliptical shape. They grow to a height of 6–12 in (about 15–30 cm) or more. The small flowers it produces in mid-spring through early summer are bluish lilac, purple or white. This species can also be aggressive and invasive.

ZONES 4–10

## VIOLA

VIOLET, PANSY

Although the sweet violet (*V. odorata*) gives one of the best loved of flower perfumes, many of the other species have little or no fragrance. Their leaves can be solitary or in clumps, lightly to heavily textured, kidney to heart shaped. The annuals are suited to summer bedding, although big beds of them are needed if you want sufficient yield to pick. The perennials are good in beds and rock gardens. Some species have runners and are invasive. Most species do best in average soil that drains well yet retains moisture, with some preferring an acidic pH. Most do best in light shade.

### *V. cornuta*

VIOLA, HORNED VIOLET

Originally a delicate, broad-faced violet with a short spur in the back,

*Vinca major*

this species has now been bred to the point that the modern viola looks like a simple version of the pansy, in a full range of solid colors. Short-lived perennials by nature, they are often grown as annuals for winter bedding in mild regions, or spring-summer bedding in areas of cool summers. Plants grow 6–12 in (about 15–30 cm) tall and wide. The flowers are 1 in (about 2.5 cm) across. Propagate from seed in spring or fall, or by division in late summer or fall.

ZONES 7–11

*Viola hederacea*

*Viola* x *wittrockiana*

### *V. hederacea*

AUSTRALIAN VIOLET

The tiny, 5-petaled, scentless flowers that bloom on short stems on this creeping perennial from the southeast of Australia are lilac or white and solitary. They appear in spring, summer and fall. The plant's stems are prostrate, suckering and mat forming, spreading widely but reaching only 2 in (about 5 cm) in height. Its leaves are rounded and kidney shaped, deep green and with irregular edges. Partially shade this creeper, and give it regular water through dry periods. Propagate by division in spring or fall.

ZONES 8–11

### *V. odorata*

SWEET VIOLET

A sweet perfume wafts from the flowers on this spreading, rhizomatous perennial from Europe, which grows 6–10 in (about 15–25 cm) tall and 12 in (about 30 cm) wide. Its dark green leaves are a pointy kidney shape with shallow-toothed edges. Spurred, flat-faced flowers in violet, white or rose bloom from late winter through early spring. Boasting many cultivars, this species readily self seeds and can be propagated by division in fall. The plants like well-composted, moist soil and a protected location in semi-shade. It is a very vigorous plant that is very easy to grow.

ZONES 6–10

### *V. reichenbachiana*

WOOD VIOLET

This perennial bears small, flattish, pink, mauve or pale blue flowers in spring and summer. Its kidney-shaped leaves are green. Although an invasive species—spreading widely but growing to only 2 in (about 5 cm)—it can serve over banks ot in natural settings.

ZONES 8–10

### *V. riviniana* Purpurea group

A neat, clump-forming perennial with rounded, purple-green leaves and purple flowers borne on short stems in spring and early summer. The leaves are usually retained through the winter. This plant thrives in part or full shade, so it is good under larger plants or for a woodland garden. They reach 2–4 in (about 5–10 cm) in height, with a spread of 9 in (about 23 cm).

ZONES 5–10

### *V. sororia* 'Freckles'

A new introduction with attractive flowers that are white and heavily speckled with blue. The flowers are borne in late winter and spring; they are shown off well by the fresh green leaves. Height and spread reach 4–6 in (about 10–15 cm). Plant in light shade.

ZONES 4–10

### *V. tricolor*

JOHNNY-JUMP-UP, WILD PANSY

Originating in Europe and Asia, this perennial or annual produces neat flowers with appealing faces from spring to fall, displaying shades of yellow, blue, violet and white. Although the flowers are only small, there will always be plenty of them. It has soft, angular, branching stems and lobed ovate to lanceolate leaves, and grows to a height and spread of 12 in (about 30 cm). It can take full sun or part shade, and readily self seeds.

ZONES 4–10

### *V.* x *wittrockiana*

PANSY

This group of predominantly bushy perennials are almost always grown as biennials or annuals. Offering flowers of a great many hues, the species bloom through the winter in mild regions and from spring into early summer elsewhere, possibly through the summer in cool areas. The flowers grow up to 3 in (about 7.5 cm) across and have 5 petals creating a flat "face" with the patterns of color and venation; violas, by contrast, have solid colors although recent hybrids have begun to erase the distinctions. Its mid-green leaves are elliptical, sometimes with toothed margins. Sedate growers, these plants reach around 8 in (about 20 cm) in spread and height.

ZONES 4–10

*Viola odorata*

*Viola tricolor*

## *XERANTHEMUM*
### *annum*

IMMORTELLE

A good source of dried flowers, this annual blooms in summer, producing heads of purple, daisy-like flowers; whites, pinks and mauves and doubles are also available. The leaves are silvery and lanceolate on this species, which grows 24 in (about 60 cm) high with a 20 in (about 50 cm) spread. Grow in well-drained soil and full sun.
ALL ZONES

## *YUCCA*

YUCCA

Huge clumps—in some species reaching to 40 ft (about 12 m)—are formed by the spear-like leaves of these evergreen plants from North and Central America. Yuccas carry showy clusters of flowers, mostly white, at the end of stalks which can measure 9 ft (about 2.7 m) or more. They need well-drained soil and full sun. If grown in containers do not over-water and ease off even more outside the growth season. Propagate from seed or root cuttings or by division in spring. Although not all are desert species, the yuccas are drought resistant. They are also resistant to frost.

### *Y. filamentosa*

ADAM'S NEEDLE

Like 3 ft (about 90 cm) long green spears, the leaves on this evergreen plant form a basal rosette. The leaves are edged with white threads. The flowers that bloom in terminal spikes from the middle to the end of summer are white and bell shaped. This species is native to southeastern North America and grows to 6 ft (about 1.8 m) high with a 4 ft (about 1.2 m) spread; it is stemless.
ZONES 4–10

### *Y. gloriosa*

SPANISH DAGGER

The stout, erect stem on this evergreen plant has a tufted crown of stiff, spear-like leaves, which start out with a grayish cast but, as they mature, turn a deeper green. The white, bell-shaped flowers appear in long, terminal spikes in summer through fall. This native of southeastern North America reaches a height of 6–8 ft (about 1.8–2.4 m) and a spread of 3–4 ft (about 90–120 cm).
ZONES 7–10

### *Y. whipplei*

OUR LORD'S CANDLE

Distinct from the other species of yucca by its very narrow, gray-green leaves that form a nearly perfect sphere. Native to the coast of California and Baja, as well as the mountains of California, this species sends up a tall, flowering spike to 12 ft (about 3.6 m) that is densely covered with creamy white flowers, sometimes tinged with purple. It is extremely drought tolerant.
ZONES 8–10

## *ZANTEDESCHIA*

CALLA LILY, ARUM LILY

These tuberous perennials, indigenous to South Africa, are characterized by the classic calla shape comprising an enfolding spathe like a funnel with a central, finger-like spadix. The leaves are glossy green and arrow shaped. Mostly evergreen in warm climates, some die to the ground after flowering. Establish in well-drained soil, but provide plenty of water to maintain foliage. Some prefer shade, others partial shade. Propagate using offsets in winter.

### *Z. aethiopica*

COMMON CALLA, CALLA LILY

The large flowers that appear on this species in spring are white, the spadix yellow. Although normally deciduous, the perennial can stay evergreen if given enough moisture. It can be grown around pools in water 6–12 in (about 15–30 cm) deep. Growing 24–36 in (about 60–90 cm) high with a 12–20 in (about 30–50 in) spread, the plant produces many large, broad leaves.
ZONES 8-11

### *Z. rehmannii*

PINK CALLA

The spathe on this summer-flowering species is rosy purple with paler margins, enclosing a yellow spadix.

*Yucca whipplei*

*Zantedeschia aethiopica*

*Yucca gloriosa*

*Xeranthemum annum*

*Yucca filamentosa*

*Zinnia angustifolia*

Its lance-shaped leaves are glossy green, semi-erect and around 16 in (about 40 cm) long. It grows 16 in (about 40 cm) high with a spread of 12 in (about 30 cm). This species likes well-composted soil, a protected location and partial shade.
ZONES 8–11

## *ZAUSCHNERIA*
### *californica*
**syn. *Epilobium canum***
CALIFORNIA FUCHSIA

The common name refers both to the species' Californian origin and to its flowers, which bear a resemblance to those of fuchsia, in whose family *Zauschneria* is placed. These are bright red, appearing in terminal spikes on erect to prostrate stems in late summer and early fall. The evergreen shrublet has lance-like, 1 in (about 2.5 cm) long leaves, and grows to a height and spread of 20 in (about 50 cm). Give it light, well-drained soil and a sunny, open location. This species is only moderately frost tolerant but thrives on the annual summer drought in the West.
ZONES 8–10

## *ZINGIBER*
### *zerumbet*

A clump-forming ginger plant from India and Malaysia with narrow, 12 in (about 30 cm) long leaves. On separate, tall stems are overlapping cones of green bracts that age to red, surrounding white and gold flowers. Used to hot equatorial areas, it is frost tender to a minimum 64°F (about 18°C) and needs a humid atmosphere in part shade with plenty of water during the growth period. Plant in moist, humus-rich soil. Propagate by division of rhizomes in spring. The rhizomes, unlike the edible ginger of *Zingiber officinale,* are bitter to eat, but can be used in pot pourri.
ZONES 10–11

## *ZINNIA*
ZINNIA

The flowerheads on these annuals are like full, double dahlias. Establish them in fertile soil that drains well in a sunny position. They need frequent dead-heading. Sow seed under glass early in spring. Found through Mexico, Central and South America, this genus is an excellent source of cut flowers.

### *Z. angustifolia*
**syn. *Z. linearis***

This native of Central America grows hairy, green leaves of elliptical shape. Its abundant flowers are orange-yellow. The plant has a loose, mounding habit with matt green leaves. A fast-growing annual, it reaches a height and spread of 12–16 in (about 30–40 cm). There is a very pretty white form.
ALL ZONES

### *Z. elegans*
COMMON ZINNIA

This sturdy annual from Mexico is the best known of the zinnias, blooming from summer until a frost. It grows fairly rapidly to 24–30 in (about 60–76 cm), with a smaller spread. Its deep green leaves are lanceolate to ovate. Grow in average soil in an open, sunny location.
ALL ZONES

*Zinnia elegans*

### *Z. haageana*
**syn. *Z. mexicana***

The $2^1/_2$–3 in (about 6.5–7.5 cm) wide single or double flowers on this annual are yellow, orange and bronze. It flowers in summer and early fall. A fast grower, this Mexican species reaches 24 in (about 60 cm) in height with an 8 in (about 20 cm) spread, its stem erect and branching. Old Mexico and Persian Carpet are old but valuable seed strains offering a variety of colors.
ALL ZONES

*Zauschneria californica*

*Zinnia haageana* 'Old Mexico'

*Zingiber zerumbet*

*Zantedeschia rehmannii*

CHAPTER 3

# Shrubs

*No garden is complete without the cohesive atmosphere that shrubs supply. With their multi-stemmed growth they fill in the garden picture between the lower growing annuals and perennials and the taller growing background trees. They unite the house and garden, make wonderful barriers for both sight and sound and can be grouped with one another to form eye-catching displays of color almost all year round.*

Shrubs are generally classified as deciduous or evergreen, although in more temperate areas some fall between these two groups and are termed partly or semi-deciduous.

Evergreen shrubs provide the permanent structure of a garden so necessary in the overall landscape design, especially in winter when the deciduous types are dormant. In this regard they make excellent backgrounds for deciduous plants. Also, consider the advantage of permanent plant foliage against a plain house or fence wall or where a division of garden space is needed.

Deciduous shrubs can provide the contrast elements of garden design. Their ever-changing attributes give continued interest. In winter their bare branches can look magnificent against green backgrounds or a winter skyline, then plants such as the bright yellow forsythias and the flowering quinces in the pink shades tell us the cold is almost over. We can look forward to an unsurpassed parade of color through spring provided by a myriad of well-loved and proven shrubs. As summer progresses the shrub garden can form a dense, cool background highlighted by spectacular show stoppers like the tibouchinas, crepe myrtles and oleanders.

Keep this continuous color show in mind when designing and choosing the plants for the shrub garden as it is possible to have a plant in bloom almost year round.

## Color through Foliage

Color is not the sole domain of flowers in the shrub garden. There are many plants clothed with a fantastic display of colored leaves. Many of these make striking accents in an otherwise green shrubbery, indeed in tropical and humid subtropical areas plants such as acalyphas and crotons take the place of flowering plants and replace those that are traditionally used to provide autumn color in colder areas.

Shrubs with silver or gray foliage can be used to create wonderful landscapes and are often combined with white flowering plants to great effect. Also there are the variegated forms, some of which need to be planted where they are sheltered from drying winds and hot afternoon sun otherwise they tend to burn. On the other hand, gold-leafed plants and those with gold markings need to be planted in full sun to retain their color. The shade loving variegated forms of *Aucuba japonica* are the exceptions to this rule.

*Roses are perhaps the best loved of all flowers.*

Remember also to include in your list of essential shrubs those plants with berries which highlight the foliage and make marvellous displays indoors. Holly is one cold country favorite. Then, in warmer climates, the pigeon berry *(Duranta repens)* with its display of bright yellow berries can be a real eye stopper as can the showy ardisias with their long-lasting red or white berries providing added interest to a deeply shaded area.

## Scented Shrubs

Plants not only give visual pleasure; a fragrant shrub can provide a subtle sense of joy as its scented foliage, if brushed against, or its flowers release their distinctive perfume. Daphne, boronias, lavenders, rosemary, gardenias and the lilacs are all beautifully scented and well worth including on your shopping list. They are examples of the many plants which can be placed near an outdoor living area where their perfume can be appreciated as you sit at leisure. Others, such as the night scented *Cestrum nocturnum*, some may find overpowering on a summer's evening and are best positioned where you pass by, such as beside a front gate or entrance path.

## Accent Points

The dramatic statements that an accent plant can provide are sometimes overlooked. These shrubs, used sparingly, act as a focal point, drawing the eye through the landscape to another section of the garden.

They are choice plants, chosen for a particular growth pattern such as a weeping standard or for their arresting shapes like those of the *Acer palmatum* cultivars. Though usually more expensive, if well positioned they give a garden that individual look.

## Soil

Most shrubs will tolerate a wide range of soil types, as long as it is well drained and reasonably fertile, however there are a number of garden favorites which need to have an acidic soil. Soil is measured on a pH scale ranging from very acid (1) to very alkaline (14) and although soil solutions don't reach these extremes a plant is considered to be acid loving if it enjoys a pH level in the low 6 range. Three that immediately come to mind are camellias, azalias and rhododendrons but there are other shrubs which will thrive in similar conditions and help to give variety to a shrub border. Other shrubs to interplant with them include the heaths and ericas, magnolias, the American laurel *(Kalmia)* and the various species of *Pieris*. These plants thrive in soils that have had loads of compost, peat moss and organic mulches added to them.

*Most of the over 30 000 varieties of camellias are descended from* Camellia japonica.

## Planting

A shrub border is best planned wide enough to accommodate at least two shrubs in depth, with the taller, easy care evergreens at the back and the plants which require more attention, in the form of pruning, or which are to be grown for cutting, planted towards the front. Often there is room to interplant these with ground-hugging shrubs to act as a mulch, keeping both weeding and watering requirements to a minimum. And it makes sound gardening sense to plant out a complete bed at the one time—not only do some plants resent being disturbed, but the ability for shrubs to establish a good root system within a well-established border is very limited.

Prepare a garden bed a few weeks prior to planting, digging it over well and adding well-rotted compost or other decayed organic matter. This humus helps to break up heavy soils making it more porous and so more easily drained and provides light, sandy type soils with moisture-retentive materials.

## Pruning

Pruning is often unnecessary for shrubs, but some do require annual attention to ensure continued high quality blooms. These shrubs can be divided into two categories—those that produce flowers on new or the current season's wood and those that form the flower buds in the previous season. Flowers that appear on last season's canes include forsythia, weigela and kerria. These and similar shrubs do best if the flowering canes are cut well back once the flowers are finished to enable the developing new shoots ample room to develop.

When shrubs produce flowers on the current season's growth, the flowers usually appear towards the end of summer on spring growth. These are best pruned in late winter, or in colder areas once all possibility of frost is over. Shaping is the main requirement here, taking thin or dead wood back to the main trunk and shortening vigorous shoots. Plants in this category include the late summer flowering shrubs such as tibouchina, fuchsias and abutilon as well as hibiscus and luculia. Bearing this in mind, it is possible to choose plants for a garden shrubbery that require very little attention and still be assured of a colorful display that is as easy care as a garden can possibly be.

*Abelia* x *grandiflora*

*Abelia schumannii*

*Acacia greggii*

*Abutilon vitifolium*

*Abutilon* x *hybridum*

*Abutilon megapotamicum* 'Variegatum'

## ABELIA

Native to Japan, the Himalayas and India, these dense, low-branching evergreens are widely grown in temperate climates the world over. They flower in summer and fall, bearing pink or white flowers with reddish brown bracts. They prefer sun or part shade, flourishing in a well-watered garden yet tolerating drought easily in summer dry climates. In colder climates they will die to the ground each winter; give them shelter from a wall or other shrubs. Plant in early spring or fall. Thin out the oldest branches and trim lightly in winter or early spring. The fine growth that follows trimming makes it an excellent choice for an informal hedge. Propagate from cuttings in summer.

### *A.* x *grandiflora*

GLOSSY ABELIA

This, the best known of the group, is a hybrid of a number of Chinese species. It has oval, glossy, bronze-green foliage and fragrant, pink-tinged, white flowers which appear from mid-summer to mid-fall. When there is new foliage, or when the flowers have fallen leaving behind reddish brown bracts, the entire bush takes on a bronze tone. It grows to a height and spread of 6–9 ft (about 1.8–2.7 m).

ZONES 6–10

### *A. schumannii*

Also from China, Schumann's abelia has larger flowers which are a deeper mauve-pink than *A.* x *grandiflora*. Its yellow-blotched, pink-and-white, bell-shaped flowers appear from mid-summer and last until mid-fall. Its dense habit makes it a suitable choice for a hedge. It grows to a height and spread of $4^1/_2$ ft (about 1.3 m).

ZONES 6-10

## ABUTILON

FLOWERING MAPLE, CHINESE LANTERN

Grown for the beauty of their maple-like leaves as much as for their delightful, colorful, lantern-shaped flowers, these leggy evergreen or semi-evergreen shrubs are grown in glasshouses in cold climates and outdoors in mild winter regions. They prefer to be shaded from the hot afternoon sun and a rich, moist, fertile, well-drained soil. Improve the flower yield by regular pinching back to ensure branching and hence budding. Tie to a support if stems are weak. Raised from seed sown at any time, *Abutilon* will germinate within 3 weeks or less and should flower within 12 months. The varieties named below however will come true only from cuttings (take these from firm, new tips later in the season and struck with heat in a sand/peat mixture). Often raised as indoor plants, they bloom best when rootbound. Popular with white flies and aphids.

### *A.* x *hybridum*

These open, soft-wooded shrubs have green, maple-shaped leaves with a slightly furry texture. They bear bell-shaped flowers in shades of white, cream, pink, yellow, orange and red (often veined in contrasting tones) from spring to fall. In the growing season, young plants may need tip pruning to promote bushy growth. Mature specimens should have the previous season's stems cut back hard annually in early spring. In the ground it grows to a height of 8–10 ft (about 2.4–3 m). Propagate from softwood or semi-ripe cuttings from summer to winter. They do well in greenhouses in cold climates.

ZONES 9–11

### *A. megapotamicum*

TRAILING ABUTILON

One of the hardiest of the genus, this sprawling evergreen is a native of Brazil. It has long, slender branches and pendent, bell-shaped, yellow and red flowers appearing in spring to fall. These appear among oval, lightly serrated leaves; 'Variegatum' has leaves with splashes of yellow. Normally it is trained against a wall, but it may be used as a dense ground cover. Prefers part shade to full sun and a well-drained but moist soil. It grows to a height and spread of 9 ft (about 2.7 m).

ZONES 9–11

### *A. vitifolium*

syn. ***Corynabutilon vitifolium***

This tall, open, evergreen shrub, native to Chile, is prized for its masses of delicate, soft lilac to white flowers in summer. It does best in full sun or partial shade with fertile, well-drained soil; it needs high humidity in summer to perform well. Tip prune new growth to encourage bushiness. Water well during growth, less at other times. It reaches a height of 12–15 ft (about 3.5–4.5 m) and a spread of 9–10 ft (about 2.7–3 m). Propagate from semi-hardwood cuttings in summer.

ZONES 8–11

## ACACIA

MIMOSA, ACACIA, WATTLE

One thousand species of evergreen, semi-evergreen and deciduous trees and shrubs, found in Africa, North America and most predominantly Australia. They grow fast and are usually short lived. The flowering season is variable and brief, with a spectacular explosion of fragrant yellow that blows away to leave dry pea pods. The flowers are actually a mass of stamens and produce pollen in abundance—birds and bees love them. Instead of leaves, many species have phyllodes—flattened, leaf-like stalks—that serve the same function. The fruits are round or extended pods containing seeds that are exceptionally resilient—they may survive for up to 30 years. Light watering in dry seasons and light pruning after flowering will prolong life. They require well-drained soil and full sun to thrive. Propagate from seed or from cuttings. Acacias suffer from few pests or diseases.

### *A. boormanii*

syn. ***A. hunterana***

SNOWY RIVER WATTLE

This small, rounded, evergreen tree or shrub grows to a height and spread of 9–12 ft (about 2.7–3.5 m), producing bright yellow balls of flowers in spring. It produces narrow, dark green phyllodes and is best propagated from the suckers that appear around the main trunk.

ZONES 9–11

### *A. greggii*

CATCLAW ACACIA

A native of southwestern United States and northern Mexico, this deciduous shrub reaches 6–8 ft (about 1.8–2.4 m) in height and spread; with training and shaping it can become a small, picturesque tree suitable for patio gardens. Tiny, gray-green leaves appear in mid-spring, followed by fuzzy yellow catkins in late spring. The stems are covered with thorns, making the shrub useful as a barrier planting but making gardening around it a challenge. It loves the heat and is very drought tolerant once established.

ZONES 7–11

### *A. pravissima*

OVENS WATTLE

This arching, evergreen shrub grows to a height and spread of 18 ft (about 5.5 m); some nearly prostrate forms are available. Its phyllodes are triangular, spine tipped and dull green. Small heads of bright yellow flowers appear in late winter or early spring.

ZONES 9–11

### *A. redolens*

Though a large, mounding shrub in its native Australia, the form most common in southwestern US gardens is a prostrate, widely spreading shrub useful as a ground cover for large areas. It reaches 24 in (about 60 cm) in height but spreads to 12–15 ft (about 3.5–4.5 m) wide. Best in sun or dappled shade. It tolerates a range of soil types as well as drought. It carries gray-green leaves and yellow flowers like puffballs in spring.

ZONES 9–11

## *ACER*

MAPLE

Maples are native throughout the cooler regions of the northern hemisphere and have been grown all over the world for centuries. The shrubby maples originated in Japan, where their cultivation reached the level of an art form. These maples are grown for the delicate beauty of their deciduous foliage, although they do have small red flowers on drooping stems which are followed by pairs of winged seeds that twirl when they fall from the tree. They prefer cool, moist conditions and fertile, well-drained soil. They do best when protected from intense sunlight, otherwise the leaves may burn. They color beautifully in the fall—particularly if the soil is neutral or slightly acid. They are propagated from seed as soon as ripe, the seed usually requiring a period of cold to encourage sprouting; cultivars should be propagated by grafting or from rooting cuttings. Avoid pruning in spring as the sap will "bleed" excessively from the pruning cuts.

### *A. palmatum* 'Dissectum Atropurpureum'

RED LACELEAF JAPANESE MAPLE

This cultivar of the deciduous Japanese mountain maple has normally reddish purple leaves that turn brilliant red in fall. The flowers are small, also reddish to purple, and appear in spring. The plant has a broad, horizontal growth habit, spreading to 15 ft (about 4.5 m) or more, with an ultimate height in great age of 10–12 ft (about 3–3.5 m). It can only be propagated by grafting and is a slow grower. It prefers a sunny site with moist soil, but protect it from the intense heat of the afternoon sun.

ZONES 7–10

### *A. palmatum* 'Dissectum Viridis'

LACELEAF JAPANESE MAPLE

The green cut-leaf maple resembles the red, but it is slightly more able to withstand the sun.

ZONES 7–10

## *AESCULUS*

BUCKEYE

Though most species of *Aesculus* are fairly large trees, the two species listed below are large, deciduous shrubs native to southeastern North America. They form broad mounds of attractive, palmately divided leaves topped with panicles of small flowers. Typical buckeye fruits mature in fall, their smooth seeds encased in a tough, leathery husk. Both are good for the large shrub border or as screening, and add a distinctive foliage texture to the garden. Give them full sun to light shade, a well-drained soil and regular garden watering during dry periods. Propagate from seed sown as soon as ripe or from softwood cuttings in early summer.

### *A. parviflora*

BOTTLEBRUSH BUCKEYE

A mounding, deciduous shrub reaching 8–12 ft (about 2.4–3.5 m) in height and spread. White flowers appear on 6–12 in (about 15–30 cm) long panicles in mid-summer. It tolerates light shade well.

ZONES 5–9

### *A. pavia*

RED BUCKEYE

This species is also a mounding, deciduous shrub to 10–20 ft (about 3–6 m) tall and wide; it may become tree like to 30 ft (about 9 m). Red flowers on 6 in (about 15 cm) panicles appear in late spring. It has excellent dark green foliage.

ZONES 6–9

## *AGAPETES*

### *serpens*

**syn. *Pentapterygium serpens***

This arching climber is native to the Himalayas. It is a squat, semi-epiphytic shrub that sends out slender, arching branches from a tuberous rootstock. The evergreen leaves are red tinted on the upper side only. Bright red tubular flowers, hanging in loose pairs, appear in spring and summer. It grows to a height and spread of just under 6 ft (about 1.8 m). *A. serpens* prefers a well-drained, humus-rich soil (neutral to acid) and full light or part shade.

ZONES 9–11

*Acacia boormanii*

*Acacia pravissima*

*Aesculus parviflora*

*Acer p.* 'Dissectum Atropurpureum'

*Acer p.* 'Dissectum Viridis'

*Aesculus pavia*

*Agapetes serpens*

## *ALYOGYNE*

### *huegelii*

**syn. *Hibiscus huegelii***

BLUE HIBISCUS

This dense, semi-deciduous desert shrub blooms in late spring through fall, bearing lilac, hibiscus-like flowers. The leaves are lobed and slightly hairy with irregularly serrated margins. It prefers full sun and well-drained soil. It needs minimal watering once established, and grows to a height of 8 ft (about 2.4 m) and spread of 4–5 ft (about 1.2–1.5 m). Propagate from semi-hardwood cuttings in summer.

ZONES 9–11

## *AMELANCHIER*

### *alnifolia*

SASKATOON SERVICEBERRY

This shrubby species of serviceberry native to the northern Great Plains and the Rocky Mountains grows from 4–20 ft (about 1.2–6 m) tall. Roundish, deciduous leaves provide good fall color. The berries are edible and are sometimes cultivated for commercial fruit production. White spring flowers cover the branches as the leaves are just emerging. Deep bluish purple fruit ripen in mid-summer. It prefers a position in full sun.

ZONES 4–6

## *ANDROMEDA*

### *polifolia*

BOG ROSEMARY

A native of subarctic areas, this dainty, spreading evergreen grows best where summers are cool. It has glossy, mid-green leaves and produces pitcher-shaped clusters of pink flowers in spring and early summer. It prefers full sun or partial shade and a moist, humus-rich, acid soil—it thrives naturally in peat bogs. It grows to a height and spread of 24 in (about 60 cm). Propagate from seed or by division of root runners.

ZONES 2–8

## *ANISODONTEA*

### x *hypomandarum*

CAPE MALLOW

Small, upright, evergreen shrubs popular in the milder regions of the US for their nearly continuous production of 1 in (about 2.5 cm), pink, hibiscus-like flowers. They make good additions to the perennial border and are fast growing but not long lived. Give them full sun for maximum flowering and a well-drained soil; they require minimal watering once established.

ZONES 9–11

## *ARBUTUS*

### *unedo* 'Compacta'

A compact selection of the strawberry tree popular on the West Coast for its white, urn-shaped flowers and strawberry-like fruits, usually appearing simultaneously. This form grows to 8–10 ft (about 2.4–3 m) tall and 5–6 ft (about 1.5–1.8 m) wide; 'Elfin King' is even more compact. Give it full sun and well-drained soil, and little water once established.

ZONES 8–11

## *ARCTOSTAPHYLOS*

MANZANITA, BEARBERRY

The manzanitas are evergreen shrubs (occasionally small trees) in the rhododendron family found mostly in California and neighboring states; the bearberry (*A. uva-ursi*) is found around the world in northern latitudes. All have small, tough leaves, clusters of urn-shaped, white to pink flowers in winter or early spring, and fruits like tiny apples ("manzanita" means little apple in Spanish). The upright forms usually have attractive, mahogany-colored bark on picturesque trunks. All prefer a well-drained, slightly acid soil, full sun to light shade and relatively little water during the summer months. *A. uva-ursi* is the exception in being very hardy and tolerant of summer moisture with good drainage. Propagate from cuttings taken in the fall. These are excellent plants for the water-conserving garden in mild regions of the West Coast.

### *A. densiflora* 'Howard McMinn'

This dense, mounding shrub is among the most adaptable and widely planted of native Californian shrubs. Ultimately growing to around 5 ft (about 1.5 m) tall and slightly wider, it is extremely useful as an informal hedge or as an addition to the middle range of a shrub border. The flowers are produced in great quantity in late winter, and are followed by dull red fruits in summer. A handsome shrub for full sun or dappled shade.

ZONES 8–10

### *A.* 'Emerald Carpet'

A valuable ground-covering form of manzanita, thought to be a hybrid of two coastal Californian species. It tops out at a height of 12 in (about 30 cm) although it may spread 6 ft (about 1.8 m) or more. The foliage is dependably bright green, even in California's hot interior regions. Pale pink flowers are relatively inconspicuous. It prefers a little shade in hotter regions and full sun along the West Coast. It is excellent as a bank cover.

ZONES 8–10

### *A. hookeri*

MONTEREY MANZANITA

A low, mounding shrub with the leaves held vertically, this manzanita is native to the dunes and pine forests around Monterey Bay in coastal central California, Clusters of pale pink flowers are showy in late winter. It is good as a ground cover or for foreground planting in a shrub border. It will need a little shade in hot interior regions. The ultimate height varies from 18 in to 4 ft (about 45 cm to 1.2 m), with the spread often exceeding 6 ft (about 1.8 m). It is most commonly grown as one of several cultivars such as 'Monterey Carpet' (only 12 in/30 cm tall but spreading very wide), or 'Wayside' (4 ft/1.2 m tall by 8 ft/2.4 m wide).

ZONES 8–10

### *A. manzanita*

COMMON MANZANITA

A large shrub or small tree, the common manzanita is a characteristic plant of the chaparral commu-

*Arctostaphylos d.* 'Howard McMinn'

*Amelanchier alnifolia*

*Arctostaphylos manzanita*

*Arctostaphylos hookeri*

*Andromeda polifolia*

*Anisodontea* x *hypomandarum*

*Arbutus unedo* 'Compacta'

*Alyogyne huegelii*

*Arctostaphylos uva-ursi*

*Athanasia parviflora*

*Artemisia tridentata*

*Aronia arbutifolia* 'Brilliant'

*Atriplex lentiformis* subsp. *breweri*

*Aucuba japonica*

*Ardisia japonica*

*Azara microphylla*

nity that once covered much of the hillside regions of interior California. Reaching 20 ft (about 6 m) tall and 10 ft (about 3 m) or more in width, this evergreen has beautiful mahogany bark on its picturesque trunk and branches. The pinkish flowers are held in pendent clusters in late winter, and are followed by deep red fruits. It is very heat and drought tolerant.
ZONES 8–10

### *A. uva-ursi*
BEARBERRY, KINNIKINNICK

Native to coastal and subarctic areas around the northern hemisphere, this delightful, prostrate shrub is the hardiest of the manzanitas. Its bright red berries are popular with bears in the wild, hence the common name. It is less drought tolerant than the other species but is adaptable over a much wider range, including the mountains of the West, the West Coast, the Great Lakes and New England. An excellent ground cover in the wild garden or on coastal dunes. It is usually under 12 in (about 30 cm), although the spread may be 10 ft (about 3 m) or more.
ZONES 2–10

## *ARDISIA*
### *japonica*
MARLBERRY

A low, evergreen shrub that spreads underground to create an attractive ground cover for shaded gardens in the Southeast. The upright stems are only 8–12 in (about 20–30 cm) tall, although the plant spreads widely. Small, white flowers are produced at the tips of the stems in fall; these are followed by red fruits that remain colorful in winter. Good for shaded areas with steady moisture and slightly acidic, loamy soils.
ZONES 8–9

## *ARONIA*
### *arbutifolia*
CHOKEBERRY

A native of eastern North America, this deciduous shrub is a common understorey plant in moist woodlands. White flowers in spring become bright red berries in fall and early winter, popular with birds. The shrubs are usually under 6 ft (about 1.8 m) tall, with many vertical stems rising from spreading clumps. Narrow, oval leaves turn bright red in the fall (best in the cultivar 'Brilliant', sometimes listed as 'Brilliantissima'). It will thrive in average garden conditions as well as in wet soils, and will tolerate full sun or part shade. Periodically cut the oldest stems to the ground to encourage vigorous new growth.
ZONES 4–9

## *ARTEMISIA*
### *tridentata*
syn. *Seriphidium tridentatum*
BIG SAGEBRUSH

This silvery shrub is one of the most characteristic plants of the mountains and basins of the West, ranging from eastern Colorado to the Sierra Nevada. The leaves have a pungent aroma; flowers are not showy. Height varies from 18 in (about 45 cm) to over 10 ft (about 3 m). It is best in natural gardens of the West and needs full sun.
ZONES 4–9

## *ASCLEPIAS*
### *subulata*
AJAMENTE, BUSH MILKWEED

An important food source for the monarch butterflies in desert regions of the Southwest, this milkweed grows along desert washes where it sends up numerous 3–5 ft (about 90–150 cm) tall, pale green stems when there is moisture present. The stems are topped by clusters of curious yellowish flowers, which develop into characteristic milkweed pods filled with cottony seeds. A very drought tolerant plant for desert gardens.
ZONES 9–10

## *ATHANASIA*
### *parviflora*
syn. *Hymenolepis parviflora*

This spreading, slightly woody shrub comes from the southwestern corner of South Africa. It grows to $4^{1}/_{2}$ ft (about 1.3 m) high and bears small, golden-yellow flowers on large, flattened heads in early summer. The leaves are needle like and finely divided. Plant in rich, well-drained soil in full sun.
ZONES 9–10

## *ATRIPLEX*
### *lentiformis* subsp. *breweri*
BREWER'S SALTBUSH

A tough, gray-leaved shrub for the hot, dry regions of the Southwest where it is native. Growing to 6–8 ft (about 1.8–2.4 m) in height and width, this makes a very serviceable shrub for screen planting, for informal hedges or for natural gardens. The flowers and fruits are insignificant, although both are attractive to birds. It takes heat, full sun, drought and even the highly alkaline soils of the arid West.
ZONES 8–10

## *AUCUBA*
### *japonica*
JAPANESE AUCUBA

Thriving in shade while producing colorful fruits under a dense cover, this cool-climate mountain native of Japan grows in all but the most barren of soils. A bushy evergreen, it has stout, green shoots and glossy, dark green, oval leaves heavily splashed or edged with gold in selected cultivars. Small, purple, star-shaped flowers appear in mid-spring. Red, egg-shaped berries ripen in fall and last into winter, but only if at least one male plant is grown to every two females (the females are the ones that bear fruit). It grows to just under 9 ft (about 2.7 m) in height and spread. Propagate from semi-hardwood fall cuttings.
ZONES 7–10

## *AZARA*
### *microphylla*
BOXLEAF AZARA

This elegant, evergreen native of Chile has $^{1}/_{2}$ in (about 1 cm), deep green, oval leaves and in spring bears tiny, vanilla-scented, creamy yellow flowers with masses of stamens. It grows to a height and spread of 15 ft (about 4.5 m), thriving in sun or shade. It requires fertile, well-drained soil. Propagate from semi-ripe cuttings in summer.
ZONES 8–10

*Berberis thunbergii*

*Begonia fuchsioides*

*Berberis darwinii*

*Bauhinia galpinii*

*Banksia ericifolia*

*Baccharis pilularis*

## BACCHARIS *pilularis*

DWARF COYOTE BRUSH

A low, mounding shrub from coastal California, this evergreen has tiny, resinous leaves and stays under 24 in (about 60 cm) in height, spreading to 6 ft (about 1.8 m) or more. Flowers like tiny shaving brushes are produced in fall; male and female flowers are produced on different plants, the females developing cottony seed heads that can be messy. Male selections are usually planted, especially 'Twin Peaks' (15 in/38 cm tall and 6 ft/1.8 m wide). Though naturally dense, the habit is enhanced by a light annual shearing in late winter. Very tolerant of coastal conditions, where it thrives with no summer water. Inland, even in the high desert, it is a dependable ground cover requiring only occasional water through the summer. Excellent on banks in full sun. Good drainage is essential.

ZONES 8–10

## BAECKEA *virgata*

This dainty, woody evergreen, native to the east coast of Australia, is prized for its elegant profusion of tiny, white, tea-tree-like flowers, which appear in summer. It bears thin leaves up to 1/2 in (about 1 cm) long and prefers well-drained, moist soil and full sun or semi-shade conditions. It grows to a height of 12 ft (about 3.5 m) with a spread to 9 ft (about 2.7 m). Propagate either from young cuttings or ripe seeds, if they can be caught before dispersal.

ZONES 9–10

*Baeckea virgata*

## BANKSIA *ericifolia*

HEATH BANKSIA

Named after the botanist Sir Joseph Banks, who discovered this evergreen in 1770, banksias are found in every state of Australia, particularly in the southwestern regions. Though common in cut-flower nurseries in coastal California, few show up in gardens. Foliage and habit vary, but all species are characterized by colorful flowerheads, odd, woody follicle fruits and adaptation to harsh conditions. The slender, tubular flowers arranged in neat, parallel rows along a spike usually appear in spring. Containerized plants need moderate watering during growth periods, but little water at other times. Do not allow pot seedlings to become pot bound prior to planting. *B. ericifolia* is a freely branching shrub with fine, glossy foliage and an upright, copper to orange, bottlebrush spike around 4–10 in (about 10–25 cm) long. It flowers in fall through winter. This is one of the more adaptable of the banksias, but is still best suited to coastal gardens. It prefers well-drained and sandy soil (free of nitrates and phosphates) and grows best in full sun or part shade conditions, to around 12 ft (about 3.5 m) in height and spread. Propagate from seed in early spring or fall. Banksias are closely related to the genus *Protea*, found in South Africa, and scientists cite this as evidence that the continents were once joined as part of the supercontinent Gondwanaland.

ZONES 9–10

## BAUHINIA *galpinii*

RED BAUHINIA

The most spectacular shrub in the genus *Bauhinia*, this low-spreading bush (occasionally a climber) is native to Africa. It has two-lobed leaves and sweet smelling, bright red flowers—borne in small racemes—which appear in late summer and fall. It prefers light, fertile, well-drained soil and full sun and dislikes cold or salty wind. It grows to a height of 9 ft (about 2.7 m) with a spread to 6 ft (about 1.8 m). Prune after flowering and propagate from seed in spring.

ZONES 9–11

## BEGONIA *fuchsioides*

This evergreen, multi-stemmed begonia has dark green, oval, serrated leaves. Small, single, white flowers are borne in spring and fall. It grows to 3 ft (about 90 cm) tall with a 12 in (about 30 cm) spread. It prefers good light and moist but well-drained soil. Best propagated from soft tip cuttings or seed if available.

ZONES 9–10

## BERBERIS

BARBERRY

Species from this genus of evergreen, semi-evergreen and deciduous shrubs from Europe, Asia and the Americas are among the most popular for cool-climate gardens. The leaves are shiny and saw toothed, and the clusters of tiny, usually golden flowers are a delight, especially when offset against the red or purple foliage, which may change color in late summer or fall. They prefer sun or part shade in any but waterlogged soil. Smaller species are excellent in rockeries while taller species make good, dense hedges. Propagate from seed in fall.

### *B. darwinii*

DARWIN BARBERRY

This is a native of Chile and Argentina. It grows to a height and spread of 9 ft (about 2.7 m), producing an abundance of orange to yellow flowers among dark green leaves from mid- to late spring. Then blue-colored berries appear in turn. Water heavily only in dry seasons. Prune lightly to shape after flowering if desired, but be prepared to lose some berries. Propagate from semi-ripe cuttings in summer.

ZONES 7–10

### *B.* × *mentorensis*

MENTOR BARBERRY

An extremely tough shrub resulting from the cross of *B. julianae* with *B. thunbergii*, this species has a dense, upright habit with many vertical stems covered with spines. The attractive foliage turns bright red in fall in colder climates, but remains evergreen in mild winter regions. Flowers and fruit are less showy than in other barberries. This is grown most frequently as an impenetrable hedge in full sun.

ZONES 5–8

### *B. ottawensis* 'Superba'

**syn. *B. o.* 'Purpurea'**

Developed at the Ottawa Experimental Station in Canada, this deciduous shrub is grown for its attractive arching habit and dark maroon/purple leaves that turn to orange-scarlet and purple in fall. Small umbels of cup-shaped, red-tinged yellow flowers appear in late spring and are followed by glossy, bright scarlet berries. It reaches a height and spread of $7^{1}/_{2}$ ft (about 2.2 m).

ZONES 5–10

### *B. thunbergii*

JAPANESE BARBERRY

This is a deciduous species from Japan. Its pale to mid-green, oval leaves turn brilliant orange-red in fall. Small, red-tinged, pale yellow flowers erupt in mid-spring. Bright red, egg-shaped fruits follow. It grows to $4^{1}/_{2}$ ft (about 1.3 m) tall and 9 ft (about 2.7 m) wide. Numerous named selections are available, such as the dwarf 'Crimson Pygmy' (18 in/45 cm tall by 30 in/76 cm wide) with deep red-purple leaves; the old-fashioned red-leaved barberry 'Atropurpurea'; and the relatively new 'Rose Glow' with new foliage that is marbled pink and purplish bronze.

ZONES 4–10

## *BERLANDIA*
### *lyrata*

CHOCOLATE FLOWER

This tough plant is a native from the hills and flatlands of western Texas through New Mexico and Arizona to Mexico, and is usually found at elevations of 4000–5000 ft (about 1220–1525 m). It produces a 12 in (about 30 cm) mound of evergreen leaves topped by bright yellow, green-centered daisies from spring through fall. The flowers release an intoxicating aroma of chocolate. This is an excellent long-flowering shrub for the prairie states and the Southwest, in a mixed border or in a natural landscape. Full sun is necessary for maximum bloom; a well-drained soil is preferred. Propagate from seed or cuttings.

ZONES 6–9

## *BOUGAINVILLEA*
### species

Bougainvilleas are popular for their brilliant papery bracts, borne for a very long period and often overpowering the foliage. They are hardy only in the mildest regions of the US, although they are very popular as container plants for summer color and can be brought indoors in winter. Semi-evergreen or evergreen in warmer climates, they can be deciduous in cooler climates. As well as being good grown in containers and tubs, they can be trained into arches and standards or can even be used as hedges and ground covers. Root restriction encourages flowering; the plants need to be cut back after blooming. They require fertile, well-drained soil, full sun and plenty of water during summer. Propagate from semi-ripe cuttings in summer or from hardwood cuttings when dormant. 'Temple Fire' is a dense, shrubby form that reaches 6–10 ft (about 1.8–3 m) in height and has bronzy-red bracts.

ZONES 9–10

*Bougainvillea* 'Temple Fire'

## *BOUVARDIA*

These evergreens come from Mexico and Central America and are grown for the spectacular beauty of their flowers, which in some species are intensely fragrant. Bouvardias are untidy and require pruning after flowering to maintain shape—cut back stems half- to three-quarters. They prefer full light and fertile, well-drained soil. Water heavily in summer and add diluted liquid fertilizer when the shrub is flowering. Propagate in spring from softwood cuttings or root cuttings. Whitefly and mealy bug may present problems.

### *B.* hybrids

There are a number of hybrid bouvardias available, mainly derived from *B. longiflora*. They are spreading shrubs to about 3 ft (about 90 cm) tall, with clusters of flowers in shades from white to bright red; some, such as the pink 'President Garfield', have double flowers. They make excellent, long-blooming pot plants and used to be very popular conservatory plants. Scent is apt to be lacking.

ZONES 9–11

### *B. longiflora*

syn. *B. humboldtii*

This thin-stemmed, spreading evergreen is the only bouvardia that is truly fragrant. It bears exquisite white flowers, each with four tubular-shaped petals, in terminal clusters during fall and winter. It has small, lance-shaped leaves and grows to a height and spread of 3 ft (about 90 cm) or more. 'Albatross' is the most commonly grown, although the more compact 'Stephanie' flowers more dependably.

ZONES 9–11

## *BRACHYGLOTTIS*
### *greyi*

syn. *Senecio greyi*

This many-branched evergreen belongs to the same family (Asteraceae) as daisies—though its petite, bright yellow, daisy-like flowers which appear in summer and fall are less interesting than the leathery, green-gray leaves with gray, woolly undersides that give a silver edge to each leaf. It prefers full sun or part shade and well-drained soil. Plants in a pot should be watered freely in summer, otherwise moderately. It grows to a height and spread of 3 ft (about 90 cm). Prune regularly and pinch back occasionally to maintain a neat habit. Propagate from cuttings in late summer.

ZONES 8–10

*Berberis ottawensis* 'Superba'

*Brachyglottis greyi*

*Bouvardia longiflora*

*Bouvardia* hybrids

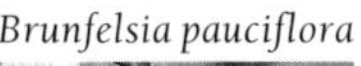

*Brugmansia sanguinea*

*Brugmansia suaveolens*

*Brunfelsia pauciflora*

*Brugmansia* × *candida*

*Brugmansia versicolor* 'Charles Grimaldi'

## *BRUGMANSIA*

ANGEL'S TRUMPET

These exotic-looking but robust, evergreen or semi-evergreen shrubs are native to the Andes mountains. They prefer full sun or half shade and fertile, well-drained soil. Propagate from seed in spring, or softwood or semi-ripe cuttings in summer. Adaptable to container culture in areas beyond their hardiness range; bring indoors in winter. Keep moist during the growing season and prune in early spring to maintain shape. Specimens in containers should be watered freely. Whitefly and spider mite may present problems. Like the wild Jimsonweed, to which they are related, all parts of the angel's trumpet are poisonous if eaten.

### *B.* × *candida*

**syn. *Datura candida***

This semi-evergreen shrub has a rounded habit, growing to 12 ft (about 3.5 m) in height with a spread of 9 ft (about 2.7 m). It is grown for its elegant, pendulous, greenish-tinted white (sometimes cream or pinkish) flowers which are extremely fragrant, especially at night. Flowers are borne from summer to fall. Leaves are oval shaped with a downy texture.

ZONES 7–10

### *B. sanguinea*

**syn. *Datura sanguinea***

RED ANGEL'S TRUMPET

This species grows cream and scarlet, trumpet-shaped flowers up to 8 in (about 20 cm) long, each with a spathe-like calyx, in summer to fall. It has oval leaves and grows to a height and spread of 12 ft (about 3.5 m).

ZONES 9–11

### *B. suaveolens*

**syn. *Datura suaveolens***

This round-headed tree or shrub produces thin, oval leaves to 12 in (about 30 cm) long and funnel-shaped, single or double, white flowers which appear in fall and winter. Green, egg-shaped berries follow. It grows to a height and spread of 6–12 ft (about 1.8–3.5 m).

ZONES 9–10

### *B. versicolor*

Similar to the other species, but with larger flowers that begin white then age to pink or apricot. Undoubtedly a parent of the pale butterscotch 'Charles Grimaldi' and the pale pink 'Frosty Pink', two of the most common cultivars available; both are extremely floriferous.

ZONES 9–10

## *BRUNFELSIA pauciflora*

YESTERDAY-TODAY-AND-TOMORROW

This stunning, rounded, evergreen shrub from South America is widely enjoyed for the varying displays of fragrant blue flowers on the one plant. In spring this tropical beauty produces rich, purple flowers which gradually fade to pale blue and then to white. The shrub has lance-shaped, glossy, leathery leaves and prefers full sun to part shade and fertile, humus-rich, well-drained soil. Water plants in containers only moderately. It grows to 6 ft (about 1.8 m) in height and spread. Propagate from summer cuttings. Mealy bug and whitefly may present problems.

ZONES 10–11

## *BUDDLEIA*

BUTTERFLY BUSH

The spicy, fragrant blooms of *Buddleia* attract butterflies from far and wide—hence the common name. Found in Asia, Africa and the Americas, there is little variation in the foliage between species—all have pointed, crepe-textured, large leaves although the bloom varies. The tubular florets may be arranged in whorls, globes, single spikes or branched racemes. Most do best in fertile, well-drained soil. Propagate these arching, deciduous shrubs and trees from semi-ripe cuttings in summer.

### *B. alternifolia*

FOUNTAIN BUTTERFLY BUSH

Forming a graceful mound, this deciduous shrub is distinct from the other species listed here in flower-

ing on wood produced the preceding year. Consequently, pruning should be done immediately after flowering in spring, cutting out the oldest stems to the ground to encourage vigorous new growth. Light purple, slightly fragrant flowers are produced in small clusters along the length of the arching stems. The leaves are smaller than on other species, and are alternate rather than opposite. Tolerant of poor soils, it prefers full sun and moderate amounts of water in summer.
ZONES 5-10

### *B. davidii*

BUTTERFLY BUSH, SUMMER LILAC

This deciduous or semi-evergreen, arching shrub is the most widely known. It has dark green, long, lance-shaped leaves with white-felted undersides. Small, honey-scented, purple, lilac or white flowers appear in long panicles in summer to fall. It grows to a height of 15 ft (about 4.5 m) and spread of 9 ft (about 2.7 m). For dense, shapely and floriferous plants, cut to the ground each spring before growth begins; all flowers are produced on wood from the current year.
ZONES 5–10

### *B. globosa*

This deciduous or semi-evergreen species from South America grows to a height and spread of 12 ft (about 3.5 m) and is valued for its fragrant, bright orange flowers in ball-like heads which appear in summer. Its leaves are long, dark green and wrinkled. It likes full sun and good drainage.
ZONES 7–10

## *BURSARIA*

### *spinosa*

BOX THORN

Sheep farmers hate this spiny, evergreen bush—they claim it is forever snagging the wool of passing sheep. However, the fragrance and charm of the tiny white flowers make it popular in gardens in California. In summer the flowers are massed in panicles toward the ends of the branches, after which attractive brown fruits appear. These contrast nicely with the small, shiny leaves, making the plant an attractive choice for flower arrangements. It is also excellent for hedging despite its thorns. It prefers full sun and well-drained soil. It grows to a height of 30 ft (about 9 m) and a spread of 18 ft (about 5.5 m). Propagate from seed or semi-ripe cuttings.
ZONES 8–10

## *BUXUS*

BOXWOOD, BOX

These densely foliaged evergreen shrubs are native to Mediterranean Europe, Japan and Central America. The flowers are insignificant but the foliage is ideal for hedging, edging and topiary; the plants have been used in this way for centuries. They thrive in sun or semi-shade and any soil that is not waterlogged. They are best set out (use semi-ripe cuttings) in early spring or late summer, watered regularly and, as they grow (which is very slowly), pinched to shape. Trim and shear regularly as separate plants grow together. Promote new growth by cutting back stems to 12 in (about 30 cm) or less in late spring.

### *B. microphylla* var. *japonica*

**syn. *B. japonica***

JAPANESE BOXWOOD

This evergreen, bushy variety bears a rounded mass of small, oblong, bright green leaves. It requires full sun and will tolerate moist soil; it is also more tolerant of the dry heat and alkaline soils of the West than is the English box. It grows to a height and spread of 7 ft (about 2 m). Perfect for hedging and screening.
ZONES 6–10

### *B. sempervirens*

ENGLISH BOXWOOD

This is almost identical to *B. microphylla* but grows to twice the height. However, the form most often seen, 'Suffruticosa', grows to only around 32 in (about 81 cm) and is the type used to make clipped edgings in formal Italian- or French-style gardens. Foliage is a darker green and has a distinct aroma not appreciated by everyone.
ZONES 5–10

## *CAESALPINIA*

These deciduous shrubs, trees and climbers are valued in warm climates worldwide for their brilliant flowers. Found in tropical and subtropical areas, they do best in soil that retains moisture and prefer full sun and plenty of water. Named after a sixteenth-century Italian botanist. Propagate from seed in fall or spring, or from softwood cuttings in summer.

### *C. gilliesii*

**syn. *Poinciana gilliesii***

BIRD-OF-PARADISE BUSH

This rather prickly deciduous shrub or small tree is grown for the short racemes of bird-like, yellow flowers with long, red stamens that appear in summer. It has finely divided dark green leaves. It prefers full sun and a well-drained soil. It grows to a height of 12 ft (about 3.5 m) and a spread of 18 ft (about 5.5 m). Propagate from seed in fall.
ZONES 8–11

*Caesalpinia gilliesii*

*Buxus sempervirens*

*Buddleia davidii*

*Bursaria spinosa*

*Buddleia alternifolia*

*Buddleia globosa*

*Buxus microphylla* var. *japonica*

### *C. pulcherrima*
**syn. *Poinciana pulcherrima***
RED BIRD-OF-PARADISE

This is the most common species of *Caesalpinia*. An erect or spreading, prickly, evergreen shrub, it has fern-like leaves and bears racemes of orange-red to yellow, cup-shaped flowers during the warm months of the year. It prefers full sun and well-drained soil. It grows to a height and spread of 9 ft (about 2.7 m) and does not tolerate cold very well. Propagate from seed in fall.
ZONES 10–11

## *CALLIANDRA*
### *tweedii*
BRAZILIAN FLAME BUSH

Native to Central and South America and related to the *Acacia*, this evergreen shrub grows to a height and spread of 9 ft (about 2.7 m). In late fall to spring it bears striking flowerheads made up of many red-stamened florets—like all species in the genus it has no petals. The bipinnate leaves each have more than 100 leaflets. This picturesque plant prefers full sun and well-drained soil, and tolerates the cold poorly. The Greek genus name reflects its characteristics (*kallos:* beauty and *andros:* stamens). Propagate from seed in spring or by semi-ripe cuttings in fall.
ZONES 9–11

## *CALLICARPA*
BEAUTY BERRY

The attraction of these upright, deciduous shrubs lies in the luxurious bunches of glossy, purplish, lilac berries they bear in fall. The pale green, crepe-textured leaves (often bronze tipped when young) and tiny, lilac flowers in spring or summer are of little interest. Ungainly plants, they should be pruned in winter. Use the fruiting stems for indoor decoration. They grow best in fertile, well-drained soil and prefer full sun or semi-shade conditions. They grow to a height and spread of 6 ft (about 1.8 m). Propagate from softwood cuttings in summer. There are several species, all very much alike: *C. dichotoma* and *C. bodinieri* are excellent; *C. bodinieri* var. *giraldii* 'Profusion' is generally considered the best.
ZONES 6–10

## *CALLISTEMON*
BOTTLEBRUSH

Native to Australia, these woody and sometimes papery-trunked evergreen shrubs are popular in Ireland, the USA, Mediterranean countries, Hong Kong and South Africa and wherever frost is not severe. Often weeping in habit, they are grown for their magnificent flowers, which closely resemble a bottle brush. From the tips of the flower spikes new leaves grow, leaving long-lasting, woody, seed capsules behind. A favorite with hummingbirds and orioles, *Callistemon* prefer full sun. Though native to seasonally wet soils, they adapt readily to the annual summer drought of California. Propagate from semi-ripe cuttings in summer. Tent caterpillar may present a problem about this time.

### *C. citrinus*
LEMON BOTTLEBRUSH

This species thrives and flowers profusely in dry or damp conditions. Its leaves have a distinct lemony fragrance. The flowers are brilliant crimson and are produced in great abundance in spring and sporadically throughout the year. Grown either as a dense shrub to 15 ft (about 4.5 m) or trained into a small-headed tree. Cultivars available include 'Splendens' (which is bright red) and 'Violaceus' (which is reddish purple).
ZONES 9–10

### *C. viminalis*
WEEPING BOTTLEBRUSH

This graceful, weeping, evergreen shrub or small tree flowers mostly in spring, producing clusters of bright red flowers. It grows to 25 ft (about 7.5 m) tall with a spread of 15 ft (about 4.5 m), producing long, narrow, oblong leaves. It tolerates most soil conditions.
ZONES 9–10

## *CALLUNA*
### *vulgaris*
SCOTTISH HEATHER

A familiar sight as natural cover on moors and heaths in northern Europe, this bushy evergreen is a native of Europe and Asia Minor. A densely spreading bush, its small leaves are arranged in pairs. It has spikes of bell- to urn-shaped, single or double flowers, usually pink, mauve or white, which appear from mid-summer to late fall. The shrub does well in rockeries and where mulched with pebbles. Though tolerant of salt and wind, heather does not thrive in areas with high summer temperatures. It makes a good ground cover, preferring a gritty, well-drained, acid soil with regular water. Grows to a height of 24 in (about 60 cm) and a width of 20 in (about 50 cm). Over 100 cultivars are available from specialists, including some with variegated or multicolored leaves such as 'Multicolor'.
ZONES 4–9

## *CALYCANTHUS*
SWEET SHRUB, SPICE BUSH

Deciduous shrubs from North America and the Orient, notable for the fragrance of their leaves and flowers which are usually maroon and resemble very small magnolia blossoms. Both species listed here prefer full sun to light shade and steady moisture. The bold foliage texture provides a good contrast in the moist shrub border. Propagate from seed.

*Callicarpa bodinieri*

*Callistemon viminalis*

*Callistemon citrinus*

*Calliandra tweedii*

*Caesalpinia pulcherrima*

*Calluna vulgaris* 'Multicolor'

*Camellia granthamiana*

*Calycanthus floridus*

*Camellia j.* 'Adolphe Audusson'

### *C. floridus*

SWEET SHRUB, CAROLINA ALLSPICE

Maroon flowers in spring and then scattered through summer are not showy but are interesting and fragrant. Clumps spread slowly to 6–10 ft (about 1.8–3 m) and reach 6 ft (about 1.8 m) or more in height. It is good as an understorey shrub in open woodland or as an informal hedge or shrub screen in full sun or part shade.

ZONES 4–10

### *C. occidentalis*

SPICE BUSH

Similar to *C. floridus* but with large flowers and slightly stronger fragrance. Native along streamsides on the West Coast, it does best with plenty of moisture. It varies from 4–12 ft (about 1.2–3.5 m) tall, spreading 6–8 ft (about 1.8–2.4 m) wide. Flowers are produced in spring and summer.

ZONES 8–10

## *CAMELLIA*

CAMELLIA

Though associated with Japanese culture, the majority of this genus of evergreen, woody shrubs and trees are actually from mainland China and the Indo-Chinese peninsula. They are found in mountainous, subtropical areas, growing in partial shade. In Japan these lush plants are grown in part for the oil content of their seed capsules, but elsewhere most camellias are cultivated for their luxurious flowers and shiny foliage. Over 30 000 varieties now exist, most of which are descendants from *C. japonica*. They prefer semi-shade in the open and a well-drained, neutral to acid soil. During frost or snow periods, move in containers to the shelter of evergreen trees. White or pink varieties need to be screened from direct sun or their flowers will discolor. Propagate from cuttings in late summer or mid-winter, or graft in spring or winter. To trim the shape, prune camellias during or immediately after flowering. *C. sinensis* is not grown for its flowers but for its leaves, which are used to make tea. Legend has it that British East India agents attempted to export some specimens out of China after tea had become fashionable in Europe. However, Chinese officials substituted *C. japonica* instead—a beautiful plant, but quite useless for tea making. Its popularity as a flowering plant took off soon after.

*Camellia japonica*

### *C. granthamiana*

This evergreen shrub from Hong Kong flowers in late fall. The flowers are single, up to 6 in (about 15 cm), white and saucer shaped, with a row of a maximum 8 petals surrounding a central boss of yellow stamens. The leaves are glossy, deep green and crinkly.

ZONES 8–10

### *C. japonica*

JAPANESE CAMELLIA

Native to Japan, Korea and eastern China, this evergreen shrub contains much variation in habit, foliage, floral form and color. The flowers may be single to very double, in shades from white to red. Its flowering season varies from late fall through mid-spring, depending in part upon climate. It grows to 20 ft (about 6 m) or more with a similar spread, but is usually kept much smaller as a shrub. It prefers a cool soil, adequate moisture and a protected environment. Shade from the burning afternoon sun. Watering is essential in dry areas, or the buds will fail to open; plants in California are remarkably drought tolerant.

ZONES 8–10

*Calycanthus occidentalis*

*Camellia japonica* 'Debutante'

*Camellia japonica* 'Elegans'

### *C. japonica* 'Adolphe Audusson'

This well-established cultivar has better resistance to cold than other varieties. It grows large, saucer-shaped, dark red flowers, sometimes with white markings, and prominent yellow stamens. They are semi-double with two or more rows of 9 to 21 petals. The leaves are dark green and are broadly lance shaped.

ZONES 8–10

### *C. japonica* 'Debutante'

Among the most popular of pink camellias, this American cultivar has a full peony form with a rounded mass of smaller petals and petaloids in the center of the flower. Medium sized, the flowers are of a clear light pink and appear early to mid-season. Foliage is light green on an upright shrub.

ZONES 8–10

### *C. japonica* 'Elegans'

Beautiful, large, rose-pink flowers are what make this cultivar so highly prized. Often the flower has white, variegated petaloids in its center. The petaloids are intermingled with a mass of stamens. The flower has surrounding rows of flat petals—the "anemone" configuration. The leaves are dark green and are broadly lance shaped.

ZONES 8–10

*Camellia sasanqua*

*Camellia sasanqua* 'Yuletide'

*Camellia reticulata* 'Captain Rawes'

*Camellia lutchuensis*

*Camellia japonica* 'Nuccio's Gem'

### *C. japonica* 'Nuccio's Gem'

A relatively recent introduction from California, this pure white cultivar is popular worldwide for the perfection of its formal double flowers. Petals present an appealing spiral pattern. Flowers are quite large and are produced mid-season on sturdy, upright stems.

ZONES 8–10

### *C. lutchuensis*

This recently introduced species from China is a little tender but well worth growing for the long display of dainty white flowers with only three petals but the strongest, sweetest perfume of any camellia. The plant is fairly fast growing, upright when young and spreading at maturity.

ZONES 9–10

### *C. oleifera*

OIL-SEED CAMELLIA

Considered about the hardiest of camellias, this species has fragrant white flowers shading to pink blooming in the fall and early winter. By crossing with *C. japonica* and other species many new hybrids are becoming available, some of which are hardy to Zone 6 or colder, particularly if they can be protected from drying winter winds.

ZONES 7–10

### *C. reticulata*

A favorite among enthusiasts, with its upright habit and handsome, serrated foliage. Found naturally in the forests of southern China, it grows slowly up to a height of 30 ft (about 9 m). The species bears large, saucer-shaped, single, rose-pink and red flowers in spring; the cultivars have large (8 in/20 cm or more) double flowers in shades of pink or red. 'Captain Rawes', the oldest, has been joined by many in recent years. The leaves are large, oval and leathery. Less cold hardy than *C. japonica*, it is a taller, more open grower. Grow in a sunny position, and provide shelter.

ZONE 10

### *C. sasanqua*

This upright native of southern Japan is another lovely evergreen and it is the most sun tolerant of all camellias. It is a fast-growing, slender and dense species which produces an explosion of fragrant, single, white (occasionally red or pink) flowers in fall. These flowers usually shatter within a day or so of opening. The leaves are lance shaped, glossy and bright green. *C. sasanqua* will thrive in a sunny spot. It grows to a height of 10 ft (about 3 m) with a spread of 5 ft (about 1.5 m).

ZONES 8–10

### *C. sasanqua* 'White Doves'

A pure white sasanqua with a graceful habit that lends itself to use as an espalier on a wall. Flowers do shatter quickly, but many are produced to give a good show against the dark green leaves.

ZONES 8–10

### *C. sasanqua* 'Yuletide'

Suitable for formal or container planting, it bears a profusion of deep red, single flowers, perfectly rectangular in shape, in great profusion throughout the winter months.

ZONES 8–10

*C. sinensis*

TEA

A variable shrub/tree, cultivated in warm, temperate parts of eastern and southern Asia; its processed young leaves are used to make tea. Some varieties are also used as ornamental hedge plants. The flowers are small, scented and white.

ZONES 6–10

*C.* x *williamsii*

This is a hybrid group between *C. japonica* and *C. saluensis,* including numerous popular and attractive cultivars. Most popular of these are 'E. G. Waterhouse' and 'J. C. Williams', but there are many others, almost all in shades of pink. Most form low mounds, flowering heavily from mid-winter.

ZONES 8–10

*C.* x *williamsii* 'Donation'

This spectacular cultivar makes both an excellent tub specimen and garden plant. It is quite prolific; a compact upright shrub, it bears large, semi-double, orchid-pink flowers in the winter months.

ZONES 8–10

*Carissa macrocarpa*

*Cantua buxifolia*

*Camellia* x *williamsii* 'Donation'

*Camellia* x *williamsii*

*Camellia sinensis*

## *CANTUA buxifolia*

MAGIC FLOWER, SACRED FLOWER OF THE INCAS

This beautiful native of the Andes mountains develops a leggy habit with slender, weeping branches. It grows to a height and spread of 9 ft (about 2.7 m). An evergreen, soft-stemmed, somewhat scraggy bush, it becomes bowed down by the sheer weight of its bright red or purplish, trumpet flowers in mid- to late spring. Preferring full sun and well-drained soil it is drought resistant, also showing a considerable resistance to cold especially in a sheltered position.

ZONES 9–10

## *CARAGANA arborescens*

SIBERIAN PEASHRUB

A shrub or small tree native to the cold reaches of Siberia and Manchuria, valued because of its tolerance of extremely harsh conditions—heat, cold, drought, wind, poor soils. Bright yellow pea flowers are produced in abundance in spring, against leaves that are divided into 8 to 12 tiny leaflets. The ultimate height may be 20 ft (about 6 m) with a spread of 15 ft (about 4.5 m).

ZONES 2–9

## *CARISSA macrocarpa*

NATAL PLUM

Native to South Africa this fast-growing, dense, thorny hedge plant grows to a height of 9 ft (about 2.7 m) and a spread of 6 ft (about 1.8 m). The leaves are leathery and glossy and in spring large, white, frangipani-like flowers appear; these are followed by fruit that is rich in vitamin C. It needs a well-drained soil (accepting nearly pure white sand on the coast), full sun to part shade and regular watering. Numerous cultivars are available, including dwarf or compact forms such as 'Boxwood Beauty', 'Green Carpet' and 'Tuttle'.

ZONES 10–11

## *CARPENTARIA californica*

BUSH ANEMONE

Like many other Californian natives, this sturdy, evergreen shrub is

*Caragana arborescens*

*Carpentaria californica*

drought resistant but dislikes the air pollution in city gardens. It thrives in full sun to part shade and requires a well-drained soil and occasional watering through the dry summers. It will do well against a south- or east-facing wall. It has glossy, long, narrow, dark green leaves and fragrant, yellow-centered, white flowers which appear in summer. Prune regularly after flowering to prevent scragginess. Grows to a height of 9 ft (about 2.7 m). Propagate from seed in fall or from cuttings in summer.
ZONES 8–10

## *CARYOPTERIS* × *clandonensis*

BLUEBEARD

This deciduous, bushy sub-shrub is prized for its masses of delicate, purple-blue flowers from late summer to fall. The leaves are irregularly serrated, oval and gray-green. Cut to the ground each spring; it will send up new shoots very rapidly. Preferring full sun and light, well-drained soil, it grows to a height and spread of 3 ft (about 90 cm). Propagate from softwood or semi-ripe cuttings in summer or from seed in fall.
ZONES 6–9

## *CASSIA*

SENNA

These shrubs and small trees from tropical and subtropical regions around the world provide a blaze of yellow and gold flowers in mild winter gardens of California and the Southwest. Pinnately divided leaves are green or gray-green, and usually evergreen. Flowers are often bowl shaped or are reminiscent of pea flowers, with the seeds produced in typical bean-like pods. Most are tolerant of heat and some drought; all need full sun and good drainage. Some species are used medicinally, while other species are used to tan leather. Propagate from seed.

### *C. artemisioides*

syn. *Senna artemisioides*
FEATHERY CASSIA, SILVER CASSIA

Native to Australia, this wiry, upright to spreading evergreen is a dry-climate, frost-tender shrub. A member of the same family (Leguminosae) as peas and beans, it bears spikes of delightful, buttercup-like yellow flowers from winter to early summer. Each leaf has 6 to 14 silver-gray leaflets covered in a fine down. It prefers an open, sunny position and fertile, well-drained soil, although it will tolerate wetter conditions if the water is allowed to drain freely. It grows to a height and spread of 3–6 ft (about 90–180 cm). Cut back hard in spring and propagate from semi-hardwood cuttings, or from seed in spring.
ZONES 9–10

### *C. corymbosa*

syn. *Senna corymbosa*
FLOWERY SENNA

This fast-growing shrub has light green foliage and large, dense clusters of bright yellow flowers that cover the shrub in fall. It grows to a height of 10 ft (about 3 m) with a spread of 6 ft (about 1.8 m). Plant in ordinary garden soil in a sunny position. Propagate from cuttings.
ZONES 9–10

## *CEANOTHUS*

CALIFORNIA LILAC

This is a genus of over 50 species, most of which originate in western North America. Despite the common name they are not true lilacs. They are grown for their small but densely clustered flowers, which develop in showy panicles or racemes not unlike the true lilacs; the colors range from blue to lavender to white, as do true lilacs. The evergreen species and their American hybrids are the most popular, but are limited in their use to the arid West. They need a sunny situation in well-drained soil with little or no summer water once they are established in the ground. A few hybrids produced in Europe are adapted to the East Coast; these have been derived from a Mexican species and *C. americanus*, one of the few species native to eastern North America. They tend to be summer flowering. All other species and hybrids are winter-spring flowering. Prune lightly to remove dead wood in spring. Propagate from seed in spring or from leafy, semi-hardwood cuttings taken in summer.

### *C.* cultivars

Nurserypeople and native plant enthusiasts are constantly discovering new forms or hybrids of ceanothus that are superior to the wild species for garden cultivation; many of the hybrids are of uncertain parentage, but those introduced into the nursery trade are generally more adaptable to garden situations (more likely to tolerate some summer water). 'Ray Hartman' is a small, broad, spreading tree with early season blooms of deep blue. 'Julia Phelps', 'Dark Star' and 'Concha' have deep, cobalt-blue flowers on large, dense shrubs with tiny, crinkled leaves. 'Percy Picton' has lavender flowers.
ZONES 8–10

### *C.* × *delilianus* 'Gloire de Versailles'

This French hybrid is a sturdy, vigorous, deciduous shrub with mid-green leaves that are broad and oval. It does best in full sun and well-drained soil, and will tolerate the moist, humid summers of eastern North America. Pale blue scented flowers in racemes are produced in mid-summer to early fall. It grows to a height and spread of 5 ft (about 1.5 m).
ZONES 6–10

### *C. griseus* var. *horizontalis*

CARMEL CREEPER

A low, broadly spreading, evergreen shrub with glossy, leathery leaves and masses of light blue flowers in late winter. Only 24–36 in (about 60–90 cm) in height this spreads to 10–15 ft (about 3–4.5 m), making an excellent ground cover for banks and rough ground, particularly along the West Coast. 'Hurricane Point' is a somewhat more refined ground cover, not so fast to grow and with deeper blue flowers. All like a well-drained soil, full sun and minimal water during the summer.
ZONES 8–10

### *C. impressus*

SANTA BARBARA CEANOTHUS

This dense, evergreen shrub is distinct for its small, deep green, crinkled leaves and for the deep blue flowers produced in spring. A broad mound, it grows to 6 ft (about 1.8 m) or more in height and up to 15 ft (about 4.5 m) across. It prefers the milder regions nearer the coast in California.
ZONES 9–10

*Cassia corymbosa*

*Cassia artemisioides*

*Ceanothus* × 'Gloire de Versailles'

*Ceanothus griseus* var. *horizontalis*

*Ceanothus* 'Percy Picton'

*Ceanothus impressus*

*Caryopteris* × *clandonensis*

*Cestrum elegans* 'Smithii'

*Ceanothus thyrsiflorus*

*Chaenomeles speciosa*

### *C. thyrsiflorus*

BLUE BLOSSOM

An upright, evergreen shrub with glossy, bright green leaves native to the coastal mountains of California. Its tall panicles of soft blue to white flowers are produced in mid-spring on plants that may reach 20 ft (about 6 m) in height and spread even wider. Fast growing, it is also one of the hardiest species. Usually found in nurseries as one of its named selections such as 'Skylark' (blue flowers) or 'Snow Flurry' (white flowers); both are more compact growers than the species.

ZONES 8–10

## *CESTRUM*

JESSAMINE

While some enjoy the scent from some species of this genus of deciduous/evergreen shrubs and semi-scrambling climbers, others find it overpowering and unpleasant. All agree that the showy flowers are a delight. These shrubs like a sunny position in fertile, well-drained soil and plenty of water during the warmer months. Plants in containers should be freely watered during active growth, less at other times. Cut out the older canes every year. Propagate from soft-tip cuttings in the summer.

### *C. aurantiacum*

ORANGE CESTRUM

Mostly evergreen, this semi-scrambling shrub is deciduous in colder climates. It grows to a height and spread of 6 ft (about 1.8 m), though it stays a rounded shrub if cut back. In summer, tubular, bright orange flowers appear in large trusses; these are followed by white berries. The leaves are oval and bright green. Prune annually, and remove older stems by cutting to the base after flowering.

ZONES 9–10

### *C. elegans*

RED CESTRUM

This arching, evergreen, almost tree-like shrub grows to a height and spread of 10 ft (about 3 m). It has large, downy green leaves and bears clusters of tubular, crimson to purplish flowers in summer and fall, followed by berries of a similar color. 'Smithii' has soft red flowers.

ZONES 9–11

*Cestrum nocturnum*

### *C. nocturnum*

NIGHT JESSAMINE

This spreading, evergreen tropical and subtropical shrub with dark green leaves comes originally from the West Indies. In summer it bears clusters of greenish white to cream flowers, which give off intense fragrance especially after dark. It prefers a position in full sun and a well-drained soil. It grows to a height of 9 ft (about 2.7 m) and a spread of 6 ft (about 1.8 m).

ZONES 9–11

## *CHAENOMELES*

### *speciosa*

FLOWERING QUINCE, JAPANESE QUINCE

This dense, thorny, many-branched shrub from China is grown not so much for its fruit as for its flowers. The spherical, greenish fruits make excellent jelly. They follow the winter–spring bloom of attractive, clustered, red, white, pink or orange flowers. The plant prefers sun and well-drained soil. After flowering, cut back side shoots on wall-trained shrubs to two or three buds and shorten shoots growing away from the wall during the growing season. Take leafy, semi-hardwood cuttings in summer or fall, the latter also being the best time to plant seed. Fireblight and chlorosis may present problems. The shrub grows to 9 ft (about 2.7 m) with a spread of 15 ft (about 4.5 m). Many named selections are available from nurseries; they offer a range in size of shrub and in flower color.

ZONES 4–9

*Cestrum aurantiacum*

*Chamaecyparis pisifera*

## *CHAMAECYPARIS*

FALSE CYPRESS

The two species listed below are usually grown in gardens as one of many dwarf or slow-growing selections that fit easily into the category of shrubs. They are evergreens with small, scale-like needles. Fruits are distinct, globular, woody cones, not always produced on the shrubby forms. All like a woodsy, well-drained soil and will take full sun or light shade but have a preference for cool summers. The smallest forms are excellent additions to the rockery, while the larger shrubs are useful for screening or as evergreen additions to a shrub border. Little pruning is needed. Propagate from cuttings.

### *C. obtusa*

HINOKI FALSE CYPRESS

A tree of 50 ft (about 15 m) or more in height in its native Japan, this attractive conifer has spawned a vast number of dwarf, shrubby forms. All have scale-like leaves arranged on fan-like branches, often swirling and spiraling in an appealing manner. 'Nana Gracilis' makes a 6 ft (about 1.8 m) tall pyramid, while 'Nana' develops into a low ball around 30 in (about 76 cm) tall and broad.

ZONES 5–10

*Chamaecyparis obtusa*

### *C. pisifera*

SAWARA FALSE CYPRESS

A tall, cone-shaped tree in the wild, this species also has a number of shrubby forms more suited to the garden. The leaves are scale like but with sharp points at their tip, usually arranged in flat sprays on branches held horizontally. Dwarf forms often display a juvenile foliage, finer textured and more needle like. 'Boulevard' has silvery blue-green foliage on a dense pyramidal shrub 6–8 ft (about 1.8–2.4 m) tall. 'Pisifera' has thread-like branchlets that droop in a graceful way; the shrubs reach 6–8 ft (about 1.8-2.4 m) tall and as wide.

ZONES 5–10

Cistus salviifolius

*Chimonanthus praecox*

*Cistus ladanifer*

*Choisya ternata*

*Cistus × hybridus*

## *CHIMONANTHUS*
### *praecox*

WINTERSWEET

This twiggy, deciduous shrub native to China and Japan is grown for the rich, fragrant scent of its dainty, brown and pale yellow flowers with purple centers. These appear on the bare wood of the branches during milder periods in mid-winter. Plant it near a doorway or sidewalk where the fragrance can be enjoyed. It has rough, glossy, oval, dark green leaves. It needs constant moisture to thrive, preferring full sun and a fertile, well-drained soil. Prune lightly to shape. Propagate from seed in late spring and early summer, and by layering in fall. It grows to 9 ft (about 2.7 m) in height and spread.

ZONES 7–10

## *CHOISYA*
### *ternata*

MEXICAN ORANGE, MOCK ORANGE

Originally from Mexico, this drought-resistant plant prefers a sunny position and a fertile, well-drained soil. It grows to a height and spread of 6 ft (about 1.8 m). Clusters of white flowers with the fragrance of orange blossoms appear in spring. The bright green, glossy leaves are also scented. Propagate from semi-ripe cuttings in summer.

ZONES 8–10

## *CHRYSOTHAMNUS*

RABBITBRUSH

Rabbitbrush is among the most characteristic plants of the mountains and basins of the West, making broad sweeps of bright yellow in early fall, one of the few native plants to flower at that season. There are numerous species, but all are very similar; they have slender, gray-green to white leaves on stems 2–6 ft (about 60–180 cm) tall, topped by fluffy heads of yellow flowers. Cottony seed heads follow and may last into winter. Best reserved for the natural garden in the mountains or high desert; it enjoys full sun and requires no water beyond the natural rainfall. It will deteriorate quickly in high summer humidity.

ZONES 2–10

## *CISTUS*

ROCKROSE

This genus of spreading evergreens is famous for its drought resistance and ability to thrive in poor or sandy conditions, such as exposed banks or seaside cliffs. Equally, it does badly in moist, humid conditions. Native to the shores of the Mediterranean, *Cistus* species produce delightful, freely borne but short-lived flowers; these only last a day, but are quickly replaced. They do not transplant easily. Regular pinching back will maintain shape—cut out deadwood in spring, but do not prune hard. Propagate by seed in fall or by softwood cuttings in summer (cultivars and hybrids by cuttings in summer only), and grow the young plants on in pots. Plant in sun in light, well-drained soil.

### *C.* × *hybridus*

**syn. *C.* × *corbariensis***

WHITE ROCKROSE

Pure white flowers cover this mounding shrub from late winter into summer and occasionally beyond. The small, slightly furry leaves have an incense-like scent, most noticeable on a warm day. Ultimate height may be 5 ft (about 1.5 m), although plants are easily kept lower with light tip pruning; the spread will be greater than the height. A good plant to use on a dry hillside with California natives and other drought-tolerant plants.

ZONES 8–10

*C. ladanifer*

CRIMSON-SPOT ROCKROSE

This open, upright evergreen bears striking, large, white flowers in summer with triangular, red markings at the base of each petal. The narrow leaves are dark green and sticky. It likes full sun and well-drained soil and grows to a height and spread of 3 ft (about 90 cm). The leaves are the source of the fragrant, medicinal resin ladanum; not to be confused with laudanum, a form of opium.

ZONES 8–10

*C. × purpureus*

PURPLE ROCKROSE, ORCHID ROCKROSE

A relatively compact hybrid rockrose notable for its soft reddish purple, 3 in (about 7.5 cm) diameter flowers with a deep red spot at the base of each petal. Flowers are produced most heavily in spring but are scattered throughout the rest of the year, especially in cool areas along the Pacific Coast. Plants reach 3–4 ft (about 90–120 cm) in height with a similar but slightly wider spread.

ZONES 8–10

*C. salviifolius*

SAGELEAF ROCKROSE

A low, spreading shrub with crinkled, gray-green, 1 in (about 2.5 cm) leaves and white flowers with yellow spots at the base of each petal. This makes an excellent ground cover, growing less than 24 in (about 60 cm) tall but spreading to 6 ft (about 1.8 m).

ZONES 8–10

## CLERODENDRUM

These picturesque flowering evergreen or deciduous shrubs are found mostly in Africa, Southeast Asia and Australia. They vary tremendously in habit, from upright tree to climbing varieties. *C. bungei*, for instance, is grown for its large, heart-shaped, coarsely serrated leaves and its rounded clusters of small, fragrant, rose-red flowers. Thriving in humus-rich, well-drained soil they all do best in full sun, with partial shade in summer. Water all year round, especially in summer. Crowded growth should be thinned out in spring. Propagate from semi-hardwood cuttings in fall. Whitefly, mealy bug and spider mite may present problems.

*C. bungei*

CASHMERE BOUQUET

A suckering shrub with many vertical stems topped in summer with wonderfully fragrant heads of rosy-pink flowers. The leaves are large and coarse, and foul smelling if crushed. The stems will reach 6 ft (about 1.8 m) unless cut to the

*Clethra alnifolia*

ground each spring; new growth will then flower on 3 ft (about 90 cm) stems. It will spread rapidly if not contained or controlled. Light shade is best.

ZONES 7–10

*C. trichotomum*

HARLEQUIN GLORYBOWER

This deciduous, upright, tree-like shrub grows to a height and spread of 9 ft (about 2.7 m). From late summer to mid-fall it bears clusters of fragrant, tubular white flowers with red calyces; these are followed by blue berries. This also travels underground, so be prepared to prune out unwanted shoots. Plant in full sun in average garden soil.

ZONES 7–10

## CLETHRA
## *alnifolia*

SUMMERSWEET, SWEET PEPPERBUSH

This bushy, deciduous, rounded shrub, native to eastern North America, has oval, serrated leaves and bears a profusion of dainty, spicily fragrant, bell-shaped flowers in summer to fall. It prefers a well-drained, moist, peaty, acid soil in semi-shade conditions and year-round watering. Prune back after bloom by removing the oldest canes. Grows to a height and spread of 9 ft (about 2.7 m). Propagate from spring seed, soft-tip cuttings or, best of all, from the suckers it produces.

ZONES 3–9

## COLEONEMA
## *pulchrum*

PINK BREATH OF HEAVEN

This spreading shrub is a native of South Africa. While not a member of the same family as heath, they do have heath-like foliage and are commonly planted along banks or alongside lawns. They can also be trained as a low hedge. The soft, bright green leaves give off a pungent fragrance when crushed. Masses of tiny pink flowers cover the shrubs from late winter through spring. *C. album* has white flowers but is otherwise identical. The shrub does best in a well-drained, neutral to acid soil and needs a

*Clerodendrum bungei*

*Clerodendrum trichotomum*

*Coleonema pulchrum*

sunny to half-shaded spot. Water potted specimens moderately during the growing season, less so at other times. Winter moisture stimulates flowering. Clip after blooming to maintain shape. Grows to a little over 3 ft (about 90 cm) in height and spread. Propagate from soft tip cuttings in summer.

ZONES 8–10

## COPROSMA

These lush, spreading, evergreen shrubs are native to New Zealand. They require both male and female plants to produce fruits, but are usually planted for their foliage. All species grow well in warm, humid conditions in a well-drained soil that is not over rich. They are salt resistant and do well in a seaside environment. Though they prefer water throughout summer, most adapt easily to the summer-dry climate of coastal California. A regular, light pruning helps maintain shape. Propagate from seed in spring or from semi-ripe cuttings in late summer.

*Coprosma × kirkii* 'Variegata'

*C. × kirkii*

The foliage of this smaller-leafed hybrid varies; most frequently narrow, oblong, glossy, bright green leaves are set opposite or in clusters. 'Variegata' has leaves that are variegated with silver and green. Squat and densely branched, this shrub is useful as a dense ground cover and for erosion control, especially on coastal sites. Grows to 16 in (about 40 cm) high with a 3–6 ft (about 90–180 cm) spread.

ZONES 9–10

# A Field Trip to the Magallanes Region

The story is told that, in the closing years of the eighteenth century, James Lee, a famous English nurseryman, was showing a client around his establishment in Hammersmith. The visitor remarked that he had seen a plant, far more beautiful than anything in Mr Lee's collection, growing in a humble house in Wapping. Lee found the house and a magnificent species of *Fuchsia*. After much negotiation he obtained the plant for the princely sum of six guineas.

The plant was *Fuchsia magellanica* and it has been one of the most important parents of our modern *Fuchsia* hybrids, thanks to its early introduction, its reputation for hardiness, the range of its different forms and color variants and, of course, its own delicate beauty.

About 95 per cent of the naturally occurring fuchsia species are native to Central and South America, mainly in the moist, cool forests of the Andes. Two of these, including *F. magellanica*, are native to Chile and that country's most southern city, Punta Arenas, is the base for our field trip.

*Torres del Paine National Park, in the Magallanes region.*

As you move south of the capital, Santiago, the climate changes progressively from dry, almost Mediterranean, to a zone of heavy rainfall around Los Lagos (the Lake Region). The rainfall becomes even heavier, the further south you go, to the point where some of the western Patagonian islands receive an astonishing 158 in (about 4000 mm) annually. *F. magellanica* occurs throughout this region and down to the southern part of the continent.

Punta Arenas, with a population of 90 000, is the capital of the Magallanes region of Chile, and the most southern city of this size in the world. It is a cold and windy place even in the warmer months from October through to March. Despite the cold, it is a good idea to time your visit for early fall, when the southern, or Antarctic, beech trees (*Nothofagus* species) are turning to red and gold. This also coincides with the later part of the flowering period for *F. magellanica.* As you travel toward the south of the Brunswick Peninsula, you will see many southern beeches covering the hillsides, some of them growing sideways due to the prevailing winds. The area around the Strait of Magellan has not changed greatly since its discovery by Ferdinand Magellan in 1520. Tierra del Fuego (Land of Fire) is but a line on the eastern horizon and looking south, you will see masses of snow-capped mountains above a green plain.

At various spots along the road south you are likely to find a delightful yellow violet *(Viola magellanica)*, the occasional Chilean fire tree *(Embothrium coccineum)*, which is a relative of grevillea and waratah and has similar red spider flowers, and a primitive flowering, glossy-leaved shrub or small tree, *Drimys winteri*.

Approximately 62 miles (about 100 km) south of Punta Arenas, in the area around Fuerte Bulnes, you will find mixed beech forests of evergreen *Nothofagus betuloides* and some

*The flowers of* Fuchsia magellanica *contrast well with its foliage.*

*Fuchsia magellanica*

deciduous *Nothofagus antarctica* and *N. pumilio.* As you glance around, you are likely to see numerous *Fuchsia magellanica* plants covered in edible black berries about ½ in (about 1.5 cm) wide. They are quite common in this open woodland, enjoying the dappled light under the beech trees, where they grow into flaky-barked shrubs 6 ft (about 2 m) high and wide. The leaves are 1½–2 in (about 3–4 cm) long, sitting in an unusual pattern on their stems—mostly in opposite pairs, but also in threes and sometimes fours. The sepals are a striking crimson and the petals themselves are a pinkish purple and form a long tube. Flowers of many unrelated plants in this part of the world are reddish and tube-like, to attract the various species of tiny hummingbird.

Other plants to be seen in this woodland include various *Acaena* species which you are likely to collect in your socks, for this ground cover member of the rose family has burrs for fruit. Some barberry shrubs *(Berberis ilicifolius)* with spiny stems and prickly leaves, are found here, as are more Chilean fire trees. Many flowering stalks of the orchid genus *Chloraea* emerge from the grazing grass that covers most of the areas between the trees.

There are patches of boggy ground where you can find a yellow-flowered *Ranunculus* (buttercup) species, and a little herb with red spikes of fruit, *Gunnera magellanica.* The treetops are home to an interesting group of shrubby parasites (*Missodendron* species) that only occur on the southern beech trees of Chile. Some look like old man's beard lichen; others resemble button mushrooms; and others are reminiscent of the unrelated European mistletoe. *F. magellanica* grows in parts of the forests that are well drained, though fairly moist. The soil here is a loamy type with a rich, organic top layer.

Although *F. magellanica* is fairly common throughout the southern region of Chile, nothing can compare with seeing it in the wild and majestic area of the Strait of Magellan—an area steeped in history, extreme in location, and the place where the plant was first recorded and collected over 200 years ago. Not a field trip for the faint-hearted, but one that will impress you with the splendor of the setting.

## *Fuchsia*

The genus *Fuchsia* comprises around 100 species, from the north to the southern tip of South America centered on the Andean mountain chain. Some species are found in eastern South America and there are five species in the Pacific, one in Tahiti and four in New Zealand. *F. excorticata*, from New Zealand, forms a tree to 40 ft (about 12 m) tall with a trunk to 2 ft (about 60 cm) in diameter! Variable in flower shape and color, *F. magellanica* is possibly the most cold-hardy species and was introduced to the British Isles as early as 1788, and has since become naturalized in some milder, wetter areas.

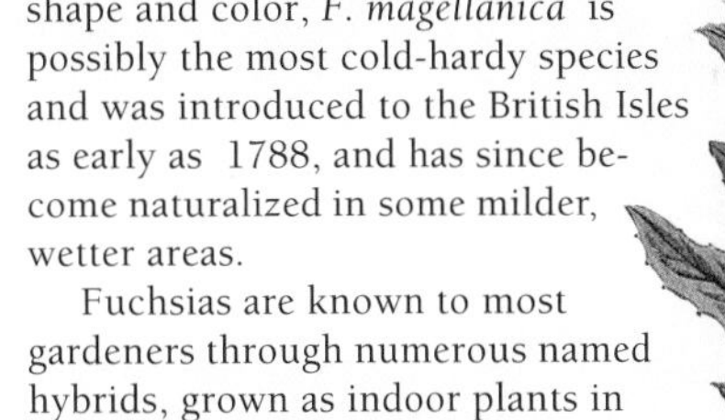

Fuchsias are known to most gardeners through numerous named hybrids, grown as indoor plants in cold climates or as outdoor shrubs in milder climates, where they are also popular in tubs and hanging baskets. These hybrids derive from South American species such as *Fuchsia magellanica* and *F. coccinea*, with some genes from *F. fulgens* and *F. arborescens*, both from Mexico.

*Fuchsia* belongs to Onagraceae, the evening primrose family, which has 21 genera worldwide, with about 640 species.

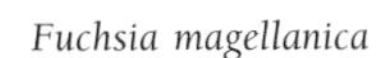

*Fuchsia magellanica*

*Cornus sericea*

*Coprosma repens*

*Cornus alba*

### *C. repens*

MIRROR PLANT

This evergreen shrub, which at first has a spreading habit and then later becomes erect, grows to a height and spread of 6 ft (about 1.8 m). It has bright, shiny, oval leaves, often with variegations. The insignificant flowers that appear in late spring are followed (on female plants only) by orange-red, egg-shaped berries from late summer to fall. It is very tolerant of drought in coastal regions and is likely to become weedy in watered gardens; it is also tolerant of all kinds of soil conditions including sandy soil. Prune back to prevent dense growth.

ZONES 9–10

## *CORNUS*

DOGWOOD

Attractive winter bark followed by a beautiful spring bloom and then by fall foliage and fruit make this genus of twiggy, deciduous shrubs a gardener's delight. Native to the cooler regions of the USA and Asia, they

*Coronilla valentina* subsp. *glauca*

*Corokia cotoneaster*

are popular in cold to cool-temperate climates. The shrubby forms have clusters of tiny white flowers followed by blue or white fruits. The various species all do best in sun or semi-shade and need a fertile, well-drained soil. Cut back stems to almost ground level annually in late winter to stimulate young growth which develops the best bark color. Propagate from seed or rooted layers struck in a humid, sand-peat mixture.

### *C. alba*

RED-BARK DOGWOOD, TATARIAN DOGWOOD

This deciduous, upright then spreading shrub from northern Europe and Asia has shoots that turn an attractive, deep red in winter. The normally dark green, oval leaves turn red-orange in fall. Star-shaped, creamy white flowers appear in late spring and early summer and are followed by round white berries, which are often blue tinted. Propagate from softwood cuttings in summer or hardwood cuttings in fall and winter. Grows to a height and spread of 9 ft (about 2.7 m). Varieties with variegated leaves or yellow stems are available. All spread slowly underground to form large thickets.

ZONES 2–9

### *C. sericea*

syn. *C. stolonifera*

RED-OSIER DOGWOOD

Similar to *C. alba* but native to North America and having a tendency to spread faster into large clumps. Winter stems are bright red, while flowers and fruit are similar as well. Both species make excellent winter accent plants against white snow or against dark green evergreens. 'Flaviramea' has yellow winter stems; 'Silver and Gold' has variegated leaves with yellow winter stems.

ZONES 2–10

## *COROKIA*
## *cotoneaster*

This sparse and hardy, evergreen bush is a native of New Zealand. It grows zigzag fashion in all directions. It has small, round, dark green leaves and fragrant, yellow flowers that appear in spring and summer. It is suitable for mild coastal areas because of its tolerance of wind and salt; give it full sun, a fertile, well-drained soil and moderate water through the summer. It grows to a height and spread of 9 ft (about 2.7 m). Shear regularly after flowering to promote dense growth, or thin to emphasize the picturesque branching pattern.

ZONES 8–10

## *CORONILLA*
## *valentina* subsp. *glauca*

syn. *C. glauca*

This dense shrub is a native of the Mediterranean region. If grown in a sunny spot in a well-drained soil it will thrive and bear yellow, fragrant, pea-like flowers from mid-spring to early summer. The leaves are a pleasant blue-gray color, each with 5 or 7 leaflets. It grows to a height and spread a little over $4^{1}/_{2}$ ft (about 1.3 m). Use seed, summer cuttings, layers or divisions to propagate this delightful evergreen shrub.

ZONES 9–10

## CORREA

AUSTRALIAN FUCHSIA

The dense, evergreen Australian natives in this genus range from ground covers to $4^1/_2$ ft (about 1.3 m) tall shrubs. Most bloom from fall through spring. Their long, bell-shaped flowers are rich in honey. They prefer a semi-shaded spot, and a moderately fertile, moist but well-drained soil. When planting out, a slightly alkaline soil is recommended. Water potted specimens moderately when in flower, less at other times. Prune to keep them well shaped and compact. They are dependably drought tolerant in shaded situations, less so in sun. Propagate from seed in spring or semi-ripe cuttings in summer. *Correa* is named for the eighteenth-century Portuguese botanist Jose Correa de Serra.

### C. *alba*

This is a low, compact, evergreen, rounded shrub with rounded, downy leaves $1^1/_2$ in (about 3 cm) long. White (sometimes pink) bell-shaped flowers, opening to star-shaped blooms, appear intermittently throughout the year but mostly in winter. It grows to a height of $4^1/_2$ ft (about 1.3 m) and a spread of 3 ft (about 90 cm). As it tolerates salt spray it does well in coastal gardens, and makes an excellent sand binder.

ZONES 9–10

### C. 'Dusky Bells'

**syn. *C.* 'Carmine Bells'**

This spreading, dense, evergreen shrub takes its name from the delightful dusky pink, bell-shaped flowers that appear from fall to spring. It grows to 24 in (about 60 cm) high with a spread of around 6 ft (about 1.8 m) and does best in shady conditions. It has bright green, oval leaves.

ZONES 9–10

### C. *pulchella*

This dense, mounding shrub flowers heavily from fall through spring. Leaves are only 1 in (about 2.5 cm) long, green and smooth; the flowers are typically pink, but may also be orange. The plants are around 3–4 ft (about 90–120 cm) tall and spread somewhat wider. They are easily grown in full sun or partial shade.

ZONES 9–10

## CORYLOPSIS

WINTER HAZEL

Native to China and Japan, these deciduous shrubs are grown for their fragrant catkins of yellow flowers, which are produced before the hazel-like leaves. The leaves often color well in fall. They require a loamy acid soil containing organic matter and semi-shady, sheltered conditions. Propagate from seed in fall or from softwood cuttings in summer; layer low branches if necessary. The flowers may be damaged by frost. Prune only to remove dead wood.

### C. *pauciflora*

Fragrant, bell-shaped flowers are borne on this dense shrub from early to mid-spring. It has a bushy habit, reaching a height and spread of 6 ft (about 1.8 m). Densely branched, it has slender, twiggy growths and bright green leaves that are bronze when young. Shelter from cold winds.

ZONES 6–10

### C. *spicata*

SPIKE WINTER HAZEL

Native to Japan, this deciduous, many-stemmed shrub is popular for its attractive foliage and late winter flowers. It grows slowly to a height of 6 ft (about 1.8 m) and a spread of 9 ft (about 2.7 m). The leaves of this spreading shrub are dull, bristle-toothed and pale green. In late winter small, fragrant, lemon-green, bell-shaped flowers appear in drooping racemes. It prefers a neutral to mildly acid soil rich in leafmold, and semi-shady conditions. Propagate from softwood cuttings in summer or from seed in fall.

ZONES 6–10

## CORYLUS

### *avellana* 'Contorta'

HARRY LAUDER'S WALKING STICK

This strange-looking form of the European hazel is at its best in winter when the leafless stems are most easily seen. It grows as a mass of contorted stems and branches clothed in broad, toothed leaves. Sleek, greenish yellow catkins around 3 in (about 7.5 cm) long appear on its bare limbs in late winter. It also produces edible brown nuts, though not as reliably as the species. It requires full sun or partial shade and deep, rich, well-drained soil. Propagate from cuttings in fall or by grafting in summer. The foliage is prone to mildew. Prune out any straight shoots from the understock to maintain the curious branching character.

ZONES 4–10

## COTINUS

### *coggygria*

**syn. *Rhus cotinus***

SMOKE TREE, SMOKE BUSH

This tall-growing, deciduous shrub, found in southern Europe and in Asia, is grown chiefly for its splendid fall color and unusual flowerheads. Its rounded, light green leaves turn a glorious yellow-red in fall, more so in colder areas. Its fruits are unimpressive, as are its flowers, but the masses of slender, silky flower stalks form pale gray clusters from late summer through fall, giving the appearance of smoke—hence the common name. Smoke tree does best in a well-drained soil that is not too rich; it needs full sun or semi-shade. It grows to a height and spread of 15 ft (about 4.5 m). Prune back to growth buds by two-thirds in winter. Propagate from softwood cuttings in summer, or from seed in fall. Cultivars such as 'Royal Purple' and 'Nutcutt's Variety' are more commonly grown for their season-long purple foliage and pinkish smoke; their fall colors are less spectacular.

ZONES 3–10

## COTONEASTER

COTONEASTER

This genus of evergreen and deciduous shrubs comes from Europe, North Africa and northern Asia. They are from the same family (Rosaceae) as the quince; the Greek *kotoneon* and *aster* together mean "like a quince", and the genus name is pronounced "kotonee-aster", not "cotton-easter". Cotoneasters are perhaps the most popular of berry-bearing shrubs anywhere—having the added attraction of tolerating almost any kind of soil condition (except waterlogged soil). They do thrive a little better, however, when the soil is dry and alkaline. They are

*Correa alba*

*Correa pulchella*

*Corylopsis spicata*

*Correa* 'Dusky Bells'

*Cotinus coggygria*

*Corylus avellana* 'Contorta'

*Cotoneaster lacteus*

*Cotoneaster microphyllus*

*Cotoneaster horizontalis*

*Cotoneaster multiflorus*

*Cotoneaster apiculatus*

*Cotoneaster dammeri*

*Cotoneaster salicifolius*

also very drought resistant. They are eminently suitable for use as an arching, specimen shrub, but may be used for hedging or for ground cover. Some of the evergreen species do well in either sun or semi-shade, but deciduous varieties and cultivars prefer full sun. Propagate from cuttings in summer or seed in fall.

### *C. apiculatus*

CRANBERRY COTONEASTER

A low, mounding, deciduous shrub, cranberry cotoneaster gets its name from the bright red cranberry-like fruits that appear in fall. The $^1/_2$ in (about 1 cm) leaves are nearly round and are wavy margined, turning burgundy in the fall. The branches are low and arching, eventually creating a mound of 24–36 in (about 60–90 cm) in height, spreading to 5 ft (about 1.5 m) or more. Pale pink flowers appear in late spring. An excellent ground cover for cold regions, for planting in large urban containers or for cascading over a wall.

ZONES 3–9

### *C. dammeri*

BEARBERRY COTONEASTER

This trailing, evergreen shrub grows to a height of 12 in (about 30 cm) with a spread of 6 ft (about 1.8 m) or more. In summer it bears striking, white flowers with purple anthers, followed in fall by red fruits. It is vulnerable at times to fireblight. The leaves are glossy, dark green and oval. The cultivar 'Lowfast' quickly spreads to 10–15 ft (about 3–4.5 m) while remaining under 12 in (about 30 cm) in height.

ZONES 5–10

### *C. divaricatus*

SPREADING COTONEASTER

A deciduous shrub from China, this has many upright, branching stems to 5 ft (about 1.5 m) with small leaves that turn red in the fall. Pale pink flowers become bright red fruits that last into winter. It can easily spread to 10–12 ft (about 3–3.5 m). Good for massing in full sun or light shade.

ZONES 5–9

### *C. horizontalis*

ROCK COTONEASTER

This low-growing, deciduous bush from China has horizontal, herringbone branches that arch along the ground; its ultimate height is under 3 ft (about 90 cm) with a spread of 6 ft (about 1.8 m) or more. From late spring to early summer it bears attractive pinkish white flowers, which are followed by bright red berries. The round, glossy green leaves turn scarlet in the fall. *C. horizontalis* is sturdy and makes an excellent addition to a rock garden.

ZONES 4–10

### *C. lacteus*

syn. *C. parneyi*

RED CLUSTERBERRY

One of the larger species, this is a large, spreading shrub (10 ft by 10 ft/3 m by 3m) or a small, umbrella-shaped tree of around 15 ft (about 4.5 m) in height and spread. Its evergreen leaves are 2–3 in (about 5–7.5 cm) long, leathery, green on top and silvery on the underside. White flowers are produced in 2–3 in (about 5–7.5 cm) clusters in spring followed by red berries that last from fall through most of winter. Best if given enough space to develop its natural arching shape; avoid shearing.

ZONES 7–10

### *C. microphyllus*

LITTLE-LEAF COTONEASTER

A low-growing, evergreen shrub useful as a ground cover, in the rockery or sheared as edging for bed or border. The tiny leaves are deep green and glossy. The white flowers are produced along the stems in few-flowered clusters, followed by bright red fruits in fall. Horizontal stems trail and root at nodes, spreading to 6 ft (about 1.8 m) or more; secondary stems rise to 24 in (about 60 cm).

ZONES 5–10

### *C. multiflorus*

syn. *C. reflexus*

MANY-FLOWERED COTONEASTER

Native from Caucasus to China, this deciduous shrub reaches a height of 10 ft (about 3 m). It has arching, pendulous branches and oval to rounded leaves. White flowers, in clusters of 3 to 12, are freely borne from late spring to early summer; these are followed by red, berry-like fruit. It prefers full sun.

ZONES 5–10

### *C. salicifolius*

WILLOWLEAF COTONEASTER

The long, slender, arching branches of this vigorous evergreen, also from China, make it a graceful addition to any garden. The small, white flowers borne in winter are not much to speak about, but the clusters of bright red berries appearing in fall are a delight. The leaves are narrow, lance shaped and dark green, with distinct veins. It grows to a height and spread of 10 ft (about 3 m). 'Fall Fire' ('Herbstfeuer') is a ground-covering cultivar only 24 in (about 60 cm) tall but spreading to 6–8 ft (about 1.8–2.4 m).

ZONES 6–10

*Cowania mexicana* var. *stansburiana*

## COWANIA

### *mexicana* var. *stansburiana*

CLIFF ROSE

A somewhat straggly shrub native to the deserts of the Southwest, this is a dependable addition to a desert garden. The rose-like, creamy white flowers in spring are followed quickly by feathery seedheads that soften the outline of the plant. The leaves are tiny, deeply toothed and evergreen. Ultimate height is around 6 ft (about 1.8 m) with a similar spread. Give it full sun, a well-drained soil and no more water than nature provides once it is established in the ground.

ZONES 5–9

## CUPHEA
### *ignea*
**syn. *C. platycentra***
CIGAR FLOWER

The most common of the cupheas, this native of Central America is popular in temperate to subtropical areas. A petite sub-shrub with bright green leaves, it can grow untidily so remove flowered shoots after bloom to maintain a compact habit. Tubular orange-red flowers appear in fall, each with a white ring at the mouth. *C. ignea* prefers fertile, well-drained soil and full sun conditions. Grows to a height and spread of 30 in (about 76 cm). In colder climates, grow as a summer annual.
ZONES 9–11

## CYTISUS
BROOM

Among the brightest and gaudiest of the pea family, this genus of flowering, arching deciduous or evergreen shrubs is native to the Mediterranean area and the islands of the Atlantic. The abundant, pea-like flowers range in color from shades of pink, red, cream and pure yellow to tan. They prefer full sun and well-drained soil that is not too rich. They do not transplant well. Brooms are ideal at the back of mixed borders or as rock plants. The species are best propagated from semi-ripe cuttings in summer or from seed in fall.

### *C.* x *praecox*
WARMINSTER BROOM

This semi-weeping, deciduous shrub bears pale yellow, pea-like flowers in spring. These have a characteristically acrid smell. The tiny, silky, gray-green leaves are quickly deciduous, but the shrubs maintain their interest through the fine texture of the twigs, also gray-green. *C.* x *praecox* prefers sunny conditions and a well-drained soil. It grows to a height and spread of $4^1/_2$ ft (about 1.3 m).
ZONES 5–10

### *C. scoparius*
SCOTCH BROOM

This deciduous, arching shrub is a native of Europe. Valued for its profusion of bright yellow flowers, which appear in spring and early summer. *C. scoparius* grows to a height and spread of $4^1/_2$ ft (about 1.3 m). In California and the Northwest this species has become a weed. Select one of the numerous cultivars, which tend to produce few seeds; 'Burkwoodii' is a garnet-red selection.
ZONES 5–10

## DABOECIA
### *cantabrica*
IRISH HEATH

This evergreen shrub, a native of Ireland, grows to a height and spread of 20 in (about 50 cm). It prefers a peaty, well-drained but moist, slightly acid soil. A slow-growing bush, it flowers throughout the year except in winter, bearing pinkish purple, urn-shaped flowers. The leaves are oval to lance shaped, dark green above, silver-gray below. It prefers full sun in cooler areas and semi-shade elsewhere. Propagate from semi-hardwood cuttings kept under glass.
ZONES 6–10

## DAHLIA
### *excelsa*
TREE DAHLIA

This woody, tuberous, bushy perennial is grown for its magnificent fall bloom of single, large, pink, slender flowers with yellow centers, which grow to 4 in (about 10 cm) across. *D. excelsa* has thick, bamboo-like stems and grows to a height of 12-15 ft (about 3.5-4.5 m). It needs well-drained soil and a sunny position. Propagate in spring from seed or basal shoot cuttings or by division of tubers. Cut the plants back hard in fall.
ZONES 8–11

## DALEA
### *pulchra*
INDIGO BUSH, BUSH DALEA

This low, shrubby native of southern Arizona has tiny, silvery green leaves and purplish flowers clustered in dense heads in spring. Butterflies and bees seek the nectar in the flowers. Useful in the dry desert garden or in the rockery, it demands a well-drained soil in full sun; it is quite tolerant of alkaline soils and does not require much fertility. Propagate from fresh seed in spring or from semi-hardwood cuttings. Ultimate height is around 5 ft (about 1.5 m) with a similar spread.
ZONES 9–10

*Daboecia cantabrica*

*Cytisus scoparius* 'Burkwoodii'

*Cytisus* x *praecox*

*Dahlia excelsa*

*Cuphea ignea*

## DAPHNE

DAPHNE

Found in Europe and Asia, these evergreen, semi-evergreen or deciduous shrubs are grown for their delightfully fragrant, tubular flowers that appear in winter and spring. Most thrive in semi-shady conditions and prefer a slightly acid, fertile, peaty soil that is well drained but not too dry. Water lightly and use a small amount of complete fertilizer after flowering. Excessive watering will cause collar rot. Transplanting is not recommended, so choose the site carefully. It is best to grow daphnes in a raised spot, with the root junction above soil level. Between summer waterings allow the soil to dry out. All parts of this plant, including the fruits, are poisonous. The genus is named after the nymph in Greek mythology who, rather than face the unwanted affections of the pursuing sun god Apollo, turned into a flowering shrub.

*Daphne odora*

*Desfontainea spinosa*

*Deutzia* 'Rosalin'

*Daphne tangutica*

*Daphne* × *burkwoodii*

*Daphne cneorum*

### *D.* × *burkwoodii*

BURKWOOD'S DAPHNE

The dense clusters of fragrant, white and pink flowers of this upright, semi-evergreen shrub appear in late spring, and sometimes for a second time in fall. Its leaves are pale to mid-green and lance shaped. It prefers a sunny spot with well-drained soil and grows to a height and spread of $4^{1}/_{2}$ ft (about 1.3 m).

ZONES 4–9

### *D. cneorum*

GARLAND FLOWER

A low-growing, evergreen native to central and southern Europe, this delightful shrub deserves a place in the rockery. Its trailing to mounding form and fragrant pink flowers in late spring are appealing. It demands excellent drainage and prefers cool summers; give it a little afternoon shade where summers are warm. It prefers peaty soil, and moderate water during summer.

ZONES 4–9

### *D. mezereum*

FEBRUARY DAPHNE

Though open and stiff this deciduous shrub looks great when planted in groups, the bare stems offering clusters of fragrant, purplish flowers in early spring. Simple leaves follow but it may be deciduous by late summer, revealing bright red berries. Give it a shady situation with a well-drained, woodsy soil.

ZONES 4–9

### *D. odora*

WINTER DAPHNE

The most popular of the genus, this evergreen, bushy shrub from China grows to a height and spread of $4^{1}/_{2}$ ft (about 1.3 m). It bears fragrant, white to purplish pink flowers from mid-winter to early spring and has glossy, dark green, oval leaves. As a cut flower, it lasts well indoors. The form with yellow-margined leaves is said to be more tolerant of cold.

ZONES 7–10

### *D. tangutica*

Native to western China, this evergreen bears clusters of perfumed, white-stained, rosy-purple flowers in mid- to late spring. It has dark leathery leaves and stout shoots and a bushy habit, growing to a height and spread of around 3 ft (about 90 cm).

ZONES 4–9

## DESFONTAINEA

### *spinosa*

This compact, evergreen native of the Andes Mountains superficially resembles a holly with its spiny, glossy, dark green leaves, but the delightful, showy, orange-scarlet tubular flowers appearing in midsummer cancel the illusion. *D. spinosa* prefers moist, peaty, preferably acid soil. In dry conditions it needs some shade and in cold areas does better in shelter. Even in these optimal conditions it will onlygrow slowly, to a height and spread of around $4^{1}/_{2}$ ft (about 1.3 m). Propagate from semi-ripe cuttings in summer.

ZONES 8–10

## DEUTZIA

These deciduous, arching bushes appear fairly nondescript until late spring or early summer, when a profusion of flowers appears—white, pink or bicolored depending on the species. Related to *Philadelphus*, which it resembles, the genus *Deutzia* is a native of China, Japan and the Himalayas. The shrubs prefer fertile, moist but well-drained soil and do best in full sun, although they require semi-shade in warmer areas. Give fertilizer in early spring to encourage a full flower yield. Prune heavily after flowering to encourage bloom—remove about half the old wood. Propagate from softwood cuttings in summer.

### *D. gracilis*

SLENDER DEUTZIA

An erect shrub with toothed leaves, this species covers itself with pure white (or occasionally pink) flowers in late spring. It blends into the background for the rest of the year, except the cultivar 'Nikko' which has maroon foliage in the fall. Best in full sun and average garden soil.

*Deutzia* × *rosea*

*Deutzia gracilis*

Height is under 6 ft (about 1.8 m) with a spread of 4 ft (about 1.2 m).
ZONES 4–9

### *D.* 'Rosalin'

This deciduous, hybrid shrub of uncertain parentage produces clusters of pink flowers from late spring through to summer. It has a rounded, bushy habit, reaching a height of 6 ft (about 1.8 m) with a spread of around $4^1/_2$ ft (about 1.3 m). It does particularly well in pots and will flower early if brought into a greenhouse in mid-winter.
ZONES 5–10

### *D.* x *rosea*

This compact, bushy, arching shrub produces massed clusters of beautiful, bell-shaped, pale pink flowers in spring and early summer. Its leaves are dark green, oval and deciduous and it grows to a height and spread of 30 in (about 76 cm). *D.* x *rosea* prefers a moist soil and partial shade.
ZONES 5–9

### *D. scabra*

This upright, deciduous shrub bears dense clusters of pink-tinged white blooms in spring. Its leaves are dark green and oval and it grows to a height of 9 ft (about 2.7 m) with a spread of $4^1/_2$ ft (about 1.3 m). It prefers a moist soil and partial shade.
ZONES 5–10

## DODONAEA
### *viscosa*
HOP BUSH, HOPSEED BUSH

This dense, fast-growing, short-lived bush is grown for the showy clusters of pinkish beige fruits in summer which follow its insignificant bloom. The sticky, glossy, pale green leaves are deciduous. Native to Australia, New Zealand, Arizona and South Africa, it succeeds in most warm, dry areas outside the tropics. *D. viscosa* grows to a height of 9 ft (about 2.7 m) or more and a spread of $4^1/_2$ ft (about 1.3 m), with reddish brown, peeling bark and thick branches. It prefers a well-drained soil, and sun or partial shade. To keep its shape, cut back in summer after flowering. Propagate from seed in spring or semi-ripe cuttings in summer; it will strike in any location. Purple-leaved forms such as 'Purpurea' are most popular in California; in Arizona use the native stock, which will be hardier and more adapted to the local conditions.
ZONES 8–10

## DRYANDRA

Native to Western Australia, these bushy shrubs are grown for the small, yellow or orange flowers in rounded domes that grow in late

*Echium fastuosum*

winter to spring. Their elongated, saw-toothed leaves are evergreen. They prefer full light or partial shade and do best in a well-drained, light, sandy soil without a large amount of nitrates or phosphates. They grow to a height and spread of 6 ft (about 1.8 m). Water moderately. Propagate from seed in spring
ZONES 9–10

## DURANTA
### *repens*
syn. *D. erecta, D. plumieri*
GOLDEN DEWDROP, SKY FLOWER

Native to Florida, Mexico, the West Indies and Brazil, this handsome, weeping shrub makes an ideal windbreak or hedge in warmer climates. It bears delightful but tiny, violet-blue flowers in summer, which are followed by a shower of yellow berries. (These are poisonous, so keep children away.) The dark green, oval leaves are evergreen. *D. repens* grows quickly to a height of 9 ft (about 2.7 m) with a spread of 6 ft (about 1.8 m). It does best in a well-drained soil and in full light or partial shade. Prune for shape (the plants can be clipped as a hedge) and water potted plants when growing. Propagate from seed in spring or from semi-ripe cuttings in summer. Whitefly can cause problems.
ZONES 9–11

## ECHIUM
### *fastuosum*
syn. *E. candicans*
PRIDE OF MADEIRA

This native of the Mediterranean is widely used in West Coast gardens for its mounds of bold, gray-green leaves and short spires of blue to purple flowers in spring. Very drought tolerant, it prefers a well-drained soil in full sun. Ultimate height and spread is around 6 ft (about 1.8 m). Prune faded flower spikes, and tip prune new growth to encourage branching and more flowers. Excellent for coastal gardens; not good where heat and humidity combine during the summer.
ZONES 9–11

*Dryandra nobilis*

*Duranta repens*

*Dodonaea viscosa*

*Deutzia scabra*

*Enkianthus campanulatus*

*Edgeworthia papyrifera*

*Eremophila glabra*

## EDGEWORTHIA
*papyrifera*

PAPERBUSH

This open, rounded shrub is native to eastern Asia. Once used in Japan for papermaking, it has tough, fibrous branches so flexible they can be knotted without breaking. In late winter and early spring it bears sweet-smelling heads of tubular yellow flowers. The oval, dark green leaves are deciduous. It likes moist, well-drained, leafy soil and full sun or partial shade. The position should be chosen carefully as it does not transplant well. It grows to a height and spread of $4^1/_2$ ft (about 1.3 m). Propagate from semi-ripe cuttings in summer or seed in fall.
ZONES 8–10

## ELAEAGNUS

These dense, spreading, mainly evergreen shrubs are favorites for hedging and as a backdrop. Found all over the northern hemisphere, they grow well in poor soil. Deciduous species prefer full sun; evergreens thrive in sun or partial shade. Hedges are best trimmed in late summer. Propagate from seed in fall or semi-ripe cuttings in summer. They are generally considered deer proof.

### *E. angustifolia*

RUSSIAN OLIVE

Large shrubs or small trees, this deciduous member of the genus has been widely planted as a hedgerow or windbreak throughout the northern states. In some areas it has become a pest by naturalizing along streamsides. Still, it is a valuable and tough plant for the low-care garden, serving as a 10–12 ft (about 3–3.5 m) tall screen or as a multi-trunked patio tree. The flowers in spring are insignificant but pleasantly fragrant; the "olives" that follow can be messy. This species is tolerant of almost any adverse condition. Prune to control size, and watch that seedlings don't appear in neighboring natural areas.
ZONES 2–9

### *E. pungens*

SILVERBERRY

This is the most common of the genus. An evergreen bush with long, prickly, horizontal branches it is excellent for hedges, growing to a height of 9 ft (about 2.7 m) and a spread of 15 ft (about 4.5 m). In fall it bears fragrant, tiny, bell-shaped, cream flowers. The glossy, oval leaves—dark green above, silvery with brown spots beneath—are evergreen. Numerous selections have been made with variegated foliage. 'Maculata' has splashes of gold in the center of each leaf; 'Marginata' has leaves that are edged in silver.
ZONES 7–10

## ENCELIA
*farinosa*

BRITTLEBRUSH, INCIENSO

A native of southwestern deserts, this mounding shrub covers itself with bright yellow daisies from late winter through spring. Well adapted to the harshness of the desert, it remains low and compact (little more than 2 in/5 cm) on natural rainfall but with irrigation it may become a lanky 6 ft (about 1.8 m) shrub. The silvery leaves usually drop during the hot summer, when it is best to cut the stems to the ground to encourage new growth for next season's flowers. It easily seeds itself around so there are usually plenty of new plants available to move into bare areas or to share with friends.
ZONES 8–10

*Elaeagnus pungens* 'Maculata'

## ENKIANTHUS
*campanulatus*

Related to azaleas and heaths, these cool-climate, tree-like shrubs are originally from China and Japan where the flowers are gathered in large numbers to celebrate New Year. In spring the open, spreading habit is gaily adorned with small, bell-shaped, red-veined, creamy flowers. The shrub is deciduous; tufts of dull green leaves turn bright red in fall. *E. campanulatus* does well in sun or partial shade in a moist, acid, peaty soil. Like all the species of *Enkianthus,* it does not tolerate air pollution well and does best in a country garden. Propagate from semi-ripe cuttings in summer or seed in fall.
ZONES 5–10

## EREMOPHILA

EMU BUSH

Native to the outback areas of Australia, this genus is appropriately named "lovers of lonely places". Evergreen, bun-shaped shrubs, they do best in a sunny, open position and require well-drained, slightly alkaline soil. They dislike moist conditions and will thrive when conditions are very dry—they can go for years without water. Throughout most of the year they bear tubular flowers of varying color. Propagate from semi-ripe tip cuttings in fall. Grow on for at least a year before planting out.

### *E. glabra*

COMMON EMU BUSH

This tenacious shrub bears red, yellow or green flowers mostly during spring. It grows to a height of $4^1/_2$ ft (about 1.3 m) and a spread

*Erica* x *darleyensis*

*Erica carnea*

*Erica cinerea*

*Erica bauera*

*Eremophila maculata*

*Erica arborea* 'Alpina'

of 3–9 ft (about 90–270 cm). Its lance-shaped, silvery gray leaves are evergreen.
ZONES 9–10

### *E. maculata*
SPOTTED EMU BUSH

From winter to spring this rounded shrub produces tubular, yellow, pink, white or red flowers with spotted throats. Evergreen, with oval or linear, gray-green leaves, it grows to a height of 3 ft (about 90 cm) and a spread of 6 ft (about 1.8 m). It prefers dry, sunny conditions.
ZONES 9–10

## *ERICA*
HEATH

This genus of evergreen shrubs is native to southern Africa, parts of northern Africa and much of western Europe. Related to azaleas and rhododendrons, it boasts some of the most popular flowering plants, partly because of the long flowering season. They are very particular, however, requiring an acid soil that is porous and moist; most will do very poorly if there is lime in the soil or water. Avoid animal manure. They bear tubular, waxy flowers of varying lengths, and small linear leaves grouped around a stem. Propagate from seed—kept moist and sheltered—or from tip cuttings taken in fall or early winter. Prune after flowering to encourage dense growth.

### *E. arborea*
TREE HEATH

This is a large shrub or small tree, 10–20 ft (about 3–6 m) tall and nearly as wide, growing from a swollen "burl" at the base of the trunk. Fragrant white flowers appear in spring. A native of southern Europe and northern Africa, the burl is the raw material from which pipes are made. 'Alpina' has vivid green foliage that contrasts well with the white flowers.
ZONES 9–10

### *E. bauera*
BRIDAL HEATH

Native to South Africa this upright, branching, evergreen shrub bears clusters of tubular white or pink flowers for most of the year, set among tiny, narrow, gray-green leaves. It grows to a height and spread of 3 ft (about 90 cm).
ZONES 9–10

### *E. carnea*
syn. *E. herbacea*
WINTER HEATH

This evergreen, spreading shrub makes good ground cover. From early winter to late spring it bears bell-shaped to tubular flowers in shades of red and pink (sometimes white). Its mid- to dark green leaves are arranged in whorls. It will withstand some lime in the soil and shady conditions. It grows to a height of 12 in (about 30 cm) and spread of around 20 in (about 50 cm) or more. There are numerous named selections available from specialty nurseries.
ZONES 5–9

### *E. cinerea*
BELL HEATH

From early summer through to early fall this compact native of Europe bears bell-shaped flowers in shades of pink, white and dark red. It has mid- to deep green, needle-like, evergreen leaves. It does best in a dry, warm position with an acid soil. Numerous attractive cultivars bear blooms of varying hue.
ZONES 9–10

### *E.* x *darleyensis*

This hybrid heath is one of the more dependable species, especially in California. Mounds 12 in (about 30 cm) tall and 24 in (about 60 cm) wide are covered with rosy-purple flowers during winter and spring. It is less demanding of acid soils than most heaths. Various cultivars are available.
ZONES 6–10

Eriogonum umbellatum

Erica vagans

Erica mammosa

### *E. mammosa*

An upright shrub from South Africa, this species flowers nearly year round in the coastal gardens of California with either pink or orange tubular flowers. Growing to a height of around 4 ft (about 1.2 m) and spread of 24–36 in (about 60-90 cm) it is one of the most dependable of the South African species, asking only a well-drained soil, full sun and moderate water during the summer.

ZONES 9–10

### *E. mediterranea*

BISCAY HEATH

As the name suggests, this attractive species is native to Mediterranean countries. An upright evergreen, it grows to 7 ft (about 2 m) high with a spread up to 6 ft (about 1.8 m). In winter and early spring it bears pinkish mauve, bell-shaped flowers. The mid-green leaves are shaped like a needle. Frost may damage the top of the plant, but it will recover from the base. Many attractive, fragrant cultivars exist; most not more than 32 in (about 81 cm) in height or width.

ZONES 9–10

### *E. vagans*

CORNISH HEATH

This summer-blooming species from Ireland, the southwest corner of England and southwestern Europe is among the hardiest of heaths. Its flowers are purplish pink against the deep green foliage. An upright mound growing to 3 ft (about 90 cm) in height with a similar spread. Numerous cultivars are available with pink, white and purple flowers.

ZONES 5–9

Erythrina x bidwillii

Erica mediterranea

## *ERIOGONUM umbellatum*

SULPHUR BUCKWHEAT

This evergreen is grown for its attractive heads of tiny bright yellow flowers, borne in summer and turning copper with time. It is a useful rock plant, growing to a height of 12 in (about 30 cm) and a spread of 24 in (about 60 cm). It has a prostrate to upright form and the dense green leaves have white, downy undersides. In cooler, wetter areas some shelter is required. Propagate from semi-ripe cuttings in summer or from seed in spring or fall. Perennial root clumps can be divided in spring. Remove spent flowerheads to prolong flowering.

ZONES 7–10

## *ERYTHRINA x bidwillii*

A bold, deciduous shrub or small trees, this hybrid coral tree has deciduous leaves divided into three nearly triangular leaflets. From early summer through fall it produces 24 in (about 60 cm) long racemes of brilliant red flowers. The stems are spiky, so take care in placement and in pruning. Plants reach 8 ft (about 2.4 m) tall and wider, or can be trained into a tree-like shape to 20 ft (about 6 m). As a shrub, the stems can be cut to the ground each winter to maintain a compact habit and to encourage more flowering. Full sun, a well-drained soil and moderate water through the summer are all that is needed for a spectacular show of flowers.

ZONES 8–11

## *ESCALLONIA*

Evergreen shrubs from South America, these plants have aromatic foliage and clusters of small, fragrant flowers over a long season. Leaves are toothed and dense; the plants will tolerate some degree of shearing, but are more graceful if left unsheared. Generally displaying an upright and arching habit, they may be used as background shrubs or for screening or may be trained as small trees; smaller forms make good informal hedges. They prefer a cool coastal situation, being very tolerant of winds, and accept a variety of soils with the exception of highly alkaline ones. Plant in full sun along the coast, part shade inland. Though drought tolerant, they are best with occasional water during the summer months. Prune after flowering to shape and control size. Propagate from softwood cuttings in summer.

### *E.* x *exoniensis*

An upright species with rose-pink flowers nearly all year round. The ultimate height is 6 ft (about 1.8 m), although plants can be kept lower with judicious pruning. Easily grown in any soil, sun or light shade and with some summer water.
ZONES 9–10

### *E.* x *langleyensis* 'Apple Blossom'

This is the most common cultivar of this hybrid species, displaying plenty of apple-blossom pink flowers from spring through summer. Dark evergreen leaves appear on shrubs of around 6 ft (about 1.8 m) in height and spread. It benefits from pinching for a dense habit.
ZONES 9–10

### *E. rubra*

This is a parent of the two hybrid forms above, but by itself is a red or crimson flowering shrub with typically deep green, glossy leaves. A large mound around 15 ft (about 4.5 m) tall and wide, it serves very well as a windbreak near the coast. Compact cultivars 'C.F. Ball' and 'William Watson' make attractive ground covers.
ZONES 9–10

## *EUONYMUS*

These evergreen or deciduous shrubs with the occasional tree and climber are prized for their foliage, their odd, spindle-shaped seed pods and the breathtaking fall color of deciduous species. Found worldwide, the deciduous shrubs are grown in cool, temperate climates while the evergreens are more suited to warmer conditions. Requirements for sun and shade vary with the species, but generally the deciduous ones need full sun and the evergreens do better with part shade. All like a well-drained soil. Propagate from semi-ripe cuttings in summer or seed in fall.

### *E. alatus*

BURNING BUSH, WINGED EUONYMUS

This slow-growing deciduous shrub from China and Japan is grown mainly for its splendid fall color and display of purple fruits with scarlet seeds. It is of stiff and open habit to around 10 ft (about 3 m) tall and wide, with pointed, oval leaves which turn brilliant crimson in fall. It has stems with corky wings and tiny, greenish spring flowers. 'Compactus' is even brighter in fall color, with wingless stems; it reaches only 6 ft (about 1.8 m).
ZONES 3–9

### *E. europaeus*

EUROPEAN SPINDLE TREE

A 20 ft (about 6 m) tall deciduous shrub or small tree, the spindle tree takes its name from the use of its hard, perfectly straight branches in weaving in the days before the mechanical loom. It is grown in gardens for its lavish display of fruits, whose carmine red calyces split to reveal orange seeds. The tiny greenish spring flowers are insignificant and the slender, pointed leaves color in the fall. 'Red Cascade' is an especially fine cultivar.
ZONES 3–9

*Euonymus alatus*

*Escallonia rubra*

*Escallonia* x *l.* 'Apple Blossom'

*Euonymus europaeus*

*Escallonia* x *exoniensis*

*Euphorbia pulcherrima*

*Euonymus j.* 'Aureomarginatus'

*Euonymus fortunei* 'Emerald 'n' Gold'

*Euphorbia fulgens*

### *E. fortunei*

WINTER CREEPER

A most important group of shrubs or climbers, popular for their evergreen leaves and for their colorful fruit. The shrubby types are dense, but are often irregular in habit; the climbers will serve as ground covers or climb a vertical surface such as a wall or tree trunk. Typical foliage color is dark green, although numerous variegated forms have been introduced; one of the most popular is the 24 in (about 60 cm) shrub 'Emerald 'n' Gold' with dark green leaves edged in gold. Fruits only develop on adult plants but have pinkish hulls that split open to reveal bright orange seeds inside. Most forms do best with some degee of shade. Scale insects seem less of a problem in the shade.

ZONES 5–10

### *E. japonicus*

JAPANESE EUONYMUS

This dense, upright evergreen grows naturally to a height of 10 ft (about 3 m). It has green, oval leaves though is more commonly seen with variegated leaves of silver, cream, yellow or gold; 'Aureomarginatus' has leaves deeply margined in yellow. The small, star-shaped flowers in summer develop into pretty coral-pink fruits containing orange seeds. Very common in the South, where they are often used for hedging or sheared into geometric topiaries. Very tolerant of heat, humidity and poor soils.

ZONES 7–10

*Euphorbia milii*

## *EUPHORBIA*

MILKWEED, SPURGE

This genus contains over 1000 widely varying species of shrubs, perennials and succulents. Each species bears a spectacular show of colored bracts rather than true flowers, and the milky sap is poisonous. The shrubs do well in sun or partial shade and in moist but well-drained soil. Propagate from seed in fall or spring, from basal cuttings in spring or summer or by division in early spring or early fall.

### *E. fulgens*

SCARLET PLUME

This evergreen, arching shrub grows to a height of $4^1/_2$ ft (about 1.3 m) and a spread of 24 in (about 60 cm). In winter to spring its long branches bear sprays of flowers, each cluster surrounded by red bracts. It has mid- to deep green, oval to lance-shaped leaves. Propagate from hardwood cuttings in summer.

ZONES 8–10

### *E. milii*

**syn. *E. splendens***

CROWN OF THORNS

This slow-growing, ferociously thorny, semi-succulent shrub is a native of Madagascar. Deciduous in cooler areas, it is drought resistant and grows to a height of 3 ft (about 90 cm) and a spread of 30 in (about 76 cm). It is excellent in rock gardens or in cavities and is often used as a low hedge in coastal areas. Throughout the year and especially in spring it bears tiny, yellowish flowers enveloped by bright red bracts whether there are pale green leaves on the branches or not. It prefers a sunny spot and well-drained soil.

ZONES 10–11

### *E. pulcherrima*

POINSETTIA

The hollow-stemmed poinsettia is the showiest and most popular of this diverse genus. A native of Mexico, it does best in well-drained soil with plenty of water. From late fall to spring small, greenish-red flowers appear surrounded by bright-red, pink or white bracts. The oval, green leaves may be evergreen or deciduous. Prune poinsettias back hard to encourage shoot growth. Grow them in pots for pleasant indoor winter decoration, although the color will not be as good as when grown outdoors in subtropical or tropical climates where it will grow 12 ft (about 3.5 m) tall and wide. Indoor plants need careful attention to a shortened day length in the fall, which encourages the development of the red bracts for the Christmas season.

ZONES 10–11

*Fatsia japonica*

## *EURYOPS*
### *pectinatus*

A native of South Africa, this shrubby evergreen grows well in the mild winter regions of the South and West; elsewhere it does well in containers. Excellent for shrub beds and borders, it likes sun or partial shade in hot conditions and a moist, well-drained, gravelly soil. From winter to spring it bears delightful, bright yellow, daisy-like flowers. It has a spreading habit, with gray-green leaves. It dislikes root disturbance so avoid transplanting. It grows to a height of 3 ft (about 90 cm) with a spread of 30 in (about 76 cm). Propagate from softwood cuttings in summer.

ZONES 9–10

## *EXOCHORDA*
### *racemosa*

COMMON PEARLBUSH

This deciduous, arching shrub, native to China, is grown for the delightful, upright clusters of white flowers it bears in late spring. These appear from bare wood and the buds resemble a string of pearls—hence the name. *E. racemosa* has oblong, deep blue-green leaves and grows to a height and spread of 12 ft (about 3.5 m). Plant the shrub in loamy but well-drained, acid soil in a sunny position. Thin out old shoots after flowering—this will improve the bloom. It needs regular watering. Propagate from softwood cuttings in summer or seed in fall.

ZONES 4–9

## X *FATSHEDERA*
### *lizei*

This bi-generic hybrid (a botanical rarity) is the offspring of *Fatsia japonica* 'Moseri' and *Hedera helix* 'Hibernica' (Irish ivy). Popular as a house plant, it is also used extensively as ground cover; otherwise it may be trained against a wall or pillar. It prefers partial shade and does best in moist but well-drained, fertile soil. It reaches 6 ft (about 1.8 m) tall with a spread of 9 ft (about 2.7 m). Small, white flowers appear in fall. It bears glossy, deep green leaves; on x *F. lizei* 'Variegata' the leaves have a narrow creamy white edge. Pinch back to keep from falling over, or support it with canes. Propagate in summer from semi-ripe cuttings.

ZONES 8–10

## *FATSIA*
### *japonica*

JAPANESE ARALIA

Japanese aralia is one of the world's most loved house plants. It may also be cultivated as a spreading bush or trained into a single-stemmed tree. It bears splendid, large, rounded, deeply lobed, glossy, dark green leaves under almost any conditions. Dense clusters of tiny, white flowers appear in fall, followed by small, black berries. It does best in sunny or shaded areas and prefers a well-drained, fertile soil. It prefers shelter from cold winds. Cut back hard if it gets too leggy. Propagate by semi-ripe cuttings in summer or from seed in fall or spring.

ZONES 8–10

## *FORSYTHIA*

FORSYTHIA

Profuse early spring displays of yellow flowers are the principal attraction of this genus. Vase shaped and deciduous, they are easy to grow in rich, well-drained soil. They prefer regions where winters are cold and are hardy to at least 13°F (minus 25°C). Propagate from semi-hardwood cuttings taken in summer. The genus was named in the eighteenth century in honor of William Forsyth, gardener to King George III of England.

### *F.* x *intermedia*

FORSYTHIA

This compact, deciduous, arching or spreading shrub bears yellow flowers in spring. Its leaves are dark green and lance shaped. Cultivars such as 'Beatrix Farrand' reach a height of 10 ft (about 3 m) and a spread of 6 ft (about 1.8 m) or more; other selections have more compact habits, but vary only slightly in flower color. Flowering is most dense on wood of the previous year's growth, which is encouraged by pruning after flowering.

ZONES 4–9

*Exochorda racemosa*

*Euryops pectinatus*

*Forsythia* x *intermedia*

x *Fatshedera lizei*

*F. suspensa*

WEEPING FORSYTHIA

The graceful, arching and weeping branching habit of this species sets it apart from other forsythias. The stems arch over until they touch the ground, where they often take root; it is often used as a tall, coarse ground cover on a bank, where the cascading effect is very attractive when in full bloom. Flowers are golden yellow in early spring; some flowers will appear in fall as well. Easily propagated from the pieces that root when a stem touches the ground.

ZONES 5–9

*Fremontodendron californicum*

## FOTHERGILLA

FOTHERGILLA

Two deciduous native shrubs of outstanding garden merit are included here; they differ primarily in the size of the shrubs and its leaves. *F. gardenii,* the dwarf fothergilla, reaches only 3 ft (about 90 cm) in height and spread, with leaves to 2 in (about 5 cm) long; *F. major,* the large fothergilla, grows to more than 6 ft (about 1.8 m) in height and spread, with leaves twice the size of the former. Both species have 1–2 in (about 2.5–5 cm) long spikes of fluffy white, fragrant flowers; in fall the leaves of both turn bright red, yellow and orange, often all on the same plant. Both are native to the mountains of southeastern North America and thrive in situations with some protection from hot afternoon sun (especially in hot summer regions), a rich, well-drained soil and regular water through the growing season. *F.g.* 'Blue Mist' has blue-green leaves. Propagate from softwood cuttings in mid-summer. These are among the most beautiful of Native American shrubs.

ZONES 5–8

*Fouquiera splendens*

*Fuchsia* 'Gartenmeister Bonstedt'

## FOUQUIERA *splendens*

OCOTILLO

One of the most distinctive shrubs of the American desert, the ocotillo is notable for its brilliant racemes of scarlet flowers so popular with hummingbirds. The unbranched stems form a graceful vase shape 12 ft (about 3.5 m) or more in height, each stem topped by a flower cluster in late spring. Tiny leaves line the spiny stems when rains have been plentiful; otherwise the stems are leafless, often appearing dead except for a hint of green in the bark. Most common in the lower deserts of California, Arizona and northern Mexico, these are excellent shrubs for the desert garden, requiring only a well-drained soil and sun. Occasional summer water will allow them to retain their leaves for a longer season. Propagate from cuttings at any time. Cut stems have been lashed together to form impenetrable fences several feet high; often the cut stems will take root, creating a beautiful living fence.

ZONES 8–10

## FREMONTODENDRON *californicum*

COMMON FLANNEL BUSH

This sun-loving, evergreen or semi-evergreen shrub is prized for its bright yellow flowers from spring through early summer. Its lobed, dark green leaves are white felted underneath. A native of California, it thrives in the arid West with full sun and a well-drained, sandy soil; once established it needs no summer water. It grows to a height of 18 ft (about 5.5 m) with a spread of 12 ft (about 3.5 m). It is advisable to wear gloves when handling the plant as it is covered in hairs which can cause allergic reactions. It does not transplant very well, so choose the final location carefully. Propagate from seed or softwood cuttings in summer or from seed in fall or spring. The hybrid 'California Glory' is the easiest in cultivation, tolerating occasional summer water.

ZONES 9–10

*Fothergilla major*

## FUCHSIA

FUCHSIA

Native to the mountain forests of Central and South America, these exotic evergreen and semi-evergreen shrubs and trees are grown for the splendid, pendulous, tubular flowers born from early summer to late fall. These hang from leaf axils, most heavily at the ends of arching branches. Each flower consists of four reflexed sepals and four or more petals, often in a contrasting color. Fuchsias prefer a partially shaded, sheltered position and will thrive in almost any soil, as long as it contains plenty of organic matter. They require plenty of water (sometimes twice a day in summer)—but avoid watering in full sun. Prune back drastically to prevent the plant from becoming too woody, and to maintain shape. Where not hardy, fuchsias make superb summer pot plants for the shaded garden. Bring indoors for the winter. Propagate from softwood cuttings in any season. Red spider mite may cause problems, as will leaf-eating caterpillars. In coastal California the fuchsia mite, introduced from Brazil, has become a serious problem, decimating many fuchsia collections; there is not yet a dependable, non-toxic control. Fortunately some species and cultivars have proven resistant to the mite.

*F.* 'Gartenmeister Bonstedt'

This lax shrub produces large, tubular, orange to brick-red flowers—abundantly, if conditions are mild with plenty of sun. It is quite useful as a garden hedge. Plant at intervals of 30 in (about 76 cm), or as a pot or garden shrub. The leaves of this cultivar are a dark, bronzed red; it is resistant to the fuchsia mite.

ZONES 10–11

*Forsythia suspensa*

*Fuchsia magellanica* var. *gracilis* 'Alba'

*Fuchsia paniculata*

*Fuchsia* 'Fanfare'

### *F.* hybrids

*F. magellanica* and various other species have been used to develop a large group of hybrid cultivars, very popular as pot plants and (in mild winter areas) as garden shrubs for a shaded spot. They can have single or double flowers in shades of white, pink, red, mauve or purple, often with the petals and sepals in contrasting colors. They range in height from less than 3 ft (about 90 cm) to more than 6 ft (about 1.8 m) when planted in the ground. Look for resistant cultivars such as 'Fanfare', 'Carnival' or 'Mrs Victor Reiter'. They are evergreen and will thrive best in fertile, well-drained soil. Prune in late winter for bushiness; propagate from softwood cuttings.
ZONES 10–11

### *F. magellanica* var. *gracilis*

This upright evergreen bears small, red, tubular flowers, with purple petals and red sepals. Black fruits follow. Susceptible to the fuchsia mite.
ZONES 7–10

### *F. magellanica* var. *gracilis* 'Alba'

If growth continues unchecked this cultivar can grow to a considerable size. Prune it back to maintain its shape. This shrub bears attractive, pale pink flowers. Susceptible to the fuchsia mite.
ZONES 7–10

### *F. paniculata*

TREE FUCHSIA

Distinct from the more common hybrid fuchsias, this species from the mountains of Mexico presents its tiny purple flowers in dense terminal panicles, looking very much like a common lilac (without the fragrance). These evergreen shrubs will reach 8-10 ft (about 2.4-3 m) in height and spread, and will flower nearly year round in coastal California. They are reliably resistant to the fuchsia mite.
ZONES 10–11

### *F. procumbens*

TRAILING FUCHSIA

Native to New Zealand this prostrate, evergreen shrub grows to a

*Fuchsia procumbens*

height of 4 in (about 10 cm) with an indefinite spread. It bears erect, orange-tipped, purple and green flowers among small, heart-shaped leaves, followed by large, red berries. It is excellent as a ground cover, or in rock gardens and hanging baskets. Not bothered by the fuchsia mite.
ZONES 9–11

## *GARDENIA*

GARDENIA

Gardenias provide some of the most attractive, fragrant blooms to be found in warm climate gardens worldwide. They do best in full sun to partial shade and like a rich, peaty, well-drained, acid soil. Shorten strong shoots after blooming to maintain a good shape. Water potted plants generously in full growth, less so at other times. Some pests can pose problems—notably aphids, scale, spider mites and whitefly. Propagate from semi-ripe cuttings in summer or from softwood cuttings in spring.

*Fuchsia magellanica* var. *gracilis*

*Garrya elliptica*

*Gardenia thunbergia*

*Gaultheria shallon*

### *G. augusta*
syn. *G. jasminoides*
COMMON GARDENIA

This Chinese species has deep green oval leaves that provide a beautiful background for its pure white, usually double flowers which fade to cream. The flowers are intensely fragrant. In cool areas give them full sun to increase heat build-up. 'Mystery' is the most common, flowering from spring to mid-summer or later but with a rangy habit to 6 ft (about 1.8 m) or more in height and requiring tip pruning to shape. 'Florida' grows to $4^1/_2$ ft (about 1.3 m) with white flowers from summer through winter. 'Radicans' is nearly prostrate, spreading to 3 ft (about 90 cm) with small flowers in summer. 'Veitchii' is a compact form (24–36 in/60–90 cm).
ZONES 8–11

### *G. thunbergia*
TREE GARDENIA

An exceptionally beautiful and desirable shrub, the tree gardenia grows to a height and spread of 10 ft (about 3 m) or more. Though less hardy than *G. augusta*, it is more tolerant of cool summer conditions and is less demanding of perfect soil conditions. In bears fragrant, large, white, terminal flowers set among glossy, deep green leaves.
ZONES 10–11

## *GARRYA*
### *elliptica*
COAST SILKTASSEL

This extraordinary, bushy, dense shrub is cultivated almost exclusively for its curtain of gray-green catkins, which grow up to 8 in (about 20 cm) in length—shorter on female plants which, however, bear decorative bluish berries. These appear in mid-winter to early spring, and may be damaged by frosts. Native to coastal California, *G. elliptica* may grow to a height of 15 ft (about 4.5 m) with a spread of 9 ft (about 2.7 m). It prefers full sun or part shade and well-drained soil to thrive, doing particularly well on the coast or inland. It has leaves that are dark green and leathery. Propagate from semi-hardwood cuttings taken in summer.
ZONES 8–10

*Gaultheria procumbens*

*Gardenia augusta* 'Florida'

## *GAULTHERIA*

These are evergreen shrubs found on the continents bordering the Pacific Ocean. They range in size from prostrate ground covers to large shrubs, nearly all with white flowers shaped like inverted urns and grouped in pendent clusters. Many produce colorful, and sometimes edible, berries. They prefer a rich, well-drained soil and regular water. Propagate from seed or cuttings, or by separating rooted prostrate stems.

### *G. procumbens*
WINTERGREEN, CHECKERBERRY

A native of the woodlands of eastern North America, this prostrate shrub grows only 6 in (about 15 cm) tall but spreads widely by trailing stems. The 1 in (about 2.5 cm) evergreen leaves are deep green and nearly round. The white flowers in early summer are followed by scarlet berries which hold their color well into winter.
ZONES 4–9

### *G. shallon*
SALAL

This species is one of the dominant understorey shrubs in the evergreen forest and coastal mountains of the West Coast of North America. Varying in height from 3 ft to over 6 ft (about 90 to 180 cm), it spreads by underground stems to form broad mounds. Oval leaves are a deep glossy green, flowers are pinkish in spring, and fruits are black and edible but bland.
ZONES 7–10

## *GENISTA*
BROOM

The members of this genus of deciduous shrubs and trees are grown for the fragrance and beauty of their blooms. Native to the Mediterranean areas of North Africa, southern Europe and Asia Minor, they make good seaside shrubs. They do well in hot, sunny conditions and are quite hardy. Grow in a not-too-rich,

*Genista monosperma*

*Genista pilosa* 'Vancouver Gold'

*Genista lydia*

well-drained soil. They will not do well if transplanted. Prune tips to encourage a bushy look. Propagate in spring from seed (soak for 24 hours first) or from semi-hardwood cuttings in summer.

### *G. aetnensis*

MT ETNA BROOM

This rounded, somewhat weeping shrub/tree is native to Sicily and North Africa. It prefers full sun and a moist soil. Growing to 30 ft (about 9 m) in height and spread it is almost leafless, but in summer bears

*Genista aetnensis*

*Grevillea* 'Boongala Spinebill'

*Genista tinctoria*

a delightful explosion of small, golden yellow flowers.
ZONES 8–10

### *G. lydia*

A dense, low mound of nearly leafless stems, this broom is covered in early summer with golden yellow flowers. It makes an excellent ground cover, only 24 in (about 60 cm) tall, and sets little seed.
ZONES 7–10

### *G. monosperma*

syn. *Retama monosperma*

BRIDAL VEIL BROOM

This deciduous, broadly bushy shrub is native to Spain and North Africa. Spectacular in spring when in full bloom, it bears fragrant, white, pea-shaped flowers on long, arching branches. It grows to a height and spread of 10 ft (about 3 m) or more. Propagate from semi-hardwood cuttings in fall.
ZONES 9–10

### *G. pilosa* 'Vancouver Gold'

A prostrate shrub of less than 15 in (about 38 cm) in height but a

*Gordonia axillaris*

spread of several feet, this selection has deeper yellow flowers than the species and a quick, uniform habit of growth. An excellent ground cover in full sun, the stems are gray-green while the leaves are deep green. It flowers in spring.
ZONES 5–10

### *G. tinctoria*

DYER'S GREENWEED, WOADWAXEN

This squat, deciduous, spreading shrub grows to a height of 30 in (about 76 cm) and a spread of 3 ft (about 90 cm). In summer golden-yellow, pea-like flowers appear set among thin, dark green leaves. It does best in full sun with a well-drained soil. Prune the tips to encourage bushiness.
ZONES 5–10

## *GORDONIA*

### *axillaris*

CRÊPE CAMELLIA

This handsome, glossy-leaved plant may reach tree size after many years—up to 30 ft (about 9 m)—in mild climates. Normally, however, it is seen as a shrub, growing to 6–9 ft (about 1.8–2.7 m). A native of China, Taiwan and Vietnam, it bears cream-white, saucer-shaped flowers with a mass of yellow stamens from fall through spring. Although evergreen, sometimes a few of its leathery, lance-shaped leaves turn rich scarlet or gold at the same time. It prefers a sunny spot with a well-drained, acid soil. Potted plants should be watered moderately, less so in winter. Propagate from late summer cuttings.
ZONES 7–9

## *GREVILLEA*

GREVILLEA, SPIDER FLOWER

One of the most popular of Australian trees and shrubs, this genus numbers some 400 species, and dozens of hybrids and cultivars. Extremely variable in habit, foliage and flowers, most grevilleas are found in the southwestern part of Western Australia; there are also a few species native to Malaysia. Well sought after as garden plants in California and the Southwest, many are adaptable and easy to grow with a long flowering period. Popular with hummingbirds, they will grow in most soils but do best in one that is well-drained, slightly dry, gravelly and neutral to acid. They appreciate the occasional addition of a light fertilizer, but avoid using phosphorus. Flowers are borne on heads, sometimes globular, sometimes elongated and one-sided, like a toothbrush. The fruits that follow are leathery capsules that split to release one or, more commonly, two seeds. Propagate from seed in spring or from firm tip cuttings taken in late summer. They can also be grafted. Strong roots develop early and it is important not to disturb these when potting on. Scale insects and leaf spot may cause some problems.

### *G.* 'Boongala Spinebill'

This attractive cultivar bears long, dense heads of deep red flowers for most of the year. A spreading, evergreen shrub, it has deeply serrated green leaves and grows to a height of 6 ft (about 1.8 m) and spread of 12 ft (about 3.5 m).
ZONES 9–10

# A Field Trip to the Cape Floral Kingdom

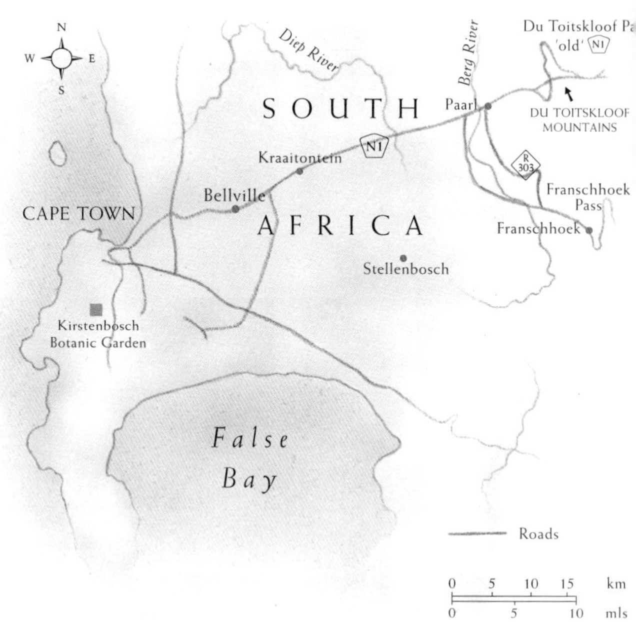


The southern tip of the African continent encompasses the "Cape Floral Kingdom," the name botanists have given to the southern Cape Province and its extraordinarily rich flora. This is a diverse region—the coastal plains are largely sand and limestone and further inland, the undulating landscape is formed from shales and clays. The Cape Fold Mountains dominate the skyline to the northeast of Cape Town and Table Mountain. They are composed of steeply tilted acid sandstones, which yield a shallow soil that is deficient in the nutrients required for plant growth and hence of no value for agriculture or even the grazing of livestock. On their slopes though, and in many areas of similar soil in the southern Cape, there has developed the famous "Fynbos" vegetation—a low scrub of extraordinary botanical diversity.

Of the world's great floral kingdoms, the Cape Floral Kingdom occupies the smallest area, but for its size it has a higher concentration of plant species (about 8500) than anywhere else on earth.

A feature of the Fynbos vegetation is the concentration of genera and species of the Proteaceae family. Richest in species are the *Protea*, *Leucadendron* and *Leucospermum* genera. In spring you can travel to any one of the mountainous areas within 160 miles (about 250 km) of Cape Town and find yourself in a world of flowers.

*Low-growing vegetation on the South West Cape Mountains slopes.*

Of the many species of *Protea*, one of the best known and most widely distributed in Cape Province is the wagon tree *(Protea nitida)*, a shrub or smallish tree of varying size and shape. It is typically small and bushy, appearing a distinct grayish white from a distance, usually 15 ft (about 5 m) high with a trunk up to 18 in (about 50 cm) in diameter. The crown of foliage is rounded and irregular. The flowerheads (inflorescences), normally creamy white, may be present all year round but their bloom peaks between May and August. They are typical protea blooms, with globes up to 6½ in (about 16 cm) wide when open.

In early colonial days in South Africa, the attractive, reddish colored wood of the wagon tree was used for furniture, wagon building and wagon brake blocks, hence the common name. The bark was also used for tanning, while the mature leaves produced a tolerably good black writing ink extracted with a solution of iron salt.

A field trip to view the wagon tree can be made at any time, as the species flowers all year round. However the best time to visit the Cape Floral Kingdom is in spring to early summer (September to December), because there is a great profusion of other flowers to be seen at this time. Head out from Cape Town along the N1 national road towards the Transvaal. Approximately 18 miles (about 30 km) northeast of Cape Town is the town of Paarl, in the heart of one of the richest and longest-settled agricultural areas in South Africa. You will pass orchards and vineyards, for this is also the center of the country's wine production.

From here there are two possible routes. If you proceed on the old N1 over the Du Toitskloof Pass, within 5 or 10 minutes you will be in the typically rugged sandstone mountains of the Cape. As you go up the pass you will have your first glimpse of the Fynbos flora and see *Protea nitida* almost on the shoulders of the road. There are many places to stop and stroll around, but the best is yet to come.

*The wagon tree, with other Fynbos plants.*

*Protea nitida*

As you continue over the pass and go slowly down the other side, you will find the sunny eastern slopes on your right are covered in groups and single specimens of both the wagon tree and another *Protea* species, the sugarbush (*P. repens*). The early Dutch settlers extracted a syrup from the nectar-rich flowers of this plant, and at times it was their only source of sugar.

The alternative route is via the R303 district road after Paarl, crossing the Berg River. This will take you to the historic town of Franschhoek (where French Huguenots settled at the end of the seventeenth century). From here continue on up the Franschhoek Pass where you will find a floral profusion equal to that of the Du Toitskloof Pass. Apart from proteas and other Proteaceae, the Fynbos on these mountain slopes contains many species of *Erica* (the heath genus), most of which have colorful flowers. This is an amazingly diverse genus with almost 600 species in the southern Cape Province alone. Although *Erica* is also well known in Europe and the Mediterranean, that far larger region has fewer than one-twentieth the number of species. Other colorful wildflowers in the Fynbos include some lovely members of the daisy family, and spring-flowering bulbs such as watsonias, to name but a couple.

From Franschhoek it is some 30 miles (about 50 km) back to Cape Town. After your field trip, it is worthwhile visiting Kirstenbosch National Botanic Garden, famous as much for its magnificent setting on the slope of Table Mountain as for its collections of South African native plants. Stroll to the magnificent Castle Rock and then walk through the Protea Garden. Here you will again find yourself in native Fynbos vegetation, rich in a number of beautiful species, including *Protea nitida* of course. Another attraction of this wonderful garden is the view, with the Cape Peninsula laid out below and, more distantly, the mountains behind Paarl and Stellenbosch where you have already been.

## Protea

When the eminent Swedish botanist Linnaeus was systematically renaming all known plant and animal species in the mid-eighteenth century, he was so impressed by the range of form in one genus of African shrubs that he named it *Protea* after the Greek god Proteus, who had the ability to change at will into any of a myriad of forms.

*Protea* later lent its name to a major plant family, the Proteaceae, which includes many genera and species in Australia as well as in Africa, with smaller numbers in South America, New Caledonia, New Guinea and Indonesia. It is one of the most clear-cut examples of a plant group that originated in the super-continent Gondwana, predating its break-up into the present southern hemisphere land masses.

The astoundingly beautiful, symmetrical and long-lasting flowerheads of many Proteaceae have contributed to their popularity as cut flowers, to the extent that they are now a major item of international trade. Foremost are species of *Protea* itself, grown in Australia, New Zealand, California and Israel as well as in their native South Africa. The more striking species of Proteaceae are all adapted to highly nutrient-deficient soils and their cultivation requirements are frequently specialized. Most are only suited to milder temperate areas.

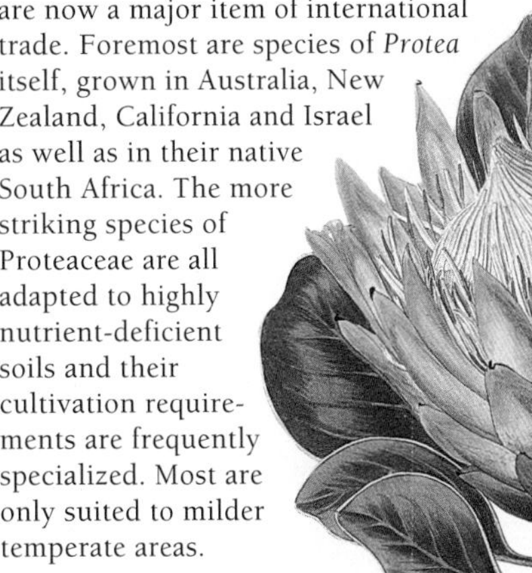

*Protea cynaroides*

*Grevillea* 'Robyn Gordon'

*Grevillea rosmarinifolia*

*Grevillea lavandulacea*

## *G. lavandulacea*

One of the most variable of the genus, this bushy, compact shrub bears small, crowded, abundant clusters of crimson to pink (sometimes white) flowers over the entire bush for most of the year. The leaves are short and broad, silvery gray, usually covered in hairs but sometimes smooth. Drought resistant, it grows to a height of 3 ft (about 90 cm) or less with a spread of 6 ft (about 1.8 m). It is suitable for hedges in parks and gardens.
ZONES 9–10

*Grewia occidentalis*

## *G.* 'Noellii'

This hybrid grevillea is the most commonly grown on the West Coast, being somwhat hardier than most species and more tolerant of a variety of soils and of summer water. Bright green, needle-like leaves cover the stems. The flowers are bright pink and white, appearing in small clusters in spring and summer. Height and spread reach around 6 ft (about 1.8 m).
ZONES 9–10

## *G.* 'Robyn Gordon'

A popular and attractive hybrid (from *G. banksii* and *G. bipinnatifida*), this sprawling, evergreen shrub bears large, rich red, drooping flowerheads all year round. It has dark green, fern-like leaves with silky undersides. It is vulnerable to leaf spot in damp conditions. Prune to encourage dense growth. It grows to a height of 3 ft (about 90 cm) and a spread of up to 6 ft (about 1.8 m).
ZONES 9–10

## *G. rosmarinifolia*

This is a variable shrub, from under 24 in (about 60 cm) to over 6 ft (about 1.8 m) in height and spread. The leaves are small and gray or gray-green. The flowers are usually pink and red, in small clusters in late winter and spring. Numerous dwarf selections have become available; they are very useful for the small garden.
ZONES 9–10

# GREWIA *occidentalis*

LAVENDER STAR FLOWER

Native to Africa this fast-growing evergreen, the most popular of the genus, is widely grown in the South and on the West Coast of the USA. In summer it bears pink and mauve star-shaped flowers. Shiny, oval, light green leaves complete the picture. It likes a well-mulched, well-drained soil, and prefers some water during the dry months. Grows to a height and spread of 9 ft (about 2.7 m). Pruning will maintain a compact habit. Propagate from seed or cuttings.
ZONES 9–11

## *GRISELINIA*
*littoralis*

This fast-growing tree or shrub is a popular seaside plant in Ireland and in New England and California in the USA. It has shining, oval, apple-green, leathery leaves. It bears insignificant tiny, yellow-green flowers in spring. Small, black berries follow the bloom. Drought resistant, it likes fertile, well-drained soil and full sun or partial shade. It grows to a height and spread of 16–36 ft (about 4.8–11 m). Propagate from semi-ripe cuttings in summer or seed in spring and fall.
ZONES 8–10

## *HAKEA*

This is a variable genus of shrubs and small trees. They do best in dry, gravelly, well-drained soil. The leaves are mostly hard and needle like. The fragrant flowers are usually small and are clustered into spheres or long heads. These plants like plenty of sun. Potted specimens should be watered moderately in full growth. Propagate from seed (pre-treated by nicking or immersion in near-boiling water) in fall or semi-ripe cuttings in summer.

### *H. laurina*
PINCUSHION TREE

A loose, gangly plant with weeping branches, this tall, smooth-barked shrub bears fragrant, crimson or cherry flowers with protruding, white styles that resemble pins in a pincushion. It grows to a height of 9–18 ft (about 2.7–5.5 m) with a spread of 9 ft (about 2.7 m).
ZONES 9–10

*Griselinia littoralis*

### *H. suaveolens*
SWEET HAKEA

With its sharply pointed, bright green leaves this hakea makes an excellent hedge. Though it will reach as much as 20 ft (about 6 m) in height and spread, it can easily be kept to under 10 ft (about 3 m) by pruning or shearing. The fluffy white flowers are hidden within the leaves, but are delightfully sweet-scented in fall. Give it full sun, a well-drained soil and little water in summer once established.
ZONES 9–10

## *HALIMIUM*
*lasianthum*
syn. *H. formosum*
SUNROSE

This spreading evergreen is a native of Spain and Portugal. It has gray-green foliage and in spring and summer bears open, golden flowers, each petal marked with a central, red blotch. Give it only occasional water during a long, dry summer, ensuring it has a well-drained soil and full sun. It grows to a height of 30 in (about 76 cm) and a spread of $4^{1}/_{2}$ ft (about 1.3 m). Propagate from semi-ripe cuttings in summer.
ZONES 8–10

*Halimium lasianthum*

## *HAMAMELIS*
WITCH HAZEL

The witch hazels are often overlooked since their flowers are not as spectacular as many of our most common garden shrubs, however the flowers appear at a time when little else is in bloom: fall, winter and very early spring. Add to that the gently lobed or toothed deciduous leaves which turn bright red, orange or yellow in fall, plus the pleasing scent that comes from the flowers and you have one of the best garden shrubs available. Native to North America and Asia, there are several species and many hybrids. All thrive in moderately moist, woodsy soil with protection from the hottest afternoon sun. Place them near a walk or window where their winter flowers can be enjoyed. Propagate from softwood cuttings in early summer; named selections are usually grafted.

### *H.* x *intermedia*
HYBRID WITCH HAZEL

This group of hybrids between two Asian species offers a broad range of flower colors from pale yellow through various shades and blends of red and orange. All bloom in winter on bare stems. Some are fragrant. Shrubs are vigorous and may reach 15 ft (about 4.5 m) tall and wide. Fall color is excellent, with the red-flowered selections often displaying the most red in their autumn leaves. Look for 'Arnold Promise' with clear yellow flowers, 'Diana' with red flowers, and 'Jelena' with coppery flowers.
ZONES 6–8

### *H. mollis*
CHINESE WITCH HAZEL

A parent of *H.* x *intermedia,* this somewhat smaller shrub from China flowers on bare stems in winter. Flowers are yellow and red-brown, and decidedly the most fragrant of the genus.
ZONES 5–8

### *H. vernalis*
VERNAL WITCH HAZEL

This extremely hardy witch hazel is a native of the woodlands of eastern

*Hamamelis vernalis*

*Hakea laurina*

*Hebe* × *andersonii*

North America. Its red to yellow flowers are produced in late winter and are fragrant. Height and spread reach around 10 ft (about 3 m).
ZONES 4–8

### *H. virginiana*
COMMON WITCH HAZEL

Fragrant flowers are golden yellow, often hidden among the yellow leaves of fall. This is a large shrub which can with time become a small tree of 25 ft (about 7.5 m) in height and spread.
ZONES 3–8

## *HEBE*
HEBE

Most of these evergreen shrubs are native to New Zealand but some species are to be found naturally in Chile and New Guinea. They are all grown for the luxurious foliage and dense spikes of tiny, four-petaled, purple, white or cerise flowers. Resistance to salt and sea winds make them eminently suited to coastal areas. They are good as dense hedges or thick ground covers. They require a well-drained but moderately moist soil and full sun to semi-shade; they do not do well where summers are hot and dry. Prune after flowering to shape and to remove faded blossoms, or to restrict growth. Propagate from semi-ripe cuttings in summer. There are a great many cultivated species and hybrids.

### *H.* × *andersonii*

This is a bushy evergreen shrub that grows to a height and spread of 6 ft (about 1.8 m). It bears dense spikes of small, lilac flowers in summer. The leaves are dark green. A form with cream variegated leaves is available.
ZONES 9–10

### *H. hulkeana*

This upright, open, evergreen shrub bears masses of small, pale lilac flowers in spring and early summer. Its attractive, oval, serrated, glossy, dark green leaves have red margins. It grows to a height and spread of 3 ft (about 90 cm). Plant in full sun in well-drained soil.
ZONES 8–10

### *H. speciosa*
SNOWY HEBE

This desirable species boasts deep green foliage and purple brushes of flowers that appear in terminal clusters in summer and winter to spring. It grows to a height of $4^1/_2$ ft (about 1.3 m) with a spread of 3 ft (about 90 cm). Numerous, brightly colored cultivars exist, with flowers ranging from purple and deep red to pale lilac, pink and white. Plant in full sun.
ZONES 8–10

## *HELICHRYSUM*
*selago*

Native to the mountain regions of New Zealand, this erect evergreen shrub grows up to 18 in (about 45 cm) in height. It has a conifer-like appearance; its rigid stems are covered with dense, triangular, scale-like foliage. Terminal clusters of downy cream flowers sporadically appear at the tips of the branchlets.
ZONES 4–10

## *HELIOTROPIUM*
*arborescens*
syn. *H. peruvianum*
COMMON HELIOTROPE

This attractive shrub is much-prized for the clusters of fragrant, purple to lavender flowers it bears from late spring to fall. A native of South America, it will grow to 6 ft (about 1.8 m) or more in mild winter regions, or to only half that size as a summer annual or pot plant in colder regions. It is a branching, evergreen species with dark green, wrinkled leaves and needs rich, fertile, well-drained soil and full sun. In very dry areas it is best raised in a semi-shady position and the soil kept moist. Potted specimens should be regularly watered in full growth, but moderately at other times. Cut back to half in early spring to promote a bushy look. Propagate from seed in spring or semi-ripe cuttings in early fall. The name comes from the unusual way the flowerheads turn towards the sun.
ZONES 9–10

## *HETEROMELES*
*arbutifolia*
syn. *Photinia arbutifolia*
TOYON, CALIFORNIA HOLLY, CHRISTMAS BERRY

This vigorous shrub is an important element of the chaparral shrub community in California, but is found in other areas of the West as well. Its glossy, evergreen leaves are sharply toothed on the margin. The large panicles of tiny white flowers appear in early summer, followed by bright red berries from fall into winter (these are popular with

*Hamamelis virginiana*

*Hebe hulkeana*

birds). A large shrub, this will often be tree like and reach 15–20 ft (about 4.5–6 m) in height and nearly as wide. Give it full sun and a well-drained soil. Fireblight can be a problem. Propagate from seed, and plant out in the garden when young. Excellent as a hedge plant, and important in natural gardens in the West.
ZONES 8–10

## *HIBISCUS*

MALLOW

These beautifully exotic, flowering, evergreen or deciduous shrubs, perennials and annuals hail from all continents, and from temperate as well as tropical regions. Popular in warm to tropical gardens they bear large, showy flowers, many of which last as little as one day, or longer with cooler temperatures. The flowering season is long, however, lasting from late spring into fall, and the range of colors is impressive. They thrive in full sun in a well-drained, rich, slightly acid, sandy soil. Water regularly and fertilize during flowering. Trim after flowering to maintain shape. Propagate from cuttings taken in spring and summer. Potential pests include aphids, caterpillars, white fly and Japanese and rose beetles. The genus is the floral emblem of Hawaii, where some of the most stunning hybrids are grown.

### *H. mutabilis*

CONFEDERATE ROSE

This delightful native of China can grow to tree-like proportions of 25 ft (about 7.5 m) in height and spread, but is usually smaller in cooler climates. It bears large, hairy, shallowly lobed leaves and single, white flowers that fade to deep rose-pink; these appear in fall. Prune regularly to maintain shape.
ZONES 8–10

*Heteromeles arbutifolia*

### *H. rosa-sinensis*

CHINESE HIBISCUS, TROPICAL HIBISCUS

Native to China, this tall shrub bears coral-red flowers virtually all year in a frost-free climate. The wild form is less often seen in gardens than the numerous dazzling cultivars, many bred in Hawaii, which come in single or double and every color but blue. Plants range in height and spread from 3–9 ft (about 90–270 cm) and have evergreen, glossy leaves. They prefer full sun in tropical or subtropical climates where they are as important in gardens as roses are in temperate climates. In cold climates they can be grown in tubs in a greenhouse or as indoor plants. Water freely in summer, prune in spring after cold weather is over, and propagate from cuttings in summer. Among the most popular cultivars are 'Agnes Gault' (red), 'Lemon Chiffon' (yellow) and 'Bride' (white/pink).
ZONES 9–10

### *H. rosa-sinensis* 'Cooperi'

Ideal for potting and excellent as an indoor decoration, this shrub bears small, light, open, scarlet flowers. It grows to a height of between $4^{1}/_{2}$–12 ft (about 1.3–3.5 m) and has variegated white, cream and pink foliage.
ZONES 9–10

*Heliotropium arborescens*

*Hebe speciosa*

*Hibiscus rosa-sinensis* 'Cooperi'

*Helichrysum selago*

*Hibiscus mutabilis*

*Hibiscus rosa-sinensis*

Hydrangea macrophylla

Hibiscus syriacus 'Ardens'

Hibiscus syriacus

### H. syriacus

ROSE-OF-SHARON

This colorful, upright, deciduous shrub is the hardiest of the genus. It flowers freely in summer in varying shades of white, pink, soft red, mauve and violet-blue. The single, semi-double and double flowers are bell shaped. It has glabrous leaves and grows to 12 ft (about 3.5 m) tall with a spread of 3-6 ft (about 90– 180 cm). Of the named selections, 'Blue Bird' is among the most popular; it bears single, violet-blue flowers with red centers and grows to a height of 6 ft (about 1.8 m). Watch out for new hybrids such as 'Aphrodite' (rose-pink) or 'Diana' (pure white), which produce no seeds.

ZONES 5–9

### H. syriacus 'Ardens'

This popular hibiscus bears large mauve flowers with crimson centers. An upright shrub, it grows to a height of 9 ft (about 2.7 m).

ZONES 5–9

Hibiscus syriacus 'Blue Bird'

## HYDRANGEA

HYDRANGEA

These lush, popular, deciduous and evergreen shrubs are native to China, Japan and North America; they grow profusely in the summer months. They need constant watering as they transpire heavily from the stems and large, saw-toothed leaves. The sun damages their foliage, so always position them in the shade or in full sun only in areas that are frequently cloudy. Hydrangeas are grown for the strikingly attractive, domed, fertile flowers which appear mid-summer. Each head consists of small flowers surrounded by larger petal-like sepals. Prune immediately after flowering—this encourages strong, vigorous growth for the following season. Propagate from softwood cuttings in summer.

### H. aspera var. aspera

syn. H. villosa

This delicate beauty, native to eastern Asia, bears broad heads of blue or purple flowers in the center of the shrub, and larger, white flowers towards the periphery. A deciduous upright shrub, it grows to a height and spread of 9 ft (about 2.7 m).

ZONES 7–10

### H. macrophylla

BIGLEAF HYDRANGEA, GARDEN HYDRANGEA

This deciduous, bushy shrub from Japan flowers in mid- to late summer, the color depending on the pH of the soil. In acid soils with a pH of 5.5 or less, flowers will be blue or purple; higher pHs will produce pink or red flowers. White cultivars are unaffected by soil pH. There are two types—hortensias, with dense, domed heads; and lacecaps, with

Hydrangea aspera var. aspera

*Hydrangea macrophylla* 'Blue Wave'

flat, open heads with tiny fertile flowers in the center. In spring, trim winter-damaged growth back to new growth; in summer, remove spent flowers and use for dried arrangements. This species has oval, serrated, green leaves and grows to a height and spread of 6 ft (about 1.8 m).
ZONES 6–10

### *H. macrophylla* 'Blue Wave'

This deciduous, bushy shrub is a good example of the lacecap type of hydrangea; it has flat heads of blue to pink flowers appearing in summer and oval, green, serrated leaves. It grows to a height and spread of $4^1/_2$ ft (about 1.3 m).
ZONES 6–10

### *H. paniculata* 'Grandiflora'
PEEGEE HYDRANGEA

This deciduous, open, upright shrub bears large, conical, terminal panicles of white flowers. Greenish to begin with, they gradually turn to pink as summer progresses. To obtain larger panicles prune back hard in spring. It grows to a height and spread of 9 ft (about 2.7 m). This hydrangea prefers full sun.
ZONES 3–9

### *H. quercifolia*
OAKLEAF HYDRANGEA

The dark green foliage of this deciduous, bushy shrub turns a brilliant red and purple in fall. It bears white flowerheads from mid-summer to mid-fall. It grows to a height and spread of 6 ft (about 1.8 m).
ZONES 5–10

## HYPERICUM
ST-JOHN'S-WORT

These showy perennials, annuals and shrubs are easy to grow in mild, temperate climates worldwide. Larger species require sun or semi-shade and fertile soil that is slightly moist. Smaller species do better in full sun and well-drained soil and make excellent rock plants. Prune annually to prevent legginess and to maintain shape. Prune seed pods to maintain vigor. Propagate small species from 2 in (about 5 cm) cuttings taken in late spring; for larger shrubs, from 5 in (about 12 cm) cuttings of non-flowering shoots in summer.

*Hydrangea paniculata* 'Grandiflora'

*Hydrangea quercifolia*

*Hypericum* 'Rowallane'

*Hypericum patulum*

### *H. patulum*

This evergreen, upright shrub bears large, golden yellow, erect flowers from mid-summer to mid-fall. It has dark green oval leaves and grows to a height and spread of 3 ft (about 90 cm).
ZONES 6–9

### *H.* 'Rowallane'

In mid-summer to mid- or late fall this attractive, arching shrub bears delightful, bowl-shaped, yellow flowers set among green, oval leaves. It grows to a height and spread of 6 ft (about 1.8 m) or more.
ZONES 8–10

## ILEX
HOLLY

These popular and well-known evergreen shrubs are grown for their green, spiny leaves and the red, yellow or black berries borne in summer, fall or winter by female plants. Male and female plants must be grown together to obtain the berries. The shrubs bear clusters of small, white or greenish blossoms, but these are not of much significance. They need a moist, well-drained soil with plenty of leaf mulch and prefer sun or partial shade. They do best when pruned hard in late spring and do not transplant successfully. Propagate from semi-hardwood cuttings in early fall. Watch for holly leaf miner and holly aphid. Holly was invested with mystical properties by Europeans during the Middle Ages as it defied the winter, retaining both leaves and berries.

*Ilex* x *altaclarensis* 'Wilsonii'

### *I.* x *altaclarensis* 'Wilsonii'
WILSON HOLLY

This hybrid is one of the most dependable and adaptable of shrubby hollies. Its large, evergreen leaves are deep green and glossy, with relatively few teeth. It fruits heavily when pollinated by *I. aquifolium*. It is normally a rounded shrub 6–8 ft (about 1.8–2.4 m) tall and wide, but can be pruned into a small tree of 20 ft (about 6 m). It is tolerant of dry conditions.
ZONES 7–10

*Ilex verticillata*

*Ilex glabra*

*Ilex cornuta*

*Ilex aquifolium* cultivar

*Ilex crenata*

### *I. aquifolium*

ENGLISH HOLLY

The bright red winter berries and glossy, spiny, dark green leaves of this European species make popular traditional Christmas ornaments. Normally a forest tree reaching 30 ft (about 9 m) or more in height with half that in spread, there are a great many selected forms grown for their more shrubby habit. All lend themselves to shearing to control their size. They do best in moist, woodsy soils and light shade, and prefer summers that are not too hot or humid (the Pacific Northwest and the mid-Atlantic states are ideal). 'Angustifolia' has small, narrow, spiny leaves on a compact pyramidal shape. 'Gold Coast' has leaves edged in yellow and reaches 6–8 ft (about 1.8–2.4 m) tall.
ZONES 6–10

### *I. cornuta*

CHINESE HOLLY

This dense, rounded species from China is self-fertile and is better suited than other species to mild

*Ilex* x *meservae* 'Blue Angel'

winter areas. It grows to a height of 12 ft (about 3.5 m) with a spread of 15 ft (about 4.5 m). The leaves are rectangular with a spine in each corner and at the tip; 'Burfordii' and a few others lack the spines. Bright red berries appear in fall. This too is excellent as a Christmas holly.
ZONES 7–10

### *I. crenata*

JAPANESE HOLLY

Among the most useful of evergreen hollies, especially for the smaller garden, the Japanese holly has tiny, dark green leaves without spines and a dense, compact habit of growth. It tolerates shearing and works well as a hedge, replacing boxwood in colder climates. The small, black fruits are not showy. 'Helleri' stays under 4 ft (about 1.2 m); 'Convexa' is taller (6 ft/1.8 m) but is more tolerant of colder, snowier winters.
ZONES 6–9

### *I. glabra*

INKBERRY

This evergreen holly is a native of wetlands in eastern North America, where it grows in broad, dense thickets. Its small leaves are dark green, and its berries are blue-black. Upright in habit, it may be leggy and bare at the base; try 'Compacta' for more dense growth. Good in damp soils in full sun or part shade. Ultimately around 8 ft (about 2.4 m) tall and wide.
ZONES 4–9

### *I.* x *meservae*

MESERVE HYBRID HOLLY

This group of hybrids was derived from *I. aquifolium* and *I. rugosa;* they are noted for their blue-green foliage, purple stems, red berries and cold hardiness. Most have a dense, pyramidal shape. 'Blue Girl', 'Blue Boy' and 'Blue Angel' are the most commonly available.
ZONES 5–9

### *I. verticillata*

WINTERBERRY

A deciduous holly native to the wetlands of eastern North America, this species is popular for the masses of tiny red berries that line the leafless stems in fall and winter; the berries are very popular with birds. Vigorous and carefree, it prefers a moist soil in a sunny situation. Prune hard to encourage more shoots and thus more fruit. It will reach 10 ft (about 3 m) in height and spread.
ZONES 3–8

### *I. vomitoria*

YAUPON HOLLY

This small-leafed, evergreen holly is native to the southeastern part of North America. Its naturally dense habit lends itself to pruning and shearing. It can be trained into a small tree, or sheared into a hedge. Dwarf selections such as 'Nana' form dense mounds, good for unsheared hedges. In fall the branches are covered with juicy red berries. More tolerant of a variety of conditions, including alkaline soils.
ZONES 7–10

## ITEA

These evergreen and deciduous shrubs, native to eastern North America and eastern Asia, are grown for their showy, fragrant, fall flowers and prickly, holly-like leaves. They are frost hardy, although in cooler areas they need the protection of a wall. They will thrive in anything but very dry soil and prefer a semi-shaded position but will tolerate full sun. Propagate from softwood cuttings in summer and plant in fall or spring. This is a useful plant for a specimen or for growing in a shrubbery.

### *I. ilicifolia*

SWEETSPIRE

This handsome, bushy, evergreen shrub, native to western China, has leaves resembling those of holly, only narrower. It bears long racemes of small, greenish or cream flowers in late summer to early fall. It does best in moist, deep, rich soil, preferring a position in partial shade. It grows to a height and spread of 6 ft (about 1.8 m).
ZONES 6–10

*Juniperus sabina*

*Jasminum nudiflorum*

*Itea ilicifolia*

*Itea virginica*

*Juniperus conferta*

*Juniperus horizontalis* 'Wiltonii'

### *I. virginica*

VIRGINIA SWEETSPIRE

This deciduous shrub is valuable for its summer flowers and bright green foliage. It develops an arching habit, reaching 5 ft (about 1.5 m) or more in height and spread. Tiny, white flowers are produced in slightly pendulous clusters with a light fragrance. Leaves turn bright scarlet to purple in the fall. Good for moist soils in full sun to part shade. It is native to the eastern United States. Propagate from softwood cuttings in summer.

ZONES 5–9

## *JASMINUM*

JASMINE

These deciduous, semi-evergreen or evergreen shrubs and woody-stemmed, twining or scrambling climbers are native to Asia, Europe and Africa. Grown for their yellow, white or pink, star-shaped flowers. Water regularly and prune occasionally to maintain their habit. The shrubs can easily be trained as climbers if their heads are not cut back. Propagate from ripe wood cuttings in summer, by layers, or from seed.

### *J. mesnyi*

**syn. *J. primulinum***

PRIMROSE JASMINE

Native to China, this evergreen, rambling shrub bears large, semi-double, golden blooms on arching canes in late winter and spring. Its dark green leaves are made up of three leaflets. It does best in warm climates and prefers full sun and a well-drained soil. *J. mesnyi* grows to a height and spread of around 9 ft (about 2.7 m).

ZONES 8–10

### *J. nudiflorum*

WINTER JASMINE

This is a rambling, deciduous, arching shrub from China. It bears masses of bright yellow flowers on slender, leafless, green shoots in winter and early spring. It prefers a well-drained soil and full sun, growing to 10 ft (about 3 m) or more in height and spread. Propagate from semi-hardwood cuttings in spring.

ZONES 6–9

## *JUNIPERUS*

JUNIPER

These evergreen conifers make excellent garden plants. Though often over-used as foundation shrubs, they make excellent ground covers, informal hedges and background plants, while the snaller forms are excellent in a rockery. Some are among the hardiest of conifers; they require full sun and a dry, sandy soil. All species and cultivars are best propagated from tip cuttings, as they root easily. Some cultivars can be propagated by grafting. Spider mites are sometimes a problem.

### *J. conferta*

SHORE JUNIPER

This shrubby, prostrate, dwarf conifer does quite well in a salty, coastal environment. It has dense, glossy, aromatic, needle-like, soft green leaves on spreading branches. It grows to a height of up to 12 in

*Juniperus* x *media* 'Pfitzeriana'

(about 30 cm) and a spread of up to 6 ft (about 1.8 m), and makes an excellent ground cover.

ZONES 6–10

### *J. horizontalis*

CREEPING JUNIPER

This spreading or trailing juniper is native to the mountains and northern parts of North America. Foliage may vary from green to blue to bronzy, especially in winter. 'Bar Harbor' is 12 in (about 30 cm) tall and up to 10 ft (about 3 m) wide, but may lose its leaves in the center as the plant ages. Silvery-blue 'Wiltonii' (also known as 'Blue Rug') hugs the ground with its dense branching, growing only 4 in (about 10 cm) tall but up to 10 ft (about 3 m) wide. 'Plumosa' has softer foliage and grows 18 in (about 45 cm) high and 10 ft (about 3 m) wide.

ZONES 2–10

### *J.* x *media*

**syn. *J. chinensis* cultivars**

These hybrid junipers are usually low, spreading shrubs, the foliage often displaying a glaucous color,

*Jasminum mesnyi*

and are among the toughest of conifers. Most familiar is 'Pfitzeriana', ultimately 10 ft (about 3 m) tall by 15 ft (about 4.5 m) wide. More manageable is 'Pfitzeriana Compacta', which grows to only 2 ft by 6 ft (about 60 by 180 cm). 'Blaauw' has blue foliage on a compact, vase-shaped shrub of 4 ft (about 1.2 m) tall by 3 ft (about 90 cm) wide.

ZONES 4–10

### *J. sabina*

SAVIN JUNIPER

The dark green leaves of this vigorously spreading, shrubby bush, a native to Europe and the Caucasus, give off an unpleasant odor when bruised or crushed. It has flaking, red-brown bark. The smaller growing named selections are more generally seen in gardens. Avoid 'Tamariscifolia' due to its susceptibility to juniper blight. Look for 'Broadmoor' or 'Buffalo', both with bright green foliage and growing 12 in (about 30 cm) or so in height and 8–10 ft (about 2.4–3 m) wide.

ZONES 3–10

*Justicia brandegeana*

*Kolkwitzia amabilis*

*Kerria japonica*

*Justicia carnea*

## JUSTICIA

These subtropical and tropical shrubs provide colorful flowers for the warm-climate garden. They are native to the southwestern corner of North America and south into Mexico and South America. The leaves may be evergreen or deciduous (especially in desert species) but are always in pairs, while the flowers are tubular and usually protrude from colorful bracts.

### *J. brandegeana*

**syn. *Beleperone guttata, Drejerella guttata***

SHRIMP PLANT

The salmon to rose-pink or pale yellow bracts surrounding the white flowers of this attractive, evergreen shrub resemble a shrimp—hence its name. Native to tropical Mexico it grows best in fertile, well-drained soil, and colors best under partial shade. It flowers mainly in summer. It can survive temperatures as low as 25°F (about minus 4°C) by behaving like a perennial when the tops are frozen back. A weak, sprawling plant, it needs regular pruning to maintain its shape and encourage new, flowering wood. Water potted plants freely when in full growth, less at other times. It grows to a height of 3 ft (about 90 cm) and a spread of 24 in (about 60 cm). Propagate from tip or semi-hardwood cuttings.

ZONES 9–11

### *J. californica*

**syn. *Beleperone californica***

CHUPAROSA

This desert shrub from southwestern North America is mostly leafless, the simple paired leaves appearing only for a short time after heavy rain. The stems are dense and green, however, creating a mounding shrub to 5 ft (about 1.5 m) or more in height and spread. In spring, masses of narrow red flowers attract hummingbirds to the garden. Give this shrub sun and heat and a well-drained soil, with no more than natural rainfall.

ZONES 9–10

### *J. carnea*

**syn. *Jacobinia carnea***

BRAZILIAN PLUME FLOWER

This strikingly handsome, evergreen shrub bears spikes of white, pink or rose-purple flowers in summer to fall. It has pointed, veined, deep green leaves. In colder climates it needs to be grown under glass, as it is a frost-tender tropical or subtropical plant. It does best in fertile, well-drained soil and needs at least partial shade. Water potted specimens freely in full growth, less so at other times. Prune back hard in early spring—this will encourage branching and prevent growth from becoming too tall and straggly. *J. carnea* grows to a height of $4^{1}/_{2}$ ft (about 1.3 m) with a spread of 30 in (about 76 cm). Propagate in spring or early summer by softwood cuttings. Caterpillars and snails can be a problem.

ZONES 10–11

*Kalmia latifolia*

## KALMIA
## *latifolia*

MOUNTAIN LAUREL

The charm and fragrance of this American native make it a favorite among shrub enthusiasts. It has dark, glossy, laurel-like leaves and bears small, purple-rose to rose-red flowers in late spring and early summer. *K. latifolia* grows to a height and spread of 10 ft (about 3 m). It thrives in a moist, peaty, acid soil and prefers sun or semi-shade. Propagate by layering in summer, otherwise (with more difficulty) from softwood cuttings in summer or seed in fall. Numerous cutting-grown named selections are available.

ZONES 4–8

## KERRIA
## *japonica*

The golden blossom of this species, the only one in its genus, will light up a garden corner in spring. The flowers, which appear along the outer reaches of the long, arching branches, are single in the species but double in 'Pleniflora', the most commonly grown form; they make delightful cut flowers. The leaves are double-toothed and bright green. It likes partial shade and a well-drained soil. Prune back heavily to promote full growth and, every now and then, give it a heavy watering. It grows to a height of 6 ft (about 1.8 m) and a spread of 9 ft (about 2.7 m).

ZONES 4–10

## KOLKWITZIA
## *amabilis*

BEAUTY BUSH

The only species in its genus, this attractive plant is native to China.

*Lantana camara*

Its deciduous, arching branches bear delightful, bell-shaped, pink flowers with yellow throats in late spring. It has peeling bark and dark green, oval leaves. *K. amabilis* likes a well-drained soil, rich in leafmold, and prefers full sun. It grows to a height and spread of 10 ft (about 2.7 m). After flowering, prune old, weak or damaged shoots. Propagate from softwood cuttings in summer. 'Beauty Bush' has white flowers with yellow throats.
ZONES 5–9

*Lavandula angustifolia*

*Lantana montevidensis*

*Lagerstroemia indica*

## *LAGERSTROEMIA*

Native to tropical Asia, north Australia and the Pacific islands, these deciduous or evergreen shrubs do best in warm climates in hot, dry situations. They are grown for their profuse creped, crinkly flowers that appear in colors from soft pink to crimson and purple according to the variety. They prefer fertile, well-drained soil, preferably light to sandy, and full sun. Prune after flowering to retain a shrubby shape, or leave to grow into a small tree. They may be grown as tub plants on patios, where they should be watered well during the full growth period but less at other times. Propagate from seed in spring, from hardwood cuttings in winter or from semi-ripe cuttings in summer.

### *L.* hybrids

Many cultivars are available in a range of colors. New hybrids have recently been created using another species, *L. fauriei*. These are dependably resistant to mildew and are therefore useful in cooler, damper climates such as along the coasts; most have Native American names such as 'Hopi', 'Sioux' and 'Natchez'.
ZONES 7–10

### *L. indica*

CRAPE MYRTLE

This deciduous, vase-shaped bush bursts into bloom in mid-summer, bearing luxuriant trusses of pink, white or purple petals. Its small, oval, short-stalked leaves are deciduous and color prettily in fall. It prefers a fertile, well-drained soil and full sun. Cut back the previous season's stems to maintain a bushy habit or allow the plant to grow unpruned into a small tree. Water potted plants freely in full growth, less at other times. It grows to 18 ft (about 5.5 m) tall with a 15 ft (about 4.5 m) spread. Propagate from hardwood cuttings in winter, semi-ripe cuttings in summer, or seed in spring.
ZONES 7–10

## *LANTANA*

These tender shrubs are grown for their generous displays of flowers throughout the warmer months. Natives of tropical America, some have become weeds in other tropic regions around the world, particularly in Hawaii. Leaves are paired, fragrant when crushed and often rough to the touch; flowers are produced in dense, flat heads of tiny flowers, each with a distinct "eye". All can be treated as annuals in cold climates, since they grow quickly and flower early and steadily. Prune permanent plants hard in spring to encourage vigorous new growth and to control size. Mildew may be a problem if grown in the shade.

### *L. camara*

This showy, flowering shrub from South America is available in a variety of colors and serves as a quick summer bedding plant in cold climates, a year-round shrub in mild climates. Growing as much as 6 ft (about 1.8 m) tall and wide, its black berries are popular with birds, which help spread seedlings in tropical areas. Many named selections are available.
ZONES 9–11

*Lagerstroemia indica* hybrid

### *L. montevidensis*

TRAILING LANTANA

The dainty, arched stems of this trailing or mat-forming evergreen shrub make a wonderful ground cover or cascading plant. Throughout the year, but particularly in summer, it bears heads of magenta or white posy-like flowers, each with a yellow eye. It grows to a height of 12 in (about 30 cm) and a spread of $4^1/_2$ ft (about 1.3 m). Native to the Americas, it does best in fertile, well-drained soil and a sunny position. To keep the habit bushy, tip prune occasionally. Propagate from semi-ripe cuttings in summer, or seed in spring. Whitefly and red spider mite may present problems.
ZONES 8–10

## *LAVANDULA*

LAVENDER

These fragrant, flower-bearing plants come from southern Europe. Cultivated commercially for the perfume industry, they are also grown for their evergreen foliage and attractive bloom. They prefer full sun and a well-drained soil that is not too rich; all are dependably drought tolerant. Excellent as hedges, they need a light trimming in spring to keep the habit neat. Propagate in summer from semi-ripe cuttings.

### *L. angustifolia*

syn. *L. officinalis*, *L. spica*

ENGLISH LAVENDER

This dense, evergreen shrub is grown mainly for the long-stemmed heads of mauve, scented flowers that appear from spring to fall—these are easily dried for lavender sachets, pot pourri and the like. It bears small, furry, gray leaves that turn green as the plant ages. It makes an excellent hedge; trim it in spring to maintain the shape. It grows to a height and spread of 3–4 ft (about 90–120 cm). Dwarf selections, only 24 in (about 30 cm) tall, are ideal for edging, low hedges, or the rockery; 'Hidcote' (deep purple) and 'Munstead' (lavender-blue) are two examples.
ZONES 5–10

*Leptospermum laevigatum*

*Lavandula stoechas*

*Leptospermum s.* 'Red Damask'

### *L. dentata*

FRENCH LAVENDER

The dense spikes of tubular, mauve-blue flowers of this bushy, evergreen shrub appear nearly year round. Its aromatic leaves are serrated and are gray-green in color. It grows to a height and spread of 3 ft (about 90 cm). *L. dentata* is drought resistant and adaptable to most soils.

ZONES 9–10

### *L. stoechas*

SPANISH LAVENDER

This evergreen, dense, bushy shrub grows to a height and spread of 24 in (about 60 cm). In late spring and summer it bears terminal spikes of fragrant, deep purple flowers. The leaves are aromatic and silver-gray.

ZONES 8–10

## *LAVATERA maritima*

**syn. *L. bicolor***

A vigorous shrub from the western Mediterranean region, this mallow is noted for its gray foliage and a

*Leucadendron salignum*

*Lavandula dentata*

nearly continuous production of hollyhock-like, soft lavender flowers with purple centers. A broad shrub, it will quickly reach 6 ft (about 1.8 m) or more in height with a somewhat greater spread. The peak of flowering is in spring, although some will always be present. Give it full sun, a well-drained, even sandy soil and only moderate water. Prune back to maintain a dense habit. It may be relatively short lived, but is easily propagated from cuttings.

ZONES 9–10

## *LEPTOSPERMUM*

TEA TREE

Ideal for the informal landscape garden, this genus of evergreen trees and shrubs is native to Tasmania and southeastern Australia, as well as New Zealand. Well suited to mild West Coast gardens, where many hybrids and cultivars have been developed. Profuse, small flowers—white, pink or red—appear in spring. Drought, wind and even salt resistant, they do well in coastal areas if not too exposed and prefer a fertile, well-drained soil and full sun. Propagate from semi-ripe cuttings in summer. History has it that Captain James Cook prepared a brew from a New Zealand species for his crew as a remedy for scurvy—hence the common name, "tea tree".

### *L. laevigatum*

AUSTRALIAN TEA TREE

Native to the eastern states of Australia, this tall, bushy shrub or tree bears attractive, small, white flowers

*Lavatera maritima*

*Leucophyllum frutescens*

in spring and early summer. The evergreen leaves are small, oval and leathery. Preferring a well-drained soil and full sun to part shade, it grows to a height of 15 ft (about 4.5 m) and a spread of just under 9 ft (about 2.7 m). It is an excellent plant for the seaside. A dwarf selection, 'Reevesii', grows to only 4–5 ft (about 1.2–1.5 m) tall and wide.

ZONES 9–10

### *L. petersonii*

**syn. *L. citratum***

LEMON-SCENTED TEA TREE

This evergreen shrub or small tree, a native of Australia, bears delightful white flowers in spring and early summer. The narrow, lance-shaped leaves turn from red to green as the plant matures, giving off a characteristic lemon scent when bruised or crushed. It prefers light to medium, well-drained soil and does best in an open, sunny position. It grows to a height of 12 ft (about 3.5 m) and a spread of 6 ft (about 1.8 m).

ZONES 9–10

### *L. scoparium*

NEW ZEALAND TEA TREE

This species is actually native to both New Zealand and Australia, though most of the material has come from New Zealand. Much hybridization and selection have taken place in California. It varies from a prostrate shrub to a small, arching tree of 15 ft (about 4.5 m) or more. It has dark green, needle-like leaves and flowers in spring and summer with masses of flowers like tiny roses in white, pink and red, sometimes double. 'Pink Cascade' is prostrate, spreading 6–8 ft (about

*Leptospermum petersonii*

1.8–2.4 m) wide with pink flowers. 'Helene Strybing' is a two-toned pink with large flowers; it reaches 12–15 ft (about 3.5–4.5 m) tall and wide. In between are many such as 'Red Damask', dense shrubs to 10 ft (about 3 m) tall and wide with double red flowers. Best in full sun and a well-drained soil.

ZONES 9–10

## *LEUCADENDRON salignum*

This evergreen shrub, a relative of the protea, is native to South Africa. Its narrow, deep green leaves are often tinged yellow or red. During winter and spring the unshowy, cone-like flowers at the tip of each stem are surrounded by brightly colored modified leaves called bracts; male and female flowers are borne on different plants. Plants may grow to 6 ft (about 1.8 m) tall and nearly as wide. Suited to coastal California, it prefers full sun and a well-drained, sandy soil, one that is low in phosphorus. It needs only occasional water during the dry summer months.

ZONES 9–10

## *LEUCOPHYLLUM frutescens*

TEXAS RANGER, SILVERLEAF, CENIZO

Of the many species of these silvery-leafed shrubs native to the Chihuahan Desert of western Texas and northern Mexico, this species is the hardiest and most commonly seen in gardens. Its dense, upright form (usually 6-8 ft/1.8–2.4 m tall and a bit narrower) is covered with lavender flowers following a good rain. Very tough and tolerant of heat and drought, nurseries are now offering selections with flowers of pink, white or purple on plants that may be low and compact or may be tall and slender.

ZONES 8–10

## *LEUCOSPERMUM cordifolium*

**syn. *L. nutans***

PINCUSHION

This well-branched evergreen shrub, a native to southwest South

Africa, is grown for the delightful profuse bloom of pinkish orange, pincushion-like flowers it bears. These are long lasting when cut and much sought after by florists; they are cultivated extensively in coastal California and Hawaii. They prefer a Mediterranean-type climate (winter rain, summer drought) and a sandy, well-drained soil with a low phosphorus level. Its leaves are green and lanceolate. It grows to a height of 3 ft (about 90 cm) with a spread of 3–6 ft (about 90–180 cm). Propagate from seed in spring. This pincushion needs little pruning, as it branches naturally to form a dense shrub.
ZONES 9–10

## *LEUCOTHOE fontanesiana*

DROOPING LEUCOTHOE, FETTERBUSH

This close relative of the rhododendron and *Pieris* bears a strong resemblance to the latter, with its slender, pendulous racemes of white, urn-shaped flowers in spring. The leaves are thick, leathery and evergreen, though turning bronze in winter. A native of southeastern American woodlands, it prefers an acid, woodsy soil, partial shade and regular water; it does not like heat or drought. Best used in masses as a coarse ground cover, the plants will grow to 3–6 ft (about 90–180 cm) tall and as wide. Propagate from seed or cuttings in winter.
ZONES 4–8

## *LIGUSTRUM*

PRIVET

These deciduous, semi-evergreen and evergreen shrubs enjoy a mixed popularity. They can be difficult to remove once established, and they spread rapidly and can easily become weeds. Some species, however, are popular as hedge shrubs. Leaf size varies among the species, but they all have small, creamy white flowers in dense clusters with a strong odor. They do best in sun or semi-shade—variegated forms require a fully sunny position. Cut back in mid-spring to restrict growth. Propagate from semi-ripe cuttings in summer.

### *L. japonicum*

JAPANESE PRIVET, WAX-LEAF PRIVET

Commonly planted, even overplanted, in the warmer areas of the US, this evergreen shrub has glossy leaves that are thin but leathery. If unsheared it will reach a height of 10–15 ft (about 3–4.5 m) and nearly as wide. Most often used as a sheared hedge, where it can be kept to 6 ft (about 1.8 m) or less in height. Tough and resilient, it tolerates most conditions including neglect. Often sold as *L.* 'Texanum', which may not be distinct from the species. Various cultivars are available including 'Rotundifolium', which is more compact in habit, and 'Silver Star', with creamy white leaf margins.
ZONES 8–10

*Leucospermum cordifolium*

### *L. obtusifolium* var. *regelianum*

REGEL'S BORDER PRIVET

Valuable for northern gardens, this hardy privet has a distinct horizontal branching pattern. Its deciduous leaves may turn purplish in fall. The typical white flowers in spring produce black berries that last into winter. This very tough plant is commonly used along highways. It will grow 5–6 ft (about 1.5–1.8 m) tall and somewhat wider. Give it full sun and average soil and water.
ZONES 3–7

### *L. ovalifolium* 'Aureum'

GOLDEN PRIVET

This upright, dense shrub, native to Japan, grows to a height of 12 ft (about 3.5 m) with a spread of 9 ft (about 2.7 m). In mid-summer it bears dense panicles of small, tubular, white flowers which give off a sickly odor. These are followed in turn by spherical, black fruits. The glossy, oval, green leaves have broad yellow borders. Prune out green shoots as soon as they appear or they will take over the shrub. Propagate from semi-ripe cuttings in summer.
ZONES 5–10

### *L.* x *vicaryi*

GOLDEN VICARY PRIVET

This hybrid of the common privet *L. vulgare* and the golden privet is just as tough as its parents, though somewhat more compact than either of them. Popular for its solid yellow leaves, the shrubs have a natural vase-like shape to nearly 10 ft (about 3 m) in height. It must be grown in full sun to ensure a good yellow color, otherwise any conditions will suit it. Shearing often reduces the impact of the yellow since the outer leaves are removed, revealing the shaded inner leaves; these inner leaves are naturally greener.
ZONES 5–9

*Ligustrum japonicum*

*Ligustrum ovalifolium* 'Aureum'

*Leucothoe fontanesiana*

*Lonicera tatarica*

*Lonicera × purpusii*

*Lonicera nitida*

*Lycianthes rantonnetii*

*Lonicera fragrantissima*

*Loropetalum chinense*

## *LONICERA*

HONEYSUCKLE

These shrubs and woody, twining climbers are grown for the delightful scented flowers and the foliage that suit them admirably as a cover for sheds and pergolas. Found worldwide in warm and temperate climates, they do best in a fertile, well-drained or moist soil in sun or semi-shade. Prune to remove dead growth or to restrict their often rampant spread—position the shrub where there is plenty of room. Mostly deciduous, the shrubby species of *Lonicera* should be propagated from cuttings taken in late summer. Aphids may pose a problem.

### *L. fragrantissima*

WINTER HONEYSUCKLE

This bushy, spreading shrub, the most fragrant of the species, is native to China. It grows to a height and spread of around 8 ft (about 2.4 m). It bears paired, creamy, tubular, sweetly fragrant flowers in winter and early spring. Its leaves are oval, heart shaped and green, and appear shortly after the flowers; bright red fruits ripen in summer and are popular with birds. Prune after flowering to control size and the plant's tendency to straggle.

ZONES 4–8

### *L. nitida*

BOXLEAF HONEYSUCKLE

This dense, semi-evergreen shrub makes an excellent hedging specimen. Growing to a height of 6 ft (about 1.8 m) and a spread of 9 ft (about 2.7 m), it bears insignificant, cream flowers in pairs in late spring. These are followed in turn by small, rounded purple berries. It has small, oval, glossy green leaves that are evergreen in mild winter regions. It can be clipped as a formal hedge.

ZONES 7–10

### *L.* × *purpusii*

This deciduous or semi-evergreen hybrid bears small clusters of fragrant, creamy white, short-tubed flowers with yellow anthers in winter and early spring. It is a dense, bushy shrub with a height and spread of up to 6 ft (about 1.8 m). The oval leaves are dark to mid-green.

ZONES 4–8

### *L. tatarica*

TATARIAN HONEYSUCKLE

This hardy, deciduous shrub from Russia is popular for its heavy production of white to pink flowers in spring, followed by bright red berries in summer. Many cultivars are available, although 'Freedom' is now recommended for is resistance to the Russian aphid which causes problems in some areas. Shrubs produce many arching stems to 10 ft (about 3 m) tall and as wide. Oval leaves are blue-green in color. One of the toughest shrubs for the cold north and the windswept prairie states.

ZONES 4–8

## *LOROPETALUM*
### *chinense*

Native to China, this well-branched, rounded, evergreen shrub is prized for the attractive, creamy white flowers it bears in clusters all along the branches during winter and spring. The 2 in (about 5 cm) oval leaves are light green. It needs full light or semi-shade, and does best in a well-drained soil that is neutral to acid. Potted specimens should be watered freely in full growth, but only moderately at other times. Little pruning is required, except to remove twiggy growth. The shrub grows to a height and spread of $4^1/_2$ ft (about 1.3 m), although it can grow larger if very happy. Propagate from semi-ripe cuttings in late summer or by layering in spring. A very attractive purple-leaved form with pink flowers has been introduced under various names, such as 'Rubrum', 'Burgundy' and 'Razzleberri'.

ZONES 7–10

## *LYCIANTHES*
### *rantonnetii*

**syn. *L. rantonnei, Solanum rantonetii***

PARAGUAY NIGHTSHADE

This South American relative of the potato is a valuable, long-blooming shrub or scrambling vine for warm-

*Mahonia lomariifolia*

climate gardens. Simple green leaves cover the branches and provide a good foil for the summer-long profusion of deep violet-blue flowers. It can be used as a 6–8 ft (about 1.8–2.4 m) tall background shrub or trained on a trellis or arbor where it may reach 12 ft (about 3.5 m) or more. 'Royal Robe' has deeper purple flowers and nearly year-round bloom in mild winter areas. Best in full sun with a well-drained soil and moderate watering. It propagates easily from cuttings.
ZONES 9–11

## *MAGNOLIA*

MAGNOLIA

These evergreen, semi-evergreen and deciduous shrubs and trees hail from Asia and North America. Grown for their pleasing, often sweet-scented, waxy, tulip-shaped flowers, they thrive in a fertile, well-drained soil. If the soil is sandy, add manure and leafmold before planting. Magnolias need shelter from strong winds, and prefer full light to shady conditions. Little pruning is required, as they continue to flower on the same wood for several years. The very old branches with woody spurs may be removed to encourage new growth. Propagate from semi-ripe cuttings in summer or from seed in fall. Alternatively, graft in winter.

### *M. liliiflora*

**syn. *M. quinquepeta***
LILY MAGNOLIA

This deciduous, bushy species is native to China. From mid-spring to mid-summer it bears handsome, purple, tulip-like flowers set among dark green oval leaves. It grows to a height of 12 ft (about 3.5 m) and a spread of 15 ft (about 4.5 m).
ZONES 6–10

### *M. stellata*

STAR MAGNOLIA

This slow-growing, deciduous shrub is a native of Japan. Prized for the delightful, white, star-like flowers it bears in late winter and early spring, it grows to a height and spread of 9 ft (about 2.7 m). It has pale green, narrow, oval leaves.
ZONES 4–10

*Mahonia aquifolium*

## *MAHONIA*

OREGON GRAPE, HOLLY GRAPE

Useful as hedges or for background plantings, these evergreens are also grown for their dense panicles of open yellow flowers. These are followed by blue-black fruits that make excellent jam. Plant in fertile soil that is well drained but not too dry. In cold conditions give them protection from winter sun and drying winds; in areas of hot summers, give shade during midday. Propagate from seed in fall or from semi-ripe cuttings in summer.

### *M. aquifolium*

OREGON GRAPE

This evergreen, open shrub, native to western North America, grows 6–8 ft (about 1.8–2.4 m) tall and spreads slowly by underground stems. 'Compacta' seldom exceeds 24 in (about 60 cm) in height and spread to make a good ground cover. In early spring it bears attractive yellow flowers, followed by blue-black, globular berries.
ZONES 6–10

### *M. lomariifolia*

This evergreen, very upright shrub is native to Yunnan Province in China. It grows to a height of 9 ft (about 2.7 m) with a spread of 6 ft (about 1.8 m), bearing bright yellow spikes in terminal clusters in late fall to winter. These are set among narrow, holly-like, spiny leaflets. Black berries covered with a pale blue powder appear after flowers fade.
ZONES 8–10

### *M. repens*

CREEPING HOLLY GRAPE

This native of North America's western mountains is a low-growing, evergreen shrub that spreads slowly by underground stems. Blue-green leaves are divided into leaflets as in other species; yellow flowers are produced in spring in small clusters, followed by blue-black fruits in fall. An excellent ground cover for the woodland or native garden in the West, it will thrive in full sun or part shade, a woodsy soil and moderate water and will grow 24–6 in (about 60–90 cm) tall but usually less.
ZONES 4–9

*Magnolia stellata*

*Magnolia liliiflora*

*Mahonia repens*

Malvaviscus arboreus

Malus sargentii

Melaleuca nesophylla

## *MALUS* *sargentii*

SARGENT CRABAPPLE

Though most crabapples are considered trees, this small-growing species is really best treated as a shrub. It will reach around 6 ft (about 1.8 m) in height and spread to 10 ft (about 3 m), covering itself with fragrant white flowers from pink buds in spring. The red fruits are small, and are popular with birds in late summer and fall. Good fall color, and attractive zigzag branching visible in winter. Give it full sun, good soil and average water.

ZONES 5–8

## *MALVAVISCUS* *arboreus*

TURK'S CAP, WAX MALLOW

This evergreen, rounded shrub, a native of Mexico, is grown for the rich, red, hibiscus-like flowers it bears in summer and for its bright green, soft-haired leaves. It prefers a well-drained but moist soil, and thrives in full sun or partial shade. Cut flower stems back hard in winter to maintain the shape. Potted specimens should be well watered in the growing season, but only moderately at other times. *M. arboreus* grows to a height and spread of 9 ft (about 2.7 m).

ZONES 8–10

Melaleuca incana

## *MELALEUCA*

HONEYMYRTLE, PAPERBARK

As well as being grown for their showy blossom, the magnificent shrubs of this genus (which also includes trees) are also useful for hedging and screening. They do best in a light, well-drained soil that is relatively free of nitrogen, but they will tolerate a wide range of soil conditions, even waterlogged soil. They do well in coastal areas and will assume interesting shapes. Many species have a fragrant honey scent from flowers rich in nectar that may attract hummingbirds. Potted specimens should be watered moderately, less so in colder temperatures. Pruning into a hedge shape will encourage a dense growth. Propagate from seed sown in spring, or from semi-hardwood cuttings any time from summer to mid-winter.

### *M. incana*

GRAY HONEYMYRTLE

This pendulous, evergreen shrub is grown for its narrow, gray-green leaves and spring appearance of dainty, creamy yellow, bottlebrush flowers. It grows to a height of 9 ft (about 2.7 m) with a broader spread. *M. incana* is native to southeastern Australia and thrives in much of California and the low deserts of the Southwest. It can be pruned into a small tree.

ZONES 9–10

### *M. nesophylla*

PINK MELALEUCA

This evergreen, bushy shrub is native to Western Australia and in summer bears terminal heads of flowers that are mauve-pink fading to white to give the plant a multicolored effect. Its leaves are oval, broad, smooth and gray-green. It grows quickly to a height and spread of 15 ft (about 4.5 m) or more. This species also does well in California and the low deserts, and adapts to drought as well as to copious water.

ZONES 9–10

## MELIANTHUS
*major*
HONEY BUSH

This sprawling, evergreen bush is a native of South Africa. Growing to a height and spread of 6–9 ft (about 1.8–2.7 m), it is prized for the luxuriant foliage and brownish-red, tubular flowers on terminal spikes that appear in spring. The leaves have oval, blue-gray, serrated leaflets. It does best in fertile, well-drained soil and will thrive in a sunny position. It can be pruned hard in early spring to keep it compact, although it will then flower less freely. Propagate from seed in spring or from greenwood cuttings in summer. The leaves have a strong, unpleasant smell when bruised, hence a common name for it in South Africa of "touch-me-not."
ZONES 9–10

## MICHELIA
*figo*
syn. *M. fuscata*
BANANA SHRUB

Native to western China, this evergreen shrub bears small, strongly scented, wine-colored flowers set among glossy, oval leaves. The flowers smell strongly of bananas. It does best in a well-drained, humus rich, neutral to acid soil in a protected spot in full light or partial shade. Pruning is not really necessary. Keep potted specimens well watered when in growth. The shrub grows to a height of 10 ft (about 3 m) or more with a spread of 6–10 ft (about 1.8–3 m). Propagate from semi-hardwood cuttings taken in summer or fall.
ZONES 8–10

## MIMULUS
*aurantiacus*
syn. *Diplacus aurantiacus*
STICKY MONKEY FLOWER

This evergreen shrub, native to western North America, is grown for the beautiful yellow to orange tubular flowers that appear in spring and summer, offset by narrow, glossy, lance-shaped leaves with margins that roll slightly inwards. It prefers full sun and a well-drained soil; it survives with little or no summer water but will flower better with occasional irrigation during the dry months. It grows to a height and spread of 3 ft (about 90 cm). Propagate from seed in fall. Prune in early spring to keep it compact.
ZONES 8–10

## MYOPORUM
*parvifolium*

This evergreen, spreading to prostrate shrub is native to southern and western Australia. It grows to a height of 6 in (about 15 cm) and spread of 6 ft (about 1.8 m) or more, and makes an excellent ground cover. Grow in an open, sunny position in a light to heavy, well-drained soil. Clusters of white, tubular flowers appear in summer, followed by purple, globular berries. A pink-flowered form is available. The semi-succulent leaves are narrow, blunt and thick. Propagate from seed in spring, or semi-ripe cuttings in late summer.
ZONES 9–10

*Melianthus major*

## MYRICA
BAYBERRY, WAX MYRTLE

These evergreen or deciduous shrubs serve beautifully as backdrops or hedges for coastal gardens. Their narrow leaves have a pleasing fragrance; although the flowers are insignificant, the fall fruits are covered with a gray, waxy substance and are popular with birds. Good drainage, full sun to part shade and only occasional water are all that they require for good growth; all are tolerant of salty coastal winds and sandy soils.

### *M. californica*
PACIFIC WAX MYRTLE

An evergreen shrub or small tree, this native of the West Coast has dark green leaves and a decidedly upright habit, except where sheared by coastal winds; it will reach 25 ft (about 7.5 m) or more in height, less in spread. *M. cerifera,* the southern wax myrtle, is similar but with light green leaves; it is native to the coasts of southeastern North America and is well adapted to gardens throughout the South.
ZONES 7–10

### *M. pensylvanica*
BAYBERRY

Like the wax myrtles, bayberry is a coastal native but is found along the northern and mid-Atlantic coast. It is a deciduous shrub only 10 ft (about 3 m) tall and wide. The wax on its berries is the source of the fragrance in bayberry candles. It spreads slowly by suckers, and does extremely well in the sand dunes of the East Coast.
ZONES 2–7

*Myrtus communis*

*Myoporum parvifolium*

*Michelia figo*

*Mimulus aurantiacus*

*Myrica californica*

## MYRTUS
*communis*
COMMON MYRTLE

Popular for hedges and screens, the evergreen myrtle also makes an elegant potted plant. From early summer it bears dainty, fragrant white flowers set among glossy, dark green leaves. The flowers are followed by purple-black berries. The leaves give off a strong scent when crushed. It grows to a height and spread of 10 ft (about 3 m), preferring full sun and a moderately fertile, well-drained soil; it is drought tolerant once established. Propagate from seed of from semi-ripe cuttings in late summer. 'Compacta' is a dwarf selection only 3 ft (about 90 cm) tall, as is 'Compacta Variegata', the leaves of which have attractive white margins.
ZONES 8–10

# A Field Trip to Mount Kinabalu

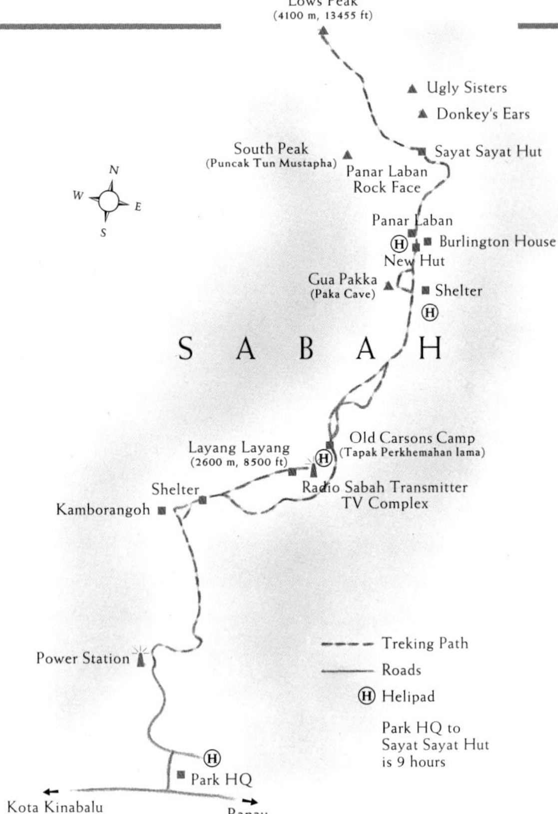


Mount Kinabalu in Sabah, on the island of Borneo, is a plant hunter's paradise. It is a bridge for the flora and fauna of both northern and southern hemispheres, and thousands of plant enthusiasts have made the pilgrimage to climb Mount Kinabalu, "the botanist's Mecca." It is also one of the places where the vireya rhododendrons can be seen. Many of these are epiphytic, and have unusual sunset coloring.

The journey from the closest town, Kota Kinabalu, takes about a day and you will then need to allow two days on the mountain, staying overnight in accommodation near the summit. You need to book an authorized guide at Kinabalu National Park Headquarters. Take warm clothing because, although this is the tropics, the upper parts of the mountain can be cold.

The journey to park headquarters will take you through typical lowland rainforest. The trees here are enormous, creating a heavy canopy that allows little or no sunlight through to the forest floor.

Park headquarters, where you start your climb, is at an altitude of 5000 ft (about 1500 m). Here in the lower montane zone, the trees, mainly oaks, are smaller than in the lowland rainforest. Lush ferns grow everywhere. The common tree fern *(Cyathea contaminans)* thrives, its graceful fronds reaching up to 12 ft (about 4 m) in length. Look up into the trees and you will see bird's nest ferns perched on forks in the branches, from which tangles of vines hang. Orchids also abound in this rich environment. The crimson and white nun's orchid *(Phaius tankervillae)* and the delicate white and gold angel orchid *(Coelogyne venusta)* are common.

After about two hours you will reach the Kamborangoh Shelter, situated at an altitude of 7500 ft (about 2286 m); then take the by-pass trail from here to Carsons Camp. The trees in this upper montane zone are smaller, up to 18 ft (about 6 m). There are more orchids here, but it is the rhododendrons which will take your breath away. The magnificent *Rhododendron lowii* is everywhere, the shrubs almost obscured by masses of bright yellow flowers. The leaves are thick and long and the waxy, funnel-shaped flowers are 3 in (about 8 cm) wide. The flowers are usually yellow but sometimes pinkish yellow in color. Along the track are located other *Rhododendron* species. *R. brookeanum* has smaller leaves and flowers, which are yellowish pink to red with white centers and often lemon-scented. You may see it growing as an epiphyte. *R. rugosum* and *R. fallacinum* have pink to apricot flowers. *R. stenophyllum* has orange to red, bell-shaped flowers and needle-like foliage. The carnivorous pitcher plant *(Nepenthes tentaculata)* also grows here.

*Rhododendron ericoides*

*Rhododendron crassifolium*

*Rhododendron lowii*

*The summit of Mount Kinabalu, seen from park headquarters.*

Mount Kinabalu is home to many rhododendrons, some of which are only found here. They are amazingly vigorous and luxuriant; if you take a moment to really study your surroundings you will see why. The soil is light but rich and covered in leaves. The rainfall and humidity are high and the rhododendrons are lightly shaded from the strong sun.

Mount Kinabalu is also rich in animal and birdlife, including the leopard, mongoose and Malay bear, but unfortunately these are unlikely to be seen as most keep well away from the tracks. Orang-utans are occasionally spotted near the trails and you may see small monkeys swinging in the trees.

Continuing on past Carsons Camp, at an altitude of 8900 ft (about 2713 m), the vegetation on either side of the track is thick with bamboo and more rhododendrons. At times the whole path will be clouded with mist and you will notice the temperature getting cooler.

After about two hours you reach Paka Cave, at an altitude of 10 500 ft (about 3200 m). This "cave," not much more than the underside of a rock, is where Sir Hugh Low and Spencer St John, two of the region's earliest explorers, sheltered for several icy nights. The trees here include twisted, gnarled forms of the manuka or tea tree *(Leptospermum)*. You may see green mountain blackeyes and the brown mountain bush warbler. You will also see the endemic *Rhododendron ericoides*, an unusual species with needle-like leaves and scarlet, ½ in (about 1 cm) long flowers.

As you climb higher the soil virtually disappears and the vegetation becomes sparse against the granite background. Very few plants can survive the fierce winds, strong sun and abundant rain. Some that do survive have adapted to the extreme conditions by assuming a bonsai-like form. Another unusual rhododendron grows at this altitude—*R. buxifolium*, which has leathery leaves and scarlet flowers.

Soon you reach the huts where you will spend the night. The best time to climb the rest of the way to the summit is at dawn; by late morning Lows Peak will be enveloped in mist. The last short leg of your climb is devoid of any vegetation but the stark granite landscape has a beauty all its own.

## Rhododendron

In 1848 the renowned botanist Professor Lindley wrote: "When Mr Hugh Low returned from his visit to Borneo, he was so obliging as to place in my hands some drawings and dried specimens of certain species of Rhododendron which occur in that island *growing upon trees*. They are found to be distinct from all previously known … "

Low's collections from Borneo contained some of the first botanical specimens of what we now call the vireya, or Malesian, rhododendrons, technically members of *Rhododendron* sect, *Vireya*. This group has around 280 recognized species (out of a total of around 800 for the genus *Rhododendron* as a whole), mostly confined to the region between mainland Asia and Australia. By far the largest number, over 150, occur on the island of New Guinea; Borneo has 34, Sumatra has 26, the Philippines has 24, and there are 15 on the Malay Peninsula. Australia has a single native species, *R. lochiae*.

Many vireyas grow as epiphytes on trees, while others grow on cliffs or rocky mountain summits, on raw clay landslips, or in high mountain bogs at altitudes of up to about 14 760 ft (about 4500 m). Both leaves and flowers range in size from tiny to very large, while flower colors tend towards yellows, oranges and scarlets, although whites and pinks are also frequent.

In the last 30 to 40 years many of the New Guinea species have been brought into cultivation and hybridized, and are popular in mild humid areas.

*Rhododendron brookeanum*

*Nerium oleander* 'Algiers'

*Nerium oleander* 'Punctatum'

*Nandina domestica*

*Nandina domestica* 'Nana'

## NANDINA

SACRED BAMBOO, HEAVENLY BAMBOO

Not a true bamboo, the stems of these mostly evergreen shrubs from China and Japan will grow to a height of nearly 9 ft (about 2.7 m) but with a spread of only about 3–4 ft (about 90–120 cm). This makes the genus popular with landscape gardeners, who also grow the species for the handsome, reddish foliage which appears in fall and winter. Small, yellow-centered white flowers appear in summer and fall, followed by glossy red fruits. They prefer a sheltered, sunny position and fertile, well-drained but not too dry soil. In spring prune untidy stems. Propagate from seed in late summer, or by division of the roots. Many cultivars are available from better nurseries. 'Compacta' is 3–4 ft (about 90–120 cm) tall with excellent fall and winter color. 'Harbour Dwarf' is a fast-growing ground cover under 24 in (about 60 cm) tall.

### *N. domestica*

SACRED BAMBOO, HEAVENLY BAMBOO

This upright evergreen shrub is a native of Japan and China. In summer it produces large panicles of tiny white flowers at the top of each stem, followed in fall and winter by bright red berries. It has compound leaves with narrow, lance-shaped leaflets, bright green during summer but usually turning purplish red in winter; the new growth in spring is bronze. It prefers a sunny situation with fertile, well-drained soil and moderate water. Each spring cut out the oldest stems to the ground to encourage new growth, but do not top the stems as they seldom branch when pruned.
ZONES 7–10

### *N. domestica* 'Nana'

This dwarf shrub is particularly popular, probably because it colors so strongly in winter. An evergreen or semi-evergreen, it grows to a height of 12 in (about 30 cm), spreading slowly as a ground cover. It rarely flowers. Given sufficient direct sun its bright green leaves will turn scarlet in fall to winter. *N. domestica* 'Nana' is eminently suitable for a mixed border or rockery.
ZONES 7–10

## *NERIUM*
## *oleander*

OLEANDER

These evergreen shrubs are grown for their delightful flowers and for their ease of growth under almost any conditions. They have dark, olive-green, spear-shaped leaves. Flowers come in a variety of colors, including red, pink, peach, salmon, white and creamy yellow, and are produced continuously throughout the warmer months. Shrubs will

*Osmanthus heterophyllus* 'Variegatus'

reach 6–12 ft (about 1.8–3.5 m) in height and spread, unless pruned in early spring to encourage branching. A native of the Mediterranean, they prefer full sun and a well-drained soil but will adapt to wet or dry soils from the tropics to warm-temperate zones; they do not like cool, moist conditions. Propagate from semi-ripe cuttings in summer or from seed in spring. All parts of the plants are poisonous, and are reliably deer proof. 'Algiers' is an excellent red cultivar, 6–8 ft (about 1.8–2.4 m) tall. 'Sister Agnes' is a vigorous white form with the potential of reaching 20 ft (about 6 m) tall and suitable for use as a tree. More compact cultivars are also available, such as 'Petite Salmon', no more than 3–4 ft (about 90–120 cm) tall with minimal pruning required.
ZONES 8–11

## *OCHNA*
### *serrulata*

BIRD'S EYE BUSH, MICKEY MOUSE PLANT

This evergreen bush is native to southern Africa. It is grown for the clusters of attractive yellow flowers set among oval, glossy, serrated leaves and for the black, glossy berries set in red calyces that follow the bloom. It prefers full light in an open, sunny position and a light, sandy, well-drained soil. Water potted plants moderately in full growth. If necessary, prune shrubs in spring. It grows to a height and spread of just under 6 ft (about 1.8 m). Propagate from semi-ripe cuttings in summer, seed in spring.
ZONES 9–10

*Ochna serrulata*

## *OSMANTHUS*

SWEET OLIVE

The slow-growing, evergreen shrubs or small trees in this genus are grown for their fragrance produced from small, almost invisible, flowers. The scent resembles that of jasmine and gardenia. They prefer fertile, well-drained soil and tolerate either sun or shade. Cut back after flowering to restrict growth, and propagate from semi-ripe cuttings in summer. The flowers of *Osmanthus* species are traditionally used by the Chinese to scent and sweeten their tea. Hybrids between *Osmanthus* and the closely related *Phillyrea* are called *Osmarea;* they look just like *Osmanthus* and are grown in the same way.

### *O. delavayi*

**syn. *Siphonosmanthus delavayi***

One of the most popular species, this evergreen, rounded, bushy shrub is a Chinese native. It has arching branches, small, glossy, dark, serrated leaves and clusters of highly scented white tubular flowers freely produced from mid- to late summer. It reaches a height and spread of around 6–9 ft (about 1.8–2.7 m). A good hedging plant whose flowering potential will increase with light pruning.
ZONES 7–10

### *O. fragrans*

SWEET OLIVE

This erect, branching, evergreen shrub is native to the Himalayas, India and Japan. It grows to a height of 15 ft (about 4.5 m) or more and nearly as wide. Sprays of small, white, very fragrant flowers appear in spring and again in fall; it has glossy, broad, green leaves. 'Aurantiacus' is an orange-flowered cultivar.
ZONES 9–10

### *O. heterophyllus*

**syn. *O. aquifolium, O. illicifolius***

HOLLY-LEAF OSMANTHUS

Native to China, this erect, branching, evergreen shrub or tree bears

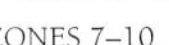

*Osmanthus delavayi*

small, white, delightfully fragrant flowers in the leaf axils in fall. It is an excellent shrub for screens or hedges or for growing in containers. It has holly-like leaves that are deep green in the species, variegated with white margins in 'Variegatus', purplish in 'Purpureus' and nearly round without any teeth in 'Rotundifolius'. It has an upright habit with a height of 8–10 ft (about 2.4–3 m) or more with age and a spread of 5–6 ft (about 1.5–1.8 m). 'Gulftide' is more compact.
ZONES 7–10

*Osmanthus fragrans*

*Paeonia suffruticosa*

*Paeonia lutea*

*Pachystegia insignis*

## PACHYSTEGIA

### *insignis*

**syn. *Olearia insignis***

This low-growing, spreading, evergreen shrub, native to New Zealand, is grown for its white, daisy-like flowers with yellow centers borne in winter. It has leathery, dark green, shiny leaves and likes a well-drained soil in a protected, sunny position. It grows to 3 ft (about 90 cm) tall with a 6 ft (about 1.8 m) spread.

ZONES 8–10

## PAEONIA

PEONY

Native to Tibet, western China and Bhutan, these shrubby "tree peonies" do best where they will get some winter chill. They are woody and deciduous, bearing brightly colored flowers that range from white to darkest red, to purple, orange and yellow. They prefer a little shade from the hot afternoon sun, especially where the climate is hot and dry; in cooler climates they will tolerate full sun. They like a moist but very well-drained soil rich with humus and preferably with some lime. These peonies are difficult to propagate—very slow from seed and tricky from cuttings; it is best to purchase plants from the nursery where most will have been grafted. Avoid botrytis by ensuring good air movement.

### *P. lutea*

A deciduous, upright shrub native to China, *P. lutea* bears single, yellow flowers in late spring to early summer. Its dark green leaves have saw-toothed edges. It grows to a height and spread of 6 ft (about 1.8 m).

ZONES 6–10

### *P. suffruticosa*

MOUTAN, TREE PEONY

This deciduous, upright shrub, a native of China, grows to a height and spread of 3–6 ft (about 90–180 cm). In spring it bears single or double, cup-shaped, huge, red, pink, white or yellow flowers set among large, compound, mid-green leaves. Most tree peonies available are actually hybrids of this and other species.

ZONES 5–10

## PARAHEBE

### *perfoliata*

**syn. *Derwentia perfoliata***

VERONICA

Found mainly in New Zealand, parahebes are dense, shrubby evergreens with a prostrate, decumbent habit, making them excellent for border edgings or for rock gardens. They are similar to *Hebe* and *Veronica*. A native of southeastern Australia, *P. perfoliata* is an evergreen shrub grown for the beautiful, five-petaled deep blue flowers occurring in long, slender, terminal spikes it bears in spring; these are set among broad, sessile, leathery, silver-gray leaves. It does best in a well-drained, peaty, sandy soil in a sunny or partially shaded position. Well suited as a rockery plant or for border edging, it grows to a height and spread of 24 in (about 60 cm). Propagate from semi-ripe cuttings in early summer.

ZONES 8–10

## PAXISTIMA

### *canbyi*

**syn. *Pachistima, Pachystima***

CANBY PAXISTIMA

This low, shrubby native from the mountains of Virginia is a useful ground cover for east coast gardens. Adaptable throughout the Midwest and Northeast, paxistima will thrive in full sun or part shade as long as the soil is well drained and on the acid side. It is grown for its narrow, evergreen leaves and mounding habit; its flowers and fruit are insignificant. It reaches around 12 in (about 30 cm) in height while spreading to around 3–5 ft (about 90–150 cm) wide.

ZONES 3–8

## *PENTAS*
### *lanceolata*

syn. *P. carnea*

STAR CLUSTERS, EGYPTIAN STAR

Native to the tropics of Africa and the Arabian peninsula, this erect, straggling shrub grows to a height of 24 in (about 60 cm) and a spread of 3 ft (about 90 cm). It is grown for the spring/summer appearance of clusters of tubular, red, pink, lilac or white flowers set among bright green, hairy leaves. It does best in fertile, well-drained, sandy soil—ideally, rich with leafmold—and an open, sunny position. Pinch back regularly to maintain a compact habit and to encourage bloom. Propagate from seed in spring or from softwood cuttings in summer.

ZONES 10–11

## *PERNETTYA*
### *mucronata*

syn. *Gaultheria mucronata*

Native to the southern tip of South America, this evergreen shrub bears white, urn-shaped, heath-like flowers in late spring and early summer set among small, pointed leaves. Small, bright berries of variable color appear in fall and winter. It does best in a moist but well-drained, acid soil and prefers sun or semi-shade. It grows to a height of 3 ft (about 90 cm) and spreads underground to create a broad clump; its spread may need to be controlled. Propagate by division or from seed in summer or spring, or from softwood cuttings in summer to be sure of the berry color.

ZONES 6–10

## *PHILADELPHUS*

MOCK ORANGE

These suckering, deciduous shrubs come from Europe, Asia and the Americas and are among the most popular of flower-bearing shrubs because of their delightful orange-blossom fragrance. Unfortunately their presence in the garden after flowering is anything but exciting. The species tend to be more ungainly than the more compact hybrids, which often flower more abundantly. Best to keep them to the background or combine with other shrubs which have more year-round interest. Hardiness varies considerably among the species. They need sun and a fertile, well-drained soil. Thin out after bloom, and propagate from softwood cuttings in summer. Keep warm and moist until the roots establish themselves. Aphids may be a problem.

### *P. coronarius*

COMMON MOCK ORANGE, SWEET MOCK ORANGE

This species is a native of Europe and Southeast Asia. It grows to a height and spread of 9 ft (about 2.7 m) and bears terminal clusters of fragrant, creamy white flowers in spring and oval leaves that have hairy veins on the undersurface.

ZONES 4–9

### *P.* hybrids

HYBRID MOCK ORANGE

Numerous named hybrids have been introduced in Europe and America, derived from *P. coronarius* and other species. Most have been selected for their abundant and fragrant flowers, although some are actually better garden plants with a more compact habit of growth. Most have white flowers in spring. 'Avalanche' has small flowers on a 4 ft (about 1.2 m) shrub. 'Belle Etoile' has larger flowers on a 6 ft (about 1.8 m) shrub. 'Lemoinei' has small, very fragrant flowers on a 4 ft (about 1.2 m) shrub. 'Minnesota Snowflake' is extremely floriferous with double flowers on an 8 ft (about 2.4 m) plant; it is among the hardiest. 'Dwarf Minnesota Snowflake' is similar but on a very compact shrub of only 3 ft (about 90 cm).

ZONES 5–8

### *P. lewisii*

MOCK ORANGE

A native of North America, this deciduous shrub grows to a height of 9 ft (about 2.7 m) with a spread of 6 ft (about 1.8 m). It has an erect, branching stem, oval green leaves and white, fragrant, 4-petaled, solitary flowers.

ZONES 5–11

*Pentas lanceolata*

*Pernettya mucronata*

*Philadelphus coronarius*

*Philadelphus* 'Lemoinei'

*Parahebe perfoliata*

*Philadelphus lewisii*

### *P. mexicanus*

EVERGREEN MOCK ORANGE

Native to Mexico, this evergreen species is really a scrambling vine bearing single, cream, very fragrant flowers set among oval green leaves. It will grow to a height of 15–20 ft (about 4.5–6 m) if it has something to climb on like a tree or trellis. It can also be grown as a trailing ground cover on a bank.

ZONES 9–11

### *P.* 'Virginal'

Fully hardy, this vigorous, upright shrub grows to a height and spread of 9 ft (about 2.7 m). From late spring to early summer it bears large, fragrant, double flowers set among dark green, oval leaves.

ZONES 5–8

## *PHLOMIS*
### *fruticosa*

JERUSALEM SAGE

This evergreen shrub, a native of southern Europe, is grown for the strikingly beautiful yellow flowers it bears in whorls, from early to mid-summer, among oval, wrinkled, woolly green leaves. It does best in full sun and a well-drained soil. Drought, frost and salt resistant, it tolerates coastal areas quite well and grows to a height of 4 ft (about 1.2 m) and a spread of slightly more. Prune back to about half in fall to keep its habit neat. Propagate from seed in spring or from cuttings in summer.

ZONES 7–10

## *PHOTINIA*

Grown mostly for their shiny foliage, species of this genus of semi-deciduous shrubs and trees make excellent hedges. They bear flat-topped clusters of white, acrid-smelling flowers followed by red or black berries. The young foliage is brilliantly colored, maturing to rich green. Photinias do best in a fertile, well-drained soil and require sun or semi-shade. Prune regularly to keep their habit dense and to promote new growth. Propagate by layering, or by grafting on to hawthorn stock.

### *P.* x *fraseri*

RED-TIP PHOTINIA

This hybrid species is widely grown in warmer regions of the US for its bright red new growth. Thriving on neglect, it is often over-used by state highway departments. The flowers are typical of the genus, but this one does not produce fruit. It quickly reaches 10–15 ft (about 3–4.5 m) in height and spread unless pruned regularly; frequent pruning encourages continual production of new red leaves.

ZONES 7–11

### *P. serrulata*

CHINESE PHOTINIA

This species, native to China, has glossy, oval, serrated, dark green leaves. In spring it bears small white flowers which are followed in turn by red berries. It grows to a height of up to 18 ft (about 5.5 m) with a spread of 12 ft (about 3.5 m).

ZONES 8–10

## *PHYGELIUS*

CAPE FUCHSIA

Related to *Penstemon* and *Antirrhinum* (snapdragon) rather than *Fuchsia,* these erect, evergreen undershrubs—perennials in some winter conditions—are native to the Cape of Good Hope, South Africa. They are grown for the handsome red flowers they bear in summer, rising on tall stems above dark green, oval leaves. They do best in sun or semi-shade and like a fertile, well-drained soil that is not too dry. Excellent in a rock garden, they grow to a height of 3 ft (about 90 cm) and a spread of 20 in (about 50 cm). Propagate from softwood cuttings in summer. *P. capensis* and *P. aequalis,* both red, are the best known species; there are several hybrids available with flowers in red, yellow or orange.

ZONES 8–10

## *PHYSOCARPUS*
### *opulifolius*

COMMON NINEBARK

Native to eastern North America, this deciduous shrub is grown for its showy leaves and spring flowers. They are good plants for the front row of a shrub border, where their attractive pendulous form can be seen to best advantage. Broadly oval, lobed, mid-green leaves change to dull yellow in fall, and clusters of tiny white, sometimes pink-flushed flowers are borne in early summer. The pale to dark brown bark peels when mature. It requires a fertile, moist, well-drained, preferably acid soil and an open, sunny position. They grow to a height of 9 ft (about 2.7 m) and a spread of 15 ft (about 4.5 m). Propagate by softwood cuttings in summer and thin established plants occasionally. 'Luteus' and 'Dart's Gold' are yellow-foliaged cultivars.

ZONES 5–9

## *PIERIS*

LILY-OF-THE-VALLEY BUSH, ANDROMEDA

These fairly dense, bushy, evergreen shrubs, native to the colder regions of North America and Asia, are

*Physocarpus opulifolius*

*Phlomis fruticosa*

*Photinia serrulata*

*Phygelius aequalis*

*Photinia* x *fraseri*

*Philadelphus* 'Virginal'

*Philadelphus mexicanus*

related to the azalea and are grown for their small, urn-shaped flowers. Slow growing, they do best in a mildly acid soil that is well drained and rich with leafmold. They prefer a sheltered spot in shade or semi-shade. They also like a humid atmosphere—this maintains the color and freshness of the foliage. Deadhead after flowering as this improves the growth. Propagate from semi-ripe or soft tip cuttings in early summer.

### *P. formosa* var. *forrestii*

**syn. *P. forrestii***

CHINESE PIERIS

This bushy, dense, evergreen species is a native of China. In spring it bears terminal sprays of white flowers set among slender, oval leaves that are bronze when young and turn dark green when older. It grows to a height and spread of 6 ft (about 1.8 m).

ZONES 7–10

### *P. japonica*

JAPANESE PIERIS, LILY-OF-THE-VALLEY BUSH

This rounded, bushy, dense, evergreen shrub is a native of Japan. In spring it bears dense sprays of pendent, white flowers that resemble lily-of-the-valley. Though flower buds develop in fall, they do not open until spring. When young, the small, oblong, glossy leaves are pink or bronze, becoming deep green as they mature. *P. japonica* grows to a height and spread of 6 ft (about 1.8 m). Plant in part sun in well-drained, fertile, organic, acidic soil; water regularly. There are selected cultivars with even more brilliant young foliage, such as 'Mountain Fire'. 'Variegata' has leaves edged in creamy white; it makes a delightful spot of brightness in a shady garden.

ZONES 5–10

## *PINUS*

### *mugo*

SWISS MOUNTAIN PINE, MUGO PINE

This shrubby, spreading conifer is native from the Pyrenees to the Balkans in Europe. It bears purple, scaly, 2 in (about 5 cm) long cones that ripen over two years. Its leaves are 2 in (about 5 cm) long, dark green needles arranged in clusters of two. It prefers a well-drained, light to medium, acid soil and an open, sunny position. It grows to a height and spread of 15 ft (about 4.5 m); various cultivars are available that are more compact and dwarf than the species. The dwarf forms are excellent as foundation plants and in small beds or rock gardens.

ZONES 3–9

## *PITTOSPORUM*

PITTOSPORUM

These handsome, evergreen, fragrant shrubs and trees are found in China, Japan, Africa, New Zealand, Australia and the Pacific. Grown for their fragrance and ornamental foliage; their fruits usually contain sticky seeds which can be troublesome with car finishes and patio furniture. They like a moderately rich, well-drained soil, moderate water and generally do best in mild winter climates. Some species prefer sun, others sun or partial shade. Propagate from seed in fall or spring, or from semi-ripe cuttings in summer. There are a great many cultivated species and hybrids.

### *P. crassifolium*

This large shrub is native to New Zealand and thrives along the West Coast, even with full exposure to the salty ocean winds and sandy soils. Gray-green leaves, woolly underneath, are clustered at the tips of each branch, nearly hiding small maroon flowers in late spring; the blue-green fruits that follow are more conspicuous. It will reach 10 ft (about 3 m) or more in height and spread.

ZONES 8–10

### *P. eugenioides*

This species is a large shrub often attaining tree-like proportions of 40 ft (about 12 m) in height and 20 ft (about 6 m) in width. Its glossy green leaves have a slight yellow cast; they provide very good, year-round handsomeness. Creamy yellow, sweetly scented flowers appear in spring. It responds well to pruning so makes a good hedge, screen or windbreak. 'Variegatum' is an engaging cultivar bearing gray-green leaves with white borders. It is usually more compact, growing only to 12 ft (about 3.5 m) tall.

ZONES 9–10

*Pittosporum eugenioides* 'Variegatum'

*Pieris japonica*

*Pinus mugo*

*Pittosporum crassifolium*

*Pieris formosa* var. *forrestii*

*Plumbago auriculata*

### *P. tenuifolium*

This evergreen tree grows to a height of 30 ft (about 9 m) with a spread of 18 ft (about 5.5 m). A native of New Zealand, it bears glossy, oval, mid-green leaves with undulating margins, and produces dark purple, honey-scented flowers in spring. There are several cultivars with variegated or purple-toned leaves much sought after by flower arrangers.
ZONES 9–10

### *P. tobira*

TOBIRA

This large shrub from Japan is commonly grown on the West Coast and in the South, where its fragrant flowers fill the air with the scent of orange blossoms during early spring. A dense mound, it will reach a height and spread of 10 ft (about 3 m) or more. It is tolerant of either full sun or part shade, and makes an excellent informal hedge (it does not respond as well to shearing as do other species). 'Variegata' is a delightful form, slightly smaller in size with gray-green leaves edged in white; it does best in light shade. 'Wheeler's Dwarf' is a miniature of the species, very dense and only 12–24 in (about 30–60 cm) tall.
ZONES 8–10

## PLATYCLADUS
### *orientalis*

**syn. *Thuja orientalis***
ORIENTAL ARBORVITAE

One of the most common evergreen shrubs in American gardens, this native of Asia is particularly adapted to the warmer regions of the South; it also adapts well to areas of low humidity in the West. Its flat sprays of scaly foliage are held vertically. Plants vary in height from 3 ft (about 90 cm) to 10 ft (about 3 m) or more, depending upon the cultivar. Give them a sunny situation with some protection from cold, drying winds in winter. A moist, well-drained soil is preferred, but it adapts to dry conditions once established. Many cultivars are available, most relatively compact and requiring little or no pruning; they are popular as specimens and for hedges and foundation plantings. Watch for spider mites in warm, dry weather.
ZONES 6–9

*Pittosporum tenuifolium*

## PLUMBAGO
### *auriculata*

**syn. *P. capensis***
CAPE PLUMBAGO

This evergreen, sprawling shrub, originally from South Africa, bears pale blue or white flowers in terminal clusters from spring to fall. It has oblong, pale green leaves. Fast growing, it likes a fertile, well-drained soil and full light or semi-shade. It is quite suitable as an informal hedge of 4-6 ft (about 1.2-1.8 m) in height, or to disguise fences and walls, where it will climb to 12 ft (about 3.5 m) or more. Water regularly to get it started; it is quite drought tolerant once established. Whitefly may pose problems. Propagate from semi-ripe cuttings in summer. *P. auriculata* 'Alba' is a white cultivar. *P. capensis* is said to have been used by the ancient Romans as a cure for lead poisoning.
ZONES 9–10

*Pittosporum tobira* 'Variegata'

## POLYGALA

MILKWORT

These evergreen shrubs are grown mainly for their masses of colorful flowers; though strongly resembling the flowers of the pea family, the milkworts are in a completely separate family. Give them full sun or partial shade in moist, well-drained soil. Cut any lanky stems back hard in late winter. Propagate from semi-ripe cuttings in late summer, or from seed in spring.

*Polygala* × *dalmaisiana*

### *P. chamaebuxus*

This evergreen shrub, a native of alpine Europe, grows to a height of 8 in (about 20 cm) with a spread of 16 in (about 40 cm). Racemes of small, pea-like, yellow and white flowers appear in spring and early summer. It has tiny, oval, dark green leaves bearing a resemblance to boxwood. *P. c.* var. *grandiflora* has rosy-purple and yellow flowers.
ZONES 6–9

*P.* x *dalmaisiana*

SWEET-PEA SHRUB

A hybrid of two South American species, this shrub flowers almost non-stop in mild regions of the South and West Coast. Its pea-like flowers are a soft magenta, sometimes difficult to use. It forms a mound around 3–5 ft (about 90–150 cm) tall and wide, with slender, light green leaves; it may become bare at the base. Use it in the middle of the border where lower shrubs can hide its bare legs; it will tolerate shearing to encourage more dense growth.

ZONES 9–10

## POTENTILLA *fruticosa*

BUSH CINQUEFOIL

The yellow or white flowers of this dense, deciduous shrub appear from early summer to fall amid flat, mid-green leaves comprising 5 or 7 narrow elliptical leaflets arranged palmately. Sow seed in fall or propagate using softwood cuttings in summer. The arching shrub reaches 24 in (about 60 cm) in height with a spread of 4 ft (about 1.2 m) or more. Numerous named selections are available including 'Tangerine', a new cultivar with golden orange flowers.

ZONES 2–9

## PROSTANTHERA *rotundifola*

MINT BUSH

This 9 ft (about 2.7 m) tall, evergreen shrub is grown for the delightful clusters of mauve or violet flowers it bears in spring. It has small, fragrant, deep green leaves. Native to southeastern Australia, it needs a fertile, well-drained soil and full light to partial shade to thrive; water moderately during the warm months. Prune after flowering. Propagate from semi-ripe cuttings in late summer, or from seed in spring.

ZONES 9–10

## PROTEA

PROTEA

The beauty of the gigantic blooms of these evergreen shrubs make them a popular choice for a sunny spot in a garden with the right soil conditions—sandy, well-drained, low on phosphates and nitrates and preferably acid (though some species tolerate an alkaline soil). Native to South Africa, the genus has relatives in South America, New Zealand and Australia. Often difficult to grow, all species need protection in the winter for a year or two after planting. Keep well ventilated if under glass. They last well after fading and after cutting—hence their popularity in both fresh and dried arrangements. Prune faded flowers off to encourage branching. Propagate from cuttings taken in summer (seed germination is erratic). The genus is named after the mythical Greek god, Proteus, who could change into any shape he desired. The flowers are widely grown in Hawaii and coastal California for cut flower shops.

*P. cynaroides*

KING PROTEA

This species bears large, open flowerheads with pink, petal-like bracts in winter, spring or summer. The leathery leaves are round and dark green. A lovely shrub, it grows to a height and spread of $4^1/_2$ ft (about 1.3 m). Like all proteas, the size of the shrub bears little relationship to that of the flowers—the flowerheads grow to 12 in (about 30 cm) wide. It is the floral emblem of South Africa.

ZONES 9–10

*Potentilla fruticosa* 'Tangerine'

*Prostanthera rotundifola*

*Protea cynaroides*

*Platycladus orientalis*

*Protea neriifolia*

### *P. neriifolia*

The flowerheads of this species are fragrant, silvery pink, black-tipped and grow to 4 in (about 10 cm) in diameter. These appear from fall to early spring. The bracts don't open very wide, although the flowers are long lasting when cut. *P. neriifolia* has narrow, oblong, oleander-like leaves. It is an evergreen, bushy, upright shrub that grows to a height and spread of around 9 ft (about 2.7 m).

ZONES 9–10

*Prunus laurocerasus* 'Otto Luyken'

*Prunus glandulosa* 'Sinensis'

## *PRUNUS*

CHERRY

Best known as a genus of popular, fruiting trees, *Prunus* also contains some delightful ornamental plants mostly from Asia and North America. Grown for the fall color of their foliage, as well as their fruits and flowers, they seem to tolerate any soil that is not excessively wet. Superficially they resemble the rose, but as would be expected in a genus with over a hundred species and cultivars there is widespread variation. All their leaves are oval to oblong. Deciduous species prefer full sun, while the evergreens do best in sun or shade. The evergreens should be propagated from semi-ripe cuttings in summer or fall, the deciduous species from seed in fall or hardwood cuttings in winter.

### *P. glandulosa* 'Sinensis'

**syn. *P. glandulosa* 'Rosea Plena'**

DWARF FLOWERING ALMOND

In late spring this dainty, suckering, deciduous shrub bears handsome, rose-pink flowers set among green, oval leaves. It grows to a height and spread of 3–4½ ft (about 90–130 cm). After flowering, prune young shoots close to the old wood.

ZONES 7–10

### *P.* 'Hally Jolivette'

HALLY JOLIVETTE CHERRY

This hybrid cherry is a large shrub or small tree, from 8–15 ft (about 2.4–3.5 m) tall and wide. A dense grower with many reddish, upright stems, it is completely covered for a two to three week period in spring with double white flowers opening from pink buds.

ZONES 5–8

### *P. laurocerasus*

CHERRY LAUREL, ENGLISH LAUREL

A dense, bushy shrub that eventually becomes spreading and open,

*Pyracantha angustifolia*

*Prunus laurocerasus*

this species bears racemes of small, white flowers in mid- to late spring. These are set among glossy, dark green, oblong to oval leaves. After the bloom period, grape-like clusters of glossy, black, cherry-like fruits make their appearance. *P. laurocerasus* grows to a height of 18 ft (about 5.5 m) with a spread of 25 ft (about 7.5 m). It responds well to clipping and makes a spendid tall hedge. Several compact cultivars are available including 'Zabeliana', which grows to under 4–6 ft (about 1.2– 1.8 m) in height.

ZONES 7–10

### *P. laurocerasus* 'Otto Luyken'

This low, spreading cultivar flowers profusely even in shade and will tolerate a position under tall trees. It grows to 4–6 ft (about 1.2–1.8 m) in height and will spread even wider.

ZONES 7–10

## *PUNICA*
### *granatum* 'Nana'

**syn. *P. granatum* var. *nana***

DWARF POMEGRANATE

This deciduous, rounded shrub grows slowly to a height and spread of 12–36 in (about 30–91 cm). Native to Asia, it bears red, funnel-shaped flowers in summer set among light green, oblong leaves. The small, orange-red fruits are dry and inedible. It does best in a sunny, sheltered position and likes a coarse, gravelly, well-drained soil. Water well in dry conditions. Prune lightly at the end of each winter to maintain its compact habit. Propagate from semi-ripe cuttings in summer, or from seed in spring.

ZONES 8–10

## *PYRACANTHA*

FIRETHORN

Though these arching, evergreen shrubs bear delightful profusions of tiny, white flowers in spring, they are mostly grown for the impressive display of berries that follows. The season and color of the fruit varies with the species and their hybrids, some lasting through winter. Dense and spiny, they do well as hedges, espaliers and ground covers. If

*Pyracantha coccinea* 'Lalandei'

grown against a wall, cut back long shoots after flowering. Grow in fertile soil in a sheltered, sunny position. Propagate from semi-ripe cuttings in summer. Scab and fireblight may cause problems.

### *P. angustifolia*

This dense shrub, native to western China, grows to a height and spread of 9 ft (about 2.7 m). In early summer it bears small, white, open flowers set among dark green, oblong leaves followed by orange berries in fall. 'Gnome' is an excellent compact selection, under 6 ft (about 1.8 m) tall.

ZONES 7–10

### *P. cocchinea*

SCARLET FIRETHORN

Upright to 8–10 ft (about 2.4–3 m) or more and sometimes erratic in branching, this species makes an excellent hedge, barrier or espalier with careful pruning. Deep green leaves set off small clusters of white flowers in spring and the red berries in fall. 'Lalandei' has orange berries on a taller plant and is the hardiest selection.

ZONES 6–10

### *P.* hybrids

A great many hybrids have been produced from the half dozen wild species. Hardiness will vary, so check with your local nursery. Cultivation is the same as for the other species listed here. 'Mohave' is tall (to 10 ft/3 m) and narrow, with great quantities of orange berries and good disease resistance. 'Teton' is also tall (15 ft/4.5 m) and narrow but with yellow-orange fruit. 'Red

*Punica granatum* 'Nana'

Elf' is a low and compact cultivar with red fruit.

ZONES 7–10

### *P. koidsumii*

FORMOSA FIRETHORN

The most commonly grown species in the Southwest and on the West Coast, this is slightly less hardy than the other species listed but is very vigorous. It is also more irregular in habit, responding less well to pruning and shaping. Good as a barrier plant or on a bank. 'Santa Cruz' is one of the best for ground cover, easily kept to under 3 ft (about 90 cm) in height and producing lots of red berries.

ZONES 7–10

## *QUERCUS*
### *gambelii*

GAMBEL OAK, ROCKY MOUNTAIN WHITE OAK

This large, deciduous shrub is native to the lower elevations of the Southern Rockies and makes a good screen planting in mountain gardens. Though it will reach 35 ft (about 10.5 m) in the wild it is usually burned periodically and develops into a thicket of 15–20 ft (about 4.5–6 m), an excellent habitat for all forms of native wildlife. Deeply lobed leaves are 3–7 in (about 7.5–17 cm) long, and turn gold and red in the fall. Give it full sun, well-drained soil.

ZONES 3–7

*Pyracantha* 'Mohave'

*Rhamnus californicus*

*Rhamnus alaternus*

*Raphiolepis* x *delacourii*

*Raphiolepis indica*

## *RHAMNUS*

BUCKTHORN

This genus of deciduous or evergreen shrubs with its inconspicuous flowers are grown for their fruits and foliage. They will grow in either sun or semi-shade and prefer a fertile soil. Deciduous species should be propagated by seed in fall, and evergreen species by semi-ripe cuttings in summer.

### *R. alaternus*

ITALIAN BUCKTHORN

This erect, branching, evergreen shrub, native to southern Europe, grows to a height of 18 ft (about 5.5 m) with a spread of 9 ft (about 2.7 m). It bears tiny, greenish flowers in axillary racemes, which are followed by black, rounded, pea-sized fruits. The leaves are dark green and oval with saw-toothed margins. *R. alaternus* likes a sunny or partially shaded situation, tolerating most soils, and adapts to generous watering or to drought. It is popular as a screening plant and is used near the coast in California. It makes an excellent clipped hedge, but looks just as beautiful unclipped. 'Argenteo-variegatus' has attractive leaves edged in white. Propagate from semi-ripe cuttings in summer.

ZONES 7–10

### *R. californicus*

COFFEEBERRY

This evergreen shrub is a native of western North America. It has oblong or oval leaves and grows to a height of 9 ft (about 2.7 m) with a spread of $4\frac{1}{2}$ ft (about 1.3 m). It produces red fruit which become purple-black as they mature.

ZONES 7–10

## *RHAPHIOLEPIS*

syn. *Raphiolepis*

These dense, evergreen shrubs, grown for their fragrant bloom and foliage, are native to subtropical Southeast Asia. They like plenty of sun but, in hot climates, prefer semi-shade. They do best in a well-drained soil with regular water, but adapt to drier conditions once established. They bear panicles of five-petaled flowers, followed by blue-black berries, among alternate, leathery, dark green, oblong leaves. They are tolerant of both coastal and interior situations. Propagate from seed or cuttings in summer.

### *R.* x *delacourii*

A rounded, evergreen shrub that grows to a height and spread of 6 ft (about 1.8 m), *R.* x *delacourii* is grown for the rose-pink flowers it bears in early summer and the blue-black berries that follow in winter. Its oval, leathery leaves are toothed at the ends. *R.* x *delacourii* is a hybrid between *R. indica* and *R. umbellata*.

ZONES 7–10

### *R. indica*

INDIAN HAWTHORN

This bushy, evergreen shrub is native to southern China. In spring or early summer it bears clusters of fragrant, star-shaped, white flowers set among serrated, oblong leaves. It grows to a height and spread of 3–5 ft (about 90–150 cm). Numerous cultivars are available with white, pink or rose-pink flowers.

ZONES 7–10

## *RHODODENDRON*

RHODODENDRON, AZALEA

The rhododendrons are an enormous genus of some 600 species (almost all garden worthy) and countless cultivars, native mainly to the temperate regions of Europe, North America and Asia although with important representatives in the highlands of tropical Southeast Asia and one species *(R. lochae)* in Australia. They are admired for their handsome leaves and showy, bell- or funnel-shaped flowers. The flowers are borne at the ends of the previous year's shoots, often in clusters, mainly in spring although both winter and summer flowers are fairly common. Just about all of them share an intense dislike of lime, but where soils suit they are among the most desirable of all flowering shrubs. As a general rule they like a shaded to semi-shaded position with a cool root run and acid, perfectly drained soil with abundant humus; none can be called drought resistant. No regular pruning is required, although they can be cut back quite severely in

*Rhododendron* 'White Gumpo'

early spring if needed. Propagation is by layering, from cuttings, or by grafting, most species being fairly slow to strike. Their usually shapely habit and compact root systems make them first rate subjects for container growing and they are among the easiest of all shrubs to transplant, even when mature. Red spider, lace bug, thrips, caterpillars and leaf miners can be troublesome, usually in dry conditions.

The genus is divided into some forty "series," but horticulturally there are three most important divisions. First there are the azaleas, formerly given a genus of their own (the distinguishing mark being that azaleas usually have 5 stamens, the rest of the genus 10 or more); then the rhododendrons proper, which are very variable in habit from dwarfs growing 10 in (about 25 cm) high or less to small trees and, generally, preferring a cooler climate than the other two groups do; and the subtropical species and their hybrids, mostly of the series Vireya and usually called vireya rhododendrons or simply vireyas. We shall deal with each in turn, illustrating merely a representative or two of each of the main types.

## AZALEAS

These divide naturally into two groups, the deciduous azaleas and the evergreen kinds. The deciduous azaleas bear their flowers either on bare branches before their leaves or with the young foliage; they are available in just about every color but blue, the yellow-to-flame range being the most distinctive and popular. The flowers are usually followed by brilliant fall foliage. They are happiest in a climate with cool to cold winters. The evergreen azaleas are on the whole less cold hardy; several of them are distinctly tender. They are of great importance in warm-temperate climates and as flowering pot plants.

### Gumpo azaleas

These are a small group of cultivars from Japan, a trifle more hardy than the Indicas. They are prostrate shrubs around 20 in (about 50 cm) tall (less with pruning) but spreading around $4^1/_2$ ft (about 1.3 m) wide. They are suitable for ground cover in mild winter climates and have 3 in (about 7.5 cm) flowers in shades from white to red. They are late bloomers and their flowers may be damaged by the sun.

ZONES 7–10

*Rhododendron*, unnamed Knap Hill-Exbury hybrid

*R.*, unnamed Knap Hill-Exbury

### Knap Hill-Exbury azaleas

These are the best known of the deciduous azaleas, derived from several species including both Japanese and American species and available in hundreds of named selections. They bear wide, open flowers in shades from white, cream and yellow to soft delicate pink and rose, to hot orange and red; flowers appear in mid- to late spring and may be fragrant. They grow 4-8 ft (about 1.2–2.4 m) tall and nearly as wide, with mid-green leaves that often turn brilliant shades in fall; the leaves may suffer from mildew in summer.

ZONES 5–9

*Rhododendron* Kurume azalea

### Kurume hybrid azaleas

Mainly derived from the Japanese *R. obtusum*, these are the most frost hardy of the evergreen azaleas. They grow to around 6 ft (about 1.8 m) high and wide, but are very slow and usually seen smaller than that. Foliage is dark green and oval, and the densely bushy plants are so smothered in bloom in their spring season that the leaves are quite obscured. The individual flowers are small, around $1^1/_2$ in (about 3 cm) across, single or double, and come in every shade from white through pink to red and purple. There are very many popular cultivars. They take their name from the province of Japan where the leading varieties originated. In Japan they are often sheared into formal shapes, although at the cost of some of the bloom.

ZONES 7–10

### *R. occidentale*

WESTERN AZALEA

A delightful fragrance is the most important feature of this deciduous azalea from the mountains along the West Coast. A variable shrub, it may grow from 6–10 ft in (about 1.8–3 m) in height and as wide. Flowers are typically white with flushes of pink or yellow, but it may be suffused with deeper colors. Many selections have been made for size, color and degree of ruffle of the flowers. Most floriferous in full sun, it needs moderate summer water.
ZONES 6–10

### *R. prunifolium*

PLUMLEAF AZALEA

This deciduous azalea is distinct for its summer flowering season, with orange-red flowers produced in abundance for July and August. Native to the southeastern corner of North America, this is a tough plant for southern gardens although it is hardy as far north as Boston.
ZONES 5–9

### Southern Indica azaleas

Derived mainly from the southern Chinese *R. simsii,* these are the most important rhododendrons in warm-temperate climates. They make rounded shrubs from 3–9 ft (about 90–270 cm) tall, according to variety, with slightly hairy, dull green leaves. There are very many named varieties. Some flower throughout winter, but most are spring blooming. Bloom is most profuse in the white to red and purple range, the flowers usually being around 3 in (about 7.5 cm) wide. These hybrids are larger growing than the Belgian indicas, from which they are derived and which are cultivated under glass as florists' potted flowering plants for Christmas and spring holiday giving.
ZONES 8–10

## RHODODENDRONS

Apart from the deciduous azaleas, all the rhododendrons are evergreen and, typically, bear their flowers in large, domed clusters. They are a very varied lot, and just a few typical species are given here to illustrate the range.

### *R. arboreum*

Native to the Himalayas, this species grows to a 50 ft (about 15 m) or more tall tree in the wild, although in cultivation it is usually only about half that. It has long, dull green leaves, often with silvery tinted undersides, and bears big clusters of red to pink flowers in spring. It is one of the chief parents of the popular Hardy hybrids.
ZONES 7–10

### *R. augustinii*

Native to central China, this bushy species can grow to about 9 ft (about 2.7 m) high and wide, although it is usually rather less in gardens. It has small leaves, giving the bush an appearance like an evergreen azalea. The wide open flowers, borne in small clusters, vary in color from blue to violet; in the best forms they are the purest blue seen in the genus. *R. augustinii* has been the parent of several very choice blue-flowered hybrids.
ZONES 6–10

### *R. auriculatum*

Another native of western China, this bushy, wide-branching shrub bears fragrant, white or pink, funnel-shaped flowers in summer. Its leaves are large, oblong and hairy. It grows to a height of 18 ft (about 5.5 m) with a spread of 12 ft (about 3.5 m). It is notable for its very late season of flowering.
ZONES 6–10

### *R. ciliicalyx*

This spreading shrub grows to a height and spread of 6 ft (about 1.8 m). It has shiny, dark green leaves. Its fragrant white or white-tinged rose flowers bloom in spring. *R. ciliicalyx* tolerates 18°F (about –8°C) or lower and grows at altitudes of up to 9600 ft (about 3000 m) in the southern China–Burma–Himalaya region.
ZONES 7–10

### *R.* 'Fragrantissimum'

In spring this rhododendron bears trusses of fragrant white flowers tinted with pink. Its lax habit of growth and quick response to pruning makes it suitable for use as an espalier on a wall or trellis. It is easily grown in a large container in colder climates and brought into a greenhouse for the winter.
ZONES 9–10

### Ironclad hybrid rhododendrons

This is an ever-growing group of extremely hardy evergreen rhodo-

*Rhododendron prunifolium*

*Rhododendron jasminiflorum*

*Rhododendron* 'Fragrantissimum'

*Rhododendron auriculatum*

*Rhododendron occidentale*

*Rhododendron arboreum*

*Rhododendron javanicum*

*Rhododendron augustinii*

*Rhododendron ciliicalyx*

dendrons, bred to tolerate the below-freezing winters of the Northeast and Midwest. The native American species *R. catawbiense* and *R. caroliniana* have been important in this breeding program. Most hybrids have relatively large flowers and large leaves on shrubs varying from 4–10 ft (about 1.2–3 m) tall. There are many named selections readily available, including the red 'America', pink 'Blue Peter' and white 'Gomer Waterer', and such compact, small-leafed hybrids as 'P.J.M.' (lavender-pink) and 'Ramapo' (violet).
ZONES 5–10

### *R. mucronulatum*

This extremely hardy species from Korea and China is deciduous except in mild winter climates. In early spring it is covered with bright rosy-purple flowers (pink in 'Cornell Pink'). It has an upright habit to 6 ft (about 1.8 m) tall.
ZONES 5–8

### *R. yakushimanum*

**syn. *R. degronianum* subsp. *yakushimanum***

This dense, mounding native of Japan bears rounded, terminal clusters of expanding, tubular flowers in late spring. It has deep green leaves with russet beneath; new leaves are covered with a silvery fur. *R. yakushimanum* grows to a height of 3 ft (about 90 cm) with a spread of 6 ft (about 1.8 m). It has been the parent of many hybrids, which retain its shapely, compact growth as well as its beautiful flowers. It is perhaps the most desirable of the rhododendrons for small gardens in temperate to cool climates.
ZONES 5–9

### VIREYAS (Malesian rhododendrons)

Native as they mostly are to such inaccessible places as the highlands of Indonesia, Borneo and New Guinea, the vireyas are still fairly new in cultivation and there is still much work to be done in sorting out which of the species are going to prove easy to cultivate and popular. They are, however, among the most exciting new developments in gardening, at least in warm-temperate and subtropical climates—in areas with more than the mildest of frosts they need greenhouse cultivation—and hybrids are already being raised. Evergreen, they are mostly shrubs around 3–4½ ft (about 90–130 cm) tall, with dark green, leathery, often glossy leaves which are apt to be tinted russet when young. They flower intermittently throughout the year, often with two or three flushes of bloom in one year. Flower size and shape varies, from 1–3 in (about 2.5–7.5 cm) and from funnels to wide open bells; some are sweetly scented. Colors range from white to orange, taking in sunset shades of gold coral and salmon pink on the way. They demand excellent drainage, growing well in containers with a fine orchid mix; in the ground, enhance the drainage with the addition of lots of bark chips or fir bark. They are more tolerant of sun and dry conditions than other rhododendrons, but benefit from plenty of water.

### *R. jasminiflorum*

This small, evergreen rhododendron bears fragrant, white flowers any time of the year among mid-green, oval leaves. It grows to a height and spread of 20 in (about 50 cm).
ZONES 10–11

### *R. javanicum*

Growing to a height and spread of 3 ft (about 90 cm), this rhododendron bears red to orange flowers with purple stamens in fall. It has oval, lightly veined green leaves.
ZONES 10–11

### *R. laetum*

This upright shrub will reach 4 ft (about 1.2 m) or more in height; it has medium green, oval leaves. It produces large trusses of deep yellow flowers that gradually fade to a soft yellow. Popular with many hybridizing programs and easily grown.
ZONES 10–11

## RHUS

SUMAC

This genus is found throughout the world, but some of its most garden-worthy shrubs are native to North America. They are either deciduous with beautiful fall color, or evergreen with lustrous leathery leaves. Flowers are usually tiny and are clustered in dense heads; the fruits may be showy and are popular with birds. Tough and adaptable within their range, there is usually a native sumac somewhere nearby. They possess none of the toxins found in their close relatives poison ivy and poison oak. All thrive in full sun, a well-drained soil and nothing more than the natural rainfall once established.

### *R. aromatica*

FRAGRANT SUMAC

This deciduous shrub of the midwestern and northeastern meadows and prairies grows as a low mound, spreading underground to as much as 10 ft (about 3 m) but only 4 ft (about 1.2 m) tall. The leaves are divided into three gently lobed leaflets, which color beautifully in red, orange or purple in the fall; they release a pleasing fragrance when crushed. Flowers are not showy, but are followed in late summer by red berries. Propagate by digging rooted segments from the edge of a clump. It thrives on infertile soils in full sun.
ZONES 3–8

*Rhododendron* 'Blue Peter'

### *R. microphylla*

LITTLELEAF SUMAC

This twiggy shrub or small tree is native to the dry Southwest, where it will reach 8–25 ft (about 2.4–7.5 m) tall depending upon the amount of moisture available to it. Normally evergreen, in cold winters it will color its leaves and drop them; it may also drop its leaves during extreme drought, but grow a new crop as soon as rain returns. The white flowers in spring are numerous enough to be showy, and the bright orange-red fruits in summer are popular with wildlife. It prefers full sun, good drainage anmd moderate water. Propagate by seed, but sow in place; it transplants only with difficulty.
ZONES 8–9

### *R. ovata*

SUGAR BUSH

A large, evergreen shrub, this native of southern California produces a sugar-coated fruit that provided native Californians with a refreshing citrus-like drink. With a height and spread of 10–12 ft (about 3–3.5 m), this makes a great background or screening plant. Its oval leaves are very tough and leathery. Clusters of tiny pink and white flowers appear in late winter. Give it full sun or part shade, good drainage and little or no water once established.
ZONES 9–10

*Rhododendron yakushimanum*

*Rhus ovata*

*Rhus aromatica*

# A Field Trip to the Blue Mountains

About a two-hour drive west of Sydney, Australia, takes you to the Blue Mountains, an area encompassing one of the country's most important national parks, and a haven for a variety of native plants, birds and animals. The Blue Mountains is also home to one of the largest populations of the waratah *(Telopea speciosissima)*, a strikingly distinctive native shrub and the floral emblem of the state of New South Wales.

The waratah blooms from October to December (spring to early summer in Australia). This is a good time to explore the Blue Mountains as it can be quite cold in winter, sometimes down to 24°F (about –4°C), and the whole area is often covered in an eerie, dense mist. In summer the average maximum temperature is a mild 73°F (about 23°C). Even when traveling in the middle of summer you should be prepared for a sudden change in the weather—a glorious warm day can suddenly turn quite cold.

A dry winter and spring can turn the whole of the Blue Mountains into a giant tinderbox and bushfires have ravaged the area many times. The waratah is a highly fire-adapted species, sprouting rapidly from a large woody underground stem (lignotuber) which withstands the fiercest bushfires and produces new growths within a month or two. Due to the fires, most wild plants are multi-stemmed with about 1–5 flowerheads per stem.

The best way to see the waratah is to start by taking the Scenic Railway at Katoomba. The railway runs the length of an almost sheer cliff face to the valley below and is so steep it is more like an amusement park ride than a train trip. It once served a coal mine and you will pass by openings to old mines and the remains of a horse-drawn tramway. A walking track at the bottom of the railway leads to a rock formation known as the Ruined Castle. The round trip on this walk will take you about 6 hours.

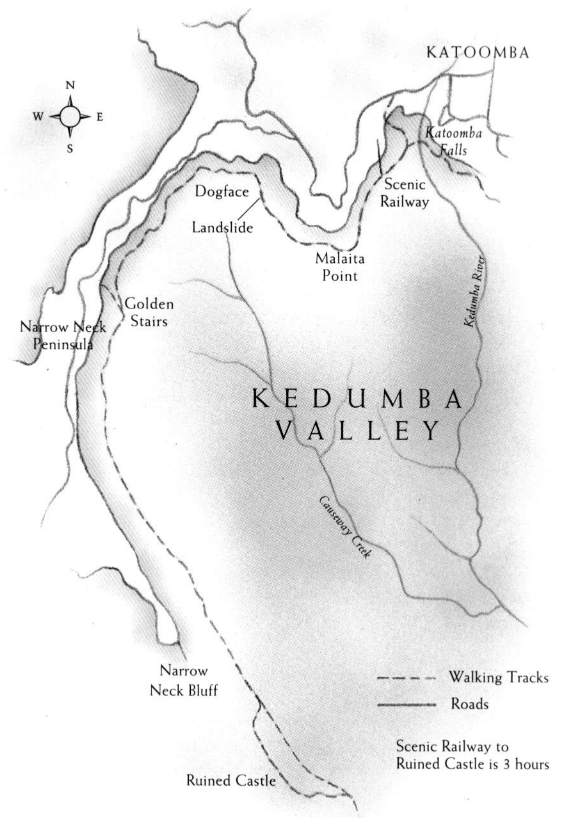

*The Three Sisters—a famous landmark of the Blue Mountains.*

The first part of the walk is through tall open forest which contains the white-trunked Blue Mountains ash *(Eucalyptus oreades)* and the smooth-barked apple gum *(Angophora costata)*, easily recognized by its twisted, bumpy trunk. The Australian bush is quite different from the forests and woodlands of Europe and America. The abundant eucalyptus trees give an overall impression of gray rather than the green of a European forest. The trees of the open forest are taller and the soil there is deeper than on the exposed ridgetops and the extra moisture due to runoff causes many of the trees to be covered in moss.

Soon you will find yourself in a rich, cool rainforest. The lush green vegetation includes the lilly pilly *(Acmena smithii)*, which bears pinkish berries in winter. These berries were once part of the local Aborigines' diet. Other plants you will see include the strap water fern *(Blechnum patersonii)* and rough tree fern *(Cyathea australis)* and rainforest trees such as the yellow sassafrass *(Doryphora sassafras)*, which has fragrantly scented leaves, and the magnificent coachwood *(Ceratopetalum apetalum)*. In this area and also in the open forest you may also be lucky enough to see a lyrebird preening its magnificent plumage. The lyrebird has a fanned tail of feathers which opens in similar fashion to that of a peacock. It is also a wonderful mimic.

*The New South Wales waratah—a colorful note in bushland.*

*Telopea speciosissima*

After the rainforest you climb a steep track leading to a ridge and the Ruined Castle. The trees here are smaller than those of the open forest and the vegetation more sparse. Walk a little further on and you will come upon the singularly striking red flowers of the waratah, which grows in profusion on the ridgetops and hillsides beneath the shelter of eucalypts such as red bloodwood *(Eucalyptus gummifera)*. The soil is very sandy and covered in leaves and twigs. The understory here contains a number of attractive shrubs including the old man banksia *(Banksia serrata)*, which has leathery leaves and creamy yellow bottlebrush-like flowers. Like the waratah, it also blooms in spring and summer.

Undoubtedly, the most distinctive plant in the area is the waratah. Both its common and botanical names mean "to be seen from afar." In 1793, Sir James Smith, President of the Royal Society, wrote in his book *A Specimen of the Botany of New Holland* (Australia): "The most magnificent plant which the prolific soil of New Holland affords is, by common consent both of Europeans and Natives, the Waratah." It grows to about 9½ ft (about 3 m) with foliage of leathery, coarsely serrated leaves. The large heads of closely packed flowers, encircled by bright red bracts and carried on strong stems, are an adaptation to bird pollination. Large nectar-feeding birds such as the wattle-bird and noisy miner are frequent visitors, their color vision enabling them to spot the flowerheads from a long way off.

Other birds commonly seen here are gray currawongs, striking crimson rosellas and white-eared honeyeaters. Bold currawongs come quite close, particularly if you have some food to share. The area is also home to the ring-tailed possum and another "bat-like" possum, the sugar glider. You may also glimpse shy wallabies.

Before you start your return journey, take time to climb to the top of the Ruined Castle and enjoy the panoramic views. The plants and wildlife alone would make this walk worthwhile but the magnificent scenery makes it unforgettable.

## *Telopea*

The waratahs belong to a remarkable group of trees and shrubs found on both sides of the South Pacific and Indian Oceans—the Proteaceae (see A Field Trip to the Cape Floral Kingdom, page 193), a family significant for its strong evolutionary association with Gondwana.

The true waratah genus *(Telopea)* consists of four or five species (an isolated population in northeastern New South Wales may be a distinct species). *T. speciosissima* is confined to a small area on the central coast of New South Wales and inland for less than 62 miles (about 100 km). The Braidwood waratah *(T. mongaensis)* is also found in New South Wales. It has bright red, loosely packed flowerheads. The Gippsland waratah *(T. oreades)* can be found in the damp ranges of southeastern New South Wales and eastern Victoria. It has small heads of crimson flowers. The Tasmanian waratah *(T. truncata)* is similar to the Gippsland waratah but has more conspicuous flowers. The latter has proved hardy under sheltered conditions in the British Isles.

Waratahs are grown for cut flowers in South Africa, Israel and California as well as in their native southeastern Australia.

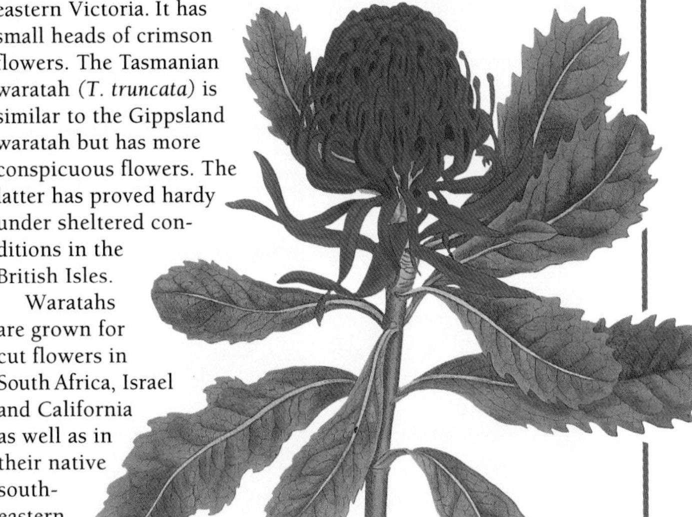

*Telopea speciosissima*

Ribes alpinum

Rosa foetida bicolor

Ribes odoratum

Ribes sanguineum

Rondeletia amoena

## *RIBES*

CURRANT, GOOSEBERRY

These are mostly deciduous shrubs found throughout Europe, North America and Asia and popular for their tasty fruits. Their leaves are usually 3 to 5 lobed and seldom give any exciting fall color. Stems on many species may be spiny, especially on those called gooseberries where the fruits are also spiny. Care must be taken to avoid planting some species near white pines as they are an alternate host for the white pine blister rust; most of the western American species are resistant to the rust. Sun or light shade suits them, along with a woodsy soil and moderate amounts of water.

### *R. alpinum*

ALPINE CURRANT

This native of the mountains of Europe is grown for its bright green leaves on dense, twiggy mounds to 5 ft (about 1.5 m) tall and wide. Excellent for hedging, either sheared or not, its flowers and fruits are inconspicuous. It does not host the blister rust.

ZONES 3–7

### *R. aureum*

GOLDEN CURRANT

Native to the mountain states of the West, this tough, drought tolerant, deciduous shrub produces masses of golden yellow flowers with a spicy fragrance in early spring. The fruits are black, purplish or orange in summer and are edible. Adaptable and hardy it will thrive with moderate water, but survives with only natural rainfall in the West. Ultimate height varies from 3–6 ft (about 90–180 cm). *R. odoratum*, the buffalo berry, is similar but is native to the prairies and high plains of the Midwest.

ZONES 2–9

Ribes aureum

Rosa glauca

### *R. sanguineum*

FLOWERING CURRANT

This deciduous shrub is native to the west coast of North America. Growing to a height and spread of around 6 ft (about 1.8 m), it bears handsome sprays of spicily fragrant, dainty, rose-pink flowers in winter or early spring, followed in turn by blue-black berries. The dark green, toothed leaves are also aromatic. Propagate from hardwood cuttings taken in fall. There are several cultivars, differing in their precise shade of pink.

ZONES 6–10

## *RONDELETIA amoena*

This erect, branching, evergreen shrub is native to Central America. Growing to a height of 9 ft (about 2.7 m) and spread of 6 ft (about 1.8 m), it is grown for the dense, rounded clusters of pink, tubular, scented flowers it bears in spring. It has dark green, oval leaves and does best in a fertile, well-drained soil in full light or partial shade. Keep potted specimens well watered in full growth. Prune back annually in early spring, taking flowered shoots back to within a few nodes of the previous year's growth. Propagate from seed in spring or semi-ripe cuttings in summer.

ZONES 10–11

## *ROSA*

ROSE

The rose is perhaps the best loved of all flowers, and it is prosaic to describe the genus as one of late spring- or summer-flowering deciduous shrubs with prickly branches, pinnate leaves and terminal inflorescences; the flowers being (in wild roses) almost always 5 petaled, usually pale pink or white, sometimes red, purple or yellow; often, although by no means always, fragrant; and followed by red or orange fruits called "hips". Such a description does not account for the charm of the flowers, which has led gardeners to develop many thousands of hybrids and garden cultivars, often flowering intermittently from late spring or early summer until fall. Most have many more petals than 5, which are arranged in a variety of flower forms and in a much wider variety of colors: every shade of red and pink, white, yellow, orange, mauve, purple, coral, in fact everything that is but true blue; many cultivars feature blends and variegations of two or more colors. Scent is variable, some cultivars offering intense fragrance, others virtually none. The plants range from under 12 in (about 30 cm) tall up to giant, long-limbed plants which are always treated in gardens as climbing plants and so are included in this book in the chapter on climbers. Names come and go from the catalogues with alarming speed, and we shall simply list here the most important classes accepted by the World Federation of Rose Societies, illustrating a typical variety or two of each and departing from strict alphabetical order to place them roughly in their historical sequence. There are roses adapted to all parts of North America; check with your local rose society for those species and hybrids that thrive in your area. They all prefer sun and rich, well-drained soil. Pruning consists of removing weak or elderly branches and shortening the rest, and is carried out either immediately after bloom (for spring-only types) or in winter (for "repeat-flowering" types). Aphids, caterpillars, scale insects, mildew, black spot, rust, and various virus diseases may prove bothersome, and it is important to seek the guidance of an experienced grower as to which varieties are most resistant in your local conditions. Roses are normally propagated by budding in summer, although many of the strongest varieties grow readily from cuttings taken in late summer or fall.

### WILD ROSES

There are between one and two hundred species of *Rosa*, distributed very widely throughout the northern hemisphere. All tend to be variable and to interbreed freely, hence the uncertainty in the number. They are mostly arching shrubs, some climbers, and probably about half are garden worthy. Only a few are described here to give an idea of the range.

### *R. foetida*

AUSTRIAN BRIAR

This deciduous, rather rangy, $4^1/_2$ ft (about 1.3 m) tall shrub from Iran is of great historical importance as the chief ancestor of the modern yellow garden roses. It comes in two forms: *R. f. lutea*, the Austrian Yellow, with brilliant deep yellow flowers around 3 in (about 7.5 cm) across; and *R. f. bicolor*, the Austrian Copper, identical except for its brilliant orange-red petals with yellow reverses. Both flower in late spring and have a strong, sharp scent which many dislike—hence the name *foetida* meaning "smelly". The name Austrian briar comes from the rose having been introduced in northern

*Rosa moyesii*

*Rosa pimpinellifolia*

*Rosa rugosa*

*Rosa gallica* 'Cardinal Richelieu'

*Rosa virginiana*

Europe from Austria in the sixteenth century. There is a double yellow version known as 'Persian Yellow', introduced from Iran in 1837. All forms are susceptible to black spot.
ZONES 4–10

### *R. glauca*
**syn. *R. rubrifolia***

This 6–9 ft (about 1.8–2.7 m) tall, arching shrub from central Europe is grown mainly for its decorative gray foliage. It is plum tinted when young and when the plant is grown in full sun; it is much sought after by flower arrangers. The small pink, late spring flowers are rather fleeting and of less account, but the red-brown hips are generously borne and decorative. Most forms are thornless or mostly so.
ZONES 3–9

### *R. moyesii*

This tall, deciduous shrub from China is grown both for the deep red color of its spring flowers and the spectacular display of large, bottle-shaped scarlet hips in fall. It is a gawky grower to around 9 ft (about 2.7 m) while several more compact selected forms have been introduced, the best known of which is the 6 ft (about 1.8 m) tall and wide 'Geranium'.
ZONES 5–9

### *R. pimpinellifolia*
**syn. *R. spinosissima***
SCOTCH ROSE, BURNET ROSE

Native from the British Isles through Europe and Asia to China and Korea, this densely thicketing shrub grows around 3 ft (about 90 cm) high. It has many straight prickles and fern-like leaves (their resemblance to salad burnet gives rise to its common name). The fragrant, 2 in (about 5 cm) wide flowers are borne in spring and are very variable in color, from white through pale yellow, and pale pink to purple. Black hips follow in fall, when the leaves assume muted tints. Double-flowered varieties have been cultivated since the eighteenth century, and in recent years the species has been used in the breeding of extremely frost-resistant garden roses.
ZONES 4–9

### *R. rugosa*
RAMANAS ROSE

This $4^1/_2$–6 ft (about 1.3–1.8 m) tall, densely thicketing (and very thorny) rose from Japan, Korea and northern China is one of the very best of all flowering shrubs. It is densely furnished with bright green, quilted (rugose) leaves and bears flowers from spring to fall. These are around 4 in (about 10 cm) across in the best forms and may be white, pink or violet. They are scented of cloves, and are followed by 1 in (about 2 cm) long globular hips. The foliage colors clear yellow in fall. In the wild it grows within sight of the sea, and is invaluable for seaside gardens and sandy soil. It is perhaps the best of all roses for hedging. There are a number of garden varieties with single and double flowers. The species has entered into the breeding lines of modern shrub roses and climbers, giving them great resistance to disease and cold.
ZONES 2–9

### *R. virginiana*
VIRGINIA ROSE

This $4^1/_2$ ft (about 1.3 m) tall, clump-forming, late spring-blooming shrub from eastern North America is one of the most desirable of wild roses. The leaves are glossy and dark green. The bright pink or white flowers, 3 in (about 7.5 cm) across, are borne in small clusters. The leaves color brilliantly in fall, and there is usually a lavish display of orange-red hips.
ZONES 3–8

## OLD GARDEN ROSES

These are the groups which were developed before the rather arbitrary date 1867, when 'La France', first of the hybrid Teas (large-flowered bush roses), was introduced. They fall into two main groups: the old European roses, mainly derived from the Mediterranean species *R. gallica* and spring- or early summer-flowering only, and including the Gallicas, Albas, Damasks and Moss roses; and those which were bred from crosses of these with repeat-flowering roses from China, bred there from the species *R. chinensis*. These include the China roses, the Teas, Bourbons, Portlands, and Hybrid Perpetuals as well as the Noisettes.

## Alba roses

These derive from the hybrid species *R.* x *alba*. They are strong, prickly bushes, usually about 6 ft (about 1.8 m) tall and wide with gray-green leaves and flowers in refined shades of white or pink, almost always very fragrant. They need only very light pruning.
ZONES 4–10

## Bourbon roses

Derived originally from crosses between China roses and Damasks, these are mainly arching shrubs around $4^1/_2$ ft (about 1.3 m) tall; a few are best treated as climbers. Flowers are mainly double, opening cupped or flat, and very fragrant. They are available in shades from white to red and purple. Most varieties are repeat flowering, although some are not very generous about it. Foliage is smooth, and the stems only lightly armed with prickles.
ZONES 5–10

## Damask roses
**syn. *R.* x *damascena***

These are thought to have originated as hybrids between *R. gallica* and the otherwise insignificant *R. phoenecia*. They are rather lax growing shrubs from $3^1/_2$–6 ft (about 1–1.8 m) in height, with matt-textured, light green leaves and flowers in shades of pink or white. Most are very fragrant. The majority flower in summer only, although there is a small group called Fall Damasks which repeat sparingly in fall.
ZONES 4–10

## *R. gallica* and varieties
GALLICA ROSES

Derived directly from *R. gallica,* these varieties are mainly upright bushes growing to around $3^1/_2$ ft (about 1 m) high and a bit less wide, with small prickled, rough-textured leaves and flowers in shades of pink, crimson and purple, often striped or blended. The flowers are usually around 3 in (about 7.5 cm) wide, carried erect, and are mainly very fragrant. The double varieties open flat and often "quartered", a style of flower common in all the European old roses. They are early summer flowering only. Mildew may be a problem.
ZONES 5–10

## Hybrid Perpetual roses

These are derived from crosses of all the old types, and were the leading garden roses from about 1840 until World War I; few of the many thousands of varieties then raised are available now. They are mostly tall shrubs to 6 ft (about 1.8 m), with long, lax branches that may be bent over horizontally and tied down to short stakes to create a great mass of summer flowers. Whether there will be a comparable fall show depends on the variety; many are distinctly stingy unless very generously manured, and the term "perpetual" is nurseryperson's salesmanship. The flowers range from white through pink to crimson and purple, and most varieties are very large in flower—to 6 in (about 15 cm) or slightly more—and fragrant.
ZONES 4–10

## Moss roses
**syn. *R.* x *centifolia* 'Moscosa'**

These arose mainly as sports of Centifolia varieties, although some are forms of the Damask roses. They resemble their parents except for the strongly developed, resinous glands on the sepals, which resemble fragrant moss. They are available in shades of white through crimson, and a few are sparingly repeat flowering. They were great favorites in Victorian times.
ZONES 5–10

## Portland roses

Derived from crosses between the Gallica types and China roses, the Portlands are mostly erect shrubs

*Rosa* 'Crested Moss' (Moss)

*Rosa* 'Celeste' (Alba)

*Rosa* x *damascena* 'Kazanlik'

*Rosa* 'Coupe d'Hébé' (Bourbon)

*Rosa* 'Monsieur Tillier' (Tea)

*Rosa chinensis*

*Rosa* x *centifolia* 'Bullata'

around $3^{1}/_{2}$ ft (about 1 m) tall with luxuriant, smooth leaves and 4–5 in (about 10–12 cm) wide flowers, usually fully double and quartered in shades of white, pink, red or purple. They are repeat blooming, although the amount of fall bloom depends on how generously the bushes are fertilized and watered.
ZONES 5–10

### Tea roses
**syn. *R.* × *odorata***

The Teas, so called because of a fancied resemblance between their scent and that of freshly prepared tea leaves, are thought to have been derived in China from crosses between *R. chinensis* and the climbing rose *R. gigantea*. They are mainly bushes growing to around $4^{1}/_{2}$ ft (about 1.3 m) high and wide (taller in mild climates) although some are climbers. Leaves are smooth and often glossy. Flowers are large, to 5 in (about 12 cm), usually carried singly on rather weak flower stalks and borne almost all year in mild climates or from late spring to fall elsewhere. They are of elegant form, and come mainly in delicate shades of pink, white, apricot or yellow. Prized by Victorian gardeners, they are outstanding in subtropical climates.
ZONES 7–10

## MODERN GARDEN ROSES

These include the types developed since the 1870s, and represent the bulk of roses grown today. They are classed as Bush roses (either large or cluster flowered) which make compact, upright bushes around 3 ft (about 90 cm) tall (although often rather more in mild climates) and flower from late spring to fall; Shrub roses, which are taller, less upright growers, mostly repeat flowering; Miniatures, which are repeat-flowering bushes growing only around 12 in (about 30 cm) tall or less, with leaves and flowers reduced in proportion; and Climbers, which may or may not be repeat flowering.

### Cluster-flowered bush roses
**syn. Floribunda roses, Hybrid Polyantha roses**

Originated in the 1920s from crosses between large-flowered Bush roses and Polyanthas, the Cluster roses rival the large-flowered roses in popularity, and interbreeding between the two has led to the division becoming rather indistinct; they can be mingled freely in beds if one so chooses. The Cluster types are generally a little shorter in growth, and bear smaller blooms in clusters of 5 to 20 or so from early summer to fall. The individual flowers range from $2^{1}/_{2}$–4 in (about 6–10 cm), and can be single to fully double, informally shaped or in the high-centered form traditional for the large-flowered roses. Most are excellent for cutting. They are available in the full range of colors, but strong fragrance is exceptional. The best varieties are disease resistant.
ZONES 5–10

### Ground cover roses

These are a very recent development, and are best thought of as prostrate or trailing shrub roses that can be used as ground cover, although very few (as yet) are really sufficiently dense or evergreen enough to smother weeds. They have flowers resembling the smaller and more informal cluster roses. Most varieties are repeat flowering. Few have much fragrance.
ZONES 5–10

### Large-flowered bush roses
**syn. Hybrid Tea roses**

Derived originally from crosses between Hybrid Perpetuals and Tea roses, but also incorporating the blood of *R. foetida* and one or two other species, these are perhaps the most important of all classes of roses. They are mainly upright bushes, displaying large, $5–7^{1}/_{2}$ in (about 12–18 cm) flowers singly on strong stems from late spring or early summer to fall, and are preeminent for cutting. Growth varies from 3 ft (about 90 cm) to twice that, depending on climate and conditions. Most are hardy, although some winter protection will be needed in extreme winter climates such as those of the Midwest and mountain states. The range of colors is enormous; just about everything but blue and bright green is available. Fragrance is variable, some varieties being very richly scented, others almost scentless. So is vigor and resistance to disease, and local knowledge should be sought in selecting varieties.
ZONES 5–10

### Miniature roses
**syn. Fairy roses**

Derived originally from exceptionally dwarf China roses crossed with Bush roses, the Miniatures are scaled down bush roses usually growing to around 14 in (about 35 cm) with flowers around $1^{1}/_{2}$ in (about 3 cm) wide. The bushes are smaller if propagated from cuttings; budded plants tend to grow larger, to around 20 in (about 50 cm). Bushes grown from cuttings are excellent for growing in containers and rockeries; the larger, budded plants are useful for giving touches of low, bright color in the garden. All the usual Bush rose colors are available, but few varieties have much in the way of scent. They are usually very free and continuous in bloom, and delightful for small flower arrangements.
ZONES 6–10

*Rosa* 'Peace' (Large-flowered)

*Rosa* 'Iceberg' (Cluster-flowered)

*Rosa* 'Jaques Cartier' (Portland)

*Rosa* 'Général Jacqueminot' (Hybrid Perpetual)

*Rosa* 'Cécile Brünner' (Polyantha)

*Rosa* 'Marlena' (Patio)

*Rosa* 'Flower Carpet' (Ground cover)

*Russelia equisetiformis*

*Ruscus aculeatus*

### Modern shrub roses

These are something of a mixed bag, with several sub-groups, but most are too tall and robust for growing in beds in the usual way; they are placed in the garden as other deciduous flowering shrubs are and can be used to great effect in mixed borders. Among the recognized groups are the Hybrid Musks, large, arching bushes with sprays of very fragrant flowers resembling cluster-flowered roses; "landscape roses", a fairly new group, mostly resembling the Cluster roses in habit but claimed by their originators to be exceptionally easy to grow and needing no pruning; "English roses", raised by the English grower David Austin who has sought to unite the grace and full petaled, scented flowers of the old European roses with the repeat flowering habit and brighter colours of the Bush roses. Hardiness varies tremendously.

ZONES 5–10

### Polyantha roses

Mainly of historical importance now, these dwarf bushes grow to around 14 in (about 35 cm) tall. They bear small, scentless flowers in large clusters from late spring to fall. They are available in shades from white through pink and salmon to red. Mildew may be a problem. The only variety to have retained general favor is the lovely pale pink 'Cécile Brünner'.

ZONES 6–10

### Patio roses

**syn. Dwarf Floribunda roses**

These are not a recognized class, but are becoming very popular. They are short-growing, cluster-flowered bush roses, usually around 20 in (about 50 cm) tall, but otherwise resemble the taller-flowered varieties. They are useful for the front of a mixed rose bed, for small spaces or for growing in pots, but their stems are rarely long enough for cutting.

ZONES 5–10

### *R. chinensis* and varieties

CHINA ROSES

Introduced from China at the end of the eighteenth century, the Chinas are mainly compact shrubs from 20–42 in (about 50–100 cm) tall, with distinctively pointed leaves. They flower very continuously from spring to fall; many will flower all year in frost-free climates. The flowers are usually around 2 in (about 5 cm) wide and are carried in clusters. They come in shades of true red or pink, with the flowers becoming deeper in color as they age; most are only mildly fragrant. They are pruned in winter.

ZONES 7–10

*Salix purpurea*

*Rosa* 'Rise 'n Shine' (Miniature)

### Centifolia roses

**syn. *R.* x *centifolia*, *R. provincialis***

CABBAGE ROSES

These are of garden origin and make floppy bushes, usually from $4^1/_2$–6 ft (about 1.3–1.8 m) tall with coarsely toothed leaves, many sharp prickles and nodding, very double flowers in white or pink; a few show deeper tones.The term cabbage roses comes from the globular flower shape. They are intensely fragrant.

ZONES 5–10

## *RUSCUS*

### *aculeatus*

BUTCHER'S BROOM

A rough, erect, branching, evergreen shrub, *R. aculeatus* is native to the Mediterranean region. In spring it bears tiny, star-shaped, green flowers followed by bright red berries. The flowers and fruit appear in the center of leaf-like structures that are actually flattened stems, each ending in a sharp point. Useful for dry, shady sites, it does well in sun or shade and prefers a heavy, moist, alkaline soil. It grows to a height of 30 in (about 76 cm) and a spread of 3 ft (about 90 cm). Propagate by division in spring. In days gone by butchers made a brush from the spiky stems to clean their chopping blocks.

ZONES 7–10

## *RUSSELIA*

### *equisetiformis*

**syn. *R. juncea***

CORAL PLANT, CORAL FOUNTAIN, FIRECRACKER PLANT

This trailing shrub is a native of Mexico. It is grown for the clusters of handsome, red, tubular flowers it bears all year round set among tiny, green leaves. *R. equisetiformis* does best in a light, humus-rich, well-drained soil and prefers a sunny spot. Fast growing, it is well suited to spilling over a wall or as a seaside specimen. It grows to a height and spread of just under 3 ft (about 90 cm). Propagate from stem cuttings or by division in spring.

ZONES 9–11

## *SALIX*

### *purpurea*

PURPLE OSIER WILLOW

Native to Europe, to Siberia and Japan, south to North Africa and

*Rosa* 'Buff Beauty' (Modern shrub)

Turkey, this deciduous, bushy species has a spreading habit and grows to 15 ft (about 4.5 m) in height and spread. It bears catkins of both sexes: the male ones have yellow anthers, while the female ones are insignificant; both are borne on slender purplish shoots in spring prior to the leaves. The narrow, oblong, deep green leaves are often borne in opposite pairs, making the species distinctive. *S. p.* 'Gracilis' is a dwarf form with a compact habit.
ZONES 3–8

## *SALVIA*

SAGE

The shrubby sages are an increasingly important group of garden plants for mild winter areas, or as summer "annuals" elsewhere. Many originate in Mexico and Central America, a few from California and the Southwest. All have paired leaves and two-lipped, tubular flowers in short or long spikes; flower colors represent the entire rainbow, including green, black and white. Easily grown in a sunny situation with good soil and moderate water, they reward with abundant flowers, usually toward the end of the season when few other plants are blooming. Hummingbirds adore most of them. Easily propagated from cuttings at nearly any time.

### *S. africana-lutea*

This dense shrub is native to southern Africa and bears brown or red-orange flowers in dense clusters nearly year round. The foliage is soft, light gray and aromatic. It does best in a sunny position with a well-drained, fertile soil.
ZONES 9–11

### *S. clevelandii*

CLEVELAND SAGE

This shrubby sage is a characteristic plant of the dry chaparral and scrublands of California, where its aromatic foliage and flowers add a distinct fragrance to the air. Usually a gray-green mound no more than 3 ft (about 90 cm) tall and 5 ft (about 1.5 m) wide, its soft lavender-blue flowers are produced on stems rising 12–24 in (about 30–60 cm) above the foliage. 'Winifred Gilman' is more compact, with deeper blue flowers. Sun and heat are preferred, along with good drainage and little or no summer water once established.
ZONES 8–10

### *S. dorrii*

DORRI SAGE, DESERT SAGE

This Southwest native is a low mound only 24–36 in (about 60–90 cm) tall, with attractive silvery foliage, evergreen except in the coldest of winters. Spring and early summer flowers are produced in dense, fluffy balls of blue and reddish purple. Great plants for softening the harshness of a desert garden, tolerating full sun to part shade and only occasional watering to extend the flowering season.
ZONES 8–10

### *S. greggii*

FALL SAGE, CHERRY SAGE

These shrubs are native from Texas into Mexico, and are long-flowering additions to dryish gardens in the Southwest and California. Leaves are small and aromatic; the plants are under 3 ft (about 90 cm) but are wider. Above the foliage rise slender stems with broad-lipped sage blossoms in red, orange, salmon, pink, pale yellow, white and blends; flowers are produced from spring through fall in coastal areas, and in fall and winter in the desert. Cut to the ground when flowering ceases to encourage new growth. Many hybrids and named selections are available.
ZONES 9–10

### *S. guaranitica*

A native of South America, this shrubby perennial is a dependable bloomer for the back of the border. Dark blue-violet flowers are produced on loose spikes from midsummer until late fall, almost year round in mild winter regions. Large, bright green, paired leaves give a bold texture to the plants, which will easily reach 6 ft (about 1.8 m) in height and spread. 'Argentina Skies' was selected for its pale blue flowers. Sun or light shade in the hottest areas, a rich soil and moderate water will ensure the best performance in the garden. Worth testing in colder zones by mulching deeply over winter.
ZONES 8–10

### *S. leucantha*

MEXICAN BUSH SAGE

This Mexican native is really a woody perannial (or sub-shrub), grown for its seemingly endless display of woolly purple and white flowers on long, aching spikes. Soft, gray-green foliage is attractive all year round. Plants will reach 3–4 ft (about 90–120 cm) in height and spread, making it suitable for the middle of the border; it is often used as a flowering hedge in mild winter regions. Sun, good drainage and occasional water suit this dependable sage.
ZONES 8–10

## *SAMBUCUS nigra*

EUROPEAN ELDER

One of the most commonly grown of the many elderberries, this species is a vigorous shrub with leaves divided pinnately into 3 to 9 leaflets. Many branching stems rise from the ground, each usually topped in spring by a flat, 8 in (about 20 cm) wide cluster of tiny, creamy white flowers. These are followed by blue-black berries, popular with birds. There are many selections with colored leaves, such as 'Aurea' (yellow), 'Purpurea' (deep maroon-black) and 'Argentea' (variegated with white). They all prefer a rich, well-drained soil and plenty of sun and will grow to a height and spread of around 18 ft (about 5.5 m), somewhat less if they are cut back every year or two to encourage young, vigorous growth. Propagate from suckers in late fall.
ZONES 5–9

## *SANTOLINA chamaecyparissus*

LAVENDER COTTON

This low-spreading, evergreen shrub, native to mild, coastal areas of the Mediterranean, grows to a height of 24 in (about 60 cm) and a spread of 3 ft (about 90 cm) or more. It bears bright yellow, rounded flowerheads on long stalks in summer set among oblong, grayish green leaves. Cotton lavender does best in a sunny spot in soil that is well drained but not too rich. Water from time to time and deadhead continually. Straggly old plants should be pruned to a neat rounded habit in early spring. *S. rosmarinifolius* (*S. virens*) is very similar but with green leaves and cream-green flowers. Propagate from semi-ripe cuttings in summer.
ZONES 7–10

*Salvia africana-lutea*

*Santolina chamaecyparissus*

*Salvia greggii*

*Salvia guaranitica*

*Salvia leucantha*

*Salvia clevelandii*

*Sambucus nigra* 'Aurea'

## *SARCOCOCCA*

### *hookeriana* var. *humilis*

syn. ***S. humilis***

SWEET BOX

This low, spreading, evergreen shrub is superb for deep shade. The shiny green leaves usually hide the clusters of tiny white flowers from mid-winter to spring, but their presence is known by the intense, honey-like fragrance they release; these are followed by small black berries. Generally carefree, sweet box needs shade except where summers are cool. Give it a woodsy soil and regular watering. Propagate by dividing clumps or by separating rooted suckers. *S. ruscifolia* is similar but is larger and less hardy (zones 9–10).

ZONES 6–10

## *SENECIO*

### *petasitis*

VELVET GROUNDSEL

This erect, branching, evergreen shrub bears large, terminal panicles of sparsely petaled, small, yellow flowers in mid-winter. The foliage is handsome and lobed. It prefers full sun in a protected position and a rich, moist, well-drained soil. It makes an excellent coastal garden shrub. Prune annually to keep its habit compact. It grows to a height and spread of 4½ ft (about 1.3 m). Propagate from semi-ripe cuttings in summer.

ZONES 9–11

## *SKIMMIA*

### *japonica*

This dense, round, evergreen shrub, native to the cooler parts of Asia, is resistant to air pollution and so is a good choice for town gardens and parks. In early spring it bears clusters of tiny, white flowers. If male and female plants have been grown together, bright red berries will follow in fall and last into winter. The leaves are aromatic, mid- to dark green and glossy. *S. japonica* prefers a well-drained, acid soil and shade or semi-shade—poor soil or too much sun will cause chlorosis. It grows to a height and spread of 4½ ft (about 1.3 m). Propagate from cuttings in summer.

ZONES 7–10

## *SOPHORA*

### *sedundiflora*

MESCAL BEAN, TEXAS MOUNTAIN LAUREL

This large shrub is a native of Texas and is valuable throughout the Southwest for its evergreen foliage and fragrant flowers. Usually with multiple trunks, it will grow to 10–30 ft (about 3–9 m) in height with a spread of at least 10 ft (about 3 m). Its leaves are pinnately divided into many rounded leaflets. The purple flowers resemble those of wisteria and have a sweet, fruity fragrance. A tough plant, it needs only a well-drained soil in full sun; it is adaptable to regular or infrequent watering.

ZONES 7–10

## *SPARMANNIA*

### *africana*

AFRICAN LINDEN, AFRICAN HEMP

This erect, spreading, evergreen shrub or small tree, native to southern Africa, bears clusters of delightful, white flowers all year round amid large, heart-shaped, light green leaves. It is available in both single- and double-flowered types. It does best in fertile, well-drained soil. Water freely when in full growth, less so at other times. Prune hard every few years to control size. *S. africana* grows to a height of 10–20 ft (about 3–6 m) and a spread of around 10 ft (about 3 m). Propagate from cuttings in spring. The genus is named after Dr Andes Sparmann, a Swedish naturalist aboard Captain Cook's historic second voyage.

ZONES 10–11

## *SPARTIUM*

### *junceum*

SPANISH BROOM

This sparse, twiggy, almost leafless, deciduous shrub is native to southern Europe. In spring it bears long, showy spikes of bright yellow, pea-shaped flowers. The leaves are very small and sparse. *S. junceum* does best in a sunny spot in soil that is well-drained but not too rich. Prune in early spring to maintain a compact habit. It grows to a height and spread of 6–10 ft (about 1.8–3 m). Too easily grown from seed, it has naturalized in most of the areas where it is well adapted, especially along the West Coast. It is best not to use it where it may escape into a natural plant community.

ZONES 8–10

## *SPIRAEA*

SPIREA, BRIDAL WREATH

Native to the northern hemisphere these thick, often arching, deciduous or semi-evergreen shrubs are grown for their beautiful spring or summer displays of pink, white or crimson flowers. They do best in a fertile, moist, well-drained soil in full sun. A layering of manure in fall and early spring will bring out the best quality bloom. Cut back spent heads to the old wood. Propagate from softwood cuttings in summer.

### *S. cantoniensis*

syn. ***S. reevesiana***

REEVES SPIREA

This deciduous shrub, with arching, slender stems, is native to China and Japan. It grows to a height and spread of 6 ft (about 1.8 m) and is prized for its showy clusters of white flowers that appear in spring. These are set among narrow, diamond-shaped leaves with saw-toothed margins.

ZONES 6–9

*Spiraea cantoniensis*

*Sparmannia africana* (double)

*Spartium junceum*

*Sarcococca hookeriana* var. *humilis*

*Senecio petasitis*

*Skimmia japonica*

*Spiraea thunbergii*

### *S. japonica*
**syn. *S.* x *bumalda***

JAPANESE SPIREA

This low, mounding, deciduous shrub bears rose-pink to red flowers from late spring to mid-summer. It grows to a height and spread of around 3 ft (about 90 cm). The cream and pink variegated new leaves turn green as they mature. 'Anthony Waterer' is the most commonly cultivated selection. 'Goldflame' has become popular for its bronze new growth which turns golden as it matures. 'Alpina' ('Nana') is more compact at only 18 in (about 45 cm). All are good additions to a shrub or mixed border, or when used as a low hedge. It has the best foliage of any in the genus.

ZONES 3–10

### *S. thunbergii*

*S. thunbergii* is a dense, deciduous shrub that bears clusters of single white flowers along the arching branches in early spring. The leaves are narrow and long and turn orange in fall. It grows to a height and spread of around 5 ft (about 1.5 m).

ZONES 4–8

### *S.* x *vanhouttei*

BRIDAL WREATH

This deciduous shrub bears dense clusters of white flowers amid dark green, diamond-shaped leaves in spring. It grows to a height of 6–8 ft (about 1.8–2.7 m).

ZONES 4–9

## *STREPTOSOLEN*
### *jamesonii*

MARMALADE BUSH

This rather lax, branching evergreen, a native of Colombia, bears terminal clusters of orange to yellow, phlox-like flowers from spring through fall (year round in frost-free areas). It has narrow, oval leaves. Full sun suits it best and it will thrive in a well-drained, humus-rich soil. Water well in full growth, less at other times. Tip prune regularly when young to help develop its shape. *S. jamesonii* is ideal as a shrub border plant. Cut back flowered shoots after the bloom. It grows to a height and spread of 6 ft (about 1.8 m). Propagate from softwood or semi-ripe cuttings in summer.

ZONES 9–11

*Streptosolen jamesonii*

## *SYMPHORICARPOS*

SNOWBERRY, CORALBERRY

These showy, cold-climate shrubs are grown for the clusters of long-lasting, pink-tinted or puffy white berries that follow their summer bloom of small, bell-shaped flowers. Native to China and North America, their arching habit bends almost double under the weight of flowers and fruit. They prefer filtered sun and a rich, acid soil. Propagate from softwood cuttings in summer or by division in fall.

### *S.* x *chenaultii*

CHENAULT CORALBERRY

This hybrid is an arching, deciduous shrub with pinkish flowers in spring followed by white fruit tinted pink. It reaches a height and spread of 3–6 ft (about 90–180 cm). 'Hancock' is a dwarf selection only 12 in (about 30 cm) tall; it is good for ground covering in a shaded area.

ZONES 5–9

### *S. orbiculatus*

CORALBERRY, INDIAN CURRANT

Native to North America, this erect, slender, deciduous shrub bears white or pink flowers in late summer set among dark green, oval leaves that turn bronze in fall. There is a variegated form. Round, purple-red berries follow the bloom. It grows to a height and spread of 3-$4^1/_2$ ft (about 90–130 cm).

ZONES 3–9

*Spiraea japonica* 'Anthony Waterer'

*Spiraea* x *vanhouttei*

*Symphoricarpos* x *chenaultii*

*Syringa patula* 'Miss Kim'

*Syringa meyeri* 'Palibin'

*Syringa* x *persica*

*Symphoricarpos rivularis*

*Syringa vulgaris*

### *S. rivularis*

**syn. *S. albus* var. *laevigatus***

SNOWBERRY

This deciduous, thicketing shrub from western North America bears pink or white flowers in summer appearing among dark green, rounded leaves. Large, white fruits follow. It grows to a height and spread of $4^1/_2$ ft (about 1.3 m). There is a form with variegated leaves.

ZONES 3–10

## *SYRINGA*

LILAC

These vigorous, open, deciduous bushes, native to Europe and northeastern Asia, are much loved. They are grown for the delightful fragrance of their flowers, which form in dense panicles in any shade of red, pink, white, mauve, purple or even yellow, most being cultivars of the Turkish *S. vulgaris*. The leaves are oval and small to medium in size. Most lilacs prefer a cold winter rest to bloom well the following spring. They do best in a deep, fertile, well-drained, preferably alkaline soil in full sun. Prune after flowering to maintain the shape. Dead-head for the first few years. Propagate by grafting or from softwood cuttings in summer. Grafted plants should be set with the graft union well below the soil surface.

### *S. meyeri* 'Palibin'

DWARF MEYER LILAC

This compact lilac has relatively small leaves, slightly hairy on the undersides. The flowers are violet to rose-pink in small, dense clusters and are delightfully fragrant; it occasionally flowers twice in a season. It will reach 6–8 ft (about 1.8–2.4 m) in height and spread.

ZONES 4–8

### *S. patula* 'Miss Kim'

MISS KIM LILAC

This is a compact selection of an excellent lilac notable for its late season flowering. It has relatively large leaves and fragrant flowers that are pale lilac. It will reach 6–8 ft (about 1.8–2.4 m) in height and spread, but is slow growing and will remain only 3–4 ft (about 90–120 cm) tall for many years.

ZONES 4–9

### *S.* x *persica*

PERSIAN LILAC

Long cultivated in western Asia and Asia Minor, this hybrid species is a deciduous, compact shrub. In spring it bears profuse sprays of small, delightfully fragrant flowers set amid narrow, pointed, dark green leaves. It grows to a height of just under 6 ft (about 1.8 m) with a similar spread.

ZONES 5–9

### *S. vulgaris*

COMMON LILAC

Commonly found around old farmhouses throughout eastern North America, these are the best known lilacs. Tall shrubs to 12 ft (about 3.5 m) or more and with many stems rising from the ground, they are topped in spring by wonderfully fragrant panicles of small flowers, typically pale lavender but with cultivars available in deep purple, blue, pink, reddish and white. Somewhat more prone to mildew and other problems than the smaller species, they are nevertheless popular for their flowers and fragrance. They flower poorly without a winter chill; select from the Descano hybrids in a mild winter region.

ZONES 4–9

## *TAMARIX*
## *parviflora*

This graceful, arching, deciduous shrub grows to a height and spread

of 12 ft (about 3.5 m). Native to Mediterranean Europe, it bears terminal racemes of tiny pink flowers set amid tiny, blue-green, sessile leaves. Being wind and salt resistant, it does particularly well in exposed, coastal positions. It will also thrive in hot interior situations, particularly where soils are heavy with salts. The shrub needs full sun and good drainage, but adapts to any watering regime. Prune back about halfway immediately after flowering to maintain dense growth and maximum flowering. Propagate from semi-hardwood cuttings in late summer or from hardwood cuttings in late fall.
ZONES 5–10

### *TAXUS*

YEW

These conifers are among the most useful of evergreen shrubs for colder regions. Their needle-like leaves are deep green, flat and softly pointed; branching is usually graceful and dense. They all adapt to shearing and are often used for hedges and topiaries. Their seeds are borne in red, fleshy fruits. They are perfectly happy in a lightly shaded situation, but will take full sun if protected from drying winds in cold winters. Give them a rich soil and regular watering.

#### *T. baccata* 'Repandens'

SPREADING ENGLISH YEW

The English yew is a large shrub becoming tree like with age; this selection is low and spreading, making an outstanding ground cover for a shaded situation. The gracefully arching branches are lined with two ranks of large, deep green, needle-like leaves. It will eventually reach 24–36 in (about 60–90 cm) in height and several feet wide. It needs little pruning.
ZONES 6–10

#### *T. cuspidata*

JAPANESE YEW

Though this species is a large, upright shrub or small tree, many selections have been made that are compact and very useful for the average garden. 'Columnaris' is narrow and is excellent for hedges. 'Nana' is low and mounded and is good for smaller hedges. 'Greenwave' is low with arching branches. All are easily sheared to control size.
ZONES 4–9

#### *T.* × *media*

These hybrids between the English and Japanese yews offer a range of sizes and shapes for the garden. 'Hatfield' is broad and upright, while 'Hicksii' is narrow and upright; both are good for hedging. 'Brownii' and 'Everlow' are low and rounded, eventually reaching 8 ft (about 2.4 m) tall and wide; it is easily kept smaller by pruning.
ZONES 5–9

### *TECOMA*

*stans*

syn. *Bignonia stans, Stenolobium stans*

YELLOW BELLS

Native to Central America, this erect, branching, evergreen shrub grows to a height of 15 ft (about 4.5 m) with a spread under 10 ft (about 3 m); in completely frost-free areas it will become a tree of 20 ft (about 6 m) or more. It bears gorgeous, golden yellow, tubular flowers right through the warmer months set among pinnately divided leaves with narrow leaflets. It thrives in a rich, well-drained soil in full sun; once established it needs relatively little water. Potted plants require an occasional watering when in full growth. Prune *T. stans* annually after blooming to maintain its habit. Propagate from soft-tip or semi-hardwood cuttings in summer.
ZONES 8–11

### *TECOMARIA*

*capensis*

syn. *Tecoma capensis*

CAPE HONEYSUCKLE

This evergreen, shrubby climber can be grown either as a shrub or as a climber. It bears tubular, fiery orange-red flowers from fall through winter, set among saw-toothed, dark green leaflets. Resistant to drought and salt it does well in coastal areas, growing to a height and spread of 6–9 ft (about 1.8–2.7 m). It does best in fertile, well-drained soil and likes an open, sunny position. It will climb if not pruned hard annually. Crowded stems should be thinned out in spring. Propagate from semi-ripe cuttings in summer or from seed in spring.
ZONES 9–11

### *TELOPEA*

*speciosissima*

WARATAH

This tree-like shrub is grown for its striking flowerhead, which consists of multiple, curved florets surrounded by common bracts. An upright, bushy evergreen, it grows to a height and spread of 9 ft (about 2.7 m); it needs a damp, sandy, neutral to acid loam and dappled shade. It is popular in floral arrangements.
ZONES 9–11

### *TERNSTROEMIA*

*gymnanthera*

This easily grown evergreen shrub is surprisingly uncommon. Its oval, leathery leaves are deep green but may take on purplish tints in winter. The softly fragrant summer flowers are small and yellow, hidden within the foliage; they are followed by red-orange berries in fall. Slow growing, this is an excellent shrub to mix with camellias and rhododendrons since it also prefers an acidic, woodsy soil and regular watering. The ultimate height and spread are around 6 ft (about 1.8 m).
ZONES 7–10

*Tecomaria capensis*

*Taxus cuspidata*

*Tamarix parviflora*

*Taxus* × *media* 'Everlow'

*Taxus baccata* 'Repandens'

*Ternstreomia gymnanthera*

*Telopea speciosissima*

*Tecoma stans*

Thevetia peruviana

Tuecrium fruticans

Tetrapanax papyriferus

Thuja occidentalis 'Rheingold'

## *TETRAPANAX*

### *papyriferus*

**syn. *Aralia papyrifera, Fatsia papyrifera***

RICE PAPER PLANT

This upright, evergreen, branching shrub is grown mainly for its large, felted, deeply lobed leaves, but the creamy white flowers it bears in late summer and fall and the small black berries that follow are added attractions. *T. papyriferus* is the only species in the genus. It prefers a humus-rich, moist but well-drained soil and does well in either full sun or partial shade. It tolerates salt-laden winds and so is excellent for coastal gardens. Too large for pots, it is suitable for courtyards. It grows to a height of 12 ft (about 3.5 m) with a spread of 15 ft (about 4.5 m). Propagate from suckers or from seed in early spring, and prune as and when it is needed to control the plant's size.

ZONES 9–11

## *TEUCRIUM*

### *fruticans*

BUSH GERMANDER

Native to southern Europe, this upright evergreen grows to a height and spread of around 4–8 ft (about 1.2–2.4 m). It is mostly enjoyed for the attractive, blue, tubular, double-lipped flowers it bears in summer and occasionally throughout the year, set among aromatic, oval, silvery gray leaves. It needs a well-drained soil and full sun. Trim old flowerheads to promote new growth. *T. fruticans* makes a good, low, neat hedge and does well in seaside gardens. Propagate from softwood or semi-ripe cuttings any time in summer.

ZONES 8–10

Ugni molinae

## *THEVETIA*

### *peruviana*

**syn. *T. neriifolia***

YELLOW OLEANDER

Native to tropical America this upright, spreading evergreen bears fragrant, yellow, funnel-shaped flowers from summer though fall, set among spidery, short-stemmed, lance-shaped leaves. It does best in well-watered, well-drained, sandy soil in full sun. Potted plants should be watered moderately in full growth, less at other times. Tip young stems in winter to promote branching. Propagate from semi-ripe cuttings in summer, or from seed in spring. *T. peruviana* is sometimes called the "be-still bush" because of the distinctive movement of its leaves in a breeze. The plant is intensely poisonous and should not be planted where it might pose a danger to children.

ZONES 10–11

## *THUJA*

### *occidentalis*

AMERICAN ARBORVITAE, EASTERN WHITE CEDAR

A tall conifer native to northeastern North America, this is most commonly seen in gardens in one of its compact forms. Flat sprays of scaly leaves have a pleasing fragrance when crushed. Woody cones are small with only 10 to 12 scales each. Arborvitae is best adapted to the cooler, more moist regions of the country—not the South or the arid West. Adapted to most soils except dry, sandy ones, it prefers a sunny situation and regular watering. The cultivars seldom need shearing but may need protection from excessive snow in winter; tie stems together to keep them from splitting apart. Spider mites are a problem in dry weather. 'Techny' keeps its good green color through the winter; it has a broad, pyramid shape to around 10–15 ft (about 3–4.5 m) tall. 'Rheingold' stays under 5 ft (about 1.5 m) in height and has a pyramidal shape and golden foliage with tints of copper and bronze. 'Woodwardii' has a rounded form and a height and spread of around 8 ft (about 2.4 m) but may lose its color in winter.

ZONES 3–9

Tibouchina urvilleana

## *TIBOUCHINA*

### *urvilleana*

**syn. *T. semidecandra***

PRINCESS FLOWER, PLEROMA

This upright, branching native of South America is grown for the delightful clusters of purple flowers it bears from summer to early winter set among prominently veined, hairy, oval leaves. It needs a rich, well-drained, acid soil and full sun. In very hot areas it will do reasonably well in dappled shade. To promote bushiness, pinch out growing tips regularly. Keep the soil moist during spring and summer. *T. urvilleana* grows to a height of 10–18 ft (about 3–5.5 m) with a spread of 6–10 ft (about 1.8–3 m). Propagate from greenwood or semi-ripe cuttings in late spring or summer. There are several cultivars available with flowers in varying shades of purple or strong pink.

ZONES 10–11

## *UGNI*

### *molinae*

**syn. *Myrtus ugni***

CHILEAN GUAVA

This handsome, upright, densely branched shrub is native to Chile. In spring it bears cup-shaped, pale pink flowers set among small, glossy, deep green leaves. The fragrant, dark red fruits are edible. It grows slowly to a height and spread of 6 ft (about 1.8 m). Give it full sun except in the hottest areas, a fertile soil and moderate water. Propagate from seed or from semi-ripe cuttings in late summer.

ZONES 9–10

## *VACCINIUM*

### *macrocarpon*

**syn. *Oxycoccus macrocarpon***

AMERICAN CRANBERRRY

Native to eastern North America, this evergreen is commercially grown in that country and several cultivars are known. It bears pink, nodding flowers in summer followed by relatively large red fruit. Prostrate in habit, it forms mats of interlacing wiry stems with alternate leaves, spreading to around 3 ft (about 90 cm) when fully mature. Grow in acid, peaty, permanently moist soil in full sun, and propagate by layers in spring or from seed when ripe. Plant in fall to spring.

ZONES 4–10

## *VIBURNUM*

ARROWWOOD

These deciduous or evergreen shrubs and trees are grown for their fragrant flowers, colorful fruits and beautiful fall foliage. The hundred-odd species and many more varieties grow best in sun or semi-shade in a rich, moist, well-drained soil. Remove spent flowerheads on those that do not produce fruit, and prune after flowering to improve shape (some fruit may be lost); old plants can be rejuvenated by pruning to the ground in late winter. Propagate from cuttings in summer or from seed in fall. Mildew and spider mite may cause problems.

### *V. acerifolium*

MAPLE-LEAF VIBURNUM

One of the lesser known viburnums but one of the most appealing for a woodland garden. Slender stems rise 4–6 ft (about 1.2–1.8 m) tall from a clump that spreads underground. Maple-shaped leaves are a soft green through the growing season, turning subtle shades of pink to purple in the fall. Yellowish flowers appear in small clusters in early summer, followed by black fruits in fall. Very tolerant of shade, forming natural colonies in the eastern American forests where it is native.

ZONES 3–8

### *V.* × *bodnantense*

A deciduous hybrid, this viburnum is one of the best frost-resistant, winter-flowering shrubs. It bears clusters of fragrant, white-flushed rose-pink flowers from late fall right through to winter. It has an upright, rather stiff habit and reaches a height and spread of 9–12 ft (about 2.7–3.5 m). The leaves, which are toothed and dull green, are bronze tinged when young. There are several forms grown, 'Dawn' being the most commonly cultivated.

ZONES 3–9

### *V.* × *burkwoodii*

BURKWOOD VIBURNUM

This bushy, open, semi-evergreen shrub bears wide, globular clusters of scented flowers that open pink but fade to white. Its oval, dark green leaves turn red in fall. It grows to a height of 8–10 ft (about 2.4–3 m) and a spread of 6–8 ft (about 1.8–2.4 m).

ZONES 3–9

### *V.* × *carlecephalum*

A deciduous, spring-flowering hybrid with large, rounded heads of fragrant, creamy white flowers that are pink when in bud. The dark green foliage often turns red in fall. It has a rounded, bushy habit and grows to a height and spread of around 9 ft (about 2.7 m).

ZONES 3–9

### *V. carlesii*

KOREAN SPICE VIBURNUM

This upright, deciduous shrub grows to a height and spread of 4–8 ft (about 1.2–2.4 m). In spring it bears intensely fragrant, snow-white flowers from pink buds, followed by round, black berries. Its dull green, woolly, oval leaves turn red in fall. 'Cayuga' has smaller leaves and similar flowers.

ZONES 4–9

### *V. davidii*

DAVID VIBURNUM

This low, mounding shrub has superb dark green, deeply veined, elliptical leaves. The creamy white flowers are unscented but are followed by metallic blue berries, more plentifully produced where there are several plants. An excellent shrub for the front or middle of a shaded border, its height is under 3 ft (about 90 cm) and it spreads somewhat wider. It needs a rich soil and water; it does best in a lightly shaded position.

ZONES 7–10

### *V. dentatum*

ARROWWOOD

This eastern North American native is one of the most serviceable and adaptable species. Its deciduous, deeply toothed leaves give good color in the fall. The flowers are creamy white in flat-topped clusters and are followed by blue-black fruits in fall. Shade tolerant, coast tolerant and tolerant of heavy alkaline soils. Height and spread reach 6–15 ft (about 1.8–4.5 m) depending upon conditions.

ZONES 3–8

### *V. farreri*

**syn. *V. fragrans***

FRAGRANT VIBURNUM

A deciduous shrub from western China, bearing the name of the great plant explorer who discovered it. It is an 8–12 ft (about 2.4–3.5 m) tall deciduous shrub whose leaves turn red in the fall. Its main feature is the fragrance of its clustered pale pink flowers produced from late fall through early spring.

ZONES 6–9

*Viburnum* × *burkwoodii*

*Viburnum* × *carlecephalum*

*Viburnum farreri*

*Viburnum carlesii*

*Viburnum* × *bodnantense*

*Viburnum davidii*

*Viburnum dentatum*

*Viburnum tinus*

*Viburnum plicatum* f. *tomentosum* 'Mariesii'

*Viburnum lantana*

*Viburnum opulus* 'Nanum'

### *V. lantana*

WAYFARING TREE

One of the larger viburnums (10–15 ft/3–3.5 m tall), with 5 in (about 12 cm) long ovate leaves, this shrub is useful for background, screening and hedging. Flowers are creamy white in flat-topped clusters and are followed by fruits that turn from yellow to red to black as they mature.
ZONES 4–8

### *V. opulus* 'Nanum'

DWARF EUROPEAN CRANBERRY BUSH

This form is very different from the snowball bush in nearly all respects. Its leaves are smaller, it seldom flowers or fruits and its size is under 24 in (about 60 cm) tall and around 24–36 in (about 60–90 cm) wide.
ZONES 3–9

### *V. opulus* 'Roseum'

**syn. *V. o.* 'Sterile'**

EUROPEAN SNOWBALL

This vigorous, bushy, deciduous shrub, native to Europe, Asia and northern Africa, grows to a height and spread of 12 ft (about 3.5 m). In spring and early summer it bears spherical heads ("snowballs") of white flowers aging to pink.
ZONES 3–9

### *V. plicatum* f. *tomentosum* 'Mariesii'

MARIES DOUBLEFIRE VIBURNUM

This is perhaps the most popular of all viburnums, with its distinct horizontal branches providing interest even in winter. In spring a double row of pure white, flat-topped clusters of sterile and fertile flowers, somewhat like the lacecap hydrangeas, floats just above the branches. Bright red fruits color by mid-summer and last for weeks until the birds eat them. The foliage turns purplish red in the fall. It grows to a height of 10 ft (about 3 m) or more.
ZONES 6–10

### *V. prunifolia*

BLACKHAW VIBURNUM

A multi-stemmed shrub or small, round-headed tree, this viburnum will grow 12–15 ft (about 3.5–4.5 m) tall and wide with a fairly stiff, branching character. The deciduous leaves are smooth and deep green, turning purplish in fall. Creamy flowers develop into edible fruits that are pink ripening to blue-black. Tolerant of both sun and shade and making a good screen, hedge or background plant.
ZONES 3–9

### *V. tinus*

LAURUSTINUS

This bushy, evergreen shrub bears clusters of honeysuckle-fragrant, pinkish white flowers in winter set amid oval, dark green, glossy leaves. It grows to a height and spread of 9 ft (about 2.7 m). Recommended as a hedge plant. The leaves tend to mildew in coastal areas, though 'Lucidum' and 'Robustum' seem resistant to the problem.
ZONES 7–10

### *V. trilobum*

HIGHBUSH CRANBERRY, AMERICAN CRANBERRY BUSH

One of America's most useful native shrubs, this species is showy in

*Viburnum trilobum*

*Viburnum prunifolia*

*Viburnum opulus* 'Roseum'

flower, fruit and fall foliage. A tall shrub (8–12 ft/2.4–3.5 m tall and wide), it is useful as a hedge or screening plant. White flowers appear in spring in flat-topped clusters. Bright red fruits in fall last through winter.
ZONES 3–7

## VITEX
*agnus-castus*

CHASTE TREE, PEPPERBUSH

Native to Europe and Asia, *V. agnus-castus* grows to a height and spread of 10–15 ft (about 3–3.5 m). This open, deciduous, spreading shrub bears dense, upright spikes of small, dark blue or white flowers in late summer. The gray-green, compound leaves are aromatic. It prefers full sun and well-drained soil.
ZONES 7–9

## WEIGELA

WEIGELA

These deciduous, fountain-shaped shrubs bear brilliant though short-lived masses of pink, white or red trumpet flowers in the warmer months. However, their leaves fall early in fall without coloring, leaving the branches bare for most of the winter. They do best in a sunny position in a rich, well-drained soil. Water well during the growing season. Propagate from softwood cuttings in summer.

### *W. florida*

A native of China and Korea, this deciduous, arching shrub bears delightful, deep rose-pink, trumpet-shaped flowers in late spring and early summer. The leaves are serrated, mid-green, small and oval. It grows to a height and spread of 8–10 ft (about 2.4–3 m).
ZONES 5–10

### *W. florida* 'Eva Ratke'

This cultivar bears deep rose-pink flowers from purplish red buds from late spring to early summer. It grows 4½ ft (about 1.3 m) tall and wide with a dense, erect habit.
ZONES 5–10

### *W. florida* 'Variegata'

This cultivar bears an abundance of funnel-shaped, deep rose-pink flowers set among green leaves.
ZONES 5–10

## WESTRINGIA
*fruticosa*

syn. *W. rosmariniformis*

COAST ROSEMARY

This evergreen Australian shrub is grown for the delicate, white to pale mauve flowers it bears in spring, set among light, grayish green, rosemary-like leaves arranged in whorls of four. It is a fast-growing, rounded shrub of 3–6 ft (about 90–180 cm) in height and spread, although it tends to be short lived. It does best in a sunny situation; it prefers a fertile, well-drained soil and needs only minimal water once established. Propagate from seed in spring or from semi-ripe cuttings in late summer.
ZONES 9–10

*Vitex agnus-castus*

*Westringia fruticosa*

*Weigela florida* 'Eva Ratke'

*Weigela florida*

*Weigela florida* 'Variegata'

CHAPTER 4

# Trees

*The backbone of a garden, trees are fundamental to the landscape. Whatever their size, these plants form the basis of the type of garden being aimed for, be it a lush rainforest atmosphere, a cold country woodland or a single specimen highlight for a small courtyard.*

A tree is a plant, either broad leafed or coniferous, with a single, woody stem reaching to a height of at least 12 ft (about 3.5 m) when mature. Palms and tree ferns, although they do not have the same type of woody stem, are generally included for horticultural purposes because their growth habit and landscape uses are similar to that of trees.

Trees can form windbreaks in larger gardens, are invaluable as noise inhibitors, provide privacy from overlooking houses or unit buildings and soften the skyline in the urban environment.

They are growing structures in gardens, chosen for a particular purpose, though many will provide bonus points to add to their initial attractiveness as they mature. Trees planted to provide shade may well provide a horizontal branch to support a swing, or branches to form a climbing frame for adventurous children. Birds will soon inhabit suitable trees for nesting or food gathering among blossom and fruits while keeping a sharp eye on the insect population in the garden below.

## Choosing the Right Tree

Never buy a tree on impulse. It is a permanent part of the garden structure, afterall trees can take around 20 years to arrive at any semblance of maturity, so it is necessary to get the selection right first time. Take time before you go to the nursery, read as much as you can about a tree's growing habits such as its estimated mature height and spread, as well as its seasonal displays. What at first appears to be a bewildering choice will soon be whittled down to a couple of possible contenders for a particular spot in the garden.

Climate and soil requirements also need to be considered. It is preferable to grow a tree climatically suited to your area. If you're new to a neighbourhood, walk through the parks and look over garden fences to see which trees are growing well.

## Evergreen or Deciduous?

Trees are most often sought after for their shade value. Consider then the choice of evergreen or deciduous. Perhaps an evergreen is what's needed in a screening situation or in the tropics where year-round sun protection over a patio is needed. A deciduous tree will provide summer shade and winter sun. There is an ever-changing display each season, ranging from the fine tracery of bare branches in winter to soft green new spring growth, a welcoming dense cover in summer then a wonderful fall display, often with flowers and colorful fruit as well.

The colorful contribution trees make to the landscape often comes because of their foliage color. Consider the soft blue-gray foliage of some of the conifers and eucalypt species or *Pyrus salicifolia* which meld so well with the white and

*Shape and height are two important considerations when selecting trees.*

pastel blues and pinks favored by cottage gardeners. Then there's the variegated foliaged trees which provide a welcome accent in an otherwise green landscape, but it's the intensity of yellow/orange/red tones that really capture a gardener's heart.

Cold country gardeners have any number of trees in all sizes and shapes from which to make a rich display of color before winter sets in. Temperate gardeners are not so fortunate. However, beautiful displays can be assured with *Nyssa sylvatica*, *Ginkgo biloba* or in larger gardens the majestic *Liquidambar styraciflua*.

## Getting the Proportions Right

For the home gardener, perhaps the most important consideration in choosing a particular tree is its mature height and spread. Proportion is the catchword here for both aesthetic and practical reasons. A large, dense tree planted too close to a house may shade it too well, making rooms very dark and cutting off any perspective view through the windows. It may also rob the surrounding garden of light and root room. In such a situation it may be better to choose a smaller, more openly branched tree which both frames the view and allows ample light into a room, for example *Cassia leptophylla*, *Betula pendula*, *Pistacia chinensis* or *Zelkova serrata*.

*Deciduous trees provide a delightful display of fall color.*

## Planting

It takes a few years for a tree to become self-sufficient even though it may be quite large when planted out. New roots need time to establish to forage for nutrients and to anchor the plant. Consequently, all trees, but in particular those planted as specimen trees, need to be given great care in their early years. Before planting, check the tree will not be hindered above by overhead wires or that underground pipes will not be invaded by vigorous root systems.

Good drainage is essential as few plants will thrive with wet feet. Wide planting holes, ample surrounding soil cultivation and even raising the bed are some ways of overcoming a drainage problem, but if the soil is very heavy the addition of gypsum or coarse sand may be required as well. As soil in the container and the surrounding garden soil are often quite different in texture, it's important to combine these two to allow new roots to venture easily into their new surrounding. Do this by digging a shallow (just a little deeper than the container) yet wide hole, at least twice the diameter of the root ball, and fill the base with a friable mixture composed of about half the existing soil and a rich humus mix. Carefully remove the plant from the container, taking special care not to damage the main trunk, and place the root ball in position, together with up to three stakes. At this point check that the roots are not tangled or wound round in circles. If they are they need to be gently teased out and straightened, otherwise they will continue in this circular fashion eventually causing the plant to wither. Continue to fill the hole with the soil mix firming it in and around the trunk by hand, but ensuring that the tree is planted only as deep as it was in the container. Once it is firmly in position water well to get rid of any remaining air pockets. The remaining soil mix can be used to form a raised circle around the plant. Then, to conserve moisture, a layer of organic mulch can be added. This mulch, weeds and low-growing ground covers should be kept well away from the trunk to discourage collar or other root rot fungus.

If planting in a lawn, cut away a circle of turf at least 3 ft (about 90 cm) in diameter to ensure the tender roots of the newly planted tree will not have to compete with those of voracious lawn grasses. Keep the surface of this area well mulched to retain as much moisture as possible and to deter weeds competing for the available nutrients.

Trees need to be staked to ensure the leader, the main trunk, is not damaged while still young and tender. Place the stakes in position at the time of planting, then attach the plant to these with tree ties or a length of old rag tied in a figure of eight to ensure the trunk remains steady when buffeted by strong winds. Don't use wire as it can cut into the trunk.

Deciduous trees are usually planted in the dormant state; evergreens, in temperate areas, are best planted out in fall while the soil is still warm. In colder areas, evergreens with new, tender growth will avoid frost damage if planted out in late spring.

## Pruning

Trees rarely need pruning in maturity except after storm damage or for the removal of diseased branches, however young trees often benefit from being given a helping hand to balance their shape or to develop a higher branching system in situations where they overhang a path. If noticed early enough, unwanted new shoots can be rubbed off very easily by hand, a technique which doesn't leave unsightly scars on the often beautiful trunks of these majestic garden plants.

*Abies concolor*

*Abies procera* 'Glauca'

*Acacia dealbata*

*Abies cephalonica*

*Acacia baileyana*

*Acer buergerianum*

## ABIES

FIR

These 50 diverse species of conical conifers are cold-climate evergreens. Prized for their aromatic wood and sap, their usefulness to the timber and pharmaceutical industries has threatened many species with extinction. Their name comes from the Latin *abeo* "I rise": some attain majestic heights of 200 ft (about 61 m) or more, growing 3 ft (about 90 cm) a year. In fall the horizontal branches display upright, seed-bearing cones, in contrast to the pendent cones of similar conifers like the spruces. The soft, spindle-shaped leaves are flat and round edged, often bearing two parallel silver lines on the underside. Most species are too large for the average garden, being better suited to a country property. They prefer a moderately moist soil, full sun and a cool summer climate. Tip prune only minimally to enhance the shape. Propagate from seed from ripened cones. Many species are used as Christmas trees.

### *A. cephalonica*

GRECIAN FIR

This upright conifer grows to 95 ft (about 29 m) high, and has a conical crown. Its cylindrical cones are 4–6 in (about 10–15 cm) long and brown when mature. The glossy, dark green leaves have white-green undersides.

ZONES 5–9

### *A. concolor*

WHITE FIR, COLORADO FIR

This native of North America's western montains is one of the most readily available in nurseries, since it is more adaptable to hotter, drier gardens than other native firs. Faster growing than most firs, it eventually reaches 100 ft (about 30 m) or more in height and 30–40 ft (about 9–12 m) wide. Needles are bluish green and around 2 in (about 5 cm) long, curving upward.

ZONES 4–8

### *A. procera*

syn. ***A. nobilis***

NOBLE FIR

The attractive bluish green foliage and smooth, silvery bark identify this upright conifer. It grows to 95 ft (about 29 m) high. Its cylindrical cones are 6-8 in (about 15–20 cm) long and purplish brown. The leaves are particularly glaucous in the cultivar 'Glauca'. It needs plenty of moisture and is best adapted near its natural range in the Cascade Mountains of western Washington, Oregon and northern California. If the tree dries out cracks will appear in the wood and bark.

ZONES 5–9

## ACACIA

WATTLE, ACACIA

This extremely diverse genus contains over 1000 short-lived, evergreen, semi-evergreen and deciduous species, mostly native to Australia and Africa. Growing 15–65 ft (about 4.5–20 m) high, they are valued for their beautiful, dense, golden blossoms and rapid growth. Most species have flattened leaf stems instead of conventional leaves; some have very finely divided leaves with tiny leaflets. The fruit is a long, bean-like pod. Heat-treated seeds may be used for propagation, mimicking the way seeds are released in bushfires. Untreated seeds have been known to last 50 years. Renowned for their ability to survive drought, acacias grow best in warm climates with well-drained soil and full sun. The fast growth of many acacias results in short-lived trees with weak and brittle wood, easily damaged in a wind storm. Thin regularly to keep them open and prune to slow their growth, usually after flowering to reduce seed production and limit unwanted seedlings. British settlers in Australia used acacias to build wattle-and-daub huts; hence the common name.

### *A. baileyana*

BAILEY ACACIA

Native to Australia, this elegant evergreen grows to 18 ft (about 5.5 m). In late winter to early spring soft, golden blossoms appear on drooping branches. The foliage is silver-blue pinnate leaves, rather than phyllodes, around 2 in (about 5 cm) long; 'Purpurea' has attractive purple new foliage in spring.

ZONES 9–10

### *A. dealbata*

syn. ***A. decurrens dealbata***

SILVER WATTLE

This evergreen produces beautiful lemon-colored flower clusters. Though tending to produce lots of weedy seedlings, it is popular and is sometimes known as mimosa. It will reach 30–50 ft (about 9–15 m) in height. Silvery-green and feathery, the compound leaves are 5 in (about 12 cm) long, contrasting with the soft pink seed pods, which are 2–4 in (about 5–10 cm) long.

ZONES 9–10

*Acer ginnala*

## ACER

MAPLE

Originating in the cool-temperate zones of the northern hemisphere, these deciduous trees and shrubs are prized for their decorative bark and magnificent foliage. Species vary considerably in size and shape, from shrubby mountain forms 15 ft (about 4.5 m) tall to 100 ft (about 30 m) tall trees dominating moist forests of eastern North America. The hand-shaped leaves of some species color dramatically in the fall, especially on those from Asia and North America. Some species produce little flowers followed by winged fruit, called samaras or keys, that "fly" long distances on the wind. Most maples prefer a rich, well-drained but moist soil and average water; they will not thrive in hot desert or tropical climates. Provide full sun or partial shade; shelter from the wind to avoid leaf burn. A neutral to acid soil encourages optimum leaf colors. Most maples require little pruning; do so after midsummer to avoid excessive "bleeding" or loss of sap. Propagate from seed in fall or by bud grafting in summer. *Acer,* meaning "sharp", has been used since the days of the Romans; the name is thought to derive from the use of the wood for spears.

### *A. buergerianum*

TRIDENT MAPLE

This medium-sized maple with three-lobed (trident) leaves has proven to be among the more drought tolerant of the species, surviving well in most areas of California with only moderate water. It has attractive bark that flakes in small patches and a rounded habit, 25–30 ft (about 7.5–9 m) high and nearly as wide. Fall color varies from gold to deep red. Plant in full or part sun.

ZONES 4–10

### *A. ginnala*

**syn. *A. tataricum* subsp. *ginnala***

AMUR MAPLE

This is a tough, shrubby maple useful for its ability to survive the climate of the northern plains and the mountains of North America. Native to northeastern Asia, it has three-lobed leaves that color nicely in the fall. It is usually no more than 20 ft (about 6 m) tall and wide, with many stems. It is tolerant of wind, cold, poor soils, heat and drought. *A. ginnala* can be used as a specimen in a lawn, or as an undemanding but colorful screen, hedge or massed planting.

ZONES 3–8

### *A. griseum*

PAPERBARK MAPLE

Among the choicest of the smaller maples this species is popular for its cinnamon and brown bark, which peels like a birch. Red fruits are fairly showy. The leaves are made of three distinct leaflets; the fall color is red. Though difficult to propagate and thus not common, this is an excellent tree for use as a featured specimen.

ZONES 5–10

### *A. japonicum*

FULL-MOON MAPLE

This bushy tree can reach 25 ft (about 7.5 m) in height with a similar spread. Originally from Japan, its mid-green leaves have 7 to 11 lobes that turn red at the tips in fall. It bears bright red flower clusters along with its spring leaves. This species needs to be protected from strong winds. *A. japonicum* 'Aconitifolium' attains much the same proportions but has deeply divided leaves that turn brilliant crimson to violet in fall.

ZONES 5–10

### *A. macrophyllum*

BIGLEAF MAPLE

This is the largest of the maples native to the West Coast, reaching 70–90 ft (about 21–27 m) in favored sites along streams. In an open situation it will be round headed, 50–60 ft (about 15–18 m) tall and nearly as wide. The leaves are often huge, epecially in woodlands of the Northwest where they reach 12 in (about 30 cm) or more across. Though adaptable to drier conditions, this species prefers a moist soil and will tolerate some shade.

ZONES 6–10

### *A. palmatum*

JAPANESE MAPLE

There are many cultivars of this popular species, both trees and shrubs, and all have striking foliage. A deciduous tree with a shapely head of horizontal branches, it will vary from 15 ft to 25 ft (about 4.5–7.5 m) in height with a similar spread. The 5-pointed leaves are deeply lobed. They turn from pink or bronze in spring to mid-green in summer to bright red, orange or yellow in fall. Named selections are available, chosen for size of tree, size of leaf, color of leaf, degree of fall color and so on. Prune only to enhance the natural branching habit and provide protection from the wind.

ZONES 5–10

### *A. platanoides*

NORWAY MAPLE

This European native is a large tree with bold leaves that turn yellow in late fall. Commonly planted throughout eastern North America, especially in one of its cultivars, it has actually become a noxious weed in some areas. Dense shade and shallow roots prevent gardening beneath. Maroon-leafed cultivars, such as 'Crimson King', are distinctive in the landscape. It grows anywhere with little attention.

ZONES 4–8

### *A. pseudoplatanus*

SYCAMORE

This fast and easily grown shade tree from Europe and west Asia will reach its greatest height of 60 ft (about 18 m) in cool, hilly country. Long clusters of yellowish flowers are conspicuous in spring, while its leaves are divided into 5 lobes with blunt teeth and are broader than they are long.

ZONES 4–8

### *A. rubrum*

RED MAPLE

This showy species has a broad natural range from northern England to northern Florida and west to the Mississippi. It is popular for its small leaves, brilliant fall color and for its red flowers and red fruits. In the swamps where it is native it will reach over 100 ft (about 30 m) tall; in gardens, most selections available stay under 75 ft (about 23 m). It is best to grow locally selected forms if possible for greater adaptability to your site. It prefers plenty of water although it tolerates average conditions. The shallow roots make underplanting rather difficult.

ZONES 3–10

*Acer platanoides*

*Acer griseum*

*Acer macrophyllum*

*Acer rubrum*

*Acer palmatum*

*Acer pseudoplatanus*

*Acer japonicum*

Acer saccharum

Aesculus × carnea

Aesculus californica

Albizia julibrissin

Aesculus hippocastanum

Aesculus flava

Ailanthus altissima

### *A. saccharum*

SUGAR MAPLE

One of North America's best-loved trees, both for the beauty of its fall color on the hills of the Northeast and for the flavor of the syrup made from its sap. An upright oval in shape and reaching over 100 ft (about 30 m) tall. The 5-lobed leaves appear on the Canadian flag. Unfortunately now suffering from acid rain, road salt, soil compaction and periodic drought.

ZONES 3–8

## *AESCULUS*

BUCKEYE, HORSE CHESTNUT

These deciduous trees are distinctive for their large, palmately compound leaves and the floral panicles that top each stem in late spring. Native throughout the northern hemisphere, the most commonly grown are those from Europe and North America. The larger species are suitable for lawns, parks and large gardens. Plant in full sun in a rich, well-drained soil; water regularly to avoid leaf scorch. Propagate from the large seeds, which resemble chestnuts but are actually poisonous.

### *A. californica*

CALIFORNIA BUCKEYE

The California buckeye is a broad, round-headed tree usually under 30 ft (about 9 m) tall and as wide, found throughout the coastal mountains of California. It leafs out in late winter, producing its creamy white flowers in late spring then often dropping its leaves due to summer drought by August. From fall through mid-winter its silvery bark and attractive branching create a beautiful sculptural effect in the garden. Hummingbirds love the nectar of its flowers. Leaves last into fall if given summer water.

ZONES 9–10

### *A.* × *carnea*

RED HORSE CHESTNUT

This deciduous hybrid between a shrubby American species and the much larger European horse chestnut is valued for its beautiful foliage and well-rounded shape. It grows slowly to 30–65 ft (about 9–20 m). The dark green, divided leaves are less prone to leaf spot than its European parent. Large, upright clusters of rich pink blossoms appear in late spring to early summer, followed by the fruit. This species prefers a cold winter to a cool-temperate climate. Suitable for parks or large gardens, it needs a rich, moist, well-drained soil and full sun or partial shade. Leaves burn easily. Propagate from seed in fall; by grafting in late winter. Pruning is generally unnecessary. 'Briottii' has larger, redder flowers.

ZONES 5–9

### *A. flava*

**syn. *A. octandra***

YELLOW BUCKEYE

A native of eastern North America, this slow-growing, deciduous tree develops a large, oval head to a height of 75 ft (about 23 m). Dark green, palmately compound leaves with 5 leaflets turn a rich pumpkin orange in the fall. Panicles of yellow flowers are produced abundantly in early spring and are followed by smooth, pear-shaped capsules containing two dark brown seeds. Deep, moist, well-drained loams are best. It is a handsome species well suited to parks, golf courses and municipal landscapes.

ZONES 3–8

### *A. hippocastanum*

COMMON OR EUROPEAN HORSECHESTNUT

Common to North American and European parks, this deciduous tree is valued for its spectacular, late spring floral display. Reaching heights of 50–75 ft (about 15–23 m) with a spread of 40 ft (about 12 m) or more, it makes a striking specimen tree for very large properties. The dark green, palmately compound leaves are comprised of 7 leaflets and can reach 12 in (about 30 cm) across at maturity. Numerous creamy white flowers are borne on upright panicles up to 12 in (about 30 cm) long in late spring. The spiny fruit capsules open to reveal smooth, chocolate brown seeds within, providing food for squirrels and ammunition for children playing "conkers". The best growth occurs in moisture-rich, well-drained soils. Leaf blotch and powdery mildew disfigure the foliage, limiting the tree's use. Easily propagated from ripe seed.

ZONES 3–7

## *AGONIS*

### *flexuosa*

PEPPERMINT TREE, AUSTRALIAN WILLOW MYRTLE

Native to Western Australia, this tree is grown for its gracefully weeping branches, very reminiscent of a weeping willow. Normally growing to a height of 35 ft (about 10 m), it will sometimes remain shrub like in extremely windy coastal situations or when frozen back periodically by temperatures below 27°F (about -3°C). It has rough, dark gray bark and shiny, evergreen, narrow leaves 2–6 in (about 5–15 cm) long. Tiny, white, 5-petaled flowers appear in profusion in late spring and early summer. Fibrous, globular fruit ripen from green to red and carry small black seeds from which the plant self-propagates. The species prefers sandy, well-drained soils and tolerates dry conditions once established. The crushed leaves give out a peppermint smell, which explains the common name.

ZONES 9–10

## *AILANTHUS*

### *altissima*

**syn. *A. glandulosa***

TREE OF HEAVEN

Native to China, this broad, deciduous shade tree reaches 18–60 ft (about 5.5–18 m). It is valued for its attractive, unusual foliage: deep green, fern-like leaves, 24 in (about 60 cm) long, with 15 to 30 oval leaflets. Inconspicuous groups of tiny green flowers, with an unfortunate odor, bloom in mid-summer; these are followed by reddish orange, winged seed pods. Able to withstand the worst city smog, this tree graces many world capitals. It does best in subtropical areas but will survive in most climates, preferring full sun or partial shade and deep, rich soil. Prune severely in spring to create a shrub. Propagate from seed in fall, and suckers or root cuttings from the female tree in winter. Because of its tendency to sucker and seed itself around it is usually considered a weed tree, yet in some inner-city regions it may be the only garden tree around.

ZONES 4–11

### *ALBIZIA julibrissin*

SILK TREE, MIMOSA

Though the genus comprises over 100 species of deciduous trees and shrubs, this is the only one commonly cultivated in the milder parts of North America. Found from Iran to Japan, this tree has a short but broad, flat-topped form and usually grows to no more than 30 ft (about 9 m) tall. It has large, doubly pinnate leaves with very tiny leaflets; they fold up at night. An abundance of translucent pink, downy blossoms appear in early summer, often covering the crown of the tree. They prefer full sun with some protection from the wind. Plant in a good, light garden soil and propagate from seed in late fall to early spring. Beware of the shallow roots and the litter from flowers and seed pods. Popular at the northerly edge of its range of adaptability for its tropical-looking foliage.

ZONES 7–11

### *ALNUS*

ALDER

These birch relatives are slender, upright, usually deciduous trees. Reaching heights of 80–95 ft (about 24–29 m), they have attractive, slightly arching branches. Highly valued for their ability to survive in extremely wet locations due to their strong root system, they are often found by rivers, in moist gullies or swamps. Pendulous catkins of male flowers appear in early spring; female flowers mature into woody "cones". The leaves are long stemmed and shiny. The genus will survive in a range of climates, from cool to warm-temperate to subtropical. Propagate from seed in fall, bud cultivars in late spring and hardwood cuttings in early winter. The timber is extremely water resistant; once prized by shipbuilders, it was also used for the wooden piles that have supported the city of Venice for hundreds of years.

*Agonis flexuosa*

#### *A. cordata*

ITALIAN ALDER

This species is popular for its glossy leaves and its greater tolerance of dry soils. Native to southern Europe, it is an upright-growing tree reaching 40 ft (about 12 m) tall and eventually spreading to 25 ft (about 7.5 m) in width. Adaptable to the drier West Coast as well as the East Coast.

ZONES 5–9

#### *A. glutinosa*

EUROPEAN ALDER, BLACK ALDER

This conical, deciduous tree grows rapidly to 30–60 ft (about 9–18 m). Hanging yellow catkins (male) and tiny upright ones (female) are borne in early spring, followed in mid-spring by shiny, heart-shaped leaves with slim stalks. The species bears round fruit like tiny pine cones in fall. It grows best by the water.

ZONES 3–9

### *AMELANCHIER*

SERVICEBERRY, SHADBUSH, JUNEBERRY

This genus of deciduous trees are native to the temperate regions of the northern hemisphere, with a few species being native to North America. White flowers in spring are followed by small, edible fruit. The foliage turns a brilliant color in the fall.

#### *A. arborea*

DOWNY SERVICEBERRY, JUNEBERRY

This multi-stemmed tree native to the eastern United States produces magnificent fall foliage colors of bright orange to cinnamon-red.

*Amelanchier arborea*

Attractive white flowers emerge with the downy leaves in early spring and are followed by sweet, dark purple fruit in mid-summer. Reaching heights of 25 ft (about 7.5 m) in height by 15 ft (about 4.5 m) in spread, it tolerates full sun to partial shade and requires a moist, well-drained, acidic soil for best growth. Ideally suited to the natural garden, it also works well around ponds and on stream banks and as a member of the forest edge. A large array of cultivars is available from nurseries.

ZONES 4–9

#### *A. laevis*

ALLEGHANY SERVICEBERRY

Of the many species of serviceberry native throughout North America, this has the widest natural distribution and, according to some, the tastiest berries. An upright, large shrub or small tree, it will eventually reach 35 ft (about 10 m) in height. Deciduous leaves appear as the clusters of white flowers are fading. Red fruit ripen in summer, but are often eaten by birds before

*Alnus glutinosa*

they can be harvested. The fall coloring foliage can be brilliant and the silvery winter bark is appealing as well. Numerous insects and diseases can cause problems, though not severe ones. The best use is in a naturalistic garden, especially at the edge of woodlands. Often used at the back of shrub borders for the early spring flowers. A moist, rich soil is preferred, along with full sun to part shade. Prune lightly only to shape. Propagate from seed in fall or from softwood cuttings in summer.

ZONES 4–8

*Araucaria bidwillii*

*Araucaria araucana*

*Araucaria heterophylla*

*Aralia elata* 'Variegata'

*Arbutus menziesii*

*Arbutus unedo*

## ARALIA
### *elata*

JAPANESE ANGELICA TREE

This deciduous Southeast Asian native is valued for its lush, tropical foliage and curious flowers. A small tree or tall shrub, it varies in height from 9 to 30 ft (about 2.7–9 m). Its enormous, shiny, deep green leaves, 3 ft (about 90 cm) long and 25 in (about 63 cm) wide, divide twice into serrated leaflets. The spiny leaf stalks, covered in fine hair, turn red in fall. Small white or pink flowers cluster together forming large, globe-shaped heads in late summer to early fall. The species has a tendency to sucker, sending out stocky, sharp, thorny shoots, and in smaller gardens is best grown in pots. It requires full sun or partial shade and protection from the wind. Plant in a rich, well-drained soil. Propagate from seed in fall; sucker and root cutting in winter. 'Variegata' is a selection with irregular, creamy leaf margins.

ZONES 3–10

## ARAUCARIA

The 18 conifers in this genus are native to the South Pacific region, where coniferous species rarely originate. These upright, slender trees grow 95–160 ft (about 29–49 m) tall and make popular indoor plants when immature. Stiff, outstretched branches which are shed periodically radiate out from the trunk. Adaptable to all but cold climates, araucarias will grow in poor soil and like full sun. Water only when the root surface appears dry. Propagate from seed in spring.

### *A. araucana*
**syn. *A. imbricata***

MONKEY PUZZLE, CHILE PINE

Brought to Europe from South America by the Spanish in the seventeenth century and popular in Victorian England, this slow-growing conifer has a very distinctive habit and can eventually reach a height of 95 ft (about 29 m). The lower branches often fall, exposing the thick gray bark. Its branchlets are covered with overlapping, dark green, flat, ½–1 in (about 1–2.5 cm) needles tipped with spines. The male and female flowers do not grow on the same tree, and cones can take up to three years to mature. This is a good tree for a windy, coastal position.

ZONES 9–10

### *A. bidwillii*

BUNYA-BUNYA

Native to the southeastern rainforests of Queensland, Australia, this slow-growing species is valued for its shapely appearance and timber. Its upright, scaly trunk supports drooping branches which umbrella out at the apex. The stiff, shiny green leaves that whorl around the ends of the radial branches are lance shaped and stalkless. This is a large tree, easily reaching more than 100 ft (about 30 m) in height with age. Heavy cones, 12 in (about 30 cm) long and 8 in (about 20 cm) wide, appear at the top of the tree every two years. These scaly, pineapple-like fruit ripen from green to brown; each scale contains an edible red seed, a traditional Aboriginal delicacy. The tree flourishes in coastal districts and reasonably moist inland areas, growing best in fertile, well-drained soils.

ZONES 9–10

### *A. heterophylla*
**syn. *A. excelsa***

NORFOLK ISLAND PINE, STAR PINE

Native to Norfolk Island and northeastern Australia, this attractive species rapidly reaches 60–95 ft (about 18–29 m) on average; some grow as high as 190 ft (about 58 m). The whorled, slightly upright branches are spaced widely apart in tiers, giving the tree a narrow, triangular shape. Deep green, scale-like triangular leaves overlap to form cylindrical branchlets up to 12 in (about 30 cm) long. The species does best in well-watered, sandy soil; a waxy layer on its foliage protects it from salt air. It can also be successfully grown in pots; it is often used as a living Christmas tree in small apartments.

ZONES 10–11

## ARBUTUS

This genus contains some 20 species of evergreen trees and shrubs. Valued for their attractive, oblong leaves and decorative bark, they are native to the Mediterranean, western North America and Mexico. Urn-shaped flowers are produced in clusters, usually in spring; these are followed by orange-red spherical fruit, ½ in (about 1 cm) in diameter, which may take up to a year to mature. Arbutus do well in both cool and warm-temperate climates. They are attractive planted in tubs, where root constriction causes earlier blooming and fruiting. Plant in a well-drained soil in full sun to light shade. Propagate from seed in spring, cuttings in summer and layering in fall or spring. *Arbutus* is Latin for "strawberry", but the raw fruit is tasteless. It is used to make wine and jam in Italy and Spain.

### *A.* 'Marina'

Found as a chance seedling in a San Francisco garden, this presumed hybrid is the showiest of the genus. Tough and relatively quick growing, it is a large shrub that can easily be trained into a small tree of 20 ft (about 6 m) or more in height. Evergreen leaves similar to *A. unedo* serve as backdrop for soft pink flowers in large clusters in fall; these are followed by fruits like those on *A. menziesii* but are larger.

ZONES 9–10

### *A. menziesii*

MADRONE, MADRONA

This native of the west coast from Canada to Mexico is valued for its bark, flowers, foliage and fruit. Moderately fast growing, it reaches 30–50 ft (about 9–15 m) on average but may grow to 95 ft (about 29 m), making it the tallest of its genus. The knotted branches are reddish, while the smooth bark a lighter red that peels away in large sheets. Smooth-edged leaves are deep-green on top and blue-gray underneath. White flowers form in triangular clusters, followed by orange or red fruit.

ZONES 8–10

### *A. unedo*

STRAWBERRY TREE

A native of Ireland and southern Europe, this small tree grows up to 24 ft (about 7 m). It is valued for its attractive foliage and its bark, used for tanning. Pink or white flowers form in clusters of 30 to 50 in fall and early winter. A species with a shrubby habit, it is suitable for hedges and backdrops.

ZONES 8–10

## *BANKSIA*
### *integrifolia*
COAST BANKSIA

This gnarled evergreen tree is a native of eastern Australia, adaptable to both coastal and mild inland regions of the West Coast. The leaves are gray-green above, white below. The lime-yellow flower spikes are up to 6 in (about 15 cm) long in late winter and spring. It will grow to 50 ft (about 15 m) tall with a 20 ft (about 6 m) spread. Give it a position in full sun, a sandy soil and occasional water during dry seasons.

ZONES 9–10

## *BAUHINIA*
### *variegata*
PURPLE ORCHID TREE

This graceful, elegant tree, originating in India and China, quickly reaches heights up to 20 ft (about 6 m) with a similar spread. Distinctive for its twin-lobed leaves, most of which drop from the tree in midwinter before the flowering season. The most popular of the many orchid trees planted in southern California, it has very showy, perfumed, orchid-like flowers; light pink to purple, they have five overlapping petals, the fifth splashed with pink or purple. This species may have a shrubby habit and benefits from regular pruning to shape. Flower buds are considered a delicacy in its native land. Give it full sun, a well-drained soil, generous water during spring flowering and moderate thereafter. Prune off seed pods for neatness; propagate from seeds sown in spring. 'Candida' has pure white flowers. *B.* x *blakeana* is a hybrid with deeper pink flowers.

ZONES 9–11

## *BEAUCARNEA*
### *recurvata*
syn. ***Nolina recurvata, N. tuberculata***

PONY-TAIL PALM, ELEPHANT'S FOOT

A slow-growing tree from southern USA and Mexico, it is not in fact a palm but is related to yuccas, adapting to the arid tropics in a similar manner.The swollen base stores water in times of drought and tapers to a smooth, palm-like trunk with 6 ft (about 1.8 m) long, thin, recurving leaves sprouting from the top. It is sparsely branched and makes an attractive plant for a dry spot. It will only grow outdoors in mild to warm climates and in well-drained, fertile soil, preferring full sun. Water well when growing, but sparingly at other times. Potted specimens need full light and moderate water; allow to dry out between waterings. Propagate from seed or suckers in spring, or from stem-tip cuttings in summer.

ZONES 7–10

## *BETULA*
BIRCH

This genus contains over 35 species, native to the northern hemisphere. Tall and elegant, these deciduous trees are valued for their slender, weeping branches and shimmering foliage. Growing to 60–95 ft (about 18–29 m), they have broad, serrated leaves that turn gold in fall. Pendent fruit contains winged seeds. Brightly colored gray, red-brown, white or yellowish black bark peels attractively. Birches will grow in any well-drained soil, provided they receive plentiful water and full sun. Pruning is unnecessary. Propagate from seed, by grafting in late winter or from softwood cuttings in early summer. Once used to make school canes and domestic brooms, birch timber is highly prized by Scandinavia's furniture industry. Native Americans traditionally used the waterproof bark to make canoes.

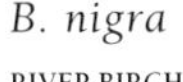

### *B. nigra*
RIVER BIRCH

Native to eastern North America, this is one of the most carefree of birches. Upright in habit to 50 ft (about 15 m) or more in height, it often grows naturally with multiple trunks. The bark is pinkish when young but ultimately an attractive cinnamon brown and black, peeling in small strips. The bright, shiny leaves turn gold in the fall. It prefers a richer soil than other species along with plenty of water; it is better adapted to hot, humid climates than the others. 'Heritage' was selected for its lighter bark.

ZONES 4–9

### *B. papyrifera*
PAPER BIRCH, CANOE BIRCH

Definitely a tree of the cold north, this species has brilliant white bark for which it is popular in its native range. Larger and less pendulous than the European white birch, it is resistant to the bronze birch borer that can destroy its relative. Best in the northern states of California.

ZONES 2–6

### *B. pendula*
syn. ***B. alba, B. verrucosa***

EUROPEAN WHITE BIRCH

This popular ornamental garden tree is native to Europe and Asia. It is widely conical and rapidly grows up to 65 ft (about 20 m). The species has silvery white bark turning to black and thinly stalked, diamond-shaped leaves 1–3 in (about 2.5–7.5 cm) long. Seed-bearing cones, lemon-green and 1 in (about 2.5 cm) long, appear in spring. If kept moist the tree will survive in most climates other than the tropics and subtropics. It is, however, happiest in cold climates.

ZONES 2–8

*Bauhinia* x *blakeana*

*Betula papyrifera*

*Bauhinia variegata*

*Beaucarnea recurvata*

*Banksia integrifolia*

*Betula nigra*

*Betula pendula*

*Carpinus betulus* 'Fastigiata'

*Calocedrus decurrens* 'Intricata'

*Betula pendula* 'Dalecarlica'

*Calodendrum capense*

### *B. pendula* 'Dalecarlica'

**syn. *B. pendula* 'Laciniata'**

EUROPEAN WHITE BIRCH

A slim and attractive tree, this cultivar is a slightly smaller tree than *B. pendula* but is equally as graceful. It has distinctive white bark and its branches are gently arching. The leaves are deeply lobed. Prune in winter to shape its form or thin for better light penetration.

ZONES 2–8

## *BRACHYCHITON*

BOTTLE TREE, FLAME TREE

This genus consists of 12 deciduous or evergreen trees native to the warm-temperate and tropical zones of Australia and New Guinea. They are extremely variable, growing to 27 ft (about 8 m) in dry, inland areas and up to 95 ft (about 29 m) on the coast. Their sturdy trunks are covered with gray or brown bark and are often swollen from moisture retained for survival during dry periods. The foliage is tough and changes in shape from youth to maturity. Attractive, bell-shaped flowers bloom erratically in spring and summer, usually after the leaves have been shed. Leathery brown pods, shaped like boats, split along a side seam to release their seeds. These trees prefer full sun or partial shade and rich, well-drained soil. Propagate from seed or cuttings; prune if necessary.

*Brachychiton populneus*

*Brachychiton acerifolius*

### *B. acerifolius*

AUSTRALIAN FLAME TREE

One of Australia's most attractive trees, this deciduous species is prized for its brilliant red flowers. It grows slowly to 18–130 ft (about 5.5–39 m), with smooth gray or brown furrowed bark. The leaves, up to 12 in (about 30 cm) long, have 3 to 7 lobes and resemble the maple's. Bright green on top, lighter underneath, foliage is shed when the tree flowers. This is when the tree earns its name, seemingly aflame with magnificent clusters of scarlet flowers 1 1/2 in (about 3 cm) long. Water regularly when in bloom.

ZONES 9–11

### *B. populneus*

**syn. *Sterculia diversifolia***

BOTTLE TREE

This cone-shaped, deciduous shade tree reaches 65 ft (about 20 m). Its gray-brown bark is orange-chocolate colored underneath. The foliage is remarkable diverse: ovate, heart-shaped and poplar-like leaves 2–4 in (about 5–10 cm) long may all grow on the same specimen. Bell-shaped flowers are cream tinged with green, spotted inside with red, purple or yellow. The spring to summer flowers are followed by clusters of brown, woody follicles. The leathery pods contain irritating hairs and red seeds. The species will survive in all soil types provided there is sufficient warmth. It is useful as a street tree or as a screen.

ZONES 9–11

## *CALOCEDRUS*

### *decurrens*

**syn. *Libocedrus decurrens***

INCENSE CEDAR

Valued for its shapely, conical habit and attractive foliage, this conifer from the mountains of the West grows slowly to 38–70 ft (about 11.5–21 m). Shiny, dark, bluish green leaves adhere to the branches in flat clusters. The small cones usually have only 6 scales. This tree likes partial sun or partial shade and a well-drained soil. It does well in the heat of summer and makes an ideal windbreak. If young plants are watered deeply they will become drought resistant in maturity. Propagate from seed. 'Intricata' is a commonly available cultivar.

ZONES 7–10

## *CALODENDRUM*
### *capense*
CAPE CHESTNUT

This warm climate evergreen is native to South Africa. Decorative and dome shaped, it grows to 24–50 ft (about 7–15 m). Its shiny oval leaves, 4–6 in (about 10–15 cm) long, are similar to those of the lemon tree. They are marked with dots, only discernible when held to the light. Clusters of light pink to pale lavender flowers appear in spring and early summer. This tree prefers warm climates but not dry exposed areas and requires regular watering. Plant in rich, well-drained soil and full sun. This species will stand pruning if necessary to keep its shape. Propagate from seed in spring or, more effectively, from semi-ripe cuttings in summer.
ZONES 10–11

## *CARPINUS*
HORNBEAM

With smooth bark and attractive foliage, these deciduous trees and shrubs of the northern hemisphere make valuable garden plants in spite of the insignificant flowers. Upright and gracefully arching branches carry flat sprays of usually toothed leaves. The fruits are nutlets held in leafy-bracted clusters, interesting but not showy. Generally woodland plants, they thrive in light shade or in full sun, with a woodsy soil and regular water. They seldom need pruning and are virtually pest and disease free. Propagate from seed sown in fall outdoors, or by cuttings in mid-summer. The wood is very hard and is valuable for making fine furniture.

### *C. betulus*
EUROPEAN HORNBEAM

This upright-growing species makes a superb small shade or street tree with its smooth gray bark, horizontal branching pattern even in winter and its general lack of litter. Most commonly grown is 'Fastigiata', which is only narrow in its youth, becoming broader and vase shaped with age. Branching is dense enough to provide good, effective screening even in winter. It can be espaliered as it doesn't mind pruning or training.
ZONES 5–10

### *C. caroliniana*
AMERICAN HORNBEAM, BLUE BEECH

A graceful, small, understory tree in the woodlands of eastern North America, this is a valuable native for lightly shaded areas in the garden. Smooth, gray bark is attractive in winter. Open branching shows off the pattern of ovate, toothed leaves which turn orange-red in fall.
ZONES 5–9

## *CASSIA*
### *leptophylla*
GOLD MEDALLION TREE

This showy tree from Brazil is notable for its nearly evergreen, pinnately compound leaves and bright golden yellow flowers. A fast-growing tree, it reaches 30 ft (about 9 m) in height and nearly as much in spread. Flowering in mid-summer with large clusters of bowl-shaped yellow flowers, the fruits that follow are brown, bean-like pods to 16 in (about 40 cm) long. It requires a sunny site with well-drained soil and moderate water during the summer. It benefits from hard pruning after flowering. Propagate from seed in spring, and from cuttings in late summer.
ZONES 9–11

## *CASTANEA*
### *sativa*
SWEET CHESTNUT, SPANISH CHESTNUT, EUROPEAN CHESTNUT

Growing to 95 ft (about 29 m), this statuesque, deciduous tree was probably introduced to Britain by the Romans from its native southern Europe. It has long, lanceolate, mid-green, toothed leaves with prominent veining. The long yellow catkins appear in summer and are followed by green, spiny husks which enclose the edible nuts, which are traditionally used for roasting and stuffings. It should be grown in a sunny position in well-drained, fertile soil. Propagate from seed in fall and grow on for up to 5 years before planting in its final site. Chestnut wood is often used for fence palings as it can withstand most weather conditions.
ZONES 5–9

## *CASUARINA*
BEEFWOOD, SHE-OAK

Originating in Australia and the South Pacific, the 70 species of evergreen trees (and shrubs) in this genus are valued for their shade and extremely tough timber. Conical, with a domed crown, they grow up to 90 ft (about 27 m) or more. Fine, spindly branchlets develop in whorls at the extremities of the rough, arching branches, giving the trees an open, pine-like appearance. The needle-like branchlets are surrounded by a variable number of tiny leaf scales, depending on the species. Small, red flowers grow among the twigs, appearing in late spring. These trees adapt to a wide range of conditions, from poor, arid soil to swampy saltwater marshes. They are excellent sand binders but are prone to suckering, which prevents other plants growing nearby. Propagate from seed in spring. Some species have become noxious weeds in the wetlands of Florida and the Gulf states.

### *C. cunninghamiana*
RIVER SHE-OAK

Reaching heights of up to 90 ft (about 27 m), this Australian native is the tallest of its genus. It has drooping, dark green, needle-like branchlets with globular cones less than 1 in (about 2.5 cm) in diameter. Flowers are reddish brown. This species is particularly useful in preventing soil erosion along rivers.
ZONES 8–11

### *C. verticillata*
syn. *C. stricta*
MOUNTAIN SHE-OAK, COAST BEEFWOOD

This is a smaller tree than *C. cunninghamiana* (only 35 ft/10m tall) from southeastern Australia with dark green, jointed branchlets resembling horsetail or scouring rush and 1 in (about 2.5 cm) diameter fruits. It is very tolerant of coastal conditions.
ZONES 8–11

*Carpinus caroliniana*

*Castanea sativa*

*Casuarina cunninghamiana*

*Casuarina verticillata*

Celtis sinensis

Cedrus atlantica

Catalpa bignonioides

## CATALPA
### *bignonioides*

SOUTHERN CATALPA, INDIAN BEAN

Native to the southeastern states, this deciduous tree is valued for its large foliage and flowers. It grows up to 50 ft (about 15 m), spreading broadly in later life. Pale green, heart-shaped leaves are $7^1/_2$–10 in (about 18–25 cm) long, grouped in threes. Bell shaped and perfumed, the flowers are white, pink or lemon, variegated with purple and yellow. They appear in summer in thick upright clusters, $7^1/_2$–12 in (about 18–30 cm) tall, later replaced by pendent, tubular seed pods to 15 in (about 38 cm) long; these can be a mess to clean up when they fall. This tree likes full sun, shelter from the wind and rich, well-drained soil. It is best grown alone. Propagate from seed in fall, cultivars by budding and cuttings in summer.

ZONES 5–9

## CEDRELA
### *sinensis*

syn. *Toona sinensis*

CHINESE CEDAR

This deciduous native of China is not a cedar, although in the timber trade its red timber is called cedar. Reaching heights of up to 70 ft (about 21 m), it is valued for its large foliage: beautiful pink, fern-like leaves, later changing to green, appear in early spring and grow 12–24 in (about 30–60 cm) long. Perfumed white flowers appear in drooping clusters in spring. This species likes full sun and rich, well-drained soil. Prune in winter to encourage shape; cutting to the ground each year results in a shrubby form with plenty of pink leaves in spring. Beware of the many root sprouts, which may invade neighboring plantings. Propagate from seed in fall, cuttings in winter. In some areas locals eat the onion-scented young leaves.

ZONES 5–10

Cedrus deodara

## CEDRUS

CEDAR

This genus of conifers contains four species of tall, conical trees greatly valued for their timber. Native from Africa to India, some species grow up to 145 ft (about 44 m) tall. The needle-like leaves are in bunches and are dark green to gray- or blue-green. They have woody, egg-shaped cones that fall apart as the seeds become ripe, leaving only the central spike on the branch. These trees prefer cool summer temperatures, full sun and rich, well-drained soil. Too large for the average garden, they are better suited to country properties. Propagate from seed; some cultivars by grafting. Cedars have an ancient lineage; their timber was used for Solomon's temple and it was greatly valued by the Greeks and by the Romans.

### *C. atlantica*

syn. *C. libanii* subsp. *atlantica*

ATLAS CEDAR

Originating in North Africa, this slow-growing species reaches heights of up to 50 ft (about 15 m). The pale green or blue-gray needles are only 1 in (about 2.5 cm) long. Female cones are erect, flowering in summer but taking two years to mature. While young this tree may be grown in a tub. Most popular is 'Glauca', with distinctly blue-gray foliage.

ZONES 6–10

### *C. deodara*

DEODAR

The largest of its genus, this magnificent Himalayan native reaches a towering 95 ft (about 29 m). Tiered branches droop slightly at the tips where the new leaves have a silvery cast. The upright cones are flat topped. This species will grow in various climates, from arid inland to cooler mountain areas. Height is determined by soil quality and also by the amount of water the tree receives.

ZONES 7–10

Cedrela sinensis

## CELTIS

HACKBERRY

The hackberries are not showy but are valuable for their ability to thrive in difficult situations: heat, drought, poor soils are not a problem for these tough trees, many of which are native in North America. Generally deep rooted, they are excellent as a street tree. The leaves resemble those of elms, to which they are related. Flowers are insignificant, but the fruits are like a hard, round berry, usually popular with wildlife. Avoid those species that are plagued by "witches' broom", congested, twiggy growths caused by a virus.

### *C. laevigata*

SUGARBERRY

This large, broad-headed tree is a favorite throughout the South, both for its cooling shade and for its ease of growth, even in poorly drained clay soils. With a height and spread of 60–80 ft (about 18–24 m), this is not one for the small garden. The leaves are a soft green, lighter below, long and with few teeth, and are presented on gracefully pendulous branches. The red-orange fruits ripen in fall and are juicier than most but are beloved by wildlife. Sugarberry is native to the southwestern quarter of North America.

ZONES 5–9

*Cercis canadensis*

*Cercidium floridum*

*Cercis occidentalis*

*Chamaecyparis lawsoniana*

### *C. sinensis*

CHINESE HACKBERRY

The glossy, scallop-toothed leaves set this species apart from other hackberries. This native of China and Japan has a height and spread under 60 ft (about 18 m). It is particularly popular in the southwestern states.

ZONES 6–10

## *CERCIDIPHYLLUM japonicum*

KATSURA TREE

With the delicate pattern of leaves like those of redbud, this tall, deciduous tree from Japan makes a beautiful specimen in the garden. Usually grown with multiple trunks it will be a wide spreading tree, 60–100 ft (about 18–30 m) tall and wide; as a single-trunked tree it remains slender and columnar. Foliage turns bright red or yellow in fall; young growth always has tints of pink or red. Flowers are insignificant. Small, round fruits remain on the branches through winter. It prefers a cold winter climate and protection from dry heat in summer. Give it good, rich soil and regular water. Little pruning is required. Propagate from seed in fall.

ZONES 4–9

## *CERCIDIUM floridum*

BLUE PALO VERDE

A popular small tree for desert gardens, this native of the Southwest is distinctive for its tiny leaves which drop quickly, leaving the blue-green branches and trunk to carry on food making with their chlorophyll-rich bark. With multiple trunks and an upright, spreading habit, this tough tree reaches a height and spread of 15–30 ft (about 4.5–9 m). Fragrant, yellow, pea-like flowers cover the spriny branches in spring; seed pods ripen in summer. Give it full sun, any well-drained soil and occasional water during the warm months to extend the life of the leaves. The light shade it gives is perfect for many cacti and succulents.

ZONES 9–10

## *CERCIS*

REDBUD

This genus consists of 7 small ornamental trees and shrubs, native to North America, southern Europe and Asia. They are grown for their beautiful, pea-like flowers. Deciduous species reach 30–35 ft (about 9–10 m) tall, with multiple trunks and delicate branching. It is straight out of these limbs that the pink, white or purple, stalkless flowers appear at the end of winter. Numerous flat seed pods, 4 in (about 10 cm) long, follow the blooms and endure until the following winter. These trees prefer rich, porous soils and full sun. They do not like being moved, so transplant when young. Propagate from seed in fall and bud cultivars in summer.

### *C. canadensis*

EASTERN REDBUD

Native to moist woodlands and streamsides in eastern North America, this spreading tree grows up to 35 ft (about 10 m) tall and nearly as wide, with heart-shaped leaves. The young, reddish purple, $^1/_2$ in wide flower buds turn light pink when open. Seed pods are brown and $3^1/_2$ in (about 8 cm) long. Several selections are available with white or clearer pink flowers; 'Forest Pansy' is distinct for its deep maroon to purple leaves. Surprisingly adaptable to the heat and drought of the West Coast.

ZONES 4–10

### *C. occidentalis*

WESTERN REDBUD

Native to hot, dry slopes in California, Arizona and Utah, this large shrub has multiple trunks and becomes tree like with age. Flowers are more magenta than pink, but are very showy on the bare branches in late winter. The leaves are heart shaped but notched at the tips. It loves the heat and needs no summer water once established. It will reach 12–18 ft (about 3.5–5.5 m) tall and wide. It flowers best where winter temperatures drop below freezing.

ZONES 7–10

*Cercidiphyllum japonicum*

## *CHAMAECYPARIS lawsoniana*

LAWSON CYPRESS, PORT ORFORD CEDAR

This native of northern California and southern Oregon is prized for its quality timber and impressive appearance. It has a conical shape, later becoming more open crowned and columnar and reaching up to 100 ft (about 30 m) or more in height. Tiny, deep green scales cover the slender, slightly arching branches, giving the tree a fine texture. Woody cones are nearly globular and plated, around 1 in (about 2.5 cm) in diameter. The species thrives best in cool conditions and rich, damp soil. There are many garden varieties with narrower habit, or silvery or golden foliage. 'Ellwoodii' is particularly hardy; 'Silver Queen' is large, fast growing and variegated.

ZONES 6–10

Cornus capitata

*Cladrastis lutea*

*Chionanthus virginicus*

*Chilopsis linearis*

*Cinnamomum camphora*

*Chorisia speciosa*

## *CHILOPSIS*
### *linearis*

DESERT WILLOW

Characteristic of the desert washes throughout the southwestern states and northern Mexico, this deciduous tree often has the multi-trunked habit of a large shrub, with branches to the ground and forming dense mounds. In garden situations, it is a tree to 30 ft (about 9 m) tall and wide. The slender leaves are willow like, while the flowers are showy trumpets in white, pink or lavender; they are produced nearly all summer in the garden. The seed pods that follow are typical of the catalpa family—long, slender and filled with milky seeds. Give it sun, heat, a well-drained soil and occasional deep soakings through the summer to extend the flowering season. Excellent for shading a patio in a desert garden.

ZONES 8–10

## *CHIONANTHUS*
### *virginicus*

FRINGE TREE, OLD MAN'S BEARD

Native to southeastern North America, this deciduous species slowly grows to 9–30 ft (about 2.7–9 m) tall, as a slender small tree or large shrub. It has an open crown and is valued for its attractive flowers. The flowers are dainty and white, and appear in late spring in drooping terminal clusters 8 in (about 20 cm) long— hence the common name "old man's beard". The large, oval leaves appear in late spring and are shiny and dark green, turning gold in the fall. Blue fruits ripen in fall on female trees; they are popular with birds. This species prefers cool temperatures and moist soil with full sun. Despite its slow growth, it needs no special care once established.

ZONES 5–10

## *CHORISIA*
### *speciosa*

FLOSS SILK TREE, BRAZILIAN KAPOK TREE

This tree is native to the subtropical zones of Brazil and Argentina. An erect species with a lofty crown, it grows to 50 ft (about 15 m). Its tapering trunk is covered with vicious spikes and its branches are long and uplifted. Compound leaves are shaped like hands, made up of saw-toothed leaflets 5 in (about 12 cm) long. Resembling the hibiscus, the variegated flowers have 5 petals and range in color from light pink to purple with white or yellow throats, marked with red or brown. The species needs full sun, a warm climate and well-drained soil. Water liberally when in flower, in fall. Propagate from seed in spring.

ZONES 10–11

## *CINNAMOMUM*
### *camphora*

CAMPHORA TREE

Originating in China, Japan and Taiwan, this evergreen is highly valued for its oil and scented timber and foliage. It grows slowly to around 50 ft (about 15 m) tall with a rounded crown and tough gray bark. New foliage is rust colored with a grayish blue underside, maturing to a shiny yellow green. The oval-shaped leaves are 5 in (about 12 cm) long, tapering to a point. These leaves release a camphor fragrance when crushed. Inconspicuous flowers appear in spring, followed by black berries. This tree requires a well-drained soil, occasional deep waterings and a warm climate with winter temperatures above 20°F (about –7°C). Shallow roots can be a problem for pavement plantings. Pruning is tolerated. Propagate from cuttings in summer, seeds in fall. Fragrant carved chests are made with the wood, which has the ability to protect their contents from moths.

ZONES 9–11

## *CLADRASTIS*
### *lutea*

syn. *C. kentukea*

YELLOW WOOD

Native to North Carolina, Kentucky and Tennessee, this deciduous tree has very fragrant flowers and thick foliage. It grows to around 50 ft (about 15 m) in height, with a broad, dome-shaped crown. The attractive compound leaves have 7 to 9 deep-green, ovate leaflets and are 4 in (about 10 cm) long. Foliage turns from deep green to vivid yellow in fall. Magnificent, white, wisteria-like flower clusters appear in early summer, but not every year. This species takes 10 years to flower. It likes cool weather and will grow in average soil provided there is good drainage. Propagate from seed in fall. The common name comes from the bright yellow color of its freshly cut timber, which is used to make dye.

ZONES 3–9

## *CORDYLINE*
### *australis*

syn. ***Dracaena australis***

CABBAGE TREE, DRACAENA PALM

A palm-like tree from New Zealand, this is the hardiest of the genus but is slow growing. The tall, central stem has a rosette of slender, strap-like leaves growing to 3 ft (about 90 cm) in length. From late spring to summer large sprays of tiny, scented, white flowers appear. This tree grows well in almost all conditions but prefers fertile, well-drained but moist soil and full sun to part shade. It makes an ex-

cellent potted plant that needs moderate watering, less in winter. Propagate from seed or suckers in spring or stem cuttings in summer. Among its many common names, it was called "cabbage tree" because early settlers in New Zealand used the leaves instead of cabbage.
ZONES 8–11

## *CORNUS*

DOGWOOD

These 50 species of deciduous and evergreen shrubs and trees originate in Asia, North America and Europe. Tree species vary up to 60 ft (about 18 m) tall; they are valued for their foliage, flowers, fall color and fruit. Small, green blossoms appear in spring surrounded by a rosette of bracts. The blooms develop into clusters of vivid red, white or pink berries that last until fall. Dogwoods are best adapted to regions with cold winters, preferring sun to part shade. Soil should be rich, porous and generally acidic; regular water is essential. Minimal pruning is needed.

### *C. capitata*

EVERGREEN DOGWOOD

This Himalayan evergreen or semi-evergreen has wide, spreading branches and grows up to 40 ft (about 12 m) high and wide. Pendent, greenish gray leaves are 3–4 in (about 7.5–10 cm) long. The bracts are creamy yellow, $2^1/_2$–3 in (about 6–7.5 cm) wide. The plump, dark pink fruit resembles strawberries. This tree does best in cool coastal climates and acid soils; once established, it is relatively drought tolerant in cool summer areas.
ZONES 8–10

### *C. controversa*

Originally from China and Japan, this deciduous species with layered branches can grow to 50 ft (about 15 m). Its ovate, alternate, bright green leaves turn purple in fall, and the 2–3 in (about 5–7.5 cm) clusters of white flowers are borne in summer. There is a variegated form, 'Variegata', which is propagated by grafting in winter.
ZONES 5–10

### *C. florida*

FLOWERING DOGWOOD

Originating in eastern North America, this deciduous species slowly reaches 20–40 ft (about 6–12 m) tall with gracefully spreading branches. It is valued for its abundant white spring flowers and deep green, oval, heavily veined leaves, around 3–4 in (about 7.5–10 cm) long, that turn vivid, reddish purple in fall. It requires a deep, rich, woodsy soil.
ZONES 5–10

### *C. kousa*

KOUSA DOGWOOD

This native of Japan and China flowers later than *C. florida,* with white, pointed bracts that age to pink. It has multiple trunks and holds its flowers above the horizontal branches. Better adapted to West Coast gardens than *C. florida,* it still needs regular irrigation.
ZONES 5–10

### *C. mas*

CORNELIAN CHERRY

Distinct for its clusters of tiny yellow flowers in late winter, this dogwood lacks the showy bracts. A deciduous shrub with a rounded habit, it has glossy leaves that turn red and gold in the fall and is likely to have many suckers from the base. It needs pruning to maintain an attractive shape.
ZONES 4–8

### *C. nuttallii*

PACIFIC DOGWOOD

This dramatic, conical, deciduous tree grows to a height of 60 ft (about 18 m). Its flowers resemble those of *C. florida* but with more and larger bracts appearing in spring; red or orange berries follow in fall, along with excellent fall foliage colors of red and gold. It is best used in areas near its natural range in the mountains of the West Coast.
ZONES 7–9

## *CRATAEGUS*

HAWTHORN

This large, diverse genus of ornamental deciduous trees and shrubs originates in the northern hemisphere. Members of the rose family, they have beautiful, 5-petaled flowers and cruel thorns. Height varies between 15 and 45 ft (about 4.5–14 m). The spiky branches, usually spreading, develop finely toothed leaves, sometimes shallowly lobed. Fragrant flowers appear in late spring, usually white but sometimes in shades of pink, followed by long-lasting ornamental fruit, white, pink, orange, yellow or bright red and of varying size. They will survive in most soils provided they are not too damp. Propagate from seed in fall; cultivars by budding in late summer. The genus name from the Greek *kratos,* "strength", refers to their durable wood.

### *C. coccinea* 'Plena'

SCARLET HAWTHORN

This species, from North America, grows to 12–21 ft (about 3.5–6.5 m) in height. It has roundish, fine-toothed leaves that turn a rich red in fall and bright pink flowers. These are followed by long-lasting red berries. Plant in full sun in well-drained soil.
ZONES 4–10

*Cornus kousa*

*Cornus mas*

*Cornus florida*

*Crataegus coccinea* 'Plena'

*Cornus nuttallii*

*Cornus controversa*

### *C. laevigata* 'Paul's Scarlet'
syn. ***C. oxyacantha***
PAUL'S SCARLET HAWTHORN

This decorative, deciduous tree reaches 25 ft (about 7.5 m). It is much admired for its flowers, ornamental fruit and dense foliage. Egg-shaped leaves with deeply cut lobes are 2 in (about 5 cm) long on spiky, broadly spreading branches. Strongly scented, double red or deep pink flowers bloom in late spring to early summer. Red fruit endures through fall. This tree prefers a cool climate, full sun and well-drained soil. Propagate by budding in late summer. Susceptible to fireblight.
ZONES 4–10

### *C.* × *lavallei*
syn. ***C.* × *carrierei***

This deciduous garden hybrid is a vigorous grower—to 20 ft (about 6 m) high with a greater spread, up to 30 ft (about 9 m). It has glossy, oval, dark green leaves which in late fall turn red and often endure on the almost thornless branches until well into winter. The white flowers appear in erect clusters in late spring, while the orange-red fruit ripen in late summer or early fall.
ZONES 4–10

*Crataegus* × *lavallei*

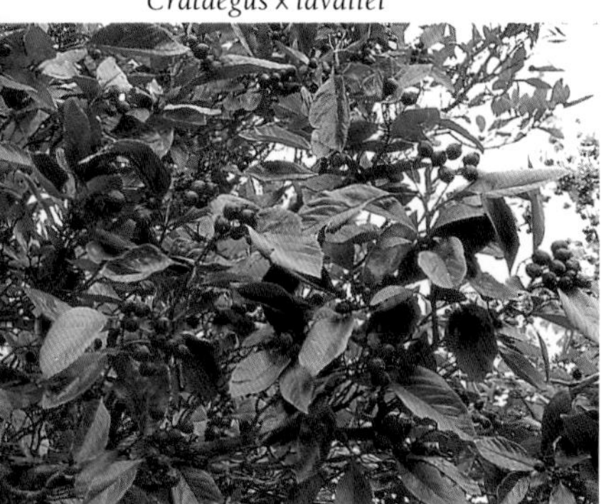

### *C. phaenopyrum*
syn. ***C. cordata***
WASHINGTON THORN

This small, attractive species has a round shape and grows up to 30 ft (about 9 m). Its shiny, deep green foliage is heart shaped and deeply lobed. Clusters of white flowers appear in early summer, followed by shiny, orange-red, spherical fruit. This species is tough, resistant to foliar diseases that may attack other hawthorns and adaptable over most of the continent.
ZONES 4–10

### *C. viridis* 'Winter King'

This is an excellent selection of a southeastern native with silvery bark, good, red fall color and bright red fruits that last well into winter. It has a vase shape to 25 ft (about 7.5 m) tall, glossy leaves and relatively few thorns.
ZONES 4–9

## *CRYPTOMERIA*
### *japonica* 'Elegans'
PLUME CEDAR

This erect, conical, Asian conifer, 40–60 ft (about 12–18 m) tall, is highly valued for its fascinating needle-like foliage that develops in soft feathery whorls and drapes to the ground. Leaves turn from deep green in summer to rich golden rust in fall. It prefers cool conditions but will survive in the heat with regular watering. Plant in cool, damp soil and shelter from cold winds; it will withstand transplanting up to a reasonable size. Propagate from cuttings. It is rare for a mature tree not to lean.
ZONES 6–10

## × *CUPRESSOCYPARIS*
### *leylandii*
LEYLAND CYPRESS

A hybrid between *Cupressus macrocarpa* and *Chamaecyparis nootkatensis*, two West Coast natives, this conifer is popular for its fast growth, sometimes reaching 20 ft (about 6 m) tall in five years (ultimately to 40 ft/12 m or more). It has a conical habit when young, becoming more open and rounded in age or where summers are hot. Often used as a quick-growing screen, it may only serve for 5 to 10 years before opening up and allowing views through. Flattened sprays of scaly leaves may be gray-green or blue-green; the cones are tiny. It prefers cool summer areas and good drainage but regular water. Propagate by cuttings.
ZONES 6–10

## *CUPRESSUS*
CYPRESS

Native to Europe, Asia, the USA and Central America, this diverse genus of evergreen coniferous trees and shrubs may be tall and slender or open and squat, ranging from 3 to 145 ft (about 90 cm to 44 m) high. They make symmetrical shade trees or hedges. Dark green, golden green or bluish gray needle-like leaves change to scale-like leaves in maturity. Their globose, scale-covered cones may hang on the branches for years. They prefer cool to warm-temperate regions and are ideal for coastal locations in full sun; some thrive in arid regions. Prune minimally to shape trees, or shear regularly for formal hedges. Propagate from cuttings in winter or cold-treated seed from the end of fall to late winter. The trees are susceptible to leaf tier caterpillars, beetles, weevils and canker.

### *C. arizonica*
ARIZONA CYPRESS

This native of the Southwest and northern Mexico is a valuable conifer for desert landscaping. Tolerant of heat and drought, it varies in its form but most commonly has a broad, conical shape, reaching 30–40 ft (about 9–12 m) tall. Foliage will vary in color as well; best forms have a silvery-blue color. Globular cones are 1 in (about 2.5 cm) in diameter. The peeling bark is a feature; usually red and smooth on young trees, it becomes thick, fibrousy and shredding on mature specimens. On *C. arizonica* var. *glabra* the bark remains smooth and red to purple. Rich soil with generous water will encourage faster growth but may shorten the life of the trees.
ZONES 7–10

### *C. macrocarpa*
MONTEREY CYPRESS

This stately tree from California is noted for its handsome habit, coni-

*Crataegus laevigata* 'Paul's Scarlet'

*Crataegus viridis* 'Winter King'

*Cupressus s.* 'Swane's Golden'

*Crataegus phaenopyrum*

*Cryptomeria japonica* 'Elegans'

× *Cupressocyparis leylandii*

cal when young and developing picturesque, spreading branches with maturity. The wild form has dark green needles, but several "golden" leaved cultivars are popular. It is not a tree for bitterly cold climates. It is very resistant to salt winds and is much used as a shelter tree and, as it takes clipping very well, for tall hedges. Propagate from cuttings or seed. It is prone to cypress canker.

ZONES 8–10

### *C. sempervirens*

ITALIAN CYPRESS

This classic Mediterranean conifer has a variable form, but trees in cultivation are usually tall, slender columns with narrowly ascending branches. Ultimate height may be 30–40 ft (about 9–12 m) tall with a spread of only 5–6 ft (about 1.5–1.8 m); some may need tying together to maintain the narrow shape. Foliage is usually dark, dull green but in some selections may be golden or silvery-blue. Cones are $1^1/_2$ in (about 3 cm) in diameter and ovoid. These trees are for hot, dry climates like California and the Southwest. 'Stricta' is the narrowest of all; 'Swane's Golden' has golden yellow foliage.

ZONES 8–10

## *DAVIDIA involucrata*

DOVE TREE, HANDKERCHIEF TREE

This native of China, the only species of its genus, is valued for its unusual white bracts. Growing to 50 ft (about 15 m) or more, this deciduous ornamental develops a rounded appearance. Its broad, egg-shaped leaves up to 6 in (about 15 cm) long are succeeded in late spring by small, deep-set, brownish red flowers. Two white bracts (commonly mistaken for petals) of unequal lengths surround the flower. The longer leaf resembles a bird or handkerchief; hence the common names. Purplish green, pear-shaped seed pods follow, each encasing a single nut. Plant in full sun or partial shade in rich, porous soil and protect the bracts from harsh winds. Propagate (with some difficulty) from cuttings in spring, or from seed in fall. The genus is named after Père David, the French missionary who discovered it.

ZONES 6–10

## *DELONIX regia*

ROYAL POINCIANA, FLAMBOYANT TREE

This tropical native of Madagascar is southern Florida's most spectacular and popular flowering tree. While it only grows up to 30 ft (about 9 m), it is often three times as broad and quickly develops a buttressed trunk and thick crown. Its extremely long, bipinnate foliage is composed of 40 light green "feathers" with numerous leaflets. These are topped by flaming red blooms, 4 in (about 10 cm) across, one petal variegated with white. The species will not survive temperatures below freezing and needs a rich, well-drained, loamy soil with plenty of moisture, and warm temperatures in summer to flower well. Prune when immature to prevent the development of multiple trunks. Propagate from seed in summer and fall.

ZONES 10–11

## *DIOSPYROS kaki*

JAPANESE PERSIMMON

Valued for its fruit, timber and stunning fall foliage, this graceful, slow-growing, deciduous tree is native to China and Japan. It may reach 40 ft (about 12 m) but is more usually 30 ft (about 9 m) tall. In fall the leathery, oval leaves turn the most striking colors: scarlet, yellow, orange and purple. Insignificant, yellowish white female flowers develop into delicious, golden red fruit, or persimmons. Up to 3 in (about 7.5 cm) in diameter, these are the size and shape of a tomato. This tree enjoys warm summers, rich, fertile soil and frequent watering. It is best propagated by grafting, though seed may be used. A relaltive of the ebony, its precious timber is used to make oriental cabinets and also to make golf "woods".

ZONES 8–10

*Diospyros kaki*

*Cupressus sempervirens* 'Stricta'

*Cupressus macrocarpa*

*Delonix regia*

*Davidia involucrata*

*Cupressus arizonica*

# A Field Trip to Norfolk Island

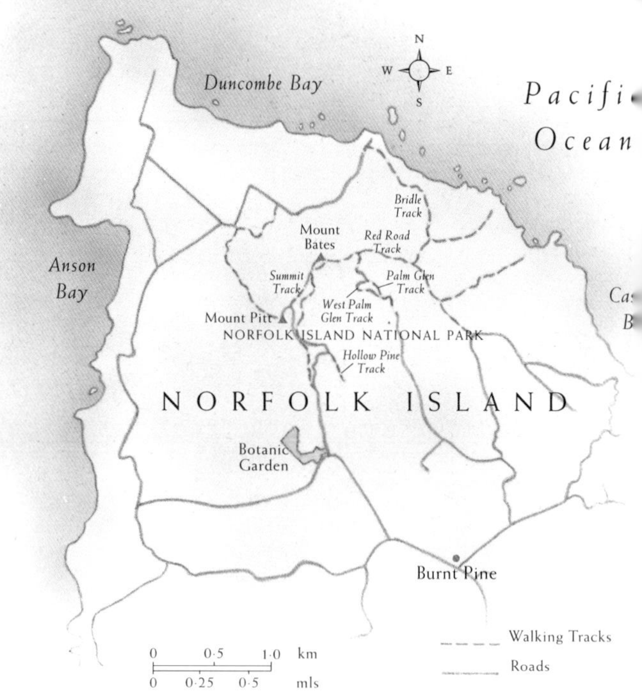


The stately splendor of Norfolk Island pines *(Araucaria heterophylla)* can't be fully appreciated until you see them growing in their own home—Norfolk Island.

Norfolk Island is a tiny island in the Pacific Ocean, about 1050 miles (about 1700 km) northeast of Sydney, Australia. You can fly to Norfolk Island from Sydney or from Auckland, New Zealand. As your aircraft approaches the island, you can see the steep basalt cliffs and gently rolling hills, and catch your first glimpse of its most dominant feature—great stands of Norfolk Island pines They can be seen both in the open and in the densely wooded areas where they are to be found towering over the canopy.

Norfolk Island has a pleasant, mild, subtropical climate with an average yearly rainfall of 52 in (about 1326 mm). The best time to visit is in summer, when the mean temperature is 77°F (about 25°C); in winter it is 65°F (about 18°C).

The best place to see the island's most interesting and beautiful flora is Norfolk Island National Park. There are up to 170 native plant species, about 40 of which are found only on Norfolk Island. It is a good idea to visit the Botanic Garden on Mission Road before you explore the National Park. Here you can familiarize yourself with some of the flora so you can more easily identify it when you are in the park. The National Park contains some 5 miles (about 8 km) of walking tracks. A good place to start exploring these is from the summit of Mount Pitt, the highest point of the island. You can walk or drive to this area from Burnt Pine.

As you wind your way up the mountain the towering pines and palms create a canopy that, in places, obscures the sky. The rich soil here is home to many fern species, including the smooth tree fern *(Cyathea brownii)*, which is considered to be the world's tallest. The view from the summit is magnificent; you can see the whole of Norfolk Island and neighboring Nepean and Phillip Islands, and all around an endless expanse of sea.

From Mount Pitt take the Summit Track to Mount Bates, winding your way through some thick forest. The trees here include the Norfolk Island hibiscus, also known as the white oak *(Lagunaria patersonii)*, which produces splendid pink flowers in spring (September to November). The pepper tree *(Macropiper excelsum)*, too, is fairly abundant. This shrub grows up to 9 ft (about 3 m), producing yellow flower spikes followed by spikes of yellow to orange fruit which was used in preserves by the early settlers.

Follow the Red Road Track from Mount Bates through more hardwood forest and large stands of Norfolk Island pines and you may see the epiphytic orchid *Taeniophyllum muellerii*, commonly known as the minute orchid, growing on the trunks and branches. On the forest floor is *Oplismenus*, a creeping native grass which has tiny reddish flowers.

*Looking south from Anson Bay, Norfolk Island.*

*Lichen covers the limbs of some pines in the island's northeast.*

*Araucaria heterophylla*

The Palm Glen Track leads you through one of the island's most attractive areas where you will see great stands of the Norfolk Island palm *(Rhopalostylis baueri)*, a magnificent tree reaching heights of 30 ft (about 10 m). The West Palm Glen Track leads through more stands of palms and a lush tree fern forest. Here you will see the smooth tree fern again, also the smaller rough tree fern *(Cyathea australis)* and the rare king fern *(Marattia salicina)*.

Wildlife in the area includes the scarlet robin, a delightful but endangered endemic bird which is black with a bright red breast. The Norfolk Island morepork (a small owl) makes its nest in a hollow of the Norfolk Island pine, as do many of the island's native birds. Another threatened species, the Norfolk Island green parrot, an attractive bird with jewel green plumage, makes its home among the branches. The white tern, a sea bird and the island's emblem, also nests here.

After you have walked back to Mount Pitt—the round trip is 2½ miles (about 4 km)—take the track to Hollow Pine. Here stands a magnificent Norfolk Island pine which is hollow at the base. An escaped convict is said to have lived for seven years in a similar pine before he was finally captured.

The area surrounding Hollow Pine is rich in native flora. Many parts of the island have been affected by the encroachment of weeds but here volunteers have assisted in the battle against unwanted introduced species.

Before European settlement, the island was almost covered in rainforest. When Captain Cook first landed, the Norfolk Island pines came right down to the water's edge. Clearing of the land started within days of settlement in 1788, and now less than 1 per cent remains as it was when Cook saw it. Planting of the pines is now being done on a large scale. These may take up to 80 years or more to reach their full height of up to 220 ft (about 70 m), but eventually the island may once again be almost covered by these magnificent trees.

As the Pitcairners of Norfolk Island say: "If we do not live to see them grow, our children will."

## Araucaria

The unique conifer genus *Araucaria* consists of 19 species, distributed in a remarkable geographical pattern. On one side of the Pacific Ocean there are two species in eastern Australia, one of which occurs in New Guinea which also has an endemic species; Norfolk Island has just one species but nearby New Caledonia has 13 species. Across the Pacific in South America there are just two species, the spectacular "monkey puzzle" in Chile and southern Argentina, and the Parana pine in south-central Brazil. This sort of distribution suggests the genus originated and diversified before Gondwana, the southern supercontinent, began splitting apart over 100 million years ago.

The araucarias make beautiful ornamental trees where space is sufficient and the climate is suitable. The most cold-hardy is the Chilean monkey puzzle *(Araucaria araucana)*, which actually requires cool climates such as that of southern England. The next most hardy is the Australian bunya pine *(A. bidwillii)*. Some of the species, such as the Norfolk Island pine and the New Caledonian pine *(A. columnaris)*, are noted for their tolerance of salt-laden winds.

*Araucaria heterophylla*

*Eucalyptus citriodora*

*Erythrina caffra*

*Eucalyptus ficifolia*

*Embothrium coccineum*

*Erythrina crista-galli*

*Eucalyptus globulus*

*Eucalyptus mannifera* subsp. *maculosa*

## *EMBOTHRIUM coccineum*

CHILEAN FIRE TREE, CHILEAN FIREBUSH

Native to Chile and Argentina, this small, evergreen tree or large, narrow shrub may reach 30 ft (about 9 m). It has shiny, dark green, leathery leaves growing up to 4 in (about 10 cm) long. Terminal clusters of scarlet, tubular flowers bloom in an impressive display from late spring to early summer. The plant will produce flowers from an early age provided it is well watered. A cool-temperate species, it enjoys a damp, cool location with acid soil and good drainage. Propagate from suckers in spring or seed in fall.
ZONES 8–10

## *ERYTHRINA*

CORAL TREE

These deciduous and semi-evergreen trees and shrubs originate in cool tropical and warm-temperate areas around the world. They are usually grown in warm winter regions as ornamentals. They vary in height between 27 and 60 ft (about 8–18 m) and usually have twisted, thorny trunks. Leaves are pinnately compound, with heart-shaped or oval leaflets; they appear on light, weak branches often prone to splitting and falling. Tubular flowers, split beneath, bloom in a mass of scarlet, crimson or orange at various times of the year; some species in mid-winter, their flowers in striking contrast to denuded limbs. Coral trees will survive in diverse conditions provided temperatures remain above 40°F (about 5°C). Many species tolerate exposed coastal locations. Provide rich, porous soil and water sparingly, especially if growing in pots. Propagate from seed in spring, cuttings in summer. Prone to attack by red spider mite.

### *E. caffra*

syn. ***E. constantiana, E. insignis***
KAFFIRBOOM CORAL TREE

This semi-evergreen African native with its spreading crown grows quickly to 35–60 ft (about 10–18 m). The compound foliage, 7 in (about 17 cm) wide, comprises three sharp, oval leaflets. Orange-red flowers appear in late winter and early spring, followed by leathery seed pods containing scarlet seeds. This species is the floral emblem of Los Angeles.
ZONES 10–11

### *E. crista-galli*

COCKSPUR CORAL TREE

Originating in Brazil, this deciduous species rapidly reaches 12–30 ft (about 3.5–9 m) and spreads broadly. Its prickly, trifoliate leaves develop at the ends of thorny stems. Rich, crimson flowers bloom in loose terminal clusters from summer to fall. The woody seed pods are 15 in (about 38 cm) long. This species requires full sun and moist soil. Prune in winter; an attractive gnarled trunk will develop without pruning but then the crown will be full of dead branches.
ZONES 8–11

### *E. lysistemon*

KAFFIRBOOM

This semi-deciduous South African native grows to 30 ft (about 9 m) tall. Terminal clusters of cylindrical red flowers often bloom from the tips of the branchlets prior to the new season's foliage.
ZONES 10–11

## *EUCALYPTUS*

EUCALYPT, GUM TREE

This diverse genus of Australian natives contains over 600 species of evergreen trees and shrubs prized for their attractive flowers, leaves and bark. Foliage varies from linear to heart shaped; young and adult leaves differ markedly, making identification difficult. All species have distinctively capped flower buds with densely packed stamens, blooming in shades of white, pink, red or yellow. Trees differ greatly in size and shape from low, multi-trunked and shrubby to extremely tall and high canopied. Their native habitat varies from coastal dunes and swamps to desert plains to mountain tops; most grown in North America are remarkably drought tolerant but tolerate little frost and are generally useful only in the mildest climates. Plant eucalypts as small as possible; their rapid root growth may lead to encircling roots if kept too long in nursery containers, and to poorly anchored trees in the garden. Give them full sun, a well-drained soil and moderate watering once established. Propagate from seed in late winter.

### *E. citriodora*

LEMON-SCENTED GUM

This species grows to 100 ft (about 30 m) or more in height and is valued for its slender beauty and lemon-scented leaves. The attractive trunk is covered with smooth, pinkish gray bark that peels in patches. The deep green foliage is rough and downy when young, becoming lanceolate and smooth when mature. Flowers bloom in thick, terminal clusters 1 in (about 2.5 cm) across.
ZONES 10–11

### *E. ficifolia*

SCARLET-FLOWERING GUM

Regarded as the most beautiful of all the flowering eucalypts, this species bears enormous terminal clusters of scarlet to orange flowers in late spring and summer. It grows up to 30 ft (about 9 m) with rough bark and a spreading crown of lance-shaped foliage. The pitcher-shaped nuts contain brown, winged seeds. This tree does best in a mild, coastal location with full sun and well-drained soil. Seeds from cultivars will produce a variety of colors. It is closely related to *E. calophylla*.
ZONES 10–11

### *E. globulus*

TASMANIAN BLUE GUM

One of the most commonly planted eucalypts in California, this tall, narrow species has naturalized in coastal areas, creating fire hazards and out-competing the native vegetation. A fast grower and weak wooded, it may exceed 200 ft (about 61 m) in height, the tall, straight trunk continually shedding its smooth, light gray bark. The young leaf is silvery-blue and oval, maturing to a green sickle shape to 12 in (about 30 cm) long and very aromatic. Creamy flowers develop from blue buds. Much over-planted in the West, this is nevertheless a

Eucalyptus leucoxylon

beautiful species when grown as a specimen but is too large for most gardens and contributes too much fuel in areas prone to fire.
ZONES 9–10

*E. leucoxylon*
WHITE IRONBARK

With smooth, bluish white bark marked with yellow patches, this erect evergreen reaches 15–30 ft (about 4.5–9 m). Its rounded crown is covered with grayish green, lanceolate leaves of varying widths. White or pink flowers (according to variety) appear in long-stemmed, triple clusters during winter and spring. The seed pods are 1 in (about 2.5 cm) long with pointed ends. This species adapts to mild coastal conditions as well as hot interior regions.
ZONES 9–11

*E. mannifera* subsp. *maculosa*
RED-SPOTTED GUM

Erect, with an open, spreading crown, this evergreen grows quickly to 30–50 ft (about 9–15 m). Its powdery white bark is pinkish red when new. The blue-green, lanceolate foliage is 3–6 in (about 7.5–15 cm) long. Creamy white flowers appear in terminal clusters of 3 to 7 blossoms in late spring and summer, or in winter in some climates.
ZONES 9–11

*E. nicholii*
NICHOL'S WILLOW-LEAFED PEPPERMINT

This fine-textured, upright eucalypt has brown, fibrousy bark and weeping branches. The juvenile leaves are very narrow and gray-green, becoming slender blue-green in maturity; crushed leaves smell of peppermint. Densely foliaged, this is an excellent shade tree for the larger garden, reaching 40 ft (about 12 m) in height and nearly as wide. Flowers and fruits are small and insignificant.
ZONES 8–10

*E. pauciflora*
GHOST GUM

This medium-sized eucalypt is one of the most attractive for its smooth white bark and blue-green, sickle-shaped leaves. Seldom more than

Eucalyptus pauciflora

35 ft (about 10 m) tall in cultivation, its open habit of growth provides dappled shade for garden or terrace. Its flowers and fruit are not showy, and it sheds very little bark. Extremely hardy for a eucalypt, it also tolerates heat and drought but may be difficult to find in nurseries.
ZONES 7–10

*E. polyanthemos*
SILVER DOLLAR GUM

This is a popular tree for its juvenile leaves which are silvery and nearly round in shape. Mature leaves are less silvery and more oval, but are still very attractive on gracefully pendulous branches. Tiny, creamy flowers are produced in large, pendent panicles in early summer. The light brown bark sometimes looks like cats have used it as a scratching post. Foliage is good for cutting.
ZONES 8–11

*E. sideroxylon*
RED IRONBARK, PINK IRONBARK

This showy eucalypt is noted for its tough, black, furrowed bark and attractive pink or red flowers. The blue-green foliage is a perfect foil for the winter flowers and emphasizes the darkness of the bark. Generally upright in habit to around 40 ft (about 12 m), occasionally more, its branches may be upright or gracefully pendent. It does well near the coast or inland, but dislikes wet, clay soils.
ZONES 9–10

## *FAGUS*
BEECH

Native to the northern hemisphere, this small, cool-climate genus includes some of the world's most popular deciduous trees. They are valued for their fall foliage and their timber, used to make furniture. Reaching up to 95 ft (about 29 m), they are well rounded with dense crowns. Foliage varies in shape, size and color, ranging from yellow to purple. Inconspicuous flowers bloom in late spring, followed in late fall by the pyramid-shaped nuts in their prickly oval seed pods. Although edible, beechnuts are not particularly tasty but are popular with wildlife. The purple-leaved trees like full sun; the yellow-leaved prefer partial shade. All species enjoy a well-drained but moist, loamy soil, preferably neutral to alkaline. Shallow roots and dense shade make it difficult for other plants to grow beneath a beech; it is best to leave lower branches to graze the ground, avoiding the need for underplanting. Propagate from seed in fall.

*F. grandifolia*
AMERICAN BEECH

One of the grandest of native North American trees, this beech is similar in most aspects to the more commonly planted European beech. Reaching well over 100 ft (about 30 m) tall in ideal situations, it is a bold tree with a dense foliage canopy and striking silvery-gray bark; it is less likely to have the symmetrical shape of its European cousin. Branches are horizontal, holding slender, elliptical leaves flat to capture the maximum sunlight. It is found growing naturally with various maples in mature forests throughout the eastern US and southern Canada.
ZONES 4–9

Eucalyptus nicholii

Eucalyptus sideroxylon

Fagus grandifolia

*Fagus sylvatica* f. *purpurea*

*Fagus sylvatica*

*Ficus microcarpa* var. *nitida*

*Ficus rubiginosa*

*Firmiana simplex*

*Franklinia alatamaha*

### *F. sylvatica*

EUROPEAN BEECH

Broadly conical in shape with gracefully spreading branches, this relatively slow grower can reach around 130 ft (about 39 m) in height, though usually less. Young foliage is oval, downy and light green, maturing to deep glossy green. Leaves turn golden in the fall. It adapts better than the American beech to urban and mild winter climates. Many named selections are available, varying in habit or in leaf color or shape: 'Atropunicea', the copper or purple beech, has deep purlish leaves; 'Tricolor' has leaves with pink, white and green markings; 'Asplendifolia' has finely cut leaves like a fern; and 'Pendula' has weeping branches.

ZONES 5–9

### *F. sylvatica* f. *purpurea*

COPPER BEECH, PURPLE BEECH

This form has purple-green leaves that turn copper in fall. It requires full sun. True color can be achieved from seed. In Germany it is considered unlucky to plant a copper beech near the house—the tree is thought to attract lightning. It stands clipping and can be used for tall hedges.

ZONES 5–9

## *FICUS*

FIG

This large and extremely diverse genus consists of about 600 evergreen or deciduous tropical trees, shrubs and root climbers. The trees are grown for their foliage or for shade; some species are also grown for their fruit. The spring or fall flowers are insignificant. They prefer a fertile, well-drained soil and sun or partial shade. Propagate from seed in spring, or from cuttings or by layering in summer. Watch out for red spider mite.

### *F. microcarpa* var. *nitida*

syn. *F. retusa*

INDIAN LAUREL FIG

This evergreen fig from India makes an outstanding street and shade tree in warm climates of the West and deep South. Native to the tropics, where it becomes a mammoth tree, under more temperate conditions its size is seldom more than 25–30 ft (about 7.5–9 m) tall and wide. Leaves are smooth, dark green and pointed oval; the trees produce very little litter from either leaves or the tiny, hard fruits. Upright, branching and dense foliage make the tree suitable for shearing and pruning to control size. *F. microcarpa* differs in its weeping branches.

ZONES 10–11

### *F. rubiginosa*

RUSTYLEAF FIG, PORT JACKSON FIG

This large evergreen, native to Australia, grows 30–50 ft (about 9–15 m) tall, its crown spreading almost as wide. The main trunk is buttressed; pendent branches drop aerial roots in moist coastal gardens that become auxiliary trunks. The foliage is shiny deep green on top, downy and rust colored underneath. Inconspicuous flowers form flapped tubes in spring and summer, followed by pairs of globular yellow fruit covered with bumps. This salt-resistant species is best along the coast, though it will tolerate some of California's warm interior valleys.

ZONES 10–11

## *FIRMIANA*
### *simplex*

syn. *F. platanifolia, Sterculia platanifolia*

CHINESE PARASOL TREE

This sturdy tree, originating in Japan and China, grows up to 50 ft (about 15 m). Valued for its shade, it has large leaves with 3 to 5 lobes. Yellowy green flowers appear in spring, clustered along the tree's thin stems. The papery fruit has 5 bracts and the seeds develop along the margins of the pods. This tree prefers a warm-temperate climate with full sun. It likes damp, well-drained soil. Prune if it becomes necessary; propagate from mature seed in spring.

ZONES 9–10

## *FRANKLINIA*
### *alatamaha*

FRANKLIN TREE

This small, showy tree is extinct in its natural range in the moist bottomlands of Georgia, but has proven to be very garden worthy and relatively easily propagated from seed. Deciduous, its leaves are large, dark green and shiny, turning crimson before dropping in fall. Fragrant, pure white flowers with a mass of golden stamens resembling small magnolias appear in late summer. Usually growing with multiple trunks of reddish brown bark, this tree reaches 20 ft (about 6 m) tall and half as wide. Not common, but worth seeking for a moist, rich, woodsy soil in full sun or part shade.

ZONES 6–9

## *FRAXINUS*

ASH

Native to the northern hemisphere, this well-known genus contains about 60 deciduous timber trees and shrubs. They are extremely variable in size, ranging from 50 to 160 ft (about 15–49 m). Dense flower clusters which are insignifi-

*Fraxinus oxycarpa* 'Raywood'

*Fraxinus uhdei*

cant in most species appear in early spring, followed by distinctive, pinnately compound leaves up to 15 in (about 38 cm) long, divided into 3 to 13 leaflets. Decorative drooping clusters of small, winged seeds develop from the flowers. These trees will endure a broad range of temperatures provided they are planted in deep, fertile soil with sufficient moisture and full sun. Propagate from heat-treated seed in fall, or by budding in the summer months.

### *F. americana*

WHITE ASH

A fast-growing native of eastern North America, this species has a tall, straight trunk and an upright oval shape, reaching 50–80 ft (about 15–24 m) in height but much narrower. Dark green leaves may be 15 in (about 38 cm) long; fall color will be gold and purple. Easily grown in average soils with regular water. Several cultivars are now available, selected for fall color or a more compact habit.
ZONES 3–9

### *F. ornus*

FLOWERING ASH, MANNA ASH

Originating in southern Europe and Asia Minor, this spreading tree can grow up to 65 ft (about 20 m) with a rounded crown. The compound foliage comprises 5 to 9 leaflets, which turn from deep green to reddish purple in fall. Fragrant white flowers appear in abundance in early spring, during which time a sweet substance called manna is exuded from fissures in the bark.
ZONES 6–10

*Fraxinus ornus*

*Fraxinus americana*

### *F. oxycarpa* 'Raywood'

**syn. *F. angustifolia* 'Raywood'**

RAYWOOD ASH

This robust and fast-growing tree, a cultivar of Australian origin, is valued for its fall leaves and attractive shape. The tree grows to 30–50 ft (about 9–15 m), developing a stocky trunk and rounded crown. The deeply lobed foliage is made up of 7 to 9 narrow leaflets which turn from shiny deep green to claret red in fall.
ZONES 6–10

### *F. pennsylvanica*

GREEN ASH

Another eastern American native, this tall, fast-growing tree is more tolerant of the heat, drought and winds of the plains than the white ash. Though naturally weedy because of its many seeds, the green ash is now available as clonally propagated male trees incapable of producing seeds and with a reliable shape and fall color. Look for 'Marshall's Seedless' and 'Summit'. In the fall the foliage turns a lovely yellow color.
ZONES 2–9

### *F. uhdei*

EVERGREEN ASH, SHAMEL ASH

This tough species is a native of Mexico and is well adapted to the Western states. Its glossy leaves are evergreen in mild winters but are deciduous where winter temperatures drop much below freezing. Fast growing at first to around 30 ft (about 9 m), then slower growth to 60 ft (about 18 m) as the trees broaden in shape. A good tree for coastal and interior California and

*Fraxinus pennsylvanica*

also for the low deserts of the Southwest.
ZONES 8–10

## GEIJERA
### *parviflora*

AUSTRALIAN WILLOW, WILGA

This evergreen, native to Australia and New Caledonia, is valued for its attractive shape and aromatic hardwood. Small and slender, with pendent branches and a spreading crown, it quickly reaches 9–30 ft (about 2.7–6 m). Its thick, lanceolate, gray-green leaves are up to 6 in (about 15 cm) long. Open clusters of creamy white flowers cover the tree in spring. Glossy black seeds follow. Propagate from seed in fall. This citrus relative enjoys full sun and grows well in dry areas.
ZONES 9–11

## GINKGO
### *biloba*

GINKGO, MAIDENHAIR TREE

The sole member of its genus, this important deciduous conifer has been found in fossils that are over 200 million years old. Native apparently to Europe, Asia, Australia and America, it is thought to be extinct now in the wild. Fortunately, it is widely cultivated. Valued for its rich fall foliage and timber, it grows up to 130 ft (about 39 m). The angular branches develop bright green, fan-shaped leaves, similar to the maidenhair fern but much larger, which turn deep golden yellow in fall. Little yellow flowers sprinkle the mature trees in spring, followed on female trees by orange-yellow fruits about the size of a small plum. This enduring tree survives both arid and wet climates and withstands urban pollution. It needs deep, fertile soil and should be propagated from seed or graft.

*Ginkgo biloba*

*Gleditsia triacanthos* var. *inermis*

Ginkgos are widely cultivated in China, where their edible seeds are considered a delicacy.
ZONES 4–10

## GLEDITSIA
### *triacanthos* var. *inermis*

THORNLESS HONEY LOCUST

This deciduous North American species grows up to 50 ft (about 15 m) and develops a broad crown. It is valued for its attractive fern-like foliage, composed of up to 32 leaflets. Insignificant, pea-like flowers appear in green, downy clusters. In the species, these are followed by large, shiny, red-ochre seed pods, slightly curved and around 18 in (about 45 cm) long; the pods are filled with a sweet pulp. The pods are very messy, and the thorns on the species are vicious. It is best to plant only the thornless cultivars, most of which are also seedless. 'Sunburst' is popular for its golden-yellow new foliage, best used against dark green foliage; 'Skyline', 'Shademaster', 'Moraine' and 'Imperial' are excellent green-leafed selections. This drought-resistant tree does best in a rich, well-drained soil in full sun. Propagate by budding.
ZONES 4–9

Hoheria populnea

Halesia carolina

Jacaranda mimosifolia

Grevillea robusta

*Ilex opaca*

## *GREVILLEA*
*robusta*

SILK OAK, SILKY OAK

Native to Australia, this cone-shaped, evergreen tree is the tallest of its large genus. It quickly reaches 50–60 ft (about 15–18 m). It is admired for its attractive flowers, foliage and timber. The pointed, bipinnately lobed leaves are dark green on top and silvery beneath. In late spring to early summer the tree is ablaze with brilliant orange, toothbrush-like flowers which are followed by small, woody capsules filled with winged seeds. It likes full sun or partial shade and can be propagated very easily from seed. Young specimens are used as indoor container plants.

ZONES 9–10

## *HALESIA*
*carolina*

syn. *H. tetraptera*

CAROLINA SILVER-BELL

A delightful, deciduous tree, native to the southeastern states, this species is grown for its bell-like, white flowers in early spring. The simple leaves barely change before dropping in fall, but the flaking bark and seed pods provide interest during the winter. Ultimately a tree of 30–50 ft (about 9–15 m) in height, it is fairly slow growing and is usually multi-stemmed. Excellent along the margin of a woodland, it favors a rich, woodsy soil, some shade and regular water.

ZONES 5–9

## *HOHERIA*
*populnea*

NEW ZEALAND LACEBARK

Native to New Zealand this slender, fast-growing evergreen reaches 24–50 ft (about 7–15 m) and is one of only five in its genus. The tree is valued for its decorative flowers, foliage and bark, which is papery, pale brown and white, shedding in patches. Its glossy, deep green leaves are elliptical and deeply toothed. Thick white clusters of lightly scented, star-shaped flowers appear in late summer to early fall. Plant in rich, porous soil with full sun or partial shade and water regularly. Propagate from cuttings in summer, seed in fall.

ZONES 8–10

## *HYMENOSPORUM*
*flavum*

SWEETSHADE

The only species of its genus, this Australian native is valued for its attractive flowers. Up to 55 ft (about 17 m) tall, it has an erect, columnar shape, spreading to triangular in maturity. The elliptical foliage is glossy deep green on sparse limbs with irregular, downturned branches. Fragrant, long-tubed flowers appear in early summer, first creamy white then golden-yellow, and are followed by odd, star-shaped capsules filled with papery seeds. This evergreen prefers a warm climate with full sun and fertile, well-drained, acidic soil. Propagate from seed in fall, cuttings in late summer.

ZONES 10–11

## *ILEX*
*opaca*

AMERICAN HOLLY

This native of deciduous woodlands of the eastern US gives winter interest with its evergreen foliage and red berries. It has a conical shape and grows slowly to a height of 50 ft (about 15 m), usually less in gardens. The leaves are sharply spined and dull green; fruits are less plentiful than on *I. aquifolium*. Excellent for use in shade gardens where the foliage can be protected from the sun and drying winds of winter. It prefers a moist, slightly acidic, woodsy soil and regular water. Various cultivars are available, both shrubby and tree like; look for 'Merry Christmas' and 'Christmas Carol' for dependable fruiting. 'Canary' has yellow fruit.

ZONES 5–10

## *JACARANDA*
*mimosifolia*

syn. *J. acutifolia, J. ovalifolia*

JACARANDA

Native to the high plains of Brazil, this fast grower is valued for its beautiful flowers, foliage and timber. It develops a broad, rounded crown and grows up to 40 ft (about 12 m) tall and wide. Vivid green, fern-like foliage is bipinnate, with 12 or more leaflets. Depending on climate, the leaves may be shed in winter or early spring before the flowers appear. These are very attractive, mauve-blue terminal clusters of tubular blossoms. Flat, leathery seed pods follow. Preferring dry and temperate climates, the juvenile tree needs protection from frosts. Plant in rich, porous soil with full sun and do not over-water; prune potted specimens in late winter. Propagate from seed in spring.

ZONES 9–11

## *JUGLANS*
*nigra*

BLACK WALNUT

This species from eastern North America is valued for its foliage, timber and edible nuts. It grows to some 95 ft (about 29 m) with an open crown and shiny green foliage comprising 15 to 25 leaflets each 4 in (about 10 cm) long. These are followed by greenish yellow male catkins, inconspicuous female flow-

ers and, finally, edible nuts. Plant in deep, rich, porous soil with full sun. Propagate from seed in fall. In Latin *Juglans* means "Jupiter's acorn", so highly did the Romans value the fruit of the walnut.
ZONES 4–9

## *JUNIPERUS*

JUNIPER

This northern hemisphere genus contains over 50 species of slow-growing conifers of extremely diverse color and habit, ranging in height from 27 to 80 ft (about 8–24 m). Adult foliage comprises short, scale-like leaves. Species are hardy, drought resistant, tolerant of most well-drained soils and either low or high pH and are able to survive extremes in temperature. They also prefer full sun and dry, sandy soil. Trees should be pruned regularly; as with most conifers, new growth will not sprout from brown wood. Propagate from seed or cuttings, or by grafting. Watch for aphids and leafrollers. The blue, berry-like fruit is used to flavor gin.

### *J. communis*

COMMON JUNIPER

This shrub or tree reaches a height of 9 to 37 ft (about 2.7–10.5 m) and is slim or cone shaped. It has brownish red bark and fragrant, yellowish green, needle-like foliage borne in groups of three. The globular fruit are blue-black, turning bluish green before finally maturing to black. These fruit are used for flavoring in cooking. The most dependably narrow cultivar is 'Stricta' ('Hibernica'), commonly known as the Irish juniper.
ZONES 2–10

### *J. scopulorum*

ROCKY MOUNTAIN JUNIPER

A shrub or small tree, this species is a characteristic conifer of the mountains of western North America, often seen in association with pinyon trees. Broadly conical in form to 40 ft (about 12 m) in height, they are often shaped by the wind; various cultivars are available with more compact habits. Aromatic, blue-green needles hold their color well during the winter. Best in their mountainous range with excellent drainage, full sun and no more water than nature provides.
ZONES 4–9

### *J. virginiana*

EASTERN RED CEDAR

Originating in eastern North America, this conifer is valued for its shade and timber. Triangular at first, the tree spreads in maturity and grows to 50–60 ft (about 15–18 m). The gray, needle-like foliage is prickly when young. Blue-black cones bear three seeds. The species is adaptable to moist or dry sites, but has poor winter color. 'Skyrocket' is a good blue-green selection with a very narrow form.
ZONES 2–10

## *KOELREUTERIA*
### *paniculata*

GOLDEN-RAIN TREE

This deciduous Asian native has a broad convex crown and grows quickly to 30–50 ft (about 9–15 m) tall. Its feathery, bipinnate foliage grows up to 18 in (about 45 cm) long and turns from green to deep golden yellow in fall, particularly in cooler climates. Large, decorative clusters of golden yellow flowers develop in summer, followed by pinkish brown seed pods swollen with black seeds. This species survives arid inland conditions and enjoys full sun and strong alkaline soil. Propagate from seed in spring; root cuttings in winter. The flowers are used in Chinese medicine.
ZONES 5–10

## *LABURNUM*
### x *watereri* 'Vossii'

GOLDEN CHAIN TREE

Native to Europe and parts of Asia Minor, this deciduous hybrid is valued for its beautiful golden chains of flowers. Elegant and erect, it grows 9–30 ft (about 2.7–9 m) tall and takes on a spreading shape in maturity. The compound foliage has three oval leaflets, shiny dark green on top and soft and downy underneath. Pendent, pea-like flowers develop in golden clusters on long stems in late spring. A few legume-like pods follow, some containing the highly poisonous seeds. This tree likes full sun and regular moisture and will tolerate most soil types but will not survive in hot climates or waterlogged soil. It is easily trained as an espalier or over an arbor. Propagate by budding in summer; species are propagated by seed in fall. Do not plant where animals graze, as all parts of this species are toxic.
ZONES 6–9

*Juniperus virginiana*

*Koelreuteria paniculata*

*Laburnum* x *watereri* 'Vossii'

*Juglans nigra*

*Juniperus communis*

Lagunaria patersonii

Maclura pomifera

Larix decidua

Liriodendron tulipifera

Ligustrum lucidum

Liquidambar styraciflua

## LAGUNARIA
*patersonii*

PRIMROSE TREE, COW ITCH TREE

Native to Australia's Lord Howe Island and Norfolk Island, this attractive evergreen is the only species of its genus. Growing to 50 ft (about 15 m), it is valued for its attractive, regular, triangular shape and for its timber and flowers. Its leathery, elliptical leaves are gray with a whitish underside. Hibiscus-like, $1\frac{1}{2}$ in (about 3 cm) wide, pink flowers appear in summer followed by large, inedible fruit. This tree prefers warm climates and is moderately drought tolerant. It is also salt resistant and enjoys coastal locations with sandy soil. It propagates simply from seed and tolerates pruning. The genus was named after the sixteenth-century botanist Andres Laguna.

ZONES 9–11

## LARIX
*decidua*

EUROPEAN LARCH

Native to northern Europe, this enduring, deciduous conifer has an attractive symmetrical, conical shape, opening out in later years. It can reach enormous heights (but can be much less in cultivation), and develops tiered, drooping branches. These are covered in pale green, needle-like foliage in spring, turning to golden brown in fall. Little upright cones with round scales become visible in winter, when all the limbs are bare. This cold-climate tree requires good rainfall, well-drained soil and full sun. It is prized by shipbuilders and is also a valuable source of turpentine.

ZONES 4–8

## LIGUSTRUM
*lucidum*

GLOSSY PRIVET

This evergreen privet from Japan makes a sturdy tree in warmer regions of the US. Its glossy leaves are produced on a round-headed tree, 30 ft (about 9 m) tall and as wide. Large panicles of tiny white flowers appear in mid-summer, their distinctive fragrance considered offensive by some. Deep blue-black berries follow and remain on the tree through fall or until the birds eat them. Tolerant of heat and drought, these trees want full sun to flower well, and appreciate an occasional soaking during the summer. Shallow roots create problems for pavements and for other plants growing beneath them.

ZONES 8–10

## LIQUIDAMBAR
*styraciflua*

SWEET GUM

This deciduous native of North and Central America has an erect, conical shape that may spread in maturity. It grows quickly: up to 122 ft (about 37 m), depending on conditions. The lustrous foliage, with 5 or 7 lobes, is 4–6 in (about 10–15 cm) wide. Young leaves are pale green, maturing to deep green and turning vivid red-purple and orange-yellow in fall. The branches develop corky ridges or "wings," most visible in winter. Plant in rich, deep, porous soil in full sun or part shade. Propagate from seed in fall or from buds in spring. This tree survives hot weather with regular watering. Select seedling trees in fall as color is very variable.

ZONES 6–10

## LIRIODENDRON
*tulipifera*

TULIP TREE, TULIP POPLAR, YELLOW POPLAR

This deciduous North American native is valued for its flowers and rich yellow fall foliage. The tree grows at moderate speed to heights of 50–100 ft (about 15–30 m), in a symmetrical pyramid; branches often do not start until halfway up. Distinctive, four-lobed leaves have a squarish shape. In late spring the tree bears green and orange tulip-like flowers at the tips of each branch. These are followed by conical seed heads containing winged seeds. It enjoys full sun and a neutral to acid soil, and does best with generous watering. It may be transplanted up to a good size and is propagated from seed in fall, budding in summer. The timber, although not very durable, is much used in the US.

ZONES 5–10

## MACLURA
*pomifera*

OSAGE ORANGE

Originating in south-central North America, this tree is valued for its tough constitution and vigorous growth in difficult situations, though many trees are far more attractive. It grows quickly to 65 ft (about 20 m) with an open, uneven crown and arching branches. Elliptical, deep green leaves turn yellow in fall. Small clusters of yellow-green flowers appear in summer followed on female trees by 4 in (about 10 cm) diamater, lumpy, yellow-green, inedible fruits. Suitable for hedges, the species requires full sun and tolerates heat, drought and neglect. Easily rooted from cuttings, fence posts made of the durable wood often root and grow into trees. The wood was once used to make bows.

ZONES 5–9

## MAGNOLIA

MAGNOLIA

This genus comprises two groups: deciduous species, mostly native to China and Japan, and evergreen species found predominantly in eastern North America and Central America. All are valued for their beautiful, often large and fragrant flowers. The leaves vary from glossy green to fuzzy on top, and from smooth to brown and furry beneath. The perfumed flowers with waxy

*Magnolia* x *soulangiana*

*Magnolia virginiana*

*Malus floribunda*

*Magnolia grandiflora*

petals and densely packed stamens bloom on deciduous trees in spring, often before the leaves appear, and on evergreen species in late spring or summer. Cone-like fruits follow, bearing brightly colored seeds. They prefer full sun or partial shade and rich, slightly acid, well-drained soil. Only *M. grandiflora* can be considered drought tolerant; others demand regular watering. Transplant with care: the roots are extremely fragile. Propagate from cuttings in summer or seed in fall, and graft cultivars in winter. The genus was named after eighteenth-century botanist Pierre Magnol

### *M. campbellii*

This deciduous Chinese native has an erect appearance when immature, broadening out later. It grows quickly to around 18–50 ft (about 5.5–15 m) tall. Scattered branches bear pointed, elliptical leaves up to 12 in (about 30 cm) long, powdery underneath. This species takes 15 to 20 years to flower. The big, scented blooms, light pink inside and darker pink outside, appear from the end of winter to mid-spring. It prefers a cool-temperate climate and open space.

ZONES 8–10

### *M. denudata*

**syn. *M. heptapeta***

YULAN

Native to China, this deciduous, spreading tree or tall shrub grows up to 30 ft (about 9 m). It has dark bark and egg-shaped leaves with a hairy underside. Naked branches bear scented, snow-white, tulip-like flowers in early spring. These are followed by rectangular cones containing orange seeds. It prefers temperate climates.

ZONES 6–10

### *M. grandiflora*

SOUTHERN MAGNOLIA, BULL BAY

This evergreen species from southeastern North America varies broadly in size and habit: 18–95 ft (about 5.5–29 m) high, it may be compact and rounded or spreading and conical. It has thick, leathery leaves, mid- to dark green above, brown and fuzzy beneath. Cup-

*Magnolia denudata*

shaped white blooms with a strong citrus scent appear from mid-summer to early fall, followed by red-brown cones. This species prefers climates with warm summers; though native to extremely moist soils, it is surprisingly drought tolerant once established.

ZONES 7–10

### *M.* x *soulangiana*

SAUCER MAGNOLIA

This deciduous tree develops slowly, reaching 9–24 ft (about 2.7–7 m), frequently growing multiple trunks and a rounded crown. Tulip-like blooms precede the foliage in early spring, even on young plants. The flower's interior varies from snow white to light pink; the exterior is a deeper pink. The dull green foliage is up to 6 in (about 15 cm) long. This species prefers a warm climate and requires shelter from hot winds. There are several cultivars, blooms ranging in color from pure white to deep red. This hybrid was bred in Paris in 1820 by Étienne Soulange-Bodin from *M. heptapeta* and *M. liliflora*.

ZONES 5–10

### *M. virginiana*

SWEET BAY

This semi-evergreen woodland native of eastern North America has flowers that have an intense lemony fragrance. The plants vary from large, deciduous shrubs in New England to evergreen trees of 60 ft (about 18 m) in the South. Flowers are creamy white and are produced in early summer with a few appearing throughout the summer. More tolerant of wet soils than other mag-

*Magnolia campbellii*

nolias, this species will grow in either sun or shade. Select nursery plants that have been propagated from local wild forms to be sure of adaptability.

ZONES 5–10

## *MALUS*

CRABAPPLE, APPLE

Native to the northern hemisphere, this diverse genus contains 25 deciduous shrubs and trees valued for their flowers, foliage and fruit. They grow 10–40 ft (about 3–12 m) tall with spreading, round crowns. Foliage ranges from bronze, hairy and wide lobed to deep green, linear and neat, while the spring blossom varies in color from deep rosy-purple to pure white. The acidic fruit also varies widely, from edible kinds that can be eaten cooked to purely ornamental crabapples. They like full sun and a cold winter climate to flower well; they tolerate any soil that is not too wet. Prune in winter to encourage symmetry; propagate by budding in summer or grafting in winter. Watch for aphids and fireblight. The cultivars recommended here are generally resistant to other diseases such as apple scab, powdery mildew and rust.

### *M.* 'Adams'

This medium-sized crabapple has reddish pink flowers in abundance, followed by $^1/_2$ in (about 1 cm) diameter red fruit. Its habit is upright and rounded, reaching 20 ft (about 6 m) in height. Excellent disease resistance.

ZONES 4–9

*Malus* 'Gorgeous'

### *M.* 'Calloway'

This is a superb cultivar of the crabapple for the deep South, growing to 25 ft (about 7.5 m) high with a rounded form. Flowers are pure white, appearing relatively late in spring. Fruits are 1 in (about 2.5 cm) in diameter and are reddish purple. Excellent disease resistance.

ZONES 5–10

### *M. floribunda*

JAPANESE FLOWERING CRABAPPLE

This expansive, thick-crowned tree grows to 30 ft (about 9 m). Its early spring buds are crimson red, blooming into light pink blossoms. The variable foliage is egg shaped to rectangular, some types with heavily saw-toothed edges and 3 to 5 lobes. Small, reddish yellow, scented crabapples appear in fall. The oldest of the decorative crabapples, this tree is thought to originate in Japan and is the parent of many hybrids.

ZONES 4–10

### *M.* 'Gorgeous'

Bred in New Zealand, this cultivar is valued for its decorative fruit, which is also used to make jellies and preserves. A small tree of only 6–12 ft (about 1.8–3.5 m), it has elliptical green leaves 5 in (about 12 cm) long. Pink buds appear in spring, opening into snow white blossoms. Between fall and winter the branches become laden with an abundance of little crabapples which mature from green-red to deep red. This selection is well adapted to the mild winter climates of the West Coast.

ZONES 6–10

*Malus hupehensis*

*Maytenus boaria*

*Melia azedarach*

*Melaleuca quinquenervia*

*Metrosideros excelsa*

### *M. hupehensis*
**syn. *M. theifera***
HUPEH CRAB

A native of China and Japan, this vigorous tree can grow to 30 ft (about 9 m). Its large, dark green, oval leaves are sharply toothed, and in spring single pink buds open to large white flowers. The fruit, yellow tinged with red, appear in early fall.

ZONES 4–10

## *MAYTENUS*
### *boaria*
MAYTEN

Originating in Chile, this handsome, willow-like evergreen grows 20–50 ft (about 6–15 m) tall and nearly as wide. Lustrous, deep green foliage growing on slender stalks is lance shaped and slightly lobed. Inconspicuous starry flowers bloom in late spring. A slow grower, this is perfect for small to medium gardens. Plant in full sun. Propagate from cuttings in summer, suckers in fall and spring. Mayten roots are shallow and may produce many suckers if they are damaged through cultivation.

ZONES 8–10

## *MELALEUCA*
### *quinquenervia*
CAJEPUT TREE

Native to Australia, New Caledonia and New Guinea, this vigorous evergreen reaches 30–50 ft (about 9–15 m). It is valued for its attractive orange-brown, tan and white bark. Small, white to pink, bottlebrush-like flower clusters appear in summer and fall. This species is able to survive in saturated soil. Plant in full sun and propagate from seed in spring, cuttings in summer. A related species, *M. leucadendron,* is a dreadful pest in the Florida Everglades.

ZONES 9–11

## *MELIA*
### *azedarach*
CHINABERRY

This expansive Asian native, growing 18–37 ft (about 5.5–10.5 m)

*Michelia doltsopa*

tall, is valued for its foliage, flowers, fruit and timber. Deep green, bipinnate leaves have numerous leaflets. Scented, star-shaped flowers bloom in spring in bluish purple clusters, resembling lilacs. The green fruit matures to yellow-orange in fall. This species flourishes in warm coastal areas, tolerates arid conditions and may be planted in any reasonable soil if given full sun. Propagate from seed in fall. Check for white cedar moth caterpillars in late summer to fall. Its fine timber is used to make furniture and its fruit, although poisonous to both animals and humans, is used to make medicines.

ZONES 7–11

## *METROSIDEROS*
### *excelsa*
NEW ZEALAND CHRISTMAS TREE

This tough New Zealand evergreen grows to 18–50 ft (about 5.5–15 m). Slow growing and compact when immature, it becomes fast growing and spreading in adult life, occasionally dropping aerial roots. The elliptical leaves are a lustrous deep green with a white, downy underside. In early summer the attractive flowers appear with erect whorls of dense, wiry, deep red stamens. This species will grow in full sun or light shade, and makes an excellent hedge or windbreak, especially along the western and Florida sea coasts. No pruning is necessary to produce a dense crown. Propagate from seed in spring, cuttings in summer. In its native country this tree flowers around Christmas time, explaining its common name.

ZONES 10–11

## *MICHELIA*
### *doltsopa*

Originating in Tibet and West China, this upright evergreen grows rapidly up to 50 ft (about 15 m). The attractive oval leaves are deep green, lighter underneath and up to 6 in (about 15 cm) long. In late winter to early spring, white to yellowish flowers appear in the leaf axils. Resembling the magnolia (to which this genus is related), they

Nothofagus solandri

Nothofagus obliqua

have 12 petals and a strong, cloying perfume. Plant in fertile, moist but well-drained soil with full sun or partial shade. Propagate from seed in fall or spring or from cuttings in summer.
ZONES 9–10

## *MORUS*
### *alba*

WHITE MULBERRY

This tough, deciduous tree is best known as the food source for the silkworms of China. In North America it is used primarily as a shade tree and as a source of tasty fruits, though many other trees are more attractive and less messy in the landscape. In hot areas of the West and South, however, this species can be useful as a shade tree since it grows in almost any soil (even gravel) and tolerates drought. Its large leaves barely turn color before falling in fall, and its rapid growth results in weak branches. For tough situations it is a serviceable tree. Fruitless cultivars, such as 'Fruitless' and 'Stribling', avoid the mess of fallen fruit on pavements. Ultimately 40–50 ft (about 12–15 m) tall and 30–40 ft (about 9–12 m) wide.
ZONES 4–10

## *NOTHOFAGUS*

SOUTHERN BEECH

Native to the southern hemisphere, this diverse genus has over 25 deciduous and evergreen species, including some extremely valuable timber trees. Dome shaped, they range from short and shrubby to tall and columnar, reaching up to 220 ft (about 67 m). The leaves, resembling those of their close relative the northern beech, are egg shaped to rectangular with distinctly wavy or toothed margins and are downy when young. Insignificant flowers develop in late spring, followed by seed pods containing three triangular beechnuts. These trees grow in cold-temperate to subtropical climates. They like full sun or partial shade and deep, rich, neutral to acid soil that is moist but porous. Protect from strong winds; propagate from seed in fall.

Nyssa sylvatica

### *N. obliqua*

ROBLÉ BEECH

This graceful, deciduous, Chilean native grows fast to 65 ft (about 20 m). It has a wide, spreading crown, pendent branches and serrated leaves that turn from deep green to orange-red in fall. It needs full sun and well-drained soil.
ZONES 8–10

### *N. solandri*

BLACK BEECH

This rapidly growing species is native to New Zealand and is valued for its appearance and timber. Up to 80 ft (about 24 m) tall, it has an erect habit with a rounded crown. The rectangular to oval leaves have slightly furled margins. Green individual blooms are followed by typical fruit.
ZONES 8–10

## *NYSSA*
### *sylvatica*

SOUR GUM, TUPELO, BLACK GUM

Native to eastern North America, this striking deciduous species is valued for its fall foliage, its timber and honey. Its shape is a wide-based pyramid, around 55 ft (about 17 m) high. Large shiny leaves are almost diamond shaped and deep green, turning vivid red and yellow in fall, though sometimes only yellow when planted away from its natural range. Little clusters of flowers, while inconspicuous, contribute to some of the finest honey in the world. Deep blue fruits in fall and a distinct, horizontal branching habit add to its charm. This tree is widely adaptable, growing naturally on the New England coast and along streams and swamps in the Midwest; it also does well in drier sites in California and the deep South. It prefers full sun and a moist, slightly acid soil. It resents transplanting.
ZONES 4–10

Oxydendrum arboreum

## *OLNEYA*
### *tesota*

DESERT IRONWOOD

A tough evergreen from the deserts of southwestern North America,the ironweed gets its name from its very heavy heartwood. Reaching 25–30 ft (about 7.5–9 m) tall with a rounded canopy, dense branching and compound leaves, it is at its best in early summer when covered with pinkish lavender blossoms like $^1/_2$ in (about 1 cm) pea flowers. Old leaves drop shortly after flowering, but are quickly replaced with a new crop. Best with occasional deep watering during the summer in a sunny situation with well-drained soil.
ZONES 9–10

## *OXYDENDRUM*
### *arboreum*

SOURWOOD

One of eastern North America's most attractive native flowering trees, the sourwood produces its white, lily-of-the-valley-like flowers in late summer in drooping panicles at the tips of nearly every branch. The attractively whorled, glossy green leaves turn a brilliant orange and scarlet in fall. An upright tree or large shrub, growing to 30 ft (about 9 m) or more in height but to only 15 ft (about 4.5 m) in width. Give it a position in full sun or light shade at the edge of a woodland, plus rich, deep, acid loam and regular water. Mulch it well.
ZONES 5–9

Morus alba

## PARKINSONIA
*aculeata*

JERUSALEM THORN, MEXICAN PALO VERDE

Native to tropical America, this small, spreading tree has a dome-shaped crown and grows 15–30 ft (about 4.5–9 m) tall and wide. Its long, narrow, bipinnate leaves have tiny oval leaflets and produce a filtered shade. In spring, pendent clusters of scented, yellow flowers with 5 petals appear, followed by slender seed pods. This tree prefers subtropical or desert climates, a rich, porous soil, full sun and little water once established. Prune minimally. It propagates easily from seed in spring; it can become weedy in a watered garden.

ZONES 9–10

## PARROTIA
*persica*

PERSIAN PARROTIA

Originating in Iran, this compact, deciduous species is valued for its decorative fall foliage. It grows to some 30 ft (about 9 m), and often has pendent limbs. Upright flower clusters of wiry crimson stamens appear on leafless branches in early spring, followed by glossy, egg-shaped foliage. The leaves have undulating margins and turn vivid red, yellow and orange in fall. The tree is fully hardy, though frosts may damage buds, and it prefers a cool climate. Plant in a protected location in deep, rich soil; it withstands lime but shows the best leaf colors in a neutral to acid soil. Propagate from seed in fall, cuttings in summer.

ZONES 5–10

## PAULOWNIA
*tomentosa*

syn. *P. imperialis*

EMPRESS TREE

This deciduous Chinese species is valued for its beautiful flowers and large leaves. Pyramidal in shape, it quickly reaches 40–50 ft (about 12–15 m). The roughly heart-shaped leaves are 12 in (about 30 cm) long and almost as wide, paired and somtimes divided into three lobes. The elegant flowers, similar to foxgloves, develop in dense, erect clusters at the stem tips before the leaves appear in early spring; the flowers are lilac and are strongly scented. Plant in rich, porous soil and full sun. Prune hard in spring after flowering to control size and encourage larger leaves. The tree can be cut to the ground annually to develop branches around 10 ft (about 3 m) tall with huge leaves, but flowers will be sacrificed. With such quick growth the wood of this tree will always be brittle; unfortunately leaves and flowers create plenty of litter.

ZONES 5–10

## PHELLODENDRON
*amurense*

AMUR CORK TREE

This deciduous Asian native grows to 37 ft (about 10.5 m), spreading widely. Its shiny, dark green foliage has a spicy aroma and turns yellow in fall. Small green flowers appear, male and female on separate trees, followed by small, black, spherical fruit. This tough tree likes a cold winter and a hot summer. Plant in full sun in rich, porous soil. Water regularly and apply a mulch during hot weather. Propagate from cuttings in summer, seed in fall and root cuttings in late winter. Rather than referring to the production of cork, the common name describes the older tree's corky bark.

ZONES 4–8

## PICEA

SPRUCE

These tall, stately conifers are trees of the cold north and the mountains of Asia, America and Europe. They usually have a very symmetrical shape, with horizontal to drooping branches. Their needles are roughly square in cross-section and are sharply pointed. Cones are pendent and do not shatter when ripe like the true firs *(Abies)*. These trees do well across the northern states and in the mountains, but not in the heat and humidity of the Southeast or the heat and drought of the Southwest. Propagate from seed in fall, or by grafting selected forms. Little pruning is necessary. All want full sun and a well-drained, neutral to acidic soil. They may be bothered by aphids and mites.

### *P. abies*

NORWAY SPRUCE

Commonly planted in the Northeast, this tall, dark green conifer has gracefully pendent branchlets festooned in season with long, slender cones. It makes a narrow cone in the landscape, up to 100 ft (about 30 m) or more in height but only 30–40 ft (about 9–12 m) wide at the base. Dense shade makes gardening difficult beneath. Makes a good windbreak, but is too large for small gardens. Plant in full sun in well-drained soil. A number of dwarf cultivars are available.

ZONES 3–7

### *P. omorika*

SIBERIAN SPRUCE

Considered the finest of the spruces, this has a tall but very narrow cone shape, sometimes only 15 ft (about 4.5 m) wide on a 60 ft (about 18 m) tree; the ultimate height may be 90 ft (about 27 m). Main branches arch upward, with gracefully pendent branchlets. It is one of the few spruces to have flat needles; white stripes on the undersides give life to the branches as they blow in the wind. Cones are only 2 in (about 5 cm) long. This is more likely to tolerate the heat and humidity of the South than other spruces.

ZONES 4–8

*Phellodendron amurense*

*Parkinsonia aculeata*

*Picea abies*

*Parrotia persica*

*Paulownia tomentosa*

*Picea omorika*

Pinus nigra

Picea pungens 'Koster'

Pinus palustris

Pinus canariensis

Pinus pinea

Pinus bungeana

Pinus patula

### *P. pungens*

COLORADO SPRUCE

This North American evergreen tree's glaucous foliage makes it one of the most attractive of all conifers. The leaves are stiff and pointed, and vary from silvery blue to deep green. Spiraled branches support tubular, scaled cones, 4 in (about 10 cm) long. It reaches 100 ft (about 30 m) or more in height in the wild, but usually under 60 ft (18 m) in cultivation. Numerous cultivars have been selected for improved or enhanced foliage color. 'Koster' is the most readily available with silvery blue needles aging to dark green; growth is sometimes irregular. Some cultivars have been selected for compact habit such as 'Fat Albert', with blue leaves but reaching only 10 ft (about 3 m) tall in ten years.

ZONES 2–7

## PINUS

PINE

This northern hemisphere genus comprises 80 variable evergreen conifers, between 18 and 190 ft (about 5.5–58 m) high. Many species are conical when immature, their crowns expanding in later life. The leaves, cylindrical needles up to 18 in (about 45 cm) long, are erect when young and develop in bundles of two, three or five. Upright, yellow-red male catkins and female flowers appear on the same tree. The latter develop into scaled, seed-bearing cones, borne singly or in bunches depending upon type. Preferred habitats range from cold high altitudes to subtropical coasts, some hardy species growing in difficult positions such as windswept cliffs. All enjoy full sun. Prune young trees' candle-like new growth if necessary to control shape; propagate from seed or by grafting. Prone to leafroller caterpillars. Pines are grown for their softwood, oil and resin.

### *P. bungeana*

LACEBARK PINE

One of the few pines grown for its bark, this species is usually seen with multiple trunks and branches pruned up to expose the sycamore-like flaking bark. Generally 50–70 ft (about 15–21 m) in height with a spread of half that. The needles are 2–3 in (about 5–7.5 cm) long in bundles of three and are bright green. Cones are only $2^1/_2$ in (about 6 cm) long. Cold tolerant, yet well adapted to the drought of the Western states.

ZONES 5–9

### *P. canariensis*

CANARY ISLAND PINE

This elegant tree, native to the Canary Islands, is valued for its bark, shade and pyramidal appearance. It grows quickly to 50–75 ft (about 15–23 m) and has tan-colored bark with black grooves. Arching branchlets are covered with long, narrow needles that mature from bluish green to a pale green. The woody cones are brown, up to 10 in (about 25 cm) long. This species prefers mild winter regions of the West Coast, and requires little water once established.

ZONES 8–10

### *P. nigra*

AUSTRIAN BLACK PINE

This slow-growing conifer has dark green needles in bundles of two, each 4–6 in (about 10–15 cm) long. Cones are small. Very hardy and well adapted to the cold northern states and Canada. Ultimate height is 40–60 ft (about 12–18 m).

ZONES 4–8

### *P. palustris*

LONGLEAF PINE

This tall, slender pine is a dominant tree of pine forests of southeastern North America, distinctive for its 12 in (about 30 cm) long needles in bundles of three. Eventually 80 ft (about 24 m) in height, its growth is spurred in the wild by fire. Common in expanding suburban developments in the Southeast. Cones are nearly 10 in (about 25 cm) long.

ZONES 7–10

### *P. patula*

JELECOTE PINE

This elegant Mexican native has a broad, pyramidal shape, sometimes with pendent branches.It grows rapidly to 50–65 ft (about 15–20 m) tall. Its foliage consists of lustrous, yellowish green, 12 in (about 30 cm) long needles hanging in bundles of three. The fruit develops in spiraled clusters of two to five egg-shaped cones. Adaptable to climates along the West Coast and the Southeast.

ZONES 9–11

### *P. pinea*

ITALIAN STONE PINE

This attractive species grows 40–80 ft (about 12–24 m) tall. The paired,

Pinus strobus

Pinus radiata

rigid needles are deep green, or blue-green when immature. The large, globular cones mature to lustrous brown and produce edible, nut-like seeds. It is prone to leafroller caterpillars.
ZONES 8–10

### *P. ponderosa*
PONDEROSA PINE, WESTERN YELLOW PINE

Native to the mountains of western North America, this is a tall pine (to 150 ft/45 m in the wild) best suited to large gardens within its natural range. Needles are 4–10 in (about 10–25 cm) long in bundles of three, usually with a yellowish green color. Cones are 3–5 in (about 7.5–12 cm) long and light brown. Prune the new growth if necessary to control shape. Propagate from seed.
ZONES 6–10

### *P. radiata*
MONTEREY PINE

The fastest growing pine, this species is commonly grown for its timber as well as its shelter and shade. It grows 80 ft (about 24 m) or more. Silky green needles, grouped in threes, grow up to 6 in (about 15 cm) long. Its long-lasting cones are 4–6 in (about 10–15 cm) long and lopsided, held tightly on the branch. Plant in a position in full sun.
ZONES 9–10

### *P. strobus*
EASTERN WHITE PINE

An attractive pine native to northeastern North America known for its soft, bluish green needles, 2–4 in (about 5–10 cm) long in clusters of five. Cones are 6–8 in (about 15–20 cm) long, slender and pendent. Mature trees have an irregular, flat-topped shape.
ZONES 4–8

### *P. sylvestris*
SCOTS PINE

One of the most popular of Christmas trees, this species also makes a picturesque landscape specimen with its orangish bark. Needles are 2–4 in (about 5–10 cm) long in bundles of two, stiff and usually twisted. Cones are small and brown. Ultimate height is around 80 ft (about 24 m), but is variable.
ZONES 3–9

### *P. thunbergiana*
**syn. *P. thunbergii***
JAPANESE BLACK PINE

Popular throughout the US for its irregular, picturesque habit. The stiff, dark green needles are 3–4 in (about 7.5–10 cm) long in bundles of two. Easily sheared in its youth, it will naturally develop a leaning trunk and horizontal branching.
ZONES 6–10

## PISTACIA
### *chinensis*
CHINESE PISTACHE

This deciduous species, prized for its fall foliage, is native to Asia. A fast grower, it averages 15–37 ft (about 4.5–10.5 m), sometimes reaching 80 ft (about 24 m). Low and spreading or erect and dome shaped, it has narrow, fern-like

Pinus thunbergiana

Pinus sylvestris

Pinus ponderosa

leaves comprising 10 or more green leaflets. These turn vivid hues of red, yellow and purple in the fall. Tiny red flowers are followed by red seed pods that ripen to blue. It will flourish in most soil types given full sun Propagate from seed in fall and winter, cuttings in summer.
ZONES 7–10

## PITTOSPORUM

This genus contains about 100 evergreen trees and shrubs that are valued for their scented blooms and decorative leaves. They have an upright habit of growth with a rounded crown, growing 20–40 ft (about 6–12 m) tall. Flowers have a strong citrus scent and the attractive seed pods contain their seeds in a sticky resin. All species prefer moderate to tropical climates. Some like dryish, well-drained soil; others prefer damp locations. They are simple to propagate, from seed in fall and spring, mature cuttings in summer and several species from semi-ripe cuttings in summer.

### *P. eugenioides*

This strongly upright growing, evergreen tree eventually reaches 40 ft (about 12 m) in height, with a spread of 25–30 ft (about 7.5–9 m). Its elliptical leaves are yellow-green in color, glossy, and have wavy margins. Small, yellow, star-like fruits are produced in clusters and have a sweet fragrance. Full sun to part shade is preferred, along with moderate watering. Light gray bark is attractive on mature trees.
ZONES 9–11

### *P. undulatum*

VICTORIAN BOX

This popular Australian native reaches 18–37 ft (about 5.5–10.5 m) tall, with a wide, domed shape. The dense, green leaves are lance shaped with scalloped edges. Clusters of intensely fragrant, creamy white, bell-shaped flowers bloom profusely in spring, followed by decorative, yellow-brown fruit.
ZONES 10–11

## PLATANUS
*x acerifolia*

LONDON PLANE TREE

This popular hybrid, from Asia's *P. orientalis* and North America's *P. occidentalis,* is robust and fast growing, reaching up to 80 ft (about 24 m) with a wide, spreading crown. Shiny, pale green leaves with 3 to 5 lobes are 10 in (about 25 cm) wide. Little red flowers appear in pendent clusters, followed by paired, spherical fruit around 1 in (about 2.5 cm) in diameter. This tree is able to withstand extremes in temperature and substantial pollution. It is a common sight lining streets throughout North America and elsewhere.
ZONES 5–10

## PLUMERIA
*rubra*

FRANGIPANI, PLUMERIA

This shrubby native of Central America grows to 25 ft (about 7.5 m) tall. It is valued for its heavily scented flowers which come in many colors and have five overlapping petals. Deep green, leathery leaves are pointed ovals with prominent mid-ribs; they usually drop briefly in winter or early spring, leaving a boldly branched, stocky shrub until new leaves appear. Flowers appear in the warmest months. Popular in southern California and throughout the tropics. It does not like cool, damp soils.
ZONES 10–11

## PODOCARPUS

FERN PINE, YEW PINE

This diverse, ornamental genus of evergreen conifers for cool to warm-temperate climates is native to Australia, New Zealand, South America and South Africa. Species vary from low and spreading to slender and erect, from 50 to 160 ft (about 15–49 m) tall. The dense foliage consists of very narrow leaves, long or short according to species. Vivid, spherical fruit, more like berries than cones, are borne individually on short stems. These trees like full sun or partial shade. Propagate from seed or cuttings.

### *P. gracilior*
**syn. *P. elongatus***

FERN PINE

Notable for their clean foliage and billowy form, this evergreen tree from East Africa is popular where its tidy habit is important. The short, slender leaves have a slight gray cast and are densely held; habit will vary from upright to gracefully pendent. Trees grow slowly, eventually reaching 60 ft (about 18 m) tall in the warmest locations.
ZONES 10–11

### *P. macrophyllus*

YEW PINE

Long, slender leaves and a narrow, upright habit set this species apart from the fern pine. Good for screening and hedging. It is tolerant of heat. It has very slow growth but may eventually reach 50 ft (about 15 m) in height and no more than 15 ft (about 4.5 m) in width.
ZONES 8–10

## POPULUS

POPLAR, ASPEN, COTTONWOOD

These deciduous trees, native to the northern hemisphere and related to the willows, are valued for their rapid growth and fall foliage colors. Reaching 40–100 ft (about 12–30 m) tall, they vary from round headed to conical or columnar in shape. Furry catkins appear in the leaf axils in late winter to early spring; leaves often turn vivid yellow in fall. These trees tolerate heat and cold, but prefer a steady supply of moisture. Plant in moisture-retentive soil with full sun. Propagate from cuttings in summer or by grafting. Some species have a strong tendency to sucker; they are unsuitable for small gardens. Cultivated for over 2000 years, they lined Roman roads and were called *arbor populi*, the tree of the people.

### *P. alba*

SILVER POPLAR, WHITE POPLAR

This central European species grows extremely quickly to 50 ft (about 15 m) or more, with a broad conical shape and silky gray bark, especially on young branches. The leaves have 3 to 5 deeply cut lobes with wavy edges. Deep green on top, frosty white and downy underneath, they turn a beautiful golden yellow in the fall.
ZONES 3–9

### *P. deltoides*

EASTERN COTTONWOOD

This lofty species from eastern North America grows rapidly to 50–100 ft (about 15–30 m) tall with an expansive crown. The cordate leaves are bright green, and turn dull yellow in fall. Pendent yellow and red catkins appear in spring.
ZONES 3–9

*Plumeria rubra*

*Pittosporum eugenioides*

*Podocarpus gracilior*

*Podocarpus macrophyllus*

*Platanus x acerifolia*

*Pistacia chinensis*

*Populus deltoides*

# A Field Trip to the Coromandel Peninsula

New Zealand's pohutukawa *(Metrosideros excelsa)* has the ability to grow where no other tree can—along the coastal cliffs of the hills, bays and beaches of northern New Zealand. The spreading roots of this tree allow it to grow on rock faces and other precipitous sites, totally out of the reach of any competition. To the people of northern New Zealand, a beach without a pohutukawa is considered no beach at all—such is the character that these trees add to the coastal landscape.

The pohutukawa's Latin name is *Metrosideros excelsa*—"ironwood of excellence"—a reference to the density of the pohutukawa's hard, reddish brown wood. Also known as the New Zealand Christmas tree, the pohutukawa flowers from December to early January, at the height of the summer holiday season. The display of crimson-red flowers brightens the headlands, cliffs and bays with splashes of color that are visible for many miles. The summer climate here is mild and pleasant, rarely getting too hot or too cold—about 77°F (about 25°C) during the day. This, with bright sunshine, provides perfect conditions both for trees and holiday makers.

Across the wide Hauraki Gulf, 25 miles (about 40 km) east of Auckland, lies the Coromandel Peninsula, home to some of the greatest pohutukawa groves. Short heavy downpours

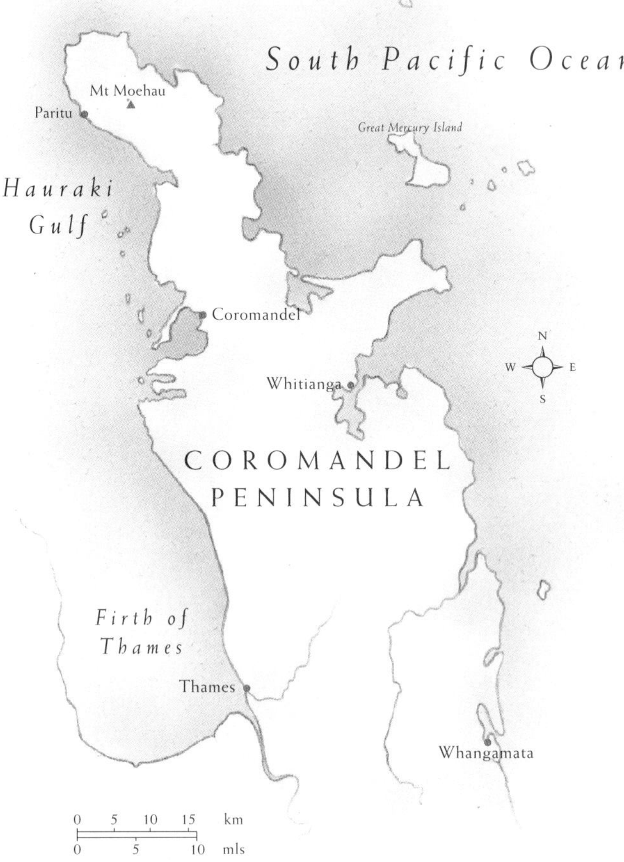


*Pohutukawa flowers add color to coastal areas in summertime.*

of rain occur regularly throughout the year, creating lush growth and almost perfect conditions for these trees. From time to time harsh storms lash the coast with salt-laden air. Winds buffet the trees, crashing the odd tree on its side, where generally they regrow with a new crop of branches.

The old miners' road between Thames and Coromandel twists and bends along the coast at the foot of the steep hills and cliffs, only a few yards above the high-tide mark. It runs around many rocky bays with oyster-encrusted rocks and 400- to 800-year old shady pohutukawas at every point.

Once you reach Coromandel—a distance of 34 miles (about 54 km) from Thames—continue up the coast to the base of Mount Moehau. Here, and right along the coastal cliffs and bays, are some of the largest pohutukawas to be found anywhere. At times they grow into huge spreading trees with great branches that bend and twist to the ground, where they re-root, encouraging even more growth. In many places the road passes under their spreading branches.

Near the base of Mount Moehau is the small hamlet of Paritu which, together with Fantail Bay just to the north, is one of the best places to view the pohutukawa. Standing slightly out to sea on the granite quarry wharves at Paritu, you can look back at the stony beaches and rocky bays, along which the pohutukawas go right down to the water's edge. Granite rocks covered in lichen add to the beauty of the coastline. At Christmas, you will see bright red carpets on the ground under the trees, where the stamens have fallen.

The crimson flowers drip with nectar, attracting songbirds such as the tui and bellbird. The introduced starlings also enjoy the nectar; the pollen from the flowers often turns their chests yellow, creating great confusion as to their identity. The road continues on until you reach Fantail Bay, where you look out to sea through the pohutukawas' contorted trunks. Fantails flit and dart about, in and under the canopy, eating insects attracted to the rich nectar in the flowers. Bees swarm to the trees, creating a persistent buzzing sound.

Other animals, plants and insects find a haven in these trees. Epiphytes festoon old pohutukawas, with great clumps of *Collospermum hastatum*, a lily-like plant, growing in the crown along the branches. *Pyrrosia serpens*, a climbing fern, scrambles up the trunks. After dark, Australian brush-tailed possums come out to devour the fresh pohutukawa shoots, killing many trees in the process. Wetas—large tree-climbing insects of the cricket family—also come out at night to eat the leaves, making loud scraping noises.

If you leave the coast road and travel inland, you will see a cousin of the pohutukawa, the northern rata (*Metrosideros robusta*). This is a tree of the inland forests, often germinating as an epiphyte high on the crown of old trees. Where the pohutukawa and rata meet—most often in the steep, hilly country of Coromandel Peninsula—hybrids are produced, sharing characteristics of both trees.

To the Maori people, the pohutukawa has been esteemed from time immemorial. At Cape Reinga, the furthest promontory of land at the northern tip of New Zealand, lies the most sacred pohutukawa tree of all. According to the Maori legend it is from this point that the souls of the dead depart from this world into the life hereafter.

*Metrosideros excelsa*

## Metrosideros

The genus *Metrosideros* consists of 20 or more species of trees and shrubs, some creeping over rocks or up trees with clinging roots. About half the species are found only in New Zealand while most of the others occur on other Pacific Islands, as far east as Hawaii. Few apart from the pohutukawa have become widely cultivated.

The beautiful pohutukawa is generally called the "New Zealand Christmas tree" in other countries, even in the northern hemisphere where it flowers from about May to July. It is only suited to milder temperate climates.

Although the twisted, contorted shape of the stout trunk and branches is too irregular to be of any great commercial value, the pohutukawa is most highly prized for seashore planting. In South Africa, Australia and California it has been found to be one of the most resistant of all small trees to continued exposure to salt spray. Popular for beachfront parks and esplanades, it will grow at reasonable speed into a low tree with a dense, rounded canopy, even in quite poor soils such as dune sands, as long as the ground is not prone to waterlogging.

Many new varieties are being produced; these have been selected for their growth and vigor. However, planted trees seldom rival those on the New Zealand seashores in the abundance of flowers and richness of color.

*Metrosideros excelsa*

### *P. nigra* 'Italica'
LOMBARDY POPLAR

This slender, stately cultivar grows up to 95 ft (29 m). Its rhomboid-oblong leaves mature from bronze tinted in spring to lustrous green before turning deep golden in fall. Red catkins appear on male trees in spring. It requires deep, damp soil.
ZONES 3–10

### *P. tremuloides*
QUAKING ASPEN

A 65 ft (about 20 m), fast-growing, deciduous tree from cold winter regions of North America, the far north and high in the mountains. It is grown within those regions for its graceful habit and the way the dark green leaves flutter in the slightest breeze.
ZONES 1–7

## *PROSOPIS glandulosa*
HONEY MESQUITE

An important tree in arid regions, where its low, spreading canopy provides needed shade for patios and garden beds. Seldom more than 30 ft (about 9 m) tall and nearly as wide, its deciduous leaves are compound with many tiny leaflets giving a fine texture to the foliage mass. Spiny stems discourage close contact. In spring, trees are covered with fluffy spikes of yellow flowers, popular with bees. It loves full sun and thrives on occasional deep waterings. It has become a problem in some regions where it develops impenetrable thickets.
ZONES 8–10

## *PRUNUS*
CHERRY, PEACH, PLUM

This large genus contains over 200 evergreen or deciduous shrubs and trees and thousands of cultivars. They are grown either for their fruit or for their ornamental foliage, flowers and bark. Reaching 15–60 ft (about 4.5–18 m) tall, their shape varies from tall ovals to broadly vase-shaped specimens. Members of the rose family, they bear sweetly scented, single or double, rose-like flowers with 5 petals ranging from white to scarlet. Most species can be widely grown, thriving in rich, well-drained soils. The evergreens tolerate some degree of shade and make excellent hedges; prune in spring and propagate from cuttings in summer and fall. Deciduous types, usually grown for their spring flowers, prefer full sun; prune after flowering and propagate from seed in fall or cuttings in winter, bud or graft cultivars in spring and fall.

### *P.* × *blireiana*

This popular deciduous hybrid grows up to 12 ft (about 3.5 m). It has a squat appearance with slender, arching branches and red-purple, elliptical leaves that change to golden brown in fall. Its red-pink, semi-double flowers, blooming in early spring, are fragrant and very attractive.
ZONES 5–10

### *P. campanulata*
TAIWAN CHERRY

This deciduous species grows up to 24 ft (about 7 m) high and wide. It late winter it bears pendent clusters of deep rose, bell-shaped flowers. These are followed by deep green leaves, sharply elliptical with heavily serrated margins, and little, spherical, red seed pods. The best cherry for mild winter regions.
ZONES 7–10

### *P. caroliniana*
CAROLINA CHERRY LAUREL

This upright, dense, evergreen tree from southeastern North America usually has a shrubby, multistemmed form, reaching 30 ft (about 9 m) at maturity. Easily pruned to a smaller size and often sheared for hedging. Tiny, white flowers are heavily scented in early spring; small, black fruits are popular with birds. It can be weedy; the leaves are often disfigured in insects. 'Bright 'n' Tight' is very compact with sturdy, glossy foliage. Best in full sun and soils that are neutral to acidic; it tolerates coastal conditions as well as the heat of deserts.
ZONES 7–10

### *P. cerasifera* 'Atropurpurea'
PURPLE-LEAF PLUM

This cultivar is commonly planted for its impressive foliage and flowers. It has an irregular dome shape to 25–30 ft (about 7.5–9 m) tall and wide. Its leaves are reddish purple, becoming bronze-green in summer. In early spring an abundance of white flowers bloom, followed by the edible cherry-plum fruit. This cherry needs full sun for the best foliage color; it accepts most soils, and is among the most drought tolerant of plums. Other cultivars may have richer purple foliage and may fruit less; look for 'Nigra', 'Newport' or 'Thundercloud'.
ZONES 4–10

### *P. ilicifolia*
HOLLY-LEAF CHERRY

This small, evergreen tree is native to the coastal mountains of California and Baja. It grows in a broad mound to 20–30 ft (about 6–9 m) tall, with small, glossy leaves resembling those of holly. White flowers

*Prunus ilicifolia*

*Prunus sargentii*

*Prunus campanulata*

*Prunus* × *blireiana*

*Prunus cerasifera* 'Atropurpurea'

*Populus tremuloides*

*Populus nigra* 'Italica'

appear in spring on slender spikes, followed by round fruit $^1/_2$ in (about 1 cm) or more in diameter and deep red-purple when ripe. Fruits are edible but contain large pits; birds love them. This tree makes an excellent screen or hedge, but develops a canopy only with age and careful pruning. It tolerates full sun or light shade, and most soils; it is drought tolerant once established.

ZONES 9–10

### *P. incisa*

FUJI CHERRY, CUT-LEAVED CHERRY

A small, deciduous tree originating in Japan, this species can reach 30 ft (about 9 m). Its oval, sharply toothed leaves are red when young, darkening to green in summer and then orange-red in fall. The pink buds, opening to white or pale pink, appear in early spring before the leaves. The form 'Praecox' flowers in early winter.

ZONES 7–10

### *P. mume*

JAPANESE FLOWERING APRICOT

This small, deciduous tree from China, Korea and Japan grows to around 18 ft (about 5.5 m). It bears abundant flowers in late winter or early spring before the leaves appear. The species is white or pink, but double-flowered cultivars in white or light or deep pink are popular. This is the "plum blossom," a favorite subject with Chinese and Japanese painters because it flowers while snow is still on the ground. It is fast growing, but for best flowering it needs annual pruning; with age it develops a picturesque, gnarled trunk.

ZONES 6–9

### *P. sargentii*

SARGENT CHERRY

A valuable tree, both for its year-round appeal in the garden and for its fine lumber, popular in its native Japan. With an upright habit, it reaches 75 ft (about 23 m) tall and around 30 ft (about 9 m) wide. It is covered with deep pink, single flowers in early spring. Its lustrous green foliage begins a bronzy green, becoming vivid red in the fall. The bark is a deep, rich mahogany, particularly effective in winter. This large tree likes full sun and a rich, moist soil.

ZONES 4–9

### *P. serrulata*

JAPANESE FLOWERING CHERRY

Originating in east Asia, this deciduous species is the parent of many cultivars. It grows quickly, up to 30 ft (about 9 m), with a dome shape and spreading habit. Its scaly bark is a glossy reddish brown. The finely toothed, glossy leaves turn from deep green to orange and yellow in fall. Long-stemmed terminal clusters of white, unscented flowers appear in spring, followed by spherical fruit. Most commonly seen in gardens as one of its many named forms, now known as the Sato-zakura group. These are smaller trees, 20–35 ft (about 6–10 m) tall and variable from upright to wide spreading. Flowers may be white or pink, fruit is seldom produced and fall color varies from yellow to orange to reddish. 'Amanogawa' is upright, 30 ft (about 9 m) tall and 12 ft (about 3.5 m) wide, with the palest pink, semi-double, scented flowers and reddish orange foliage in fall. 'Kwanzan' ('Kanzan') has fully double, deep pink flowers on a broadly vase-shaped tree. 'Mt Fuji' is pure white and sweetly scented on a broad, dome-shaped tree to 20 ft (about 6 m) tall and wide; fall color is orange-red. Many other cultivars are available.

ZONES 6–10

### *P. subhirtella* 'Pendula'

WEEPING HIGAN CHERRY

This deciduous, spreading tree has a wide crown and arching branches. It grows 18–37 ft (about 5.5–10.5 m) tall and develops sharply elliptical, serrated, deep green leaves which turn yellow in fall. Light pink flowers, predominantly single with 5 petals, appear from winter to early spring before the foliage. These are followed by little, spherical, brown-red fruit. The cultivar 'Fallalis' is more reliably winter flowering.

ZONES 5–10

### *P.* × *yedoensis*

YOSHINO CHERRY

This Japanese hybrid is an elegant, deciduous tree. It grows up to 24 ft (about 7 m) tall and spreads up to 30 ft (about 9 m) wide, with a convex crown and pendent limbs. White or light pink flowers with an almond fragrance open in early spring, preceding the deep green foliage. This tree prefers full sun and a well-drained soil. It is much planted in Washington DC. 'Akebano' is particularly popular on the West Coast; it has slightly softer pink flowers.

ZONES 5–10

## *PSEUDOTSUGA*

### *menziesii*

syn. *P. taxifolia*

DOUGLAS FIR

This majestic species, one of North America's most impressive conifers, grows 65–220 ft (about 20–67 m) in an attractive pyramid shape. Its deeply grooved, gray-brown bark is set off by the bluish green foliage, which comprises needles $1^1/_2$ in (about 3 cm) long. The woody brown cones hang down and are 3–4 in (about 7.5–10 cm) long. Mountain forms will be hardier than those from coastal regions. It grows quickly in fertile soil. Plant in open spaces in full sun or partial shade; propagate from cold-treated seed. The Douglas fir is America's leading Christmas tree. Its valuable timber is known as Oregon pine.

ZONES 6–10

*Prunus* × *yedoensis*

*Pseudotsuga menziesii*

*Prunus serrulata* 'Mt Fuji'

*Prunus serrulata*

*Prunus subhirtella* 'Pendula'

*Prunus serrulata* 'Amanogawa'

*Prunus mume*

*Pterocarya fraxinifolia*

*Pyrus calleryana*

*Quercus agrifolia*

## PTEROCARYA *fraxinifolia*

CAUCASIAN WINGNUT

This rapidly developing deciduous tree, native to the Caucasus and Iran, is a relative of the walnut. It grows up to 110 ft (about 33.5 m) with a spreading, convex crown. Its fern-like, compound foliage consists of up to 20 lance-shaped leaflets. Pendent, yellowish green chains of attractive male and female catkins appear in summer. These are followed by drooping clusters of green, winged nuts with red markings. This species prefers warm climates and waterside locations. Prune suckers frequently and propagate from cuttings or suckers in summer; seed in fall.

ZONES 5–10

## PYRUS

PEAR

This genus contains small, evergreen and deciduous species native to Europe, Asia and Africa. They are valued for their foliage and flowers, and some for their edible fruit.

*Pyrus salicifolia* 'Pendula'

Foliage is diverse, from ovate and hairy to linear and smooth, and in many species assumes brilliant color in fall. White flowers are followed by plump fruit in various shades of brown, yellow and green. Species vary in their hardiness, but all enjoy a well-drained soil with full sun. Propagate from seed in fall; bud cultivars in summer, graft in winter. Some are quite susceptible to fireblight.

### *P. calleryana*

CALLERY PEAR

This tough Asian native grows up to 50 ft (about 15 m). It has shiny, elliptical leaves that turn from deep green to red in fall. An abundance of white blossoms appear in mid- to late spring, followed by little brown fruit. A number of selected cultivars are available, including 'Aristocrat', 'Bradford' and 'Chanticleer'.

ZONES 4–9

### *P. kawakamii*

EVERGREEN PEAR

A graceful, evergreen tree to 25 ft (about 7.5 m) tall and wide, with somewhat pendulous branches, this is a native of Japan. White flowers are produced in quantity in late winter, attractive against the glossy green leaves. Fruits are tiny and hard. Easily trained as an espalier, but susceptible to fireblight.

ZONES 8–10

### *P. salicifolia* 'Pendula'

WEEPING WILLOW-LEAFED PEAR

Native to southeastern Europe and the Caucasus, this tree grows to 30 ft (about 9 m) with a domed shape and gracefully arching branches.

*Pyrus kawakamii*

*Quercus kellogii*

The tasseled, lanceolate foliage, similar to the willow's but silver-gray, emerges soon after the flower buds. Flat-topped clusters of small white flowers appear in abundance in spring, followed by small, yellowish brown fruit.

ZONES 4–9

### *P. ussuriensis*

USSURIAN PEAR

Originating in Asia, this tough, deciduous species has a pyramidal crown and spreading habit. It grows 50–65 ft (about 15–20 m) tall and has rigid lower limbs. The roundish leaves are 2–4 in (about 5–10 cm) across and shiny green, turning to vivid red, orange and yellow in fall. The tree is powdered with small, pink-budded, white flowers in spring, followed by insignificant fruit. This is the hardiest of the pears, and is valuable for its flowers and fall color where other species cannot be grown.

ZONES 4–9

## QUERCUS

OAK

This extremely diverse genus contains some 45 species of evergreen and deciduous trees and shrubs, mostly native to the northern hemisphere. Ranging from small and shrubby to very tall and erect, they grow slowly. Foliage varies from wide, multi-lobed and leathery to lustrous, thin and papery. All species bear nut-like fruits called acorns, partially enclosed with a cup-like cap. The acorns differ from species to species: slender and sharp or stubby and flat; sleek shelled or downy and rough. The many species of oak vary little in their climatic preferences, but generally like a deep, well-drained soil. Some like alkaline soils and full sun; others prefer semi-shade. Propagate from seed in fall—also a time to guard against oak-leaf miner. The heavily grained timber, moisture and salt resistant, is prized by boatbuilders and carpenters.

### *Q. agrifolia*

COAST LIVE OAK

Perhaps the most characteristic of California's evergreen oaks, this species is found in the coastal hills and valleys from north to south. A wide-spreading, picturesque tree in the open, reaching 80–100 ft (about 24–30 m) across, it will be narrow and upright to 80 ft (about 24 m) tall in dense groves. Sturdy, holly-like leaves are around 1–3 in (about 2.5–7.5 cm) long; acorns have a shallow cap. Very drought tolerant, they are likely to succumb to oak root fungus if irrigated during the summer. A mature tree is worth cherishing, though gardening opportunities beneath are limited. Keep turf grass away from the trunk, and underplant with other drought-tolerant natives.

ZONES 9–10

### *Q. gambelii*

GAMBEL OAK

This shrubby oak from the foothills of the Rockies is an important tree for the mountain regions of the West. Normally 15–30 ft (about 4.5–9 m) tall and growing in a thicket, it can be pruned up into a small tree form. Its deciduous leaves have deeply cut, rounded lobes. Very adaptable to the dry climate of the mountains, it serves many forms of wildlife as a source of food and shelter.

ZONES 3–7

### *Q. kellogii*

CALIFORNIA BLACK OAK

This deciduous oak is found throughout the mountains of California and Oregon, where it provides some of the best fall color of any native tree in the region. Leaves resemble those of the eastern deciduous oaks, with pointed lobes. It grows to 90 ft (about 27 m) tall in the wild, less in cultivation. It prefers a very well-drained site with plenty of sun.

ZONES 7–10

### *Q. macrocarpa*

BUR OAK

One of the largest of American oaks, this is native from the prairies to New England and northeastern Canada. Though large (to 80 ft/24 m tall and 100 ft/30 m wide) for a small garden, it is one of the most

adaptable for prairie landscapes, tolerating the drought and persistent winds. Leaves are up to 10 in (about 25 cm) long, with irregular, rounded lobes. Acorns have a distinctive cap with curled scales.
ZONES 2–8

*Q. palustris*
PIN OAK, SWAMP OAK

Originating in eastern North America, this popular deciduous tree is valued for its branching habit, shade, fall color and ease of transplanting. A fast grower, it reaches 75 ft (about 23 m) in height with a spread of 40 ft (about 12 m), though often larger in its native swamplands. Slender branchlets bear glossy green, deeply lobed leaves that turn scarlet in fall; like many deciduous oaks, the leaves turn brown but remain on the tree through much of the winter. Small, globe-shaped acorns are half covered by their cup. This tree's dense root system means transplanting is quite easy.
ZONES 4–9

*Q. phellos*
WILLOW OAK

This large oak, popular in the southeastern US, differs from most species in having long, slender leaves like a willow (5 in/12 cm long, 1 in/2.5 cm wide). Reaching 40–60 ft (about 12–18 m) high and 30–40 ft (about 10–12 m) wide, it serves well as a relatively fast-growing shade or street tree. Its bright green leaves turn yellow to russet in the fall. It is easily transplanted, preferring an acid soil but tolerating poorly drained sites.
ZONES 5–9

*Q. robur*
ENGLISH OAK

This species, like others native to Europe, Asia or North Africa, is less frequently planted in North America due to its lack of good fall color. It grows quickly, ranging widely in height between 30 and 110 ft (about 9–33.5 m), with an expansive crown and large, heavy branches. The leaves are shallowly lobed with a very short petiole. Egg-shaped acorns are one-third covered by their cup and develop in small bunches on slender stems. Most valuable selection is the nearly columnar 'Fastigiata'.
ZONES 5–9

*Q. rubra*
RED OAK, NORTHERN RED OAK

Among the most attractive of trees native to eastern North America, this oak is notable for its tall trunk and sturdy branching, fall color and relatively fast growth. It reaches 75–100 ft (about 23––30 m) tall and half as wide, with large, deeply lobed leaves turning red in fall. Acorns are usually oval with a thick, saucer-like cap. Best in well-drained soils, they transplant readily.
ZONES 4–9

*Q. suber*
CORK OAK

Valued for its soft, deeply ridged bark (the original source of cork), this evergreen has a broad, spreading crown up to 50 ft (about 15 m) high. The glossy deep green leaves are egg shaped and serrated with a fleecy underside. Single, oval acorns are half covered by their cup. Best adapted to drier regions of the West, Southwest and South.
ZONES 7–10

*Q. virginiana*
LIVE OAK, SOUTHERN LIVE OAK

Native from the southeastern US south to Mexico, this evergreen grows rapidly to 60 ft (about 18 m) or more in height with a spread of over 100 ft (about 30 m). Rigid, spreading branches bear deep green leaves with a fleecy white underside. These are predominantly oval with erratically serrated margins. Elliptical acorns are a quarter covered by their cup. In humid coastal areas trees are usually draped with Spanish moss, a type of bromeliad.
ZONES 7–10

## RHUS
SUMAC

This genus contains over 150 species of small, deciduous and evergreen trees, shrubs and climbers, some of which are valued for their vibrant fall foliage. They grow 18–27 ft (about 5.5–8 m) tall with wide, spreading crowns. The foliage varies from simple ovals to pinnately compound leaves with serrated margins on each leaflet. Small flowers appear in dense to open terminal clusters, followed by pendent bunches of fruit on the female tree only. Sumacs require full sun and a porous soil. Propagate from seed in fall, cuttings in summer or root cuttings in winter. Poison oak, poison ivy and sumac are now placed in a related genus called *Toxicodendron*.

*R. lancea*
AFRICAN SUMAC

This small, evergreen tree has only three slender leaflets per leaf, each a glossy green, creating a fine texture. The tree reaches 25 ft (about 7.5 m) tall and as wide, often with multiple trunks. Well adapted to the desert and to drier regions of the West, it makes a delightful patio tree although the fruits of the female tree can cause a litter problem. It prefers full sun, tolerates drought and is virtually pest free.
ZONES 9–10

*Quercus macrocarpa*

*Quercus robur*

*Quercus virginiana*

*Rhus lancea*

*Quercus suber*

*Quercus rubra*

*Quercus palustris*

*Rhus typhina* 'Laciniata'

*Sapindus drumondii*

### *R. typhina*

STAGHORN SUMAC, VELVET SUMAC

This North American species has a broad crown, growing quickly to a height and spread of 15–23 ft (about 4.5–7 m). Its long, pinnately compound leaves have up to 31 light green leaflets which turn beautiful shades of red and orange in fall. Dense clusters of tiny, greenish flowers appear at the top of each stem, followed by woolly red fruits. This species provides a strong silhouette in winter, although its tendency to sucker can be a problem. Plant in full or part sun in average garden soil; it tolerates heat and drought once established. 'Laciniata' has leaflets further divided into delicate segments, giving a lacy pattern.

ZONES 4–9

## *ROBINIA*

BLACK LOCUST

This deciduous genus contains 20 species of trees and shrubs, native to North America but now common worldwide. They grow up to 80 ft (about 24 m) with a rounded shape and spreading habit. The scented flowers and fruit are typical of the legume family, the pods resembling those of the locust tree (hence the common name). The species will survive in a broad range of temperatures and soils but dislikes saturated soil. Plant in full sun and protect the fragile limbs from strong winds. Propagate from seed and suckers in fall, cultivars by grafting. The genus was named after seventeenth-century herbalist Jean Robin, who first cultivated it.

### *R.* × *ambigua* 'Idahoensis'

IDAHO LOCUST

This hybrid of *R. pseudoacacia* and *R. viscosa* was selected for its deep reddish purple, fragrant flowers. Other features are similar to *R. pseudoacacia,* though its height is usually no more than 40 ft (about 12 m). It is equally tolerant of difficult soils, heat and drought, and also spreads by suckers. It is a good, tough tree for mid-western and drier mountain regions.

ZONES 3–9

*Robinia pseudoacacia*

*Salix babylonica*

### *R. pseudoacacia*

BLACK LOCUST

This erect tree grows to 75 ft (about 23 m) and has a tough, grooved trunk and thorny branches. Its fern-like leaves, composed of up to 23 elliptical leaflets, turn yellow in fall. Pendent clusters of scented, wisteria-like flowers appear in spring, followed by sleek seed pods that endure until the following spring. This species has a strong suckering habit; avoid planting near pathways.

ZONES 3–10

### *R. pseudoacacia* 'Frisia'

This expansive deciduous cultivar is thornless and grows up to 15 m (about 50 ft) high and 10 m (about 30 ft) wide. Its feather-like foliage has rounded leaflets and changes from gold in spring to yellowish orange in fall. Plant this fully hardy tree in well-drained soil with full sun.

ZONES 3–10

## *SALIX*

WILLOW

There are approximately 300 species of willow in the northern hemisphere, varying from dwarf Arctic shrublets to large trees with rough, twisted trunks and weeping branches. The latter make bold shade trees, their slender-leaved, pendent branches draping to the ground. Pendent male and female catkins usually develop on different trees and may be slender and soft or thick and leathery. Most willows prefer waterside locations, where eroded banks benefit from their strong suckering habit. They will grow in all except arid soils and require full sun, or partial shade in hot regions. Prune in spring to control their size, or to encourage plenty of new shoots which often are attractively colored the following winter; propagate from cuttings in summer and winter. The long, fast-growing young shoots are used for making wicker furniture.

*Salix alba*

### *S. alba*

WHITE WILLOW

This fast-growing though rather short-lived upright willow from Europe reaches as much as 75 ft (about 23 m) tall; in Europe it is often pollarded to gain long, flexible shoots for basket making. The leaves are lance shaped and turn yellow rather fitfully in fall. This is a popular tree for wet ground, holding riverbanks and the like, but its roots are greedy so it is not very popular as a garden tree.

ZONES 2–9

### *S. alba* var. *tristis*

**syn. *S. babylonica aurea*, *S.* 'Niobe' and others**

GOLDEN WEEPING WILLOW

This French cultivar, possibly a hybrid, grows rapidly up to a height and spread of 60 ft (about 18 m) or more.

ZONES 2–10

### *S. babylonica*

WEEPING WILLOW, BABYLON WEEPING WILLOW

This very attractive, popular tree is native to China and grows up to 50 ft (about 15 m). It has a broad dome and erect trunks that support distinctively weeping branches. The light green, lanceolate leaves, brushing the ground, are slender and thinly lobed. Like other species, this tree is best when planted near waterways or in heavily irrigated areas. The name comes from the unlikely story that these were the trees growing in Babylon under which the Hebrews sat and wept.

ZONES 6–10

### *S. caprea*

GOAT WILLOW, FRENCH PUSSY WILLOW

This species grows well in damp marshlands but its very strong

Schinus molle

suckering habit can cause problems in the garden. A dense shrub or tree, it grows 9–30 ft (about 2.7–9 m) tall. The rounded, deep green leaves are 2–4 in (about 5–10 cm) long with a fleecy gray underside. Decorative, gray, male catkins with yellow stamens appear in spring before the foliage.
ZONES 4–8

### *S. matsudana* 'Tortuosa'

CORKSCREW WILLOW, TWISTED HANKOW WILLOW

This popular northern Asian tree resembles *S. babylonica*, but is smaller growing to only 30 ft (about 9 m) tall and wide. Its branchlets and shiny green leaves are tortuous and twisted (as the cultivar name implies). Catkins appear at the same time as the lanceolate, serrated foliage. A curiosity for the garden, its branches are popular with flower arrangers.
ZONES 4–9

## SAPINDUS *drumondii*

SOAPBERRY

This native of southwestern North America is a deciduous tree with pinnately compound leaves that turn yellow in fall. Relatively fast growing, it reaches 40–50 ft (about 12–15 m) in height and 23–30 ft (about 7–9 m) in width and serves well as a shade tree. Tiny, greenish flowers in summer are not showy, although yellow fruits the size of grapes last into the winter. An excellent tree for harsh conditions in the arid Southwest. Give it full sun and dry soil.
ZONES 6–9

Salix matsudana 'Tortuosa'

Schinus terebinthifolius

## SAPIUM *sebiferum*

CHINESE TALLOW TREE

This variable deciduous tree, native to China and Japan, grows 18–40 ft (about 5.5–12 m) tall. Its dense crown is composed of pointed leaves, oval to diamond, which turn a beautiful lustrous crimson or orange-red in fall. Slender, yellow catkins are followed by white, waxy fruit, their three seeds held together with wax. Plant this species in rich, porous soil in a position with full sun; fall color is more vivid in hotter areas. Prune if necessary and propagate from seed in spring, semi-ripe cuttings in summer. This tree is sometimes cursed for its invasion of pastures and forests. Wax from the fruit of *S. sebiferum* is used to make soap and candles.
ZONES 7–10

## SASSAFRAS *albidum*

SASSAFRAS

This erect, deciduous, eastern North American native reaches up to 18 ft (about 5.5 m), widening to 3 ft (about 90 cm) in maturity. The foliage, either egg shaped or with two or three deep lobes, turns from lustrous deep green to striking red and yellow in fall. Inconspicuous, yellow-green flowers bloom in spring, followed by blue fruit. This species likes full sun or partial shade and rich, porous, slightly acid soil. Propagate from seed or suckers in fall, or from root cuttings in winter. Sassafras oil is extracted from the bark and roots of these trees.
ZONES 4–8

Salix alba var. tristis

Sassafras albidum

Sapium sebiferum

## SCHINUS

This genus consists of about 28 species of evergreen trees and shrubs, usually grown for their foliage and as shade trees. They prefer a sunny position with some protection from winds. Plant in moist, well-drained, well-composted soil. Propagate from semi-ripe cuttings in summer or seed in spring.

### *S. molle*

CALIFORNIA PEPPER TREE, PERUVIAN PEPPER TREE

Native to South America, this handsome evergreen grows quickly to 50 ft (about 15 m) with a broad, rounded crown and elegant, arching branches. Pendulous, pinnate foliage is a dark glossy green, comprising up to 40 slender, lance-shaped leaflets. Little yellow flowers appear in branched racemes from late winter to summer, followed by drooping "necklaces" of small, shiny, reddish pink berries; these can be used as a substitute for pepper. This species endures extreme drought. The Incas planted this tree to shade their royal roads.
ZONES 9–10

Salix caprea

### *S. terebinthifolius*

BRAZILIAN PEPPER TREE, FLORIDA HOLLY

This stout, evergreen, bushy, small tree is native to tropical America; it can become a pest in some areas. It has oval, mid- to deep green leaflets, 3 to 13 on each leaf, and bears panicles of insignificant greenish flowers. Dense clusters of round, orange berries follow the bloom, but only if male and female plants have been grown together. This species grows to a height and spread of 30 ft (about 9 m).
ZONES 9–10

*Sequoia sempervirens*

*Sciadopitys verticillata*

*Sophora tetraptera*

*Sophora japonica*

## *SCIADOPITYS verticillata*

UMBRELLA PINE, JAPANESE UMBRELLA PINE

Native to Japan, this evergreen conifer is valued for its perfect pyramid shape and unusual foliage. It grows very slowly up to 40 ft (about 12 m) in cultivation, and up to 130 ft (about 39 m) in the wild. Its horizontal, open spirals of dark green needles look like the ribs of an umbrella. Ovate, woody cones with numerous wide, curved scales mature for two years before dispersing their seeds. This tree prefers cold mountain locations with damp, acid soil and will not tolerate lime or urban smog. Plant in a protected site in full (but not hot) sun and water liberally. It will benefit from yearly mulching with composted leaves. Propagate from seed and transplant when young. The genus name comes from two Greek words: *skias*, "shade," and *pitys* "fir tree."
ZONES 4–9

## *SEQUOIA sempervirens*

COAST REDWOOD

This tough, evergreen conifer, native to the coastal mountains of California and southern Oregon, is prized for its timber. It averages 100 ft (about 30 m) in cultivation, reaching well over 300 ft (about 91 m) in the wild. It is either pyramidal or columnar in shape, with gracefully drooping branches. Branchlets are lined with two rows of small green needles which are narrow and flattened, with two frosty bands underneath. The oblong cones seem too small for such a large tree. This tree prefers a cool, moist climate without prolonged freezing temperatures in winter. Root suckers may be pruned off for neatness; young trees can be sheared into hedges. Redwoods are extremely long living, with some specimens estimated to be about 3500 years old. The genus boasts the world's tallest tree, at 362 ft (about 110 m).
ZONES 8–10

## *SEQUOIADENDRON giganteum*

syn. *Sequoia gigantea, Wellingtonia gigantea*

BIG TREE, GIANT SEQUOIA, SIERRAN REDWOOD

This long-living, evergreen conifer, native to California's Sierra Nevada Mountains, has an attractive pyramidal shape and an extremely massive trunk. This vigorous tree averages 65–160 ft (about 20–49 m) tall and, like its coastal relative, grows taller in the wild. The scaly needles are bluish green. Lower branches drape to the ground in its youth but eventually fall off, leaving a bare lower trunk. Cylindrical cones endure for 20 years—not very long, given that some trees are 3000 years old. These trees like cool climates, full sun and damp soil. Propagate from seed.
ZONES 7–9

*Sequoiadendron giganteum*

## *SOPHORA*

This diverse and widespread genus belongs to the pea family and contains semi-evergreen and deciduous species. They are valued for their shape, leaves and flowers. They vary in height, from 15 to 80 ft (about 4.5–24 m), and have fern-like foliage with differing numbers of oval leaflets. The pea-like flowers hang in thick, terminal clusters during summer, generally in shades of white and yellow. Plant in rich, porous soil with full sun. Pruning is tolerated. Propagate deciduous species from seed or cuttings in fall; semi-evergreens from softwood cuttings in summer.

### *S. japonica*

PAGODA TREE, SCHOLAR TREE

Native to Japan, China and Korea, this deciduous species grows 50–75 ft (about 15–23 m) tall and 50 ft (about 15 m) wide. Its round crown is composed of deep green foliage with up to 16 oval leaflets. Older trees bear big, open clusters of little yellowish white, pea-like flowers in late summer, followed by green, elliptical seed pods. This species enjoys hot summers and tolerates urban conditions. 'Regent' is the best cultivar, selected for more uniform growth and earlier flowering. The leaves of *S. japonica* are said to have medicinal qualities.
ZONES 4–9

### *S. tetraptera*

KOWHAI, YELLOW KOWHAI

This semi-evergreen New Zealand species varies between 15 and 30 ft (about 4.5-9 m), a compact shrub or broad, pyramidal tree. It has slender, deep green foliage with up to 40 leaflets. Golden-yellow, pea-shaped flowers 2 in (about 5 cm) long appear in spring, followed by winged seed pods. It prefers a moist situation and tolerates light shade. *S. tetraptera* is the national flower of New Zealand.
ZONES 8–10

## *SORBUS*

This member of the rose family has deciduous and semi-evergreen species native to Europe, North America and temperate Asia. Shrubs or trees, growing 27–85 ft (about 8–26 m) tall, are valued for their foliage, flowers and fruit. Leaves may be either pinnate or simple ovals; color varies from green to purplish, with good fall color on the deciduous species. Little, white, 5-petaled flowers appear in spring, followed in summer by enduring, pendent bunches of berries. These trees thrive in regions with cool summers and cold winters, preferring full sun and a moisture-retentive soil. Propagate by grafting in winter, from buds and cuttings in summer or from seed in fall. Susceptible to fireblight. Some species' edible fruit is used to make cider.

### *S. aucuparia*

EUROPEAN MOUNTAIN ASH, ROWAN

Originating in Europe and Asia, this erect, broad-crowned tree grows 18–37 ft (about 5.5–10.5 m) tall and is valued for its flowers, foliage and edible fruit. The green, pinnate leaves comprise up to 15 leaflets and change to yellowish red in fall. Big, dense sprays of white spring blossoms are followed by a profusion of elliptical, orange-red, late summer berries, turning golden yellow in fall. The fruit is used to make rowan jelly. This deciduous species is suited to northern climates, where it has become naturalized. Subject to many insect problems. Numerous cultivars are available.

ZONES 3–7

### *S. cashmiriana*

A native of Kashmir, this spreading, deciduous tree can attain a height of 27 ft (about 8 m), though it is often smaller. Its mid-green leaves are made up of 17 to 19 elliptical leaflets, and are gray-green underneath. The pendent clusters of white to pale pink flowers appear in early summer and are followed by $^{1}/_{2}$ in (about 1 cm) wide, globular, white fruits, which endure into winter.

ZONES 5–8

### *S. commixta*

A strong-growing, deciduous native of Japan, this species has an erect habit when young but spreads with maturity. It grows to 30 ft (about 9 m) in height. The lustrous, mid-green leaves have 6 to 7 pairs of oblong leaflets and take on bright red and orange hues in fall. White flowers in panicles 4 in (about 10 cm) wide appear in spring, and are followed by bright scarlet fruit.

ZONES 5–8

### *S. hupehensis*

CHINESE ROWAN

This small, elegant, Chinese species reaches up to 50 ft (about 15 m) tall and 40 ft (about 12 m) wide. It is good for small gardens. The bluish green deciduous foliage, with up to 17 slightly serrated leaflets, turns reddish orange in fall. Open sprays of spring blossom are replaced by big clusters of egg-shaped, white to pink fruits in fall and winter. 'Coral Cascade' is the most commonly available cultivar, selected for its brilliant fruit and fall color.

ZONES 6–8

## SPATHODEA
### *campanulata*

AFRICAN TULIP TREE

This handsome, flowering evergreen, native to West Africa, grows to 55 ft (about 17 m) with an upright, spreading habit. The pinnate foliage comprises 10 to 20 dark green, lanceolate leaflets up to around $5^{1}/_{2}$ in (about 13 cm) long. Vivid green, downy spring buds unfurl to reveal stunning, long-lasting flowers; tulip like and orange to deep red, their lacy edges are tinged yellow inside. This tropical tree prefers the warm, frost-free climates of southern California and southern Florida, but will not tolerate stiff sea breezes. Plant it in rich, damp, sandy soil with full sun. Propagate from semi-ripe cuttings in summer, seed in spring.

ZONES 10–11

## STEWARTIA

**syn. *Stuartia***

These aristocrats among small flowering trees are suitable for even small gardens, particularly since they are attractive at any season. Deciduous leaves offer beautiful fall color, camellia-like blossoms add excitement in summer, attractive bark provides winter interest. They are all forest dwellers, tolerant of shade though flowering better in sun; plant when small in rich, moist soils where afternoon shade can be provided. Propagate *Stewartia* from seed in fall, or from cuttings in summer.

### *S. ovata* var. *grandiflora*

MOUNTAIN STEWARTIA

This native of the mountains of southeastern North America is a large shrub to 15 ft (about 4.5 m) tall that can easily be trained into a small tree. The oval leaves are dark green above, grayish green below, and around 5 in (about 12 cm) long, turning orange or scarlet in fall. In summer the plants are dotted with 3–4 in (about 7.5–10 cm) wide white flowers with purple stamens, resembling big, single camellias. It is a showy plant that is not commonly used but should be.

ZONES 5–9

### *S. pseudocamellia*

**syn. *Stuartia pseudocamellia***

JAPANESE STEWARTIA

This deciduous Japanese native is valued for its foliage, flowers and decorative, scaly bark. Compact or open, it can reach 60 ft (about 18 m) in height but usually remains much less in cultivation. Leaves are elliptical, sparsely toothed and turn attractive shades of yellow, red and purple in fall. Large, snow white, camellia-like flowers with dense yellow stamens appear in summer, followed by downy seed pods. It prefers moderate temperatures and rich, acidic soil. Provide partial shade and protect from stiff winds.

ZONES 5–8

## STYRAX
### *japonica*

JAPANESE SNOWBELL

This delightful small tree from Japan and China is too little planted in North America. It has a tidy habit with more or less horizontal branches; leaves seem to float above each branch, revealing the bell-shaped, white flowers hanging from the underside. Leaves turn red or yellow in fall. Flowers appear in late spring and are slightly fragrant. This tree will reach 30 ft (about 9 m) tall and 20 ft (about 6 m) or more wide. Give it a position in full sun, a rich soil and regular water for best growth and flowering.

ZONES 6–9

*Sorbus commixta*

*Stewartia pseudocamellia*

*Spathodea campanulata*

*Sorbus hupehensis*

*Sorbus aucuparia*

Tabebuia chrysotricha

Tamarix aphylla

Syzygium paniculatum

Taxus baccata

Taxodium distichum

## *SYRINGA reticulata*

JAPANESE TREE LILAC

The largest of the lilacs, this Asian species develops into a broad, canopied tree-like form 30 ft (about 9 m) tall and 25 ft (about 7.5 m) wide. Large, ovate leaves clothe the stems, each one topped by a large, branched panicle of tiny white flowers. Fragrance is musk like, different from the typical shrubby lilacs. Among the toughest of lilacs, tolerating winter cold and summer heat. Give it full sun, any well-drained soil and moderate water.

ZONES 3–8

## *SYZYGIUM paniculatum*

**syn. *Eugenia myrtifolia, E. paniculata***

AUSTRALIAN BRUSH CHERRY

This Australian native, one of hundreds of species of evergreen shrubs and trees from the southern hemisphere, is a quick-growing tree 30–60 ft (about 9–18 m) tall, typically with an erect habit. Branches are densely covered with shiny green, elliptical leaves; new leaves are bronzy. The creamy white flowers are followed by deep crimson, globular fruits that are lightly scented and edible but with little taste. Adaptable to sun or shade they are also tolerant of shearing, and are often used as tall, narrow hedges. Give it a well-drained soil and moderate water. Propagate from semi-ripe cuttings in summer. Psyllids have become a serious pest in California; researchers are working on biological controls for the insect.

ZONES 10–11

## *TABEBUIA*

These showy members of the catalpa family are deciduous trees from the dry tropics of Central and South America. Leaves are palmately compound, and drop for a short period just as the flowers are produced. Flowers are trumpet shaped in short racemes and are very showy. Fruits are fuzzy, bean-like pods as much 12 in (about 30 cm) long and are filled with silky

Styrax japonica

Tabebuia impetiginosa

Syringa reticulata

seeds. These are trees for the warmest regions of the country, demanding summer heat to flower well and suffering in temperatures much below freezing. Well-drained soils in full sun suit them best; they are drought tolerant once established. Propagate from cuttings or seed.

### *T. chrysotricha*

GOLDEN TRUMPET TREE

The bright yellow flowers of this species are produced in mass during mid-spring, and occasionally during summer. Pods are brown and furry. The leaves have golden-brown hairs on their margins. Trees reach 25 ft (about 7.5 m) tall and wide. It is very showy.

ZONES 9–11

### *T. impetiginosa*

**syn. *T. ipe***

PINK TRUMPET TREE

A more upright tree than *T. chrysotricha,* this species reaches 50 ft (about 15 m) or more in height. It is very striking when its bare branches are covered with flowers in early to mid-spring; flowers vary from rose to deep purple, with a yellow throat fading to purple. The leaves are smooth and dark green.

ZONES 9–11

## *TAMARIX aphylla*

**syn. *T. articulata***

ATHEL TREE

This short, tough evergreen originates in Africa and Asia. It reaches 18–30 ft (about 5.5–9 m) with an upright, slender habit and is an excellent hedge tree. Minute, grayish green leaves form in whorls around its branchlets. Racemes of pinkish white flowers bloom profusely during summer and fall. This species prefers warm regions but is extremely resilient, surviving stiff sea breezes and arid sandy soil. For optimum growth, plant in full sun in a rich, porous soil; with insufficient drainage it is prone to borer. Propagate from hardwood cuttings in winter, semi-ripe cuttings in late spring.

ZONES 8–10

## *TAXODIUM distichum*

BALD CYPRESS, SWAMP CYPRESS

Originating in the southern USA, this deciduous conifer quickly reaches 100 ft (about 30 m) or more in height; it is erect to broadly pyramidal in shape but eventually with a flat crown. Soft green sprays of slender needle leaves turn orange-brown in fall. Purplish brown cones are fragrant. "Cypress knees" are the cone-shaped growths that rise 12 in (about 30 cm) or more from the roots to help them breathe when submerged in their native swamplands. This species loves sun and water, but grows well even when soil is not saturated. Propagate from seed and cuttings; prune young trees to encourage symmetry. The valuable timber resists moisture and termites.

ZONES 5–10

## *TAXUS baccata*

ENGLISH YEW

This long-living evergreen conifer originates in Europe, North Africa

*Thujopsis dolabrata*

and Asia. It grows slowly to 40 ft (about 12 m) or more, its irregular, conical shape becoming flat topped in maturity. Its slender needles are deep green with a greenish yellow underside. Small, pollen-rich bunches of male flowers and green, globular, female flowers develop on separate trees. Unusually, this conifer has no cones; the female flower develops instead into an individual seed partly enclosed in a fleshy red case. This tree likes full sun and tolerates pruning; it is greatly favored for hedging and topiary. It propagates simply from seed and cuttings in spring and is prone to scale insects. The Irish yew is a narrowly upright cultivar of Irish origin. Both it and the regular type prefer moist climates.
ZONES 6–10

## *THUJA*

ARBORVITAE

This small genus comprises 5 species of evergreen conifers, native to North America or Asia. They grow up to 220 ft (about 67 m) in the wild, with a pyramidal shape. They have heavily grooved trunks and flat, compound foliage. Woody, green, seed-bearing cones of varying size mature to brown before releasing their seeds. Trees tolerate pruning and will grow in most soils but prefer moist climates and full sun. Propagate from seed or simply from cuttings. Several of the species are among the world's most valuable softwood timber trees.

### *T. occidentalis*

AMERICAN ARBORVITAE, EASTERN WHITE CEDAR

This North American native reaches up to 50 ft (about 15 m), its triangular shape becoming columnar in later life. Its bark is orange-brown and its aromatic foliage develops in flat, V-shaped sprays of deep green scales with blue-green undersides. This species does not do well in hot, dry climates.
ZONES 3–8

### *T. plicata*

WESTERN RED CEDAR, GIANT ARBORVITAE

Native from northern California to Alaska, this species grows quickly to

*Tilia americana* 'Redmond'

50–95 ft (about 15–29 m), and up to 220 ft (about 67 m) in the wild. Conical to columnar, it has brownish red, scaly bark and upstretched limbs. Sprays of shiny green scales, backed with silver, hang from their extremities. Its very small, erect cones open like flowers to disperse their seeds. Its wood is used for shingles and other construction elements, but it is also a beautiful specimen tree, particularly in its natural range.
ZONES 5–7

## *THUJOPSIS dolabrata*

FALSE ARBORVITAE, HIBA CEDAR

This handsome Japanese evergreen grows slowly to 18–45 ft (about 5.5–14 m). Pyramidal or low and spreading, this conifer is valued for its thick foliage: large, flat fans of shiny needles, dark green with frosted white undersides. Its little rounded cones are bluish gray and consist of fleshy scales. This tree prefers cool climates and damp soil. Prune to encourage shape or restrict size. Propagate from cuttings or cold-treated seed.
ZONES 6–9

## *TILIA*

LINDEN, LIME

This genus is made up of over 25 deciduous species native to Asia, Europe and North America. These elegant trees grow fast to 100 ft (about 30 m) or more in height. They are generally upright with extremely wide, buttressed trunks and noticeable suckers. Their heart-shaped foliage has slightly saw-toothed, furled edges and frosted downy undersides. Five-petaled, yellowish green, star-shaped flowers appear in pendent clusters in spring or early summer; they are highly scented, proving irresistible and sometimes deadly to bees. These trees prefer cool weather and rich, porous soil. However, they will grow in most soil types given regu-

*Thuja plicata*

*Tilia* 'Petiolaris'

lar water and full sun or partial shade. Propagate from seed in fall; some species and cultivars are propagated by grafting and layering in late summer. The versatile timber—a pale honey color— is used for wood carvings, musical instruments, clogs and blinds.

### *T. americana*

AMERICAN BASSWOOD

This tall woodland tree from eastern North America has the biggest leaves of the genus—4–6 in (about 10–15 cm) long and heart shaped. The flowers are yellowish white and fragrant in early summer. At 120 ft (about 36.5 m) tall, too large for the small garden, it is worth keeping if present in a wood lot. 'Redmond' is more dense and compact, with a conical shape.
ZONES 3–8

### *T. cordata*

LITTLELEAF LINDEN

One of the most commonly planted street trees in North America and elsewhere, this European native adapts well to urban conditions. Small, heart-shaped leaves are smooth and glossy, creating a fine texture. Flowers are small and fragrant. Numerous cultivars available have been selected for their narrower habit (such as 'Greenspire'), columnar habit (such as 'Erecta'), or for greater production of flowers (such as 'June Bride').
ZONES 3–9

*Thuja occidentalis*

*Tilia cordata*

### *T.* 'Petiolaris'

**syn. *T. tomentosa* 'Petiolaris'**

WEEPING SILVER LINDEN

This weeping tree, native to southern Europe and west Asia, reaches between 60 and 80 ft (about 18–24 m) high. It has a narrow, conical shape which expands with age. The pointed, cordate leaves are 2–4 in (about 5–10 cm) long, deep green on top and silver felted underneath. Creamy yellow flowers bloom in terminal clusters, followed by bumpy, nut-like seed pods.
ZONES 5–9

*Ulmus glabra* 'Camperdownii'

*Ulmus americana*

*Tipuana tipu*

### *TIPUANA*
### *tipu*

TIPU TREE, YELLOW JACARANDA

Native to subtropical and tropical South America, this predominantly evergreen genus is valued for its shade, flowers and timber. The tree grows quickly to around 25 ft (about 7.5 m), eventually reaching 50 ft (about 15 m) or more in height, with a broad, spreading, flat-topped habit. The dense crown is covered with attractive, feather-like foliage, composed of up to 25 rounded leaflets. In summer an abundance of pea-like, yellowish orange blooms appear on short, slender stalks. These are followed by leathery, brown pods up to $2^1/_2$ in (about 6 cm) in diameter. Plant in full sun with a rich, well-drained soil. This tree prefers a subtropical climate; it refuses to bloom in a tub. Prune immature plants in winter and propagate from seed in spring. The timber is marketed as Brazilian rosewood.

ZONES 10–11

### *TRISTANIA*
### *confertus*

**syn. *Lophostemon confertus***

BRISBANE BOX

This evergreen Australian species is a fast grower, reaching 145 ft (about 44 m) in its rainforest habitat, but only 50–95 ft (about 15–29 m) in the average garden. The brown bark is shed in strips. It has a domed crown and deep green foliage, lanceolate and woody. Little cream flowers with dense, prominent stamens bloom in spring. It is adapted only to mild winter regions without significant frost. Plant in rich, well-drained soil with full sun; prune saplings in winter to encourage shape. Propagate from seed in spring, cuttings in summer. There is a handsome cultivar with variegated leaves.

ZONES 10–11

### *TRISTANIOPSIS*
### *laurina*

**syn. *Tristania laurina***

WATER GUM

From the east coast of Australia, this small, erect evergreen grows 15–50 ft (about 4.5–15 m) and has sleek, light brown bark. Its dense, rounded crown bears lance-shaped foliage up to 4 in (about 10 cm) long. Leaves are shiny deep green with a pale green underside, occasionally turning reddish in cooler weather. During summer, clusters of small, fragrant yellow flowers appear in the leaf axils. It adapts to full sun or part shade, and though it prefers a rich, moist but well-drained soil it tolerates drought once established. Prune when required and propagate from seed. Suitable for small gardens and hedges, the flowers make for fine honey.

ZONES 10–11

### *TSUGA*
### *canadensis*

CANADIAN HEMLOCK, EASTERN HEMLOCK

This elegant conifer is native to northeastern North America. It is somewhat variable in color and shape, but generally grows to 80 ft (about 24 m) or more in a broad, conical shape, often with multiple upstretched trunks. The bark is dark and heavily grooved and the foliage is deep green, comprising two ranks of flat, narrow leaves. These are lightly serrated and often twist to reveal silvery white stripes underneath. Pale brown, egg-shaped cones contain little winged seeds from which the tree is propagated. It responds very well to pruning and can be easily shaped into a dense hedge. The "hemlock" in the common name apparently derives from the leaves' resemblance to those of the poisonous plant.

ZONES 3–7

*Tristania confertus*

*Ulmus parvifolia*

### *ULMUS*

ELM

This genus contains over 15 species of deciduous trees and shrubs native to Asia, Europe and North America. The majestic, round-crowned trees have attained heights of up to 160 ft (about 49 m). The elliptical foliage varies: from slender, deep green and shiny to broad, mid-green and roughly textured; heavily or finely serrated; with or without prominent parallel ribs. Inconspicuous flowers appear in spring or fall, followed by dense clusters of flat, roundish, winged seeds. These trees like a rich, well-drained soil with full sun. Propagate from seed or cuttings or by grafting the numerous suckers. The Dutch elm disease has wiped out much of the beautiful American elms that once lined streets throughout the eastern half of the continent. Researchers are still looking for disease-resistant forms; check local regulations, which may prohibit the planting of some elms.

*Tsuga canadensis*

### *U. americana*

AMERICAN ELM

An old favorite among native trees in eastern North America, the 100 ft (about 30 m) tall, vase-like shape of this species lined many city streets, creating cathedral-like spaces. The Dutch elm disease has nearly wiped out the species, since treatment is expensive and not always successful. Naturally a swamp dweller, this tree adapted easily to the drier urban conditions, though its shallow roots often caused problems with pavements and water lines. New selections and hybrids are continually being tested for resistance to the disease.

ZONES 3–9

### *U. glabra* 'Camperdownii'

CAMPERDOWN ELM

This distinctive weeping elm is selected from the Wych or Scotch elms. It is usually grafted to the top of an erect elm sapling; the weeping habit creates a dense curtain of foliage, making a secret hideaway beneath the tree. A dramatic specimen tree, it is best in a park or large gardens.

ZONES 5–10

### *U. parvifolia*

**CHINESE ELM**

Native to China, Japan, Korea and Taiwan, this species grows fast to 30–50 ft (about 9–15 m). Its trunk and pendent branches are covered with an attractive gray, white and yellow-brown bark. Small, glossy, elliptical leaves are serrated. It is reliably evergreen in mild winter climates, deciduous elsewhere. This adaptable tree is useful throughout much of the continent. Propagate from seed or root cuttings in fall.

ZONES 5–10

### *U. pumila*

**SIBERIAN ELM**

Generally considered a weed tree, this species is nevertheless valuable in the windswept prairie states where few trees are really happy. Very fast growing and as a result weak wooded, it will reach 50 ft (about 15 m) or more in just a few years. Tiny leaves offer no fall color; seedlings need constant weeding. It tolerates most soil conditions, heat, drought and cold.

ZONES 3–9

## *UMBELLULARIA*
### *californica*

**CALIFORNIA BAY, OREGON MYRTLE, PEPPERWOOD**

This single-species North American genus is a valuable shade tree that reaches up to 80 ft (about 24 m). Variable in habit, it may be compact and shrubby in exposed coastal areas, or tall and slender in damp forests. Its glossy, bright green leaves are lanceolate and aromatic when crushed. Little clusters of insignificant yellow blossoms are followed by small, inedible purple fruit. This species is found in cool, coastal regions from California north to Washington, yet adapts to gardens in hotter interior areas and will take full sun to full shade on well-drained soils. The spicy leaves of *U. californica* are similar to bay leaves, but stronger, and may be substituted for them in cooking.

ZONES 8–10

## *VITEX*
### *lucens*

**NEW ZEALAND CHASTE TREE**

Reaching up to 60 ft (about 18 m) in height, this attractive New Zealand evergreen develops a broad, rounded crown with palmately divided leaves composed of up to 5 glossy, dark green leaflets. From late winter to mid-spring, racemes of small, red, cup-shaped flowers appear in profusion. This species prefers full sun and porous soil. Propagate from seed in fall and spring, or semi-ripe cuttings in summer.

ZONES 9–10

## *YUCCA*
### *brevifolia*

**JOSHUA TREE**

Native to the deserts from southern California to southwestern Utah, this is the tallest of the yuccas; it has only a few branches, each ending with a dense rosette of the typical stiff, narrow, sharply pointed leaves. Found only in the higher deserts, it is well adapted to intense heat, extreme drought and the frosty nights of winter. Reaching 25–30 ft (about 7.5–10 m) tall, it creates a distinct silhouette, best suited to use in desert gardens. Short, dense clusters of waxy white flowers appear in spring.

ZONES 7–9

## *ZELKOVA*
### *serrata*

**JAPANESE ELM**

Native to Japan, this broad-spreading, deciduous tree rapidly reaches 37–60 ft (about 10.5–18 m). Erect, with sculpted limbs, it is valued for its shade and timber. The slender, elliptical leaves, similar to those of other elms', are fine pointed and gently serrated; fall color varies from soft golds and oranges to dull reds. Little, inconspicuous green flowers, the males in clusters, appear in spring and are followed by enduring leathery fruit. This attractive tree is widely adapted across North America. Plant in deep, damp, well-drained soil and allow full sun. Propagate from seed in fall. The timber is highly regarded in Japan.

ZONES 4–10

*Tristaniopsis laurina*

*Vitex lucens*

*Zelkova serrata*

*Umbellularia californica*

*Ulmus pumila*

CHAPTER 5

# *Bulbs, Corms & Tubers*

*The history of bulbs and how they came to western Europe to be hybridized into the plants we grow today makes fascinating reading. Most of the bulbs we think of as being indigenous to Europe can be traced back to their native habitat much further east in the mountainous regions of Asia Minor, while others were gathered initially from southern Africa.*

In the centuries of European worldwide exploration bulbs, as well as other exotic plants, were prized by naturalists and form the basis of modern strains of the bulbs marketed today. Narcissus for instance were grown by the ancient Egyptians, tulips came from Turkestan while gladiolus and nerines originated in the mountains of the southwestern Cape of South Africa.

As bulbs have differing flowering times, there is no limit to the type and number which can be included in the garden to provide for almost year-round color. The term bulb, horticulturally speaking, includes true bulbs, corms and tubers.

## Bulbs

True bulbs, of which the onion is an easily identified example, are made up of a series of scales joined at the base which enclose and protect a central bud. These scales collect and store food for the following year's growth and flowering and it's for this reason that it is necessary to allow the leaves of true bulbs to die down naturally as they continue to manufacture and store food for the following season, well after the flower has finished. This process also makes it possible for true bulbs such as hyacinths, narcissus and tulips to flower successfully in pots or jars as they use this stored energy to produce the current season's flowers. True bulbs reproduce by forming bulbils around the base of the plant and these can be easily removed when bulbs are lifted, even though they may take several years to flower.

## Corms

A corm has a swollen base of solid storage tissue. Once flowering is over a new corm develops on top and the original one dies, often producing new corms or pips around the perimeter before it withers completely. Gladiolus and freesias are good examples of a corm.

## Tubers

Again a food storage system, a tuber can be formed from stems or roots. "Eyes" are produced from these swollen areas and form new plants. Dahlias are easily identified as being this type of bulb as is the common potato, which has been sitting in the vegetable drawer too long.

## Creating Effects with Bulbs

Basically bulbs have evolved in the above ways because of environmental factors. They are able to store food for long, dry, dormant periods then, in very quick time when the climate is right,

*The elegant flower of the tulip has made it one of the most popular bulbs in the world.*

shoot, flower then gather enough food for the following year. Some northern hemisphere bulbs like crocus and fritillaria wait for the watering they receive as the snow melts to suddenly burst upon the scene. These and many other bulbs are very particular regarding their environment as many temperate climate gardeners have realized when they have omitted to "refrigerate" their tulip bulbs to chill them before planting. Other bulbs are far more accommodating and will often naturalize in the most unlikely places because the soil, combined with the surrounding ecosystem, is to their liking.

Even in small gardens a natural effect can be created, especially under lightly foliaged deciduous trees as the roots of the trees ensure adequate drainage and there's less competition from grass. These woodland companions need to be chosen with consideration to their dormant period. Choose bulbs like trilliums and scillas and many of the narcissus species which are early to shoot and bloom; as their dormancy approaches, the overhead canopy is beginning its active growth.

The informality of a woodland bulb display relies to a great extent on the naturalistic way in which the bulbs are planted. Planting in drifts, random scatterings of the bulbs whereby they are left to grow where they land when thrown by the handful, is the best method of ensuring this. Size of the drift is governed by available space, of course, yet it is the very randomness of the display rather than its size that is the eye-catching element. Often a gardener in cold areas relies on bulb drifts to give a welcome color display in early spring and is tempted to mix different species and colors. However, a more pleasing effect is achieved by having drifts of different color or species flowering on from one drift to the next rather than a "hundreds and thousands" look. Bluebells look good in such a design with the blue species in the lighter, more open areas and the white flowering ones grouped closer to, say, the dark green background of evergreen shrubs.

There are many hardy bulbs which we often associate with "old" gardens. Long left to their own devices, they surprise us each year with their colorful appearance amid the shrubbery. Some of these, like *Amaryllis belladonna*, send up tall, single stems holding clusters of pale pink trumpets at the cusp of the summer–fall season, while the snowflake with its dainty, green-tipped, white bells gives us a good indication that spring is almost here.

*The sunny narcissus flowers are ideal for indoor decoration.*

Planting bulbs among shrubs usually needs careful consideration because we can very easily lose track of where they are while they are dormant, and gardeners everywhere always have the tendency to fill any vacant space with something new which takes their fancy. As discussed earlier, competition from overhanging shrubs also has to be taken into account.

Many of the more delicate bulbs are overpowered by surrounding plants and are ideally suited to rock gardens where individual pockets can be given over to one particular species. Rockeries really need to be placed on an existing slope or where a change of level is being designed into the garden, otherwise dwarf bulbs can be placed in a brick or stone paved outdoor area where they can pop up in unpaved pockets from under a fine gravel scree. Provided drainage has been catered for, these pockets are ideal for dwarf tulips, crocus, freesias, ixias, sparaxis, babianas, lachenalias and other delicate bulbs which would be lost in the general shrubbery.

Raised beds filled with good quality, free-draining soil are a sure way of providing the bulbs with the freedom from competition and drainage they need. These beds can be made using treated logs, railway sleepers or a couple of rows of old bricks. For a gardener wishing to perfect the hobby of growing prized, delicate bulbs rather than opting for a general garden display, these beds may well be the answer. Alternatively these raised beds can be filled with free-draining sand and pots of bulbs plunged into them to ensure that they don't dry out, then when the flowers appear each individual pot can be taken indoors or placed in a prominent position in the garden or even on the patio where the blooms can be appreciated.

## Growing Conditions

Generally bulbs prefer well-drained, slightly acidic soil. Most have evolved in areas with prolonged dry periods followed in the growing season by melting snow or good rains. Therefore, most are unable to withstand prolonged periods of waterlogged soil, but there are always exceptions to the rule and the arum lily thrives in moist sites as do the Japanese and flag iris.

Similarly there are very few bulbs which can be grown in really shady areas and still flower well. Again, luckily for the gardener looking to highlight a shady spot with yearly color there is *Clivia miniata,* which produces bright orange flowers each spring, or the more delicate lily of the valley and snowflakes, providing that wonderful flowering highlight of white blooms against green foliage so often employed by professional landscapers to such good effect.

Allium christophii

Allium narcissiflorum

Amaryllis belladonna

Allium moly

Anemone blanda

## ALLIUM

Garlic and onions belong to this large genus of over 700 species, native to Asia, Africa and America. There are many very attractive ornamental species as well as edible ones. Many species have a pungent onion or garlic scent but this is usually only noticeable when parts of the plant are bruised or crushed. Most are easy to grow; some are so vigorous they can become difficult to control. They vary greatly in size: from 2 in (about 5 cm) high to 3 ft (about 90 cm). Smaller species are ideal in a rockery. Bulbs should be planted in fall in well-drained soil 2–6 in (about 5–15 cm) deep, depending on the size of the bulb. Flowering time varies from spring to fall. Propagation can be from offsets, which multiply freely, or from seed sown in fall; seedlings may take several years to reach flowering size.

### *A. christophii*

**syn. *A. albopilosum***

STAR OF PERSIA

This attractive species grows up to 24 in (about 60 cm) high. The broad leaves are glaucous blue-green above and hairy beneath. The sturdy stem bears a rounded umbel of flowers up to 12 in (about 30 cm) wide. The individual violet flowers borne in spring are star shaped. They turn silvery as the seeds ripen and are very useful for dried flower arrangements. Bulbs should be planted in fall, 6 in (about 15 cm) deep in well-drained soil. *A. christophii* grows best in full sun.

ZONES 4–10

Allium giganteum

### *A. giganteum*

GIANT ALLIUM

Among the tallest of flowering onions, this species has 4–6 ft (about 1.2–1.8 m) stems topped with dense, 4–6 in (about 10–15 cm) diameter umbels of violet to deep purple flowers in mid-summer. Leaves are gray-green, 18 in (about 45 cm) long and usually fade by flowering time. The flowers dry well for later use indoors. Plant bulbs 4 in (about 10 cm) deep.

ZONES 6–10

### *A. moly*

GOLDEN GARLIC

Native to Spain, *A. moly* grows up to 14 in (about 35 cm). Broad, gray-green basal leaves surround stems which each bear an umbel of up to 40 flowers. The bright yellow, star-shaped flowers appear in late spring. It can be planted in full sun or partial shade. Bulbs should be planted 2 in (about 5 cm) deep in fall in well-drained soil. The Spanish once regarded this plant as a sign of prosperity if they discovered it in their gardens.

ZONES 2–9

### *A. narcissiflorum*

This delightful species grows up to 12 in (about 30 cm) high. Slender, gray-green leaves surround a stem bearing an umbel of up to 12 flowers. The bright pink to purple, nodding flowers appear in early summer. Plant bulbs 3 in (about 7.5 cm) deep in fall in full sun.

ZONES 8–10

### *A. neopolitanum*

NAPLES ONION, DAFFODIL ONION

This easily grown flowering onion produces fragrant white flowers in loose heads in early spring. Flowering stems are 12 in (about 30 cm) tall. This species spreads by seed where it is happy. Plant 3 in (about 7.5 cm) deep in fall. It can also be potted up and forced for indoor bloom.

ZONES 7–9

## AMARYLLIS

### *belladonna*

NAKED LADY, BELLADONNA LILY

This outstanding plant is a gardener's dream: easy to grow and, as the name *belladonna* ("beautiful lady") implies, very beautiful. Native to

*Anomatheca laxa*

South Africa, it flowers in late summer or early fall. A sturdy, fast-growing stem up to 20 in (about 50 cm) high is topped with a glorious display of white, pale pink or rosy pink, lily-like flowers. The strap-like basal leaves appear after the flowers fade; leaves die by the following summer. Plant large bulbs in late summer at soil level or just below, in well-drained soil. A fairly sunny position is best in cool areas, but they may need light shade in very warm areas. Cut down flower stalks once flowering is finished but ensure the plant is well watered through winter. Grown easily from seed, it often self-sows freely. The genus *Amaryllis* once contained many species, including hippeastrums. Now, *A. belladonna* is considered to be the only true *Amaryllis* and other species have been reclassified.

ZONES 8–10

## ANEMONE

WINDFLOWER

This highly varied genus is mainly native to southern Europe and the Middle East. Size and flower color vary greatly, as do flowering times; the planting of tubers can be staggered to provide a succession of glorious blooms. Most species do well in rich, well-drained soil in a sunny or lightly shaded situation. Flowers usually appear about 4 months after planting. Grow from seed planted in summer, being careful to protect the seedlings from hot sun. Plant tubers 2–3 in (about 5–7.5 cm) deep and take care that each tuber's "fingers" are pointing down.

*Arum italicum*

### *A. blanda*

GRECIAN WINDFLOWER

This delicate-looking species is native to Greece; it grows to 8 in (about 20 cm) with green, deeply divided leaves. The daisy-like flowers which appear in spring can be white, pink or blue and are around 1½ in (about 3 cm) wide. *A. blanda* self-seeds freely and, given moist, slightly shaded conditions, should spread into a beautiful display of flowers.

ZONES 5–9

### *A. coronaria*

POPPY-FLOWERED ANEMONE

Many hybrids have been developed from this Mediterranean species, the most commonly planted anemone. It grows up to 10 in (about 25 cm). The poppy-like flowers are up to 4 in (about 10 cm) wide and can range in color from red to purple to blue. *A. coronaria* is usually treated as an annual. 'De Caen' is a single and 'St Brigid' is a popular semi-double, with colors ranging from pink to purple to scarlet to blue.

ZONES 8–10

### *A. nemorosa*

WOOD ANEMONE

This spreading species grows to 6 in (about 15 cm). The green leaves are deeply divided, while the delicate white flowers are star shaped and 1½ in (about 3 cm) wide; they appear in spring. Plant in a lightly shaded spot in moist, woodsy soil.

ZONES 5–10

## *ANOMATHECA*

*laxa*

**syn. *Lapeirousia laxa***

SCARLET FREESIA

This freesia-like native of South Africa grows 6–10 in (about 12–15 cm) tall with narrow, sword-shaped, erect, basal leaves, and produces one-sided spikes bearing up to 12 flowers. The star-shaped, salmon, red or white flowers, less than 1 in (about 2.5 cm) wide, appear in spring. Corms should be planted in fall in well-drained soil in a sunny or partially shaded situation. In very cold areas corms should be lifted and dry stored for

*Anenome nemorosa*

the winter. It needs little or no water during summer. If left undisturbed, it should self-seed freely. It can be propagated from offsets or from seed sown in late summer, which may flower the next spring but will usually produce a much better display in the second year.

ZONES 7–10

## *ARISTEA*

*ecklonii*

This iris relative from South Africa produces loose panicles of 1 in (about 2.5 cm) blue flowers in late spring and early summer. Clumps of sword-like leaves are up to 24 in (about 60 cm) long and are evergreen. Flattened flowers stems rise above the foliage; each flower is short lived, although many are produced. Rhizomes should be planted in well-drained soil in full sun or partial shade. They thrive in a moist soil but do well in average garden conditions. Propagate from seed in the fall or spring. It resents transplanting or dividing once established.

ZONES 9–10

## *ARUM*

*italicum*

ITALIAN ARUM

Although many plants are commonly called arums, only a few truly belong to this genus. *A. italicum*

*Asphodeline lutea*

grows to 12 in (about 30 cm). Broad, arrow-shaped, marbled leaves appear in fall. The flower is a light green, hooded spathe with a yellow spadix which appears in early spring and is followed by stout clusters of orange-red berries which last until late summer; the berries are held just above the ground on short stalks. Tubers should be planted in fall in rich, moist soil in partial shade, with plenty of water during the growing season. They need protection in cold areas. They can be divided from big clumps once the foliage has died, or propagated from seed in the fall.

ZONES 6–10

## *ASPHODELINE*

*lutea*

YELLOW ASPHODEL, KING'S SPEAR

A native of the Mediterranean, this neat, clump-forming perennial is a fragrant plant that grows to 3 ft (about 90 cm) or more. Furrowed, gray-green leaves appear below spear-like stems bearing racemes of yellow, star-shaped flowers, some 1½ in (about 3 cm) long. Plant in full sun in well-drained soil and keep moist before the flowering period in spring. Can be propagated by dividing the roots carefully in late winter, or from seed in fall or in spring.

ZONES 7–10

*Anemone coronaria*

## BABIANA
### *stricta*
BABOON FLOWER

Popular with baboons for their edible bulbs, these South African plants grow to 12 in (about 30 cm) tall. The hairy, slender leaves are strongly ribbed and spikes bearing up to 10 cup-shaped flowers appear above the foliage. The freesia-like flowers, which appear in spring, are blue to violet but there are pale-colored forms of white or cream; some are fragrant. Plant the corms in fall in sandy soil in a sunny position. They look best planted in large clumps. Provide plenty of water during the winter growing season, little or none during the summer. Propagate from offsets or seed in the fall.

ZONES 8–10

## BEGONIA
BEGONIA

These immensely popular plants are grown worldwide for their exotic summer blooms and beautiful foliage. Large-flowered, tuberous begonias are usually called *B.* x *tuberhybrida.* They are available with flowers in every color of the rainbow, as singles or doubles, with many variations of frills and ruffles. They like temperate to warm conditions. The tubers should be planted in spring in partial shade in a rich, moist soil. Sometimes they are planted in pots and started indoors in winter and transferred outside when the weather is warmer. They may need to be staked as the large flowers are heavy. Water should be decreased after flowering, and when the leaves have started to yellow the tuber should be lifted and dried very carefully before storage. Propagate from seed or from stem or leaf cuttings.

### *B.* x *tuberhybrida* 'Camellia' and 'Rose' flowered types
TUBEROUS BEGONIA

The most popular of the tuberous begonias, these bear large to enormous, 10 in (about 25 cm) or more, double flowers in every color but blue. To have the biggest flowers they should be disbudded, sacrificing the small female flowers that grow on either side of the central male. There are many named varieties in an ever-changing selection.

ALL ZONES

### *B.* x *tuberhybrida multiflora*

Usually single flowered, these are grown not so much for the individual flowers as for the massed effect. They are available in the same range of colors as the others and are grown in the same way, except that they need no disbudding. Plants can be floppy and will benefit from staking.

ALL ZONES

### *B.* x *tuberhybrida pendula*
BASKET BEGONIA

The basket begonias carry their flowers in pendent sprays, which look very good cascading from hanging baskets. The flowers are single or double, and usually smaller than the large-flowered types. They come in the same range of colors as the others and are grown in the same way.

ALL ZONES

## BELAMCANDA
### *chinensis*
BLACKBERRY LILY, LEOPARD LILY

This little known native of China and Japan is a member of the iris family. Growing to 3 ft (about 90 cm) or more, the foliage is sword shaped like that of an iris. Branched spikes of orange-red, spotted flowers appear in summer, giving it the name "leopard lily." The flower produces clusters of black, shiny seeds, hence the other name, "blackberry lily." Tubers should be planted in spring just below the soil level in rich, well-drained soil in full sun or partial shade. Water well in summer. They need some protection in very cold winters. Propagate by division or from seed.

ZONES 6–10

## BRIMEURA
### *amethystina*
syn. ***Hyacinthus amethystinus***

This hyacinth-like native of Spain grows to 10 in (about 25 cm). Slender, strap-like foliage surrounds stems which bear up to eight delicate, $^1/_2$ in (about 1 cm), bell-shaped flowers ranging in color from white to blue. Plant bulbs in fall in rich, well-drained soil in full sun or partial shade. Propagate by division or from seed in fall.

ZONES 5–10

## BRUNSVIGIA

Members of this South African genus are similar in character to the belladonna lily. However, they are far more tender and can be quite difficult to grow. Tall stems bear a dazzling mass of flowers in fall. The scented flowers radiate from the top of the stem like a candelabra. The bulbs are huge, up to 10 in (about 25 cm). They should be planted in rich, sandy soil in full sun. Water well in the growing season but keep dry when dormant. Propagation is

*Begonia* x *tuberhybrida*

*Begonia* x *tuberhybrida pendula*

*Babiana stricta*

*Begonia* x *tuberhybrida multiflora*

*Brimeura amethystina*

*Belamcanda chinensis*

slow. Seedlings can take up to 4 years to flower. Offsets must be fairly large before division and may take years to flower.

*B. josephinae*

JOSEPHINE'S LILY

The beautiful Josephine's lily grows up to 30 in (about 76 cm). The stout stem bears a mass of bright red, funnel-shaped flowers in late summer. The 2 in (about 5 cm) wide flowers are scented and radiate out from the top of the stem. Strap-like leaves appear after flowering. The large bulbs should be planted with the top half exposed above the soil line.

ZONES 9–10

*B. orientalis*

The sturdy stem grows up to around 18 in (about 45 cm) and bears a flowerhead which can be up to 16 in (about 40 cm) wide. The small crimson flowers appear in late summer before the leaves. The foliage often lies flat on the ground.

ZONES 9–10

## *BULBINELLA floribunda*

CAT'S-TAIL

This native of South Africa produces 24 in (about 60 cm) flower stalks in late winter to early spring. The stalk is topped with a 4 in (about 10 cm) spike crammed with tiny yellow to orange flowers. Long, narrow basal leaves appear in fall. The plant disappears completely in summer. Bulbs should be planted in well-drained soil with the top of the bulb at soil level. It likes a sunny situation and plenty of water during the growing season, but can be allowed to dry out in summer. Propagate from seed or by division. Excellent as a long-lasting cut flower.

ZONES 8–10

## *CALADIUM bicolor*

syn. *C.* x *hortulanum*

FANCY-LEAVED CALADIUM

These tropical plants from South America can be grown as summer bulbs throughout North America. Ideal for moist, shaded portions of the garden, they will tolerate full sun in very humid climates. Their arrowhead-shaped leaves vary from plain green to intricate combinations of green, white, pink and red. The flowers are arum like and inconspicuous, held beneath the foliage. Plants reach 12–15 in (about 30–38 cm) high, with a similar spread. In tropical climates they can remain in the ground year round, and may naturalize in damp areas. Elsewhere they âre planted in spring and lifted before the first killing frost. Store in a dry place indoors over winter. Give plenty of water through the growing season. Divide rhizomes before planting in spring.

ALL ZONES

## *CALOCHORTUS*

MARIPOSA LILY, FAIRY LANTERN

*Mariposa* is Spanish for butterfly, which aptly describes this richly varied genus with its beautifully colored and patterned flowers. Native to the West Coast of North America and Mexico, they produce goblet-shaped flowers above grass-like foliage in spring and summer. They are best adapted to the summer-dry climates of the West, where they should be planted in full sun to light shade. Plant bulbs in fall in a gritty, well-drained soil. A raised bed is ideal as good drainage is essential. Water through the growing season but allow them to dry out for the summer. They can be propagated by division or from seed.

*C. albus*

FAIRY LANTERN

A delightful spring-flowering species growing up to 20 in (about 50 cm). White or pink, nodding, bell-shaped flowers around 1 in (about 2.5 cm) wide can sometimes have a brownish blotch.

ZONES 7–10

*C. venustus*

MARIPOSA LILY

A late spring/early summer flowering species. The wiry, branched flower stem grows to 20 in (about 50 cm) and bears up to 4 poppy-like, three-petaled flowers, usually white, cream or yellow with a maroon blotch in the center.

ZONES 7–10

## *CAMASSIA quamash*

syn. *C. esculenta*

CAMASS, QUAMASH

This North American native grows to 24 in (about 60 cm) and produces a densely covered flower

*Bulbinella floribunda*

*Calochortus venustus*

*Camassia quamash*

*Calochortus albus*

*Caladium bicolor*

*Brunsvigia orientalis*

*Brunsvigia josephinae*

*Canna* x *generalis*

*Clivia miniata*

spike above an erect stem; it has slender basal leaves. The blue, star-shaped flowers which appear in spring have 6 petals and measure 1 in (about 2.5 cm). Bulbs should be planted in late fall in loamy, rich, moist soil. Position in partial shade or full sun if the soil is very moist. It does well in cool temperatures. Propagate by division or from seed; the latter may take up to five years to produce flowers. North American Indians once ate the large bulbs of quamash.

ZONES 4–9

## CANNA
### x *generalis*

Cannas are amongst the easiest of perennial bulbs to grow, with flower color varying from bright red, orange, salmon pink, yellow to white, and appearing from early summer to fall. These hybrids grow to a height of 2–6 ft (about 24–180 cm). Plant in full or part sun in good soil with steady moisture.

ZONES 8–11

## CARDIOCRINUM
### *giganteum*
**syn. *Lilium giganteum***

GIANT LILY

A magnificent, summer-flowering plant reaching up to 12 ft (about 3.5 m) in height. Unfortunately, the giant lily is not for the gardener who needs to see overnight results. A small bulb planted today is unlikely to flower for 5 years. The tall, sturdy stem bears up to twenty 10 in (about 25 cm) flowers, tubular at

*Cardiocrinum giganteum*

*Chasmanthe aethiopica*

the base and trumpet shaped at the top. The cream flowers are striped with maroon-red blotches at the throat and are heavily scented. The large bulbs should be planted in rich, acid soil in partial shade. Water and fertilize well once shoots appear. The main bulb dies after flowering but propagation is possible from offsets (which flower in 3 or 4 years) and seed. A good plan is to buy three sizes of bulbs, to ensure some flowers each year.

ZONES 7–9

## CHASMANTHE
### *aethiopica*

This South African native shares some characteristics with gladiolus. Ribbed, sword-shaped leaves fan out from the base, and the stems rise to 4½ ft (about 1.3 m). Yellow to red, slender, tubular flowers, 1 in (about 2.5 cm) long, are borne fan like on one side of the stem in late winter and spring. Plant corms in the fall in sun or partial shade in well-drained soil. Keep moist during the growing season and allow to dry out after flowering. Propagate from offsets or from seed sown in the fall.

ZONES 9–10

## CHIONODOXA
### *luciliae*
**syn. *C. gigantea***

GLORY-OF-THE-SNOW

These delicate-looking flowers are seen emerging from the melting snow in Europe and parts of Asia, giving the name *Chionodoxa*, Greek for snow glory. Ideal for a rock garden in a cool climate, they grow

*Chionodoxa luciliae*

to 6 in (about 15 cm), flowering in early spring. Narrow, basal leaves surround a slender stem which bears up to six, ½ in (about 1 cm), mauve to blue star-shaped flowers with white centers. Bulbs should be planted in well-drained soil, dressed with a layer of mulch, in fall. They will spread well of their own accord and can be propagated from seeds or offsets in the fall.

ZONES 3–8

## CLIVIA
### *miniata*

CLIVIA, KAFFIR LILY

This South African native produces a glorious spring display of funnel-shaped, 3 in (about 7.5 cm) orange-red flowers, paler at the throat, in clusters of up to 12. This species grows to 18 in (about 45 cm) tall and as wide. The foliage is glossy, thick and strap like. Plant in a sheltered position in rich, well-drained soil. The foliage burns in direct sunlight. Give regular water year round. Propagate by division after flowering; seed can also be used but this can be slow to flower. In cooler areas they can be grown in pots; they flower better when pot bound. Yellow and cream varieties are also available, and hybrids are becoming very popular.

ZONES 9–11

## COLCHICUM

AUTUMN CROCUS, MEADOW SAFFRON

This genus of flowering corms is native mainly to Europe and Asia. Masses of crocus-like flowers appear in fall, followed by the strap-like basal foliage. They are very easy to grow. Plant the corms in late summer in well-drained soil in sun or partial shade. Corms will also usually flower without any soil, so they can be kept inside for display and planted after flowering. Propagate from seed or by division in summer. The plants are poisonous, although their active ingredient colchicine is used in the treatment of certain forms of cancer. *C. speciosum* is one of the most striking of the autumn crocuses, producing beautiful mauve-purple, goblet-shaped flowers.

*Convallaria majalis*

*Colchicum autumnale*

### *C. autumnale*

The best known of the species, this grows to 6 in (about 15 cm) and has rosy pink to white, goblet-shaped flowers up to 4 in (about 10 cm) long. Each corm produces masses of flowers and multiplies freely. There is also a double-flowered form.
ZONES 5–10

### *C.* 'Lilac Wonder'

As the name suggests, this hardy cultivar produces large, up to 8 in (about 20 cm) long, lilac flowers. The tulip-like flowers appear in fall and are followed by the strap-like foliage.
ZONES 4–10

### *C. speciosum*

This very attractive species has reddish purple flowers, usually with a white throat. Flowers can be 4 in (about 10 cm) wide and reach 12 in (about 30 cm) high, appearing in fall ahead of the foliage.
ZONES 6–10

## CONVALLARIA
### *majalis*
LILY-OF-THE-VALLEY

Renowned for its glorious perfume, this beautiful plant is native to the northern hemisphere and does best in cool climates. It is low growing, up to 8 in (about 20 cm), with thick, oval to oblong, dark green leaves. The dainty, white, bell-shaped flowers appear in spring. The rhizomes, or "pips" as they are commonly known, should be planted in fall in a partially shaded position. Soil should be rich and moist, and a dressing of mulch will give good results. Water well during the growing period. Given the right conditions *C. majalis* spreads freely, sometimes becoming overcrowded when it will need to be divided.
ZONES 2–7

## *CRINUM*

Natives of warm climates around the world, crinums are valued for

*Crinum moorei*

their large, lily-like flowers and the ease with which they grow. Up to 20 scented flowers are borne on a tall, thick stem, usually in summer to early fall. The large bulbs should be planted in rich, moist soil with the neck of the bulb above ground level. Partial shade is best, particularly in very hot areas. Propagation is best from seed as dividing the plants is difficult. Flowers usually take a few seasons to develop with either method. They are susceptible to caterpillars, slugs and snails.

### *C. bulbispermum*

This species reaches up to around 3 ft (about 90 cm). Glossy, oblong leaves are borne on a thick leaf stalk. The sturdy scape rises beside the stem and is topped with a cluster of large, 10 in (about 25 cm), funnel-shaped flowers in white to pink, sometimes striped with dark pink. It does well in damp soil.
ZONES 7–10

### *C. moorei*

This popular species grows up to 30 in (about 76 cm). The strong stem bears a cluster of 4 in (about 10 cm), funnel-shaped flowers. The semi-pendent blooms are pale pink with white at the throat. The foliage is glossy and strap like.
ZONES 8–10

### *C.* x *powellii*
CRINUM

This well-known and easily grown hybrid between *C. bulbispermum*

*Crinum bulbispermum*

*Crinum* x *powellii*

and *C. moorei* grows up to 3 ft (about 90 cm). Strap-like foliage is produced on a thick stalk and the bare scape is crowned with up to 10 scented, pink flowers. There is also a white form. Plant in sun or shade in average garden soil.
ZONES 7–11

## *CROCOSMIA*
MONTBRETIA

These South African natives bear attractive displays of flowers in summer. Tall, pleated leaves form a fan of foliage, similar to a gladiolus. A branched spike of brightly colored flowers sits atop the tall stem. Plant the corms in spring in any soil with adequate drainage in a position that receives plenty of sun. Little or no summer water is needed once established. They will multiply freely and should not be divided unless overcrowded. This should be done in spring if necessary.

*Colchicum* 'Lilac Wonder'

*Crocosmia* x *crocosmiiflora*

### *C.* x *crocosmiiflora*
MONTBRETIA

Growing to 30 in (about 76 cm), the stem bears a branching spike of up to 40 orange-red, gladiolus-like flowers of around 1 in (about 2.5 cm). Bayonet-shaped foliage forms a fan from the base of the plant. This species needs a protected situation in cold climates. Plant in full sun in ordinary, well-drained garden soil.
ZONES 6–10

### *C. masonorum*

A tall species, growing up to 4 ft (about 1.2 m). The branched stem is topped with an arched display of vermilion flowers. The 6-petaled flowers are quite large, up to 3 in (about 7.5 cm) wide. The narrow, bayonet-shaped foliage is pleated. It is useful as a cut flower. Recently, larger-flowered hybrids in a wider range of colors (yellow to red) have been introduced from England. These hybrids have names like

*Crocus,* Dutch hybrids

*Crocus flavus*

*Crocosmia masonorum*

*Cyclamen coum* subsp. *coum*

*Crocosmia* 'Lucifer'

*Crocus tomasinianus*

'Lucifer' (flame red) and 'Solfatarre' (golden-apricot with bronzy leaves). They may be a bit hardier than are the species.
ZONES 6–10

## *CROCUS*

CROCUS

Heralding the beginning of spring in Europe, crocuses pop up through the snow, the cheerful displays a sign that winter is over. Other species flower in late summer or fall. The goblet-shaped flowers vary greatly in color. The foliage is grass like, with a silver-white stripe along the center of the leaf. In warmer climates the corms may flower in the first year but may not flower again. They can be grown in pots in warmer areas, in a cool spot. Corms should be planted in early fall in moist, well-drained soil in full sun or partial shade. Keep well watered until the foliage begins to die. They do not spread very fast but clumps can be divided if they are overcrowded. Seed can be planted in fall, although plants grown from seed usually will not flower for three years.

### *C.*, Dutch hybrids

The Dutch hybrids are vigorous plants with large flowers up to 6 in (about 15 cm) long. The color range is varied, with white to yellow to purple to blue. There are also some striped varieties. Many of these hybrids derive from *C. vernus.* They should be planted in fall in well-drained soil at a depth of around 4 in (about 10 cm).
ZONES 4–9

### *C.* species, autumn blooming

AUTUMN-BLOOMING CROCUS

Some of the most delicate of the crocus are those that flower in late summer or during the fall. All are native to regions around the Mediterranean. Springing directly from the ground with no foliage present, their effect in the garden is magical. All need to be planted in late summer in a sunny, well-drained situation. *C. speciosus* is one of the easiest to grow, producing lavender-blue flowers in September. Mauve-colored *C. sativus* is the source of the flavoring saffron.
ZONES 7–10

### *C.* species, spring blooming

SPRING-BLOOMING CROCUS

These Mediterranean natives begin the season in late winter, various species offering flowers into mid-spring. Generally of easy growth and tolerating the summer shade of a deciduous tree, they often multiply readily, creating enchanting drifts in the garden. Colors vary from white and yellow to blue, purple and pink. *C. flavus* is an early-flowering yellow species. *C. tomasinianus* is typically lavender to purple in color, sometimes with a white throat.
ZONES 5–9

## *CYCLAMEN*

CYCLAMEN

The flower of the cyclamen must be one of the most elegant of all plants. These natives of the Mediterranean region are often cultivated in pots indoors but can also be grown in the garden. Florist's cyclamen (*C. persicum*) is usually bought already in flower for an indoor display. Keep the pot in good light but out of direct sun in an unheated room. It is less hardy than the other species. Tubers should be planted in late summer or fall in light, fibrous soil rich in organic matter with excellent drainage, in partial shade. Water regularly during growth but allow to dry out during summer. The tubers are best left undisturbed and should grow larger each year, flowering more abundantly each season. Propagate from seed in fall. Plants should flower in a year.

### *C. coum*

This popular, Middle Eastern species grows to 4 in (about 10 cm) with leaves that are round to heart shaped, dark green and may be marbled with light green or silver. The abundant flowers vary from pale mauve to deep pink, often stained crimson at the base. Flowering is from January to March. *C. coum* subsp. *coum* has elegant, pink to crimson flowers.
ZONES 6–10

### *C. hederifolium*

syn. *C. neapolitanum*

This later summer- or fall-flowering species can produce corms up to 6 in (about 15 cm) wide. Growing to 4 in (about 10 cm), it has dark green, marbled, ivy-shaped foliage. The flowers are white to rose-pink, darker at the base; some strains are perfumed.
ZONES 6–10

### *C. repandum*

This is the latest flowering species, producing pink, crimson or white, fragrant flowers in spring. The broad, heart-shaped leaves are usually patterned with bands of dark green, light green and silvery gray. It grows to around 4 in (about 10 cm) in height.
ZONES 7–10

## *DICHELOSTEMMA*

syn. *Brodiaea*

These native West Coast bulbs are quite adaptable to garden cultivation. Needing only the normal winter rains of their natural range, they quickly develop leaves and stems with the warming days of spring. Flowers are produced in mid- to late spring, after which the foliage withers; the bulbs remain dormant until the next winter's rains. Best adapted to the wild garden, they can also be used in a dry border but will be enhanced by the placement of plants with evergreen foliage around them. They prefer full sun and a well-drained soil. Propagate from seed sown in fall, or by separating the young bulbs from their parent bulb.

*Eranthis hyemalis*

*D. ida-maia*
**syn. *Brodiaea maia***
FIRECRACKER FLOWER

This Californian native is distinct for its gentle twining habit, looping its way up through sturdier perennials and small shrubs. Topping each stem in late spring is a loose cluster of pale green and bright red tubular flowers. Stems may reach 3 ft (about 90 cm) in height.
ZONES 7–10

*D. pulchellum*
**syn. *Brodiaea pulchella***
BLUE DICKS, WILD HYACINTH

This easily grown bulb has flowers resembling a blue-purple *Allium,* with loose umbels of star-shaped flowers in spring. It naturalizes easily in a dry garden or meadow, but is also useful in the border. Flower stems reach 18 in (about 45 cm) or more.
ZONES 5–10

## *DRACUNCULUS*
*vulgaris*
**syn. *Arum dracunculus***
DRAGON LILY, STINK LILY

This relative of the arum is not a plant you would want to grow beside your front door. It emits a potent, foul odor which attracts flies for pollinating. A native of the Mediterranean region, it grows to around 3 ft (about 90 cm). The large leaves are red veined and deeply divided. In late spring a thick stem bears one or more large, up to 16 in (about 40 cm) spathes, like that of the arum, green on the outside and red to purple to black on the inside with a purple to black spadix. Plant the large tubers in winter in well-drained soil in partial shade. Water well through the growing season but allow to dry out after flowering. In cold areas protect with a dressing of mulch in winter. Propagate from seed or offsets in the fall.
ZONES 9–11

## *ERANTHIS*
*hyemalis*
WINTER ACONITE

This delightful, ground-hugging native of Asia and Europe flowers in

*Cyclamen hederifolium*

late winter to early spring. Sunny yellow, goblet-shaped flowers around $1^1/_2$ in (about 3 cm) wide are perched on a ruff of green, divided leaves. Plant the tubers in early fall in rich, slightly damp soil. The species likes full sun to partial shade and does best in cooler areas, naturalized under a deciduous tree or in a rock garden where it will spread quite rapidly. Propagate by division in summer or from seed in the fall.
ZONES 4-8

## *ERYTHRONIUM*
DOG-TOOTH VIOLET, TROUT LILY

Native to Asia, Europe and North America, these little plants bear delicate, reflexed, star-shaped flowers in spring. The dark green foliage is often attractively mottled. *Erythronia* do best in cooler areas. Plant the tubers in fall in well-drained soil that is rich in organic matter. Keep plants moist in partial to full shade. They multiply easily and should be left undisturbed until overcrowding occurs. Propagate from offsets in summer or from seed in fall.

*E. americanum*
TROUT LILY, ADDER'S TONGUE

A native woodlander from eastern North America, this species has mottled leaves (like its aquatic namesake) and pendent, pale yellow flowers, often bronze on the outside, in spring. It forms clumps by stolons; the stems reach 9 in (about 22 cm) in height. It thrives in sandy soil in shady situations.
ZONES 3–9

*Dracunculus vulgaris*

*Freesia*, Florist's hybrids

*Freesia alba*

*Fritillaria imperialis*

*Erythronium revolutum* 'Pagoda'

*Eucomis comosa*

*Erythronium dens-canis*

### *E. dens-canis*

DOG-TOOTH VIOLET

The most widely grown species, reaching to 8 in (about 20 cm), it has beautiful, oval, marbled foliage. The reflexed, star-shaped flowers are white to lilac, around 2 in (about 5 cm) wide. The common name refers to the shape of the corm.

ZONES 3–8

### *E. revolutum* 'Pagoda'

This is an excellent selection of a West Coast native. It grows to 16 in (about 40 cm) and has marbled green foliage. The creamy yellow flowers are star shaped, reflexed and nodding, around 2 in (about 5 cm) across.

ZONES 5-9

## *EUCOMIS*

### *comosa*

PINEAPPLE LILY

This native of South Africa has a spike of flowers which looks very similar to a pineapple; it is even topped with a tuft of pineapple-like leaves. It grows to 28 in (about 71 cm). Dark green, crinkly, strap-like leaves surround the tall, purple spotted scapes. The hundreds of star-shaped flowers, white to green and sometimes spotted with purple, are borne on a spike in fall. Plant bulbs in spring in full sun in well-drained soil. Water well through the growing season. Propagate by division in winter or from seed in spring, but it takes a long time to flower. It may need to be lifted in very cold winters. Makes an excellent, long-lasting cut flower.

ZONES 8–10

## *FREESIA*

FREESIA

These South African natives are extensively grown for their brightly colored and deliciously scented spring flowers. Slender, sword-shaped leaves surround wiry stems which bear spikes of goblet-shaped flowers. The weight of the flowers can be too much for the stems so they may need to be supported by twigs or wire. Plant the corms in fall in full sun in well-drained soil. They look best in a massed display. Water well through the growing season but allow to dry out once flowering is finished. The clumps are best left undisturbed for three years; they can then be divided in fall. Seed should be sown in late summer. In cold climates they grow very well in pots in a cool greenhouse.

### *F. alba*

**syn. *F. refracta alba***

This widely grown species flowers in early spring. The creamy white, goblet-shaped, highly scented flowers are 2 in (about 5 cm) long and are borne on a spike. Slender, bayonet-shaped leaves surround wiry stems up to 12 in (about 30 cm) long.

ZONES 9–10

### *F.*, Florist's hybrids

There are many named strains of hybrid freesias available; they come in shades of white, pink, blue, red or yellow and grow from 6–14 in (about 15–35 cm) in height. Some have semi-double flowers whose weight makes the plant top heavy enough to need staking. None is difficult to grow, although they need glasshouse culture in frosty climates or if blooms outside of their natural spring season are desired. Some strains are well scented, others almost scentless.

ZONES 9–10

## *FRITILLARIA*

FRITILLARY

These relatives of the lily and tulip are native to Asia, Europe and North America. They are not easy to grow, but their nodding, bell- to goblet-shaped flowers which appear in spring are worth the trouble. Plant bulbs in early fall in partial shade in well-drained soil rich in organic matter. Water well through the growing season but allow to dry out after flowering. In areas which have high summer rainfall the bulbs may need to be lifted. Handle the rather soft bulbs gently, and keep them out of the ground for as short a time as possible. Propagate from offsets in summer, although clumps are best left undisturbed for a few years. Seed can be sown in fall but will take 4 or 5 years to bloom.

### *F. affinis*

**syn. *F. lanceolata***

CHECKER LILY

This is one of the easier species to grow of the West Coast natives, and is a charmer as well. Stems reach 30 in (about 76 cm) tall, carrying whorls of leaves topped by bowl-shaped flowers of a curious purple brown mottled with yellow spots. Give it particularly well-drained soil in light shade.

ZONES 6–10

### *F. imperialis*

CROWN IMPERIAL

This is the tallest species and also the easiest to grow. The stems reach up to 3 ft (about 90 cm) or more and the leaves are borne in whorls along the stem. The flowers are also arranged in a whorl or crown at the top of the scape, and above the flowers is a bunch of leaves. The bell-shaped flowers are $1^1/_2$ in (about 3 cm) long and can be yellow to orange to red.

ZONES 4–9

*F. meleagris*

CHECKERED LILY, SNAKESHEAD LILY

Slender stems reach to 14 in (about 35 cm), each bearing one to two nodding, goblet-shaped blooms. The maroon, green or white flowers are 1 in (about 2.5 cm) long and are blotched or checkered. A few slender leaves are found along the stem. Does well naturalized under deciduous trees or in a rock garden, provided it has plenty of moisture while growing.

ZONES 4–9

*F. persica*

This Mediterranean species can be grown in warmer areas than most other species. It grows to around 3 ft (about 90 cm) and bears up to 25 nodding, bell-shaped flowers on a spike. The 1 in (about 2.5 cm) flowers that appear in spring are dark purple to brown to blackish purple. Dozens of narrow, green leaves appear along the stem.

ZONES 5–10

## *GALANTHUS*

SNOWDROP

These natives of Europe and western Asia flower in late winter and herald the coming of spring. They do best in cold areas. Delightful nodding flowers appear above daffodil-like foliage. Plant bulbs in autumn in rich, moist soil in partial shade. In very cold areas they may be planted in full sun. Divide or transplant immediately after flowering, before the leaves start to die off. They can be grown from seed, which will bloom a few years after sowing. Snowdrops do well in a rockery and are an excellent cut flower. Avoid buying the rarer species, many of which are dug up from the wild, leaving behind depleted natural populations.

*G. ikariae*

**syn. *G. latifolius***

Fine stems reaching to 4 in (about 10 cm), each bear one delicate, 1 in (about 2.5 cm), nodding, bell-shaped flower. The outer petals are pure white, the inner petals are green at the throat. The blue-green foliage is narrow and strap like. It does well in a rock garden.

ZONES 4-8

*G. nivalis*

SNOWDROP

Nodding, 1 in (about 2.5 cm), bell-shaped flowers appear on 9 in (about 22 cm) stems above slender, star-shaped, blue-green leaves. The outer petals are white and the tubular inner petals are green and white. There are many cultivars derived from this species, including a double-flowered one.

ZONES 4–8

## *GALTONIA*

*candicans*

SUMMER HYACINTH

This South African native produces delightful, bell-shaped flowers for 6 weeks in the middle of summer. The flower spike bears up to 20 white blooms that are sometimes green at the tips. Broad, blue-green, strap-shaped leaves surround stems which can reach up to 6 ft (about 1.8 m). Plant bulbs in late fall around 6 in (about 15 cm) deep in well-drained, compost-rich soil in a sunny position. Water well through the growing season and allow to dry out after flowering. Propagate from offsets in fall or from seed which will usually bloom in three years. Protect from slugs and snails.

ZONES 5–10

## *GLADIOLUS*

GLADIOLUS

Gladioli are native to Africa, Europe and the Middle East. They vary greatly in size, color, flowering time and even the arrangement of the blooms on the flower spike. Most of the widely cultivated hybrids originate in South Africa. The hybrids are divided into several groups, including Large-flowered, Primulinus and Butterfly. The Large-flowered types are those that are usually seen in florist's arrangements, sometimes with ruffled flowers which are arranged alternately either side of the 6 ft (about 1.8 m) long stem. The Primulinus group has smaller flowers, often blotched and arranged irregularly on a 3 ft (about 90 cm) stem. The Butterfly group has blotched, ruffled flowers on 40 in (about 1 m) stems. Corms should be planted around 5 in (about 12 cm) deep in very well-drained, sandy soil in a sunny position. In cold climates, plant in spring; in warm winter climates, plant in late fall to early spring for a succession of blooms. The tall stems may need staking. Water well through summer and cut off spent flower stems. Corms will need to be lifted in cold areas; Large-flowered gladioli are best lifted in all areas, especially those that have a high winter rainfall. Make sure they are perfectly dry before storing. Gladiolus can be propagated from offsets, although these may take a few years to bloom.

*G.*, Butterfly hybrids

These resemble the Large-flowered hybrids but have slightly smaller, ruffled flowers, usually with contrasting blotches in the throat. They come in the same range of colors and are grown in the same way.

ALL ZONES

*G. byzantinus*

**syn. *G. communis byzantinus***

BYZANTINE GLADIOLUS

A Mediterranean species reaching to around 3 ft (about 90 cm). The slender stem bears up to 15 pink to magenta blooms. Plant in a position in full sun in average garden soil; water regularly.

ZONES 5-10

*Galanthus nivalis*

*Gladiolus*, Butterfly hybrids

*Fritillaria persica*

*Galtonia candicans*

*Fritillaria meleagris*

*Gladiolus byzantinus*

*Galanthus ikariae*

*Haemanthus coccineus*

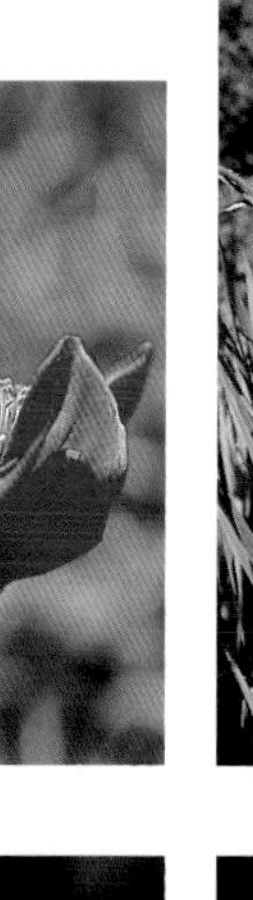

*Gladiolus callianthus*

*Habranthus robustus*

*Gloriosa superba*

*Herbertia drummondii*

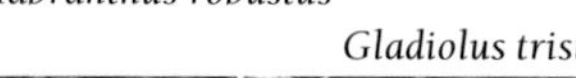

*Gladiolus tristis*

*Gladiolus carneus*

*Gladiolus* x *colvillei*

*Gladiolus*, Large-flowered hybrids

### *G. callianthus*
**syn. *Acidanthera bicolor***
ABYSSINIAN SWORD LILY, FRAGRANT GLAD

This scented species grows to around 3 ft (about 90 cm). The mainly white flowers often have a crimson blotch at their base and grow to 4 in (about 10 cm) in length; they appear in late summer or early fall. Protect from thrips, and water lavishly while in growth.
ZONES 7-10

### *G. carneus*
**syn. *G. blandus***
PAINTED LADY

A lovely, spring-flowering plant with arching spikes of white, funnel-shaped flowers stained with purple or yellow blotches. It is easily grown, multiplying vigorously.
ZONES 8–10

### *G.* x *colvillei*
BABY GLADIOLUS

Up to 10 elegant, 3 in (about 7.5 cm) dark pink, yellow or white blooms on an 18 in (about 45 cm) spike. This species usually flowers in late spring.
ZONES 8–10

### *G.*, Large-flowered hybrids

These are the familiar gladioli of the flower shops. They grow up to 6 ft (about 1.8 m) tall with one-sided flower spikes that can carry up to 24 wide open flowers. The individual flowers are normally around 4 in (about 10 cm) wide, although they may be as large as $5^1/_2$ in (about 13 cm). Every color but blue is available. They are best planted in spring and lifted in late fall to be stored for the winter. Rich soil, sun and vigilant protection from thrips are needed. Propagate by growing on offsets, which take 3 years to flower.
ALL ZONES

### *G. tristis*

In late winter or early spring each 24 in (about 60 cm), slender stem carries up to 6 white, cream or pale yellow 3 in (about 7.5 cm) wide flowers; their strong fragrance is only released at night. It prefers a rich soil, but adapts to most situations; when happy it self-sows freely. Many spring-flowering hybrids derive from this popular species.
ZONES 7–10

## *GLORIOSA*
### *superba*
GLORIOSA LILY, GLORY LILY, CLIMBING LILY

This is a tropical species from Africa, only suitable for the garden where there is no chance whatever of frost. However, it does grow very well as a pot plant while greenhouse grown flowers are popular with florists. They resemble tiger lilies but are brilliant in red and gold. The plants climb by means of tendrils on the ends of the leaves and needs support. Plant the tubers in spring, laying them horizontally under 24–36 in (about 60–90 cm) of soil. *G. rothschildiana* is very similar and some authorities consider it merely a variety of *G. superba*.
ZONES 9–11

## *HABRANTHUS*
### *robustus*

This beautiful plant is a relative of the *Hippeastrum* and comes from the Argentine pampas. A trumpet-shaped flower around 4 in (about 10 cm) long appears on each 12 in (about 30 cm) stem. The flowers, which appear in summer, are rose-pink, often fading to white. The glossy, green basal foliage is strap like. It is easily grown in warm to temperate areas. Plant the bulbs in a sunny position in fall in well-drained soil rich in organic matter. Water well through the growing season. Can be propagated from offsets when dormant or from seed, which will usually flower in the third year.
ZONES 9–11

## *HAEMANTHUS*
### *coccineus*
BLOOD LILY

The *Haemanthus* genus, with its brightly colored flowers, originates in Africa and prefers mild to warm conditions. This fall-flowering species grows to 14 in (about 35 cm). The two broadly oval, dark green leaves are hairy on the underside, and they lie on the soil. A sturdy, purple-spotted stem bears a cluster of slender, bright red flowers enclosed by scarlet to pink bracts; these are followed by red berries. Plant bulbs in fall or spring in partial shade in a compost-rich, well-drained soil. Water and feed well during the growing season, but allow it to get completely dry during its summer dormancy. The plants are best left undisturbed for a few years when they can then be propagated from offsets, or from seed, which takes a few years to flower. The common name has no sinister connotations; it merely refers to the red spots on the bulb.
ZONES 9–11

## *HERBERTIA*
### *drummondii*
BLUE TIGER FLOWER

This spring-flowering South American native is a relative of the *Tigridia* and the iris. The foliage is like that of an iris, sword shaped and pleated. The stems reach to 12 in (about 30 cm) and bear short-lived, triangular flowers around 2 in (about 5 cm) wide. The outer petals are violet-blue and the smaller inner

*Hyacinthoides hispanica*

*Hippeastrum* 'Red Lion'

*Hippeastrum* 'Apple Blossom'

*Hyacinthoides non-scripta*

*Hyacinthus orientalis*

petals are often spotted. It does best in temperate to warm areas. Plant the corms in fall in a sunny to partially shaded position. The soil should be light and well drained but enriched with compost. Water well through the growing season but allow to dry out after flowering. Propagate by dividing corms in winter or from seed in fall.
ZONES 9–11

## *HERMODACTYLUS*
### *tuberosus*
**syn. *Iris tuberosa***
SNAKE'S HEAD IRIS

This relative of the iris gets its common names from the appearance and unusual colors (often black and green) of its flowers. Native to the Middle East and Mediterranean region, it grows to 16 in (about 40 cm). The tall, blue-green foliage is slender and squarish. The perfumed, iris-like flowers, yellow-green and purple-black, appear in early spring. Plant the tubers in early fall in very well-drained soil in a sunny spot. Leave clumps undisturbed for a few years, then divide in spring or summer. Alternatively, grow from seed, but this may be difficult to obtain.
ZONES 8–10

## *HIPPEASTRUM*
### cultivars
DUTCH AMARYLLIS

These magnificent plants with their showy, trumpet-shaped flowers are native to tropical South America. They have been widely hybridized and it is these cultivars which are usually grown by the average gardener. Named selections are available in red, pink, orange, soft yellow, white and combinations. 'Apple Blossom' is the most popular of the Dutch-bred hippeastrums. A sturdy stem reaching to 18 in (about 45 cm) bears clusters of up to 6 stunning, pale pink and white blossoms. Trumpet-shaped flowers up to 8 in (about 20 cm) wide appear in winter indoors or in spring outdoors, followed by slender, strap-shaped foliage. 'Red Lion' has up to 6 blood-red, trumpet-shaped flowers appearing all through spring. Hippeastrums are most commonly grown in a glasshouse or inside as a pot plant. A single bulb in a pot will produce a display that any florist would be hard pressed to match. Outdoors in warm winter climates, bulbs should be planted in fall. Use a well-drained soil rich in organic matter, with just the tip of the bulb exposed, and plant in full sun or partial shade. Water and feed well through the growing season and allow the bulb to dry out after the foliage dies down. Clumps are best left undisturbed for a few years when they can then be divided. They can also be grown from seed sown in spring. Protect from snails.
ALL ZONES

## *HOMERIA*
### *collina*
**syn. *H. breyniana***

Among the easiest of the South African bulbs for warm winter climates, this species presents a glorious display of yellow to salmon, cup-shaped flowers in spring. Each bulb produces only one narrow leaf which quickly disappears after flowers fade. The stems are 18 in (about 45 cm) tall, the flowers 2 in (about 5 cm) across. Plant in fall, giving it full sun, a well-drained soil and little or no summer water. It spreads quickly by seed.
ZONES 9–10

## *HYACINTHOIDES*
**syn. *Endymion, Scilla***
BLUEBELLS

The hardy, European bluebells with their attractive, scented flowers are popular with gardeners all over the world. Equally at home in a rock garden, naturalized under deciduous trees or in the flower border, they thrive in partially shaded conditions. Bulbs should be planted in fall in rich, moist soil. Water well until the flowers start to die. They should multiply freely but are best left undisturbed for a few years, then divided in late summer.

### *H. hispanica*
**syn. *Endymion hispanica, Scilla campanulata***
SPANISH BLUEBELL

The most popular and most easily grown species, it grows to around 18 in (about 45 cm) and flowers in spring. The 1 in (about 2.5 cm), nodding, bell-shaped flowers are lilac to blue. The bright green foliage is strap like. It multiplies freely.
ZONES 4–10

### *H. non-scripta*
**syn. *Endymion non-scripta, Scilla non-scripta***
ENGLISH BLUEBELL

The English bluebell flowers in early to late spring. The very fragrant, nodding, bell-shaped flowers in

*Hermodactylus tuberosus*

lavender-blue, pink or white are $^1/_2$ in (about 1 cm) long on fine stems reaching to around 18 in (about 45 cm). The slender, strap-like foliage is glossy green. Plant in a partially shaded position in moist soil.
ZONES 5–10

## *HYACINTHUS*
### *orientalis*
HYACINTH

Favorites with gardeners all over the world, the popular named varieties of hyacinth are cultivars of *H. orientalis*, which originally comes from the Middle East and Mediterranean region. A spike of flowers is massed on top of a 12 in (about 30 cm) stem. The sweetly perfumed spring flowers vary enormously in color. 'King of the Blues' is a favorite, along with the newer 'Gipsy Queen' (soft salmon-orange), but many others are available in white, pale yellow, pink, red or purple. The glossy green foliage is strap like. Plant the bulbs in clumps in fall in rich, well-drained soil in full sun or partial shade. Hyacinths do best in cooler climates, or in pots

anywhere. It is best to buy new bulbs each year, as the flowers are never so magnificent as in that first spring; but, planted in a congenial spot, they will continue to bloom each spring for years.
ZONES 4–9

## HYMENOCALLIS

SPIDER LILY, SEA DAFFODIL

The unusually beautiful flowers of the spider lily resemble daffodils except for the delicate, spider-like petals surrounding the inner bloom. Mainly native to South America they are not too fussy about conditions, but usually do best in temperate or warm areas. Bulbs should be planted in spring, around 6 in (about 15 cm) deep in well-drained soil. A partially shaded position is best. Water very well during growth and never allow to dry out completely. Offsets form quickly and should be divided in spring before growth begins. In cold climates, they can be lifted in fall and stored indoors over winter.

### *H.* × *festalis*

This hybrid species grows to around 24 in (about 60 cm) and has deliciously scented flowers. The glossy green foliage is slender and strap like. Each stem bears up to five 4 in (about 10 cm) white flowers. The inner trumpet-shaped cup of petals is surrounded by 6 slender, spider-like petals.
ZONES 8–10

### *H. littoralis*

Pure white, trumpet-shaped flowers surrounded by 6 thread-like petals are borne on 30 in (about 76 cm) stems. The almost strap-like foliage is bright green.
ZONES 10–11

### *H. narcissiflora*

syn. ***Ismene calathina***
PERUVIAN DAFFODIL, BASKET FLOWER

This is the most widely grown species, often planted as a summer bulb like gladiolus in the North. Its broad, deep white flowers are very showy, with wide petals reflexed behind the green-tinged cup. It is native to the Andes, but is at home in gardens of the South. Flowers appear in early summer. A pale yellow form exists.
ZONES 9–11

## IPHEION

### *uniflorum*

syn. ***Tristagma uniflora, Triteleia uniflora***
SPRING STAR FLOWER

This relative of the iris gets its common names from the appearance and unusual colors (often black and green) of its flowers. Native to the Middle East and Mediterranean region, it grows to around 16 in (about 40 cm). The tall, blue-green foliage is slender and squarish. The perfumed, iris-like flowers, yellow-green and purple-black, appear in early spring. Plant the tubers in early fall in very well-drained soil in a sunny spot. Leave clumps undisturbed for a few years, then divide in spring or summer. Alternatively, grow from seed.
ZONES 6–10

## IRIS

IRIS

This wide-ranging genus, named for the Greek goddess of the rainbow, is valued all over the world for its beautiful and distinctive flowers. Size, color and growing conditions vary greatly but the unusual flowers are easily recognized. Each flower has 6 petals: 3 outer petals, called "falls," droop away from the center and alternate with the inner petals, called "standards." Irises are divided into two main groups, rhizomatous (which we have included in the chapter on annuals and perennials) and bulbous. The bulbous irises include several groups, of which the following two are the most important: the Xiphium, which includes the Dutch irises of florist shops as well as their parent species *I. xiphium, latifolia, lusitania* and *tingitana* (they are mostly native to Spain, Portugal and North Africa); and the Reticulatas, which bear small winter and spring flowers and are mainly native to the Middle East. Both groups are of easy cultivation, demanding only a sunny position with ample moisture during growth but very little during their summer dormancy. A third group is the Juno irises also from the Middle East and central Asia, noteworthy for their handsome foliage and spectacular flowers; these are generally difficult in cultivation and are not commonly grown. All are planted in fall.

### *I. bucharica*

syn. ***I. orchiodes***

This species of Juno iris grows to around 18 in (about 45 cm). The $2^{1}/_{2}$ in (about 6 cm) scented flowers can be varied in color. Standards and falls can be both white or yellow, or standards can be white and falls yellow. It requires a rich soil and is slow to increase. Take care not to damage the thick lateral roots when transplanting.
ZONES 6–10

### *I.*, Dutch hybrids

These are the best known of the bulbous irises; florists keep them in bloom just about all year by chilling

*Hymenocallis* × *festalis*

*Iris reticulata*

*Ipheion uniflorum*

*Iris* 'Professor Blauw' (Dutch hybrid)

*Iris* 'Symphony' (Dutch hybrid)

*Iris bucharica*

*Hymenocallis littoralis*

the bulbs and planting in greenhouses. In the garden they flower in mid- to late spring. They grow to around 30 in (about 76 cm) in flower, with rather straggly, gray-green leaves, and bear one or two flowers on long stems. Easy to grow, they like rich, well-drained soil and sun. Water freely while they are in growth and keep them dry in summer. Propagate by division in autumn. Handle the bulbs gently as they bruise easily. There are many named varieties, in shades of white, blue, violet or yellow. The blue 'Professor Blauw' and yellow and white 'Symphony' are typical. The blue and white 'Wedgwood' is a hybrid with *I. tingitana*.
ZONES 6–10

### *I. latifolia*

**syn. *I. xiphioides***

Most of the bulbous English irises (so called because of their great popularity in eighteenth-century England) are derived from this species from Spain. It grows to 30 in (about 76 cm), and the 4 in (about 10 cm), Dutch iris-like flowers which appear in summer are purple-blue or white. The falls are "winged" and often have a golden blotch.
ZONES 6–10

### *I. reticulata*

**NETTED IRIS**

This is the best known species in the Reticulata group, a native of central Asia. It grows to 4 in (about 10 cm) high in flower, its flowers in various shades of blue: several named varieties are available, differing mainly in the precise color of the flowers. Foliage is short during the late winter/early spring-flowering time, becoming longer after bloom. It likes sun and perfectly drained soil and is propagated from seed or by division. It does best in cold winter climates and will make a delightful pot plant.
ZONES 3–10

### *I. xiphium*

The Spanish iris is similar to the English and to its hybrid offspring, the Dutch iris. Flowers may be blue to mauve, white or yellow; the falls have a yellow or orange blotch and are not winged like the English iris. Flowering is in late spring.
ZONES 6–10

## *IXIA*

**AFRICAN CORN LILY**

The South African corn lily produces masses of delightful, star-shaped flowers on wiry stems in spring. These flowers close in the evening and on cloudy days. The tallest species grows to around 24 in (about 60 cm). The leaves are usually long and slender. They are easy to grow in mild winter climates. The bulbs should be planted in early fall in well-drained soil. Blood and bone mixed into the soil before planting will help produce good blooms. A sunny position is ideal except in warm areas, where they will need protection from hot sun. Water well through winter and spring but allow to dry out after flowering. Propagate from offsets in fall.

### *I. maculata*

**YELLOW IXIA**

This is the most commonly grown species. The wiry stems grow to around 18 in (about 45 cm), with 2 in (about 5 cm) flowers clustered along the top; these have brown centers and orange to yellow petals, sometimes with pinkish red undersides. Garden forms come in white, yellow, pink, orange or red.
ZONES 8–10

### *I. paniculata*

The slender stems grow to around 24 in (about 60 cm) and are topped with spikes of yellow to pink blooms. The 2 in (about 5 cm) flowers, which are star shaped and tubular at the base, appear in late spring.
ZONES 8–10

### *I. viridiflora*

**GREEN IXIA**

The exquisite, jewel-like flowers make this a popular species. The 2 in (about 5 cm) flowers are borne on a spike atop the 24 in (about 60 cm) stem. The star-shaped flowers are a pale turquoise with a purple-black center.
ZONES 9–10

## *LACHENALIA*

**CAPE COWSLIP**

Massed in clumps or planted in window boxes, these South African natives make a striking display. Spikes of pendulous, tubular flowers stand erect above narrow, sometimes marbled, strap-like foliage. Plant bulbs in fall in well-drained soil enriched with organic matter. They like a sunny position and lots of water until the foliage begins to die off, usually in summer. They need to be kept dry when dormant and may need to be lifted in areas with a high summer rainfall. They are sensitive to frost and can be planted in pots or window boxes in cool areas. They spread quite freely and can be divided in fall.

### *L. aloides*

**syn. *L. tricolor***

This species grows to around 12 in (about 30 cm). Flowers appear on a spike in winter to spring above strap-like foliage. The nodding, tubular flowers flare out at the tips, and are usually golden yellow and green at the tips. The base of the petals is sometimes red to orange. Plant in full sun or partial shade. There are various forms and many hybrids derived from this species.
ZONES 9–10

*Iris* 'Wedgwood'

*Ixia maculata* hybrid

*Iris latifolia*

*Ixia viridiflora*

*Lachenalia aloides*

*Ixia paniculata*

*Lilium*, Asiatic hybrid

*Leucocoryne ixioides*

### *L. bulbifera*

**syn. *L. pendula***

This species grows to around 10 in (about 25 cm), with a spike of flowers appearing in winter to spring. The pendulous, tubular flowers are pink to red to yellow and the flared tips are violet to purple. The green foliage is strap like.
ZONES 9–10

## *LEUCOCORYNE* *ixioides*

GLORY-OF-THE-SUN

This native of Chile is a bit of a gamble for the gardener. One year you may get a magnificent display of blooms and the next spring it may refuse to flower at all. Flowers are borne in clusters on wiry stems up to 18 in (about 45 cm) tall. The 2 in (about 5 cm), sweetly scented flowers are reflexed and star shaped, white in the center and graduating to blue at the tips with prominent yellow anthers. The foliage is long and slender. Plant bulbs in fall in full sun in light, well-drained soil with plenty of

*Leucojum aestivum*

*Lilium* 'Bright Star' (Aurelian hybrid)

*Lilium* 'Royal Gold' (Trumpet hybrid)

water in winter and spring and allow to dry out over summer. Propagate from seed in fall.
ZONES 9–10

## *LEUCOJUM*

SNOWFLAKE

The snowflakes are easily grown bulbs flowering either in spring or fall. Their white, bell-like flowers are usually tipped with green at the end of each petal. Leaves may be narrowly strap shaped or reed like. All need a rich, well-drained but moist soil and full sun, except in the hottest areas where the shade of a deciduous tree will be preferred; in the wild they are often found near streams. Their faint fragrance is appealing. Plant bulbs in the fall; propagate from seed or offsets in fall or spring. Clumps perform best if allowed to grow undisturbed for several years.

### *L. aestivum*

SUMMER SNOWFLAKE

These dainty, spring-flowering bulbs are native to Europe and Asia.

*Leucojum autumnale*

*Lachenalia bulbifera*

The fragrant flowers are white with a green spot near the tip of each petal and are borne in clusters atop 20 in (about 50 cm) stems. The blue-green leaves are long and slender. 'Gravetye Giant' has larger flowers with as many as 9 per stem.
ZONES 4–10

### *L. autumnale*

AUTUMN SNOWFLAKE

Far more delicate in appearance than the summer snowflake, this species flowers in fall. Its 9 in (about 22 cm) stems are topped by a single flower usually lacking the typical green spot but often flushed with pale pink. They very narrow leaves resemble those of reeds or rushes. An excellent bulb for the fall rock garden.
ZONES 6–10

## *LILIUM*

LILY

Many plants are commonly called lilies but the "true" lilies are the many species and hybrids of the magnificent genus *Lilium*. The elegant flowers possess a breathtaking beauty often accompanied by a glorious perfume. The flowers have 6 petals arranged in a variety of ways, and 6 stamens. The scaly bulbs should be planted in fall, but in very cold areas they are best planted in spring. The soil should be rich with excellent drainage and the bulbs planted fairly deep as they like a cool root run. A dressing of mulch in spring helps keep the roots cool. A partially shaded position is best as the flowers need protection from hot afternoon sun. Tall species may need staking. Dead flowers should be removed but leaves and stems should not be cut back until fall. Clumps are best left undisturbed for a few years; they can then be lifted and divided. In recent years many hybrids, easier to grow than many of the species, have been created and have become very popular. The most important groups are the Asiatic or Mid-Century hybrids, the Trumpet hybrids, the Aurelians which have trumpet or bowl-shaped flowers, and the spectacular Oriental hybrids. They need lime-free soil, although *L. candidum* prefers an alkaline soil and *L. regale* and *L. lancifolium* will put up with a little lime.

### *L.*, American hybrids

As the name suggests, these hybrids are all derived from lilies native to North America, including *L. parryi* and *L. pardalinum*. They are characterized by whorled leaves, pendent flowers with reflexed petals, good garden tolerance and resistance to viruses. The best known group is the Bellingham hybrids, available in soft pinks and buff oranges, usually spotted. They flower in early summer on stems reaching 7 ft (about 2 m) tall.
ZONES 5–10

### *L.*, Asiatic hybrids

Raised from *L. lancifolium*, *L. bulbiferum*, *L. croceum* and other Asiatic species. These are summer flowering and mostly grow to around 3 ft (about 90 cm) tall. Most have upward-facing, flat flowers in shades from white through yellow and pink to orange and russet-red. They have no scent and do best in a sunny position. They are first-rate cut flowers, much grown in greenhouses by florists for out-of-season bloom. Propagate by division. There are many named varieties: the yellow 'Connecticut King' and orange 'Enchantment' are popular and typical.
ZONES 4–10

### *L.*, Aurelian hybrids

The name comes from the Latin name for Orléans in France where the earliest varieties were bred. They derive from crosses between the Chinese *L. henryi* and trumpet lilies and resemble the Trumpet hybrids, except the flowers may be flat or bowl shaped. Some cultivars are well scented, others scentless.
ZONES 4–10

### *L.*, Oriental hybrids

Most glamorous of all lilies, the Oriental hybrids grow to 6 ft (about 1.8 m) tall and bear many bowl-shaped flowers as much as 10 cm (about 25 cm) wide in shades from white to crimson. They are powerfully scented and very desirable (and expensive) cut flowers. De-

rived from crosses of *L. auratum*, *L. speciosum* and *L. rubellum*, they like a mild climate, light shade and perfectly drained acid soil. They are subject to virus and care needs to be taken to obtain clean stock. There are many cultivars.
ZONES 5–10

### *L.*, Trumpet hybrids

Deriving from *L. regale*, the Trumpet hybrids flower in late summer. They can reach 6 ft (about 1.8 m) and carry as many as 30 outward-facing trumpets in shades from white through pink to yellow, usually with purple shadings on the outside. They are usually fragrant and are easily grown in light shade and lime free, well-drained soil.
ZONES 4–10

## SPECIES

### *L. auratum*
GOLDEN-GAND LILY

This magnificent species grows up to 6 ft (about 1.8 m). Each stem bears 8 open-faced blooms, 8 in (about 20 cm) wide. The flowers are white, sometimes red spotted, and have a yellow or red stripe down the center of each petal.
ZONES 5–10

### *L. canadense*
MEADOW LILY

This eastern North American lily prefers light shade and moist soil. Its stems rise up to 5 ft (about 1.5 m) tall with whorled leaves. Gracefully drooping flowers in early summer are bell shaped with widely spreading petals. Flower color ranges from yellow to orange or red, usually spotted with darker colors.
ZONES 4–9

### *L. candidum*
MADONNA LILY

This beautifully scented species is thought to be the oldest lily in cultivation. It grows to 7 ft (about 2 m) and bears up to 20 trumpet-shaped blooms in early summer. The pure white flowers can be 6 in (about 15 cm) wide and slightly reflexed. Unlike most, this lily should be planted in early fall with only 1 in (about 2.5 cm) of soil over it; a rosette of leaves will develop and remain through the winter, producing a flowering stem in spring. Better adapted to warm, dry climates than most lilies.
ZONES 4–10

### *L. formosanum*

This is an elegant lily which grows to 6 ft (about 1.8 m). The flowers that appear in late summer are trumpet shaped and reflexed. The petals are pure white on the inside and pink to purple-brown on the outside. It is easily grown from seed. Mature bulbs are prone to viruses so they should be replaced every few years.
ZONES 5–10

### *L. henryi*

This lily from Central China grows to around 6 ft (about 1.8 m), with each stem bearing as many as 40 reflexed flowers in pale apricot. The bulbs can be 8 in (about 20 cm) in diameter, an indication of the great vigor of the species. It tolerates lime and is resistant to viruses.
ZONES 4–10

### *L. lancifolium*
syn. *L. tigrinum*
TIGER LILY

One of the most popular species and also one of the oldest in cultivation, the tiger lily grows to around $4^1/_2$ ft (about 1.3 m). It produces masses of bright orange, trumpet-shaped, sharply reflexed flowers. The $7^1/_2$ in (about 18 cm) blooms are spotted with purple and are usually pendent. The tiger lily can harbor viruses without showing any ill effects and for this reason is best grown away from other lilies.
ZONES 4–10

### *L. longiflorum*
EASTER LILY

A lovely, pure white lily which grows to 4 ft (about 1.2 m). Up to 8 slender, trumpet-shaped flowers are borne on each stem. The fragrant blooms, 8 in (about 20 cm) long, appear in summer; they are forced in greenhouses for Easter bloom.
ZONES 7–10

### *L. martagon*
TURK'S-CAP LILY

Native to Europe, this species flowers in summer and bears many reflexed flowers in mauve-pink or white, with a strong fragrance. Flower stems can reach 6 ft (about 1.8 m) tall. It does best in cool climates and thrives in the dappled shade of an open woodland. Tolerant of alkaline soils.
ZONES 4–10

*Lilium henryi*

*Lilium martagon*

*Lilium formosanum* (white form)

*Lilium auratum*

*Lilium* 'Wildfire' (Oriental hybrid)

*Lilium candidum*

*Lilium lancifolium*

*Lilium longiflorum*

# A Field Trip to Darling and Malmesbury

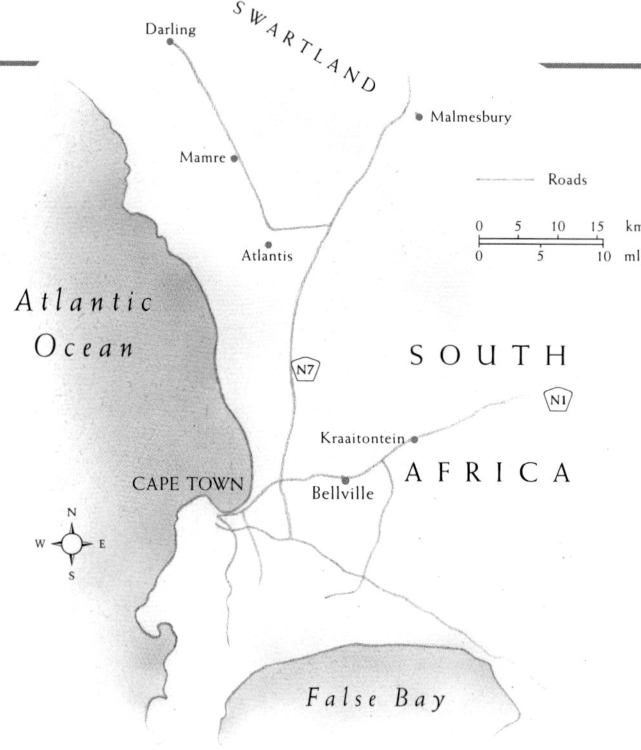


Southwestern Cape Province, in the southern tip of Africa, is known to botanists worldwide as the "Cape Floral Kingdom." Unlike the rest of sub-Saharan Africa this region has a Mediterranean climate—cold, wet winters and hot, dry summers. It is also geologically and topographically diverse—a coastal plain of largely sand or limestone and, further inland, a gently undulating landscape made up of shale and clay. Rising abruptly from this are the rugged parallel ranks of the Cape Fold Mountains, whose jagged and forbidding slopes dominate the skyline. The soil here is deficient in nutrients due to the acid sandstone formation of the mountains. *Gladiolus* is one of many genera of plants that have adapted and thrive in this region of contrast.

*Gladiolus* species are bewildering in their variety and have been beloved by colonists from the earliest days of European settlement. A number of species common in the vicinity of Cape Town have acquired picturesque names, and one of the best loved of these is the kalkoentjie or little turkey *(Gladiolus alatus)*. This delightful little plant derives its name from the appearance of the flowers, which resemble a brilliantly hued turkey head, resplendent with wattles. The flowers are predominantly bright reddish orange, but the lower two petals are yellowish green with orange tips. Other similar species, also sharing the common name of kalkoentjie, are variously colored in greens and browns and all have a delightful scent, but none has quite the impact of *G. alatus*. You cannot see a colony of these plants without feeling a little cheerier for the experience.

*In springtime the meadows near Cape Town are a beautiful sight.*

*G. alatus* is a small plant, usually 6–10 in (about 15–25 cm) tall, with four strap-shaped leaves. The spike bears up to six flowers 1–2 in (about 3–5 cm) in diameter. The dorsal petal is the largest and forms a shallow hood arching forward, while broad lateral petals curve back like wings. The three stamens, arched together in front of the flower, are pollinated by long-tongued bees of the Anthophoridae family.

Although it is widespread in the southwestern Cape, one of the best places for a field trip to see the kalkoentjie is only half an hour's drive from Cape Town. And the best time to see them in bloom is spring, particularly September. As the flowers of a number of showy plants, particularly the annual daisies and the bulbs *Oxalis* and *Romulea*, close in the late afternoon and only open again in the warmth and light of mid-morning, you need not rush off early in the morning to start your trip.

With your back to the splendid massif of Table Mountain, which guards Table Bay and Cape Town harbor, drive towards Malmesbury on the N7 national road. Soon you will see the narrow flats of the west coast and, inland, the gently rolling country of the Swartland. In winter much of this flat, sandy land near the coast is inundated with water. Snowy white arums *(Zantedeschia aethiopica)*, thrusting their heads out of clumps of dark, arrow-shaped leaves, are a common sight along drainage lines and roadside ditches.

Clay soil on the rising ground in this area supports a natural vegetation dominated by a gray, small-leaved shrublet which is covered by a confetti of small white flowers in winter, followed by a similar scattering of fluffy white seeds. This is known as the renosterbos or rhinoceros bush *(Elytropappus rhinocerotis)*, and as the name suggests, it was once a favorite food of the (now rare) rhinoceros. During spring, annuals

*The little turkey, or kalkoentjie*

*Gladiolus dalenii*

*Gladiolus priorii*

and bulbous plants emerge in abundance, and along the road verges and in patches of undisturbed veld a haze of color greets your eyes. Some introduced Australian mimosas, the Sydney golden wattle *(Acacia longifolia)* and the golden wattle *(A. cyclopis)*, create a magnificent sea of fragrant, yellow blossom in spring but, unfortunately, also form impenetrable woodlands, almost suffocating all other plant growth.

Continue along the N7 towards Malmesbury for 22 miles (about 35 km), and when you reach the turnoff to Atlantis and Mamre stop the car and breathe in the beauty around you. On either side of the road, bordering a small stream, are meadows as resplendent with flowers as an oriental rug. Tall orange bugle lilies *(Watsonia meriana)* stand at attention in serried ranks along the road. Beyond them in the meadows, *Gladiolus alatus* forms orange patches among the velvet blue of bobbejaantjie or little baboon *(Babiana angustifolia)*, and the glistening pink of the large sundew *(Drosera cistiflora)*. Some 22 miles (about 35 km) to the northwest, a blood red form of *D. cistiflora* grows near the village of Darling, which holds a justifiably famous wildflower show each spring. A host of smaller species are scattered about with profligate generosity, including various sorrels *(Oxalis)* of different colors, the brick red form of the small iris *(Moraea tricolor)*, the quaintly formed orchids, *Holothrix villosa* and *Satyrium odorum*, and the heavenly scented *Gladiolus tenellus*—this one is a favorite with the local children, who gather it for their posies.

Further north in Namaqualand, also well known for its spectacular displays of spring flowers, you will see another orange-flowered kalkoentjie *(Gladiolus equitans)*. This species is not nearly as common as *G. alatus*, and is a larger plant with much broader leaves. Also, the green kalkoentjie *(G. orchidiflorus)*, a taller and more slender species with lovely dove-gray flowers marked with maroon, is common here.

Seeing the kalkoentjie or little turkey in its natural environment, surrounded by other equally colorful flora, is a pleasure you are unlikely to forget.

## Gladiolus

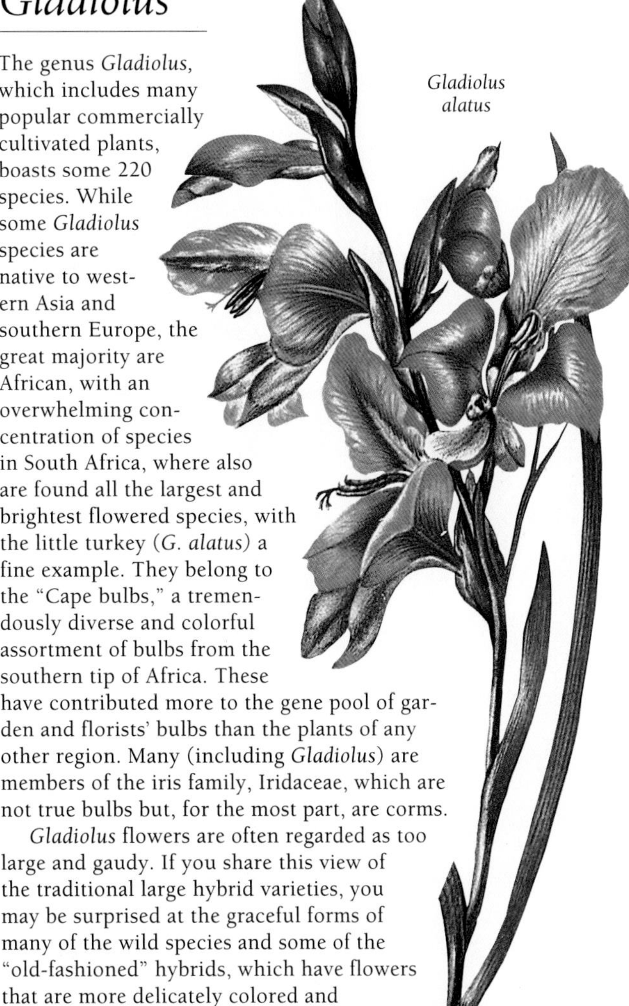

*Gladiolus alatus*

The genus *Gladiolus*, which includes many popular commercially cultivated plants, boasts some 220 species. While some *Gladiolus* species are native to western Asia and southern Europe, the great majority are African, with an overwhelming concentration of species in South Africa, where also are found all the largest and brightest flowered species, with the little turkey (*G. alatus*) a fine example. They belong to the "Cape bulbs," a tremendously diverse and colorful assortment of bulbs from the southern tip of Africa. These have contributed more to the gene pool of garden and florists' bulbs than the plants of any other region. Many (including *Gladiolus*) are members of the iris family, Iridaceae, which are not true bulbs but, for the most part, are corms.

*Gladiolus* flowers are often regarded as too large and gaudy. If you share this view of the traditional large hybrid varieties, you may be surprised at the graceful forms of many of the wild species and some of the "old-fashioned" hybrids, which have flowers that are more delicately colored and loosely arranged.

*Lilium speciosum*

*Lycoris radiata*

*Lycoris aurea*

*Lilium regale*

### *L. pardalinum*
**LEOPARD LILY**

This Californian native gets its name from the maroon dots against the gold to orange background color of the flowers. On 4–8 ft (about 1.2–2.4 m) stems the early summer flowers are beautifully pendent, with petals strongly reflexed. It spreads quickly underground by rhizomes, soon forming a large colony. It tolerates moist and alkaline soils.
ZONES 5–10

### *L. regale*
**REGAL LILY**

Growing up to 7 ft (about 2 m), this easily grown lily from western China bears from 3 to 20 fragrant blooms on each stem. The trumpet-shaped flowers, up to 6 in (about 15 cm) long, appear in summer. The inside of the petals is white, the outside carmine. There is also a pure white form.
ZONES 4–10

### *L. speciosum*

This popular, fragrant species grows up to $4^1/_2$ ft (about 1.3 m). The flat, nodding flowers with reflexed petals may be 4–6 in (about 10–15 cm) wide. There are many forms, varying from white to crimson, some spotted. It flowers late summer to early fall.
ZONES 5–10

## *LYCORIS*
**SPIDER LILY**

The spider-like flowers of these natives of China and Japan appear in late summer to early fall. The 20 in (about 50 cm) flower stems appear before the foliage. Each scape carries 4 or 5 blooms. The flowers are trumpet shaped but the petals are very slender and sharply reflexed. It has slender, strap-like leaves. Plant the bulbs in a sunny position in rich, well-drained soil. They like plenty of water during growth but need warm, dry conditions when dormant. Clumps are best left undisturbed for a few years; they can then be divided when dormant at the end of summer. This genus is named for Marc Antony's actress mistress.

### *L. aurea*
**syn. *L. africana***
**GOLDEN SPIDER LILY**

This lily grows to 16 in (about 40 cm) and bears a cluster of 4 or 5 tea-rose yellow flowers. The 3 in (about 7.5 cm) flowers have narrow, sharply recurved petals and prominent stamens. The slender leaves are strap like.
ZONES 7–10

### *L. radiata*
**RED SPIDER LILY**

This is the most common species. The 16 in (about 40 cm) stems bear clusters of 4 or 5 red blooms. The 4 in (about 10 cm) flowers have slender, sharply reflexed petals, with prominent red stamens. Well adapted to the Southeast, where it has occasionally naturalized. Provide lots of water.
ZONES 8–10

### *L. squamigera*
**MAGIC LILY**

The hardiest of the spider lilies, this species has pink flowers resembling those of *Amaryllis belladonna*. The 24 in (about 60 cm) flower stems appear before the leaves at the end of summer. The leaves last until late the following spring, but may look tattered at the end of winter. Plant in full sun in rich, well-drained soil.
ZONES 6–10

## *MUSCARI*
**GRAPE HYACINTH**

The popular grape hyacinths are natives of the Mediterranean region. A short spike bears grape-like clusters of bright blue or white flowers in early spring. They thrive in cool climates. They look best planted in clumps and need a rich, well-drained soil. Plant the bulbs in fall in a sunny position, but protect from hot sun in warm areas. The slender, strap-like leaves appear soon after planting, as the summer dormancy period is very short. The clumps should spread freely and are best left undisturbed for a few years. Divide the bulbs if they become overcrowded. They can also be grown from seed.

*Muscari comosum*

*Muscari armeniacum* 'Blue Spike'

*Narcissus* (Unnamed) (Div. 3)

*Narcissus* 'Tahiti' (Div. 4)

### *M. armeniacum*

GRAPE HYACINTH

Growing to around 6 in (about 15 cm), this is one of the best loved of spring bulbs. The flowers may be blue or white, and there are several named cultivars of which 'Heavenly Blue' is the best known.

ZONES 4–10

### *M. armeniacum* 'Blue Spike'

This fairly new cultivar grows to 8 in (about 20 cm). The flower spikes bear clusters of rounded, bell-shaped double blooms. The flowers are blue, sometimes rimmed with white. The foliage is slender and strap like.

ZONES 4–10

### *M. comosum*

TASSEL HYACINTH

This unusual plant grows to 12 in (about 30 cm). It has strap-shaped leaves and curious flowers whose petals are so elongated that the inflorescence looks like a plume of lavender feathers. It is as easily grown as other *Muscari* species.

ZONES 4–10

*Narcissus* 'Fortune' (Div. 2)

*Muscari armeniacum*

*Narcissus* 'Ptolemy' (Div. 1)

## *NARCISSUS*

DAFFODIL, JONQUIL, NARCISSUS

The sunny yellow spring flowers of the daffodil are popular all over the world. They are easy to grow, multiply freely and bloom year after year. Native to the northern hemisphere the genus is extremely varied, but all flowers have 6 petals which surround a cup or corona. They are grouped into 11 "divisions" or classes, the most important of which are: the Trumpet daffodils (Div. 1) which have trumpets as long as the outer petals or perianth; the Large-cupped daffodils (Div. 2), with trumpets at least one-third as long as the petals; the Small-cupped daffodils (Div. 3), with trumpets less than one-third the length of the petals; and the Double-flowered daffodils (Div. 4) with double flowers, either one or several per stem. Divisions 5 to 9 cover hybrids of important species such as *N. tazetta, triandrus, cyclamineus, jonquilla* and *poeticus*. Div. 10 covers the miscellaneous species. Div. 11 holds the new hyrid forms, the split-coronas, which are not included in the other divisions. Color ranges from white to yellow, although individual varieties may have white, yellow, red, orange or pink trumpets and each group is further subdivided according to colors. Most are adapted to areas with cold winters; some, however, do very well in the South and on the West Coast. Bulbs are usually planted in fall, 4–6 in (about 10–15 cm) deep in rich, well-drained soil. Full sun is fine in cool areas, but they will need some shade in warmer areas. Water well during growth and allow to dry out once the leaves die down. Remove spent flowers. Clumps will multiply freely and should be left undisturbed for a few years. Lift and divide them in fall. The common names daffodil, jonquil and narcissus are rather loosely applied, usage varying widely from place to place.

### *N.*, Trumpet daffodils (Div. 1)

These are the best known of all daffodils with their large flowers and long trumpets. There are innumerable named cultivars, which may be all yellow, white with yellow trumpets, all white, or white with pale pink trumpets. They are the first of the big daffodils to flower. The all-gold 'King Alfred', raised in 1890, is the classic cultivar, but its name has been very loosely applied and some authorities consider the original variety may be extinct.

ZONES 4–10

### *N.*, Large-cupped daffodils (Div. 2)

Flowering a week or two later than the trumpets, this is a large class with many named varieties. The popular pink-cupped cultivars with their white perianths mostly belong here but there are many others, in various combinations of white or yellow perianths with cups in white, yellow, orange or red.

ZONES 4–10

### *N.*, Small-cupped daffodils (Div. 3)

These resemble the first two groups except for their smaller cups, and like them come in many named cultivars. They flower at the same time as the Div. 2 types.

ZONES 4–10

### *N.*, Double-flowered daffodils (Div. 4)

These can have either a solitary large flower or several smaller ones, and either the whole flower can be double, with extra petals with segments of the corona intermixed; or the corona is doubled, like a pompon set against the outer perianth. They tend to be late flowering and must not suffer drought when the buds are developing or they will not open properly.

ZONES 4–10

*Narcissus tazetta* (Div. 8)

*Narcissus* 'Pink Pageant' (Div.11)

*Narcissus jonquilla* (Div. 7)

*Narcissus poeticus* (Div. 9)

*Narcissus* 'Tête-à-Tête' (Div. 6)

*Narcissus cyclamineus* (Div. 6)

*Narcissus* 'Silver Chimes' (Div. 5)

*Narcissus bulbocodium* (Div. 10)

### *N. triandrus* hybrids (Div. 5)

ANGEL'S TEARS

The type species *N. triandrus* is native to Spain, however it is not usually cultivated. This division is represented by garden forms which have pendent, nodding flowers, a straight-edged cup and slightly reflexed petals. The blooms appear in spring, and there are usually several per stem. The forms vary in height from 6-18 in (about 15-45 cm). 'Hawera' grows to 8 in (about 20 cm) and thrives in the sun. With its light yellow flowers it makes a good pot plant. 'Silver Chimes' is creamy white and delicately scented. The popular 'Thalia' has pale yellow petals and a white cup with 3 or more blooms per stem.

ZONES 4–10

### *N. cyclamineus* hybrids (Div. 6)

These hybrids grow to 15 in (about 38 cm). Their trumpet-shaped cups are longer than those of *N. triandrus*, and their petals are narrow and strongly reflexed. They flower in early to mid-spring. Good examples are: 'February Gold', an early bloomer that naturalizes well and has single, lasting flowers with yellow petals and slightly darker yellow trumpets; 'Dove Wings', a mid-spring bloomer with small flowers comprising white petals and a long, primrose-yellow trumpet; and 'Tête-à-Tête', one of the most popular with golden flowers on 12 in (about 30 cm) stems.

ZONES 4–10

### *N. jonquilla* hybrids (Div. 7)

JONQUIL

Possessing the characteristics of the wild jonquil of southern Europe and northern Africa, this group of daffodils are scented, with the cups shorter than the flat petals. Spring flowering, there are often 2 blooms on a stem that grow to 16 in (about 40 cm), while the leaves are dark green. 'Suzy' flowers in mid-spring and has 2 or more fragrant blooms on its sturdy stem, the flowers having golden petals and a deep orange cup. 'Stratosphere' has 3 blooms with a cup of a deeper golden yellow than its petals. 'Trevithian' flowers early in spring and produces up to 3 large, rounded blooms of a primrose yellow color.

ZONES 4–10

### *N. tazetta* hybrids (Div. 8)

BUNCH-FLOWERED NARCISSI

These daffodils have many-flowered stems and grow up to 16 in (about 40 cm). The cup is small and straight sided, with broad, often frilled petals. The sweetly scented blooms appear from late fall to spring. The leaves are dark green. This class can be further subdivided into those similar to *N. tazetta* and which are generally too frost tender to be grown outdoors but often flourish in indoor pots, and those resulting from a cross between *N. tazetta* and *N. poeticus* and referred to as poetaz daffodils. 'Grand Soleil d'Or' is a late fall- to early spring-flowering bulb. Growing to 14 in (about 35 cm), the petals are a rich yellow and the cup orange; this is a good variety for cutting. 'Paper White' is best grown indoors; in winter to mid-spring it produces 10 or more strongly scented blooms with white petals per stem. 'Minnow' is a mid-spring bloomer with 4 fragrant flowers per stem; the cups are lemon yellow and the petals a lighter yellow; growing to 7 in (about 17 cm), it is often planted in a rockery.

ZONES 4–10

### *N. poeticus* hybrids (Div. 9)

POET'S NARCISSUS

This is a late-spring to early-summer flowering division. The plants grow to 16 in (about 40 cm) and produce one, occasionally two, blooms per stem. The petals are white and the small cup often has a frilled red or orange rim. 'Actaea' produces fragrant flowers in late spring with a flat yellow cup rimmed with orange. 'Cantabile' is completely white. 'Pheasant's Eye', also known as *N. poeticus* var. *recurvus*, has a red cup and reflexed white petals.

ZONES 4–10

### *N.*, miscellaneous species (Div. 10)

This division covers the miscellaneous species, which flower any time from early fall to early summer. They usually bear single flowers; some are trumpet shaped, others funnel shaped. A well-known example of the funnel-shaped daffodils is *N. bulbocodium*, the hoop-petticoat daffodil.

ZONES 4–10

*Nerine sarniensis*

### N., Split-corona daffodils (Div. 11)

This group of recent introductions are a break from the typical form in having the cup, or trumpet, split into several segments that lie flat against the petals. Colors are white, yellow or orange, with the cup often different from the petals. They generally flower mid- to late season. 'Baccarat', 'Cassata' and 'Pink Pageant' are good, very dependable selections.
ZONES 4–10

## *NECTAROSCORDUM*

### *siculum* subsp. *bulgaricum*

**syn. *Allium bulgaricum***

The genus name means "nectar-bearing onion," and this is a relative of the *Allium* (onion). In spring it bears elegant, pendent, bell-shaped flowers, pale pink tinged with purple and green. The upright foliage dies off quickly. It likes most soils and semi-shade. Keep drier in summer. Propagate from offsets in summer. It makes a lovely cut flower.
ZONES 6–10

## *NERINE*

These South African bulbs bear a strong resemblance to the spider lilies in the genus *Lycoris*. The colorful flowers are borne in spider-like clusters at the top of tall stems, usually in fall. The foliage is strap like. The bulbs should be planted in sandy soil with good drainage in a sunny position. Water well during growth but allow to dry out over the summer dormancy period. They are not suitable for areas with high summer rainfall or severe frosts. They can be propagated from seed or offsets, but the plants do not like being disturbed and may take a couple of years to flower. They are good plants for pots, and can be brought inside when in flower.

### *N. bowdenii*

A sturdy stem of 24 in (about 60 cm) bears up to 12 pink blooms. The flowers are trumpet shaped but the narrow petals are split and reflexed. They have a crimson rib running along their center and the edges are frilled. There is also a white form.
ZONES 8–10

### *N. filifolia*

This plant grows to 10 in (about 25 cm) and bears a 3 in (about 7.5 cm) cluster of rosy pink blooms. The flowers are trumpet shaped with slender, reflexed petals. The foliage is grass like and almost evergreen.
ZONES 9–10

### *N. sarniensis*

**GUERNSEY LILY**

This delightful species was discovered growing wild on the Isle of Guernsey, south of England, where it had washed up following the wreck of a ship from South Africa. Sturdy, 24 in (about 60 cm) stems bear up to 20 bright red, 3 in (about 7.5 cm) blooms. The trumpet-shaped flowers have sharply reflexed petals and prominent stamens. The strap-shaped leaves usually appear after flowering. Recently, breeders in North America and Europe have begun introducing hybrids in an array of electric colors from pink to orange.
ZONES 9–10

## *ORNITHOGALUM*

This large genus of spring- to summer-flowering plants is native to Asia, Africa and Europe. Clusters of star- to cup-shaped flowers are borne along the top of tall stems. Plant bulbs in fall or spring in well-

*Nerine bowdenii*

*Nectaroscordum s.* subsp. *bulgaricum*

*Nerine filifolia*

*Ornithogalum arabicum*

*Rhodohypoxis baurii*

*Ornithogalum thyrsoides*

*Polianthes tuberosa*

*Ornithogalum umbellatum*

*Ranunculus asiaticus*

*Oxalis adenophylla*

drained soil. They like full sun but will need partial shade in warm areas. Keep the plants moist until the leaves begin to die off. They need to be kept dry when dormant. Frost-tender species should be lifted in winter. They multiply quite freely and clumps should be divided every one to two years to prevent overcrowding.

### *O. arabicum*

STAR OF BETHLEHEM

Dense racemes of black-centered, pure white, fragrant flowers, 2 in (about 5 cm) wide, top 24 in (about 60 cm) stems in spring on this species from the Mediterranean. Adapted to climates with dry summers, the long, narrow leaves disappear soon after flowering as the bulbs begin their dormancy. Flowering is best where summer heat is available.
ZONES 9–10

### *O. thyrsoides*

CHINCHERINCHEE

This species from South Africa grows to 18 in (about 45 cm). A cluster of up to 20 star- to cup-shaped white flowers is borne on a spike. The basal leaves are strap shaped. The cut flowers last for weeks, even out of water. The flowers absorb dye and bunches of chincherinchees are sold in a myriad of colors.
ZONES 8–10

### *O. umbellatum*

STAR OF BETHLEHEM

This, the hardiest species, can become a pest if it naturalizes. White flowers are produced in broad racemes atop 12 in (about 30 cm) stems in spring; a green stripe marks the outside of each petal. It likes plenty of water during the growing season. Excellent as a cut flower.
ZONES 5–10

## *OXALIS*

SORREL, SHAMROCK

Though found around the world, the greatest number of *Oxalis* are native to South Africa and South America. Many have become garden and greenhouse weeds which, though pretty in flower, have given a bad name to the genus. The two species listed here are more restrained in growth and make choice additions to the garden. The leaves are always divided into three or more leaflets in a palmate arrangement (like clover). Simple, star-shaped flowers are usually pink, white or yellow. Many species grow from bulbs, which multiply readily. A position in sun or part shade suits most, along with a woodsy but well-drained soil and moderate water. Propagate from division of the bulbs or from seed in fall.

### *O. adenophylla*

A choice selection for the rock garden, this species is native to the Chilean Andes, and hence more cold tolerant than most. Gray-green leaves are divided into many leaflets, folded in a fan shape and only 4 in (about 10 cm) high. Pink flowers rise above the foliage in spring. Excellent drainage is the prime concern; full sun and moderate water are best.
ZONES 6–10

### *O. purpurea*
**syn. *O. variabilis***

One of the showiest species, this has been improved in the Grand Duchess series with larger flowers in pink, rose, lilac or white; all have soft yellow centers. Clover-like leaves grow in a mound only 4 in (about 10 cm) tall; the bluish-green leaves provide a good background for the flowers which appear from late fall until early spring. Spreads slowly by bulbs and rhizomes, but is not invasive.
ZONES 9–10

## *POLIANTHES*
### *tuberosa*

TUBEROSE

This native of Mexico produces a mass of sweetly scented blooms in summer or early fall. A tall stem up to 3 ft (about 90 cm) is topped with a spike bearing clusters of tubular, star-shaped, creamy white flowers. A double variety, 'The Pearl', is more widely available than the single. The slender leaves are strap shaped. The tubers should be planted in spring when there is no chance of frost, in a sheltered, sunny position with rich soil and good drainage. Water well once leaves appear and allow to dry out when the leaves start to die off. The tubers only bloom once, so they should be lifted in fall and the offsets stored for planting in spring. In zones 9 and 10, tubers can be left in the ground all year, although flowering may not always be as good as the first year with fresh tubers. Tuberoses are first-rate cut flowers.
ALL ZONES

## *PUSCHKINIA*
### *scilloides*

These little spring bulbs bear a strong resemblance to *Scilla* and *Chionodoxa*, with pale blue to white flowers on 4–8 in (about 10–20 cm) spikes. Native to southwest Asia, it thrives where winters are cold and prefers a very well-drained soil. It is an excellent bulb for spring color in the rockery. Plant in fall and give it a position in full sun to very light shade. Propagate by division of the bulbs in early fall.
ZONES 3–9

## *RANUNCULUS*
### *asiaticus*

PERSIAN BUTTERCUP

This native of the Mediterranean region is parent to many hybrids and cultivars popular all over the world. Masses of single or double flowers are borne on 14 in (about 35 cm) stems in spring. The gorgeous blooms are available in many colors, yellow, orange, red, pink, white and more. The corms should

*Scilla peruviana*

*Sprekelia formosissima*

*Sternbergia lutea*

*Sparaxis tricolor*

be planted in fall in a sunny position in well-drained soil enriched with organic matter. Water well through the growing season and allow to dry out after flowering. The rhizomes are usually lifted after flowering and should be stored in a cool, dry place. In cold winter climates, start in pots in early spring for planting out after the danger of severe frost has passed; flowering will be quick but will end with hot weather. Propagation is by division or from seed sown in spring.
ZONES 9–10

## *RHODOHYPOXIS*
### *baurii*

This charming dwarf plant comes from the mountains of South Africa and appreciates a warm spot in cold areas. It produces masses of star-shaped flowers in late spring to early summer. The small stems grow to around 4 in (about 10 cm) and each bears one 6-petaled, red, pink or white flower. The hairy foilage is grass like. The bulb-like tubers should be planted in early spring in rich, acidic, well-drained soil. It needs plenty of water during the growing season but should be kept dry in winter. Plant in full sun, but protect from direct hot afternoon sunlight. Propagate by division or from seed in spring.
ZONES 9–10

## *SAUROMATUM*
### *venosum*
**syn. *S. guttatum***
VOODOO LILY

This curious bulb resembles *Dracunculum* in its bold, tropical foliage and strange, yellow, arum-like flower; the purple-spotted, 12 in (about 30 cm) tall flower releases a foul odor for a short time after opening. Usually grown as a pot plant, its origin in India suggests it adaptation for garden cultivation in the warmest parts of the South and Southwest. The 5 in (about 12 cm) bulbs should be planted just below the surface in rich soil kept moist while in growth. Foliage appears after flowering. Propagate from the tiny bulbs that develop on top of the mother bulb.
ZONES 10–11

## SCILLA
SQUILL

These bulbous plants from Europe, Asia and Africa are dependable for their blue flowers in spring. Varying from 6 to 12 in (about 15–30 cm) in height, their tiny, star-shaped flowers are clustered on racemes above strap-shaped leaves. Most are adaptable to cold winter climates and naturalize with ease in lawns and gardens. All should be planted in fall in average garden soil in full sun to light shade. Divide in fall when clumps become crowded.

### *S. peruviana*
PERUVIAN SCILLA

This plant, actually native to southwest Europe, has a dense cluster of up to 50 star-shaped flowers which are borne in summer on a 12 in (about 30 cm) stem. The 1 in (about 2.5 cm) flowers are usually blue, sometimes white or purple. The dark to olive-green foliage is glossy and strap like. Plant bulbs in fall in well-drained soil. Water well during the growing season. Clumps are best left undisturbed for a few years. In colder climates, grow in pots. Propagate by division or from seed in fall.
ZONES 9–10

### *S. siberica*
SIBERIAN SQUILL

Rich blue flowers on loose racemes are produced in such quantity from established patches as to color the ground blue. Flowers appear in early to mid-spring on 6 in (about 15 cm) stems. Foliage dies soon after flowering finishes. It spreads rapidly by division of bulbs and by seed. It does not do well where winters are mild.
ZONES 3–8

## *SPARAXIS*
### *tricolor*
HARLEQUIN FLOWER

This native of South Africa is easily grown in warm areas. The 12 in (about 30 cm) wiry, drooping stems bear a spike of up to 5 funnel- to star-shaped blooms in spring. The 2 in (about 5 cm) flowers are red to pink or orange. The center is usually yellow, outlined in black. The flowers close at night and on dull days. The stiff leaves are lance shaped. Plant corms in fall in a sunny spot in well-drained soil. Water well during the growing season, but allow to dry out when dormant. The corms should be lifted in areas which have wet summers. Propagate from the freely produced offsets or from seed in early fall.
ZONES 9–10

## *SPREKELIA*
### *formosissima*
AZTEC LILY, JACOBEAN LILY, ST JAMES LILY

This beautiful Mexican native grows to 18 in (about 45 cm). In summer it produces bright red, 5 in (about 12 cm) long flowers. The lower 3 petals form an open tube and the upper petals curve upwards and outwards. The green leaves are strap shaped. Plant the bulbs in fall in sun or light shade; the flowers will last longer in hot areas if lightly shaded. The soil should be rich with good drainage. Water well during the growing season but keep dry when dormant. It is sensitive to severe frosts and should be grown in pots in cold areas. It does not like being disturbed, so clumps should be left for a few years, then divided in fall.
ZONES 9–11

## *STERNBERGIA*
### *lutea*
AUTUMN CROCUS, AUTUMN DAFFODIL

The delightful fall-flowering lily-of-the-field is native to the Mediterranean region. The buttercup-yellow, crocus-like flowers are 2 in (about 5 cm) long and are borne singly on 6 in (about 15 cm) stems. The slender leaves are strap shaped. Bulbs should be planted in late summer or early fall in rich, well-drained soil in full sun. It likes to be warm and dry when dormant in summer so is best grown in pots in areas with wet summers. Clumps should be left undisturbed and only divided (in summer) when they are overcrowded. Makes an excellent plant in a rock garden.
ZONES 7–10

*Tritonia crocata*

*Tulbaghia violacea*

*Triteleia laxa*

*Tigridia pavonia*

*Tricyrtis hirta*

## TIGRIDIA
*pavonia*
TIGER FLOWER, MEXICAN SHELL FLOWER

This brightly colored Mexican native blooms in summer. The triangular flowers are short lived, often lasting for only a day, but a succession of new blooms will keep appearing for weeks. The 5 in (about 12 cm) flowers may be red, orange, pink, yellow, cream or lilac, usually with a heavily spotted center, borne on 24 in (about 60 cm) stems. The foliage is iris like, sword shaped and pleated. Plant bulbs in spring in a sunny position in rich, well-drained soil. Water well during the growing season. In areas of colder winters, lift bulbs in fall and store dry until spring. Propagate from freely formed offsets or from seed.
ZONES 7–10

## TRICYRTIS
*hirta*
HAIRY TOAD LILY

Native to cool, mountainous areas of Asia, the toad lily produces curious star-shaped flowers in late summer to fall. The 12–36 in (about 30–90 cm) tall, gently arching stems have hairy, stem-clasping leaves; the 1–2 in (about 2.5–5 cm) flowers, borne at the axils of the upper leaves, are white, heavily spotted with purple. Plant the rhizomes in spring in rich, moist soil in a partially shaded spot. It can be propagated from offsets in spring or from seed sown in fall.
ZONES 5–10

## TRITELEIA
*laxa*
syn. ***Brodiaea laxa***
GRASS NUT, ITHURIEL'S SPEAR

This native of California and Oregon grows to 24 in (about 60 cm). In late spring it produces a scape of up to 30 purple to blue flowers; 'Queen Fabiola' is a selection with light lavender flowers. The 2 in (about 5 cm) flowers are funnel shaped; the leaves are slender and grass like. Plant the corms in a sunny position in well-drained soil. In very warm areas it should be planted in partial shade. Water well during the growing season, less during the summer dormancy period. It should be grown in pots in cold areas. Propagate from offsets in the fall.
ZONES 7–10

## TRITONIA
*crocata*
FLAME FREESIA

This freesia-like plant is native to South Africa. The wiry stems grow to 20 in (about 50 cm) and bear a spike of pretty, cup-shaped blooms. The 2 in (about 5 cm) flowers which appear in late spring to summer are bright orange to red with yellow throats and purple anthers. The erect green leaves are sword shaped. Plant the corms in fall in a sunny position in light, well-drained soil. Water well during the growing season but allow to dry out after flowering. It multiplies quite freely and can be divided in fall, or grown from seed. It make a good cut flower.
ZONES 9–10

## TULBAGHIA
*violacea*
SOCIETY GARLIC

This easily grown South African native is delightful to look at but smells strongly of garlic. Spherical clusters of star-shaped, mauve flowers appear nearly all year round on 24 in (about 60 cm) stems above the mounds of slender, grassy or onion-like leaves. The fleshy roots can be divided any time and planted in average soil in either a sunny or a partially shaded situation. They appreciate regular water but are drought tolerant once established. Society garlic is good in a border, as an edging or in a rockery; it is also a pretty little plant for containers. The leaves and flowers are both edible.
ZONES 9–11

## TULIPA
TULIP

The elegant flower of the tulip has, with good reason, made it one of the most popular bulbs in the world. Tulips originated in the Middle East and Asia and have been cultivated for hundreds of years. The genus contains about 100 species, but the most commonly grown tulips are the highly developed cultivars grouped under *T. gesneriana* which vary in color, shape and flowering time. There are very many cultivars which were formerly grouped into a large number of classes. Recently the classification has been simplified, the main groups being: Early, Mid-season, Late and Species tulips with subdivisions in each group. Tulips do best in cold winter regions, but can be grown in pots in warmer climates. The bulbs should be planted in late fall, around 6 in (about 15 cm) deep, in a sunny position in rich, well drained soil. Water well during the growing season. Spent flowers can be removed but allow the leaves to die off naturally. It is usually preferable to lift the bulbs in areas with a wet summer and store in a dry, well-ventilated spot; the species and species hybrids are often better adapted to leaving in place and will usually bloom well and increase in numbers each year. Propagate by division in fall.

### GARDEN TULIPS

These are of complex hybrid origin and are grouped into a number of classes, which follow. They are very popular and delightful for cutting, but are best adapted to cold winter climates. In mild winter areas they are best treated as annuals, by chilling the bulbs for 6 weeks in the vegetable drawer of the refrigerator before planting in late fall. They come in a vast range of colors, everything but true blue; the virus-infected striped varieties are now illegal to import and as a result less popular than they used to be.

### SINGLE EARLY TULIPS

These are the first of the garden tulips to flower, and bear their flowers on stems around 16 in (about 40 cm) tall. They are the best varieties for forcing for early bloom in a greenhouse and come in the full range of colors.
ZONES 5–9

### DOUBLE EARLY TULIPS

These have mostly arisen as sports of single varieties and flower at the same time. The range of colors is wide, but it is a matter of taste whether you like these multi petaled flowers. They are long-lasting cut flowers.
ZONES 5–9

### MID-SEASON TULIPS

As the name suggests, these hybrids flowers after the Early tulips but about 10 days before the Late tulips begin. They are generally midway in height between the Early and Late tulips, around 20–24 in (about 50–60 cm) on average.
ZONES 5–9

### Darwin hybrid tulips

Derived from crosses between the Darwins and *T. fosteriana*, these tulips grow to around 24 in (about 60 cm) in height, and despite their rather limited color range—red, yellow and orange—rival their parents in popularity. The flowers can be very large, though they are not as long lasting as the Darwin tulips. They are more reliable in mild-winter areas.
ZONES 5–10

### SINGLE LATE TULIPS

These are the most widely grown tulips flowering in late spring. They are taller, to 26 in (about 65 cm), than the early varieties and are divided as follows:

### Cottage tulips

These are more egg shaped and open wider than the Darwins, to give a more graceful effect. Most are around 24 in (about 60 cm) tall.
ZONES 5–9

### Darwin tulips

The most popular group, growing around 24 in (about 60 cm) tall with flowers almost rectangular in profile and coming in the full range of colors. There is a sub-group with fringed petals. All are excellent for cutting.
ZONES 5–9

### DOUBLE LATE TULIPS

These have their admirers, but they are less desirable than the Double Earlies, the many petaled flowers often proving too heavy for the 24 in (about 60 cm) tall stems. They are essentially cut flowers.
ZONES 5–9

### LILY-FLOWERED TULIPS

These are the most graceful of all tulips, with long, slender petals curved outwards in the fashion of a lily. Stems are 18–24 in (about 45–60 cm) tall, and flowering is late. All colors are available, including two-tones.
ZONES 5–9

### PARROT TULIPS

Sports of Darwin and Cottage tulips, these are grown for their fantastically fringed and ruffled flowers. They grow to around 20 in (about 50 cm) and are available in the usual colors.
ZONES 5–9

Single late tulip, 'Queen of Night'

Darwin hybrid tulip, 'Golden Oxford'

Double early tulip, 'Peach Blossom'

Single late tulips

Parrot tulip, 'Flaming Parrot'

*Tulipa gesneriana*

Single early tulip

Cottage tulips

Double late tulips

*Tulipa fosteriana*

Rembrandt tulips

*Tulipa greigii*

*Tulipa clusiana*

*Tulipa tarda*

*Tulipa acuminata*

*Tulipa saxatilis*

### REMBRANDT TULIPS

Though the great Dutch master is not known to have painted tulips, his name is attached to all the striped tulips. These striped or broken flowers were indeed very popular in Holland in his time, so much so that speculation in tulip bulbs nearly upset the Dutch economy and the government of the day had to step in to stop the "tulipomania." Since discovering that the stripes are caused by a virus, they have become less popular and are no longer permitted to be imported into the US. Many newer cultivars are available with stripes and "feathering" that has been genetically induced; they are safe to plant with other tulips. An evenly broken flower in red or pink and white can be very pretty.

ZONES 5–9

### SPECIES OR BOTANICAL TULIPS

#### *T. acuminata*

A most curious tulip, thought not to be a true species but an ancient cultivar of Turkish origin. It grows around 16 in (about 40 cm) tall, and is distinguished by its curious long, narrow petals in colors of red and yellow.

ZONES 5–9

#### *T. clusiana*

LADY TULIP

This tulip has 10 in (about 25 cm) stems which bear one or two cup-shaped blooms which eventually open out almost flat. The flowers are white, the outside petals and inside base stained dark pink. It flowers in mid-spring.

ZONES 5–10

#### *T. fosteriana*

This low-growing, mid-season tulip from Central Asia is rarely grown, but it has a number of garden varieties much admired for their enormous, 10 in (about 25 cm) wide flowers. They are almost all red.

ZONES 5–9

#### *T. greigii*

This early to mid-season species has given rise to a popular group of hybrids, which mostly grow around 12 in (about 30 cm) tall. It has wide-open flowers in the usual tulip colors, often with contrasting edges to the petals. The foliage is variegated with red-brown or purple on a green background.

ZONES 5–10

#### *T. kaufmanniana*

WATER LILY TULIP

This early-flowering species is admired for the elegant form of its pale yellow flowers, strongly marked with red on the outside. There are several named varieties in shades of red, pink and yellow. They mostly grow around 10 in (about 25 cm) tall.

ZONES 5–10

#### *T. saxatilis*

A species originating in Crete, it does well in warmer climates. The 12–18 in (about 30–45 cm) stems bear up to 3 goblet-shaped flowers which eventually open out almost flat. The purple-pink flowers have bright yellow centers. It flowers in early spring.

ZONES 6–10

#### *T. tarda*

syn. *T. dasystemon*

This small tulip grows to 6 in (about 15 cm). Each stem bears up to 6 white flowers with yellow centers. The pointed petals sometimes have a red or greenish tinge. It flowers in early spring.

ZONES 5–10

## *VALLOTA*

### *speciosa*

syn. *Cyrtanthus purpureus*

SCARBOROUGH LILY

This beautiful plant, with its showy red flowers, is originally from South

Africa. The stout, 12 in (about 30 cm) stem bears up to 5 orange-red, trumpet-shaped blooms. The flowers appear in summer to fall and are around 4 in (about 10 cm) wide. The thick, green leaves are strap shaped. Plant the bulbs in late winter in rich, well-drained soil, and in partial shade in very warm areas. Water well through the growing season but allow to dry out over winter. Remove spent flowerheads. The small offsets can be removed from the parent bulb and planted out in late winter. It makes a glorious display as an indoor pot plant.
ZONES 9–11

## *VELTHEIMIA*

These unusual natives of South Africa produce a dense spike of pendent, tubular flowers in winter or spring. Bulbs should be planted in fall in moist, rich, well-drained soil in partial shade. Reduce watering when flowering is finished. They should be grown in pots in cold areas. Propagate from offsets in the fall.

### *V. bracteata*
**syn. *V. viridiflora***

Found in the wild in the eastern Cape area of South Africa, *V. bracteata* has wavy, glossy green leaves growing in a rosette. Rocket-like inflorescences on strong, erect stems are produced in spring and early summer. The drooping, tubular flowers are pink, red or pale yellow. It thrives in semi-shade beneath trees or shrubs. Plant in rich, well-drained soil and water occasionally.
ZONES 9–11

### *V. capensis*
**syn. *V. glauca***

A strong stem growing up to 18 in (about 45 cm) bears a dense spike of pendent, tubular, 1 in (about 2.5 cm) blooms. The rosy pink to red flowers are sometimes tipped with green. The glossy, dark green leaves have wavy edges.
ZONES 9–11

## WATSONIA

These beautiful natives of South Africa produce fragrant flowers in spring or summer. They appear quite similar to the gladiolus and have lance-shaped leaves and a tall flowering spike. The corms should be planted in fall in light, well-drained soil in a sunny spot. They like plenty of water during the growing season. Clumps are best left undisturbed and they should spread freely. They can be propagated from seed or by division.

### *W. beatricis*

This evergreen species grows to 4 ft (about 1.2 m). The flower spike bears 3 in (about 7.5 cm) long, tubular, star-shaped flowers that are orange to orange-red. The green foliage is sword shaped. There is some doubt about whether this plant, common in nurseries under this name, is the true wild species, which is now correctly known as *W. pillansii*. Hybrids of this and other species are available with flower colors ranging from white to pale pink to red and coral.
ZONES 8–10

### *W. borbonica*
**syn. *W. pyramidata***

This delightful species grows to $4^1/_2$ ft (about 1.3 m). The stem bears a spike of lilac to pink, 2 in (about 5 cm), funnel-shaped flowers. The slender green leaves are sword shaped and deciduous. It flowers in spring.
ZONES 9–10

## *ZEPHYRANTHES*

ZEPHYR FLOWER, FAIRY LILY, RAIN LILY

These charming natives of the Americas often appear quite suddenly after summer rain. The widely trumpet-shaped flowers are borne singly on short stems. They are easy to grow and should be planted in late fall to early winter in a sunny position. Soil should be rich with excellent drainage. Give plenty of water during the growing season but reduce this after flowering. They can be grown in pots in very cold climates. Clumps are best left undisturbed for a few years. Propagate from offsets in fall or from seed sown in spring. They are excellent in rockeries or borders.

### *Z. atamasco*

ATAMASCO LILY

Among the hardiest of the zephyr lilies, this native of southeastern North America has pure white to purple-tinged fragrant flowers. Its stems are up to 12 in (about 30 cm) tall, amidst grassy, dark green leaves. Flowers appear in late spring and early summer.
ZONES 8–11

### *Z. candida*
**syn. *Argyropsis candida***

This vigorous species grows to 6 in (about 15 cm). The starry, cup-shaped, white flowers are 2 in (about 5 cm) wide and are borne singly on the slender stems. The grass-like foliage is evergreen.
ZONES 9–11

### *Z. grandiflora*
**syn. *Z. carinata***

This popular species grows to 10 in (about 25 cm). The 4 in (about 10 cm) flowers are dusky pink. The slender leaves are strap shaped. Some forms have smaller flowers.
ZONES 9–11

*Vallota speciosa*

*Veltheimia capensis*

*Watsonia* hybrid

*Zephyranthes grandiflora*

*Veltheimia bracteata*

*Zephyranthes candida*

*Watsonia borbonica*

CHAPTER 6

# Lawns, Ground Covers & Ornamental Grasses

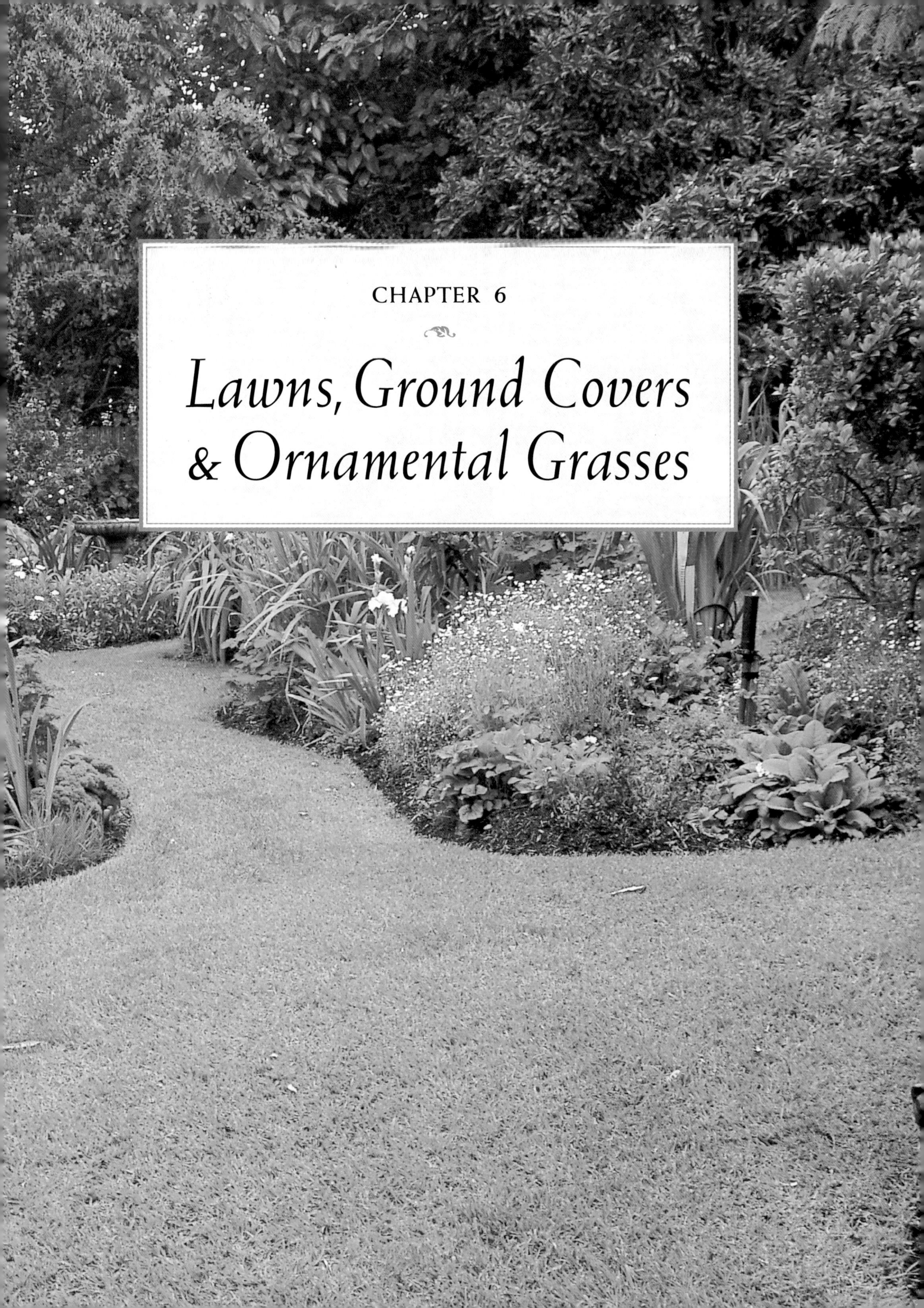

*The soil is the mother of the garden, and a gardener treats it with all due respect; but bare earth, mud when it rains and dust when it does not, makes a most unsuitable floor for a garden. We can, of course, lay paving or gravel, but they are hard, expensive and reflective of heat and glare. The universal favorite for flooring the main part of a garden is lawn. It is soft and quiet underfoot, it doesn't reflect glare, and its greenness is the most flattering backdrop imaginable for plants and flowers.*

No one species will give a perfect, year-round sward—the finest lawns are the result of careful blending. Every area has its favorite lawn grass species, and these are the ones you should choose. We do suggest that if you choose the finest, slow-growing types you'll have less work to do in the long run, even if they are more trouble to establish than the faster growing meadow and pasture grasses.

## Looking After a Lawn

Nonetheless the meadow grasses can become an acceptable lawn if they are regularly shorn, and that brings us to the least loved of all gardening tasks—mowing. No one enjoys it, and many shortcuts are devised by the lazy in the hope of having to take the mower out less frequently. Most common is cutting too short or leaving it to grow too long. Alas, none works. All weaken the grass and encourage the weeds, and so the time saved is spent (with interest) on weeding. A weedy lawn actually needs mowing more frequently than a clean one—the weeds grow faster than the grass so that unacceptable shagginess sets in sooner.

It's best to encourage a good, dense growing turf by watering as needed, fertilizing at least once a year (in spring) and cutting short enough for neatness but not so short as to scalp the grass. With most fine grasses, 1 in (about 2.5 cm) is short enough, and it is desirable not to let the grass get more than about twice as long as that so it won't be unduly shocked when it is cut. When you come to mow you'll be grateful for having kept the lines of the lawn simple—getting the mower around wriggly edges and island flowerbeds is time consuming and frustrating. Whether you choose a rotary mower or a reel-cut type is up to you; the reel does give a more velvety finish (and is the only way to get that smart striped effect, caused by the way it "lays" the grass like the pile of a carpet) but it is more trouble to maintain. Untidy edges will spoil the effect of the most immaculate mowing; allow time for trimming them, either with shears or a powered edging clipper. And don't be careless about safety. Turn the mower off whenever you leave it unattended, even for a minute; keep your hands and feet well away from the blades; and usher small children safely out of harm's way.

It can be tempting to allow the clippings to lie, to rot down and return the nourishment they contain, but this doesn't really work. They'll just make half-rooted "thatch" and clog up the crowns of the grass plants. Off to the compost heap with them!

In nature, grass tends to grow in the spring and then brown off with summer's heat, to return green with the

*A well-manicured lawn can provide a flattering backdrop to flowers and foliage plants.*

spring; however, in gardens we want spring green all year. Except in the moistest of climates, this means watering. It is amazingly easy to do this wastefully—just sprinkle lightly until the lawn looks refreshed and repeat when it looks tired again. This will be pretty soon; light watering encourages the grass roots to linger near the surface. It is much better to water infrequently—even in the hottest, driest climates, this means no more than every ten days or so—but do it thoroughly so the water penetrates right into the soil and the roots go down deep after it.

The constant removal of foliage from the grass strips it of nutrients, and these ought to be made up to it by an occasional dose of fertilizer. This is easy: just buy a ready-made lawn fertilizer, sprinkle it on, and water heavily at once to wash it into the soil—if you don't it can burn the leaves. You can apply it at the manufacturer's suggested rate in one go, but it is more effective to divide the quantity in half and give two doses a fortnight apart.

If you started out with clean soil and keep the grass flourishing, weeds should cause little headache. If any get in, just dig them out (an old kitchen knife is a useful implement here) or spot treat them with glyphosate. The lawn should soon grow over the resulting bare patch, especially if you assist it with water and fertilizer.

## Woodland Gardens

There is, however, one currently fashionable style of lawn to which all these rules don't apply, and that is the flowering woodland. Here, the grass is deliberately inter planted with "weed" —primroses, small bulbs, cornflowers, Flanders and Californian poppies, daisies and the like—the aim being to create an effect like the carpets of flowers you see in old tapestries. Very pretty and romantic it can be too. Here, you don't want the grass to flourish so much it smothers the flowers, so you start with rather poor soil, apply fertilizer with a sparing hand, water very judiciously, and mow only a few times a year.

Precisely when depends on your chosen flowers, but as a guide you'll probably mow in late winter to give the spring flowers a setting of short grass; again when they have shed their seeds and died down; and perhaps again in fall. Always keep the mower as high as it will go.

*The golden hues of pampas grass can brighten a winter garden.*

## Ground Covers

It is a short step from the flowering woodland to leaving out the grass and carpeting the ground entirely with low-growing, easy-care plants known, naturally enough, as ground covers.

You can use annuals as temporary ground cover—nasturtiums are excellent—but the best ground covers are spreading, evergreen perennials or dense, low-growing shrubs. Flowers are a feature of many, but far more important is the ability to make a carpet dense enough to smother weeds without growing too tall—ankle height is about right. Then a good ground cover needs to be presentable all year; to need little in the way of trimming or spraying; and to be easy to propagate to cut down on cost. It is possible to weave patterns with several species, but the stronger will tend to crowd out the weaker—and simplicity usually looks better anyway. Ground covers cannot be walked on.

Prepare your bed as thoroughly as for any other plant, plant at the appropriate season, and mulch at once; the last thing you want is weeds getting in between the young plants. If you like, you can plant some low-growing annuals between your permanent plants—and they will remind you to water and fertilize. Ground covers may be low, low maintenance when they are established, but when young they need care!

## Ornamental Grasses

You can supplement the flowers in your meadow with grasses chosen for their ornamental foliage and flowers rather than their ability to stand cropping into lawn: but you will need to place them with care as many are quite tall. They can be placed anywhere in the garden that you want their airy grace, and it is currently fashionable to include them in plantings with more orthodox annuals and perennials. The important thing is to choose species that stay in sedate clumps; those that run about will turn themselves into weeds as soon as your back is turned. Most retain their form as they die off for the winter, and their golden and brown tints can be a lovely feature of the fall and winter garden—but if they might be a fire hazard, by all means cut them down when they dry off. (You can use them in dried flower arrangements indoors.)

*Agrostis tenuis*

*Asarum caudatum*

*Asarum canadense*

*Aegopodium podagraria* 'Variegatum'

*Festuca elatior*

## LAWNS AND GROUND COVERS

### AEGOPODIUM

*podagraria* 'Variegatum'

VARIEGATED GOUTWEED, VARIEGATED BISHOP'S WEED

An aggressive spreader, this coarse-textured, herbaceous perennial ground cover can become weedy if not controlled. The variegated green and white, compound foliage reaches 12 in (about 30 cm) in height and lightens up a dark, shady site. Tiny white flowers are borne on umbels, which rise above the foliage to 18 in (about 45 cm) in mid-summer. Easy to grow in sun or shade in ordinary soil, it is best suited for embankment cover. Divide and replant in early spring.

ZONES 3–9

### AGROSTIS

*tenuis*

COLONIAL BENT, BROWN TOP, BENT GRASS, NEW ZEALAND BENT

Regarded highly for its tolerance of the cold, this attractive and durable annual grass is widely grown in New Zealand, the cooler Australian states and in parts of North America. It is resistant to frost. Left unmown, this New Zealand native grows to 16 in (about 40 cm) in height. A recommended mowing height is ¾ in (about 2 cm). A prodigious spreader, it has a creeping stem with bright green, narrow leaves. It prefers moist soil that drains well in a sunny, open location, although it will grow in light shade. Compared with other bent grasses, this more erect species needs less care. Propagate from seed in spring.

ZONES 3–10

### ASARUM

This genus consists of over 70 rhizomatous perennials, both evergreen and deciduous, which are commonly called wild ginger. Originating in temperate areas of the northern hemisphere, these tufted plants make very good ground covers. The leaves are either kidney shaped or cordate, and the small tubular flowers that arise to 2 in (about 5 cm) are often hidden below the leaves. These plants prefer a shady site in moist, well-drained soil and can be planted out any time between fall and spring. They spread rapidly; divide the clumps every few years in spring. They can also be propagated from seed.

#### *A. canadense*

CANADIAN SNAKEROOT, WILD GINGER

This deciduous perennial native to the woodlands of eastern North America forms tufted mats of coarse-textured leaves reaching 8 in (about 20 cm) in height. Inconspicuous brown, bell-shaped flowers are hidden beneath the 2–7 in (about 5–7 cm) wide heart-shaped leaves. Grow as a ground cover in shady sites with moisture-holding, organic soils. It is ideal in the woodland garden or as an edging plant for shady areas. It is a hardy species although it is prone to attack from slugs and snails. Propagate by division in spring.

ZONES 3–8

#### *A. caudatum*

BRITISH COLUMBIA WILD GINGER

Native to the coastal mountains from California to British Columbia, this ground-hugging, evergreen perennial grows in relatively deep shade on the forest floor. Spreading by rhizomes, it forms colonies of irregular, open patches. Flowering in late spring through summer, the large, 6 in (about 15 cm) long, heart-shaped leaves rise to 7 in (about 17 cm) above ground and hide the brownish purple blooms. Plant in organic rich, humusy soil in shady areas.

ZONES 6–9

### BOUTELOUA

*gracilis*

BLUE GRAMA GRASS

This densely tufted perennial is native to the short-grass prairies of the North American Great Plains. An eye-catching grass, it withstands heat, drought and extreme cold. Delicate, wiry stems rise to 24 in (about 60 cm) above the narrow, gray-green foliage and terminate in flower clusters which resemble dust brushes. Able to succeed with little irrigation, it has been used extensively as a water-saving lawn grass for dry climates.

ZONES 3–9

### BUCHLOE

*dactyloides*

BUFFALOGRASS

A native of the short-grass prairies from North Dakota to Texas, this stolonizing grass forms dense stands of turf which perform well in low-water sites. Tolerant of heat and cold, its gray-green leaves provide a nice contrast to other grasses mixed with it for lawns.

ZONES 4–9

### FESTUCA

FESCUE

A native of Asia and temperate Europe, this genus provides good grassed areas requiring little maintenance and are ideal for playing fields, street-side plantings and parks in cold through to moderate climates. They grow deep roots and forms tufts, with short rhizomes and bright green leaves ¼ in (about 6 mm) wide. The turfs have a loose texture, wear well and tolerate semi-shade. They also withstand drought and frost well. A mowing height of 2 in (about 5 cm) is recommended for these lawns. Disease and pests rarely affect the fescues.

### *F. elatior*

TALL FESCUE

This is a species with a tendency to clump, making it more suited to coarser lawns such as those grown for playing fields. It is also good for controlling erosion. Its leaves are tough and it will grow in compacted soil. As it does not send out runners, sow thickly to ensure a close turf. Lightly fertilize each month through summer, only once or twice in fall and spring. Sow seeds in fall.

ZONES 4–10

### *F. rubra*

CREEPING RED FESCUE

A meadow grass native to the Rocky Mountains, this species is easily identified by the red or purplish sheath circling the base of the stem. Wiry, slender, green leaves rise to 6 in (about 15 cm), overtopped by narrow panicles of purple-tinged flowers. Rhizomatous, it is suited for use as a lawn grass where low maintenance and drought tolerance are required.

ZONES 3–6

*Festuca rubra*

### *F. rubra* 'Commutata'

NEW ZEALAND FESCUE, CHEWINGS FESCUE

A tuft-forming grass, this species is often sown with bent grasses, with which it shares common needs and preferences. Established on steep slopes and left ungroomed it makes for an appealing cover. Propagate from seed.

ZONES 3–10

*Lolium perenne*

*Fragaria chiloensis*

## *FRAGARIA*

### *chiloensis*

BEACH STRAWBERRY

The low, bushy plants of this West Coast North American native form dense carpets to 9 ft (about 2.7 m) in spread and thrive in full sun and slightly acidic garden soils. The glossy green, compound leaves with silky, bluish white undersides provide the perfect foil for the bright white flowers which appear in spring. An excellent ground cover in sunny locations, the edible pink fruit attract birds and other wildlife. Remove and replant the young, rooted plantlets that are at the end of the runners.

ZONES 5–10

## *LOLIUM*

### *perenne*

PERENNIAL RYE GRASS

This perennial grass grows in clumps up to 20 in (about 50 cm) high and 12 in (about 30 cm) in spread. The linear leaves are glossy, smooth and dark green. The yellowy green flowers, which appear in late spring and summer, are narrow, spike-like blooms 6 in (about 15 cm) long. It has smooth, whippy stems that tend to lie down under the lawnmower, springing back up later. This fast-sprouting species from Europe thrives in most well-drained soils in open, sunny locations. Propagate from seed. It is a coarse grass needing frequent mowing and is best for rough areas.

ZONES 3–8

## *MENTHA*

### *requienii*

CORSICAN MINT

This ground-hugging, semi-evergreen species of mint native to the Mediterranean grows to only ½ in (about 1 cm) and forms dense mats to 12 in (about 30 cm) in diameter. The tiny round leaves are bright green and, when crushed, smell strongly of peppermint. In late summer, pale purple flowers appear on short, erect spikes above the foliage. Best grown in partial shade on well-drained soils, it is ideally suited to fill the spaces between paving stones. Propagate by division.

ZONES 7–10

## *OPHIOPOGON*

### *japonicus*

MONDO GRASS

Not a true grass, this evergreen member of the lily family is native to Japan and Korea. The narrow, dark green foliage arises from rhizomes, spreading to form dense, lush mats. Pale purple flowers appear among the leaves in mid-summer, followed by bright blue, pea-sized fruit. Propagate by division in spring.

ZONES 8–11

*Ophiopogon japonicus*

## *PACHYSANDRA*

### *terminalis*

JAPANESE SPURGE

This evergreen perennial, native to Japan, has leathery, glossy green leaves with saw-tooth tips clustered at the ends of short stems. Tiny white flowers appear in terminal clusters in early summer. Growing to a height of 8 in (about 20 cm), it makes a good ground cover in well-drained, moisture-holding soil. Propagate by division in spring.

ZONES 4–10

*Pachysandra terminalis*

*Thymus serpyllum*

*Poa pratensis*

*Carex elata* 'Aurea'

*Thymus pseudolanuginosus*

### *POA*
#### *pratensis*

KENTUCKY BLUE GRASS, MEADOW GRASS

Although producing an appealing blue-green lawn, this native of central Europe will not take the heavy traffic of playgrounds or playing fields and does not survive dry conditions. It does well in cooler climates but is slightly frost tender. This perennial has smooth, erect stems and small, flat, pointed leaves. If left ungroomed, it will grow to 6 in (about 15 cm) in height and spread. In spring and mid-summer it bears spikelets in spreading panicles. Establish in light, sandy soil that drains well. Although it tolerates shade, a sunny, open location is best. It needs ample watering. Propagate from seed or by division. It is vulnerable to attack by rust and other diseases brought on by a hot summer.

ZONES 3–10

### *RUBUS*
#### *calycinoides*

This carpet-forming, evergreen sub-shrub roots along the stems where they touch the ground, spreading to 3 ft (about 90 cm) and only 2 in (about 5 cm) in height. The shiny, dark green leaves are deeply veined above and silky white beneath. Small, white, strawberry-like flowers appear in mid-summer. Requiring good drainage, it thrives in full sun or partial shade. Propagate from stem tip cuttings or by division.

ZONES 3–10

### *THUNBERGIA*
#### *gregorii*

**syn. *T. gibsonii***

ORANGE CLOCKVINE

Performing as a perennial in mild climates and as an annual in harsher ones, this twining vine climbs to 6 ft (about 1.8 m) or sprawls as a ground cover to 6 ft (about 1.8 m) in diameter. The very showy, brilliant orange, tubular flowers are borne nearly all year round where climates permit, or only in summer when treated as an annual. Easy to grow, it should be planted in a position in full sun and given adequate moisture. Propagate from cuttings or from seed.

ZONES 9–11

### *THYMUS*

THYME

This genus consists of over 300 evergreen species of herbaceous perennials and sub-shrubs, ranging from prostrate plants to 8 in (about 20 cm) high. Chosen for their aromatic leaves, these natives of southern Europe and Asia are frequently featured in rockeries, grown between stepping stones, or for a display on banks. Some species are also used in cooking. The flowers are often tubular and vary from white through pink to mauve. For thick, dense plants, the flowerheads should be removed after flowering. Plant out from early fall through to early spring in a sunny site with well-drained soil. Propagate by division in spring or late summer.

#### *T. pseudolanuginosus*

**syn. *T. lanuginosus***

WOOLLY THYME

This extremely low-growing thyme accentuates the contour of the ground below as it spreads to form broad, oval mats of densely hairy, gray-green foliage. It grows best in full sun and well-drained, relatively infertile soils. Excellent as a filler between paving stones, it is easily propagated by division.

ZONES 3–9

#### *T. serpyllum*

WILD THYME, CREEPING THYME

A smaller plant than garden thyme, this native of Europe grows to a height and spread of 4 in (about 10 cm), to form a useful ground cover. Its creeping stem is woody and branching, and the scented, bright green leaves are elliptical to lanceolate. The bluish purple flowers are small and tubular with two lips, and are borne in spring and summer in dense terminal whorls. This species prefers alkaline soil, while full sun intensifies the aroma of the leaves. Propagate from cuttings or by root division. It will take moderate foot traffic, but needs replanting every few years to maintain a dense cover.

ZONES 3–9

*Butomus umbellatus*

*Thunbergia gregorii*

### *ZOYSIA*
#### *japonica* 'Meyeri'

MEYER ZOYSIA

This very drought-tolerant, rhizomatous perennial grass from Japan is extensively used for lawns in the arid zones of southern and southwestern states where frosts are of short duration. Resembling bluegrass, the wide blades are dark green to 5 in (about 12 cm) in length. Meyer's is the first zoysia to brown in winter and the last to green up in spring. Propagate by division.

ZONES 8–11

*Rubus calycinoides*

## *ORNAMENTAL GRASSES*

### *ANDROPOGON*
#### *gerardii*

BIG BLUESTEM

A native of the American prairies, this clump-forming grass is extremely drought and heat tolerant. Easily identified by the blue color at the base of the stems, the narrow, erect foliage reaches 4 ft (about 1.2 m) in height and is tinged red. Turning a rich orange wheat color in the fall, it is useful in native plantscapes or where low-water input is essential.

ZONES 3–8

### *ARUNDO*
#### *donax*

GIANT REED

This giant perennial grass is one of the most striking of summer foliage plants. Growing to a height of 18 ft

*Arundo donax*

(about 5.5 m) and spread of 3 ft (about 90 cm), it is an excellent ornamental plant for large gardens. In mild areas it can grow very vigorously and will need confining. Floppy, blue-green leaves are borne on thick stems, and dense panicles of creamy spikelets appear in summer. It prefers a sunny situation and moist soil. In winter, when the foliage becomes untidy, it should be cut to the ground, creating luxuriant new spring and summer growth. *A. donax* 'Versicolor' is a popular variegated cultivar with broad, creamy white–striped leaves.
ZONES 7–11

## *BRIZA*
### *media*
QUAKING GRASS

An evergreen, tuft-forming, rhizomatous, perennial grass that grows to a height of 12–24 in (about 30–60 cm), with a spread of 3–4 in (about 7.5–10 cm). It has mid-green leaves and in summer bears open branched flower clusters of about 30 hanging, brownish purple spikelets. They make very good dried flower decorations and are excellent for dyeing. Plant in a position in full sun in well-drained, poor soil. Propagate from seed in spring or fall, or by division any time in spring. Fungus diseases may cause problems.
ZONES 5–11

## *BUTOMUS*
### *umbellatus*
FLOWERING RUSH

This elegant, marginal water plant is the only member of its genus. Related to the lilies, it is a rush-like, deciduous perennial with razor-sharp, narrow, twisted, mid-green leaves and tall stalks of rose-pink flowers in summer. It grows to a height of 3 ft (about 90 cm) and spread of 18 in (about 45 cm). Plant in a warm, sunny area in a shallow pool or boggy soil. Propagate from seed in spring or late summer, or by division in spring. The plant's name translates as: "a plant that cuts the mouth of oxen when grazing."
ZONES 4–9

## *CALAMAGROSTIS*
### *acutiflora* 'Stricta'
FEATHER REED GRASS

A strong-growing, clump-forming perennial from Europe, this species makes a dense, stiffly upright mass of arching, medium green leaves to 4 ft (about 1.2 m). The pale white, delicate flowers appear in midsummer from the center of the clump, rising well above the foliage. Changing from white to purple, the flowers turn to gold by fall and should be left on over winter to provide a unique focal point. Drought tolerant, it grows well in any soil and full sun. Well suited to stream and pond edges, it provides a strong, vertical element in the garden. Divide the clumps in spring after removing the previous year's foliage and flowers.
ZONES 5–10

## *CAREX*
SEDGE

This large genus contains over 1500 temperate perennials with grass-like foliage. Predominately clump forming and evergreen, they make resilient decorative potted plants. Many species have sharp, pendent leaves and catkin-type flowers. Male and female blooms may appear on the same head or on the same stem. Plant in full sun or partial shade and only water when surface roots seem dry. Propagate by division in spring. These sedges are a characteristic feature of the New Zealand landscape, with more than 70 species native to that country.

### *C. elata* 'Aurea'
syn. *C. stricta* 'Aurea'
GOLDEN SEDGE

This evergreen, tuft-forming perennial sedge is useful for growing in damp places and beside ponds. It has golden-yellow leaves, and blackish brown flower spikes that are borne in summer. It reaches a height of 16 in (about 40 cm) and spread of 6 in (about 15 cm). It grows best in a sunny situation in fertile, wet soil.
ZONES 5–10

### *C. morrowii* 'Variegata'
VARIEGATED JAPANESE SEDGE

This striking, mound-forming sedge native to the moist woodlands of Japan forms a tidy, low, evergreen tuft of bright green and white striped leaves. Becoming 12 in (about 30 cm) tall and 18 in (about 45 cm) wide at maturity, it is ideally suited as an edging to a border or pond, or in a damp spot in the rock garden. Fertile, moist loam and full sun or partial shade are required for best growth. Plant the divisions 15 in (about 38 cm) apart to ensure each clump remains distinct. 'Aureo-variegata' has bright yellow and green striped leaves.
ZONES 5–10

## *CORTADERIA*
### *selloana*
syn. *C. argentea*
PAMPAS GRASS

Native to Argentina and Brazil, this perennial, clump-forming, stately grass grows to a height of 9 ft (about 2.7 m) and spread of $4^1/_2$ ft (about 1.3 m). Its stems are tall and reed like and the leaves are long and slender, growing outwards from the base. In summer, erect, silvery, plume-like panicles appear above the leaves. Pink varieties are also available. Propagate from seed or by division. It can be invasive, and in some areas is considered a noxious weed.
ZONES 8–11

## *DESCHAMPSIA*
### *caespitosa*
TUFTED HAIR GRASS

This mound-forming, evergreen perennial reaches 24–36 in (about 60–90 cm) in height with a 24 in (about 60 cm) spread. The flowers are borne in open panicles which rise above the coarse, arching foliage. Flower colors range from pale greenish yellow to gold (in the cultivar 'Goldgehaenge'), to silver and bronze ('Bronzeschleier'). Best grown in partial shade, it tolerates a wide range of soil conditions provided adequate moisture is available. Plant it in groups to achieve a delicate, airy mass of blooms in the garden.
ZONES 4–10

## *FESTUCA*

This is a genus of evergreen, tuft-forming perennial grasses with rounded flower stems and basal, alternate, long, narrow leaves. They bear panicles with flowerheads comprised of spikelets with one or more florets. These grasses are fully hardy and will do best in full sun in any well-drained soil.

*Carex morrowii* 'Variegata'

*Briza media*

*Cortaderia selloana*

*Deschampsia caespitosa*

*Calamagrostis acutiflora* 'Stricta'

### *F. amethystina*

A native of the Alps and southern Europe, this fescue takes its name from the deep purple panicles of flowers that appear in late spring and early summer. It grows to 10 in (about 25 cm) high with a similar spread. A dense evergreen, its slender leaves are blue-green and rough edged. It will thrive in full sun in well-drained soil and looks good planted on a bank.

ZONES 3–10

### *F. ovina* var. *glauca*

BLUE SHEEP'S FESCUE

This clump-forming perennial grass grows to a height and spread of around 8–12 in (about 20–30 cm). The narrow, rolled leaves range in color from blue-green to silver-blue. The flowers are of little value and should be removed to encourage foliage growth. Very useful as a decorative edging or massed, it is best planted at very close spacing to ensure a solid cover. Drought tolerant, it thrives in full sun and average soils. Propagate by division or from seed. 'Sea Urchin' and 'Elijah's Blue' have silver-blue leaves.

ZONES 3–10

## *HAKONECHLOA*

### *macra* 'Aureola'

GOLDEN VARIEGATED HAKONECHLOA

This slowly spreading, deciduous, perennial grass from the mountains of Japan provides a striking accent to the garden. The narrow, 8 in (about 20 cm) long, bright yellow leaves are lined with fine green stripes that make it a great candidate for use as a specimen or ground cover in light shade. Reaching heights of 24 in (about 60 cm), it grows best in organic, rich, well-drained soil in partial shade.

ZONES 5–11

## *HELICTOTRICHON*

### *sempervirens*

BLUE OAT GRASS

The flowers of this species are borne on long, slender stems that stand well above the leaves. Initially blue when they appear in spring, they turn a deep, golden yellow by fall. It grows well in full sun and a well-drained soil.

ZONES 4–11

## *IMPERATA*

### *cylindrica* 'Red Baron'

JAPANESE BLOOD GRASS

The deep red leaves of this Japanese import grow to 12 in (about 30 cm) tall and provide a striking contrast in the garden. At least 4 to 6 hours of sun and moisture-holding, loam soil make ideal growing conditions. The best effect is to mass a number of plants together and allow them to slowly colonize the site. Propagate by division in spring.

ZONES 5–11

## *MILIUM*

### *effusum* 'Aureum'

BOWLES' GOLDEN GRASS, MILLET GRASS

An evergreen, tuft-forming perennial grass grown for its yellow foliage and flowers. Good for growing in perennial borders, water gardens or as a ground cover, and effective when planted under white variegated shrubs. Its flat leaves are golden-yellow in spring and fade to yellowish green in summer. Panicles of greenish yellow spikelets are produced in summer; these can be cut and used for dried arrangements. It grows to a height of 3 ft (about 90 cm) and spread of 12 in (about 30 cm). It grows best in the shade in a well-drained, rich, moist soil. Propagate from seed in spring or fall, or by division in spring. It also self seeds readily. The Bowles in question in the common name was a very influential English gardener of the Edwardian period. He was particularly fond of plants with unusual leaves.

ZONES 5–11

## *MISCANTHUS*

### *sinensis* 'Variegatus'

JAPANESE SILVER GRASS

This large, herbaceous perennial grass grows to a height of 6 ft (about 1.8 m) with a spread of 18 in (about 45 cm). One of the most popular ornamental grasses, it is grown for its overall plant form and is good for perennial borders, water gardens, naturalized areas, screens and specimen planting. Clump forming, it has linear leaves with silvery white stripes and margins. Long-lasting beige, red-tinged flowerheads are borne in fall—they are good for drying and dyeing. It requires a sunny situation and well-drained, moist soil. Divide every 5 to 7 years to keep the plants growing vigorously. Propagate by division any time in spring.

ZONES 5–11

## *MOLINIA*

### *caerulea*

A native of acid heathlands in Europe, and southwest and northern Asia, this tuft-forming, deciduous, perennial grass forms large tussocks growing up to 18 in (about 45 cm) when in flower. It has broad, flat, mid-green leaves and in summer bears panicles of purplish spikelets. It grows best in acid soils in full sun. It has swollen stem bases which at times have been used as pipe cleaners and toothpicks. It is one of the most attractive garden grasses, especially in its finest variegated forms. 'Variegata' has yellow-striped, mid-green leaves. Propagate by division in spring.

ZONES 5–11

## *PENNISETUM*

This genus of tuft-forming, herbaceous, perennial grasses has species with narrow, green basal leaves and rounded flower stems. Dead foliage may be cut back on herbaceous perennials when dormant. Propagate species from seed in spring or fall or by division in spring.

### *P. alopecuroides*

FOUNTAIN GRASS

This hardy perennial grass from Asia produces broad clumps of gracefully arching foliage that reaches 3–4 ft (about 90–120 cm) in height. Of easy care, it grows well in full sun or partial shade and most well-drained soils. Flowers emerge

*Helictotrichon sempervirens*

*Festuca ovina* var. *glauca*

*Pennisetum alopecuroides*

*Molinia caerulea* 'Variegata'

*Festuca amethystina*

*Imperata cylindrica* 'Red Baron'

*Miscanthus sinensis* 'Variegatus'

*Pennisetum setaceum*

in late summer, producing 6 in (about 15 cm) long pink to magenta heads. Fall foliage colors of pink to rust fade to gold and almond for winter appeal. Very useful as a specimen in the perennial border, in water gardens or massed for ground cover, it provides wide-ranging garden appeal. Space plants widely to accommodate the mature growth. Divide clumps every 5 to 10 years in early spring.
ZONES 5–11

### *P. setaceum*

FOUNTAIN GRASS

Native to tropical Africa, this mound-forming species belongs to the same genus as many cereal grasses. Arching, pink to purple-red spikes of bearded blooms form brush-like flower clusters to 4 ft (about 1.2 m) above narrow, arching, 24 in (about 60 cm) long leaves. A herbaceous perennial in frost-free zones, it is grown as an annual in harsher climates. The 9–12 in (about 22–30 cm) long flowers appear in mid-summer and last well into winter, creating additional seasonal interest. The bristly textured stems and leaves are rusty green, whereas 'Atropurpureum' has purple foliage and 'Cupreum' has bronze-red. Drought tolerant, it should be grown in well-drained soil in full sun. Propagate by division in spring or from seed.
ZONES 8–11

## *PHALARIS*

### *arundinacea* var. *picta*

GARDENER'S GARTERS, REEDY GRASS

This clump-forming perennial grass is easily grown, bearing reed-like leaves with white stripes and, in summer, terminal panicles of purplish or pale green spikelets on stout, upstanding stems. Indigenous to North America and Europe, it can grow to $4^1/_2$ ft (about 1.3 m) but is generally kept lower in a garden. This evergreen likes well-drained soil and semi-shade; it can prove invasive. Propagate by division of the clumps.
ZONES 3–11

## *PLEIOBLASTUS*

### *pygmaeus*

syn. *Arundinaria pygmaea, Sasa pygmaea*

DWARF BAMBOO

This spreading, rhizomatous bamboo can be used to help control erosion. Left uncut, the dark green foliage (variegated in most of the commonly available strains) of this evergreen will grow to 20 in (about 50 cm) and spread indefinitely. Cut back almost to the ground in early spring to ensure a lush crop of fresh new leaves.
ZONES 5–10

## *SASA*

This genus consists of over 150 species of rhizomatous, woody grasses. They are found in eastern Asia, especially Japan. They are usually not very tall. Propagate from seed in fall or by division in spring.

### *S. palmata*

This spreading, evergreen bamboo grows to a height of 6 ft (about 1.8 m) with an indefinite spread. Its flowers are insignificant but the wide, rich green leaves make it an excellent foliage plant, adding grace and contrast to borders and rock gardens. *S. palmata* does best in a sheltered, not too dry situation in sun or shade. Its hollow stems are streaked with purple and bear one branch at each node.
ZONES 6–11

### *S. veitchii*

syn. *S. albomarginata*

This bamboo grows to a height of 5 ft (about 1.5 m) and spreads indefinitely. Its 10 in (about 25 cm) long leaves turn white at the edges. Its stems, which branch from each node, are generally purple with a whitish powder beneath the node. Grow in a position with well-drained soil in full sun.
ZONES 6–11

## *SCHIZACHYRIUM*

### *scoparium*

LITTLE BLUE-STEM

A native of eastern North America across to Arizona, this tufted perennial bunchgrass produces stiffly upright, slender, purplish stems to 5 ft (about 1.5 m).
ZONES 3–10

## *SCIRPUS*

### *lacustris* subsp. *tabernaemontani* 'Zebrinus'

syn. *S. tabernaemontani* 'Zebrinus'

This is an evergreen sedge with white-banded, leafless stems. In summer, it carries brown spikelets. Growing $4^1/_2$ ft (about 1.3 m) high, this perennial spreads widely. It likes full sun, wet soil and is not deterred even by brackish water; however, it is invasive and will need regular division.
ZONES 5–10

## *SESLERIA*

### *autumnalis*

AUTUMN MOOR GRASS

This perennial, clump-forming grass produces bright green, narrow foliage with a slight yellow cast to 12 in (about 30 cm). The narrow, 3 in (about 7.5 cm) long, silvery-white inflorescences are borne among the foliage in late summer to early fall. Grow in full sun or partial shade; it is useful massed, in rockeries or as a border.
ZONES 5–10

## *SINARUNDINARIA*

### *nitida*

syn. *Arundinaria nitida*

This medium-height bamboo from China is grown for its purplish gray stems and deep purple sheaths. Reaching heights of 4–6 ft (about 1.2–1.8 m), the canes emerge erect and eventually arch gracefully to show off the abundance of small, greenish leaves. Best grown in full sun and well-drained, fertile soils, it needs to be rejuvenated when the crowns begin to push themselves above the soil. Propagate by division.
ZONES 5–10

## *STIPA*

### *gigantea*

FEATHER GRASS

This densely tufted native of the Iberian peninsula and northern Africa grows to 4 ft (about 1.2 m) and forms a lovely mound of gently arching, narrow foliage. The large, open, many-branched panicles rise above the leaves, creating a light, airy effect in the garden. Deep golden yellow fruit with long, twisted awns are produced in mid- to late summer, making it ideal as an eye-catching specimen in the middle or back of a border. Best grown in full sun in light, well-drained, moderately fertile soil. Propagate by division.
ZONES 5–11

*Sasa palmata*

*Phalaris arundinacea* var. *picta*

*Stipa gigantea*

*Sinarundinaria nitida*

*Pleioblastus pygmaeus*

*Sesleria autumnalis*

*Sasa veitchii*

CHAPTER 7

# *Vegetables & Herbs*

*There's nothing to quite match the flavor of home-grown vegetables or herbs. They can be picked at the moment of perfection and eaten or preserved within hours to the benefit of both the family's health and budget. What's more, vegetables like spinach and rhubarb, or herbs are always bunched for sale and we often have to buy more than is immediately needed for a meal. Home grown, these are readily available by the sprig or leaves can be cut as required.*

To be grown successfully, vegetables do need to be chosen with consideration to climate. Vegetables such as beans, tomatoes and the ground vine crops like cucumbers and squash are frost sensitive and therefore need to be planted out when the prospect of frost is over. They like temperatures of around 68°F (about 20°C) to set fruit. On the other hand, many of the root crops (those with the edible parts underground), like spinach and peas, grow well in temperatures of between 53 and 64°F (about 12–18°C) and are not as susceptible to frost. Then there are the cabbages, cauliflowers and Brussels sprouts, all members of the same family, which revel in cool temperatures and are quite frost hardy.

All vegetables must have ample sunlight and this factor, more than any other, can dictate the positioning of a vegetable garden. Other points to consider include competition from tree or shrub roots, prevailing winds and drainage, although this last factor is usually able to be rectified by raising the beds or by underground piping.

The size of the garden also needs careful thought. Depending on space available and the time you are prepared to spend in the garden, any number of beds can be made, but it's a good idea to begin small. Beds are easily extended or new ones made. A bed of up to $3\frac{1}{2}$ ft (about 1 m) wide is easily cultivated from both sides. Length can be determined by available space, but 6 ft (about 1.8 m) gives ample room for the compact and quick growers. Others, like the vine crops, take up a lot more garden space and need the use of a bed the whole season to complete their cycle. The perennial plants such as rhubarb and asparagus, as well as many of the herbs which occupy the same space for many years, need a bed of their own or to be grouped at one end of a highly cultivated bed so that they are not interfered with when the rest of the garden is being prepared for the new season's crop.

Consider too the choice of vegetables you plan to grow. Yield per plant is a very important factor when space is limited. For instance beans take up relatively little space and their yield is tremendous over a season. Salad vegetables and the leaf crops too are worth considering before, say, a plot given over to potatoes, which don't really spoil when left on the greengrocer's shelf.

One very practical way to overcome limited space is to build a trellis towards the back of a garden to hold climbing beans, peas, even cucumbers. Sited correctly, this trellis will not shade the lower growing vegetables and it can act as a windbreak to a row of corn or some tomatoes.

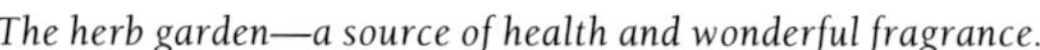

*The herb garden—a source of health and wonderful fragrance.*

Pots too can be used. They need not be restricted to growing herbs; they are also ideal for such long-cropping vegetables as capsicums, tomatoes, eggplant or the "bush" varieties of cucumbers or pumpkins. Placed on a sunny patio they can be easily observed and given immediate attention if this is required.

## Planting

Some seeds, like the quick growing radish or beans, melons and carrots, can be sown directly into their permanent garden positions. Finer seeds are better planted into seedbeds or frames where germination and early growth can be closely monitored. A seedbed needs to have soil of a fine consistency, perfect drainage and to be placed where it receives adequate sunlight and warmth and is well protected from any drying winds. The surface should be flat so that fine seeds are not washed away. Shallow grooves can be made with a length of dowel or similar, then the seeds carefully dropped into these miniature farrows and covered with a light soil layer. Water with a fine mist or spray, ensuring the surface is neither too wet nor allowed to dry out.

Gardeners in colder areas can sow seeds in frames in protected areas while it is still too early to plant outdoors. These plants are then transplanted into their permanent positions when all possibility of frost is over. When the weather warms up then it may be possible to sow another batch or two in a well-prepared, outdoor seedbed in the successive weeks. By making these regular small sowings the household won't be inundated by a glut of vegetables all maturing at the one time.

Many gardeners prefer to buy their seedlings at the nursery. Transplanting should be done in the cool of the evening. Using a garden knife or small trowel, and holding the plants by their leaves, loosen them gently from the seedbed or punnet and place a bunch of them on a board—covering them with a cloth or damp kitchen paper towel will prevent them drying out. Use a piece of dowel to make a row of holes sufficiently deep so the tiny roots will not be bent or broken, then gently prise the seedlings apart and place single plants in the prepared holes, pushing the soil firmly around them with two fingers. Water each plant to ensure any air pockets are filled with soil. The seedlings do benefit from being given some protection in the form of a leafy branch, cut down milk carton or similar until they have time to become accustomed to their new surroundings.

*Nothing can beat the flavor of home-grown vegetables.*

Planting the same vegetables in the same position each year is not good garden practice as the plants of the same family are often prone to similar diseases and this only accentuates the problem. And, although chemicals can be used, one of the benefits of growing vegetables is that you can decide which, and indeed if any, chemicals to use. Plants of the same family also take up similar nutrients and it was for this reason that crop rotation was first introduced. Today these nutrients can be replaced by commercial fertilizers.

Different crops require different types of fertilizers; the green plants grown for their leaves need a high nitrogen content, while plants grown for their fruit need a more balanced diet. When a garden is as intensively used as it is for vegetable growing it pays to supplement the use of chemical fertilizers with organic material to ensure its continued good health. Organic fertilizers such as compost can be dug into the soil at the changeover of the seasons. Straw or similar material used as a mulch during the growing season is usually sufficiently decomposed to be dug into the garden at the end of summer. You'll be amazed at the difference in soil texture and general health of the soil when this is done.

Vegetables need to be grown quickly to promote maximum quality in both leaf and fruiting types. To ensure this rapid, uninterrupted development it is necessary to keep soil adequately moist at all times. It follows then that sandy soil, which dries out more rapidly than heavy soil, needs to be watered more frequently. Many of the vine crops and tomatoes are prone to leaf diseases if leaves are subject to continued moisture, so in beds where these types of vegetables are to be grown a trickle hose or a depression running the length of the bed and filled with water each morning could be used instead of sprinklers, which spray moisture indiscriminately over foliage and ground alike.

Close planting and mulching are two ways to ensure moisture is conserved. Close planting may produce less vigorous plants or a marginally less prolific crop, but the home gardener can progressively use, and so thin out, rows as plants mature. Mulching saves the gardener time and energy in other ways as well. It helps the soil temperature control at both extremes and stops heavy rain washing away soil from around the fibrous roots, which are often very near the surface of many of the annual vegetables. Mulching also limits weed growth. Many gardeners today rely solely on mulched or "no dig" beds for successful vegetable growing.

Do try gardening with vegetables and herbs as it really is the most satisfying of the stress reducing hobbies and you'll glow with pleasure at the bountiful results of your leisure!

Allium ascalonicum

Allium cepa var. aggregatum

# VEGETABLES

## ALLIUM

This is a large genus consisting of more than 700 species of perennials and biennials that grow in temperate climates around the world and range in size from 4–60 in (about 10–150 cm). Some species are edible, including the onions, garlic and chives. The most ornamental species, which are brightly colored with beautiful flowers, are found in the northern hemisphere. Common to the genus is the oniony smell emitted when the leaves are bruised or pinched. The onion species may need the protection of a cold frame if the soil is cold. Both the onion and ornamental species have the same pest and disease enemies. The name derives from the Celtic, *all*, meaning hot.

### *A. ascalonicum*

SHALLOT

A carefully thinned bed of shallots will self-perpetuate by dropping seeds or generating new clusters of bulbs. Like all onions, shallots like a light, fertile, weed-free soil. They are usually propagated by dividing the clumps of bulbs.

ALL ZONES

### *A. cepa*

ONION, SCALLION

Onions need a cool climate and a sunny, open position in a well-drained bed of soil. Sow the seeds or immature onions in mid-spring in holes $^1/_2$ in (about 1 cm) deep and 12 in (about 30 cm) apart, and water moderately. Harvest in late summer when the leaves have begun to turn a yellow color. The onion was a popular vegetable among the Greeks and Romans but was never eaten by the Egyptians, who regarded it as sacred. The scallion is an immature onion which has not yet made a bulb. It likes the same conditions as the other onions. Sow seed any time of the year in warm climates.

ALL ZONES

### *A. cepa* var. *aggregatum*

TREE ONION

Otherwise known as golden shallots or the Egyptian onion, these have a more delicate taste than scallions and can be used instead of chives. Propagate from the small bulbs that grow among the flowers or by division.

ALL ZONES

### *A. porrum*

LEEK

Easier to grow than the onion and more suited to cold climates, the leek likes a sunny spot and a moist light soil. Sow seeds in spring or summer or plant seedlings 8 in (about 20 cm) apart with 12 in (about 30 cm) between rows, filling each hole gently with water. Keep clear of weeds and, once the base of the leek is at least 1 in (about 2.5 cm) thick, harvest as needed.

ALL ZONES

## APIUM

CELERY

Native to the Mediterranean, this leafy vegetable is a boon to any salad, but a challenge for the home gardener to grow well. It needs a

Allium cepa

well-prepared, loamy soil that can drain water but still hold the desired amount. It also commands a lot of space and regular doses of liquid fertilizer. Prior to some hard work put in by Italian gardeners some 400 years ago celery was nothing more than a bitter-tasting weed, and even now its stalks need to be blanched to remove bitterness. This is done by shoring the soil up around them to exclude the light when they reach a height of 12 in (about 30 cm). You can also bundle the plant up in black plastic.

### *A. graveolens* var. *dulce*

CELERY

Prepare the bed for celery by adding plenty of compost or animal manure. Space plants 12–16 in (about 30–40 cm) apart. It is a shallow rooted plant that needs regular watering—every day or so in hot weather. It prefers a mild to cool climate.

ALL ZONES

### *A. graveolens* var. *rapaceum*

CELERIAC

Easier to grow than celery and with a longer growing season, this is similar to the turnip (often called turnip-rooted celery) but with a celery flavor. Keep well watered even when cool, and harvest the roots when around 4 in (about 10 cm) across. The leaves are edible but inferior to regular celery.

ALL ZONES

## *ASPARAGUS officinalis*

ASPARAGUS

A perennial member of the lily family, this vegetable seems to have been cultivated and eaten all over the world as far back as the ancient Egyptians. Sow seed in spring or set young plants in winter in 10 in (about 25 cm) deep trenches in a sunny part of the garden. Give asparagus a good 12 in (about 30 cm) between each plant so that its fleshy roots can wander freely. The soil should be well drained and rich with compost or manure. Do not harvest the young shoots (spears) until the third spring, and always stop in time to allow sufficient shoots to mature to keep the plants going. The red berries should be picked before they go to seed.

ALL ZONES

## *BETA*

BEET

A relatively easy vegetable to grow, beet is fast growing and should be given space and an open position. It needs a deep, fertile soil that has been previously cultivated. It is adaptable to most climates, although plants may run to seed.

### *B. vulgaris*

BEET, GARDEN BEET

Sow seeds in the fall in 1 in (about 2.5 cm) holes 8 in (about 20 cm)

*Beta vulgaris*

*Apium graveolens* var. *rapaceum*

*Allium porrum*

*Asparagus officinalis*

*Apium graveolens* var. *dulce*

*Brassica oleracea* var. *acephala*

*Brassica oleracea gonglyoides*

*Brassica oleracea* var. *botrytis*

*Beta vulgaris* var. *cicla*

apart. When the first leaves appear weed out the weaker seedlings. Keep the soil moist and pull out the beet by hand. In warm climates it can be harvested almost all year round, but in cold climates bulbs will need to be picked and then stored over winter. It is susceptible to boron deficiency and white fly. It was once valued by the Romans and Greeks for its leaves rather than the root itself.

ALL ZONES

### *B. vulgaris* var. *cicla*

LEAF BEET, SWISS CHARD

Similar to spinach, but better in warm climates, it has the same requirements as beet. It is easy to grow and will tolerate shade or sun. Sow in mid-spring and summer. Snails and slugs are the only real problem. Harvest the leaves, a few at a time, as needed. Propagate from seed sown from spring to early fall.

ALL ZONES

## *BRASSICA*

There are 30 species of this annual or biennial vegetable, some grown for cooking, oilseed and mustard, others for animal fodder. It is native to the Mediterranean and parts of Asia. Most of the *Brassica* species love a lime-rich, moist, well-drained soil. Seedlings should be raised in flats or pots and then carefully replanted 6 to 8 weeks later in a sheltered spot in soil that has been prepared previously for an earlier crop. Brassicas are more prone to pests and diseases than other vegetables so ensure all soil is weed free and not wet. Crop rotation should be practised.

### *B. campestris* var. *rutabaga*

RUTABAGA, SWEDE

Similar to turnips but larger and sweeter, rutabagas prefer a fertile soil. Sow seeds in late spring to early summer in 1 in (about 2.5 cm) deep holes 18 in (about 45 cm) apart. Harvest in mid-fall.

ALL ZONES

### *B. oleracea gonglyoides*

KOHLRABI, CABBAGE TURNIP

With characteristics of both the turnip and cabbage, this is a versatile vegetable with a slightly nutty flavor that can be eaten raw or cooked. Sow seeds in holes $^1/_2$ in (about 1 cm) deep and spaced 8 in (about 20 cm) by 30 in (about 76 cm) apart. Weed very lightly as root disturbance will slow growth.

ALL ZONES

### *B. oleracea* var. *acephala*

KALE

A variety of flat-leafed or curly-leafed, headless cabbage that is prolific in northern Europe because of its tolerance to cold. Plant out the seedlings in 1 in (about 2.5 cm) holes 18 in (about 45 cm) apart. Sow the flat-leafed variety from seed as they do not tolerate transplanting.

ALL ZONES

### *B. oleracea* var. *botrytis*

WHITE CAULIFLOWER

Mark Twain scathingly labeled the cauliflower "a cabbage with a college education," but time has proved this to be a very popular vegetable with a long history. It prefers a humus-rich soil for large compact head production. Plant seedlings 24 in (about 60 cm) apart and across with care as they hate being transplanted. Ensure the right amounts of boron, magnesium and potassium.

ALL ZONES

### *B. oleracea* var. *bullata*

SAVOY CABBAGE

This variety is extremely tolerant to frost and will thrive in very cold

conditions. It is larger and stronger in flavor than European cabbage.
ALL ZONES

### *B. oleracea* var. *capitata*
EUROPEAN CABBAGE

Water this species regularly and mulch well, keeping the soil well drained. Space seedlings between 12–20 in (about 30–50 cm) apart, depending on variety. Red cabbage, with its purple leaves, is a slow maturing cabbage that needs a long growing season. However it is the best of all the cabbage species for pickling and frying.
ALL ZONES

### *B. oleracea* var. *cymosa*
BROCCOLI

Sow seeds in late spring. Plant seedlings in late summer 20 in (about 50 cm) apart in 24 in (about 50 cm) rows. It is ideally grown in raised beds. Keep clear of weeds and do not allow to flower as it will stop growing. Harvest 10 or 11 weeks after planting.
ALL ZONES

### *B. oleracea* var. *gemmifera*
BRUSSELS SPROUTS

Brussels sprouts need to mature in the coldest part of the year in order to form compact hearts. In warm climates sow or plant in summer. In cold climates sow or plant in mid-spring. In the fall remove any yellowing leaves and make sure the soil stays firm around the stem of the plant.
ALL ZONES

### *B. pekinsensis*
CHINESE CABBAGE, WOM BUK

Resembling lettuce more than cabbage, this fast-growing species is native to China and was only introduced to Europe in the nineteenth century. Sow seeds 4 in (about 10 cm) apart with 16 in (about 40 cm) between rows. This species is easy to grow as long as it is kept moist. Tie the leaves together after they begin to form their heart shape. Harvest the whole plant as you would a regular cabbage.
ALL ZONES

*Brassica oleracea* var. *cymosa*

*Brassica oleracea* var. *capitata*

*Brassica oleracea* var. *bullata*

*Brassica oleracea* var. *gemmifera*

*Brassica pekinsensis*

*Capsicum annuum* (Chilli pepper)

*Brassica rapa*

*Brassica sinensis*

### *B. rapa*

TURNIP

The turnip was a staple food of the northern European working classes until the potato upstaged it. It is suited more to the cooler regions of the world. In order to produce a quick crop, grow turnips in fertile soil in rows approximately 15 in (about 38 cm) apart. Keep the young plants moist at all times during the growing period. Harvest the turnips when they are golfball size.

ALL ZONES

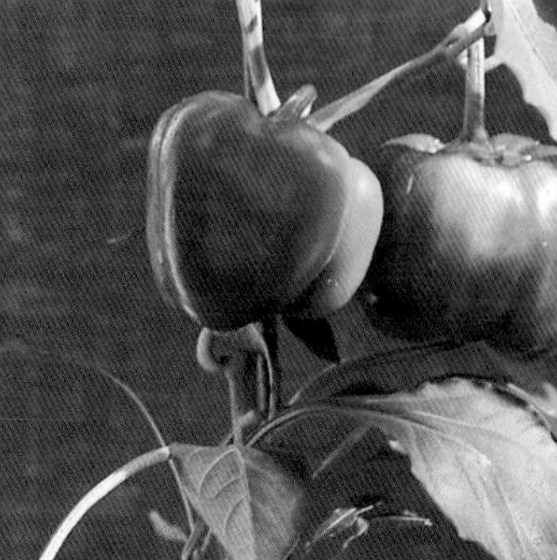
*Capsicum annuum* (Bell pepper)

### *B. sinensis*

BOK CHOY, CHINESE WHITE CABBAGE

This species looks like silver beet and is also known as Chinese mustard. The plants run to seed quickly so sow them in small groups every 10 days. Harvest the entire plant or take a few leaves as needed after 6 to 8 weeks.

ALL ZONES

## *CAPSICUM*

Closely related to the tomato, and like it native to Central America and a lover of hot, humid summers. The genus contains both ornamental species, grown for their brightly colored fruit—they are far too hot to eat—and edible types, which divide into the sweet or bell peppers. They can be cooked as a vegetable and eaten raw in salads. The chilli peppers are used fresh or dry to add a sharp flavor to cooking.

GROSSUM GROUP

### *C. annuum*

SWEET BELL PEPPER, CAPSICUM

Extremely high in vitamin C and available in lots of different hybrids. Sow the seeds in containers in a compost-rich soil and then leave in a greenhouse for 8 weeks until late spring. This plant is quite tender to frost and, once planted outside, seedlings may need to be covered with a cold frame to keep warm. Keep plants well watered. Bell peppers contain more vitamin C and vitamin A if they are left to mature until they turn a deep red color, but they are good eating when green. Red spider mites are common pests.

ALL ZONES

LONGUM GROUP

### *C. annuum*

CHILLI PEPPER, CAPSICUM

A much smaller fruit than the sweet bell pepper and a more profuse grower, this plant needs the same conditions as the green bell pepper and can be sun dried and stored in jars. Wash your hands after handling, as the "hot" substance capsicain is present in all parts of the plant.

ALL ZONES

## CICHORIUM

This genus of perennials from the Mediterranean and the Middle East is distantly related to the lettuce. The two species in gardens, however, have little in common except their family relation—they are grown and used in the kitchen quite differently.

### *C. endivia*

ENDIVE, CURLY ENDIVE

This is a relative of chicory, grown for its leaves. As with most salad vegetables, it needs a humus-rich soil which is kept moist so that it won't run to seed. Sow the seeds 12–14 in (about 30–35 cm) apart in a shaded position in late summer. Use liquid fertilizer every now and then as the plants are growing. The leaves are usually eaten green as a bitter salad; they rather resemble lettuce but are more sharply flavored.

ALL ZONES

### *C. intybus*

CHICORY

The plants are usually grown from spring-sown seed, allowed to grow through the summer and then lifted a few at a time during winter to be replanted in boxes of moist earth in a dark warm place. The resulting shoots (chicons) will be almost pure white and sweet in flavor; they are ready to harvest when they are 10 in (about 25 cm) long, about 3 or 4 weeks from transplanting. The whole procedure succeeds best in a cool climate; in warm winter areas chicory is a gourmet luxury. Chicory root is used to make caffeine-free coffee and can also be eaten raw or grated. It is a common weed along highways with its bright blue flowers.

ALL ZONES

## COLOCASIA
### *esculenta*

TARO

Widely grown throughout the tropical regions for the edible tubers, it has large, heart-shaped, mid- to dark green leaves often with prominent veins. It likes a well-drained acid soil and will flourish in tropical, hot, wet conditions; in cold areas in can be grown in a greenhouse. Keep the soil around the base of the plant firm to support the slender stem. Propagate from young suckers or sections of tuber. Harvest 8 months after planting.

ALL ZONES

## CUCUMIS
### *sativus* cultivars

APPLE CUCUMBER, ENGLISH CUCUMBER

The cucumber is a native of India. In cold areas sow seeds in containers and then transfer the seedlings to a greenhouse or cold frame. In warm areas sow into high-compost soil in the garden in late spring and cover with a light layer of soil. Ensure seedlings are free of weeds and that the ground is moist and not hot as this will destroy cucumber vines. The vines have to be trained on a frame or outdoor trellis in warm areas, to keep the fruit away from the soil. Harvest in summer, removing the small cucumbers to encourage further production. Apple cucumber cultivars are compact and can be grown hydroponically, however they are quite vulnerable to mildew. English cucumbers are more resistant to mildew; pick them when they are a deep green color. Both vining and compact (bush) cultivars are available.

ALL ZONES

*Cucumis sativus* cultivar

*Colocasia esculenta*

*Cichorium intybus*

*Cichorium endivia*

*Cynara scolymus*

Summer squash

Pumpkin

Zucchini

## CUCURBITA

This is an ancient vegetable genus that dates back to 7000 BC in Central America and 1000 BC in North America. So hybridized are the species that applying Latin names can be quite arbitrary. There are squashes, pumpkins, marrow, zucchini, trombones, butternuts and many others. Most species of this genus are easy to raise and have the same need of a warm, rich soil. In warm areas sow from early spring to late summer. In cold areas sow indoors in early summer. To prepare the garden for seedlings dig holes 12 in (about 30 cm) square, 36 in (about 90 cm) apart for bush varieties and $3^1/_2$ ft (about 1.3 m) apart for the trailing varieties of pumpkin. Fill with a good fertilizer mix. Plant out seedlings in spring, watering well beforehand. Watch for slugs and keep well irrigated as they are water hungry. Harvest in fall. The genus has been grown and interbred in gardens for so long that its botany is rather confused; most types are usually given as forms of *C. pepo*, but some authorities loudly disagree. The issue has been sidestepped by simply listing them under the common names used in gardens. However, the common name may also vary.

### Zucchini, courgette, vegetable marrow

Marrow used to be eaten when fully ripe and about the size of a large cucumber; but in recent years the fashion has been to eat them when very small when they are called zucchini or courgettes. There are varieties selected to be at their best when immature (i.e. as zucchini) and others that are best when mature; but you can in fact eat all of them at either stage. They need fertile soil, sun and lots of moisture. Plant seedlings 20 in (about 50 cm) apart and feed with liquid manure as the first fruit forms.

ALL ZONES

### Pumpkin

Food for pigs in much of Europe but a delicious vegetable for the table elsewhere. The pumpkin is a sprawling vine which ripens its fruit in fall. They will keep all winter if left until cold withers the vine before harvesting, but they can be taken earlier as soon as they are ripe. There are many varieties ranging greatly in size and weight. They like rich soil, warmth and water.

ALL ZONES

### Summer squash

This is a trailing vine that likes rich, well-drained soil in full sun. Grown during the warm weather, summer squash are eaten while young.

ALL ZONES

### Vegetable spaghetti

This delightful marrow cultivar is easy to grow and features bright yellow fruit whose flesh looks much like spaghetti when boiled.

ALL ZONES

### Winter squash

More hardy than summer squash, this vegetable needs rich soil and plenty of sunlight. Make sure it has enough space for sunlight to filter through otherwise blossoms may drop. Winter squash are allowed to mature on the vine and eaten in winter.

ALL ZONES

## CYNARA

ARTICHOKE

The artichoke is a thistle-like plant that grows to a height of 3 ft (about 90 cm) or more. They take up a lot of space, but once planted they will flourish for a couple of years. They prefer mild winters with no frost and cool summers.

### *C. cardunculus*

CARDOON

Resembling its relative the artichoke, cardoon produces broad, fleshy, edible stems in a similar manner to celery. Cardoon is most often grown from offsets, though seed may be started indoors and planted out after all danger of frost has passed. Space plants 5 ft (about 1.5 m) apart in rows in well-drained, organic-rich soil. Harvest the stems by slicing under the crown through the roots and remove all of the bitter leaves.

ALL ZONES

### *C. scolymus*

GLOBE ARTICHOKE

Native to the Mediterranean, the globe artichoke is one of many vegetables once considered to be an aphrodisiac. It has delicate, gray-green leaves and is easy to grow in most soils and positions. Make sure it has enough space (one or two plants are enough in a small garden)

and a rich soil. Plant suckers 3 ft (about 90 cm) apart in early spring. Remove any yellowing leaves and stems in fall. Cut the plump flower buds from the plants in spring and summer before the flowers begin to open.

ALL ZONES

### *DAUCUS*
*carota*

CARROT

This famous root vegetable is native to Afghanistan and was introduced to Europe 600 years ago. Sow in deep, warm, aerated soil that is loamy, in rows 10 in (about 25 cm) apart, making sure the earth is firmly compacted around the seeds. Keep the earth moist around the seedlings and thin the rows out when they are 1 in (about 2.5 cm) high. The carrot gives a high yield even in a small garden and can be stored easily in bins or boxes between layers of sand.

ALL ZONES

### *ELEOCHARIS*
*dulcis*

CHINESE WATER CHESTNUT

Grown like rice in flooded fields, the tubers of the Chinese water chestnut are harvested and eaten fresh or cooked as a vegetable in many Asian dishes.

ALL ZONES

### *HELIANTHUS*
*tuberosus*

JERUSALEM ARTICHOKE

A relative of the sunflower, this plant has nothing whatsoever to do with Jerusalem, and is in fact a native of North America. It is grown for its pleasant-flavored tubers. This is a very enthusiastic plant which in some conditions may need controlling. It will grow in any soil as long as it is well watered and should be placed in a sunny corner. Plant divisions of the tuber 6 in (about 15 cm) deep and 12 in (about 30 cm) apart in late winter. Hoe when necessary during the year and harvest when the tops have died.

ALL ZONES

### *HIBISCUS*
*esculentus*

OKRA, GUMBO

This attractive plant with pale yellow flowers with a red heart is similar to the ornamental hibiscus. The edible part of the plant is the starchy seed pod which is used for general flavoring as well as in Indian curries and Cajun cooking. It does best in warm climates. Sow 3 or 4 seeds together in early summer in aerated, fertilized soil. Ensure there are 16 in (about 40 cm) between each clump of seeds and that rows are 28 in (about 71 cm) apart. Thin seedlings out and weed soil throughout the year. Pick the pods after the flowers have opened or when they are 4 in (about 10 cm) long.

ALL ZONES

### *IPOMOEA*
*batatas*

SWEET POTATO

This native of Central America and the Pacific islands comes in both a white-fleshed or, more recently, orange-fleshed variety. Plant cuttings in rows 3 ft (about 90 cm) apart in soil that has been fertilized and dug thoroughly. In a frost-free area sweet potato can be planted at any time, but it is not recommended for planting in cool climates. Keep the young plants clear of weeds until the vines are big enough to cover the ground. Keep the soil moist while the tubers grow. Harvesting depends on the variety of sweet potato and ranges from 16 to 40 weeks after planting.

ALL ZONES

### *LACTUCA*
*sativa*

LETTUCE

From the Latin, *lac*, meaning milk, referring to its milky white sap, this biennial originated in the Middle East and the Mediterranean. Praised through history for its healthy or sleep-inducing properties, lettuce is a salad plant with a very delicate root system. It grows up to 3 ft (about 90 cm) high. Sow lettuce seeds in spring or summer in the open ground or sow in flats for later transplanting. Ensure that the seed is right for the climate as there are many kinds of lettuce to suit different areas. The soil must be humus rich and evenly moist. Thin the seedlings gradually until they are 12 in (about 30 cm) apart. Sudden

*Hibiscus esculentus*

*Daucus carota*

*Ipomoea batatas*

*Helianthus tuberosus*

*Lactuca sativa* (mignonette type)

*Lycopersicon esculentum*

*Nasturtium officinale*

*Phaseolus vulgaris*

*Pastinaca sativa*

*Phaseolus coccineus*

*Pisum sativum*

changes in temperature can leave the lettuce open to disease. Ensure they do not flower. Water regularly over summer, avoiding excessive water on leaves. Winter growers will need little water. Watch for slugs and mold. Popular types include the common iceberg with globular heads like pale green cabbages, romaine lettuce with more open darker heads, and mignonette with ruffled pink-tinted leaves. All come in an array of cultivars.

ALL ZONES

## LYCOPERSICON *esculentum*

TOMATO

This native of South America was regarded with suspicion for centuries because of its infamous relative, the deadly nightshade. Its basic needs are sunshine, moist, well-drained soil and an area free from frost. In cold areas use a cold frame to keep the soil warm. In open ground plant seedlings in rows 3 ft (about 90 cm) apart and keep 12–24 in (about 30–60 cm) between each plant. Seedlings can be grown in pots and then gently planted out when 5 in (about 12 cm) high. It is essential that tomatoes are supported by stakes as they grow and are sheltered from strong winds. Prune secondary shoots and keep soil moist, mulching if necessary.

ALL ZONES

## NASTURTIUM *officinale*

WATERCRESS

An aquatic plant, watercress will flourish in a damp, shaded corner of the garden as well as in a pond. Plant from cuttings 4 square in (about 10 square cm) apart in early fall. Make sure the soil has been thoroughly and deeply fertilized. Water thoroughly and constantly and prune the shoots to keep growth thick. Cut back any flowers that appear.

ALL ZONES

## PACHYRHIZUS *tuberosus*

JICAMA

Native to the Amazon Basin, jicama is a frequently used root vegetable in the American Southwest where Mexican food is popular. A twining, herbaceous vine, it requires staking in the garden. Sow seed in sandy soil in a sunny, dry site, thinning to 12 in (about 30 cm) between plants. Remove all flowers clusters to promote a large tuber size. Harvest the tubers 8 to 10 months after seed emergence. Each plant produces only one tuber. The seeds are poisonous.

ALL ZONES

## PASTINACA *sativa*

syn. *Peucadeneum officinale*, *P. sativum*

PARSNIP

A hardy root vegetable that is related to the carrot, parsnip is nutritious and sweet and able to be grown year round in warm areas and from mid-spring in cold areas. It needs a sunny position and deep, fertile soil. Water well in dry weather and thin out the weak seedlings. Hoe or mulch to keep weeds off. Harvest when the leaves start to yellow. Watch for slugs.

ALL ZONES

## PHASEOLUS

BEANS

This genus, native to the warm-temperate to tropical regions of the Americas, contains more than 20 species of mostly twining climbers. Beans are grown for their edible pods and seeds. Tender to frost, they grow best in enriched, well-drained soil. They are also suitable for planting in tubs and flowerbeds.

### *P. coccineus*

SCARLET RUNNER BEANS

This vigorous climber can grow up to $10^1/_2$ ft (about 3.1 m) high. It needs a rich, deep, slightly acid soil in a sheltered position. Sow seeds in late spring in double rows 2 in (about 5 cm) deep and 12 in (about 30 cm) apart. Water well in dry weather. Pick the bean pods when they reach 5–7 in (about 12–17 cm) long.

ALL ZONES

### *P. limensis*

LIMA BEANS

Lima beans come in both climbing and bush varieties. They require a well-drained loam soil and full sun location and a long growing season. Sow seed 2–3 in (about 5–7.5 cm) apart and $1–1^1/_2$ in (about 2.5–3 cm) deep after the danger of spring frost has passed. Water frequently in dry weather and apply nitrogen fertilizers sparingly for best fruit production. Watch for bean beetles. Harvest the beans when they are around 3–4 in (about 7.5–10 cm) long.

ALL ZONES

### *P. vulgaris*

FRENCH BEANS

The annual French beans, known as kidney beans, string beans or haricot beans, come in dwarf or climbing varieties that need staking. They prefer a warm, rich soil in a sunny, sheltered spot. Mulch with straw to keep off weeds and to keep the soil moist. Harvest 10 to 12 weeks after sowing, picking every 2 to 3 days.

ALL ZONES

## PISUM

PEA

There is an enormous range of peas, from the bush type which is good for humid climates, tall climbing plants which need trellising to the newer snap pea that can be eaten when immature or fully developed. Peas need a sunny, well-drained, rich, previously manured soil bed that contains some lime and dolomite for a good yield.

ALL ZONES

### *P. sativum*

PEA, BUSH AND CLIMBING VARIETIES

Plant seedlings 2 in (about 5 cm) apart in rows 4 in (about 10 cm) apart. When the seedlings are 3 in (about 7.5 cm) high stake them with short twigs. The tall varieties will need wire or plastic netting to support them as they grow.

ALL ZONES

### *P. sativum* var. *macrocarpum*

SNOW PEA, MANGETOUT PEA

This variety prefers a temperate climate and a moist sandy soil. Sow 2 in (about 5 cm) deep when the garden is likely to be frost free. Use a trellis for climbing varieties.

ALL ZONES

## PSALLIOTA *campestris*

syn. *Agaricus campestris*

MUSHROOM

This common fungus is happy to grow indoors or outdoors, under houses or in sheds, as long as it is dark, dry and the temperature is constant. Plant mushroom spawn in lumps 1 in (about 2.5 cm) deep and 10 in (about 25 cm) apart. Keep moist and humid at this stage. After 2 weeks cover the compost with a layer of soil (this is called casing) which must be pre-sterilized to avoid the lethal fungus diseases that prey on mushrooms. Do not firm it down: keep it moist but not soaking. Mushrooms will appear 3 weeks after casing. Pick them by twisting out, not pulling.

ALL ZONES

## RAPHANUS *sativus*

RADISH

The well-traveled radish has a winter variety and a summer variety. The summer radish is easily and quickly grown in a rich, moist soil out of full sun. Sow directly into rows 12 in (about 30 cm) apart and thin out seedlings so that the roots aren't competing. In hot weather keep well watered. Harvest 4 weeks after sowing in warm areas. In cooler areas wait for a further 3 weeks.

ALL ZONES

## RHEUM *rhabarbarum*

RHUBARB

Grow rhubarb from roots in a fertile, phosphorous-rich soil. Choose a cool position and plant the roots firmly with 3 ft (about 90 cm) between each row and each plant. Leave it to get established in the first year and start harvesting in the second and third years, making sure not to pull off too many sticks. The leaves are poisonous.

ALL ZONES

## RUMEX *scutatus*

SORREL

This is a low-growing perennial with pale green, oval-shaped leaves and yellow-red flowers. Sorrel's tart flavor is suitable for sauces, salads or in soups. Sow in spring or plant from divisions, leaving 12 in (about 30 cm) between each plant. Remove flowers to encourage new growth. Sorrel contains oxalic acid, which is toxic in large amounts.

ALL ZONES

## SOLANUM

*Solanum* includes the eggplant (aubergine) and the potato and used to include the tomato too, though the latter is now usually given a genus of its own: *Lycopersicon*. There are several ornamental species and many tropical weeds, but they should be approached with caution as it is the exception rather than the rule for them to be edible.

### *S. melongena*

EGGPLANT

This tropical vegetable native to Asia has large, purple fruit. It is a relative of the potato and tomato, and needs warm conditions and low level humidity. Cold frames should be used in cold areas to protect young plants. Plant seedlings in spring in well-drained soil that is free from frost. The rows should be 3 ft (about 90 cm) apart with 24 in (about 60 cm) between each seedling. Feed young plants with liquid fertilizer.

ALL ZONES

### *S. tuberosum*

POTATO

Native to South America and one of the most widely eaten vegetables, the potato was preceded to the Western world by the sweet potato. Potatoes can be scatter grown. Prepare the soil with well-rotted manure or compost. Plant tubers when the soil is frost free, usually late summer in cool areas or late winter in hot ones. If planting in rows keep them 12 in (about 30 cm) apart and cover with 3 in (about 7.5 cm) of soil. For best results plant in sloped mounds for good drainage. Protect shoots from frost with straw or soil. Do not expose potatoes to the light as they will turn green and toxic. (They can be restored by putting them in the dark for a couple of weeks.) Harvest in dry conditions when foliage turns yellow.

ALL ZONES

*Solanum melongena*

*Rheum rhabarbarum*

*Pisum sativum* var. *macrocarpum*

*Solanum tuberosum*

*Rumex scutatus*

*Psalliota campestris*

*Raphanus sativus*

*Zea mays*

*Valerianella locusta*

*Spinacia oleracea*

*Taraxacum officinale*

*Tetragonia tetragonioides*

*Vicia faba*

*Tragopogon porrifolius*

## SPINACIA
*oleracea*

SPINACH

Native to the Middle East and partial to cool climates, spinach can be a challenge to grow well. It prefers well-drained soil and a cool position in the garden, so find a spot in part shade and dig in generous amounts of manure. Sow in fall or in spring in cool climates, spacing plants 4 in (about 10 cm) apart. Keep the soil free of weeds and well watered so that the plant will not run to seed. Harvest the first leaves 8 weeks after sowing and then as needed.

ALL ZONES

## TARAXACUM
*officinale*

DANDELION

Regarded highly in Europe where it is cultivated or grows wild, these plants feature toothed leaves, large yellow flowers and round seed heads. The roots, flowers and leaves are all edible. Grow scattered in the lawn or any corner of the garden. For a good, juicy plant ensure the soil is rich and moist. Sow in early summer 12 in (about 30 cm) apart. Cut off the flowers when plants have matured and harvest the roots in fall.

ALL ZONES

## TETRAGONIA
*tetragonioides*

syn. *T. expansa*

NEW ZEALAND SPINACH

Sir Joseph Banks brought this plant back to England from New Zealand, but it became more popular in the US and Europe. Unlike true spinach, it prefers warm summers and a humus-rich soil. Soften the seeds overnight and sow them in groups of 3 in spring, making sure to leave 3 ft (about 90 cm) between each group. Thin the weaker seedlings out and keep weeds away from the remaining young plants. Water regularly and harvest the leaves as they are needed.

ALL ZONES

## TRAGOPOGON
*porrifolius*

SALSIFY

Also known as the vegetable oyster, this plant belongs to the daisy family and is valued for its edible, white tap roots. It prefers a light soil free from stones. It grows best in temperate climates. Sow the large seeds in lots of 3 in spring. Keep 8 in (about 20 cm) between each group and 12 in (about 30 cm) between each row. Mulch with compost to keep weeds down and water to maintain moisture. Harvest the root from fall onwards. It can be baked, roasted, boiled or made into soup. It is fairly pest and disease free.

ALL ZONES

## VALERIANELLA
*locusta*

CORN SALAD, LAMB'S LETTUCE

Rampant in corn fields in cool to cold climates and a hardy grower, this is a good substitute for lettuce in winter. Sow the seeds in late summer and early fall in a sunny spot in the garden. Place seeds 10 in (about 25 cm) apart. Make sure the soil is lightly raked and forked. Ideally it should be situated where another crop was previously grown. Keep the soil moist and harvest the leaves as they are needed. Watch for slugs. There are two types, not always labeled distinctly by seedsmen: one forms loose hearts like a small lettuce, the other just makes clumps of loose leaves.

ALL ZONES

## VICIA
*faba*

FAVA BEAN, BROAD BEAN

A good source of protein, the fava bean is native to the Mediterranean and Far East. It prefers a temperate climate and a sunny position in rich, well-drained soil, preferably where no beans were previously grown. Ensure good bean production by digging in organic fertilizer some weeks before sowing. Sow seeds in mid-fall in double rows 8 in (about 20 cm) apart and leave 4 in (about 10 cm) between each plant. In cold areas sowing can be left until early spring. Shelter seedlings from the wind with stakes. Make sure that the soil is not too wet as this may encourage root rot. Beans are ready to be picked 2 or 3 months after planting. Do not wait until the pods are too large or they will be tough and unappetizing. Fava beans are vulnerable to aphids.

ALL ZONES

## ZEA
*mays*

CORN, MAIZE

Originating in ancient Mexico, corn is a most popular vegetable. Although it has sometimes been seen more as fodder than as human fare, every part of the corn plant can be put to use. Corn needs an open, spacious position and is a dramatic addition to the home garden. It likes a nitrogen- and lime-rich soil and needs hot weather to grow well. Sow in early summer in short rows 24 in (about 60 cm) apart. Weed gently and water thoroughly in really dry weather. Tie the stems to stakes as they grow taller and be sure to keep the soil firm around the plant base. Harvest when the corn kernels are yellow by twisting the cobs firmly from the stem.

ALL ZONES

# HERBS

## ALLIUM

See genus entry under Vegetables, page 336.

### *A. sativum*

GARLIC

There are two main types of garlic. The mauve-flowered variety known as 'Giant Russian' (*A. giganteum*) or 'Jumbo' is very much larger and milder than the more potent, small or common garlic (*A. sativum*), which has dainty white flowers. Individual cloves are planted 2 in (about 5 cm) deep in fall in warmer areas or in spring where there is a risk of frost. Good drainage, a rich, organic soil and a sunny position are its requirements. Harvest when the leaves have turned yellow and fallen over. Handle gently to avoid bruising and allow to dry off and harden thoroughly before storage. For at least 5000 years garlic has been used for culinary, medicinal and strength-giving purposes as well as a plague preventative and charm against vampires and witchcraft.

ZONES 3–11

### *A. schoenoprasum*

CHIVES

Chives are grown for their narrow, cylindrical leaves which are used for flavoring and garnishing savory dishes. It is a perennial plant which grows up to 10 in (about 25 cm) high in small, neat clumps. It bears numerous balls of mauve flowers in late spring and summer that are edible and can be added to salads. Chives do best in a fertile, well-drained soil in full sun or part shade and should be kept well watered. They are easily grown by seed or division of small bulbs. Bulbs should be spaced around 4 in (about 10 cm) apart because they will quickly multiply and develop into clumps. Lift and divide the clumps every 2 or 3 years to invigorate the tufts. Chives make an attractive edging for the herb garden and can be grown in window boxes, troughs and flower pots.

ZONES 3–11

## ALOYSIA
*triphylla*

**syn. *Lippia citriodora***

LEMON VERBENA

This wonderfully fragrant perennial shrub from South America is valued for its delicious, lemon-scented leaves. It grows up to 9 ft (about 2.7 m) and is partly deciduous in winter. Very small, white or lilac flowers are borne at the ends of the stems in late summer and fall. It is best positioned in full sun in a warm, sheltered position and prefers a well-drained, fertile soil and regular watering in summer. Propagate from soft tip cuttings in spring or semi-hardwood cuttings in summer. Lemon verbena is commercially cultivated for its fragrant oil used in the cosmetics industry. The leaves are also used to flavor tea.

ALL ZONES

## ANDROPOGON
*nardus*

**syn. *Cymbopogon citratus***

LEMON GRASS

This aromatic, grass-like plant has very long, gray-green leaves reaching to 6 ft (about 1.8 m). From the tropics, it does best in warm areas where it will multiply readily and quickly form large clumps. A rich soil, good drainage, full sun and plenty of water are its requirements. Propagate by division. The fleshy white part at the base of the plant is used in Southeast Asian cooking and is best when fresh. The leaves are used fresh or dried to make a herbal tea.

ZONES 10–11

## ANETHUM
*graveolens*

DILL

This deliciously aromatic annual grows to around $4^1/_2$ ft (about 1.3 m) high with pretty, feathery, thread-like leaves. Yellow flowers are borne on umbels in summer followed by the pungent dill seeds. Dill requires a humus-rich, well-drained soil and a sunny position. The seed is best sown in spring where it is to grow, as seedlings are difficult to transplant. Both the leaves and seeds are used as flavorings.

ALL ZONES

## ANGELICA
*archangelica*

ANGELICA

A fast-growing, robust biennial, angelica grows to 6 ft (about 1.8 m) high and will live longer if emerging flowerheads are removed before the seed develops. It has handsome, deeply divided, bright green leaves and umbels of small, green or white flowers in late summer. Soil should preferably be rich, moist and well drained. Propagate from seed in late summer. The roots, leaves, stalks and seeds of angelica are all used in cooking and liqueurs such as chartreuse, Benedictine and vermouth.

ZONES 4–11

## ANTHRISCUS
*cerefolium*

CHERVIL

Resembling parsley, chervil grows to 12 in (about 30 cm) and is grown as a cool-season annual for early spring or late summer planting. Direct seed in well-drained soil in full sun or partial shade, thinning seedlings to 6 in (about 15 cm) apart. The light green, finely textured leaves and stems are harvested 2–3 in (about 5–7.5 cm) above the crown for use in French cooking for its delicate licorice flavor. Easily grown in boxes in sunny windows.

ALL ZONES

*Allium schoenoprasum*

*Anethum graveolens*

*Aloysia triphylla*

*Angelica archangelica*

*Andropogon nardus*

*Allium sativum*

## ARTEMISIA
*dracunculus*

TARRAGON

Essential in French cuisine, tarragon is grown for its narrow, aromatic leaves which have a delicate, peppery aniseed flavor. It grows up to 3 ft (about 90 cm) high in the warmer months then dies back to a perennial rootstock over winter. It needs full sun and a fertile, well-drained soil. As it produces no seed, propagate by division in early spring. The tarragon seed sometimes offered is the flavorless *A. dracunculordes,* known as Russian tarragon. Tarragon loses most of its flavor during drying. Before the plant dies down for a winter's rest, gather the leaves and make tarragon vinegar and butter.

ZONES 3–11

*Coriandrum sativum*

*Artemisia dracunculus*

## BORAGO
*officinalis*

BORAGE

This decorative, annual herb is grown for its cucumber-flavored leaves and pretty, lilac, star-shaped flowers. It grows to around 30 in (about 76 cm) high and bears clusters of nodding flowers in spring and summer. It requires full sun to part shade, good drainage and a light, porous soil. Propagate from seed in spring. Protect from snails. The fresh young leaves are used raw in salads and cool drinks or cooked with vegetables. The edible, blue flowers have been used to decorate salads from the early seventeenth century. Flowers may also be crystallized for cake decoration. It used to be said that eating borage flowers gave you courage.

ALL ZONES

## BRASSICA
*juncea*

BROWN MUSTARD

This Eurasian native is cultivated for its pungent seeds used to flavor many dishes. An annual that grows to 3 ft (about 90 cm), it requires full sun and ordinary, well-drained soil. Bright yellow flowers mature to $1^1/_2$ in (about 3 cm) long pods which house the smooth brown seeds. Occasionally the young leaves are used in salads.

ALL ZONES

*Carum carvi*

## CAPPARIS
*spinosa*

CAPERS

Capers are the unopened flower buds of a small shrub native to the Mediterranean. Most successfully grown as a container plant overwintered in cold climates, it can be grown as a perennial in frost-free zones. Requiring full sun and well-drained soil, capers are best started as stem cuttings from new growth. Harvest the flower buds before they show any color. Often pickled in wine vinegar, capers are used as garnish and in sauces and butters.

ALL ZONES

## CARUM
*carvi*

CARAWAY

Since ancient Egyptian times, caraway has been cultivated for its condiment and medicinal properties. It is an attractive biennial plant growing to 24 in (about 60 cm) high with finely cut, lacy leaves rather like its relative, the parsley. In its second year small, white flowers are produced in umbels, followed in late summer by a crop of seeds. It will grow well in a light, moist, but well-drained soil in full sun. Propagate from seed in early fall in mild winter areas or in spring. The small black seeds are used to flavor cakes, breads, sauces and pickles. Their flavor is best when dried. Caraway has also been used as an ingredient of love potions.

ALL ZONES

## CHAMAEMELUM
*nobile*

CHAMOMILE

This is a delightfully aromatic, mat-forming perennial which grows to 12 in (about 30 cm) tall and has fine, bright green leaves and masses of small, white daisies in spring, summer and fall. Non-flowering varieties are used in chamomile lawns. It grows best in full sun in a moist, but well-drained fertile soil. It creeps along the ground by runners which take root as they spread. Propagate by division or from seed in spring. Dried chamomile flowers can be used in pot pourri, sleep pillows, hair rinses and facials. Renowned as a herbal tea, chamomile has been credited with the power to treat dyspepsia, flatulent colic, fever, stomach cramps, wounds, swelling and also calluses.

ZONES 4–11

## CORIANDRUM
*sativum*

CORIANDER

This herb is grown mainly for its seed and aromatic leaves, although in Thai cuisine the whole of the coriander plant, including the roots, is used. Coriander is a fast-growing annual reaching to 30 in (about 76 cm) high with parsley-like leaves and umbels of tiny, white flowers in summer. The flowers are followed by small, round, aromatic seeds. It requires a light, well-drained soil and full sun. Propagate from seed in early spring. The dried seeds are used in curry powders, chutneys, confectionery, cakes and sauces.

ALL ZONES

## CUMINUM
*cyminum*

CUMIN

Cumin is grown commercially in India, China, Japan and the Middle East for its powerfully flavored seeds. It is a small annual which grows to 12 in (about 30 cm) high with finely divided leaves and small, white flowers in summer, followed by aromatic seeds. It grows best in warm climates. Grow in a light, well-drained soil in a sunny position. Propagate from seed sown in spring in a warm situation. The dried seed is an important ingredient in curry powders. Both the Dutch and Germans flavor cheese with it, and it is used in many Mexican and Middle Eastern dishes.

ALL ZONES

*Chamaemelum nobile*

*Borago officinalis*

*Capparis spinosa*

## *CURCUMA*
*domestica*
syn. *C. longa*
TURMERIC

A tropical member of the ginger family, turmeric is grown for its bright orange, underground stems or rhizomes. This perennial herb can grow to 3 ft (about 90 cm) in hot areas. It forms clumps of lance-shaped leaves and dense clusters of pale yellow flowers in summer. It prefers the warmth of tropical regions but can be successfully grown in warm-temperate areas. In cooler areas, grow in a glasshouse. It requires a rich, moist, well-drained soil and lots of sun. Propagate by division. Turmeric has been used in the East since antiquity. The dried root provides color and pungent fragrance to chutneys, pickles and curry powders. It is used as a substitute for saffron *(Crocus sativas)*, the world's most expensive spice and one very rarely grown in home gardens.
ZONES 6–11

## *ELETTARIA*
*cardamomum*
CARDAMOM

An important and pungent oriental spice, cardamom seeds come from a perennial shrub which originated in southern India. It grows to 9 ft (about 2.7 m) tall and has large, dark green, lance-shaped leaves. The flowering stems spread horizontally near the ground and bear small, yellow flowers during spring. These are followed by gray-green, oblong pods which contain dark reddish brown seeds. Cardamom is for tropical and warm regions only where it requires a rich, moist soil and a shaded position. In cooler areas, grow in a glasshouse. The seed pods are gathered before they ripen and are then dried before storage. Propagate by division. Cardamom is used in curry powders, pastries, baked apples and fruit salads.
ZONES 10–11

## *FOENICULUM*
*vulgare*
FENNEL

Common fennel is a tall, graceful perennial which grows to 6 ft (about 1.8 m) with thick, glossy stems, masses of feathery foliage and flat clusters of yellow flowers on tall, erect stems during summer. The flowers are followed by aromatic, brown seeds. Bronze fennel is similar but has rich bronzy green leaves and grows to around $4^1/_2$ ft (about 1.3 m) high. In cool climates it will die back to the roots over winter and is sometimes grown as an annual. It prefers full sun to part shade, a rich, alkaline, well-drained soil and regular watering during dry periods. Propagate from seed in mid- to late spring. Both the leaves and seeds have a pleasant aniseed flavor and are used for flavoring fish and other savory dishes. The seeds are also used in breads and biscuits.
ZONES 4–11

*Foeniculum vulgare* var. *dulce*

*Hyssopus officinalis*

### *F. vulgare* var. *dulce*
FLORENCE FENNEL, FINOCCHIO

Florence fennel is distinct from common fennel in having a pronounced swelling at the base of the leaves where the stems overlap. It is an annual and needs to be grown from seed each year. The crisp, white bulb, with the texture of celery, is cooked as a vegetable or grated raw for salads.
ZONES 4–11

## *GLYCYRRHIZA*
*glabra*
LICORICE

This perennial, native to southern Europe, is grown commercially for the juice of its sweet roots, used in the production of licorice. The plant has large, mid-green leaves and bears pea-like, bluish purple and white flowers on short upright spikes in late summer. It grows to a height and spread of 3 ft (about 90 cm). It requires a sunny position and a deep, rich, moist but well-drained soil.
ZONES 7–11

*Foeniculum vulgare*

## *HYSSOPUS*
*officinalis*
HYSSOP

This bushy perennial grows to 24 in (about 60 cm) and has narrow, pointed, dark green leaves. Spikes of rich blue flowers, attractive to bees and butterflies, are borne in late summer. Hyssop is evergreen in mild climates; in cool areas it dies down for the winter. It prefers a light, well-drained, alkaline soil and full sun. Propagate from seed, cuttings or by division in spring. The slightly bitter leaves are used in small quantities with fatty meats and fish.
ZONES 3–11

*Elettaria cardamomum*

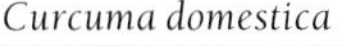
*Curcuma domestica*

*Mentha* × *piperita*

*Mentha* 'Citrata'

*Levisticum officinale*

*Lavandula angustifolia*

*Melissa officinalis*

## *JUNIPERUS*
### *communis*

JUNIPER

An evergreen, bushy shrub or small tree, juniper grows to 9 ft (about 2.7 m). There are a number of ornamental forms in varying shapes, sizes and foliage color. It has sharply pointed, needle-like leaves, small, yellow flowers and bears fleshy, green berries that take up to 3 years to ripen to black. To ensure berry production grow both male and female plants. Juniper requires excellent drainage and a sunny position. In warm climates provide a cool, moist root run. Propagate from semi-hardwood cuttings in late summer or early fall. The berries have a resinous flavor and are used to flavor gin. A few berries make an excellent addition to stews and stuffings for poultry.

ZONES 4–11

## *LAURUS*
### *nobilis*

BAY

This medium-sized, evergreen tree which reaches 21 ft (about 6.5 m) is slow growing and can be kept in a pot for a number of years. It withstands clipping and makes an excellent topiary subject. It can be grown in a tub and brought indoors where winters are frosty. In warm areas grow in a humus-rich, well-drained, sunny position. Protect from both dry winds and scorching sun in hot areas. Propagate from cuttings. Watch for scale insects. Bay leaves are best used fresh in cooking to flavor marinades, soups, sauces, stews and meat dishes. Dried leaves

*Laurus nobilis*

may be used in cooking, though they lose flavor quickly; they add scent to pot pourri.

ZONES 8–11

## *LAVANDULA*
### *angustifolia*

syn. *L. officinalis*

LAVENDER

This beautiful, small, rounded shrub, native to southern Europe, is valued for its perfumed, lavender flowers and aromatic gray-green foliage. It thrives in cool-temperate areas in a light, rather alkaline, well-drained soil. Grow in an open, sunny position to avoid fungal disease. Propagate from cuttings in fall or spring. The best quality essential oil is extracted from this plant, but many other species and varieties of lavender can be grown for their fragrant flowers. Dried lavender flowers are used in pot pourri mixtures, lavender bags and moth repellent sachets. The herb can be used sparingly in cooking, but it is an acquired taste.

ZONES 5–11

*Juniperus communis*

## *LEVISTICUM*
### *officinale*

LOVAGE

From southern Europe, this robust, coarse-growing perennial reaches 6 ft (about 1.8 m) tall and looks and tastes like a large celery. It has deeply lobed, dark green leaves, umbels of small, yellow flowers in summer and brown seeds which ripen in late summer or early fall. It prefers a fairly cool climate and does best in full sun or part shade in a rich, moist soil. Propagate by root division in spring or from seed in late summer. The stems are cooked and eaten and tender young leaves can be added to salads and savory dishes. *Levisticum americanum* and *Ligusticum scoticum* are also called lovage.

ZONES 3–11

## *MELISSA*
### *officinalis*

LEMON BALM

A native of southern Europe, this hardy perennial, 24 in (about 60 cm) high, is grown for its fresh, lemony scented and flavored leaves. Small, white flowers that appear in late summer attract pollinating bees into the garden. Lemon balm will thrive in a rich, moist soil in full sun or part shade. It spreads rapidly. It will die down in winter but shoot again in spring. Propagate from cuttings or by root division. The lemon-scented leaves are valued as a calming herbal tea. They will give a light, lemon flavor to fruit salads, jellies, iced tea and summer drinks, and can be used as an emergency substitute for lemon in cooking.

ZONES 5–11

## *MENTHA*

MINT

This is a large genus of herbs, some evergreen and some deciduous, from just about all the continents. They vary in size from tiny creeping ground covers to bushy plants around 16 in (about 40 cm) high, and in flavor from refreshing to so strong they must be used with circumspection. As a rule they like sunshine and rich soil and need lots of moisture (poor drainage matters not at all) and are invasive growers, spreading rapidly by runners. To keep them from taking over, try growing them in large pots, watering them regularly and then repotting annually.

### *M.* 'Citrata'

EAU DE COLOGNE MINT

Of garden origin and thought to be a variety of peppermint, this mint is too strong and bitter to use in cooking. It is grown for the delicious fragrance of its dark green leaves; perhaps the sweetest and most flower like of any scented-leafed plant. It has purplish stems and mauve flowers in early summer. Like all the tribe it is a rampant spreader by underground runners.

ZONES 5–11

### *M.* × *piperita*

PEPPERMINT

This spreading perennial, grown for its aromatic foliage and culinary uses, grows to a height and spread of 24 in (about 60 cm). Spreading by means of underground stems, it

forms a carpet of oval, toothed, mid-green and reddish green leaves. Purple flowers appear in spring. Plant this herb in sun or shade in moist, well-drained soil. Propagate by division in spring or fall.
ZONES 5–11

### *M. spicata*

SPEARMINT

This fast-growing perennial, reaching 24 in (about 60 cm), is the most popular mint used in cooking. It has crinkly, dark green leaves and as it has a tendency to put down roots all over the garden is often best grown in a separate bed or container. It thrives in a sunny or partially shaded position in a moist, but well-drained soil. Plants should be cut back regularly to encourage fresh growth. Propagate by root division. This is the mint used in mint sauce and to flavor new potatoes, green peas and ice-creams. Fresh sprigs are used as a garnish in fruit drinks or desserts.
ZONES 5–11

## *MONARDA*
### *didyma*

BERGAMOT, BEE BALM

Native to North America, this herb was used by the American Indians and early colonists as a tea. With its spidery flowers in white, pink or red borne in late summer, bergamot is one of the showiest of the culinary herbs. The showiest variety is 'Cambridge Scarlet'. It is a hardy perennial growing to 3 ft (about 90 cm) tall with dark green, slightly toothed leaves that when crushed or brushed against emit an exotic, citrus-like scent. It prefers part shade and a rich, moist soil with a cool root run in hot climates. Cut plants back periodically to keep compact. Propagate by division in spring. The young leaves may be used in salads, but mainly it is used as a soothing tea. Add a few leaves to China or Indian tea for an Earl Grey flavor.
ZONES 4–11

## *NEPETA*
### *cataria*

CATNIP, CATMINT

A native of Europe, catnip is a hardy perennial with branching, upright stems growing up to 3 ft (about 90 cm). It has aromatic, gray-green leaves and whorls of white flowers from late spring through to fall. Provide a light, rich soil in sun or part shade and moderate water for best results. Cut back each year to prevent the plant from becoming straggly. Propagate by root division or from seed in spring. Cats are attracted to this plant and will lie in it or play in it and sometimes dig it up. Fortunately, their interest is only in the spring growth; once the plants start to flower they lose interest. Its tea is said to be relaxing.
ZONES 3–11

## *OCIMUM*
### *basilicum*

BASIL

A favorite with cooks, basil is one of the most widely used herbs in Mediterranean cooking. It is a tender, annual plant growing to 12 in (about 30 cm) with light green, oval leaves that have a delicious, warm, spicy fragrance. Small white flowers are carried in whorls towards the ends of the stems in late summer. Full sun and a moderately rich, moist, but well-drained soil are its requirements. Grow in a warm, protected position. There are a number of varieties of basil including a compact small-leaf type; a crinkled, lettuce leaf variety and the beautiful 'Dark Opal' with rich purple stems and leaves. There are perennial varieties also, but their flavor is inferior. Regularly pinch back all basil plants to encourage bushy growth and to prevent them going to seed quickly. Propagate from seed sown when there is no frost. Watch for chewing insects or snails.
ALL ZONES

## *ORIGANUM*

Native to the Mediterranean region and parts of Europe and India, these perennials are often grown as annuals in cooler climates. They like sun and rich, well-drained soil. Trim regularly and propagate from seed in spring or by root division.

### *O. hortensis*

syn. *Majorana hortensis*
SWEET MARJORAM

A highly aromatic plant up to 24 in (about 60 cm) high, marjoram is grown for its sweet and spicy, small, gray-green leaves. The flowers consist of tiny, white, knot-like clusters from which the plant gets another common name, knotted marjoram. Leaves are used fresh or dried for savory foods and are said to aid digestion.
ALL ZONES

### *O. vulgare*

OREGANO, WILD MARJORAM

A close relative of marjoram, oregano has a sharper, more pungent flavor. It has a sprawling habit and grows to 24 in (about 60 cm) high with dark green, oval leaves and small, white or pink flowers in summer. The leaves, fresh or dried, are used in many Mediterranean-inspired dishes. In Italy oregano is used in pizza toppings and pasta dishes.
ZONES 5–11

*Ocimum basilicum*

*Mentha spicata*

*Nepeta cataria*

*Monarda didyma*

*Origanum vulgare*

*Origanum hortensis*

Salvia officinalis

Polygonum odoratum

Salvia elegans

Rosmarinus officinalis

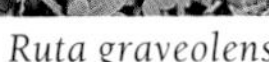

Ruta graveolens

Petroselinum crispum

## *PETROSELINUM*

*crispum*

PARSLEY

Cultivated for thousands of years for its flavor and health-giving properties, parsley is still one of the most popular herbs grown. It is a biennial plant which grows to 12 in (about 30 cm) high. The most commonly used are the curly-leaved form and the stronger, flat-leaved Italian variety. Parsley does best in full sun or light shade in warm climates. It likes a moist, well-drained position and regular feeding. For best flavor, harvest the leaves before the plant flowers. Propagate from seed. To speed up germination soak the seeds in warm water overnight before planting.

ALL ZONES

## *POLYGONUM*

*odoratum*

VIETNAMESE MINT

A native of Indochina, this fast-growing perennial, 24 in (about 60 cm) high, has long, dark green leaves with a distinct hot, spicy taste. Pink flowers in slender spikes appear in late summer and fall. Vietnamese mint prefers partial shade, a rich soil and plenty of moisture. It can die back in winter frosts but will reshoot in spring. Propagate from cuttings or by division. The leaves are used as a garnish in many Vietnamese dishes including salads and soups.

ZONES 5–11

## *ROSMARINUS*

*officinalis*

ROSEMARY

A beautiful, aromatic shrub, rosemary has been cultivated for centuries for flavoring food and for medicine. It will grow to 3 ft (about 90 cm) high, has resinous, narrow, needle-like leaves and small flowers in shades of mauve-blue, off and on all year. Rosemary can be grown outdoors in warm climates, but should be taken in for winter where temperatures fall much below freezing. In the garden it will flourish in a light, well-drained soil in a sheltered position with plenty of sun. It will withstand salt-laden air. Propagate from cuttings or by layering. Rosemary leaves can be used fresh or dried to flavor meat dishes, chicken, fish and vegetables. Dried branches can be used in wreath-making and leaves in pot pourri.

ZONES 8–11

## *RUTA*

*graveolens*

RUE

One of the bitter herbs used for warding off insects and disease, rue is also one of the most decorative herbs with its very pretty, gray-green, lacy leaves. It is a hardy perennial growing 24 in (about 60 cm) high with clusters of small, yellow-green flowers in summer. Grow in a slightly alkaline, well-drained soil in full sun. Protect from strong winds and severe frost in cold climates. Trim after flowering. Propagate by division in spring or from stem cuttings in late summer. The leaves and flowers are used in small posies. Rue has been used in the past for medicinal purposes, but can be dangerous if taken in large doses and during pregnancy.

ZONES 5–11

## *SALVIA*

This mainly northern hemisphere genus includes an enormous number of species. Almost all are aromatic and many are grown just for their brightly colored flowers (see "Annuals & Perennials"). The following are the most important kitchen species.

### *S. elegans*

**syn. *S. rutilans***

PINEAPPLE SAGE

This shrub reaches 3 ft (about 90 cm) and is grown for its light green foliage, which has a distinct pineapple scent and flavor. Its whorls of red flowers are borne in late summer and fall. It likes full sun and a moist, well-drained soil. Propagate from cuttings. Leaves are used in fruit salads, summer drinks and tea.

ZONES 9–11

### *S. officinalis*

SAGE

Sage is a decorative perennial plant which grows to 24 in (about 60 cm) high, with downy, gray-green, oval leaves and mauve-blue flowers on tall spikes during summer. There are several forms of sage, those with plum-red leaves, greenish-purple variegated leaves, tricolored leaves and golden variegated leaves. All are attractive and edible. Grow in an open, sunny, well-drained position. In hot areas plants are best in light shade. Trim frequently, but never into hard wood, to keep shapely. Propagate from cuttings. Sage is highly valued for its medicinal qualities and has been used for centuries for curing all manner of ailments and is reputed to give longevity.

ZONES 5–11

## *SATUREJA*

Native to the Mediterranean, savory was much loved by the Ancient Greeks and Romans for the refreshing flavor. Among many of its uses savory is added to dishes featuring mildly flavored meats like chicken and pork.

### *S. hortensis*

SUMMER SAVORY

This bushy annual grows 16 in (about 40 cm) high and has narrow, dark green leaves and pale lavender flowers in late summer. Grow in a humus-rich, well-drained soil in full sun and provide plenty of water. Propagate from seed in spring where it is to grow. The leaves have a sweet, spicy flavor with a hint of thyme and are traditionally used as a flavoring for bean dishes. Use also to flavor vinegar, salad dressings and butter.

ZONES 6–11

### *S. montana*

WINTER SAVORY

A low, spreading perennial which grows to 12 in (about 30 cm), winter savory has dark green, pointed leaves and tiny white flowers with pink markings in summer. Winter savory prefers a light, well-drained, alkaline soil and less moisture than summer savory. It may need winter protection in cold climates. It benefits from regular cutting back to stimulate fresh growth and prevent legginess. Propagate by division or from cuttings. It makes a good edging or border plant. The leaves, sharper and more peppery than summer savory, are used to flavor meat casseroles and roasts.

ZONES 6–11

## *SYMPHYTUM*
## *officinale*

COMFREY

This robust, clump-forming perennial grows to 3 ft (about 90 cm) with large, lance-shaped leaves and clusters of pretty, mauve, pendent flowers in late spring and summer. Grow in part shade and a humus-rich, well-drained soil. It may die down to the roots in cold areas. Propagate by root division. It is an excellent companion plant in the garden, where it keeps the surrounding soil rich and moist. Wilted leaves are used as a mulch and when added to the compost heap will help activate decomposition. In the Middle Ages, comfrey's chief claim to fame was its ability to aid in knitting fractured and broken bones. It is mildly poisonous if eaten in sufficient quantities.

ZONES 6–11

## *THYMUS*

THYME

No herb garden should be without at least one variety of thyme. There are many species and varieties, all are perennials with tiny, aromatic leaves and small flower spikes that appear at the end of the stems during summer. Thyme likes a light, well-drained soil and full sun if possible. It may need winter protection in very cold areas. Keep well trimmed for compact growth. Propagate by division or layer stems. Historically thyme has been associated with courage, strength, happiness and well-being.

### *T.* × *citriodorus*

LEMON-SCENTED THYME

This delightful, rounded shrub grows 12 in (about 30 cm) high and has tiny, oval, lemon-scented leaves and pale lilac flowers. Leaves are used fresh or dry in poultry stuffings or to add lemon flavor to fish, meat and vegetables.

ZONES 4–11

### *T. vulgaris*

COMMON THYME

This is the most popular culinary thyme, producing the strongest aromatic leaves. It grows to 12 in (about 30 cm) high. The tiny, mid-green leaves are used in vinegars, butters and to flavor a variety of meat or vegetable dishes. Thyme tea is used to aid digestion, sore throats and coughs.

ZONES 4–11

## *ZINGIBER*
## *officinale*

GINGER

Originating in southern Asia, this tender, perennial plant is grown for its spicy, tuberous roots. It can reach up to 6 ft (about 1.8 m) high in hot areas, has long, lance-shaped leaves and bears spikes of white flowers with purple streaks in summer. Ginger prefers the warmth of tropical regions but can be successfully grown outdoors in warm, frost-free, temperate areas. A humus-rich, well-drained soil and light shade are its requirements. Propagate from small pieces of root cuttings. The fresh root is peeled and finely chopped or grated and used to flavor many Asian dishes, curries and chutneys. Dried and powdered ginger is used in sweet dishes and cakes. It is often recommended as a therapeutic infusion for colds and travel sickness.

ZONES 8–11

*Satureja montana*

*Zingiber officinale*

*Thymus* x *citriodorus*

*Satureja hortensis*

*Symphytum officinale*

*Thymus vulgaris*

CHAPTER 8

# *Fruit Trees, Nut Trees & Other Fruits*

*Scholars have been arguing for centuries over the identity of the most famous fruit tree of all, the one that caused so much trouble for Adam and Eve. Tradition says it was an apple; some learned people say no, it was an apricot; still others point out that it was called the Tree of Knowledge, a species rarely met with now.*

Let us leave them to it and content ourselves with the thought that the author of *Genesis* knew what he was about when he described the chief attraction of the Garden of Eden as its fruit trees, with no mention of lawns, flowers or other frivolities.

There are few things so delightful as picking your own fruit, and if it comes from a tree you planted yourself the pleasure is all the greater. The delight won't be just at harvest time either: fruit trees tend to be comely in habit and often beautiful in flower. And few are large, so they take up little space.

## Choosing a Fruit Tree

They can be classed into two broad groups: the tropical fruits, members of several plant families, mainly evergreen, and often rather stately growers; and the temperate fruits, deciduous and almost all cousins of the rose. The citrus are a kind of link between the two, evergreen and with members that like hot climates and others that don't mind it coolish. Which to choose? Your own favorite, that goes without saying, but you need to take your climate into account. There is no joy in pining after mangoes if you suffer frost or cherries if you can't provide them with the cold winters they need. Then, there is no point in growing just any sort of variety. Just about all types of fruit have been bred and improved by gardeners for centuries, and come in a bewildering number of varieties. Some of the tropical types (citrus too) can be easily grown from seed, but seedling trees almost always turn out inferior. Insist on a top-quality named cultivar, and check that it is suited to your purpose. (Apples, for instance, come in "dessert" and "cooking" varieties, and so do mangoes, cherries and bananas.) It sometimes happens that the very choicest varieties are rather weak growers and therefore not popular with orchardists; but why grow an ordinary pear that you can buy at the greengrocer's when you could have the incomparable 'Buerre Bosc'?

The named varieties are almost always grafted, and you may be offered the same one on several different understocks. Usually this is because by choice of a more or less vigorous stock you can tailor the final size of the tree, but sometimes one stock will be better than another in different soils. If in doubt ask your supplier for advice, bearing in mind that bigger isn't necessarily better—you may prefer to have two smaller trees instead of one large one. That way you might have both a dessert and a cooking apple, or have an early-ripening variety and one that ripens later to spread your crop. (You can even buy ultra-dwarf strains of such fruit as apples and peaches, which are great if your gardening is confined to

Malus domestica *'Red Delicious', an excellent dessert apple.*

containers on an apartment balcony, unfortunately their crop is proportionately tiny too.)

With some of the temperate fruits, notably apples, pears and sweet cherries, you need two trees in any case, as they are not "self-fertile"—the flowers must receive the pollen of a different variety or there will be no fruit. Not that pollinating insects respect fences; the spouse tree could be in the garden of a co-operative neighbor. Or you might graft a branch of a compatible variety on to your main tree, being careful not to accidentally prune it off later.

Then, before you make your final choice, check with your local horticultural expert about whether your favorites are subject to pests or diseases that you are required by law to spray against. Alas, the number of enemies of fruit is legion (indeed, in different countries there are different enemies), and neglected backyard fruit trees can be a potent source of infestation not only to the neighbors' trees but to commercial orchards—which is why the law takes an interest. The horticulturist can give you all the details, but take heart—the job isn't as burdensome as all that, and there will be some fruit that you can grow that doesn't suffer unduly from problems.

*'Valencia' is the best known variety of* Citrus sinensis, *the sweet orange.*

## *Growing Fruit Trees*

Almost all fruit trees need sun and fertile soil, and are best if they don't suffer undue drought while the fruit is ripening. They benefit too from some fertilizer in spring, but there is no need to grow them in mulched beds like vegetables; they can be grown in association with flowers and shrubs, in any way that suits your garden design. Careful and regular pruning will control the size of the tree and increase its fruitfulness, but you only have to come across some ancient apple tree, untouched by the shears for years yet groaning with fruit, to realize that pruning is optional. Most warm climate fruits need little pruning in any case. A specialised form of pruning is training the tree espalier, that is flat against a wall. The idea was originally that the warmth reflected from the masonry encourages the fruit to ripen earlier. It is a lot of work, as you will need to prune each year, but worth doing if you are short on space or want to grow a variety that is on the borderline of hardiness in your climate. (Peaches and figs, for instance, are almost always grown against walls in Britain, and mangoes and loquats are trained similarly elsewhere.) Choose a tree grafted on a "dwarfing" rootstock or it will be too vigorous.

All the above applies to nut trees too; after all they are just fruit trees where we eat a different part of the fruit—the seeds rather than the fleshy covering. They aren't so popular, perhaps because we tend to regard nuts as an occasional luxury, but they are well worth growing and the crop keeps without having to be preserved. As a group, they are less subject to pests and need less care generally.

Not all fruit grows on trees. There are for instance those that grow on vines, of which the grape is the supreme example, others being the kiwifruit or Chinese gooseberry and the passionfruit, sometimes called the granadilla and a great favorite in warm climates. All are great for covering fences and pergolas, and all are handsome plants. However, selection of varieties is just as important as ever, especially with grapes; not only are varieties specially designed for wine, for eating fresh or for making raisins, they have very marked likes and dislikes about climate. All the vine fruit need regular pruning to keep them under control, but no more than any other vigorous climber does.

Then there are the bush fruits, fruit shrubs rather than fruit trees. They can be the answer if you are short on space (although most like cool climates) and they are well worth growing, as their fruit tends to be soft and easily damaged on the way to market. Grow your own, and you can have the very best. This is particularly true of strawberries, everyone's favorite—and everyone can grow them, for this is a creeping perennial to be tucked in at the front of any convenient bed or even in containers.

When is a fruit not a fruit? When it is a vegetable. The tomato is a fruit, but the plant is an annual to be grown in the vegetable patch rather than the orchard; and the fruit a savory one, for main course dishes rather than dessert. The same is true of zucchini, bell peppers, squashes, even melons. Everyone calls them vegetables, and so shall we.

*Castanea sativa*

*Carya illinoinensis*

# FRUIT TREES AND NUT TREES

## ANNONA
*squamosa*

CUSTARD APPLE, SUGAR APPLE

There are many varieties of the custard apple, a popular fruit that originated in the tropical regions of

*Ceratonia siliqua*

Africa, Asia and the Americas. Its flowers are pale green and pleasantly scented. The large fruit has a custard-like texture and is delicious when eaten fresh. This is a semi-deciduous tree growing to 15 ft (about 4.5 m). Plant in a warm, sheltered position as the fruit yield may be damaged by low temperatures and the tree itself is frost tender. Propagate by grafting.
ZONES 10–11

## ASIMINA
*triloba*

CUSTARD APPLE, PAPAW

Native from New York to Florida, west to Nebraska, this multi-stemmed small tree with a dense, rounded head will grow to 30 ft (about 9 m). Deep purple flowers are borne in the spring, followed by 2–5 in (about 5–12 cm) long edible berries, brownish black at maturity. The fruit taste similar to a banana

*Annona squamosa*

and have a custard-like texture. It requires moisture-holding organic soils for best culture. Easily propagated by seed.
ZONES 4–9

## CARICA
*papaya*

PAPAYA, PAWPAW

This is an evergreen, frost-tender tree, native to South and Central America, which grows to 24 ft (about 7 m) high and is topped with a cluster of large, deep-lobed leaves that drop away as the soft stem grows up. Plant in a position where it will receive lots of warmth and shelter in a well-drained, moist, organic soil. The large fruit, which weigh up to 4½ lb (about 2 kg), will reduce in size after 4 years of harvesting. Before picking the fruit let it ripen as long as possible on the branch. Propagate from seed and plant the seedlings in summer, watering regularly. Watch for powdery mildew, fruit rot (especially if the tree is in a warm-temperate climate and exposed position) and fruit bugs.
ZONES 10–11

## CARYA
*illinoinensis*

PECAN

A native of the United States, and from the same family as the walnut, the pecan tree's large size may make it impractical for the average garden. The nuts have a smooth, brown shell and a large kernel. Moderately hardy to frost, these trees prefer dry summers and because of their large taproot need deep, well-drained soil. The fruit will fall early if there is insufficient water or nutrition. Prune the young tree to encourage it to grow to a single, upright stem. Selected cultivars have fruit that is much larger and with thinner shells that are easier to crack. Once they are collected, nuts should be allowed to dry out for several weeks before they are stored.
ZONES 5–8

## CASTANEA
*sativa*

SPANISH CHESTNUT, SWEET CHESTNUT

This deciduous Mediterranean native is valued for its timber, shade and edible fruit which is delicious roasted. It grows slowly to 50 ft (about 15 m), with dark green foliage and an open crown. The leaves, which turn brown in fall, are egg shaped and heavily serrated, 5–8 in (about 12–20 cm) long, with a hairy underside. Creamy golden, malodorous flowers bloom in early to mid-spring. In late summer to early spring, glossy brown chestnuts develop inside spiny, spherical pods. This species enjoys warm summers and a rich, well-drained, acid soil, otherwise it can be prone to root rot. Propagate mainly from seed in fall. It is prone to chestnut blight and has a tendency to sucker. The tree is very long lived and some English specimens were reputedly planted by the Romans.
ZONES 6–10

## CERATONIA
*siliqua*

CAROB

Native to the eastern Mediterranean, this evergreen tree or shrub can

*Carica papaya*

grow to 40 ft (about 12 m) but can be pruned to a more suitable garden size. It has glossy, green leaves and long, brown, bean-like pods 10 in (about 25 cm) long. It prefers full sun but can tolerate light shade. It requires hot summers to perform well. Fertilizing is usually not necessary and the tree is remarkably resistant to summer drought. Because of its tolerance to heat and drought it does well as a low-maintenance durable hedge. The carob pods are ready to be picked in fall when they are dark brown. When eaten fresh they are sweet and chewy. Roasting and powdering them for use as a chocolate substitute can be arduous but rewarding, and the branches can be used as emergency fodder for stock in times of drought. Do not plant the tree too close to the house as many people find the odor of the flowers objectionable.

ZONES 9–11

## *CITRUS*

Native to Southeast Asia, it is thought citrus fruit trees were introduced to the Middle East and Europe in the time of the Romans. They do best in a warm, humid climate with mild winters. The attractive white flowers in spring and fruit in winter make them a valued tree. A nitrogen-rich, well-drained soil and a sunny position are their requirements. Water and fertilize well. They are prone to attack by a number of pests. Although citrus are more reliable when grown from seed than most fruit trees, they are almost always budded to ensure the perpetuation of the desired variety. Understocks vary with type; the most common is *Poncirus trifoliata,* which gives greater resistance to cold and to certain viruses.

### *C. aurantifolia*

LIME

Known as the West Indian or key lime, this is a small, slender, thorny evergreen which reaches 9 ft (about 2.7 m) high and wide. Native to Malaysia this tree can only be grown in tropical and subtropical areas as it is frost tender. In cooler areas grow in a glasshouse. It makes a perfect tub tree when put in a sheltered, sunny spot and will produce lots of fruit. The fruit is best in cool drinks and is acidic and strongly flavored. Propagate by grafting or budding.

ZONES 9–11

### *C. aurantium*

BITTER ORANGE, SEVILLE ORANGE

These small trees originated in China and are grown as ornamental shrubs or providers of fruit for marmalade and jelly. The heavy-fruiting variety 'Seville' with its glossy, dark-green leaves and small growth habit is excellent in containers or as a border grower. Propagate from seed.

ZONES 9–11

### *C. limon*

LEMON

Native to Pakistan and India, this tree or shrub is an attractive evergreen that grows to 12 ft (about 3.5 m) high and 9 ft (about 2.7 m) wide. The most common cultivar is 'Eureka', a smooth-stemmed tree with a year-round display of fruit and flowers if grown in frost-free climates; it is an excellent choice because of its culinary versatility and because of its ability to ripen in cool summers. 'Meyer' is smaller than most lemons with a less acidic flavor, and is rather hardier than other lemons. Plant in well-drained soil and fertilize regularly with nitrogen. Propagate by budding. The lemon is less prone to disease than other citrus trees.

ZONES 9–11

*Citrus medica*

*Citrus paradisi*

*Citrus aurantifolia*

### *C. medica*

CITRON

The fruit is like a lemon, but has a rougher, highly fragrant skin. The young foliage has a purplish tinge; the flowers have a purplish tinge as well. Propagate by budding. Because it produces very little juice, *C. medica* is an excellent choice for use as marmalade or as candied peel. The tree is about as hardy as a sour orange. Grow in a nitrogen-rich, well-drained soil in a position in full sun.

ZONE 10–11

### *C. paradisi*

GRAPEFRUIT

Native to the West Indies where it was called forbidden fruit, grapefruit is relatively large for a citrus tree at 15 ft (about 4.5 m) high. The fruit is prominently displayed on the tree's outer section, hanging in golden yellow clusters that should be left until fully ripe before being picked. If it is grown in a cool climate the fruit takes up to 18 months to ripen. Propagate by budding.

ZONE 9–11

*Citrus aurantium*

*Citrus limon*

*C. reticulata*

MANDARIN, TANGERINE

This is the largest citrus group and has a wide range of climate tolerance among its varieties: the hardiest can take an occasional light frost. It grows to 9 ft (about 2.7 m) high and is a good fruit tree for the suburban garden. The fruit is similar to oranges, but smaller and looser skinned. It is slow growing with heavily perfumed flowers. Prune to remove dead wood. Propagate by budding.
ZONE 9–11

*C. sinensis*

SWEET ORANGE

The sweet orange traveled the trade routes as far back as the mid-fifteenth century and was introduced to the Western world by Arab traders. A large evergreen, it is grown commercially in subtropical climates. It can be grown in cooler climates if it is grafted *Poncirus trifoliata* rootstock, which helps it tolerate cold winters and also gives it greater resistance to certain virus diseases. Propagate by budding. Humidity encourages fungal diseases. Orange blossom is traditionally worn by brides in their hair. 'Valencia' is the best known variety of sweet orange, and is much grown commercially.
ZONE 10–11

*C. sinensis* 'Washington Navel'

NAVEL ORANGE

This small, slow-growing tree grows best away from hot summer coastal areas as this climate does not suit it. It has a distinctive, button-like growth on its seedless fruit, which many consider superior in mildness and sweetness to 'Valencia'. It is a mutation of the sweet orange.
ZONES 10–11

*C.* x *tangelo*

TANGELO

An evergreen tree growing up to 12 ft (about 3.5 m) high and 9 ft (about 2.7 m) wide, it is derived from a cross between mandarin and grapefruit. Tangelo is renowned for its juicing properties and as a superb dessert fruit with its tart yet sweet flavor. Plant in well-drained soil in a warm spot sheltered from frost. As with all citrus trees, regular watering is essential, especially when the tree is fruiting. Apply nitrogen fertilizer from early spring until mid-summer. Propagate by budding.
ZONES 10–11

## *CORYLUS*
### *avellana*

HAZELNUT, FILBERT

A small deciduous tree that grows up to 12 ft (about 3.5 m) high and wide. It will grow in a wide range of climates, but prefers mild summers. The tree should be placed in full light where it is sheltered from strong winds. It produces the best crop of nuts, which grow in clusters and ripen in fall, in fertile, well-drained soil. Propagate by layering or from cuttings. The hazelnut has long been steeped in mystic lore; parts of the plant were supposedly used for rituals in ancient times. In modern days it is eaten as a dessert and much used in the making of sweets and chocolates.
ZONES 4–9

## *CYDONIA*
### *oblonga*

QUINCE

Native to the Middle East, this is a deciduous tree growing 9–12 ft (about 2.7–3.5 m) high and 9 ft (about 2.7 m) wide. Its soft green leaves turn an attractive golden yellow before falling and it is not fussy about soil, making it an ideal ornamental for potting or for borders. Its highly aromatic fruit can be left on the tree for a few weeks after it ripens without harm. Pick with care as it bruises easily. Prune minor branches or shoots which have produced fruit. Propagate from cuttings. Quinces cannot be eaten raw and are best cooked for jellies or sauces. Quinces are thought to be the "golden apples" that feature in Greek mythology.
ZONES 5–11

## *CYPHOMANDRA*
### *betacea*

TAMARILLO, TREE TOMATO

This is an evergreen shrub or small, shrubby tree from South America with large, green leaves and, depending on the variety, dark red or yellow-orange fruit. Train it up against a wire fence or stake it to protect from the wind, as it is very inclined to top heaviness. This is a shallow-rooted plant which prefers

*Corylus avellana*

*Citrus sinensis* 'Washington Navel'

*Cydonia oblonga*

*Citrus reticulata*

*Citrus* x *tangelo*

*Citrus sinensis*

a subtropical or temperate climate and moist but not wet soil. It grows to 9 ft (about 2.7 m) in height. Prune lightly after fruiting and take cuttings at 3 ft (about 90 cm) high to encourage more shoots. Propagate from cuttings and plan to replace the trees after 5 years or so as they are short lived. The fruit will mature throughout the year and can be used for jam or on ice-cream.
ZONES 10–11

## *DIOSPYROS*
### *kaki*
JAPANESE PERSIMMON

This attractive, deciduous tree is common in Japan and China and grows to 15 ft (about 4.5 m) high and wide. The leaves are dark green and glossy, changing color in fall to a handsome russet and gold. The tree can be kept in a large container and even if pruned will continue to fruit happily. The fruit is golden orange and is either astringent (in which case it should be eaten when quite ripe), or non-astringent (eat while still firm and crunchy or dry for future use, as is done in Japan). Plant in well-drained soil; no pruning is needed beyond the removal of dead or awkwardly placed branches. Take care not to plant this tree near sidewalks as the fruit can be messy when it drops.
ZONES 8–11

## *ERIOBOTRYA*
### *japonica*
LOQUAT

In its natural state this tree will grow to 20 ft (about 6 m) high but in domesticity can be kept quite small by regular post-harvest pruning. Large, dark green leaves have a silver-gray underside and the scented, creamy colored flowers form in multiple clusters. It prefers a temperate to subtropical climate; it will survive cold spells although there may be some fruit damage. Its fruit are pear shaped, small and sweet. Prune the more fragile shoots after the first fruiting; this will improve future harvests and make the tree more compact. Birds can be a problem. Remove the bitter seeds and stew for jam or eat the fruit raw in salads. The tree can be propagated easily from seed, but grafted, named varieties give superior fruit.
ZONES 7–11

## *FEIJOA*
### *sellowiana*
FEIJOA, PINEAPPLE GUAVA

Native to Brazil and Argentina, this evergreen grows to 9–12 ft (about 2.7–3.5 m) high and wide and features green foliage and, in early summer, attractive red and white flowers. It makes a good windbreak or can be pruned to make a tall hedge. Keep well watered, especially while fruiting. The fruit is large and pale green, with a similar taste to pineapple, and should not be stored for too long before consumption. Plant in pairs of different varieties to ensure pollination. 'Unique' is a good cultivar for the domestic garden, being self-fertile.
ZONES 8–11

## *FICUS*
### *carica*
FIG

Originally from the Mediterranean and Asia, this deciduous tree varies in height from 9–27 ft (about 2.7–8 m). It flourishes in deep, lime-rich soils and a mild, dry climate and ideally should bear fruit twice a year. A distinguishing feature of this plant is the way the flower is formed and held within the fruit itself. May be trained as a wall plant. The yield is greater when its root range is limited or it is containerized. Propagate from cuttings. Figs have few natural enemies although wasps and birds might find the near-ripe fruit very tempting. There are several named varieties, varying in their tolerance of cold and whether their fruit are best eaten fresh or dried. Little pruning is needed.
ZONES 8–11

*Diospyros kaki*

*Cyphomandra betacea*

*Ficus carica*

*Feijoa sellowiana*

*Eriobotrya japonica*

*Juglans regia*

*Malus domestica* 'Golden Delicious'

## *FORTUNELLA*
### *japonica*

KUMQUAT

This small, evergreen, ornamental shrub made the journey from the Orient to the West in the nineteenth century. It is excellent in a large tub and its glossy, green foliage and small, golden fruit can also be a highlight in a flower border. There is a pretty variety with variegated leaves also. It will survive fairly open spaces on patios and courtyards. Propagate from seed. Kumquats are used in marmalades and liqueurs.

ZONES 9–11

## *JUGLANS*
### *regia*

WALNUT

A forest tree, this species grows 30–80 ft (about 9–24 m) high and 65 ft (about 20 m) wide. It can take several years before the tree starts to bear any nuts so patience is required. A silver-gray trunk ends in a canopy of arching branches, making this a good source of shade in a spacious garden. Prune early to form a central branch and a well-spaced system of boughs. It is cold and wind hardy, although young trees may be damaged by harsh frost. Ensure that the soil is deep, loamy and well drained. Water well to increase nut production and pick the nuts from the ground after they have fallen. Large birds can be a problem.

ZONES 7–10

## *MALUS*

A member of the rose family, this genus contains the crabapple and the garden apple (*M. domestica*); there are many species and varieties of both. The genus is extremely hardy, tolerating subtropical to subarctic conditions, though they do best in temperate climates with cold winters. Well-drained soil is essential for growth. They prefer deep, humus-rich, sandy loams in full light, although shade is tolerated. Plant in early spring in colder areas and fall in warmer ones. Pruning consists basically of thinning out branches to allow plenty of air and light around the fruit, though the fruiting apples are subjected to various detailed systems. Once established, it is rarely necessary to do more than shorten (in summer) the current season's over-long shoots. Apple trees are not fertile to their own pollen, so it is necessary to grow two or more varieties to have a crop. The size of the tree depends on the understock.

*Malus* 'Bramley's Seedling'

### *M.* 'Bramley's Seedling'

This well-known cooking apple bears its large green fruit, occasionally flushed red, between October and March. Its flowers, which appear in early spring, can be damaged by frost.

ZONES 3–8

*Fortunella japonica*

### M. 'Discovery'

This tasty dessert apple appears in late summer. It is a small, deciduous tree that grows to a height of 6–12 ft (about 1.8–3.5 m).

ZONES 3–8

### M. x 'Dolgo'

**DOLGO CRABAPPLE**

Introduced in 1917 by the South Dakota Agricultural Experimental Station, this extremely hardy crabapple produces a spreading head around 20 ft (about 6 m) high and 25 ft (about 7.5 m) across. The pure white flowers are succeeded by glossy, red, teardrop-shaped fruit $1^1/_2$ in (about 3 cm) in diameter. The crabapples are used extensively for making jellies and wine.

ZONES 2–6

### M. *domestica* 'Delicious'

'Golden Delicious' is a prolific tree with juicy golden fruit, while 'Red Delicious' is an excellent dessert apple. Neither keeps very well after being picked.

ZONES 3–8

*Malus* 'Discovery'

### M. *domestica* 'Granny Smith'

This Australian-bred apple was a lucky seedling in the garden of a woman called Granny Smith. The pale green fruit is excellent for cooking or for eating fresh.

ZONES 3–10

### M. *domestica* 'Gravenstein'

A medium to large aromatic apple native to Germany which is striped red and yellow. This is a large tree which should be placed with care in the home garden. Partly self-fertile, it is the best choice where only one apple tree is grown, though fruit production will be more abundant if it has a mate.

ZONES 3–9

### M. *domestica* 'Jonathan'

This American-raised cultivar is very popular in that country and elsewhere for its sweet bland flavor and bright red color. It is sometimes a rather weak-growing tree.

ZONES 3–9

*Malus domestica* 'Granny Smith'

*Malus domestica* 'Jonathan'

*Malus domestica* 'Gravenstein'

*Musa paradisiaca* 'Cavendish'

*Musa paradisiaca*

### M. 'Golden Hornet'

FLOWERING CRAB

An attractive erect tree with an open habit, this species can grow to 15 ft (about 4.5 m). Its oval leaves are mid-green, and in spring it is covered with single white flowers around 1 in (about 2.5 cm) wide. The bright yellow fruit which follow remain on the tree well into fall, after the foliage has dropped. Plant in full sun in well-drained soil.

ZONES 3–9

### M. 'James Grieve'

This tasty eating apple is available in late summer. Yellow and red, it is prone to disease and easily bruised. Its blossom appears in spring.

ZONES 3–9

### M. 'John Downie'

This large crabapple grows to 15 ft (about 4.5 m). It yields an abundant crop of red fruit in fall. The spring flowers are white.

ZONES 3–8

## *MORUS*

### *nigra*

BLACK MULBERRY

From the same family as the fig tree, the deciduous mulberry has a 15–30 ft (about 4.5–9 m) tall trunk and wide-spreading branches. This slow-growing species is native to Iran and is valued for its ornamental, heart-shaped leaves and black fruit. This tree commands a lot of space in the garden but can be grown in tubs or trained espalier as long as it has been pruned and shaped from early growth. It loves a temperate climate and the fruit will ripen in early summer, becoming easy prey for passing birds. Propagate from seedlings. The white mulberry *(M. alba)* is more suitable for warm winter climates, however fruit is not quite as good. Its leaves are fed to silkworms. Do not plant either species where the fruit can fall on paving, as it will stain it.

ZONES 5–10

## *MUSA*

### *paradisiaca*

BANANA

The banana tree is really a herbaceous perennial that needs frost-free tropical or subtropical climates. It has exotic, orange-yellow or red flowers and needs a lot of water for fruit production. Plant in loamy soil in a spacious position away from wind. Give regular doses of nitrogenous fertilizer. Propagate from suckers or by a bud from part of the tuber. Cut down the fruit when semi-ripe and allow to ripen in a warm place indoors.

ZONES 10–11

### M. *paradisiaca* 'Cavendish'

This small banana tree, growing to 6–9 ft (about 1.8–2.7 m) high, bears fruit reliably. Plant in sun or partial shade in a position protected from wind and in humus-rich, well-drained soil.

ZONES 10–11

### M. *paradisiaca* 'Lady Finger'

This tree grows up to 15 ft (about 4.5 m) in height and is particularly well suited for domestic gardens; it also tolerates cooler, more temperate weather than other species. The fruit is very sweet.

ZONES 10–11

*Morus nigra*

*Musa paradisiaca* 'Lady Finger'

*Malus* 'Golden Hornet'

## *OLEA*
### *europaea* subsp. *europaea*
OLIVE

This is a hardy, evergreen tree that grows to 20 ft (about 6 m) high. It originates in the eastern Mediterranean where it is grown mostly for its oil but also for its fruit, eaten green or ripe but always pickled. It has glossy, narrow, green leaves, small yellow-white flowers and attractive spreading branches. It prefers warm summers and cool winters. It should be potted and grown in a greenhouse for protection in colder climates and tolerates most soils as long as they are well drained. Water thoroughly in summer to ensure good fruiting. Fruit will not appear for at least 8 years but the tree is ornamental in its own right, developing an interestingly gnarled trunk as it ages. There are several named varieties, some being better for eating while others are better for oil. "Virgin" olive oil is that from the first pressing of the fruit, and is the best quality.
ZONES 8–11

## *PERSEA*
### *americana*
syn. *P. gratissima*
AVOCADO

Native to Central America and reaching a height of 24 ft (about 7 m) and 18 ft (about 5.5 m) wide this large, evergreen tree has glossy, dark green leaves and tiny spring flowers. It prefers warmth and shelter in the garden (young trees are frost tender) and may be grown indoors providing it is exposed to 4 hours of sunlight each day. Water regularly and ensure the soil is salt free and aerated. Avocados are not self-pollinating and it is best to plant more than one. Pollinate the flowers by hand if only one tree is growing. The best-known varieties are 'Fuerte', with large, green-skinned fruit in summer and early fall; and 'Hass', which bears dark-skinned fruit in winter and spring. Gardeners with room for both can have avocados virtually all year round.
ZONES 10–11

## *PINUS*
### *pinea*
PINE NUT, ITALIAN STONE PINE

This tall pine tree is a native of Italy and one of the most popular nut bearers there, the pine nuts (pignons or pignolias) being much used in cooking. They are very rich in protein. The tree is easily grown in a subtropical or temperate climate. The pines contain an average of 100 nuts and should be picked when slightly green and left to open in a warm, dry spot. When the pine opens out, the nuts can be shaken out. Eat them raw or roasted. Propagate from seed or cuttings.
ZONES 8–10

## *PISTACIA*
### *vera*
PISTACHIO

Belonging to the same family as the mango and cashew, this tree is valued as an ornamental garden tree as well as a nut bearer. It features red-gold leaves in fall, and red male and white female flowers on separate trees; at least one of each is needed for a crop of nuts although bisexual, grafted trees are sometimes available and grafted trees of known sex are always to be preferred to seedlings. It prefers hot, dry summers and mild to cold winters. Loamy, organic soil is best for quick growth of the tree. The pistachio's long, deep roots make it drought tolerant but it should be well watered to ensure a good crop. *Pistacia chinensis*, the Chinese pistachio, is grown solely for its dazzling fall colors, its fruit being too small to be worth eating.
ZONES 9–11

## *PRUNUS*

This genus contains over 400 species of deciduous and evergreen shrubs or trees grown for their fruits or nuts and as ornamentals. Most species prefer a well-drained soil. Propagate from seed in summer, from cuttings, or by grafting or budding. Prune regularly.

### *P. armeniaca*
APRICOT

This deciduous tree grows to 18 ft (about 5.5 m) high and 15 ft (about 4.5 m) wide. Dwarf varieties are now available which may be grown in pots. Apricot trees flourish in warm summer areas with well-drained, alkaline soil. A wet spring will mean a smaller crop. Prune for the first 4 years to a vase shape with 6 or 7 main branches. In areas with spring frost, the tree is best given a position with the shelter of a warm wall. Early spring flowers are a pale pink in color.
ZONES 4–9

*Pistacia vera*

*Olea europaea* subsp. *europaea*

*Prunus armeniaca*

*Pinus pinea*

*Persea americana*

### *P. avium*

SWEET CHERRY

This tree grows to 30 ft (about 9 m) tall and has white blossoms. Dwarf hybrids that grow to only a few yards high are available and these will live and fruit happily in tubs. It is suited to fan training against a high wall or fence. Otherwise, prune gradually to an open vase shape with 10 or so main branches. Do not prune in winter or during wet weather as cherry wood is prone to fungus. While cherries are ripening, cover the tree with plastic netting to keep birds away. Cherries are generally not self-fertile so two trees will be necessary. They need a cold winter to fruit.

ZONES 4–9

### *P. cerasus*

SOUR CHERRY

This species is suitable for the domestic garden, being smaller, more compact and naturally self-fertilizing. The fruit ripens in late summer, but is acidic and needs to be cooked or preserved. Like the sweet cherry, it needs cold winters.

ZONES 4–9

### *P. domestica* and *P. salicifolia*

PLUM

The plums are of mixed origin but the European varieties are usually assigned to *P. domestica* and the Japanese (many of which were bred in the US) to *P. salicifolia.* The main distinction is that the European plums are lovers of cooler climates than the Japanese. Both types come in many named varieties, but whereas just about all the Japanese plums are dessert fruit, the European plums include varieties best suited to cooking (jam making, pies, etc.) or drying for prunes. Damsons are European plums with rather small but very sweet fruit; greengages are similar but green-yellow even when ripe. Plum blossoms are quite lovely and some species of trees are grown purely for their display of beautiful red leaves. Plum trees are generally very easy to grow and will tolerate different soil types; these species prefer a potash-rich mixture which is well watered. They like a temperate climate with dry summers and should be planted in a sunny sheltered position. Prune regularly in summer to slow growth and pick the plums only when fully ripe. Use netting to protect the trees from birds.

ZONES 5–10

### *P. dulcis*

syn. *P. amygdalus*

ALMOND

A deciduous tree from Southeast Asia that grows to 18 ft (about 5.5 m) high and 15 ft (about 4.5 m) wide. This is a stone fruit which is closely related to the peach. However, the flesh of the fruit is inedible while the kernel is sweet. Pink blossoms grow in clusters of 5 and 6. Ideally, this tree should be grown in a dry summer climate in a well-drained, salt-free soil. Young trees are frost tender. As with other stone fruit, weed the base area well and feed the young tree nitrogen. Prune to an open vase shape encouraging 3 or 4 main branches. Almonds are not self-fertile and two varieties that blossom at the same time are needed to produce fruit.

ZONES 7–10

### *P. persica*

PEACH

This deciduous tree grows to 15 ft (about 4.5 m) high and wide, and is the most commonly grown of the stone fruit. Most feature pink-tinged blossoms, yellowish red-skinned fruit and should be grown in a warm climate. Cultivated dwarf varieties are perfect for placing in tubs or among flower beds and shrubberies. Peach trees must be planted in well-drained soil as waterlogging can be fatal. Plant where the tree, including the interior branches, will receive the most light and shelter from frosts. If new shoots aren't pruned the tree will overbear and the fruit will be small and of poor quality. Pick the peaches when they just start to soften. Propagate from seed. They are officially self-fertile, but crops will be better if two varieties are grown. The trees are not long lived, 25 years or so.

ZONES 5–10

### *P. persica* var. *nectarina*

NECTARINE

The nectarine is almost identical to the peach in habit and flowers but needs more attention as it is less hardy than the peach. Its fruit is usually smaller and smooth skinned. There are several named varieties; seedlings often give rise to normal peaches.

ZONES 5–10

## PSIDIUM
### *cattleianum*

CHERRY GUAVA, STRAWBERRY GUAVA

Native to tropical Central and South America, this medium-sized evergreen is related to the feijoa. It is fast growing with a smooth trunk and large, white flowers. Its pear-shaped fruit has dark red flesh which is high in vitamin C. It prefers a warm, frost-free climate, plenty of water for good fruit production and some shelter from the wind when it is young. The tree should be pruned to encourage flowering. Guavas are excellent for juicing, or for jams and jellies.

ZONES 10–11

## PUNICA
### *granatum*

POMEGRANATE

This very attractive, compact but very thorny tree is from the Middle East where about 20 named varieties, varying in flavor from acid to very sweet, are grown. It is valued not only for its sweet fruit but for its

*Prunus avium*

*Prunus cerasus*

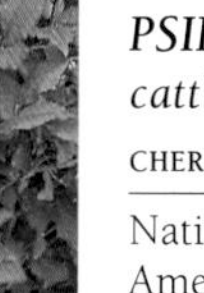

*Prunus domestica*

*Prunus persica* var. *nectarina*

*Prunus persica*

*Prunus dulcis*

large, red blooms which appear in late spring and early summer. It grows to 15 ft (about 4.5 m) and its glossy leaves, showy scarlet flowers and orange fruit make it popular as an ornamental, long-living shrub. Pomegranates require hot summer conditions to produce good crops. Prune lightly in winter to encourage new growth. Pomegranates start to bear fruit after 5 to 6 years; the fruit should be harvested when it becomes an orange-brown color. Do not leave it too long on the tree as it tends to split. Propagate from cuttings or rooted suckers. Watch out for fungal rot. Use the fruit kernels in salads or desserts and eat the pulp fresh. A warm summer is needed for the fruit to ripen, and the double-flowered varieties (red, pink or white) are mostly sterile.
ZONES 8–11

## *PYRUS*

PEAR

Thousands of years of cultivation have produced many different shapes, sizes and fruit of pear trees, some more suitable for the domestic garden than others. Usually a large tree, it is thought to have originated in the Mediterranean. It flourishes in a moist, mild climate. Plant in a warm, protected spot where it will receive maximum sunlight. In a small garden, train it to grow on a lattice or wire frame. Alternatively, pear trees grafted on to quince stock are good for home gardens. It can stand a reasonable amount of water and responds well to loamy soil with the occasional boost of nitrogen-rich fertilizers. Cross-pollination is needed for productive fruiting.

### *P. communis* 'Beurre Bosc'

This is popular worldwide for its large, soft, sweet pears that are ideal for baking.
ZONES 5–10

### *P. communis* 'William's Bon Chrétien'

BARTLETT PEAR

This is a sweet, musky-flavored, medium-sized pear which bears the name of an English schoolteacher but is thought by some to have been cultivated by the Ancient Romans. It is the most widely grown Bartlett pear cultivar for canning.
ZONES 5–10

### *P. pyrifolia*

ASIAN PEAR

Native to China but also much cultivated in Japan, this tree is an excellent, compact, fruit bearer. Plant among garden shrubs where its white blossoms and glossy, green leaves can be seen to advantage. It has two types: the Japanese Asian pear, which is more apple shaped with green or brown skin, and the Chinese Asian pear, which is more traditionally pear shaped. The Asian pear is easier to grow than the European pear in mild winter areas, and more suited to domestic use. Grow on a trellis and prune excess shoots. It is more disease hardy than the European pear, and not so dependent on cross-pollination for fruit, although crops will be better if the tree does have a mate; a European pear will be perfectly adequate.
ZONES 6–10

## *SAMBUCUS*
*canadensis*

AMERICAN ELDERBERRY

This dense, multi-stemmed, deciduous shrub native to the eastern seaboard across to Texas and Manitoba grows to a height of 12 ft (about 3.5 m). It produces broad trusses of creamy white flowers which cover the plant in mid-summer. Lustrous, purple-black fruit mature in late summer and are often used for pies. It needs a position in sun in fertile, moist soil.
ZONES 3–9

## *ZIZIPHUS*
*jujuba*

CHINESE DATE

This tree is native to an area stretching from southeastern Europe to China. It grows quickly up to 50 ft (about 15 m) and ranges in habit from compact and shrubby to open and spreading. The leaves are rectangular to elliptical with angled teeth. Little creamy flowers develop in clusters in spring, succeeded by the lush, reddish orange fruit. Edible and sweet, they ripen in winter. Plant this frost-tender tree in light, porous soil with full sun or partial shade and water frequently. Prune to encourage dense growth and propagate from seed or stem cuttings. Chinese dates are a delicacy in Middle Eastern countries and are delicious cooked or uncooked.
ZONES 9–11

*Sambucus canadensis*

*Pyrus pyrifolia*

*Ziziphus jujuba*

*Pyrus communis* 'Buerre Bosc'

*Pyrus communis* 'William's Bon Chrétien'

*Psidium cattleianum*

*Punica granatum*

# OTHER FRUITS

## ACTINIDIA
*chinensis*
**syn. *A. deliciosa***
KIWIFRUIT, CHINESE GOOSEBERRY

This deciduous vine is native to the Yangtze Valley in China and is now grown in warm areas around the world. It should be planted on a sturdy trellis or pergola (as it grows quickly and quite wildly) in deep soil which is high in nitrogen. It prefers a sheltered spot away from the winds, early frosts and hot sun that can damage the fruit. Prune regularly in summer and winter to ensure large, good quality fruit. Water abundantly in summer. The first fruit will appear after 4 to 5 years. Both male and female vines (named varieties are superior) are needed to produce fruit; grafted plants carrying both sexes are often available. Prune annually after the leaves have fallen to control growth.
ZONES 8–11

*Arachis hypogaea*

## ARACHIS
*hypogaea*
PEANUT

This is an herbaceous annual with bright green, clover-like leaves and small, pea-shaped, yellow flowers that blossom in summer. Native to Brazil, it grows to a height of 12 in (about 30 cm) with a spread of 16 in (about 40 cm). It can be planted to good effect in flower borders or in containers, but is frost tender so grow only where it will enjoy a long, hot summer. They need a long growing season with consistently warm soil, as in mild summer areas the nuts will not ripen. The peanuts themselves are actually seeds that grow underground, so make sure that the soil (which should be slightly acid) is loose enough for the peanut to grow productively. Keep the soil well drained and well composted. Peanut plants should be ready to pull up when the foliage turns yellow in fall.
ALL ZONES

## CITRULLUS
*lanatus*
**syn. *C. vulgaris***
WATERMELON

This is a large, heat-loving vine with crinkled leaves similar to rather large ivy leaves. Sow seeds in spring in rich, well-drained soil in a sunny position. (Mostly it grows rampantly, and without much encouragement, from compost heaps in the back garden.) The rind can be pickled and of course the sugary, red-pink flesh inside is delicious. The longer and hotter the summer the better the crop will be.
ALL ZONES

*Cucumis melo* (cantaloupe)

*Citrullus lanatus*

*Actinidia chinensis*

## CUCUMIS
MELON

Native to Africa where there are 40 species, most melons grow on vines and are grouped according to the characteristics of their fruit. They need a long, hot growing season to produce sweet fruit, and in a cooler climate the vines should be encouraged to grow over concrete or rocks, or trained over black plastic in order for heat to circulate around the plant. Plant in humus-rich soil and water generously but not too much. Humid conditions can affect the quality of the fruit and make the plant more prone to the fungus anthracnose. Hand pollinate if growing melons on a small scale. Propagate from seed.

### CANTALUPENSIS GROUP
*C. melo*
CANTALOUPE

This is a compact plant with oval-shaped or round fruit with netted rinds and orange flesh.
ALL ZONES

### INDORUS GROUP
*C. melo*
HONEYDEW MELON

A small, bushy plant with a harder rind than most melons, making it suitable for long storage. The skin is usually smooth and the flesh is pale green or yellow.
ALL ZONES

### RETICULATUS GROUP
*C. melo*
NETTED MELON

This melon has net markings on the rind, orange flesh and is widely grown in the United States.
ALL ZONES

## FRAGARIA
STRAWBERRY

This small perennial grows no more than 8 in (about 20 cm) high and 16 in (about 40 cm) wide. These plants are capable of growing all over the world in all sorts of climates, including the Arctic. The strawberry itself is a false fruit made up of tiny pips. Modern, more robust strawberry plants can produce fruit for 6 months if grown properly; some will bear fruit year round in a warm climate. Plant in tubs, pots, garden beds or even boxes that have been lined with straw, potting mix and fertilizer. Ensure the soil is free draining and acidic. The plants need sun and protection from wind, and in cold climates should be grown in slits in sheets of plastic. Propagate from runners and replant with fresh, virus-free stock every few years. Snails and birds are a nuisance. There are many named varieties of the garden strawberry, varying in their preferred climates and especially in flavor.

### *F. alpina*
ALPINE STRAWBERRY

The fruit from this variety is small and hardy and tastes very tangy. Alpine strawberries make a good ground cover under trees or near walls and are less susceptible to attack by birds. The fruit can be red or yellow, and plants usually don't make runners. They are propagated from seed.
ZONES 4–10

### *F. ananassae*
GARDEN STRAWBERRY

The name means "pineapple flavored," a curious description for the garden strawberry which arose from crossing American species.
ZONES 4–10

### *F. vesca*
WOODLAND STRAWBERRY

Native to Europe, this was originally a wild woodland berry, the fruit of which is larger than that on the alpine strawberry. It is a spreading perennial to 12 in (about 30 cm) in height.
ZONES 4–10

*Humulus lupulus* 'Aureus'

*Fragaria ananassae*

## *HUMULUS lupulus*

HOP

This perennial, twining vine from Eurasia produces fruit used as flavoring in beer making. Very fast growing, easily attaining heights of 18 ft (about 5.5 m), it should be supported by a trellis to facilitate the fruit harvesting. Large, 3- to 5-lobed, bright green leaves clothe the bristly stems, creating a dense, nearly impenetrable screen. Hops produce male and female flowers on separate plants, the fruit being formed on the females. The cultivar 'Aureus' is readily available.

ZONES 2–10

## *PASSIFLORA*

This genus contains over 400 species of evergreen or semi-evergreen, tendril-climbing vines, primarily, though not exclusively, native to tropical America. They are grown as ornamentals or for their pulpy fruit. Flowers range from pale pink to purple-red and fruits from pale yellow through to purple-black, depending on the species. Plant in rich, well-drained soil in full sun and provide support. Propagate from seed or cuttings. Most species are frost tender.

### *P. edulis*

PASSIONFRUIT

This species of passionfruit vine is a common sight in gardens in temperate climates and is valued for its glossy, bright green leaves, purple-white flowers and flavorsome fruit. Train on a pergola or trellis and prune into shape to prevent tangling, which encourages insect infestation. It likes a well-drained, sandy soil and occasional doses of nitrogen fertilizer. The fruit will grow quickly and should be picked when its skin has turned purple and is still smooth. This species is self-fertile. Propagate from seed or by grafting a selected, named variety. The Spanish conquistadors regarded the flower of the passionfruit as a symbol of the crucifixion.

ZONES 10–11

### *P. mollissima*

syn. *Tacsonia mollissima*

BANANA PASSIONFRUIT

This attractive, fast-growing vine does well in cool climates and features pink flowers and long, golden yellow fruit. Train against a trellis or fence, or over a supporting tree where the fruit and flowers can be seen to advantage. Drought hardy and generous in its crop, it often fruits in the first year. The fruit is not as sweet as the ordinary

*Passiflora edulis*

*Fragaria alpina*

*Rubus* 'Boysen'

*Passiflora mollissima*

*Ribes nigrum*

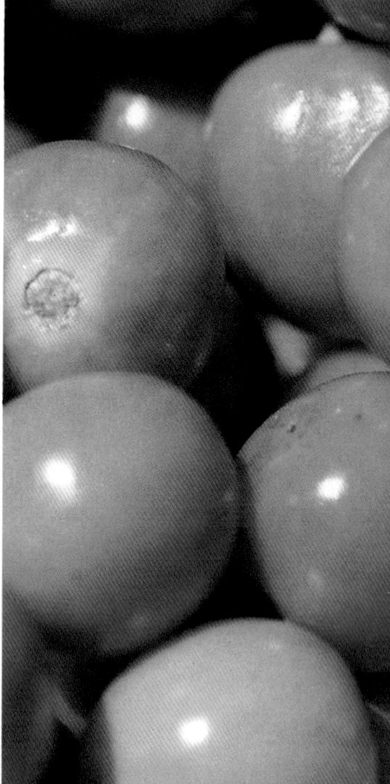
*Physalis peruviana*

*Ribes grossularia*

*Ribes sativum*

passionfruit but can still be used for cakes and fruit salads.
ZONES 10–11

## PHYSALIS

### *peruviana*

CAPE GOOSEBERRY

This edible species of *Physalis* is an attractive bush with gray-green leaves and gold berries. It is frost tender so it is best grown in the shelter of another bush or tree. Hot weather usually means that the fruit will be sweet, while a cooler, temperate climate can lead to sour-tasting berries. Propagate from cuttings. Use for chutney or jam or in fruit salads.
ZONES 10–11

## RIBES

A member of the Grossulariaceae family, this genus contains about 150 species of deciduous, fruit-bearing shrubs. They grow to a height of 3–6 ft (about 90–180 cm) and spread of 3–4$^1/_2$ ft (about 90–130 cm). Frost hardy, they are unsuited to warm winter climates. Most species prefer deep, rich, well-drained, slightly acidic soil. Plant in sun or partial shade, and water well during summer. Prune annually to shape as required by the species. Diseases, insects and birds can be a problem.

### *R. grossularia*

GOOSEBERRY

The thorny-stemmed gooseberry bush grows to 3 ft (about 90 cm) high. It can tolerate quite poor soil as long as it is salt free and grows best in cool, moist positions in sun or partial shade. The thorny stems should be kept in mind when placing it in a small garden. Shape as a short-stemmed bush or tie the shoots against a fan-shaped wire support. Pick the fruit while it is still hard if using for cooking, but wait until it is soft if eating it fresh. Propagate from cuttings. Botrytis, birds, caterpillars and mildew are problems; only mildew-resistant varieties should be grown.
ZONES 4–10

### *R. nigrum*

BLACKCURRANT

This very popular garden shrub reaches up to 6 ft (about 1.8 m) and produces green-white flowers and sweet, black fruit high in vitamin C. Frost hardy, it prefers a rich, loamy soil which can hold water. Plant it deep in the soil and enrich wood growth with potash and nitrogen-rich fertilizer. Put it in a position in full sun or partial shade. Weeds must be controlled and preferably eradicated before planting the blackcurrant bush. Prune old shoots to encourage new growth. The fruit should be picked when the upper berries are starting to fall from the cluster. Propagate from cuttings. Watch for spider mites and leaf spot.
ZONES 4–10

### *R. sativum*

REDCURRANT

This is very similar to the blackcurrant and prefers the same conditions. Its beautiful, glossy, red berries ripen earlier and are less likely to fall prematurely. They are usually used in cooking. White currants are a form of the red, and are grown in exactly the same way.
ZONES 4–10

## RUBUS

This genus includes a large number of the berry fruits, including raspberries and blackberries. The plants produce long, trailing shoots known as canes which bear fruit in their second season and then die. These plants need supporting frames to keep the fruit away from the ground, and to keep the plants under control—any shoot that lies on the ground will take root. In a small garden the plants can be trained against a wall or trellis. Cool climates are best and an acidic, well-drained soil that holds water well. Make sure that the ground is well clear of weeds before planting. Propagate from pieces of root or root suckers.

### *R.* 'Boysen'

BOYSENBERRY

Like all bramble berries this is a rampant grower with long canes that are either thorny or smooth, the thornless variety being much easier to manage. It prefers a warm-temperate climate and depending on the fertility of the soil it may need vigorous pruning. The large, purple-red berries take 6 weeks to

ripen, when they can be quite black. The best variety is 'Thornless', the merits of which are indicated by its name.
ZONES 4–10

*R. fruticosus*

BRAMBLE, BLACKBERRY

This British native rambler is found growing wild in woods, hedgerows and also as a weed in the garden. The species consists of an aggregate of over 2000 micro-species, all differing minutely. The cultivated blackberry's stems will grow to 9 ft (about 2.7 m) with a similar spread and will need support. The prickly, arching stems bear deep green leaves with 3 to 5 leaflets which are felt like on the undersides. The white or pink flowers, up to 2 in (about 5 cm) across, appear during summer and are followed by the purple blackberries. The canes that bear fruit should be pruned immediately after harvesting.
ZONES 4–10

*R. idaeus*

RASPBERRY

*R. idaeus* from Europe (especially it is said from Mt Ida in Greece where Zeus was born) is the main parent of the garden raspberries, though most modern cultivars have various American species in their background. All make tall lax bushes with delicious red fruit, much used for jam but also eaten fresh. There are both summer and fall fruiting varieties; be sure to buy certified virus-free stocks and control aphids, which spread virus diseases.
ZONES 3–10

*R.* 'Logan'

**syn. *R. logan baccus***

LOGANBERRY

This is a hybrid between a blackberry and a garden raspberry, said to have originated in the garden of Judge Logan in California in 1881. It has a crimson, tart fruit highly suitable for cooking. The plant is raspberry like in growth.
ZONES 6.10

## *SECHIUM*

### *edule*

CHAYOTE

Native to South America and from the same family as the melon and cucumber, this is strictly a perennial fruit that grows on a strong, bright green vine. It requires sun and plenty of space to grow, as its tendrils will grip on to and climb almost anything. In a temperate climate chayotes are frost tender. Propagate from a shooting chayote fruit in spring. The large, hairy green fruit can be boiled, baked or stewed but do not overcook or it will be tasteless. Steamed chayote with white sauce is a pleasing accompaniment to meat; and chayote pie, with plenty of sugar and cinnamon, rivals apple pie.
ZONES 9–11

## *VACCINIUM*

### *corymbosum*

BLUEBERRY

A fast-growing, deciduous shrub with lovely, small white flowers and handsome fall colors. It looks best when planted as a thick hedge so that the flowers and berries form a mass of white or blue, depending on the season. It does well in cold climates and prefers a well-drained but constantly moist, loamy, acidic soil. It is self-fertile. Clear away weak branches in winter and shape so that light and air can reach the inner bush. The cooler the climate the tastier the fruit will be. Propagate from cuttings. The blueberry is quite difficult to reproduce.
ZONES 4–10

## *VITIS*

GRAPE

The grapes need cool winters and low summer humidity or mildew will be a major worry; in humid summer, coastal climates hybrid American varieties like 'Isabella' or 'Concord' are the most reliable. Train on a pergola or fence where it is sunny, and in deep soil so that the vine can dig its roots down. Pruning depends on grape type and upon the way the vine is being grown. For pergola vines, train on a single trunk until it reaches the horizontal beams, then allow it to spread out. Birds are a problem, so cover the vines with bird netting or put paper bags around the grape clusters. Cut the grapes with sharp scissors when fully ripe. Grapes need annual pruning after the leaves have fallen to control the vine's growth and encourage heavy fruiting. They are traditionally propagated by cuttings.

*V. labrusca*

FOX GRAPE

The parent of most of the cultivated grapes in the United States, this native of the eastern seaboard produces long, woolly young shoots that require trellising for support. The large, shallowly 3-lobed leaves are deep green above and white-woolly beneath. Full sun locations and well-drained, fertile soils are ideal for the production of the large, purple-black fruit, which has a musky or "foxy" flavor. 'Concord', 'Niagara' and 'Catawba' are commonly grown cultivars in areas where winters are cold and summers are cool and short.
ZONES 4–9

*V. vinifera*

GRAPE

This species is native to Europe and the Mediterranean and has been cultivated since remote antiquity. A vigorous, frost-hardy, deciduous vine, it has given rise to a multitude of varieties with either black or white (pale green or yellow) fruit, some being designed for wine, others for eating fresh or dried. It is best grown where summers are dry.
ZONES 6–10

*Vitis labrusca*

*Vitis vinifera*

*Vaccinium corymbosum*

*Sechium edule*

*Rubus idaeus*

*Rubus* 'Logan'

CHAPTER 9

# Indoor Plants

*You'd be forgiven for thinking that in an art as ancient as gardening, there was nothing new; yet house plants are quite a recent idea. True, the Victorians grew fuchsias on their windowsills and ferns in miniature greenhouses called Wardian cases; but the idea of using growing plants as major features in interior design—and growing a large range of species too—had to wait for several things to happen.*

First, modern architecture had to increase the size of our windows, so that rooms would be bright enough for plants to flourish. Then, electric light had to supersede gas, whose fumes will kill off just about anything except aspidistras and parlor palms. Even now, if you cook with gas you may well find plants don't flourish in your kitchen. Finally, central heating had to make our houses consistently warm enough for tropical plants, for tropical forests are among the few natural environments where decorative plants grow in gloom comparable to the interior of a building.

Hardiness zones have not been included, as it is considered these plants will always be grown indoors.

## The Importance of Light

We humans can adjust our eyes to an extraordinary range of brightness, but then we don't need light to photosynthesize. Plants do; and the first rule in growing any plant in the house is to give it adequate light. We almost always place our furniture in the best-lit places in the room—and why not, rooms are designed for our own comfort first of all—but that often means that the corners where plants fit the decor best are the darkest in the room. The brightest place is in front of or just next to a window, but if you habitually keep your curtains drawn during the day for privacy your room can be dim no matter how large your windows. There are plants that can take very low levels of light, but the range is limited and pretty well confined to plants with plain green leaves. (Variegated leaves are almost always short on chlorophyll, and flowering takes a lot of energy which the plant can only derive from light.) It is a matter of cutting your cloth according to your measure, but remember that a flourishing plant, no matter how plain, is an asset to a room; a struggling one, all weak, pale and drawn, isn't. You can overcome the forces of darkness by placing the plant under a lamp, but it will have to be fitted with a special bulb (a "grow-light" or fluorescent bulb, to be bought at most plant nurseries) that maximizes the frequencies of light that plants use—ordinary lights are of little use. Alternatively, have two plants and rotate them weekly or fortnightly between the garden or greenhouse.

## Humidity

The next requirement is adequate humidity, and here there can be real conflict between our ideas of comfort and those of our plants, many of which would be happier in a Turkish bath than

*It's very important to provide adequate light for indoor plants.*

the average living room. If you have a well-lit bathroom or kitchen they can be good places for plants, but you can assist by growing several plants together—they will help humidify the air for each other—and by standing your pots on saucers filled with pebbles which you keep constantly moist (on, not in; you don't want the roots standing in water).

Air conditioning and central heating can dry the air out to desert-like levels. It is often said that house plants dislike air-conditioning, but this isn't strictly true. If they are standing on wet pebbles they should be fine—and you'll be more comfortable too, and the piano will stay in better tune, for their presence. But you must keep your rooms at a reasonably even temperature. If you save energy by setting your system to come on and adjust the temperature by 18°F (about 10°C) in the half-hour before you come home, your plants will resent it. Happily, the 64–70°F (about 18–21°C) that most people find comfortable will suit most plants too, and if it falls by a couple of degrees during the night they'll appreciate it.

*The peace lily (*Spathiphyllum *'Mauna Loa'), one of the most popular indoor plants.*

## Watering

More house plants drown than die of thirst—water with care. Just about all should be allowed to dry out a little between waterings; if you can't be so hard hearted, pot them in terracotta pots, whose porosity makes it harder to over water than impervious plastic. It looks better too. You can then use the best method of testing: tap the pot and if it rings, the plant needs water; if you hear a dull thud, it doesn't. This doesn't work with plastic! Alternatively, try one of the various self-watering pots, which allow the plants to draw just the water they need from a reservoir in the bottom. Or try concentrating on spathiphyllums, which are among the very few house plants that like constant damp feet!

## Temporary Plants

It is all very well to say that happiness comes from concentrating on the easy plants, but you would be less than human if you were not to fall sometimes for one of the difficult but spectacular flowering types like cyclamen, gloxinias or poinsettias. They aren't impossible—just difficult, needing warmer or cooler conditions than usual, high humidity and great care in watering—but they really aren't happy in the average room. Unless you have a greenhouse or sheltered, totally frost-free place in the garden to use as a convalescent home, resign yourself to their being temporary delights. They'll still last longer than a bunch of cut flowers.

## Fertilizing and Repotting

Sooner or later, if a plant flourishes the question of fertilizing or repotting will arise. The advent of slow-release fertilizers has made fertilizing easy. Just buy one formulated for indoor plants, and apply it in spring as growth begins (it's astonishing how, even indoors, plants remain aware of the seasons) according to the directions on the packet. As always, don't overdo the dosage. Fertilizer will usually allow you to at least put off the decision about repotting—but if you feel the plant's shoes really are getting too tight, do the job in spring, handle the plant gently, and don't go up to a pot more than a size bigger than the old one. If you like, you can tease off some of the old soil from the roots to allow more fresh soil, which should be the best, premium grade potting mix you can buy. Naturally, you won't be tempted to put your plant in a container, no matter how beautiful, which has no drainage holes. If you can't resist put some pebbles in the bottom, and use it purely as a decorative mask for the holey-bottomed one in which the plant is actually growing.

## Pests

Alas, pests sometimes follow house plants indoors. The worst are mildew and root rot (almost always a result of over watering), red spider and mealy bug. All can be controlled by spraying with insecticides and fungicides, but who would be crazy enough to spray such poisons indoors, quite apart from the mess? If you can't take the plant outside to spray, you can use a systemic insecticide which is stirred into the soil. Fungi are more difficult, and if a plant really is severely infested it might be wise to consider disposing of it, soil and all. (Wash the pot out with bleach and you can re-use it.)

A final word—dust. This settles invisibly on house plants and robs the leaves of light. Wipe it off regularly with a damp cloth and, better yet, stand your plants out in the summer rain every so often. If you can bear to forgo their company, a few weeks outside in the shadiest place in the garden each summer will do them a power of good; but bring them back in the instant you sense fall in the air.

*Anthurium scherzerianum*

*Aspidistra elatior*

*Alocasia macrorrhiza*

## AESCHYNANTHUS
*radicans*

LIPSTICK PLANT

Grown for its bright red flowers held by a deep purple, tubular calyx, this trailing plant is ideal for hanging baskets. An epiphyte native to Indonesian jungles, it requires bright but filtered light, high humidity and regular fertilizing during flowering. Water regularly while allowing the soil to dry between waterings. Propagate by taking 4 in (about 10 cm) cuttings after flowering. Regular pinching will produce bushier plants.

## ALOCASIA
*macrorrhiza*

GIANT ELEPHANT'S EAR, CUNJEVOL, GIANT TARO

This is a member of a genus of plants from Sri Lanka and tropical Southeast Asia which are grown for their spectacular foliage of large leaves with highlighted veins on long stalks. This species has 3 ft (about 90 cm) long stalks which carry the broad, arrowhead-shaped, glossy green leaves which grow to 3 ft (about 90 cm) in length. It produces insignificant but fragrant flowers on a spadix enclosed in a leaf-like, yellowish-green spathe. It can be grown outdoors only in warmer climates as it is frost tender, and does best indoors in cool climates. If potted, grow in a rich, peaty mixture. Outdoors, grow in well-drained soil in a shady position with high humidity. Water heavily and feed regularly with diluted fertilizer. May be propagated from suckers which root easily or by division of rhizomes or stem cuttings planted in spring.

## ANTHURIUM
*scherzerianum*

FLAMINGO FLOWER

Grown for its attractive flowers and foliage, this tropical plant from Columbia grows to 24–32 in (about 60–81 cm), often in a greenhouse or indoors, but given the right conditions will grow outdoors. Anthuriums have long-stalked, heart-shaped leaves and long-lasting, graceful, glossy, bright red or pink spathes with yellow or red spadices. Indoors, they need bright light, high humidity and constant warmth and moisture to flower. *A. scherzerianum* has red flowers and curled orange to yellow spadices. Plant outdoors in a humid position in well-drained, peaty soil in full or part shade out of the wind. Water well, keeping the soil moist but not soggy. The temperature must not fall below 59°F (about 15°C). Propagate from rhizomes in early spring. Potted plants need dividing and repotting every few years. *A. andraenum* and its hybrids are larger and warmer growing.

*Aphelandra squarrosa* 'Louisae'

## APHELANDRA
*squarrosa* 'Louisae'

ZEBRA PLANT

Native to South America, this popular indoor plant takes its common name from its large, glossy, dark green leaves, heavily striped by white veins. It grows to 3 ft (about 90 cm). It is sometimes called "Saffron spike" due to the bright yellow flower bracts which surround the tiny white flowers and which appear in spring. Needs bright light, but not direct sunlight, and warm, reasonably humid conditions, especially when flowering. For high humidity stand the pot on a tray of pebbles and water. It is best in a rich, porous soil and can be grown in relatively small pots as it prefers to be slightly pot bound. Keep well watered in the warmer months and less in winter, but never let soil ball dry out, and fertilize regularly. As it tends to become leggy, prune back after flowering, leaving one or two pairs of leaves. Propagate by cutting off side shoots that have roots. Leaf drop can be caused by dry roots, low or sudden drops in temperature, or by direct sun. Browning of leaf tips or brown leaf spots may be caused by low humidity.

## ARDISIA
*crispa*

CORALBERRY, SPICEBERRY

This shrub native to the subtropical regions of Asia grows to around 3 ft by 3 ft (about 90 cm by 90 cm). Preferring cool temperatures and high humidity, they also require high light levels to ensure prolific blooming and fruit production. Keep the soil evenly moist during active growth and fertilize regularly. Fragrant white or pink, star-shaped flowers are followed by berries that turn bright red at Christmas time.

## ASPIDISTRA
*elatior*

CAST-IRON PLANT

This is a species of evergreen perennials from Japan, China and the Himalayas, and was one of the most famous house plants of the Victorian era. The tough, long, narrow, dark green leaves are pointed at the tips and arch elegantly on a clump of 6 in (about 15 cm) stems to a length of 24 in (about 60 cm). There is also a handsome variegated form. The cream to dark purple, bell-shaped flowers grow at soil level and are screened from view by the leaves; it is something of an event to see them, as indoor plants seldom flower. It is known with good reason as the "cast-iron plant," for its ability to withstand neglect makes it one of the toughest and most adaptable house plants. It can be kept in bright to very low light, but direct sunlight burns the leaves. Water lightly when soil is dry and do not stand the pot in water. Feed occasionally and regularly wipe leaves with a damp cloth to maintain the gloss. When the plant becomes very crowded, divide the root crown and repot in late winter to early spring.

## BEGONIA

BEGONIA

Begonias are native to all tropical regions except Australia and there are over 1500 known species. They are prized for their beautifully colored foliage and attractive flowers, making an ideal indoor plant with a number of varieties readily available. This diverse group includes rhizomatous, fibrous-rooted and tuberous plants. They all have waxy leaves and a succulent form. They do well in indoor potting mix with either peat moss, leafmold or decomposed cow manure added to increase acidity. Grow in bright to moderate light with fresh air, above average humidity and temperatures of 60–85°F (about 15–30°C F). Humidity can be maintained by standing the pot on a tray of pebbles and water. Keep soil moist but not soggy. Fertilize in the spring growing season. Pinch back young plants to stop them becoming gangly and to encourage flowers. Most begonias can be propagated from stem and leaf cuttings in spring, by division of rhizomes or from seed. Begonias are susceptible to gray mold, powdery mildew and botrytis from late spring to early fall if conditions are too damp.

### *B. auriculata*

CATHEDRAL WINDOWS

This evergreen rhizomatous begonia grows to 12–15 in (about 30–38 cm) high and the spreading trunk to a width of 16 in (about 40 cm). The green and red leaves are thick and ear shaped. It has tall spikes of pink flowers.

### *B.* x *cheimantha* 'Gloire de Lorraine'

CHRISTMAS BEGONIA, LORRAINE BEGONIA

The single, white to pale pink flowers appear in winter on this round-leafed plant. The leaves are bright green and it grows to a height of 12 in (about 30 cm).

### *B.* 'Cleopatra'

This is a popular, easy-to-grow plant with 2 in (about 5 cm) wide, star-shaped leaves. The yellow-green leaves have brown markings with a reddish underside. Clusters of pale pink flowers bloom in early spring.

### *B. masoniana*

IRON CROSS BEGONIA

This plant's name is derived from the bold, brown, iron cross mark on the bright green, puckered leaves. This evergreen, rhizomatous plant grows to a height of 18–24 in (about 45–60 cm) and a spread of 12–18 in (about 30–45 cm). The single, pinkish white flowers are insignificant.

### *B. rex* 'Merry Christmas'

**syn. *B. ruhrtal***

*Rex* are the most common foliage begonias and are available in many cultivars. This evergreen, creeping, rhizomatous variety has a band of emerald green with a rose-red center and silver highlights on the leaf. The leaves are 6–8 in (about 15–20 cm) long with the plant growing to 10–12 in (about 25–30 cm) high.

## *BILLBERGIA*

VASE PLANT

This genus, comprising about 50 species and many garden varieties, was originally from the jungles of the American tropics where most grew on rocks or suspended in trees. With their exotic foliage of long, thin, stiff leaves, often edged with small teeth, and showy flowers, they are easy to grow and make an ideal indoor plant. The rosette of leaves form a cup and it is by filling this cup that the plant should be watered. A porous, fast-draining soil mix is required, but they will grow sitting in a pot of stones. The plant multiplies quickly and can be propagated by division. Brown leaves may be due to too much sun.

### *B. leptopoda*

The striking gray-green leaves are heavily powdered with silver and framed by small spines or teeth. Dark blue flowers enclosed in salmon-pink bracts appear in winter. A height of 12 in (about 30 cm) is reached. This is one of a number of similar species, all spectacular.

### *B. nutans*

QUEEN'S TEARS, FRIENDSHIP PLANT

Almost hardy, this species can be grown out of doors in shady places where it will only have to endure the occasional light frost. Indoors it likes a rich potting mix and good light. The leaves are long and narrow, plain olive green, and the pendent clusters of flowers appear in spring. They are a unique combination of pale green and navy blue, but it is the pink bracts that grow along the flower stems that catch the eye.

### *B. pyramidalis* var. *concolor*

A showy, erect spike of pyramid-shaped, rose-red and purple-tipped flowers appears from late summer to mid-winter. Broad, apple-green leaves form rosettes, sometimes with silver banding. It grows to 12–20 in (about 30–50 cm).

*Begonia* 'Cleopatra'

*Begonia rex* 'Merry Christmas'

*Billbergia nutans*

*Begonia* x *c.* 'Gloire de Lorraine'

*Begonia masoniana*

*Billbergia pyramidalis* var. *concolor*

*Begonia auriculata*

*Billbergia leptopoda*

*Costus speciosus*

*Calathea makoyana*

*Cordyline terminalis* 'Imperialis'

*Codiaeum variegatum*

*Callisia navicularis*

*Calathea zebrina*

## CALATHEA

PEACOCK PLANT

Native to South America and the West Indies, this large genus of plants are grown for their decorative foliage. The long-stalked, mostly upright leaves are usually large with beautiful colorings in shades of green, white, pink, purple and maroon, with contrasting markings. Many leaves have purple undersides. Calatheas require moderate to bright light, but never full sun, and high humidity achieved by misting frequently or standing the pot on a tray of pebbles and water. Do not allow to dry out completely and feed with half-strength fertilizer every 4 to 5 weeks, when conditions are warm and growth is active. A standard potting mix, with sand added to the mix for good drainage, is needed. Repot annually as they exhaust the soil and do not like to be overcrowded. Propagate by division in early spring.

### *C. makoyana*

PEACOCK PLANT

This dwarf species has oval, pale yellow-green leaves with a feathery design of darker green markings. The underside has the same markings in purple.

### *C. zebrina*

ZEBRA PLANT

The large, velvety, floppy leaves on short stems are deep green, marked by parallel stripes or bars of pale chartreuse. The undersides are purplish red. In winter the leaves turn yellow and can be removed to reveal clusters of chocolate brown bracts which are the spring flowers.

## CALLISIA *navicularis*

syn. *Tradescantia navicularis*

Grown for its decorative foliage, this low-growing perennial reaches 2–3 in (about 5–7.5 cm) high and has creeping shoots which root where they touch the soil. Two rows of oval, keeled, reddish green leaves enclose the stem. In summer to fall clusters of small, stalkless, 3-petaled, pink to purple flowers appear in the leaf axils. Grow in well-drained, moist, fertile soil in full light but not direct sunlight. Propagate from tip cuttings inserted into light compost in mid-spring or summer.

## CLERODENDRUM *thomsoniae*

BLEEDING HEART VINE, BLEEDING GLORY BOWER

A climbing, woody shrub from western tropical Africa, the popularity of this species derives from the clusters of crimson flowers emerging from white, bell-shaped calyces contrasted by large, oval, deep green leaves. Reaching 10 ft (about 3 m) in height, it requires high humidity and full though indirect sun. Keep the soil evenly moist during active growth and prune stems back after blooming has subsided. Propagate from stem cuttings.

## CODIAEUM *variegatum*

CROTON

Originally from Malaysia and Polynesia, this tropical, well-known indoor plant is grown for its brilliantly colored foliage. The glossy, leathery leaves come in a range of shapes and are variegated in red, yellow, pink and orange, with only the new leaves in green. The small flowers are insignificant. It reaches a height of 3–6 ft (about 90–180 cm). Grow outdoors only in warm climates in half- to full shade with a minimum temperature of 50–55°F (about 10–13°C). If grown indoors it requires bright light, a moist atmosphere and rich, well-drained soil. Water well during the warm season but allow to dry out between waterings when the temperature is low. To encourage branching, remove tips from very young plants. Repot in spring in a peaty compost. Propagate from stem cuttings in spring or summer.

## COLUMNEA *gloriosa*

GOLDFISH PLANT

Similar to its relative the lipstick plant, this Central American native produces an abundance of erect, brilliant yellow to red tubular flowers along the leaf axils.

## CORDYLINE *terminalis* 'Imperialis'

TI TREE, TI PLANT, HAPPY PLANT

Most plants of this species are started from "logs," which are small sections of mature branches imported from Hawaii. It resembles a palm with lance-shaped leaves on cane-like stems. The ti tree needs plenty of room indoors to grow to its full height of 6–12 ft (about 1.8–3.5 m). It prefers filtered sunlight and needs higher temperatures and humidity than others of the genus. To increase humidity, stand the plant on a tray of pebbles and water. It can be allowed to dry out in winter, but keep moist during the growing season from spring to fall. Fluoride in the water or perlite in the potting mix can cause browning of the leaves.

## COSTUS

SPIRAL FLAG, SPIRAL GINGER

This genus of clump-forming perennials comprises 150 species scattered throughout the tropics, particularly Asia and South America. They have attractive flowers carried in heads whose bracts are arranged rather like a pine cone. Preferring temperatures above 65°F (about 18°C), they are suitable for planting outdoors only in tropical or subtropical regions, but they make a showy indoor plant. Grow in humus-rich soil in a well-lit position, but not direct sunlight, and a humid atmosphere. It requires an abundance of water. Propagate by division or from seed in spring. Plants grown indoors may be bothered by red spider mite. *C. speciosus* bear white, sometimes pinkish, flowers with yellow centers.

## *CRYPTANTHUS*
### *zonatus*
ZEBRA PLANT, EARTH STAR

*Cryptanthus* have earned the name "earth star" because of the unusual shape of the low growing rosettes. *C. zonatus* is a native of Brazil, growing to 4–6 in (about 10–15 cm) high. The attractive foliage resembles a zebra skin with sepia-green leaves that are wavy edged and banded crosswise with ivory and tannish brown markings. In summer, a cluster of tubular, white flowers appears in each rosette. Grow in a standard potting mix with some sphagnum moss or peat added. Propagate from offsets which are liberally produced in late spring to summer.

## *CTENANTHE*
### *lubbersiana*
BAMBURANTA

Originally from Brazil, this splendidly marked, foliage plant is an erect, leafy perennial. It produces insignificant flowers. This variegated species grows to 30 in (about 76 cm) or more. The lance-shaped, green leaves are patterned in irregularly shaded bands of pale yellow-green with pale green undersides. The attractive leaves grow on tall, branching stems. Small, white flowers on one-sided spikes are produced intermittently. Grow in a standard potting mix; add coarse sand to aid drainage. A humid atmosphere is important, so mist foliage occasionally. Propagate by division or from basal offsets in spring, but do not repot too often as it likes to be crowded.

## *CYCLAMEN*
### *persicum*
FLORIST'S CYCLAMEN

From the woodlands of the Middle East, this is the most common species grown indoors and is readily available. From the heart-shaped leaves, which are often marbled light and dark green with silver markings, rise waxy flowers in shades of white and pink, sometimes ruffled or edged with a contrasting tone. There is profuse flowering over a long period in winter. Needs high humidity so stand on a tray of pebbles. To continue flowering it must be kept cool at night. Thoroughly water, avoiding getting water in among the bases of the leaves for fear of rot, then let the surface become just dry. In summer leave in the pot but do not

*Cyperus involucratus*

*Dieffenbachia* 'Amoena'

water. Repot in fall in potting mix with a sprinkling of lime and blood and bone; resume watering.

## *CYPERUS*
### *involucratus*
**syn. *C. flabelliformis***

Grass-like plants, *Cyperus* come from tropical and subtropical areas. *C. involucratus* grows to around 3 ft (about 90 cm) and sends up triangular, hollow stalks crowned by a whorl of leaf-like bracts. The green flower spikes appear in summer. Grow in rich compost and water well by standing the pot in a dish of water. Direct sunlight is tolerated. Repot when the plant fills the container.

## *DIEFFENBACHIA*
DUMB CANE

These decorative foliage plants from tropical America reach ceiling height when mature. The large, variegated leaves are oval-shaped. Popular indoor plants, they are easy to grow provided humidity is maintained by mist spraying, and extremes of temperatures are minimized by keeping them away from windows in winter. Bright to moderate light suits them. Allow the surface soil to become dry in between waterings as root rot may occur if over-watered. Propagate in spring or summer from cuttings or stems laid horizontally in compost,

*Cyclamen persicum*

*Cryptanthus zonatus*

but be careful to wash your hands. The common name is due to the poisonous sap which causes the mouth and tongue to swell, rendering speech impossible.

### *D.* 'Amoena'
**syn. *D. seguine* 'Amoena'**

This robust plant of up to 6 ft (about 1.8 m) has large, sword-like, deep green leaves marked with cream-white bars and blotches along the lateral veins. It has insignificant, greenish white flowers and flourishes in poor light.

*Ctenanthe lubbersiana*

*Drosera capensis*

*Episcia cupreata*

*Episcia* 'Pink Brocade'

*Epipremnum aureum*

*Dizygotheca elegantissima*

*Dieffenbachia s.* 'Rudolph Roehrs'

*D. seguine* 'Rudolph Roehrs'
**syn. *D. seguine* 'Roehrsii'**

Slightly smaller, growing to 3 ft (about 90 cm) or more, this plant has sword-like, chartreuse leaves with mid-rib and edges in green.

## DIZYGOTHECA
*elegantissima*
**syn. *Aralia elegantissima***
FALSE ARALIA, FINGER ARALIA

An elegant, erect plant from the New Hebrides which can grow to 6 ft (about 1.8 m) indoors. When young, the leaves are bronze-green changing to a lustrous, dark green with maturity. Between 7 and 10 thin, finger-like leaflets with saw-toothed edges grow from slender, mottled green stems. Grow in an all-purpose soil mix in bright, indirect light with no direct sun. Water well during growing period, and at other times only when the top soil is dry—it is extremely sensitive to the level of moisture in the soil, developing leaf drop if it is too high. Difficult to propagate, it prefers to be pot bound; repot every 2 to 3 years in spring. Susceptible to red spider mite and mealy bug. It can be grown outdoors in warm, frost-free climates, where it grows to an 18 ft (about 5.5 m) tree with coarse adult foliage—very different from the way it looks indoors.

## DROSERA
*capensis*
CAPE SUNDEW

This insect-eating plant grows to 6 in (about 15 cm) with small rosettes of narrow leaves covered in sensitive, red, glandular hairs which secrete fluid. It attracts insects which get stuck to the leaves and are digested by enzyme secretions. In summer there are many small, purple flowers on leafless stems. Frost tender and delicate to grow it should be planted in a pot, preferably in a greenhouse, in a mixture of peat and sphagnum moss, standing the pot on a saucer of water. If grown outdoors plant in the sun in a similar mixture; do not let the soil dry out. Water only with rainwater as it is very sensitive to the impurities found in tapwater. Propagate from seed or by division of rhizomes in spring.

## EPIPREMNUM
*aureum*
**syn. *Scindapsus aureus***
POTHOS, DEVIL'S IVY

This evergreen root climber is sometimes mistaken for a philodendron. It is a fast-growing plant which can be kept in water for months or planted in good, rich, moisture-retentive soil. The apple-green, heart-shaped leaves are marbled with creamy white or gold. It needs bright, indirect light and a humid and draught-free location. Water regularly during spring and summer, less in winter. Pinch out shoot tips to encourage branching. Propagate in late spring from leaf bud or stem cuttings, which are kept in barely moist soil in a dark position until they have rooted. Poor light may cause a lack of variegation.

## EPISCIA

From the jungles of tropical America and the West Indies, this relative of the African violet makes an ideal plant for hanging baskets. The attractive, ornamental leaves cascade from runners down the sides of the pot or basket with, given the right conditions, long-lasting, colorful flowers. Plant in African violet mix or porous, peaty, indoor plant mix in bright light (no direct sun). They require constant warmth and humidity, so are well suited to a sunny bathroom or glassed area. Keep moist at all times, but take care not to over-water as it leads to rotting. Pinch back stems after flowering to encourage branching, and repot every year in spring. Propagate in summer by laying runners in compost, from stem cuttings or by division. Lack of flowers may be due to poor light.

*E. cupreata*
FLAME VIOLET

The attractive, felted, bronze leaves have silver veins. This plant intermittently produces tubular, scarlet flowers with yellow centers.

*E.* 'Pink Brocade'

The runners bear deep, copper-green leaves variegated in silver and pink. Small pink flowers appear in summer but not freely.

## FERNS

Their love of shady places makes ferns eligible for indoor culture, and many species do very well. For recommendations check the chapter "Ferns, Palms & Cycads."

## FICUS

A genus of great variety, with some of the most reliable and adaptable house plants, grown for their foliage and tropical effect. Their leathery leaves allow them to tolerate a dry atmosphere. They need bright light, but will tolerate low light and an average room temperature and a winter temperature of at least 55°F (about 13°C). Water moderately, keeping moist in the warmer months, and very little when the temperature is low. Over-watering may lead to leaf drop. Sponge leaves with a damp cloth. Propagate from stem or leaf bud cuttings and repot when roots fill the pot, but remember, figs like to be slightly cramped.

*F. benjamina*

WEEPING FIG

One of the most popular of the indoor figs beause of its graceful, slightly weeping habit. The 2–4 in (about 5–10 cm) long glossy green leaves taper to a long point and are quite leathery. The leaves of 'Variegata' are edged with white. Bushy young plants are often 2–3 ft (about 60–90 cm) and at maturity will reach 15–18 ft (about 4.5–5.5 m). It grows well in medium to bright light and temperatures above 50°F (about 10°C). Avoid drafty locations and sudden temperature changes.

*F. elastica* 'Decora'

INDIA RUBBER TREE, RUBBER PLANT

One of the most foolproof of all indoor plants, this strong-growing *Ficus* has broad, leathery, glossy, deep green leaves 8–12 in (about 20–30 cm) long. New leaves are encased in rosy pink sheaths that wither and drop, the emerging leaves having a pinkish bronze hue. They can grow to 9 ft (about 2.7 m) or more and tolerate less light than most plants of this size.

*F. lyrata*

FIDDLE-LEAF FIG

A handsome indoor plant, particularly when young, it has huge, lustrous, dark green leaves shaped like a fiddle. The leaves are 12 in (about 30 cm) or more long and are prominently veined. It may grow to 9 ft (about 2.7 m) indoors and will tolerate low light.

## *GESNERIA*

*cuneifolia*

FLORAL FIRE CRACKER

The genus *Gesneria* is native to the islands of the Caribbean and are ideal for growing in terrariums. The dark green leaves have light green undersides, are spoon shaped and serrated, and can grow to a length of 6 in (about 15 cm). The bright orange, tubular flowers appearing from leaf axils are the size of small Chinese crackers. They bloom mostly in summer and the duration of the bloom depends on temperature. They like a well-drained, leaf-rich soil, bright light and high humidity. Keep well watered and propagate in spring from leaf cuttings or by division of rooted runners.

## *GRAPTOPHYLLUM*

*pictum*

CARICATURE PLANT

This evergreen shrub grows to over 3 ft (about 90 cm) in height and has oval, pointed, green leaves; the leaves have yellow variegation in the center. In spring and summer red to purple tubular flowers appear on terminal spikes. It likes a position in well-drained, fertile soil in part shade. *Graptophyllum pictum* can be grown outdoors in subtropical climates. Give plenty of water when growing in the warmer months and less in cooler weather. It requires temperatures above 60°F (about 15°C). To promote branching, tip prune young plants and cut back hard after flowering. Propagate from semi-ripe cuttings in spring or summer.

## *GUZMANIA*

The plants in this genus of bromeliads are known for their formation of rosettes of smooth leaves and attractive flowers. The long-lasting bracts in red, green or yellow surround a spike of white flowers. Grow in a pot of open, rubble-filled compost. Water moderately during the growing season, less at other times, but always keep the leaf vases filled with water. Propagate in spring or summer from suckers on the parent stem; the original plant usually dies after flowering. *G. lingulata* is the most common of the genus, with basal rosettes of broadly strap-shaped, apple-green leaves growing to a height of 12–18 in(about 30–45 cm). The much showier orange-red bracts surround the clusters of tubular, white to yellow flowers.

## *HEDERA*

COMMON ENGLISH IVY

There are several species of ivy, but the most famous and the only one to thrive indoors is *H. helix*, which is available in many named varieties. As a trailing plant it makes an excellent hanging basket, but it can also be trained to climb almost any kind of support. It comes in a wide array of leaf shapes and colors. Use an all-purpose potting soil and place in a cool, bright spot. It will tolerate some direct weak sun, and likes extra humidity by misting or placing on a tray of pebbles and water. Keep moist, but not soggy, and do not let the soil dry out completely. In spring, prune to encourage bushy growth. Propagate from stem cuttings or rooted runners.

*H. helix* 'Cripsii'

VARIEGATED IVY

There are many cultivars of ivy with variegated leaves, suitable for growing indoors. 'Cripsii' has attractive marblings of dark gray-green with cream; 'Glacier' and 'Gloire de Marengo' are similar in color. 'Goldheart' is perhaps the best of the green-and-gold cultivars.

*Gesneria cuneifolia*

*Guzmania lingulata*

*Graptophyllum pictum*

*Ficus elastica* 'Decora'

*Hedera helix* 'Crispii'

*Ficus lyrata*

# A Field Trip to Fortin de las Flores

The little town of Fortin de las Flores is about a one-day drive east from Mexico City. Set in lush tropical jungle, Fortin is a mecca for bromeliad lovers in general, and more particularly a major native habitat for the epiphytic bromeliad, *Tillandsia ionantha*. This is one of the "air plants," so-called because they do not use roots to obtain nutrients and appear to survive on nothing but air. The trip to Fortin takes you comfortably along the toll roads that radiate from Mexico City to outlying areas. You will pass through a wide variety of landscapes—green valleys, desert vegetation, mountain country, tropical jungle and pine forests—in abrupt and striking succession.

The toll road following highway F190 and then F150 takes you through the states of Puebla and Veracruz in the heart of Mexico, a region rich in churches and pyramids as well as orchids and bromeliads. On the way you will have the rewarding experience of seeing four of the country's most famous mountains (Popocatepetl, Ixtaccihuatl, Malinche and Orizaba), all snow-capped and in stark contrast to the surrounding jungle.

This route also takes you through the city of Puebla, one of Mexico's oldest and yet most progressive centers. Continuing on past the Tehuacan turn-off, the road climbs the Sierra Madre Oriental mountain range, at an altitude of 7200 ft (about 2200 m), and there are spectacular views of the valley of Acultzingo. At the peak you can find broad leaf air plants of the genus *Tillandsia* thriving in the moist and cloudy atmosphere. Soon however, you will quickly descend to an oak forest which is home to the succulents *Echeveria nuda* and coral-beads *(Sedum stahlii)*.

*Mexican landscapes vary from desert to jungle to mountainsides.*

If you have time, a side trip to the Tehuacan Valley provides an ideal opportunity for cactus lovers. In areas uncleared by farming you can find many huge cacti colonies of the genera *Opuntia*, *Stenocereus*, *Ferocactus* and *Mammillaria*, and also various *Agave* species. It is also home to some of the drier-growing air plants, including the ball moss *(Tillandsia recurvata)* and several related species.

On the road to Fortin is the home of Dr Alfred Lau, an evangelist and leading world cacti expert whose interests extend to the conservation of orchids, bromeliads, passion flower vines and other tropical plants. A visit to his garden is a must. There you can wander through 3 acres (1.2 ha) of landscaped garden, featuring epiphytes landscaped on to citrus and other trees. A nearby motel, the Posada Loma, is the usual stopping point for bromeliad enthusiasts, as it too has an excellent garden.

The town of Fortin de las Flores is a beehive of people, bars, open-style shops, livestock, and even a resort hotel. The town is surrounded by jungle, and trails run into it from the edges of town. It is possible to walk these trails, starting at the edge of the tropical fruit orchards or roadsides, to study the rich variety of flora, bird life and, occasionally, animals. It is a delight to sit quietly and watch the humming birds feeding from the flowers and you may even catch sight of the elusive toucan or bands of spider monkeys.

In the jungle around Fortin the blushing bride *(Tillandsia ionantha)* can be found growing on the trees both above and in front of you. Fallen branches make the best studies as recently fallen branches will still have plants intact and alive. Usually no more than 2 in (about 5 cm) across, *T. ionantha* grows either singly or in clumps, forming a rosette of fleshy pointed leaves frosted with silver scales. Its common name, blushing bride, refers to the way the leaves turn red when the plant is in bloom, in contrast to the blue of its flowers.

*Tillandsias growing on tree trunks in the jungle.*

*Tillandsia ionantha*

Ball moss *(T. recurvata)* grows here too, with other air plants. This small, clumping plant with small blue flowers grows in ball formations on trees, power lines and house roofs. Another air plant that grows in association with *T. ionantha* is Spanish moss *(T. usneoides)*, which has long, gray strands and small, scented, green flowers. Its habit of tangling around tree branches makes it popular as bird nest material.

Be careful when examining the larger air plants. They hold quantities of water between their leaves, and a plant tipped on to the ground is likely to reveal cockroaches, salamanders, frogs, spiders and other insects that could sting and bite. As well, watch out for paper wasp nests in the trees as even a slight tap on these can disturb the wasps.

A short trip north on highway F139 will bring you to the town of Huatusco, where *T. ionantha* was first recorded in 1898. The jungle in this area is also home to many beautiful broad leaf air plants including *T. deppeana*, *T. multicaulis* and *T. lieboldiana,* which has bright red bracts and blue tubular flowers which attract pollinating birds and butterflies. If you study the moss-covered branches you will also find many different orchids, cacti and ferns, as well as various *Columnea* and *Anthurium* species. On the floor of the jungle grow giant *Spathiphyllum* species, including elephant ears, which are used as rain hats by the Indian children. Fruit salad plant *(Monstera deliciosa)* is common in all its trailing and compact forms. The color-changing chameleon and brightly colored iguana are among the many lizards seen scuttling across the roads and walking tracks. The jaguar and ocelot, both magnificent cats, can occasionally be spotted in the area.

The best time to visit this area is during the earlier months of the year, when the average temperature is around 64°F (about 18°C), and before the rainy season which lasts from June to September.

The whole region covered in this field trip is botanically very rich, but for those who love bromeliads, particularly the epiphytic ones, the jungle around Fortin is the botanic equivalent of heaven.

## *Tillandsia*

Tillandsias are members of the Bromeliaceae family. With 1500 or more species divided among about 60 genera, the family is almost entirely confined to the Americas, the majority South American.

*Tillandsia* is the largest bromeliad genus, and it is best represented in Mexico and the adjacent countries. Its over 400 species include the most extreme epiphytes, or "air plants," which appear literally to subsist on nothing but air. Most tillandsias have leaves clothed in minute silvery scales which behave like sponges, soaking up water from rain or mist and absorbing it into the plant's tissues. The scales also trap dust and fine organic debris, from which the plants derive their nutrient minerals; rainwater also contributes essential nitrogen, converted to soluble form by tropical thunderstorms. Successful cultivation of tillandsias requires high humidity combined with high light levels.

Many new forms of *T. ionantha* are emerging, especially from countries in which they are grown for the commercial horticultural market. Popular for its unusual appearance and its adaptability, *T. ionantha* is exported in huge quantities from Mexico and other Central American countries to satisfy a growing world market.

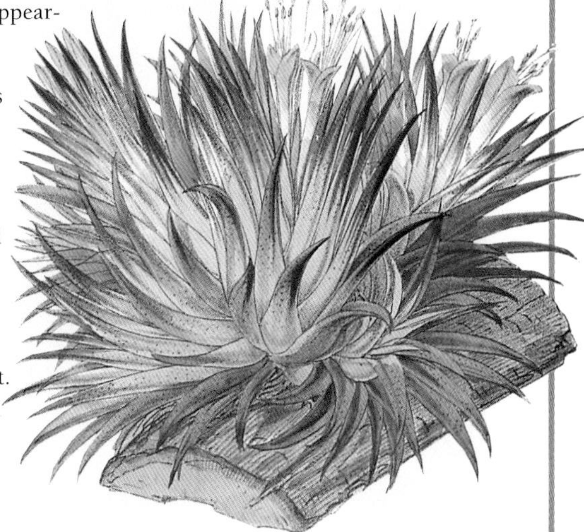

*Tillandsia ionantha*

*Hoya carnosa*

*Hoya bella*

*Nematanthus gregarius*

*H. helix* 'Pittsburgh'

**syn. *H. helix* 'Hahn's Self-branching'**

A dense, branching plant, this cultivar has closely set, small, deep green leaves.

## *HEMIGRAPHIS*

### *alternata*

RED IVY

This creeping or trailing plant has wonderful foliage of ivy-like, heart-shaped or oblong, deeply puckered, metallic, purplish gray leaves with wine-red undersides and stems. The white summer flowers hardly show at all. Grow in an all-purpose potting mix in bright light, but not direct sunlight. They like average room temperature and humidity. Keep moist and water frequently in the growing season, less in winter. Cut back the spindly stems and pinch off the growing tips to encourage a bushy shape. Propagate from stem cuttings in spring or summer. It is rarely bothered by pests.

*Hedera helix* 'Pittsburgh'

*Maranta leuconeura* var. *kerchoviana*

*Monstera deliciosa*

## *HOYA*

Twining and/or root climbers with waxy foliage, native to Malaysia, China, India and tropical Australia. They all bear clusters of scented, star-shaped flowers in summer. If the plant is supported on a frame and also slightly pot bound it is more likely to flower, but may not do so for several years. Plant in any potting soil that drains well, in bright to very bright light, with moderate temperatures and humidity. Allow the soil surface to become quite dry between waterings. As the new flowers come from the same spurs as the old ones it is best not to prune or pick. Propagate from semi-ripe cuttings in summer. Be careful where you place the plant as sticky honeydew drips from the flowers.

*H. bella*

BEAUTIFUL HONEY PLANT

From India, this shrubby species has pendulous stems and bright green, narrow, lance-shaped leaves. It looks best when grown in a hanging pot or basket where the summer flowers can be easily admired. The star-shaped white flowers, with red or purplish pink centers, hang in flattened clusters.

*H. carnosa*

WAX PLANT

Native to Australia, this twining plant can be grown against a small framework. From summer to fall it has dark green, glossy, oval leaves and scented, star-shaped flowers, white to pink in color and with dark pink centers.

## *HYPOESTES*

### *phyllostachya*

POLKA-DOT PLANT

A native of Madagascar, this popular indoor plant is grown for its colorful lavender-pink spotted leaves. Though it can grow to 3 ft (about 90 cm), it is best kept pruned to 12–18 in (about 30–45 cm). Average temperatures and filtered to bright light produce the most colorful leaves. Allow the soil to dry between waterings and fertilize every 2 weeks during active growth periods. Propagate from stem tip cuttings.

## *MARANTA*

### *leuconeura* var. *kerchoviana*

RABBIT TRACKS, PRAYER PLANT

*Maranta* is a genus from tropical America, containing plants grown for their strongly patterned, colored foliage. Variety *kerchoviana* has oval, light green leaves with brown blotches on either side of the central vein. The insignificant white to mauve flowers appear intermittently. *Maranta* in general are called "prayer plants" because they fold their leaves into a vertical or upright position, as in prayer, to funnel the condensing dew down to the roots. Grow in humus-rich, well-drained soil, using a shallow container, in moderate to low light. They need even, warm temperature and high humidity, but avoid mist spraying as the leaves are easily marked. Keep continually moist. Propagate from stem cuttings or by division in spring or summer. Dry soil or low humidity may cause browning of leaf tips.

## *MONSTERA*

### *deliciosa*

FRUIT SALAD PLANT, SWISS-CHEESE PLANT

A close relative of *Philodendron* and a native of the West Indies and tropical America, the huge, broad, glossy, perforated and deeply cut leaves of *M. deliciosa* grow from woody stems with aerial roots. Mature plants bear thick, cream spathes, followed by sweet-smelling, cone-like, edible fruits that take about a year to ripen and usually only outdoors. They are easy to grow and adjust to all but the coldest indoor conditions. Plant in an all-purpose mix in large containers with a stout support for the aerial roots. Some roots can be planted back into the container to help support the plant. Requires bright, indirect light and a high degree of humidity. Water when soil is dry to touch, and feed monthly with a soluble plant food during warm conditions. As *M. deliciosa* prefer to be pot bound, repot every 2 to 3 years in spring. Prune tops off tall plants to limit growth. The lower leaves will drop, but serious leaf drop may result if the plant is moved or there is a sudden environmental change.

## *NEMATANTHUS*

### *gregarius*

**syn. *N. radicans*, *Hypocyrta radicans***

CLOG PLANT

A relatively easy to grow, trailing plant, it has closely set, glossy, dark green leaves. The dark yellow or orange flowers look puffy and bloom throughout the year, es-

*Nidularium fulgens*

*Neoregelia carolinae* 'Tricolor'

*Pedilanthus tithymaloides*

pecially if it is slightly pot bound. It prefers an African violet potting soil mix and bright light with some cool morning sun. Keep the soil moist and the atmosphere humid by placing on a tray of pebbles and water, or mist frequently. It can be grown outdoors in partial shade but is frost tender.

## NEOREGELIA

About 50 species and many varieties comprise this spectacular genus of bromeliads. They produce some of the largest rosettes of colorful, thick, shiny leaves, designed to attract fertilizing insects to the tiny flowers blooming deep within the vase. They need bright light with some direct sunlight to maintain color, and a humid atmosphere. Water regularly and keep the rosette centers full at all times. Propagate from offsets in spring or summer.

### *N. carolinae*

HEART OF FLAME, BLUSHING BROMELIAD

A spreading rosette of 16–24 in (about 40–60 cm) across, composed of light olive-green, strap-shaped, saw-toothed leaves. Just before flowering, which can be at any time of the year, the youngest, inner leaves turn crimson. The cluster of small, inconspicuous, blue-purple flowers is surrounded by crimson-red bracts. The cultivar 'Tricolor', with cream-striped leaves, is seen more often than the species itself.

### *N. marmorata*

Spreading to 20–24 in (about 50–60 cm), the rosettes of red-tipped, pale green leaves are mottled in reddish brown. White flowers bloom deep in the vase in spring to summer.

## NEPENTHES

PITCHER PLANT

These insectivorous plants have adapted leaves which form pendulous, colored pitchers with lids. Insects are attracted to these and drown in the liquid in the pitcher before being absorbed into the plant as food. In rainforests, plants climb via tendrils on the leaf ends. They are suitable for hanging baskets in a

*Peperomia caperata*

garden where the minimum temperature is 65°F (about 18°C), or for a greenhouse in a temperate climate. Grow as an indoor plant in moist, fertile soil with peat and moss added, in filtered sun and a very humid atmosphere. Propagate from stem cuttings in spring or summer, or from seed in spring.

## NIDULARIUM
### *fulgens*

BIRD'S NEST BROMELIAD

Sometimes called "friendship plants" and resembling the genus *Neoregelia*, *N. fulgens* has dense rosettes of strap-shaped, saw-toothed, glossy, yellow-green foliage with dark green spots. A rosette of scarlet bracts surrounds the white and violet flowers, which appear mainly in summer. The plant is happy in any open, fibrous mix. Position in an area of bright light for good foliage and color. Water regularly, keeping the rosettes full at all times. Propagate from offsets in spring or summer.

## PALMS

Many of the smaller species of palm—and some of the larger, at least in their youth—grow very happily indoors. For recommendations check the chapter "Ferns, Palms & Cycads."

## PEDILANTHUS
### *tithymaloides*

ZIGZAG PLANT, DEVIL'S BACKBONE, JACOB'S LADDER

Popular as a greenhouse plant in Britain in the nineteenth century,

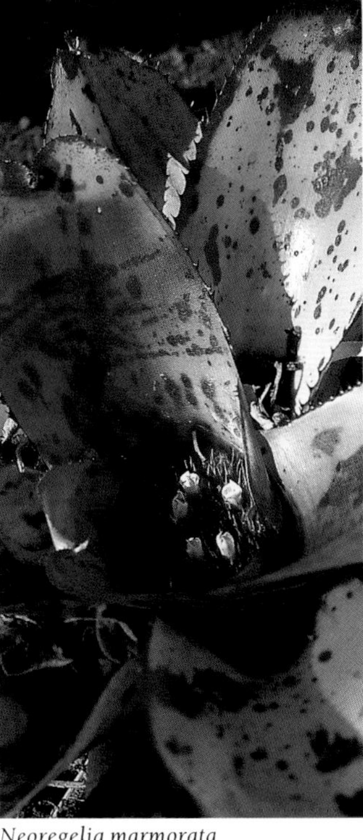
*Neoregelia marmorata*

this slow-growing succulent from the West Indies usually grows to around 18 in (about 45 cm). The fleshy, erect stems change direction at each node, hence the name "zigzag plant." Leaves are mid-green and sprout from the stems in two rows, resembling ribs on a backbone. (Variegated cultivars are popular.) Showy red bracts shaped like a bird's head encase small, scarlet flowers, but such flowers are rarely produced indoors. Water sparingly, allowing the soil surface to dry out between waterings. The plant needs very bright light with some direct sun and a dry atmosphere, so it is well suited to wintering in heated rooms. Propagate from seed or summer cuttings, hardened thoroughly. The stems, when cut, secrete poisonous, milky sap. Mildew may be caused by a humid atmosphere.

## PEPEROMIA

RADIATOR PLANT

Most of these small plants come from the tropical rainforests of Central and South America. Ideal in terrariums or dish gardens, they have diverse and beautifully marked and shaped leaves. They produce long-stemmed spikes of flowers. Well suited to the average home environment, peperomias like bright light (but not direct sun), especially near a window, with high humidity in summer. Keep moist in warm weather, and be sure to water the plants from below as the leaves mark easily; in winter it is best to allow the plants to dry out between waterings. Use a half-strength, soluble fertilizer once a month in spring and summer. Peperomias are easily propagated from leaf or from stem cuttings in spring or summer. Repot annually.

*Nepenthes*, hybrid

### *P. caperata*

EMERALD RIPPLE

From the pinkish stems of this species grow oval, deeply corrugated and veined, dark green leaves. Tight clusters of white flower spikes appear irregularly. Propagate from leaf or stem cuttings in spring or summer.

*Pisonia umbellifera* 'Variegata'

*Philodendron selloum*

*Peperomia obtusifolia* 'Royal Gold'

*Philodendron bipennifolium*

*Philodendron oxycardium*

*Peperomia* 'Sweetheart'

### *P. obtusifolia*

BABY RUBBER PLANT

This is a bushy perennial with fleshy leaves and occasional spikes of minute flowers. The plain green species is a handsome plant growing about 12 in (about 30 cm) tall. More common are the variegated cultivars with the leaves marbled in gray-green and cream or gold. Good light but not direct sun is needed. Cut back if the plants grow straggly and propagate from cuttings.

### *P.* 'Sweetheart'

Typical of the hybrid peperomias that appear from time to time, 'Sweetheart' is named for its heart-shaped leaves. *P. marmorata*, the silver-heart peperomia, resembles it except that the leaves have silver markings. Both are a shade larger than *P. caperata*.

## *PHILODENDRON*

PHILODENDRON

Shrubs or climbers native to the tropical forests of Central and South America, these are adaptable, strong plants with handsome leaves and a long life expectancy, making them successful and popular indoors. Arum-like flowers are produced on mature plants in optimum conditions. Grow in bright light with a warm, moist atmosphere, as high humidity improves growth. Water when the surface soil dries out and sponge any dust from the leaves. They need support by tying the aerial roots to a stout pole or moss-covered netting. Remove young stem tips to encourage branching. Philodendrons like to be crowded, so do not plant in too large a pot. Most will drop their lower leaves. Propagate from stem or leaf bud cuttings in summer. They are free from pests and diseases.

### *P. bipennifolium*

**syn. *P. panduriforme***

FIDDLE-LEAF PHILODENDRON

This climber attaches itself to suitable supports by means of aerial roots. A decorative plant, it is unusual for the guitar-like shape of the lobed, bright green leaves. It likes medium light, and in a large pot will grow 6–9 ft (about 1.8–2.7 m) tall. Cut back if necessary; it will drop its lower leaves.

### *P. oxycardium*

**syn. *P. scandens***

SWEETHEART VINE, MONEY PLANT

A rapid climber with glossy, heart-shaped, rich green leaves. It may either grow up a column or trail down. It grows to a height of 10 ft (about 3 m) or more. The aerial roots on the trailing stems will attach to anything. This is the most common and popular of the genus.

### *P. selloum*

Officially a climber, but in effect a clumpy perennial with a short stem from which the huge, deeply lobed leaves are carried on stalks 24 in (about 60 cm) or more long. It is a magnificent specimen plant, though as a full-grown specimen it can reach $4^1/_2$ ft (about 1.3 m) high and wide, a bit big for all but the largest rooms. Several cultivars are available, some smaller than usual, others with variegated leaves, and there are several even larger hybrids of which 'Sao Paolo' is most notable. The flowers are insignificant.

## *PISONIA*

### *umbellifera* 'Variegata'

BIRDCATCHER TREE, MAP PLANT

Known in its native New Zealand as "Para para," the 12–16 in (about 30–40 cm) oval leaves of this plant are beautifully patterned in tones of pale to dark green and creamy white, resembling a map (hence the common name). The small, greenish flowers rarely appear indoors. The fruit that forms when grown in its native habitat gave it the other common name of "birdcatcher tree." Grow in a standard indoor mix in warm temperature and bright light, but keep out of direct sun, wind or warm draughts. Water freely and regularly during the growing season, but in winter allow to dry out between waterings. Mist the plant, and wipe the leaves with milk and water when dull. To encourage bushing, pinch out the growing tips while the plant is young. Propagate from semi-ripe cuttings in summer.

## *POLYSCIAS filicifolia*

FERN-LEAF ARALIA, MING ARALIA

*P. filicifolia,* from tropical Asia and Polynesia, is an unusual house plant with large, 12 in (about 30 cm) long leaves divided into bright green, serrated leaflets. They are not easy to grow as they are fussy plants. Grow in a container of standard peaty mix with sand and a little charcoal added. It needs bright light (but not direct sunlight) and warm temperature—keep away from glass windows in cool climates. Keep humidity high by misting or standing on a tray of pebbles and water, and keep out of draughts. Water freely in summer; keep drier at other times. Feed monthly with half-strength, soluble fertilizer during the warm months. *P. filicifolia* is at its best when the plants are young as the stems tend to grow straggly. These, however, can be cut back in spring. It prefers to be pot bound so repot only when roots emerge from the pot hole. Propagate from stem tip or stem section cuttings in summer. Watch for red spider mites and scale.

## *PROTASPARAGUS*

**syn. *Asparagus***

ASPARAGUS FERN

These climbers are grown for their foliage. They are related to the asparagus of the kitchen table, but their shoots are too skinny to eat. They need a fertile, well-drained soil. Propagate in spring by division or from seed.

### *P. densiflorus* 'Sprengeri'

This is a sprawling, trailing perennial which grows from small tubers. Its stems grow around 32 in (about 81 cm) long and, being well clad with bright green leaves, they look charming trailing from a hanging basket, despite the occasional sharp thorns. In early spring it bears abundant tiny, white, heavily scented, flowers, usually followed by red berries. Remove spent stems for neatness. Requires good light and regular watering.

### *P. setaceus*

**syn. *Asparagus plumosus***

A slender, climbing perennial with leaves divided many times into tiny segments, giving an ultra-ferny appearance. It is very easy to grow, provided it is never allowed to quite dry out and receives good light. Old leaves need to be removed for neatness, and over-long stems can be cut to the base in early spring to encourage new growth. Handle with care as the plant has some hooked and razor-sharp thorns. Propagate by division or from seed, in spring.

## *SAINTPAULIA*

AFRICAN VIOLET

A native of East Africa, saintpaulias were originally collected in the late nineteenth century by Baron von Saint Paul. The several thousand varieties are some of the most popular flowering indoor plants because of their attractive foliage, compact nature, long flowering periods and wide range of flower colors. Although African violets have a reputation for being difficult to grow, given the right conditions this is generally not the case. They do demand certain soil, however, so it is easiest to plant in commercial African violet mix. Constant temperature, moderate humidity and maximum, bright, indirect light will ensure prolonged flowering. In winter this may need to be supplemented with artificial light. Use room temperature water, allowing the surface soil to dry out a little between waterings. Avoid splashing the foliage. Feed once a month in the warm season with half-strength, soluble fertilizer. If the plant is overleafy flowers may not appear, so remove some of the leaves. African violets prefer to be slightly pot bound to bloom well, but repot when very leafy and no longer flowering well. They are easy to propagate from leaf cuttings stuck in a layer of pebbles on top of a moist sand and peat mixture, so that leaves do not rot. African violets are vulnerable to attack by powdery mildew.

### *S. ionantha*

*Ionantha* means "with violet-like flowers" in Greek, and this species has clusters of tubular, 5-lobed, violet-blue flowers of semi-succulent texture, growing on the stems above the leaves. The mid-green leaves, with reddish green undersides, are scalloped, fleshy and usually have a hairy surface. There are thousands of cultivars available, now far removed from the species. The flowers can be single or double, usually 1–2 in (about 2.5–5 cm) across, and come in shades from white through mauve and blue to purple, and pale and deep pink to crimson. Some cultivars are particolored and others have ruffled, scalloped or variegated leaves. Named cultivars are available, but they change constantly and most growers simply offer a selection by color and flower type. Fully grown plants are normally 10 in (about 25 cm) wide.

### *S.* miniature and trailing types

These African violets are derived from crosses of *S. ionantha* and other lesser known *Saintpaulia* species. They can be compact rosettes, no more than 3 in (about 7.5 cm) across with leaves and flowers in proportion—effectively miniatures of the *S. ionantha* cultivars and available in the same range of colors—or trailing types, which may develop stems as much as 4 in (about 10 cm) long. The leaves and flowers are equally tiny; some flowers are bell shaped rather than flat. These miniature types have the reputation of being easier to grow than the large ones, but their tiny pots dry out quickly and they do need regular watering. Repot when very leafy and no longer flowering well.

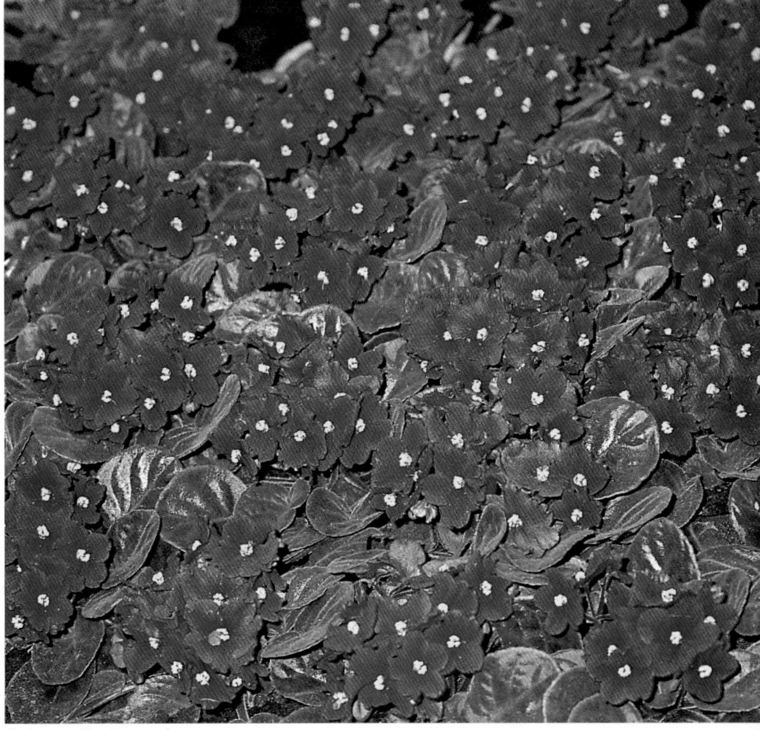

*Saintpaulia ionantha*

*Protasparagus densiflorus* 'Sprengeri'

*Polyscias filicifolia*

*Saintpaulia* (miniature)

*Protasparagus setaceus*

## SANSEVIERIA

BOWSTRING HEMP, MOTHER-IN-LAW'S TONGUE

Native to India and to southern and tropical Africa, these popular and resilient indoor plants are grown for their stiff, fleshy, patterned 12–24 in (about 30–60 cm) tall leaves. Stems of greenish white flowers appear in late spring if conditions have been warm enough during the previous year. The flowers have a slight fragrance. Grow in standard, indoor potting soil with a deep layer of pot rubble for drainage. For good growth, place in bright light with average house temperature and humidity. Sansevierias look their best, however, when the humidity is high, so mist occasionally. Water enough to moisten the soil but allow to dry between waterings in warm weather and, in cool weather, only enough to prevent the soil drying out completely. Over-watering may cause rotting at the base of the leaves and roots. Feed monthly in spring and summer with half-strength, soluble plant food. Repot only when the plant fills the pot. Propagate from leaf cuttings or by division in spring or summer. In Africa the fibers are a source of hemp.

### *S. trifasciata*

From the central rosette emerge stiff, lance-shaped leaves, 2–4 ft (about 60–120 cm) long, and 2 in (about 5 cm) or more wide. The dark green leaves are banded with gray-green and yellow. The plant sometimes has racemes of tubular, green flowers.

### *S. trifasciata* 'Hahnii'

This plant has rosettes of banded, gray and green leaves, and is smaller than the other two sansevierias mentioned.

### *S. trifasciata* 'Laurentii'

The narrow upright leaves resemble *S. trifasciata* but they have broad, yellow margins. It sometimes has pale green flowers. Propagate by division.

## SCHEFFLERA

**syn. *Brassaia, Heptapleurum***

These attractive, subtropical and tropical trees can grow to 6–12 ft (about 1.8–3.5 m) indoors and much taller outdoors. The glossy foliage is split into leaflets. They are easy to grow (but rarely flower) indoors. Plant in a standard indoor potting soil, in bright light but no direct sunlight, with average to warm temperatures. Keep humidity high by misting or placing on a tray of pebbles and water. Water freely when in full growth, less at other times, allowing the top of the soil to dry out between waterings. Feed every 6 to 8 weeks in warmer weather with soluble plant food. Propagate by taking 4 in (about 10 cm) long stem cuttings from just below the node in early spring. Falling leaves may be due to low temperature or too little water.

### *S. actinophylla*

UMBRELLA TREE

The most common indoor species, its glossy foliage resembles segments of an umbrella. Long green stalks are crested by light green leaves divided into 5 to 16 leaflets, the whole being as much as 20 in (about 50 cm) wide. In summer spikes of small red flowers arise from the top of the tree, but this rarely happens indoors where it usually grows to about 6 ft (about 1.8 m) tall. If the plant gets too big, cut it back in spring.

### *S. arboricola*

MINIATURE UMBRELLA TREE

This plant resembles *S. actinophylla*, but the leaves are only around 5 in (about 12 cm) wide, and it grows into a bushy shrub approximately 32 in (about 81 cm) tall and wide. It can be cut back if it grows straggly. (Outdoors in tropical climates it becomes a 30 ft/9 m tree.) Variegated-leaved cultivars are available. The insignificant flowers and brown-orange fruit are rarely seen indoors.

### *S. digitata*

This species has rich green leaves that are shaped like a hand and are divided into 5 to 10 oval leaflets. In spring there are tiny greenish flowers followed in fall by small, globular, dark violet fruit, but this happens rarely indoors.

## SERISSA
### *foetida*

From Southeast Asia, this evergreen shrub has small, oval, deep green leaves that have an unpleasant smell if they are bruised. From spring to fall 4- or 5-lobed, funnel-shaped, white flowers appear. It is a most attractive garden shrub for frost-free areas; indoors it needs high humidity and good light. Water moderately when growing and less at other times. Propagate from semi-ripe cuttings in summer.

## SINNINGIA
### *speciosa*

FLORIST GLOXINIA, VELVET SLIPPER PLANT

This native of Brazil is highly prized for its large, trumpet-shaped flowers available in whites, reds, blues, purples and pastels. Nearly stemless with long, velvety leaves, they thrive in bright, indirect light, high humidity and warm temperatures. Extremely popular as a seasonal potted plant, they are propagated from seed or leaf cuttings.

## SPATHIPHYLLUM

Most species of this genus come from tropical America, but some are native to Malaysia. They are lush, with dark green, oval leaves that stand erect or arch slightly, and beautiful white, cream or green flowers, resembling arum lilies, that bloom reliably indoors. Grow in loose and fibrous, porous potting soil in filtered light away from the sun. (To re-create tropical conditions, increase the humidity by placing the plant on a tray of pebbles and mist regularly.) Water the plants regularly, and allow them to dry out a little in winter. Feed every 4 to 6 weeks with half-strength, soluble fertilizer in spring and summer. Propagate by division in spring or summer.

*Serissa foetida*

*Schefflera actinophylla*

*Sansevieria trifasciata* 'Laurentii'

*Sinningia speciosa* hybrid

*Schefflera arboricola*

*Sansevieria trifasciata*

*Schefflera digitata*

*Sansevieria trifasciata* 'Hahnii'

*S.* 'Mauna Loa'

PEACE LILY

The leathery, lance-shaped, glossy, mid-green leaves reach lengths of 18–24 in (about 45–60 cm). Oval, white, papery spathes, surrounding white spadices, are borne intermittently, turning green with age. It is the best known of a fairly large number of large-flowered cultivars; others are 'Clevelandii', which is shorter, and 'Aztec'.

*S. wallisii*

WHITE SAILS

This is a dwarf species with clusters of glossy green, lance-shaped leaves on reed-like stems growing to 12 in (about 30 cm). A white spathe encloses tiny, creamy white spadices of fragrant flowers tightly packed around an upright spike. The color changes to green with age.

## *SYNGONIUM podophyllum*

**syn. *Nephthytis triphylla***

ARROWHEAD VINE

This plant closely resembles its relative, the climbing *Philodendron*, with its handsome climbing or trailing foliage. It has an unusual feature of changing leaf shape with maturity. The young, arrowhead-shaped leaves on the end of erect stalks become, with age, lobed with 7 to 9 glossy leaflets growing to 12 in (about 30 cm) long. There are several varieties with variegated leaves in cream or pink. Grow in an all-purpose potting soil in a warm, moist environment. This species tolerates fairly low to bright light, but no direct sunlight. Water thoroughly, allowing the surface to dry out between waterings. Feed when conditions are warm every 4 to 6 weeks with half-strength, liquid fertilizer. Propagate from stem cuttings in spring or summer. To encourage branching and more young leaves, pinch off long stems.

## *TILLANDSIA*

This genus contains over 350 species of mainly epiphytic plants. Commonly called "air plants," these bromeliads are grown for their unusual flowers. The flowers are usually carried on spikes, heads or panicles and range in color from white to purple and green to red. Plant in well-drained sphagnum moss or they may be grown on slabs of bark or driftwood. They are often positioned high up in hanging baskets in order to catch the rising heat. Mist regularly and water moderately in summer and sparingly at other times. Propagate from offsets or by division in spring to summer.

*T. cyanea*

PINK QUILL

Dense rosettes of grass-like, arching leaves are usually deep green and often reddish brown when new. In summer to fall the spectacular, paddle-shaped flowerheads rise on tall stems from among the foliage. They consist of overlapping pink or red bracts with deep violet-blue flowers emerging. This variety needs maximum humidity and is best grown in a compost of tree fern fiber, peat and sand.

*T. lindenii*

The thin, smooth, pointed, arching leaves with red-brown lines grow in a typical rosette. In fall a large flower spike of crimson or pink-tinted bracts overlaps dense clusters of pansy-shaped, deep blue or purple-blue flowers arising just above the leaves.

## *TOLMIEA menziesii*

PICK-A-BACK PLANT, PIGGYBACK PLANT, MOTHER-OF-THOUSANDS, YOUTH-ON-AGE

Native to the West Coast of North America, this popular house plant is suitable for both pots and hanging baskets. Bright green, hairy leaves that are ivy shaped with toothed edges, send out new plantlets at the junction of the leaf and stalk. There is also a form with variegated leaves. In spring there are spikes of nodding, tubular to bell-shaped, rich brown and green flowers. Hot, dry air can harm these plants so grow in a cool area in bright to moderate light in an all-purpose potting mix. Keep soil moist but not soggy, and water sparingly in winter. Feed every two months in the warmer season with half-strength, soluble fertilizer. Propagate by planting leaf cuttings or plantlets in spring or summer. Frequent attacks by spider mite create brown or brittle leaves, requiring immediate treatment.

*Tillandsia cyanea*

*Tillandsia lindenii*

*Syngonium podophyllum*

*Spathiphyllum* 'Mauna Loa'

*Tolmiea menziesii*

*Spathiphyllum wallisii*

CHAPTER 10

# Cacti & Succulents

*One of the most intriguing of horticultural statistics comes from Britain. There, nurseries sell more cacti during the school holidays than at any other time of year. The industry interprets that to mean that they appeal strongly to what used to be known (rather pretentiously) as "junior gardeners." And why not? A collection of cacti (and other succulents) is just as much fun as a collection of stamps.*

You don't have to be an adolescent to find them different and appealing. Nor do you have to have hectares of garden to indulge. Sure, there are giants in the succulent world, but there are many beautiful species that will happily spend their entire lives in a small flower pot.

Some might find them an example of that beauty that resides in grotesqueness; but no one can deny that they are wonderful examples of how life adapts to flourish in the most unpromising of environments. While there are a few cacti that have migrated to the forests where they live as epiphytes in the manner (and often in the company) of orchids, most of these are plants of the desert, where their lifestyle revolves around the need to conserve water from the rare but copious desert rains.

The cacti, a family from the Americas and distantly related (believe it or not) to the carnation, show the succulent habit at perhaps its most wonderful. They have dispensed with leaves which would only transpire precious water, carrying out the vital business of photosynthesis in the green skin that covers their stems. The stems themselves are enormously swollen and spongy, often being almost spherical so they provide nearly as much light-catching area as leaves would. Many have developed ribbed forms, the ribs ensuring that at least part of the plant is in its own shade. A fat and tender plant full of stored water would be irresistible to thirsty desert animals (at least some of the stories of people lost in the desert saving themselves by breaking open a cactus and sucking the water from it are true), so the typical cactus has given itself an armory of thorns. Some have so many that they also serve to shade the body of the plant from the sun, almost as though the plant were aware that its thorns were the last vestiges of its leaves.

Handling the plants may put one in mind of the old joke about how porcupines make love (very carefully), but you don't have to be a devoted cactophile to admire their often dazzlingly beautiful flowers. Dazzling is literally true: they need their brilliant sheen and color to show up in the bleaching desert light.

## Other Succulents

The Cactaceae are not the only family of succulent plants, although perhaps they are the only one to be comprised exclusively of succulents. There are succulent members of such well-known garden families as the lilies (agaves, aloes, gasterias) and even the daisies (kleinias, the succulent senecios) as well as families like the Crassulaceae and Mesembryanthemaceae, which are predominantly succulents. Most depart

Echinopsis *species are highly valued for their brilliant flowers.*

from the cacti in preferring to store their reserves of water in succulent leaves rather than stems, and these are often wonderfully shaped, colored and marked. Their habit varies from shrubby to just a few leaves on ground-hugging stems, and their flowers vary from the sheer brilliance of the mesembryanthemums and aloes to almost complete insignificance.

Notocactus *are ideal for beginners as they are very easy to grow.*

## *Growing Cacti and Succulents*

For all their diversity, cacti and succulents are surprisingly uniform in their cultural needs, and their built-in tolerance of extreme drought makes them invaluable in arid climates. They ask only to be given sun, the more the better; perfectly drained but rich soil (desert soils are usually very fertile, as the prodigious crops they can yield under artificial irrigation show); and to be allowed to dry out completely while they are dormant in winter. Never mind that then they may shrivel alarmingly; they will recover almost fast enough to watch when you water them again in spring. Most can take a degree or two of frost as long as they are dry, but they are best considered tender and grown outdoors only in mild-winter climates.

They differ so much in appearance from conventional plants that they need careful placement in the garden. Most people find it easiest to grow them on their own, but you don't have to grow them as single specimens; mass and group them, taking their different heights and colors into account just as you would in creating a border of more conventional perennials or shrubs. If you care to add a few desert-type (xerophytic) shrubs like *Cassia artemisioides* as background and some carpeting annuals like portulacas, you'll find it easier to integrate the planting with the rest of the garden; but you need to exercise restraint—such lush growers as petunias would simply look silly planted with cacti and succulents.

Succulents grow perfectly happily in pots and can be the ideal answer for a situation where it is troublesome to water pots frequently—on a roof or balcony for instance. In fact apart from the Southwestern states most of the cacti and succulents on the following pages will be grown as pot plants, and therefore no hardiness zones have been given. Some exceptions have been noted. Suit the size of the pot to the plant, and avoid plastic pots if you can—terrracotta allows the soil to dry out faster. An open but still rich potting mix is best—you can try adding sand to a regular commercial mix, and mulching the plants with gravel to keep their collars dry. Give the plants as much sun and fresh air as you can, water and fertilize (artificial fertilizer is best) lavishly in spring and early summer while the plants are growing, and then tail off the watering gradually until by the return of cold weather the plants are bone dry.

Almost all can be very easily propagated from cuttings of side shoots, spring being the best time; the only thing to watch is that you don't over water until the new roots are well developed. Indeed, over watering is the main thing you can do wrong; it encourages the fungus, botrytis, to rot the roots and even the bases of the plants, and you can't always save them by making cuttings of unaffected parts of the plant after drenching everything in a strong fungicide. Mealy bug is the other main pest; it can eat out the growing point of a cactus but can also infest the roots of just about any succulent. As soon as you see it, spray the top and soak the roots in a powerful insecticide.

The only exception to this regime is the epiphytic forest cacti—the epiphyllums, the Christmas cacti, and their ilk. These are definitely tender, needing winter temperatures no lower than around 46°F (about 8°C); they are best grown in hanging baskets, as their usually flattened, leaf-like stems tend to weep. They like a fertile, well-drained soil and to be watered in warm weather but, again, don't water in winter.

All indoor grown cacti and succulents will benefit greatly from being taken outdoors for the summer, but bring them in the moment the weather forecast hints of cold and damp.

*Adenium multiflorum*

*Agave victoriae-reginae*

*Aeonium arboreum* 'Schwarzkopf'

*Agave americana* 'Variegata'

*Aeonium canariense*

*Adenium obesum*

## ADENIUM

Originating in tropical and subtropical Africa and the Middle East, these semi-succulent shrubs have dense, bloated trunks with woody bases and bright, deep green leaves. The foliage sheds naturally during the dry season but endures for at least another year on cultivated plants. The cylindrical flowers are vividly colored and have 5 petals. Total sun or semi-shade, porous soil and warm temperatures are required. Propagate from cuttings in summer or seed in spring. They are susceptible to rot. The genus name is derived from Aden, home of the first recorded species.

### *A. multiflorum*

IMPALA LILY

This deciduous, succulent shrub originated in South Africa and reaches to 9 ft (about 2.7 m) in height. Whorls of silky, lance-shaped to oval leaves appear at the tips of its multiple branches. The decorative, trumpet-shaped blooms are white with deep pinkish red margins.

POT CULTURE

### *A. obesum*

DESERT ROSE

Valued for its flowers and foliage, this species grows to 6 ft (about 1.8 m). Whorls of shiny, green, leathery leaves (downy when immature) develop at the ends of plump stems. In mid- to late winter and spring terminal clusters of vivid, pink-red, tubular flowers appear. This shrub is frost tender and should be planted in full sun or partial shade. Water sparingly. Propagate from seed or cuttings in summer.

POT CULTURE

## AEONIUM

Native to the Canary Islands, the Mediterranean and northern Africa, this genus contains 40 short-lived, perennial or evergreen succulents. The species develop either as one large (or several smaller), compact, stemless rosette, or as several long, leathery stalks with rosettes on top. The lush, egg-shaped foliage ranges from vivid green to greenish blue and sometimes purple. Attractive, star-shaped, pink, red, white or yellow flowers appear from the center of the leaf whorls, usually in spring. These succulents prefer full sun or partial shade, light, well-drained soil and warmer temperatures. Prune stems after the bloom although the flowering rosette will usually die. Propagate from seed or leaf stem cuttings in spring and summer.

### *A. arboreum* 'Schwarzkopf'

This shrubby plant from southern Europe grows up to 24 in (about 60 cm) in height and 3 ft (about 90 cm) in width. Its striking, stemmed rosettes have lance-shaped, purple-black leaves. In spring, after 2 or 3 years, little, starry, golden yellow flowers develop from the center of each rosette.

ZONES 10–11

### *A. canariense*

This low-growing, frost-tender perennial is native to the Canary Islands where it is typically found growing on rocky outcrops. The species reaches 6 in (about 15 cm) in height and spreads to 20 in (about 50 cm) in diameter. Each rosette has lush green, spoon-shaped leaves with red-tinted edges. After 2 or 3 years the center rises to form a flower stem. In spring, yellow, starry flowers develop in a terminal cluster; after blooming the whole plant expires.

ZONES 10–11

## AGAVE

This genus consists of over 300 species native to South and Central America. The small species flower after 5 to 10 years; the tall species may not flower until they are 20 to 40 years old. They all like well-drained, gritty soil, but will grow in poor soil. Although they need a very sunny position, young plants should be sheltered if in a frost area. They are drought tolerant, but need regular watering. Propagate from offsets or from seed in spring or summer.

### *A. americana*

CENTURY PLANT

This large succulent makes a very good accent plant in the garden, with a 9 ft (about 2.7 m) high and wide rosette of thick, fleshy, strap-shaped, gray-green leaves edged with sharp spines and pointed tips; a variety with variegated leaves is popular. It flowers when 10 or more years old with a stalk up to 21 ft (about 6.5 m) of yellow flowers. The plant dies after flowering, leaving offsets which can be used for propagation.

ZONES 9–10

### *A. victoriae-reginae*

ROYAL AGAVE

Originating in Central America, this slow-growing succulent is considered by many to be the most beautiful of all. Stalkless and up to 24 in (about 60 cm) in height and breadth, its single rosette has dense, narrow, keeled foliage with white edges and surface lines. After 20 years, creamy yellow flowers develop in spring and summer. This extremely resilient species is seldom attacked by pests and requires full sun. If grown in a tub make sure it is a good size, otherwise the species will refuse to bloom and the foliage will be stunted. Plant in rich, well-drained soil and water sparingly. Propagate from seed in spring or from offsets after the rosette has perished.

ZONES 9–11

## ALOE

ALOE

This diverse genus of rosetted plants is native to Africa and the Middle

East. They range widely in habit, from low and shrubby to tall and tree like, with several types of vines and creepers also included. The whorled, lush, grayish green foliage is usually lanceolate and marked with white lines or patches. In spring and summer attractive, red, yellow or orange, cylindrical flowers appear in long-stemmed racemes. These plants prefer moderate temperatures. The larger types prefer full sun, while the dwarf species enjoy semi-shade. Plant in rich, extremely porous soil and only water when the roots appear dry. In spring or summer propagate from seed or stem cuttings.

### *A. arborescens*

CANDELABRA PLANT, OCTOPUS PLANT, TORCH PLANT

This popular, South African species has a shrubby habit and reaches up to 6–9 ft (about 1.8–2.7 m) in height when in flower. Its short-stemmed rosettes are composed of lush, grayish blue leaves up to 24 in (about 60 cm) long, slightly inward curving and thorny edged. Thick clusters of scarlet-red or yellow, cylindrical flowers develop along an upright stem in late winter to early spring. This tough aloe is both salt and drought resistant.

ZONES 9–10

### *A. aristata*

TORCH PLANT, LACE ALOE

Native to South Africa, this enduring, stemless species forms a single, basal rosette, 4 in (about 10 cm) tall, and up to 12 in (about 30 cm) wide. Its long, deep green, lanceolate leaves have white surface spots, soft, serrated margins and a curved, short spike on each tip. Clusters of orange-red flowers develop in racemes in spring.

ZONES 9–10

### *A. barbadensis*

UNGUENTINE CACTUS, MEDICINAL ALOE, MEDICINE PLANT, BURN PLANT

Renowned for its medicinal qualities, this widely cultivated, short-stemmed species is thought to have originated in the Middle East or northern Africa. It grows up to 24 in (about 60 cm) in height and develops dense rosettes composed of long, thick, lance-shaped, grayish green leaves with thorny margins. In summer, small yellow flowers appear in racemes up to 3 ft (about 90 cm) in height. This frost-tender species is excellent in window boxes. The flesh of the foliage has soothing qualities and is used in the treatment of scalds.

ZONES 10–11

### *A. ciliaris*

DUNNY VINE

The common name comes from the popular use of this climbing species for hiding outhouses in the Australian outback; it is one of the few climbing plants able to resist semi-desert drought. It prejudices gardeners in more favored climates against the plant, but it is an attractive evergreen climber with bright green leaves and scarlet and yellow flowers from spring to fall. Propagate from cuttings.

ZONES 10–11

### *A. ferox*

TAP ALOE, BITTER ALOE

Originating in South Africa, this lofty species may grow up to 15 ft (about 4.5 m) tall. Its single, woody stem produces a dense rosette composed of lance-shaped leaves up to 3 ft (about 90 cm) long. These bluish green leaves have a spiny surface with reddish brown spines on the margins. In spring, vivid orange-red blooms appear in a thick, terminal cluster atop a single, slender stalk.

ZONES 9–10

### *A. variegata*

TIGER ALOE, PARTRIDGE-BREASTED ALOE

Native to South Africa, this thicket-forming species grows up to 12 in (about 30 cm) tall and 6 in (about 15 cm) in diameter. The overlaying, pyramidal leaves are boldly marked with white, horizontal bands and have slightly serrated margins. In spring clusters of funnel-shaped, rose-orange flowers appear at the ends of slender stems.

ZONES 9–11

## APTENIA *cordifolia*

This mat-forming, enduring succulent is quick growing and up to 2 in (about 5 cm) in height. The creeping stems are covered with lustrous, green, oval leaves. Small, vivid, pink flowers bloom in summer and are daisy like in appearance with dense stamens. There is also a red-flowered form, and one with variegated leaves. This species makes good ground cover. It requires extremely porous soil with full sun. Propagate from seed or cuttings in spring or summer.

ZONES 9–10

## ARGYRODERMA *delaetii*

LIVING STONES

This bizarre species has two succulent, frosted-green leaves, joined at the base. It appears as a rectangular mass $1^1/_2$ in (about 3 cm) high with a scooped out center. In winter a single, deep crimson, daisy-like flower emerges from the middle of the plant, often covering the leaves. Plants require total sun and extremely porous soil. Propagate by division or from seed in summer.

ZONES 9–10

*Argyroderma delaetii*

*Aloe ferox*

*Aloe ciliaris*

*Aloe variegata*

*Aloe arborescens*

*Aptenia cordifolia*

*Aloe aristata*

*Aloe barbadensis* (*Echinocereus* behind)

## ASTROPHYTUM

This popular genus contains 6 diverse species of slow-growing cacti, native to Mexico. They range widely in size and their form varies from star shaped, hence the Greek genus name, to elongated and globular. The plants are divided into 5 to 10 prominent ribs, some with a smooth appearance, some covered in thick hair, others patterned with white, tufty areoles. Individual, large, yellow or red, trumpet-shaped flowers appear from the top of the plant in summer or fall. The species prefer porous, alkaline soil. Full sun and dry conditions are also preferred, except during mid-summer. Propagate by grafting and from seed in spring and summer.

### *A. asterias*

SEA URCHIN CACTUS, SAND DOLLAR CACTUS

Looking very much like a sea urchin, this highly valued, grayish green, globular cactus grows to 3 in (about 7.5 cm) in height and 4 in (about 10 cm) in diameter. It is alternately divided by smooth, vertical ribs and bands of little white areoles. Completely covered with fine, white scales, this cactus is unusual because it has no spikes. Yellow flowers with red interiors bloom in summer.

ZONES 9–10

### *A. myriostigma*

BISHOP'S CAP, BISHOP'S MITRE

This odd-looking species grows up to 12 in (about 30 cm) in height and 4 in (about 10 cm) in diameter. It has a grayish green, globular body, divided into 4 to 8 prominent ribs and covered with tiny, white scales. Glossy, yellow blooms appear in summer.

ZONES 9–10

## *AZUREOCEREUS hertlingianus*

Native to Peru, this erect cactus is tree like in habit, growing up to 12 ft (about 3.5 m) when cultivated. A slow-developing species, it has a column-shaped, frosted, grayish blue stem with up to 20 ribs and numerous, tufted areoles sprouting rust-colored spikes. White, tubular, night-blooming flowers appear in summer on larger specimens. This species requires full sun and rich, porous soil. Propagate from seed or cuttings in spring and summer.

POT CULTURE

## *BESCHORNERIA yuccoides*

MEXICAN LILY

A spectacular member of the lily family, this plant makes clumps of sword-shaped, gray-green leaves around 32 in (about 81 cm) long, rather like a yucca but much less prickly. In spring it sends up $4^1/_2$–6 ft (about 1.3–1.8 m) tall flower stems with pendent, apple-green flowers and bright pink bracts. As the flower stalk is itself pink, it is a spectacular sight. It prefers full sun and rich, well-drained soil. Propagate from seed or offsets.

ZONES 10-11

## *BORZICACTUS celsianus*

OLD MAN OF THE ANDES, OLD MAN OF THE MOUNTAINS

Native to South America, this slow-growing cactus reaches heights of up to around $4^1/_2$ ft (about 1.3 m). The body and branches have 10 to 18 ribs and rust-colored spikes. Elliptical areoles sprout long, white hairs which completely cover the younger cacti. Older specimens produce reddish pink summer flowers that close up at night. The species is simple to grow if allowed full sun, porous soil and occasional water. Propagate any time in spring or summer from seed.

ZONES 8–10

## *CARNEGIA gigantea*

SAGUARO

This is the most famous of all cacti—the 18 ft (about 5.5 m) tall one that raises single or branched columns in the background of just about every early cowboy movie. It is native to the deserts of California and New Mexico, where changes to the ecology and the depredations of tourists are seriously endangering its future as a wild plant. It grows very slowly, a seedling taking many years to be tall enough (9 ft/2.7 m) to flower; but the white, sweetly scented, night-blooming, summer flowers are worth seeing.

ZONES 9–10

## CARPOBROTUS

Valued for their abundance of vivid flowers, the 30 species in this genus of carpet-forming succulents are predominantly native to South Africa, with some found in Australia, North America and the Pacific Islands. The vigorous, 2-angled stems vary in length up to 6 ft (about 1.8 m) and become leathery with age. The deep green, extremely pulpy leaf pairs vary from cylindrical to triangular, and often have serrated margins and clear surface markings. The large, daisy-like flowers are borne individually in varying shades of purple, and occasionally yellow. These are followed by lush, sometimes edible fruit from which the genus name is derived—*karpos*: fruit and *brota*: edible. These species are easy to grow, requiring full light and porous soil. They are suited to hanging baskets and make excellent sandbinders. Propagate from stem cuttings or seed in spring to early fall.

### *C. edulis*

HOTTENTOT FIG

Originating in South Africa, this prostrate, mat-forming, perennial succulent is an excellent sandbinder. It produces long, spreading, narrow stems covered with deep green, erect foliage with serrated, reddish margins. In spring and summer, bright yellow, red or purple flowers appear. Edible, brown, fig-like fruit follows the bloom. This species prefers mild temperatures and is ideal for a hanging basket. It requires full sun, porous soil and light water.

ZONES 10–11

### *C. muirii*

REAL SOUR FIG

This fast-growing species is native to South Africa and in spring bears

*Borzicactus celsianus*

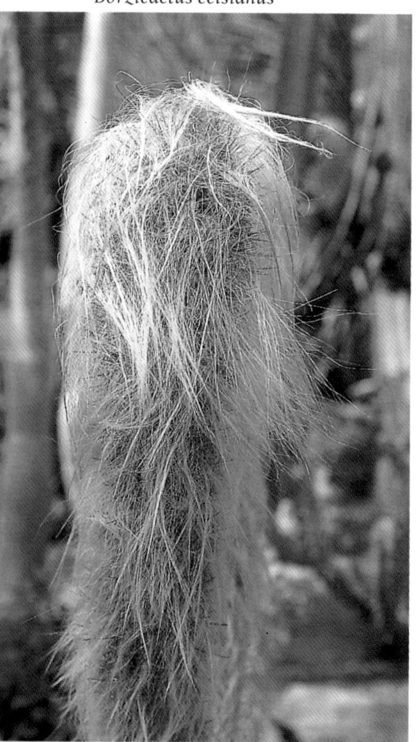

*Astrophytum myriostigma*

*Astrophytum asterias*

*Carnegia gigantea*

*Azureocereus hertlingianus*

*Carpobrotus edulis*

*Beschorneria yuccoides*

pinkish purple flowers up to 3½ in (about 8 cm) in diameter, followed by tasty fruit.
ZONES 9–10

## *CEPHALOCEREUS senilis*

OLD MAN CACTUS

This erect, South American cactus grows slowly to 40 ft (about 12 m) tall in the wild but only 20 in (about 50 cm) in pots. It has up to 30 ribs, fine, short, yellowy white spines and a profusion of gray-white fleecy hair (hence the common name) which completely covers the body and can be washed and combed similarly to one's own. Mature plants develop thorny crowns from where trumpet-shaped, reddish pink spring flowers appear, but not usually on cultivated specimens. This cactus is suitable for the greenhouse and requires full sun or partial shade and sandy, slightly alkaline soil.
ZONES 9–10

## *CEREUS peruvianus*

PERUVIAN APPLE, PERUVIAN TORCH

Originating in South America, this popular cactus grows up to 15 ft (about 4.5 m) in height. It has an erect habit, deep green-blue stems with up to 10 ribs and brown, downy areoles with yellow spines. Scented, brown-green flowers open at night during summer and are followed by red, globular fruit. This species prefers total sun and porous soil. Propagate from seed or stem cuttings in spring.
ZONES 9–10

## *CEROPEGIA woodii*

ROSARY VINE, HEARTS-ON-A-STRING

An excellent plant for hanging baskets, this native of South Africa produces an abundance of slender, thread-like branches with small, "bead-like" tubers produced at the nodes. The small, heart-shaped leaves are bluish green mottled white. Purple, hairy, tubular flowers appear in summer and are ¾ in (about 2 cm) long, poking out from among the leaves at the nodes. Rosary vine requires several hours of sunlight and moderate water. Propagate from stem cuttings.
POT CULTURE

## *CHAMAECEREUS silvestrii*

PEANUT CACTUS

This well-known Argentine cactus has a prostrate carpeting habit and reaches to 4 in (about 10 cm) in height. It is composed of clusters of initially erect, peanut-shaped "finger" stems with numerous soft, white bristles. Readily flowering indoors from an early age, this species produces vivid, orange-red flowers in spring and summer. It requires porous soil and full sun or partial shade. Propagate by planting the small fingers, which are easily broken off at their joints, in spring and summer.
ZONES 9–10

## *CLEISTOCACTUS strausii*

SILVER TORCH

This erect columnar cactus is native to Bolivia and reaches to 9 ft (about 2.7 m) in height. Quick and simple to grow, it has numerous, ribbed, gray-blue stems that distinctively taper toward the base. These are covered with areoles sprouting fine white hair. An abundance of deep red, cylindrical flowers develop straight from the stems in late summer, but only on older cacti. This species likes full sun and extremely porous soil. Propagate from seed or cuttings in summer.
ZONES 9–10

## *COPIAPOA*

This genus of cacti, all native to Chile, are slow developing and vary in habit from single and erect to multi-stemmed and spreading, and from gray to light green with brown shadings. All species have numerous areoles sprouting long spines and fleecy crowns from where the blooms emerge. These yellow or red flowers are wide and trumpet or bell shaped. Some enjoy full sun, while others prefer semi-shade. Propagate from seed in spring, offsets in summer, or by grafting in summer and spring.

### *C. cinerea*

This unusual species is single-stemmed up to 24 in (about 60 cm) when young, forming colonies up to 6 ft (about 1.8 m) wide in maturity. Gray, downy areoles sprouting pointed spines cover silver-gray stems. These stems have numerous ribs and a thick, fleecy, white crown from where the flowers emerge. The wide, yellow blooms develop only on cacti 4 in (about 10 cm) or more in diameter.
ZONES 9–10

### *C. echinoides*

Reaching a height of up to 6 in (about 15 cm) and 4 in (about 10 cm) in diameter, this solitary-stemmed, frost-tender perennial has a flat, globe-shaped appearance. Its green-gray body has ten outstanding ribs and large areoles producing seven whorls and a central spine. Light, yellowish green flowers bloom in summer.
ZONES 9–10

*Carpobrotus muirii*

*Cereus peruvianus*

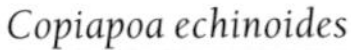

*Copiapoa echinoides*

*Copiapoa cinerea*

*Chamaecereus silvestrii*

*Cleistocactus strausii*

*Cephalocereus senilis*

Dioscorea elephantipes

Cyphostemma juttae

Crassula ovata

Crassula arborescens

Crassula coccinea

Cotyledon orbiculata

## COTYLEDON

### *orbiculata*

PIG'S EAR

This evergreen, succulent shrub is native to northern Africa and reaches to 20 in (about 50 cm) in height and breadth. Egg-shaped, gray-green leaves with a white wax coating and occasionally red margins form in opposite pairs along plump, multiple stems. In fall terminal clusters of orange, cylindrical or bell-shaped, hanging flowers appear. This succulent requires total sun or partial shade and very porous soil. Avoid watering flowers from the top. Propagate from seed or cuttings in summer.

ZONES 9–10

## CRASSULA

This large, diverse genus comprises about 300 species of annual and perennial, mostly evergreen, succulent shrubs. Predominantly native to South Africa, they range widely in habit from prostrate and carpet forming to tall and erect. Star-shaped flowers form in terminal clusters. Species require full sun or partial shade, very porous soil and slight watering only in winter. Propagate from cuttings or by division in spring and summer, from seed in spring.

### *C. arborescens*

SILVER JADE PLANT, SILVER DOLLAR

Reaching up to 12 ft (about 3.5 m) in height and 6 ft (about 1.8 m) in diameter, this perennial succulent has strong, thick stems that develop broad, pulpy, silver-gray leaves with contrasting red margins. This succulent requires full sun and well-drained soil. It makes an excellent potted specimen but is then unlikely to flower.

ZONES 10–11

### *C. coccinea*

syn. *Rochea coccinea*

This evergreen succulent from South Africa reaches 24 in (about 60 cm) in height. Five-petaled, pink flowers appear from fall to winter. Its numerous, upright, leathery stems produce pairs of pulpy, flat green leaves with red undersides and downy edges. In summer to fall an abundance of cylindrical, deep red flowers appear in thick, terminal sprays. This succulent needs warmer temperatures, total sun and porous soil. This species is easily cultivated from seed or cuttings in spring and summer.

POT CULTURE

### *C. ovata*

JADE TREE, FRIENDSHIP TREE, MONEY TREE

This quick-growing, shrubby, perennial succulent grows to 12 ft (about 3.5 m) in height and 6 ft (about 2 m) in diameter. It has thick, leathery stems that are covered with shiny, pulpy, egg-shaped leaves edged with red. In fall and winter small, pink, starry flowers appear. This species prefers full sun, and makes a good potted plant.

ZONES 10–11

## CYPHOSTEMMA

### *juttae*

syn. *Cissus juttae*

Native to southern Africa, this deciduous, perennial succulent grows to 6 ft (about 1.8 m) in height when mature. It has a distinctively bloated trunk which branches near the top and is covered with yellow, peeling bark. The wide, shiny green foliage is roughly saw toothed and has a downy underside that emits droplets of resin. Small, greenish yellow flowers appear in summer, followed by red or yellow fruit which look very much like small bunches of grapes. Plant in porous soil in full sun. Propagate from seed in spring.

POT CULTURE

## DIOSCOREA

### *elephantipes*

ELEPHANT'S FOOT, HOTTENTOT BREAD

Many species of the genus *Dioscorea* are cultivated for yams, which make up the tuberous storage roots. Although *D. elephantipes* was originally cooked and eaten by the Hottentots of southern Africa, it is now grown primarily as a decorative garden plant. It is a twining species with circular to kidney-shaped leaves abruptly pointed at the ends, but its most striking feature is the truly enormous rootstock. Insignificant, yellow flowers appear in spring. Requiring a position in deep soil with good drainage and semi-arid conditions, it is also suitable as a greenhouse plant. Propagate from seeds, cuttings or root section at any time of the year.

POT CULTURE

## DROSANTHEMUM

This genus contains approximately 95 species of perennial succulents native to South Africa. They have a spreading habit and vary in height, some reaching 3 ft (about 90 cm). The numerous leaves are fleshy and irregularly shaped. The yellow to deep purple flowers range in color from pink and yellow to deep purple. They require bright sunlight for the flowers to open fully. Potted specimens can be kept indoors in winter in a warm, sunny position. Plant in well-drained, compost-enriched soil. Water sparingly in summer and keep fairly dry in winter. Propagate from seed or cuttings and replace plants about every 3 years.

### *D. bicolor*

BICOLORED ICE-PLANT

This fast-growing but short-lived perennial has a stiffly branched, thick, rounded form. Spectacular, golden centered, purplish red-tipped flowers are borne in spring. Plant in a position in well-drained, compost-enriched soil.

ZONES 10–11

### *D. floribundum*

This small, cushion-forming, succulent, perennial plant reaches to 6 in (about 15 cm) in height with an indefinite spread. Its creeping branches take root as they grow and are covered with pairs of pale, gray-green, cylindrical leaves. A profusion of little, pink, daisy-like flowers are borne in summer. Excellent for hanging baskets or pots.

ZONES 10–11

## *ECHEVERIA*

HEN AND CHICKS

Native to the Americas, this large genus contains over 150 species of ornamental, perennial succulents valued for their habit, foliage and flowers. The species form in perfectly symmetrical, basal rosettes or in multi-stemmed bushes up to 3 ft (about 90 cm) tall. These plants have pulpy, sleek-edged leaves which are particularly vivid during the colder months. Bell-shaped to cylindrical flowers bloom at different times of the year. They require full sun or semi-shade, very porous soil and light watering. Propagate from seed, offsets or cuttings, or by division in spring and summer.

### *E. elegans*

PEARL ECHEVERIA

This clump-forming, perennial succulent develops in a thickly foliaged, basal rosette up to 2 in (about 5 cm) tall and 20 in (about 50 cm) in diameter. Its lush leaves are frosted blue-green with red margins. The bell-shaped, pinky red flowers have yellow petal tips. It makes a good bedding plant and should be kept dry in winter.

ZONES 9–10

### *E. pulvinata*

PLUSH PLANT, CHENILLE PLANT

This shrubby perennial produces multiple, brown, downy stems crowned with open rosettes up to 4 in (about 10 cm) in diameter. These whorls are composed of dense, inversely egg-shaped leaves, silky soft and covered with white down. In winter to spring red or yellowish red flowers appear along stems up to 12 in (about 30 cm) tall.

ZONES 9–10

## *ECHINOCACTUS*

### *grusonii*

GOLDEN BARREL CACTUS

Originating in Mexico, this popular, slow-growing cactus reaches up to 6 ft (about 1.8 m) in height and breadth. It has a single, globe-shaped, pale green body that stretches upwards in maturity, becoming barrel shaped. This stem is heavily ribbed with numerous areoles sprouting radial, yellow spines. In summer, larger cacti produce a circle of vivid, yellow flowers from a crown at the top of the plant. Drought resistant, the species requires a position in full sun with well-drained soil.

ZONES 9–10

## *ECHINOCEREUS*

This large and popular genus of small, North American cacti has a varying habit. The stems are numerously ribbed and spiny with new stems bursting forth from inside existing ones. In spring to summer large, brightly colored, trumpet-shaped, enduring blooms appear, followed by small thorny, globular fruit. Species need extremely porous soil with full sun or semi-shade. Propagate from seed or cuttings in spring and summer.

### *E. reichenbachii*

LACY CACTUS

Native to the southern USA and to Mexico, this typically single-stemmed cactus is globe shaped when immature, becoming elongated and cylindrical with age. It reaches a height of up to 8 in (about 20 cm) and 4 in (about 10 cm) in diameter. Close-set areoles sprout abundant yellow or white spines, giving the species a lacy appearance. In spring large, vivid, rose-pink to purple flowers appear.

ZONES 7–10

### *E. subinervis*

This attractive species from New Mexico grows around 12 in (about 30 cm) in height, usually as a single, fluted, gray-green plant. It bears lovely cream or yellow flowers in spring.

ZONES 9–10

### *E. viridiflorus*

This thicket-forming, globe-shaped cactus is native to the southern USA and to Mexico. The shortest species in the genus, its 3 in (about 7.5 cm) high stems spread in colonies up to 6 in (about 15 cm). The stems are covered in red-brown or white spines with up to 16 ribs. Vivid, green flowers bloom in spring.

ZONES 7–10

*Drosanthemum floribundum*

*Echeveria pulvinata*

*Echinocereus reichenbachii*

*Drosanthemum bicolor*

*Echinocereus viridiflorus*

*Echinocereus subinervis*

*Echeveria elegans*

*Echinocactus grusonii*

## ECHINOPSIS

This popular genus contains over 35 species of cacti native to South America. Ranging from single, basal, globe-shaped stems to readily colonizing, tubular and erect, these cacti are densely covered with spines and have pronounced ribs. Species are highly valued for their funnel-shaped, brilliantly colored flowers which are up to 8 in (about 20 cm) long. The blooms open at night and are very short lived. These plants will survive in varying degrees of shade and require rich, well-drained soil and light water. This genus has been extensively crossed with *Lobivia* to produce many hybrids, all of which have large flowers in a great many color varieties. Propagate in spring and summer from seed and readily produced offsets.

### *E. arachnacantha*
syn. *Lobivia arachnacantha*

This short, spherical, perennial cactus is up to $1\frac{1}{2}$ in (about 3 cm) tall, with a spread of 2 in (about 5 cm). Numerous undulating, cream-white ribs cover the deep green stem. An abundance of downy, golden yellow flowers 2 in (about 5 cm) in diameter bloom from the crown in late spring.
ZONES 9–10

### *E.* 'Green Gold'

This is a neat, clump-forming cactus grows to around 8 in (about 20 cm) high with abundant lime-yellow flowers in summer. It prefers a position in rich, well-drained soil with light watering; it is easy to grow and will survive long periods of neglect.
ZONES 9–10

### *E. oxygona*
EASTER LILY CACTUS, BARREL CACTUS

Originating in Brazil, this spherical, multi-branched cactus grows to 6 in (about 15 cm) in maturity and forms dense thickets up to 3 ft (about 90 cm) in diameter. Long, slender, tapering, ribbed branches are covered with brown, black-tipped spines. These asparagus-like stems are inwardly curving and sprout fragrant, pinkish blue flowers from the tips. Propagate in spring and summer from seed or from readily produced offsets.
ZONES 10–11

## EPIPHYLLUM
ORCHID CACTUS

This genus from tropical South America and Mexico contains 35 species and over 3000 hybrid, epiphytic cacti. The species have a shrubby, prostrate or pendent habit and are virtually spineless in maturity. Multiple flattened stems develop from a leathery base with heavily undulated margins often mistaken for leaves. In spring or summer large, funnel-shaped flowers bloom. These appear from the edges of the stems and vary from nocturnal to daytime opening. The species require a dry, cold spell during winter, light, sandy soil and full sun for optimum flowering. These cacti are ideal hanging basket plants, their trailing stems seeming to grow better if the roots are restricted. Propagate from seed in spring, stem cuttings in summer.

### *E.* hybrids

Growing usually to 24 in (about 60 cm) in height and width, these plants come in a wide range of flower colors—white through pink to red and through yellow to orange. The flowers can be as much as 6 in (about 15 cm) across, and open during the day. Often the plants are simply sold by flower color.
POT CULTURE

### *E. oxypetalum*
DUTCHMAN'S PIPE, BELLE DE NUIT

Native to Mexico and Guatemala, this popular perennial cactus has an upright habit to 6 ft (about 1.8 m) in height, arching in maturity. Its multiple stems are up to 4 in (about 10 cm) wide and tapering. The night-opening, 6 in (about 15 cm) wide, white flowers have slightly curved tubes. They are most intensely fragrant. It does very well as a house plant.
POT CULTURE

*Echinopsis arachnacantha*

*Echinopsis* 'Green Gold'

*Echinopsis oxygona*

*Epiphyllum oxypetalum*

*Epiphyllum* 'Pink Nymph'

*Euphorbia caput-medusae*

## EUPHORBIA
SPURGE, MILKWEED

This massive genus contains over 2000 species of shrubs, perennials and succulents naturally occurring worldwide. These slow-growing species have distinctive yet diverse forms and are popular as house plants. The succulents have complex, cup-shaped bracts which encase two to three male flowers and a single, 3-toothed female ovary. These are followed by leathery, 3-lobed seed pods which burst open to disperse the seeds. The plants require a cool, dry resting period. Plant in damp, porous soil with full sun or partial shade. Propagate from seed or dry cuttings in spring, or by division in early spring or early fall. Many types contain a milky white, toxic sap which is extremely skin irritant, and it is by this, as well as the insignificant flowers, that they can be distinguished from the true cacti which many of them superficially resemble.

### *E. caput-medusae*
MEDUSA'S HEAD

This South African perennial succulent has a thick, leathery base up to 6 in (about 15 cm) tall, out of which develop a number of gray-green, pulpy stems 18 in (about 45 cm) long that look like the tentacles of an octopus. Short-lived, narrow, lance-shaped leaves grow only at the branch extremities, where green flowers with white, lacy margins appear in summer. It is best propagated from seed or offsets.
ZONES 9–10

*Furcraea foetida*

*Fenestraria aurantiaca*

*Faucaria tigrina*

*Euphorbia obesa*

*Gasteria verrucosa*

*Ferocactus hamatacanthus*

### *E. obesa*

GINGHAM GOLF BALL, BASEBALL PLANT

Perfectly spherical, becoming elongated, this unusual and popular perennial succulent is native to South Africa. It grows up to 8 in (about 20 cm) tall and 6 in (about 15 cm) in diameter, and is spineless. The pale green stem has eight depressed ribs and red-brown, horizontal and vertical lines, making a check pattern similar to gingham. Little, yellow-green, cup shaped bracts bloom from the apex in summer.

POT CULTURE

### *E. trigona*

AFRICAN MILK TREE

This 3 ft (about 90 cm) tall cactus-like succulent from eastern Africa is a popular indoor plant—it looks prehistoric with its bolt-upright, 3-angled stems and oval leaves standing horizontally at intervals from the angles. By the end of summer, most of the leaves drop. The insignificant green flowers are not often seen on indoor plants. It needs good light indoors or light shade in the garden, and prefers damp, porous soil. Give it a cool, dry resting period.

ZONES 9–10

## FAUCARIA
### *tigrina*

TIGER'S JAW

Clump forming, this easy to cultivate, attractive, stemless, perennial succulent is native to South Africa. It grows to 4 in (about 10 cm) and spreads out to 20 in (about 50 cm). The triangular, vivid, fleshy, gray-green leaves form in rosettes and are dense and pulpy with a keeled reverse. They are covered with white dots, occasionally tinted red and bear up to 10 erect, white teeth on their margins. Large, deep yellow, daisy-like flowers, 2 in (about 5 cm) across, bloom in fall, only opening in the afternoon. This species likes full sun, little water in winter and porous soil. Propagate from seed in spring, cuttings in summer.

ZONES 9–10

## FENESTRARIA
### *aurantiaca*

WINDOW PLANT

This small, clump-forming, perennial succulent, native to South Africa, grows up to 2 in (about 5 cm) tall and 8 in (about 20 cm) across. The basal rosettes are composed of upright, club-shaped, shiny, gray-green foliage approximately $1^{1}/_{2}$ in (about 3 cm) long. These slender, smooth leaves have a curved underside and permeable gray tips. Large, vivid yellow, daisy-like flowers appear from late summer to fall or in winter. The distinctive leaves enjoy a position in full sun with porous soil and scant water; in fact they should be kept bone dry over the winter period. Propagate from seed in spring and summer or by careful division in spring.

POT CULTURE

## FEROCACTUS
### *hamatacanthus*
**syn. *Hamatocactus hamatacanthus***

TURK'S HEAD

Originating in Mexico, this fiercely spined, globe-shaped cactus reaches

*Euphorbia trigona*

25 in (about 63 cm) in height and diameter. Elongating with age, it has up to 20 prominent ribs and numerous tubercles sprouting extremely sharp, brownish red spines with yellow tips. In spring to summer a single yellow flower, with a red interior, blooms from the crown, followed by a pulpy, globe-shaped seed pod. Plant in full sun and porous soil. Blackened areoles, which occur on some species, should be treated with a systemic fungicide. To prevent the problem occurring, ensure plants have adequate ventilation. Propagate from seed in spring and summer.

ZONES 9–10

## FURCRAEA
### *foetida*
**syn. *F. gigantea***

This giant false agave is the largest of the *Furcraea* genus and, like the agave, is a perennial succulent. It has a rosette of broad, sword-shaped, fleshy, green leaves and in summer fragrant, bell-shaped, white-centered, green flowers on a 24 ft (about 7 m) stem appear. It has a spread of 15 ft (about 4.5 m ). Grow in a position in well-drained soil in full sun. Propagate from bulbils which grow on the lower stem of the flower.

ZONES 10–11

## GASTERIA
### *verrucosa*

WARTY ALOE, OX TONGUE

Native to South Africa, this fan-shaped, perennial succulent grows up to 4 in (about 10 cm) in height and 12 in (about 30 cm) wide. Its long, sharply pointed, lance-shaped leaves are deep green and coated with white, wart-like tubercles. They form in two opposing ranks and have slightly furled edges. In spring racemes of cup-shaped, orange and green flowers appear from the center. This succulent is simple to cultivate, requiring well-drained soil with full sun or partial shade. Propagate in spring and summer from leaf cuttings or seed, or by division.

ZONES 9–10

# A Field Trip to the Anza-Borrego Desert State Park

The Anza-Borrego Desert State Park in southern California is part of a remarkable landscape—and the setting for many a Hollywood western. The park lies in a rain shadow shielded from the coast by the Sierra Nevada Mountains, and takes in an area of high desert approximately 50 miles (about 80 km) east of San Diego.

The road from the San Diego–Carlsbad area, where your trip begins, to Mount Palomar, takes in a breathtaking array of mountain and desert scenery. Leaving the urban areas near the coast you wind through willows and oaks along shaded watercourses. The canyons and hills are home to a number of bulbs and perennials such as blue dicks (*Dichelostemma* sp.), various *Allium, Lilium* and *Penstemon* species, the spectacular red delphinium *(Delphinium cardinale)* and many others. As you travel further into the foothills, the area is dominated by chaparral vegetation (dense, tangled brushwood). An outstanding feature here is the manzanita (*Arctostaphylos* sp.), a shrub or small tree which has a beautiful, smooth, rusty colored bark and clusters of white to pink bell-shaped flowers in spring. If you get out of the car you may be joined by roadrunner birds (made famous by the cartoon character).

Continue along the highway to Mount Palomar; it reaches an imposing 10000 ft (about 3000 m). Here you can walk through the tranquil conifer forests. The atmosphere will be slightly damp, as this area on the coastal side of the Sierra Nevada is subject to mists from the Pacific Ocean. The walking trails around Mount Palomar are delightful and the conifer forest provides a majestic backdrop for mountain wildflowers such as wild roses, liliums, columbines *(Aquilegia formosa)* and a host of other bulbs and perennials. You are also likely to hear and see the famous woodpecker bird.

*Plants can grow even in this harsh desert environment.*

Crossing to the other side of the mountains you wind your way down fairly steep roads and, as you travel further east, the vegetation changes rather dramatically—trees give way to cacti, yuccas and agaves. The air is drier, and is accompanied by strong winds whipping off the mountains. Any plant that thrives here is extraordinarily tough.

The visitors' center at the Anza-Borrego Desert State Park is a suitable place to start a walk which takes you to the most interesting flora and fauna in this unique area. The center is near Borrego Springs on the floor of the desert and is surrounded by hills and canyons. The 2–3 miles (about 3–4 km) Palm Canyon walk winds through a mountain chasm and rises to 400 ft (about 120 m). The mountains are predominantly granite which, as they erode, forms a sandy and, in places, gravelly soil, providing an ideal medium for the various cacti and other plants that grow here.

The desert of the Anza-Borrego experiences extremes of temperature and low rainfall. The average annual rainfall is 5 in (about 125 mm) but this is erratic and there are years when there is virtually no rain. During the winter period, from November through to April, temperatures go down to 32°F (0°C). Spring arrives in April and lasts a fairly short time, the floral display depending very much on the rainfall. Various ephemerals such as sunflowers and godetias (satin flowers) as well as the perennials ocotillo, agave, and various barrel cactus species can also be found in flower at this time. During the long, hot, desert summer temperatures can reach over 110°F (about 43°C) for days or even weeks on end. Hot dry winds often lash the countryside.

*A variety of desert plants in rocky soil.*

*Ferocactus acanthodes*

As you walk along the trail you gradually climb up the canyon, and here the red barrel cactus *(Ferocactus acanthodes)* can be found thriving on the sandy, gravelly slopes. The best time of year to see the red barrel cactus is when it flowers, in spring. One of the most spectacular of the cactus species in the area, it can grow up to 4½ ft (about 1.5 m) tall, which makes for an impressive plant, especially when in flower. Its preference for growing on sloping gravelly ground gives it an almost surreal quality, as if perched ready to roll down the hill. The plant itself is fascinating, with rows of curved spine clusters presumably standing guard to intercept any predator foolish enough to try to feed on it. The curved spines were once used as fish hooks by the local Indians. Arachnophobics should be wary of getting too close to the plant as colonies of tarantula spiders are often found at the base.

While a number of animals such as the mountain lion and kit fox inhabit this area, you are unlikely to encounter them. However, you can occasionally hear the howls of coyotes. The silence of the desert is also sometimes broken by the terrifying sound of the rattlesnake. Although this is rare, if you see one treat it with respect as they have been known to aggressively pursue people.

On the same slopes as the red barrel cactus are other interesting plants such as the ocotillo *(Fouquieria splendens)*. In spring it bears tight clusters of spectacular red flowers. The cholla (pronounced choya) cactus and prickly pear (*Opuntia* sp.) grow here in abundance, producing pleasing floral displays. Agaves can also be found with their tall, stout stems and clusters of yellow flowers on the branches. The ubiquitous yuccas are also here and are reminiscent of agaves in their overall form.

A trip to the Anza-Borrego Desert is a unique experience for the plant lover. It certainly does not have the lushness of a tropical rainforest or the wildflower displays of the prairie meadows, but there is an exhilarating feeling of wilderness in the desert, an experience not easily forgottem.

## Ferocactus

The 20 to 30 North American species of *Ferocactus* show characteristics typical of many cacti—the stem is a fleshy, succulent, vertically ribbed cylinder, armed with very fierce spines arranged in small radiating groups. The term cacti refers to members of the large plant family Cactaceae. Nearly all the species of Cactaceae are succulent plants, or "succulents," but there are many succulents which are not be cacti, such as euphorbias, aloes and agaves.

The family Cactaceae consists of at least 1000 species, divided among 80 or more genera. They occur as natives only in the Americas (including the West Indies and the Galapagos Islands), except for a few rainforest epiphytes in West Africa and Madagascar. Their popular image as desert plants is a very incomplete picture: in fact they are rare or absent in the driest American deserts, while on the other hand they may be common in other habitats, for example North American prairies, Brazilian rainforests, West Indian vine thickets, and high Andean hillsides. It is true, though, that cacti are adapted for survival in places where a deficiency of moisture is regularly experienced.

*Ferocactus acanthodes*

Gymnocalycium mihanovichii

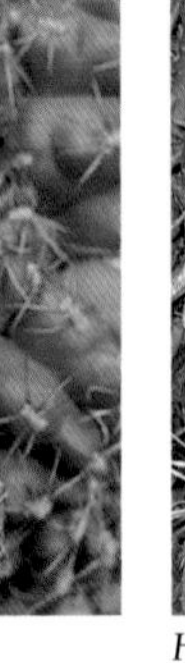

Gymnocalycium andreae

Hylocereus undatus

Haworthia fasciata

Hatiora salicornioides

Graptopetalum paraguayense

Haageocereus versicolor

Haworthia bolusii

## *GRAPTOPETALUM* *paraguayense*

GHOST PLANT, MOTHER-OF-PEARL PLANT

In spite of its specific name implying it is native to Paraguay, the mother-of-pearl plant is actually native to Mexico and is closely related to the echeverias. Dense rosettes of thick, blunt-tipped leaves are borne on long, fleshy stems at first erect then becoming decumbent with age. The leaves are reddish gray cast with a silvery blue bloom. Showy cymes of white flowers bloom in the spring, rising well above the rosette; they are very long lasting. Provide bright light and sandy, well-drained soil. Propagate by rooting detached leaves or rosettes directly in sand.

ZONES 9–10

## *GYMNOCALYCIUM*

CHIN CACTI

Native to South America, these small cacti grow to 10 in (about 25 cm) in height and vary in habit, from single and globe shaped to clump forming and cylindrical. All are distinguished by a chin-like prominence just below the areoles, hence the common name. In spring and summer numerous, trumpet-shaped flowers appear from the crown. The cacti grow well indoors, requiring a cool spell in winter. Plant in porous soil with full sun or semi-shade. Propagate from seed in spring or offsets in summer. The genus name comes from the Greek *gymnos*: naked, and *kalyx*: bud, referring to the sessile flowers.

### *G. andreae*

From Argentina, this colonizing cactus reaches 2 in (about 5 cm) in height and spreads to 4 in (about 10 cm). The shiny, green-blue stems are globe shaped and bear eight ribs. Seven yellowish, radial spines and three upwardly curving, central spines sprout from whitish areoles. Vivid yellow, trumpet-shaped flowers appear from the flat crown in spring and summer. This species requires total sun.

ZONES 10–11

### *G. mihanovichii*

PLAID CACTUS

This species, native to Paraguay, has flattened, grayish green, globular stems up to 2 in (about 5 cm) in diameter. These have eight ribs and horizontal grooves above and below the areoles. Brownish, yellow spines develop in whorls but there are no central spines. Numerous light-yellow tinted, green flowers appear early on. A number of red and yellow natural varieties occur that are without chlorophyll; the best known is the scarlet 'Hibotan'.

ZONES 10–11

## *HAAGEOCEREUS* *versicolor*

Under cultivation, this Peruvian cactus forms in clumps of upright, tubular stems to $4^1/_2$ ft (about 1.3 m) tall and 3 in (about 7.5 cm) in diameter. The compact, downy stems have about 20 light ribs and are thickly covered with areoles bearing up to 30 golden yellow-red, whorled spines. At night during summer, long, white, trumpet-like flowers appear. This cactus requires porous soil with full sun and light water. Propagate from cuttings in summer, or from seed in spring.

ZONES 9–10

## *HATIORA* *salicornioides*

DRUNKARD'S DREAM, BOTTLE PLANT

Native to Brazil, this little, perennial, epiphytic cactus has a narrow, shrubby habit and reaches 16 in (about 40 cm) in height and spread. The slender, jointed, tubular stems readily branch and are totally spineless. In spring tiny, deep-yellow, cup-shaped flowers appear at the bloated stem tips. This species needs extremely porous soil and semi-shade. Maintain moisture during the hotter months and only water occasionally during winter. Propagate from cuttings in spring and summer.

ZONES 9–11

## *HAWORTHIA*

This genus of 150 dense, dwarf-like, perennial succulents originated in South Africa and grow to 12 in (about 30 cm) tall. They are predominantly thicket forming, developing in basal or short-stemmed rosettes. The decorative, lush foliage is lanceolate to triangular and marked with distinctive, white spots. Racemes of rather insignificant white, or occasionally yellow, six-lobed flowers appear in summer. These succulents require semi-shade to maintain healthy leaves. Keep slightly moist during the hotter months and totally dry in winter. Propagate by division or from offsets during spring to fall.

### *H. bolusii*

Growing to $2^1/_2$ in (about 6 cm) in height and 4 in (about 10 cm) in diameter, this extremely attractive succulent develops in a compact, stemless rosette. The plentiful, silvery, gray-blue leaves are triangular and are slightly serrated. Slender racemes of typically white flowers appear from spring to fall.

POT CULTURE

### *H. fasciata*

This more or less stemless succulent is grown for its interesting leaves which stand upright in neat ro-

settes, the better to show off the white dots on their undersides—the whole effect is of gray and white. The tiny white flowers are carried in early summer on 16 in (about 40 cm) tall, bare stems but are not very interesting. It is propagated by removing offsets in spring.
POT CULTURE

## *HYLOCEREUS undatus*

NIGHT-BLOOMING CEREUS, MOON FLOWER, HONOLULU QUEEN, QUEEN OF THE NIGHT

Of unknown origin, this tropical, scaling cactus develops long, multiple stems up to 15 ft (about 4.5 m) in length. These fragile, vivid green stems have two to three angles and tough, undulating margins with widely spread, single-spined areoles. In late spring to summer enormous, creamy white, fragrant flowers appear at the leaf tips. These are followed by red, edible, egg-shaped fruit. This cactus requires moist, fertile soil and partial shade. Propagate from stem cuttings in spring and summer. The species is easy to cultivate.
ZONES 9–10

## *KALANCHOE*

This genus comprises approximately 200 species of perennial succulents native mostly to southern Asia and tropical and subtropical Africa. The species range in habit from erect and bushy to spreading and prostrate, and grow up to 9 ft (about 2.7 m) in height and width. The succulent pairs of opposing leaves vary from slender to rounded. The tubular or bell-shaped flowers have four petals and appear in branched terminal clusters. These succulents only require light watering in the colder months. Propagate from stem or leaf cuttings in late spring to summer, seed at the end of spring, or pot up plantlets that may form along leaf margins.

### *K. blossfeldiana*

FLAMING KATY

This small, shrubby perennial is native to Africa and reaches 12 in (about 30 cm) in height and width. Its multiple, upstretched branches are covered with round to rectangular, deep green leaves with red margins and notched tips. Thick racemes of little, deep red, cylindrical flowers appear from winter to early summer; cultivated strains may be pink, yellow or orange. The species requires partial shade. It is a very popular florist's pot plant.
ZONES 9–10

### *K. fedtschenkoi*

SOUTH AMERICAN AIR PLANT

This compact succulent of uncertain origin grows to 12–20 in (about 30–50 cm) in height and width, readily producing multiple branches and trailing stems. The glossy, blue-green leaves are rounded to rectangular and have deeply undulating margins; a form with cream edges is very popular. Terminal panicles of reddish orange, bell-shaped flowers appear in late winter. This species requires total sun, with only light watering in the cooler months.
ZONES 10–11

### *K. tomentosa*

PANDA PLANT

This small, shrubby African native grows gradually up to 20 in (about 50 cm) tall. It has dense, spoon-shaped, light green leaves that are covered with white felt and often have brown, rounded tips. Creamy yellow flowers appear in fall, though flowering is very rare in cultivation. Give it a position in full sun with well-drained soil.
ZONES 10–11

## *LAMPRANTHUS*

These small, perennial succulents originated in South Africa and have an erect habit, usually spreading in maturity. Full sun and a well-drained soil are preferred and dry conditions are withstood; however the plants become straggly after several years and should be replaced. Simple to grow, these succulents are propagated from cuttings in late spring and summer and from seed in spring.

### *L. aurantiacus*

Reaching up to 20 in (about 50 cm) in height and 30 in (about 76 cm) in width, this species has small, green-gray, tubular foliage which narrows towards the tip. In summer an abundance of vivid, dark orange, daisy-like flowers with a spot of purple at their centers appear.
ZONES 9–10

### *L. aureus*

ORANGE VYGIE

Native to South Africa, this upright, perennial, succulent shrub reaches to 16 in (about 40 cm) tall. The bluish green leaves are up to 2 in (about 5 cm) in length and are covered with clear spots. In summer vivid yellow or orange, daisy-like flowers up to $2^{1}/_{2}$ in (about 6 cm) in diameter appear.
ZONES 9–10

### *L. coccineus*

This spectacular South African plant resembles *L. aurantiacus* except that the leaves are a little shorter; in its late spring season it is a dazzling sight—literally so, as the red flowers are iridescent and flash purple or pink or orange as the sun strikes them. Plant in full sun.
ZONES 9–10

*Kalanchoe blossfeldiana*

*Lampranthus aureus*

*Kalanchoe fedtschenkoi*

*Lithops dorotheae*

*Kalanchoe tomentosa*

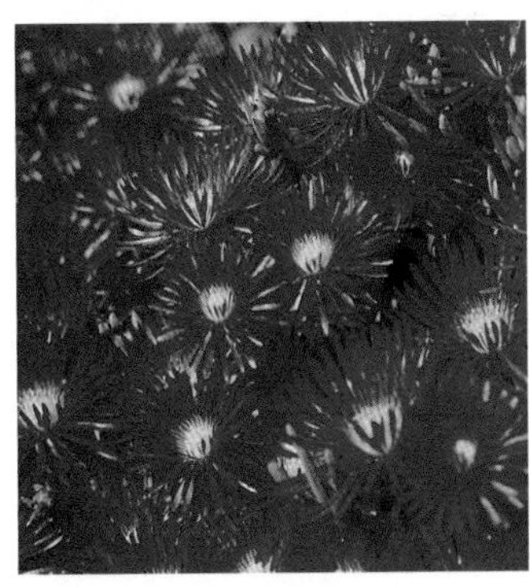

*Lampranthus coccineus*

*Lampranthus aurantiacus*

## LITHOPS

LIVING STONES, STONEFACE

Originating in South Africa, this fascinating genus contains over 50 perennial succulents which develop singularly or in colonies. They are composed of pairs of extremely lush, upright leaves compressed together to form a hemispherical mass with a deep crevice running across the top. New growth and white or yellow, daisy-like flowers grow up through the fissure. The old leaves split and dry away to paper-like skin to reveal a pair of new leaves growing at right angles to the old ones. The plants look like smooth river stones, and have translucent upper surfaces. These succulents are easy to grow and are drought resistant. Plant in light soil and allow full sun. Water only in spring and propagate in summer from seed or by dividing bodies.

### *L. dorotheae*

This cushion-forming species is up to $1^1/_2$ in (about 3 cm) tall and 4 in (about 10 cm) in diameter. Its light, gray-blue, egg-shaped body is made up of two pulpy, asymmetrical leaves. The top surface has deep green "windows," red and white markings and a deep, transversal slit. Yellow flowers appear from this crevice in summer to fall.

POT CULTURE

### *L. glesinae*

Not a common species, *L. glesinae* is typical in the way the egg-shaped, spotted leaves mimic the stones among which they grow. A pebble or gravel mulch is appreciated by just about all succulents; it keeps their crowns dry.

POT CULTURE

### *L. karasmontana* var. *bella*

syn. *L. bella*

This cluster-forming perennial has egg-shaped bodies up to $1^1/_2$ in (about 3 cm) tall and 1 in (about 2.5 cm) in diameter. These are composed of yellowish brown, compressed leaves with dark brown lines on the markedly curving crown. In summer to fall snow white flowers appear from the crown's crevice.

POT CULTURE

### *L. turbiniformis*

This South African succulent forms in small clumps of paired leaves. Egg shaped and orange-brown in color, these lush leaves grow to 1 in (about 2.5 cm) in height. The flattened surface is scored with a shallow, transverse crevice and brown, linear markings. Vivid yellow flowers up to 2 in (about 5 cm) in diameter bloom from white buds.

POT CULTURE

## LOBIVIA

COB CACTUS, HEDGEHOG CACTUS

This genus contains over 70 species of thicket-forming cacti ranging in habit from basal and globular to erect and cylindrical, up to 12 in (about 30 cm) in height. Large, bell-shaped or funnel-like flowers are borne on short, downy stems. These decorative blooms come in vivid orange, yellow, purple or red and frequently have deeper-colored throats. Species need porous soil, total sun or semi-shade and light water. They are simple to grow and make beautiful pot plants. Propagate from seed or stem cuttings in spring and fall.

### *L. backebergii*

A smaller growing species with an almost spherical body, tufts of whitish spines and profuse, magenta flowers in spring. It sometimes refuses to make clumps.

ZONES 9–10

### *L. bruchii*

GOLDEN BARREL OF THE ANDES

This is one of the larger species, the many-ribbed stems growing to be as much as 12 in (about 30 cm) thick. The spines are yellow, the flowers brilliant red.

ZONES 9–10

## LOPHOCEREUS

### *schottii*

WHISKER CACTUS

Native to Mexico and the southern USA, this erect cactus grows up to 15 ft (about 4.5 m) tall. Its sallow to bright green stem tends to branch out from below after several years. The body has five to seven ribs and varying areoles. The higher, flowering areoles sprout bristly, gray spines radiating around one central spine. The smaller, non-flowering areoles bear up to 10 dense, cone-shaped, grayish black spines. Small, tubular, night-opening flowers appear in spring and summer, followed by globular fruit. This species enjoys full sun and porous soil. Propagate from seed in spring, cuttings in summer.

ZONES 9–10

## LOPHOPHORA

### *williamsii*

PEYOTE, MESCAL BUTTONS, DUMPLING CACTUS

This flat-crowned cactus is native to Mexico and the southern USA. It is extremely slow growing up to 2 in (about 5 cm) tall and may be singular or colonizing. The dumpling-like, bluish green, ribbed stem is lightly covered with areoles sprouting short, bristly, white hair. Beautiful, light pink flowers sprout from the crown center in summer. This cactus, perhaps the most cold tolerant of the tribe, needs full sun and porous soil. Propagate from seed in spring and summer. It is the source of the dangerous and illegal drug mescaline. Consumption of the cactus induces hallucinations and it has been used for thousands of years by American Indians in their spiritual ceremonies.

ZONES 9–10

*Lobivia backebergii*

*Lophophora williamsii*

*Lithops glesinae*

*Lithops karasmontana* var. *bella*

*Lobivia bruchii*

*Lophocereus schottii*

*Lithops turbiniformis*

## MAMMILLARIA

PINCUSHION CACTI

This is one of the largest genus of cacti, containing over 300 dwarf-like species native to Mexico and southwestern North America. The short, globular or clump-forming, erect columns up to 12 in (about 30 cm) tall have stems with raised, horny tubercles and downy areoles sprouting either silky bristles or tough, curving spines. In spring and summer funnel- or bell-shaped flowers appear near the crown, followed by reddish pink fruit. These cacti require full sun to maximize flowering. Easy to grow, they prefer light, sandy soil and occasional water. Propagate from seed in spring and summer, or from offsets in summer.

### *M. bombycina*

SILK PINCUSHION

Native to Mexico, this single, spherical cactus has short, pillar-like stems that grow up to 8 in (about 20 cm) tall, and have spirally arranged tubercles with numerous whorls of white spines and yellowish brown, central spines. If allowed full sun, purple-pink flowers bloom around the fleecy crown from winter to spring.

POT CULTURE

### *M. elegans*

This Mexican species is singular and globular, later clustering in short columns up to 8 in (about 20 cm) in height. Four black-pointed, central spines and numerous shorter, white bristles densely cover the blue-green stems. In spring this cactus develops vivid, deep reddish purple flowers.

POT CULTURE

### *M. plumosa*

FEATHER CACTUS

This curious cactus is native to Mexico and readily forms a thick, woolly, mound-like cluster 6 in (about 15 cm) high and 16 in (about 40 cm) wide. The stems are blanketed with feather-like, overlaying, radial spines which sprout from downy areoles. In winter creamy green, pink or yellow flowers appear, but rarely under cultivation. Grow in a fertile, alkaline soil.

POT CULTURE

### *M. zeilmanniana*

ROSE PINCUSHION

Originating in Mexico, this cactus has globular stems up to 6 in (about 15 cm) in height and colonizing out to 12 in (about 30 cm). Silky brown and white radial spines and reddish brown, central spines cover the green stems. Rings of dark purple flowers appear around the crown any time in spring.

POT CULTURE

## MESEMBRYANTHEMUM *crystallinum*

This annual, carpet-forming succulent grows to 4 in (about 10 cm) high and has dense, pulpy foliage with undulating edges. Glossy glands cover the leaves, flower stems and cups. Groups of 4 white flowers appear in summer. It requires a position with extremely light soil and total sun. Propagate from seed in spring.

ZONES 9–10

## NOPALXOCHIA

This genus of epiphytic cacti is native to Central America. The species have flat, ribbon-like, spineless stems with heavily undulating margins. Pinkish red flowers appear from the edges of the stems, then both flower and stem perish. These species are readily cultivated and require porous, fertile soil in semi-shade. Propagate from stem cuttings in spring and summer.

### *N. ackermannii*

**syn. *Epiphyllum ackermanii***

RED ORCHID CACTUS

Originating in southern Mexico, this freely branching cactus grows up to 12 in (about 30 cm) tall and spreads up to 24 in (about 60 cm). Its succulent, arching stems can be up to 16 in (about 40 cm) long with notched margins. Bright red, trumpet-shaped flowers that close up at night bloom from these notches in spring to summer.

POT CULTURE

### *N. phyllanthoides* 'Deutsche Kaiserin'

**syn. *Epiphyllum* × 'Deutsche Kaiserin'**

This epiphytic cactus grows up to 24 in (about 60 cm) tall and spreads to 3 ft (about 90 cm). The cylindrical base bears vivid green, pendulous stems with wavy margins. Numerous pink, tubular-stemmed flowers bloom in spring.

POT CULTURE

## NOTOCACTUS *apricus*

SUN CUP

This small, ball-shaped cactus is native to South America and grows up to 4 in (about 10 cm) in diameter. Its single, multi-ribbed, light green stem has deep, transverse grooves and downy areoles. Colorful, yellow-brown, radial spines and red, central spines completely cover the cactus. In summer, rich yellow flowers with purple stamen readily appear from the crown. It likes porous soil, semi-shade and occasional water at all times. Propagate from seed in spring and summer.

ZONES 9–10

*Nopalxochia phyllanthoides* 'Deutsche Kaiserin'

*Mammillaria zeilmanniana*

*Mammillaria elegans*

*Mammillaria plumosa*

*Notocactus apricus*

*Mammillaria bombycina*

*Mesembryanthemum crystallinum*

*Nopalxochia ackermannii*

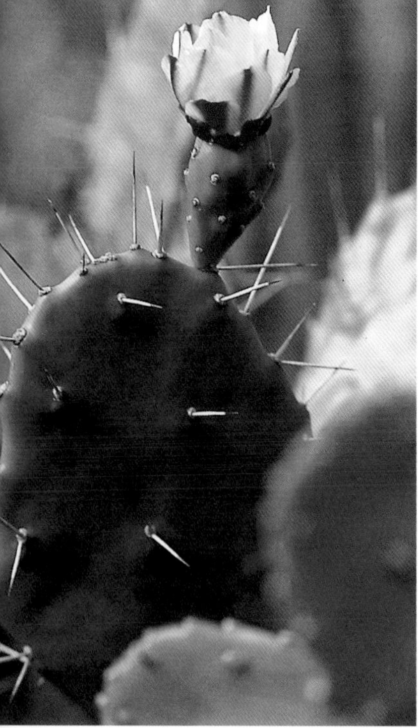
*Opuntia ficus-indica*

*Orbea variegata*

*Pachypodium lamerei*

*Pachyphytum oviferum*

*Parodia formosa*

*Pachypodium baronii* var. *windsori*

*Opuntia violacea* var. *macrocentra*

## OPUNTIA

PRICKLY PEAR

This large, diverse genus is native to the United States, South America and the West Indies. Varying from prostrate to erect, and typically compact and branching, these cacti either develop flat, pad-like, jointed stems or branches with little tubular or three-angled leaves. Most species are covered with sharp spines and soft, hooked, bristles, called "glochids." Open-petaled, mostly yellow flowers appear on larger plants (except under cultivation) in spring and summer. These are followed by the frequently edible fruit. They require total sun and porous soil. Propagate from seed or cuttings in spring and summer.

### *O. ficus-indica*

syn. ***O. engelmannii, O. megacantha***

INDIAN FIG

With an upright, open habit, becoming compact and multi-stemmed in maturity, this popular species reaches 15 ft (about 4.5 m) in height and breadth. It has jointed stems composed of gray, oval pads up to 18 in (about 45 cm) long and usually covered with spines. Funnel-like, vivid yellow flowers appear from the stem tips in summer, followed by reddish yellow-purple, bristly but edible fruit. A useful hedge cactus in its native South America. Spineless varieties are cultivated (where legal) for the delicious fruit.

ZONES 9–10

### *O. violacea* var. *macrocentra*

BLACK-SPINED PRICKLY PEAR

Native from west Texas to Arizona into northern Mexico, this shrubby cactus reaches heights of 7 ft (about 2 m) with a similar spread. The obovate, dark green segments are 7 in (about 17 cm) long and are covered on both sides with nearly black, 7 in (about 17 cm) long spines. The showy yellow flowers have brilliant orange-red bases and appear in late spring. Of easy culture, it thrives in sandy, gravelly soil in full sun with little irrigation. Propagate by planting individual segments or from seed.

ZONES 9–10

## ORBEA

### *variegata*

TOAD CACTUS, STAR FLOWER, STARFISH FLOWER

Highly valued for its stunning flowers, this South African colonizing, perennial succulent has multiple, finger-shaped, upright stems up to 4 in (about 10 cm) tall. These deep green-gray stems are often marked with purple and have 4 notched angles. From summer to fall striking, starfish-shaped flowers appear individually or in clusters with a kaleidoscopic pattern of reddish brown, yellow and purple. The beauty of the flower contrasts with its unpleasant smell. Porous soil is preferred with full sun or partial shade. It is propagated from seed or stem division in spring or summer.

ZONES 10–11

## PACHYPHYTUM

### *oviferum*

SUGAR ALMOND PLANT, MOONSTONES

Originating in Mexico, this beautiful, perennial succulent colonizes in stemless rosettes of bloated, spoon-shaped, blue-green leaves with a whitish red, powdery coating. Deep red-orange flowers appear in short-stemmed, pendent clusters from the end of winter to early spring. This succulent requires full sun, porous soil and light water. Propagate in late spring or summer from stem and leaf cuttings.

ZONES 19–10

## PACHYPODIUM

These upright, perennial succulents reach heights up to 18 ft (about 5.5 m); most species have spines and swollen stems and are native to Madagascar. They require full sun, porous soil, occasional water during summer months and a dry spell during winter. Propagate from seed in spring and summer.

### *P. baronii* var. *windsori*

This is a most attractive small species, with an almost spherical main stem and short, spiny branches. The flowers are distinct and a beautiful shade of scarlet.

POT CULTURE

### *P. lamerei*

This species has a spiny, triangular, light green trunk and develops multiple stems which readily divide after each flowering. Slender leaves sprout from the crown and white, scented, summer flowers appear from the stem tips.

POT CULTURE

## PARODIA

BALL CACTUS

Mostly native to the mountains of equatorial South America, the species in this genus vary from singular and globe shaped, to colonizing in dense clusters of short cylindrical stems. These stems are ribbed with transverse rows of prominent tubercles with fleecy areoles sprouting brilliantly colored, curving spines. From a relatively young age red, yellow and orange, trumpet-shaped flowers bloom from the crown. Some species prefer full sun, others semi-shade. Easy to grow, these cacti require well-drained soil and plentiful water during the summer months. Propagate from seed in spring, cuttings in summer.

### *P. formosa*

A rather pleasing cactus from South America, less flamboyant in bloom than other species of the genus—the orange flowers are small in comparison with the 12 in (about 30 cm) diameter body—but noteworthy for its spiral ribs and short, white spines.

ZONES 9–10

### *P. mutabilis*

Originating in Argentina, this quick-growing cactus has a spherical stem

that reaches 3 in (about 7.5 cm) in diameter and height. The lightly ribbed, green body is covered with white, downy areoles producing numerous, fine, whorled spines and longer, extremely sharp, red central spines with brown tips. Vivid, yellow summer flowers grow out of the fleecy crown. A fertile, neutral to acid soil is recommended.
ZONES 9–10

### *P. nivosa*

This multi-ribbed, egg-shaped cactus reaches up to 6 in (about 15 cm) in height and 4 in (about 10 cm) in diameter. The stem is covered with white, fluffy areoles sprouting rigid, white spines. Brilliant red flowers appear from the crown in summer. It enjoys full sun and porous soil.
ZONES 9–10

## *PILOSOCEREUS*
### *palmeri*

This upright, pillar-like cactus is native to Mexico and grows to 9–18 ft (about 2.7–5.5 m) tall and up to 3 ft (about 90 cm) in diameter. The silvery, blue-green stem readily branches and is prominently ribbed. Areoles sprouting brown spines line the ribs and white, radially spined areoles cover the apex. Glossy, pink, nocturnal flowers develop near the crown on taller trees. It requires total sun, porous soil and plentiful water only during the hotter months. Propagate from seed and stem cuttings in spring or summer.
POT CULTURE

## *PORTULACARIA*
### *afra*

JADE PLANT, ELEPHANT FOOD

This small, succulent shrub has an upright habit, reaching up to 9 ft (about 2.7 m) tall, and a dense rounded crown. The stiff, level branches are covered with little, oval, blue-green leaves. This succulent prefers a sunny location (though it will grow in light shade) with porous soil and will not tolerate the slightest frost. Lightly water during the hotter months and propagate from semi-ripe cuttings in summer. It makes a fine pot plant. The common name comes from the popular belief that the shrub is eaten by elephants in Africa where it grows wild.
ZONES 9–11

## *REBUTIA*

CROWN CACTUS, HEDGEHOG CACTUS

This genus, native to South America, contains over 25 very small, predominantly cluster-forming species varying from hemispherical to erect and cylindrical. The plants develop tubercles around their bases from where the flower buds emerge after one or two years. Relatively large, vivid orange, pink, purple, red, yellow or white flowers readily bloom in late spring to early summer. Easily grown in most soil types, the species require total sun and adequate water only during the budding and blooming period. Propagate from seed and cuttings in spring or summer.

### *R. aureiflora*

Originating in Argentina, this mound-forming cactus averages 2 in (about 5 cm) in height. Its deep green-purple body is covered with lateral rows of tubercles and rigid, brownish white radial and central spines. At the end of spring an abundance of yellow, or occasionally purple, flowers with white interiors bloom in abundance around the base.
POT CULTURE

### *R. muscula*

Native to Argentina, this globular, deep green cactus has a mound-forming habit spreading out to 6 in (about 15 cm). White, silky, short spines and light green tubercles thickly cover the body. Vivid orange flowers blossom at the end of spring.
POT CULTURE

### *R. pseudodeminuta*

WALLFLOWER CACTUS

This is one of the most desirable of all miniature cacti. The plant is just a cluster of $1^1/_2$ in (about 3 cm) thick, 4 in (about 10 cm) or so tall stems with whitish prickles; in early summer it disappears under the scarlet flowers with their prominent golden stamens.
POT CULTURE

## *RHIPSALIDOPSIS*
### *gaertneri*

EASTER CACTUS

This pendent cactus with its leaf-like, thornless stems resembles the popular Christmas cactus (*Schlumbergera* × *buckleyi*) and is grown in the same way. The points of difference are that the Easter cactus has symmetrical, starry flowers instead of asymmetrical ones; that it is rarely more than 12 in (about 30 cm) high and wide; and that it flowers later, in early spring. Garden varieties come in a range of colors: white, light and deep rose pink, salmon, orange and red. Propagate from cuttings in summer.
POT CULTURE

*Rebutia aureiflora*

*Rebutia pseudodeminuta*

*Rebutia muscula*

*Parodia mutabilis*

*Parodia nivosa*

*Pilosocereus palmeri*

*Rhipsalidopsis gaertneri*

*Portulacaria afra*

*Sedum* x *rubrotinctum*

*Sedum acre*

*Sedum morganianum*

*Schlumbergera* x *b.* 'White Christmas'

*Sedum aizoon*

## RHIPSALIS
*paradoxa*

Native to South America, this epiphytic cactus has a compact habit up to 3 ft (about 90 cm) tall, then developing multiple, trailing, chain-like stems. In winter to spring little, trumpet-like, white flowers appear along the margins of the "chains" followed by resinous, spherical fruit. It requires a dry rest during fall and should be planted in fertile, porous soil with partial shade. It prefers a warm, damp atmosphere. This pendent cactus makes an ideal hanging basket specimen and is propagated from cuttings in summer, or from seed in spring or summer.

POT CULTURE

## SCHLUMBERGERA
x *buckleyi*

**syn.** *Zygocactus truncatus*

CHRISTMAS CACTUS

Originating in Brazil, these epiphytic, readily branching cacti produce upright stems, which arch in maturity. They are composed of flat, rectangular pads or lush, cylindrical links, covered with bristly areoles, often with notched edges. Prominent, cylindrical flowers bloom from the tops of the stems in fall and winter. These species need porous, fertile soil and full sun or partial shade. They make ideal hanging baskets and should only be watered when the surface roots completely dry out. Propagate in summer from stem cuttings.

POT CULTURE

*Selenicereus grandiflorus*

## SEDUM

STONECROP

This extremely large genus contains over 500 species of predominantly evergreen succulents native to the northern hemisphere. These quick-growing plants widely vary in habit from carpet forming to upright up to 3 ft (about 90 cm) tall. Their lush, whole leaves may be tubular, lanceolate, egg shaped or elliptical and the five-petaled flowers appear in terminal sprays. They make excellent hanging basket or pot plants. Fertile, porous soil is preferred; however some types are extremely robust and will grow in most soil types. Propagate from seed in spring, from stem cuttings in summer or by division in spring or summer.

### *S. acre*

STONECROP, GOLD MOSS

This little plant is one of the hardiest of all succulents. It is native to Europe and eastern Asia; its creeping stems hug the ground between rocks or grow in the chinks of old walls. The whole plant is only around $1\frac{1}{2}$ in (about 3 cm) high and, with its bright green leaves, looks like a lush patch of moss—until it covers itself in spring with zillions of tiny yellow flowers. It has an indefinite spread and can be invasive. Give it a position with sunshine and sharp drainage and propagate by removing offsets.

ZONES 5–9

### *S. aizoon*

Native to Siberia and Japan this is a fully hardy plant, differing from the usual run of succulents in not being evergreen—it dies down each winter, to return in spring with 20 in (about 50 cm) tall stems with fleshy, toothed, lance-shaped, mid-green leaves and crowned with clusters of yellow flowers in summer. It grows well in any soil but prefers one that is fertile and well drained.

ZONES 7–10

### *S. morganianum*

DONKEY'S TAIL, BURRO TAIL

Native to Mexico, this popular, readily branching, evergreen succu-

*Rhipsalis paradoxa*

lent has a compact, upright habit, becoming weeping as the stems lengthen. Growing up to 3 ft (about 90 cm), the attractive stems are composed of bluish green, interlocking leaves that have a plump, lanceolate form. In cultivation clusters of long, pinkish red, starry flowers may bloom at the stem tips in summer. This pendent species makes an ideal hanging basket but should be handled with care as leaves readily detach.

POT CULTURE

### *S.* x *rubrotinctum*

PORK AND BEANS, JELLY BEANS

Little and semi-evergreen, this fully hardy, perennial succulent grows up to 8 in (about 20 cm) in height and has yellow winter blooms. Readily branching, its slender, multiple stems are wide spreading and develop pulpy, obovate leaves in grape-like bunches that turn red and yellow under arid conditions. The leaves will be bright green if the plant is grown in cool, wet conditions. This ideal climate will also maintain the leaf luster.

ZONES 9–10

### *S. spathulifolium*

This fully hardy, evergreen succulent has a carpet-forming habit with tiny rosettes to 2 in (about 15 cm) high, composed of plump, circular, green or frosted gray, intermingled with brownish red leaves. In summer star-shaped yellow flowers appear on short stems. Grow in a position in full sun.

ZONES 7–10

## SELENICEREUS
### *grandiflorus*
QUEEN OF THE NIGHT

*Selenicereus* is a genus of perennial cacti with climbing, 4–10 ribbed, green stems growing to 1 in (about 2.5 cm) in width. *S. grandiflorus* is a vine-like, climbing cactus that reaches up to 9 ft (about 2.7 m) in height and is native to Jamaica and Cuba. It is highly valued for the large, pure white, nocturnal flowers, up to 12 in (about 30 cm) in diameter, to which the common name refers. They are very sweetly scented. Quick growing and readily branching, its deep bluish green, slender stems bear needle-shaped, short yellow spines. It likes full sun and fertile, porous soil. Propagate from seed or stem cuttings in summer.

ZONES 9–11

## SENECIO
### *articulatus*
**syn. *Kleinia articulata***
HOT DOG CACTUS, CANDLE PLANT

Native to South Africa, this deciduous, succulent shrub grows up to 24 in (about 60 cm) tall. Its mutiple, grayish blue stems are tubular and weakly jointed. Terminal sprays of yellow-white flowers, similar in appearance to daisies, bloom from spring into summer. It is well suited to coastal climates and makes an ideal tub or large pot specimen. It prefers full sun and extremely porous soil. Propagate from semi-ripe stem cuttings, simply removed at the joint, in summer.

ZONES 9–10

## STAPELIA
### *leendertziae*

Native to South Africa, this species is one of a genus which comprises 90 species of clump-forming, perennial succulents highly valued for their unique flowers. Growing to 12 in (about 30 cm) tall, it has lush, slender, upright stems with 4 angles and indented or winged margins. The hairy, deep purple flowers are bell-shaped and bloom in summer on tubes up to 2½ in (about 6 cm) long. While extremely beautiful, the flowers unfortunately have an unpleasant carrion odor which attracts flies for pollination, making them unsuitable for indoors. The plants may be grown in the greenhouse. They prefer total light or semi-shade and porous soil. Propagate this species from seed in spring, from cuttings in spring or summer or by division in spring and fall.

POT CULTURE

## SULCOREBUTIA
### *arenacea*

This extremely attractive, small, globular cactus grows up to 2 in (about 5 cm) in height and the same in diameter. Its greenish brown body is thickly covered with tubercles which are arranged in spirals and bear buff-colored spines. Beautiful, rich golden yellow flowers, similar to daisies, bloom around the base of the stem. It prefers full sun, though partial shade should be provided in hotter regions. Propagate in summer and spring from stem cuttings.

POT CULTURE

## THELOCACTUS
### *bicolor*
**syn. *Ferocactus bicolor***

This perennial cactus is native to Mexico and the southern US. It has a spiny, globe-shaped to erect, pillar-like, singular body up to 8 in (about 20 cm) in height and diam eter. This stem has over 10 prominent ribs lined with pronounced tubercles sprouting yellow and red, twisted, radial spines and four longer, yellow, central spines. Easily flowering, pinkish purple, trumpet-shaped flowers bloom from the crown and are up to 2½ in (about 6 cm) long. It enjoys full sun, porous soil and light watering. Propagate from seed in spring and summer.

POT CULTURE

## TRICHOCEREUS

This genus (which is sometimes included in the genus *Echinopsis)* consists of about 25 species of ribbed, cylindrical cacti native to South America. Well-drained soil and full sun are required. Propagate in spring and summer from seed or stem cuttings.

### *T. bridgesii*

Originating in the Andes of South America, this cactus has an erect, cylindrical stem up to 12 ft (about 3.5 m) in height. The greenish blue body freely branches from its base and has up to 8 ribs, sparsely lined with areoles bearing up to 6 spines. In summer white, trumpet-shaped flowers open widely at night and emit a very strong, sometimes overpowering fragrance. Spreading only to 3 ft (about 90 cm), this cactus makes an excellent conservatory specimen. It is of easy culture, frequently being used for grafting.

ZONES 9–10

### *T. huascha*
**syn. *Lobivia huascha***

An example of how imperfect knowledge on the part of botanists can make life difficult for cactus lovers, this Argentine species is found in some books under *Lobivia*, in others under *Trichocereus* or even *Echinopsis*. It is an attractive plant with stout stems, symmetrically ribbed and spiny, and brilliant red or yellow flowers in summer.

ZONES 9–10

*Trichocereus bridgesii*

*Stapelia leendertziae*

*Senecio articulatis*

*Sulcorebutia arenacea*

*Thelocactus bicolor*

*Trichocereus huascha*

CHAPTER 11

# Orchids

*Orchids have a reputation for being glamorous, expensive and difficult. Glamorous they certainly are; but new methods of propagation have made plants much more affordable than they used to be—and few are really difficult to grow: wherever you garden, there will be at least a few you can grow just as easily (well, almost) as any other flower.*

The family is an enormous one (second only to the grasses as the largest in the plant kingdom) and wild orchids grow just about everywhere except in the Arctic and the Antarctic. The most admired and coveted may be those from the tropics and subtropics of the Old and New Worlds, but the more modest temperate climate orchids are delightful too and not as well known as they should be.

## Growing Orchids in the Garden

Most of these temperate orchids are terrestrial, that is they grow in the ground the way other plants do; however the glamorous, warm-climate genera are mostly epiphytes, growing perched in trees (or on rock faces) where they derive nourishment from such debris as they manage to accumulate around their roots—fallen leaves, the odd dead insect, that sort of thing—and storing water from rainy seasons in fleshy, almost succulent, stems called pseudobulbs. They can thus be grown very effectively in gardens where the climate is suitable, and it's not difficult to do. A not too shady tree, preferably with rather rough bark to which the roots can cling, is best. Attach the young plant in a suitable fork with twine, and pack sphagnum moss around its roots; water and fertilize as needed. The important thing is to match the orchid to the climate; on the other hand, although we always think of epiphytic orchids as tropical plants, many grow in rather cool mountain regions and there is a surprisingly large range that can be grown outdoors wherever the temperature rarely falls to freezing and summer humidity is fairly high.

It is assumed that most orchids will be grown in containers in protected coditions everywhere except the Southern coast of California and the Southern tip of Florida, and therefore no hardiness zones have been given. Some exceptions have been noted. As long as it has ample drainage holes, the type of pot is immaterial. However, terracotta not only looks better than plastic, it makes it easier to control the amount of water the roots receive. This is the most important aspect of growing orchids: most take rest periods both in winter and for a short while after flowering and dislike being over watered while they are not in active growth.

It is critical in coolish climates or in an unheated greenhouse, for orchids can't cope with being both cold and wet—the roots go quite dormant in winter and will rot if they aren't kept dry. (That does mean dry—don't worry if the pseudobulbs shrivel a little.) Don't pot them in soil or the roots will suffocate. Rather, choose a specially formulated orchid potting mix. Most of these are based on chopped up bark, the different types varying in how finely it is chopped. (Phalaenopsis and cattleyas, for instance, prefer a coarser mix than cymbidiums or paphiopedilums. If in doubt, choose the coarser mix.) The bark doesn't contain much nourishment for the plant, and you will need to fertilize. You can buy special orchid fertilizers, but a bit of well-rotted manure will be just fine.

*Species of the evergreen, epiphytic orchid* Zygopetalum *are ideal for cold conditions.*

Fertilize while the plants are growing, either making new leaves or flower buds, but not when the plants are resting. You can divide the plants like any other perennial when they outgrow their pots, after flowering being the best time, or you can just put the plant (pot and all if its roots are clinging to the old one) into a bigger pot. Pests are few: the main ones are snails and caterpillars, which adore orchid flower buds; mealy bugs; and red spider.

## Growing Orchids Indoors

If you can arrange the fairly high humidity they enjoy, there is no reason why you can't try orchids as house plants too, although it has to be admitted that out of flower few of them are especially decorative. Don't let direct sun strike them, but give them lots of bright light or they may grow furiously but never flower. Indoors or out it's best to err on the side of too much light, even if the leaves then look a bit bleached. Lots of fresh air is desirable too—open the windows wide in warm weather.

If the orchid bug bites, you will want to consider a greenhouse. It is hard to do without one in cold climates, but even in mild areas it will considerably enlarge your scope. Whether it be timber or aluminum framed, plain or architecturally elaborate is up to you, but take as many ventilators as the makers offer. Not only do orchids like fresh air, you need to be able to keep the greenhouse temperatures from soaring on warm days, when the humidity should be kept up; spraying the plants with water every couple of days in summer is a good idea. Make sure too that the roof can be shaded from spring to fall. Heating can be by any means you find economical and convenient, the amount of heat needed depending on the plants. Orchids are classified according to the minimum winter (night-time) temperatures they need, the convention being that "cool growers" need around 46–50°F (about 8–10°C), "intermediate growers" around 55–59°F (about 13–15°C), "warm growers" as much as 68°F (about 20°C), with daytime (winter) temperatures around 10°F (about 5°C) higher. (These classes are useful in determining the most suitable types to grow out of doors too, remembering that almost all orchids can take a couple of degrees less if they are kept dry in winter.)

*Orchids are grown for their large, showy, often brilliantly colored flowers.*

## Propagation

For all their variety, orchid flowers are built to a common pattern—three petal-like sepals and three petals, the lowest (the lip or labellum) being different in size, shape and often in color too. Above it, the stamens and stigma are fused into a single column, and the often fantastic shapes of column and labellum are designed to ensure that only the orchid's favorite insect gets a chance to pollinate it.

Therefore orchid hybrids are rare in the wild; but when gardeners perform the act, orchids interbreed with startling freedom and hybrids uniting two, three, or even four genera (unheard of in other families) are common. These are usually given names combining those of their parents; for instance cattleyas and their close relatives the laelias, brassavolas and sophronitis will cross among themselves, giving rise to brassocattleyas, brassolaeliocattleyas, sophrolaelias and so on. (When all four get into the act a new name, *Potinara*, is used.) Actually making the pollination is easy, but germinating the seeds is not; it needs laboratory conditions beyond the scope of most of us, who must rely on division. (Some tall growers such as vandas can be air-layered.)

Still, seed is the best way to propagate orchids in quantity, and this gives rise to a peculiarity in their nomenclature. If a breeder makes a particular cross, all the seedlings of that cross constitute a "grex" and the grex is given a name, which by convention is not given the usual single quotes. The seedlings will be all of a kind, but some will likely be superior to their fellows; and if one of these is propagated vegetatively, it will be given a further (clone) name of its own, which does get quotes: and thus you get double-barrelled names such as *Brassolaeliocattleya* Sylvia Fry 'Supreme' or *Vuylstekeara* Cambria 'Plush'. (The system is sometimes used for rhododendrons and lilies too, as in *Rhododendron* Loderi 'King George'.)

These selected clones used to be frighteningly expensive, propagation by division being slow, but in recent years the technique of tissue culture has been applied to orchids with stunning success, enabling them to be quickly made available in large numbers. More than anything else, this has brought orchids from the gardens of the very rich to being flowers for all of us.

*Aerides mitratum*

x *Ascocenda* Flambeau

*Bifrenaria harrisoniae*

*Ada aurantiaca*, hybrid

x *Angulocaste* Olympus

*Ascocentrum curvifolium*

*Angraecum superbum*

## *ADA*
### *aurantiaca*

This cool-growing epiphyte originating from Colombia is notable both for its lovely clear orange color and its habit of flowering in late winter and early spring; it has no real rest period and should never be allowed to quite dry out. It is a compact plant, with sprays of small, bell-shaped flowers, and grows and looks best when it is allowed to make clumps—do not be in too great a hurry to divide the plants and don't over-pot it. An open, cattleya-type compost suits it best. It will interbreed with odontoglossums, bringing its bright color, but hybrids are not commonly grown.

## *AERIDES*
### FOXTAIL ORCHID

There are about 50 species in this genus from tropical Asia, called foxtail orchids because of the way the sprays of flowers hang down from a rather upright plant which resembles a vanda in growth. They come in several colors, mostly in the delicate white to pink range; are usually very pleasantly scented; and can appear at any time from spring to fall. They need intermediate to warm conditions and a coarse open compost; a hanging basket shows the pendent flowers to best advantage. They should be allowed to dry out a bit in winter.

## *ANGRAECUM*
### COMET ORCHID

There are 200 or so species from tropical Africa and Madagascar, but relatively few are grown in gardens; best known are *A. superbum*, *A. angraecum* and *A. sesquipedale*, in which last the characteristic nectar spurs can be as much as 14 in (about 35 cm) long; they are pollinated by night-flying moths with exceedingly long tongues. There are several hybrids available too; all are classed as warm growing and have scented flowers in white or combinations of white and pale green. They grow into 3 ft (about 90 cm) tall plants and like year-round warmth, humidity and moisture (which makes them difficult to keep as house plants) and a coarse potting mix. Give them plenty of light but not direct sunshine, and propagate from offsets.

## X *ANGULOCASTE HYBRIDS*

This hybrid genus is derived from crosses between species of *Lycaste*, from Central America, and the less well known *Anguola*, from South America. The plants are rather like large lycastes in habit, with fat pseudo-bulbs that usually lose their leaves in winter; the large flowers, which may be white, cream or yellow, appear from the bases of the naked pseudo-bulbs at the same time as the new shoots and last for several weeks. The plants are best grown into large clumps, dividing only infrequently. Give them bright, filtered light, and keep them dry in winter. Avoid wetting the leaves, which mark easily. Propagate by division after flowering. They are classed as cool growing.

## X *ASCOCENDA HYBRIDS*
### MINIATURE VANDA

These hybrids, developed from crosses of ascocentrums and vandas, resemble small-growing vandas (to about 24in/60 cm tall) and have very long-lasting flowers around 2 in (about 5 cm) wide in clusters, in just about any color except green; the blues and purples are especially admired. They are popular with gardeners as they take up less room in the greenhouse than full-size vandas, and they often feature among the bunches of "Singapore orchids" imported from there and from Thailand and sold in flower shops. Mostly summer flowering, they are warm growing and are cultivated in the same way as vandas.

## *ASCOCENTRUM*
### *curvifolium*

This is the best known of this genus of 9 or 10 species from Southeast Asia. It makes a bushy plant around 14 in (about 35 cm) tall with leathery leaves; it carries its clusters of 1 in (about 2.5 cm) wide flowers in late spring or summer. The flower color varies between red and orange; they are very long lasting. The warm growing genus is closely related to the vandas and will interbreed with them; it is grown in the same way.

## *BIFRENARIA*
### *harrisoniae*

There are 30 or so species in this genus from Central America; *B. harrisoniae* is both typical and the best known. It is an epiphyte, making a single large leaf from the top of each round pseudo-bulb, and the flowers are carried one to a stem but several to a bulb on bare stems from the base in early summer. They look a little like cream-colored cymbidiums, but the purple labella are delicately fringed. They like cool to intermediate conditions, an open compost, and to be left undisturbed; though the plants can be propagated by division after flowering, they hate it and take several years to settle down and flower again. Give them plenty of fresh air and a winter rest.

## *BLETILLA*

*striata*

**syn. *B. hyacinthina***

CHINESE GROUND ORCHID

This charming plant from China and Japan is perhaps the prettiest, certainly the easiest to grow, of the temperate climate terrestrial orchids. It likes a cool, lightly shaded spot with plenty of organic matter in the soil and ample moisture during the growing season; it shouldn't be allowed to quite dry out even after the leaves have died down for the winter. Mid-green and distinctively pleated, these are an attractive feature in their own right, an unusual characteristic among orchids. In spring, the plant bears 12–16 in (about 30–40 cm) tall sprays of small bright mauve-pink flowers. There is a white variety of great beauty but this is rare and expensive. Propagate by careful division in early spring, but the plants are best left undisturbed to develop into clumps. Plants can be grown in a cymbidium mix with a little well-rotted manure added.

## *BRASSAVOLA*

*nodosa*

LADY OF THE NIGHT

This epiphytic orchid from Central America earns its common name from its sweet fragrance, wafted mostly at night. The plant is clumpy, with cylindrical leaves that look like green extensions to the pseudo-bulbs, and the pendent sprays of white (or white and pale green) flowers with their big white labella can appear at any time from spring to fall. It is cool growing and is usually grown attached to a piece of tree-fern trunk, but a hanging basket with a coarse, cattleya-style compost suits it also. Give it plenty of light and fresh air and keep it on the dry side during winter. Propagate by division in early spring. The glamorous *B. digbyana*, parent of most *Brassocattleya* hybrids, is now officially *Rhyncolaelia digbyana*.

## *BRASSIA*

*verrucosa*

This is the most popular of this genus of cool-growing epiphytes from South America. It makes a clump of round pseudo-bulbs with strap-shaped leaves above which the graceful sprays of spidery flowers rise in early summer. These are pale green (or green and cream) and fragrant, though some people find the scent a bit heavy for their taste. Give it coarse compost, fairly bright light and a winter rest, though it shouldn't be allowed to dry out enough to cause the leaves to shrivel. Propagate by division. There are other species and hybrids available, all rather similar to this one; all are among the easiest of orchids to grow as house plants.

## X *BRASSOCATTLEYA HYBRIDS*

This hybrid genus is derived from crosses between cattleyas and *Rhyncolaelia (Brassavola) digbyana*. The result is usually sumptuous flowers with the rich colorings of the cattleyas and extravagantly frilled and ruffled labella derived from the rhyncolaelia. Often the flowers are fragrant, though usually only at certain times of the day. Cultivation is the same as for cattleyas; most like cool to intermediate conditions.

## X *BRASSOLAELIOCATTLEYA HYBRIDS*

Another hybrid genus, this time derived from *Rhyncolaelia digbyana*, cattleyas and laelias. They resemble the brassocattleyas, the laelia influence showing up in more richly colored labella and broader petals; the result is some of the most sumptuous of all orchid flowers. They are mostly intermediate growers and are cultivated exactly as cattleyas are. (Often, these multi-generic cattleya hybrids are simply sold as cattleyas.)

## *CALYPSO*

*bulbosa*

CALYPSO ORCHID

This terrestrial orchid is found from Russia and Scandinavia to the northern parts of North America. In spring a stem to 4 in (about 10 cm) or more rises above a single leaf; the stem is topped by a single, 1 in (about 2.5 cm) wide lady's slipper–type flower. The twisted, magenta petals of the flower frame a white to pink pouch, often spotted with purple. A delicate flower, the plants are nevertheless fairly tough, requiring a humus-rich soil and plenty of water in a shaded garden situation. Most commonly found in cool, damp, conifer forests.

ZONES 5–9

## *CATTLEYA*

This large genus of epiphytes from Central and South America is perhaps the most admired of all orchids. The big ruffled hybrids of the flower shop, usually orchid-pink or white, are the best known: but there are more than 60 species and countless hybrids, the flowers ranging from miniatures only 2 in (about 5 cm) or so across to giants of 6 in (about 15 cm) or more. Just about every color but blue is available, though the brighter yellow to red shades tend to have smaller flowers. The genus is divided into two types: the bifoliate cattleyas, which have two thick leaves atop their stem-like pseudo-bulbs and are mostly cool growing; and the unifoliates, which have only one and tend to prefer intermediate conditions. They mostly grow around 14 in (about 35 cm) tall, though they can spread into clumps as much as 3 ft (about 90 cm) wide, and the flower sprays (1 or 2 to as many as 10 flowers) arise from the tops of the pseudo-bulbs. They appear, according to variety, in spring or fall. All prefer good light but not strong sunshine, a coarse potting mix and a winter

x *Brassocattleya,* unnamed hybrid

*Brassia verrucosa*

x *Brassolaeliocattleya* Sylvia Fry

*Brassavola nodosa*

*Bletilla striata*

*Cattleya bowringiana*, hybrid

*Cattleya* Bob Betts

*Cattleya bifoliate* hybrid

*Cattleya trianaei*

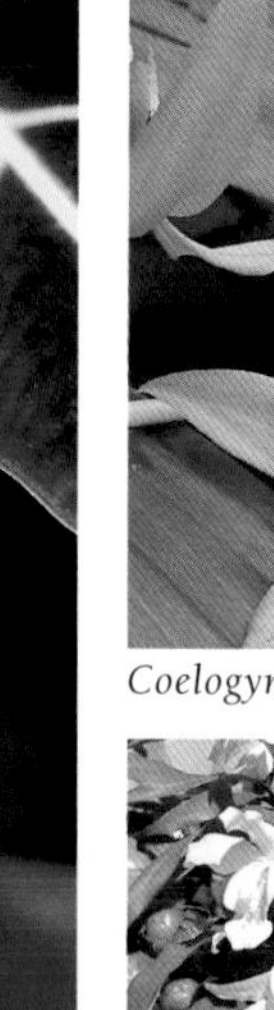

*Coelogyne pandurata*

*Coelogyne cristata*

*Cymbidium* Atlantis

rest. They are propagated by division just as growth begins, which may be either in spring or in early fall. This can be a messy job, as the roots tend to stick to the pot; if in doubt, simply transfer pot and all to a larger one. The genus hybridizes very easily with the related *Laelia*, *Rhyncolaelia* and *Sophronitis*, and the resultant hybrids are often sold simply as "cattleyas." They are cultivated in the same way. The genus is named after an English orchid fancier, William Cattley, which should be a guide to pronunciation—they are not "cattle-ay-as."

### *C. bifoliate* hybrids

CLUSTER CATTLEYA

There are many of these available with mostly rather small flowers in clusters, and almost all cool growing; they can be grown out of doors in any frost-free, humid summer climate. They can be spring or fall growing; colors range from white through pink to magenta. Some in the yellow to coral range carry genes derived from the dainty orange *C. aurantiaca*.

### *C. bowringiana*

This delightful fall-flowering, bifoliate cattleya from Central America is one of the most popular and easy to grow of the cattleya species. It is a cool grower and looks best when allowed to make a large clump, when it will bear many clusters of 3 in (about 7.5 cm) wide, orchid-pink flowers of beautiful shape. It is the parent of several hybrids, some of which are rather optimistically described as "blue."

### *C. labiata*

The name is now taken to cover a large group of unifoliate cattleyas from South America, including *C. mossiae* (the national flower of Venezuela), *C. warneri*, *C. trianaei*, *C. gatskelliana* and *C. warscewiczii*, all pink or white, as well as the yellow *C. downiana*. They are all intermediate growers with large flowers in spring or fall, and are collectively the most important parents of the cattleya hybrids of the flower shops. Pure-bred species of the group are not often available, but they are well worth growing.

### *C. unifoliate* hybrids

These are the big, ruffled flowers of the flower shops, mainly in shades of pink or white, the white flowers being especially prized by florists. They prefer intermediate conditions and can flower either in spring or fall; some grexes will bloom at both seasons if they are well looked after. The flowers, which can be as much as 5½ in (about 13 cm) wide, are usually borne singly or in twos or threes. Many of these big cattleyas are more or less hybridized with laelias and rhyncolealias, but famous names to look out for among the pure-bred cattleyas are Bow Bells, Suzanne Hye and Bob Betts.

## COELOGYNE

There are 120 species of these epiphytic orchids from Southeast Asia, Indonesia and the Pacific Islands. Relatively few are grown in gardens, perhaps because they are all best encouraged to grow into large, rather bulky plants and their usual colors—white, pale green or brown—seem tame beside larger and brighter orchids. They are, however, well worth growing, and many are happy in cool conditions. They like a cymbidium-type compost and plenty of water while they are in active summer growth, but they demand a winter rest if they are to flower freely. They can be propagated by division after flowering.

### *C. cristata*

ANGEL ORCHID

This is the most popular of the genus, and one of the loveliest of all orchids. The angel orchid is a specimen plant with dozens of sprays of scented white flowers touched with gold among the glossy leaves; it is a wonderful sight. Cool growing, it likes summer shade and is one of the easiest orchids to grow as a house plant. It flowers at the end of winter and on into spring.

### *C. pandurata*

BLACK ORCHID

The black is only on the labellum; otherwise the scented flowers are pale green. They are borne on arching, 20 in (about 50 cm) tall sprays in summer, among large leaves which spring from egg-shaped pseudo-bulbs. The black orchid prefers intermediate conditions.

## CYMBIDIUM

There are nearly 300 species, mostly epiphytic, in the Orient and extending through Indonesia to the east coast of Australia. Relatively few are seen in gardens, though *C. ensifolium*, a fragrant, spring-flowering miniature, is a popular subject with Chinese artists: it is the many showy hybrids that rank among the most widely grown of all orchids. These make rather bulky plants with clumps of pseudo-bulbs from which spring long, dull green leaves. The leafless flower stems, which can be more than 3 ft (about 90 cm) tall in the largest hybrids, arise from the foot of the pseudo-bulbs to carry as many as 30 flowers. Though scentless, these are of elegant form and last for several weeks. They are available in green, yellow, white, pink or dull reds and browns, the labella usually marked in red. They appear mainly in spring, and are excellent for cutting. In recent years mericlonal propagation has brought the price of the best clones down to the point where plants can be bought in flower at the florist and used as temporary house plants, to be discarded when the flowers are over; however, there is no need to do this as the plants are easy to grow and they do quite well as house plants. In frost-free areas they can be grown out of doors in the ground in shaded places and lime-free soil liberally enriched with organic matter. In pots, they should be given a fairly coarse, soil-free compost, light shade and a winter rest, when they can be allowed to almost dry out. They can be divided after flowering. The hybrids are divided into large and miniature types; most species are best classed as miniatures, and some species are fragrant.

### *C.*, large-flowered hybrids

These are the best known cymbidiums, and innumerable

*Dendrobium falcorostrum*

grexes and clones are available. Atlantis, with 3 in (about 7.5 cm), cream and pink flowers, is typical. The largest types can have flowers as much as $5^1/_2$ in (about 13 cm) wide, and their top-heavy flower stems benefit from staking.

### *C.*, miniature hybrids

These cymbidiums usually grow around 20 in (about 50 cm) tall, with many flowers around 2 in (about 5 cm) wide or less; some have the broad petals and rounded shape of the larger types, others are more spidery. All are charming, cool-growing plants that look best when allowed to grow into large, many-flowered clumps. Many tend to have weeping flower stems, which may need to be staked.

### *C.* species

There are many of these available from time to time; most grow around 20–24 in (about 50-60 cm) tall, with flowers in various subtle colors. They mainly flower in spring and some are sweetly fragrant. They are mostly cool growing and need the same treatment as the hybrids though some, such as the red and green *C. devonianum*, have pendent flower spikes and look best in hanging baskets. The red-brown *C. caniculatum* is more upright. Like all the cymbidium species, they both look their best grown into large, many-flowered clumps. They are charming cut flowers.

## CYPRIPEDIUM

LADY'S SLIPPER ORCHID

These terrestrial orchids are an exception in the orchid world: they are rarely cultivated in pots but most often in beds, like any other herbaceous plant. They take both their common name and the scientific one which mean "slipper of Venus" from the way the labellum folds over at the end to form a pouch. They come from Europe and North America and like cool temperate climates, rich, leafy, rather moist soil and a shaded position. They are propagated by division of the tubers in spring, but with care, as like all terrestrial orchids, they resent being disturbed.

*Cypripedium reginae*

*Cymbidium caniculatum*

### *C. calceolus*

Native to Europe and North America, this herbaceous perennial has bold, bright green leaves and small clusters of yellow and brown (or yellow and purple) flowers on 3 ft (about 90 cm) tall stems in summer.

ZONES 5–9

### *C. reginae*

This rather rare plant is often thought to be one of the most beautiful of all American wildflowers, but though fully hardy it is difficult in cultivation. It must have acid, very leafy, well-drained soil, shade and a cool position where there is no chance of its drying out; and it is resentful of having its roots disturbed. Where it is happy it spreads into clumps, its fresh green leaves adorned with large white flowers with rose pink labella and borne singly on 20 in (about 50 cm) tall stems in early summer.

## DACTYLORHIZA

syn. *Orchis*

MARSH ORCHID, MAY ORCHID

The genus *Orchis*, native to southern Europe, is the one from which the whole tribe takes its name (from the Greek for a testicle, because of the way the egg-shaped tubers tend to grow in pairs). It has some pretty members, but the most garden worthy are now usually classed in the genus *Dactylorhiza*. They are herbaceous perennials with bold green leaves and 20 in (about 50 cm) tall spikes of small, magenta or white flowers in early summer. The best known species are *D. latifolia*, which has spotted leaves, and the slightly taller *D. elata*, also known as *D. majalis*, which has plain green ones. Both like a semi-shaded position in moist, leafy but well-drained soil and prefer to be left undisturbed; they hate being transplanted and often take 1 or 2 years to recover and start flowering.

ZONES 7–9

*Dactylorhiza elata*

*Dendrobium*, cane-stemmed hybrid

## DENDROBIUM

This is one of the largest of all the genera of orchids, with some 1500 species ranging from India, to China and Japan, Indonesia, New Guinea, Australia (where there are many) and New Zealand. It is also one of the most diverse, and here we have illustrated only a few of the more easily grown species, ignoring most of the many hybrids. They can be evergreen or deciduous: most are epiphytic, but they vary in habit from clump formers that make fat pseudo-bulbs rather like those of a cattleya, to those whose bulbs have grown long and stem like and which often carry their flowers in sprays in the axils of the fallen leaves. These last are divided into "hard-" and "soft-caned" types: but though the hard types tend to be more upright in habit, the soft more floppy, even pendulous, the distinctions are not very consistent. The species and hybrids range from cool to warm growing: but in these days of high fuel costs, the warm-growing types are more often seen in bunches of imported "Singapore orchids" than in what the orchid trade patronizingly calls "amateur" greenhouses. There are innumerable hybrids, both natural and man-made.

*Cypripedium calceolus*

*Cymbidium*, miniature hybrid

### *D.*, cane-stemmed hybrids

*D. nobile* gives you an idea of what to expect from these; they are mostly upright growers bearing sprays of flowers along the canes in spring or summer, in a wide variety of colors from white and cream through yellow and pink to magenta red. *D. nobile* itself has entered into the parentage of many, but such other species as *D. infundibulum* from India, the purple *D. biggibum* and the yellow *D. signatum* have had great influence too. They are mostly cool to intermediate growing and are propagated by division after flowering.

### *D. falcorostrum*

This epiphyte from eastern Australia makes a clump of thick pseudo-bulbs around 8 in (about 20 cm) tall and topped with leathery leaves; in summer sprays of many dainty flowers, beautifully shaped and fragrant, appear. They are white, often with red on the labellum.

### *D. kingianum*

Photographs are apt to make this enchanting plant from eastern Australia look more imposing than it is; it is in fact a miniature, and a clump filling a 6 in (about 15 cm) pot counts as a large one. It will certainly be large enough to carry at least a hundred of its ½ in (about 1 cm) wide, beautifully formed flowers, which may be in any shade from white to deep pink. It is cool growing and likes shade and an open, well-drained compost. It is a very reliable species for growing out of doors. It flowers in spring.

### *D. nobile*

This species from northern India is one of the most popular of all dendrobiums, both in its own right and as a parent of fine hybrids. Cool growing, it is classed as a soft-cane type. The pseudo-bulbs shoot up in summer to around 14 in (about 35 cm) high; in winter they lose their leaves and then the following spring are garlanded from top to bottom with shapely flowers, pale pink with maroon and gold on the labellum; some forms are richer and darker in color, some white and gold. They are fragrant, the scent being stronger at certain times of day. It likes shade in summer, an open compost, and must have a winter rest to flower—don't start watering again until the flower buds are well developed.

### *D. speciosum*

ROCK LILY

Though the individual flowers are quite small—1 in (about 2.5 cm) across at the most—they are borne in huge sprays of as many as 80 from the big, cattleya-like pseudo-bulbs, and a large clump with many flower clusters of white or cream flowers is a magnificent sight in spring. The flowers are scented too, though they are not very long lasting, fading in a fortnight or so. The plant grows around 18 in (about 45 cm) tall and does best when allowed to multiply into generous clumps. It comes from eastern Australia, likes cool to intermediate conditions, an open compost, and a complete winter rest. A little summer shade is desirable.

### *D. thyrsiflorum*

BACON AND EGGS

The common name comes from the yolk-yellow labella and white petals of the flowers, which are borne in large, pendent sprays in spring; the bacon is presumably the white pseudo-bulbs and green leaves. It is in fact a species of very great beauty and is classed as intermediate to warm growing.

## *DISA*

This genus of terrestrial orchids comes from central and southern Africa and is notable for the beauty of its flowers, which are normally borne several to a stem in summer. They have the labellum at the top, and this is normally white or cream and heavily veined with the color of the remaining petals. Notoriously difficult to grow and propagate, they need mild climates with freedom from extremes of temperature, constant moisture (but perfect drainage), light shade and high humidity. They are classed as cool growing.

### *D.*, hybrids

Derived from crosses of *D. uniflora* with several other species, these are considerably easier to grow, and make splendid, long-lasting cut flowers. The flowers are usually rather smaller than *D. uniflora*, but are borne with as many as 8 to the stem, in shades of red, pink or lilac with white. They like a cool, shaded, but airy position and as long as they are in no danger of frost there is no need to heat the greenhouse. Pot the tubers in any standard, rather rich orchid compost, and then plunge the pots in damp sphagnum moss to keep them evenly moist—they should never be allowed to dry out, even during their winter dormancy. They can be divided with care in early spring.

### *D. uniflora*

PRIDE OF TABLE MOUNTAIN

Often held to be the most beautiful of all South Africa's native flowers, this orchid with its large scarlet and white, scented flowers on 3 ft (about 90 cm) tall stems is native to the cloud forests of the high mountains of the Cape, whose even temperatures, constant cloud and light rain are far from easy to duplicate in gardens. It is thus a very difficult plant to grow away from its native home, and only very skilled orchid cultivators should attempt it.

## *DRACULA*
### *bella*

The name has nothing to do with Count Dracula of horror-movie fame, but means "a little dragon," referring to the curious formation of the flowers with their long-tailed sepals and their mahogany red color. They appear in spring and summer from the base of the 8 in

*Disa uniflora*

*Dendrobium kingianum*

*Dracula bella*

*Disa*, hybrid

*Dendrobium thyrsiflorum*

*Dendrobium nobile*

*Dendrobium speciosum*

*Encyclia cochleata*

*Eulophia speciosa*

*Gongora galeata*

*Laelia* Coronet

(about 20 cm) tall plant which looks best grown in a hanging basket. Warm growing, it likes an open compost and regular watering even in winter, as the plant forms no water-storing pseudo-bulbs. Fungus can mark the leaves unless they get plenty of fresh air. Propagate by division after flowering.

## ENCYCLIA
### *cochleata*

COCKLE-SHELL ORCHID

This cool-growing epiphyte comes from Central America, and is one of the best orchids to try as a house plant. It makes clumps of strap-shaped leaves attached to round pseudo-bulbs, with flower stems arising from their summits. The flowers themselves are green with purple, shell-shaped labella; each stem carries 3 or 4 at any one time, but continues to open a succession of flowers for months; it is not unknown for a flower stem to bloom continuously for two years, so you can have last year's stems flowering beside this summer's. Give the plant a coarse compost and light shade and do not let it get too dry in winter. Propagate by division, which is best done in spring even if the plant is still in flower. There are several other desirable species such as *E. vitellina* (bright orange), *E. citrin* (yellow) and *E. mariae* (green and cream). They resemble small cattleyas and are grown in the same way.

## EPIDENDRUM
### *ibaguense*
**syn. *E. radicans***

CRUCIFIX ORCHID

This is one of the easiest of all orchids to grow, suiting cool, intermediate or warm conditions and flowering profusely out of doors in any frost-free climate in sun or light shade. It is an epiphyte, but will grow happily in the ground if the soil is lavishly enriched with organic matter; as a pot plant it will accept any standard orchid compost. It makes a rather straggly plant, with long, thin pseudo-bulbs 25 in (about 63 cm) tall that have leathery leaves all along them—staking and

*Laelia anceps*

the occasional trimming back will help keep it neat. The flowers, which can appear at any time of year, are only around 1 in (about 2.5 cm) wide, but each flower stem will have up to 20 open at any one time and continue to produce new flowers for months. The common name comes from the shape of the yellow labellum that stands upright in the center of the orange star of the petals and sepals. There are red- and mauve-flowered varieties available also, but the orange is the commonest. Water and fertilize from spring to fall, and propagate by division or removing rooted offsets. Less often seen, other species are more like small flowered cattleyas in appearance and need the same treatment.

## EPIPACTIS
### *gigantea*

STREAM ORCHID

This tall, streamside orchid is native to western North America, from San Francisco north. It prefers the constant moisture of a stream or lake margin, but adapts to a damp spot in the garden in full sun to part shade. Stems rise 12–36 in (about 30–90 cm) in clumps, each stem graced by several strongly veined, elliptical leaves whose bases clasp the stems. The terminal spike may present up to 15 oddly colored flowers less than 1 in (about 2.5 cm) wide; the green, purple and orange flowers apear in late spring or early summer. Selections are sometimes available with maroon leaves and stems.

ZONES 6–10

*Laelia purpurata*

## EULOPHIA
### *speciosa*

A terrestrial species from Africa, this orchid bears vivid yellow flowers in spring, when the new foliage also appears. It is warm growing and needs constant moisture and light shade; it can be propagated by division of the dense clumps of tubers in early spring before growth begins. There are over 200 species in the genus, but very few are known in gardens; even *E. speciosa* is something of a rarity.

## GONGORA
### *galeata*

There are about 12 species of these Central and South American epiphytes, of which *G. galeata* is the most likely to be found at specialist growers. It needs to be grown in a hanging basket, as the 2 in (about 5 cm) wide flowers, on their wire-thin, zigzag stems dangle below the evergreen foliage. Of most intricate and curious form, they are a pleasing tawny yellow color and strongly fragrant. They appear in summer. The plant is cool growing and likes shade, a coarse compost and regular summer water and fertilizer, but should be kept dry in winter. Propagate by division in early spring.

## LAELIA

The laelias are closely allied to the cattleyas and rather resemble them, both in growth and the shape and colors of their flowers. They have always suffered by comparison with their more glamorous relatives, but are in their own right a most attractive group of South American epiphytes and many of the 75 species and their hybrids are well worth growing. They interbreed easily with the cattleyas, bringing to the hybrids their richly colored labella and also a neater flower shape—some of the larger cattleya species have distinctly floppy petals. They are cultivated in the same way as the cattleyas. *L. purpurata* has been much used in crossing with cattleyas.

*Epidendrum ibaguense*

### *L. anceps*

Important in cattleya breeding but a most attractive species in its own right, this cool-growing species resembles a unifoliate cattleya in habit, though its 3 in (about 7.5 cm) wide lilac pink flowers with their purple labella are carried several together on rather long flower stems; a plant in full fall bloom can be 26 in (about 66 cm) tall. There are several named clones available.

### *L.* Coronet

This is representative of a group of miniature hybrids raised from *L.*

x *Laeliocattleya,* hybrid

*Masdevallia,* unnamed hybrid

*Odontoglossum crispum* hybrid

*Miltoniopsis,* hybrid

*Odontoglossum grande*

*Lycaste virginalis*

*cinnabarina* (itself well worth cultivating) which have dainty sprays of 2 in (about 5 cm) wide flowers in shades of deep yellow or orange. The plants grow about 10 in (about 25 cm) tall, and look best when allowed to form generous, many-flowered clumps. It prefers a coarse potting mix. Intermediate conditions suit them and they flower in spring or summer. Some have cattleya genes and thus are officially classed as laeliocattleyas, but you usually have to read the label to discover this.

### *L. purpurata*

This evergreen, epiphytic orchid well deserves the honor of having been selected as the national flower of Brazil, a country with many beautiful wildflowers. It grows to a height of 20 in (about 50 cm). Its 6 in (about 15 cm) wide flowers with their white or pale mauve petals and vivid purple labella are quite magnificent. They appear in small clusters in early spring. The plant likes intermediate conditions and a winter rest.

## X *LAELIOCATTLEYA* HYBRIDS

The laelias have been much crossed with the cattleyas, and this hybrid genus has over 2000 named members. They vary from cool to intermediate growing, and can have dainty, almost miniature flowers or enormous ruffled ones in the full range of "cattleya" colors. They are cultivated in exactly the same way as cattleyas.

## *LYCASTE*

### *virginalis*
syn. *L. skinneri*

The name *virginalis* might suggest a white flower, however most forms of this Central American epiphyte, the national flower of Guatemala, are pink, sometimes quite deep in tone. At first sight they seem to be three petaled, and can be as much as 6 in (about 15 cm) wide; they are carried on bare stems 14 in (about 35 cm) long which arise from the base of the round pseudo-bulbs, which are often quite naked at the spring flowering time, the broad leaves having fallen during the winter. Others, such as the bright yellow and intensely fragrant *L. aromatica* and *L. deppei*, are also much admired, and there are a number of handsome hybrids available. All are cool growing and need a coarse compost; give them light shade and do not overwater—keep them quite dry in winter and on the dry side in summer.

## *MASDEVALLIA*

These epiphytes come from the mountains of South America and are classed as cool growing. The dainty, 2 in (about 5 cm) wide flowers are notable for their shape; the petals and labella are tiny so the sepals give the effect of a triangular flower, held on a slender stem around 14 in (about 35 cm) above the lowly foliage. The petals are iridescent so that as you change your point of view they glitter with different spectrum colors. The effect is seen even in the white varieties, but is still more wonderful in the red and orange types such as *M. coccinea* and *M. veitchii*. There are a number of hybrids available in the red to yellow range also. The plants are evergreen and flower from winter to spring. It is important therefore that winter temperatures do not fall near freezing or the plants will be damaged. They can be propagated by division after flowering.

## *MILTONIOPSIS*
syn. *Miltonia*
PANSY ORCHID

The several species of *Miltonia* are worth growing, but the popular pansy orchids are now reclassified in a genus of their own. There are about 5 species, but much more commonly grown are the many hybrids. These make round pseudo-bulbs with strap-shaped, rather pale green leaves; the flowers are carried in small clusters, mostly in mid-summer—a time when there are not many orchids in flower—though they can appear at any time from spring to fall. Usually around 4 in (about 10 cm) wide, they are quite flat like pansies though the colors, white through clear pinks to red with flashes of gold on the labella, are not really pansy like. They like an open compost, light shade, and to be kept growing all year—a winter rest is not desirable. Propagate by division after flowering.

## *ODONTOGLOSSUM*

The most widely grown species of this genus of 200 species from Central and South America are epiphytes, though terrestrial species are known. They are admired for their usually ruffled flowers borne in long sprays, and the wonderful variety of colors and markings displayed thereon. Few are difficult to grow: most are cool growing and need only the usual orchid cultivation of coarse compost, plenty of water in summer and light shade. They don't need as definite a winter rest as, say, cattleyas do, but should not be overwatered then. They make egg-shaped pseudo-bulbs from the bases of which the flower stems appear. Flowering is from early spring to fall, depending on variety. They can be divided after flowering. The closely related genus *Cochlioda* is very similar but has smaller flowers in shades of red; it has been crossed with odontoglossums to bring in this color, and some of the more brilliantly colored hybrid odontoglossums are more properly known as odontiodas. This only affects orchid breeders with an eye on bloodlines.

### *O. crispum* and hybrids

This species and its many hybrids are the best known of the genus. *O. crispum* itself is white, though it is very common for the flowers to be patterned and marked in shades of red or pink; some of the hybrids are almost striped, in a range of colors that may blend white with cream, yellow, red, pink or purple, or they may be entirely of any of these colors. The ruffled, flat flowers can be as much as 5 in (about 12 cm) wide and borne 20 to the stem. They don't have a definite flowering season, flowers appearing whenever the plant feels like it; spring and fall are the peak periods. They dislike too-hot conditions in summer, when they should be given fresh air.

### *O. grande*

This species differs from the *O. crispum* group in that it definitely flowers in fall and needs a winter rest, but otherwise its cultivation is similar. The huge (to 6 in/15 cm wide) flowers are a blend of yellow and russet with white on the labella, and are borne half a dozen to the stem. It can be divided in spring.

## *ONCIDIUM*

This is a huge and varied genus (over 700 species) from Central and South America, allied to the odontoglossums and miltonias (though different in appearance) and able to be crossed with them to give odontocidiums and such multigeneric hybrids as wilsonaras. The ones usually grown are epiphytes, and they vary in their temperature requirements. They all like light shade and only a short winter rest; open, coarse potting mix and high humidity, but most intensely dislike being overwatered. Many have a tendency to climb up their host tree, and are best potted with a slab of tree-fern trunk to cling to. They can be propagated by division in spring.

### *O. papilio*

BUTTERFLY ORCHID

This much-admired species is atypical in that it bears its flowers singly, though the 20 in (about 50 cm) tall flower stem carries several buds which open in succession over many weeks in summer. The flowers are $5^1/_2$ in (about 13 cm) across, of unusual shape, and marbled with bronze on a gold background. Give it a very coarse compost and keep it on the dry side, relying on a very humid greenhouse to give it the moisture it needs; keep vigilant for red spider mites. It can be propagated by division, but it is so difficult to please that few growers, having persuaded it to grow, would dare. It is warm growing.

### *O. varicosum*

DANCING LADIES

This species from South America is typical of a large group that bears small flowers in large branched sprays, which dance in the slightest movement of air. The most prominent feature of each flower is the labellum, the other parts being tiny; in *O. varicosum* and *O. flexuosum* this is yellow, but other species can be yellow and chestnut-brown, and some of the hybrids are almost red or pink though always with a russet tinge. Flowering season runs from spring to fall. Most are cool growing, and not at all difficult to grow if given their winter rest and bright light but not direct sun. They are very popular with florists, as the airy sprays last for weeks in water.

## *PAPHIOPEDILUM*

SLIPPER ORCHID

The tropical slipper orchids used to be classed with the temperate ones in the genus *Cyprepedium*, but now they have been given a genus of their own. There are about 60 species from Indo-China and Indonesia, and though all are distinctive enough to be worth cultivating the most important is the cool-growing *C. insigne*. This has been the parent of many hybrids and selected forms, but there are other hybrids available developed from other intermediate- or even warm-growing species. As a general rule, types with spotted leaves need warmer conditions than those with plain green leaves, but none is difficult to grow. All are clump-forming perennials, mostly terrestrial in habit, with no pseudobulbs; the leaves hug the ground and the flowers are borne above them, one to a stem. They all like a rich compost. They are propagated by division; mericlonal propagation does not suit them, so selected clones and hybrids remain expensive.

### *P.*, hybrids

The aim in breeding hybrids has been to achieve a rounder flower than the rather spidery one of *P. insigne*, and the unnamed flower in the picture gives a good idea of the ideal. Colors range from green and bronze to yellow and white, often in combination but always subtle; they are not brilliant.

### *P. insigne*

This cool-growing species from Bangladesh and the nearby Himalayas is rather variable; there are many different named forms in cultivation. They are normally 12 in (about 30 cm) tall in flower, and the waxy flowers combine shades of green, russet, cream and white in various patterns and markings; all-green forms are much admired. They all look best when allowed to form generous clumps, and the flowers last for several weeks.

## *PHAIUS*

### *tankervillae*

NUN'S HOOD ORCHID, SWAMP ORCHID

This orchid from northern Australia is perhaps the most magnificent of all terrestrial orchids, its 3 ft (about 90 cm) tall stems of glossy leaves being crowned in spring with clusters of $5^1/_2$ in (about 13 cm) wide flowers in an unusual and attractive combination of purple, brown and white. It is grows quite readily outdoors wherever temperatures rarely fall to freezing. Give it rich, leafy soil, light shade and constant moisture, and propagate by division of the tubers in early spring. In cooler areas it needs a cool greenhouse, a large pot and a cymbidium-type compost; potted plants can be allowed to dry out a little in winter when the foliage dies down.

*Phalaenopsis amabilis*

*Oncidium varicosum*

*Paphiopedilum*, hybrid

*Oncidium papilio*

*Phaius tankervillae*

*Paphiopedilum insigne*

## *PHALAENOPSIS*

### *amabilis*

MOTH ORCHID

There are nearly 60 species in this Oriental genus, but by far the most important is *P. amabilis* from the Philippines and its many garden forms and hybrids. They do not make pseudo-bulbs; rather, the leaves, which may be plain green or spotted, spring directly from the rootstock and the arching flower stems rise clear above them. In the best forms, the stem can be 25 in (about 63 cm) tall and bear as many as 20 shapely, 5 in (about 12 cm) wide flowers, usually shining white but sometimes pale pink. They can appear at almost any time of year. They should be treated as temporary house plants, to be discarded when the flowers fade unless you have a greenhouse to retire them to. Warm growing, the plants need shade, constant moisture and a rich but open and perfectly drained compost. They are apt to send roots out over the top of the pot which then attach themselves to the greenhouse staging, and these should be left undisturbed.

## PLEIONE
*bulbocodioides*

This species is the best known of this genus of herbaceous terrestrial orchids from China. It is a lovely, dainty plant, bearing its shapely, 3 in (about 7.5 cm) wide pink flowers in early spring before the new leaves appear. It will grow out of doors in a temperate climate, though it is best given the shelter of a frost-free greenhouse. A cymbidium-type compost suits it, and it looks best when the tubers are allowed to multiply undisturbed to form clumps. Water well in summer while it is growing, hardly at all in winter after the leaves have died down. There are several other, rather similar species and now a range of hybrids, which extend the color range to white, yellow and deeper pinks; they are all grown in the same way.
ZONES 8–10

*Sarcochilus falcatus*

x *Sophrolaeliocattleya*, hybrid

*Sophronitis coccinea*

*Renanthera coccinea*

*Pterostylis banksii*

*Pleione bulbocodioides*

*Rhyncolaelia digbyana*

## PTEROSTYLIS
GREENHOOD

A fairly large genus of diminutive terrestrial orchids from Australia and New Zealand, notable for their unusually shaped, pale green flowers that rise on bare stems around 6 in (about 15 cm) tall in late spring. The foliage is ground hugging and dies off for the winter. Cool growing, they can be grown outdoors in a frost-free climate, in leafy soil and shade; in pots they can be allowed to dry out a bit in winter but should be watered freely while growing. Propagate by careful division after flowering. There are several species, all very much alike.

## RENANTHERA
FIRE ORCHID

This is a small genus from the tropical Far East, allied to the vandas and grown in the same way. They make tall, vanda-like plants and bear, at various times of the year, branching sprays of as many as 100 small, brilliant red or orange flowers. A plant in full cry is a dazzling sight, and as the flowers last very well when cut they are exported from Singapore and Thailand to appear in high-class flower shops elsewhere. There are several species, of which *R. coccinea* and *R. imschootiana* are the best known, and a number of hybrids; they have been crossed with the vandas and ascocentrums to lend them their dazzling color. They are outdoor plants only in humid, tropical climates.

## RHYNCOLAELIA
*digbyana*
**syn. *Brassavola digbyana***

Its reputation for being difficult has cost this orchid from Central America popularity with gardeners, but it is a very beautiful plant and important in orchid breeding. It grows like a large unifoliate cattleya and bears its lemon-scented flowers, one per pseudo-bulb, in summer. They are 5 in (about 12 cm) wide and pale green or pinkish; their outstanding feature is their enormous, deeply fringed labella. Crosses with cattleyas are still known as brassocattleyas, the name *Rhyncolaelia* having been adopted only in 1971; with their splendidly ruffled labella they probably now outnumber the pure-bred cattleyas in gardens. *R. digbyana* itself is classed as intermediate growing and is grown in the same way as cattleyas, though it loves bright sunshine and fresh air and must never be overwatered. Keep it quite dry in winter and on the dry side when it is not actually growing or flowering, and propagate by division in spring.

## SARCOCHILUS
ORANGE-BLOSSOM ORCHID

This is a genus of very pretty dwarf epiphytic orchids from the rainforests of northeastern Australia. They make low clumps of leathery foliage and in spring bear sprays of 1 in (about 2.5 cm) wide flowers which do resemble orange blossom in size and shape, though not in scent. The best known are the white *S. falcatus* and *S. hartmannii*, white with a small crimson labellum: *S. fitzgeraldii* is pink, and there are a number of hybrids and selected forms of all three, of which the white Blue Nob is perhaps the best known. All are cool growing and like a coarse, open compost and light shade. They appreciate constant moisture, and shouldn't be allowed to get quite dry even in winter.

## X SOPHROCATTLEYA AND SOPHROLAELIOCATTLEYA HYBRIDS
RED CATTLEYA

These two hybrid genera derive from infusions of *Sophronitis coccinea* genes into the cattleya and laeliocattleya breeding lines, creating beautifully colored red or orange, rather small-flowered "cattleyas." Here they are grouped together because the laelia influence is not always very obvious without consulting the label and they are grown in the same way—exactly as intermediate-growing cattleyas are, though perhaps with a little more water in winter. When *Rhyncolaelia digbyana* gets into the act the resultant flowers are not called *Sophrobrassolaeliocattleya* but *Potinara,* in honor of the great French horticulturist Julien Potin. Their cultivation is the same.

## SOPHRONITIS
*coccinea*
**syn. *S. grandiflora***

This is a most dainty epiphyte from Brazil. It makes a low-growing clump of dark green leaves, adorned in spring with beautifully shaped, 1½ in (about 3.5 cm) wide flowers like small cattleyas. They can be pink, orange, red or violet, but it is the scarlet forms that are most admired and which have been crossed with cattleyas to lend them their beautiful color. It likes intermediate conditions; culture is the same as for cattleyas, but it dislikes being divided and is best left to multiply. Don't let it dry out too much in winter, as it is never quite dormant.

## STANHOPEA
*wardii*
UPSIDE-DOWN ORCHID

There are several species of this South American genus of epiphytes, all rather similar in habit: the cream-flowered *S. wardii* and the yellow and brown *S. tigrina* are the best known. (There are several hybrids available also.) All have the

*Vuylstekeara* Cambria 'Plush'

*Thunia marshalliana*

*Stanhopea wardii*

*Vanda* Rothschildiana

*Wilsonara*, unnamed hybrid

*Vanda* Nellie Morley

*Zygopetalum mackayi*

peculiarity that the flower buds burrow down through the potting compost to hang in the air beneath the roots, so they must be grown in hanging baskets. The extraordinarily shaped flowers appear in summer. As orchid flowers go they are not very long lasting, but they are very strongly fragrant. The pseudo-bulbs are round and the leaves broad and luxuriant. Cool to intermediate conditions suit, and they will grow happily outdoors in a shaded position in frost-free climates. Keep the plants dry in winter, and propagate by division in spring.

## *THUNIA marshalliana*

BAMBOO ORCHID, ORCHID OF BURMA

This is the most commonly grown of the 9 species, which all come from Indo-China. It is a terrestrial and, having no pseudo-bulbs, is effectively a regular, frost-tender, herbaceous plant. The pendent clusters of 5 in (about 12 cm) wide, white flowers with pink and gold veins on the labellum are carried atop the 3 ft (about 90 cm) tall stems. The stems die down after the summer flowering, when the plants can be divided if desired. It likes intermediate conditions, summer shade and regular watering; it should not be allowed to get quite dry even in winter. Give the plants fairly large pots of any ordinary orchid compost, and allow them to build up into generous, many flowered clumps.

## *VANDA*

The most celebrated species of this epiphytic genus from Southeast Asia to northern Australia is *V. caerulea,* the blue orchid from the mountains of Thailand and Burma, where it used to be quite common. Sadly, the greed of Western gardeners has brought it to an endangered state—and it is not often seen in gardens either, its place having been taken by more easily grown hybrids. It is typical of its genus in its 3 ft (about 90 cm) tall, stem-like pseudo-bulbs with leathery leaves, from which the sprays of as many as twelve 4 in (about 10 cm) wide flowers appear in early fall. Some of the 70 or so species are spring or summer flowering, and the color range is from white through cream and pink to orange—the blue is in fact rare. Many have interesting markings and mottlings of other colors. They are all warm-growing epiphytes, liking a very coarse compost and strong light, though preferably not full sunshine; they are outdoor plants only in the tropics. Keep them warm and watered all year as they rarely take a winter rest, and propagate by removing rooted offsets. Most will need staking; if this is a piece of tree fern trunk they will cling to it by aerial roots.

### *V.* Nellie Morley

Derived, as so many good vanda hybrids are, from the not now often cultivated (except by orchid breeders) *V. sanderana*, Nellie Morley has become perhaps the most popular of the vanda hybrids, with many named clones available, usually with 4 in (about 10 cm) wide flowers in some shade of rich pink or coral. It has the unusual habit of flowering twice a year, in spring and again in fall. It likes warm conditions but plenty of fresh air and an open potting mix; don't dry off in the winter.

### *V.* Rothschildiana

BLUE ORCHID

This hybrid between *V. coerulea* and *V. sanderana* is easier to grow than *V. caerulea* itself, and hence more often encountered in gardens. It bears sprays of 5 in (about 12 cm) or larger flowers in winter; they range in the different clones from light to deep violet-blue, the flowers being distinctly veined with a deeper shade; a well-grown plant can carry several sprays of flowers. Its cultivation is the same as that of Nellie Morley, and it has itself given rise to further hybrids, many of startlingly intense blue.

## *VUYLSTEKEARA*

CAMBRIA 'PLUSH'

There are many other members of this hybrid genus, but Cambria 'Plush' is by far the most famous—and, thanks to mericlonal propagation, one of the most widely available. It is a compact plant, with round pseudo-bulbs each carrying a few long leaves; the flowers can appear at any time from spring to fall. They are around 3 in (about 7.5 cm) wide, carried in sprays of a dozen or so, and an attractive shade of dull red with very pretty white markings on the labellum. Like almost all the group it adapts to cool, intermediate or warm conditions, likes a coarse compost and regular watering—it needs no winter rest—and flowers even when the plants are very young and small. Propagate by division in spring. The name *Vuylstekeara* honors the Flemish orchid grower C. Vuylsteke, who originated the genus early in the twentieth century from crossings of species and hybrids of *Odontoglossum, Miltonia* and *Cochlioda.* (The last are like small, red-flowered odontoglossums.)

## *WILSONARA HYBRIDS*

This hybrid genus, which combines the genes of *Oncidium, Odontoglossum* and *Cochlioda*, goes in and out of fashion but does have some rather charming members that are rather like vividly red- or chocolate-striped odontoglossums and given such appropriate names as Tiger Talk. They are grown and propagated in the same way as the *Odontoglossum crispum* hybrids are and like them can flower at any time. They dislike conditions that are too hot in summer, when they should be given plenty of fresh air.

## *ZYGOPETALUM mackayi*

syn. *Z. intermedium*

This is the best known of several rather similar species from Central and South America. It makes a low-growing plant with mid-green leaves and carries its 24 in (about 60 cm) tall flower stems in fall or early winter. The flowers are chiefly notable for their unusual color—the petals and sepals are green, spotted with red, and the labellum is purple and white. The effect is much more attractive than it sounds and the flowers are fragrant. The plant likes intermediate to cool conditions, and needs a winter rest after flowering. Give it good light and plenty of fresh air; if the leaves get damp they will develop unsightly black blotches. Propagate by division in spring.

CHAPTER 12

# *Ferns, Palms & Cycads*

*That these three groups of plants come together here in this book is a coincidence of horticulture rather than botany—it would be hard to select three groups so unrelated to each other.*

Except for moss, cultivated only in Japanese gardens and their imitations elsewhere, ferns are the most ancient, "primitive" plants we grow. Far more ancient than the flowering plants, they have been around for hundreds of millions of years. The palms on the other hand are among the most recent and highly evolved flowering plants, although their flowers are not such that gardeners take much notice of them. The cycads, often hard to distinguish from palms at a little distance, are a kind of bridge between the ferns and the most primitive flowers, the conifers; they aren't even flowering plants.

Yet they play similar roles in gardens: all are admired mainly for their leaves, characteristically long but divided into small segments (although there are many exceptions); all are invaluable plants for shade; their most glamorous varieties are lovers of warm climates; some species at least provide food in their native lands; and they can find their place among indoor plants.

## Ferns

Let us take the ferns first. They are all perennials, mainly growing from creeping or clumpy rootstocks—although the tree ferns array their leaves atop palm-like trunks—and none has flowers. Their sex life is in fact rather complex and interesting. On the underside of their leaves (sometimes on special leaves which differ from the usual) they bear an array of what look like blisters. These are called sori; they release spores, tiny clusters of cells which blow away on the wind. If they land in a favorable place they germinate into curious little plants called prothalli, which usually look like little bits of leaf lying on the ground. These in turn bear male and female organs, the male releasing sperms which *swim* to the female ones to fertilize them. Then, and only then, the fern plant grows from the prothallus into its familiar form. The swimming sperms need water to swim in, of course, and that is why ferns are almost all lovers of moist ground and shady places—the sun dries up the needed moisture too fast.

They fall into two broad groups, the tropical and the temperate climate species, in each of which the variety of foliage forms and even colors is staggering. You can have the usual once-divided fronds, twice or three times divided, crested, or even severely plain with no divisions at all. And they can be any shade of green or marked with color; in some species the sori are silver or gold and so abundant they color the leaf. The plants can be sedentary in habit or running about by their rhizomes, and they range from just a couple of inches in height to over 3 ft (about 90 cm)—and they can be deciduous or evergreen. No wonder the Victorians adored them

*Ferns are greatly admired for their beautiful and diverse foliage.*

and devoted whole gardens to them. The tree ferns are mostly natives of warm-temperate to tropical climates and dislike frost, but they share the tribe's fondness for shade, fertile soil and moisture. Few have big root systems, which makes them wonderful pot plants, although you need to choose your varieties with care if you want to grow them as house plants—most need more humidity than living rooms offer. They can be propagated from the spores, which are sown in pots of moist soil like seeds, and most can be divided like any other perennial.

Food? The very young leaves of many species can be gathered and cooked as a vegetable—if you see fiddlehead ferns on a restaurant menu, do try them. (The term fiddlehead doesn't designate a species; it refers to the way the young leaves are scrolled like a crosier or the end of the pegboard of a violin.)

*Palms and ferns can be used to create an oasis in the suburban garden.*

## Palms

The palms are, by contrast, trees, although usually they grow on a single unbranched trunk with a crown of large leaves at the top. (Some form clumps of stems, but these are normally unbranched.) These leaves can be long and divided, like giant fern leaves, or they can be rounded and fan shaped, the two types being called "feather" or "fan" palms. They mostly grow in the company of other trees so they like the shade, at least when they are young, but there are few among the taller palms that insist on it.

Palms vary enormously in height: some of the clump formers grow to only around 6 or 9 ft (about 1.8 or 2.7 m) tall and can be placed in the garden like shrubs; others can reach 90 ft (about 27 m) and are sufficiently stately for the largest gardens. Alas, the most magnificent palms are strictly for frost-free climates, and the delights of a palm avenue is denied to the temperate climate gardener. (There are a few species that will grow in cold areas, but they aren't very exciting.) He or she will have to be content with growing some of the more modest palms indoors; however, they are among the most attractive of all house plants. They are mostly easy to grow; give them a position in reasonable light, don't over-water them, and don't over- pot them—they rather like tight shoes.

There are few groups of trees as useful as palms in the countries where they grow. Some people make thatch from the leaves, the trunks provide timber, and dates and coconuts are both borne by palms. Some species can have their sap tapped to make palm wine or toddy (which in turn can be distilled into arrack, one of the most head-spinning liquors known). There are those whose young shoots can be cut out and cooked like cabbage; not the sort of thing for the backyard vegetable patch, but you can buy canned palm hearts, also known as millionaire's salad. They are nearly always imported from Brazil.

## Cycads

Cycads also produce food; they bear large, nut-like seeds that are very rich in starch. But again they are not for the vegetable plot—the raw seeds contain poisonous alkaloids, which have to be destroyed by long and elaborate preparation. This varies with the species but may involve pounding the seeds, steeping them in water for long periods or both. This is an art perfected by the indigenous peoples of Australia and Africa, where most species grow. Some species contain a great deal of starch (called sago) in their growing shoots, although as cycads grow extremely slowly it is not economic to harvest the sago. In fact, commercial sago (tapioca) comes from a different, totally unrelated plant.

It is their agonizingly slow growth that limits the popularity of cycads in gardens; sow a seed and it will be years before you are rewarded with a fully developed clump of glossy, palm-like leaves let alone the curious flower cones, which can be huge—far larger than any pine cone. The plants bear male and female cones, usually on the same plant, and the female cones can be a striking sight when the seeds ripen. Eventually, most will grow up on to a short, thick trunk, but don't hold your breath waiting—the magnificent specimens you see in botanic gardens have almost all been transplanted fully grown from the wild. Cycads must be the most easily transplanted of all woody plants, but we must discourage you from going cycad hunting—they are not exactly abundant and are usually protected by law. If you do acquire one, give it a climate free of frost, or almost so, a place in light shade, and fertile soil. Grow it in a big pot by all means, and if you like you can bring it inside to a sunny room.

Adiantum pedatum

*Athyrium filix-femina*

*Asplenium bulbiferum*

*Adiantum capillus-veneris*

# FERNS

## ADIANTUM

MAIDENHAIR FERN

Common throughout the tropics and subtropics, these ferns look delicate but grow vigorously in the right conditions. There are over 200 species worldwide, mostly ground dwellers with an even greater number of cultivars. They grow well in gardens with filtered sunlight and make perfect ground cover where there is any decaying organic matter such as leaf litter to keep the surface moist. Their fronds vary in length from 2 in (about 5 cm) to 3 ft (about 90 cm) and turn from red to green as they grow. They have creeping rhizomes and polished, black-brown leaf stalks. Most species need repeated watering during summer.

### *A. capillus-veneris*

SOUTHERN MAIDENHAIR FERN

Found almost worldwide, this species grows to 18 in (about 45 cm) with bipinnate or tripinnate fronds. It does well with a little lime added to its potting mixture. There are several cultivars which grow best away from direct sunlight; they also prefer a sheltered position.
ZONES 8–10

### *A. pedatum*

NORTHERN MAIDENHAIR FERN

This deciduous, cold-hardy fern is native across North America. Thin, black stipes hold delicate, airy, fan-shaped fronds radiating from tight crowns. The shell-shaped, overlapping, pinnae emerge pale green and mature to a deep blue-green. Rhizomatous, they form broad, dense patches in moist, humus-rich soil in partial to full shade. Fronds grow 12–36 in (about 30–90 cm) tall and are deciduous. Propagate by spores or division.
ZONES 3–9

## ASPLENIUM

SPLEENWORT

Commonly found in rainforests all over the world, this fern genus has approximately 650 species that differ greatly in size and frond shape (simple, pinnate or bipinnate). Many hybrids have developed in the wild. Most of them are fast, hardy growers and tend to grow in clumps with creeping or tufted rhizomes. Species may be ground dwelling, rock dwelling or epiphytic. Avoid placing these ferns under direct sun under glass. Propagate from spore or by division.

### *A. bulbiferum*

MOTHER SPLEENWORT, MOKU, HEN-AND-CHICKEN FERN

This large rainforest fern is common to Australia, New Zealand and the islands of East Africa and the Pacific. It generally grows to more than 3 ft (about 90 cm) high. It varies greatly in the wild, so there are many widely differing subspecies. It will grow well indoors, as well as in a sheltered garden if the rhizome is placed in a well-drained position. Propagate from the plantlets that grow on the mature fronds.
ZONES 10–11

### *A. nidus*

BIRD'S-NEST FERN

This pantropical, epiphytic fern colonizes trees, rock faces and boulders in humid, tropical rainforests. The glossy green, thin, tongue-like fronds have wavy margins and a prominent, almost black midrib. The spreading fronds arise fom a densely hairy crown in a radial fashion, somewhat resembling a bird's nest. Provided warmth and ample humidity, it is easily grown as a container plant in coarse, well-

drained potting media. Easily propagated from fresh spores.
ZONES 10–11

## ATHYRIUM

This is a genus of deciduous and sometimes evergreen ferns. Tender to frost, they need shade and a humus-rich, moist soil. Fading fronds should be removed. Propagate from spores in late summer or by division in winter or fall.

### *A. filix-femina*

syn. *Asplenium filix-femina*

LADY FERN

The lady fern was a great favorite in Victorian ferneries, and a number of garden varieties with variegated or unusually shaped and feathered leaves and names like 'Fritzelliae', 'Pulcherrimum' and 'Victoria' were developed. The wild plant, which comes from Europe and America, is as pretty as any, with much divided leaves in a delicate shade of green. It can vary in height from 14 in (about 35 cm) to three times that, according to variety, and gradually spreads into wild clumps. It is frost hardy and likes the usual fern treatment of shade, fertile soil and moisture.
ZONES 3–8

### *A. nipponicum* var. *pictum*

JAPANESE PAINTED FERN

Prized for its soft metallic gray new fronds, which are suffused with bluish or reddish hues, this Japanese native grows to 20 in (about 50 cm) in height. Locate in humus-rich loam with adequate moisture in a semi-sunny exposure; this will ensure the richest foliage color. Divide mature plants in early spring or in late fall.
ZONES 4–8

## BLECHNUM

WATER FERNS

This genus is found in temperate to tropical climates, mostly in the southern hemisphere. Size and growth vary according to species. Most are ground dwellers that prefer moist soil, and propagate via their runners to form clumps. The new fronds on most species are pinnate and fishbone shaped; some are brightly colored. They are mostly frost tender and happiest in subtropical climates.

### *B. fluviatile*

RAY WATER FERN

This colonising, semi-upright, evergreen fern has a squat, leathery crown which has both decorative rosettes of sterile fronds and erect, fertile fronds. These are up to 20 in (about 50 cm) high and 3 ft (about 90 cm) in spread. The rigid, slender, pinnate fronds are densely foliaged. Frost hardy, it requires total shade and light, fertile soil.
ZONES 6–10

### *B. penna-marina*

ALPINE WATER FERN

A native of New Zealand, Australia, South America and the subantarctic islands, this fern is often found where snow and frost are common. Growing in quick bursts in the summer, its slender, dark green fronds grow up to 8 in (about 20 cm). It prefers bright light and, although not soil sensitive, needs a temperate climate with cold periods. It makes an ideal ground cover.
ZONES 6–10

## CYATHEA

syn. *Alsophila, Sphaeropteris*

TREE FERN

These evergreen tree ferns, from tropical to subtropical areas of the world, can reach a height of 50 ft (about 4.5 m), although they are usually not as tall as that in gardens. Their palm-like trunks, from the summits of which the fronds spring, are composed of knitted-together aerial roots; below ground they have normal roots. Established plants need care in transplanting—ensure that the normal, subterranean roots are not damaged. The genus is characterized by its arching rosette of weeping or erect, bipinnate or tripinnate fronds. Tree ferns prefer a warm climate, needing plentiful water in warm weather and protection from the hot sun. Plant in humus-rich, moisture-retentive but well-drained soil. They do well in tubs but eventually need replanting. Propagate from spores.

### *C. australis*

ROUGH TREE FERN

A popular garden plant for mild climates, this majestic fern grows up to 35 ft (about 10 m) high. The fronds may grow up to 12 ft (about 3.5 m) long; they are deep green in dark positions and yellowish in open areas. A very adaptable fern which will tolerate sun or shade and a whole range of soil conditions, but requires regular watering.
ZONES 10–11

*Cyathea australis*

### *C. dealbata*

SILVER KING, PONGA, SILVER TREE FERN

New Zealand's national emblem, this fern is instantly identifiable by the silver white underside of the fronds. This is a hardy plant that grows to around 15 ft (about 4.5 m), although it is often taller in the wild. It likes shelter, humidity and a moist soil.
ZONES 9–11

## CYRTOMIUM

### *falcatum*

HOLLY FERN

A native of Southeast Asia, its common name derives from the small, shiny, holly-shaped leaves that grow upright on wiry stems. Its spores are easily carried by the wind, so it has naturalized in many countries and is widespread on the cliffs of coastal areas. It grows well in greenhouses and indoors in a well-lit position, ideally growing up to 20 in (about 50 cm). Although it is frost hardy, its upper fronds can burn; just clip them if this happens. The plant will form new growth in warmer

*Blechnum penna-marina*

*Blechnum fluviatile*

*Cyathea dealbata*

*Davallia trichomanoides*

*Dicksonia squarrosa*

*Dicksonia antarctica*

*Cyrtomium falcatum*

weather. It likes shade, although it is one of the most sun tolerant of the ferns.
ZONES 9–10

## DAVALLIA *trichomanoides*

HARE'S-FOOT FERN, SQUIRREL'S-FOOT FERN

Popular among fern enthusiasts, this species is native to Malaysia, New Guinea and Indonesia, where it grows as an epiphyte in rainforests. Furry, yellowish brown rhizomes produce lacy, glossy green, pinnate fronds around 16 in (about 40 cm) long. Easily cultivated in hanging baskets and pots, it demands a coarse, very well-drained, organic growing medium. Though deciduous for a short period, it quickly reproduces new fronds. Propagate from rhizome cuttings.
ZONES 9–11

## DICKSONIA

This genus contains 30 large species of evergreen to semi-evergreen tree ferns native to the region stretching from Malaysia to Australia. Reasonably fast growing, these attractive ferns develop trunks in maturity and have arching, lance-shaped, multi-pinnate fronds with downy bases. The plants range from frost hardy to frost tender and require protection from the wind. Plant in peaty, damp soil with full or partial shade. Withered fronds should be frequently pruned. Propagate from spores in summer. The genus was named after the eighteenth-century British botanist James Dickson.

### *D. antarctica*

SOFT TREE FERN

Native to southeastern Australia and the giant of its genus, this tree fern can grow to 50 ft (about 15 m) with a trunk diameter of 6 ft (about 1.8 m). It is a fast and hardy grower that does well in tubs and favors a moist, sheltered position in the garden. Its lance-shaped fronds are long—up to 13 ft (about 4 m)—and its huge trunk is made of fibrous roots. Sections of trunk are used to make hanging baskets. Possums often make a meal out of the young fronds, and the pith of the trunk is a traditional food source for Australian Aborigines. As the severed trunk will grow when replanted, it is easy for unscrupulous persons to steal it from its rainforest habitat. Propagate from spores in summer.
ZONES 10–11

### *D. squarrosa*

WHEKI, ROUGH TREE FERN

One of the most popular tree ferns, this robust New Zealand species develops in colonies, prohibiting the growth of other plants. The trunk is covered in brownish red down and grows to over 15 ft (about 4.5 m) tall and 9 ft (about 2.7 m) in diameter. The rough, deep green 3 to 4 pinnate fronds, forming in a rough crown, have a lighter colored underside and are over 3 ft (about 90 cm) long. This fern needs a humid climate, partial shade, damp soil and shelter from frost and wind.
ZONES 10–11

## DOODIA

This genus contains 15 thicket-forming, evergreen dwarf ferns native to Sri Lanka, some Pacific islands and Australia. The rough, slender pinnate fronds have heavily

*Doodia media*

*Doodia aspera*

serrated leaflets and are vivid red-pink when immature. Species range from fully to half-hardy and prefer a cool, but not cold, climate. Plant in any reasonably fertile, damp soil and avoid direct sunlight. The plants in this genus grow well in an extremely humid atmosphere and are suitable for rockeries or as ground cover. Dry conditions are withstood after they have become well rooted. Do not overwater as they are susceptible to rot. Propagate from spores or by division in spring. The genus was named after English chemist and botanist, Samuel Doody.

### *D. aspera*

PRICKLY RASP FERN

This small, hardy fern proliferates in open forests in tropical and temperate climates. Its light green, pinnate fronds are lance shaped and, as the common name suggests, have a rough, raspy texture. New growth is an attractive pink or red. A moderate grower, this fern does well in shade and sun provided it is kept moist. It will do well in hanging baskets and makes excellent ground cover for steep banks or slopes. Propagate by division or from spores.

ZONE 11

### *D. media*

COMMON RASP FERN

This low-tufted New Zealand fern has upright rhizomes growing 8–12 in (about 20–30 cm) tall and spreading up to 24 in (about 60 cm). The immature, rich reddish pink, lanceolate fronds are covered in scales and hairs. They are at their most vivid in full sun, turning deep green in maturity. This species prefers a heavy clay soil. It is much more restrained in its spread than *D. aspera*.

ZONE 11

## DRYOPTERIS

This is a genus of deciduous or semi-evergreen ferns with regular crowns. They require shade and moist soil. Remove fading fronds regularly. Propagate from spores in summer or by division in fall or in winter.

*Dryopteris filix-mas*

### *D. erythrosora*

AUTUMN FERN

Native to eastern Asia, this evergreen fern produces new fronds that range in color from coppery to very bright red. As the fronds age they become glossy green and contrast handsomely with the colorful emerging ones; they persist well into winter. Bright red sori dot the undersides of the pinnules. A mature height of 18 in (about 45 cm) can be expected; it spreads to 12 in (about 30 cm). Of easy culture, it succeeds in deep shade to partial sun and a wide range of soils provided drainage is adequate. Propagate from spores.

ZONES 5–9

### *D. filix-mas*

MALE FERN

Common to the temperate and tropical areas of the northern hemisphere, this fern features lanceolate, pinnate fronds. It grows up to 12 in (about 30 cm) high and spreads out to the same width. A hardy ground dweller with short rhizomes, it prefers moist, well-drained soils. The common name survives from the days when herbalists thought that plants came in male and female, the ivy and the oak being one such "couple". The lady fern is *Athyrium filix-femina*. It is a graceful plant, very similar in culture to the male fern.

ZONES 3–9

### *D. marginalis*

MARGINAL SHIELD, WOOD FERN

This native of eastern and Central North America thrives in well-drained, acidic to neutral, humus-rich soil in part to full shade. The stiffly upright, slightly arching, olive-green fronds grow from a tight, central crown to heights of 12–24 in (about 30–60 cm). The sori are borne along the margins of the pinnules. Propagate from spores.

ZONES 4–8

## HUMATA

### *tyermannii*

SILVER HARE'S-FOOT FERN

Native to the tropical parts of China, this hardy fern is easily identified by the small, silvery scales on its rhizomes. It has thick, leathery, tripinnate fronds. One of the hardiest of its genus, this plant flourishes when maintained in moist soil and placed in a hanging basket. It is rather frost tender and is really only a garden plant in subtropical climates, where it makes pleasing ground cover and will do very well on shaded rocks. It grows around 12 in (about 30 cm) tall.

ZONES 10–11

## *MATTEUCIA*

### *struthiopteris*

**syn. *M. pensylvanica***

OSTRICH FERN

Native to the temperate regions of the northern hemisphere, this rhizomatous fern produces clusters of tall, plume-shaped, sterile fronds 24–60 in (about 60–150 cm) in height. Each cluster eventually forms a dense, raised crown. Persistent, fertile fronds arise from the crown and provide engaging winter scenery. Grow in moisture-holding, neutral to acidic loam soil in partial to full shade. Clumps can spread rapidly and become invasive. Propagate by division.

ZONES 2–8

## *NEPHROLEPIS*

SWORD FERN

Commonly found in the tropics and subtropics on the edges of rainforests or in open forests, this genus of hardy ferns features fishbone-shaped fronds with short, upright rhizomes. They are extremely tolerant to drought and also to being waterlogged and are fast growing, provided they are given enough room to spread out. Since they are sensitive to cold these ferns are ideal for indoor placement, but be sure to provide lots of water in warm conditions. Fading fronds should be removed and the plant should be divided regularly. Propagate from spores or tissue culture, or by division.

*Nephrolepis exaltata*

### *N. cordifolia*

**syn. *N. cordata***

FISHBONE FERN, HERRINGBONE FERN, SWORD FERN, LADDER FERN

Naturally found among rocks at the edge of rainforests this fern can grow in fairly dry and dark positions as well as in full sun. It is one of the toughest species in cultivation. Fronds grow to 3 ft (about 90 cm). It is a very easily grown, fast-growing plant—so much so that it can become a pest.

ZONES 9–11

### *N. exaltata*

SWORD FERN

Native to tropical America, this species is less often grown than its many cultivars, which have more luxuriant foliage that is sometimes lacy or yellow tinted. These cultivars are sterile and must be propagated by division or from tissue culture. All are suitable for hanging baskets. They are first-rate indoor plants and do well outdoors in frost-free climates. Give them rich soil, light to heavy shade and regular moisture; clean the fronds of outdoor plants occasionally.

ZONES 9–11

## *ONOCLEA*

### *sensibilis*

SENSITIVE FERN

Native to the United States and east Asia, this deciduous, water-loving fern is the only member of its genus. Hardy and quick spreading, with creeping rhizomes, it has two types of fronds, one sterile and one fertile. The sterile, bipinnate fronds are large and wide while the fertile fronds look like a small group of green balls growing on the leaf stalk. Suitable for cool climates.

ZONES 5–10

## *OSMUNDA*

These hardy, deciduous ferns require a position in shade, with the exception of *O. regalis*, which tolerates sun and very wet conditions. Propagate by division in fall or winter or from spores as soon as they ripen.

### *O. cinnamomea*

CINNAMON FERN

This hardy fern produces 2–4 ft (about 60–120 cm) tall, sterile fronds that arch gracefully from a stout, crown-forming rhizome. From the center of the crown emerge stiffly erect clusters of deep green fertile fronds that turn bright cinnamon brown as they mature. The sterile fronds are bluish green from spring to summer, turning golden to russet in the fall. Used in clumps or drifts in consistently moist to wet, acidic, humus-rich soils in sun or shade. Though slow to establish and gain stature, they are long-lived ferns. Sow fresh spores to propagate.

ZONES 3–10

### *O. claytonia*

INTERRUPTED FERN

This fern resembles the cinnamon fern but has much broader pinnae that are pale green in color. The unusual name for this North American native derives from the fertile fronds bearing normal, sterile segments among the fertile segments on the same frond. As the frond matures the fertile pinnae fall off, in mid-summer, giving an "interrupted" appearance to the frond. Growing from 1–5 ft (about 30–150 cm) in height, the young fiddleheads emerge covered with pinkish hairs. Requiring moist, acidic, organically rich soils, they will grow in sun or shade. Sow spores as soon as they mature.

ZONES 3–8

### *O. regalis*

ROYAL FERN

Native to Asia, the United States, Africa and Europe and varying slightly in each country, this is the

*Onoclea sensibilis*

*Nephrolepis cordifolia*

largest of its genus. It grows to a height of 6 ft (about 1.8 m) with long, bipinnate fronds. Deciduous and frost hardy, it is commonly found in large groups in swamps and other boggy areas and so is suitable for wet gardens as long as it is shaded. Propagate from spores. It has brown, clustered, spore-bearing fronds which grow among the regular ones.
ZONES 3–8

## *PELLAEA*
### *rotundifolia*

BUTTON FERN, ROUND-LEAFED FERN, TARAWERA

Native to New Zealand, this species is very popular as a garden plant. It is a small, dark green, ground-dwelling fern found in damp, open forests or drier woodlands. It has pinnate fronds with deep green, glossy round leaflets and long-creeping rhizomes. Suitable for a garden or fernery with filtered sunlight, protected from draughts, it also does well in rock gardens.
ZONES 10–11

## *PHYMATOSORUS*
### *diversifolius*

KOWAOWAO

The most common and variable of its genus, this prostrate, epiphytic species has distinctive, pulpy green stems covered with brownish black scales. Slender, undivided fronds, becoming woody and pinnate with age, grow to 10 in (about 25 cm) long and bear up to 12 shiny green leaflets with conspicuous veins, smooth or undulating margins and rounded tips. This species grows well in total shade, as ground cover or over logs.
ZONES 10–11

## *PLATYCERIUM*

A genus of epiphytes common to the tropics and subtropics of Africa, Southeast Asia and Australia, some species can tolerate quite cool temperatures though not frost. They are valued for their showy, staghorn-like appearance and are easily grown as epiphytes when tied on to the tree on slabs of board, or grown in baskets. The sterile nest leaves are used to catch leaf litter and other vegetable matter so that the roots eventually grow into the debris and are protected from winds. The base of the plant should be kept moist. Fertilize with blood and bone or old manure. Propagate by division in spring. Watch for beetles and moths.

### *P. bifurcatum*

ELKHORN FERN

Native to Australia, New Guinea and New Caledonia, the elkhorn fern is an easily grown plant that does well in sheltered gardens. It grows to a height and spread of approximately 3 ft (about 90 cm).
ZONES 10–11

### *P. superbum*
**syn. *P. grande***

STAGHORN FERN

The enormous size (up to 6 ft/1.8 m high and wide) that this epiphyte reaches as it clings to a rainforest tree can cause it to fall to the ground from sheer weight.
ZONE 11

*Osmunda regalis*

*Phymatosoros diversifolius*

*Pellaea rotundifolia*

*Platycerium superbum*

*Platycerium bifurcatum*

Polystichum setiferum

Polypodium aureum

Pteris cretica

Polystichum proliferum

## POLYPODIUM

These hardy deciduous, semi-evergreen or evergreen ferns are grown for their sculptural fronds. Grow in a position in semi-shade and a moist but well-drained soil. Propagate by division in spring or by spores in late summer.

### *P. aureum*

RABBIT'S-FOOT FERN

This evergreen fern has creeping rhizomes with golden scales. The mid-green fronds have orange-yellow sporangia on the undersides. The plant grows to $4^1/_2$ ft (about 1.3 m) high and spreads to 24 in (about 60 cm). Frost tender, it is happiest in partial shade and a moist, well-drained soil. It is ideal for growing in hanging baskets.

ZONES 10–11

### *P. californicum*

CALIFORNIA ROCK FERN

This evergreen, epiphytic fern is native to California and grows along rock ledges in humusy soil. Emerging from low, creeping rhizomes, the fronds reach heights of 12 in (about 30 cm) and are deeply incised. Grow this fern in rock crevices filled with humus and water during dry spells. Propagate from spores or by division.

ZONES 8–11

### *P. virginianum*

AMERICAN ROCK FERN

Native to eastern and central North America, this hardy, evergreen fern forms colonies atop rocks, in rock crevices and along woodland banks. Creeping rhizomes produce glossy green, deeply incised, leathery fronds that grow to 14 in (about 35 cm) tall. Bright orange sori are borne in rows along each side of the mid-veins of the lobes. Requiring excellent drainage, the rhizomes should be planted very shallowly in humus-rich, moist, neutral to acidic soil in partial to full shade. Propagate from spores or by division.

ZONES 2–8

### *P. vulgare*

COMMON POLYPODY

The European counterpart of *P. virginianum*, it is clearly identical to it in all respects. Cultivars such as 'Bifidum' and 'Cristatum' are very popular both as garden and container plants.

ZONES 4–8

## POLYSTICHUM

SHIELD FERN

This genus of ground- or rock-dwelling ferns is found in tropical and subantarctic regions worldwide. Their fronds are either pinnate or simple and ribbon shaped and they are known as shield ferns because groups of spores are covered with a fragile, shield-shaped growth. Some of these ferns are very ornamental and have become popular with gardeners and enthusiasts. The plants prefer moist soil and partial shade, although some grow well in direct sunlight. There is usually an abundance of small buds on the tips of fronds that become plantlets in their own right when conditions are favorable.

### *P. acrostichoides*

CHRISTMAS FERN

A native of eastern North American woodlands, this terrestrial fern grows from tufted crowns arising from slowly spreading rhizomes. The leathery, evergreen fronds emerge as silvery white "fiddleheads" in early spring and mature to lustrous, dark green, pinnately divided leaves 12–36 in (about 30–90 cm) tall. Easily grown, provide it with well-drained, acidic to neutral soil and partial shade. An excellent fern for naturalizing among low- to medium-height shrubs. Propagate from spores or by division.

ZONES 3–9

### *P. munitum*

WESTERN SWORD FERN

Resembling *P. acrostichoides* but much taller, the 3–5 ft (about 90–150 cm) fronds are dimorphic, the fertile fronds standing erect at the outer extremity of the sterile fronds. Native to coastal North America, it grows naturally in moist, coniferous woods so it is well suited to gardens with cool, shady, moist sites in very humusy soil.

ZONES 5–9

Polystichum munitum

### *P. proliferum*

MOTHER SHIELD FERN

This is one of the most easy growing and reliable of the shield ferns, growing to a height of 3 ft (about 90 cm) and lasting for a long time in tubs or the ground.

ZONES 5–9

### *P. setiferum*

SOFT SHIELD FERN

Native to the damp woodlands and valleys of Europe, this large fern grows to 18 in (about 45 cm) high. With its long, soft, bipinnate fronds, it is extremely popular in ferneries or gardens.

ZONES 5–9

## PTERIS

BRAKE FERN, BRACKEN

This genus is native to the shady, damp gullies of subtropical and tropical rainforests but can also be found growing out of rock crevices in full sunlight. They are usually hardy and can adapt to various positions but they need a great deal of water during the early growth period and should be kept out of direct sunlight. Keep an eye out for aphids. These ferns are often grown indoors and are generally best propagated from spores. The common bracken is considered a weed, but there are several species which are well worth cultivating.

### *P. cretica*

CRETAN BRAKE FERN

One of the many hardy cultivars of the Cretan brake fern, this grows to 20 in (about 50 cm) high. A bushy

yet delicate fern, it prefers a moist, sheltered garden or fernery and makes a very pretty indoor plant. There are several cultivated varieties, the best known being 'Albolineata', which has almost gray leaves with broad central margins of white. They are all very pretty indoor plants.
ZONES 10–11

*P. ensiformis*

SLENDER BRAKE FERN

This dainty little fern originates in Southeast Asia's moist lowland forests. It grows to some 12 in (about 30 cm) high and its small fronds are pinnate or bipinnate, with narrow segments rounded at their tip. Cultivars are variegated. This species prefers a warm climate, so in cool areas it should be well sheltered.
ZONES 10–11

### *TODEA*
*barbara*

KING FERN

From a genus of large tree ferns, this majestic fern features a black, fibrous trunk that grows to $4^1/_2$ ft (about 1.3 m) and bipinnate, dark green fronds that can reach 6 ft (about 1.8 m) in length. Although it prefers wet sites such as gullies, creeks and rainforests, it is a tough plant that tolerates some sun and grows well in tubs or gardens, provided the soil is kept moist. Propagate from fresh spores.
ZONES 10–11

### *WOODWARDIA*

CHAIN FERN

These evergreen or deciduous ferns prefer semi-shade and moist, fibrous, peaty soil. Faded fronds should be removed regularly. Propagate by division in spring.

*W. fimbriata*

GIANT CHAIN FERN

Native from British Columbia, this evergreen fern produces large, oval to lanceolate fronds from a stout, creeping rhizome. Growing to 6 ft (about 1.8 m) in height, the dark green fronds have deeply incised, ragged-edged pinnae with pointed lobes. The sori are borne in chain-like formations on the undersides of fertile fronds. Requiring constantly wet, acidic, humus-rich soil, they grow well in full sun or shade.
ZONES 7–9

*W. virginica*

VIRGINIA CHAIN FERN

A smaller version of *W. fimbriata*, this eastern North America native produces deep green, 3–4 ft (about 90–120 cm) tall fronds with striking shiny black stripes. Found growing in bogs in nature, provide them with acidic, humus-rich soil in full sun to shade. Deciduous and rhizomatous, they form large clumps that are easily divided.
ZONES 4–10

## PALMS

### *ARCHONTOPHOENIX*

This genus of palms are grown for their majestic and stately appearance. They should be planted in a position in full sun in humus-rich soil; they will tolerate shade, and need shelter from frost when young. Propagate from seed in spring.

*A. alexandrae*

ALEXANDER PALM

This graceful, un-armed palm is distinct from its sister species by its swollen trunk at the base. Native to eastern Australia, it reaches 50–80 ft (about 15–24 m) in height with a slender habit. The 8–10 ft (about 2.4–3 m) leaves drop neatly, leaving behind a smooth trunk.
ZONES 10–11

*A. cunninghamiana*

BANGALOW OR PICCABEEN PALM

Native to tropical Australia, this tall, slender, pinnate palm grows to 70 ft (about 21 m) high and is popular with landscape gardeners. The leaves are 6–10 ft (about 1.8–3 m) long, upright to spreading, and green to rust-brown at the crown shaft. This palm will tolerate an indoor position and some shade, but humidity must be maintained or its leaf tips may go brown. This is the most frost hardy of the genus. Propagate from seed—germination takes six weeks to three months.
ZONES 10–11

### *ARECASTRUM*
*romanzoffianum*

**syn. *Syagrus romanzoffianum*, *Cocos plumosa***

QUEEN PALM, COCOS PALM

In its native South America this palm grows in forests and along rivers. The 80 ft (about 24 m) trunk is smooth, gray and clearly ringed. There is no crown shaft; the crown is dense with leaves that grow to 15 ft (about 4.5 m). This fast-growing palm is perfect for a large tub in subtropical areas and flourishes in full sun in its mature stages; it is a very popular palm for avenues and clumps in large gardens in frost-free climates, although it grows best where it is sheltered from the wind. Like almost all palms, it transplants easily even when mature. It adapts well to different conditions as long as plenty of water reaches the roots and the climate is not too cool. Seed germination takes two months;

*Todea barbara*

*Archontophoenix alexandrae*

*Archontophoenix cunninghamiana*

*Pteris ensiformis*

*Brahea armata*

*Butia capitata*

*Arecastrum romanzoffianum*

allow enough room for the roots to run deep. The trunks of the mature plant are sometimes hollowed out and used as irrigation pipes and its leaves provide cattle fodder during droughts.
ZONES 9–11

## BRAHEA

These palms, sometimes thorny and usually with an upright trunk, are grown for their foliage and for their stately appearance. They need full sun and will tolerate stony soil.

### *B. armata*

FAN PALM

Originally found in Mexico on hillsides or in deep gullies, this attractive but very slow-growing palm has a stout trunk, eventually 50 ft (about 15 m) high and 18 in (about 45 cm) in diameter. The tree features bluish gray, fan-shaped blades, brown-yellow fruits and yellow flowers clustered in groups of three on the branchlets. The flowers can be up to 15 ft (about 4.5 m) in length. Avoid rich acidic soils when planting in wet climates. Propagate from seed; germination is slow (up to six months).
ZONES 10-11

### *B. edulis*

GUADALUPE PALM

This native of an island off the coast of Baja California differs from *B. armata* in having light green leaves, a stout trunk and also being shorter in height (to only 30 ft/9 m). The flowers are similar but are more likely to be held within the foliage mass. It seems to be equally happy in sites in the low desert or in beach situations.
ZONES 9–11

## BUTIA

### *capitata*

syn. *Cocos capitata*

JELLY PALM

Native to central Brazil, Uruguay and Argentina, this species varies in appearance, with a variable trunk height of 3–15 ft (about 90–450 cm). It is characterized by its overlapping leaf bases, which make the palm's trunk quite spiky and rough. Its flowers are creamy yellow and the orange-yellow fruits are egg shaped. This palm grows well in areas of high or low rainfall. The sweet flesh of the fruit can be strained and used to make jelly or, when fermented, wine.
ZONES 10–11

*Caryota urens*

## CARYOTA

FISHTAIL PALM

Native to the hill slopes and rocky outcrops of Malaysia, eastern Asia and northern Australia, this genus has bipinnate leaves rather than the pinnate or palmate leaves that are common to most palms. These smaller leaflets are triangular and form a fishtail shape. The flower-bearing branches have a short stalk and numerous pendulous, smaller branches. Some species are multi-stemmed and others are taller and single trunked. *Caryota* are generally fast growers and trouble free in tropical and subtropical, frost free areas; they are often grown as indoor plants. Fiber from the leaves is used to make brooms. The fruit contain caustic crystals and should not be eaten. *C. urens* has a distinctive gray trunk that thins out as it gets higher. Once established it grows fast and may reach 65 ft (about 20 m) tall. In some Asian countries it is used to make palm sugar, or jaggery. It flowers only once in its life, but flower clusters follow in succession down the trunk for several years, after which the tree dies.
ZONES 10–11

## CHAMAEDOREA

This genus comprises more than 130 species and most of these are native to Central America. They are slender, ornamental palms with smooth, green, bamboo-like stems that grow to just below the forest canopy rather than towering above it. The stems can grow singly or in clusters. The leaves are slender and green and may be whole or pinnate. When leaflets die they leave bare, gaping leaf veins visible below the palm's apex. These palms make good garden plants in shady positions. Propagate from seed.

### *C. elegans*

PARLOR PALM

Native to Mexico and Guatemala, this dwarf palm has dark green, pinnate leaves that arch upwards, with shiny leaflets up to 20–30 in (about 50–76 cm) long. A popular indoor plant, as the common name implies, it may be grown outside in a cool position if protected from sun and wind. Insignificant yellow flowers are borne, followed by small black fruit. The leaves are fairly frost sensitive.

ZONES 9–11

### *C. erumpens*

BAMBOO PALM

This palm has sickle-shaped leaflets that form part of shiny leaves 20 in (about 50 cm) long. Growing up to 12 ft (about 3.5 m) in height and spreading up to 7 ft (about 2 m), it forms a nice cluster in gardens and does best in tropical and subtropical climates; it grows very well indoors.

ZONES 9–11

## *CHAMAEROPS*

### *humilis*

EUROPEAN FAN PALM

Europe's most widespread native palm (native to southern Europe and the Mediterranean), this single-species genus is varied in its habit: it can have many trunks or one solitary trunk and be small or large, depending on its position. It is very resilient and perfect for temperate regions, being frost hardy. It has been found covered in snow at high altitudes. It prefers a sunny position and well-drained soil. A big clump makes a good lawn specimen and it can also be grown in a tub for long periods of time. Carpet fibers known as "African hair" are manufactured from the leaf sheaths, and leaf fibers have also been used as a substitute for flax.

ZONES 8–11

## *COCOS*

### *nucifera*

COCONUT PALM

A palm highly valued as a source of food, drink, and housing and other materials throughout the tropics. The only species in its genus, it has long been a symbol of tranquillity and recreation for exhausted city workers. It grows up to 95 ft (about 29 m) high and has a crown of long, pinnate leaves. Male and female flowers grow on the same plant. Despite the popular coastal image, this palm can be grown inland as long as it has an underground water supply and a warm climate. It is not frost hardy and will not fruit away from tropical or warm subtropical climates.

ZONE 11

## *CYRTOSTACHYS*

### *renda*

syn. *C. lakka*

SEALING WAX PALM, MAHARAJAH PALM

The contrast between the rich green of the leaves and the brilliant scarlet of the glossy leaf bases makes this clumping feather palm from Malaysia one of the most ornamental of all palms. Alas, it is rarely a success away from the tropics—although it will grow in subtropical climates, it needs constant hot weather for the color to develop properly. It likes rich, constantly moist soil, grows to around 12 ft (about 3.5 m) tall and has the reputation of being rather difficult to transplant. Propagate from absolutely fresh seed.

ZONE 11

*Cyrtostachys renda*

*Chamaedorea elegans*

*Chamaerops humilis*

*Chamaedorea erumpens*

*Cocos nucifera*

# A Field Trip to Tengchong

Near Tengchong in Yunnan Province, China, you can observe the Chusan or Chinese windmill palm *(Trachycarpus fortunei)* in a setting that closely resembles its native origin. This widespread species has been so widely cultivated over the centuries that its origin is now uncertain. However, it was probably native to southern and central China, northern Burma, and possibly the island of Kyushu in southern Japan.

Tengchong is situated in the extreme west of China, and has only been open to tourists since the late 1980s. You start your trek at Kunming, the provincial capital and administrative hub of Yunnan. A short flight from Hong Kong, Kunming is a picturesque city surrounded by mountains and situated on the shores of China's sixth largest lake, Dian Chi. It has a reputation for being the most pleasant of Chinese cities because of its mild, subtropical climate. Tengchong is some 460 miles (about 750 km) to the northwest of Kunming.

Leaving Kunming you then travel along the Burma Road. Dali, the next stop on your trek to Tengchong, is about a twelve-hour drive to the northwest. Along the way you will pass through small villages, over mountain passes and along denuded hillsides. The road is lined with Tasmanian blue gums *(Eucalyptus globulus)* and a relative of the American tupelo or sour gum *(Camptotheca acuminata)*. The tree trunks are whitewashed, as guideposts.

*Yunnan Province, a region of contrasts.*

Dali, like Kunming, is situated on the Yunnan–Guizhou Plateau at about 6000 ft (about 1900 m) above sea level. It has an idyllic setting at the foot of the Cang Shan, or "Tali Range," which is a 30 miles (about 50 km) long mountain range to the west of Dali, attaining an altitude of about 13 000 ft (about 4100 m).

Numerous collections of plants have been made from the Cang Shan by European and American botanists, but the most extensive collections were made by George Forrest between 1904 and 1932. Of the 30 000 plants he collected, many came from the Cang Shan, and he was responsible for introducing many fine garden plants from this area to the West. Some notable examples include a yellow-flowered orchid *(Pleione forrestii)*, the fragrant, white-flowered *Rhododendron edgeworthii*, the silver fir *(Abies delavayi)*, and the pink-flowered *Magnolia campbellii*.

Leaving Dali and traveling for about 220 miles (about 350 km), you descend from the crest of the plateau into a broad, open valley. If you go in the fall, the landscape will glow with ripened grain and straw ready for the rice harvest. The only impediment to the view is a somber range of mountains with some distinctly conical peaks. These are volcanoes, remnants of the county's volatile geological history, and were active as recently as 700 years ago.

Very few tourists have visited this region so, whether you stay at the Tengchong Hotel or choose other accommodation, do not be surprised if you are the object of great interest.

Tengchong has a mild, subtropical climate with a mean annual temperature of about 63°F (about 17°C) and an average annual rainfall of approximately 43 in (about 1100 mm). The southwest monsoon influences the climate, and the rain falls mostly from July to October.

North of Tengchong on the road to the Goaligong Shan, a copse of about twenty Chusan palms grows in an exposed hillside corn field. The soil is a deep, red earth. The palms are very old and most probably have been cultivated for many

Dense vegetation in a valley near Luxi.

The Chusan palm fibers have many uses.

Trachycarpus fortunei

decades. They are 30 ft (about 10 m) high with 4 in (about 10 cm) diameter trunks, the uppermost sections of which are clad in coarse, black-brown fibers which are the remnants of old leaf sheaths. You can sometimes see irregularly shaped, bluish fruits either on the ground or on the upper leaf axils. However, this is unlikely as the flowers of the Chusan palm are considered a culinary delicacy throughout the region and are regularly harvested by the villagers. The immature flower spikes resemble cauliflower and are used in a similar way to bamboo shoots.

From here, drive on to the Goaligong Shan and its botanical treasures. Some plants to be observed there include the pink-flowered *Rhododendron stenaulum*, *Michelia doltsopa* (a white-flowered magnolia relative), and last but not least *Gordonia chrysandra* (a relative of the camellia).

You can also see the Chusan palm near a series of small volanic lakes located on the outskirts of Tenchong, on the way to Mount Yunfeng. Near the lakes is a small village surrounded by well-constructed, dry-packed, basalt stone walls. Behind these walls about twelve Chusan palms grow in rich, deep, red-brown loam which is very acidic. Again, it is unlikely that you will find flowers or fruits in evidence. Drive on to Mount Yunfeng, where you can walk to the summit and view a Taoist temple. This involves a climb up 2000 steps which are in places quite steep and precarious. Nevertheless, the walk is worthwhile for the spectacular views and the chance to explore the richness and almost untouched serenity of the forest surrounding the temple. The forest includes Yunnan pine *(Pinus yunnanensis)* and *Quercus*, *Lithocarpus* and *Castanopsis* species.

Whether you visit Yunnan to observe the spectacular scenery or experience its tourist attractions, much of the province's significance lies in the many and varied plants that occur here. By a combination of topographic, geologic and climatic factors, Yunnan has definitely proved its claim to be "The Kingdom of Plants."

## Trachycarpus

Palms belong to the Arecaceae family, which contains almost 3000 species. These are largely confined to the tropics; only a handful being adapted to moderately cool conditions. Among these are the six species of the small Chinese-Himalayan genus *Trachycarpus*, which all occur in regions receiving winter snow. Most widely grown is the Chusan palm *(Trachycarpus fortunei)*; it regularly withstands winter temperatures of 14°F (about −10°C) and has been known to survive at 5°F (about −15°C). This palm will grow almost anywhere between these colder limits and a few degrees of latitude short of the tropics (or highlands even within the tropics), thriving in most soils and tolerating both fierce sun and winter gales. However, neither this nor any palm can survive outdoors in climates in which the soil becomes frozen.

*Trachycarpus* has been prized in China for many centuries, both as an ornamental plant and for its many uses. Apart from a variety of fiber and similar products from the trunk and leaves, there is a high quality wax, used in polishes, obtained from the fruit skin, and a blood-clotting drug, "hsuen an," extracted from the seed. Both of these are now processed on an industrial scale. *T. fortunei* has been widely cultivated in Southeast Asia for its fiber.

*Trachycarpus fortunei*

*Euterpe edulis*

## *EUTERPE*
### *edulis*

ASSAI PALM

Originally from Brazil, this forest-dwelling palm has a tall, slender trunk and a crown of dark green, pinnate fronds. It bears small, round, brown-black fruit. It is easy to grow in a warm, humid climate but be sure to keep the young plant sheltered from direct sunlight for a few years. It prefers well-drained soil. Seeds germinate quickly, especially if leached in warm water for three days. Brazil harvests and exports palmito, the edible, sweet white tissue of the palm hearts; it is taken from the young shoots.
ZONES 10–11

## *HEDYSCEPE*
### *canterburyana*

UMBRELLA PALM, BIG MOUNTAIN PALM

From Lord Howe Island, Australia, this solitary feather palm grows to heights of 12–30 ft (about 3.5–9 m) and features a thick crown of dark green leaves and a silver crown shaft. It is slow growing but has potential as an ornamental palm, with its dramatic crest of dense leaves and contrasting brown to red fruit. It prefers shade, humidity and subtropical climates. Avoid placing it in full sun, especially when young. Propagate from seed.
ZONES 9–11

## *HOWEA*
syn. *Howeia, Kentia*

This genus of small palms has only two species, both native to Australia's Lord Howe Island and both widely cultivated. They have feathered leaves on long, smooth stalks and a smooth, ringed, single trunk. Flowers are male (light brown) or female (green). The plants are frost-sensitive and need moist humid conditions and shade if they are to be kept outdoors. They are more commonly grown indoors as they tolerate less light and need less heat than a lot of other palms. They can be kept in the same pot or tub for years, as long as the potting mix is well drained and contains some humus. Provide partial shade while they mature.

### *H. belmoreana*

CURLY PALM, SENTRY PALM

This is of great value as an indoor palm as it tolerates a substantial amount of neglect. Outdoors, it may grow to 24 ft (about 7.5 m) high.
ZONES 10–11

*Howea forsteriana*

*Hedyscepe canterburyana*

*Howea belmoreana*

*Livistona chinensis*

### *H. forsteriana*

THATCH PALM, KENTIA PALM

This is the more popular and faster growing of the two species in the *Howea* genus. An excellent palm for a small garden, it is widely grown in the United States, as well as Europe and Australia.

ZONES 10–11

## *JUBAEA*
### *chilensis*

COQUITO PALM, CHILEAN WINE PALM

Now very rare in its natural habitat of coastal Chile, this palm grows to 80 ft (about 24 m) with a very thick trunk and a dense mass of long, straight, deep green leaves spanning 12–15 ft (about 3.5–4.5 m). Flowers are yellow and 2 in (about 5 cm) long. This is a very slow-growing tree, suitable to a temperate climate and full sun. The soil should be well drained and deep. Seeds may take up to 6 months to germinate. Chileans once tapped the trunks of this palm for up to two years, then made wine or palm honey from its sugary sap, but this practice is now banned as it weakens the trees.

ZONES 8–10

## *LACCOSPADIX*
### *australasica*

ATHERTON PALM

An Australian native from the rainforests of northeastern Queensland, this feathered palm is found either in clumps or standing alone. It has a 6–24 ft (about 1.8–7.5 m) trunk and single cascading spikes of yellow to red fruit. It prefers the dense canopies of rainforests and so is best placed in shade in a rich, organic soil. It makes an excellent indoor plant but is also good for landscaping as long as it can be sheltered from full sun. It is moderately frost hardy. Propagate from seed or divisions of suckers.

ZONES 9–11

## *LIVISTONA*

A genus of medium to tall fan palms found in the wetter parts of Malaysia, south China and Australia. They feature very large, round, pleated fronds $4^1/_2$ ft (about 1.3 m) across

*Laccospadix australasica*

and a dense crown from which dead leaves may remain hanging for a short time. The leaf stalks are usually long and edged with sharp teeth. These palms are good for outdoor landscaping: their clusters of purple-black fruit and tapering leaves are shown to great effect. Most species prefer a moderate amount of light and are hardy enough to survive cool and subtropical climates, although they do better in mild climates. They prefer a deep, sandy soil and are slow growing. Propagate from seed.

### *L. australis*

AUSTRALIAN CABBAGE-TREE PALM

This is one of the tallest species, reaching heights of up to 85 ft (about 26 m) in the wild. It does well in coastal areas. Australian Aborigines traditionally ate the fleshy part of this palm's young leaves and made spearheads from the hard wood.

ZONES 10–11

### *L. chinensis*

FOUNTAIN PALM, CHINESE FAN PALM

A smaller, very attractive palm with glossy green, tapering leaves, this species can be grown in tubs. In the garden it may grow to some 24 ft (about 7.5 m) and tolerates full sun or partial shade. It has been grown outdoors in sheltered gardens in colder countries.

ZONES 10–11

## *NEODYPSIS*
### *decaryi*

This palm is native to Madagascar and has an unusual three-sided trunk, formed by the leaf bases that

*Neodypsis decaryi*

*Livistona australis*

*Jubaea chilensis*

arrange themselves in three rows. Both the trunk and leaflets feature a chalky white growth. The pinnate leaves grow upright and curve at the tips only. It grows quickly and well in a sun-filled location in tropical and subtropical areas but is not commonly cultivated. Propagate from seed.

ZONES 10–11

## *PHOENIX*

DATE PALM

Tropical Africa, southern China, Asia and the Philippines are where this genus originates. They are feather palms that feature a dense crown of long, pinnate leaves with stiff, sharp spines and a very rough trunk where the leaf base has broken away and left scarring. The flowers grow in clusters of thousands on some species. The bright red or golden fruit is usually edible. These palms are sun lovers, very popular as landscape subjects on main streets and in parks and are among the hardiest palms in cultivation. They are not commonly grown in containers. They tolerate hot winds and poor soil and the various species hybridize freely when grown together. Propagate from seeds. Species of *Phoenix* are valued not only as ornamental palms but also as a source of palm sugar, used in Asian cooking.

Phoenix dactylifera

Phoenix canariensis

### *P. canariensis*
CANARY ISLAND DATE PALM

Native to the Canary Islands as the name implies, this shorter, heavier species has large, dark green fronds. Its 1 in (about 2.5 cm) orange fruit is inedible.
ZONES 9–11

### *P. dactylifera*
DATE PALM

Able to make do with less water than almost any other tree, this palm grows to 95 ft (about 29 m) in height and grows succulent fruit in dry tropical and subtropical conditions.
ZONES 9–10

### *P. reclinata*
SENEGAL DATE PALM

An African species, this palm is smaller than *P. canariensis* and *P. dactylifera*, reaching only 20–30 ft (about 6–9 m) in height. It is distinct for its multiple trunks, each gracefully curving out from the center of the clump. Small fruits are yellow to red.
ZONES 10–11

Rhapis excelsa

Sabal palmetto

Serenoa repens

### *P. roebelinii*
PYGMY DATE PALM

The smallest of the date palms, this species from Laos makes a suitable house plant. Only 6 ft (about 1.8 m) tall, this single-stemmed palm prefers a shaded site in the garden. Its fruit is black, and the foliage has a finer texture than other species. Propagate from seed.
ZONES 10–11

## *RHAPIDOPHYLLUM*
### *hystrix*
NEEDLE PALM

This low-growing, shrubby palm is native to the southeastern coast of North America. Its stem may be sprawling or upright to no more than 5 ft (about 1.5 m). The stiff, palmate leaves are around 3 ft (about 90 cm) wide and are silvery on the undersides. It prefers moist soil and full sun to part shade. The wine-red flower clusters are tucked within the foliage mass. The leaf sheaths are well protected by long, sharp spines.
ZONES 8–11

Rhopalostylis sapida

## *RHAPIS*
### *excelsa*
LADY PALM, BAMBOO PALM

Native to southern China, this is a dwarf palm with several hundred slender stems that form very large, leafy clumps. Its leaves are 24–28 in (about 60–71 cm) long, pale green, randomly scattered along the stem and divided into rigid, finger-like segments. An excellent tub plant, it must be kept away from full sunlight as the leaves burn easily. It makes a neat, attractive indoor palm and can live in the same pot for years with infrequent breaks outside. If planted in the garden, it is happiest under a large tree where the ground is more easily kept moist and shady; it is frost tender. Propagate by division.
ZONES 8–11

## *RHOPALOSTYLIS*

This genus comprises three attractive, evergreen feather palms with upright, gray-green, solitary trunks and erect or pendent pinnate fronds. The leaflets have a smooth surface, fleecy underside and scaly mid-rib. Both male and female flowers are borne along semi-upright or arching, branched stems. These are followed by smooth, red, round to elliptical fruit. The species range from frost hardy to frost tender, surviving in temperatures down to 37°F (about 3°C). They require a humid atmosphere and reasonably fertile soil with protection from full sun and wind. Swampy conditions are tolerated and propagation is from seed in spring.

### *R. baueri*
NORFOLK PALM

This palm originates in Norfolk Island, Australia, and has a gray, closely ringed trunk growing up to 38 ft (about 11.5 m) high, a wide-spreading crown and leaves that grow to 12 ft (about 3.5 m) long. The crown shaft of this tree is stout, very pale green and easily recognizable. Young plants have a distinct reddish toning in their leaves. It bears panicles of white to mauve flowers. The fruit is small, red and slightly conical. Suited to a moist

Rhopalostylis baueri

and frost-free climate, this palm should be kept out of the wind as the leaves very easily become shredded and ragged looking. Easily propagated from fresh seeds.
ZONES 10–11

### *R. sapida*
NIKAU PALM, FEATHER DUSTER PALM

The only palm native to New Zealand, this slow-growing species reaches 35 ft (about 10 m) in height and 16 in (about 40 cm) in diameter. It has a slender, unbranched trunk encircled by prominent rings. The pinnate, rigid fronds are upstretched and 3–9 ft (about 90–270 cm) in length. Light bluish purple-pink to cream flowers are followed by vivid red fruit.
ZONES 10–11

## *SABAL*

This is a genus of palms with fern-like fronds that are often used in basketry or for thatched roofs. They are native to the southeastern United States to South America and prefer positions in full sun.

### *S. mexicana*
OAXACA PALMETTO, TEXAS PALMETTO

A fan palm from south of the border, this species grows slowly to 30–50 ft (about 9–15 m) tall. The leaves fall naturally to reveal a clean, slender trunk.
ZONES 9–11

### *S. palmetto*
PALMETTO, CABBAGE PALM

Native to the southeastern United States, this tall, thick palm grows up to 80 ft (about 24 m) tall and 12–18 in (about 30–45 cm) in diameter. The trunk is covered with continuous, interlaced leaf bases and the fan-shaped leaves have an idiosyncratic twist initiated by the leaf stalk, making this plant easy to recognize. It flowers and bears fruit while it is still young. This is a sun lover, as are most species of the *Sabal* genus, and should be planted in sandy soil in subtropical and tropical areas. Large group plantings are particularly showy and many of the famous palm avenues in Miami are of their species. Propagate from seed.
ZONES 9–11

## *SERENOA*
### *repens*

SAW PALMETTO

A single-species dwarf genus, this low-growing fan palm appears in large colonies in the southeastern United States. It has stiff, spiky, variable-colored leaves ranging from yellow to bluish green or silvery white and the trunk often grows below the ground. Plant in a sunny position as it can tolerate full sun even when immature and is quite frost tender. It grows well along coastlines and can withstand salt-laden winds. Its egg-shaped, dark purple fruit was eaten by the local American Indians for its therapeutic properties and is valued now as a health food. Propagate from seed.
ZONES 8–10

## *TRACHYCARPUS*
### *fortunei*

CHUSAN PALM, HEMP PALM, WINDMILL PALM

This is perhaps the most frost hardy of all the palms, surviving even in cold-climate gardens. In a mild climate it can grow 30 ft (about 9 m) tall, its trunk covered in the shaggy, fibrous remains of the old leaf bases and crowned with splendidly slashed, fan-shaped leaves. It is a solitary grower, but looks best in groups; in China and Japan the fibrous leaf sheaths are made into rope—hence the name "hemp palm." The specific name honors Robert Fortune, who first brought the plant from China to England in the 1840s; it is said that several of his original specimens are still growing.
ZONES 8–10

## *WASHINGTONIA*

Native to the rocky, dry areas of the southern United States and Mexico, there are only two species in this genus, both large, single-standing fan palms. The trunk is fatter at the base and, in older trees, may be covered with a thick thatch of old leaves which extends almost to the ground. If you dislike the appearance, the palm will come to no harm if the dead leaves are cut off; they can be a fire hazard. The crown is dense with no crown shaft and the stalks of the finely bladed leaves are broad and toothed. The fruit is small, brown and egg shaped. These are versatile landscaping plants, appropriate for planting in avenues or as potted ornamental palms. Suited to a sun-filled position in warm-temperate areas or dry tropical climates. Ensure soil is well drained. Propagate from seed.

### *W. filifera*

WASHINGTON PALM, DESERT FAN PALM, CALIFORNIA FAN PALM

The more frost hardy of the two species, this has long, gray-green leaves and bears small white flowers in summer. It grows up to 50 ft (about 15 m) high. One of the common names refers to the white, cotton-like threads on the leaf segments. This is the palm that lends its name to the city of Palm Springs, California.
ZONES 8–10

### *W. robusta*

WASHINGTON PALM, MEXICAN FAN PALM

At 80 ft (about 24 m) high this is the taller species, with a more slender trunk and greener leaves. Its flowers are creamy white.
ZONES 9–10

# CYCADS

## *CYCAS*
### *revoluta*

SAGO PALM, JAPANESE SAGO CYCAD, JAPANESE FERN PALM

Native to the islands of southern Japan, this evergreen suits temperate and subtropical regions. The trunk grows slowly to 10 ft (about 3 m), with a wide, flat crown of numerous, glossy green leaves. Male cones are narrow cylinders up to 16 in (about 40 cm) long; female cones, brown and hairy, are half as long. The hairy vermilion seeds, $1^{1}/_{2}$ in (about 3 cm) long, appear in fall. Grow in a glasshouse or outdoors in full sun. Water well in dry weather and fertilize lightly. Propagate from seed, basal suckers or trunk offsets. Widely grown as an ornamental, this is a very popular bonsai subject in Japan.
ZONES 9–11

## *ENCEPHALARTOS*
### *horridus*

BREAD TREE

Originating from South Africa, this evergreen cycad forms dense, impenetrable thickets because of its suckering habit and rigid, extremely spiny leaves. Suited to temperate and subtropical regions, it grows to 3 ft (about 90 cm) from short, thick trunks. The leaves emerge lustrous silvery blue and mature to glaucous blue-green. Reaching 3 ft (about 90 cm) in length, the leaves are straight near the crown, becoming strongly recurved at the apex. Grow in full sun and well-drained soils. Easily propagated from seed and suckers.
ZONES 10–11

## *MACROZAMIA*

This is a genus of slow-growing, evergreen cycads with or without trunks. They prefer to be planted in a position with some shade. Mature female plants may produce several pineapple-like cones every couple of years or so.

*Macrozamia communis*

*Washingtonia robusta*

*Cycas revoluta*

### *M. communis*

This evergreen cycad, native to southeastern Australia, forms colonies in gravelly, loam soils in open forests. One of the most popular species for cultivation in tropical and temperate regions, its graceful, open form makes an excellent specimen for containers. Reaching 5 ft (about 1.5 m) in height, the strongly arching, bright green leaves grow to 6 ft (about 1.8 m) in length. The male cones are cylindrical while the female cones are barrel shaped, producing bright red, orange or yellow seeds. This species thrives in full sun to partial shade and tolerates moderate to heavy frosts. Propagate from seed. A note of caution: the seeds are poisonous.
ZONES 10–11

### *M. spiralis*

BURRAWANG

This evergreen cycad is native to eastern Australia, where it grows in open forests in sandy soils. A stumpy plant, it grows mostly underground, reaching 3 ft (about 90 cm) in height above with a spread of around 3 ft (about 90 cm ) also. The spiraling, deep green leaves grow up to 3 ft (about 90 cm) long, developing a full crown in fertile conditions, and limited to one or two leaves in poor conditions. The male cones are cylindrical while the female ones are ovoid and bear brilliant scarlet seeds the size of bantam eggs. Both are 6–8 in (about 15–20 cm) long, and appear only sporadically. Suitable for temperate and tropical regions, this plant will thrive best in full or filtered sun and

*Washingtonia filifera*

tolerates moderate to heavy frosts. Propagate from seed but be prepared to be patient. Australian Aborigines developed a long, complex method of processing the poisonous, starchy seeds to make them edible. Some early white settlers tried eating the unfamiliar seeds unprocessed, with disastrous results.
ZONES 10–11

## *ZAMMIA*
### *pumila*

A native of the grasslands and open forests of the Caribbean, this small cycad grows from freely branching, underground stems. The dark green, stiff, leathery leaves stand erect to slightly angled from the crown. The male cones are cylindrical while the female cones are ovoid, both being rusty-red colored. Seeds are orange to orange-red. Best grown in full sun, this species makes an attractive addition to a border or as a container specimen. Propagate from seed.
ZONES 10–11

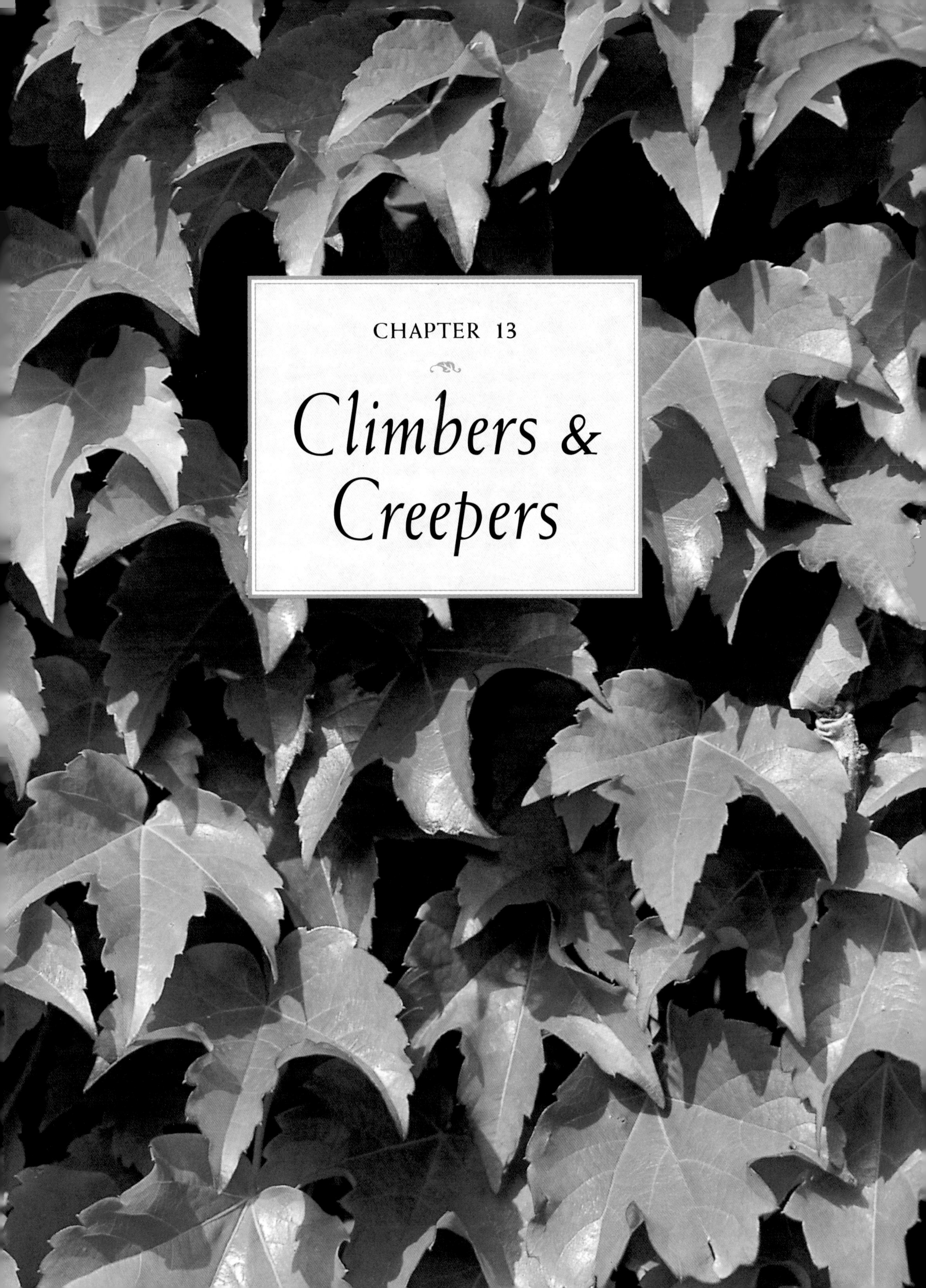

CHAPTER 13

# Climbers & Creepers

*There's nothing as welcoming as a vine-covered arch over a front gate or a delicate rambler twining its way in and around window shutters to display its perfumed flowers to perfection. In these and other subtle ways climbers play an important role in the overall garden landscape.*

By their very nature climbers set out to reach the high spots where there's less competition for light. Some can be used as explanation points in small gardens, or in a tight spot as they need very little ground or wall space; other, more adventurous types will sprawl over a garden shed, camouflaging it in no time. Climbers come mainly from temperate or tropical forests where competition has forced them to evolve various means of ensuring their lax stems reach the light that is essential for manufacturing food. These modifications allow some vines to twine around a host while others have thorns or hooks, tendrils, sucker disks or even aerial roots to reach out for an anchorage on supporting plants.

The most common climbing mechanism is simply for a vine to twine; *Pandorea jasminoides* and *Phaseolus caracalla* are among the most accommodating. All they need is a post or open support such as lattice or a wire frame. Plants with thread-like tendrils such as sweet peas or the wonderful range of clematis need fine supports to allow the slender, modified leaf parts to grip. Those with sucker pads, like parthenocissus, are ideal for solid masonry walls although their position should be chosen with care as the pads will leave unsightly marks on the masonry should they ever need to be removed.

*Hydrangea petiolaris*, the climbing hydrangea, and the temperate garden climber *Campsis grandiflora* are two vines which rely on their aerial roots to grip on to a solid surface, as does the true ivy, *Hedera helix*. Be warned though: true ivy is fine contained on walls but its brush-like roots can very soon help in a takeover bid for the complete garden if allowed ground space. The scramblers, like roses and some tropical plants such as bougainvillea, have thorns or hooks by which to hoist their branches even higher—in a garden with the correct support and a little time spent on training they are docile and most rewarding to grow.

Once these characteristics are known and understood, climbers can be chosen to suit any existing garden situation or be coupled with a new structure to add a wonderful softening effect.

## Arbors, Pergolas and Balcony Gardens

Arbors and pergolas are generally firm, solid structures built to last and can take strong-growing twiners such as wisteria and the ornamental grapes. Both of these are deciduous, providing shade in summer and allowing the sun to penetrate during the colder months. However, pergolas can be "double planted" with less vigorous plants to give a combined show. For instance, a delicate, soft look can be achieved by highlighting the single, yellow flowers of *Rosa* 'Mermaid' against the small, starry, white flowers of the dainty *Solanum jasminoides*. These delicate twiners can also be used on a growing frame such as an established flowering fruit tree, then when the

*A climbing rose—the perfect complement to a timber pergola.*

blossoms synchronize there are few more beautiful sights that a gardener could look forward to.

One of the joys of sitting under a pergola is being able to enjoy the flowers of the covering vine. Those with pendulous sprays such as *Akebia quinata* and *Thunbergia grandiflora* as well as the superb wisterias will certainly delight. However, some other vines will provide a carpet of fallen petals but the flowers remain hidden to all but those looking out from balconies or windows above. For this reason many vines are best grown on a vertical surface such as a trellis or lattice or strands of wire stretched between two vertical posts to form a screen or fence. Here the complete surface area of the plant provides a breathtaking display while taking up very little actual garden space. Aspect needs to be taken into account when growing climbers in this way. In cold areas tender plants can be damaged if frozen tissue is thawed rapidly against a wall receiving early morning sun, while in warmer areas both the last rays of the sun and reflected heat from nearby paved areas can scorch new summer growth on plants that have been trained against a wall.

Often the very reason for choosing to plant a vine against a wall is because it takes up very little space, yet this also could mean the root run is limited. Take care here with soil preparation and fertilizing to provide the best possible conditions for what is to be a feature plant. Often in these conditions, protected by eaves or next to a concrete slab, the climber is best planted away from the house then trained back against it. Then again in cases like this you could consider using a decorative tub filled with a good quality potting mix. Tubs can be used to grow cascading plants like the colourful nasturtiums or dwarf sweet peas with some branches allowed to tumble over the edge while others trained upwards to camouflage the lower twiggy sections of the main vine.

Many balcony gardens rely solely on tub culture to produce stunning effects with cascading vines and shady canopies. The risk of these tubs overheating and drying out can be greatly reduced by "mulching" the surface area and sides of the pots with a growing veil. In these often exposed situations care should be taken never to allow the pots to dry out or its contents to become overheated—one cunning method to overcome this is to drop a plastic pot containing the plant into a more decorative one so the pot is insulated. Grouping say three or five pots together to generate shade for one another is another way to ensure a successful high-rise or balcony garden.

Clematis montana *'Rubens' provides a spectacular spring display.*

## Soil Preparation and Planting

As most climbers will be permanent, time spent preparing the soil well by digging it over will certainly be welcome. Like most plants, climbers need good drainage; this is especially important in those pockets against house walls. In these spots it is very often worthwhile to dig deep and wide to unearth any leftover builder's rubble buried just beneath the surface. These positions are often a lot drier than the open garden, so be generous with garden compost or animal manure to help with moisture retention.

## Pruning

General pruning rules apply equally to climbers as to any other plant. In the very early stage of a climber's growth, finger or tip pruning encourages a single stem to branch out, giving more than one stem to be trained up a trellis—this can become the basis for an informal or stylized espaliered effect, say for a rose growing on stretched wire supports. Then as the climber matures flowering can be encouraged by pruning, but as in the case of shrubs you have to become aware of the flowering characteristics of your chosen plant. Most will flower at the tips of branches so by pruning at nodes and allowing two or three extra branches to be formed, flowering can be increased. But, it must also be remembered that some vines flower on new or the present season's growth, while others take till the next season to produce their blooms and pruning needs to be carried out keeping this in mind. Of course rambling-type roses, for instance, flower on long new canes, and in general these can be cut well back after flowering. However, many of the climbing roses form a permanent mainframe of branches that adhere to horizontal trellising, then each year flowering side shoots appear and in turn these are pruned back to make way for further flowers. Even though they are thorny, roses trained in this way are very easily managed and are very long lived.

If a vine is tied on to a support, be sure to check the ties regularly, particularly in the growing season, as they can very easily injure the plant if they become too tight. Vines may take that little bit more of a gardener's time but it is very satisfying to see the end results.

*Antigonon leptopus*

*Akebia quinata*

*Allamanda cathartica*

## AKEBIA
### *quinata*

FIVE-LEAF AKEBIA

Deciduous (or semi-evergreen in areas where winters are mild), this decorative, twining climber from China is grown for its attractive habit, leaves and flowers. The gray-green leaves are divided into 5 leaflets and fragrant, purple-mauve, drooping, vanilla-scented flowers appear in late spring. Male and female plants are needed for the female plants to produce interesting sausage-shaped, edible fruit in mild climates. The plant likes full sun, good drainage and plenty of water during summer. It will do very well when used to shade an entryway or arbor or if allowed to scramble over a dead tree or tree stump. It will grow to 30 ft (about 9 m) or more and requires a strong support. Prune after flowering and cut down to the base every 3 or 4 years to remove tangled growth. Pinch when young to encourage plentiful stems. Be careful that it does not smother small shrubs. Propagate from cuttings or by layering in spring.

ZONES 5–9

## ALLAMANDA
### *cathartica*

GOLDEN TRUMPET VINE

Native to South America, this vigorous, evergreen climber, fast growing to 15 ft (about 4.5 m), bears large, yellow, trumpet-shaped flowers up to 5 in (about 12 cm) across in summer. It has whorls of lance-shaped leaves and makes a luxuriant cover for walls and strong fences in frost-free areas. Grow in full sun or partial shade in humus-rich, neutral to acid, well-drained soil and water well during the growing period, less so when not in full growth. Regular tip pruning improves its appearance. Propagate from softwood cuttings in spring and summer, and watch for red spider mites. It will take heavy pruning and can be grown in a large container.

ZONES 10–11

*Ampelopsis brevipedunculata* var. *maximowiczii*

## AMPELOPSIS
### *brevipedunculata* var. *maximowiczii*

**syn. *A. heterophylla, Vitis heterophylla***

PORCELAIN BERRY

This vigorous, deciduous climber will twine with the aid of tendrils 15 ft (about 4.5 m) or more. It has grape-like, lobed leaves, small greenish flowers in summer, and in fall bunches of berries like miniature grapes that ripen from pale green to turquoise, bright blue and violet. Grow in a sunny or partially shaded position in a moisture-retentive but well-drained soil. It grows rapidly and needs strong support and plenty of room to spread; it will provide almost instant cover over a trellis, arch, wall or pergola. Cut back hard to the main branches when berries have finished. Japanese beetles may decimate it; otherwise it has few other problems. Propagate from cuttings in summer or by layering in fall.

ZONES 5–9

## ANTIGONON
### *leptopus*

CORAL VINE, QUEEN'S-WREATH

A dainty, fast-growing, showy creeper that climbs by tendrils and may grow to 21 ft (about 6.5 m) or more. It bears masses of deep pink, heart-shaped flowers from early summer to fall and is easily grown in warm, frost-free areas. In cool areas it can be grown as a summer-flowering annual. The plant does best in a sunny situation in well-drained, fertile soil. Keep well watered during spring and summer. It is ideal for trellises, pergolas and arbors where a light cover is desirable. Remove spent flowerheads and cut out old twiggy growth in early spring. Propagate from seed sown in spring or from cuttings taken in late spring.

ZONES 8–11

## ARISTOLOCHIA

BIRTHWORT, DUTCHMAN'S PIPE

This large genus of over 500 species comprises evergreen and deciduous, climbing and herbaceous perennials, native to many different climatic regions. The climbers are most often cultivated, chosen for their cordate leaves and unusually shaped flowers, which have a globe-shaped swelling at the base and a hood above. Insects are attracted into the mouth of the flowers by a strong scent, and pollen is scattered over their bodies. The plants require well-drained, humus-rich soil in a sunny position with some shade in summer, and support for their climbing habit. In spring, prune the previous year's growth to 2 to 3 nodes. Propagate from seed in spring or from semi-hardwood cuttings in summer. Watch out for red spider mites.

### *A. durior*

DUTCHMAN'S PIPE

This vigorous, eastern North American, deciduous, twining vine reaches height of 20–30 ft (about 6–9 m), crowding out other plants as it matures. The large, dark glossy green, heart-shaped leaves tend to cover the pipe-shaped, purple-brown and yellow-green bicolor flowers borne in the leaf axils in late spring and early summer. Tolerant of a wide variety of soil types, it grows well in sun or shade and is most often propagated from seed, though division and semi-hardwood cuttings are also recommended. Useful as a quick cover for unsightly objects, as a dense screen or rambling over the top of a pergola.

ZONES 4–9

### *A. elegans*

CALICO FLOWER

This creeper, fast-growing to 18 ft (about 5.5 m), is native to Brazil and needs high humidity and protection from frost. It has fleshy, heart-shaped leaves and in summer bears strangely shaped, maroon flowers with white, thread-like markings. Plant in humus-rich, well-drained soil in a partially shaded position. An interesting plant for verandah columns or a pergola. Propagate from semi-ripe cuttings in late summer, or seed in spring. It can be grown as an annual in cool climates.

ZONE 11

## *ASARINA*
### *erubescens*

CLIMBING SNAPDRAGON

This dainty, semi-evergreen climber has velvety, heart-shaped leaves and bears pink, tubular flowers resembling snapdragons in late spring and early summer. It has twining stems up to 9 ft (about 2.7 m) tall and adapts well to hanging baskets and window boxes. It requires full sun, good drainage and regular watering in summer. Easily propagated from seed in spring.

ZONES 10–11

## *BEAUMONTIA*
### *grandiflora*

HERALD'S TRUMPET

This beautiful, large, woody, evergreen climber growing to 24 ft (about 7.5 m) needs strong support for its thick, twining stems. It is valued for its large, fragrant, white, trumpet flowers, which appear in late spring and summer, and handsome, deep green leaves. It is best suited to subtropical areas, but it can also be grown in a protected position in warm-temperate districts. Soil should be deep and fertile with good drainage. It requires full sun and regular watering in summer. Prune immediately after flowering. Propagate from cuttings in late summer.

ZONES 10–11

## *BIGNONIA*
### *capreolata*

CROSS-VINE, TRUMPET-FLOWER

A rampant grower, this dense, woody vine native to the southeastern United States climbs by tendrils with adhesive discs, achieving heights of 50–60 ft (about 15–18 m). Orange-red, trumpet-shaped flowers blanket the plant in late spring, providing a vivid display of color. The evergreen, compound leaves, composed of two leaflets, are bright green in summer, turning reddish purple is fall and remaining through the following spring. Grow in well-drained, rich loam soil in a sunny or partially shaded site. Though it has a tendency to become a nuisance, it is useful for covering walls, fences and buildings and for scrambling over banks and hillsides.

ZONES 6–10

## *BOMAREA*
### *caldasii*
**syn. *B. kalbreyeri***

CLIMBING ALSTROEMERIA

This attractive, evergreen, twining climber to 9 ft (about 2.7 m) bears large clusters of bright orange, pendulous bell flowers in summer. Grow in well-drained, humus-rich soil and water regularly in summer.

*Aristolochia elegans*

It is ideal for a warm environment in a sunny or partially shaded position. It needs strong support and will form an attractive dense screen on a fence or trellis. Cut back hard after flowering to encourage fresh growth. Propagate by division of underground stems in early spring.

ZONES 9–11

## *BOUGAINVILLEA*

BOUGAINVILLEA

Native to South America, bougainvilleas are valued for their glorious, flamboyant flowers and their ability to cover a large area. There is a large range of different kinds and colors to choose from, but all do best in warm to hot climates in full sun. They are evergreen in the tropics, but may be deciduous in cooler climates. The flowering period is early spring and can extend well into fall. The true flowers are insignificant, but the surrounding bracts are brilliantly colored, often changing color or shade as they age. Only water when needed and do not over-fertilize, particularly with nitrogen as this will produce luxuriant leaf growth but very little in the way of colorful bracts. Bougainvilleas need strong support for vigorous growth but can be controlled by pruning after flowering, when rampant plants can be ruthlessly cut back without harm. Flowers appear on the new wood. Propagate from semi-hardwood cuttings in summer. With regular, heavy pruning they can be grown in large containers.

### *B.* cultivars

There is an enormous number of cultivars available. 'Texas Dawn' produces pink flower bracts and grows to 30 ft (about 9 m). 'Magnifica Traillii' has brilliant crimson bracts. 'Barbara Karst' has brilliant red flowers.

ZONES 9–11

### *B. glabra*

This is the parent of several varieties. A vigorous shrubby vine growing to 30 ft (about 9 m), with masses of bright purple floral bracts in spring and summer.

ZONES 10–11

*Bomarea caldasii*

*Beaumontia grandiflora*

*Asarina erubescens*

*Bougainvillea glabra*

*Bougainvillea* 'Magnifica Traillii'

### *B. spectabilis*

Native to Brazil, this evergreen species produces a profusion of large, red-bracted blooms along its gracefully arching, spiny branches from early spring through fall. Flowers are borne on new wood, so prune in spring before growth begins. A rapid grower, it reaches heights of 20–30 ft (about 6–9 m) and requires a sturdy support for tying up the branches. Grow in a humus-rich, well-drained soil and avoid over-watering in fall and winter. Fertilize sparingly to maximize blooms. Most effective as a specimen climbing along a trellis-covered wall, over a pergola or cascading over a wall.

ZONES 9–11

## *CAMPSIS*

TRUMPET CREEPER, TRUMPET VINE

This genus contains two species of deciduous root climbers that used to be part of the *Bignonia* and *Tecoma* genera, but are now differentiated because of the leaf shape—the leaves have between 7 and 11 leaflets, arranged oppositely in pairs. Originally from the temperate regions of the northern hemisphere, the plants are grown for their orange-scarlet, trumpet-like flowers which appear in summer. They require a sunny site, preferably with some shelter, with well-drained soil. They will need to be watered in summer. They can be propagated in winter from root or hardwood stem cuttings or by layering, and in sum-

*Campsis grandiflora*

*Campsis* x *tagliabuana* 'Madame Galen'

*Celastrus scandens*

*Celastrus orbiculatus*

*Campsis radicans*

mer from semi-hardwood cuttings. Established plants should be pruned hard in late winter or early spring, removing the previous season's flowering wood to within 2 in (about 5 cm) of the ground.

### *C. grandiflora*

**syn. *C. chinensis*, *Bignonia grandiflora***

CHINESE TRUMPET CREEPER

This vigorous, woody-stemmed climber from China will reach up to 30 ft (about 9 m) with the aid of aerial rootlets clinging to a support. Deciduous and fast growing, it produces eye-catching clusters of trumpet-shaped scarlet to orange flowers up to 4 in (about 10 cm) long in late summer and fall. It requires full sun in a well-drained, humus-rich soil. Water generously during the growing season. Prune in spring and propagate from semi-ripe cuttings taken in summer, or from layers or suckers.

ZONES 8–11

### *C. radicans*

TRUMPET CREEPER

This vigorous, deciduous, woody vine native to the central and southern United States reaches heights of 30–50 ft (about 9–15 m). Athough aerial rootlets are produced along the branches, they are not strong enough to support the weight of the vine, especially in strong winds, so additional support is required. The showy clusters of orange and scarlet, trumpet-shaped flowers blanket the plant from July to September, providing a stunning focal point in the garden. It is best grown in a rich, moist, well-drained loam in full sun for maximum bloom production. Considered a weed in the southeastern United States, it is a popular garden specimen in midwestern and northeastern states and throughout the Southwest and Pacific Coast states.

ZONES 4–10

### *C.* x *tagliabuana* 'Madame Galen'

MADAME GALEN TRUMPET CREEPER

This cultivar produces spectacular salmon-red flowers clustered in loose, open racemes throughout the summer months. As vigorous but not as hardy as *C. radicans*, it reaches heights of 25–30 ft (about 7.5–9 m).

ZONES 4–10

## *CELASTRUS*

This genus consists of 30 species of deciduous shrubs and woody climbers which are grown mainly for their unusual and striking fruits. Native to Asia and North America, the climbers can reach 30–45 ft (about 9–14 m) in height. The most commonly grown species carry the male and female flowers on separate plants, so one of each sex must be grown to produce the brilliantly colored fruits. They are an excellent choice to cover an old tree stump or grow over a wall as they will need support. Plant in well-drained soil in full sun or partial shade any time from fall to spring. Plants will benefit from a spring pruning of old wood and a general tidy up, and from an occasional feed. Propagate from seed or by layering in spring, or from cuttings in summer and fall.

### *C. orbiculatus*

**syn. *C. articulatus***

ORIENTAL BITTERSWEET

From China, this deciduous, vine-like climber is valued for its brilliantly colored, red and gold, pea-like berries which are retained through winter. Grow in humus-rich, moisture-retentive soil in sun or partial shade and provide good, roomy support for the twining stems as they can reach 10 ft (about 5.5 m) or more. It is not fussy about its water requirements. Pruning is only necessary to maintain shape, and is best done in late winter. Be careful that it does not smother small trees and shrubs to death. Propagate from root cuttings or layering in fall, or from seed sown in spring.

ZONES 5–9

### *C. scandens*

AMERICAN BITTERSWEET

Native to the southern United States, this deciduous, woody vine produces heavy, intertwining stems which can become quite invasive if left unchecked. Reaching heights of 15–20 ft (about 4.5–6 m), it is tolerant of many soil types, drought and wind. Of easy culture, it grows well in sun or shade. Male and female flowers are borne on separate plants, necessitating the planting of both sexes to produce the spectacular display of vivid orange-yellow and crimson fruit in fall and winter on female plants. Often discounted because of its rampant, voracious habit, it is best sited in the outlying reaches of the garden, covering rocky ground, banks or hillsides. Bittersweet makes a valuable addition to the natural or woodland garden.

ZONES 3–10

## *CISSUS*

### *antarctica*

KANGAROO VINE

This vigorous inhabitant of Australian rainforests is grown for its handsome, rich green, oval leaves and its ability to cover large areas. When given support it will climb by tendrils up to 15 ft (about 4.5 m) or more in the garden. Without support it will effectively scramble over rocky slopes and banks. This plant grows well in partial shade or full shade in humus-rich, well-drained soil with some water retention. It is frost tender and in cool areas can be grown as a house plant as it will accept reasonably dark situations. Regular pruning improves its appearance. Propagate from stem cuttings or fresh seed. In warm areas it can be used as a ground cover, although its tendency to climb any tree or shrub within reach will need to be controlled.

ZONES 10–11

## *CLEMATIS*

VIRGIN'S BOWER, TRAVELER'S JOY

This large genus of twining vines and sub-shrubs is distributed throughout the northern hemisphere. Most are woody, while some are treated as herbaceous perennials. All vines require some form of support that provide sites for the nodal tendrils to twist around. Each flower consists of 4 to 6 showy sepals, which are either pendulous and lantern like or fully open and flat faced. The flowers are followed by masses of fluffy-tailed seed heads that persist through winter. The most important cultural requirement is a well-drained, permanently cool soil with ample moisture retention. The foliage and flowers require full sun for best development while the roots are in the shade. Eastern exposures are best.

### *C. armandii*

EVERGREEN CLEMATIS

A native of China, this vigorous, evergreen climber will reach heights of 15–25 ft (about 4.5–7.5 m) provided it has a suitable support to twine around. The leathery, ternately compound leaves emerge coppery colored, becoming dark lustrous green with age. The relatively large (2 in/5 cm in diameter), highly scented, white flowers are borne in dense, auxillary clusters, providing a spectacular display throughout spring. Since the flowers are produced on the previous year's wood, pruning is done after blooming ceases. Plant in sun or shade and well-drained soil; once established it will quickly cover an unsightly landcape feature, scramble over an arbor or pergola, or simply cover an unwanted view. It can become invasive and require serious pruning. The cultivars 'Snowdrift' (pure white flowers) and 'Appleblossom' (white with a pink blush) are worth pursuing.

ZONES 8–10

### *C.* 'Jackmanii'

Produced in 1862, this is still the most popular large-flowered cultivar. It climbs up to 9 ft (about 2.7 m) and produces spectacular purple flowers, 6 in (about 15 cm) across, in summer and fall. It is deciduous.

ZONES 3–9

### *C.* × *lawsoniana* 'Henryi'

Moderately vigorous, this twining vine produces large (to 6 in/15 cm in diameter), white flowers that have a contrasting "eye" of brown-tipped stamen. Young foliage emerges bronze and matures to a deep green. A repeat bloomer, the initial floral display is in mid-summer.

ZONES 3–9

*Clematis tangutica*

*Clematis* 'Jackmanii'

*Clitoria ternatea*

*Clematis montana*

### *C. montana*

ANEMONE CLEMATIS

This vigorous, deciduous species from the Himalayas will reach up to 30 ft (about 9 m) or more. It bears prolific, sweetly perfumed, pure white flowers with yellow anthers in clusters in late spring. Fast growing, it is ideal for covering a small shed or wall. It was introduced to England in 1831 by Lady Amherst, wife of the Governor-General of India. *C. m.* 'Rubens' is a popular pink form. Prune hard after flowering.

ZONES 6–9

### *C. tangutica*

GOLDEN CLEMATIS

This long-flowering species from China grows up to 18 ft (about 5.5 m). It bears curious, nodding, lantern-shaped flowers, with clear yellow "thick-skinned" petals, in summer and early fall. The flowers are followed by decorative silky seed heads.

ZONES 3–9

### *C. viticella*

ITALIAN CLEMATIS

This Eurasian species of clematis produces clusters of 1–2 in (about 2.5–5 cm) diameter flowers in mid- to late summer in the violet to reddish purple color range. The delicate blooms hang like lanterns from long, slender stalks, providing a light, airy visual appeal in the garden. Cultivars of note include: 'Alba Luxurians', white with dark purple anthers; 'Kermesina', deep wine red; and 'Purpurea Plena', deep violet purple double flowers.

ZONES 4–9

*Cissus antarctica*

## *CLITORIA*

### *ternatea*

BUTTERFLY PEA

A lovely evergreen twining vine that reaches up to 12 ft (about 3.5 m) with slender stems and fresh green leaves divided into 3 or 5 oval leaflets. Large, dark blue, pea-like flowers with yellow centers bloom in summer, followed by flat pods. There is also a double-flowered form. It is frost tender, growing best in full sun in warm, sheltered sites in humus-rich, well-drained soil. Provide good support for twining stems and thin out growth with annual spring pruning. Propagate from seed or from cuttings.

ZONES 10–11

## *CLYTOSTOMA*

### *callistegioides*

VIOLET TRUMPET VINE

This evergreen creeper native to tropical South America is grown for its showy, trumpet-shaped flowers. Fast growing and densely foliaged, it climbs to 12 ft (about 3.5 m) by

Clytostoma callistegioides

Distictis buccinatoria

means of tendrils and needs good support. In late spring and summer the pale lavender flowers with purple streaks are carried atop long, drooping stems, making it ideal for training over fences and tall tree stumps in warm areas. It prefers a sunny position, humus-rich soil, good drainage and regular watering in summer. It is frost tender. Thin out less vigorous canes after flowering. Propagate from cuttings taken in summer.
ZONES 8–10

Dolichos lablab

## COBAEA
*scandens*

CUP-AND-SAUCER VINE

This herbaceous, perennial, climbing vine from Mexico produces tendrils that tenaciously cling to rough surfaces. The large cup-and-saucer-shaped flowers emerge green, becoming dull rose-purple on maturity. Flowers are produced in profusion and the blooming season is long, mid-summer through frost. A rapid grower, it does best in rich, well-drained loams in sunny, hot sites. Most useful in the outlying regions of the garden as a temporary screen or as a filler plant while others mature. Easily propagated from seed. Hardy in mild climate zones, it is treated as an annual in colder regions.
ZONES 8–11

## COMBRETUM
*bracteosum*

This climbing, evergreen shrub grows to a height and spread of over 9 ft (about 2.7 m). In summer it bears a profusion of orange-red flowers with rounded heads. Plant in a position in full sun in a rich, well-drained soil and water frequently in summer.
ZONES 10–11

Ficus pumila

Cobaea scandens

## DISTICTIS
*buccinatoria*

syn. *Phaedranthus buccinatorius*

BLOOD-RED TRUMPET VINE

A native of Mexico, this evergreen, woody climber reaching 15 ft (about 4.5 m) bears large clusters of trumpet flowers in bright shades of red in early spring and summer. This vigorous vine clings with tendrils to surfaces such as rough brick and stone. It grows best in sun or semi-shade in fertile, well-drained soil and needs regular watering in summer. Prune in spring. Propagate from softwood cuttings in early summer.
ZONES 9–11

## DOLICHOS
*lablab*

syn. *Lablab purpureus*

HYACINTH BEAN

This deciduous, twining plant with a spread of around 18 ft (about 5.5 m) is often grown as an annual for quick cover to hide unattractive fences, walls and sheds. Frost tender, it will die down in winter. It is easily grown in full sun in any well-drained soil. Pink to mauve pea-like flowers appear from early summer to fall, followed by many large seed pods which can make the plant unsightly. The plant can be removed and easily replaced by sowing the seed in late winter; in other words, growing it as an annual. In some parts of the world it is grown as a forage or green manure crop.
ZONES 6–10

## ECCREMOCARPUS
*scaber*

CHILEAN GLORY FLOWER

This native of Chile and Peru is a lightweight, sub-shrubby, tendril climber grown for its attractive flowers, blooming over a long season from summer into fall. It is evergreen, with dainty leaves and racemes of small, orange-red, tubular flowers, followed by fruit pods containing winged seeds. Grows sparsely to a height of 6–9 ft (about 1.8–2.7 m). It can be grown as an annual in areas prone to frost. It grows best in full sun in a light, well-drained soil. Keep moist during the growing season and support with small sticks until attached to the main trellis. Propagate from seed in early spring.
ZONES 10–11

## FICUS
*pumila*

CREEPING FIG

From Japan and China, this decorative creeper is a useful evergreen climber for covering walls or fences. It clings by aerial roots along the stems and, although often slow to get started, it later grows very vigorously. It has small, bright green, heart-shaped juvenile leaves and a neat habit. Young growth is an attractive bronze. Remove any mature woody branches that stand out from the support to retain juvenile leaves. It is best grown in full sun or semi-shade in a well-drained, fertile soil. Propagate from semi-hardwood cuttings. A tiny-leaved form, *F. p.* 'Minima', is less rampant.
ZONES 8–11

## GELSEMIUM
*sempervirens*

CAROLINA JASMINE, YELLOW JASMINE

A well-behaved, evergreen twiner with glossy green leaves and fragrant, yellow trumpet flowers, which appear for many months in spring and again in fall. It likes a sunny, warm, sheltered position

and a fertile, well-drained soil. It grows quickly but tidily to 9 ft (about 2.7 m) and can be trained on fences, walls or a pergola near the house, where the perfume can be enjoyed. All parts of the plant are poisonous and should be kept away from children. Thin out older growth after flowering. Propagate from semi-hardwood cuttings in summer.
ZONES 8–11

### *HARDENBERGIA violacea*

syn. *H. monophylla*
PURPLE CORAL PEA, FALSE SARSAPARILLA

Used as a ground cover for scrambling over banks or as a climber when given support, this beautiful twining plant from Australia can grow under adverse conditions. It will withstand dry conditions, some frost and will grow in most soils with good drainage. Semi-shade or a fairly sunny position is preferred. Lovely sprays of purple pea flowers are borne in spring. Propagate from presoaked seed.
ZONES 10–11

### *HEDERA*

IVY

Useful for enhancing many a situation, ivies have long been well-loved, hardy evergreen creepers. Their firmly clasping habit was once considered a lucky love charm. They can be used for ground cover, clothing walls and fences, covering tree stumps and arches, growing up pillars and posts, edging borders and masonry work, trailing from containers and as indoor specimens. In sun or shade they are adaptable to a wide variety of conditions, soils and climates. Regular pruning is recommended so that the attractive, lobed juvenile leaves are retained and no flowers are produced. If the mature growth (which produces tiny green flowers in fall, followed by black berries) is struck as cuttings, the resultant plants remain as shrubs. This is called "arborescent ivy." Propagate from cuttings or rooted stems. The charming fashion of ivy topiary has been revived and wire topiary frames are now available in many garden centers. As the ivy grows over the shape the side shoots are regularly clipped to produce a dense cover.

*H. canariensis* 'Variegata'
ALGERIAN IVY

A handsome, popular ivy with broad, leathery leaves, dark green in the middle shading to silver-gray and bordered with cream or white. Some leaves are completely white or cream. This slightly frost-tender ivy is particularly showy and looks good covering large areas of walls or fences.
ZONES 9–11

*H. helix*
ENGLISH IVY, COMMON IVY

This hardy species will produce a dense, dark green cover. It is often used as a ground cover in shade where grass has difficulty thriving, and is also excellent for climbing up walls and hiding paling fences. There are innumerable named varieties with unusually shaped and/or variegated leaves. They are often grown as house plants.
ZONES 5–11

### *HIBBERTIA scandens*

GUINEA FLOWER, GUINEA GOLD VINE

A native of Australia, this soft twining climber or trailing plant can grow up to 12 ft (about 3.5 m) high or be trained along the ground as an effective ground cover. It has broad, dark green leaves and large, showy buttercup yellow flowers from spring through the warmer months. Any moderately fertile, well-drained soil is suitable. It will grow in full sun or semi-shade and is a good choice for sandy, coastal gardens, as it tolerates salt spray. It is ideal for warm climates. Lightly prune to shape in spring and propagate from semi-ripe tip cuttings in late summer.
ZONES 10–11

### *HYDRANGEA petiolaris*

syn. *H. anomala* subsp. *petiolaris*
CLIMBING HYDRANGEA

This deciduous, self-clinging climber grows up to 50 ft (about 15 m) or more and bears beautiful, flattened heads of small white flowers in summer. It has oval, finely toothed leaves. Plant in humus-rich, well-drained, moist soil in full sun with some protection from hot afternoon sun, and water regularly in summer. Propagate from semi-hardwood cuttings in summer. Prune after flowering, trimming close to the support.
ZONES 5–10

*Hedera canariensis* 'Variegata'

*Hydrangea petiolaris*

*Hibbertia scandens*

*Hedera helix*

*Hardenbergia violacea*

*Gelsemium sempervirens*

## IPOMOEA

MORNING GLORY

Care should be taken when choosing these ornamental climbers, as some rampant species can become extremely invasive in warm districts. Native to tropical and warm-temperate regions, most species have a twining habit and masses of funnel-shaped flowers which are at their best in the early morning. They are best suited to warm coastal districts or tropical areas. Any moderately fertile, well-drained soil is suitable and they prefer a sunny position. These plants are useful for covering sheds, fences, trellises and banks. They may also be grown in pots. Propagate in spring from seed which has been gently filed and presoaked to aid germination, or from cuttings (for all perennial species).

### *I. alba*

syn. ***Calonyction aculeatum***

MOON FLOWER

From tropical America, this fast-growing, soft-stemmed, perennial vine grows up to 21 ft (about 6.5 m) and is cultivated for its large, white, fragrant flowers, 6 in (about 15 cm) across, which open at night during summer.

ALL ZONES

### *I. nil*

WHITE-EDGE MORNING GLORY

This twining, perennial vine native to the tropical regions of the world produces an abundance of funnel-shaped flowers up to 6 in (about 15 cm) in diameter. Single or double, the edges are often ruffled or scalloped, and the flower color ranges from purples and blues to rose-reds. The large, heart-shaped, 3-lobed leaves provide a strong backdrop to the magnificent blooms. It is treated as an annual in colder climates. The Japanese Imperial morning glories are of this species.

ZONES 10–11

### *I. quamoclit*

CYPRESS VINE, CARDINAL CLIMBER

A vigorous, annual vine with finely dissected, pinnately compound leaves, this native of the American tropics produces trumpet-shaped, 3 in (about 7.5 cm) diameter blooms in shades of deep rose and scarlet from mid-summer through fall.

ALL ZONES

*Ipomoea alba*

*Jasminum officinale*

*Jasminum polyanthum*

### *I. tricolor*

MORNING GLORY

This annual, twining vine produces an abundance of large, trumpet-shaped flowers which stand out from the dark green, heart-shaped leaves. The flowers are deep blue at the outer extremities, fading to white at the base of the throat. Thriving in full sun and fertile, well-drained soil, it will easily reach heights of 15 ft (about 4.5 m) during the growing season. Propagate from seed.

ALL ZONES

## JASMINUM

JASMINE

These mostly woody stemmed, climbing plants are valued for their showy, fragrant flowers. Most like a sunny or lightly shaded position with a moderately fertile, well-drained soil. They must have adequate water during spring and summer. Some species are easily propagated by layering, others can be raised from semi-ripe cuttings in summer. The flowers of some species are used in making essential oils for perfume, as well as scenting jasmine tea.

### *J. officinale*

COMMON JASMINE, POET'S JASMINE

Introduced to Europe from the East during the Tudor period, this vigorous, deciduous or semi-evergreen climber can reach up to 27 ft (about 8 m) high. Sweetly fragrant, white flowers are borne in terminal clusters throughout summer and fall. Elizabethan poets referred to its common use on arbors, and it also provides beautiful covering for pergolas, arches, bowers or trellises.

ZONES 10–11

### *J. polyanthum*

This vigorous, scrambling, evergreen climber from China is fast growing but tender and easy to grow in mild climates only. In cool areas it makes a pretty pot plant. Very fragrant, white flowers with pink buds are produced in spring. It grows to around 18 ft (about 5.5 m) and requires a good pruning after flowering to keep tidy and under control.

ZONES 10–11

*Kennedia rubicunda*

## KADSURA

*japonica*

Valued for its bright red berries in fall, this evergreen, twining climber grows up to 9 ft (about 2.7 m) tall. It has attractive, rich green, oval leaves and lightly perfumed, small, cream flowers in summer. This plant does best in semi-shade in a well-drained soil. Male and female flowers grow on separate plants, so both are needed to produce berries. Propagate from cuttings in summer.

ZONES 9–11

## KENNEDIA

*rubicunda*

RUNNING POSTMAN

Endemic to Australia, *Kennedia* are climbing or scrambling plants that were named after John Kennedy, a London nurseryman. They are widely cultivated for their showy, pea-like flowers which attract birds. They thrive in a light, well-drained soil in a sunny situation, but will tolerate light shade. *K. rubicunda* is an extremely vigorous species that grows up to 15 ft (about 4.5 m) and should be kept well away from nearby shrubs and trees as it will quickly climb over anything in reach. It bears showy, dark red pea flowers in small sprays in spring and early summer. In spring or after flowering invasive growth can be cut back reasonably hard without harming the plant, but keep well watered until new growth is established. Propagate from presoaked seed.

ZONES 10–11

## LAPAGERIA

*rosea*

CHILEAN BELLFLOWER

Native to Chile (where it is the national flower) this beautiful evergreen climber can reach 15 ft (about 4.5 m) on support. The oval leaves are bright glossy green. Waxy, pinkish red, bell-like flowers, faintly spotted within, are borne for a long period through summer and fall. It needs a warm, sheltered spot in cool climates. Grow in humus-rich, well-drained soil in partial shade, and keep fairly dry in winter. Propagate from presoaked seed in spring or layers in fall. Watch for red spider mite and thrips.

ZONES 10–11

*Lapageria rosea*

*Lathyrus latifolius*

*Lonicera hildebrandiana*

## LATHYRUS

SWEET PEA, EVERLASTING PEA

This genus takes its name from the Greek for "pea." It has over 130 species of annuals, sub-shrubs and perennials, most of which are climbers. Originating in the temperate regions of the northern hemisphere and also found in Africa and South America, the climbers vary in height from 3–9 ft (about 90–270 cm), and have pinnate leaves (one of which becomes a twining tendril). The racemes of flowers appear between spring and summer. Easily recognized by their wing-shaped petals, the flowers are excellent for cutting. They are followed by long, slender seed pods. Sweet peas require well-drained soil that has been enriched with humus, and need plenty of sunlight with a cool root run. For all but the lower-growing species, support should be provided. Dead-head frequently and pick the seed pods to prolong the flowering period. Tip pruning will encourage bushiness, and the perennials' growth should be cut back in late fall. Propagate the annuals from seed in either early spring or fall, and the perennial species by division in spring or by seed in fall. These beautiful plants are subject to various diseases such as mildew, mold and rust, while slugs and aphids can be a problem.

### *L. latifolius*

PERENNIAL PEA, EVERLASTING PEA

This perennial, tendril climber from Chile grows to around 6 ft (about 1.8 m) high. It has dull green foliage and dense heads of pink, rose or white, scentless pea flowers in spring and summer. It is easily grown in a humus-rich, well-drained soil. It needs the support of a sunny fence or trellis. The plant responds to regular feeding and also to watering when the buds are forming.

ZONES 3–10

### *L. odoratus*

ANNUAL SWEET PEA

A native of Italy, this annual climber grows to 6 ft (about 1.8 m) on a supporting structure such as a trellis or fence. An old-fashioned garden favorite, it has long been in cultivation and hundreds of cultivars and strains are now available for the gardener. It produces an abundance of fragrant, pea-shaped flowers in an amazing range of colors. They do best in cool weather, suffering in prolonged heat waves. The Cuthbertson strain is intended for hot weather sites. Sow chitted seed in early spring in well-drained, fertile, loam soil and a sunny, sheltered location for the best bloom production. Grown primarily for cut flowers, sweet peas are also useful as a temporary colorful screen and to brighten up a void in the garden. Remove faded blooms to encourage more flowers.

ALL ZONES

## LONICERA

HONEYSUCKLE, WOODBINE

Grown for their masses of perfumed flowers, these are perhaps the most romantic climbers of all. They are perfect for covering arches, arbors and bowers, where they will provide a sweet summer evening fragrance. Grow in a well-drained, moisture-retentive soil in sun or semi-shade. Propagate from cuttings in summer or late fall.

### *L. caprifolium*

HONEYSUCKLE, WOODBINE

A deciduous, twining climber growing up to 15 ft (about 4.5 m) with light green, oval, pointed leaves that are joined at the base. Highly scented, yellow flowers, tinted with pink on the outside appear in summer and fall.

ZONES 5–9

### *L. heckrottii*

EVERBLOOMING HONEYSUCKLE, GOLDFLAME HONEYSUCKLE

The garden appeal of this deciduous, woody vine rests in its magnificent flower colors and exceptionally long bloom period; late spring through summer with an occasional recurrent bloom in fall. In bud, the flowers are brilliant carmine red, revealing a lustrous yellow throat as the corolla opens. Once opened, the outside changes to a true pink, harmonizing nicely with the yellow interior. The foliage is also quite handsome, emerging reddish purple and maturing to a lustrous blue-green. Its reaches 10–20 ft (about 3–6 m).

ZONES 5–9

### *L. hildebrandiana*

GIANT HONEYSUCKLE, BURMESE HONEYSUCKLE

This deciduous climber from Burma reaching up to 65 ft (about 20 m) bears large, creamy flowers in summer that turn orange with age; they are only faintly scented. It needs strong support and is frost tender.

ZONES 10–11

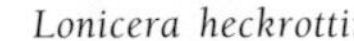

*Lonicera heckrottii*

*Lathyrus odoratus*

*Mandevilla laxa*

*Mandevilla* x *amabilis* 'Alice du Pont'

*Mandevilla splendens*

*Macfadyena unguis-cati*

*Lonicera japonica*

### *L. japonica*

JAPANESE HONEYSUCKLE

This vigorous climber from east Asia, growing to 30 ft (about 9 m), has glossy, dark green leaves. Pairs of fragrant, white flowers aging yellow or sometimes purple-tinged, appear in late summer to fall. This species can become an invasive weed although it is very useful as a ground cover or to quickly hide fences and posts. Provide support if it is used as a vine.

ZONES 4–10

### *L. sempervirens*

TRUMPET HONEYSUCKLE, CORAL HONEYSUCKLE

Superb flower and foliage colors make this twining, woody vine from the eastern United States ideal for growing on open latticework, along a grapestick fence, or scrambling over a sunny bank. The glaucous, blue-green leaves unite to form a disk at the terminal ends of the thin stems where clusters of orange to red tubular flowers are produced. The throat of the tube opens to reveal a bright yellow to yellow-orange interior. Climbing to 20 ft (about 6 m) or more, it is evergreen in milder climates but deciduous in colder regions. 'Superba' produces brilliant crimson blooms, while 'Sulphurea' produces a pure yellow flower inside and out.

ZONES 4–10

## *MACFADYENA*

### *unguis-cati*

syn. ***Doxantha unguis-cati***

CAT'S CLAW CREEPER

A beautiful, evergreen vine grown for its large, bright yellow flowers in the shape of a flattened trumpet up to 4 in (about 10 cm) across. These are borne in profusion in late spring. It clings by tiny, 3-pronged tendrils, like little claws, and climbs to a mature height of up to 30 ft (about 9 m). An excellent climber for covering a high fence or garden shed, it likes a sunny, well-drained position and is frost tender. Prune back hard after flowering to keep in check. Propagate from semi-ripe cuttings in late summer.

ZONES 9–11

*Lonicera sempervirens* 'Superba'

## *MANDEVILLA*

Native to tropical America, these woody-stemmed climbers are grown for their profusion of showy, trumpet-shaped flowers which are sometimes fragrant. They do best in warm, frost-free climates with partial shade in summer. Soil should be deep, rich and well drained. Provide ample water on hot days. Propagate from semi-ripe cuttings in summer. In cool areas they grow very well in frost-free greenhouses.

### *M.* x *amabilis* 'Alice du Pont'

syn. ***Dipladenia* x *amabilis* 'Alice du Pont'**

A twining climber growing up to 12 ft (about 3.5 m) with handsome, oval, glossy leaves and clusters of large, deep pink, scentless, trumpet flowers over a long period in summer. It is frost tender and needs a warm protected position with light shade. Give it plenty of water on days that are hot.

ZONES 10–11

*M. laxa*
**syn. *M. suaveolens***
CHILEAN JASMINE

From Argentina, this fast-growing, woody vine reaches 18 ft (about 5.5 m) or more and is deciduous in cool areas. In summer it produces heavily perfumed, white trumpet flowers in profusion—these make good cut flowers. Grow in full sun or afternoon shade in fertile soil, provide regular watering. The plants can be pruned heavily in early spring to keep it tidy and encourage new growth.
ZONES 8–11

*M. splendens*
**syn. *Dipladenia splendens***

One of the showiest species of its genus, this evergreen, twisting climber is native to Brazil and climbs to 9 ft (about 2.7 m). Its lustrous green leaves are wide and elliptical to rectangular, reaching a length of 8 in (about 20 cm). At the end of spring to the beginning of summer attractive, deep reddish pink, trumpet-shaped flowers with yellow middles appear. This species prefers temperatures above 50°F (about 10°C).
ZONES 10–11

## PANDOREA

Named after Pandora of Greek mythology, this is a small genus of beautiful twining climbers native to Malaysia and Australia. They are grown for their spectacular, long-lasting displays of tubular bell flowers and make excellent pergola or trellis subjects. Frost tender, they are ideal for warm-temperate or tropical areas; where the temperature reaches freezing, *P. pandorana* may survive if given a warm, sheltered spot. The soil should be well drained and enriched with humus. Most require abundant moisture and a sunny position protected from strong winds. Propagate from fresh seed in spring or semi-ripe cuttings in summer.

*P. jasminoides*
**syn. *Tecoma jasminoides***
BOWER CLIMBER

This very attractive climber grows up to 15 ft (about 4.5 m) and has lush, deep green, glassy leaflets. Showy, pale pink trumpet flowers with a deep carmine throat are borne from late spring to fall in warm climates. A pure white flowering form is also in cultivation, and there is a form with variegated leaves is available.
ZONES 10–11

*P. pandorana*
**syn. *Tecoma australis***
WONGA-WONGA VINE

This robust, woody climber up to 18 ft (about 5.5 m) bears masses of very showy, tubular flowers in spring and summer. The flowers are usually creamy white with reddish throats; a number of cultivars are available, one with pure white flowers and another with gold and brown flowers. This is a very good climber for covering arches, and pergolas and for disguising unattractive sites such as wire mesh fences.
ZONES 10–11

*Pandorea jasminoides*

*Parthenocissus tricuspidata*

*Passiflora caerulea*

*Pandorea pandorana*

*Parthenocissus quinquefolia*

*Passiflora coccinea*

## PARTHENOCISSUS

These charming climbing plants from North America and Asia have deciduous, attractively cut leaves, some with magnificent fall coloring. The genus name is from the Greek *parthenos*, meaning "virgin," and *kissos*, "creeper." They climb by tendrils with tiny, disk-shaped suckers and are the perfect climbers for growing on buildings and walls. They will grow best in humus-rich, well-drained soil in filtered sunlight with protection from hot winds. They are hardy to heat and to cold. Propagate from hardwood cuttings in late winter or early spring.

*P. quinquefolia*
VIRGINIA CREEPER

A high climber growing 50 ft (about 15 m) or more. The handsome leaves divided into 5 leaflets make an attractive green wall cover in summer and turn a brilliant red color in fall.
ZONES 2–8

*P. tricuspidata*
BOSTON IVY, JAPANESE IVY

Ideal for covering large walls, this ivy will reach up to 65 ft (about 20 m). The 3-lobed leaves, 8 in (about 20 cm) across, turn spectacular shades of red and purple in fall.
ZONES 4–8

## PASSIFLORA

PASSIONFLOWER

Native chiefly to tropical South America, these showy, tendril climbers are treasured for their ornamental blossoms and their delicious fruit, notably the well-known passionfruit. They are best suited to warm areas. A humus-rich, well-drained soil and a sunny aspect are preferred. Water regularly in summer and provide good support. Prune congested or overgrown plants in spring. Propagate from seed or semi-ripe cuttings or by layering in summer.

*P. caerulea*
BLUE PASSIONFLOWER

In summer this fast-growing evergreen or semi-evergreen climber to 30 ft (about 9 m) produces beautiful flowers with pale pink petals, banded with blue or purple. These are followed by edible but not especially delicious egg-shaped, yellow fruit.
ZONES 10–11

*P. coccinea*
RED PASSIONFLOWER

A robust, evergreen climber to 12 ft (about 3.5 m) grown for the brilliant, large, scarlet flowers borne in summer and fall, set among large, dark green, crinkly leaves. It is frost tender and also needs protection from hot winds.
ZONES 10–11

*Rosa* 'America'

*Phaseolus caracalla*

*Pyrostegia venusta*

*Rosa banksiae lutea*

## PHASEOLUS
*caracalla*
**syn. *Vigna caracalla***
SNAIL CREEPER

A decorative, evergreen, twining climber with soft green foliage composed of 3 leaflets and curiously twisted, pea-like flowers in shades of purple, white and yellow. The flowers have a delightful perfume and are produced from mid-summer to early fall. Frost tender, it is best suited to warm-temperate and tropical areas, where it will grow rapidly to 9 ft (about 2.7 m), scrambling over everything in reach. Grow in full sun in humus-rich, well-drained soil and protect from drying winds. Prune tangled growth in spring.
ZONES 9–11

## POLYGONUM
*aubertii*
SILVER LACE VINE, SILVERVINE FLEECEFLOWER

This is an extremely fast-growing, vigorous vine native to China which makes an effective screen quickly in almost any growing situation. The heart-shaped foliage emerges bronze red and matures to bright green, showing off the cloud-like masses of delicate white flowers produced in late summer through mid-fall. Of easy culture, it will reach heights of 25–35 ft (about 7.5–10 m) and grows well in sun or shade; it also tolerates drought. Having a passion for spreading by rhizomes, care must be taken to ensure it is contained in the desired garden location.
ZONES 4–9

## PYROSTEGIA
*venusta*
FLAME VINE, GOLDEN SHOWER

From South America, this magnificent creeper will reach great heights of 30 ft (about 9 m) or more in warm climates. This climber is grown chiefly for its brilliant display of orange-gold flowers in fall, winter or spring, depending on the climate. Frost tender, it will thrive in most well-drained soils but will only flower well in full sun. Water well in summer and grow on a strong pergola or arch where the flowers can droop down freely. After flowering prune out old shoots and spent flowers. Propagate from semi-hardwood cuttings in summer or fall.
ZONES 10–11

## ROSA
ROSE

Climbing roses vary greatly in their habit from short-stemmed, rambling or pillar roses to tall vigorous climbers capable of reaching up to 30 ft (about 9 m) high. They beautifully decorate fences, walls, trellises, pergolas, arches, pillars and columns, and are ideal for small gardens where there is not enough room for a conventional rose bed. Species growing to around 12 ft (about 3.5 m) are useful for covering walls and fences; those short-stemmed roses held close to the foliage are best for growing on pillars; and miniature climbers look pretty cascading down retaining walls and tall containers. Most roses require humus-rich soil, full sun and ample water. Give climbers room to develop and tie back canes as they grow. Some of the pillar roses need only light pruning, but old, vigorous climbers may need more severe cutting back. Always remove spent blooms to prolong flowering. Aphids, black spot and mildew can cause problems.

### *R.* 'America'

The All-America Rose Selection for 1976, this vigorous climber attains heights of 6-9 ft (about 1.8–2.7 m) and produces slightly fragrant, 3–4 in (about 7.5–10 cm) wide salmon pink, double blooms. Main flower production is mid-season, followed by a good repeat bloom into late season. Good disease resistance.
ZONES 7–10

### *R. banksiae* 'Alba Plena'

Reaching 12–18 ft (about 3.5–5.5 m) in height, the masses of very fragrant, double white, 1 in (about 2.5 cm) diameter flowers that clothe this vining rose from late spring through mid-summer make it an ideal backdrop for early summer-

blooming perennials. Of easy care, it requires trellising and grows best in full sun and well-drained soil. It is relatively pest free. It is deciduous to semi-evergreen in the northern reaches and evergreen in the south.
ZONES 7–9

### *R. banksiae lutea*

This extremely vigorous, thornless climber will reach up to 30 ft (about 9 m). Clusters of small, white or yellow, double flowers are borne in spring. Light green foliage is small and pointed. It needs warmth and protection. As flowers are borne on permanent spurs produced on older wood, remove only dead wood when pruning.

### *R.* 'Blaze'

An old-fashioned favorite that blooms all summer with red, semi-double flowers to 3 in (about 7.5 cm) wide and produces canes up to 9 ft (about 2.7 m) tall. Train it on a trellis or a post and beam fence.
ZONES 7–10

### *R.* 'Climbing Cécile Brünner'

A sport of the bush form of 'Cécile Brünner', this vigorous climber grows to 20 ft (about 6 m). Lustrous green leaves provide the ideal backdrop for the profusion of small, clear pink, fully double flowers. Not a repeat bloomer, optimum flowering occurs in early summer. The flowers, looking like miniature tea roses in bud, are sweetly fragrant, making it an ideal candidate for an arbor or for trellises near seating.
ZONES 7–10

### *R.* 'Climbing Peace'

This hybrid tea climbing rose produces masses of large, fully double, yellow flowers edged with pink. Slightly fragrant, it blooms all season on canes up to 10 ft (about 3 m) in height.
ZONES 7–10

### *R.* 'Golden Showers'

Upright canes to 10 ft (about 3 m) bear fragrant, semi-double, yellow flowers 3–4 in (7.5–10 cm) wide. Blooming freely throughout the growing season, it makes a good pillar or wall rose.
ZONES 7–10

### *R.* 'Joseph's Coat'

A "changing colors" rose, the double flowers open yellow and gradually turn red. A mid-seaon bloomer with good repeat blooming, flowers are 3–4 in (about 7.5–10 cm) wide and slightly fragrant. Mature height is 8–10 ft (about 2.4–3 m).
ZONES 7–10

### *R.* 'Madame Alfred Carrière'

This is the most popular white climber among the old garden roses (it is classed as a Noisette); it bears scented, medium-sized, double flowers, white with faint touches of pink, all season. It grows to around 18 ft (about 5.5 m).
ZONES 7–10

### *R.* 'Mermaid'

This extremely vigorous climber, reaching 24 ft (about 7.5 m), is for large areas only. Its stiff, thorny canes are rather awkward to train and tie. It makes an impressive climber for walls, as its flowers are large, prolific and continuous from spring to fall. The single flowers are yellow with prominent stamens. The glossy foliage is oval and dark green. It is frost resistant.
ZONES 7–10

### *R.* 'New Dawn'

A sport of 'Dr Van Fleet', this vigorous rose produces fragrant, semi-double, light pink flowers 3 in (about 7.5 cm) wide on canes reaching 15 ft (about 4.5 m). The majority of blooms occur mid-season, with good repeat blooming.
ZONES 7–10

*Rosa* 'Climbing Cécile Brünner'

*Rosa* 'Golden Showers'

*Rosa* 'New Dawn'

*Rosa* 'Mermaid'

*Rosa* 'Madame Alfred Carrière'

*Rosa* 'Climbing Peace'

### R. 'Zéphirine Drouhin'

A semi-climbing bourbon rose growing to $7^1/_2$ ft (about 2.2 m), noted for its lack of thorns and recurrent, fragrant blooms. The long, pointed buds open to semi-double, deep pink blooms from spring to fall.
ZONES 7–10

## *SCHIZOPHRAGMA hydrangeoides*

JAPANESE HYDRANGEA

From Japan and Korea, this vigorous, deciduous, woody-stemmed climber clings by aerial roots for support. It will grow to 27 ft (about 8 m) or more and makes a spectacular cover for pergolas and large walls. The large, flattened flowerheads, 12 in (about 30 cm) across, are composed of very small white flowers surrounded by ornamental, white bracts and are borne in summer. It has attractive, deep green, toothed leaves 5 in (about 12 cm) long on long, red stalks. Grow in a humus-rich, moist but well-drained soil in full sun. Train young plants on the support until established. Propagate from semi-ripe cuttings in summer.
ZONES 5–10

## *SOLANDRA maxima*

CUP OF GOLD, HAWAIIAN LILY, GOLDEN CHALICE VINE

A giant Mexican climber valued for its huge flowers and ability to cover very large areas. It is a rampant, woody vine growing to 30 ft (about 9 m) or more requiring plenty of space and a sturdy support. The yellow flowers, up to 10 in (about 25 cm) across, with a near purple stripe down the center of each petal, are produced in spring and summer. It requires fertile soil, good drainage and full sun. It is an excellent plant for seaside gardens. Prune in summer to keep the plant in bounds and promote more flowers. Propagate from semi-ripe cuttings in summer.
ZONES 10–11

## *SOLANUM*

With a worldwide distribution, this very large genus of annuals, perennials, shrubs, trees and climbers includes potatoes, tomatoes and other food plants, as well as a few medicinal and poisonous plants. The climbers are valued for their ornamental flowers, foliage and fruit. They are fast growing. They do best in a warm, sunny position in fertile, well-drained soil. Cut back congested growth in spring. Propagate from seed.

### *S. jasminoides*

POTATO VINE

From South America, this quick-growing, semi-evergreen climber reaches 15 ft (about 4.5 m) and bears showy clusters of pale blue flowers in summer and fall, followed by small, purple berries. In cool areas it can be potted up in fall to spend the winter under glass. The cultivar 'Album' has masses of star-shaped, white flowers.
ZONES 10–11

### *S. seaforthianum*

A showy vine growing to 18 ft (about 5.5 m) and bearing large clusters of violet-blue flowers with yellow stamens in summer, followed by small, scarlet berries.
ZONES 10–11

## *STEPHANOTIS floribunda*

WAX FLOWER

This evergreen climber can grow to a height and spread of 9 ft (about 2.7 m). It is grown for its pleasant fragrance and its attractive foliage of paired, waxy, deep green leaves. The pendulous, tubular, white flowers have widely flared lobes, and appear in clusters of about 4 blooms from spring to fall. The flowers are very popular as bridal decorations. Plant in well-drained soil in partial shade. This climber may be grown indoors and forced into flower throughout the year. Propagate by layering.
ZONES 10–11

*Solandra maxima*

*Solanum jasminoides*

*Solanum seaforthianum*

*Stephanotis floribunda*

*Thunbergia alata*

*Thunbergia grandiflora*

*Trachelospermum jasminoides*

*Vitis californica* 'Roger's Red'

## *THUNBERGIA*

CLOCK VINE

This genus contains 200 species of annual twisting climbers and perennial, evergreen, clump-forming shrubs native to Africa, Asia and Malagasy. Their leaves, which are entire, have up to 5 lobes. The cylindrical blooms are borne individually from the leaf axils or in trusses. The species prefer temperatures above 50°F (about 10°C). They will grow in any reasonably rich soil with adequate drainage. Full sun is preferred, except during the summer months when partial shade and liberal water should be provided. Support stems and prune densely packed foliage during early spring. Propagate from seed in spring and semi-ripe cuttings in summer. This genus was named after Swedish botanist Dr Carl Peter Thunberg, who worked in Africa.

### *T. alata*

BLACK-EYED SUSAN

Native to the tropics of Africa, this vigorous, annual or perennial twisting climber grows quickly to 9 ft (about 2.7 m). Its deep green, cordate leaves grow to 3 in (about 7.5 cm) long. It bears masses of 2 in (about 5 cm) wide orange flowers with black throats from early summer to early fall. It is perennial in frost free areas. Plant in fertile, well-drained soil and thin out crowded stems in early spring.

ALL ZONES

### *T. grandiflora*

BLUE TRUMPET VINE, SKY FLOWER

Originally from India, this quick-growing, vigorous climber to 15 ft (about 4.5 m) is grown for its drooping clusters of large, sky-blue trumpet flowers, borne in summer and fall. It has large-toothed, heart-shaped leaves up to 8 in (about 20 cm) long and looks best when grown on a trellis, fence or pergola. It requires humus-rich, well-drained soil, lots of water and protection from dry summer winds. Propagate from seed in spring or from semi-hardwood cuttings in summer.

ZONES 10–11

## *TRACHELOSPERMUM jasminoides*

CONFEDERATE JASMINE, STAR JASMINE

Valued for its perfumed, star-shaped flowers, this attractive, evergreen, twining climber from China grows up to 21 ft (about 6.5 m) high. It has lance-shaped leaves, and hanging clusters of white flowers are produced in summer. This plant does best in a sunny position in well-drained, fertile soil. Although it is slow growing during the early stages, it will flourish once established and is excellent for training on pillars, pergolas and arches. It can also be used as a ground cover. Prune congested or straggly branches in fall. Propagate from semi-ripe cuttings in summer or fall.

ZONES 8–11

## *TROPAEOLUM speciosum*

FLAME NASTURTIUM

A herbaceous, perennial climber with slender stems reaching up to 9 ft (about 2.7 m). It has a tuberous rhizome and attractive, bright green foliage composed of 6 oval leaflets. Scarlet flowers in summer are followed by blue fruit. Grow in partial shade in a humus-rich, moist, but well-drained soil. Native to China. Propagate from seed or by division of tubers.

ZONES 10–11

## *VITIS*

This genus consists of deciduous, woody-stemmed, tendril climbers. They are grown for their foliage (on trellises and the like as ornamentals) and fruits (grapes). Grow in humus-rich, moisture-retentive but well-drained soil in full sun or partial shade. Propagate from hardwood cuttings taken in late fall or winter.

### *V. californica* 'Roger's Red'

ROGER'S RED CALIFORNIA GRAPE

Native to central California into Oregon, this cultivar is grown for its rich red fall foliage color. The small leaves are dull green above and gray beneath, distinctly toothed and of variable size. Vigorous, it will attain

*Wisteria sinensis*

*Vitis coignetiae*

*Wisteria venusta*

heights of 14–20 ft (about 4–6 m) in full sun. Small, greenish flowers produce tiny black fruit suitable as wildlife attractants. Propagate from stem cuttings taken in late fall or winter or by grafting.

ZONES 6–10

### *V. coignetiae*

CRIMSON GLORY VINE

A rapid-growing climber reaching 50 ft (about 15 m), with green, slightly lobed leaves which change to deep crimson, orange and scarlet in fall. Clusters of small, black berries with a glaucous bloom are borne in late summer. Its tendrils coil around supports and need plenty of room to spread. The leaf color is best in cool climates. Prune

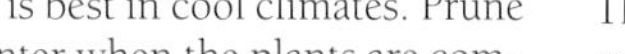

in winter when the plants are completely dormant.

ZONES 5–10

### *V. vinifera* 'Purpurea'

TEINTURIER GRAPE

This cultivar of grape is prized for its highly ornamental foliage, which emerges a rich claret red and deepens to a lustrous purple at maturity. The bright crimson fall color is spectacular. It is shown to its best advantage when grown in combination with gray or silver-leaved shrubs. It does best in the mild climates of California and the West Coast, where the summers are warm and dry.

ZONES 5–10

## *WISTERIA*

WISTERIA

The deciduous wisteria is one of the most popular plants for pergolas, where the large, drooping sprays of perfumed flowers are best displayed. Providing welcome summer shade, the soft, light green, luxuriant foliage is particularly attractive. Wisterias like a sunny position and a humus-rich, well-drained soil. Although they take some time to establish, they become large, vigorous plants and need strong support for healthy future growth. Prune after flowering and again in late winter; only prune in winter if really necessary to control size. Propagate from cuttings or by layering in late summer. With regular pruning and some support in the early years, wisteria can be grown as a large, free-standing shrub or standard. Take care, as all parts of the wisteria plant are poisonous.

*Wisteria floribunda*

### *W. floribunda*

JAPANESE WISTERIA

This vigorous, woody-stemmed climber up to 30 ft (about 9 m) bears pendulous, purple-blue flowers of around 20 in (about 50 cm) or more long. The flowers are fragrant and are often produced after the leaves in spring.

ZONES 5–10

### *W. sinensis*

**syn. *W. chinensis***

CHINESE WISTERIA

Native to China, this vigorous, woody-stemmed climber will reach up to 95 ft (about 29 m) high. The sprays of slightly fragrant, lavender-blue flowers up to 12 in (about 30 cm) long appear in spring on bare branches before the leaves, creating a magnificent sight.

ZONES 5–10

### *W. venusta*

SILKY WISTERIA

The earliest of the wisteria to bloom, its slightly fragrant, 1 in (about 2.5 cm), white flowers are borne in 4–6 in (about 10–15 cm) long racemes followed by velvety, 8 in (about 20 cm) long fruit pods. Flowering occurs in early spring before the foliage emerges. It obtains heights of 30 ft (about 9 m). The cultivar 'Violaceae' has lavender-blue flowers with a pale white standard.

ZONES 5–9

*Vitis vinifera* 'Purpurea'

# Tables

## Keys

The following lists are keys to the Cultivation Guidelines and Seasonal Calenders that follow. If, for example, you wish to find out how to propagate *Ageratum houstonianum*, you simply locate it in the keys below (Annuals, low growing, spring–fall flowering), find that group in the Cultivation Guidelines (page 504), then move across the column until you reach the one headed "Propagation." For ease of reference each plant is also listed in the Index to Plants, with page numbers referring to where it occurs in the text and where it occurs in these keys.

### ANNUALS & PERENNIALS

The cultivation of annual and perennial plants is rewarding as a large variety of flowering plants can be grown to appear throughout the year. To grow the more unusual flowers from seed requires patience, as germination can be erratic, and constant attention, as seedlings need an even light source and must never be allowed to dry out. In other words, their best chance of healthy development requires daily care.

Perennials, on the other hand, are not called hardy for nothing. Different perennials can be found for cold, mountainous climates, for salt-spray coastal gardens and for excessively dry, wet or shady positions. Simple maintenance practices such as removing spent flowers, checking under leaves for pests and a tidy up during winter are all they need. Regular mulching and fertilizing during the growing and flowering seasons helps maintain their vigor, and before long there will be excess plants to give away to friends.

#### Annuals, low growing, spring–fall flowering

*Ageratum houstonianum*
*Begonia* Semperflorens-Cultorum hybrids
*Bellis perennis*
*Browallia americana*
*Calceolaria* x *herbeohybrida*
*Calendula officinalis*
*Celosia argentea* var. *cristata*
*Convolvulus tricolor*
*Dianthus barbatus*
*Dianthus chinensis*
*Dorotheanthus bellidiformis*
*Echium vulgare* [dwarf]
*Eschscholzia californica*
*Exacum affine*
*Gomphrena globosa*
*Iberis amara*
*Iberis umbellata*
*Impatiens balsamina*
*Lobelia erinus*
*Lobularia maritima*
*Malcolmia maritima*
*Mimulus* x *hybridus*
*Nemesia strumosa*
*Nemophila menziesii*
*Nierembergia hippomanica* var. *violacea* 'Purple Robe'
*Papaver nudicaule*
*Papaver rhoeas*
*Petunia* x *hybrida*
*Phacelia campanularia*
*Phlox drummondii*
*Portulaca grandiflora*
*Primula malacoides*
*Reseda odorata*
*Sanvitalia procumbens*
*Tagetes patula*
*Tagetes tenuifolia*
*Torenia fournieri*
*Tropaeolum majus*
*Verbena* x *hybrida*
*Viola cornuta*
*Viola* x *wittrockiana*
*Xeranthemum annum*

#### Annuals, medium growing, spring–fall flowering

*Agrostemma githago*
*Anagallis monellii*
*Anchusa capensis* 'Blue Angel'
*Antirrhinum majus*
*Argemone platyceras*
*Callistephus chinensis*
*Campanula medium*
*Catharanthus roseus*
*Centaurea cyanus*
*Centaurea moschata*
*Chrysanthemum carinatum*
*Clarkia amoena*
*Clarkia unguiculata*
*Coleus blumei*
*Coreopsis tinctoria*
*Cosmos sulphureus*
*Dianthus caryophyllus* cultivars
*Dimorphotheca sinuata*
*Erysimum cheiri*
*Eustoma grandiflorum*
*Gaillardia pulchella*
*Gilia capitata*
*Gypsophila elegans*
*Helichrysum bracteatum*
*Impatiens wallerana*
*Kochia scoparia* f. *trichophylla*
*Limonium sinuatum*
*Linaria maroccana* 'Fairy Bouquet'
*Linum grandiflorum* 'Rubrum'
*Lunaria annua*
*Lupinus hartwegii*
*Lupinus texensis*
*Matthiola incana*
*Myosotis sylvatica*
*Nigella damascena*
*Rudbeckia hirta*
*Salpiglossis sinuata*
*Salvia farinacea*
*Salvia splendens*
*Scabiosa atropurpurea*
*Schizanthus pinnatus*
*Senecio cruentus*
*Silene coeli-rosa*
*Tagetes erecta*
X *Venidio-arctotis* cultivars
*Zinnia angustifolia*
*Zinnia haageana*

#### Annuals, tall growing, spring–fall flowering

*Abelmoschus moschatus* 'Mischief'
*Alcea rosea*
*Amaranthus caudatus*
*Amaranthus tricolor* 'Joseph's Coat'
*Calceolaria integrifolia*
*Canna* x *generalis*
*Cleome hassleriana*
*Consolida ambigua*
*Cosmos bipinnatus*
*Delphinium* x *belladonna*
*Delphinium* x *cultorum* hybrids
*Delphinium grandiflorum*
*Digitalis purpurea*
*Echium wildpretii*
*Euphorbia marginata*
*Helianthus annuus*
*Hibiscus moscheutos*
*Hunnemannia fumariifolia*
*Lavatera trimestris*
*Matthiola* 'Mammoth Column'
*Mina lobata*
*Mirabilis jalapa*
*Moluccella laevis*
*Nicotiana alata*
*Nicotiana* x *sanderae*
*Oenothera biennis*
*Papaver somniferum*
*Rhodochiton atrosanguineum*
*Tithonia rotundifolia* 'Torch'
*Tropaeolum peregrinum*
*Verbena bonariensis*
*Verbena canariensis*
*Zinnia elegans*

#### Annuals, dahlias

Cactus dahlias
Collarette dahlias
Decorative dahlias
Dwarf or bedding dahlias
Pompon dahlias
Waterlily dahlias

#### Annuals, pelargoniums

*Pelargonium crispum*
*Pelargonium* x *domesticum*
*Pelargonium graveolens*
*Pelargonium* x *hortorum*
*Pelargonium odoratissimum*
*Pelargonium* 'Orange Ricard'
*Pelargonium peltatum*
*Pelargonium tomentosum*

#### Perennials, spring–early summer flowering

*Adonis aestivalis*
*Anigozanthos* Bush Gems series
*Aquilegia canadensis*
*Aquilegia chrysantha*
*Centranthus ruber*
*Corydalis lutea*
*Dianella tasmanica*
*Dianthus* 'Allwoodii'
*Dianthus deltoides*
*Dianthus gratianopolitanus*
*Dianthus plumarius*
*Diascia rigescens*
*Dicentra eximia*
*Dietes grandiflora*
*Dietes vegeta*
*Epimedium grandiflorum*
*Epimedium pinnatum* subsp. *colchicum*
*Epimedium* x *rubrum*
*Epimedium* x *warleyense*
*Erodium reichardii*
*Euphorbia characias* subsp. *wulfenii*
*Euphorbia myrsinites*
*Galium odoratum*
*Gentiana acaulis*
*Geranium maculatum*
*Geranium phaeum*
*Geum chiloense* 'Mrs Bradshaw'
*Lupinus*, Russell hybrids
*Meconopsis cambrica*
*Penstemon barbatus*
*Penstemon digitalis* 'Husker's Red'
*Penstemon* hybrids
*Potentilla* 'Gibson's Scarlet'
*Potentilla nepalensis*

*Silene vulgaris* subsp. *maritima*
*Sisyrinchium angustifolium*
*Sisyrinchium striatum*
*Tanacetum coccineum*
*Trillium chloropetalum*
*Veronica gentianoides*
*Veronica incana*
*Viola reichenbachiana*
*Viola riviana* Purpurea group

**Perennials, spring–early summer flowering, short lived**

*Anchusa azurea*
*Aquilegia caerulea*
*Aquilegia*, McKana Giants
*Aquilegia vulgaris*
*Dimorphotheca pluvialis*
*Erysimum* x *allionii*
*Linum narbonense*
*Myosotis* 'Blue Ball'
*Oenothera missouriensis*
*Papaver alpinum*
*Papaver orientale*

**Perennials, summer flowering, sun**

*Acanthus mollis*
*Acanthus spinosus*
*Achillea filipendulina* 'Gold Plate'
*Achillea millefolium*
*Achillea* 'Taygetea'
*Achillea tomentosa*
*Agapanthus praecox* subsp. *orientalis*
*Alstroemeria aurea*
*Alstroemeria*, Ligtu hybrids
*Amsonia tabernaemontana*
*Anaphalis margaritacea*
*Arisaema triphyllum*
*Artemisia lactiflora*
*Artemisia* 'Powys Castle'
*Artemisia stellerana*
*Asclepias tuberosa*
*Astrantia major*
*Baptisia australis*
*Catananche caerulea* 'Major'
*Centaurea dealbata*
*Centaurea hypoleucha* 'John Coutts'
*Cephalaria gigantea*
*Coreopsis grandiflora*
*Coreopsis verticillata*
*Crambe maritima*
*Dictamnus albus*
*Dierama pulcherrimum*
*Echinacea purpurea*
*Echinops ritro*
*Epilobium angustifolium*
*Eremurus* x *isabellinus* Shelford hybrids
*Erigeron glaucus*
*Erigeron speciosus*
*Erodium absinthoides*
*Eryngium alpinum*
*Eryngium* x *oliverianum*
*Eryngium variifolium*
*Erysimum* 'Bowles Mauve'
*Gaillardia* x *grandiflora*
*Gaura lindheimeri*
*Gazania rigescens* var. *leucolaena*
*Geranium incanum*
*Geranium* 'Johnson's Blue'
*Geranium sanguineum*
*Gerbera jamesonii*
*Gypsophila paniculata* 'Bristol Fairy'
*Hesperis matronalis*
*Heuchera* x *brizoides*
*Ipomopsis aggregata*
*Lavatera thuringiaca*
*Leucanthemum* x *superbum*
*Liatris spicata*
*Limonium latifolium*
*Linum perenne*
*Lychnis coronaria*
*Lychnis* x *haagena*
*Macleaya cordata*
*Malva moschata*
*Mimulus cardinalis*
*Oenothera speciosa*
*Origanum laevigatum*
*Osteospermum ecklonis*
*Osteospermum jucundum*
*Oxypetalum caeruleum*
*Paeonia lactiflora* hybrids
*Penstemon pinifolius*
*Phlomis russeliana*
*Phormium cookianum* 'Tricolor'
*Phormium* hybrids
*Physostegia virginiana*
*Platycodon grandiflorus*
*Rodgersia aesculifolia*
*Rodgersia pinnata*
*Salvia azurea*
*Salvia* x *superba*
*Salvia uliginosa*
*Scabiosa caucasica*
*Sedum spurium*
*Sidalcea malviflora* 'Rose Queen'
X *Solidaster luteus*
*Stachys coccinea*
*Stokesia laevis*
*Tradescantia virginiana*
*Verbascum olympican*
*Veronica spicata*
*Viola tricolor*
*Yucca whipplei*
*Zantedeschia rehmannii*

**Perennials, summer flowering, shade to part shade**

*Aruncus dioica*
*Astilbe* x *arendsii*
*Astilbe chinensis* 'Pumila'
*Begonia grandis*
*Campanula lactiflora*
*Campanula persicifolia*
*Cimicifuga racemosa*
*Codonopsis clematidea*
*Diascia barberae*
*Digitalis* x *mertonensis*
*Filipendula rubra*
*Gentiana andrewsii*
*Heuchera micrantha* 'Palace Purple'
*Heuchera sanguinea*
*Lamiastrum galeobdolon* 'Variegatum'
*Ligularia dentata* 'Desdemona'
*Ligularia tussilaginea* 'Aureomaculata'
*Lobelia* x *gerardii* 'Vedrariensis'
*Lysimachia punctata*
*Meconopsis betonicifolia*
*Phlox paniculata*
*Polemonium caeruleum*
*Rheum palmatum* 'Atrosanguineum'
*Rodgersia podophylla*
*Roscoea cauteloides*
*Thalictrum aquilegiifolium*
*Thalictrum delavayi*
*Veratrum nigrum*

**Perennials, winter–early summer flowering**

*Bergenia cordifolia*
*Bergenia* hybrids
*Bergenia stracheyi*
*Brunnera macrophylla*
*Campanula carpatica*
*Dicentra formosa*
*Dicentra spectabilis*
*Helleborus argutifolius*
*Helleborus foetidus*
*Helleborus niger*
*Helleborus orientalis*
*Mertensia virginica*
*Osteospermum fruticosum*
*Paeonia officinalis*
*Pulmonaria angustifolia*
*Ranunculus aconitifolius*
*Ranunculus gramineus*
*Smilacena racemosa*
*Trillium grandiflorum*
*Trollius europaeus*
*Viola odorata*
*Viola sororia* 'Freckles'

**Perennials, summer–fall flowering**

*Aconitum napellus*
*Agapanthus africanus*
*Agastache cana*
*Anemone* x *hybrida*
*Aster* x *frikartii* 'Mönch'
*Aster linariifolius*
*Aster novi-angliae*
*Aster novi-belgii*
*Chelone obliqua*
*Cosmos atrosanguineus*
*Dendranthema* x *grandiflora*
*Eupatorium purpureum*
*Francoa apendiculata*
*Gentiana asclepiaea*
*Geum cocchineum* 'Werner Arends'
*Helenium* 'Moorheim Beauty'
*Helianthus salicifolius*
*Heliopsis helianthoides* 'Light of Lodden'
*Hemerocallis fulva*
*Hemerocallis* hybrids
*Hosta fortunei*
*Hosta lancifolia*
*Hosta plantaginea*
*Hosta sieboldiana*
*Kirengeshoma palmata*
*Kniphofia* hybrids
*Kniphofia uvaria*
*Liriope muscari*
*Lobelia cardinalis*
*Rudbeckia fulgida* var. *sullivantii* 'Goldsturm'
*Sanguisorba canadensis*
*Schizostylis coccinea* 'Grandiflora'
*Sedum* hybrids
*Sedum spectabile*
*Solidago* species and hybrids
*Verbascum nigrum*
*Veronica austriaca* subsp. *teucrium*
*Yucca filamentosa*
*Yucca gloriosa*

**Perennials, ground covers & rock plants, temperate climate**

*Aethionema armenum* 'Warley Rose'
*Anthemis tinctoria*
*Arabis caucasica*
*Arctotis* x *hybrida*
*Armeria maritima*
*Aubrieta deltoidea*
*Aurinia saxatilis*
*Brachycome*
*Cerastium tomentosum*
*Convolvulus sabatius*
*Duchesnea indica*
*Erigeron karvinskianus*
*Gazania* hybrids
*Globularia cordifolia*
*Iberis sempervirens*
*Lotus berthelotii*
*Nepeta* x *faassenii*
*Phlox stolonifera*
*Phlox subulata*
*Saponaria ocymoides*
*Scaevola aemula*
*Scaevola* 'Mauve Clusters'
*Stachys byzantina*
*Viola hederacea*

**Perennials, alpines, ground covers & rock plants, cool climate**

*Aster alpinus*
*Dodecatheon meadia*
*Erinus alpinus*
*Gentiana acaulis*
*Gentiana sino-ornata*
*Geranium dalmaticum*
*Geranium macrorrhizum*
*Incarvillea delevayi*
*Mazus reptans*
*Mimulus moschatus*
*Nertera granadensis*
*Pachysandra terminalis*
*Podophyllum peltatum*
*Pratia angulata*
*Prunella grandiflora*
*Pulsatilla vulgaris*
*Raoulia australis*
*Saxifraga caespitosa*
*Saxifraga paniculata*
*Saxifraga stolonifera*
*Sempervivum arachnoideum*
*Sempervivum tectorum*
*Tanacetum ptarmicifolium*
*Tiarella cordifolia*
*Veronica prostrata*

**Perennials, sub-shrubs, sun**

*Artemisia arborescens*
*Ceratostigma plumbaginoides*
*Convolvulus cneorum*
*Felicia amelloides*
*Gentiana lutea*
*Helianthemum nummularium*
*Helichrysum petiolare*
*Hypericum calycinum*
*Hypericum cerastoides*
*Leonotis leonurus*
*Penstemon heterophyllus* subsp. *purdyi*
*Perovskia atriplicifolia*
*Plectostachys serphyllifolia*
*Romneya coulteri*
*Solanum pseudocapsicum*
*Zauschneria californica*

**Perennials, sub-shrubs, shade to part shade**

*Ajuga reptans*
*Alchemilla mollis*
*Campanula isophylla*

Campanula portenschlagiana
Campanula poscharskyana
Glechoma hederacea
Lamium maculatum
Parochetus communis
Polygonatum × hybridum
Polygonum affine
Soleirolia soleirolii
Vinca major
Vinca minor

### Perennials, water garden plants

Acorus calamus
Caltha palustris
Cyperus papyrus
Houttuynia cordata 'Chamaeleon'
Lysichiton camtschatcensis
Myosotis scorpioides
Nelumbo nucifera
Nymphaea alba
Nymphaea 'Aurora'
Nymphaea candida
Nymphaea × helvola
Nymphaea Laydeckeri hybrids
Nymphaea marliacea 'Carnea'
Nymphaea odorata
Peltiphyllum peltatum
Pontederia cordata
Thalia dealbata
Zantedeschia aethiopica

### Perennials, for tropical effect

Alpinia zerumbet
Baileya multiradiata
Begonia metallica
Begonia 'Orange Rubra'
Coleus thyrsoides
Hedychium coronarium
Hedychium gardnerianum
Impatiens, New Guinea hybrids
Impatiens sodenii
Phormium tenax
Ricinus communis
Sarracenia flava

### Perennials, irises

Iris bearded hybrids
Iris cristata
Iris ensata
Iris japonica
Iris Lousiana hybrids
Iris Pacific Coast hybrids
Iris pallida 'Variegata'
Iris pseudacorus
Iris pseudacorus 'Variegata'
Iris siberica
Iris spuria hybrids
Iris unguicularis

### Perennials, primulas

Primula denticulata
Primula florindae
Primula japonica
Primula obconica
Primula × polyantha
Primula viallii
Primula vulgaris

## SHRUBS

The cultivation of shrubs will only be successful if they are correctly located. A sun-loving shrub will never flower brilliantly in a dark, damp corner; instead, it will sulk for years and produce only one or two flowers.

Always provide adequate water during dry spells as water stress often leaves shrubs vulnerable to insect attack. Using plenty of mulch around plants will help to conserve water. Conversely, planting in waterlogged soils may result in shrubs suffering root rot or fungal diseases, so an even balance needs to be found.

Regular, controlled pruning after flowering will result in healthy, well-formed shrubs. Deciduous shrubs should *not* be cut back when the leaves drop off as the next season's flowers may be inadvertently removed as well. If you don't have the time for regular pruning plant the same shrub in groups of three or five, as this will look much better than one straggly individual. Also, lightly fertilize every few months rather than in one big hit; avoid heaping animal manures up around plants' main stems.

Wander through a botanic garden to see shrubs growing in their prime. At the same time you can discover which shrubs might be suitable for your garden.

### Low growing, frost hardy, evergreen

Andromeda polifolia
Arctostaphylos 'Emerald Carpet'
Arctostaphylos uva-ursi
Berberis × mentorensis
Brachyglottis greyi
Buxus microphylla var. japonica
Buxus sempervirens
Calluna vulgaris
Cassia artemisioides
Coleonema pulchrum
Coprosma × kirkii
Daboecia cantabrica
Daphne × burkwoodii
Daphne cneorum
Daphne odora
Eremophila glabra
Euryops pectinatus
Gaultheria procumbens
Halimium lasianthum
Helichrysum selago
Leucadendron salignum
Mahonia repens
Mimulus aurantiacus
Myoporum parvifolium
Nandina domestica 'Nana'
Pachystegia insignis
Parahebe perfoliata
Paxistima canbyi
Pernettya mucronata
Phlomis fruticosa
Polygala chamaebuxus
Prunus laurocerasus 'Otto Luyken'
Pyracantha coccinea
Pyracantha hybrids
Raphiolepis indica
Ruscus aculeatus
Santolina chamaecyparissus
Sarcococca hookeriana var. humilis
Taxus baccata 'Repandens'
Thuja occidentalis
Vaccinium macrocarpon

### Low growing, frost tender, evergreen

Agapetes serpens
Anisodontea × hypomandarum
Arctostaphylos densiflora 'Howard McMinn'
Arctostaphylos hookeri
Ardisia japonica
Baccharis pilularis
Begonia fuchsioides
Bouvardia hybrids
Bouvardia longiflora
Brunfelsia pauciflora
Cantua buxifolia
Cuphea ignea
Encelia farinosa
Heliotropium arborescens
Justicia carnea
Lantana montevidensis
Pentas lanceolata
Pyracantha koidsumii
Russelia equisetiformis
Senecio petasitis
Streptosolen jamesonii

### Low growing, frost hardy, deciduous

Abelia schumannii
Berberis thunbergii
Berlandiera lyrata
Caryopteris × clandonensis
Cytisus scoparius
Deutzia × rosea
Eriogonum umbellatum
Hypericum patulum
Hypericum 'Rowallane'
Justicia brandegeana
Justicia californica
Lavatera maritima
Phygelius
Potentilla fruticosa
Prunus glandulosa 'Sinensis'
Punica granatum 'Nana'
Rhus aromatica
Symphoricarpos × chenaultii
Symphoricarpos orbiculatus
Symphoricarpos rivularis

### Medium to tall growing, frost hardy, evergreen

Abelia × grandiflora
Abutilon × hybridum
Abutilon megapotanicum
Abutilon vitifolium
Alyogyne huegelii
Arctostaphylos manzanita
Aucuba japonica
Azara microphylla
Baeckia virgata
Berberis darwinii
Bursaria spinosa
Carpentaria californica
Ceanothus cultivars
Ceanothus × delilianus 'Gloire de Versailles'
Ceanothus griseus var. horizontalis
Ceanothus impressus
Ceanothus thyrsiflorus
Chamaecyparis obtusa
Chamaecyparis pisifera
Choisya ternata
Coprosma repens
Corokia cotoneaster
Coronilla valentina subsp. glauca
Daphne tangutica
Desfontainea spinosa
Dodonaea viscosa
Dryandra
Elaeagnus pungens
Eremophila maculata
Escallonia × exoniensis
Escallonia × langleyensis 'Apple Blossom'
Escallonia rubra
Euonymus fortunei
Euonymus japonicus
× Fatshedera lizei
Fatsia japonica
Fremontodendron californicum
Garrya elliptica
Gaultheria shallon
Grewia occidentalis
Griselina littoralis
Heteromeles arbutifolia
Itea ilicifolia
Jasminum mesnyi
Jasminum nudiflorum
Kalmia latifolia
Leucothoe fontanesiana
Ligistrum japonicum
Ligustrum ovalifolium 'Aureum'
Lonicera fragrantissima
Lonicera nitida
Loropetalum chinense
Mahonia aquifolium
Mahonia lomariifolia
Melianthus major
Michelia figo
Myrica californica
Myrtus communis
Nandina domestica
Photinia × fraseri
Photinia serrulata
Pieris formosa var. forrestii
Pieris japonica
Pinus mugo
Pittosporum eugenioides
Pittosporum tenuifolium
Pittosporum tobira
Platycladus orientalis
Polygala × dalmaisiana
Prostanthera rotundifolia
Prunus laurocerasus
Pyracantha angustifolia
Rhamnus alaternus
Rhamnus californicus
Rhaphiolepis × delacourii
Skimmia japonica
Spartium junceum
Taxus cuspidata
Taxus × media
Tecoma stans
Ternstroemia gymnanthera
Tetrapanax papyriferus
Teucrium fruticans
Westringia fruticosa

### Medium to tall growing, frost tender, evergreen

Arbutus unedo 'Compacta'
Asclepias subulata
Athanasia parviflora

*Atriplex lentiformis* subsp. *breweri*
*Banksia ericifolia*
*Bauhinia galpinii*
*Bougainvillea* species
*Brugmansia* × *candida*
*Brugmansia sanguinea*
*Brugmansia suaveolens*
*Brugmansia versicolor*
*Caesalpinia pulcherrima*
*Calliandra tweedii*
*Carissa macrocarpa*
*Cassia corymbosa*
*Clerodendrum bungei*
*Cowania mexicana* var. *stansburiana*
*Dalea pulchra*
*Duranta repens*
*Echium fastuosum*
*Fouquiera splendens*
*Gordonia axillaris*
*Lantana camara*
*Leucophyllum frutescens*
*Leucospermum cordifolium*
*Lycianthes rantonnetii*
*Malvaviscus arboreus*
*Nerium oleander*
*Ochna serrulata*
*Pittosporum crassifolium*
*Plumbago auriculata*
*Rhus microphylla*
*Rhus ovata*
*Rondeletia amoena*
*Sophora secundiflora*
*Sparmannia africana*
*Tecomaria capensis*
*Thevetia peruviana*
*Tibouchina urvilleana*
*Ugni molinae*

### Medium to tall growing, frost hardy, deciduous

*Acer palmatum* 'Dissectum Atropurpureum'
*Acer palmatum* 'Dissectum Viridis'
*Aesculus parviflora*
*Aesculus pavia*
*Amelanchier alnifolia*
*Aronia arbutifolia*
*Artemisia tridentata*
*Berberis ottawensis* 'Superba'
*Caesalpinia gilliesii*
*Callicarpa*
*Calycanthus floridus*
*Calycanthus occidentalis*
*Caragana arborescens*
*Chaenomeles speciosa*
*Chimonanthus praecox*
*Chrysothamnus*
*Clerodendrum trichotomum*
*Clethra alnifolia*
*Cornus alba*
*Cornus sericea*
*Corylopsis pauciflora*
*Corylopsis spicata*
*Corylus avellana* 'Contorta'
*Cotinus coggygria*
*Cytisus* × *praecox*
*Dahlia excelsa*
*Daphne mezereum*
*Deutzia gracilis*
*Deutzia* 'Rosalin'
*Deutzia scabra*
*Edgeworthia papyrifera*
*Elaeagnus angustifolia*
*Enkianthus campanulatus*
*Erythrina* × *bidwillii*
*Euonymus alatus*
*Euonymus europaeus*
*Exochorda racemosa*
*Forsythia* × *intermedia*
*Forsythia suspensa*
*Fothergilla*
*Hamamelis* × *intermedia*
*Hamamelis mollis*
*Hamamelis vernalis*
*Hamamelis virginiana*
*Itea virginica*
*Kerria japonica*
*Kolkwitzia amabilis*
*Lagerstroemia* hybrids
*Lagerstroemia indica*
*Ligustrum obtusifolium* var. *regelianum*
*Ligustrum* × *vicaryi*
*Lonicera* × *purpursii*
*Lonicera tatarica*
*Magnolia liliiflora*
*Magnolia stellata*
*Malus sargentii*
*Myrica pensylvanica*
*Paeonia lutea*
*Paeonia suffruticosa*
*Physocarpus opulifolius*
*Prunus* 'Hally Jolivette'
*Quercus gambelii*
*Ribes alpinum*
*Ribes aureum*
*Ribes sanguineum*
*Salix purpurea*
*Sambucus nigra*
*Tamarix parviflora*
*Vitex agnus-castus*

### Acacia

*Acacia boormannii*
*Acacia greggii*
*Acacia pravissima*
*Acacia redolens*

### Buddleia

*Buddleia alternifolia*
*Buddleia davidii*
*Buddleia globosa*

### Callistemon

*Callistemon citrinus*
*Callistemon viminalis*

### Camellia

*Camellia granthamiana*
*Camellia japonica*
*Camellia japonica* 'Adolphe Audusson'
*Camellia japonica* 'Debutante'
*Camellia japonica* 'Elegans'
*Camellia japonica* 'Nuccio's Gem'
*Camellia lutchuensis*
*Camellia oleifera*
*Camellia reticulata*
*Camellia sasanqua*
*Camellia sasanqua* 'White Doves'
*Camellia sasanqua* 'Yuletide'
*Camellia sinensis*
*Camellia* × *williamsii*
*Camellia* × *williamsii* 'Donation'

### Cestrum

*Cestrum aurantiacum*
*Cestrum elegans*
*Cestrum nocturnum*

### Cistus

*Cistus* × *hybridus*
*Cistus ladanifer*
*Cistus* × *purpureus*
*Cistus salviifolius*

### Correa

*Correa alba*
*Correa* 'Dusky Bells'
*Correa pulchella*

### Cotoneaster

*Cotoneaster apiculatus*
*Cotoneaster dammeri*
*Cotoneaster divaricatus*
*Cotoneaster horizontalis*
*Cotoneaster lacteus*
*Cotoneaster microphyllus*
*Cotoneaster multiflorus*
*Cotoneaster salicifolius*

### Erica

*Erica arborea*
*Erica bauera*
*Erica carnea*
*Erica cinerea*
*Erica* × *darleyensis*
*Erica mammosa*
*Erica mediterranea*
*Erica vagans*

### Euphorbia

*Euphorbia fulgens*
*Euphorbia milii*
*Euphorbia pulcherrima*

### Fuchsia

*Fuchsia* 'Gartenmeister Bonstedt'
*Fuchsia* hybrids
*Fuchsia magellanica* var. *gracilis*
*Fuchsia magellanica* var. *gracilis* 'Alba'
*Fuchsia paniculata*
*Fuchsia procumbens*

### Gardenia

*Gardenia augusta*
*Gardenia thunbergia*

### Genista

*Genista aetnensis*
*Genista lydia*
*Genista monosperma*
*Genista pilosa* 'Vancouver Gold'
*Genista tinctoria*

### Grevillea

*Grevillea* 'Boongala Spinebill'
*Grevillea lavandulacea*
*Grevillea* 'Noelli'
*Grevillea* 'Robyn Gordon'
*Grevillea rosmarinifolia*

### Hakea

*Hakea laurina*
*Hakea suaveolens*

### Hebe

*Hebe* × *andersonii*
*Hebe hulkeana*
*Hebe speciosa*

### Hibiscus

*Hibiscus mutabilis*
*Hibiscus rosa-sinensis*
*Hibiscus rosa-sinensis* 'Cooperi'
*Hibiscus syriacus*
*Hibiscus syriacus* 'Ardens'

### Hydrangea

*Hydrangea aspera* var. *aspera*
*Hydrangea macrophylla*
*Hydrangea macrophylla* 'Blue Wave'
*Hydrangea paniculata* 'Grandiflora'
*Hydrangea quercifolia*

### Ilex

*Ilex* x *altaclarensis* 'Wilsonii'
*Ilex aquifolium*
*Ilex cornuta*
*Ilex crenata*
*Ilex glabra*
*Ilex* × *meservae*
*Ilex verticillata*
*Ilex vomitoria*

### Juniperus

*Juniperus conferta*
*Juniperus horizontalis*
*Juniperus* × *media*
*Juniperus sabina*

### Lavandula

*Lavandula angustifolia*
*Lavandula dentata*
*Lavandula stoechas*

### Leptospermum

*Leptospermum laevigatum*
*Leptospermum petersonii*
*Leptospermum scoparium*

### Melaleuca

*Melaleuca incana*
*Melaleuca nesophylla*

### Osmanthus

*Osmanthus delavayi*
*Osmanthus fragrans*
*Osmanthus heterophyllus*

### Philadelphus

*Philadelphus coronarius*
*Philadelphus* hybrids
*Philadelphus lewisii*
*Philadelphus mexicanus*
*Philadelphus* 'Virginal'

### Protea

*Protea cynaroides*
*Protea neriifolia*

### Rhododendron, Azalea

*Rhododendron arboreum*
*Rhododendron augustinii*
*Rhododendron auriculatum*
*Rhododendron ciliicalyx*
*Rhododendron* 'Fragrantissimum'
*Rhododendron*, Gumpo azaleas
*Rhododendron*, Ironclad hybrid rhododendrons
*Rhododendron jasminiflorum*
*Rhododendron javanicum*
*Rhododendron*, Knap Hill-Exbury azaleas
*Rhododendron*, Kurume hybrid azaleas

*Rhododendron laetum*
*Rhododendron mucronulatum*
*Rhododendron occidentale*
*Rhododendron prunifolium*
*Rhododendron*, Southern Indica azaleas
*Rhododendron yakushimanum*

### *Rosa*

Alba roses
Bourbon roses
Centifolia roses
Cluster-flowered bush roses
Damask roses
Ground cover roses
Hybrid Perpetual roses
Large-flowered bush roses
Miniature roses
Modern garden roses
Modern shrub roses
Moss roses
Old garden roses
Patio roses
Polyantha roses
Portland roses
*Rosa chinensis* and varieties
*Rosa foetida*
*Rosa gallica* and varieties
*Rosa glauca*
*Rosa moyesii*
*Rosa pimpinellifolia*
*Rosa rugosa*
*Rosa virginiana*
Tea roses
Wild roses

### *Salvia*

*Salvia africana-lutea*
*Salvia clevelandii*
*Salvia dorrii*
*Salvia greggii*
*Salvia guaranitica*
*Salvia leucantha*

### *Spiraea*

*Spiraea cantoniensis*
*Spiraea japonica*
*Spiraea thunbergii*
*Spiraea* × *vanhouttei*

### *Syringa*

*Syringa meyeri* 'Palibin'
*Syringa patula* 'Miss Kim'
*Syringa* × *persica*
*Syringa vulgaris*

### *Viburnum*

*Viburnum acerifolium*
*Viburnum* × *bodnantense*
*Viburnum* × *burkwoodii*
*Viburnum* × *carlecephalum*
*Viburnum carlesii*
*Viburnum davidii*
*Viburnum dentatum*
*Viburnum farreri*
*Viburnum lantana*
*Viburnum opulus* 'Nanum'
*Viburnum opulus* 'Roseum'
*Viburnum plicatum* f. *tomentosum* 'Mariesii'
*Viburnum prunifolia*
*Viburnum tinus*
*Viburnum trilobum*

### *Weigela*

*Weigela florida*
*Weigela florida* 'Eva Ratke'
*Weigela florida* 'Variegata'

## TREES

Choosing the right tree for a location requires careful consideration—the tiny seedling tree you admire in a pot may grow to overwhelm a small garden or cause major problems to building foundations and underground pipes. Always check the mature height of a tree before purchase and allow plenty of room for it to fully develop. Visit an arboretum to see trees growing at their best when choosing one for your garden.

At planting time dig a hole at least three times the root volume and add compost and a complete fertilizer. To help the tree get off to a good start, cut off any coiled or damaged roots, plant firmly and leave a slight depression around the main stem to allow rainwater to collect. Although many trees are drought tolerant, they still require a good supply of water. As the tree grows, avoid root disturbance at all times and remove any crossing or rubbing branches. Fertilize to the dripline of trees during rainy weather.

When pruning mature trees always cut flush to a branch or trunk, leaving no stubs—these look unsightly and give insect pests and diseases an easy entry to the tree. Seasonal checks for insect pests may be necessary. Small holes or sawdust on the trunk indicate the presence of borers.

### Evergreen

*Acacia baileyana*
*Acacia dealbata*
*Agonis flexuosa*
*Arbutus* 'Marina'
*Arbutus menziesii*
*Arbutus unedo*
*Banksia integrifolia*
*Beaucarnea recurvata*
*Calodendrum capense*
*Cinnamomum camphora*
*Cordyline australis*
*Eucalyptus citriodora*
*Eucalyptus ficifolia*
*Eucalyptus globulus*
*Eucalyptus leucoxylon*
*Eucalyptus mannifera* subsp. *maculosa*
*Eucalyptus nicholii*
*Eucalyptus pauciflora*
*Eucalyptus polyanthemos*
*Eucalyptus sideroxylon*
*Ficus microcarpa* var. *nitida*
*Ficus rubiginosa*
*Geijera parviflora*
*Grevillea robusta*
*Hoheria populnea*
*Hymenosporum flavum*
*Ilex opaca*
*Lagunaria patersonii*
*Ligustrum lucidum*
*Magnolia grandiflora*
*Magnolia virginiana*
*Maytenus boaria*
*Melaleuca quinquenervia*
*Metrosideros excelsa*
*Michelia doltsopa*
*Nothofagus obliqua*
*Nothofagus solandri*
*Olneya tesota*
*Pittosporum eugenioides*
*Pittosporum undulatum*
*Quercus agrifolia*
*Quercus suber*
*Quercus virginiana*
*Schinus molle*
*Schinus terebinthifolius*
*Spathodia campanulata*
*Syzygium paniculatum*
*Tamarix aphylla*
*Tristania confertus*
*Tristaniòpsis laurina*
*Umbellularia californica*
*Vitex lucens*
*Yucca brevifolia*

### Semi-deciduous

*Bauhinia variegata*
*Brachychiton acerifolius*
*Brachychiton populneus*
*Cornus capitata*
*Erythrina caffra*
*Erythrina lysistemon*
*Firmiana simplex*
*Jacaranda mimosifolia*
*Plumeria rubra*
*Prosopis glandulosa*
*Sophora tetraptera*
*Tipuana tipu*

### Deciduous, 30 feet or shorter

*Acer buergerianum*
*Acer ginnala*
*Acer griseum*
*Acer japonicum*
*Acer palmatum*
*Albizia julibrissin*
*Amelanchier arborea*
*Amelanchier laevis*
*Aralia elata*
*Carpinus caroliniana*
*Cercidium floridum*
*Cercis canadensis*
*Cercis occidentalis*
*Chilopsis linearis*
*Chionanthus virginicus*
*Cornus florida*
*Cornus kousa*
*Cornus mas*
*Crataegus coccinea* 'Plena'
*Crataegus laevigata* 'Paul's Scarlet'
*Crataegus* × *lavallei*
*Crataegus phaenopyrum*
*Crataegus viridis* 'Winter King'
*Erythrina crista-galli*
*Franklinia alatamaha*
*Halesia carolina*
*Koelreuteria paniculata*
*Laburnum watereri* 'Vossii'
*Magnolia* × *soulangiana*
*Oxydendrum arboreum*
*Quercus gambelii*
*Rhus lancea*
*Rhus typhina*
*Salix caprea*
*Sapium sebiferum*
*Sorbus cashmiriana*
*Sorbus commixta*
*Stewartia ovata* var. *grandiflora*
*Stewartia pseudocamellia*
*Styrax japonica*
*Syringa reticulata*
*Tabebuia chrysotricha*

### Deciduous, taller than 30 feet

*Acer macrophyllum*
*Acer platanoides*
*Acer pseudoplatanus*
*Acer rubrum*
*Acer saccharum*
*Aesculus californica*
*Aeculus* × *carnea*
*Aesculus flava*
*Aesculus hippocastanum*
*Ailanthus altissima*
*Alnus cordata*
*Alnus glutinosa*
*Betula nigra*
*Betula papyrifera*
*Betula pendula*
*Betula pendula* 'Dalecarlica'
*Carpinus betulis*
*Castanea sativa*
*Catalpa bignonioides*
*Cedrela sinensis*
*Celtis laevigata*
*Celtis sinensis*
*Cercidiphyllum japonicum*
*Chorisia speciosa*
*Cladrastis lutea*
*Cornus controversa*
*Cornus nuttallii*
*Davidia involucrata*
*Diospyros kaki*
*Fagus grandifolia*
*Fagus sylvatica*
*Fagus sylvatica* f. *purpurea*
*Fraxinus americana*
*Fraxinus ornus*
*Fraxinus oxycarpa* 'Raywood'
*Fraxinus pennsylvanica*
*Fraxinus uhdei*
*Gleditsia triacanthos* var. *inermis*
*Juglans nigra*
*Liquidambar styraciflua*
*Liriodendron tulipifera*
*Maclura pomifera*
*Magnolia campbellii*
*Magnolia denudata*
*Melia azedarach*
*Morus alba*
*Nyssa sylvatica*
*Parrotia persica*
*Paulownia tomentosa*
*Phellodendron amurense*
*Pistacia chinesis*
*Platanus* × *acerifolia*
*Populus alba*
*Populus deltoides*
*Populus nigra* 'Italica'
*Populus tremuloides*
*Pterocarya fraxinifolia*
*Quercus kellogii*
*Quercus macrocarpa*
*Quercus palustris*
*Quercus phellos*
*Quercus robur*
*Quercus rubra*

*Robinia* × *ambigua* 'Idahoensis'
*Robinia pseudoacacia*
*Robinia pseudoacacia* 'Frisia'
*Salix alba*
*Salix alba* var. *tristis*
*Salix babylonica*
*Salix matsudana* 'Tortuosa'
*Sapindus drumondii*
*Sassafras albidum*
*Sophora japonica*
*Sorbus aucuparia*
*Sorbus hupehensis*
*Tabebuia impetiginosa*
*Tilia americana*
*Tilia cordata*
*Tilia* 'Petiolaris'
*Ulmus americana*
*Ulmus glabra* 'Camperdownii'
*Ulmus parvifolia*
*Ulmus pumila*
*Zelkova serrata*

### Conifers

*Abies cephalonica*
*Abies concolor*
*Abies procera*
*Araucaria araucana*
*Araucaria bidwillii*
*Araucaria heterophylla*
*Calocedrus decurrens*
*Casuarina cunninghamiana*
*Casuarina verticillata*
*Cedrus atlantica*
*Cedrus deodara*
*Chamaecyparis lawsoniana*
*Cryptomeria japonica* 'Elegans'
× *Cupressocyparis leylandii*
*Cupressus arizonica*
*Cupressus macrocarpa*
*Cupressus sempervirens*
*Ginkgo biloba*
*Juniperus communis*
*Juniperus scopulorum*
*Juniperus virginiana*
*Larix decidua*
*Picea abies*
*Picea omorika*
*Picea pungens*
*Pinus bungeana*
*Pinus canariensis*
*Pinus nigra*
*Pinus palustris*
*Pinus patula*
*Pinus pinea*
*Pinus ponderosa*
*Pinus radiata*
*Pinus strobus*
*Pinus sylvestris*
*Pinus thunbergiana*
*Podocarpus gracilior*
*Podocarpus macrophyllus*
*Pseudotsuga menziesii*
*Sciadopitys verticillata*
*Sequoiadendron giganteum*
*Sequoia sempervirens*
*Taxodium distichum*
*Taxus baccata*
*Thuja occidentalis*
*Thuja plicata*
*Thujopsis dolabrata*
*Tsuga canadensis*

### Ornamental, blossom & fruit

*Malus* 'Adams'
*Malus* 'Calloway'
*Malus floribunda*
*Malus* 'Gorgeous'
*Malus hupehensis*
*Prunus* × *blireiana*
*Prunus campanulata*
*Prunus caroliniana*
*Prunus cerasifera* 'Atropurpurea'
*Prunus ilicifolia*
*Prunus incisa*
*Prunus mume*
*Prunus sargentii*
*Prunus serrulata*
*Prunus subhirtella* 'Pendula'
*Prunus* × *yedoensis*
*Pyrus calleryana*
*Pyrus kawakamii*
*Pyrus salicifolia* 'Pendula'
*Pyrus ussuriensis*

### Tropical & subtropical

*Cassia leptophylla*
*Delonix regia*
*Embothrium coccineum*
*Parkinsonia aculeata*

## BULBS, CORMS & TUBERS

Bulbs are one of the easiest groups of plants to grow, as they are adaptable to a wide range of climates and growing conditions. Select firm, healthy bulbs when buying and check around the surface or under the outer papery casing for any sign of insects or grubs. Soft, damp spots or gray mold may indicate damage from a fungus. Many bulbs in or near flowering time are now available in pots.

If you live in a warm climate and wish to grow cold-climate bulbs, you may have to give the bulbs an artificial winter in the refrigerator crisper for six weeks before planting. In a cold climate, lift frost-tender bulbs over winter, grow them in pots and plant them out in spring when the danger of frost has passed.

Certain bulbs are known as "garden escapees." Freesias in lawns or on roadsides in spring are popular with everyone, however, other bulbs appearing in prime country pasture cause heartache to farmers. Check with a reputable dealer if in doubt about the suitability of any bulb.

### Summer flowering, sun

*Amaryllis belladonna*
*Aristea ecklonii*
*Belamcanda chinensis*
*Crocosmia masonorum*
*Galtonia candicans*
*Gloriosa superba*
*Habranthus robustus*
*Lycoris aurea*
*Lycoris squamigera*
*Oxalis adenophylla*
*Polianthes tuberosa*
*Sauromatum venosum*
*Scilla peruviana*
*Sprekelia formosissima*
*Tigridia pavonia*
*Triteleia laxa*
*Tritonia crocata*
*Vallota speciosa*
*Watsonia beatricis*

### Summer flowering, part shade

*Caladium bicolor*
*Cardiocrinum giganteum*
*Crinum bulbispermum*
*Crinum moorei*
*Crinum* × *powellii*
*Dracunculus vulgaris*
*Hymenocallis* × *festalis*
*Hymenocallis narcissiflora*

### Fall flowering

*Brunsvigia josephinae*
*Brunsvigia orientalis*
*Colchicum autumnale*
*Colchicum* 'Lilac Wonder'
*Colchicum speciosum*
*Crocus* species, autumn blooming
*Haemanthus coccineus*
*Hymenocallis littoralis*
*Leucojum autumnale*
*Lycoris radiata*
*Nerine bowdenii*
*Nerine filifolia*
*Nerine sarniensis*
*Sternbergia lutea*
*Tricyrtis hirta*

### Winter flowering

*Galanthus ikariae*
*Galanthus nivalis*

### Winter–spring flowering

*Bulbinella floribunda*
*Chasmanthe aethiopica*
*Cyclamen coum*
*Eranthis hyemalis*
*Oxalis purpurea*

### Spring flowering, sun

*Anomatheca laxa*
*Asphodeline lutea*
*Babiana stricta*
*Calochortus albus*
*Chionodoxa luciliae*
*Crocus*, Dutch hybrids
*Crocus* species, spring blooming
*Dichelostemma ida-maia*
*Dichelostemma pulchellum*
*Freesia*, Florist's hybrids
*Freesia alba*
*Herbertia drummondii*
*Hermodactylus tuberosus*
*Hippeastrum* cultivars
*Homeria collina*
*Hyacinthus orientalis*
*Ipheion uniflorum*
*Ixia maculata*
*Ixia paniculata*
*Ixia viridiflora*
*Lachenalia aloides*
*Lachenalia bulbifera*
*Leucocoryne ixioides*
*Leucojum aestivum*
*Muscari armeniacum*
*Muscari armeniacum* 'Blue Spike'
*Muscari comosum*
*Ornithogalum arabicum*
*Ornithogalum umbellatum*
*Puschkinia scilloides*
*Ranunculus asiaticus*
*Rhodohypoxis baurii*
*Scilla siberica*
*Sparaxis tricolor*
*Zephyranthes atamasco*

### Spring flowering, shade to part shade

*Anemone blanda*
*Anemone coronaria*
*Anemone nemorosa*
*Arum italicum*
*Camassia quamash*
*Convallaria majalis*
*Cyclamen repandum*
*Erythronium americanum*
*Erythronium dens-canis*
*Erythronium revolutum* 'Pagoda'
*Hyacinthoides hispanica*
*Hyacinthoides non-scripta*
*Nectaroscordum siculum* subsp. *bulgaricum*

### Summer–fall flowering

*Crocosmia* × *crocosmiiflora*
*Cyclamen hederifolium*
*Eucomis comosa*
*Zephyranthes candida*

### Spring-summer flowering, sun

*Ornithogalum thyrsoides*
*Tulbaghia violacea*
*Watsonia borbonica*
*Zephyranthes grandiflora*

### Spring–summer flowering, shade

*Calochortus venustus*
*Clivia miniata*
*Veltheimia bracteata*
*Veltheimia capensis*

### Allium

*Allium christophii*
*Allium giganteum*
*Allium moly*
*Allium narcissiflorum*
*Allium neopolitanum*

### Begonia

*Begonia* × *tuberhybrida* 'Camellia' and 'Rose' flowered types
*Begonia* × *tuberhybrida multiflora*
*Begonia* × *tuberhybrida pendula*

### Fritillaria

*Fritillaria affinis*
*Fritillaria imperialis*
*Fritillaria meleagris*
*Fritillaria persica*

### Gladiolus

*Gladiolus*, Butterfly hybrids
*Gladiolus byzantinus*
*Gladiolus callianthus*
*Gladiolus carneus*
*Gladiolus* × *colvillei*
*Gladiolus*, Large-flowered hybrids
*Gladiolus tristis*

### Iris

*Iris bucharica*

*Iris*, Dutch hybrids
*Iris latifolia*
*Iris reticulata*
*Iris xiphium*

### *Lilium*

*Lilium*, American hybrids
*Lilium*, Asiatic hybrids
*Lilium auratum*
*Lilium*, Aurelian hybrids
*Lilium canadense*
*Lilium candidum*
*Lilium formosanum*
*Lilium henryi*
*Lilium lancifolium*
*Lilium longiflorum*
*Lilium martagon*
*Lilium*, Oriental hybrids
*Lilium pardalinum*
*Lilium regale*
*Lilium speciosum*
*Lilium*, Trumpet hybrids

### *Narcissus*

*Narcissus cyclamineus* hybrids
*Narcissus*, Double-flowered daffodils
*Narcissus jonquilla* hybrids
*Narcissus*, Large-cupped daffodils
*Narcissus*, miscellaneous species
*Narcissus poeticus* hybrids
*Narcissus*, Small-cupped daffodils
*Narcissus*, Split-corona daffodils
*Narcissus tazetta* hybrids
*Narcissus triandrus* hybrids
*Narcissus*, Trumpet daffodils

### *Tulipa*

*Tulipa acuminata*
*Tulipa clusiana*
*Tulipa*, cottage tulips
*Tulipa*, Darwin hybrid tulips
*Tulipa*, Darwin tulips
*Tulipa*, double early tulips
*Tulipa*, double late tulips
*Tulipa fosteriana*
*Tulipa*, garden tulips
*Tulipa greigii*
*Tulipa kaufmanniana*
*Tulipa*, lily-flowered tulips
*Tulipa*, mid-season tulips
*Tulipa*, parrot tulips
*Tulipa*, Rembrandt tulips
*Tulipa saxatilis*
*Tulipa*, single early tulips
*Tulipa*, single late tulips
*Tulipa tarda*

## LAWNS, GROUND COVERS & ORNAMENTAL GRASSES

Cultivating the perfect lawn is the aim of every gardener; it can even develop into an obsession. The key to success is a fine, even, well-drained surface that is free from weeds. The chosen grass or ground cover must be suitable for the climate and be able to withstand its intended use. Softer grasses or ground covers are suitable for occasional foot traffic, while tough grasses are more able to withstand sport, children and dogs.

Regular watering is essential to keep a nice green surface but is fairly wasteful of a valuable resource. A brown lawn will quickly recover after adequate rain. Light, frequent applications of fertilizer during the growing season will gain the best results.

Always weed and mow on a regular basis, never mowing the lawn to lower than around 1 in (about 2.5 cm) in height. Groundcover lawns may just need the occasional once over with hedge shears if the area is small.

Ornamental grasses, sedges and bamboos grow best in garden conditions that are not overly fertile. Add some moisture-retaining compost to the soil and give them plenty of space to develop. However, some form of barrier may be necessary to stop the spread of vigorous species. Few pests worry them.

Propagation is from seed or by division of clumps in spring. When dividing clumps or cultivating soil near them, be sure to wear protective clothing as the sharp leaf blades and fine hairs can irritate the skin.

### *Lawns & ground covers*

*Aegopodium podagraria* 'Variegatum'
*Agrostis tenuis*
*Asarum canadense*
*Asarum caudatum*
*Bouteloua gracilis*
*Buchloe dactyloides*
*Festuca elatior*
*Festuca rubra*
*Festuca rubra* 'Commutata'
*Fragaria chiloensis*
*Lolium perenne*
*Mentha requienii*
*Ophiopogon japonicus*
*Pachysandra terminalis*
*Poa pratensis*
*Rubus calycinoides*
*Thunbergia gregorii*
*Thymus pseudolanuginosus*
*Thymus serpyllum*
*Zoysia japonica* 'Meyeri'

### *Ornamental grasses, sedges & bamboos*

*Andropogon gerardii*
*Arundo donax*
*Briza media*
*Butomus umbellatus*
*Calamagrostis acutiflora* 'Stricta'
*Carex elata* 'Aurea'
*Carex morrowii* 'Variegata'
*Cortaderia selloana*
*Deschampsia caespitosa*
*Festuca amethystina*
*Festuca ovina* var. *glauca*
*Hakonechloa macra* 'Aureola'
*Helictotrichon sempervirens*
*Imperata cylindrica* 'Red Baron'
*Milium effusum* 'Aureum'
*Miscanthus sinensis* 'Variegatus'
*Molinia caerulea*
*Pennisetum alopecuroides*
*Pennisetum setaceum*
*Phalaris arundinacea* var. *picta*
*Pleioblastus pygmaeus*
*Sasa palmata*
*Sasa veitchii*
*Schizachyrium scoparium*
*Scirpus lacustris* subsp. *tabernaemontani* 'Zebrinus'
*Sesleria autumnalis*
*Sinarundinaria nitida*
*Stipa gigantea*

## VEGETABLES & HERBS

It is not practicable to include vegetables in the Seasonal Calendars in this book. For detailed information refer to books specifically dealing with vegetables.

Herbs are ideally suited to cultivation in cool-temperate climates where summers may be hot but not humid. They can tolerate a range of growing conditions within a garden, from dry, gravelly, limy positions in full sun to cool, moist, partly shaded positions.

Herbs don't need a special garden of their own although this is often more convenient. Prepare the garden position by adding plenty of compost and a light application of fertilizer, or else grow in pots with a good-quality potting mix and some slow-release fertilizer.

Annual herbs grown from seed need to be sown regularly to ensure a constant supply for the kitchen. They tend to bolt to seed when fluctuations of temperature occur. Perennial herbs should be tip pruned regularly for compact growth, checked occasionally for invasions of leaf-eating insects or snails and tidied up in late winter before spring growth starts.

Cuttings strike readily during spring and summer, or herbs can be divided during the cooler months. Frost-tender herbs may need to be moved to a sheltered position during winter in cold climates. Otherwise, their demands are few.

Herbs make good companion plants and mix happily with flowers, vegetables and fruit or they can be used as a ground cover among shrubs.

### *Herbs*

*Allium sativum*
*Allium schoenoprasum*
*Aloysia triphylla*
*Andropogon nardus*
*Anethum graveolens*
*Angelica archangelica*
*Anthriscus cerefolium*
*Artemisia dracunculus*
*Borago officinalis*
*Brassica juncea*
*Capparis spinosa*
*Carum carvi*
*Chamaemelum nobile*
*Coriandrum sativum*
*Cuminum cyminum*
*Curcuma domestica*
*Elettaria cardamomum*
*Foeniculum vulgare*
*Foeniculum vulgare* var. *dulce*
*Glycyrrhiza glabra*
*Hyssopus officinalis*
*Juniperus communis*
*Laurus nobilis*
*Lavandula angustifolia*
*Levisticum officinale*
*Melissa officinalis*
*Mentha* 'Citrata'
*Mentha* × *piperita*
*Mentha spicata*
*Monarda didyma*
*Nepeta cataria*
*Ocimum basilicum*
*Origanum hortensis*
*Origanum vulgare*
*Petroselinum crispum*
*Polygonum odoratum*
*Rosmarinus officinalis*
*Ruta graveolens*
*Salvia elegans*
*Salvia officinalis*
*Satureja hortensis*
*Satureja montana*
*Symphytum officinale*
*Thymus* × *citriodorus*
*Thymus vulgaris*
*Zingiber officinale*

## FRUIT TREES, NUT TREES & OTHER FRUITS

The basic requirement for fruit and nut trees is a good, deep, fertile soil that is well drained. Have your soil tested in a laboratory to see if it is deficient in certain elements; this will save a lot of problems later on after planting. As well, check with a reputable dealer for varieties suitable for your area and for the pollination requirements.

Remember to always choose virus-free or organically grown trees. Prune to allow light and air into the tree and to encourage continuous cropping. Keep the area around trees free from weeds and mulch and fertilize regularly.

Pest and disease problems may be numerous, so always seek expert advice on the safest way of dealing with them. Plant companion plants that are beneficial for insect control and fruit and nut production. Do not attempt to grow cool-temperate fruits in warm climates. If you follow these simple procedures you will soon be able to enjoy the "fruits" of your labor.

### *Tropical to subtropical*

*Annona squamosa*
*Arachis hypogaea*

*Carica papaya*
*Cyphomandra betacea*
*Musa paradisiaca*
*Musa paradisiaca* 'Cavendish'
*Musa paradisiaca* 'Lady Finger'
*Persea americana*
*Psidium cattleianum*

### Cool-temperate

*Castanea sativa*
*Corylus avellana*
*Cydonia oblonga*
*Fragaria alpina*
*Fragaria ananassae*
*Fragaria vesca*
*Humulus lupulus*
*Juglans regia*
*Malus* 'Bramley's Seedling'
*Malus* 'Discovery'
*Malus* × 'Dolgo'
*Malus domestica* 'Delicious'
*Malus domestica* 'Granny Smith'
*Malus domestica* 'Gravenstein'
*Malus domestica* 'Jonathan'
*Malus* 'Golden Hornet'
*Malus* 'James Grieve'
*Malus* 'John Downie'
*Morus nigra*
*Pyrus communis* 'Beurre Bosc'
*Pyrus communis* 'William's Bon Chrétien'
*Pyrus pyrifolia*
*Ribes grossularia*
*Ribes nigrum*
*Ribes sativum*
*Rubus* 'Boysen'
*Rubus fruticosus*
*Rubus idaeus*
*Rubus* 'Logan'
*Sambucus canadensis*
*Vaccinium corymbosum*
*Vitis labrusca*

### Warm-temperate

*Actinidia chinensis*
*Asimia triloba*
*Carya illinoinensis*
*Ceratonia siliqua*
*Citrullus lanatus*
*Cucumis melo*, Cantalupensis group
*Cucumis melo*, Indorus group
*Cucumis melo*, Reticulatus group
*Diospyros kaki*
*Eriobotrya japonica*
*Feijoa sellowiana*
*Ficus carica*
*Fortunella japonica*
*Olea europaea* subsp. *europaea*
*Passiflora edulis*
*Passiflora mollissima*
*Physalis peruviana*
*Pinus pinea*
*Pistacea vera*
*Punica granatum*
*Sechium edule*
*Vitis vinifera*
*Ziziphus jujuba*

### Citrus

*Citrus aurantifolia*
*Citrus aurantium*
*Citrus limon*
*Citrus medica*
*Citrus paradisi*
*Citrus reticulata*
*Citrus sinensis*
*Citrus sinensis* 'Washington Navel'
*Citrus* × *tangelo*

### Prunus

*Prunus armeniaca*
*Prunus avium*
*Prunus cerasus*
*Prunus domestica*
*Prunus dulcis*
*Prunus persica*
*Prunus persica* var. *nectarina*
*Prunus salicifolia*

## INDOOR PLANTS

Cultivation of indoor plants is simple if they are given positions with reasonable light and warmth, kept evenly moist (but slightly drier in winter), and have regular weak doses of liquid fertilizer. Check regularly for pests such as mealy bug, scale insects and mites on the stems and undersides of leaves, as these bugs thrive in warm, enclosed conditions. Also, take plants outside occasionally to wash the dust from the leaves, never allowing them to sit in the sun for long as they will quickly burn.

If you live in a warm climate, don't be tempted to plant indoor plants in the garden if they have become too big—they may grow even bigger outside and cause real problems.

Propagation is fairly easy, particularly from stem or leaf cuttings during the warmer months. Clump-forming types can be divided once they have outgrown their pots. Seasonal flowering plants such as cyclamen are best discarded after they flower, as they rarely perform as well the next year.

### Indoor foliage plants

*Alocasia macrorrhiza*
*Aspidistra elatior*
*Calathea makoyana*
*Calathea zebrina*
*Callisia navicularis*
*Codiaeum variegatum*
*Cordyline terminalis* 'Imperialis'
*Cryptanthus zonatus*
*Ctenanthe lubbersiana*
*Cyperus involucratus*
*Dieffenbachia* 'Amoena'
*Dieffenbachia seguine* 'Rudolph Roehrs'
*Dizygotheca elegantissima*
*Epipremnum aureum*
*Ficus benjamina*
*Ficus elastica* 'Decora'
*Ficus lyrata*
*Hedera helix* 'Cripsii'
*Hedera helix* 'Pittsburgh'
*Hypoestes phyllostachya*
*Maranta leuconeura* var. *kerchoviana*
*Monstera deliciosa*
*Neoregelia carolinae*
*Neoregelia marmorata*
*Nepenthes*
*Nidularium fulgens*
*Pedilanthus tithymaloides*
*Peperomia caperata*
*Peperomia obtusifolia*
*Peperomia* 'Sweetheart'
*Philodendron bipennifolium*
*Philodendron oxycardium*
*Philodendron selloum*
*Pisonia umbellifera* 'Variegata'
*Polyscias filicifolia*
*Protasparagus densiflorus* 'Sprengeri'
*Protasparagus setaceus*
*Sansevieria trifasciata*
*Sansevieria trifasciata* 'Hahnii'
*Sansevieria trifasciata* 'Laurentii'
*Schefflera actinophylla*
*Schefflera arboricola*
*Schefflera digitata*
*Syngonium podophyllum*
*Tolmiea menziesii*

### Indoor flowering and foliage plants

*Aeschynanthus radicans*
*Anthurium scherzerianum*
*Aphelandra squarrosa* 'Louisae'
*Ardisia crispa*
*Begonia auriculata*
*Begonia* × *cheimantha* 'Gloire de Lorraine'
*Begonia* 'Cleopatra'
*Begonia masoniana*
*Begonia rex* 'Merry Christmas'
*Billbergia leptopoda*
*Billbergia nutans*
*Billbergia pyramidalis* var. *concolor*
*Clerodendrum thomsoniae*
*Columnea gloriosa*
*Drosera capensis*
*Episcia cupreata*
*Episcia* 'Pink Brocade'
*Graptophyllum pictum*
*Guzmania*
*Hemigraphis alternata*
*Nematanthus gregarius*
*Serissa foetida*
*Sinningia speciosa*
*Spathiphyllum* 'Mauna Loa'
*Spathiphyllum wallisii*
*Tillandsia cyanea*
*Tillandsia lindenii*

### Indoor flowering plants

*Costus*
*Cyclamen persicum*
*Gesneria cuneifolia*
*Hoya bella*
*Hoya carnosa*
*Saintpaulia ionantha*
*Saintpaulia* miniature and trailing types

## CACTI & SUCCULENTS

Most of these weirdly decorative, fascinating plants are native to arid regions of the world and their cultivation requirements are fairly simple: that is, a warm, dry atmosphere and protection from too much moisture. The misconception arising from this, unfortunately, is that they should all be planted in the hottest, most desolate site in a garden or be allowed to languish in pots without any attention. This simply is not true.

Species such as *Epiphyllum*, *Haworthia* and *Kalanchoe* prefer shade and more fertile soil, and they will tolerate humidity. As a general rule, water well only during the growing or flowering periods then give them a rest.

Propagation is from seed or cuttings in spring and summer. The stored moisture inside leaves and stems in mucilaginous, or jelly like, and should be allowed to dry out slightly before propagation. Wear thick gloves when handling cacti with sharp spines and protect your eyes. Watch for pests such as scale insects, mealy bugs and aphids, which tend to hide between cacti spines or in the closely packed rosette leaves of succulents.

Cacti and succulents are fun to collect, so join a cacti and succulent society to obtain the more unusual ones or visit a specialist nursery and talk to an expert.

*Adenium multiflorum*
*Adenium obesum*
*Aeonium arboreum* 'Schwarzkopf'
*Aeonium canariense*
*Agave americana*
*Agave victoriae-reginae*
*Aloe arborescens*
*Aloe aristata*
*Aloe barbadensis*
*Aloe ciliaris*
*Aloe ferox*
*Aloe variegata*
*Aptenia cordifolia*
*Argyroderma delaetii*
*Astrophytum asterias*
*Astrophytum myriostigma*
*Azureocereus hertlingianus*
*Beschorneria yuccoides*
*Borzicactus celsianus*
*Carnegia gigantea*
*Carpobrotus edulis*
*Carpobrotus muirii*
*Cephalocereus senilis*
*Cereus peruvianus*
*Ceropegia woodii*
*Chamaecereus silvestrii*
*Cleisocactus strausii*
*Copiapoa cinerea*
*Copiapoa echinoides*
*Cotyledon orbiculata*
*Crassula arborescens*
*Crassula coccinea*
*Crassula ovata*
*Cyphostemma juttae*
*Dioscorea elephantipes*
*Drosanthemum bicolor*
*Drosanthemum floribundum*
*Echeveria elegans*
*Echeveria pulvinata*
*Echinocactus grusonii*
*Echinocereus reichenbachii*

*Echinocereus subinervis*
*Echinocereus viridiflorus*
*Echinopsis arachnacantha*
*Echinopsis* 'Green Gold'
*Echinopsis oxygona*
*Epiphyllum* hybrids
*Epiphyllum opypetalum*
*Euphorbia caput-medusae*
*Euphorbia obesa*
*Euphorbia trigona*
*Faucaria tigrina*
*Fenestraria aurantiaca*
*Ferocactus hamatacanthus*
*Furcraea foetida*
*Gasteria verrucosa*
*Graptopetalum paraguayense*
*Gymnocalycium andreae*
*Gymnocalycium mihanovichii*
*Haageocereus versicolor*
*Hatiora salicornioides*
*Haworthia bolusii*
*Haworthia fasciata*
*Hylocereus undatus*
*Kalanchoe blossfeldiana*
*Kalanchoe fedtschenkoi*
*Kalanchoe tomentosa*
*Lampranthus aurantiacus*
*Lampranthus aureus*
*Lampranthus coccineus*
*Lithops dorotheae*
*Lithops glesinae*
*Lithops karasmontana* var. *bella*
*Lithops turbiniformis*
*Lobivia backebergii*
*Lobivia bruchii*
*Lophocereus schottii*
*Lophophora williamsii*
*Mammillaria bombycina*
*Mammillaria elegans*
*Mammillaria plumosa*
*Mammillaria zeilmanniana*
*Mesembryanthemum crystallinum*
*Nopalxochia ackermannii*
*Nopalxochia phyllanthoides* 'Deutsche Kaiserin'
*Notocactus apricus*
*Opuntia ficus-indica*
*Opuntia violacea* var. *macrocentra*
*Orbea variegata*
*Pachyphytum oviferum*
*Pachypodium baronii* var. *windsori*
*Pachypodium lamerei*
*Parodia formosa*
*Parodia mutabilis*
*Parodia nivosa*
*Pilosocereus palmeri*
*Portulacaria afra*
*Rebutia aureiflora*
*Rebutia muscula*
*Rebutia pseudodeminuta*
*Rhipsalidopsis gaetneri*
*Rhipsalis paradoxa*
*Schlumbergera* x *buckleyi*
*Sedum acre*
*Sedum aizoon*
*Sedum morganianum*
*Sedum* x *rubrotinctum*
*Sedum spathulifolium*
*Selenicereus grandiflorus*
*Senecio articulatus*
*Stapelia leendertziae*
*Sulcorebutia arenacea*
*Thelocactus bicolor*
*Trichocereus bridgesii*
*Trichocereus huascha*

## ORCHIDS

There is a large and varied selection of orchids for warm-temperate climates, or cooler climates if extra protection is given over winter. You don't need a special glasshouse to cultivate orchids as they can be successfully grown outdoors in pots, in garden beds or on the trunks and branches of trees.

There is no great mystery to growing orchids, as their requirements are similar to those of other groups of plants. The correct temperature is the most important factor for success, although lighting, atmosphere, water supply and food should also be taken into consideration. Propagation is usually carried out in spring by division of well-established clumps. Methods of division will vary depending on the species.

Terrestrial orchids grown in gardens or pots need good drainage and plenty of leaf mold and well-rotted cow manure at planting time. Epiphytes can be grown in pots or on trees; if planting on a tree make sure it is one with rough, fibrous bark that does not shed. Pests and diseases will be kept to a minimum if plants are well fertilized and well watered and there is good air circulation around them.

If you want to include orchids in your garden, gauge your success rate by trying just one or two types first before considering a large and expensive collection.

*Ada aurantiaca*
*Aerides*
*Angraecum*
X *Angulocaste* hybrids
X *Ascocenda* hybrids
*Ascocentrum curvifolium*
*Bifrenaria harrisoniae*
*Bletilla striata*
*Brassovala nodosa*
*Brassia verrucosa*
X *Brassocattleya* hybrids
X *Brassolaeliocattleya* hybrids
*Calypso bulbosa*
*Cattleya bifoliate* hybrids
*Cattleya bowringiana*
*Cattleya labiata*
*Cattleya unifoliate* hybrids
*Coelogyne cristata*
*Coelogyne pandurata*
*Cymbidium*, large-flowered hybrids
*Cymbidium*, miniature hybrids
*Cymbidium* species
*Cypripedium calceolus*
*Cypripedium reginae*
*Dactylorhiza*
*Dendrobium*, cane-stemmed hybrids
*Dendrobium falcorostrum*
*Dendrobium kingianum*
*Dendrobium nobile*
*Dendrobium speciosum*
*Dendrobium thyrsiflorum*
*Disa*, hybrids
*Disa uniflora*
*Dracula bella*
*Encylcia cochleata*
*Epidendrum ibaguense*
*Epipactis gigantea*
*Eulophia speciosa*
*Gongora galeata*
*Laelia anceps*
*Laelia* Coronet
*Laelia purpurata*
X *Laeliocattleya* hybrids
*Lycaste virginalis*
*Masdevallia*
*Miltoniopsis*
*Odontoglossum crispum* and hybrids
*Odontoglossum grande*
*Oncidium papilio*
*Oncidium varicosum*
*Paphiopedilum*, hybrids
*Paphiopedilum insigne*
*Phaius tankervillae*
*Phalaenopsis amabilis*
*Pleione bulbocodioides*
*Pterostylis*
*Renanthera*
*Rhyncolaelia digbyana*
*Sarcochilus*
X *Sophrocattleya* hybrids
*Sophrolaeliocattleya* hybrids
*Sophronitis coccinea*
*Stanhopea wardii*
*Thunia marshalliana*
*Vanda* Nellie Morley
*Vanda* Rothschildiana
*Vuylstekeara*
*Wilsonara* hybrids
*Zygopetalum mackayi*

## FERNS, PALMS & CYCADS

Ferns thrive in quite unusual places and often appear on moist rock ledges or among rotting tree trunks where no soil seems to be present, which should give an indication of how best to grow them. They need fairly moist conditions, and plenty of leaf humus compost should be added to the soil before planting. Apply a weak solution of liquid fertilizer in the warmer months. During dry spells ferns may brown off or disappear completely, only to reappear after rain. Inspect new fronds for any signs of pests such as caterpillars, aphids or snails, which may congregate around the fresh young foliage and distort their growth before they get a chance to unravel.

Palm trees promote the image of carefree days on tropical islands. On a practical level, palms are ideal for growing close to swimming pools and structures as their root systems are not extensive or destructive. Add plenty of compost and a slow-release fertilizer at planting time. Mature palms are heavy feeders and enjoy frequent applications of nitrogenous fertilizer along with an adequate water supply. Pest and disease problems are more likely to occur on dry, underfed palms. Certain caterpillars and grasshoppers can sew the leaves of palms together, resulting in a ragged appearance. Control caterpillars with a bacterial pesticide, while grasshoppers can be controlled with a strong insecticide.

To propagate ferns, collect mature spore by placing older fronds in a paper bag until dry, or carefully divide older plants in spring. Propagation of palms is from seed, although this can be slow and erratic. Prune off old or dead fronds of both ferns and palms regularly to create a neat appearance, although many palms are "self-cleaning." Frost can cause considerable damage in cold districts, even to mature specimens, and will cause the fronds of ferns to blacken. In these areas choose hardy specimens and plant out in sheltered sites protected from wind.

### Ferns

*Adiantum capillus-veneris*
*Adiantum pedatum*
*Asplenium bulbiferum*
*Asplenium nidus*
*Athyrium filix-femina*
*Athyrium nipponicum* var. *pictum*
*Blechnum fluviatile*
*Blechnum penna-marina*
*Cyathea australis*
*Cyathea dealbata*
*Cyrtomium falcatum*
*Davallia trichomanoides*
*Dicksonia antarctica*
*Dicksonia squarrosa*
*Doodia aspera*
*Doodia media*
*Dryopteris erythrosora*
*Dryopteris filix-mas*
*Dryopteris marginalis*
*Humata tyermannii*
*Matteucia struthiopteris*
*Nephrolepis cordifolia*
*Nephrolepis exaltata*
*Onoclea sensibilis*
*Osmunda cinnamomea*
*Osmunda claytonia*
*Osmunda regalis*
*Pellaea rotundifolia*
*Phymatosorus diversifolius*
*Platycerium bifurcatum*
*Platycerium superbum*
*Polypodium aureum*
*Polypodium californicum*
*Polypodium virginianum*
*Polypodium vulgare*
*Polystichum acrostichoides*
*Polystichum munitum*
*Polystichum proliferum*
*Polystichum setiferum*
*Pteris cretica*
*Pteris ensiformis*
*Todea barbara*
*Woodwardia fimbriata*
*Woodwardia virginica*

### Palms & cycads

*Archontophoenix alexandrae*
*Archontophoenix cunninghamiana*
*Arecastrum romanzoffianum*
*Brahea armata*
*Brahea edulis*
*Butia capitata*
*Caryota*
*Chamaedorea elegans*
*Chamaedorea erumpens*
*Chamaerops humilis*
*Cocos nucifera*
*Cycas revoluta*
*Cyrtostachys renda*
*Encephalartos horridus*
*Euterpe edulis*
*Hedyscepe canterburyana*
*Howea belmoreana*
*Howea forsteriana*
*Jubaea chilensis*
*Laccospadix australasica*
*Livistona australis*
*Livistona chinensis*
*Macrozamia communis*
*Macrozamia spiralis*
*Neodypsis decaryi*
*Phoenix canariensis*
*Phoenix dactylifera*
*Phoenix reclinata*
*Phoenix roebelinii*
*Rhapidophyllum hystrix*
*Rhapis excelsa*
*Rhopalostylis baueri*
*Rhopalostylis sapida*
*Sabal mexicana*
*Sabal palmetto*
*Serenoa repens*
*Trachycarpus fortunei*
*Washingtonia filifera*
*Washingtonia robusta*
*Zammia pumila*

## CLIMBERS & CREEPERS

Climbers and creepers are adaptable to a wide range of climates, and even exotic-looking subtropical ones may adapt to cold, frosty areas. They will look ragged, tattered or even leafless over winter, but will spring back into growth once the weather warms up.

Be prepared to work hard with climbers and creepers, pruning, training and tying them up to shape them the way you want; even self-clinging types will wander if they are not controlled. Be careful not to leave training for too long, as brittle stems will break.

Carefully prepare the soil before planting climbers and creepers by digging in plenty of compost and a complete fertilizer to ensure healthy results. Adequate water during the growing season and mulching are also essential practices. Check the Seasonal Calendars for information on propagation and pest and disease problems.

### Warm-temperate to cool-temperate

*Akebia quinata*
*Ampelopsis brevipedunculata* var. *maximowiczii*
*Aristolochia durior*
*Aristolochia elegans*
*Asarina erubescens*
*Bignonia capreolata*
*Bomarea caldasii*
*Campsis grandiflora*
*Campsis radicans*
*Campsis* x *tagliabuana* 'Madame Galen'
*Celastrus orbiculatus*
*Celastrus scandens*
*Cissus antarctica*
*Clematis* 'Jackmanii'
*Clematis* x *lawsoniana* 'Henryi'
*Clematis montana*
*Clematis tangutica*
*Clematis viticella*
*Clitoria ternatea*
*Clytostoma callistegioides*
*Dolichos lablab*
*Eccremocarpus scaber*
*Gelsemium sempervirens*
*Hardenbergia violacea*
*Hedera canariensis* 'Variegata'
*Hedera helix*
*Hibbertia scandens*
*Hydrangea petiolaris*
*Jasminum officinale*
*Jasminum polyanthum*
*Kadsura japonica*
*Lapageria rosea*
*Lathyrus latifolius*
*Lathyrus odoratus*
*Lonicera caprifolium*
*Lonicera heckrottii*
*Lonicera japonica*
*Lonicera sempervirens*
*Mandevilla* x *amabilis* 'Alice du Pont'
*Mandevilla laxa*
*Mandevilla splendens*
*Parthenocissus quinquefolia*
*Parthenocissus tricuspidata*
*Polygonum aubertii*
*Rosa* 'America'
*Rosa banksiae* 'Alba Plena'
*Rosa banksiae lutea*
*Rosa* 'Blaze'
*Rosa* 'Climbing Cecile Brunner'
*Rosa* 'Climbing Peace'
*Rosa* 'Golden Showers'
*Rosa* 'Joseph's Coat'
*Rosa* 'Madame Alfred Carriere'
*Rosa* 'Mermaid'
*Rosa* 'New Dawn'
*Rosa* 'Zephirine Drouhin'
*Schizophragma hydrangeoides*
*Solanum jasminoides*
*Solanum seaforthianum*
*Stephanotis floribunda*
*Trachelospermum jasminoides*
*Tropaeolum speciosum*
*Vitis californica* 'Roger's Red'
*Vitis coignetiae*
*Vitis vinifera* 'Purpurea'
*Wisteria floribunda*
*Wisteria sinensis*
*Wisteria venusta*

### Tropical to subtropical

*Allamanda cathartica*
*Antigonon leptopus*
*Beaumontia grandiflora*
*Bougainvillea* cultivars
*Bougainvillea glabra*
*Bougainvillea spectabilis*
*Clematis armandii*
*Cobaea scandens*
*Combretum bracteosum*
*Distictis buccinatoria*
*Ficus pumila*
*Ipomoea alba*
*Ipomoea nil*
*Ipomoea quamoclit*
*Ipomoea tricolor*
*Kennedia rubicunda*
*Lonicera hildebrandiana*
*Macfadyena unguis-cati*
*Pandorea jasminoides*
*Pandorea pandorana*
*Passiflora caerulea*
*Passiflora coccinea*
*Phaseolus caracalla*
*Pyrostegia venusta*
*Solandra maxima*
*Thunbergia alata*
*Thunbergia grandiflora*

# Seasonal Calendars

| | SUMMER | | |
|---|---|---|---|
| **PLANT** | **JUNE** | **JULY** | **AUGUST** |
| ***ANNUALS & PERENNIALS*** | | | |
| *Annuals, low growing, spring–fall flowering* | Mulch plants to conserve water • Deadhead to prolong flowering • Add spent plants to compost • Practise crop rotation • Keep beds free of weeds • Sharpen and oil garden tools • Clean seed flats | Compost spent flowers • Watch for aphids, white fly; spray with pyrethrum • Peak flowering time • Store saved seed in dry place • Practise crop rotation • Keep beds free of weeds • Look for seed suppliers in garden magazines • Plan next spring's color scheme | Check for nematodes • Cut back straggly growth or replant with fresh seedlings • Spray powdery mildew with a fungicide or wettable sulfur • Add spent plants to compost • Practise crop rotation • Keep beds free of weeds • Sow seed in seed-raising mix in well-lit sheltered position |
| *Annuals, medium growing, spring–fall flowering* | Water and liquid fertilize regularly, paying particular attention to hanging baskets and containers • Compost to conserve water, suppress weeds and keep roots cool • Cut back flowering stems of *Lupinus* to prolong flowering into fall • Allow *Nigella* to produce decorative seed pods • Collect *Centaurea* seed when ripe | Remove spent flowers regularly to prolong flowering • Pick *Zinnia* flowers regularly to prolong flowering • Protect *Impatiens* from afternoon sun | Spray powdery mildew with a fungicide • Prune *Coleus* flower-heads as these are not required • Sow seed • As seedlings emerge drench soil with a fungicide to prevent damping off |
| *Annuals, tall growing, spring–fall flowering* | Remove spent flowers • Spray rust, leaf spot and powdery mildew with a fungicide or wettable sulfur • Mulch • Break down organic matter with liquid fertilizer • Spray black aphids with pyrethrum | Remove spent plants and add to compost heap • Practise crop rotation • Water well in dry weather • Spray mildew with a fungicide or wettable sulfur • Protect *Tropaeolum* from aphids and caterpillers | Sow seed in seed-raising mix • Protect seedlings from damping off using a fungicide • Cut back overgrown plants to continue flowering • Store saved seed in dry location • Add summer weeds to compost before seed sets |
| *Annuals, dahlias* | Mulch around plants to conserve water • Plant *Tagetes* around plants to discourage nematodes | Liquid fertilize before flowering and then at 2-week intervals • Protect plants from strong wind • Restake | Remove spent flowers to encourage continuous flowering • Spray mold/stem rot or mildew with a fungicide |
| *Annuals, pelargoniums* | Mulch around plants to conserve water • Water only during very dry spells | Spray bud caterpillars on flowers with an insecticide • Water early morning to discourage black stem rot • Treat soil with a fungicide | Spray rust on *P.* 'Orange Ricard' with a fungicide or wettable sulfur • Dead-head to keep plants tidy |
| *Perennials, spring–early summer flowering* | Prune dead flower stems of *Anigozanthos* and liquid fertilize • Divide *Geum* | *Dianella* produces blue berries after flowering—leave for their decorative value | Water *Anigozanthos* sparingly in humid weather to prevent root rot • Collar rot may occur in *Dianthus* • Gravel mulch |
| *Perennials, spring–early summer flowering, short lived* | Plants can be allowed to seed—scatter seed to produce new plants | Provide a mulch of compost but keep away from plant stems | Provide gravel mulch for those that need sharp drainage |
| *Perennials, summer flowering, sun* | Flowering begins • Liquid fertilize regularly • Keep surrounding area free of weeds | Remove spent flowers and add to compost • Ensure adequate water • Soak plants once a week if dry | Tidy up plants, removing old foliage • Liquid fertilize to encourage continuous blooming |
| *Perennials, summer flowering, shade to part shade* | Protect plants from hot drying winds • Ensure plentiful supply of water • Pick flowering stems to encourage more blooms | Liquid fertilize regularly • Check plants for snail or slug damage | Take cuttings from flowering stems of *Lobelia* • Remove old flowers of other plants |
| *Perennials, winter–early summer flowering* | Ensure adequate water • Provide a leaf compost and light dressing of blood and bone fertilizer • Protect plants from hot winds | Ensure adequate water • Provide a leaf compost and light dressing of blood and bone fertilizer • Protect plants from hot winds | Ensure adequate water • Provide a leaf compost and light dressing of blood and bone fertilizer • Protect plants from hot winds |

# Seasonal Calendars

## FALL

| SEPTEMBER | OCTOBER | NOVEMBER | PLANT |
|---|---|---|---|
| | | | ***ANNUALS & PERENNIALS*** |
| Liquid fertilize at 2-week intervals • Peak flowering time • Watch out for snails and caterpillars • Sow seed • Mix seed with sand for even coverage • Dress soil with dolomite/ lime; and/or add compost • Protect seedlings with a fungicide | Add spent flowers to compost• Peak flowering time • Store saved seed in dry place • Protect young seedlings from snails, avoiding products harmful to cats and dogs | Practise crop rotation • Use green manure crops • Wear safety equipment if you plan to spray • Protect seedlings from transplant shock by drenching soil with liquid fertilizer | *Annuals, low growing, spring–fall flowering* |
| Allow *Lunaria* to go to seed for decorative seed pods • Sow seed of *Anchusa* and *Eustoma;* keep moist until germination •Plant *Lupinus* with a minimum of fertilizer to encourage flowers • Plant seedlings • Apply lime when planting out *Matthiola* and *Gypsophila* | Cut back *Salvia* and *Catharanthus;* treat as biennials • Add spent annuals to compost heap • *Campanula, Senecio* and *Schizanthus* need cool, semi-shaded positions • Plant seedlings • Plant *Dianthus* with crown above soil level to avoid *Phytophthora* collar rot | Sow seed • Keep sheltered • For hard-to-get seeds contact a reputable seed supply company • Thin seedlings to avoid overcrowding and diseases | *Annuals, medium growing, spring-fall flowering* |
| Sow seed • Protect from damping off using a fungicide • Lightly apply dolomite/lime to soil; and/or add compost or waste from worm farm and slow-release fertilizer • Store saved seeds in dry location | Plant seedlings • Give weak solution of liquid fertilizer once established • Protect from snails • Add spent plants to compost heap • Practise crop rotation • Remove fall weeds as they appear | Plant seedlings • Give weak solution of liquid fertilizer once established • Investigate companion planting to reduce spraying with chemicals | *Annuals, tall growing, spring–fall flowering* |
| Flowering continues into fall • Give extra protection to flowers for exhibition • Water well in dry weather | Flowering continues into fall • Give extra protection to flowers for exhibition | Lift tubers as foliage dies • Dust with fungicide and store in cool, dry place • Leave tubers in well-drained soil | *Annuals, dahlias* |
| Take cuttings from overgrown summer growth; strike in sand • Keep cuttings in warm, dry location • Flowering of *P. peltatum* continues | Remove spent flowers and dead leaves | Remove old foliage and tidy up plants | *Annuals, pelargoniums* |
| Divide *Anigozanthos* and *Sisyrinchium* • Take cuttings of *Dianthus* • Sow seed of *Potentilla* and *Geum* | Plant *Lupinus*, Russell hybrids now but only in a cold climate • Plants begin winter dormancy • Plants may be divided now | Dig in compost and complete fertilizer • Apply low-phosphorus fertilizer to native plants • Divide *Lupinus*, Russell hybrids every 3–5 years | *Perennials, spring–early summer flowering* |
| Cut back old foliage of *Aquilegia* and mulch with compost • Liquid fertilize to encourage new growth | Prepare a cool site for *Anchusa, Aquilegia, Myosotis* and *Papaver,* apply compost and a complete fertilizer | Prepare a cool site for *Anchusa, Aquilegia, Myosotis* and *Papaver*; apply compost and a complete fertilizer | *Perennials, spring–early summer flowering, short lived* |
| Collect seed from flower stems and store in cool, dry place | Order new plants for summer flowering • Check heights and spread • Organize a color scheme | Cut down old flower stems to ground level • Plants may be divided now • Prepare soil as for March | *Perennials, summer flowering, sun* |
| Prepare soil with generous amount of compost, leaf mold, cocopeat • Order new plants • Collect seed and store in cool, dry place | Divide established plants | Tidy up plants of old flowering stems • Allow leaves from deciduous trees to gently cover established plants | *Perennials, summer flowering, shade to part shade* |
| *Bergenia* produces colored foliage in fall | Divide plants • Prepare soil with good quantity of compost and complete fertilizer | Plant together for spring display *Mertensia, Dicentra,* and *Ranunculus aconitifolius* in cool, shady spot | *Perennials, winter–early summer flowering* |

# Seasonal Calendars

| | WINTER | | |
|---|---|---|---|
| PLANT | DECEMBER | JANUARY | FEBRUARY |
| *ANNUALS & PERENNIALS* | | | |
| *Annuals, low growing, spring–fall flowering* | Sow seed in hot districts • Sharpen and oil garden tools • Tidy glasshouse • In frosty areas protect plants with loose straw or sow seed in protected position then plant when danger of frost is over | Join a garden club to discuss your success with others • In frosty areas protect plants with loose straw or sow seed in protected position then plant when frost is over • Flowering begins in warm districts | Sow seed • Lightly apply dolomite/ lime to soil; and/or add compost and apply complete or slow-release fertilizer • In shaded positions add extra cocopeat • In frosty areas protect plants with loose straw or sow seed in protected position then plant when frost is over • Spray with pyrethrum if aphids appear • Check underside of leaves |
| *Annuals, medium growing, spring–fall flowering* | Use loose straw to protect against frost, or plant seedlings in spring • Sow seed in hot districts • Protect seedlings from wind | Sow seed in warm districts • Plant a children's summer garden • Do not use sprays in gardens where children play • Use loose straw to protect against frost, or plant seedlings in spring • Protect seedlings from wind | Sow seed in warm districts • Plant a children's summer garden • Do not use sprays in gardens where children play • Avoid planting *Argemone* in warm districts where it can be a weed |
| *Annuals, tall growing, spring–fall flowering* | Protect seedlings from frost in cold districts or plant out when danger of frost is over • Look for seed suppliers in garden magazines • Sow seed in hot districts | Apply loose straw around plants to help protect from cold • Start a worm farm for valuable humus and summer fishing | Protect plants from cold winds • Give weak solution of liquid fertilizer • Sow seed, ensuring good light and even moisture • Lightly apply dolomite/lime to soil; and/or add compost and complete or slow-release fertilizer |
| *Annuals, dahlias* | Join a horticultural society and exhibit your dahlias at their meetings and shows | Join a horticultural society and exhibit your dahlias at their meetings and shows | Join a horticultural society and exhibit your dahlias at their meetings and shows |
| *Annuals, pelargoniums* | Protect plants in frosty areas • Move to warm location over winter | Prepare soil for summer display • Dig in compost and complete fertilizer • Ensure good drainage | Protect plants from strong winds |
| *Perennials, spring–early summer flowering* | Protect plants over winter with loose straw | Protect plants over winter with loose straw | Divide clumps of *Epimedium* and protect from snails |
| *Perennials, spring–early summer flowering, short lived* | Take root cuttings of *Papaver orientale*; plant pieces upright in pot | Protect plants in frosty areas with loose straw | Protect plants in frosty areas with loose straw |
| *Perennials, summer flowering, sun* | Protect plants with loose straw in frosty areas | Take root cuttings of *Acanthus, Echinops, Eryngium, Gaillardia, Verbascum* | Take root cuttings of *Acanthus, Echinops, Eryngium, Gaillardia, Verbascum* |
| *Perennials, summer flowering, shade to part shade* | Winter dormancy | Winter dormancy | Winter dormancy |
| *Perennials, winter–early summer flowering* | Lift *Dicentra* and divide with sharp knife into pieces with leaf bud and root attached | New foliage begins to appear • *Viola* and *Helleborus* in flower in warm districts • Take root cuttings of *Paeonia officinalis* | New foliage begins to appear • Some may start to flower • Apply a weak solution of liquid fertilizer |

# Seasonal Calendars

## SPRING

| MARCH | APRIL | MAY | PLANT |
|---|---|---|---|
| | | | *ANNUALS & PERENNIALS* |
| Sow seed or plant seedlings • Water regularly • Protect from snails • Apply liquid fertilizer at 2-week intervals to increase humus level and prevent transplant shock • Pinch out growing tips to encourage bushy growth • Spray leaf spot with a fungicide • Plant seedlings in cool districts • Remove spent flowers to encourage more blooms | Thin seedlings if too close • Plant seedlings in cold districts • Protect seedlings from damping off with a fungicide • Spray caterpillars with a pesticide • Check undersides of leaves • Dead-head *Viola* to prolong flowering • Flowering continues • Keep surrounding area free of weeds | Collect rainwater to water garden • Tip prune • Liquid fertilize buds at 2-week intervals • Plant up containers • Flowering continues • If growth is poor, check soil for nematode activity • Keep surrounding area free of weeds | *Annuals, low growing, spring–fall flowering* |
| Plant seed in cold areas after danger of frost has passed • Cultivate soil for direct sowing to fine tilth and add sand • Check *Senecio* for leaf miner and spray with an insecticide | Protect young seedlings from snails and slugs • Practise crop rotation • As buds appear liquid fertilize at 2-week intervals | Lightly trim *Kochia* • As flower buds form, liquid fertilize at 2-week intervals • Spray rust on foliage underside with a fungicide • Spray budworm on *Dianthus* buds with an insecticide • Pick flowers for indoor decoration | *Annuals, medium growing, spring–fall flowering* |
| Provide support for flower stems using lightweight stakes • Plant seedlings in cold districts • Sow seed direct or plant out seedlings when danger of frost is over • Protect from snails • Apply liquid fertilizer when transplanting seedlings | Spray pests with pyrethrum or use biological control • Liquid fertilize regularly to promote flowering • Thin out seedlings and support with stakes or tripods • Spray caterpillars with an insecticide | Remove spent flowers • Spray rust and powdery mildew with a fungicide or wettable sulfur • Mulch • Break down organic matter with liquid fertilizer • Spray cutworms with an insecticide • Control weeds to reduce cutworm population • Sow extra seed to fill in gaps of planting | *Annuals, tall growing, spring–fall flowering* |
| Order dahlia tubers from a reputable grower • Apply compost, complete fertilizer or slow-release fertilizer; avoid high nitrogen fertilizer | Plant tubers • Provide a stake at planting time | Tip prune new growth to encourage bushy, compact growth • Set traps to control earwigs • Check for snails in foliage | *Annuals, dahlias* |
| Flowering • Remove dead flowers | Tip prune regularly • Plant *P. crispum* or *P. tomentosum* near a path so they release fragrance when brushed against | Liquid fertilize regularly to encourage flowers | *Annuals, pelargoniums* |
| Main flowering season begins • Plant *Centranthus* in or near rock walls so it can establish in cracks or crevices • Divide *Tanacetum* | Take cuttings of *Silene* • Spray budworm on *Dianthus* with an insecticide | Collect seed as it matures • Allow *Euphorbia* to self-seed | *Perennials, spring–early summer flowering* |
| Main flowering period • Dead-head flowers to encourage continuous blooming • Fresh seed may be sown | Main flowering period • Dead-head flowers to encourage continuous blooming • Fresh seed may be sown | Cut back plants after flowering • Use for cuttings | *Perennials, spring–early summer flowering, short lived* |
| Take stem cuttings • Divide plants • Lightly dress soil with lime; dig in compost, complete fertilizer or slow-release fertilizer for perennials | Protect new foliage from snails and slugs • Take stem cuttings from established plants | Mulch around plants to conserve water and suppress weeds • Add water-storing granules in dry areas • Side dress plants with blood and bone | *Perennials, summer flowering, sun* |
| Plant seed and keep moist until germination in warm, sheltered place | Side dress with blood and bone as weather warms up | Mulch garden and compost around plants | *Perennials, summer flowering, shade to part shade* |
| Divide clumps of *Pulmonaria* • Plants in flower | Collect and sow seed as it ripens • Stake tall-flowering stems • Spray paeony wilt with a fungicide | *Mertensia* dies down • Pot on self-sown seedlings | *Perennials, winter–early summer flowering* |

| | SUMMER | | |
|---|---|---|---|
| PLANT | JUNE | JULY | AUGUST |
| ***ANNUALS & PERENNIALS*** *(continued)* | | | |
| *Perennials, summer–fall flowering* | Mulch around plants to conserve water and suppress weeds • Watch for snails and slugs | Liquid fertilize regularly • Flowering stems appear • Ensure adequate water | Flowering • Provide stakes for tall flower stems • Ensure adequate water |
| *Perennials, ground covers & rock plants, temperate climate* | Mulch plants with compost; side dress with blood and bone fertilizer • Remove spent flowers • Cut back hard plants that overgrow others | Keep surrounding area free of weeds | Provide gravel mulch in humid conditions to prevent root rot diseases of *Gazania*, *Lotus*, *Arctotis* and *Phlox* • Take semi-ripe cuttings |
| *Perennials, alpines, ground covers & rock plants, cool climate* | Plan a drystone wall for plants such as *Erinus alpinus*, *Tanacetum* and *Sempervivum* • Cut back spring-flowering plants | Take semi-ripe cuttings • Provide shade and extra water if required • Remove dead sections from rosette plants | Take semi-ripe cuttings • Provide shade and extra water if required • Remove dead sections from rosette plants |
| *Perennials, sub-shrubs, sun* | Mulch plants with compost; side dress with blood and bone • Cuttings may be planted out | Spray leaf miner on *Argyranthemum* with an insecticide • Ensure adequate water during dry spells | Remove flowering stems of *Hypericum* when spent |
| *Perennials, sub-shrubs, shade to part shade* | Flowering season • Ensure adequate water during summer months • Apply liquid fertilizer regularly | Flowering season • Ensure adequate water during summer months • Apply liquid fertilizer regularly | Spray powdery mildew on *Ajuga* with a fungicide |
| *Perennials, water garden plants* | Feed water plants with slow-release fertilizer | Cut back plants which crowd out others • Take softwood cuttings | Collect ripe seed from water plants • Sow and keep covered |
| *Perennials, for tropical effect* | Mulch with compost and ensure adequate water for summer flowering • Keep *Sarracenia* wet during summer months | Spray stem borer on *Hedychium* with an insecticide • Remove toxic flowers from *Ricinus* | Spray stem borer on *Hedychium* with an insecticide • Remove toxic flowers from *Ricinus* |
| *Perennials, irises* | Fertilize and mulch | Divide and replant bearded irises | Divide and replant bearded irises |
| *Perennials, primulas* | Liquid fertilize regularly • Remove old leaves around base of plants | Keep plants moist during summer • Shelter from hot winds | Remove plants after 3 years if flowering diminishes • Spray two-spotted mite with an insecticide • Plant seed of *P.* × *polyantha* |
| ***SHRUBS*** | | | |
| *Low growing, frost hardy, evergreen* | Provide adequate water during dry spells • Prune after flowering • Mulch and fertilize | Take semi-ripe cuttings • Tip prune regularly | Check for insect pests • Prune after flowering • Mulch and fertilize |
| *Low growing, frost tender, evergreen* | Check for summer pests • Provide adequate water during dry spells | Mulch • Fertilize | Ensure good drainage in hot, humid weather |
| *Low growing, frost hardy, deciduous* | Take softwood cuttings • Mulch and fertilize • Check for summer insect pests | Provide adequate water during dry spells • Mulch | Prune after flowering • Mulch and fertilize |
| *Medium to tall growing, frost hardy, evergreen* | Provide adequate water during dry spells • Prune after flowering • Mulch and fertilize | Take semi-ripe cuttings • Tip prune regularly | Check for insect pests • Prune after flowering • Mulch and fertilize |
| *Medium to tall growing, frost tender, evergreen* | Check for summer pests • Provide adequate water during dry spells | Mulch • Fertilize | Ensure good drainage in hot, humid weather |
| *Medium to tall growing, frost hardy, deciduous* | Take softwood cuttings • Mulch and fertilize • Check for summer insect pests | Ensure adequate water during dry spells • Mulch | Prune after flowering • Mulch and fertilize |
| *Acacia* | Check older plants for signs of borer, sawdust or small holes in trunk | Ensure adequate water during dry spells • Remove galls if they appear at ends of stems | Lightly prune to shape |

| FALL | | | |
|---|---|---|---|
| **SEPTEMBER** | **OCTOBER** | **NOVEMBER** | **PLANT** |
| | | | ***ANNUALS & PERENNIALS*** *(continued)* |
| Peak flowering • Cut flower stems for indoor decoration | Peak flowering | Flowering may continue until frosts • Cut spent flower stems to ground level • Divide established plants | *Perennials, summer–fall flowering* |
| Take cuttings of *Gazania* and place in peat/sand mix in warm position • Second flush of flowers as weather cools | Plants may be divided • Liquid fertilize plants in warm districts • Sow seed of *Globularia* | Reset stones in rock gardens to protect plants during winter • If gravel mulch is used replenish bare patches | *Perennials, ground covers & rock plants, temperate climate* |
| Take cuttings now • Sow seed and keep moist until germination | Divide mat- and clump-forming plants • If gravel mulch is used replenish bare patches | Protect plants from winter wet if necessary • Plan a raised bed to display alpine plants | *Perennials, alpines, ground covers & rock plants, cool climate* |
| Plant seed collected during summer; keep moist until germination • Light pruning of plants | *Solanum* produces bright, decorative fruit • Spot flowering occurs on other plants | *Solanum* produces bright, decorative fruit • Spot flowering occurs on other plants | *Perennials, sub-shrubs, sun* |
| *Campanula* continues to flower • Cut back rampant growth of *Vinca* and *Glechoma* | Plants may be divided now | Allow leaves from deciduous trees to protect plants over winter | *Perennials, sub-shrubs, shade to part shade* |
| Divide established clumps of waterside plants • Secure loose edging stones around ponds | Remove all dead or dying foliage from submerged plants | Cover ponds to keep out leaves from deciduous trees • Move frost-tender plants to warm position | *Perennials, water garden plants* |
| Add plenty of manure and compost to soil • Establish plants in pots then plant in spring | Cut down flowering stems of *Alpinia, Begonia, Coleus* and *Hedychium* after they have finished flowering • Tidy up plants | Cut down flowering stems of *Alpinia, Begonia, Coleus* and *Hedychium* after they have finished flowering • Tidy up plants | *Perennials, for tropical effect* |
| Sow seed and keep moist until germination | Divide overcrowded clumps • Do not damage rhizomes when digging up • Cut foliage down before replanting | Divide overcrowded clumps • Do not damage rhizomes when digging up • Cut foliage down before replanting | *Perennials, irises* |
| Apply blood and bone to existing plants • Remove plants that flower poorly | Prepare garden site with compost and old manure • Select site with heavy or clay soil | Set out new plants • Divide old plants; trim old roots and excess foliage • *P. × polyantha* begins to flower | *Perennials, primulas* |
| | | | ***SHRUBS*** |
| Choose shrub for right location • Prepare planting site with compost and complete fertilizer | Water well until established • Mulch | Water well until established | *Low growing, frost hardy, evergreen* |
| Lightly prune • Mulch • Lightly fertilize | Add compost and complete fertilizer at planting time | Add compost and complete fertilizer at planting time | *Low growing, frost tender, evergreen* |
| Mulch • Lightly fertilize for winter hardiness | Fall color on some plants | Fall color on some plants | *Low growing, frost hardy, deciduous* |
| Choose right shrub for right location • Prepare planting site with compost and complete fertilizer | Water well until established • Mulch | Water well until established | *Medium to tall growing, frost hardy, evergreen* |
| Mulch • Lightly prune • Lightly fertilize | Add compost and complete fertilizer at planting time | Add compost and complete fertilizer at planting time | *Medium to tall growing, frost tender, evergreen* |
| Mulch • Lightly fertilize for winter hardiness | Leaves on some plants color in fall | Leaves on some plants color in fall | *Medium to tall growing, frost hardy, deciduous* |
| Top up mulch around plants • Lightly fertilize with blood and bone • Ensure soil is moist before applying fertilizer and water in well | Plant new specimens • Prepare soil by digging in compost and slow-release fertilizer | Plant new specimens • Prepare soil by digging in compost and slow-release fertilizer | *Acacia* |

| | WINTER | | |
|---|---|---|---|
| **PLANT** | **DECEMBER** | **JANUARY** | **FEBRUARY** |
| **ANNUALS & PERENNIALS** *(continued)* | | | |
| *Perennials, summer–fall flowering* | Winter dormancy | Winter dormancy | Protect emerging foliage from snail damage |
| *Perennials, ground covers & rock plants, temperate climate* | Protect plants with loose straw in frosty areas • Provide minimum water over winter | Protect plants with loose straw in frosty areas • Provide minimum water over winter | Prepare soil for spring planting with compost and general-purpose fertilizer • Prepare heavy soil with gypsum and drainage material |
| *Perennials, alpines, ground covers & rock plants, cool climate* | Protect plants from winter wet if necessary • Plan a raised bed to display alpine plants | Apply loamy soil, cocopeat and sharp sand. Provide extra cocopeat for acid-loving plants such as *Gentiana* | Apply loamy soil, cocopeat and sharp sand. Provide extra cocopeat for acid-loving plants such as *Gentiana* |
| *Perennials, sub-shrubs, sun* | Take root cuttings of *Romneya*; plant upright in a pot • Protect plants in areas of severe frost | Take root cuttings of *Romneya*; plant upright in a pot • Protect plants in areas of severe frost | Take root cuttings of *Romneya*; plant upright in a pot • Protect plants in areas of severe frost |
| *Perennials, sub-shrubs, shade to part shade* | Allow leaves from deciduous trees to protect plants over winter | Allow leaves from deciduous trees to protect plants over winter | Allow leaves from deciduous trees to protect plants over winter |
| *Perennials, water garden plants* | Cover ponds to keep out leaves from deciduous trees • Move frost-tender plants to warm position | Cover ponds to keep out leaves from deciduous trees • Move frost-tender plants to warm position | Clean and drain pond or water garden in preparation for spring planting |
| *Perennials, for tropical effect* | *Coleus thyrsoides* in flower • Reduce watering and allow plants to rest | Propagate *Coleus thyrsoides* from seed under glass | Propagate *Coleus thyrsoides* from seed under glass |
| *Perennials, irises* | Divide overcrowded clumps, if necessary | Divide overcrowded clumps, if necessary | Divide overcrowded clumps, if necessary |
| *Perennials, primulas* | Take root cuttings of *P. denticulata* in 2 in (about 5 cm) pieces; propagate in sharp sand | *P. obconica* flowering for indoor use; those with sensitive skin may have allergic reaction to this plant | Remove old flowers from *P. obconica* • Move outdoors as weather warms up |
| **SHRUBS** | | | |
| *Low growing, frost hardy, evergreen* | Protect young plants in frosty areas | Protect young plants in frosty areas | Protect young plants in frosty areas |
| *Low growing, frost tender, evergreen* | Provide some winter protection if growing in cold districts | Provide some winter protection if growing in cold districts | Prune after flowering in warm districts • Mulch and fertilize |
| *Low growing, frost hardy, deciduous* | Take hardwood cuttings | Flowering may begin in warm districts | Flowering may begin |
| *Medium to tall growing, frost hardy, evergreen* | Protect young plants in frosty areas | Protect young plants in frosty areas | Protect young plants in frosty areas |
| *Medium to tall growing, frost tender, evergreen* | Provide some winter protection if growing in cold districts | Provide some winter protection if growing in cold districts | Prune after flowering in warm districts • Mulch and fertilize |
| *Medium to tall growing, frost hardy, deciduous* | Take hardwood cuttings | Remove dead wood • Flowering may begin in warm districts | Flowering may begin |
| *Acacia* | Flowering begins | Flowering | Flowering |
| *Buddleia* | Plants may be deciduous in very cold districts | — | Cut out old or woody stems |

| SPRING | | | |
|---|---|---|---|
| **MARCH** | **APRIL** | **MAY** | **PLANT** |
| | | | ***ANNUALS & PERENNIALS*** *(continued)* |
| Divide plants • Take root cuttings of *Verbascum* • Take care in handling *Aconitum* as it is very poisonous | Add compost around plants • Side dress established plants with blood and bone | Side dress plants with blood and bone | *Perennials, summer–fall flowering* |
| Flowering • Take stem cuttings • Keep surrounding area free of weeds | Flowering • Remove spent blooms regularly • Keep surrounding area free of weeds | Flowering • Plants may be divided or cut back after flowering • Liquid fertilize regularly to prolong flowering into summer | *Perennials, ground covers & rock plants, temperate climate* |
| Plant out rock garden plants • Fertilize lightly with complete plant food or slow-release fertilizer | Plants begin to flower and continue into summer • Plants may be divided now | Flowering continues • Plants may be divided | *Perennials, alpines, ground covers & rock plants, cool climate* |
| Liquid fertilize as plants come into bud • For planting out choose a sunny, well-drained, light soil | Main flowering period through to late summer • Take cuttings and strike in sand/peat mix | Flowering • Prune after flowering to maintain good shape • Water well in dry weather | *Perennials, sub-shrubs, sun* |
| Divide overgrown clumps • Replant with addition of compost | Place flat rocks near plants for them to grow over and keep roots cool • *Polygonum* in flower | Mulch around plants with leaf mold compost; side dress with blood and bone | *Perennials, sub-shrubs, shade to part shade* |
| Prepare planting site • Use compost and well-rotted cow manure • Plant marginal, shallow, deep water plants | Divide overcrowded plants • Plant water plants in heavy loam with compost and slow-release fertilizer | Provide gravel mulch over water plants if fish are active | *Perennials, water garden plants* |
| Divide established clumps of *Alpinia, Hedychium* and *Phormium* • Take stem cuttings of *Begonia* | Divide established clumps of *Alpinia, Hedychium* and *Phormium* • Take stem cuttings of *Begonia* | Liquid fertilize *Impatiens* to produce good flowers | *Perennials, for tropical effect* |
| Fertilize and mulch | Visit a specialist grower to choose correct iris for your garden • Apply generous compost • Check soil pH before planting | Check plants for any sign of pests and disease, especially discolored or streaked foliage • Iris may suffer from fungus disease | *Perennials, irises* |
| Sow seed in seed-raising mix • *P. vulgaris* in flower • *P.* × *polyantha* in full flower | Treat gray mold botrytis with a fungicide • *P. viallii* in flower | Mulch around plants • Remove spent flowers • *P. florindae* in flower • Plant seed of *P.* × *polyantha* in summer months | *Perennials, primulas* |
| | | | ***SHRUBS*** |
| Prune after flowering | Sow seed and keep moist until germination | Take semi-ripe cuttings • Mulch • Lightly fertilize | *Low growing, frost hardy, evergreen* |
| Fertilize established shrubs • Add compost and complete fertilizer at planting time | Add compost and complete fertilizer at planting time | Take semi-ripe cuttings • Mulch | *Low growing, frost tender, evergreen* |
| Flowering | Prune after flowering • Mulch and fertilize | Prune after flowering • Mulch and fertilize | *Low growing, frost hardy, deciduous* |
| Prune after flowering • Mulch and fertilize | Prune after flowering • Mulch and fertilize • Sow seed and keep moist until germination | Take semi-ripe cuttings • Mulch • Lightly fertilize | *Medium to tall growing, frost hardy, evergreen* |
| Fertilize established shrubs • Add compost and complete fertilizer at planting time | Add compost and complete fertilizer at planting time | Mulch • Take semi-ripe cuttings | *Medium to tall growing, frost tender, evergreen* |
| Flowering | Prune after flowering • Mulch and fertilize | Prune after flowering • Mulch and fertilize | *Medium to tall growing, frost hardy, deciduous* |
| Flowering | Collect ripe seed as covering turns brown • Treat with boiling water before sowing | Lightly prune • Apply mulch • Side dress with slow-release fertilizer | *Acacia* |
| Cut back plants • Add compost and complete fertilizer | Give plenty of space when planting | *B. globosa* begins to flower | *Buddleia* |

| PLANT | SUMMER<br>JUNE | JULY | AUGUST |
|---|---|---|---|
| ***SHRUBS*** *(continued)* | | | |
| *Buddleia* | *B. davidii* in flower | Prune spent flowers regularly to encourage continuous blooming | Ensure adequate water during dry spells, although all are drought tolerant |
| *Callistemon* | Take cuttings of semi-ripe wood • Apply mulch around plants • Fertilize lightly with complete or slow-release plant food | Ensure adequate water during dry spells • Mulch well • Tip bug may cause wilting and death of young shoots | Check for pests: sawfly larvae may defoliate shrubs, thrip damage may cause deformed leaves |
| *Camellia* | Sunburn may cause brown patches on leaves; move plant to cooler location | Check for aphids, thrips and mealy bug • Cut out variegated leaves • Ensure adequate water in hot weather | Check for aphids, thrips and mealy bug • Cut out variegated leaves • Ensure adequate water in hot weather |
| *Cestrum* | Take semi-ripe or softwood cuttings • Main flowering time | Prune old or recently flowered branches • Collect seed from mature specimens | Provide adequate water to encourage continuous flowering |
| *Cistus* | Apply gravel mulch to imitate natural habitat | Ensure adequate water during dry spells, although *Cistus* is drought tolerant | *Cistus* resents humid weather • Ensure soil is well drained • Allow free air movement around plants |
| *Correa* | Keep moist during dry spells | Keep moist during dry spells | Propagate from semi-ripe cuttings |
| *Cotoneaster* | Take cuttings from semi-ripe wood • Flowering now | *Cotoneaster* is drought tolerant | Lightly fertilize, watering in well |
| *Erica* | *E. cinerea* in flower • Lightly prune after flowering | *E. bauera* in flower | Take cuttings now |
| *Euphorbia* | Take cuttings of semi-ripe wood • Ensure adequate water | Ensure adequate water | Ensure adequate water |
| *Fuchsia* | Liquid fertilize regularly to promote continuous flowering | Provide adequate water during dry spells | Cuttings may be taken • Check leaves for two-spotted mite damage |
| *Gardenia* | If growth is stunted dig up plants and check roots for nematode infestation; treat soil with a nematicide or plant *Tagetes* | Ensure adequate water during dry spells or buds may drop • Check for scale insects and mealy bug on leaves and stems | Some leaves will turn yellow and drop off • If foliage is yellow or pale green add iron or magnesium |
| *Genista* | Take cuttings now | Prune lightly after flowering | Prune lightly after flowering |
| *Grevillea* | Check leaves for caterpillar larvae, especially on tip growth • Spray with pyrethrum • Tip prune regularly | Check plants for scale insects; spray with white oil • Take cuttings of semi-ripe wood | *G.* 'Robyn Gordon' may develop leaf spot disease in humid weather |
| *Hakea* | Take cuttings of semi-ripe wood • Fungal leaf spot may occur | Spray caterpillar larvae with pyrethrum | Root rot diseases may occur • Ensure sharp drainage |
| *Hebe* | Ensure adequate water during dry spells, although most are drought tolerant | Check for damage by scale insects or leaf miner • *H.* × *andersonii* in flower | Downy mildew may occur in humid weather; spray with a fungicide |
| *Hibiscus* | Check for insect pests but spray only when necessary | Hibiscus spray will control aphids, caterpillars | Do not apply mulch around stem or collar rot may occur |
| *Hydrangea* | Protect from hot dry winds, as foliage and flowers may burn | Provide adequate water and mulch well • Two-spotted mite may cause silvery leaves | Powdery mildew may occur in humid weather; spray with a fungicide • Take cuttings |
| *Ilex* | Watch for holly leaf miner and holly aphid | Watch for holly leaf miner and holly aphid | Apply plenty of leaf mulch |
| *Juniperus* | — | Check for aphids and scale insects | Check for aphids and scale insects |

| FALL | | | |
|---|---|---|---|
| SEPTEMBER | OCTOBER | NOVEMBER | PLANT |
| | | | ***SHRUBS*** *(continued)* |
| Prune old flowers • Apply compost around plants | Prune lightly | Prune lightly | *Buddleia* |
| Sow seed collected from previous season; keep moist until germination • Lightly fertilize with blood and bone | Mulch well and check again for insect pests | Watch for web worm in dry districts | *Callistemon* |
| Lightly fertilize; water well before and after • Apply compost mulch around plants; keep away from main stem | Debud large flowering varieties to encourage better size and color • *C. sasanqua* in flower • Established plants may be moved | Debud | *Camellia* |
| Mulch around plants • Lightly fertilize | Tip prune regularly | Tip prune regularly | *Cestrum* |
| Prune lightly • Tip prune | *Cistus* tolerates coastal conditions | *Cistus* tolerates coastal conditions | *Cistus* |
| Mulch with gum leaves • Tip prune regularly • Lightly fertilize with blood and bone | *Correa* are suitable for coastal gardens | Flowering begins and continues to spring | *Correa* |
| Red fruits appear • Cut branches for indoor decoration | Collect and sow seed; keep moist until germination | Keep seed moist | *Cotoneaster* |
| Provide well-drained soil for planting • Check soil pH | Cut old flowering stems and lightly prune to shape | — | *Erica* |
| Mulch around plants and fertilize | Mulch around plants and fertilize | Leaves fall from *E. pulcherrima* as flowers form | *Euphorbia* |
| Plant in sites sheltered from strong wind • Apply compost and complete fertilizer before planting • Lightly fertilize established plants | Flowering continues in warm districts | Flowering may continue in warm districts | *Fuchsia* |
| Tip prune regularly • Lightly fertilize with blood and bone | Second flush of flowers may occur | Second flush of flowers may occur | *Gardenia* |
| Sow seed now; keep moist until germination | Keep seed moist | — | *Genista* |
| Top up mulch after summer and lightly fertilize | Flowering most of the year • Lightly prune regularly | Flowering most of the year • Lightly prune regularly | *Grevillea* |
| Top up mulch after summer and lightly fertilize | Top up mulch after summer and lightly fertilize | — | *Hakea* |
| Mulch • Lightly fertilize with complete fertilizer | Remove spent flowers of *H.* × *andersonii* | — | *Hebe* |
| Select a warm location for planting • Ensure good drainage • Dig in compost • Fertilize once established | Flowering continues | Flowering continues | *Hibiscus* |
| Flowering | Remove spent flowerheads | Remove spent flowers • Prune out dead wood | *Hydrangea* |
| Propagate from semi-hardwood cuttings | Propagate from semi-hardwood cuttings | *I. verticillata* has masses of tiny red berries | *Ilex* |
| — | — | Foliage may start to change color | *Juniperus* |

| | WINTER | | |
|---|---|---|---|
| **PLANT** | **DECEMBER** | **JANUARY** | **FEBRUARY** |
| ***SHRUBS*** *(continued)* | | | |
| *Callistemon* | Watch for web worm in dry districts | — | — |
| *Camellia* | Select camellias while in flower • Sun may damage flowers in morning if wet with dew | Prepare planting site • Dig in plenty of compost • Add cocopeat • Ensure soil is well drained to deter root rot | Prune while blooming to remove dead, diseased or straggling branches |
| *Cestrum* | Protect plants in very cold districts from frost damage with hessian | Protect plants in very cold districts from frost damage with hessian | Prune frost-damaged stems when all danger of frost is over |
| *Cistus* | Protect from very cold winds | Protect from very cold winds | Protect from very cold winds |
| *Correa* | Flowering | Flowering | Flowering |
| *Cotoneaster* | *C. horizontalis* is deciduous in cold climates | *C. horizontalis* is deciduous in cold climates | *C. horizontalis* is deciduous in cold climates |
| *Erica* | — | *E. carnea* in flower • Tolerates a position with some lime | *E. carnea* in flower |
| *Euphorbia* | Protect flowering stems from strong winds | Protect flowering stems from strong winds | Protect flowering stems from strong winds |
| *Fuchsia* | Provide some shelter from cold winter winds | Frost may damage some stems but growth will recommence in spring | Frost may damage some stems but growth will recommence in spring |
| *Gardenia* | Provide shelter from cold winds • Move plants in pots to warm location in frosty areas | Provide shelter from cold winds • Move plants in pots to warm location in frosty areas | Provide shelter from cold winds • Move plants in pots to warm location in frosty areas |
| *Genista* | — | — | — |
| *Grevillea* | Protect young plants in frosty areas; provide gravel mulch and hessian cover at night | Protect young plants in frosty areas; provide gravel mulch and hessian cover at night | Protect young plants in frosty areas; provide gravel mulch and hessian cover at night |
| *Hakea* | Protect plants when young in frosty areas; provide gravel mulch and hessian cover at night | Protect plants when young in frosty areas; provide gravel mulch and hessian cover at night | Protect plants when young in frosty areas; provide gravel mulch and hessian cover at night |
| *Hebe* | *H. speciosa* flowering | *H. speciosa* flowering | *H. speciosa* flowering |
| *Hibiscus* | In warm districts cut back by half deciduous hibiscus, *H. mutabilis* and *H. syriacus* • After pruning mulch and fertilize with complete fertilizer | As for June in cooler districts • Use prunings for cutting material | — |
| *Hydrangea* | Frost may cause some damage in cold districts; wait until spring to prune | Prune *H. macrophylla* in warm climates; prune to flowering buds | Prune *H. macrophylla* in cool climates; prune to flowering buds |
| *Ilex* | *I. aquifolium* has bright red berries; use as Christmas ornaments | Ensure soil is moist but well drained | Ensure soil is moist but well drained |
| *Juniperus* | Foliage may change color | Take hardwood cuttings | Take hardwood cuttings |

## SPRING

| MARCH | APRIL | MAY | PLANT |
|---|---|---|---|
| | | | **SHRUBS** *(continued)* |
| Flowering period | Flowering period | Prune off all spent flowers; retain some for seed collection | *Callistemon* |
| Test soil pH if growth is unsatisfactory | Prune long or straggly growth • Lightly fertilize with azalea/camellia food | Mulch around plants as weather warms up • Spray scale insect attack with white oil | *Camellia* |
| Sow seed in seed-raising mix; keep moist until germination • Cut old or woody shrubs back hard to encourage new growth | Mulch around plants • Apply light application of complete fertilizer | Tip prune regularly to encourage bushy shape | *Cestrum* |
| Ensure perfect drainage when planting • Dig in compost and slow-release fertilizer | Flowering • Prune lightly after flowering | Take cuttings • Apply light application of fertilizer | *Cistus* |
| Sow seed; keep moist until germination | Prune over lightly | Mulch well and keep moist during dry spells | *Correa* |
| Lightly prune • Fertilize with complete fertilizer | When planting ensure soil is well drained | Mulch plants to conserve water | *Cotoneaster* |
| Dig in plenty of compost and complete fertilizer before planting | Sow seed; keep moist until germination | Fertilize and mulch | *Erica* |
| Choose a warm, sunny location for planting • Prune as flowers fade | Mulch and fertilize • Prune as flowers fade | Ensure adequate water, although most are drought tolerant | *Euphorbia* |
| Prune • Fertilize with complete fertilizer | Tip prune young plants for good shape | Mulch around plants with compost • Train as standards if desired | *Fuchsia* |
| Dig in plenty of compost and complete or slow-release fertilizer • Check soil pH: it should be slightly acid | Prune old or woody plants hard • Fertilize and mulch | Remove spent flowers regularly • Check for thrips | *Gardenia* |
| Prune lightly • Fertilize lightly with complete fertilizer | *Genista* are suitable for coastal conditions | Ensure soil is well drained • Avoid root disturbance; do not cultivate around *Genista* | *Genista* |
| Prepare planting site with compost and slow-release, low-phosphorus fertilizer • Ensure excellent drainage | Tip prune regularly or pick bunches of flowers • Fertilize established plants • Sow seed; keep moist until germination | *G. lavandulacea* is suitable for hedges • Mulch plants with gum leaf mulch | *Grevillea* |
| Prepare planting site with compost and slow-release, low-phosphorus fertilizer | Sow seed • Avoid root disturbance of established plants; do not cultivate around roots | Mulch plants with gum leaves or leaf litter | *Hakea* |
| *H. hulkeana* flowering | Prune back old flowering stems • Fertilize and water well | Mulch around plants • Take semi-ripe cuttings | *Hebe* |
| In warm districts prune *H. rosa-sinensis* • Prune by a third; use for cuttings • Mulch and fertilize after pruning | In warm districts prune *H. rosa-sisensis* • Prune by a third; use for cuttings • Mulch and fertilize after pruning | Flowering season May to November • Fertilize regularly with a high-potassium fertilizer • Mulch well but keep away from stem | *Hibiscus* |
| Prune *H. paniculata* 'Grandiflora' and *H. quercifolia* by a half • Mulch and fertilize well | Select a cool, moist location for planting • Dig in plenty of compost and complete fertilizer • Take cuttings | Liquid fertilize as buds develop • Take cuttings | *Hydrangea* |
| *I. crenata* and *I. vomitoria* suitable for shearing as a hedge | Prune hard to control size | Prune all species back hard • Do not transplant | *Ilex* |
| Choose a sunny, well-drained site for planting • Sandy soil and coastal conditions are fine | Prune regularly and lightly but growth is naturally compact • Fertilize lightly with complete plant food | — | *Juniperus* |

| PLANT | SUMMER<br>JUNE | JULY | AUGUST |
|---|---|---|---|
| **SHRUBS** *(continued)* | | | |
| *Lavandula* | Take semi-ripe cuttings • Provide gravel mulch | Ensure good drainage and air flow around plants • Fertilize lightly | Stems may blacken and die in humid weather • Prune out dead wood |
| *Leptospermum* | Take semi-ripe cuttings | Watch out for scale insects which may result in sooty mold on stems | Web-spinning moth larvae may cause damage; remove affected branches |
| *Melaleuca* | Sawfly larvae may defoliate plants; spray with pyrethrum • Take semi-ripe cuttings | Ensure adequate water during dry spells, although most will tolerate dry weather | Spray scale insects with white oil • Root rot diseases may occur in humid weather |
| *Osmanthus* | Propagate from semi-ripe cuttings | Provide adequate water during dry spells • Propagate from semi-ripe cuttings | Check for summer pests |
| *Philadelphus* | Take softwood cuttings | Provide some shade in warm districts | Ensure adequate water • Mulch • Lightly fertilize |
| *Protea* | Take semi-ripe cuttings | Take semi-ripe cuttings | Ensure good drainage in humid conditions |
| *Rhododendron, Azalea* | Apply compost or leaf litter around plants • Supply adequate water • Do not dig around plants as root system may be damaged | Protect plants from hot afternoon sun • Propagation may be carried out by layering | Remove unsprayed plants badly damaged by insect attack • Check for mildew during humid weather; spray with a fungicide |
| *Rosa* | Soak plants heavily once a week • Spray scale insects on stems with white oil plus an insecticide • Main flowering period commences | Spray rust spores with sulfur; remove and destroy affected leaves • Prune back sucker growth from base rootstocks • Propagate by budding | Spray black spot at 2-week intervals • Allow good air movement |
| *Salvia* | Raise seedlings in flats for transplanting or sow seed direct • Flowering begins | *S. dorrii* and *S. guaranitica* in flower • Water occasionally | *S. dorrii* and *S. guaranitica* in flower • Water occasionally |
| *Spiraea* | Provide adequate water during dry spells • Take softwood cuttings | Provide adequate water during dry spells • Take softwood cuttings | Provide adequate water during dry spells • Take softwood cuttings |
| *Syringa* | Mulch around plants and keep moist during dry spells | Take softwood cuttings or buy grafted specimens for greater hardiness | Lightly prune to shape |
| *Viburnum* | Take softwood cuttings of deciduous plants • Take semi-ripe cuttings of evergreens • Prune old flower stems • Mulch and fertilize | Ensure adequate water during dry spells • Mulch and fertilize | Two-spotted mite may cause silvering on leaves of *V. tinus*; control may be difficult |
| *Weigela* | Take softwood cuttings • Prune after flowering | Ensure adequate water during dry spells • Mulch • Lightly fertilize | Ensure adequate water during dry spells |
| **TREES** | | | |
| *Evergreen* | Take semi-ripe cuttings | Watch for summer insect pests | Watch for summer insect pests |
| *Semi-deciduous* | Take semi-ripe cuttings | Mulch and fertilize | Watch for summer insect pests |
| *Deciduous, all heights* | Mulch and lightly fertilize | Watch for summer insect pests | Watch for summer insect pests |
| *Conifers* | Ensure adequate water during dry spells • Check stems for scale insect damage | Thrips may cause brown or dead foliage in patches | Thrips may cause brown or dead foliage in patches |

| FALL | | | |
|---|---|---|---|
| **SEPTEMBER** | **OCTOBER** | **NOVEMBER** | **PLANT** |
| | | | ***SHRUBS*** *(continued)* |
| Some species still flowering | Some species still flowering | Prune off dead flowers to encourage continuous blooming of *L. dentata* | ***Lavandula*** |
| Top up mulch • Lightly fertilize | Tip prune regularly | — | ***Leptospermum*** |
| Top up mulch • Lightly fertilize | Prune out any old or woody growth | — | ***Melaleuca*** |
| Mulch and lightly fertilize | Flowering commences | Flowering | ***Osmanthus*** |
| — | — | — | ***Philadelphus*** |
| Prepare planting site • Ensure good drainage • Dig in compost • Check soil pH | *P. neriifolia* flowering | *P. neriifolia* flowering | ***Protea*** |
| Apply light application of fertilizer and water in well • Take cuttings of semi-ripe wood • Pot on layer-grown plants | Apply mulch of compost or well-rotted animal manure | Spot flowering occurs | ***Rhododendron, Azalea*** |
| *R. moyesii* flowering • Lightly dress soil with dolomite/lime; and/or dig in compost or well-rotted manure, especially in sandy soil • Improve drainage in heavy soil | Allow rose hips to develop on *R. rugosa* • Pick rose hip stems for decoration • Check rose catalogs for varieties suitable for your area | Do not prune old-fashioned roses • Clip annually; shorten back flowering canes • Take cuttings | ***Rosa*** |
| Flowering continues in warm-temperate climates | Flowering continues in warm-temperate climates | Flowering continues in warm-temperate climates | ***Salvia*** |
| Prune lightly to shape | In cold districts leaf color may occur in fall | In cold districts leaf color may occur in fall | ***Spiraea*** |
| Mulch around established plants with compost | Mulch around established plants with compost | Prepare soil for planting with light application of dolomite/lime and/or compost • Ensure good drainage | ***Syringa*** |
| Mulch and fertilize lightly | Leaves of *V. burkwoodii* color in fall • Berries may remain on some species | Leaves of *V. carlesii* color in fall | ***Viburnum*** |
| — | Plants begin to lose leaves | Plants continue to lose leaves | ***Weigela*** |
| | | | ***TREES*** |
| Plant new trees in areas of fall rains • Lightly fertilize established trees | Plant new trees in areas of fall rains • Lightly fertilize established trees | Plant new trees in areas of fall rains • Lightly fertilize established trees | ***Evergreen*** |
| Prepare planting site for new trees; dig in plenty of compost and complete fertilizer • Be sure soil is well drained | Water well until established if no rain is present | Leaves may fall in cool districts | ***Semi-deciduous*** |
| Prepare planting site 2 months ahead if planting bare-rooted young trees | Dig in plenty of compost and complete fertilizer | Transplant established trees | ***Deciduous, all heights*** |
| Prepare soil for planting; dig in compost and complete fertilizer | Water new plants until established | Take hardwood cuttings from young plants | ***Conifers*** |

| | WINTER | | |
|---|---|---|---|
| PLANT | DECEMBER | JANUARY | FEBRUARY |
| **SHRUBS** *(continued)* | | | |
| *Lavandula* | *L. dentata* produces purple bracts with its flowers | *L. dentata* produces purple bracts with its flowers | *L. dentata* produces purple bracts with its flowers |
| *Leptospermum* | — | — | — |
| *Melaleuca* | Give some protection to young plants in frosty areas | Give some protection to young plants in frosty areas | Give some protection to young plants in frosty areas |
| *Osmanthus* | Flowering | Flowering | Cut back after flowering to restrict growth |
| *Philadelphus* | Protect *P. mexicanus* from frost; grow in pot and move to sheltered location | Protect *P. mexicanus* from frost; grow in pot and move to sheltered location | — |
| *Protea* | Provide protection for young plants in frosty areas | *P. cynaroides* flowering | Pick flowers for indoor decoration |
| *Rhododendron, Azalea* | Protect young plants in frosty areas • | Ensure adequate water if cold, dry winds occur | Flowering in warm districts |
| *Rosa* | Main pruning time for hybrid Tea and Floribunda roses • Prune back dead, weak or spindly growth • Prune to outward pointing bud | Pruning continues • Bare-rooted roses may be purchased • Water well after planting • When planting, do not allow roots to be bent | Spray scale insects with white oil • To exhibit roses, join a horticultural society |
| *Salvia* | Protect from strong winds | Protect from strong winds | Protect from strong winds |
| *Spiraea* | — | — | — |
| *Syringa* | Select grafted, bare-rooted, healthy specimens for planting | Prune out dead or weak shoots on established plants | Some species may flower again |
| *Viburnum* | *V. tinus* begins to flower | *V. tinus* flowering | *V. tinus* flowering |
| *Weigela* | Deciduous | Deciduous | Deciduous |
| **TREES** | | | |
| *Evergreen* | Mulch around young trees with gravel to protect from frost, or cover with hessian tent overnight | Mulch around young trees with gravel to protect from frost, or cover with hessian tent overnight | Mulch around young trees with gravel to protect from frost, or cover with hessian tent overnight |
| *Semi-deciduous* | Some loss of leaves in all districts | Some loss of leaves in all districts | Some loss of leaves in all districts |
| *Deciduous, all heights* | Protect young trees with gravel mulch in frosty areas | Take hardwood cuttings | Remove old or dead branches • Shape trees if not flowering species |
| *Conifers* | Frost damage may occur on young plants of *Abies* | Take hardwood cuttings | Take hardwood cuttings |
| *Ornamental, blossom & fruit* | Purchase bare-rooted trees • Do not let roots turn up when planting • Prune branches lightly after planting | Water well until established, but not excessively | Water well until established, but not excessively |

| SPRING | | | |
|---|---|---|---|
| MARCH | APRIL | MAY | PLANT |
| | | | **SHRUBS** *(continued)* |
| When planting add light application of dolomite/lime to soil; and/or compost and complete fertilizer | Tip prune young plants to ensure compact habit | Prune lightly after or during flowering | *Lavandula* |
| Sow seed; keep moist until germination | Ensure good drainage • Fertilize and mulch | Tip prune regularly or use hedge shears over plants | *Leptospermum* |
| Ensure good drainage; all enjoy some moisture in soil • Lightly fertilize with blood and bone | Tip prune regularly, especially young plants • Prune old flowering stems and collect seed • Sow seed; keep moist until germination | Mulch around plants to conserve water | *Melaleuca* |
| — | Ensure good drainage | — | *Osmanthus* |
| Prepare planting site • Dig in compost and complete fertilizer | Provide part shade in hot districts | Prune after flowering, especially older shoots • Mulch and fertilize | *Philadelphus* |
| Prune lightly after flowering | Fertilize only with fertilizer recommended for proteas | Keep mulch away from main stem | *Protea* |
| Main flowering period • Apply compost or well-rotted animal manure and a complete plant food for rhododendrons • Water well before planting | Main flowering period • Do not water directly on to flowers • Spray petal blight with a fungicide • Take cuttings 6 weeks after flowering | Prune lightly after flowering • If growth is poor, check soil pH • Use a systemic insecticide regularly to combat insect damage on leaves | *Rhododendron, Azalea* |
| Protect new foliage from wind damage • In warmer districts some roses begin to flower • Choose roses by perfume | Use commercial preparations on insect pests and diseases; or plant garlic or onion chives and encourage birds • Prune after flowering | *R. glauca* flowering • Mulch thickly with straw or old cow manure; keep mulch away from plant stems • Lightly apply fertilizer every 6 weeks | *Rosa* |
| Liquid feed occasionally with soluble fertilizer • Provide a friable, well-drained soil | Raise seedlings in flats for transplanting or sow seed if the weather is warm | Pinch back established plants to encourage lateral shoots | *Salvia* |
| Cut out old or dead wood | Prune after flowering • Cut out old or dead wood | Fertilize and mulch well | *Spiraea* |
| — | Fertilize young plants with complete fertilizer once established • Flowering commences | Prune old flowers; prune to shape after flowering | *Syringa* |
| *V. carlesii* flowering • Prepare planting site • Dig in plenty of compost and complete fertilizer | Ensure adequate water as flower buds develop | Prune out any old or dead wood • Pick flowering branches for indoor decoration | *Viburnum* |
| Hard prune overgrown or straggly specimens • Mulch and fertilize | Prepare planting site • Dig in plenty of compost and complete fertilizer | Tip prune young plants regularly • Flowering commences | *Weigela* |
| | | | **TREES** |
| Sow tree seed and keep moist until germination | Mulch well as weather warms up • Fertilize during periods of good rain | Mulch well as weather warms up • Fertilize during periods of good rain | *Evergreen* |
| Prune new trees to shape or after flowering | Mulch and fertilize • Water well | Sow seed and keep moist until germination | *Semi-deciduous* |
| Plant container specimens | Prune blossom trees after flowering • Mulch and fertilize | Ensure adequate water during dry spells | *Deciduous, all heights* |
| Prune new growth (not old wood) to shape • Sow seed after giving cold treatment if necessary | Mulch and fertilize | Mulch and fertilize | *Conifers* |
| Cut flowering branches for indoor decoration | Mulch and fertilize well | Prune after flowering | *Ornamental, blossom & fruit* |

| | SUMMER | | |
|---|---|---|---|
| **PLANT** | **JUNE** | **JULY** | **AUGUST** |
| **TREES** *(continued)* | | | |
| *Ornamental, blossom & fruit* | Provide cool, moist conditions over summer • Mulch and fertilize | Prune back suckers near ground level • Watch for insect pests during warm weather | Watch for insect pests during warm weather |
| *Tropical & subtropical* | Prune young trees to shape • Mulch | Mulch to conserve water | Watch for summer insect pests |
| **BULBS, CORMS & TUBERS** | | | |
| *Summer flowering, sun* | Provide adequate water during summer months while plants are in active growth and producing flowers | Flowering • Provide adequate water | Flowering • Provide adequate water |
| *Summer flowering, part shade* | Flowering | Flowering | *Cardiocrinum* produce decorative seed pods after flowering |
| *Fall flowering* | Allow summer sun to bake bulbs in the ground | Plant bulbs • Prepare soil with plenty of compost and slow-release fertilizer for bulbs • Select *Colchicum* for a cool climate | Foliage dies down • Reduce watering • Plant bulbs just below ground in hot districts or with neck exposed in cool districts |
| *Winter flowering* | — | — | Order bulbs from a reputable grower • Sow seed of *Galanthus* in compost seed-raising mix • Pot on when large enough |
| *Winter–spring flowering* | Dormancy | Plant out *Bulbinella* with top at ground level in humus-rich soil | Dig in plenty of compost and well-rotted cow manure • Make sure soil is well drained or bulbs may rot • Order bulbs |
| *Spring flowering, sun* | Dry off over summer • Bulbs may be lifted and stored in a cool, dry place or left to naturalize | Dry off (bake) bulbs in ground | Divide clumps of *Hermodactylus* • Sow seed of *Freesia* • Add light dressing of lime/dolomite compost and blood and bone fertilizer to soil |
| *Spring flowering, shade to part shade* | — | — | Sow *Anemone* seed in sandy loam or seed-raising mix • Add compost, leaf mold and a low-nitrogen fertilizer to soil |
| *Summer–fall flowering* | Maintain adequate water during dry spells | Bulbs begin main flowering season and continue through to fall | Plant *Cyclamen* bulbs 4 in (about 10 cm) deep, 6 in (about 15 cm) apart; choose a partly shaded site |
| *Spring–summer flowering, sun* | Allow bulbs to dry off during summer • A hot, dry summer will help bulbs mature | Allow bulbs to dry off during summer • A hot, dry summer will help bulbs mature | Allow bulbs to dry off during summer • A hot, dry summer will help bulbs mature |
| *Spring–summer flowering, shade* | Plant offsets of *Veltheimia* | Sow seed of *Calochortus* and keep in a cool, moist position until ready to plant • Reduce watering of *Veltheimia* over summer | In warm climates choose *Calochortus* for fall planting • Add plenty of compost and fertilizer to soil |
| *Allium* | *A. moly* and *A. narcissiflorum* in flower through summer • Provide adequate water during flowering period | Leave foliage to die down • Pick flowers for indoor decoration | Divide plants of *A. christophii* |
| *Begonia* | Liquid fertilize regularly • Do not water foliage if possible, just fine spray occasionally • Support flowering stems with thin wire stakes | Plan a visit to begonia festivals | Plan a visit to begonia festivals |

| FALL | | | |
|---|---|---|---|
| **SEPTEMBER** | **OCTOBER** | **NOVEMBER** | **PLANT** |
| | | | **TREES** *(continued)* |
| Prepare planting site 2 months ahead for bare rooted trees | Dig in plenty of compost and complete fertilizer | Ornamental fruit appear on *Malus* • Leave on tree for winter or until fallen | *Ornamental, blossom & fruit* |
| Mulch and lightly fertilize | Prune out dead or diseased limbs • Plant new trees during rainy weather | Prune out dead or diseased limbs • Plant new trees during rainy weather | *Tropical & subtropical* |
| | | | **BULBS, CORMS & TUBERS** |
| Plant *Amaryllis* bulbs just below soil surface • Plant *Habranthus* 3 in (about 7.5 cm) deep, 6 in (about 15 cm) apart • Divide established clumps of *Scilla* | Plant *Scilla* bulbs in warm climates or divide clumps • Plant just below soil surface • Plant *Watsonia* 3½ in (about 8 cm) deep | Divide clumps of *Polianthes* and store in dry sand | *Summer flowering, sun* |
| — | Divide *Dracunculus* roots • Plant 12 in (about 30 cm) apart • Plant *Cardiocrinum* in rich, moist soil | Mulch planting area with compost or allow leaves from deciduous trees to gently cover bulbs | *Summer flowering, part shade* |
| Flowering • Top dress areas of naturalized bulbs with compost • Liquid fertilize regularly | Flowering • Divide established clumps • Replant healthiest bulbs • Plant *Nerine filifolia* in a rock garden | Flowering • Fertilize bulbs as foliage begins to die down • *Nerine* foliage appears after flowering | *Fall flowering* |
| Select a cool, moist, partly shaded site under deciduous trees or shrubs • Add compost, leaf mold and slow-release fertilizer • Plant bulbs 2 in (about 5 cm) deep | Select a cool, moist, partly shaded site under deciduous trees or shrubs • Add compost, leaf mold and slow-release fertilizer • Plant bulbs 2 in (about 5 cm) deep | — | *Winter flowering* |
| Keep *Bulbinella* moist • Plant *Crocus* under deciduous trees in cold climates • In warm areas plant in pots of bulb fiber | Plant *Chasmanthe* in a rock garden or as path edging • Plant *Bulbinella* and *Oxalis* together for brilliant color combination | Divide *Eranthis* when overcrowded | *Winter–spring flowering* |
| Bulb planting time • Keep moist during growing season • Plant *Babiana*, *Freesia* and *Hermodactylus* | Bulb planting time • Plant *Leucocoryne* and *Sparaxis* | Bulb planting time | *Spring flowering, sun* |
| Choose a cool, moist spot for *Arum* and *Hyacinthoides* | Plants left in ground may be divided • Plant *Anemone*, *Arum* and *Hyacinthoides* | Spot flowering of *Anemone* occurs if plants have been left in ground • Allow deciduous leaves to fall over bulb planting area | *Spring flowering, shade to part shade* |
| Choose a sunny spot, well-drained soil enriched with compost and low-nitrogen bulb fertilizer for bulb planting • Plant *Cyclamen* bulbs | Water bulbs well once foliage appears • Liquid fertilize when flower buds appear • Protect from snails | Plant *Zephyranthes* bulbs 4 in (about 10 cm) deep, 3 in (about 7.5 cm) apart | *Summer–fall flowering* |
| Plant *Ornithogalum* in well-drained soil | Plant bulbs of *Tulbughia* and *Watsonia* 3 in (about 7.5 cm) deep • Lightly apply compost, but average soil is tolerated | Plant *Zephyranthes* 4 in (about 10 cm) deep • Plant *Ornithogalum* bulbs or sow seed | *Spring–summer flowering, sun* |
| Plan a woodland garden in a partly shaded site with plenty of leaf compost for *Calochortus* and *Clivia* | Plant out *Veltheimia* bulbs; mass plant in large groups in sunny position • Main bulb planting time | Plant bulbs • Foliage on *Clivia* should be glossy green • Plant *Veltheimia* in warm climates, place in pots in cold climates | *Spring–summer flowering, shade* |
| Plant all seed varieties; sow in seed-raising mix and pot when ready • Top dress with blood and bone as flowering dies down | Plant bulbs of all varieties when available | Plant bulbs of all varieties when available | *Allium* |
| Plan a visit to begonia festivals | Lift tubers and allow to dry off in a cool position • Do not remove soil from around tuber until dry | Glasshouse-grown plants are available for indoor use most of the year • Store dry tubers in sand or dry peat moss | *Begonia* |

| | WINTER | | |
|---|---|---|---|
| **PLANT** | **DECEMBER** | **JANUARY** | **FEBRUARY** |
| ***TREES*** *(continued)* | | | |
| *Tropical & subtropical* | Protect trees from cold wind if growing in cooler climates | Protect trees from cold wind if growing in cooler climates | Protect trees from cold wind if growing in cooler climates |
| ***BULBS, CORMS & TUBERS*** | | | |
| *Summer flowering, sun* | Bulbs are hardy but give some protection in areas of severe frost with mulch of loose straw or dry leaves | As for December • Plant *Galtonia* bulbs in warm climates 6 in (about 15 cm) deep, 8 in (about 20 cm) apart; add compost and slow-release bulb food | Plant *Tigridia* corms 3 in (about 7.5 cm) deep, 6 in (about 15 cm) apart • Divide established clumps after several years |
| *Summer flowering, part shade* | Grow *Hymenocallis* in pots in cold areas | Protect *Caladium* in cold areas | Sow seed of *Crinum* |
| *Fall flowering* | Flowers die down • Allow leaves from deciduous trees to cover areas of naturalized bulbs | Protect bulbs with loose straw in areas of severe frost | Protect bulbs with loose straw in areas of severe frost |
| *Winter flowering* | Main flowering period • Pick flowering stems of *Galanthus* | Main flowering period • Fertilize to prolong flowering | Leave bulbs to naturalize |
| *Winter–spring flowering* | Protect *Bulbinella* bulbs in frosty areas with mulch of loose straw • Bulb flowering time from now until April | Protect *Bulbinella* bulbs in frosty areas with mulch of loose straw | Plant bulbs in pots for indoor decoration • Liquid fertilize regularly |
| *Spring flowering, sun* | Provide shelter from cold winds • Protect bulbs in frosty areas with mulch of loose straw or dry leaves | Provide shelter from cold winds • Protect bulbs in frosty areas with mulch of loose straw or dry leaves | Flowering may start in warm climates |
| *Spring flowering, shade to part shade* | Protect *Anemone* in frosty areas with mulch of loose straw | *Arum* foliage looks good in association with *Galanthus* | Ensure adequate moisture if cold dry winds occur |
| *Summer–fall flowering* | Plant *Crocosmia* bulbs 4 in (about 10 cm) deep, 6 in (about 15 cm) apart; confine bulbs as they may be invasive | Protect *Eucomis* bulbs in frosty areas | Plant *Zephyranthes* bulbs 4 in (about 10 cm) deep, 3 in (about 7.5 cm) apart |
| *Spring–summer flowering, sun* | Plant *Zephyranthes* tubers in sheltered position | In frost-prone areas grow potted bulbs in sheltered positions; plant out in spring • If left in ground protect with straw | Divide and separate corms of *Watsonia* |
| *Spring–summer flowering, shade* | *Veltheimia* requires water during winter to ensure good flowering • Reduce watering of *Clivia* to encourage flower production | Keep *Calochortus* dry over winter | Liquid fertilize as buds develop in spring |
| *Allium* | — | — | — |
| *Begonia* | Turn potted specimens on their sides to dry off | Prepare a soil mix for begonias with equal parts loamy soil, leaf mold or cocopeat, cow manure and blood and bone | Tubers available until May; begin in pots of sand/peat before transferring to garden; ensure tubers are firm |
| *Fritillaria* | Watch for winter weeds | Watch for winter weeds | Watch for winter weeds |
| *Gladiolus* | Lift bulbs in cold areas or wet areas • Dust bulbs with sulfur fungicide and store in a cool, dry place | Store bulbs in a cool, dry place | Store bulbs in a cool, dry place |

# SPRING

| MARCH | APRIL | MAY | PLANT |
|---|---|---|---|
| | | | **TREES** *(continued)* |
| Mulch and fertilize • Plant seed and keep moist until germination | Prune established trees after flowering • Take cuttings | Prepare planting site if good rains have fallen • Dig in compost and complete fertilizer | *Tropical & subtropical* |
| | | | **BULBS, CORMS & TUBERS** |
| Plant *Belamcanda* bulbs just below soil surface • Add compost and blood and bone fertilizer • Plant *Polianthes tuberosa* 2 in (about 5 cm) deep, 5 in (about 12.5 cm) apart | Protect plants from snails and slugs | Mulch bulbs with compost and liquid fertilize regularly • Give *Vallota* plenty of room to grow | *Summer flowering, sun* |
| Plant *Cardiocrinum* just below soil surface • Allow plenty of space for it to develop | Liquid fertilize as weather warms up and plants emerge or grow | Keep soil evenly moist over summer | *Summer flowering, part shade* |
| Divide bulbs if overcrowded • Sow seed from previous fall flowering | Plant fresh bulbs | Provide adequate water while foliage is growing; reduce watering once foliage has died down | *Fall flowering* |
| Allow bulbs to dry off after flowering • Mulch area with compost • Bulbs may be divided | — | — | *Winter flowering* |
| Cut off old flower stalks of *Bulbinella* • Divide *Eranthis* after flowering • Thin and replant healthiest bulbs | Sprinkle over blood and bone fertilizer as bulbs die down | Dormancy | *Winter–spring flowering* |
| Main flowering period • Pick flowers regularly for indoor decoration | Main flowering period | Cut off flower stems after flowering • Collect seed for fall sowing | *Spring flowering, sun* |
| Bulbs in full flower • Pick flowers for indoor decoration | Flowering continues • When flowering finishes lift *Anemone* and store in a cool, dry place | Leave bulbs in ground to die off • Mulch with compost • Leave flowering stems of *Arum* to produce berries for decoration | *Spring flowering, shade to part shade* |
| Plant *Eucomis* bulbs 2 in (about 5 cm) deep, 12 in (about 30 cm) apart | Sow seed of bulbs in pots until planted out • Divide large clumps of bulbs if overcrowded • Give away excess bulbs | Maintain adequate water during dry spells | *Summer–fall flowering* |
| Plant bulbs of *Ornithogalum* | Main flowering period begins and continues into summer | *Tulbaghia* flowers emit a strong odor; do not plant near open windows | *Spring–summer flowering, sun* |
| Flowering time begins and continues to early summer | Pick flowers regularly for indoor decoration | Remove spent plants of *Calochortus;* save the best tubers for replanting next fall | *Spring–summer flowering, shade* |
| *A. christophii* in flower | Divide clumps of *A. moly* and *A. narcissiflorum* | Save seed of *A. christophii* for dried flower arrangements | *Allium* |
| Sow seed with fine sand for even distribution; sow in moist, fine compost and cover with thin layer of sand | Pot seedlings in sand/peat; mix 50:50 with slow-release fertilizer • Don't overpot • Keep in glasshouse or warm position | If planting out acclimatize plants gradually • Prepare position with well-rotted cow manure and compost | *Begonia* |
| Flowering in cold climates | Flowering | Lift bulbs from areas with high summer rain or bulbs may rot • Store in cool, dry place | *Fritillaria* |
| Plant bulbs in cool climates • Add compost and lightly apply blood and bone fertilizer • Discard insect-damaged bulbs | *Gladiolus* hybrids flowering in warm climates • *G. carneus* and *G. tristis* in flower | Thrips may cause silver streaks on leaves and deformed flowers • Spray with an insecticide • Stake flowering stems in windy sites | *Gladiolus* |

| | SUMMER | | |
|---|---|---|---|
| **PLANT** | **JUNE** | **JULY** | **AUGUST** |
| ***BULBS, CORMS & TUBERS*** *(continued)* | | | |
| *Fritillaria* | Store bulbs in a cool, dry place | Store bulbs in a cool, dry place | In cold climates prepare partly shaded, moist sites with compost, cocopeat and leaf mold • *Fritillaria* tolerate slightly limey soil |
| *Gladiolus* | *G.* × *colvillei* in flower • Leave 3 or 4 leaves when flowers are cut | Lift when foliage starts to fade • Cut off stems when dry | Add compost and complete fertilizer • Dig sandy loam into heavy soils • *G. callianthus* in flower |
| *Iris* | *I. bucharica* requires a hot, dry summer | Order bulbs • Deeply cultivate and add compost, old manure and bulb fertilizer to soil | Chill bulbs in refrigerator if planting in warm climates |
| *Lilium* | *L. formosanum* in flower until October • Mulch with compost and fertilizer • Cut flower stems for decoration • Remove seed capsules as flowers fade | *L. longiflorum* the most reliable in warm climates • *L. regale* and *L. martagon* in flower • Take scales from flowering plants for propagation | Plant bulbs in a sunny spot in well-drained, rich, neutral soil • Allow plants to die down naturally after flowering |
| *Narcissus* | Cut down yellow foliage • Lift bulbs and store in cool, dry place in warm climates | Order bulbs from catalog of reputable grower | Planting may start in cool districts • Lightly dress soil with dolomite/lime; and/or add compost, well-rotted manure and small amount of complete fertilizer |
| *Tulipa* | Check stored bulbs for any insect damage • Keep only large, healthy bulbs • Use insecticide granules to control insect attack | Order bulbs from reputable grower • Plan a garden display, keeping same variety together for mass planting | In warm climates store bulbs in refrigerator before planting • Lightly dress soil with dolomite/lime; and/or add compost and well-rotted manure |
| ***LAWNS, GROUND COVERS & ORNAMENTAL GRASSES*** | | | |
| *Lawns* | Mow on a regular basis and never lower than 1 in (about 2.5 cm) | Insect pests active | Fungal diseases common during humid weather |
| *Ground covers* | Mow on a regular basis and never lower than 1 in (about 2.5 cm) | Insect pests active | Fungal diseases common during humid weather |
| *Ornamental grasses, sedges & bamboos* | Cut out dead or overcrowded stems • Cut back vigorous creeping grasses | If planting out, restrict growth around bamboos by placing barrier | If planting out, restrict growth around bamboos by placing barrier • Sow annual grasses |
| ***HERBS*** | Harvest and dry leaf herbs • Place paper bag over annual herbs to collect seed | Mulch garden to conserve water • In cooler districts semi-woody cuttings may be taken of *Aloysia, Laurus* and *Thymus* | Take cuttings of all perennial herbs • Plant seed of *Borago, Carum, Coriandrum, Cuminum* and *Satureja hortensis* for fall harvest |
| ***FRUIT TREES, NUT TREES & OTHER FRUITS*** | | | |
| *Tropical to subtropical* | Establish plants during or after good summer rain • Add plenty of compost and a complete fertilizer to soil | Fertilize established plants • Buy virus-free stock, or from an organic grower | Check for seasonal pests • Identify common problems and treat with safe methods |
| *Cool-temperate* | Practise fruit thinning so that branches are able to support crop • Mulch well to inhibit summer weeds | Use trickle irrigation in dry spells • Summer prune where appropriate to encourage fruit • Bud graft tree fruits on to suitable rootstocks • Take softwood cuttings of *Vaccinium* | Bud graft tree fruits on to suitable rootstocks • Take softwood cuttings of *Vaccinium* • Check for branches rubbing against stakes |
| *Warm-temperate* | Use netting to protect developing fruit from birds • Mulch well with compost to inhibit summer weeds | Fertilize regularly with appropriate fertilizer • Water well during dry spells • Summer prune where appropriate to encourage regular crops of high yields | Check for pests and diseases weekly • Allow good air circulation to discourage mildew in humid weather |

| FALL | | | |
|---|---|---|---|
| **SEPTEMBER** | **OCTOBER** | **NOVEMBER** | **PLANT** |
| | | | ***BULBS, CORMS & TUBERS*** *(continued)* |
| In cold climates only plant *Fritillaria* 4 in (about 10 cm) deep, 8 in (about 20 cm) apart • Choose *F. persica* for warmer climates | — | — | *Fritillaria* |
| Plant *G. carneus* for spring flowering | Plant *G.* × *colvillei* in a rock garden | Corms can be planted in subtropical or warm climates • Plant at intervals to flower over a long period | *Gladiolus* |
| Plant bulbs 4 in (about 10 cm) deep, 4 in (about 10 cm) apart | Plant bulbs 4 in (about 10 cm) deep, 4 in (about 10 cm) apart | Plant bulbs 4 in (about 10 cm) deep, 4 in (about 10 cm) apart | *Iris* |
| Sow seed in seed-raising mix mulched with organic matter • Raise in pots • Divide and plant new bulbs in conditioned soil | Try growing *L. auratum* and *L. speciosum* from bulblets found around the main underground stem • Plant bulbs immediately; do not store | Avoid using garden forks as bulbs damage easily • Glasshouse-grown plants available in flower • After flowering, plant out in spring | *Lilium* |
| Plant *N. cyclamineus* hybrids in rock gardens or pots 2 in (about 5 cm) deep, 2 in (about 5 cm) apart • Plant others 2 in (about 5 cm) deep, 4 in (about 10 cm) apart | Lightly fertilize bulbs with blood and bone if naturalized in garden position | Over-watering bulbs may cause bulb rot • Watch for aphids when buds form • Otherwise few problems | *Narcissus* |
| Planting time • Overplant with *Viola, Myosotis* or *Matthiola* • Plant same varieties *en masse* • Add slow-release bulb fertilizer | Planting time | Planting time | *Tulipa* |
| | | | ***LAWNS, GROUND COVERS & ORNAMENTAL GRASSES*** |
| Lightly fertilize in warm districts or prepare site for planting | Lightly fertilize in warm districts or prepare site for planting | Check for appearance of winter weeds | *Lawns* |
| Lightly fertilize in warm districts or prepare site for planting | Lightly fertilize in warm districts or prepare site for planting | Check for appearance of winter weeds | *Ground covers* |
| If planting out, restrict growth around bamboos by placing barrier • Sow annual grasses | Remove flowerheads if grass presents a weed problem | Collect seed when fully ripe for sowing | *Ornamental grasses, sedges & bamboos* |
| Continue to take cuttings • Harvest ripening seed • Cut back flowering stems and old foliage of *Petroselinum* | Harvest and dry last of summer herbs • Remove spent annual herbs and add to compost heap | Cut back overgrown plants • Dig up and pot *Andropogon, Curcuma, Elettaria* and *Zingiber* in frosty areas • Shelter over winter | ***HERBS*** |
| | | | ***FRUIT TREES, NUT TREES & OTHER FRUITS*** |
| Prune to allow light into tree or shape for good fruiting | Mulch • Fertilize lightly | Mulch • Fertilize lightly | *Tropical to subtropical* |
| Prepare ground for planting bare-rooted trees and soft fruit canes • Dig in compost or well-rotted manures • Check soil pH, ideal 6–6.5 except *Vaccinium*, 4–4.5 | Check pollination requirements of new plants • Provide stakes or trellis support where appropriate • Take hardwood cuttings from established plants | Check pollination requirements of new plants • Take hardwood cuttings from established plants | *Cool-temperate* |
| Prepare ground for planting container-grown speciments • Dig in compost or well-rotted manure • Avoid over-rich soil • Check pollination requirements | Provide sturdy trellis or stake where necessary • Take hardwood cuttings from established plants • Remove spent annual summer fruit plants and add to compost | Check pollination requirements • Take hardwood cuttings from established plants • Remove spent annual summer fruit plants and add to compost | *Warm-temperate* |

| | WINTER | | |
|---|---|---|---|
| PLANT | DECEMBER | JANUARY | FEBRUARY |
| ***BULBS, CORMS & TUBERS*** *(continued)* | | | |
| *Iris* | Watch for winter weeds | Provide shelter from strong winds as bulbs sprout • Mulch with compost • Liquid fertilize regularly | Mosaic virus may cause yellow-green streaks on new foliage; destroy bulbs/rhizomes • Spray for aphids with an insecticide • Bulbs begin to flower |
| *Lilium* | Do not water bulbs over winter | Frost hardy over winter | Frost hardy over winter |
| *Narcissus* | Protect plants from strong wind • Odd flowers of *N. jonquilla* hybrids may appear in warm climates | Liquid fertilize as flower stems appear • *N. tazetta* hybrids in flower | *N. cyclamineus* hybrids and *N. jonquilla* hybrids in flower |
| *Tulipa* | Watch for winter weeds | Watch for winter weeds | — |
| ***LAWNS, GROUND COVERS & ORNAMENTAL GRASSES*** | | | |
| *Lawns* | Warm-climate grasses may lose green color in cool winters • Oversow with cool-climate grass | Warm-climate grasses may lose green color in cool winters • Oversow with cool-climate grass | Warm-climate grasses may lose green color in cool winters • Oversow with cool-climate grass |
| *Ground covers* | Warm-climate ground covers may lose green color in cool winters • Oversow with cool-climate ground covers | Warm-climate ground covers may lose green color in cool winters • Oversow with cool-climate ground covers | Warm-climate ground covers may lose green color in cool winters • Oversow with cool-climate ground covers |
| *Ornamental grasses, sedges & bamboos* | Leave flowers for winter decoration in cold districts | Leave flowers for winter decoration in cold districts | Leave flowers for winter decoration in cold districts |
| ***HERBS*** | *Allium* and *Artemisia* go dormant • Divide established clumps of *Glycyrrhiza, Melissa* and *Symphytum* | Mulch plants with loose straw over winter | Sow annual seeds under glass or in protected position • Lightly apply dolomite/lime to soil; and/or dig in compost and complete fertilizer |
| ***FRUIT TREES, NUT TREES & OTHER FRUITS*** | | | |
| *Tropical to subtropical* | Protect plants from cold winds if growing in warm-temperate climates | Protect plants from cold winds if growing in warm-temperate climates | Protect plants from cold winds if growing in warm-temperate climates |
| *Cool-temperate* | Soak bare-rooted plants well before planting out; do not plant below graft level • Protect young plants from severe frost with hessian tent • Prune established plants to maintain high yields | Protect young plants from severe frost with hessian tent • Prune established plants to maintain high yields • Prune to open structure to allow light to reach ripening fruit | Protect young plants from severe frost with hessian tent • Prune established plants to maintain high yields • Prune to open structure to allow light to reach ripening fruit |
| *Warm-temperate* | Prune young trees to shape, selecting three main branches to form a framework • Cut back current season's fruited shoots | Cut back current season's fruited shoots • Remove crossing or rubbing branches or dead wood • Protect young plants from cold winds or frosty spells | Remove crossing or rubbing branches or dead wood • Protect young plants from cold winds or frosty spells |
| *Citrus* | Choose citrus species by cold tolerance; some are frost tender | Cold winds and frost can cause foliage to curl up | Fertilize and mulch |

| SPRING | | | |
|---|---|---|---|
| **MARCH** | **APRIL** | **MAY** | **PLANT** |
| | | | ***BULBS, CORMS & TUBERS*** *(continued)* |
| Main flowering period • Pick flowers in early morning | Main flowering period • Remove spent flowers | Flowering continues in cold districts • Leave bulbs in ground for 3–5 years or lift and store in cool, dry place | *Iris* |
| Avoid over-watering as bulbs may rot • Mulch soil with compost and water infrequently • Apply a liquid fertilizer once growth starts | Plant glasshouse-grown bulbs after flowering | *L. longiflorum* and *L. lancifolium* in flower • Cucumber mosaic virus may cause reflexing and streaking of leaves; destroy affected plants | *Lilium* |
| *N. triandrus* hybrids in flower • Pick flower stems just before they open | Main flowering period for hybrids | Liquid fertilize as bulbs die down • Tie up untidy foliage • Divide bulbs every 2–3 years • Reduce watering | *Narcissus* |
| Rock garden tulips *T. clusiana, T. saxatalis* and *T. tarda* in flower • Save seed of species tulips for sowing | Spray aphids with an insecticide • Spray tulip fire botrytis with a fungicide • Do not water overhead • Practise crop rotation | Remove spent flowers and let bulbs die down naturally • Lift bulbs and store in cool, dry place | *Tulipa* |
| | | | ***LAWNS, GROUND COVERS & ORNAMENTAL GRASSES*** |
| Lightly fertilize • Ensure adequate water | Prepare planting site • Ensure good drainage • Cultivate to fine tilth and even surface • Water well until established | Top dress with sandy loam • Lightly fertilize • Check for appearance of summer weeds | *Lawns* |
| Lightly fertilize • Ensure adequate water | Prepare planting site • Ensure good drainage • Cultivate to fine tilth and even surface • Water well until established | Top dress with sandy loam • Lightly fertilize • Check for appearance of summer weeds | *Ground covers* |
| Clumps may be divided and planted out • Sow annual grasses | Cut out dead or overcrowded stems • Cut back vigorous creeping grasses | Cut out dead or overcrowded stems • Cut back vigorous creeping grasses | *Ornamental grasses, sedges & bamboos* |
| Lightly apply dolomite/lime; and/or dig in compost and fertilize with complete or slow-release fertilizer • Prune dead wood • Sow seed of annuals in seed-raising mix | Plant out established plants in pots • Harvest young, fresh leaves • Apply a weak solution of liquid fertilizer | Tip prune plants regularly to ensure compact growth • Give extra water to *Andropogon* during dry spells | ***HERBS*** |
| | | | ***FRUIT TREES, NUT TREES & OTHER FRUITS*** |
| Provide adequate water during dry spells • Mulch well | Ensure good pollination of flowers | Apply mulch • Suppress weeds • Plant companion plants | *Tropical to subtropical* |
| Plant out container grown fruit/nuts; choose healthy, sturdy plants, less than 2 years old • Spread a balanced fertilizer just beyond where branches grow • Check weekly for signs of pest or disease problems | Mulch established plants with compost and manure • Check for leaf discoloration as a nutrient deficiency may be present • Protect buds and developing fruit from birds | Spread a balanced fertilizer just beyond where branches grow • Check weekly for signs of pest or disease problems • Protect buds and developing fruit from birds | *Cool-temperate* |
| Fertilize established plants to encourage fruit • Mulch heavily as weather warms up with compost or manure | Fertilize established plants to encourage fruit • Lightly prune *Ficus* and *Fortunella* to shape • Take softwood cuttings where appropriate | Check for any sign of aphids or scale insects and take necessary action • Lightly prune *Ficus* and *Fortunella* to shape • Take softwood cuttings where appropriate | *Warm-temperate* |
| Choose a sheltered position for planting • Prepare site with compost and a complete fertilizer • Ensure good drainage | Mulch and fertilize • Keep away from main trunk | Keep trunk free from weeds | *Citrus* |

| PLANT | SUMMER JUNE | JULY | AUGUST |
|---|---|---|---|
| ***FRUIT TREES, NUT TREES & OTHER FRUITS*** *(continued)* | | | |
| *Citrus* | Check for pests • If leaves are discolored check for signs of deficiency in soil | Leaf miner a common problem; cut off damaged section or spray weekly with an insecticide in cool of day | Mulch and fertilize |
| *Prunus* | Provide adequate water during dry spells | Clear summer weeds away from trees | Clear summer weeds away from trees |
| ***CACTI & SUCCULENTS*** | Check for pests on spines or under leaves | Protect tender specimens from really hot sun | Root rot diseases occur in humid weather • Top up gravel mulch and ensure good drainage |
| ***ORCHIDS*** | Mist spray daily • Water daily as required in late afternoon • Fertilize weekly with weak solution of orchid food | Control pests and diseases as noticed • Allow air circulation around pots • Fertilize weekly with weak solution of orchid food | Ensure plants are dry before watering • Check for fungal diseases in humid weather |
| ***FERNS, PALMS & CYCADS*** | | | |
| *Ferns* | Provide cool, misty water during dry spells • Mulch around plants with leaf litter • Lightly apply liquid fertilizer | Protect fronds from hot dry winds • Check under leaf hairs for insect pests; use weak strength insecticides or hand remove | Aphids may cause deformed fronds • Check stems for scale insects |
| *Palms & cycads* | Transplant palms during rainy weather • Clean up old fronds | Ensure adequate water during dry spells | Ensure adequate water during dry spells |
| ***CLIMBERS & CREEPERS*** | | | |
| *Warm-temperate to cool-temperate* | Mulch around climbers as weather heats up • Ensure adequate water during dry spells • Frequent wilting indicates dryness | Cut overgrowth back drastically • Fertilize, mulch, water well and growth should recommence • Spray caterpillars on large-leafed climbers with a pesticide | Prune back early summer-flowering climbers • Lightly apply complete fertilizer • If soil is badly drained root rot diseases may occur |
| *Tropical to subtropical* | Plant evergreen climbers, especially during or after rain periods • Check foliage for damage by caterpillars; spray with a pesticide | Mulch around plants | Prune back excess or rampant growth regularly |

| FALL | | | |
|---|---|---|---|
| **SEPTEMBER** | **OCTOBER** | **NOVEMBER** | **PLANT** |
| | | | ***FRUIT TREES, NUT TREES & OTHER FRUITS*** *(continued)* |
| Mulch and fertilize | Ensure adequate water at all times | Ensure adequate water at all times | *Citrus* |
| Prepare planting site for new trees several months in advance | Dig in compost and a complete fertilizer • Ensure soil is well drained | Check with a reputable dealer for trees suitable for your area • Spray bacterial canker with a fungicide at leaf fall | *Prunus* |
| Root rot diseases occur in humid weather • Ensure perfect drainage | Remove old dry leaves around succulents • Repot crowded specimens | Tidy up plants and move to a sunny location • Give weak solution of liquid fertilizer for those with flower buds | ***CACTI & SUCCULENTS*** |
| Provide a well-lit position but not direct sunlight | Protect flower spikes from insect damage | Reduce watering in deciduous species | ***ORCHIDS*** |
| | | | ***FERNS, PALMS & CYCADS*** |
| Check for caterpillars on young fronds • Lightly fertilize | Remove old fronds • Tidy up plants | Reduce watering during cooler weather | *Ferns* |
| Mulch and fertilize | Check leaf tips of potted specimens—they turn brown if humidity is low • Spray foliage | If trying palms in cold districts, protect well when young • Move potted specimens to warm, sheltered location | *Palms & cycads* |
| | | | ***CLIMBERS & CREEPERS*** |
| Check undersides of leaves for snails • Spray scale insects with white oil • Ants climbing up stems indicate presence of scale insects | Deciduous climbers show fall color • Prune after all leaves have dropped or growth may recommence while weather is still warm | Dig plenty of compost and a complete fertilizer into soil • Allow adequate space and strong support • Ensure soil is well drained | *Warm-temperate to cool-temperate* |
| Summer flowering species continue to flower in warm districts | Second flush of flowers for spring flowering species | Mulch well around plants and ensure adequate water during dry spells | *Tropical to subtropical* |

| | WINTER | | |
|---|---|---|---|
| **PLANT** | **DECEMBER** | **JANUARY** | **FEBRUARY** |
| ***FRUIT TREES, NUT TREES & OTHER FRUITS*** *(continued)* | | | |
| *Prunus* | Buy virus-free stock from an organic grower | Buy virus-free stock from an organic grower | Water young plants well until established but not excessively • Check for blossom diseases on established trees |
| ***CACTI & SUCCULENTS*** | Some are frost hardy but most will require protection over winter • Move pots to sheltered location | Reduce watering for all except those in flower | Bring potted specimens indoors for brief periods and place in a well-lit location |
| ***ORCHIDS*** | Maintain warmth during winter months where appropriate • Reduce watering • Clean glasshouse to prevent disease | Maintain warmth during winter months where appropriate • Reduce watering | Maintain warmth during winter months where appropriate • Reduce watering |
| ***FERNS, PALMS & CYCADS*** | | | |
| *Ferns* | Protect ferns in very cold districts • Fronds may blacken when frost damaged | Protect from cold, dry winds in all districts | Protect from cold, dry winds in all districts |
| *Palms & cycads* | Check for appearance of scale insects • Use very weak solution of white oil and an insecticide | Water containerized plants sparingly | Water containerized plants sparingly |
| ***CLIMBERS & CREEPERS*** | | | |
| *Warm-temperate to cool-temperate* | Add gypsum to badly drained heavy soil or use gravel at bottom of planting hole • Protect frost-tender species with hessian | Planting time for deciduous climbers • Prune climbing roses and *Vitis* • Prune *Wisteria* to flowering buds | Wait until all frost danger is passed before cutting back damaged climbers |
| *Tropical to subtropical* | Mulch well around plants and ensure adequate water during dry spells • Protect with hessian blanket if growing in cold districts | Frost may kill tropical species or damage subtropical ones • Growth may recommence from base in spring | Prune back cold- or wind-damaged stems in warm districts • Side dress established plants with blood and bone or complete fertilizer |

| SPRING | | | |
|---|---|---|---|
| **MARCH** | **APRIL** | **MAY** | **PLANT** |
| | | | ***FRUIT TREES, NUT TREES & OTHER FRUITS*** *(continued)* |
| Check for blossom diseases on established trees | Check for blossom diseases on established trees | Mulch and fertilize | *Prunus* |
| Sow seed or take cuttings • In garden, build up soil to allow good drainage; add sand, gravel and slow-release fertilizer | Divide established clumps and repot or replant • Give weak solution of liquid fertilizer | Cut off old flowering stems • Watch for snails—they enjoy the fleshy leaves | ***CACTI & SUCCULENTS*** |
| Repot overcrowded specimens • Trim dead or damaged roots from plants if repotting | Water regularly during growing period • Fertilize regularly • Divide established plants | Apply extra leaf mold and well-rotted cow manure on garden specimens | ***ORCHIDS*** |
| | | | ***FERNS, PALMS & CYCADS*** |
| Prepare planting site with plenty of compost and leaf litter • Use slow-release fertilizer at planting time | Propagate spore from mature fronds under moist conditions • Side dress established plants with blood and bone • Divide established ferns with rhizomes | Remove dead fronds • Cut them up and use as mulch around ferns • Lightly apply liquid fertilizer | *Ferns* |
| Mulch well • Fertilize | Collect fresh seed when ripe and sow; for successful germination high temperatures and high humidity are required | Mulch well and apply nitrogenous fertilizer • Dig in plenty of compost and a slow-release fertilizer when planting new palms | *Palms & cycads* |
| | | | ***CLIMBERS & CREEPERS*** |
| Prepare evergreen climbers planting position as for November • Spring climbers in flower • Cut back frost-damaged shoots and leaves on tender plants | Plant evergreen climbers • Prune established climbers after flowering • Side dress with blood and bone • Sow fresh climbers seed in seed-raising mix | Tie new growth into growing position • Spray aphids with pyrethrum • Take semi-hardwood cuttings from vigorous plants • Strike in coarse sand/peat mix 3:1 | *Warm-temperate to cool-temperate* |
| Sow fresh seed in seed-raising mix • Prune summer–fall flowering climbers • Apply blood and bone or complete fertilizer | Dig plenty of compost and a complete fertilizer into soil • Ensure strong support for holding growth • Tip prune regularly | Take semi-hardwood cuttings from vigorous young plants • Train climbers where you want them to grow • Tie up with soft material | *Tropical to subtropical* |

# Cultivation Guidelines

| PLANT | ORIGIN | LIGHT | SOIL PREPARATION | MAINTENANCE | PLANT PROTECTION | PROPAGATION |
|---|---|---|---|---|---|---|
| ***ANNUALS & PERENNIALS*** | | | | | | |
| *Annuals, low growing, spring–fall flowering* | Warm to cool-temperate | | Loose, well-drained loam with good organic matter component • Add compost and fertilizer | Pick flowers to encourage more blooms • Liquid fertilize regularly • Mulch | Aphids, caterpillars, snails, slugs, damping off, leaf spot, root rot | Seed, seedlings |
| *Annuals, low growing, spring–fall flowering* | Temperate | | Loose, well-drained loam with good organic matter component • Add compost and fertilizer | Pick flowers to encourage more blooms • Liquid fertilize regularly • Mulch | Aphids, caterpillars, snails, slugs, damping off, leaf spot, root rot | Seed, seedlings |
| *Annuals, medium growing, spring–fall flowering* | Cool-temperate to warm-temperate | | Loose, well-drained loam with good organic matter component • Add compost and fertilizer | Shelter from strong winds • Pick flowers regularly to encourage continuous flowering • Liquid fertilize regularly • Mulch | Rust, aphids, snails, mites, budworm, leaf miner | Seed, seedlings |
| *Annuals, tall growing, spring–fall flowering* | Temperate | | Loose, well-drained loam with good organic matter component • Add compost and fertilizer | Provide tripods if necessary or stakes • Remove spent flowers • Liquid fertilize at regular intervals • Mulch | Rust, mildew, aphids, snails, two-spotted mite | Seed, seedlings |
| *Annuals, tall growing, spring–fall flowering* | Cool-temperate to warm-temperate | | Loose, well-drained loam with good organic matter component • Add compost and fertilizer | Provide tripods if necessary or stakes • Remove spent flowers • Liquid fertilize at regular intervals • Mulch | Rust, mildew, aphids, snails, two-spotted mite | Seed, seedlings |
| *Annuals, dahlias* | Warm-temperate | | Well-drained, moderately rich soil | Stake plants • Remove spent flowers | Snails, slugs, mites, earwigs, wilt, stem rot, mildew, mold, nematodes | Tuber |
| *Annuals, pelargoniums* | Warm-temperate | | Average garden soil enriched with compost and complete fertilizer | Regular pruning | Caterpillars, rust, stem rot | Cuttings, seed |
| *Perennials, spring–early summer flowering* | Temperate | | Compost • Fertilizer • Drainage material | Remove spent flowers | Few problems | Division, seed, cuttings |
| *Perennials, spring–early summer flowering, short lived* | Warm-temperate | | Compost • Fertilizer • Sharp sand or grit for drainage | Remove plants after several seasons or allow to self-seed | Root rot diseases | Cuttings, seed, root cuttings |
| *Perennials, summer flowering, sun* | Temperate | | Dolomite/lime; and/or compost and complete fertilizer • Well-drained soil | Stake tall-flowering plants • Dead-head old flowers | Snails, slugs, few problems | Division, seed, root cuttings, stem cuttings |
| *Perennials, summer flowering, shade to part shade* | Cool-temperate | | Moist, humus-rich soil | Divide every few years | Snails, slugs | Division, seed, stem cuttings |
| *Perennials, winter–early summer flowering* | Temperate | | Moist, humus-rich soil | Divide every few years | Snails, slugs, wilt disease | Division, seed, root cuttings |

| PLANT | ORIGIN | LIGHT | SOIL PREPARATION | MAINTENANCE | PLANT PROTECTION | PROPAGATION |
|---|---|---|---|---|---|---|
| ***ANNUALS & PERENNIALS*** *(continued)* | | | | | | |
| *Perennials, summer–fall flowering* | Temperate | Sun or part shade | Compost • Fertilizer | Remove spent flowers • Divide every few years | Snails, slugs, few problems | Division, seed, root cuttings |
| *Perennials, ground covers & rock plants, temperate climate* | Cool-temperate to warm | Sun | Tolerant of average, well-drained soil conditions | Prune overgrown plants | Few problems | Cuttings, division |
| *Perennials, alpines, ground covers & rock plants, cool climate* | Cold-temperate | Sun or part shade | Garden loam with a little compost and sharp sand in a 3:2:1 ratio • Fertilizer | Winter protection from wet soils | Few problems | Seed, cuttings |
| *Perennials, sub-shrubs, sun* | Cool to warm-temperate | Sun | Average garden soil enriched with compost and a complete fertilizer | Remove spent flowers • Prune to shape | Few problems | Cuttings, seed, root cuttings for *Romneya* |
| *Perennials, sub-shrubs, shade to part shade* | Temperate | Part shade to shade | Humus-rich, cool, moist soil | Cut back overgrown plants | Mildew, root rot | Division, cuttings |
| *Perennials, water garden plants* | Cool to warm-temperate | Sun or part shade | Moist or wet conditions as recommended | Divide every 3–5 years | Few problems | Division, seed |
| *Perennials, for tropical effect* | Tropical to subtropical | Sun or part shade | Moist, humus-rich soil | Remove spent flower stems | Stem borer, snails | Division, cuttings, seed |
| *Perennials, irises* | Cool-temperate | Sun, part shade or shade | Soil requirements as specified for species or variety in plant descriptions | Remove spent flowers • Divide when overcrowded | Rust, collar rot | Division in fall to spring, seed in fall |
| *Perennials, primulas* | Temperate | Part shade | Moisture-retaining, humus-rich soil | Cool site required • Mulch | Snails, mold, mites | Division, seed, root cuttings for *P. denticulata* |
| ***SHRUBS*** | | | | | | |
| *Low growing, frost hardy, evergreen* | Warm-temperate to cool-temperate | Sun or part shade | Well-drained, humus-rich soil, pH adjustment | Mulch • Prune regularly • Some protection for young specimens in very cold conditions | Insect damage as noted in separate plant descriptions | Seed, cuttings, layering |
| *Low growing, frost tender, evergreen* | Subtropical to warm-temperate | Sun or part shade | Average, fertile, humus-rich soil, pH adjustment | Prune to shape or after flowering • Mulch | Insect damage as noted in separate plant descriptions | Seed, cuttings |
| *Low growing, frost hardy, deciduous* | Cool-temperate | Sun or part shade | Well-drained, fertile, humus-rich soil, pH adjustment | Mulch regularly • Prune regularly | Insect damage as noted in separate plant descriptions | Seed, cuttings |
| *Medium to tall growing, frost hardy, evergreen* | Warm-temperate to cool-temperate | Sun, part shade or shade | Well-drained, fertile, humus-rich soi, pH adjustment | Mulch regularly • Prune regularly • Some are able to withstand dry periods | Insect damage as noted in separate plant descriptions | Seed, cuttings |
| *Medium to tall growing, frost tender, evergreen* | Subtropical to warm-temperate | Sun or part shade | Average, fertile, humus-rich soil, pH adjustment | Prune to shape or after flowering • Mulch • Protect from wind and cold | Insect damage as noted in separate plant descriptions | Seed, cuttings |
| *Medium to tall growing, frost hardy, deciduous* | Temperate | Sun or part shade | Compost • Complete fertilizer • Well-drained soil, pH adjustment | Prune regularly • Mulch | Insect damage as noted in separate plant descriptions | Cuttings, grafting |
| *Acacia* | Temperate | Sun or part shade | Average, well-drained soil | Prune regularly • Mulch | Borers, galls | Seed, cuttings |
| *Buddleia* | Temperate | Sun | Average, well-drained soil | Prune regularly • Mulch | Few problems | Cuttings |
| *Callistemon* | Temperate | Sun | Average moisture-retaining soil | Prune after flowering; prune heavily after 3–4 years for best flower/fruit production | Tip bugs, thrips, borers | Seed, cuttings |

| PLANT | ORIGIN | LIGHT | SOIL PREPARATION | MAINTENANCE | PLANT PROTECTION | PROPAGATION |
|---|---|---|---|---|---|---|
| **SHRUBS** *(continued)* | | | | | | |
| *Camellia* | Temperate | Sun or part shade | Moist, well-drained, humus-rich soil, acidic pH | Provide shelter from weather extremes • Mulch • Disbud | Scale insects, mites | Cuttings |
| *Cestrum* | Warm-temperate | Sun | Average, well-drained soil | Tip prune regularly | Few problems | Seed, cuttings |
| *Cistus* | Warm-temperate | Sun | Well-drained, light soil, slightly acidic pH | Prune after flowering | Few problems | Cuttings |
| *Correa* | Temperate | Sun or part shade | Well-drained, light soil | Prune regularly | Few problems | Cuttings |
| *Cotoneaster* | Temperate | Sun or part shade | Average, well-drained soil | Prune regularly | Few problems | Seed, cuttings |
| *Erica* | Temperate | Sun | Acid, well-drained soil | Prune after flowering | Few problems | Cuttings |
| *Euphorbia* | Warm-temperate to subtropical | Sun | Average, well-drained soil | Prune regularly | Few problems | Cuttings |
| *Fuchsia* | Temperate | Part shade | Moist, well-drained, humus-rich soil | Protect from strong winds | Thrips, mites, mealy bug | Cuttings |
| *Gardenia* | Warm-temperate | Part shade | Moist, well-drained, humus-rich soil, acid pH | Prune and fertilize regularly • Correct iron or magnesium deficiency • Mulch | Mealy bug, scale insects, nematodes | Cuttings |
| *Genista* | Temperate | Sun | Average, well-drained soil | Prune after flowering | Snails | Cuttings |
| *Grevillea* | Warm-temperate to subtropical | Sun | Acid, well-drained soil, sandy | Tip prune | Borer, caterpillars, plant bugs | Cuttings, seed |
| *Hakea* | Warm-temperate | Sun | Acid, well-drained, soil, sandy, gravelly | Tip prune | Borer, caterpillars, plant bugs | Seed, cuttings |
| *Hebe* | Temperate | Sun | Moist, well-drained soil | Prune after flowering | Scale insects, leaf miner, downy mildew | Cuttings, seed |
| *Hibiscus* | Warm-temperate to subtropical | Sun | Well-drained, fertile soil with compost added | Prune in spring to encourage more blooms | Aphids, scale insects, mealy bug, collar rot | Cuttings, seed |
| *Hydrangea* | Temperate | Part shade | Cool, moist, humus-rich soil | Prune regularly | Mildew, two-spotted mite | Cuttings |
| *Ilex* | Temperate | Sun or part shade | Moist, well-drained soil | Prune hard in spring • Mulch • Fertilize as required | Leaf miner, aphids | Cuttings |
| *Juniperus* | Temperate | Sun | Average, well-drained soil | Prune to shape | Few problems | Cuttings |
| *Lavandula* | Temperate | Sun | Well-drained, fertile soil, neutral to alkaline pH | Tip prune regularly | Few problems | Cuttings |
| *Leptospermum* | Temperate | Sun | Acidic, well-drained soil | Tip prune regularly • Mulch | Borer | Seed, cuttings |
| *Melaleuca* | Warm-temperate | Sun | Moist, well-drained, soil | Tip prune regularly | Wax scale | Seed, cuttings |
| *Osmanthus* | Temperate | Sun or part shade | Fertile, well-drained soil | Prune after flowering | Few problems | Cuttings |
| *Philadelphus* | Temperate | Sun or part shade | Moist, humus-rich soil | Prune hard after flowering | Few problems | Cuttings |
| *Protea* | Warm-temperate | Sun | Well-drained, organic-rich, acid soil | Water in winter • Prune after flowering | Contact a reputable dealer about *Protea* diseases and their control | Cuttings |

| PLANT | ORIGIN | LIGHT | SOIL PREPARATION | MAINTENANCE | PLANT PROTECTION | PROPAGATION |
|---|---|---|---|---|---|---|
| ***SHRUBS*** *(continued)* | | | | | | |
| *Rhododendron, Azalea* | Temperate | Sun, part shade to shade | Well-drained, humus-rich soil, acid pH | Water regularly • Mulch | Two-spotted mite, thrips, caterpillars, leaf miner, petal blight, mildew | Layering, cuttings |
| *Rosa* | Temperate | Sun | Well-drained, organic, humus-rich soil | Water regularly • Lightly apply fertilizer • Remove dead or unproductive branches • Mulch • Allow good air circulation | Thrips, aphids, scale insects, mildew, rust, black spot, caterpillars | Budding, cuttings |
| *Salvia* | Warm-temperate | Sun | Well-drained, fertile soil | Water moderately • Mulch • Trim spent flowers | Few problems | Cuttings, division |
| *Spiraea* | Temperate | Sun | Average soil | Prune straggly growth to shape | Few problems | Cuttings |
| *Syringa* | Cool-temperate | Sun | Average, well-drained soil | Remove sucker growth • Prune after flowering | Keep under cool conditions | Grafting |
| *Viburnum* | Temperate | Sun or part shade | Fertile, humus-rich soil | Prune after flowering | Two-spotted mite, thrips | Cuttings, seed |
| *Weigela* | Temperate | Sun | Fertile, humus-rich soil | Prune older branches | Few problems | Cuttings |
| ***TREES*** | | | | | | |
| *Evergreen* | Subtropical to cool-temperate | Sun to part shade | Well-drained, humus-rich, fertile soil | Regular pruning when young to shape • Mulch • Fertilize as required | Seasonal insect pests, root rot diseases on poorly drained soils | Seed, cuttings, grafting |
| *Semi-deciduous* | Subtropical to cool-temperate | Sun to part shade | Well-drained, humus-rich, fertile soil | Regular pruning when young to shape • Mulch • Fertilize as required | Seasonal insect pests, root rot diseases on poorly drained soils | Seed, cuttings, grafting |
| *Deciduous, 30 feet or shorter* | Temperate | Sun to part shade | Well-drained, fertile soil | Regular pruning when young to shape • Mulch • Fertilize as required | Seasonal insect pests, root rot diseases on poorly drained soils | Seed, cuttings, grafting |
| *Deciduous, taller than 30 feet* | Temperate | Sun to part shade | Well-drained, fertile soil | Regular pruning when young to shape • Mulch • Fertilize as required | Seasonal insect pests, root rot diseases on poorly drained soils | Seed, cuttings, grafting |
| *Conifers* | Temperate | Sun | Well-drained soil | Prune to shape if necessary • Mulch • Fertilize as required | Thrips, two-spotted mite, beetles | Seed, cuttings, grafting |
| *Ornamental, blossom & fruit* | Temperate | Sun | Well-drained, humus-rich, deep soil | Prune after flowering to shape • Mulch • Fertilize with high-potassium fertilizer as required | Rust, leaf curl, pear and cherry slug, aphids | Cuttings, grafting |
| *Tropical & subtropical* | Tropical to subtropical | Sun to part shade | Well-drained, humus-rich, fertile soil | Regular pruning when young to shape • Mulch • Fertilize as required | Seasonal insect pests, root rot diseases on poorly drained soils | Seed, cuttings |
| ***BULBS, CORMS & TUBERS*** | | | | | | |
| *Summer flowering, sun* | Warm-temperate to cool-temperate | Sun or part shade | Rich, organic, well-drained soil | Provide adequate water during growing season • Protect plants with loose straw in frosty areas | Few problems; slugs on *Galtonia* | Seed, division, offsets |
| *Summer flowering, part shade* | Cool-temperate | Part shade | Cool, moist, humus-rich soil | Mulch with compost once or twice a year | Few problems | Seed, division |
| *Fall flowering* | Temperate | Sun or part shade | Well-drained, humus-rich soil• Add compost, fertilizer or bulb food | Leave to naturalize or lift and store when dormant | Aphid, snails, bacterial rot | Seed, division |
| *Winter flowering* | Temperate | Sun or part shade | Humus-rich, well drained soil | Leave to naturalize | Few problems | Division |

| PLANT | ORIGIN | LIGHT | SOIL PREPARATION | MAINTENANCE | PLANT PROTECTION | PROPAGATION |
|---|---|---|---|---|---|---|
| ***BULBS, CORMS & TUBERS*** *(continued)* | | | | | | |
| *Winter–spring flowering* | Cool-temperate | Sun or part shade in warm districts | Prepare soil with compost and complete fertilizer • Soil should be well drained | Remove spent flowers • Lift and divide every 3–5 years | Snails | Seed in fall, or offsets, divide clumps |
| *Spring flowering, sun* | Warm-temperate | Sun | Average, well-drained soil • Add compost before planting and complete fertilizer | Keep moist during growing season; dry off in summer • Protect with loose straw in zones with harsh winters | Few problems | Seed, division, offsets |
| *Spring flowering, shade to part shade* | Temperate to cool-temperate | Part shade to shade | Moist, humus-rich, well-drained soil • Add compost and complete fertilizer | Lightly mulch in summer | Few problems | Seed, division |
| *Summer–fall flowering* | Temperate | Sun or part shade | Average, well-drained garden soil enriched with compost and complete fertilizer | Water during growing season • Allow to dry out when dormant | Snails | Seed, division |
| *Spring–summer flowering, sun* | Warm-temperate to cool-temperate | Sun or part shade in all zones | Average, well-drained soil enriched with compost or bulb food | Protect bulbs with straw in zones with harsh winters • Lift and store in areas with wet, humid summers | Few problems | Seed, offsets, division |
| *Spring–summer flowering, shade* | Temperate | Sun, but most prefer cool shade | Well-drained, fertile soil enriched with compost and bulb food | Naturalize or replant each year • Protect bulbs with loose straw in zones with harsh winters | Few problems | Seed, bulbs, tuber claw |
| *Allium* | Temperate | Sun | Well-drained, fertile soil | Remove spent flowers • Divide every 5 years or so | Few problems | Seed, division |
| *Begonia* | Subtropical | Part shade | Moist, gritty compost in pots or garden • Good drainage necessary | Keep dry over winter • Liquid fertilize regularly | Damping off, bulb rot | Seed or tubers in spring |
| *Fritillaria* | Cold-temperate | Sun or part shade | Deep, rich, well-drained soil, alkaline pH | Provide adequate moisture during summer • Mulch | Bulb rot | Seed, offsets |
| *Gladiolus* | Warm-temperate | Sun | Well-drained, light, sandy loam | Lift and divide in cool, dry spot in cold climates • Lift and divide every few years where perennial | Thrips | Corm, cormlets |
| *Iris* | Cold-temperate | Sun | Well-drained soil with compost added | Lift and divide every 3–5 years | Stem rot | Division |
| *Lilium* | Temperate | Sun or, preferably, part shade | Well-drained, fertile soil; neutral pH | Minimal disturbance of established plants • Mulch in spring/summer • Allow stems to die down before removal | Bulb rot, cucumber mosaic virus | Seed, offsets, bulb scales |
| *Narcissus* | Temperate | Sun or part shade | Well-drained soil • Dolomite/lime; and/or compost and low-nitrogen fertilizer | Provide shelter from strong winds • Lift and divide in warm climates | Bulb rot, aphids | Offsets |
| *Tulipa* | Temperate | Sun | Well-drained soil • Lightly apply dolomite/lime; and/or add compost and blood and bone fertilizer • Add coarse sand in heavy soils | Disease control in spring | Tulip fire botrytis, aphids | Seed, division |
| ***LAWNS, GROUND COVERS & ORNAMENTAL GRASSES*** | | | | | | |
| *Lawns* | Warm-temperate to cool-temperate | Sun or part shade | Average, well-drained soil • Smooth, even surface | Regular mowing • Fertilizing • Pest control • Aerating | Insect damage as noted in plant descriptions | Seed, turf |

| PLANT | ORIGIN | LIGHT | SOIL PREPARATION | MAINTENANCE | PLANT PROTECTION | PROPAGATION |
|---|---|---|---|---|---|---|
| ***LAWNS, GROUND COVERS & ORNAMENTAL GRASSES*** *(continued)* | | | | | | |
| *Ground covers* | Warm-temperate to cool temperate | Sun to shade | Well-drained, average soil | Mulch • Regular fertilizing | Pest problems as noted in plant descriptions | Runners, division, cuttings |
| *Ornamental grasses, sedges & bamboos* | Cool-temperate to warm-temperate | Sun to part shade | Average soil plus compost; dry to poorly drained depending on species | Remove seed heads before dispersal • Restrict spread of bamboos using a barrier | Few problems | Seed, division |
| ***HERBS*** | Warm-temperate to cool-temperate | Sun or part shade | Dolomite/lime; and/or compost and fertilizer | Tip prune regularly • Harvest spring and summer | Few problems | Cuttings, seed, division |
| ***FRUIT TREES, NUT TREES & OTHER FRUITS*** | | | | | | |
| *Tropical to subtropical* | Tropical to subtropical | Full sun | Topsoil at least 24 in (60 cm) deep • Compost • Complete fertilizer | Training • Pruning • Fertilizing • Shelter from climatic extremes | Seasonal pest problems, root rot diseases | Seed, cuttings, grafting |
| *Cool-temperate and warm-temperate* | Temperate | Sun | Well-drained, humus-rich soil | Regular pruning for maximum fruit production • Mulch • Fertilizer • Weed control • Check pollination requirements | Root rot diseases, insects, various bacterial canker | Grafting, budding, cuttings |
| *Citrus* | Warm-temperate to cool-temperate | Sun | Humus-rich, well-drained soil | Regular fertilizer • Mulch • Prune to encourage fruit production | Scale insects, leaf miner, aphids, caterpillars | Grafting, *trifoliata* or *citronelle* root stocks |
| *Prunus* | Warm-temperate to cool-temperate | Sun | Humus-rich, well-drained soil | Correct pruning for maximum fruit production • Check pollination requirements • Weed control • Mulch | Leaf curl, brown rot, rust, bacterial canker, various insects | Grafting |
| ***INDOOR PLANTS*** | | | | | | |
| *Indoor foliage plants* | Subtropical to temperate | Good light to part shade • Warm to humid conditions | Humus-rich, well-drained potting media | Even moisture; less in winter • Liquid fertilize regularly • Remove dead foliage | Mealy bug, mites, scale insects | Seed, cuttings |
| *Indoor flowering & foliage plants* | Subtropical to warm-temperate | Good light to part shade | Humus-rich, well-drained potting media | Keep soil evenly moist • Dry in winter • Warm conditions • Remove dead flowers/foliage | Mealy bug, mites, scale insects | Seed, cuttings |
| *Indoor flowering plants* | Cool to warm-temperate | Part shade | Humus-rich, well-drained potting media | Remove spent flowers • Liquid fertilize regularly | Root rot, mealy bug, scale insects | Seed, cuttings |
| ***CACTI & SUCCULENTS*** | Tropical to subtropical | Sun or part shade | Light, gritty potting media • Good drainage essential | Water during flowering, then allow to dry | Root rot diseases, mealy bugs, scale insects, aphids | Seed, cuttings |
| ***ORCHIDS*** | Tropical to subtropical, temperate | Part shade | Open, free-draining potting media containing bark/leaf litter/charcoal peatmoss mixture for epiphytes and terrestrials | Regular fertilizer when not in flower • Maintain high humidity where appropriate • Good air circulation | Aphids, scale, mealy bug, beetles, bulb rot | Seed, seedlings, division |
| ***FERNS, PALMS & CYCADS*** | | | | | | |
| *Ferns* | Subtropical to cool-temperate | Sun or part shade | Well-drained, humus-rich, moist soil | Cut back old fronds • Leaf litter mulch • Regular application of weak solution of liquid fertilizer | Aphids, mealy bug, scale insects, snails, staghorn, fern beetle | Spores, cuttings, division |

| PLANT | ORIGIN | LIGHT | SOIL PREPARATION | MAINTENANCE | PLANT PROTECTION | PROPAGATION |
|---|---|---|---|---|---|---|
| ***FERNS, PALMS & CYCADS*** *(continued)* | | | | | | |
| *Palms & cycads* | Tropical to warm-temperate | Sun or part shade | Compost • Humus-rich, moist, well-drained soil • Complete or slow-release fertilizer | Some wind protection when young • Nitrogenous fertilizer • Mulch • Remove old fronds | Mealy bug, mites, palm dart caterpillars, scale insects, grasshoppers | Seed |
| ***CLIMBERS & CREEPERS*** | | | | | | |
| *Warm-temperate to cool-temperate* | Warm-temperate to cool-temperate | Sun or part shade | Average, well-drained soil • Complete fertilizer | Regular pruning • Mulch | Few problems | Seed, cuttings |
| *Tropical to subtropical* | Tropical to subtropical | Sun or part shade | Compost • Rich, well-drained soil • Complete fertilizer | Regular pruning • Mulch | Few problems | Seed, cuttings |

# Glossary

× (multiplication sign) A sign placed in front of the name of plants with Latin names to show that they are not true wild species but are of hybrid origin, whether natural or artificial; as in *Camellia* × *williamsii* or × *Brassolaeliocattleya* Sylvia Fry.

+ (plus sign) Though grafts do not usually hybridize, it does happen on very rare occasions, and the resulting plant is designated with the + sign, as with + *Laburnocytisus adamii*, a freak that occurred in a Paris nursery last century when a purple broom was grafted to laburnum stock to create a standard broom.

**Acid** (of soils) Containing relatively little lime, to give a pH reaction of less than 7, the sort of soil needed to grow such plants as azaleas, camellias, rhododendrons and the like, and in which hydrangeas flower blue. A very acid soil is described as "sour."

**Aerial root** A root that springs from the stem of a plant above ground. The aerial roots of ivy are short and used by the plant to cling to its support. In such plants as monsteras, philodendrons or some of the tropical figs they eventually reach the ground; before they do they draw moisture from the air.

**Air-layering** A method of propagation applicable to a wide range of trees and shrubs which involves wounding the stem and then packing the wound with damp sphagnum moss. This is all held in place with string and plastic. When roots show, the new plant can be severed and transplanted.

**Alkaline** (of soils) Containing a great deal of calcium (lime) to give a pH reaction of more than 7. It is the sort of soil preferred by such plants as bearded irises and the cabbage tribe, and in which hydrangeas flower pink. Some gardeners refer to alkaline soils as "sweet."

**Alternate** (of leaves) Springing, one by one, from first one side of the stem and then the other. Whether the leaves are alternate or opposite is an important aid in plant identification.

**Annual** A plant that lives for only a year—often less—or which is customarily treated as such in gardens.

**Anther** The part of the stamen that actually produces the pollen, usually carried on a thin stalk called the filament. *Lilium auratum* has the largest anthers of any flower.

**Apex** The growing tip of a shoot, or the very end of a leaf, which may take a variety of shapes.

**Arbor** A structure, usually free standing, designed to be covered with climbing plants to provide shade. The term is more or less interchangeable with pergola.

**Areole** The swelling on the stem of a cactus which bears the spines. It is actually the vestigial remains of a shoot.

**Axil** The "armpit" of a leaf, where it joins the stem, and where there is usually a growth bud to be found.

**Bedding plant** A plant, usually low growing, suitable for a mass planting display of flowers or foliage. Most are annuals or short lived perennials.

**Berry** In normal use, a small juicy fruit which is eaten entire and unpeeled; to the botanist, a fleshy fruit containing several seeds which does not open when ripe—including citrus fruits and the tomato.

**Biennial** A plant which flowers and dies in its second year after germination, producing only roots and leaves in the first. Parsley is the best known example.

**Bifoliate** (of cattleyas and their hybrids) Plants which have two leaves per pseudo-bulb.

**Bipinnate** (of leaves) Twice pinnate, as in many ferns and such tropical trees as the jacaranda.

**Blade** The flat part of a leaf, where most photosynthesis occurs.

**Bloom** A general term for a flower, much used in flower show schedules. Also, a waxy or powdery coating on the skins of leaves or fruits, as on a grape.

**Bole** The lowest part of the trunk of a tree, from the ground to the lowest branches.

**Bract** A leaf-like organ, usually associated with a flower or cluster of flowers, but not part of the flower itself. Bracts are smaller and a different shape to ordinary leaves, as in roses; or they may be brightly colored and resemble petals, as in bougainvilleas and poinsettias.

**Bud** An immature, unopened flower. Also, an embryo shoot, usually small and pointed, found normally in the axils of the leaves or at the ends of shoots, but also occurring on rootstocks, tubers and the like. It is usually protected by small, waxy scales.

**Budding** A form of grafting, where the scion consists of a piece of bark carrying a single growth bud, inserted into the bark of the understock. It is used especially for the propagation of roses and fruit trees.

**Bulb** An underground (usually) organ, consisting of a reduced stem (the base plate) surrounded by modified leaves that store food for the plant's dormancy. The onion is the classic example.

**Bulbil** A small bulb, carried in the axil of a leaf, as in certain lilies. It offers a convenient means of propagation.

**Bulblet** A small bulb developing from the base of a mature one and used for propagation. The term "offset" is sometimes used.

**Cactus** The most significant family of succulent plants, all perennial and native to the Americas.

**Calyx** The outermost part of a flower, which encloses and protects the rest while in bud. It is made up of sepals, usually small, green and leaf like, but sometimes colored and the showiest part of the flower, as in clematis and anemones.

**Capsule** A fruit which when ripe dries and opens to release the seeds, such as the fruits of lilies and petunias.

**Carpel** The female organ of the flower, also known as the pistil. A flower may have several or only one.

**Catkin** The type of flower cluster, usually pendulous, found on such plants as willows or alders. The individual flowers, usually one sex only, are tiny and generally have no petals, being pollinated by the wind.

**Caudex** The thickened base of the stem of certain plants such as some ferns and *Dioscorea elephantipes*.

**Cladode** A flattened stem rather like a leaf and performing the same functions, as in the butcher's broom *(Ruscus aculeatus)*. Similar organs in acacias are called phyllodes.

**Climber** A plant with stems too long and flexible to be self supporting and which raises itself to the light by climbing into and over other plants. It may attach itself to its support by twining around it, as jasmine or honeysuckle do; by means of tendrils (grapes, peas); by short aerial roots (ivy); or by suckers (Virginia creeper). The latter two need no trellis and are termed self-clinging climbers. Some climbers attach themselves only loosely to their supports and need to be tied in place. The term "vine," while applicable only to the grape, is often used for any climbing plant, especially in the USA.

**Clone** A group of plants propagated asexually (that is, by cuttings, grafting, division, etc.) from a single individual and thus genetically all identical, such as roses and fruit trees.

**Cold frame** A miniature, portable greenhouse placed over crops in the open ground to protect them from cold or encourage early development. Traditionally made from two or four pieces of glass in a wire frame, but can be simply a wire frame clad in transparent plastic.

**Common names** The names by which plants are commonly known, as distinct from their Latin or scientific ones (which, unlike common names, are universally recognized). Sometimes the two coincide and, as a plant can have several common names, it is usual for books to list the plants they describe under their scientific names. The American nursery industry has for some years been attempting to standardize common names, by no means an easy task.

**Composite** The botanist's term for a daisy, from the way the "flowers" are in fact made up of many small flowers.

**Compost** The most effective of all fertilizers, it is made from organic matter such as leaves, grass clippings and manure which has been allowed to rot for a few weeks or months until it has turned black and crumbly; in orchid growing, the soil-free medium, which may or may not contain compost from the compost heap, in which the plants are grown.

**Compound** (of leaves) Subdivided into several leaflets, as in a rose or palm leaf. Leaves not so subdivided are called "simple."

**Cone** The structure that encloses the primitive flowers and then the seeds of conifers (pines, cypresses, etc.) and cycads. It is made up of overlapping scales, which become woody when the seeds ripen.

**Conifer** A member of a primitive order of flowering plants (the Gymnospermae), characterized by their cones and usually needle-like leaves. They are all shrubs or trees, usually evergreen, and the hardiest trees in cold climates; they supply the bulk of the world's timber. Pines, cypresses, sequoias and junipers are examples.

**Cordate** (of leaves) Heart shaped, as in the European lime *(Tilia cordata)*.

**Corm** A bulb-like organ, usually growing underground but without the scales (fleshy modified leaves) of a bulb, and often simply called a bulb by gardeners, such as gladiolus and freesias. When a corm flowers the old corm dies and the plant creates a new one on top of it; bulbs are usually more or less permanent structures.

**Cormlet** A small corm that grows from around the base of a corm, usually in fair numbers and used for propagation.

**Corolla** The whole collection of petals that forms the eye-catching part of most flowers. The petals can be separate, as in the rose, or fused together in a bell or trumpet, as in rhododendrons or campanulas.

**Corona** The cup or trumpet-shaped outgrowth in the center of the flower of narcissi and its relatives. It is formed from the bases of the stamens.

**Creeper** A plant that makes long shoots that grow along the ground, usually rooting as it goes, such as *Convolvulus sabatius*. The distinction between a climber and a creeper is not clear cut—many creepers will climb if given the chance, and some climbers will creep if there is nothing to climb on, such as ivy and Virginia creeper.

**Crown** The more or less permanent base of a herbaceous plant from which the leaves and flower stems grow upwards and the roots downwards; the upper part of a tree, consisting of the branches and top section of the trunk; the corona of a narcissus or narcissus-like plant.

**Cultivar** A variety of plant which has arisen as the result of cultivation, that is, not naturally, usually by means of hybridization. It may be propagated by any suitable means, and the rules of botany state that it must not be named in Latin but should be given in Roman type with single quotes, for example 'Queen Elizabeth', 'Model of Perfection'. Cultivars that arose before these rulings and were given Latin names are treated similarly, giving rise to such names as *Acer palmatum* 'Dissectum Atropurpureum'.

**Cutting** A piece of stem or root cut from a plant and used for propagation. According to the state of maturity of the stem from which it is taken, a cutting may be classed as a softwood, semi-mature or hardwood cutting.

**Dead-head** To remove dead flowers, with the twofold aim of tidying up the plant and preventing it wasting energy in unwanted seed.

**Deciduous** (of trees and shrubs) Losing all the leaves each year, growing a fresh set later. Typically the leaves are shed in the fall, sometimes assuming brilliant colors before they do so, and new leaves grow in spring. Many tropical trees drop at any time of the year in anticipation of a prolonged dry season. A tree that doesn't drop all its leaves is called semi-deciduous.

**Die-back** The death of the tips of shoots or branches, sometimes followed by the death of the entire shoot. It can be caused by frost or by disease.

**Diffuse** Growing into many branches, usually used of shrubs to suggest an open, rangy habit of growth rather than a compact one.

**Division** The simplest method of propagation, whereby a clump of plants is dug up and broken up into several pieces which are then replanted.

**Dorsal** Situated on the back of an organ.

**Double** (of flowers) Having more than the "natural" number of petals. The extra petals are formed from stamens, and where these are completely transformed the flower is apt to be sterile. A flower with only a few extra petals and enough stamens for fertility is described as "semi-double."

**Elliptic** (of leaves) More or less oval in shape.

**Entire** (of leaves) Having smooth margins, that is, without lobes or serrations, such as an aspidistra or privet leaf.

**Epiphyte** A plant that grows on, and usually in the branches of, another, but does not steal nourishment from its host; many orchids are examples.

**Espalier** The technique of training a tree or shrub, most typically a fruit tree such as a peach or a fig, to grow flat against a wall or trellis. It was originally designed to encourage earlier ripening by holding the fruit close to the reflected warmth of the wall, but can also be used for decorative effect.

**Evergreen** Any plant that retains foliage all year. Evergreen trees and shrubs do drop old leaves, though not until after the new ones have been formed and usually only a few at a time.

**F1 hybrid** A hybrid strain created by pollinating two very carefully selected parents. The resulting seedlings usually show great vigor and uniformity and many strains of annuals and vegetables are F1 hybrids. It is useless to save seeds from these, as the original cross must be made afresh every time seed is wanted.

**Fall** The lower three petals of an iris, which project out and down (the upright ones are called "standards").

**Family** A group of genera which are considered to be closely related. The cacti (family Cactaceae) are one such; the rose family (Rosaceae) includes not only the rose but such fruits as the peach, blackberry, strawberry and apple.

**Fan palm** A palm with roughly circular (palmate) leaves, so called because they can be used to make fans. A palm with pinnate leaves is called a "feather palm."

**Fertilizer** Anything added to the soil to maintain or increase its fertility. Fertilizers may be organic, that is, derived from once-living matter, as are manure, compost, and blood and bone; or inorganic (artificial), such as sulphate of ammonia or superphosphate, which are prepared in chemical factories.

**Fibrous root** A fine, young root, usually one of very many. These are the roots that take up moisture and nourishment from the soil.

**Filament** The stalk of a stamen, which carries the anther.

**Floret** A single, small flower in a head or cluster of many, as in a delphinium or cluster-flowered rose.

**Flower** The organ of reproduction, basic in determining to what genus and species the plant belongs. They are normally composed of three parts: the calyx, the corolla, and the sexual organs proper, the male stamens and the female carpels. Not all may be present in any given flower (clematis, for instance have no petals), and they may be, as in orchids or cannas, modified into the most fantastic forms.

**Flowerhead** A cluster of flowers, which may be so compact as to look like a single flower, as in a daisy.

**Frame** A miniature greenhouse, designed mainly for propagation. The traditional style is an enclosed bed with wood to a height of around 16 in (about 40 cm) with an old window across the top. A hot frame is heated, a cold one not.

**Frond** The leaves of a fern. Fronds carrying spore-bearing organs (sori) are called "fertile" fronds; if not, they are called "sterile" fronds. In some species the two types are of different appearance. The term frond is also used for the leaves of feather palms; the Latin *frondosa* when applied to many plants means "leafy."

**Fruit** The part of the plant which carries the seed or seeds, and which arises after the flower is pollinated. It may or may not be edible.

**Fungus** A very large group of evolutionary primitive plants, of which the most relevant to gardeners are mushrooms and the many parasitic fungi that cause most plant diseases.

**Genus** A group of species which have sufficient in common to be classed as closely related; the name is always Latin. For example, roses are members of the genus *Rosa,* and both the smoking and ornamental tobaccos are of the genus *Nicotiana.*

**Glabrous** (of leaves and stems) Smooth and non-hairy; a hairy plant is described as "hispid."

**Glasshouse** A structure, traditionally roofed and clad with glass but now often with plastic sheeting, designed to trap the sun's heat and thus allow warmth loving plants to be grown in cool climates. Supplementary heating may be provided.

**Glaucous** (of leaves) Bluish gray, a more accurate description for the many conifers sold as having "blue" leaves.

**Grafting** A method of propagation which involves the uniting of a piece of stem of a desirable plant, the "scion," to that of a less desirable one, the "stock" or "understock," to give a stronger root system than the scion would have naturally. Many different techniques for grafting have been employed.

**Greenhouse** Originally a lavishly windowed structure where evergreen plants were placed to keep them from winter cold; but now synonymous with "glasshouse."

**Green manure** A crop of annual plants grown to be dug into the soil at maturity to improve or restore its fertility, for instance legumes such as clover, alfalfa or lupins.

**Grex** A group of hybrid plants of the same parentage; the term is used mainly in the context of orchid breeding. Grex names are given without quotes, such as Vanda Nellie Morley.

**Ground cover** An extensive planting of a single species of low-growing plants, intended to carpet the ground with foliage and suppress weeds. Also, a plant suitable for such use.

**Habit** The complete picture of the way a plant grows; a species may be described as being of "compact," "weeping" or "upright" habit, for instance.

**Hanging basket** A container designed to be suspended in order to show trailing plants such as ivy, Christmas cactus or fuchsias to their best advantage.

**Heel** A sliver of old wood retained at the base of a cutting. It is traditional in taking cuttings of carnations and roses.

**Herb** In botany, any plant that does not have permanent woody stems, such as petunias and zinnias. In gardening, a plant whose leaves or shoots are added to food to enhance its flavor or used in the preparation of medicines.

**Herbaceous** A perennial plant which dies down to the ground each year; a herbaceous border is a planting composed entirely of such plants, for example delphiniums and chrysanthemums.

**Humus** The final product of rotting organic matter, whether of plant or animal origin.

**Hybrid** A plant originating from the cross-pollination, either in the wild or as the result of match-making by the gardener, of two different species. If hybrids are crossed, the resulting plants may carry the genes of several species. Hybrids between plants of different genera are rare, though quite common among orchids.

**Inflorescence** The structure that carries the flowers. It may take any one of a number of forms—a spike (as in gladioli), a raceme (as in delphiniums), a panicle (as in lilacs), an umbel (as in onions); gardeners often refer simply to a "cluster." Inflorescences are described as "terminal" when they grow at the ends of shoots, or axillary, when they arise in the axils of the leaves.

**Insectivorous plant** The strict term for carnivorous plants; they trap and digest insects to supply them with extra nitrogen, which is difficult to obtain from the swampy soils where they usually grow.

**Irregular** (of flowers) Having the petals arranged in some way other than radial symmetry, though almost always bilaterally symmetrical, such as on orchids and violets. The scientific term is "zygomorphic."

**Labellum** The lowest of the three petals of an orchid, usually larger or more elaborately shaped and colored than the others. Also called a "lip."

**Lanceolate** (of leaves) Long and narrow; lance or sword shaped, such as gladiolus and iris leaves.

**Lateral** A side shoot, growing from the axil of a leaf of the main stem. In many fruit trees it is these shoots that bear the flowers and ultimately the fruit.

**Lax** Of rather floppy habit, for instance *Philadelphus mexicanus,* the opposite of upright or stiff.

**Layering** A method of propagation by which a branch of a plant is bent down to the ground where it takes root; the rooted section can then be severed from its parent and transplanted. It is most useful for plants that can be slow or reluctant to root from cuttings; some plants will layer themselves naturally.

**Leaflet** One of the several leaves in which a compound leaf such as a rose leaf is divided. A leaf has a bud in its axil; a leaflet does not.

**Legume** A member of the large pea family, which includes peas, beans, clover, lupins, wisteria, acacias, the various brooms, and some trees such as the cassias. They all share the ability to draw nitrogen straight from the air, by courtesy of bacteria that live in nodules on their roots.

**Lime** A compound of calcium added to soil to make it more alkaline, and also to improve the structure of clay soil; a tropical fruit of the genus *Citrus;* deciduous trees of the genus *Tilia,* also known as lindens.

**Linear** (of leaves) Very long and narrow, so that they look as though they could be drawn with a single line, such as the leaves of chives.

**Lip** See *Labellum.*

**Lithophytic** (of orchids and some primitive plants) Growing on the naked surfaces of rocks and deriving nourishment from any litter they can accumulate around their roots.

**Lobe** One of the divisions in which a scalloped leaf, such as a maple or ivy leaf, is not quite divided; similarly in the corollas of flowers with united petals such as campanulas.

**Manure** The dung of animals, used as fertilizer. Like all materials of organic origin it adds humus to the soil.

**Marginal plant** One which in the wild grows in the swampy margins of ponds or lakes, and which can be cultivated in similar positions around a garden pond, such as *Iris ensata.* Most don't mind having their roots submerged for at least part of the year.

**Midrib** The main central vein of a leaf; the central stalk to which the leaflets of a pinnate leaf are attached.

**Monocarpic** A plant which flowers only once in its life and then dies, for example *Agave americana* and the fishtail palm *(Caryota urens).*

**Monopodial** (of orchids) One that does not naturally form a clump of shoots growing from a creeping rhizome, for example the vandas. (Clump-forming orchids such as cattleyas and cymbidiums are described as "sympodia.")

**Moss** A large group of species of primitive non-flowering plants which need moist soil to grow. Most are of very diminutive stature; some are cultivated as ground cover.

**Mulch** A blanket spread over the bare surface of soil to block the loss of moisture and to discourage the growth of weeds. Most mulches are of such organic matter as manure, compost, straw, bark chips, etc. which eventually rot and add humus to the soil, thus enhancing its fertility. Inorganic materials are also used.

**Nectar** The sweet, sugary liquid secreted by glands at the base of the petals of some flowers. Bees gather it and concentrate it into honey.

**Neutral** (of soils) Neither acid nor alkaline, that is having a pH of 7.

**Node** The point on a stem where a leaf and its axillary bud grows. It is the place to cut when pruning, and also where the base of a cutting should be cut.

**Obovate** (of leaves) More or less oval in shape.

**Offset** A shoot arising from the base of a plant which can be detached and used for propagation.

**Opposite** (of leaves) Arising in pairs, one on either side of the stem. See also *Alternate.*

**Organic matter** Material derived from things that were once alive, such as manure and compost, and which breaks down to form humus. The addition of organic matter improves the structure and fertility of any soil.

**Ovary** The lowest part of a carpel where the embryo seeds are. Ovaries found above the calyx are called "superior," while those found below the calyx are called "inferior."

**Ovate, ovoid** (of leaves and petals) Oval in shape.

**Palm** Members of the family Palmae or Arecaceae, that is, trees characterized by a normally unbranched trunk topped by a bunch of large leaves and a distinct preference for warm climates.

**Palmate** (of leaves) Divided into lobes or leaflets that spread out from the end of the leaf stalk like the fingers of a hand, as in a maple leaf.

**Panicle** A type of inflorescence, strictly a compound raceme, as typified by that of the lilac.

**Parasite** A plant which grows upon another, stealing moisture and nourishment from its host. Mistletoe is an example; more common and less welcome are the parasitic fungi that cause plant diseases.

**Pendent** Hanging, the way the flower sprays of the wisteria do.

**Perennial** A plant that lives for three years or more. In botany, the term includes trees and shrubs, while in horticulture it is normally limited to plants that do not produce permanent woody stems, such as irises, peonies or ginger lilies.

**Persistent** A structure that stays on the plant after it serves its purpose, instead of falling off. The sepals of the rose which stay on the ripening rose hip are an example.

**Petal** The colorful part of most flowers. Petals are in fact modified leaves, and there are some flowers that have green petals, for example the green zinnia 'Envy'.

**Petiole** The stalk of a leaf.

**pH** The scale on which the acidity or alkalinity of soil is measured. It ranges from 1, an acid of fearsome strength, to 14, an alkali of equal ferocity, with 7 being the neutral point. Most garden soils fall somewhere between about pH 5.5 to about 8.6.

**Phyllode** See *Cladode.*

**Pinch out** The operation of removing the tip of a growing shoot, usually with the fingers, to encourage lateral shoots to grow and make the plant bushier.

**Pinna, pinnule** Another term for the leaflet of a pinnate or bipinnate leaf.

**Pinnate** A leaf divided into leaflets arranged on either side of the leaf stalk, as in a rose leaf or those of many palms and ferns.

**Pollen** The tiny grains of plant substance containing DNA which unite with the embryo seeds contained in the ovary to create the fruit and hence a new generation of flowering plants—a process termed pollination. The transfer is usually carried out by insects, but can also be carried out by nectar-eating birds and sometimes by the wind.

**Prostrate** A plant of low-growing, ground-hugging habit, such as the prostrate junipers.

**Pruning** The art of cutting off parts of a plant to encourage more of the sort of growth the gardener desires, or to maintain a compact habit of growth.

**Pseudo-bulb** The fleshy, bulb-like stem found on many orchids.

**Raceme** A type of inflorescence, where the flowers are arranged on a long, usually upright stem, each flower having a separate flower stalk as in delphiniums.

**Revert** To return to normal, as when a variegated plant starts producing plain green leaves.

**Rhizomatous** A plant that grows from rhizomes.

**Rhizome** A creeping stem, growing either at ground level, or just below, and swollen with starch and nutrients to nourish the shoots and roots that grow from it. The rhizomes are the edible part of the ginger plant.

**Root** The underground parts of a plant which anchor the plant and draw up water and nourishment from the soil.

**Rootstock** The understock of a grafted plant; the base of a perennial where the roots grow.

**Rosette** A group of leaves radiating from the same point on a short stem, to give an effect like a green flower, as in sempervivums.

**Runner** A horizontally growing stem that roots at each node where it touches the ground, as in strawberries and violets.

**Scape** A leafless flower stem that arises directly from the base of the plant, especially common in bulbs. Narcissi and agapanthus are examples.

**Scarify** To break or soften the hard coat on the seeds of certain plants, especially legumes such as sweet peas and wattles, to allow water to penetrate and thus speed up germination. It can be done by rubbing carefully with fine sandpaper or soaking the seed for a little while in hot water.

**Scientific name** The internationally recognized Latin name of a plant which often gives a potted description of the plant or commemorates some person connected with it. The name consists of two parts, the genus name and the species name. The system was first devised by the Swedish botanist Linnaeus in 1753.

**Seed** The organ of propagation of flowering plants. Seeds are not immortal, and it is not worth saving left-over seeds of vegetables and flowers for the following year; the percentage that will germinate decreases markedly.

**Seed head** A general term for a dry, inedible fruit that contains seeds.

**Seed leaf** The leaves contained in the seed which are the first to appear when a seedling germinates; they are different from those that follow. Plants are classified according to whether there are one or two.

**Self sow, self seed** A plant's habit of shedding seeds around itself which germinate without the gardener's assistance.

**Sepal** One of the parts of the calyx, usually green, leaf like and sometimes colored and showy, as in hellebores and clematis. In many one-seed-leaf plants the sepals are almost indistinguishable from the petals, as in lilies and tulips.

**Series** (also **strain**) A group of plants raised from seed and thus not genetically identical but sufficiently alike to be treated as a garden variety, for example most cultivars of annuals and vegetables.

**Sessile** Having no stalk, as the flowers of most camellias for example.

**Sheath** An organ, usually vaguely leaf like, that encloses another, such as a shoot or cluster of flower buds. The sheath that encloses the buds of an agapanthus is an example.

**Shoot** Any aerial part of a plant that bears leaves.

**Shrub** A plant with several permanent woody stems that arise from ground level. A tree has only one, but in gardening the distinction is not quite clear cut—many plants such as the larger cotoneasters or bottlebrushes can be treated equally well as large shrubs or small, multi-stemmed trees.

**Spadix** A fleshy flower stalk which bears many tiny flowers—a specialty of the arum family.

**Species** A population of wild plants which are sufficiently alike to carry the same name, and which will freely breed with one another to give rise to offspring like themselves. The honor of naming a species goes to the scientist who discovers or describes it.

**Sphagnum** A type of rather luxuriant growing moss, normally an inhabitant of boggy ground and much used when dried as an ingredient in potting mixes, especially for orchids. Live plants often grow from spores in the dried material, and are welcomed by orchid growers as a sign that conditions are right.

**Spike** A type of inflorescence where the flowers are borne on a long, usually upright stem. Unlike a raceme, a spike has no separate flower stalks, as in gladioli.

**Spikelet** The basic unit of the flowers of grasses, consisting of one or more petal-less flowers and an accompanying bract or two.

**Spore** The equivalent of a seed in non-flowering plants such as ferns and fungi. Much tinier than seeds, they are produced in great numbers and blow about on the wind.

**Spreading** A plant which grows much wider than it does tall, perhaps with mainly horizontal branches, perhaps by rooting in the ground and making an ever-expanding clump.

**Spur** A hollow projection from a petal, often containing nectar; the short flowering shoots on such plants as apples, pears or hoyas, which normally continue to flower and fruit for several years.

**Stalk, stem** The two terms are almost interchangeable, but in horticulture a stem usually has leaves growing from its sides while a stalk does not.

**Standard** The big petal that stands up at the back of a pea flower; a tree or shrub with a single, rather tall stem before the branches begin. Many trees grow thus naturally; shrubs like roses or fuchsias have to be trained to the form artificially. A half-standard has a shorter stem than usual.

**Sterile** Incapable of bearing seeds or pollen or both (flowers) or spores (the fronds of ferns). A plant may produce perfectly normal flowers but not mature fertile seed due to some aberration in its genetic make-up, something which often occurs in hybrids; or the reproductive parts of the flower may have been transformed into the extra petals of a double flower.

**Stigma** The business part of a carpel, where the pollen lands and is captured.

**Stipule** Leafy outgrowths that grow at the base of a leaf stalk, as in roses, and on the leaves of sucker shoots.

**Stratify** A technique used to break the dormancy of seeds of such plants as roses and apples, which need a period of cold before they can germinate. In its simplest form, it involves bundling them up in damp sphagnum moss and putting them in a refrigerator for a few weeks.

**Striate** (of leaves) Ridged or fluted down the length, as in *Sisyrinchium striatum*.

**Sub-shrub** A perennial with more or less permanent but not woody stems, such as geraniums or *Phlomis fruticosa*.

**Subspecies** A group of plants within a species, different from the norm but not sufficiently so to rank them as a species in their own right.

**Succulent** A plant which has evolved swollen water-filled organs, either stems or leaves, which help it to survive in arid climates. Cacti are the extreme example, but other plants show succulence to a lesser degree, as most orchids do in their pseudo-bulbs.

**Sucker** A shoot or stem that arises from the roots of a tree or shrub or, undesirably, from the understock of a grafted specimen.

**Synonym** (usually abbreviated to "syn.") A scientific name which, though no longer valid, still lingers in use, for example *Plumbago auriculata* syn. *P. capensis*.

**Taproot** The main root of a plant, which plunges straight down to anchor it; the swollen taproots of carrots are the most familiar. Most trees have them too, and resent their being damaged.

**Tendril** A string-like structure which some climbing plants wrap around a branch or trellis to support themselves. Peas have them, as do grapes.

**Terminal** (of inflorescences and flowers) Appearing at the end of a shoot, as with roses, marigolds and poinsettias.

**Terrestrial** (of orchids) Growing in the ground, the way most plants do, rather than perched in trees.

**Throat** The inside part of a trumpet- or tube-shaped flower, often carrying, as in foxgloves and gloxinias, a different pattern or color to guide insects.

**Tooth, teeth** The serrations on the edges of a leaf or leaflet, as in rose leaves.

**Topiary** The art of clipping suitable trees or shrubs such as yew, privet or box into artificial shapes, such as pyramids, globes, peacocks, etc.

**Tree** A woody plant, often very tall and large but not always, with only one main stem and very rarely more. See also *Shrub*.

**Tri-** In compound words, indicating three, as trifoliate, tripinnate, etc.

**Tuber** A fat, starchy underground organ designed to store food for a plant during its dormancy. Many tubers, such as those of the potato, provide food for humans too.

**Umbel** A type of inflorescence where several flower stalks arise from one point, as in onions, agapanthus and parsley.

**Upright** A growth habit whereby main branches grow more or less vertically.

**Variegated** Variegated plants have patterns of other colors as well as green on their leaves, and usually grow less strongly than their plain leaved counterparts as they have less chlorophyll. They are usually the result of cultivation and are sometimes caused by viruses though some species, notably *Coleus blumei*, are variegated naturally.

**Variety** Strictly speaking, a group of plants arising in the wild which though not sufficiently different from the norm of their species to be of great interest to botanists (they may only differ in flower color, for instance) are different enough to be of interest to gardeners. A variety is designated as, for instance, *Buxus microphylla* var. *japonica*, the var. being short for *varietas*. Varieties created by gardeners are supposed to be called cultivars and not given Latin names.

**Ventral** Situated on the front of an organ.

**Virus** A disease in plants which is incurable and may be fatal. However, some viruses are relatively benign, such as the one that makes tulips "break" into stripes.

**Whorl** Usually of leaves, an arrangement where three or more arise at the same node, as in rhododendrons. Flowers can grow in whorls around the stalk also, as in *Primula malacoides*.

**Wood, woody** A stem which may not be big enough to use as timber but which contains hardened cells and is more or less permanent. It is characteristic of trees and shrubs, but some climbers, such as the grape, are also woody.

# General Index

# Index to Plants